W9-CKF-973

PSYCHOLOGY APPLIED TO LIFE AND WORK

Fourth Edition

PSYCHOLOGY

APPLIED TO LIFE AND WORK

Harry Walker Hepner

Syracuse University
and
Management Consultant

Prentice-Hall, Inc. Englewood Cliffs, New Jersey

Psychology Applied to Life and Work, 4th Ed.

Harry Walker Hepner

Current printing (last digit):
10 9 8 7 6 5 4 3 2 1

Prentice-Hall International, Inc., *London*
Prentice-Hall of Australia, Pty., Ltd., *Sydney*
Prentice-Hall of Canada, Ltd., *Toronto*
Prentice-Hall of India (Private) Ltd., *New Delhi*
Prentice-Hall of Japan, Inc., *Tokyo*

Library of Congress Catalog Card No.: 65–13457

PRINTED IN THE UNITED STATES OF AMERICA
73347-C

PREFACE

This edition is more than an updating of the previous edition. It also offers the perspectives and background developed during several decades of teaching and reading of journals in psychology. The topics selected and emphasized are those which have passed the test of classroom use with a wide variety of students. Entirely new chapters have been added on automation and psychological climates. Recent research studies on mental health, psychological needs, illumination, the adoption of new products, and animal experiments of significance in child development and executive stress are some of the topics that have been given special attention.

As in the previous editions, the basic framework for the reader's thinking about the dynamics of the individual's behavior—the adjustment concept—is still central; it is the binding thread of theory running through the work in a pattern strong enough to provide some integral unity.

My interviews with individual students, counseling sessions with employees and executives in industry, and the comments of colleagues have confirmed my belief that the reader should be offered information and viewpoints that may contribute to effective dealing with both personal problems and relations with others. Many a reader will not have opportunity to extend his formal acquaintance with psychology beyond the scope of this book, and I have therefore tried to present those psychological principles that are fundamental and significant in life and work. The reader should obtain some sound bases for better insight into psychodynamics as he lives and works with others. He should also gain some foundation of social philosophy that is applicable to the changing social order and thereby be able to function more effectively in a position of leadership.

Of course, a teacher-writer has a tendency to think in terms of those behavioral and instructional patterns which he has found fruitful. Another teacher in the same field may follow somewhat different patterns in his thinking and procedures. Any teacher should, however, find it easy to adapt the text contents to fit his unique needs. Sometimes a teacher becomes especially effective when he modifies the treatment of a topic in a text.

A text such as this deals with so many subjects that the reader must not imagine that he has been given final or conclusive information. Rather, he should feel that the present treatment of topics has opened the way for further exploration on his own initiative.

No man can produce a text such as this only by his own effort. One of the functions of an author is to obtain from other teachers and researchers the fruits of their work for presentation to students. I am indebted to Karen Bowles who abstracted hundreds of published articles in order that I might select appropriate findings to update the book. Lura Jackson, of the National Institute of Mental Health, kindly suggested the most recent data available from the Department of Health, Education, and Welfare. My secretary, Gladys K. Kennedy, not only typed and edited the manuscript but also made numerous inspections and corrections to insure accuracy.

HARRY W. HEPNER

CONTENTS

"I like to study people" *is a very common expression. Those who say it are apt to refer to unusual personalities. Furthermore, their interest in people is likely to be merely the entertainment variety. Actually, all people, including the everyday varieties of normal people, are interesting, too, but they should be given systematic study as in a course in psychology.*

PART I

INTRODUCTION

CHAPTER ONE

REASONS FOR STUDYING PSYCHOLOGY

People study psychology for various reasons. A few want to appreciate its influence in the big affairs of historical significance, but most people study it as an aid in dealing with their own problems of life and work. This chapter reviews some of these personal problems and indicates how psychologists deal with them.

We all like to study people. Psychology is surely among the most useful of all our sciences. Its importance is constantly impressed upon us by the delightful and the not-so-delightful behavior of our associates as well as of ourselves. Examples of psychological influences are as numerous as people—ourselves, our friends, our work associates, and our leaders. Every human being, no matter how low or high his position on whatever scale of values we choose, is a living example of the subject matter of psychology.

Somehow many people seem to think that psychology is more or less limited to the study of odd or atypical persons, such as the feeble-minded, the neurotic, the insane, the genius, the problem child, or other deviates. They fail to appreciate that the so-called ordinary individual, the member of the great majority, is just as interesting as the most unusual personality. Furthermore, they are apt to assume that the outstanding leaders in business, political, and other affairs are motivated by logical, not by psychological, influences.

Actually, the leader is just as good (or poor) a subject for study as anyone else. Sometimes he deserves special study on our part because his behavior is likely to have wider effects on more people than that of the non-leader.

Recent events in world affairs have revealed to us some marked differences in the mental maturity and balance of leaders. The members of this generation are gradually learning about the close relation between the psychological characteristics of individual leaders and some effects those characteristics have on everyday human affairs. Many of us are beginning to realize that a leader may be so immature psychologically that he seeks to satisfy himself at the expense of other people, or he may be so mature as to promote the satisfactions of his people in such a way as to foster their personality development. Whenever we study the many historical influences in the shifting boundaries on maps of the world, we note how, in some instances, millions of lives have been affected by the impulsions of some maladjusted dictator to satisfy his complexes and those of his blind followers. The study of psychology shows us how we, as individuals, as well as our leaders, at times cling to immature and unintelligent patterns of behavior.

When a person trained in psychology listens to a business executive, labor union official, politician, preacher, or reformer, he says to himself: "Has this man analyzed the conditions of which he speaks and come to a sound objective solution, or is he merely giving vent to the impulsions or perhaps even the venom of his own mind?" The dictators and the tyrants in all human affairs, whether of nation, corporation, school, or home, will continue to blight the lives of others until people learn enough applied psychology to recognize the personality differences between tyrants and statesmen, between bosses and leaders, between schoolmasters and educators, and between neurotic females and well-adjusted women.

Most thinking persons look out upon a sorely troubled world. The problems of international relations are baffling, and the influences of leaders in international affairs are often discouraging. Furthermore, we can do little or nothing about many of the most discouraging problems at home or beyond our own shores. Even with the best of psychological training, we could not teach the people of a foreign nation to choose or direct their leaders more intelligently. However, through the aid of psychological insight, we, in our own nation and niche in life, can often interpret the most hopeless of situations; and this ability to interpret the mental factors helps to lift us to a more intelligent plane of living.

The ability to recognize psychological currents everywhere and to interpret them intelligently is a most desirable accomplishment. Young people, particularly those who seek to train themselves for the positions of leadership of today, want to see more clearly the human problems in our time. The complexities of our industrial civilization call for a wisdom which the members of this generation have not as yet fully attained.

The stimulating nature of the college situation forces the alert student to ask himself questions such as "How can I get my place in this world straight?" "How can I become a mature adult in the midst of all the possibilities around me?" and "How can I attain a satisfying *identity* of my own?"

Two counselors of college students have pointed out one of the growth tasks of adolescence as

> defining a cognitive map of the universe so that the self, when developed, will have a place to stand. This part of the problem generates the adolescent's brooding interest in abstractions and absolutes: God, Communism, creativity, right, wrong, evolution, relativity and a host of other ideas that are somehow personally important to the boy. By sorting them out, he sorts himself out. This aspect of his growth task is little emphasized in psychodynamic literature; psychiatrists and psychologists both usually tend to overvalue human relations and to understate the importance of purely cognitive understanding of the nature of things.[1]

The psychological problems around us and in our own lives require the aid of all that psychological research can contribute. Fortunately, most students want to become familiar with fundamental facts about themselves as emotional beings and as developing persons in this changing world.

Outstanding Problems That Are Partly of a Psychological Nature

One important kind of psychological problem arises from the fact that our magnificent industrial and technical development has not resulted in equally magnificent emotional satisfactions for many of our citizens. Engineers, scientists, and inventors have produced a technological age which is truly marvelous, but which has not always satisfied the hearts and minds of the men who operate its machines, nor of the customers who benefit from its products. We are like children playing with powerful but somewhat dangerous toys.

Economic insecurity, whether caused by political or other conditions, certainly has an important bearing on emotional insecurity. We must also recognize, however, that economic security does not imply emotional security. Many persons with high incomes feel insecure because of psychological problems that wealth does not solve. Furthermore, unemployment is not entirely an economic problem; many unemployed people have a psychological immaturity which would cause them to be unemployed in any economic system.

Feelings of insecurity may arise from a wide complex of sources as indicated by findings of investigators who have studied emotional problems of students:

> One hears a great deal about security. It has become the golden calf of today. When one stops to analyze what is meant by it, one soon learns that it has little to do with jobs, with income or social status, but is a subjective feeling derived usually from a certain sense of approbation and depending more on self-approbation than on anything else.[2]

The state of mind of any individual is often more important to him than his relationship to the state of the nation or the international situation. When a person is filled with feelings of inadequacy, worry, and anxiety, the lowered self-esteem is likely to produce overwhelming declarations of dependence or as one man phrased it, "a muted cry for help."

The presence in a nation of many persons who have these needs suggests that some are apt to look to some stronger person or to some political system which promises to play the role of all-providing father.

When people lose faith in themselves and their ability to cope with life's problems, they are likely to turn to an untried system of government, a dominant cure-all type of leadership, or to "escape" from the intolerable situation, as is exemplified by some of the drug addicts in this country.

Problems of Students Who Were Not Having Academic Difficulties

When we ask people about their own psychological problems, we find that almost all appear to be living with bothersome worries.

One of the best studies of personal problems of special interest to college students was made of 259 healthy, "normal" students, sophomores at Harvard from four entering classes. The problems reported were either raised by the students themselves or were recognized by the investigating staff. These students were selected for good health, satisfactory academic status, and overtly good social adjustment. They participated voluntarily in the research. With regard to such factors as socio-economic status and race or creed, these students were representative of a fair cross section of the college population. The investigations consisted of the coöperative observations of a physician, several psychiatrists, a physiologist, an anthropologist, a psychologist, and a social case-worker (who interviewed practically all the families as well as the young men themselves).

...In the first place, the students were made to feel that they were helping in the investigation by talking about themselves or asking questions, and that they were not encroaching on anyone's time. In the second place, each participant knew that he would be put through certain routine examinations by different observers: the medical examination, the anthropological measurements, the psychometric tests, the psychiatric interviews, etc. In this way he became aware of different fields in the study of man, and his interest in his personal characteristics was aroused. We could observe a certain educational advantage in the system. Thirdly, he could voluntarily choose any one of the various examiners to discuss matters of concern to him.[3]

The report of the investigators omitted aspects of a boy's life which occurred before college or during postgraduate years and purely medical or other technical aspects that would not be in the sphere of a counselor. Problems resulting from military service, or that could be solved without too much trouble by the person concerned, were also omitted. Ninety per cent, 232 students, had problems they wanted to talk over. See Table 1.1. Twenty-seven men (10 per cent) seemingly had none.

The kinds of problems varied greatly according to individual situations. Most of them centered around social or family relationships. Many men revealed multiple interconnected problems, such as personality difficulties, adjustment to family and friends, college finances, and career. Others revealed only isolated problems in a setting of very sound personality.

The authors pointed out that in an unselected group of college students, more problems would be likely to occur than did in this study, as the selection of students eliminated obvious cases of poor adjustment.

Studies of students of several colleges have been reported. At Brooklyn College, for example, one counselor of students found the following types whom he met with regularly:

(1) The student who cannot study, who complains of inability. (2) The student who is lonely, who cannot make friends. (3) The student who is unable to speak in class. (4) The student without any purpose or vocational aim. (5) The habitual evader, obstructionist, and complainer. (6) The student in acute conflict with his family. (7) The student with a physical defect. (8) Special problems of veterans.[4]

At Bennington, another counselor reported:

One-third came for help because of neurotic or psychosomatic symptoms obviously suggesting an emotional basis.... A quarter came to ask for advice or support in the midst of emancipation battles with the family.... A sixth appeared because of difficulties in college work, varying from almost total failure to take hold of college tasks in spite of good ability to complaints of dawdling and mind-wandering when papers had to be written. Approximately the same number reported maladjustment in the college community or in personal relations....The remainder consulted the psychiatrist for vocational or other practical perplexities...and because of general interest in a personality review.[5]

The classifications used and the emphases in counseling differ somewhat in the reports of studies made over the years but the emotional problems of students seem to be essentially the same in most colleges and time periods.

A common estimate of the proportion of students who require professional psychological or psychiatric assistance is 10 per cent. These seek help. Perhaps an equally great number need such assistance but do not seek

TABLE 1.1

KINDS OF PROBLEMS RAISED

(including both self-offered problems and those recognized by the Staff)

	Number of 259 Participants
1. *Social adjustment* (shyness, feelings of inferiority, social sensitivity, making friends, meeting and getting along with girls, immaturity *per se,* roommates, class dissatisfactions)	113
2. *Adjustments to family*	
a. Parental discord, separation, divorce, remarriage	14
b. Antagonism to parents, reaction to domination or discipline, family criticism, lack of understanding, family relations in general	69
c. Advice concerning physical or mental health of parent	18
d. Adjustment to death of parent	6
3. *Career and life work*	67
4. *Finances in college*	35
5. *Need for discussions centering around subject's personality*	
a. Emotional instability, tenseness, excitability, fears and concerns, "psychoneurotic" symptoms	50
b. Discussions of personality in general, integration of personality, handling of arrogance and egotism	47
c. Need for directions, objectives, purpose, and values	32
d. Mood swings	21
e. Rigidity, "just-so" personality	12
f. Possible mental illness	6
6. *Academic*	
a. Adjustment to Harvard, dissatisfactions with Harvard	20
b. Academic help needed, organization of time and work	14
c. Intellectual lacks for college or career	6
d. Field of concentration (majoring)	3
7. *Sex*	
a. Marriage, love affairs, sex relations	39
b. Problems arising from masturbation	17
c. Need for information concerning homosexuality	3
d. Information about venereal disease	2
8. *Others*	
a. Anti-Semitism, anti-Nazism	8
b. Religious conflict, search for religious belief	8
c. Alcohol	7
d. College scrapes	6
e. General advice needed	6
f. Help in getting job	5
g. Stammering, speech	4
h. Insomnia	3
i. Handwriting	2
j. Extracurricular activities	2
k. Revolt against New England	2
l. Extreme wealth	1

From Clark W. Heath and Lewise W. Gregory, "Problems of Normal College Students and Their Families," *School and Society,* Vol. 63, 355–358.

it. Recently, certain present and former staff members: psychiatrists, psychologists, and other specialists of the Harvard University Health Service, available to those students who present cases of poor adjustment, have written a book about the psychiatric and other problems of students and the ways in which the problems are dealt with by the Health Service. Some of the chapter titles are "Distinguishing Patterns of Student Neuroses," "Problems Connected with Studying," "Student Apathy," and "Emotional Disturbances Among College Women."[6]

Problems That Led to Discharge of Employees

Personal problems that are related to personality also have considerable bearing on one's effectiveness and adjustment to work. In a study at a major oil company, character traits were said to represent 90 per cent of the causes for discharge and 76 per cent of the reasons for which promotion was not granted.[7]

When Alanson H. Edgerton had spent over twelve years in an extensive study of vocational education, he too found that personality and character traits are often more important than skill or intelligence for success in employment. He and his colleagues examined 144,279 actual jobs in 2,630 fields and followed 15,824 youths through ten years of school and work.

Successful employees, he reported, must be versatile. Three-fourths of the employers he questionnaired wanted youths skilled in at least two kinds of work (such as lawyers who also knew banking, or stenographers who could keep books).

But more important than skill or intelligence, he found, is personality. In one sub-survey, studies were made of 3,607 men and women who had lost their jobs. It turned out that 77 per cent had been fired for tactlessness, unfairness, irritability, bad manners, etc. Again, Dr. Edgerton rated a group of job holders for (1) intelligence and (2) personality. The most intelligent 33 per cent earned only $139.44 more per year than the least intelligent; but the highest 33 per cent in personality earned $842.73 more than the lowest.

Specifically, well-liked employees are co-operative, loyal, polite, tactful, friendly, patient, alert, daring, confident, and cheerful.[8]

Psychological Problems of Businessmen

The employees of business are not the only workers who have psychological problems, some of which result in discharge. Executives, too, have their unique problems, both as individuals and as executives.

Business and industrial job failure due to psychological problems is not limited to the lower ranks of workers; many of their problems are shared by those in executive positions, although the greater responsibilities of such jobs create additional psychological hazards.

When we talk about businessmen and their psychological problems, we should recognize that the principles and problems of the mental life are common to all people of our civilized society. Students, business executives, employees, and customers have essentially the same emotions, feelings, and traits as individuals of other classifications. The psychological principles that apply to the person in the school and the home also apply to the same individual in the office and the factory. Basic principles are universal; only settings differ. As students of human behavior, we can be alert to the meanings in a person's behavior regardless of where he may be active.

When a man speaks to us he is always telling us two stories at once even though we commonly attend to but one of them. One is the tale he actually tells, and it may be about anything. The other is a story about himself—the story constituted by the fact that he, under the circumstances present, does tell us just that tale and tells it to us in just the way he does. The style and the matter of a man's speech or of his writings, it has been said, is a picture of what the man is—of his point of view, his character, his intellectual resources, his tastes, his temperament, et al. And all this is exhibited to us, if we but give it our attention, not only when a man expresses himself in language but equally where this mode of expression is of other sorts. How a man walks or sits, what sort of clothes he wears and how he wears them, what sort of house he builds, how he spends his leisure and his money, what he fights for and how he does it, the undertakings to which he devotes himself, the sort of gods he worships, which books he reads, the arts he cultivates and the sorts of products he makes them yield, the modes of conduct and the social institutions which he approves or disapproves—all these things provide us with a picture of the man and of his environment into which we can project ourselves in imagination as effectively as we can into the characters and situations represented in the stories he tells, the plays he acts, or the books he writes.[9]

The person who studies human behavior extensively wherever he finds it learns to see the patternful nature of the individual's activities, and how certain acts in behavior are related to other acts. The person's behavior becomes more meaningful as it fits into basic patterns that characterize the individual. For example, the executive who failed as a youth to learn how to compete in games with other boys is also apt to be unable to endure the presence of rivals in his business relations. Such an executive seldom hires subordinates or assistants who are as able as he. The department head who has ability but surrounds himself with weak personalities is harmful to the business concern and also is a problem to the college graduate who seeks to advance in that executive's department. The student, therefore, should seek to know psychological principles and patterns in behavior wherever he may find them in order that he may be able to use them when needed in business and other settings.

What Psychology Is Not

In Greek mythology, Psyche was represented as a beautiful maiden having the wings of a butterfly. Psyche symbolized the soul. The butterfly symbolized human immortality. Originally psychology, from the root words *psyche,* soul, and *-logy,* a combining form meaning a science—the science of the soul—was a branch of philosophy.

A generation ago psychology severed its formal relations with philosophy and became a science in itself. It no longer studies the soul, nor is it interested in such problems as communication with the dead. Psychology and psychical research are two different fields, and the psychologist does not have very much hope of successful discoveries in *psychic* realms. Psychology has lost its mystical quality. It is not interested in cults or in magical influences on people who happen to be about us. It does not take the place of the witch doctor.

Psychologists are not interested in character analysis from observation of superficial physical signs, except to report that such methods of analyzing people are largely fallacious. Many sales managers mistakenly think that they are psychologists when they try to predict a man's selling ability from the color of his hair or the shape of his chin.

Most psychologists are not interested in mind reading or in thought transference. They have not found that mental telepathy has sound foundations. Investigations of those incidents in the lives of their friends which indicated that mental telepathy might exist usually showed that such experiences were coincidences which occur in the life of everyone. When the psychologists have checked or examined phenomena of this sort, they have found that the apparently mystical should be treated in terms of natural laws.

Nor is psychology a short cut to success in business or in life. Many people who study psychology do so with the hope of finding a talisman for success. It will not make a mentally strong and powerful individual out of a weakling. It is of assistance, of course, in bringing out the latent possibilities of people and in enabling them to adjust themselves to one another; but we should look upon psychology as a science.

What Psychology Is

Psychology is method applied to mental phenomena, not magic. The outstanding approach to the problems of our modern age is our highly developed technique for gaining insight into all aspects of our experiences—namely, the scientific method. Steps in a scientific method are: (a) observation of a chosen phenomenon, (b) accumulation of the facts, (c) noting a pattern among the facts, (d) finding a plausible explanation of the pattern within these facts (hypothesis), (e) making a new prediction on the basis of the plausible explanation, and (f) checking the prediction experimentally—hence increasing or decreasing the belief in the plausible explanation, depending upon whether the new findings agree or disagree with the prediction. Albert Einstein once put it:

> The scientific way of forming concepts differs from that which we use in our daily life, not basically, but merely in the more precise definition of concepts and conclusions; more painstaking and systematic choice of experimental material; and greater logical economy. By this last we mean the effort to reduce all concepts and correlations to as few as possible logically independent basic concepts and axioms.[10]

The use of the scientific method does not reveal absolute laws or ultimate truth. Rather, scientifically developed principles are descriptive statements of relationships observed between events. Each principle, though useful in describing relationships, is subject to further improvement. Scientists do not expect to discover final laws but they do seek progress toward continued enlightenment.

Delicate instruments have been invented to aid the observer in detecting and measuring variations of the phenomena under study. Involved statistical techniques have been developed for treatment of the data. The thousands of scientific studies being made by psychologists and other scientists are slowly modifying our daily work and living. They have already revealed possibilities for utilizing human and physical forces that were not dreamed of by our forefathers. The use of the scientific method for gaining insight has partially displaced unsound methods such as those of superstition and occultism.

Several organizations furnish those research and consulting services which bring various social sciences and management techniques to bear on problems of human relations. F. F. Bradshaw, president of one of these concerns—Richardson, Bellows, Henry & Company, Inc.—stated:

> It has been said that chemistry is the result of the marriage of alchemy with mathematics. Whether or not that is true historically, it is true that the essence of science lies in measurement. Common sense told us that the world was flat, but measurement sent Columbus on his voyage of discovery. Painstakingly, piece by piece, patient scholars have taken man's experience and analyzed, defined, and measured. This is the history of science, and science is a foundation of modern civilization.
>
> Sometimes people mistakenly assume that science is a body of fact. It is more than fact—it is measurement, prediction, and control. Sometimes ignorant people have insisted that science was fiction, especially wherein it was not fact. There is a vast difference, however, between fiction and theory—between simple prediction based on hunch and wish and scientific prediction based on measurement.[11]

We now define psychology as the "study of human behavior by scientific methods." *Behavior,* as used here, refers to more than conduct, deportment, or manner. It includes all normal and abnormal activities of the whole organism, even those of feeblemindedness and insanity. *The aims of applied psychology are the description, prediction, and control of human activities in order that we may understand and direct intelligently our own lives and influence the lives of others.*

Psychology is a most useful study because every man must live with himself and with others. Even though a person never studies it as a science, his every thought and act illustrate its principles. To live means to function, and behavior is the material of psychology. The unit of study is the individual.

Of course, a person may live a pleasant life and never study himself or his behavior. An angleworm and a cow are presumably content, but we have no evidence to indicate that they are intelligently happy. Happiness for the modern man demands more than mere organismic contentment. He wants to be physically comfortable, but he also wishes to know the laws of mental life, the principles of human behavior, so that he may utilize them for new satisfactions. Our present civilization rests upon the basis: "Let us study life and its conditions so that we may utilize our findings to rise to new and more intelligent levels of personal satisfactions and social relationships."

Every person is something of a psychologist. The roots of the subject are as old as the human species. However, modern scientific psychology is a relatively recent development. The first American laboratory was started in 1883 at Johns Hopkins University, and in 1889 the first title of "Professor of Psychology" was bestowed upon William James by Harvard University.[12]

Present-day psychologists pride themselves on their use of the scientific method. Formerly, it was not unheard of to set up a law after making a hypothesis. Now the accent is on objectivity and quantitative data. Statisticians and psychologists have collaborated to achieve scientific methodology. They have made possible the objective appraisal of facts with a minimum of subjectivity by devising methods of treating quantities of data to ascertain whether they have any real significance. A classic example is the concept of correlation, by which it is possible to compute what relationship one factor or group of factors bears to another factor or group of factors. The last chapter of this book presents a few of the more simple statistical techniques in use today.

Another method by which experiments are made more scientific and yield dependable conclusions is the use of control groups in experimental groups of subjects. Use of a control group with an experimental group makes it possible to learn which factors under investigation have a bearing on the findings. Animals are used frequently as subjects by some experimental psychologists because of the impracticability of running certain types of experiments on human beings. Through such experiments it has been possible to learn about important aspects of drives and motivations, effects of thwarting, and problem-solving behavior, for example. Caution must always be exercised, however, in generalizing that results obtained from animal experiments apply also to human beings.

In addition to the basic methodological tools already mentioned, such as statistics and experimental and control groups, there are secondary tools such as rating scales, morale and attitude surveys, readership surveys, the polling of selected samples or panels, and objective and projective tests.

Some psychologists who are particularly interested in personality and characteristic behavior have developed schools of thought or theories regarding it. Other psychologists are inclined to an eclectic view, and take some phase from each school or theory into their own thinking. There is much general agreement, however; as, for example, on the viewpoint that all types of personality deviate from the statistical "average" to a greater or lesser extent, and that all behavior is adjustive, although not necessarily successfully so.

Each person adjusts himself to his world in his own way. Average or so-called normal behavior is really only theoretical. There is no sharp division between normal and abnormal behavior. Behavior considered normal might be said to represent that of more than half of the people in a society. The other people differ more and more from the normal. Although such a definition would be but one of several possible and arbitrary ones, it should be understood that atypical behavior refers to the less common methods of adjustment in a particular culture.

When a person's behavior is so far removed from the norm of his society as to make him or society uncomfortable, psychotherapy is often indicated. This is a job for clinical psychologists, who utilize the work of experimental and other psychologists. To guide the process of therapy, clinical psychologists employ various diagnostic methods—tests to aid in ascertaining the dynamics underlying behavior, and devices that yield specific information, such as the encephalogram, a record of brain waves that reveals whether certain disorders are functional or due to epilepsy or brain tumors.

So much work has been done by psychologists that only certain major divisions can be treated in any course in applied psychology. The divisions chosen for consideration here, because of their probable value to the student as a student and as a potential leader, are the following:

Personality

Students who are interested in improving their personalities—and most students are—are especially interested in principles that underlie personality development. Much serious work has been done in this field to ascertain relationships between environment, experience, natural endowments, the physical (organic) state of the individual, and his personality. As yet there are few final answers, although many hypotheses are being explored.

The oft-used terms "introvert" and "extravert" usually intrigue students. If they have come by some means to believe that they are either introverts or extraverts, they want to know whether it is possible for them to change. Here again they should be warned that extraversion and introversion represent positions on a continuum. Most people are neither one type nor the other; they have some introverted characteristics and some extraverted ones. It is the tendency to display more of one characteristic pattern of behavior than the other that makes a person introverted or extraverted. In view of this fact, is a person doomed to remain one personality type, or can he change? The answer is that he can change, provided he can acquire new insights that enable him to develop new behavior patterns.

Personal Problems

Mental Efficiency and Effective Study

Also of special interest to the student are his problems in mental efficiency and effective study habits. Since these are largely a function of the personality in action, a person with new insights can improve his habits in this area of activity. Experiments on the nature and methods of learning have revealed some helpful suggestions for every student.

Vocational Adjustment

The psychological problems of the student do not end with the completion of his college work. He must earn a living, as a professional worker or a businessman, most probably as an employee who has ambitions for himself as a supervisor, manager, or owner.

Vocational guidance has become more successful with the improvement of counseling techniques and the development of interest, aptitude, and achievement tests. Many schools require the student to take a battery of tests to ascertain wherein his abilities and interests lie and whether they are compatible with his educational record. Likewise, many employers test job applicants before hiring them to ascertain whether they are qualified for the job they desire and whether they meet the company's standards. Improved testing procedures to estimate the potentialities of applicants are becoming available.

Test-score profiles have been developed in an attempt to derive objective standards of interests, aptitudes, and abilities for various types of jobs. These profiles show certain characteristics that are typical of workers in the various types of occupations. Success in a vocation, however, cannot be guaranteed or predicted absolutely on the basis of test results alone. Again, success is a function of the whole personality.

Tests of ability and aptitude that are used in hiring are too numerous to mention here (see Chapter 16). The trend, however, is in the direction of trying to make sure that new employees will fit harmoniously into the organization from the personality standpoint as well as be able to do the work.

Courtship and Marriage

Although a few psychologists have tried to develop criteria for ascertaining in advance whether a marriage will be successful, it has proved to be a difficult task. Some remarkably interesting studies have been made, however, and certain trends characteristic of successful and unsuccessful marriages have been found. Marriage is no different from any other social situation in which a person may find himself. He must adjust himself, not depend on outside forces to do it for him.

Child Guidance

Most students, unless they are already parents, have little interest in child psychology. And yet one of the best ways to understand the adult is to understand the child. Research centers and individuals concentrating on the study of child psychology are responsible for many valuable contributions to the field of psychology as a whole. Of primary importance is the growing appreciation of the importance of childhood experience because of its effects on character and personality. Also highly important is the conclusion that no matter what the overt behavior pattern of the child, it is his way of adjusting to his world. This is as true of the "naughty" child as of the "good" child. Psychologists have also taught parents the importance of maturation in the child's learning and activities, so that children are now less likely to be pushed beyond their stage of development than they formerly were.

Dealing with Employees

Interviewing

Although applied industrial and business psychologists have done a great deal of work to determine the criteria of successful interviews and to ascertain how they can be made more diagnostic, most interviews are still conducted in a casual manner and without a basic framework of thinking on the part of the interviewer. Such unsystematic ways of interviewing permit only subjective analyses, whereas new interview procedures make the evaluation of interview findings more objective and significant. (See Chapter 15.)

Merit Ratings

Various methods of deriving appraisals of employees and of informing them about their work have been studied. Anyone who aspires to become a responsible executive should become acquainted with these findings.

Motivating Employees

To give management the "know-how" to motivate employees in the direction of improved efficiency and greater productivity, the American Management Association and other organizations are bringing to the attention of management the results of psychological investigations that deal with human motivations. By this means psychologists are giving managements the opportunity to make employees happier and more productive with improved results for both. Psychologists in collaboration with progressive managements have made time studies and measured fatigue, effects of noise, lighting, and so forth. They have studied accident control, job evaluation, and values of different wage payment systems. Training courses for supervisors have been developed by psychologists.

Communications and Group Dynamics

Years ago when one man owned and managed a company, an employee could walk into his office and get a decision or the boss' point of view in a hurry. But that was before the days of mass production. Now the man at the roll-top desk is only a memory. His counterpart today is the management chart—indicative of the many groups which participate in running a plant. Decisions are influenced and made at many different points in the complex structure of management, production, engineering, and sales. As a result, many members of the organization are uninformed or misinformed. Unexpected dynamic forces arise

***New American Psychological Association Headquarters** building at 17th and M Streets, Washington, D.C., occupied in the fall of 1964.*

The American Psychological Association maintains an office in Washington, D.C. It is the coordinating center for all APA activities. Journal subscriptions, membership applications, personnel placement requests, and general APA business procedures are handled in this office. The staff is always glad to answer inquiries from the members and the general public.

*The American Psychological Association, founded in 1892 and incorporated in 1925, is the major psychological organization in the United States. With approximately 22,000 members as of January 1, 1965, it includes most of the qualified psychologists in the country. The purpose of the APA is to advance psychology as a science, as a profession, and as a means of promoting human welfare. It attempts to further these objectives by holding annual meetings, publishing psychological journals, and working toward improved standards for psychological training and service. It also publishes a monthly **Employment Bulletin** containing notices of vacancies and situations wanted, and an annual **Directory** of members.*

In order to give recognition to the specialized interests of different psychologists, the APA includes appropriate Divisions: Any person, after becoming a member of the APA, may apply for membership in as many Divisions as he wishes. The Division numbers and the number of members in each are: 1. Division of General Psychology, 857; 2. Division on the Teaching of Psychology, 1287; 3. Division of Experimental Psychology, 863; 5. Division of Evaluation and Measurement, 698; 6. Division of Physiological and Comparative Psychology, 353; 7. Division of Developmental Psychology, 690; 8. Division of Personality and Social Psychology, 2392; 9. The Society for the Psychological Study of Social Issues, 1030; 10. Division on Esthetics, 137; 12. Division of Clinical Psychology, 2737; 13. Division of Consulting Psychology, 510; 14. Division of Industrial Psychology, 832; 15. Division of Educational Psychology, 1317; 16. Division of School Psychologists, 840; 17. Division of Counseling Psychology, 1189; 18. Division of Psychologists in Public Service, 363; 19. Division of Military Psychology, 323; 20. Division on Maturity and Old Age, 235; 21. The Society of Engineering Psychologists, 316; 22. Division on Psychological Aspects of Disability, 819; 23. Division on Consumer Psychology, 215; 24. Division of Philosophical Psychology, 344.

within work groups. Supervisors and workers develop misunderstandings and frictions.

Methods of improving communication between modern managements and workers are becoming increasingly essential. Group dynamics require special attention. The team approach to industrial relations has grown with mass production technology.

Dealing with Consumers

Automation and related technological advances are increasing our production potentials to so high a level that it is becoming increasingly necessary for us to develop new and bigger markets. Psychologists are therefore being called upon to assist in finding markets through the discovery and stimulation of consumer wants. Consumers are being studied as never before by means of improved interviewing and other research techniques.

Advertising and Selling

The most effective methods of advertising, from the standpoint of both the consumer and the advertiser, are being studied. Readership reports directed by such psychologists as Daniel Starch, and new mechanical methods such as eye cameras, have increased advertising effectiveness for each dollar spent.

These are a few examples of the kinds of positive contributions that psychologists have been making to daily life and work.

The very fact that more than one thousand psychologists were called upon to help solve wartime problems of a practical nature indicated that abstract knowledge of psychology and scientific methods is not a useless luxury in a desperately chaotic world. Rather, consulting psychologists in business are increasing in numbers and importance because of the contributions they can make toward the solutions of current problems.

The applied psychologist is a specialist who integrates the principles and other findings of psychologists who have special interests, such as those of experimental, social, and educational psychology. He adapts and uses these principles and findings in practical situations. He applies them to personal problems of the individual and to the problems of other specialists, such as the executive in business.

Psychologists in Business

Corporate hiring has not sought as intensively to fill the need for psychologists as it has to recruit its other professionals, such as engineers. In recent years, however, some business executives have called with increasing frequency upon psychologists and have invited them to assist in dealing with business problems, to act as consultants, and to work full-time in their organizations.

Gradually, managements are recognizing that they need more information on how people and groups in business interact. Businessmen today rely on data concerning cost-of-living, turnover, car loadings, retail sales and many other varieties of economic conditions. Eventually, business managements will also depend upon behavioral data concerning human conditions for guidance in making decisions.[13]

Accurate data on the number of psychologists who are now employed on a full-time basis in business is not available.

The professional interests of American psychologists can be deduced to some extent from data on their memberships in the several divisions of the American Psychological Association. As shown by the data on page 12, the number of psychologists who are members of the Division of Industrial and Business Psychology is considerably smaller than the number who belong to the Division of Clinical Psychology.

The several divisions of The Psychological Corporation's services are also indicative of the interests of psychologists and the areas of business in which they operate.

About one half of all Association members are employed by colleges and universities. In comparison with a generation ago, the number of applied psychologists is growing but the number of professionally trained psychologists in business will continue to be a small percentage of the total number of trained workers.

It is obvious that very few college students will become *business psychologists*. Few psychology majors will ever wear the label, occupationally speaking, which they had as a major in their college studies. In this respect, psychology is similar to mathematics. Very few students who major in mathematics ever have the occupational designation of

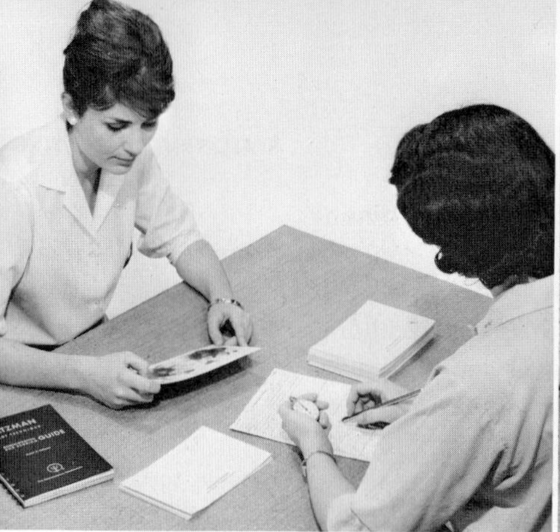

Aptitude tests *help business and industry find the right person for the right job and aid individuals in selecting the kinds of educational programs and careers in which they are most likely to be successful. Here a young man is taking the mechanical reasoning part of the Differential Aptitude Test.*

Administration *of the Holtzman Inkblot Technique, a relatively new projective technique published by The Psychological Corporation. These inkblots offer the clinical sensitvity of the original Rorschach blots combined with more objective scoring based on analysis of large numbers of protocols using modern computer processes.*

Here a counselor *is talking about the profile of scores obtained by a high school student on The Psychological Corporation's widely used Differential Aptitude Tests.*

The Psychological Corporation *was founded in 1921 by 20 eminent psychologists to extend applications of psychology in business, industry, education, government, and welfare. It is directed and managed by professional psychologists and its ownership is shared by more than 400 psychologists in business and industry, schools and colleges, clinics, public agencies, and private practice.*

Test Division*—Develops, publishes, and distributes educational and psychological tests, for example—Academic Promise Tests, Differential Aptitude Tests, Minnesota Multiphasic Personality Inventory, Wechsler Intelligence Scales, Miller Analogies Test, Mechanical Comprehension Tests, and Edwards Personal Preference Schedule—for use in schools, colleges, industry, psychological clinics, and social agencies.*

Professional Examinations Division*—Conducts the Medical College Admission Test and Dental Hygiene Aptitude Test programs; conducts entrance examination programs for schools of nursing, practical nursing, veterinary medicine, and pharmacy; conducts the Evaluation Program for Biological Sciences Curriculum Study; provides testing services to scholarship agencies, certification boards, and industrial organizations.*

Industrial Division*—Specializes in professional psychological services to business and industry designed to help utilize manpower resources most effectively; services include psychological evaluations, interviewer training, and management and personnel surveys.*

Personnel and Marketing Research Division*—Applies psychological principles and the results of research studies in the areas of personnel selection and training, attitude and morale, job evaluation and compensation; in addition, continues marketing and social research services in the broad fields of consumer motivation and behavior, and communication.*

Experimental Laboratory*—Undertakes research projects in applied psychology; principal current activities are the development of digital test scoring machines, research in logical abilities including the validation of methods of identifying individuals who are especially qualified for assignment to problem-solving tasks such as computer programming.*

The offices of The Psychological Corporation are located at 304 East 45th Street, New York 17, New York.

mathematician, even though they use mathematics in their work. They are more likely to be called engineers, accountants, statisticians, or clerical workers; although they use mathematics constantly, they think of themselves, and their employers think of them, as trained in some business field, such as accounting, production, or selling. Similarly, students of psychology who go into business are likely to find many applications of their psychological knowledge even though they are not classified on a payroll as psychologists.

Very few students can ever hope to become expert psychologists who will solve psychological problems for business firms, but all who enter business should hope to improve their knowledge of psychological principles and techniques, to become more intelligent mem-

Applied psychology *has become so useful in modern industry that several organizations of consulting psychologists have offices in industrial centers. Rohrer, Hibler Replogle, founded in 1945, is an international firm of professional psychologists serving management. It operates offices in some twenty cities of this country as well as in several foreign cities. The photograph above was taken at the sixteenth annual staff meeting.*

Compare the ages of the men in the foreground with those in the back row—some of the members of the back row will probably move to the front as their abilities mature. Minimum professional training is the doctoral degree. Additional requirements are broad, rather than narrow, training in psychology, sincere interest and skill in teaching others, service mindedness, and intellectual honesty.

bers of the business team. Human relations problems in industry are rarely solved by lone experts—they are solved by the members of a team. As one industrial psychiatrist has stated:

But how *do* you deal with people? Where and when do you deal with people? I want to nail down once and for all the fact that the problem of human relations in any industry, department store, government agency, educational institution or any other place where there is supervision of people, is solved by a team approach. Everybody in management is responsible at some time for the development of effective human relationships. . . .

The determining factor in what people feel and think is the kind of treatment they get on the daily job in millions of work places. Their satisfaction or dissatisfaction with the spiritual take-home as well as the financial take-home, will be their criteria for judging the worth of working.[14]

Each member of the team can, of course, improve his sensitivity to the ways people feel and think. He can improve his knowledge and skills as well as his awareness of psychological factors in daily situations. He can become acquainted with the findings of researches as reported in current texts and in journals such as *The Journal of Applied Psychology.*

Psychology Should Contribute toward Adjustment to Change

Certainly, we cannot stop changes such as those of automation any more than we can stop time. Almost every change which benefits some persons or industries brings new psychological problems to others. No one can prevent these changes which, in the long run, seem to spell progress. Nor would many care to turn back to the former modes of living, when life was simpler but everyone worked seventy hours a week and had to amuse himself by attending funerals and spelling bees. Every individual, stupid or intelligent, is jostled by the technological and social forces that surround him. What then can the intelligent individual do about it, if anything? What can he gain for this purpose from a study of psychology? A suggested major objective for the educated person of today is personal development in two important respects:

(a) To learn about the *modern techniques*

involved in dealing with people, such as the clinical method of analyzing personalities, tests in hiring applicants, rating scales in promoting employees, recent developments in supervising employees, predicting consumers' wants, influencing groups of people, using clarifying statistics, and other factual methods. These are examples of knowledge that may be learned through college classroom approaches.

(b) To gain something more important than knowledge only, namely, the mental quality which we term *adaptability on the part of the individual himself.* This means that he must catch the spirit of the age in which he lives and become an intelligent participant in the changes taking place about him.

Of course, no man can foresee all the great changes that will occur in the later years of his life, but he can adapt himself to the changes occurring in his own time and place. His guiding attitude should be that of expecting changes and preparing to meet them. A fundamental psychological purpose for the intelligent individual, regardless of sex, vocation, or environment, is that of adjusting himself to the accelerated rates of change taking place about him.

Adaptability is far more than knowledge. It is a mental habit that can be acquired by anyone who really seeks it. *Adaptability is the habit of finding and using opportunities in the environment and following not the lines of least resistance but those of greatest opportunity.* The habit of acquiring new points of view, new skills, new facts, and new habits can be learned. Everyone can to some extent travel, attend classes, read books, see moving pictures, listen to the radio, talk with others, and learn new ideas from various other available sources. However, more besides travel, education, and social contacts is necessary to bring about adaptability in one's self. Conscious recognition of one's mental habits or adjustments and intelligent direction of self-growth are most important. These principles will be treated in Chapters 2 to 8.

Once a person recognizes the importance of adaptability and then studies the principles of adjustment, he will discover how his psychological tendencies and habits can be modified in the direction of greater adaptability. The age-old laws of evolution are still with us. The struggle for existence is not new; only its form has changed. The machine has only accelerated the rate of change and accentuated the need for a certain kind of psychological development in order to capitalize the changes for individual benefit.

The individual who recognizes these rapidly changing conditions and their mental requirements may have two sustaining convictions. These are that the world still has many unsolved problems, and that determination to help solve an immediate problem always has been and always will be a worthwhile goal. Anyone can find self-expression in solving a near-by problem in his work through the three following channels of direct attack:

1. Improving the mechanical equipment.
2. Improving the methods of operating the equipment or of doing the work.
3. Improving the human relationships.

The fact that the worker in the past got much of his feeling of worthful participation from his craftsmanship does not mean that the present-day worker cannot achieve the same feeling. Anything now being done could be done better, more easily, more economically, or more pleasingly. For example, a stenographer cannot hope to improve the typewriter or office machine she uses, but she can always improve her methods of work.

The same situation applies to businessmen, teachers, and students. Many young people have not learned how to gain creative self-expression through the three general channels of improvement because the books they have read, the courses they have taken, and the diplomas they have earned do not require development of adaptability. Some of their studies have taught them to criticize life as it is. Few have learned to recognize the rapidly changing conditions under which we live, to feel in control of themselves, to tackle sys-

***Psychologists often work with** industrial relations and other executives. Here is an example from the International Harvester Company plant. The members of the group include, left to right around the table: a division superintendent; works auditor; the company psychologist who is in charge of personnel research and testing; works manager; a consulting psychologist, Prof. C. H. Lawshe, of Purdue University; the plant training director; and another company psychologist on the extreme right of the table. The meeting dealt with an attitude survey and ways of gaining employee and company benefits from it.*

tematically the problems of the immediate job, and to become adaptable. Every man with a job and a steady income should assume that he may some day lose the job and his income. Every girl who marries should assume that she may some day become a widow and have to earn her own living. No one can prevent catastrophe, but every intelligent person can prepare himself psychologically to deal with catastrophe.

Our ultimate dependence cannot be on systems of government or business, but on ourselves as individuals. Life and civilization always have been and always will be dangerous. Dangers change only their form. The entire history of civilization is one long series of crises. Some individuals who survived were only fortunate; others were intelligent. The spirited man is still master of his fate.

Some years ago when the *Titanic* sped across the Atlantic on her maiden voyage, she struck an iceberg and sank. One American newspaper cartoonist of unusual insight drew two contrasting illustrations of the tragedy. One drawing showed the ship broken and about to sink. Underneath that picture were the words: "The weakness of man—the supremacy of nature." The other drawing illustrated how a certain passenger stepped aside to give his place in the last lifeboat to a woman with a child. This picture had the words: "The weakness of nature—the supremacy of man."

Adaptability is far more than knowledge. It depends upon the ability to control one's habits and to change them intelligently. To do this, the individual needs the self-knowledge which psychology can often contribute. In the next few chapters we shall examine certain mental habits that inhibit and others that facilitate adaptability and thereby gain that insight which contributes to man's supremacy over himself as well as over nature.

ACKNOWLEDGMENTS AND REFERENCES

1. Graham B. Blaine, Jr., and Charles C. McArthur, *Emotional Problems of the Student* (New York: Appleton-Century-Crofts, 1961), p. 94.
2. *Ibid,* p. 175. From Chapter 10, by Carl A. L. Binger.
3. Clark W. Heath and Lewise W. Gregory, "Problems of Normal College Students and Their Families," *School and Society,* 63 (1946), 355–358. This whole investigation was part of the Grant Study, 1938–1942.
4. P. Blos, "Psychological Counseling of College Students," *American Journal of Orthopsychiatry,* 16 (1946), 571–580.
5. Joseph Chassell, "Individual Counseling of College Students," *Journal of Consulting Psychology,* November-December, 1940. For summaries of this and related studies, see next reference, No. 6, below.
6. Graham B. Blaine, Jr., and Charles C. McArthur with 12 Contributing Authors, *Emotional Problems of the Student* (New York: Appleton-Century-Crofts, 1961).
7. Karl A. and W. C. Menninger, *Business Week,* Nov. 5, 1955, p. 94.
8. *Newsweek,* April 1, 1940, p. 39.
9. C. J. Ducasse, "Are the Humanities Worth Their

Keep?" *American Scholar,* 6, No. 4 (1937), 467–468.
10. Albert Einstein, "The Fundaments of Theoretical Physics," *Science,* 91 (1940).
11. F. F. Bradshaw, "Management Science—Neither Fiction Nor Fact," *Advanced Management,* September, 1955, p. 4.
12. Emily S. Dexter and Katharine T. Omwake, *An Introduction to the Field of Psychology* (Englewood Cliffs, N. J.: Prentice-Hall, Inc., 1938), p. 1.
13. See statement by Mason Haire, *Business Week,* June 2, 1956, p. 126.
14. Ralph T. Collins, M.D., Psychiatrist, Medical Dept., Eastman Kodak Company, "Psychiatry and Industry," *Mental Hygiene News,* New York State, November, 1954, p. 4.

PROJECTS

1. No single textbook can possibly supply all the information now published in the field of applied psychology. Hence you should examine and note differences in the tables of contents of any of the following applied psychology textbooks that may be available in your library:

   Bellows, Roger M., *Psychology of Personnel in Business and Industry,* (3rd ed.). Englewood Cliffs, N.J.: Prentice-Hall, Inc., 1961.

   Burtt, H. E., *Applied Psychology,* (2nd ed.). Englewood Cliffs, N.J.: Prentice-Hall, Inc., 1957.

   Fleishman, Edwin A., *Studies in Personnel and Industrial Psychology.* Homewood, Ill.: The Dorsey Press, Inc., 1961.

   Ghiselli, Edwin E. and Clarence W. Brown, *Personnel and Industrial Psychology.* New York: McGraw-Hill Book Company, 1955.

   Gilmer, B. von Haller, *Industrial Psychology.* New York: McGraw-Hill Book Company, 1961.

   Harrell, Thomas Willard, *Industrial Psychology.* New York: Holt, Rinehart & Winston, Inc., 1958.

   Maier, Norman R. F., *Psychology in Industry.* Boston: Houghton Mifflin Company, 1955.

   Poffenberger, A. T., *Principles of Applied Psychology.* New York: Appleton-Century-Crofts, Inc., 1942.

   Smith, Henry Clay, *Psychology of Industrial Behavior.* New York: McGraw-Hill Book Company, 1955.

2. Visit your library and examine the periodicals that might be of special value to the person who studies applied psychology. List the titles and content of several articles that appeal to you. Quote parts which you find interesting or of value to you. Be prepared to describe your findings to other students.

3. Do you know an adult who has been unemployed or irregularly employed for several years? Describe his psychological characteristics. Did unemployment cause his psychological problem, or did psychological problems cause his unemployment? Discuss.

4. Examine books and journals for descriptions of the work done by The Psychological Corporation. Perhaps you can obtain a copy of a recent year-end annual report.

5. Examine biographies and autobiographies of famous contemporary leaders. Point out any relationships between the leader's psychological characteristics and his policies or achievements. Read books such as E. S. Bogardus, *Leaders and Leadership,* New York: Appleton-Century-Crofts, Inc., 1934.

6. How does training to be a business technician differ from training to be a business leader?

7. A professor of astronomy in a large university frequently receives letters asking for astrological advice, such as: "My son was born under the sign of Taurus. He is contemplating joining the Navy. Will his life be safe?" Assume that you are the astronomer and compose a brief letter to the mother.

8. Many scientists believe that human nature and the social sciences have not kept pace with the physical and chemical sciences. Some have suggested that we should retard certain sciences until human beings catch up with them. What arguments can you present for or against the suggestion? Should we choose the goal of improving human adaptability to keep pace with developments in all fields?

COLLATERAL READINGS

Bellows, Roger M., *Psychology of Personnel in Business and Industry,* (2nd ed.). Englewood Cliffs, N.J.: Prentice-Hall, Inc., 1954, Chapters 1 and 2.

Harrell, Thomas Willard, *Industrial Psychology.* New York: Holt, Rinehart & Winston, Inc., 1958, Chapters 1 and 3.

Meltzer, H., "Industrial Psychology in Psychological Abstracts," *Journal of Applied Psychology,* April, 1960.

Shaffer, Laurance F. and Edward J. Shoben, Jr., *The Psychology of Adjustment.* Boston: Houghton Mifflin Company, 1956, Chapter 1.

Smith, Henry Clay, *Psychology of Industrial Behavior.* New York: McGraw-Hill Book Company, 1955, Chapter 1.

The Psychologist in Industry. New York: Research Institute of America, Inc., 1959.

The "bundle of nerves" *person may need medical or psychological treatment, and should consult trained specialists in those fields; unfortunately, those who have to live with emotionally unstable, neurotic, or poorly adjusted persons do not have specialists from whom they can learn how to live comfortably in these relationships. The normally healthy and well-adjusted persons have to adapt themselves as best they can. To make the adaptation, a great deal of insight and patience must be acquired. Eventually, too, it often becomes necessary for the healthier individuals to develop a personal philosophy which recognizes that our associations with difficult personalities force us to strengthen our own personalities. We grow through positive adjustments to our problem friends and situations. The strengths we acquire through our relations with them enable us to attain satisfactions that would not come to us through ease. Furthermore, our insight into their adjustments helps us gain greater insight into our own, and we therefore evaluate our psychological kinships more intelligently and more highly.*

PART II

UNDERSTANDING THE INDIVIDUAL'S BEHAVIOR THROUGH THE ADJUSTMENT CONCEPT

CHAPTER TWO

THE PROBLEM PERSON IS A PERSON WITH A PROBLEM

The forms of behavior which we are apt to classify as inappropriate or abnormal really have important meanings for dealing with ourselves as well as others. The behavior of the problem person is not merely the effect of environment or the age in which he lives. It always has purpose for the individual. It is part of his pattern of adjustment to his problems. A first step in appreciating the real meaning of the behavior patterns that characterize an individual's personality is to become aware of the problems in his psychological development. When we recognize patterns of adjustment we can improve the appreciation of our best potentials for our own development. And we should be able to deal more intelligently with the problem persons whom we meet in life and work.

The people of this nation have made some very great gains in bodily health and personal comforts in recent years. Material advantages, such as ownership of automobiles and indoor plumbing, have increased tremendously. The expectation of life at birth has steadily increased since the turn of the century, largely as a result of the control of infectious diseases, which formerly took a heavy toll of lives among infants, children, and young adults. Educational opportunities have improved for the boy and girl. In 1900, the average American youth's chances of going to high school were one in ten. Fifty years later, they were eight in ten. These and numerous other advancements might be cited as evidence of the progress of the American people. But what about their mental health?

Some Figures on Mental Maladjustment

At least one person in every ten has some form of mental or emotional illness (mild to severe) that needs therapeutic treatment. Mental or emotional maladjustment is also known to be an important factor in many physical illnesses—at least 50 per cent of all medical and surgical cases treated by private physicians and hospitals have a mental illness complication. There are as many people in hospitals with mental illnesses, at any one time, as with all other diseases combined. And the number of persons admitted for psychiatric treatment in mental hospitals and in the psychiatric sections of general hospitals each year is greater than the number of students who receive earned degrees from our colleges.

Of course mental health and illness should be viewed in terms of degree rather than as complete presence or absence. An eight-year psychiatric study of a midtown Manhattan area was made by a Cornell University Medical College team of researchers. The study involved a cross-section of an East Side residential neighborhood adjoining the central business district. Approximately 175,000 persons lived in the 190-block area surveyed.

Using a detailed and carefully prepared questionnaire, specially trained interviewers probed into the backgrounds and symptoms of 1,660 residents of the area. The interviews were evaluated on a scale from zero for "well" to six for totally incapacitated. The evaluating psychiatrists came within one step (out of seven ratings) of each other in 86.7 per cent of the cases. Complete agreement was found 47.2 per cent of the time.

Only 18.5 per cent of those aged 25–59 were sufficiently free from symptoms to be considered "well." Impairment of life functioning was found in 23.4 per cent who had marked, severe, or incapacitating symptoms.

Personal data were used to assess the relationship to mental illness and defect of such factors as age, sex and marital status, socioeconomic status, rural-urban origins, and national and religious origins. Some of the findings follow.

Well	18.5%
Mild symptom formation	36.3
Moderate symptom formation	21.8
Marked symptom formation	13.2*
Severe symptom formation	7.5*
Incapacitated	2.7*
*Impaired	23.4%[1]

One of the most striking facts revealed by the Midtown study is that of those persons who fell into the last three categories and could therefore be classified as "impaired," approximately three-fourths never received any professional care, nor were they even known to professionals. Twenty per cent of these people may have received some professional treatment, but it was never adequate for complete cure. Only five per cent of the impaired had received relatively constant aid and treatment. Just as the base and largest part of an iceberg lies submerged beneath the surface of the water, the great mass of persons suffering from acute mental disorders and in need of help are hidden from the view of professional care.[2]

Many persons who read statistics such as

1903 vs. 1960, Table 2.1, regarding the increasing numbers of people who are in need of treatment for mental disorders assume that the causes of mental illness stem from the fast tempo of modern life.

The idea that the hustle and bustle of modern life are responsible for the occurrence of mental diseases is not so convincing when explorers report that the natives of many primitive societies with more simple cultures suffer from the same mental diseases that are found among us.

Researchers have found it difficult to prove that the "faster pace" of city living in this country is an important factor in causing mental illness. However, in a study to see if the rates of crime, suicide, and psychiatric illness would be greater in an urban community than in a rural one, it was discovered that the rates were higher in the city, although by a small margin: 3.8/1,000 vs. 2.6/1,000. This study also revealed that in the urban community, society is more likely to commit the mentally ill to institutions or to professional care. Perhaps this is because the city dwellers have less time to spend in taking care of the less seriously disturbed mentally ill, or because they have greater access to mental health facilities. In general, people of the rural areas seem more tolerant of mental illness in the community, and this may account for the difference in the figures. The most unusual fact revealed by this study, and one which it could not explain, was that in the rural areas, women outnumbered men in all categories of mental illness except suicide.[3]

Statistical changes that occur in our national picture from time to time can be attributed to factors such as (1) our increased awareness of mental illness has led to the discovery of more cases; (2) a larger proportion of our population is now reaching the higher-age groups where the rates of admission are also highest (see the accompanying chart); (3) more of those who need it can now be hospitalized because the space available has been increased; and (4) an increasing proportion of old people are being hospitalized in nursing and convalescent homes. Formerly, many of these were sent to hospitals for the mentally ill.

Mental Hospital Patients

Resident patients in hospitals for psychiatric care totaled 602,558 in 1961. Between 1903 and 1955 resident patients rose from 185.5 to 388.7 per 100,000 civilian population. This rate, however, decreased each subsequent year to 332.6 in 1961. This decrease has occurred largely in the resident patient population of the state and local government hospitals.

TABLE 2.1

RESIDENT PATIENTS BY TYPE OF HOSPITAL FOR MENTAL ILLNESS

		Rate per 100,000 population	
Fiscal Year	*Number of Mental Patients at End of Year*	*All Hospitals*	*State and Local Government Mental Hospitals*
1903	149,596	185.5	178.7
1940	477,907	363.7	330.0
1950	578,639	384.9	339.9
1960	611,432	343.2	300.6
1961	602,558	332.6	291.1

Source: "New Approaches to Mental Retardation and Mental Illness," *Health, Education and Welfare Indicators,* U.S. Department of Health, Education, and Welfare, November, 1963.

Current hospitalization trends for both public and private mental hospitals give some idea of the task to be accomplished in mobilizing our resources in the battle against mental illness. (See chart and Table 2.1). Since 1956, the public (state and local) mental hospital population has been decreasing steadily by an average annual rate of 1.1 per cent to 516,000 at the end of 1962. During this same period (1956–1962) the total number of admissions rose by 85,000—46 per cent—to a high of 271,000, while net live releases from public mental hospitals increased by 86,000, or 59 per cent, to 231,000. However, public mental

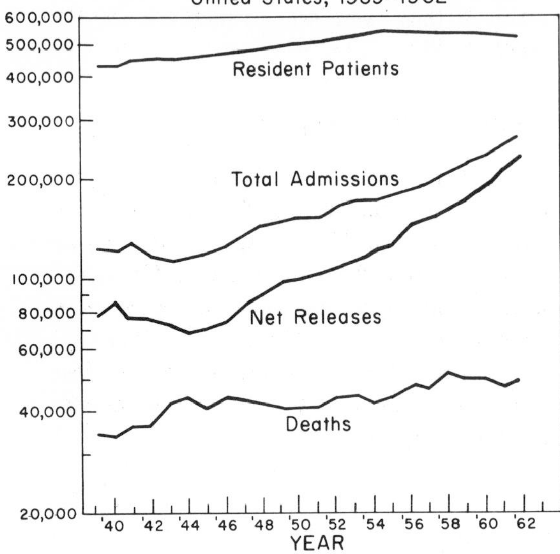

hospital facilities are actually being utilized to a greater extent than ever before due to a steady increase in both first admissions and readmissions. The over-all decline in resident hospital population, while encouraging, must be viewed in terms of the entire context of the needs in the field of mental disorders.

Recent declines are attributable in large measure to the new knowledge derived from research, improved treatment techniques including drug therapy, plus greater availability of community facilities.

The mental hospital population is very heavily weighted with patients for whom release rates are quite low, and more than half (55 per cent) have been hospitalized longer than five years. The patient's chances of discharge vary sharply with length of stay.

Studies of the statistics on mental disease indicate that the highest incidence rates are not found among persons in the adolescent and adult years, the age-periods often regarded as of greatest psychological stress, but among those over 50 years of age.

Certainly, some of the increases in the incidence of mental illness can be attributed to our improved facilities for discovering persons having mental ailments, the increased number of mental hospitals, and decrease in the social stigma formerly—and to some extent still—attached to mental disease.

Obviously, the costs in happiness and adequate living of mental illness, whatever the causes may be, are very great. In addition to the patients in hospitals for mental disorders, we might also consider drug addicts and the inmates of our prisons as examples of mental maladjustment.

The Real Challenge to the Student

The figures cited above are impressive and give emphasis to the enormity of the problems of mental maladjustment that are on the in-

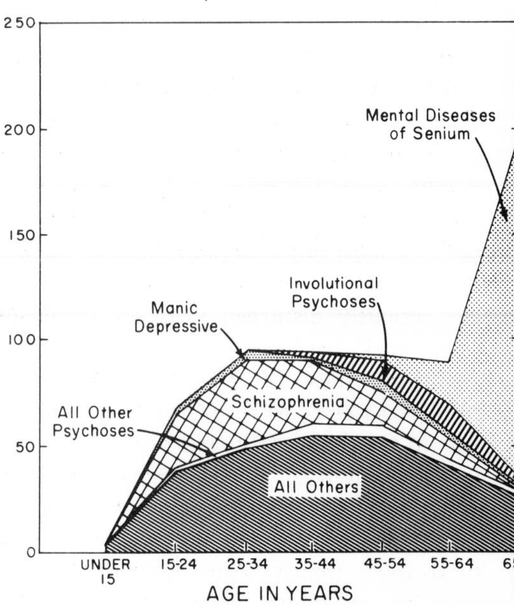

The relationship between *a person's age when he is first admitted to a mental hospital and the kind of mental illness he is likely to have is shown in the graph. Different psychoses are associated with different ages. For example, schizophrenic and manic-depressive psychoses are most frequent among those in the age range of 15-44 years. There is a sharp rise in mental disease associated with aging, especially in the sixties and later.* ***Source:*** *U. S. National Institute of Mental Health: Patients in Mental Institutions, 1959 (Part II) Public Health Service Publication No. 820. U. S. Bureau of the Census, Current Population Reports, Series P25 No. 212. Prepared by Hospital Studies Section, Biometrics Branch of the National Institute of Mental Health, February 1964.*

stitutional level. It is, however, the far greater numbers who suffer from minor mental or non-hospital varieties of maladjustment who offer the student of psychology his real challenge. Every student at times is confronted by classmates, relatives, and friends who are so unhappy or so poorly adjusted as to irritate or worry their colleagues. Some workers of the shop and office have sudden emotional outbursts that baffle their friends and supervisors. Husbands and wives sometimes are unable to meet the mental demands of married life. Sometimes, too, our own unhappiness or emotional disturbance may arouse us to our own need for a systematic approach to the study of adjustment and maladjustment.

We all meet peculiarly behaving people whom we should like to understand. Undoubtedly you have had some annoying experiences with friends, relatives, fellow employees, or students in college whom you consider queer, or sullen, overconscientious, over-suggestible, mentally twisted, disturbing, misfit, sexually perverted, and so on. How did their personalities become warped? What, if anything, might be done to help them?

What facts and points of view are needed by friends, parents, and executives to facilitate the development of strong personalities? How can you and I direct our own mental habits in order to facilitate our happiness and mental health? Perhaps we should begin our study of mental ailments by first noting their place among all human illnesses.

Human illnesses, maladjustments, and adjustment mechanisms cannot be classified into nonoverlapping or mutually exclusive categories, but the reader's background for further discussion may be aided by means of the following groupings:

A. ORGANIC. The tissues have been impaired.

1. TRAUMATIC—Mechanical injuries or wounds, such as broken bones or cuts.
2. TOXIC—Poisons in the body, such as alcohol or drugs.
3. MICRO-ORGANIC—popularly called germ infections, these include illness caused by microscopic organisms such as protozoa, bacteria, and the viruses.
4. GLANDULAR—These may involve glands that pour their secretions into body cavities or the endocrines which pour their secretions into the blood stream.
5. TISSUE CHANGES—Cancer, tumor, arteriosclerosis, and so on.
6. PSYCHOSES, ORGANIC—So far as insanity is concerned, approximately 42 per cent of the cases are caused by organic conditions. These diseases with their percentages of total admissions are mainly senile dementia (8 per cent), cerebral arteriosclerosis (10 per cent), general paresis (7 per cent), and alcoholic psychoses (5 per cent). In these disorders a definite physical or organic basis is known to be present. In business, these organically caused disorders are seen in the occasional cases of brain tumor, epilepsy, sleeping sickness, strokes, general paresis or syphilis of the central nervous system, hardening of the arteries, and senile dementia.

B. FUNCTIONAL. These ailments do not involve any measurable impairment of the tissues. About 58 per cent of all psychopathic or mentally ill cases appear to have a functional origin.

1. PSYCHOSES, FUNCTIONAL—Pronounced mental disorders, which unfit the individual for adjustment to his usual environment, principally dementia praecox (23 per cent), manic-depressive psychoses (9 per cent), involutional melancholia (4 per cent), and others.*

* The percentages of total admissions, given in parentheses above, should be differentiated from vital statistics of this kind which usually show first admissions, readmissions, and resident population in state mental hospitals. The percentages in parentheses do not total 100 per cent because of difficulty in classifying many patients who are placed under headings such as "other psychoses."

2. PSYCHOPATHIC PERSONALITY—A general classification for persons who are neither psychotic nor neurotic. It is a convenient borderline term for social misfits that includes the pathological liars, sex perverts, vagrants, eccentrics, misanthropes, troublemakers, moral defectives, and criminals who commit crimes without extenuation. The psychopaths constitute about 2 per cent of first admissions to mental hospitals and 15 to 20 per cent of incarcerated criminals.
3. PSYCHONEUROSES—Mild mental disturbances or patterns of behavior which do not wholly unfit the individual for his usual environment. Often called "nervous cases" in the home and in business offices.

C. COMMON ADJUSTMENT "MECHANISMS" OR "DYNAMISMS." These are found among all normal persons and are not evidence of abnormality. They become maladjustments only when extremely inappropriate manifestations handicap the individual who uses them too frequently or too extensively. Examples of terms used for some of the more common adjustment mechanisms or behavior dynamisms are:

1. OVERCOMPENSATION—The behavior resulting from the extreme motivation is much greater than necessary for the situation. If expressed indirectly and to an appropriate degree, it may be a positive substitute activity.
2. DEFENSE MECHANISM—Maintaining a sense of personal worth by resorting to behavior that guards some aspect of the personality from scrutiny by others or by one's self.
3. IDENTIFICATION—A mental process which expresses itself in the form of an emotional tie with other persons (or situations) in which the individual behaves as if he were the person with whom he has this tie. "Before I do anything, I always ask myself what my 'hero' would want me to do." Also, basking in reflected glory.
4. REGRESSION—Reverting to the role of a child or living in an earlier, easier world as a means of escape from present situations of a frustrating or unsatisfying nature; returns to infantile types of behavior. "If I can't be a big businessman in the city, I can go back to the farm of my childhood."
5. RATIONALIZATION—Reasoning in regard to the problem is distorted to justify an act or opinion which is actually based on other grounds, as in the "sour grapes" or "sweet lemon" or Pollyanna interpretations.
6. NEGATIVISM—Resisting suggestions from others, doing the opposite of what is expected, or, in some cases, doing nothing at all.
7. CONQUERING HERO MECHANISM—Role-playing, in imagination, in which the individual is superior or successful.
8. SUFFERING HERO MECHANISM—Role-playing, in imagination, in which the individual is inferior or attains superiority through his "superior" inferiorities.
9. PROJECTION—The tendency to ascribe to other persons or situations drives and complexes that belong to oneself. Ideas of reference and delusions of persecution are examples.
10. INTROJECTION—The tendency or act of absorbing the personality of others, or situations, into one's own mental life to the extent of reacting to external events as though they were internal ones. By some, this behavior is considered an extreme form of identification.
11. EGOCENTRISM—The observer is so tightly tied to his own personality that he is

unable to share directly the experiences of others. The term is used also in regard to an act to overcome being ignored and to get attention, even if unfavorable, as a symbol of social approval.

12. HABIT SPASM—A convulsive involuntary contraction of a muscle or set of muscles that helps to reduce tension. An unconscious purpose may be attention-getting: "People will notice my twitches."
13. SEXUAL ANOMALIES, such as homosexuality, sadism, masochism, and exhibitionism.
14. INVALIDISM—Habitual ill health or exaggerated ailment resorted to as a means of dealing with one's problems. It offers the individual an apparently acceptable excuse in his failure to meet his own or others' expectations.

Most persons need not concern themselves about the organic psychoses—the severe breakdowns of the human machinery; or the functional psychoses—the extreme cases of mismanagement of oneself. The physician and psychiatrist must deal with these. In a brief survey of this kind, we must relegate cases which require hospital or institutional treatment to experts who specialize in those problems. Every person, however, has frequent dealings with the psychoneuroses and common adjustment mechanisms. At times every person exhibits symptoms of abnormality, in a mild degree, as 100 per cent management is not common among individuals any more than it is among businesses. "Qualitatively, we are all about the same; quantitatively, we differ widely." This old saying simply means that we all have the same behavior tendencies or traits, but we differ in the extent or degree to which we have them.

A study of the more common adjustment mechanisms—psychodynamisms—should enable us to recognize when we are using them, to avoid using them excessively, and to abandon inappropriate ones for more effective methods of dealing with our problems. We want to view the individual's experience as a continuous process and when possible, to recognize his "life style."

We Need a Basic Pattern for Our Study of People

We want to learn to think of human behavior in its dynamic aspects—strivings, motivations and adjustments. These of course cannot be observed directly but they can often be correctly inferred if we study behavior systematically.

The human being operates in as natural a manner as do other parts of the physical world. Every human act could be understood if we knew all the pertinent facts. True, we do not know all the important facts needed to understand each person, but we believe that a person's behavior can be understood on the basis of principles that can be learned. To understand an individual we need a pattern for our thinking. Furthermore, we need a pattern for our thinking which is far more meaningful than a mere classification of the individual's behavior. Giving a person a label such as "introvert" does not indicate his other characteristics that are equally or more important. The label may even deter us from understanding him more completely. Nor does telling a person how we classify his behavior help him: it usually annoys him; furthermore, it sometimes harms him, because he may unconsciously accept the descriptive classification as a model from which to pattern his own behavior.

A classification of human maladjustments and common mechanisms such as the ones we have listed is somewhat convenient for discussion purposes and record, but in handling people we need a scheme of thinking that is more meaningful. A human being is a living, responding organism and can be understood only when we visualize him as an active, adjusting personality that evolves over a period of years. The use of the adjustment concept means that we view the individual's

"I simply can't stand being cooped up here any longer!"

The environment is incidental; *the way the individual adjusts to the environment is most important. Reproduced by special permission from Ralph Fuller, the artist, and* ***The Saturday Evening Post;*** *copyright 1933 by The Curtis Publishing Company,*

experience as a continuing process. Each person constantly responds to a complex of forces, within and external to himself. This means specifically that we can gain little help from statements such as, "He has an inferiority complex," or, "That's a defense mechanism." Such terms should be used mainly as points of departure for our thinking about the individual's problems and the ways he characteristically deals with them.

Nor is a knowledge of hereditary factors of much value to anyone who deals with problem persons. We may know, for example, that if one parent has a certain mental disease, the expectancy rate of mental disease for the offspring is 16 per cent; if both parents are so afflicted, the expectancy rate for the children is 68 per cent. This knowledge does not help us in practical situations, because we are always dealing with a specific individual. For example: if we know that both parents of a person have a particular mental ailment, is the subject of our analysis a member of the 68 per cent group who become afflicted or the 32 per cent group who never do become afflicted? Such statistics are of little aid to the educational advisor or the employment man. Often a knowledge of them does much harm, because the man who guides his human relations by means of statistics only is apt to be unfair to the many people to whom the figures do not apply.

Furthermore, many vital statistics have a kind of fatalistic effect on the individual to whom they seem to apply in part. He assumes that, his ancestry being what it is, there is little that he can do about or for himself through his own intelligent effort. This is a most unfortunate notion, because everyone can direct his own psychological development to a surprisingly great extent.

A knowledge of environment has some value in dealing with people but only a very limited value when we deal with a person. The old arguments about heredity versus environment are usually beside the point, because the individual is not a sum of the two. He is the *product* of the two in interaction. The individual is not a rubber stamp of his background. Rather, he is more like a live rubber ball. He not only rolls in the grooves of his environment but he also bounces away from parts of it. And, like those of a football, his "bounces" are often unpredictable, though a knowledge of the field or area where the "bounce" takes place often enables the experienced observer to predict the direction of some of the "bounces."

Sometimes a football bounces just as one would expect; at other times it veers off in a wholly unexpected direction. On some few occasions, too, it scarcely bounces at all but comes to rest very quickly. This football analogy is somewhat helpful whenever we study a person's environment. To understand any individual in relation to his environment, we should ask three general questions:

1. *To what influences of the environment did he learn to react as expected?* That is, what influences has he adopted? Which ones does he now follow habitually in his life? For example, if he was reared on a farm, does he have a typical farmer's work habits and points of view? Or, if he was reared in the home of a Democrat, is he a Democrat? If he was reared in the slums, does he feel at home in the slums?

2. *To what influences of the environment did he learn to react in an unexpected or opposing manner?* For example, if he was reared on a farm, does he now despise farming and rural life? Similarly, does he dislike Democrats, and does he feel out of place in the slums?

3. *What influences of the environment might ordinarily be expected to affect the personality but have really had no effect?* Some people fail to react to certain influences in terms of acceptance or rejection; they react neither favorably nor unfavorably. Some farmers' sons grow up and neither like nor dislike the farm. The same principle can be noted when we study any person's background. His early environmental history may have had very little effect on many of his present habits. The external conditions of life do not determine inescapably man's psychological development. Man is an active agent in the world around him. He selects the facets of the complex environment to which he reacts.

These three concepts regarding the environment—*acceptance, rejection,* and *indifference*—compel us to seek for more than a knowledge of the peculiar person's environment.

The employment man who collects bulging files of data about his applicants should know how to organize and interpret the data. The college personnel man who has extensive card records of facts about each student needs a method of viewing the facts. The parent who learns the hundreds of incidents in the development of his children needs a pattern for his thinking in order to arrange the facts into psychological significance. Anyone who associates with people in business, in school, or in their homes should have a systematic approach to the interpretation of human personalities. The approach described here is known as the adjustment concept.

The Adjustment Concept

We can, if we wish, explain human behavior by many different systems of thinking, as shown by the several schools of thought in modern psychology. Each school makes its unique contributions by virtue of the fact that, when we study anything in terms of a given system of thinking, we often gain a new perspective of related matters. This particular system of thinking, the adjustment concept, is used by this writer because it is easily grasped and is most meaningful to persons who do not plan to become highly trained psychologists through years of graduate work in clinics and universities.*

To understand a person, we may first think of him as in a state of activity. He is always active, whether he is sleeping, thinking, daydreaming, resting, playing, or working. Even dying is an activity. Some ongoing activities are always present, because the motive of life is to function. For us to think of a living individual who is totally inactive would be impossible, for he would be frozen, mummified, or calcified. Basic to our thinking of human beings is the point of view of interaction, the adjustment concept. To say that an individual is always active and that through his activity he develops may be trite, but to appreciate how a personality grows in the adjustment process is not always so simple as it sounds.

In his activities, the individual is always trying to achieve a satisfying state. In his functioning, his activity frequently is blocked or delayed by difficulties or barriers, and so he must learn how to overcome the difficulties or go around them.

A woodsman exploring in a forest exemplifies the adjustment idea. When he finds an obstruction in his path, he may use direct attack upon it, that is, remove it or go through it. Or he may go around it by means of a substitute or indirect route. Or he may decide to make a different kind of exploration, or even return to his home and do no more exploring at all.

* The treatment of the adjustment concept in this book must of necessity be limited to a few chapters as a background for dealing with certain selected aspects of the individual's life and work situation. Students who wish to read a comprehensive scholarly treatment of adjustment are referred to Laurance Frederic Shaffer and Edward Joseph Shoben, Jr., *The Psychology of Adjustment.* Boston: Houghton Mifflin Company, 1956.

Obviously, if the woodsman has once used a route, he will be apt to use it on the second and succeeding trips over the territory. He may use an old route even though he has found a better or easier one. An important part of the concept is that the woodsman does, at times, make new paths as a result of obstructions in his way. The barriers, often called frustrations, cause him to develop new mental habits and new urges to act.

Let us apply this barrier-adjustment idea to a few everyday situations. Assume that you are a student who is sitting comfortably in class and looking forward to a pleasant school experience. Suddenly the instructor announces an examination on some part of the course which you do not understand. You are annoyed by the barrier to your pleasant ongoing activity. You must make an adjustment. The adjustment you make will be one or more of the four general varieties:

Of course, the student who deals with the examination barrier by *direct attack* also prepares himself to deal more effectively with new or later examinations in the same and other courses. He builds up efficient study habits. His ego or feeling of self-worth is increased in a sound way. He achieves a more satisfying state. His personality is stronger than it was previous to his dealing with the barrier. His behavior is integrative in the sense that it facilitates growth toward greater adequacy in the meeting of new and more difficult problems. Accomplishments and satisfactions are increased.

A *substitute act* of positive value, at times, may be a more logical adjustment than direct attack. Although the decision to choose a substitute act may result in a feeling of failure with regard to the barrier thus avoided, it is likely to cause the individual to put extra energy into the substitute act. Not every student who fails in his school work and decides to go into business works harder in business than he did in school, but some do. A sense of failure in one field may stimulate the individual to put forth extra effort in another field.

The student who chooses to make an

Adjustment by direct attack upon the barrier or problem. The individual is in a state of ongoing activity, such as attending college. He finds that he must take a difficult examination. He studies diligently for the examination and overcomes the difficulty. If he fails in his first attempt, he persists until he succeeds. The original goal is kept and the successful adjustment tends to build up the ego—the individual's feeling of self-worth. His personality is strengthened and he is, to that extent, better prepared to meet future problems that involve volitional effort.

Adjustment by substitute activities, positive and negative: Instead of taking the difficult examination, the student may develop a new goal, such as going into business. If he does this, his feeling of self-worth may or may not remain the same, depending upon the extent to which the original goal was associated with pleasant emotional patterns. The evasive substitute activity of negative value is represented by subterfuge. This type of adjustment tends to weaken the personality and to lessen the feeling of self-worth. The reacting person's ability to meet similar problems is decreased by the latter variety of adjustment.

1. DIRECT ATTACK. Examples:
   a. Study for the examination.
   b. Prepare for the examination by having someone quiz you on the accuracy of your present knowledge.
   c. Outline the subject matter, recite to yourself all parts which you understand, and learn the important parts which are not clear to you.
2. SUBSTITUTE ACT OF POSSIBLE POSITIVE VALUE. Examples:
   a. Change to another course.
   b. Transfer to another school.
   c. Decide to quit school and find a job in the business world.
3. SUBSTITUTE ACTS OF NEGATIVE VALUE. Examples:
   a. Arrange to sit near a good student who will help you during the examination.
   b. Prepare a "crib" for the examination.
   c. Feign illness at the time of the examination and thus postpone or avoid taking it at the designated time.
   d. Accuse the teacher of unfairness.
   e. Berate or ridicule the students who study for the examination.
4. ADVANCED STAGES OF NEGATIVE VALUE ADJUSTMENT. Examples:
   a. Imagine yourself the hero of fiction or motion picture adventures and ignore your problem.
   b. Contemplate suicide.

evasive adjustment weakens himself for the next problem. His ability has been lessened. The evasive experience has weakened his personality. In this sense, his behavior is non-integrative.

Obviously, no person makes direct attack or intelligent substitute act adjustments in every situation. Everyone uses evasion and retreat at times, but the strong personality tends to use the first two habitually and the

Adjustment by retreat. *A photograph of a state hospital patient whose emotional life has been turned wholly inward. He lives in a world of fantasy rather than of reality. His adjustment is of the retreat type.*

weak man ordinarily uses the latter two in dealing with life's problems.

If a given adjustment habit is once firmly established, it is easily repeated in dealing with the same or related barriers. Adjustments begin very early in life and are made every day until the end of life. Each time we deal with a problem, great or small, we contribute toward or detract from the effectiveness of our personalities. The employee who has worked in an unsatisfactory position for a year, a day, or even an hour is no longer quite the same employee that he was when he first began to work. In the course of his employment he has developed new mental habits or tendencies toward new habits. In his reacting he may have acquired either hatred or admiration for a department manager, or for certain kinds of work.

To repeat the adjustment concept, but to apply it to the worker who finds himself in an uncongenial job, the outline elaborates the idea further (on page 33).

The worker who habitually deals by direct attack with the problems of his job increases his ability to deal with more difficult jobs. He may never attain any famed expertness, but he tends to feel in control of himself in relation to the problems around him. He earns his own self-respect. He finds that life offers him many opportunities for growth and genuine happiness. He is confident about the future. Furthermore, in the process of adjusting himself to the barriers in his job, he acquires new behavior patterns, such as a dislike for certain types of supervision or a liking for certain kinds of work.

If, however, the individual's habitual methods of solving his problems fail to give him satisfaction, he feels frustrated. In *frustration,* continuing or recurrent strong motivation forces the individual to search for a solution to this problem. This searching, largely unconscious, results in highly emotionalized or unorganized behavior that lasts until some effective or seemingly effective solution is found. Frustrated persons are apt to be unusually forceful, persevering, and immune to appeals of logic and reason concerning the area of mental life colored by the frustration. As we shall see later, frustration-motivated individuals are a problem not only to themselves but also to those leaders who try to direct social movements rationally and objectively.

Predisposing and Precipitating Influences

Every person has many *predisposing tendencies* when confronted by a new problem. He may be young in years, but he is "old" psychologically. He is a member of a human race which is really millions of years old in terms of biological influences. Furthermore, his bodily equipment—sex, size, glands, muscular and other structures—all contribute predisposing influences in behavior. *Conditionings* (*a*) from a single intense emotional experience, such as a fright, or (*b*) from repeated experiences of the same kind, such as customs, habits, beliefs, education, parental training, and the whole culture where he has lived, are additional predisposing influences.

***The employee who finds** his job uncongenial and wishes that he could get a new job can make any one or more of several types of adjustment. He can remain on the job he has, but utilize it for his personal growth. He may also make the adjustment by a substitute act of positive value such as seeking and obtaining another job. He may also remain on the job, but compensate for his dissatisfaction through a hobby, athletics, church work, art, etc. Substitute acts of negative value are of numerous kinds, such as finding fault with the world, criticizing others unnecessarily, acquiring functional illnesses, immersion in a cult, longing for death, etc. In this illustration, the negative substitute act is illustrated by the individual in the "gimme" response, getting unearned money from others.*

1. DIRECT ATTACK. Examples:
   a. Study the mechanical equipment used in the work, if any is used. Improve its design or invent new equipment.
   b. Study methods of doing the work. Practice the methods and improve them.
   c. Study the fellow workers and improve the human relationships. Influence the fellow employees and supervisors in order to have them like him as well as enjoy their work more fully.
2. SUBSTITUTE ACTS OF POSSIBLE POSITIVE VALUE. Examples:
   a. Obtain or continue to seek a transfer to another job.
   b. Obtain or continue to seek employment elsewhere.
   c. Compensate for dissatisfaction through a hobby, athletics, church work, art, etc.
3. SUBSTITUTE ACTS OF NEGATIVE VALUE. Examples:
   a. Criticize the job, the boss, the fellow workers, or industry as a whole.
   b. Feign illness or, as a result of subconscious maladjustment, become too ill to work.
   c. Adopt an air of superiority toward the job.
   d. Feel inferior in the job and avoid thoughts of the work as much as possible.
4. ADVANCED STAGES OF NEGATIVE VALUE ADJUSTMENT.
   a. Immerse himself in some mystical cult or pseudo-science such as a Hindu philosophy, astrology, palmistry, etc.
   b. Isolate himself and avoid any possible failure by making no attempts to change his status.
   c. Long for death and release from all life's problems.

These have affected him over relatively long periods of time. They will be discussed further in Chapters 7 and 14.

Precipitating factors are influences which act over a short period of time. These are likely to be emotional or exciting states, such as a recent threat, thwarted habit, ridicule, failure, success, fatigue, or disappointment. Obviously, the child who has just been scolded is likely to react to frustration somewhat differently from the way he would react at another time.

No one can unravel all the strands in the web of human personality. Life is too complex. We can, however, collect available facts about ourselves or others and try to see how the known facts arrange themselves into patternful relationships. A knowledge of psychology and the ability to use intelligently such concepts as adjustment often contribute to the art of dealing with people. It is especially useful to those who have counseling, guidance, or executive responsibilities. A starting point in this kind of analysis of a person is the sources of frustration or barriers.

Barriers

When we note the peculiar behavior of a maladjusted individual, we observe his peculiarity and then try to think of the way it originated. We try to think of the person's problems.

The sources of frustration in the lives of different individuals vary greatly, but we can mention typical barriers that necessitate adjustment. The problems or difficulties that stimulate the individual to seek adjustment may be a part of the external environment or within the personality. The particular nature of the barrier is not especially important. Any environmental situation or characteristic of a person may constitute a barrier. The important factor is the meaning of the situation or characteristic to the individual who is adjusting. A feeling of resentment, inadequacy, or inferiority toward the situation often indicates the presence of a barrier.

The two broad classes of barriers are (*a*) those owing to lack of capacity and (*b*) those owing to the necessity for abrupt changes in behavior (see Table 2.2). Obvious examples of capacity difficulties that demand adjustment are organic or physical conditions such as poor health or a crippled limb. Or there may be a chronic ailment or disability such as asthma, tuberculosis, heart murmur, epilepsy, color-blindness, or flat feet.

In the mental group may be found capacity problems such as low general intelligence, specific inaptitudes, emotional conflicts, bad habits, feelings of insecurity, lack of opportunity for training, and convictions of one's inferiority. Perhaps the most common personal difficulties are those which result from a lack of recognition for sincere efforts. This last type often occurs among children and students who think that they are doing well and then later find through comparisons with others that they appear to be inferior.

Bodily and mental punishment may accentuate the feelings of inadequacy. Many an introverted adult represents the effects of too many or too severe lashings of rod or tongue by the parent of the child. Any activity or situation may become a barrier if the individual is given punishment, neglect, or no approval in connection with it. Conversely, any activity may be satisfying if praise and prestige follow or accompany the activity.

Environmental barriers may be poverty, inhibiting customs or laws, and lack of opportunity for expression of the biological tendencies. However, the barrier objectively considered is not nearly so important as the interpretation that the person gives it. The same situation that is a barrier to one person may be a challenge or an opportunity to another. Among nations, a sterile soil and a harsh climate may result in the development of a virile nation, whereas a land of plentiful resources may have a race of fruitless people. Similarly, a poverty-stricken home may stimulate a child to achieve eminence while the son of the rich man on the hill becomes a weakling. It is significant that neither the poor boy nor the rich boy necessarily becomes strong or weak. The way each adjusts to his situation determines whether he will be strong or weak.

Nor can we hope to remove all difficulties from the life of anyone. To do so would only handicap him for life as it is. As Herbert Spencer said: "The ultimate result of shielding men from the effects of folly is to fill the world with fools."

Throughout infancy, childhood, youth, and

adulthood, the individual is constantly bombarded by experiences in which he is shown his inferiorities and inadequacies. For many people, a few experiences of inadequacy cause them to develop habits, through their adjustments, which make ordinary activities, such as the study of certain school subjects, very difficult. Reasons for many inabilities and peculiarities can be traced to the early experiences of the child.

One girl could not be convinced that she was pretty enough to make a favorable impression on others. She had two sisters who were praised frequently for their beauty. One day a wealthy aunt visited the home and again praised the two sisters for their beauty. On one occasion, however, the aunt realized that she should make a favorable comment regarding the plain child and so she said to her: "And you, my dear, have a kind face." In spite of the fact that many people would rather have a kind face than mere beauty, this girl, who is now a woman, prefers work that isolates her from other people, especially those who are attractive in appearance. Any vocation that would require emphasis upon personal beauty or attractive attire is out of the question for her. She has given up all hope of making herself attractive to others.

Any Situation May Be a Barrier to One Person but a Means of Satisfaction to Another

Personal appearance became a great barrier to the above-mentioned girl because her own appearance was associated with feelings of inferiority. However, to some women their personal appearance is an outstanding means of attaining satisfactions. Similarly, the study of music is a barrier to many children whose parents compel them to practice on the piano for hours. To other children, music is the one satisfying outlet for self-expression. Hundreds of school subjects, jobs, and activities are "meat for some and poison for others." The nature of the activity is incidental. What the activity means, represents, symbolizes, or is associated with in the mind of the individual is the important factor.

Tasks that are easy to perform tend to be satisfying but are not necessarily so. Tasks that are difficult to perform tend to be annoying but are not necessarily so. Many students can learn certain school subjects far more easily than their classmates but prefer to study other subjects that are more difficult for them. Many housewives can do their housework with ease but dislike it. Many employees can do the tasks in their jobs with ease but prefer to change their vocations. We should not assume that easily performed acts are always satisfying.

How Executives Contribute to the Better Adjustments of Employees

Every executive can, and many do, facilitate the direct-attack adjustments of individual employees. The executive may apply the adjustment concept when he finds that a salesman's volume has fallen off suddenly in a territory where the business activity of other companies has increased.

The manner of the failing salesman may indicate that something is bothering him. The astute manager tends to make inquiries regarding the failing salesman's habits, health, home conditions, and so on. If he finds that the salesman's wife has learned to consider her husband's job a socially inferior one since her nagging mother moved into the home, the manager can discuss the situation sympathetically and prove that the husband's job is important. A few special assignments that include a title may be all that is necessary to build up the salesman's self-respect and social prestige with the wife and mother-in-law.

Psychological insight and skill are applied in business whenever an executive feels with, thinks with, and works with employees who have disturbing emotional problems. The executive may not be able to give a technical psychological name to the employee's variety of inappropriate adjustment, but if he discovers the bothersome problem, notes the kind of evasive adjustment being made, and then instills confidence in the employee by showing him the possible direct-attack methods, the employee's behavior is likely to improve.

The adjustment concept causes us to recognize that we should not think of an employee as *being* this or that—as, for example, being conceited or sarcastic when dealing with difficult customers. The individual is not conceited or sarcastic, but he *uses* conceit or sarcasm when dealing with another personality. He has acquired the habit of using certain evasive methods, "personality tools," when dealing with other personalities.

Similarly, when an executive's stenographer becomes irritable, the psychologically minded executive tries to discover her problem. Perhaps her father has lost his job and makes little attempt to find another because he assumes that his employed daughter will support him. Or the girl's boyfriend may have become interested in someone else. Or any one of thousands of other problems may have occurred, each of which might necessitate that the stenographer make an adjustment. During the process of adjustment, the insight and encouragement of the executive may be very helpful.

Of course, many men have attained the kind of growth characterized by the personality tools of direct attack and intelligent substitute acts even though they have never studied psychology. The psychologists have so clarified the process of adjustment that people who lack psychological insight may the more quickly acquire it.

The significance of the classification of problem-solving methods has been ably stated by Robert H. Seashore:

It has thus far been implied that in dealing with any maladjustment it is first essential to determine the nature of the problem being faced. The next step is to determine what the individual is doing about the problem, and if his efforts are not successful, to consider the other methods of problem solving that might be considered as desirable alternatives. The writer has employed this classification in several ways, the simplest being a discussion designed to assist students of elementary psychology in starting to plan a career. In this case they were asked to describe what they would like to achieve (either in general terms or by giving illustrations of other people's similar achievements) in each of five areas of endeavor: 1. educational, 2. vocational, 3. avocational, 4. leadership, 5. personal development. It was found that the students could do this fairly easily, particularly when they were urged to set goals which they would really be willing to work for if they thought there was some reasonable possibility of success. After listing the advantages and handicaps which they had for achieving each of the five goals they were then asked to describe what methods, if any, they had employed up to the present time to achieve each goal. If these did not appear productive of the desired results, they were then to examine the classification for alternative methods which might overcome the difficulties so far encountered. This procedure is based on the idea that the formulation of a problem is often more than half of the total process of solution, and that a systematic method of procedure may save both the student and his advisors a great deal of time and wasted effort.

Perhaps the greatest importance of this classification for clinical psychology is that of attempting to analyze personality characteristics in terms of *habitual methods of responding to the principal types of situations which every person faces.*

. . . Furthermore, the classification in terms of problem solving behaviors is an operational one which tells what the person has been doing so far and lists the principal alternative things which he or his consultants could do in the future to provide a more satisfactory solution. The fact that such a classification is not a static one is perhaps one of its most hopeful features, in that it breaks down such large and vague concepts as social maladjustment into things which the person can do about particular problems in his social situation. In this it parallels the work of all individualized remedial education such as athletic coaching, time and motion studies on industrial operations, where it is already recognized that technical skill and guidance can often produce marked improvements in individual performance. From this point of view clinical psychology gets beyond the problem of diagnosis and endeavors to place a greater emphasis on the provision of technical facilities for assisting the individual to deal with his problems more accurately. Both the consultant and the client can contribute actively to such counseling, and if the method is made clear, there should be greater probability of the client's being able to develop skill in the methods of handling future problems himself, or at least recognizing when he needs expert assistance.[4]

Adjustments Are More Important than Environment

From the standpoint of the incidence of mental disease, as discussed in the early part of this chapter, the adjustment concept means that the environment is often an incidental part in our important mental habits. The environment may be paced slowly or rapidly and be relatively simple or complex. The individual's adjustment to the pace, whatever it is, is what counts. In other words, it is just as easy to drive an automobile at fifty miles an hour as to drive a horse at twenty—once the driver has learned the art. The art of living is an individual matter and must be learned by the individual regardless of when or where he lives.

Whenever we compare the lives of those who succeeded in dealing with the conditions of life with those who have failed, we find that the strong persons developed good adjustment habits and the failures developed evasive and retreat habits. The same observation applies to the people of a nation. The strength of a nation does not wholly depend upon natural resources nor on geographical location but mainly upon the strength of personality of its people. We need only compare the resources and people of the various nations, as, for example, Switzerland versus Russia, to see ample evidence of this axiom. The leaders and citizens of the United States must recognize this basic truth or suffer through the lack of its application. If too many individuals learn to lean upon charity or other artificial aids rather than upon their own strong adjustment habits, this nation will become weaker and the eventual prey of the stronger. This means that everyone, regardless of race, culture, or age, can benefit from a thorough study of the adjustment process in order that he may guide his own adjustments intelligently.

Good adjustment means that the person to whom it is ascribed is one who *usually* uses the direct-attack and positive-value mechanisms in dealing with his problems. He deals effectively and satisfyingly with life and its problems without bringing about disturbing feelings of anxiety, hostility, or dependence on his own part or on the part of others. He feels that he has attained or is attaining goals that are satisfying to him and approved by society. When he helps to solve problems of value to society, he does not exploit or injure other persons to attain his ends. He believes in and seeks to enhance those values which the race has found necessary for survival and for spiritual growth, such as truthfulness, altruism, and objective thinking. He feels that he "belongs" and that he is needed where he finds himself. He utilizes the immediate situation for further growth in his ability to deal with new and more difficult problems that befall him. He enjoys life intelligently and shares his enjoyments.

He is cooperative and an effective member of a team. He identifies with his immediate social groups: the work gang, office force, neighbors, and church, club, or association members.

He is master of himself. He does not unnecessarily upset the smooth tenor of his relations with others nor allow his own impulsive or ill considered acts to interfere with his plans or his social adjustments. He is consistent and stable without too many continuous bothersome tensions from conflicts and frustrations.

If he has learned to live creatively and effectively, he is not perfectly adjusted but he has learned to live well in spite of bothersome problems and some inadequate adjustments. See Chap. 8.

One purpose of education in general and of psychology in particular is to assist the individual in learning those adjustment habits which are of the positive variety. You and I, as laymen in the field of mental hygiene, can do very little to assist the psychotic, but we can do a great deal toward the development of sound mental habits in ourselves and our associates.

Of course many persons confuse the adjustment concept and the social desirability concept. Actually, the two differ somewhat as shown by one researcher. He pointed out that we can define personal adjustment as psychological health and social desirability as the attainment of certain superficial goals imposed on the individual by society. The two are not synonomous, although the adjusted person usually behaves in a socially desirable manner. He will have certain characteristics which are socially desirable simply because society would reject him if his behavior were contrary to its mores. However, the tests used in the research study indicated that the adjusted individual is more critical, more aggressive, more admittedly egocentric, more interested in others and more at ease with them, and less prone to despondency than the socially desirable person.

In his attempt to conform to what he feels are the demands of society, the person oriented toward social desirability may sacrifice his personal adjustment, his psychological health. Therefore, while good adjustment entails social desirability, the latter can and does exist without the former. It is possible for an individual to conform to society and thereby seem adjusted, while in reality, he may have weakened his psychological health and failed to adjust.[5]

Every living person has troubles and problems. The important consideration in bringing about personal effectiveness is not the number or kinds of problems a person encounters, but how he responds to them. Do they overwhelm him or challenge him? We have to realize that the ability to deal intelligently with misfortunes, to endure suffering, and to face loss without breaking down completely, all contribute to the kind of mental strength we seek and admire. This was especially well stated by a mature woman writer who described some problems of her early life:

> A woman said to me once so proudly, "My family never quarrels." I was young at the time and our children were young and I thought, "How wonderful! If only I could say that." But I'm not young now and I know better. When I look back on that family who never quarreled I remember their passivity; the slow eyes that did not flash; on the parents' faces, no grooves that tears had scoured. I know now that it takes passion and energy to make a quarrel...of the magnificent sort. Magnificent rows, magnificent reconciliations; the surging and soaring of magnificent feeling.[6]

Tables 2.2 and 2.3 will enable the reader to see a general outline of the adjustment concept. This list of barriers and adjustments is not intended to be exhaustive, nor is the classification of any one item of behavior supposed to be fixed. The adjustment activities mentioned are not mutually exclusive kinds of reactions to barriers, but only frequently-met or modal varieties. As previously stated, any variety of behavior can be classified only in relation to its context or setting. However, a brief examination of these tables should help the reader in developing an alertness to the kinds of adjustment which he can observe in his everyday experiences.

TABLE 2.2

EXAMPLES OF BARRIERS TO WHICH THE INDIVIDUAL ADJUSTS

I. "Capacity" barriers:
- A. *Insufficient capacity* to perform satisfactorily the activities that others expect the individual to perform or that he himself expects to perform:
  - 1. Organic or physical:
    - a. Poor health.
    - b. Atypical body shape or size.
    - c. Endocrine imbalance.
    - d. Lack of athletic ability.

TABLE 2.2 (cont.)

e. Defective sensory equipment, such as deafness.
f. Defective motor equipment, such as stiff joints.
g. Unattractive personal appearance, real or fancied.

2. Intellectual:
a. Intelligence too low; for example, inability to do satisfactory school work or to handle jobs requiring brain work.
b. Ability evaluated too high; for example, individual's parent expects him to be an honor student or an accomplished musician.
c. Specific inabilities, such as lack of ability in mathematics.

3. Social:
a. Lack of friends and inability to make friends.
b. Lack of ability to maintain ego in the face of bullying, ridicule, snubs, nicknames, and so forth.
c. Competing with superiors; for example, an average student rooms with a bragging superior student.

B. *Capacity too great* for required or present activities:
1. Rating of individual's capacity by parent, teacher, mental examiner, or supervisor much lower than it actually is.
2. Constant association with inferiors in education, health, or social development.
3. Environment unstimulating, as among children of foreigners and among fellow workers who set poor examples; working hours too long for normal development, and so forth.

II. Barriers arising from a *change* in activities:

A. Barriers arising because the individual is compelled to change his activities *abruptly:*
1. Birth of another child in a family in which the individual was an only child and a transfer of affection from the older child to the newborn.
2. Adoption into a strange family.
3. Death of a loved person.
4. Sex experiences that occurred too early in life and could not be continued satisfactorily.
5. Disappointment in love; betrayal of confidence.
6. Conflicts in love that require immediate adjustment.
7. Sudden change from a higher to a lower standard of living.
8. Sudden change from a lower to a higher standard of living.
9. Loss of a job; new job not satisfactory.

B. Barriers resulting from the individual's *lack of training or preparation* to meet his problems and his being thus compelled to accept new activities:
1. Normal associations with other children forbidden by parents; consequently, child or adult now adapts himself to new environments or contacts with great difficulty.
2. Puritanical, austere, or unsympathetic parents.
3. Parents who have been too lenient and have not trained their child to solve adult problems, such as the wise spending of money, the acquisition of proper habits, freedom of choice, etc.
4. Teachers who do not understand their pupils.
5. Disinterest of parents in the child; broken home; mother who is employed or who is interested in other activities more than in the child's development.
6. Compulsion to continue an unwanted education or to study subjects of no interest, such as music, languages, etc.
7. Compulsion to take an unsatisfactory job.
8. Association with superiors in studies or in work.
9. Association with persons of greater wealth, refinement, ability, or charm, and a feeling of inferiority caused by the differences.
10. Association with others of assumed superior race or nationality.

C. Barriers arising from the *continuance of activities* that should have been superseded by other activities:
1. Remaining in a social environment too long for personal development.
2. Remaining in a job too long.
3. Continuation into adulthood of inefficient or childish habits, such as poor study habits, lisping, temper tantrums, sullenness.
4. Continuation into adulthood of childhood emotional tendencies, such as parent fixations: *Oedipus complex, Electra complex.*
5. Clinging to outmoded religious creeds that appear to be out of harmony with new experiences—a condition found among some college students.

TABLE 2.2 (cont.)

D. Frequent *interruptions* of ongoing activities:
  1. Frequent change of school.
  2. Frequent changes in the home.
  3. Frequent changes of home town.
  4. Frequent shiftings of tasks or of instructions in work.
  5. Reprimands by superiors.
  6. Naggings by mate.
  7. Frequent inhibition of desired acts that are not approved by society and the aroused energy of which is not directed into satisfying channels but accumulates from repeated thwartings.

TABLE 2.3

EXAMPLES OF ADJUSTMENT ACTIVITIES OF THE INDIVIDUAL

I. Adjustment by *direct attack* upon the problem:
  A. As applied to any problem:
    1. Repeated attempts to solve the problem.
    2. Stoicism.
    3. Enjoyment of difficulty.
    4. Refusal to accept defeat.
    5. Admission of the problem, recognition of its true nature, and treatment of it through intelligence and insight.
  B. As applied to an employee's situation when he wishes to grow through his work:
    1. Study and improve the equipment of the job.
    2. Study and improve the methods of work.
    3. Study the fellow workers and improve the human relationships.

II. *Positive substitute activities* that often enable the individual to go around a barrier or a problem:
  A. Activities in dealing with people:
    1. Doing favors for others.
    2. Taking positions of leadership.
    3. Being active in organizations, such as the church, a club, a lodge.
    4. Being socially popular.
    5. Speaking in public.
    6. Attending social functions.
    7. Debating.
    8. Making new acquaintances.
    9. "Playing politics."
    10. Playing games with people.
    11. Analyzing others.
    12. Supervising others.
    13. Associating with inferiors.
    14. Associating with superiors.
    15. Doing stunts or tricks.
    16. Persuading people.
    17. Selling things to people.
    18. Entertaining or amusing others.
    19. Improving or correcting others.
    20. Helping those who are weaker.
    21. Taking care of children.
    22. Impressing the opposite sex.
    23. Seeking the approval of others.
    24. Teaching others.
    25. Identification with another personality.
  B. Intellectual activities:
    1. Studying.
    2. Developing money-making schemes.
    3. Collecting stamps, books and so forth.
    4. Creative writing.
    5. Creating mechanically.
    6. Inventing new systems, such as for production control.
    7. Studying and developing philosophies.
  C. Physical or manual activities:
    1. Mechanical work.
    2. Household work, such as sewing, cooking, etc.
    3. Physical labor.
    4. Outdoor work.
    5. Athletic activities.
  D. Emotional activities:
    1. Painting, or studying art.
    2. Studying music, vocal or instrumental.
    3. Writing or reading poetry.
    4. Religious activities.
    5. Impersonating others, acting.
    6. Symbolical behavior.

III. *Negative substitute* or *evasive* activities:
  A. Handicaps to the individual:
    1. Criticizing others.
    2. Annoying or teasing others.
    6. Bluffing, conceit.
    7. Cynicism.

TABLE 2.3 (cont.)

3. Rowdyism.
4. Bullying.
5. Air of superiority.
8. Sarcasm.
9. Argumentative responses.
10. Refusal to make decision.

B. Mere annoyance to others, or not positively developmental when carried to extreme degree:
1. Distinctive mannerisms.
2. "Show-off" behavior.
3. Doing tricks or stunts.
4. Joining organizations merely "to belong."
5. Mimicry.
6. Personal adornment.
7. Emphasis on clothing.
8. Talkativeness.
9. Exaggeration.
10. Fictionizing.
11. Overagreeableness.
12. Travel in order to get away from difficulties.
13. Exaggerated attempts to impress the opposite sex.
14. Attending movies frequently.
15. Excessive reading of fiction.
16. Ancestry worship.

C. Serious evasive habits indicating minor maladjustments:
1. Excessive daydreaming.
2. Regression.
3. Projection.
4. Introjection.
5. Invalidism.
6. Sulkiness.
7. Extreme introversion.
8. Alcoholism.

IV. *Retreat* adjustments:
A. Solitude, stay-at-home habits to avoid ordinary problems.
B. Mysticism.
C. Living in another world—pronounced escape from reality.
D. Death wish and suicidal tendencies.

ACKNOWLEDGMENTS AND REFERENCES

1. Leo Srole, Thomas S. Langner, Stanley T. Michael, Marvin K. Opler, Thomas A. C. Rennie, *Mental Health in the Metropolis: The Midtown Manhattan Study* (New York: McGraw-Hill Book Company, 1962), p. 138.
2. *Ibid.,* p. 147.
3. G. M. Carstairs and G. W. Brown, "A Census of Psychiatric Cases in Two Contrasting Communities," *Journal of Mental Science,* January, 1958, pp. 72–81.
4. Robert H. Seashore, "Problem Solving Behavior in Conflict Situations," *The Training School Bulletin,* March, 1947, pp. 202–210.
5. Jack Block, "Some Differences Between the Concepts of Social Desirability and Adjustment," *Journal of Consulting Psychology,* December, 1962, pp. 527–530.
6. Sylvia Ashton-Warner, *Teacher* (New York: Simon & Schuster, Inc.), 1964.

PROJECTS

1. Read Table 2.2 and check the barriers you have had in the course of your adjustment history. Select one of your barriers, preferably of the kind that would not embarrass you if a description of it were read by a friend or teacher.
   a. Write a brief description of the barrier or problem and the adjustment you made to it.
   b. State how the barrier and your adjustment to it have affected your own personality in dealing with others, in doing school work, or in earning your living.
   c. If you have a friend available for the purpose, ask him to read your description of your barrier and your adjustment. To what extent does he agree or disagree with your interpretation of your own psychological conclusions?
2. Hendrik Willem Van Loon was reported as having said:

   "The purpose of education is to get a perspective of yourself so that you can understand yourself in relation to those around you. It enables you to have an active and pleasant life. It enables you to go through the world with the least amount of friction and a proper amount of understanding. That is all education is supposed to do. . . .

   Let's look at our colleges and see what is going on. We find that they are doing little in the way of educating students. The colleges in the United States are simply big play pens where the incompetent can send their children for four years."

a. Do you agree with Van Loon that colleges "are simply big play pens"?

b. What evidence can you offer to refute his statement?

3. Magazine and newspaper articles often publish pictures of physically handicapped persons who achieve a high level of skill in some activity, such as the one-armed stenographer who turns in perfect copy in a typing contest or a one-legged swimmer who wins an aquatic contest. Can you describe examples of this kind from your own acquaintances?

COLLATERAL READINGS

Barron, Frank, *Creativity and Psychological Health*. Princeton, N.J.: D. Van Nostrand Company, Inc., 1963, Chapters 9–13.

Dunlap, Knight, *Personal Adjustment*. New York: McGraw-Hill Book Company, 1946, Chapter 7.

Lehner, George F. J. and Ella Kube, *The Dynamics of Personal Adjustment*. Englewood Cliffs, N.J.: Prentice-Hall, Inc., 1964, Chapter 1.

Moment, David and Abraham Zaleznik, *Role Development and Interpersonal Competence*. Boston: Harvard University, Division of Research, Graduate School of Business Administration, 1963.

Passamanick, Benjamin, *et al.*, "Home vs. Hospital Care for Schizophrenics," *The Journal of the American Medical Association*, Jan. 18, 1964.

Patty, William L. and Louis S. Johnson, *Personality and Adjustment*. New York: McGraw-Hill Book Company, 1953.

Shaffer, Laurance F. and Edward Joseph Shoben, Jr., *The Psychology of Adjustment*. Boston: Houghton Mifflin Company, 1956, Chapters 1 and 2.

"American Gothic." *How would you describe the probable adjustments of these two characters so excellently portrayed by Grant Wood?* ***(Courtesy of Grant Wood and the Art Institute of Chicago.)***

CHAPTER THREE

ADJUSTMENT BY SUBSTITUTE ACTIVITIES THAT ARE OFTEN OF SOME POSITIVE VALUE

Frustrations and feelings of inadequacy often result in adjustments such as compensation, radicalism, or identification. Certain adjustments, though rather unusual, give the individual the motivation which enables him to apply himself to a life program or vocation. If the object of the motivation becomes a program that serves others, the motivated person is likely to become successful or even famous.

Whenever we study the lives of famous men and women, we are likely to find that their chief psychological assets were their adjustments to severe handicaps. The important point for us to keep in mind is not that a man has problems or failures but how he adjusts to his barriers, and whether his adjustments have value for other people as well as satisfaction for himself.

Beethoven was handicapped by deafness but wrote some of the world's best music. Byron's clubfoot and his poverty-stricken neurotic parents gave him a sense of inadequacy for which he compensated by writing poetry. Demosthenes and Moses are supposed to have been stutterers and yet both became famous leaders. Benjamin Disraeli suffered from ozena, a degenerative disease of the mucous membrane of the nose that produces a constant stench from the nostrils, but he became a prime minister of England. Arturo Toscanini, successively conductor of the Metropolitan Opera Company, the New York Philharmonic-Symphony Orchestra, the National Broadcasting Company Symphony Orchestra, compensated for his near-sightedness by developing a remarkable memory. Steinmetz, though deformed in body, left an imprint on our civilization by means of his genius for pure research.

The great men of the world have had all kinds of personal problems—some severe, some minor. Many factors entered into their success—too many for us to unravel clearly and completely. The nature of their handicaps is less important than the intensity of effort which resulted from adjustment to the handicaps. Certain it is that many of life's biggest prizes go to those with physical* or mental handicaps, real or imaginary. Perhaps if the progress of the world depended upon only the purely normal people (if such exist!) we would all still be living in primitive fashion.

* Alfred Adler has stressed the idea and given many examples of compensation brought about by some organ inferiority. See "A Study of Organ Inferiority and Its Psychical Compensation," *Nervous and Mental Disease Monograph,* 1917, for his early writing in this field.

Compensatory Mechanisms

Many people of no great importance illustrate the compensatory mechanisms as well as do the famous. For example, many sculptors, musicians, speed typists, experts in fine needlework, men who write name cards with flourishes, and others whose work demands delicateness of touch developed their skills as the result of an effort to compensate for left-handedness. Many of these persons were potentially left-handed but were compelled to change to the right hand.* Of course, the right-handed person can achieve success in skilled movements just as readily as the left-hander, but the former often lacks the urge. A study of the ability to grasp the meanings of American Indian sign language gestures, for example, showed that deaf high school students of both sexes scored significantly higher than the nondeaf.[1] Such extra abilities appeared to be clearly compensatory.

The compensatory mechanism is easily recognized when we recall the example of anyone who, being little in stature or having physical defects, habitually assumes a haughty air, a cold gaze, a pompous manner, or a loud voice. Consider some of the military and political leaders of history who are known for their bombast as well as their short stature or physical defects.

Compensatory mechanisms are characterized by extra effort or aggressive conduct in order to defend the ego or feeling of self-worth. The individual's compensatory behavior enables him to reduce the tension

* The child's stuttering which occasionally accompanies the shift from the use of the left hand to the use of the right hand is not caused by the inability of the brain to make the change but by a sense of inferiority brought about by the parent's or teacher's harsh treatment of left-handedness. When a person loses the use of his writing hand through accident and changes to use of the other hand, no speech defect arises; he has not been criticized for his awkwardness.

caused by feelings of inadequacy. Confronted by a barrier to his ongoing activities, the individual naturally seeks to react in ways which appear to overcome the deficiency, decrease feelings of tension, and give increased feelings of self-worth.

Every person has some defects, and so we expect him to have the desire to feel superior in one or more respects. Each man wants to be worthwhile in his estimation of himself. If he is frustrated in the attainment of his goals so that he cannot meet his obstacles in a positive manner, he will do so in an indirect manner.* Inferiority cannot be endured. Superiority, or at least a sense of adequacy, must be achieved. A sense of failure, guilt, or shame is hard to accept. For example, the woman who feels inferior may ape the cultured or the rich and attend functions for which she does not care or lectures which she does not understand. Attendance at the opera may be imperative for her, because it puts her into the desired class of those who are admired.

When the individual is confronted with barriers to which he cannot make a direct adequate adjustment, he may seek satisfactions through substitute activities that have positive values. For example, pupils who cannot attain satisfaction in scholarship may do so on the athletic field. Girls who do not find their personal appearance attractive may become good students. High school students who find their studies very difficult are apt to quit school and seek jobs. The employee who feels disgraced because his father has been convicted as a criminal may achieve satisfaction by taking up art, athletics, church work, stamp collecting, or by inventing new machinery.

When we study the lives of some labor leaders, we find that certain barriers confronted them in their earlier years of employment. They were not successful in becoming members of management and so they dealt with their failure by helping the workers whom they believed to be as unhappy as themselves. Likewise, businessmen who cannot succeed in business often make an adjustment by entering another type of work, such as teaching. Teachers who cannot attain satisfactions in teaching may make an adjustment by going into business.

Compensations or substitute activities may be useless, even harmful, or they may be of great value to the individual and to society. The man who goes into the business world and finds that he is not a good businessman can substitute for that lack of attainment the satisfactions of church work and fraternal activities. Of course, the normal individual takes some interest in his community, his home, and other phases of good citizenship; but, if he remains in business and makes his outside activities a heavy sideline, he shows that he is not really well adjusted to his job. He is seeking compensation for some lack that he feels in his personality. It is usually well, therefore, that the general manager should frown upon outside activities of employees when those activities absorb very much time without bringing better adjustments to the man's job.

In this connection, we may ask whether every person goes into a chosen vocation in order to compensate for some inadequacy. Do not education and the examples of others have any influence in the choice of work? Of course they have some bearing with many individuals, as when a father tells his son about the money to be made in the legal profession and then has the son talk with some enthusiastic lawyer who convinces the lad that law is the most honorable and remunerative profession. Law, as a vocation, becomes associated with other desirable ideas of prestige, fame and wealth. However, it is also evident that many of the vocations we select are chosen as an avenue of expression for

* An excellent treatment of frustration with examples of adjustments is presented in *Frustration and Aggression,* by Dollard, Doob, Miller, Mowrer, Sears, *et al.,* published for The Institute of Human Relations, Yale University Press, 1939. See pages 12–17 for six good illustrations of the concept of frustration. Page 53 presents a summary of principles.

thwarted tendencies. If a boy is a poor athlete, he may take refuge in his books. If he cannot be worthwhile as a physical specimen, he may become a college professor, a scientist, a statistician, or an accountant.

Many positive or desirable substitute activities are compensations for inadequacies in social relations. The individual who meets barriers that make him feel inadequate may learn to obtain personal satisfactions from being kind to others, public speaking, playing politics, doing tricks, taking care of children, or teaching others. All these habits or tendencies are desirable and may be utilized vocationally. The understanding employer tries to give the employee the type of work that utilizes adjustment tendencies which are already well established.

To the counselor, adjustment by positive substitute activity is very important because evidence of such adjustment is likely to mean that the individual has a strong inner drive. When Daniel Starch studied the life histories of one hundred and fifty men by personal interview, analysis of their characteristics indicated that one important factor in the success of the ablest men was their inner drive. These men were divided into three groups: Fifty top executives, heads of America's leading enterprises, whose salaries ranged from $50,000 to over $200,000; fifty second line, mid-level executives, whose salaries ranged from $7,000 to $20,000; and fifty small businessmen, whose incomes were lower than those of the mid-level executives.

> ...Of two men with equal intellect, of equal capacity to take on responsibility, or equal skill in handling people, the one with twice the drive will achieve twice as much, or six times as much.
>
> Is it true that most men get to important positions because of wealth or luck?
>
> I carefully searched the careers of our 150 men and found that 9 per cent of the men in the top groups went into their father's business; whereas, 20 per cent of the men in the low group did so.
>
> Two facts are plain: Only one in eight men steps into his father's business, and actually twice as many do so in the low group as in the top group.
>
> As to work, I have also diligently searched the careers of our executives and found that 78 per cent of the men in the top level worked hard and long; whereas, only 20 per cent of the men in the low group did so.
>
> There are two powerful forces behind the inner drive in great men.
>
> The first is their all consuming purpose—the goal from which there is no swerving—the preconceived destination which drives the locomotive on and on.
>
> "Great souls have wills, feeble ones have only wishes" is an old Chinese saying.
>
> The second force behind the inner drive of great men is not money or material reward. It is emotional—it is the anticipated satisfaction of achievement.[2]

The trained personnel man, vocational counselor, executive, and teacher are all interested in studying the individual in order that behavior tendencies may be utilized for greater self-expression. When a personnel man refuses to hire an applicant for a selling job and says to the applicant, "I will not hire you for the sales department because you really would not be happy there," the interviewer has recognized that the applicant's adjustments are not of the kind that would make him satisfied in sales work.

A man may be capable of selling and even have a good record in salesmanship work but still decide that he must do something else because his friends regard salesmanship as Babbitty and he feels inferior as a salesman. Hence, he wishes he were an artist or something respected by his friends. This principle is often important in labor problems.* Many dissatisfied employees are trying to find forms of self-expression whereby they may escape their feelings of social inferiority and appear superior in the estimation of their associates. The job or experience that causes one man to feel socially superior may cause another to feel inferior. A man's reactions to a job often depend upon how he is attempting to adjust

* Of course, a great deal of labor unrest comes from well-adjusted workers who believe they have a right to a larger share of the income from the business, better conditions of work, and so on. These desires may be no more evasive than those of a merchant who tries to get the highest possible price for his goods.

his inner mental life rather than upon the job itself.

Many positive or desirable substitute activities are compensations for personal inadequacies, real or imagined. The person who has difficulty in admitting to others or himself some inadequacy in his personality may try to guard it from scrutiny by others. He develops some modes of behavior that shield or appear to shield him. He often protects himself from anxieties by such *defense mechanisms,* and his associates may learn to avoid any mention of his inadequacy. They know that any mention of his defect, real or imagined, is likely to result in exaggerated behavior or withdrawal from the social situation. Sometimes the individual's tendency to exaggerate some trait in order to draw attention away from a weakness and turn it in another direction results in *overcompensation.*

Usually, individuals who overcompensate are unable to accept defeat. Those who overcompensate work their way out of a difficulty by vigorous attacks. Sometimes the individual even accomplishes what appears to be impossible. One man, for example, was born with a very large clubfoot. Walking was difficult for him but he became an expert golfer who invariably walked faster than his teammates. When walking on the street with a friend, he always set a rapid pace in spite of obvious difficulty in walking at all.

When, however, an individual discovers that it is impossible for him to attain success in the defeating activity, his overcompensation may take a substitute direction. The individual seeks success in some other activity. The new activity may be obviously related to the one in which defeat has been experienced. An unsuccessful concert violinist may, for example, resort to clowning by means of the violin. Similarly, an unsuccessful actor may become a teacher of public speaking.

Of course the substitute compensation may also lead to a different field. This is especially likely to happen when the frustration arises out of a lack of opportunity to exercise one's talent. A factory worker of high intelligence, for example, operates a machine that requires a great deal of manual skill. The worker lacks the muscular coordination necessary to develop a high level of skill. He therefore studies accounting in evening school until he overcomes his feelings of defeat.

Unfortunately, too, some persons overcome the reality of defeat by immersing themselves in projects. When the feeling of defeat is so unpleasant as to approach the painful, the individual may concentrate on some unusual project, preferably one that few people know much about. The project may have little real value. It may seem merely time-frittering to others, but to the individual it overcomes the painfulness of defeat in some other area. To observers, the individual is escaping *from* reality. If, however, the substitute activity opens up new emotional satisfactions as in the case of the fine arts, he may later find that he escaped *into* reality.

A sense of adequacy, however achieved, often enables a person to "endure" or adjust happily to numerous frustrations or problems that beset him as indicated by this example:

> I once heard of a blind piano tuner whose disposition was so unfailingly even that the man whose piano he had come to tune set out intentionally to ruffle him, just to see if he could.
>
> "What's that note you just struck?" he asked.
>
> "That's C," said the blind man.
>
> "Oh no, that isn't C," said the owner. "You must be slipping. Hit it again."
>
> The piano tuner struck the note again.
>
> "See?" said the man. "It's a little off."
>
> "No," the blind man said with a smile, "that's C all right."
>
> At this the owner gave up.
>
> "Look here," he said, "I know that's C, right on the nose. I've just been trying to see if I could ruffle you. You know your business, and here I was, trying to tell you how to do it. Why didn't you get mad?"
>
> "Why should I get mad?" asked the piano tuner mildly. "My wife loves me. Why should I get mad?"[3]

The Messiah Complex

Any person who finds himself in a predicament because his life is unsatisfying is likely to try to solve his own problem by attempting to alleviate the predicaments of others. The student who plans to do college teaching and then later finds that he cannot do so may adjust himself by helping others who are in a difficulty similar to his. This type of adjustment is, perhaps, one of the most common psychological origins of the professional adviser. Teachers and executives who find their work unsatisfying or difficult often enter the advisory field as counselors, college deans, assistants to principals, welfare workers, or personnel men. Such counselors become engrossed in their work and are likely to be sympathetic toward those who seek their advice. This kind of adjustment is both psychologically sound and socially desirable. When people make comments about a clinical psychologist to the effect that he is trying to help others make better adjustments because he really is trying to help himself make better adjustments, the comments are complimentary. The adjustment is beneficial to both the advisees and the adviser. Personality development should be reciprocal rather than one-sided.

If the person who has made such an adjustment in the direction of helping others has had an intensely unpleasant experience in connection with his problem, he may develop an extreme form of the Messiah complex—the radical reformer's tendency. The radical wishes not only to help those toward whom he is sympathetic, but also to destroy all persons and features connected with the hated situation. He wants a new educational system, or a new economic order, or a new religion, or even an entirely new civilization. Back of those fanatics analyzed is an emotional history that explains the fanaticism. Most malcontents have had very unhappy childhoods which have a direct relation to their radical ideas.

Identification with the underprivileged. *Some persons make adjustments in the direction of identification with the misunderstood or unappreciated. Such individuals are apt to seek vocational expression through positions that enable them to be kind and helpful to the unsuccessful members of society. This kind of "uplift" tendency is often found among sons of very successful men, especially when the son feels that he has not met his father's expectations of him.*

Rowdies and Radicals

The rowdy and the radical, who like to annoy or shock their associates, may have their desires to be noticed directed into worthy channels. Any skillful teacher knows that she can direct a rowdy pupil's impulsions into better channels by assigning to him the task of controlling the other rowdies in the room. Or she may give him recognition by appointing him traffic patrol leader. Or he may be induced to protect the girls instead of teasing them. His rowdiness may be an attempt to gain the limelight, and any personal recognition accompanied with an assignment of responsibility is likely to be more satisfying to him than a continuation of his annoying conduct.

Similarly, the college student who has radical tendencies toward the economic order is likely to moderate his extreme points of view if he is assigned the job of helping some of the chronic down-and-outers. Few experiences are so likely to change the young industrial radical into a conservative as the task of hiring some of the industrial misfits, supervising their work, and then paying their wages out of his own money. When he goes into business for himself and observes many a worker's carelessness, tardiness, and irresponsibility toward the employer's needs, he is apt to decide that his former panacea for economic disorders is impracticable.

The college student who realizes that he

is considered a radical by his acquaintances often has difficulty in getting a job. Many employers shy away from him. He imagines that they deny him employment because of his "advanced" ideas which clash with their interests. Actually many intelligent employers have little fear of so-called advanced ideas but they realize that the radical employee is rarely a good teamworker. He is likely to be either a free lance or, if in a group, a disturber of the group. Most employers like to feel that their employees like each other and function smoothly as a "team." Hence many avoid the radical as much for his lack of group integration as for his ideas as such.

The small number of students who can be classified as radicals usually have problems in adjustment and are more in need of a clinical psychologist's services than a policeman's club.[4] Radicals reveal important personality changes in their histories, but the exact nature of the relationship between the changes and the radical political activity can be revealed only through analysis of each individual's adjustments.[5]

Radicals, rowdies, and reformers need the same constructive treatment which we should accord to others who are seeking adjustment to their problems. The business executive who finds that he has hired radicals should think of them as stimulating critics and decide whether the benefits from their criticism outweigh the annoyances they cause him. If their actions become a burdensome task for the executive, he should recognize that the normal employees also deserve attention. When the normal employees are neglected so that maladjusted radicals may be given more time and thought, the executive should refer the maladjusted employees to the specialists of a clinic and devote his best efforts to the more ordinary members of his organization.

Identification

Identification means that the individual *feels* that he is part of another person, situation, or institution. In some cases, he feels that he is part of the purpose of the institution, activity, or person. The process is one of feeling rather than of intellect. (It should not be confused with "identity," the individual's psychological definition of himself.)

The person who, when at the theater, identifies himself with the hero, fights his battles, endures his hardships, conquers the villain, and finally marries the heroine, is not, for the time being, a mere observer or onlooker, but is the character in the picture or the play, psychologically speaking. Such a person makes many incipient movements that give reality to his imaginary acting. In like manner, the loyal college student attending the football game of his alma mater gives the player who is carrying the ball many a vigorous "shove" from the grandstands. For the moment the spectator carries the ball. He has identified himself with the team and is mentally doing the same things that the team is trying to do.

Every sport fan knows that the successful football team is the one in which the members identify themselves with the team as a whole. Each player does not play an individual game but integrates his playing with that of the entire team.

Through the achievements of other persons, groups of persons, and institutions, the individual may reduce tensions arising from his own inadequacies. Identification may be made with social and political organizations or reform movements as a compensation. An individual may also identify himself with his material possessions, as exemplified by the housewife who cleans and protects her home so well that it becomes uncomfortable to others. Possessions such as the house, clothing, automobile, office desk, or factory machine may be used to gain many subconscious satisfactions as well as obvious prestige values.

Positive identification is one of human nature's most valuable means of making wholesome adjustment. It is present in the life of every well-balanced personality; it is absent from the mental lives of certain

Identification with one's superiors. *Some persons make adjustments in the direction of identification with the able, competent, and successful. Such individuals are apt to seek vocational expression through managerial positions.*

patients in hospitals for the mentally ill. In other patients, the identifications are carried to an extreme degree. They identify themselves so completely that they become "Napoleons," "Hitlers," "Messiahs," and so on. The well-balanced person of any age is the one who has learned the art of identifying himself intelligently with the people and the tasks of his daily contacts. The factors of his personality are integrated into an effective working unit. He feels at home with his associates, his supervisors, his family. Unlike the cynic, he finds the age in which he lives reasonably admirable because he has identified himself with its admirable movements.

Identification is the important fundamental of a happy married life. Ideally and typically, two people marry, not mainly for sexual gratification but for more complete identification of their personalities. In the course of history, society has developed many institutions in order to enable its members to identify themselves with satisfying personalities. In addition to marriage, we have the church, which aims to have the individual identify himself with the cosmic power.

The good citizen identifies himself with his community and his nation. The well-adjusted pupil identifies himself with his school and his teacher. The great teacher first acquires a strong personality and then enables his students to live partially within his personality in order that they may thus develop their own personalities.

Teachers and business executives should try to assist their pupils and employees in identifying themselves with the age in which they live, the institutions of which they are a part, the social groups in which they are nurtured, and the employers or others who give them employment. The true educator and builder of men instructs not by teaching subject matter only but by showing people their places in the scheme of things; by pointing out the trends of the past and the possible trends of the future; by discussing the problems of today that challenge us to excel our forefathers, and the beauties of the machines, of nature, and of man, in addition to their cruelties.

The skillful executive who enables employees to identify themselves with his personality must also help them to transfer their identifications to other tasks, persons, and institutions. He may direct them so well that they wish to become a boss "like him." Later, the employees may find they are really interested not in the intrinsic values of their tasks but in the person who happened to supervise them. The able executive who has insight into the processes of identification among his employees is careful to see that they clearly differentiate between interest in him and interest in their work. Each worker should be led to find the intrinsic values of his work and to feel that he is a worthwhile member of the institution to which he belongs. The same admonition applies to the teacher in relations with his pupils.

How We Can Help People Acquire Identifications

Complex influences enter into the development of identifications and no one can control their development in any one person. Those who are in positions of leadership often seek to develop positive identifications with an organization such as a political party, with a company, or a person. They use the following kinds of procedures:

1. They provide goals for the individual that are worthwhile to him. Politicians talk about lower taxes, more jobs, and world peace. Astute managements talk about job security and advancement for the employee. They know that when management talks about the things that interest management—higher profits, lower costs, and better competitive position—the employee is not impressed. Such goals are not especially worthwhile to him as an employee. To make the goals worthwhile to an employee, they should be stated in terms such as the greater number of people, usually customers, who are benefited by the bigger production and lower costs.

2. The people emphasized as likely to benefit are the kind whom the individual likes or respects, usually people who are similar to himself. The politician may describe himself as "one of the people." The executive depicts himself as a worker. This principle is commonly seen in advertising. Housewives who view television commercials identify readily with other housewives of refinement but not with society matrons, crude comic characters, or sexy models. Children lose interest in programs when there is an emphasis on adults. Instead, they like to hear children's voices and to see children of their own age participating in children's activities.

3. Identification is developed through shared experiences. Its strongest forms are often found among men who have endured mutual suffering as in the case of soldiers who have been together in combat or in rigorous training as exemplified in our Marine Corps. Their shared hardships cause them to identify lastingly with members of their group. In like manner, children who are reared in families where all members of the family share to the point of personal sacrifice for the family life often have deeper family loyalty than children of families where the parents do all the sacrificing. In business, the executive who inspires employees to sacrifice their own comfort in order to make a contribution to the business develops far stronger identification of the employees with the company than the executive who thinks mainly in terms of what he or the company can do for the employees. The identifications of most persons are intensified when they learn how to "give of themselves" to ideals, persons, and institutions outside themselves.

Initiation rites that involve pain or embarrassment have been used for centuries by peoples on the assumption that the suffering will cause the neophyte to identify more thoroughly with the organized group. An experiment was conducted by psychologists to learn about the effects of severity of initiation. They tested the hypothesis that persons who undergo an unpleasant initiation increase their liking for a group; that is, find the group more attractive than do persons who become members without going through a severe initiation. Three conditions were employed: reading embarrassing material before a group, reading mildly embarrassing material, and no reading. The results clearly verified the hypothesis.[6]

Managements have learned that they need not insist on having employees suffer for the benefit of the company but they must give the employee ego involvement toward the products and operations of the company. One method is to challenge the employee to make or help make products that are better than those made by competitors. Most workers want to be good craftsmen and to prove their competence in competition. We fail them when we do not supervise them in that spirit. This means that managements have to learn how to give the worker a feeling of colleagueship in the attainment of objectives. The inability of managements to give the employee emotional as well as economic identification with the company has been an important factor in causing employees to form associations of their own and through those associations, to compel employers to bargain with them.

4. Symbols of status within a company

such as job titles and achievement awards are helpful. Think of all the titles, diplomas, and badges that people treasure. If these have a direct tie-in with a company, the identification is enhanced.

5. Constant communication is essential. Executives, particularly those in top management, are authority symbols to employees. Employees like to see these men, to feel that they are personally acquainted with them, and that the executives know them. One of the most common complaints on the part of employees in large companies is "no one in top management ever bothers to come through the shop just to see us." Executives who appreciate the importance of a strong "company spirit" usually spend a great deal of time in visiting and talking with employees.

When an employee identifies with his company, he learns to realize that the management is similar to the head of a family—the head must withhold some desired rewards and earnings in order to distribute the available income where it is needed most. The head of a family cannot afford to give each child everything he wants, nor can a management give each employee everything he wants, but frequent communication with employees is essential if management wishes to have employees think "with management."

Most people are emotionally happier when they identify with authority figures such as political leaders, supervisors, teachers, and parents. When employees, for example, have no authority figure for identification where they work, they tend to leave or to seek such identifications elsewhere as among leaders of community organizations.

One of the most important reasons for promoting men to executive positions from the employees within a company is that the subordinate employees usually find it easy to identify with a colleague who has worked with them. The executive who is brought into a company from the outside usually realizes that he must enable his new subordinates to gradually learn to identify with him. He must do this to prove that he is worthy of their identifications.

The Alert Executive Recognizes Adjustment Tendencies and Directs Them into Positive Channels

Some executives are very sensitive to the feeling tones in the lives of their employees; others are unaware of them. The important action-channels of employees are not always those which are obvious to the observer. Such obvious emotions as the hysterical or angry expressions of the aroused worker are likely to be mere surface ripples. The really significant emotions are hidden beneath the surface—they are undercurrents in the inner basins of the individual personality. People suffer in silence for years. They brood over injustices. Their resentments are cumulative. Their reservoirs of emotional energy are recognized only by the executive who is alert to human emotions and their meanings. Once these reservoirs are revealed to the capable analyst, he may be able to direct the energies of the employee into channels of activity that lead to a more satisfactory and constructive life.

The executive who is alert to the barriers and adjustments in the lives of his employees is also likely to be alert to their strong qualities. If he notices that an office employee is especially skillful in persuading others but also has some show-off tendencies, the executive can direct the employee into salesmanship and train him properly for the work.

Another employee may not have the knack of persuading people but likes to entertain them by clowning, being the "life of the party," and by telling stories. Such an employee is likely to be invited to many social affairs where he amuses others but fails to achieve anything valuable for the employer or for himself. Accordingly, the employer may counsel him regarding training for public relations work that will build goodwill in the community for the company. The entertaining ability can be focused for a purpose which benefits both employer and employees.

The employee who is legally minded may be given the responsibility of keeping in touch with governmental rulings that affect the business.

The employee who is fussy, meticulous, and overly careful can usually be placed in work which requires those habits, such as handling cash or performing an operation requiring manual skill.

Most employees are somewhat adaptable. Their adjustment tendencies, whatever they are, can often be directed for the advantage of both employer and employee. But to do so means that the executive must be alert to the potentialities within the individual, his deep-seated emotional tendencies, his adjustment history. Furthermore, the executive should have the manner of a leader who can, through a definite vocational program, inspire men by showing them visions of their better selves.

ACKNOWLEDGMENTS AND REFERENCES

1. F. B. Rowe, S. Brooks, and B. Watson, "Communication Through Gestures," *American Annals of the Deaf,* 105 (1960), 232–237.
2. Daniel Starch, *How to Develop Your Executive Ability* (New York: Harper & Row, Publishers, Inc., 1943).
3. Frederick G. Vosburgh, "If You Have Goodwill," *Phi Kappa Phi Journal,* March, 1956.
4. Students of radicalism may wish to refer to Edward G. Benson, "Three Words," *Public Opinion Quarterly,* 2 (1938), 130–134, and to E. S. Dexter, "Personality Traits Related to Conservatism and Radicalism," *Character and Personality,* 7 (1939), 230–237.
5. Solomon Diamond, "A Study of the Influences of Political Radicalism on Personality Development," *Archives of Psychology,* October, 1936, p. 53.
6. Elliot Aronson and Judson Mills, "The Effect of Severity of Initiation on Liking for a Group," *Journal of Abnormal and Social Psychology,* September, 1959.

PROJECTS

1. How would you classify the adjustments evident in the main characters described in the following paragraphs:
   a. Samuel is an office employee of a lumber company. He is intensely loyal to his employer, Mr. Brown. The town where they live is small, and Samuel and Mr. Brown have mutual acquaintances. Whenever Samuel can possibly do so, he praises his employer. Samuel's expressions of loyalty have become so extreme that Mr. Brown is often embarrassed.
   b. Marylee says that she won't marry until she finds a man as nice as her daddy.
   c. Robert Burns resented the repressions of the Scotch and wrote literature to express his own revolt.
   d. An injury resulting from a hemorrhage at birth left Earl Carlson with a permanent scar on his brain, an area the nerve currents could not bridge. Hence, if Earl wished to eat his soup, his brain would dispatch the message but the message would never arrive. Only a convulsive flood of energy with a series of haphazard muscular movements would result. The soup would never reach his mouth.

   When Earl became an adult, he managed to go through college and became a physician. Later he became Director of the Department of Corrective Motor Education for the Birth-Injured and Allied Problems, the Neurological Institute, Columbia-Presbyterian Medical Center, New York, where he treated children with handicaps similar to his former handicap. (See Harry W. Hepner, *Finding Yourself in Your Work.* New York: Appleton-Century-Crofts, Inc., 1939, Chapter III.)
2. Consider the extent of a person's identification with an institution or company in spite of frequently voiced criticisms of it. Can a student, for example, identify with his college even though he often criticizes it? Does a mother identify with a son even though she frequently criticizes him?
3. How do status symbols in authoritarian governments differ from those found in democratic forms of government?
4. What differences in identifications have you noticed in college groups such as athletic teams, student political organizations, classes and among members of non-teaching groups?

COLLATERAL READINGS

Fleishman, Edwin A., *Studies in Personnel and Industrial Psychology*. Homewood, Ill.: The Dorsey Press, Inc., 1961.

Hepner, Harry W., *Perceptive Management and Supervision.* Englewood Cliffs, N.J.: Prentice-Hall, Inc., 1961, Chapter 6.

Leavitt, Harold J. and Louis R. Pondy, (Editors), *Readings in Managerial Psychology.* Chicago: The University of Chicago Press, 1964, pp. 331–351.

Lehner, George F. J. and Ella Kube, *The Dynamics of Personal Adjustment.* Englewood Cliffs, N.J.: Prentice-Hall, Inc., 1964, Chapters 4 and 5.

Patty, William L. and Louise Snyder Johnson, *Personality and Adjustment.* New York: McGraw-Hill Book Company, 1953, Chapter 10.

Shaffer, Laurance F. and Edward J. Shoben, Jr., *The Psychology of Adjustment.* Boston: Houghton Mifflin Company, 1956, Chapters 4 and 5.

Smith, Henry Clay, *Psychology of Industrial Behavior.* New York: McGraw-Hill Book Company, 1955, Chapter 7.

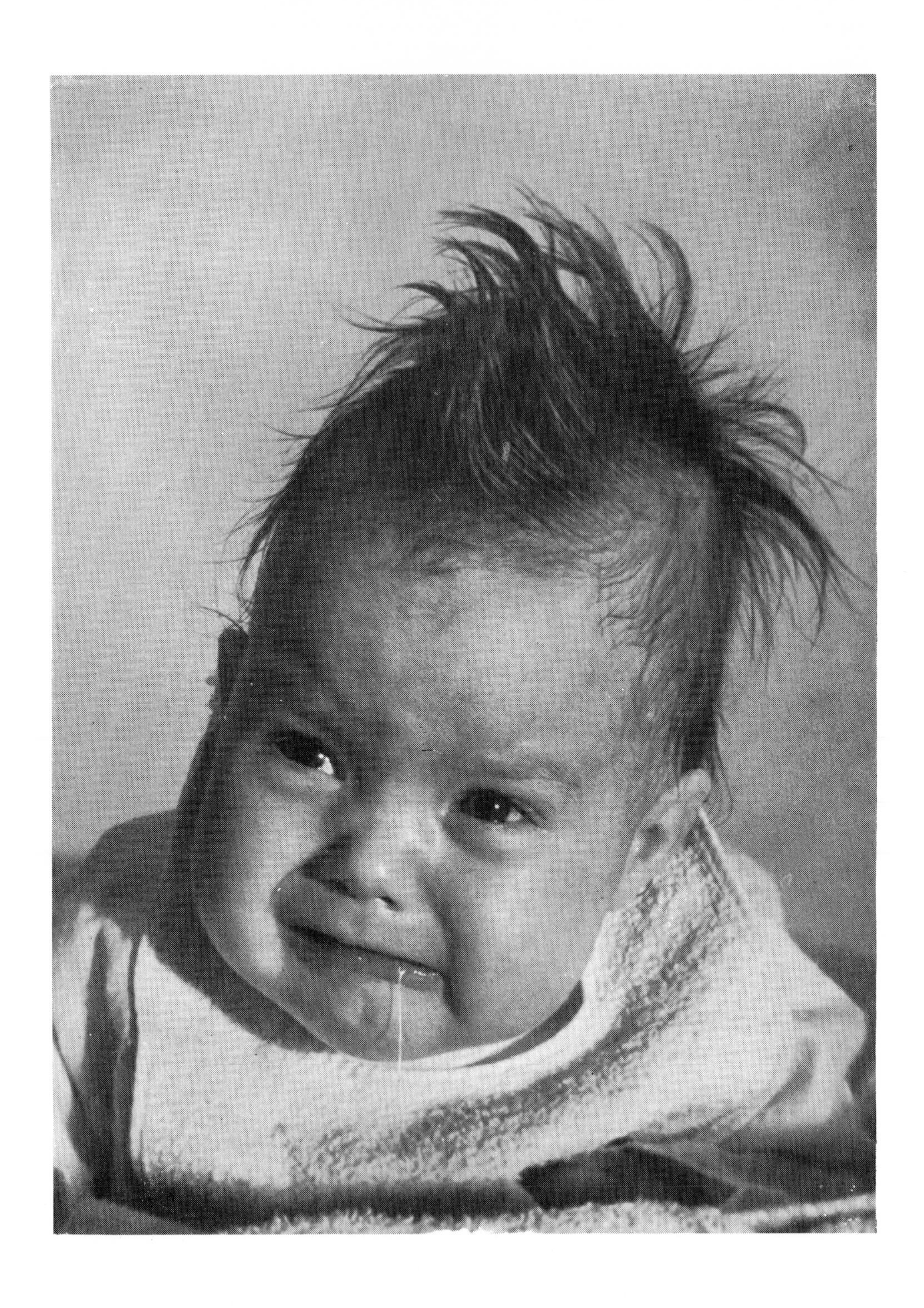

Frustration is as old as life. *The picture was taken in the morning just before feeding time. The mother was standing at the side of the bassinet holding the bottle. The baby was annoyed at the delay and began to cry. There is only one time when the human being has no frustrations, and that is in the period before birth. Frustration begins at birth and ends at death.* **(Photograph by Kenneth P. Marsh, Detroit, Michigan.)**

CHAPTER FOUR

ADJUSTMENT BY SUBSTITUTE ACTIVITIES THAT ARE USUALLY OF NEGATIVE VALUE

"Do you enjoy novel reading, Miss Prim?"
"Oh, very much. One can associate with people in fiction that one wouldn't dare to speak to in real life."—Speed.

When happiness is difficult to attain and the individual lacks intelligent perspective of his barriers and adjustments, he is apt to seek happiness through fictions, psychological returns to childhood, blaming others for his situation; or to make some other form of evasive adjustment. These habits of evasion tend to weaken the individual for dealing with future problems.

A simple example of adjustment by evasion is the cashier who steals money from the cash register. Fundamentally, stealing is wrong; not because of the laws against it, but because it weakens the personality for dealing with future situations. This is a major criterion of the positive or negative values of an act of adjustment: Does it strengthen or weaken the individual for dealing with future problems?

Certain kinds of evasive adjustments are very common and so have been given names, such as regression, projection, and invalidism. Giving a type of adjustment a name has little value except as a convenience for discussion. However, the individual who knows the names of typical forms of evasion is likely to be more alert in recognizing and dealing with them.

Evasive and retreat forms of behavior have meaning; they indicate purpose and the use of poor habits in accomplishing the purpose. A discussion of typical evasive habits should increase our ability to appreciate what the maladjusted individual is trying to accomplish by means of his evasive behavior. Perhaps we can suggest or otherwise encourage the substitution of good habits for poor ones. The following discussion of evasions should also help us increase our psychological alertness in recognizing typical evasions on our part and possibly suggest methods of improving our own mental habits.

Defense Mechanisms

The individual who has failed to develop adjustment habits that enable him to feel at home in his social situations may resort to excessively aggressive conduct and make himself a nuisance to others. More typically, however, he acquires habits of inferiority. He reacts with pronounced fear responses to most

Adjustment by substitute activity *of negative value may eventually lead to adjustment of positive value. The youth who has problems to which he first adjusts by escape into the "arty" or Bohemian aspects of the artist's life may thereby also find himself and eventually devote himself to art in its most meaningful and enduring forms. Similarly, the boy who escapes into the study of nature may thereby become interested in the best aspects of science. The adjustments of evasion do not always remain on the negative value level; many persons rise to positive levels from the negative value levels.*

social situations. His mannerisms of inferiority enable him to avoid much competition and criticism. His habits of personality in social situations are poor because he chose poor adjustive techniques when confronted by barriers such as severe punishment by parents, criticisms by teachers, and the competitiveness of his playmates.

The pattern of convictions, attitudes, and overt behavior of social inferiority is indicated by the symptoms: a tendency to derogate others, preoccupation, to rationalize inadequacies, seclusiveness, and over-susceptibility to flattery.[1]

The most common description of the defensive person is "He has a chip on his shoulder." This pattern is self-protective. The person who has difficulty in admitting to others or himself some inadequacies in his personality may try to guard it from scrutiny by others. He develops some modes of behavior that shield or appear to shield him. These protective forms of behavior are called *defensive mechanisms*. He uses them to protect himself from his own anxieties and his associates soon learn to avoid any mention of those inadequacies for which he adjusts by defensive behavior. They know that any mention of his defect, real or imagined, is likely to result in exaggerated behavior or withdrawal from the social situation.

Painful and unpleasant topics of importance to us are likely to bring out defense mechanisms, as exemplified in a person's anger over a situation in which he has played an unintelligent part.

"Never talk to Oliver Gaskel about his son!" one of the new executives of the pottery plant was warned. "If you want to get along with the old man, don't mention Junior unless he brings it up first."

Why should Gaskell, Sr., become angry when someone discusses the son? Does he, perhaps, realize that he is responsible for wrecking his son's life, when he forced him away from medicine as a career in order to have his son enter and carry on the pottery business? Or does he secretly think of his son as a weakling, a failure? In either case, is he now trying to close his mind to a painful idea? When someone mentions his son, he uses anger as a defense.

The one situation in work life where defensiveness is often evident is in the ways certain employees react to criticism of their work. When the supervisor points out an error, the non-defensive person accepts it objectively. In contrast, the defensive employee tightens up and refuses to admit the error, however small. He may even refuse to admit the error when it is clearly evident that he made it, and offers far-fetched explanations instead.

The defensive person asserts his innocence even when not accused as exemplified by one executive who said of his secretary: "She is so defensive that if you told her it was raining outside, she'd say it wasn't her fault."

A common example of defensiveness in social situations is the very dignified gentleman who seems to wear an armor plating of dignity as a protection against criticism and social inadequacy. As one humorist said: "Don't mistake dignity. Lots of times it enables a man who says nothin', does nothin', and knows nothin' to command a lot of respect!"

Everyone is certain to meet this type of dignity. It is protective. The individual avoids risks of social failure by means of a manner which causes others to treat him with the kind of respect his manner demands. In business, his associates sense his sensitiveness. They defer to him when in his presence but they avoid his presence whenever possible. He is a lonely person and can be "reached" only when he is in circumstances where he feels secure from criticism. In previous generations, many of these dignified gentlemen held executive jobs. Today, if circumstances place them in executive positions, they are likely to be poor leaders. Modern business requires the ability to give and take criticism without excessive defensiveness.

The cliché, like dignity, is a device for avoiding anxiety, withholding information, and concealing ignorance. The cliché often enables the individual to reduce the turmoil in his life to a series of simple formulae.[2]

Anxiety

Anxiety is an emotional response to a situation such as a conflict or a problem that seems to have no acceptable solution. It evokes a sense of helplessness. All of us experience it at various times, and in different degrees of severity. It is, in fact, the most common form of personality disturbance. We have all experienced anxiety in some form: a sense of anticipatory dread, unfocused and not quite localizable; the cold, sweaty palms; the palpitation; the urgent and ill-timed call of nature; or the tense headache.

Anxiety is a fear response to anticipated situations that threaten self-esteem. Neurotic anxiety is an over-response to such threats. It often occurs in adults who, as a result of not being accepted and intrinsically valued as children, do not enjoy a full sense of adequacy independent of their performance and success in fields outside the immediate threat.[3] This helps us understand why our compliments to the anxiety-ridden adult usually have little or no effect on his anxiety when he finds himself in another situation that threatens his self-esteem. It also suggests that when we deal with an overly anxious response to a simple situation, we should examine the individual's early background.

Anxiety crops up frequently among people attempting to make an adequate adjustment to the real world. It can be defined as an individual's fear-laden over-reaction to an adjustment situation. The threatening implications of the situation are felt because the individual already senses that he cannot cope with the situation. It becomes a threat to his self-esteem. Because anxiety is so prevalent, it is important to gain insight into the characteristic techniques of adjustment that anxious individuals adopt.

In an attempt to determine what these are, 50 high- and 50 low-anxiety students in an undergraduate course in education were given two tests: In one they were blindfolded and asked to trace a stylus through a maze. The other test was mirror tracing. Some from each group were given prior orientation to the tests. Others were not.

In those cases where there was no prior training given, the low-anxiety group was significantly superior to the high-anxiety

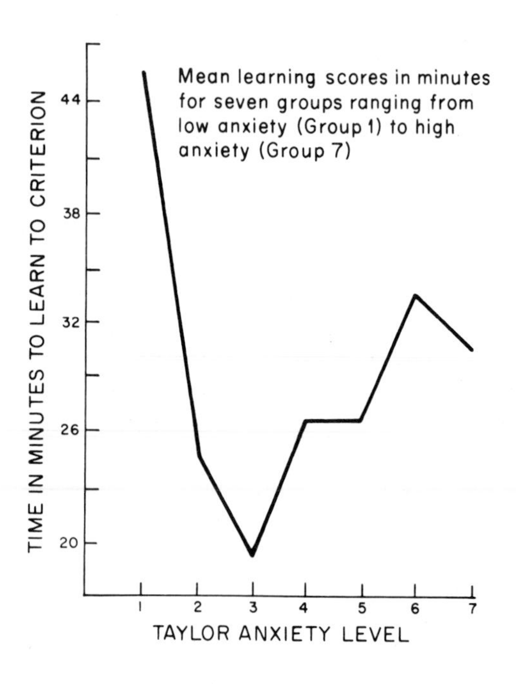

The student who wonders whether he should ever have any anxiety in regard to his work should study the above chart.

An anxious individual can learn to do a job, such as tracing a stylus maze, more easily than a person who exhibits little anxiety according to one series of experiments. Matarazzo grouped subjects into seven divisions based on the subject's level of anxiety according to the Taylor Manifest Anxiety Test. Those who were in Group 7 were the most anxious; those in Group 1, least anxious. The subjects who were midway—in Group 3—learned most efficiently. It took them only 19.33 minutes as compared with Group 1 who took almost 50 minutes. Those who were in Groups 6 and 7 took a long time to learn to perform the task efficiently. Still, they learned in a much shorter time than those who recorded very little anxiety. —From Matarazzo, Joseph, George Ulett and George Saslow, "Human Maze Performance as a Function of Increasing Levels of Anxiety," ***Journal of General Psychology,*** *1955, pp. 79–85.*

group on the first trial of the maze. This superiority was not maintained over ten trials, however. The highly anxious subjects greatly benefited by successful repetitions of the maze. Because they had less intrinsic self-esteem they also clung to their initial goals more than did the low group after experiences of failure. Their need for high achievement made them less flexible in lowering their level of aspiration. They also performed better when they had received prior orientation to the test.

There was no difference between the two groups in mirror tracing ability.

The results may mean that the reason the high-anxiety group reacted as they did was because they could not improvise readily in a novel learning situation. Tracing a stylus, while blindfolded, through a maze is unlike most other experiences an individual has. The highly anxious individuals tended to cling to stereotyped responses which had been useful in other learning situations. Only when it was apparent that these would not work were they discarded. Both practice and advance preparation produced better results, for they reduced novelty and unfamiliarity. Thus, the threat of failure and the danger of lowered self-esteem were mitigated. Anxiety was reduced, and performance improved when the elements of improvisation and newness were removed from the situation.[4] (See chart on opposite page for results of another experiment on relation of anxiety to maze learning.)

For some individuals, anxiety can be a useful and a facilitating force which helps them overcome difficult situations. For others, anxiety only impairs their ability to perform. We call these types of anxiety facilitating and debilitative, respectively.

The student who finds that he works best under pressure, who does better on his examinations than on his regular daily work, and enjoys the challenge of an examination is the one who profits from his anxiety. On the other hand, the student who always does poorly on exams, who never overcomes his feelings of nervousness during any kind of test situation, and dreads examinations is hindered by anxiety.[5]

Students who feel anxious or worried sometimes think that their feelings will affect intelligence test scores adversely. According to one study this does not appear to be true. Anxiety, in this test situation, did not affect intelligence levels. College sophomores, 101 in number, were tested using three criteria of intelligence. The subjects took intelligence tests while they were experiencing different levels of anxiety (as measured by the Taylor Scale of Manifest Anxiety). No relationship was found between the student's grade point average and his score on non-timed intelligence tests. Although anxiety levels affected scores on a timed intelligence test only slightly, the difference was large enough to be statistically significant. This may mean that efficiency, but not intelligence, is reduced when a certain level of anxiety is reached.[6]

Anxiety, though usually unpleasant, has considerable motivating value. A student, for example, thinks of low grades as incompatible with his self-esteem and becomes anxious about his grades. The resultant drive causes him to study. A positive adjustment has been made and tension is reduced.

Anxiety is also a frequent motivating factor in negative value adjustments. We see examples every day in the various forms of trial-and-error types of adjustive behavior. These may seem irrational to the observer, as in the example of the woman who feels anxious because of her imagined social inferiority and then treats sarcastically those whom she admires. Much of the so-called senseless behavior that we see, particularly the kind that obviously results in disadvantage for the individual, does have tension-reducing benefits.

Anxieties which are deep seated aspects of an individual employee's life style cannot, of course, be eliminated by counseling or supervisory skills on the part of the executive. Fears concerning situations outside the employee and anxieties within can, in some cases, be reduced by the executive. He can assure the employee of management's confidence in and respect for him, provide facts about the company's favorable business prospects, keep the employee busy at important tasks, and invite him to discuss his situation with other members of the organization.

Anxiety is one of the basic elements in some varieties of humor. The main themes in humor are sex and aggression because they are primary sources of most human conflicts and tensions. Anxiety often arises from inner conflicts over the inhibition of strong drives or impulses. Hence, a story or situation seems funny when it arouses anxiety and at the same time relieves it.

This interpretation of humor is Freud's. He found that humor gives pleasure by permitting the momentary gratification of some hidden and forbidden wish and at the same time reducing the anxiety that normally inhibits the fulfillment of the wish. A contemporary explanation of these views follows.

By making light of the forbidden impulse, treating it as trivial or universal, a joke or cartoon releases inner tension. The sudden release of tension comes as a pleasant surprise, while the unconscious source of the individual's tension is so disguised in the joke that it is usually not disturbing. . . .

From this theory we can derive a hypothesis that there are three types of reaction to a joke or humorous happening. If it evokes no anxiety at all in an individual, either because he has no conflict over the subject or because his conflict is too deeply repressed, he will be indifferent to the joke. If the situation calls forth anxiety and immediately dispels it, the individual will find it funny. But if it arouses anxiety without dissipating it, he will react to the ostensibly humorous situation with disgust, shame, embarrassment or horror. . . .

Psychotic patients tend to be either indifferent to cartoons or disturbed by them; when they do find one funny, they are likely to laugh uproariously at some totally irrelevant interpretation of their own. For example, a female schizophrenic was greatly amused by a cartoon of a fat man standing on a weighing machine with his back to the dial (his belly protruded too far to allow him to stand facing it). When asked why she found it funny, she explained: "The man is pregnant. . . ."

Mental patients and many relatively normal people resist laughter because it means a loss of self-control, which they fear. . . .The unfortunate individuals who cannot laugh (have "no sense of humor") are restrained, we believe, by a strong and vigilant guard against the release of unacceptable thoughts or wishes.

Play, according to psychoanalytic theory, is a way of mastering anxiety which most people develop very early in childhood. After a particularly frightening experience at the dentist's, a child is apt to go home and play dentist with a doll. The violent fantasies of the comics provide a release of aggressive impulses which the child can enjoy with impunity. . . .

It is no accident that comedians are often basically sad, depressed persons. For them, humor serves as a defense against anxieties arising from their relations with people. The wish to make people laugh becomes a pervasive and consuming drive; they must have laughter and applause as an expression of love. Alone or when not performing, they are apt to be withdrawn, melancholy, preoccupied. . . .

It is no easy matter to predict what cartoons will seem funny to a given person. But psychiatrists have found that they can predict pretty reliably which cartoons will disturb their patients. Undisguised sex, gruesome aggression, extreme prankishness and irreverence toward accepted authority are most often disturbing. However, persons whose sexual problems are close to the surface of awareness are apt to laugh boisterously —too readily and too loudly—at jokes about sex. . . .

Humor serves as a tension-releaser for most people. The more sorely troubled, who cannot relax in this way, may seek release in alchohol or pathological flights from reality. The capacity to laugh is a measure of one's adjustment to his environment. It follows that inability to appreciate humor, or deviant responses to it, can be regarded as a sensitive indicator of maladjustment and inner disturbance.[7]

These views are now applied in a psychological test which has proved to be a useful instrument for clinicians in bringing out emotional problems. Responses of the subject are studied in relation to what is known about his background and personality.

Those who score high on certain anxiety scales are somewhat more likely to be described by their peers as less frank, less good-natured, less conscientious, and less generous than those who score low.[8] Obviously, anxiety, motivation, and defensiveness often function in a very complex interacting relationship.

Regression

We occasionally meet the man who acts and dresses in the manner of several decades ago. We have also known the type of adult who talks of the "good old days when boys were gentlemanly and girls were virtuous." Such expressions may mean that he is simply giving evidence of having partly outlived his age. The problems of his present are too great for him to solve satisfactorily and he regresses mentally to a former happier state when life was more satisfying.

The employee who once had a good job but lost it may make an adjustment by living in that former happy state, or he may react to his present situation in an aggressive manner and look toward the future rather than the past. Psychologically, old age sets in just as soon as the past appears to be more pleasant than the present and the future. There is but one stage in the life of man when all his wants are satisfied just as soon as they occur, and that is when he is an embryo. As soon as he is born he begins to have wants which are not always satisfied when they occur. He must adjust himself to his world until death overtakes him and ends the process of adjustment.

The unmarried woman may regress to the days when she had a lover but lost him, or she may face the future with a zest for new loves and new adventures. Barriers such as a broken engagement, failure in studies, bankruptcy in business, or discharge from a good job should cause no tears, but should motivate the individual for a stronger attack upon new ventures. Failure to do this is illustrated when an older employee has failed in a hard job or a business for himself, and the remark is made: "The experience took the heart right out of him." In some forms of insanity, regression takes place to an extent that is almost unbelievable. The patient goes back to childhood in talk and conduct.

Regression, of the kind which is a form of relaxation that leads to possible later attack on one's problems, is found in childish hobbies and games. Toy trains are an example.

Children as well as adults regress. An older child, for example, who must adjust to the arrival of a new infant in the home may regress by losing previously well-established toilet habits or by crying a great deal. Parents who do not recognize the meaning of the regressions are apt to scold or punish the child. Instead, the understanding parents will show the child that he is wanted and loved.

Adults who regress are unhappy because they are no longer children. The world has moved on but they are left behind. In trying to adjust themselves to modern problems they take refuge, through their imaginations, in the mental life experienced when they were happy, carefree children. They find it satisfying to regress at times:

> Backward, turn backward, O Time, in your flight!
> Make me a child again, just for to-night!

The girl who longs for the ignorance and the innocence of pre-adolescence finds adjustment difficult. It would be better for her to prepare for motherhood or, if unmarried, to sublimate her sex energies into socially acceptble channels. Also, the middle-aged married woman who has not developed a deep-seated interest in her own family or in a career is apt to take an excessive interest in young men, especially if she was attractive when young. The poor adjustment to her increasing age and declining beauty causes her to regress to her youth when boys admired her. Many middle-aged women grow bitter when they can neither achieve an acceptable relationship with young men nor develop another interest that is intrinsically sound. Well-adjusted women grow old gracefully.

Regression to childish mannerisms, *infantilism,* is exceedingly common. The average grown-up frequently shows his infantilism by his temper tantrums, pouting, dawdling, weeping, clowning to attract attention, making grimaces, or noisy nasal and throat habits.

Adjustment by regression or return to a former happier state is very common. Many of our nostalgic songs stress the scenes of childhood and youth.

These childish mannerisms are so common and meaningful that we can often recognize what a maladjusted person is trying to do if we say to ourselves: "What would the person's behavior signify if it were performed by a four-year-old child?"

The college student who suffers from "homesickness" demonstrates that he has a barrier in the form of being too closely attached to the members of his family and that he must turn to them to shield him and make his decisions for him. In the new college environment, he finds barriers in the form of strangers among faculty and student body who pay little attention to him, and so he develops fears and anxieties which result in physiological imbalances that lead to such physical symptoms as headaches, indigestion, or loss of appetite. His physical symptoms now "prove" to himself and to others that he should return home at once!

Regression is a serious problem to the new executive who has been hired to put a money-losing company back into the profit-making column. Many of the old employees have fixed habits which once were sound but are now inefficient in comparison with modern methods. The old employees may be pursuing methods the very opposite of those pursued by the man who is in tune with the new American tempo. What should be the attitude of the new executive toward an organization that is antiquated in methods and attitude? Should he "clean house" and "fire" most of the old employees and executives, replacing them with new blood? Or should he try to revitalize the old members? We must remember that adjustment habits cannot be erased and new ones formed at a moment's notice. The behavior patterns that are in the nervous systems of the old employees were put there by many thousands of repetitions, and new ones are difficult to produce. Shock is the only quick method, but this also does much harm. To rebuild an old organization may require so much time and effort on the part of the key executives that the end does not justify the means. However, this does not imply that all the old timber of the structure is bad. Certain employees bearing the scars of battle may have become better because of having withstood the onslaughts of competition. The ideal policy would be to save the good men and to retrain those who do not fit into the new situation but this may not always be feasible.

Rigidity

Rigidity can be defined as a pervasive personality trait that restricts the range of behavior. It is protective. The rigid individual avoids many problems, particularly conflicts,

"Here's Mr. Apgar, Ed—set your watch for 7:32." Source: by Jeff Keate. Reproduced by permission of the McNaught Syndicate, Inc.

by ignoring them—he lives in a world of "blacks" and "whites," no "greys." He holds strictly to some personal philosophy, set of ethical principles, or dogma. His behavior is usually quite predictable but he is likely to be limited in leadership ability, socially introverted, lacking in social presence, anxious, and unoriginal.[9]

One research study of rigidity was made by comparing the 10 most rigid and the 10 most flexible individuals from a pool of 500 persons whose rigidity had been measured by a test for the trait. The study indicated that the flexible individuals married older, had had more education, had higher income, attained higher occupational levels, and rated themselves as happier, more successful, and more socially responsible than the rigid subjects. The young flexible group changed residence more often than the young rigid group.[10]

The employment interviewer who wants to hire applicants for jobs that require adaptability as in selling does not usually test the candidates for their degree of rigidity but he often estimates it from the interview behavior. For some jobs, he typically prefers the rigid personality as in accounting, engineering, and laboratory research.

The supervisor of rigid employees usually notes their behavioral patterns and gives them the kinds of assignments they prefer. He lets them alone but he himself usually seeks the camaraderie of the flexibles and helps them to develop themselves for greater responsibility.

Rigidity has several well-known manifestations as in fixed ideas and negativism.

Fixed Ideas

Every businessman has met the employee who was reprimanded for some slight infraction of the rules and who brooded over the reprimand for months—his feelings being wholly out of proportion to the seriousness of the affair; or the employee who had to be discharged and who returned again and again for a reconsideration of his case; or the old employee who demanded a pension even though the company has not given pensions to other employees and has never consciously given the impression that pensions were granted; or the executive who wants a decision in his favor, and, if it is not rendered wholly in his favor, reopens the case at each conference and insists upon discussing it, to the disgust of his fellows; or the person who loses a lawsuit and then carries the case to higher courts until the lawyers decide to neglect it or to postpone it indefinitely.

Why do these individuals persist in their fixed ideas? One reason may be that the ego of the complainant has been assailed. The concession demanded in his favor is desired, not for its intrinsic worth, but, as he calls it, "the principle of the thing." He wants the decision in his favor because he needs it to make himself appear worthwhile in his own estimation. The complaint often indicates that the individual is adjusting to a barrier of a failure type and he resents that his desired success cannot be achieved through normal channels. The really big man is willing to make concessions to others and does not feel that he has compromised his own integrity or worth. It is the little fellow who cannot accept anything less than complete surrender from others. The person who has some great achievement to his credit is not likely to feel the need of small concessions. It is well, therefore, to try to make the complainant feel satisfied by showing him that you admire him for certain other qualities and that he really does not need what he desires—you like him as he is.

Most of the persons who develop these fixed ideas lead so routine or narrow a life that they lack practice in making the daily little adjustments which we learn to make when we associate with many people. The employee who operates a semi-automatic machine for five days of the week and then goes home to a lonely room where he sleeps until the next day is a fit victim for fixed ideas.

Sometimes managers wonder whether they are supplying too many side activities and forms of recreation for their employees. The danger from these extra activities lies in the fact that they are often patronized by one group or clique, and the backward employees who need more contacts do not take an active part. To prevent this, it is well to see to it that each employee does take an active part in the company's recreational activities or in some other activities not sponsored by the employer. Employees should appoint committees to look after the retiring fellows who have no stimulating forms of recreation. Each and every employee should be encouraged to attend some company recreational affairs.

Executives themselves may lead too narrow lives. Of all the men whom the writer has ever met, the one most fixed in his ideas is an executive who lives only for his business, which he inherited. His two-year-old baby and his wife are merely incidental parts of the home, like the furniture. His mental and emotional life is too circumscribed, and, when he attends a conference where he can talk, his associates become angry and disgusted with his harping upon nonessentials that were considered settled long ago. To be normally adjusted, everyone needs many varied intellectual, emotional, and physical exercises.

Negativism

One of the greatest problems of the executive is that of securing the coöperation of his associates and subordinates. Whenever any program of action is suggested that involves some absent member of the organization, the question arises as to how to handle the absent but important individual. The point is raised as to how to sell the idea to him. Some member of the group may suggest: "Let's ask him to do the opposite of what we want, and then he'll want to do it." A few employees always seem to carry a negative attitude toward any ideas that are proposed to them. How did they acquire such reaction patterns?

Negativism is a defense. In many cases the habit pattern was established by the persons who reared the individual as a child. If we observe a mother rearing her child, we may find that she is constantly setting up barriers to the child by telling him what to do and what not to do. The commands flow in rapid succession: "Wash your face," "Say 'Thank you,' " "Give the toy to little brother," "Come here," "Stop that," and so on. Most of these demands from the adult come at times when the child is busily engaged in some absorbing activity, such as building a castle, flying an airship, or slaying a giant. Small wonder that he feels that adults are tyrants who spoil his fun and can be dealt with only by opposing them through breaking valuable articles or by other forms of naughtiness. Sometimes the repressions of childhood lead to later expressions of opposition to authority as in kleptomania or exhibitionism. These are simply adult varieties of "naughtiness" which the individual cannot explain.

Children who have the barrier of too much discipline from parents may withdraw into themselves and daydream rather than play active games, or they may voice their resistance in their dreams at night when they talk to themselves and say: "I don't have to," or "I won't do it." Boys who are reared by a mother and several older sisters who supervise every act of the child often acquire a negative attitude toward all women, and, if they marry, their wives are apt to say: "My husband loves me and I love him, but he does just the opposite of anything I tell him to do." Small wonder that he is negatively set toward any woman's requests, when women have "lorded" it over him for years!

Adjustment by negativism may be expressed passively, as in doing nothing when something is expected, or it may be active negativism—doing the opposite of what is expected. In some forms of insanity the individual may be so negative as to refuse to obey the normal promptings of the bodily processes, such as swallowing the saliva.

In industry, negativism may find an outlet when employees perform duties to the point ordered but no farther. The executive who finds that his employees are quarrelsome or do what is asked of them but no more may take stock of himself to learn whether he has hired a group of employees who were negative when hired or whether he has made them negative in attitude by the tone of his voice and the manner in which he gives orders. The dictatorial type of executive may get results by cowing his employees or by brilliant tactical strategy, but he seldom gets that teamwork which gives joy to the executive who knows that "the boys are with him to the utmost." The great leader of men has learned that it is best to explain the reasons for his requests in a straightforward but friendly tone and manner which convinces the employees that he believes in and likes them.

Fantasy or Daydreaming

The imaginary representation of satisfactions which the individual would like to attain but does not attain in everyday life is called *fantasy* or daydreaming. It is so easy an adjustment to make when a barrier arises that everyone daydreams to some extent.

In the *conquering hero* mechanism, the individual does not successfully face his situations in direct attacks, but pictures himself doing the deeds or possessing the things he desires. The boy who is thwarted in his attempts to do as he pleases at home can soar away in his imagination to wonderful lands of cannibals and kings, where he can conquer armies and achieve honor. As he becomes older, he daydreams of financial success, with several large automobiles, a magnificent estate, a yacht, plenty of money, and then, to cap the climax, he will become a member of the board of education and fire all the teachers whom he does not like! On other days he may picture himself as a great prize fighter, a football player, a bandit, or a preacher. The girl daydreams of the social approval of others about her, where she is a great singer, a social worker, a missionary, or a Joan of Arc. Daydream frequency declines with age from the late teens to the fifth decade.[11] Those who score high on a daydream inventory differ from those who score low along a dimension which might be termed self-awareness, the acceptance of inner experience.[12]

A certain amount of daydreaming is normal and natural for all persons; but when it becomes a substitute for reality, it eliminates the necessity of actual achievement and causes the individual to live in a world of fantasy. In hospitals for the mentally ill, we find patients who are satisfied to live within their imaginations. Some of them imagine they are great men and women, such as Napoleon or Queen Victoria. As Kipling said, if one can dream and not make dreams his master, he is a successful man.

G. H. Green[13] has suggested four types of fantasy which are varieties of the conquering hero daydream. In the *display* fantasy, the dreamer gains social recognition for some act of ability or daring. In the *saving* daydream, the dreamer pictures himself performing some brave deed under extreme difficulties and thereby gaining the affection of the person rescued. In the fantasy of *grandeur,* the individual imagines himself a great person such as a king or even a god. In the *homage* daydream, the dreamer imagines himself performing a service for someone whose love he desires. Many other kinds of daydreams are used by individuals as a means of adjusting themselves to problems, such as the *destruction* daydream in which enemies may be put to death, injured, or destroyed in the fantasy.

The *suffering hero* or *martyr* type of escape is also common, as in the small boy who, because he is reprimanded, decides that he will be a very wicked bandit, rob trains, be put in jail, and eventually be hanged. His body will be brought home, and all his parents, relatives, friends, and teachers will be sorry that they mistreated him.

This type of behavior is also expressed on a milder level by the stenographer who becomes peevish and sullen. Usually she can be stimulated in several different ways. Her supervisor may approach the issue in a direct frontal attack and tell her to "snap out of it" because she is making the day unpleasant for everyone around her, or he may give her so much work to do and demand it so soon that she simply will not have time to think about herself. However, a very sensitive girl may be paralyzed by a severe scolding. It is well, therefore, to treat each employee as an individual rather than as one of a class. One rule should govern the executive: The employees must be stimulated to deal with situations as they are rather than as they would prefer them to be.

Important questions for the executive are: "What are my employees really thinking? What kinds of daydreams are they having? Are their minds filled with pleasant imagery?" The employees may apparently be busy at their tasks, but their minds may be filled with unvoiced curses for the boss and wishes that they were a thousand miles away from him and his picayune job.

Factory workers who perform repetitive jobs usually overcome boredom by means of daydreams. Mind-wandering of the fantasy variety is a protection against monotony.[14] It compensates for the deficiencies of life in general, and many a poorly adjusted person has sought a repetitive job so that he might enjoy his fantasies without the interruptions of the alert thinking which would be a part of a more varied job. Many machine tenders are very happy while at work—their minds are roaming about in delightful worlds of fantasy.

All persons like to get away from monotony and routine in order to enjoy vicarious adventures. When we go to the moving picture show and throw ourselves into the emotionality of the plot, we not only escape from our humdrum world but also "experience" worlds which we can never hope to enjoy in actuality. One reason why we do not care to see moving pictures or plays that describe life in its daily routine is that we want to escape our own realities and live in a new world rather than in the kind we have each day. Those of us who have routine jobs want to identify ourselves, for example, with the young man who was reared in the country but went to the city and there beat the captains of finance at their own game. We want to see beautiful women in the moving picture; women who are never troubled by boresome problems of taking care of crying babies and mending socks. We want the ideal pictured in the dramatizations to help us escape our problems. The happy ending is the only satisfying one, because we experience realistic living every day and do not find it sufficiently thrilling.

> ...the movie...notoriously furnishes an antisocial "escape" that takes mere murder in its stride and delightfully threatens maid, matron, and debutante with the fate that is worse than death. All this in a theater darkened just enough to enjoy the moral support of one's beshadowed neighbors without actually suffering their active chaperonage. Motion pictures thus become, in a milder degree, a recognized mechanism for multiple defrustration, like mixed bathing and the country club drink-and-dance.[15]

Withdrawal or Escape

Of course, one of the most universally-used methods of adjustment to unpleasant situations is withdrawal or escape. The individual simply refuses to deal with the problem. He treats it as though it did not exist. Or, if that is not possible, he may escape from it temporarily by concentrating his thinking on some other activity such as reading "escape" literature. If that kind of activity is not attractive to him, he can resort to the use of tranquilizer drugs.

The fact that so large a proportion of people turn to these avoidance types of adjustment indicates that some persons need release from their problems even though the respite may be for short periods of time only. Then too, those who have developed the tendency toward using the strengthening adjustments of the positive variety often find that their occasional *escape from* one kind of activity leads to an *escape into* a new and developmental interest. Certainly, not all adjustments by escape are detrimental to mental health. They may help us deal with stress as exemplified by a study of marital dissatisfaction. Some marriage partners deal with their dissatisfactions by fantasy rather than real involvement.[16]

Projection

Every individual, at times, shifts blame for his own incapacities upon some other person or institution. He does this as a defense against anxiety-producing drives.

The process of ascribing to another person or institution the burden of our own repressions is commonly referred to as projection. The person who perceives in other people the traits and motives which he cannot admit in himself is probably using the mechanism of projection.

Occasionally we hear unjustified rumors of immorality as a result of projection. A woman accuses some reputable and important member of the community of gross immoralities. Such stories throw undeserved suspicion upon the accused individual. The suspicion should really be directed toward the accuser, for the accusing woman is merely projecting to someone else the impulses that she herself is trying so hard to combat. She could not bear to admit to herself her terrible impulses and so she built up pictures of others who did the things that shamed her self-respect. Many a reformer has retained the integrity of his selfhood by joining an organization to combat the same tendencies that he had to fight in his moral life.

The fanatical reformer and chronic accuser are often unpopular among intelligent people, and the unpopularity is partly deserved. If one has a normal desire to improve the world, he will tend to do it in a quiet and tactful manner rather than by beating his chest and crying his aims from the housetops. The clinical psychologist who visits so-called liberal clubs is often amused by the large percentage of members who have not grown up emotionally and are projecting their own maladjustments upon a conjured monster, such as the economic or political system.

"He spends most of our vacations scolding his office help. He's getting even with a boss he used to have."

From "The Neighbors," by George Clark.

Many of these club members are so maladjusted that they are unable to analyze modern problems objectively. Some prate glibly about coöperation and sharing with others when they themselves are rank individualists who emotionally could not coöperate even though they might intellectually wish to do so. We can rest assured that when our economic or political system does evolve into a better stage, its evolution will have been brought about by balanced personalities, and not by the self-styled projecting liberals. True, occasionally we all do some projecting, because admission of our own deficiencies is painful, but we cannot solve our personal problems by "jumping on somebody's neck." The well-adjusted personality does not condemn his environment; he analyzes it objectively and utilizes it in new ways.

The student who has the barrier of failure in an examination often projects the cause to the unfairness of the teacher. The man who slips in his marital relations tends to cover up his digressions by accusing others of infidelity. The man who fails in business does not, as a rule, blame himself, but imputes his losses to the "powerful forces of Wall Street" or governmental interference. The production foreman who falls down on his schedule may have sound reasons for so doing; but it is to be expected that he will suggest that the blame should be placed on some other executive. Forceful executives often develop the habit of asking their subordinates to perform certain jobs and of implying, when the orders are given, that excuses are not going to be even considered. This method has decided benefits, because it causes the subordinate executives to spend their mental efforts in working out schemes for the accomplishment of the desired end rather than in seeking excuses of the projectionist's kind. The executive who insists upon results and results only may develop the reputation of being hard-boiled, but his methods are sounder psychologically than those of the other man who accepts the excuses of poorly adjusted employees. Any organization that is made up of a large number of "projectors" is also a red ink organization.

The executive himself often projects his failures to factors other than himself. If the balance sheet figures are unsatisfactory, he can blame his employees, competitors, or government interferences; or he can calmly analyze the situation for the causes of failure and then busy himself on an improved plan of procedure for the next fiscal period. "Passing the buck" satisfies the "passer" but does not bring objective results.

Repression

An everyday example of repression arises when we have injured someone. We "forget" our shameful act toward him because we repress the memory. Some repressed memories, however, often produce an energy much stronger than those trivial experiences we forget because they are unimportant to us.

The energy developed by a repressed experience seeks an outlet. The repressed experience may appear in symbolical form in fantasy, dreams, or situations unconsciously related to the earlier shameful act. Irrational fears, dislikes, and strong emotions develop even though we are quite unaware of their origin. The person whom we injured becomes a scapegoat for our repressed memory. We find many apparently logical reasons for disliking him. We imagine that our dislike for him arises from his acts, not from our own. If, for example, we borrowed money from him years ago and felt ashamed because we never paid him back, we may eventually "discover" that he has become so despicable a character that he no longer deserves our friendship! The debt is forgotten and he is now so low a personality that we no longer want to associate with him.

A person represses something when he unconsciously denies that it exists, or when he fails to see its relevance to him. Although he may actually look at an object, or hear words, these make no impression upon his conscious mind. Or he may see the object or hear the words but fail to understand their real personal significance for him. This has been illustrated in many experiments, including one in which respondents were shown sentences describing sexual and aggressive feelings toward parents. They were asked to read these under varying degrees of illumination. The results: Different individuals found certain sentences more difficult to read, or distorted their meaning, although all were shown with the same degree of legibility. In general, this experiment showed that all subjects tend to repress aggressive and sexual material but women repress aggressive material to a greater extent than they do sexual and men repress sexual material to a greater extent than they do aggressive.[17]

The student who has cheated in past examinations and has a guilty reaction to it may be anxious lest he cheat again. He represses the memories of his past cheating and his impulsion to cheat again. He becomes scrupulously honest about cheating but projects the idea of cheating upon his fellow students. Even though his colleagues do not cheat, he believes that they do and he conjures up "evidence" to prove it. He may even head a reform movement for overcoming the evil of cheating in his college. This kind of common mechanism has given rise to the old adage, "There's no one so virtuous and anxious to impose upon others his idea of virtue as the reformed sinner!"

Scapegoating

All through history primitive peoples have transferred their own guilt and suffering to other living creatures. Civilized man continues to do the same today. Now, however, transfer is usually made to a person or a group of persons, whereas in ancient times an animal was often selected. Probably the most famous transfer ceremony on record is the one described in the Old Testament wherein the Hebrews, anxious to rid themselves of their feelings of guilt, transferred their sins to a live goat. (Leviticus 16:22.)

"Frankly, we need someone to act as a sort of goat around this office —think you can qualify?"

From "Grin and Bear It," by Lichty, courtesy of Chicago Sun-Times Syndicate. Reprinted by permission.

To rid themselves of feelings of guilt and suffering, people of today use similar methods. They find a scapegoat—an object, institution, person, or group of persons—on whom they can project their aggressions. These aggressions may be wholly undeserved. Although scapegoating is an ever-present phenomenon, it is particularly noticeable in times of social strain, such as during war, famine, revolution, or depression.

Aggression includes verbal and physical abuse, and the victim seldom retaliates because the scapegoat is invariably weaker than the persecutors. In eighteenth-century American history the Salem witches served as scapegoats, because to the accusers of that day the witches personified the devil whom the sin-ridden wished to attack.

There are other reasons for scapegoating. When people are deprived of what they want or what they have, they adjust by aggression, not necessarily against the source of their deprivation, but against any object, person, or group that is convenient. Although the chosen scapegoat may be partially blameworthy, the extent to which it is blamed is out of all proportion to its deserts. Usually, too, the scapegoat must take blame not only for immediate conditions, but for long-standing and deeply rooted frustrations.

The demagogue who seeks political power often encourages scapegoating. By pointing out a scapegoat, an unscrupulous person may achieve a unity among diverse elements who have only the scapegoat as a focal point.[18] Propagandists know that it is easier for most people to blame their own troubles on some persons or institutions, such as financiers, religionists, the educational system, foreign organizations, or any other popularly accepted "devil." The political opportunist finds out who the unpopular "devils" are at the moment and speaks for the projectionists in demanding reforms.

Experiments show that frustration such as a ruined evening may bring anger toward faraway people.

> This was revealed when two psychologists learned that a group of young men at a camp was to be given a series of tests which would be boring to them and which were so difficult that everyone was bound to fail miserably. The time taken to give the tests forced the men to miss what they considered the most interesting event of the week at the local theater. The men, it was anticipated, would be frustrated and made angry by this situation.
>
> Before the men knew the nature of the tests and the fact that they would miss Bank Night, their attitude toward the people of a far-away nation was measured by means of rating-scales.
>
> After they had taken the tests and realized that they could not enjoy the evening at the theater, they were once again asked to rate this nation. It was found that their attitudes after the frustrating tests were reliably more hostile toward the nation than before.
>
> Similar groups who were not frustrated by the tests and who rated the same nation twice revealed no such change. . . .
>
> The psychologists who turned the test evening into an experiment were Dr. Neal E. Miller, of Yale University, and Richard Bugelski, of the University of Toledo. They see in the results an expression of the tendency to blame someone else for an individual's own misfortunes, known to psychologists as the scapegoat device. . . .
>
> "In ordinary social living," Dr. Miller points out, "men and women suffer frustrations especially when they are unemployed or are compelled to accept a reduction in pay. Their anger can spread to scapegoats in the same way that the anger of the men in the camp spread to the people of a foreign country. It is one of the functions of propaganda to induce people to use as scapegoats innocent foreigners who, even though not necessarily responsible for the frustration, are made to serve as targets for aggression.[19]

Somewhat veiled hostility characterized men who were subjected to frustrating situations while being deprived of their night's sleep, Sears, Hovland and Miller found in an exploratory study. In order that the subjects, male college students, might not know the true nature of the experiment, they were told that the purpose was to study reflexes and motor activities of sleep-deprived men.

After attending classes during the day, the subjects reported to the laboratory at 7:30 P.M. where they were kept under close observation until eight o'clock the following morning. During the evening they studied and read. Games and cards were to be brought in about midnight to relieve the monotony, but the materials for these diversions never arrived. At 3 A.M. the experimenter who was to have brought them came in, but had "forgotten" the games. At midnight the subjects were suddenly told not to smoke any more, while the experimenters continued to smoke in their presence. A group discussion from which the men were getting some enjoyment was arbitrarily halted, and a period of silence was maintained. When the men became hungry in the late evening, they were told that a hot breakfast would be brought in at 5 A.M. At 6 A.M. the experimenter who had gone out to get the promised breakfast had failed to return, so the two remaining experimenters "decided" not to wait for him. They therefore tested the men's reflexes and motor activities to maintain the ostensible purpose of the experiment.

During all these frustrations an "in-group" was formed among the subjects, and the cleavage between it and the experimenters was obvious. Aggressive reactions to the frustrations were directed largely at the experimenters; however, they were almost entirely in the form of jocular references to the dullness of the experiment and wisecracks about the uncoöperativeness of the experimenters. The tone of voice and inflection the subjects used in making their "cracks" made their aggressiveness unmistakably clear. Typical of the remarks made by subjects are the following:

3:40 A.M. An experimenter ostentatiously lit a cigarette. Group of five subjects sitting together. "Where's this partial entertainment you offered us? How about some stories?" (E told dull joke; no laughter.) "We discussed cannibalism earlier in the evening." (E: "Would you eat human flesh?") "We may yet tonight." (Meaningful look at one of the E's; much snickering among S's.)

3:50 A.M. "What would happen if we would walk out?" "I suppose you'd blackmail us." "I bet it would wreck your experiment if we did. Let's leave."

5:15 A.M. "Are all psychologists mad?" "They're all queer. I've been watching 'em for a couple of hours."[20]

One piece of aggression that was not a joke or wisecrack was done by the most out-

Spontaneous drawings *revealing the hostility aroused in a deprivation experiment situation. Note the sarcasm in the title!—From R. R. Sears, C. I. Hovland, and N. E. Miller, in the* ***Journal of Psychology,*** *Vol. 9 (1940), pp. 275-295.*

spokenly aggressive subject. The sheet of sketches which he drew to represent psychologists amused the other subjects highly. His sketches are reproduced in "The Joys of Affection."

It must be pointed out that hostility and aggression might have been expressed differently had the relationship between experimenters and subjects not been one of professors and students.[21]

Hostility and Aggression

The hostile person is one who often expresses aggressive behavior or attitudes toward others and reacts to minor frustration, social restrictions, and other people with spiteful anger.[22]

Feelings of hostility have many forms. Examples are irritability, resentment, suspicion, negativism, assault, verbal hostility, and guilt. Some of these are attitudinal, others have a "motor" component.[23]

Feelings of hostility can develop from almost any ordinary life situation, depending upon how much the individual reacted to it with a feeling that he was wronged. A simple example often takes place when a small boy takes music lessons. If the teacher is a frustrated concert artist, she tends to see in the boy the fulfillment of her lost dreams and she pushes him to the point where his love of music is replaced with lifelong hostility to it.

Feelings of hostility have numerous likely components. Studies indicate, for example, that persons high on the personality dimension of authoritarianism exhibit greater overt hostility than persons lower on that dimension.[24]

The self-righteous person who has refused to yield to temptation is likely to be especially severe in his reactions to those who have yielded. One researcher obtained some objective evidence of this well-known principle by conducting an experiment with sixth grade pupils.

He measured their attitudes before and after a contest which presented them with a decision to violate or comply with the moral standard against cheating. Motivation to cheat was manipulated by offering different rewards for winning the contest. Generally, the findings indicated that pupils who decided not to cheat when tempted became more severe in their attitudes toward cheating, those who cheated became more lenient. The greater the motivation to cheat, the more the attitude of severity increased on the part of those who resisted the temptation.[25]

The expressions of aggression in reactions of a hostile nature are too numerous to describe here. They range from physical destruction of the person or situation as in war to the more conventional forms of behavior such as gossip and litigation. They are evident in the rebel who as a child regarded himself superior to his parents and other authority figures. Actually, the typical rebel suffers from ego-weakness and makes unrealistic self-appraisals.[26] We see many examples of hostility, both veiled and overt, whenever we make observations of human behavior. We even see instances where the individual cannot identify a suitable target for his hostility and then turns his aggressions against himself.

In colleges, we often observe the Bohemians who cultivate the bizarre and deviant. They engage in activities which they do not enjoy in the hope that they may thereby be able to overcome their own feelings of inadequacy and loneliness. Many of these rebels are troublemakers to the administration. The reviewer of a book by Everett Lee Hunt, Dean Emeritus of Swarthmore College, has described the college rebel, in part:

> Dean Hunt takes proper pride in the reputation of his college but he also tells us another side of the story. Swarthmore has had its problems. The students attracted by its reputation not only are highly verbal, hard-working, and good grade-getters—they also are prone to arrogance, adolescent varieties of nonconformity, and rebellion against all authority. Though Swarthmore administrators have been both more competent and more tolerant than those of most colleges, the students spend so much time staging protests against the administration that one wonders how they manage to find time to study.
>
> Fortunately, Swarthmore students are capable of criticizing each other. In response to a questionnaire one said: "I can only think of three things that I dislike, and these concern the attitudes of some of the students. Number one is the search for a controversial issue at all costs, be the problem ever so slight. Number two: Why must there be this lurking suspicion that the diabolical administration is plotting against the student body? The very presence of a rule turns them rabid with anger. Number three: I fear some of our much-lauded intellectuality is simulated. A real scholar among the students is the exception, not the rule."[27]

Of course the mature person recognizes that these rebels confuse individualism with self-assertiveness and antisocial behavior. They fail to make the essential distinction between intelligent initiative and the warped drive of the unhappily maladjusted.

Introjection

In projection, we shape the world to suit ourselves—to the satisfaction of the ego. In introjection, we do the opposite. The world shapes us in the images of itself. The intro-

***Many persons erroneously believe** that the typical business executive prefers employees of the introjectionist kind. Only the rather inappropriately adjusted employers prefer them. Most well-balanced executives prefer employees who have ideas and express them tactfully. Of course if the employee is defensive in manner and becomes assertive when he presents his ideas, the listener is likely to be irritated rather than pleased.*

jectionist follows the surge of the crowd. In time of war, he believes all the propaganda that is put out by his side. In politics, he remains within the party lines and cheers without mental reservation for his candidate. He does not calmly analyze and then choose the better of two or more courses of action, but he adopts one course with all his emotional power. In business, he is the "carbon copy" man, the "yes" man. He tries to anticipate the slightest wishes and beliefs of his boss and then adopts those as his own. He likes to be dictated to and ordered about. He dwells within the shadow of his superior and scrapes and bows to the fiddling of those above him. His coöperation is as blind as it is devoted.

Certain executives seem to prefer an organization of introjects. They are easy to handle. They satisfy the ego of the executive and he imagines that he is in full control of his employees, but his organization is one that neither thinks nor analyzes. It is too pliable. Too many companies are headed by men who like a pliable personnel. One business consultant claimed that he had one basic criterion for sizing up the strength or weakness of any business concern. His evaluation of the management was determined by comparing the top executive's ability with the ability of his associates. "If the top executive chooses associates, vice-presidents and department heads, who are as able as he, the whole organization is bound to be a strong one," according to this consultant.

What can the executive do when he finds that an otherwise good employee is too willing to imitate him? He can make at least one attempt to readjust him by explaining the situation very frankly and telling the "yes" man to agree less and to make more suggestions. The slavish employee may have been conditioned in that way by some other executive who fired him for disagreeing with the boss. An executive cannot "jump" on employees for an honest questioning of his decisions and then expect them to be filled with helpful suggestions the next day. The fear of losing their jobs will give them introjective characteristics. Employees are not always to be blamed for "putty" minds. Certain executives have so strong an inferiority complex that they cannot endure the presence of subordinates who are their equals in ability.

Many introjectionists develop their introjective habits in their adjustments to cruel parents, stern teachers, or executives who resent suggestions. Through such experiences, the individual learns to cater to people at all times, rather than to cater to them some of the time and to oppose them when opposition is appropriate. An executive's study of the employee's past history will often reveal experiences which brought about the introjective behavior.

Compulsion Neuroses and Phobias

In the compulsion neurosis, the individual cannot explain why he feels that he must perform a given act, but he dreads failure to follow the ritual which he has set up in his own mind. In its mild forms, it is found among normal people and is generally treated as an idiosyncrasy or a superstition, as in the individuals who tap wood in order to avoid a calamity which they have escaped thus far. Such compulsive acts are trivial and do not affect emotional health.

The more serious compulsions are known as *manias* and are given specific names to indicate their type as *kleptomania,* the impulse to steal things that are not needed; *pyromania,* the impulse to set fire to things; *onomatomania,* the impulse to say a word again and again or to hunt for it in the memory; *dipsomania,* the periodic uncontrollable craving for alcoholic beverages; and *arithmomania,* the obsessive tendency to count everything, such as the stones in the sidewalk or the objects in a room. A mania is an exaggerated predilection toward a type of activity and is often contrasted with extreme dread of some specific type of situation as in a phobia.

A *phobia* is a persistent and irrational fear of a harmless object or situation. The individual may know quite well that he has no logical reason to fear the thing that he fears. Examples are *claustrophobia,* fear of closed places; *acrophobia,* fear of high places, such as the tenth floor of an office building; *agoraphobia,* fear of open spaces, such as fields or wide streets; *pyrophobia,* fear of fire; *misophobia,* fear of dirt; and *aelurophobia,* the fear of cats, Napoleon's well-known fear. The phobia usually comes on very suddenly and overwhelms the patient, who is seized with trembling, sweating, pallor, and all the usual signs of extreme fear. All this, in spite of the fact that the patient knows quite well that his fears are merely morbid and under irrational control. Some persons having phobias are able to continue their daily work by avoiding the situations which stimulate the phobia responses. Others have phobias which unfit them for certain forms of economic life.

The woman who was afraid to look into a mirror for fear that she would find a hair on her face knew that the finding of a hair was no real cause for alarm; but still she became so fearful of seeing her reflection that she refused to handle silverware or to open her eyes in a room where there were windows. The executive who was seized with fear whenever he was in a building higher than the second floor knew that the building was perfectly safe; he simply could not go up to any height. The stenographer who spent most of her time washing her hands knew that her hands were reasonably clean, but still she feared they might be soiled. The bookkeeper who feared to make the figure five knew that figure was harmless, but still he feared it.

What are the barriers which give rise to such apparently irrational adjustments as manias and phobias?

Means studied the fears of a thousand college women and found that only 38 per cent of them indicated any knowledge of the origin of their fears.[28] About 70 per cent of the fears of known origin were due to some personal experience. The first five fears in their relative importance were: snakes, cancer, death of loved ones, death by burning, and bulls.

At least three of these fears are considered by psychoanalysts to be sexual in nature: snakes, burning, and bulls. If we accept the explanation of some psychoanalysts, we shall interpret these manifestations of abnormal fears and impulses as symbols of barriers which are inadmissible impulses. The woman who could not look into a mirror for fear she would see a hair on her face was unable to do so because hair symbolized some sexual wish that she refused consciously to admit to herself. The executive who could not go higher than the second floor of a building was fearful of a moral fall which might be brought about if he yielded to an immoral impulse.[29] The stenographer's fear of contamination was caused by the fear of repressed desires to yield to an immoral impulse such as the sexual entreaties of her lover. The figure five represented the five fingers of the bookkeeper's hand which were used in a sex perversion. And so on for other impulsions, such as the oversolicitude for the health of a wealthy aunt which disguised the wish for her death.

In most analyses of phobias, phychiatrists find that the origin of the fear is closely coupled with a sense of guilt or shame. That is why Freud and his disciples can find many illustrations of his theory that the phobia masks a repressed sex desire. Sex, to most people, is something terrible and unmentionable rather than a perfectly normal impulse.

An urge to do something considered reprehensible by the individual, with an anticipation of punishment, is especially frequent in the phobia. In many cases, too, the patient exhibits a history of early frustrations, aggressive impulsions that were suppressed, and unappreciated fears of punishment. Many individuals whose behavior is restricted by a phobia are lonely and seek the security of being protected by adults.[30]

As soon as the phobia-bound individual understands the origin of his fear and is allowed to express the repressed impulse that it symbolizes, the phobia is likely to disappear. Scolding him will not banish the fear, but uncovering the origin of it may. If the fear persists, the cause has not been found or the process of readjustment is incomplete. A complete "cure" takes place only when the individual has achieved a readjustment to the anxiety-producing experience. Of course, this process of readjustment is one for the attention of the clinical psychologist.

Some phobias are more easily and logically thought of in terms of conditioned responses or as associative linkages. It is certain that some of the maladjustments of the individual are brought about through simultaneous associations, as in the case of the man who, during a heart attack, collapses in an open section of the city. He may then have an agoraphobia for certain areas.

Parents can do much to prevent abnormal fears. The main form of instruction given to children by some parents seems to be "Shame on you"; "Nobody will like you if you are so naughty"; "You know that you are a naughty little boy, don't you?"; and "God will punish little girls who tell lies." No wonder the children of oversolicitous parents often grow up to become fearful retiring nobodies while roughnecks of the slums develop into business and professional leaders. Fears do not dog the roughneck's every step. We must remember that the child fears in silence. Shame may be so strong that it is difficult to obtain admission. Cowardice may develop, and all because the father and mother and teacher have held up the bogey of shame. Every unnatural fear has a natural cause, and the attitude of the executive toward his employees and his children should be that of the analyst who sympathetically discovers the origin of the fear and aids the individual in gaining a better adjustment. A knowledge of what fears really mean is the first step in aiding the phobia-bound person.

Alcoholism

There are several million alcoholics, perhaps five million, depending upon the criteria used. Of these, approximately three-quarters of a million adults in this country have become alcoholics to such a degree that they have impaired their physical or mental health. These are the chronic alcoholics. We do know that on the average, three per cent of the members of our work force are problem drinkers.

It is generally accepted that there is no alcoholic personality as such. Rather, numerous individuals cannot manage their lives in sobriety; they continue to resort to alcohol as a means of dealing with their psychological problems, such as feelings of insecurity and inferiority. Many are depressed because they labor under the unconscious fantasy that they were not loved sufficiently by their mother in childhood.[31] The craving for alcohol is more a craving for the habit pattern that relieves tensions than for anticipated sensory enjoyment. The fact that when individuals take too much alcohol on a social occasion, certain ones become aggressive, elated, or "weepy"; indicates that the imbibing is related to the person's adjustment tensions.

Several intensive investigations of chronic

alcoholics are now under way. One of these, at the Laboratory of Applied Physiology, Yale University, has found that alcoholics can be studied in terms of the following classifications of excessive drinkers:

1. The neurotic.
2. The psychotic.
3. The feebleminded.
4. Those who gravitate into drink as a means toward solving their problems.

Among 100 excessive drinkers, about 40 are neurotic, 10 are psychotic, and 10 are feebleminded. The personality patterns may be briefly described as follows:

The *neurotic* lacks patience with his world. He needs many props to support him. He will seek conditions under which the conflict between his wishes and reality are endurable. In order to escape from his world he resorts to daydreaming, but he fully realizes the difference between the real world and his imagined world. He may try, for instance, to obviate the conflict between his two worlds by adopting a job which permits seclusion, by a hobby, or by intoxication. His general conduct may be thought "peculiar" by others, but his overt conduct usually conforms to the standards of the real world. In other words, he is in touch with reality.

The *psychotic,* on the other hand, resolves the conflict between his dream world and the world of reality by retreating entirely into his dream world. He loses contact with the world of reality, and cannot distinguish between it and the dream world, or between right and wrong. For these reasons he is segregated from society.

In the incipient stage of the illness, some psychotics drink heavily to shut out such phenomena as auditory hallucinations. After a few months the psychosis becomes so fully recognizable as to necessitate hospitalization. Observers are apt to conclude that the psychosis was caused by the drinking, whereas actually the drinking was a symptom of the psychosis. Only over a period of years could heavy drinking in itself cause a psychosis.[32]

It has been noted that alcoholism is sometimes the symptom of a mental disorder. If drinking bouts occur periodically, perhaps at intervals of several months, there is a possibility that the patient is drinking during one or the other stages of a manic-depressive psychosis; if the drinking is steady and wild, there is a possibility of early schizophrenia or early general paresis. Other deep-seated maladies are sometimes the real cause of heavy drinking. In almost all such cases the patient needs hospitalization.

With the majority of alcoholics, however, the root of the trouble isn't so deep. It is the patient's inability to adjust himself to life as he finds it. Perhaps he has always been lonely; or dominated by the family; or tortured by fears—that he won't make good, that people don't like him, that he isn't manly. Or he may be a business and social success, yet hate his work and the people he goes around with. For a variety of reasons he may hate himself.[33]

On the whole, about 60 per cent of all inebriates come to their excessive habits through some "ailment," including feeblemindedness as an ailment. This means that at least 40 per cent cannot attribute their inebriety to disease.

The fourth group of the 100 inebriates who are not in the neurotic, psychotic, or feebleminded categories are persons who have been drinking large amounts of alcoholic beverages as a form of social relaxation.

In the course of their drinking they have found, however, that intoxication will help them over situations which otherwise would take some effort to adjust to. Some minor misadventure may be a sufficient reason to "let themselves go" and to let intoxication "do the job"; they solve their troubles with drink. As they get "pampered" by intoxication, they may take recourse to it more and more frequently until they become as dependent upon alcohol as the neurotic, compulsive drinker. While they did not start from a disease, they become diseased. . . . Ultimately, then, all inebriates are diseased persons. But it is important to distinguish those who were brought to inebriety through disease and those whose inebriety brings about the disease. These latter excessive drinkers are usually gregarious persons, good mixers, and easy-going in contrast to the neurotic drinkers who, as a rule, are persons who never found their place among others, who always were lone travelers. When the "normal excessive drinker" becomes an habitual inebriate, he appears to be much like the neurotic drinker. By necessity he too becomes a "lone traveler," for he loses his friends and becomes isolated. Because of that he becomes as suspicious, sensitive, and selfish as the neurotic inebriate. But he can be helped. As he has arrived at his dependence through habituation, he can be trained away again from this habit. This can be done successfully if it is recognized that he is not of the neurotic type and that he, therefore, needs to be handled differently.[34]

The man who drinks for social relaxation should analyze his drinking habits as a precaution against becoming an alcohol dependent. Dr. Abraham Myerson, Boston psychiatrist, suggests seven test questions:

1. Can you enjoy a party only if there is liquor to release your social instincts?
2. Do you long for the time of day when you can drink without hurting your job?
3. Do you consider drink necessary to relaxation and enjoyment of life?
4. Do you turn reflexively to alcohol each day to overcome anxiety, disgust, fatigue or frustration?
5. Do you tend to drink to offset difficulties with your wife, your boss, your children or employees?
6. Is the goal of your drinking something other than the drink itself?
7. Do you *need* this drink?

If the answer to any of the questions is yes, the individual is in danger of becoming an alcohol dependent. The last question epitomizes the questionnaire. When a person feels that he *needs* a drink, he is drinking to escape. He craves the anesthesia which alcohol supplies.[35]

Alcoholics Anonymous, formed in 1934, is a nonprofit organization of former alcoholics who want to help other alcoholics stop drinking. Its purpose: To help the sick alcoholic recover if he wishes to do so. A drinker's honest desire to recover normal health and habits, and his belief in some form of Supreme Power, are the prerequisites for membership.

Members of Alcoholics Anonymous actively help the patient in his fight to regain normal health, and as his condition improves he in turn helps others in their fight. Thousands of former habitual drinkers, members of A.A., understand better than anyone else the problems of other alcoholics and ex-alcoholics, so a fellowship is thereby created which acts as a mainstay when regression threatens. The organization and its methods are endorsed by many physicians and clergymen.[36]

In view of the alcoholic's deep-seated inability to deal effectively with his problems, effective treatment is usually very difficult. The employer, wife, or friend of the alcoholic can seldom hope to overcome the victim's failures in adjustment. Psychiatric treatment is, however, likely to be far more effective than mere legislation. The businessman who finds that an employee or colleague is a chronic alcoholic must usually decide whether he should sever their business relationship or get along with the victim in spite of his annoying derelictions. Some alcoholic employees have qualities which compensate the employer for their recurring deficiencies; others can only be discharged, in the hope that they will find their way to an institution where positive treatment will be given them. Many will continue to drink until their adjustment problems have been removed and they have developed new mental habits.[37]

Many companies now look upon alcoholism as a form of illness. They think of alcoholics as sick rather than morally corrupt individuals. They believe that many can be cured, and that the company can assist in the curing process. They believe that it is better policy to try to rehabilitate the problem drinker than to fire him. They think in terms of therapy rather than punishment. They have worked out specific personnel programs and procedures toward this end.[38]

Several big corporations have created their own rehabilitation programs or joined with other companies in community-type clinics. Consolidated Edison Co. of New York, has been one of the pioneers. In 1952, they underwrote the cost of setting up a consultation clinic at New York University-Bellevue Medical Clinic. In later years, they have been joined by other companies such as Bell Telephone Laboratories, Metropolitan Life Insurance, and *The New York Times*. Several companies of other areas also have extensive programs of their own for rehabilitating alcoholics. Some companies have informal programs or they refer their workers to clinics, to psychiatrists, and to organizations such as Boston's Committee on Alcoholism, and Cleveland's Center on Alcoholism.

Companies that have set up in-plant programs to salvage alcoholics usually have a program that includes these interrelated phases: (1) recognition of the problem drinker and getting him to want to do something about his situation; (2) rehabilitation of the person through psychiatric, psychological, and counseling help; and (3) prevention of alcoholism—perhaps through education of the employees as to the nature and causes of this illness. Some of these programs by industrial firms appear to have produced beneficial results but it is still too early to know just how beneficial or lasting the effects really are.

Sexual Anomalies

The sex customs of modern civilization are the most remarkable illustration of the strength of the cortical control over the instinctive or animal nature of man. Bear in mind that throughout the millions of years of evolution of man's forebears, no males took part in that whole line of descent except those who had some sex impulse. Small wonder then that it is a strong force in the life of man. Freud and his followers have considerable evidence whereon to build their brand of psychology. With so strong a force, we need not wonder that perversions or anomalies take place in the sex lives of a significantly large percentage of the people. The occasions when it is necessary for the executive to deal with serious sex problems, such as perversions, are few in number. Many businessmen think that they can recognize a sex pervert when he applies for a job. This is not true. At least, no evidence has ever been obtained which indicates that it is possible to recognize the homosexual pervert. When someone meets a stranger and classifies him as a sex pervert merely on the basis of appearances, such as the gaze of the eyes, he is just guessing. The stranger may accidentally give him such an impression because of some characteristic of clothing or voice that unconsciously reminds him of a pervert whom he met previously.

In terms of Freud, the tendencies of the child are *polymorphous,* or many-form. The sexual sense has not developed in the young child. Later, as it develops, it tends to center its aim in some special direction, usually toward the opposite sex and normal conduct in sex life. However, the child's sex tendencies may be developed in any direction according to the influences that take place in the educational and adjustment process.

Nature has given man a strong sex impulse, but civilization has fenced in the impulse with dozens of taboos. It is only natural, therefore, that masturbation should be common. A passing addiction to it in infancy is considered normal by many psychologists. Contrary to popular interpretation, masturbation is not to be considered as a cause of insanity.

When Malamud and Palmer found an abnormal mental state coupled with the masturbation habit, they found people who usually differed from the average in other ways too, e.g., by constitutional peculiarities, lack of proper sex knowledge, misinformation regarding masturbation, unsatisfactory environmental situation, and so on. In those cases where masturbation was believed to be of prime etiological importance, psychotherapy was highly satisfactory, indicating "that the disturbances were due to the conflict rather than the effects of the practice in itself."[39]

Nearly all studies of masturbation have indicated that it is an important mental hygiene problem which may have serious effects on personality and should be handled by persons who have both intelligence and emotional balance regarding sex practices. It is especially important to avoid giving the youth a feeling of guilt or inferiority in regard to sex.[40] Such feelings are almost certain to give rise to defense mechanisms of the withdrawal-from-people variety. Or, in potentially more dangerous cases, mechanisms of aggression.

Sadism (the *a* pronounced as in *say*) refers to some few individuals who do not express their sexual tendencies in a normal direction but gratify sexual feelings by the infliction or sight of pain. The pain may be real or it may be simulated, in which case it is symbolic. This anomaly is found among men more often than among women, as we would naturally expect. In any large organization, one is likely to find mild expressions of the sadistic variety expressed by persons who like to pinch others or stick pins into them.

Masochism is the opposite of sadism. The individual's sexual feelings are gratified when he suffers pain. The pain may be real or simulated. The latter is symbolic.[41] The masochistic tendency is found among women more often than among men.

Exhibitionism is the gratification of sex by the exposure of the body, especially erogenous parts. It is the showing-off tendency in the extreme. The exhibitionist cannot explain why exposing his body brings sexual pleasure. He is not a sex-crazed rapist, but he is an infantile, impotent person. Imprisonment does not deter or reform him. The use of drugs to reduce potency are valueless. He needs psychotherapy.[42]

Some analysts claim that the desire of some leaders in business and public affairs to be the "whole show" in the presence of others is merely substituting a mild form of this type of exhibitionism for a more perverted and unacceptable variety of showing off.

Voyeurism, a minor mental maladjustment which contrasts with exhibitionism, is the tendency to derive sexual satisfaction from looking at sexual objects and acts. The "Peeping Tom" who is occasionally caught by campus policemen is an extreme case of voyeurism.[43] (The word comes from the French *voir,* to see.)

Less extreme are those people who show unusual interest in case histories from medical books, who insist upon knowing the intimate details of their friends' lives, and who are happy in listening to a particular kind of gossip about movie stars and other famous people. Some business concerns have "old maids" who are forever curious about what their associates do after working hours. These employees can make an office rather unpleasant for other workers.

This unusual type of adjustment is used largely by people whose own lives are drab. They are more or less unable to make a satisfactory normal social adjustment, and so they devote time to watching and hearing about others whose activities are nearer normal.

Homosexuality, when used as signifying a perversion, is the term given to the desire for sexual relations with persons of the same sex. In this connection we must bear in mind that no man is wholly male, nor is any woman wholly female. Sexness is a relative trait. We are mixtures of physical and mental traits. Many women have a general bodily conformation and pilosity which is characteristic of the male, and many men have some typically female traits. But such physical attributes do not appear to be as important in bringing about the maladjustment as the psychological factors. An examination of current clinical psychological and psychiatric literature will show that numerous researches are being conducted on the problem of homosexuality. Its origins and causes are still largely unknown. However, a typical finding of some studies has been reported in an investigation of 50 male homosexuals whose psychological situations were compared with those of 50 normal controls. The homosexuals showed the presence of a typical parental constellation significantly more often than the controls, namely, an over-intense mother and unsatisfactory father relationship.[44]

Unfortunately for young people who are still searching for their values and basic adjustment patterns, some of our writers of plays and novels try to portray homosexuality as superior to heterosexuality. The more mature view has been expressed succinctly by a leading interpreter of literature: "Many of our unhappy geniuses defend homosexuality. From that we are sometimes prone to assume that homosexuality has made them geniuses. Perhaps it is only what has made them unhappy."[45]

A predisposing influence in some cases of homosexuality is that of isolation of the sexes as in penitentiaries, on shipboard, and in one-sex boarding schools. "Crushes" are likely to develop where the sex impulse has no normal outlets. Coeducational colleges are more in harmony with the mental life of human beings than one-sex schools. In the coeducational institutions the two sexes mingle with each other in a normal manner. The family type of social contacts is present. A boy is not some heroic sexless knight in armor to the girl who sees him each day in the classroom and notes his humanness when asked a question by the instructor. Boys and girls will continue to fall in love with each other until human nature changes, and the best preventive of sexual anomalies is to give the child and youth a sane and normal sex environment where parents are not shocked by sexual digressions but are intelligent in redirecting them.[46]

ACKNOWLEDGMENTS AND REFERENCES

1. John Perry, *Human Relations in Small Industry,* Small Business Administration, Washington, D.C., March, 1954, p. 8.
2. Martin H. Stein, "The Cliché: A Phenomenon of Resistance," *Journal of the American Psychoanalytical Association,* **6** (1958), 263–277.
3. David P. Ausubel, "Some Comments on the Nature, Diagnosis, and Prognosis of Neurotic Anxiety," *Psychiatric Quarterly,* **30** (1956), 77–88.
4. See David P. Ausubel, Herbert M. Schiff, and Morton Goldman, "Qualitative Characteristics in the Learning Process Associated with Anxiety," *Journal of Abnormal and Social Psychology,* October, 1953, pp. 537–547. For report of another study with grade school children, see Hayne W. Reese, "Manifest Anxiety and Achievement Test Performance," *Journal of Educational Psychology,* **52,** No. 3 (1961), 132–135.
5. Richard Alpert and Ralph N. Haber, "Anxiety in Academic Achievement Situations," *Journal of Abnormal and Social Psychology,* **61,** No. 2 (1960), 207–215.
6. For further information see Joseph D. Matarazzo, *et al.,* "The Relationship between Anxiety Level and Several Measures of Intelligence," *Journal of Consulting Psychology,* June, 1954, pp. 201–205.
7. Jacob Levine, "Responses to Humor," *Scientific American,* February, 1956, pp. 31–35.
8. Joel R. Davitz, "Manifest Anxiety and Social Behavior," *Journal of Consulting Psychology,* December, 1960.
9. John M. Rehfisch, "Some Scale and Test Correlates of a Personality Scale," *Journal of Consulting Psychology,* October, 1958.
10. K. Warner Schaie, "Differences in Some Personal Characteristics of 'Rigid' and 'Flexible' Individuals," *Journal of Clinical Psychology,* **14** (1958), 11–14.
11. J. L. Singer and Vivian G. McCraven, "Some Characteristics of Adult Daydreaming," *Journal of Psychology,* **51** (1961), 151–164.
12. J. L. Singer and Rosalea A. Schonbar, "Correlates of Daydreaming: A Dimension of Self-Awareness," *Journal of Consulting Psychology,* **25** (1961), 1–6.
13. G. H. Green, *Psychoanalysis in the Classroom* (New York: G. P. Putman's Sons, 1922), Chapter II.
14. Morris S. Viteles, *Industrial Psychology* (New York: W. W. Norton and Company, Inc., 1932). Chapter XXIV presents an excellent summary of specific influences in monotonous work.
15. Kenneth M. Goode, *What About Radio?* (New York: Harper & Row, Publishers, Inc., 1937), p. 30.
16. See Gerhard Neubeck and Vera M. Schletzer, "A Study of Extramarital Relationships," *Marriage and Family Living,* **24,** No. 3 (1962), 279–281.
17. For further information see Irwin M. Rosenstock, "Perceptual Aspects of Repression," *Journal of Abnormal and Social Psychology,* July, 1951.
18. "ABC's of Scapegoating," Central Y.M.C.A. College, Chicago, Illinois, undated, presents a summary of the types of practices of scapegoating today.
19. This article is one of a series on the psychology of war and propaganda prepared by the Society for the Psychological Study of Social Issues especially for release through Science Service. *Science News Letter,* March 9, 1940, p. 157.
20. Robert R. Sears, Carl I. Hovland, and Neal E. Miller, "Minor Studies of Aggression: I, Measurement of Aggressive Behavior," *Journal of Psychology,* **9** (1950), 275–295.
21. Norman R. F. Maier, "The Role of Frustration in Social Movements," *Psychological Review,*

American Psychological Association, Inc., 1942, Vol. 49, and Emory L. Cowen, Judah Landes and Donald E. Schaet, "The Effects of Mild Frustration on the Expression of Prejudiced Attitudes," *Journal of Abnormal and Social Psychology,* **58** (1958), 33–38 present additional aspects of frustration in behavior.
22. K. Edward Renner, Brendan A. Maher and Donald T. Campbell, "The Validity of a Method for Scoring Sentence Completion Responses for Anxiety, Dependency, and Hostility," *Journal of Applied Psychology,* August, 1962, p. 286.
23. Arnold H. Buss and Ann Durkee, "An Inventory for Assessing Different Kinds of Hostility," *Journal of Consulting Psychology,* **21** (1957) 343–349.
24. See Saul M. Siegel, "The Relationship of Hostility to Authoritarianism," *Journal of Abnormal and Social Psychology,* **52** (1956), 368–372.
25. Judson Mills, "Changes in Moral Attitudes Following Temptation," *Journal of Personnel,* December, 1958.
26. Eva Maria Shippee-Blum, "The Young Rebel: Self-Regard and Ego-Ideal," *Journal of Consulting Psychology,* February, 1959.
27. "The Editor's Bookshelf," *Saturday Review,* Dec. 21, 1963, p. 53. A review by P. W. of book, *The Revolt of the College Intellectual,* Human Relations Aids, 104 E. 25th St., New York, 1963.
28. M. H. Means, "Fears of One Thousand College Women," *Journal of Abnormal and Social Psychology,* **31** (1936), 291–311.
29. Edmund Bergler, "Fear of Heights," *Psychoanalytical Review,* **44** (1957), 447–451, reports a depth psychoanalytical study that is more insightful than the explanation given in the text. This kind of explanation requires clinical training to understand it.
30. O. Fenichel, "Remarks on the Common Phobias," *Psychoanalytical Quarterly,* **13** (1944), 313–326.
31. E. Bergler, "Contributions to the Psychogenesis of Alcohol Addiction," *Quarterly Journal of Studies on Alcohol,* **5** (1944), 434–449.
32. *The Drinker and the Drunkard,* Lay Supplement No. 10, pp. 11–12. *Quarterly Journal of Studies on Alcohol,* 1944.
33. Herbert Yahraes, *Alcoholism Is a Sickness,* Public Affairs Pamphlet No. 118, Public Affairs Committee, Inc., New York, 1946, p. 19.
34. *The Drinker and the Drunkard, op. cit.,* p. 15.
35. Charles Stevenson, "Rebellious Liquors in My Blood," *Nation's Business,* September, 1947, pp. 60–66.
36. A.A.: *An A. A. Publication,* The Alcoholic Foundation, Inc., P. O. Box 459, Grand Central Annex, New York, N. Y., 10017.
37. W. R. Miles, "Psychological Factors in Alcoholism," *Mental Hygiene,* **21** (1937), 529–548.
38. For further information about current developments in this field, see "Catalog of Publications," The National Council on Alcoholism, Inc., 2 East 103rd St., New York, N. Y., 10029.
39. W. Malamud and G. Palmer, "The Role Played by Masturbation in the Causation of Mental Disturbances," *Journal of Nervous and Mental Diseases,* **76** (1932), pp. 220–233 and 366–379.
40. See Don D. Jackson, "Guilt and the Control of Pleasure in Schizoid Personalities," *British Journal of Medical Psychology,* **31** (1958), 124–130.
41. C. Brenner, "The Masochistic Character: Genesis and Treatment," *Journal of the American Psychoanalytical Association,* **7** (1959), 197–226.
42. John McLeish, "Exhibitionism," *Medical World,* London, **93,** No. 8 (1960), 126–128.
43. Irvin D. Yalom, "Aggression and Forbiddenness in Voyeurism," *Archives of General Psychiatry,* **3** (1960), 305–319.
44. D. J. West, "Parental Figures in the Genesis of Male Homosexuality," *International Journal of Social Psychiatry,* **5** (1959), 85–97.
45. Joseph Wood Krutch, "Confessions of a Square," *Saturday Review,* May 9, 1964, p. 26.
46. For an excellent treatment of homosexuality, see Graham B. Blaine, Jr., and Charles C. McArthur, *Emotional Problems of the Student* (New York: Appleton-Century-Crofts, 1961), Chapter 6, "Basic Character Disorders and Homosexuality."

PROJECTS

1. Study any tendencies you may have toward fantasy or daydreaming. Which of the following types seems to be dominant: Display fantasy; Saving daydream; Fantasy of grandeur; Homage daydream; Suffering hero daydream? Can you suggest possible causes for the direction the tendency takes?
2. Consider people whom you have known and list any examples of fixed ideas you may have noted. Can you discover rational relationships between the fixed ideas and their adjustment background?
3. Make a collection of newspaper clippings concerning persons whose peculiar behavior has gotten them mention in the newspapers. Compare any explanations given in the clippings with hypotheses of your own.
4. Read some recent articles on "Alcoholics Anonymous." Evaluate the benefits and limitations of the methods of this group.
5. Analyze, for his compensatory behavior, an acquaintance of middle age who has never married. To what extent has such activity resulted in satisfactory adjustment?
6. Draw up a list of beneficial and possibly harmful adjustment influences in coeducational and

non-coeducational schools. Check those which you can substantiate from your own or your friends' experiences.

7. Read several reports of experiments on rat behavior to note some of the ways in which frustration seems to affect animals.

   In an experiment made to ascertain the effects of irregular and insufficient feeding in infancy, it was found that rats that had been subjected to infantile feeding frustration in infancy hoarded more than two and one-half times as much as their freely fed litter-mate controls. Hunt concluded that the "results tend to substantiate the psychoanalytic claim that infantile experience is an effective determinant of adult behavior, and they are interpreted in terms of learning theory."

8. To realize how energy may be dammed up, conduct this experiment. Have a person time you for ten trials of thirty seconds each. During each trial make the figure 5 as rapidly as you can in the usual manner of making a 5. Then make the figure 5 in an inverted manner as rapidly as possible for the same number of trials and the same number of seconds to each trial. Then make the 5 right side up as rapidly as you can for about five trials of the usual thirty seconds each. Do not allow more than ten seconds rest between any of the trials. Plot a curve of the number of 5's made in each of the 25 trials. Note the waves of efficiency and the release of the dammed-up energy.

COLLATERAL READINGS

Kinsey, Alfred C., Wardell B. Pomeroy, Clyde E. Martin, *Sexual Behavior in the Human Male*. Philadelphia: W. B. Saunders Co., 1948, Parts Two and Three.

Lehner, George F. J. and Ella Kube, *The Dynamics of Personal Adjustment,* (2nd ed.). Englewood Cliffs, N.J.: Prentice-Hall, Inc., 1963, Chapter 6.

London, Perry and David Rosenhan, Anxiety as a section in "Personality Dynamics," in *Annual Review of Psychology,* Vol. 15, 1964, Annual Reviews, Inc., Palo Alto, Cal., 479–483.

Maier, Norman R. F., *Psychology in Industry*. Boston: Houghton Mifflin Company, 1955, Chapter 4.

Shaffer, Laurance F. and Edward J. Shoben, Jr., *The Psychology of Adjustment.* Boston: Houghton Mifflin Company, 1956, Part Two.

Smith, Henry Clay, *Psychology of Industrial Behavior*. New York: McGraw-Hill Book Company, 1955.

"What to Say to an Alcoholic," *Management Review,* American Management Association Inc., January, 1964.

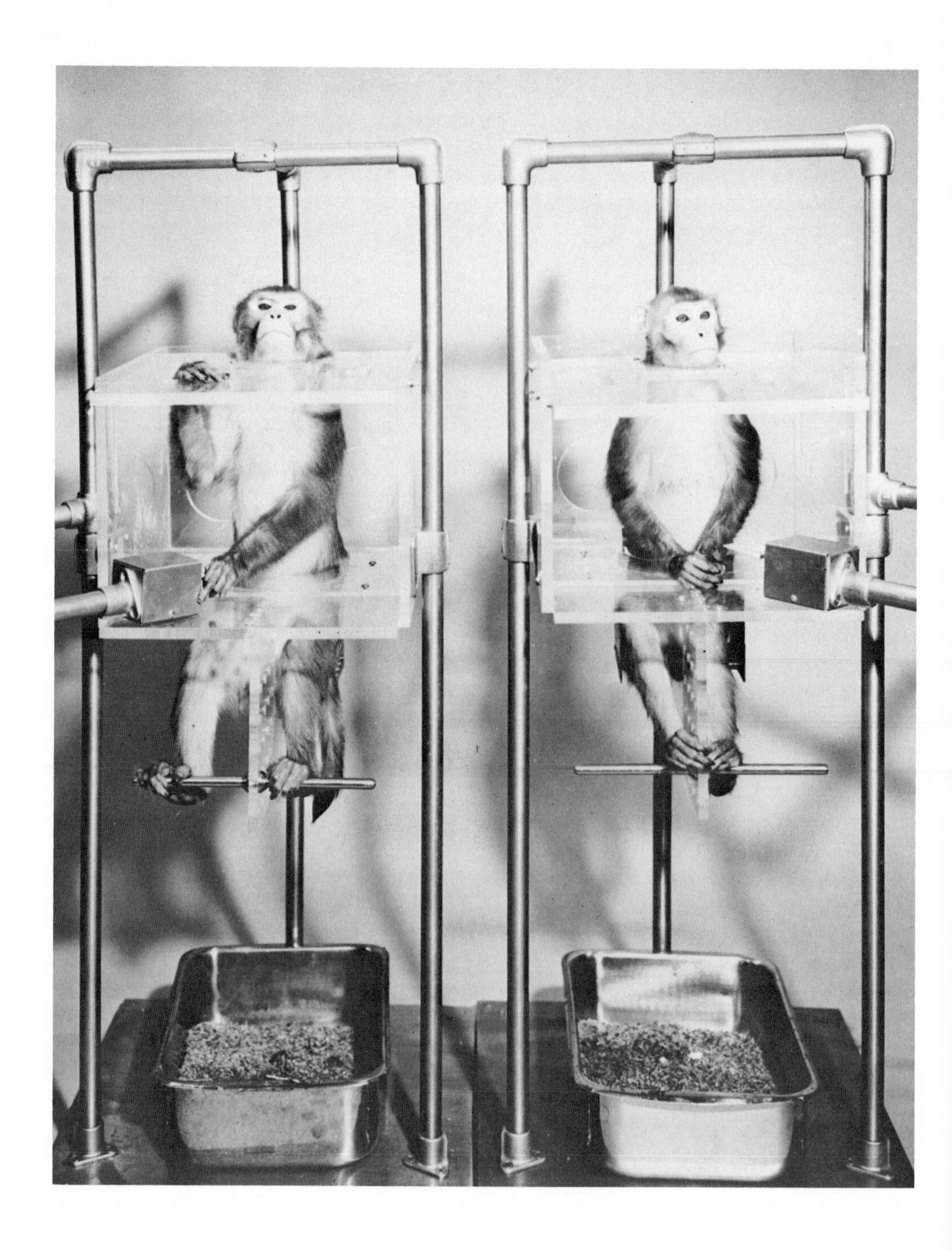

Stress is often believed to be a factor in the development of some of our functional ailments. *Experiments with animals have revealed interesting findings that may be significant in understanding effects of stress in human beings. The experimental monkey on the left must press a switch at regular intervals; otherwise he and the control monkey on the right will receive a mild electric shock.* *See pages 100-101 for further explanation.* ***Source:*** *Medical Audio-Visual Dept., Walter Reed Army Institute of Research, Washington 12, D.C. Property of U.S. Government. Reproduced by special permission.*

CHAPTER FIVE

ADJUSTMENT BY FUNCTIONAL AILMENTS

Patient: "Oh, doctor,
I have the most awful pain somewhere in my shoulders."
Doctor: "And when did you first notice the pain, madam?"
Patient: "About two months ago,
I think. Yes, it was two months ago. It was just about
the time Mrs. Neighbor got her new fur coat; the snob."

A psychiatrist reported the case of a woman who claimed that she had stomach trouble because of a frog in her stomach. She "knew" she had swallowed a frog egg while on a picnic. Her physician ridiculed the idea but she was so insistent that he finally agreed to operate for the removal of the frog. Accordingly, he sent her to a hospital to be prepared for the operation and he, at the same time, hired a small boy to catch a frog for him. To give the woman the impression that she had really had an operation, an incision was made in her abdomen, and the doctor showed her the "frog," in a bottle of alcohol, which had presumably been removed from her stomach. The woman was delighted and at once recovered, but only temporarily. Three months after the psuedo-operation, she claimed that the first frog had laid some eggs and that she now had two frogs in her stomach!

This amusing example illustrates the uselessness of ordinary logical thinking in the consideration of the many ailments which are functional rather than organic.

When a surgeon is prevailed upon to operate for a functional disturbance, the operation does not, as a rule, result in permanent cure. A physician may occasionally give "placebos," pills which have no medicinal value, in order to satisfy a patient temporarily. However, physicians who treat the functionally ill realize that certain patients need an improved adjustment to their problems more than they need pills.

How Illness Often Becomes a Means of Adjustment

Any form of invalidism is likely to be useful as a means of adjustment to problems. Almost every child learns that he can avoid unpleasant duties such as mowing the lawn, washing dishes, or studying his lessons, by feigning illness.

Jo is a boy of twelve who has been feeling very much out of the family picture. He is the youngest child. His sister is soon to be married and his brother has just started to work, but Jo is at an age when he is not particularly interesting to any member of the family. He has been doing only fairly well in his school work and he has definitely neglected his arithmetic.

One morning he went down to breakfast and ate rather heartily: he had oatmeal with cream, eggs, bacon, jam, and milk; and while he was eating he recalled that he was going to have an arithmetic test that morning. He had a queer, twitchy feeling of excitement in his stomach at the thought of the arithmetic test. He started walking slowly to school, thinking more about the test, and his stomach felt queerer and the oatmeal weighed very heavily on it. He had a vague feeling, which was hardly a thought, that if his breakfast were to come up he wouldn't have to go to school, and the arithmetic test came to mind again. Suddenly he found it hard to keep the breakfast down.

Shortly after his arrival at school, it did come up. He was sent home by the principal with a clear conscience to have a day in bed. The principal telephoned his mother, who immediately became concerned. She put Jo to bed in the guest room and made a fuss over him such as he had not experienced since he was quite a small boy. His sister came in and showed him her wedding presents; his brother stopped and had a talk with him before going out in the evening, an event which had not occurred for months; and his father spent the evening reading to him.

This upset stomach had a high value: no arithmetic test, and solicitude from all the people from whom he had been wishing attention for some time. The next time Jo was faced with a difficult situation and there was a queer feeling in his stomach, it was no longer necessary to go through all the preliminary steps. Now meals just come up without further consideration on his part.[1]

The child's convenient illness often brings about considerable sympathy and attention. Later the same child meets problems for which he lacks requisite skills or energies to solve. The poorly adjusted individual cannot admit to himself his own lack of courage to make direct attack upon his problems or duties. That would lower his sense of self-worth. However, the old habits of evasion through ailment take place subconsciously because the pattern for that kind of adjustment has been used in the past. His ego is sustained because he himself is not aware of the true cause of his ailment. He believes that he is ill. In fact he is ill, but the origin of the illness has been forgotten. He repressed the recognition of his inabilities or deficiencies.

We must not confuse *Repression* with *Suppression.* The latter is a conscious process; we use it when we force an idea out of our minds by deliberately attending to something else. A person gets a letter containing bad news on the morning of an important examination; he forces himself to put it aside and go through with the examination. In other words, he suppresses his tendency to grief or anxiety for the time being. If it were *repressed,* he would forget that he had ever had the letter. Such repression does occur, especially in certain neurotic types of personalities, but not out of a clear sky; that is, the matter repressed is connected with earlier conflicts which underwent repression. A young woman stenographer lost her job because she forgot to transcribe an important letter, and when she maintained that she had not taken it she was thought to be lying. The letter was addressed to a man whose name was that of a former sweetheart who had jilted her. The normal adult, apparently, does not make much use of repression; he handles his conflicts, his griefs and disappointments, in other ways.[2]

The executive whose office boy reports on the first day of the baseball season that he is too ill to work but at the same time winks knowingly to the boss, who himself enjoys baseball, has insight into the "illness." In contrast to the office boy, the stenographer, an introverted spinster, may have a splitting headache and find it necessary to go home and go to bed. She probably lacks insight into her adjustments because she fails to recognize that her illness is her subconscious method of avoiding a visit from a former classmate who always could capture more boy friends than she could.

Many ailments do have an organic basis, but some are wholly or partially functional. We must bear in mind that a pain is felt through the mechanisms of the brain rather than only at the point of injury. We say that the pain of the psychoneurotic is in his "head." Well, all pains are felt in the head. Surgeons tell us that, when they sever the foot of a soldier, the soldier can still "feel" the ache of his corns or the bedclothes pressing on his "foot." The war veteran who had both feet cut off and yet predicted the weather from the aches of his corns was not merely "joshing" his hearers. Stimuli passed over certain nerve tracts which formerly conveyed impulses from his corns, and the response in his brain was quite the same as it had been before he had had his feet cut off. A psychological pain, therefore, is just as painful as an organic pain. We do our friends an injustice when we tell them that they only imagine the pain and that, if they wanted to do so, they could forget it. They are not helped by scoldings. Rather, they become worse. But, on the other hand, we should not coddle the patient.

Some pains are conditioned responses, as we can readily see in many children. If father sits down to the table and tells mother that spinach gives him indigestion, the little members of the family tend to develop the same symptoms when required to eat their spinach. Mothers who suffer from painful menstruation condition their daughters to the same pains when they reach maturity. Epidemics of various sorts have been reported in schools, after one child had a real or a functional ailment that impressed the other children. For this reason, intelligent teachers and parents do not discuss their aches and pains in the presence of children.

Medical students often develop the symptoms of the patients whom they study. When the writer arranges tours through state hospitals for the benefit of his students, he usually finds that one or two students develop enough symptoms to require some form of treatment. In some cases the student must be sent to a psychiatrist for mental treatment before he recovers. Suggestion, no doubt, plays an important part in many of our functional illnesses.

Functional Illness Enables the Individual to Evade Barriers

In this discussion, we want to give emphasis to the part that illness plays as a means of escape from unpleasant problems. The classic case of the girl who was engaged to the man she loved and became totally deaf when she realized that he no longer loved her is illustrative of a definite attempt to escape reality through illness. She became deaf on the evening when her sweetheart called with the express purpose of telling her that he no longer loved her and wished to be released from the engagement. Deafness enabled her to evade the problem.

Illness may be an escape from an unpleasant situation even though such an adjustment will not be admitted or recognized by the patient. One businessman of unusual honesty borrowed money from his relatives and friends and earnestly expected to be able to pay it back from anticipated profits. Unfortunately, the business did not prosper and the money was lost. The debtor could not face his creditors; nor could he commit suicide because he loved his wife and child. Suddenly he became totally blind and has remained blind for several years. The examining physicians are convinced that the blindness has no organic cause. Strange as it may seem, his blindness is not a barrier to him but is an acceptable mode of adjustment to an otherwise unbearable situation.

Sickness not only keeps fearful men out of battle but also enables new employees to seek to evade failure on the new job, as reported by one executive:

> In this connection I might say that it has been a continual source of amazement to me how frequently men stay home during the first few weeks on a new position. One would imagine that nothing short of serious illness would prevent prompt and regular attendance on the job until it was thoroughly mastered and a competent understudy was on hand to keep things properly moving. But such is not the case.[3]

Thousands of employees are uncertain regarding their abilities and, being unable to admit their limitations, they may make an adjustment by becoming sickly. Sickness is often an acceptable excuse for vocational mediocrity or failure. Many executives, too, realize that they cannot achieve outstanding business success, and so their desk drawers are filled with pills and medicine bottles. Sickness, conscious and subconscious in nature, is an acceptable excuse for our inability to achieve the eminence we desire. People who evade their barriers by means of illness feel that employers, teachers, parents, friends, and relatives have no right to expect the "sick" to accomplish very much when they are "too ill" to work. At the same time, they have the satisfaction of knowing that they do drag through the day's work when others tell them that they really ought to be home in bed!

Most members of our American culture are sympathetic toward persons who are organically sick and toward those who use illness as a means of evading problems. Almost everyone is practically encouraged to use illness as an excuse for failure. This situation should lead us to be suspicious of the real reason for any illness which is not obviously caused by some organic condition. Furthermore, a knowledge of common adjustment patterns which include illness should enable us to choose more intelligently the person with whom we work or live, such as the employee or the mate.

The young man or woman in love as well as the executive should be able to recognize the more common patterns for maladjustment such as neurasthenia. A neurasthenic wife, for example, is the kind of spouse who keeps her mate busy propping up a partner who insists upon being hard to live with. The neurasthenic mate is a true psychological "ball and chain." For the lover, the time to recognize the neurasthenic is before marriage; not after. For the executive, the best time to deal with psychoneurotic employees is before they are hired. Of course, if the prospective neurasthenic mate or employee has compensating qualities, the marriage or employment may be satisfactory, but the one who must bear the effects of their maladjustments should be aware of the extra load he will have to carry. The person who knows the *syndrome* (pattern of symptoms) of the more common psychoneurotic ailments has an important advantage in human relations.

The Psychoneuroses

Many experts refuse to classify the ineffective adjustment patterns that are commonly found in the behavior of psychoneurotic personalities. Their objection is that few cases of "perfect" patterns of symptoms are found among clinical patients. Combinations of certain symptoms are common, however, and our discussion will include the use of the more common terms in this division of psychological literature.

The terms *psychoneurosis* and *neurosis* are used interchangeably by many psychologists. In this book the term psychoneurosis is used the more often. It does not designate a specific disease. Rather, it indicates a level or degree of severity in maladjustment. It refers to a level between the psychosis, or insanity, and an inappropriate adjustment, such as a simple defense mechanism of little seriousness. A psychotic is incapacitated for his world. The neurotic is poorly adjusted to it. A humorous distinction between the psychotic and the neurotic is that "To the psychotic, 2 and 2 make 5. To the neurotic, 2 and 2 make 4, but he's unhappy about it!" Generally, it is believed that neuroticism and psychoticism are separate dimensions of personality and that the former seldom leads to the latter state.[4] We should realize that many psychoneuroses provide the patient with relief from his anxieties. This is especially true of the psychosomatic and psychophysiologic disorders—they hardly ever mature into psychoses.[5]

Some experts classify the psychoneuroses with organic ailments. Psychoneuroses often do involve many physical symptoms, such as headache, backache, indigestion, constipation, and dysmenorrhea. The extent to which these bodily symptoms are cause or effect or mere accompaniments of maladjustments is unknown. However, we shall describe these symptoms for the benefit of the psychological neophyte so that he can recognize them when he finds himself, his friends, or his employees having the reactions characteristic of the psychoneurotic.

Neurasthenia means literally *asthenia,* or exhaustion, of the nerves. It is often called nervous exhaustion or nervous breakdown. However, it is really not so much an exhaustion of nerve energy as a case of misplaced energy. It is more common among women than among men. The main symptoms in the syndrome are (a) chronic bodily fatigue, (b) irritability (occasionally the patient exhibits pronounced exhilaration, but this is soon followed by fatigue and irritability), (c) inability to concentrate attention on any one task, (d) bad temper, (e) moodiness, (f) self-analysis and self-pity and (g) *hypochondria,* or excessive attention to the functioning of the bodily organs, with continued functional pains, is a frequent accompaniment. As soon as the doctor shows the neurasthenic that she cannot have that kind of pain where she has located it, she then claims that the pain has moved to some other part of the body. The more attention the pain receives, the worse it becomes. Some people easily develop symptoms of various ailments when they read descriptions of the different maladies.

For this reason it is well to keep medical books in the physician's office and the public library. They should not be in most homes. If the housewife is tempted to buy medical books, let her buy, instead, a book on how to operate a tourist home or how to rear her children.

What are the causes? Some men attribute neurasthenia to heredity, but it is generally considered to be due very largely to an inability to face reality. It is an evasional device. As in most psychoneurotic ailments, the evading individual is likely to be in a state of conflict between his instinctive tendencies and his intelligent strivings. A housewife, for example, has instinctive urges to meet and enjoy

the company of handsome men whom she likes, but she also knows that she must obey the rules of conduct of our culture. In her conflicts, physiological imbalances arise in her nervous system. Freud concluded that neurasthenia was nothing more nor less than the expression of suppressed sexual excitement.[6]

Neurasthenia may be accentuated by bad habits such as late hours, sexual excesses, and alcoholism. The endocrine glands may be a factor in the psychoneurosis, but that has not been demonstrated as yet. The strenuous life of the present age is supposed to be responsible in many cases. This is hardly correct. The stress of modern life for many people lies in the fact that they do not have enough important things to do. This applies particularly to the women of the middle and upper income classes. Labor-saving devices have eliminated most of the hard but beneficient labor of the American home. In addition to finding themselves more or less useless, many women have a kind of indefinable, unfulfilled longing to be something or to do something worthwhile. Many are out of the general scheme of things except as spectators or as they concoct something to do.

A device commonly chosen by an idle woman to escape neurasthenia and to make herself a part of the scheme of things is to "take up a cause." She hears that certain factory workers are underpaid and so starts a home for them; or she finds that some dogs do not have homes, so she starts a home for homeless dogs. Some of these "causes" are quite worthy and legitimate, but they are not a natural part of the lives of these women. As the term expresses it, "the cause is taken up."

Attaching one's self to a cause is better, however, than seeking relief in a continuous round of social pleasures. When a woman has a so-called nervous breakdown, because she has dashed from one meeting to the next meeting, then to a show, and then to a dance and supper at breakfast time, the breakdown is really caused by mental factors that caused her to dash around in circles. The rushing around to functions is merely the expression of a lack of adjustment to life, and the breakdown is just a nice name for a maladjustment. When effort is the result of conflict or disturbing anxiety and not a part of an integrative plan of living, then the effort becomes fatiguing and unsatisfying. The individual becomes irritable and moody. Life is futile.

What are the remedies? The usual method suggested by physicians is to take a rest cure at home or in a sanatorium. A rest cure of the right kind—a cure that builds up the integrative adjustments as well as the body—is desirable. Many cures, however, are more harmful than beneficial for neurasthenics. If the patient merely goes to a new environment where she sits down and does nothing, she is not helped to build a new philosophy of life that will revitalize her. Temporarily the rest is helpful if it removes the patient to an environment which does not have some of her old problems, and in so far as the maladjustment may be accentuated by a rundown physical state.

If the attention is directed to the bodily organs or functions, harm is done. Sensations of pain and discomfort are soon established even though the organic state is perfect. Detailed attention to the diet often makes the indigestion worse. The physician's questions regarding symptoms are interpreted to mean that the symptoms are present and suggestibility runs wild.

Pains and aches should be minimized by friends and associates, and the patient should be given mental pictures of health and strength rather than pity and sympathy. Make her feel that she is missing fun by her illness. Social contacts should be with those of dynamic, positive personalities. The mental imagery should be of a very happy sort. Autosuggestion is of value if the patient can be trained to apply it with complete belief. If she can do so with conviction, it is well for her to renew her interest in some religion and to acquire a philosophy of her own.

The real problem is that of getting the patient to live outside herself rather than within her own feelings. She should acquire absorbing and satisfying work that fits into some plausible scheme for her own philosophy of life. Work which necessity forces her to do is the main help. Mental re-education is the best route to attain this end of a healthy outlook; but the whole scheme of treatment is more easily applied on paper than to the patient. Most of these patients are not ill enough for scientists to spend much time and effort on them, and so they are neglected and allowed to grow worse. Neurasthenia is exceedingly difficult to relieve for any great length of time, and it is much harder to cure. One lesson that the neurasthenics indicate to the parent is that his son and daughter should be required to work at some steady occupation which is worthwhile to society and to the individual. From the standpoint of sound mental adjustment, we should have many women going into business or some other kind of work, unless they are, of course, needed in the home. If business will not accept them, then we must expect to have more neurasthenic wives and daughters and to supply institutions and "causes" to take care of them.

It is difficult to secure data to prove that women are more afflicted with neurasthenia than are men, but many physicians judge this to be true. If so, it may be partly caused by the fact that we are more solicitous of girls than of boys. When Johnnie, aged six, comes into the house, crying because of a skinned nose, we tell him, "Be a man and stop crying." When his sister, aged eight, comes into the house crying because of a skinned knee we tell her, "Well now, that is too bad. Let's see that knee. Maybe we can put something on it to make it feel better." We still give women the impression that they are weaker than men and, therefore, that we must defer to them because they are women. Daughters should be required to work just as much as sons. The work may be different, but they should sense the joy of a positive productive life rather than the negative attitude of attention through illness.

Psychasthenia is a group term used for tendencies such as obsessions, manias, impulsions, and phobias.[7] In recent years the general term has been almost discontinued, because it is more accurate to treat these tendencies as specific forms of maladjustment. The individual with a mania may have a strong impulse to set fire to his home, to steal money, or to injure someone. Some psychoneurotics wonder whether they are alive and whether they are really themselves. Sometimes the world seems to be closing in about them and crushing them. They know that their fears and impulsions are without any real basis, but still they continue to fight them. We are not concerned here with the true or completely psychasthenic patient, but rather with the psychasthenic tendencies that are found among the members of the office, the school, and the home.

Many physicians consider the *anxiety syndrome* the most frequently observed form of the various functional illnesses. Typical symptoms are a constant feeling of tension and apprehension, headache, irritability, insomnia, desire to be alone, mental weariness, and feelings of unreality. Psychosomatic symptoms are dilated pupils, tremor of outstretched hands, increased pulse pressure, flushing, giddiness, perspiration, breathlessness, and feelings of suffocation. No one patient has all symptoms.[8] The presence of many of them, however, is recognized by those trained in psychosomatic medicine as a signal to treat the emotional as well as the organic causes.

In addition to psychoneurotic symptoms such as manias and phobias, we have other milder and more common negative-value tendencies.

Worry is the most common tendency under this heading. In general, we consider worry an unpleasant mental state, and yet, like any other habit that is continued, it may become agreeable in its own way. A worry may hide a symbolic wish, as does the excessive worry regarding the health of a wealthy uncle whose money we hope to inherit, but we never discuss the wish with ourselves. A boy worries about the welfare of his mother when she goes away from home. Inasmuch as she has kept him tied to her apron string, he experiences a sense of relief and may secretly hope that the train will be wrecked in order that he may be completely free. A mother sends her children out to play, and when they do not come home at the usual time, she worries; partly because of the fact that some neighbor's child was lost or killed, but also because she will have a greater thrill when the children do come back. In many cases the worry is a kind of thrill or a preparation for a thrill. It relieves the monotony of housework. Worry may also be a kind of mental random movement which can be made for the solution of a problem when physical attention is impossible.

Temporary worry is not so great a problem as the persistent apprehensive variety of worry regarding one's financial status, health, or studies. In many cases there is just cause for worry on these subjects, but the psychasthenic does nothing about it. If a student is failing in his studies, he should not worry about it but get to work. If a person worries about his health, the answer is to have a thorough physical examination and then, if the worry is unjustified, stop it. But here comes the difficulty. When the chronic worrier is told all about the fact that he has no real reason to worry, he still continues to worry. For this reason, it is well to ask the expert in worry whether he really wants to stop worrying. Even if he answers, "Of course I do," he should have the idea emphasized most strongly that he must really want to stop worrying before he can reduce his worries. He must determine to picture in his mind positive, healthful, pleasant images rather than the expected unpleasant imagery. Furthermore, he must put into effect definite schedules of work and recreation which will help to develop new mental habits in dealing with his problems. He must achieve insight. If he cannot gain insight into the basic cause of his worry, such as the pressure of a conflict, he will need the assistance of a clinician.

Stage fright is a common negative-value tendency. Why should anyone be fearful when he speaks before others? If he has nothing worth saying, he can simply say so and sit down; but, if he has a message of any importance, he ought to be glad to give it to his fellows. Of course, a talk in public puts one in a position where the ego is liable to be assailed. The speaker knows that some members of the audience may know more about the subject than he does, and he fears their disapproval. This can be overcome by the speaker's frank acknowledgment that he is presenting his own experiences or views and that he would like others there to tell him wherein he is wrong. This does not mean that the speaker who is called upon for a five-minute report or discussion should then spend a half-hour in making apologies. Nor need his talk begin with an apology. But his attitude should be that of the student and learner rather than that of the polished expert. In fact, very many of our psychological difficulties, particularly our self-conscious feelings and fears, would vanish if we could only get ourselves into the mental state of the true student. The true student seeks truth and the facts. Whatever his searches may uncover, it will not jeopardize his ego, because his ego is not involved. The true scientist is interested in finding the things that fail as well as the things that succeed, because he wants to know all aspects of the problem—not just those that give him prestige.

If the speaker makes up his mind that speaking in public is an opportunity for him to exchange ideas with his fellows and at the same time an opportunity to learn more than he can give, he is likely to have little trouble in speaking anywhere, unless he has had a serious shock while speaking in public. If he has had a decidedly unpleasant experience while speaking in public, then he will have to regain his ease of speaking by gradual steps. He should begin on small and sympathetic audiences. He should practice on people who know much less than he does of the subject he talks about. He should get away from the idea that he is competing with anyone. He is just going to tell what he knows as clearly and as well as he can, and thereby he hopes to learn more himself.

Abulia or the *abulic obsession* is also a common negative-value tendency. This term is applied to the inability to get started on the job that awaits our action. We have a report to prepare or a call to make. We often find ourselves postponing it and procrastinating until we are too embarrassed to do it. This is one reason why operating a business according to a definite schedule is better than trusting to the initiative of the employees. A large part of the executive's work consists of setting schedules for his associates and then seeing that the schedules are followed. Almost everyone often finds himself unable to do the things that he wants to do but somehow never gets done. The answer is to make a schedule for his annoying hang-over tasks. The student, for example, should set a definite date when an assignment is to be completed, and at once start a small part of the task. He should not plan to complete the whole job or a large part of it at one sitting, but should make the outline, and then he will find that he can continue for a reasonable length of time.

Another help is "whenpecking." By this is meant enlisting the coöperation of one's colleagues. The businessman can, for example, tell his wife or secretary that he wants to finish a task by a certain date and request her to jog his memory occasionally. Some evening when he may have made up his mind to go to a stag party, his wife will say: "*When* are you going to finish that fourth lesson in business management?" He may be more or less offended at the insinuation, but he will know that she is right and probably will get busy on the important task.

When dangerous and irrational negative-value tendencies are persistent, such as the handicapping phobia, compulsion neurosis, impulsions to say indecent words in public, and the desire to injure some person who is loved and admired, then it is well to consult the psychiatrist. These impulsions are symbolic of patterns which have been connected with the adjustment of the individual to some unrecognizable and inadmissible impulse, such as the sex impulse.

Hysteria is a word used in many different ways by the psychiatrists, but it is most frequently applied to certain unstable emotional states that come and go without apparent cause. An example is that of a housewife who, while busily engaged in her housework, such as sweeping the kitchen floor, suddenly breaks forth into a fit of intense weeping. She may cry bitterly for a few minutes and then pick up her broom and resume her work. When she is asked why she cried she says that she did not cry. She is unable to recall the incident because of her mental dissociation. In many cases the individual also acquires a paralysis of a limb or an area of anesthesia, or has tics and tremors, or may be in a state of mental stupor and have strong delusions.

Hysteria is a mental disorder which is characterized not by hysterical behavior such as crying but by mental dissociation. One famous case of hysteria had a history of five different personalities.[9] Hysteria often includes pronounced disturbances in bodily and mental activity and may result in illnesses such as hysterical blindness, as in the case of the businessman who became blind after he was unable to pay back money borrowed for his failing business, mentioned on page 92.

In some cases of hysteria the patient seems to acquire his functional ailment as an accompaniment of an emotional outburst. In the ordinary case of invalidism, the patient acquires the chronic ailing more slowly. Invalidism is more common among intelligent persons. Hysteria is more common among children and adults of low intelligence than among persons of high intelligence. The hysteria patients have a tendency toward simulation and delusions. Many of them have falsely accused those whom they love. Children have caused their parents to be brought into court, because they claimed that their parents had locked them in the attic or the cellar and had given them no food for days at a time.

The chief suggestion for all of us is the fact that disease may be truly organic, functional, or a combination of the two. If it is functional, it is just as serious as if it were organic, but it must be dealt with along psychological lines.

About one fourth of all adult patients consecutively admitted to Mayo Clinic during the course of a study received a diagnosis solely of some type of neurosis. Most of the neurotic patients were somewhat younger than the other members of their occupational groups, probably because people tend to become less emotional as they grow older. Figures also revealed a somewhat higher incidence of neurosis among women patients.[10]

For supervisors in American industry, neuroticism among female workers has been reported as an especially difficult problem. Dr. Sylvia A. Sorkin in an address before a yearly conference of the National Office Management Association gave results of a questionnaire sent to office managers. Approximately 900 responded. She told the conference delegates that from a listing of nine common office management "headaches" mentioned in the survey, the problem of dealing with neurotic female workers was rated second only in importance to the problem of securing well-trained clerical workers.

Although a third of the executives who gave their opinions said that securing trained help was their biggest problem, nearly a quarter of them ranked the neurotic female as their most difficult problem. Neurotic male workers, on the other hand, got top billing as a problem by only 3 per cent of the executives.[11]

These findings for women in industry are not very unusual when we realize that the incidence among college students is similarly evident. An analysis of almost 600 cases seen by Harvard's psychiatric service in the academic year, 1956–1957, indicated that about one quarter of the students who consulted the Health Service were diagnosed as having neuroses.[12]

Also, in the Midtown Manhattan Study mentioned in Chapter 2, the study of the random sample of 1660 revealed that all but 18.5 per cent had some degree or kind of psychiatric symptoms. Slightly over half the population was classified as probably neurotic in combination with other symptoms. Of the total number of Midtowners classified as to mental health, "neurotic types" constituted 34.3 per cent; "neurotics showing psychosomatic symptoms," 5.7 per cent; "neurotics having personality trait disorders," 16.0 per cent or a total of 56.0 per cent of population sample. This, however, is actually not quite as frightening as one might think. As the authors pointed out: the average person in Midtown functions with little or no difficulty but he has mild symptoms.[13] Obviously, too, the members included in classifications of this kind vary with the inclusiveness of the definitions.

Malingering versus neurosis. The executive who supervises large numbers of factory employees sooner or later has the problem of deciding whether an employee who claims compensation is suffering from an organic ailment or is merely malingering. True malingering places a premium on fraud. Both malingering and neurosis may spring from maladjustments of personality, so that differentiation between the two is very difficult.[14]

An analysis of 1,000 consecutive disability insurance claims for psychoneurosis was made five years after disability had commenced. Almost 30 per cent of the cases had been incorrectly diagnosed. The mortality rate for these neurotics also showed that neurotics have a distinctly greater life expectancy than normal persons and that suicide is very rare among them.[15]

The fact that many neurotics, especially hysteria cases, do not have an organic ailment is often indicated by their ability to use muscles or limbs in certain situations but not when they are at work. One telegrapher, for example, could send messages perfectly when he knew that his key was connected to a testing machine, but he developed a cramp as soon as his key was attached to the main line. Many of these occupational neurotics can use their muscles very effectively at play but are unable to use them in work. The expert in diagnosis uses various tests to determine whether the claimant for compensation is malingering or neurotic. Important tests are willingness to take medicine regularly, to undergo surgical operations, to submit to repeated examinations, and the content of dreams and conversation.[16]

The occupational neurotic is usually very unhappy in his work or hates some part of it. Sometimes he merely associates some personal emotional problem with his work. Neuroses of this kind are more likely to occur when the worker is unable to quit his job because of his geographic isolation, requirements of a long-term contract, or enlistment in the army. An injury, fatigue of certain muscles, or an example of a fellow-worker may suggest the way in which the maladjustment can be made to disappear or how the patient's emotional problems can be corrected through systematic psychological treatment.

Allergies

Allergy may be defined as a special sensitivity to a substance that is harmless to most individuals. We all know persons who cannot eat certain foods without distress. Others cannot be in the presence of furry or hairy animals without developing asthma or skin eruptions. About 10 per cent of the people of the United States are allergic to a marked degree and another 40 per cent to a minor extent. Wheat foods, eggs, and milk are the most common causes of food allergies. The victims develop certain itches, aches, sneezes, and wheezes.

Some allergies are undoubtedly of organic origin, but many appear to be psychological. For example, one woman always suffered from asthma when she went to a certain railroad station. Someone told her that the station dust was of an unusual chemical nature and that she could be cured by having an injection of the dust. Her doctor injected her with a solution of common salt. After that the attacks of asthma ceased.[17]

An interesting study of totemism and allergy among inhabitants of Ponape, a North Pacific island, has been reported. Physical symptoms of allergy types were found in a fair proportion of those Ponapeans who violated totemic food taboos, the symptoms resembling those found in the United States among persons who felt guilty about violating prohibitions established by parents in regard to sexual and aggressive behavior. Increases in hostile feelings among some individuals brought out both an increased tendency to eat forbidden fruits and an increased tendency to react to them. Thus, some allergists believe that true food allergies are rare in adults and that both in the United States and the island of Ponape, food allergies are caused by emotional disturbances resulting from engaging in tabooed activitiy.[18]

"Darling, this is our last night together. Tomorrow my hay fever starts." Courtesy of Crowell-Collier Publishing Co.

"Psychosomatic" Illnesses

Every newspaper reader has become acquainted with the term "psychosomatic." To many people, unfortunately, it implies that the mind causes the ailment of the body. They imagine that psychological and physiological functions are separated. To overcome this erroneous dualistic assumption, the Army psychiatric classification system uses the term *somatization reactions*. Reactions of this kind are brought about by interactions of nonseparable organic and psychological factors. Measurable damages are caused by the tissues and structures of the body. Peptic ulcers are an example.

Psychosomatic disorders may be regarded as somatic symptoms which, in some cases, can be successfully treated by methods effective in treating psychic symptoms.[19]

There is still much question about the cause and effect relationship between the so-called psychologically induced ailments and emotional problems of people suffering from these afflictions. Does the emotional state of an individual precipitate his illness, or does the illness itself bring about personality changes?

While the etiology (origins) of a disease may differ some diseases are not to be approached exclusively through treatment of the mind and others exclusively through treatment of the body. Ideally, all medicine should be psychosomatic, with the mind and body being treated as a unit.

Studies of patients having arthritis, colitis, and obesity indicate that many have deep-seated resentments or feelings of guilt. Their resentments are likely to be directed against employers, members of the family, or teachers. When primitive men were aroused to anger against an enemy, they could expend their aroused energies against the enemy. Although civilized men are also aroused to anger, their heightened bodily activities cannot be promptly expressed, so they suffer a prolonged state of anxiety. When a man loses his job, he has the same fears experienced by his caveman ancestors who needed food, but the stronger heartbeat and extra secretions are now superfluous. The biochemical changes which facilitate adjustive action must be suppressed, but suppression does not remove them. The aroused bodily resources find expression in protective and aggressive reactions of asthma, arthritis, duodenal ulcer, allergies, and hundreds of other apparently unrelated manifestations.[20]

A tension-wrought individual may have need for the satisfaction of unbearable feelings of hunger. Unbearable hunger may be a displacement of a generalized need for pleasure, a substitute gratification of sexual drives, or for a tendency toward self-destruction. Other neurotic needs which may be connected with the development of obesity are feelings of boredom, loss of love, lack of challenge, or limitless greed. Flight into obesity may be a way of avoiding contact with people. However, it is erroneous to assume that overweight is always an abnormal condition that should be removed by dietary restrictions. For many people, acquiring excess weight is an important factor in their adaptation to life and may serve as a protection against more serious maladjustment or illness. The assessment of the psychological factors that contributed to the weight should be made before initiating marked changes in the weight pattern of the individual.[21]

Stress as a Factor in Psychosomatic Ailments

Most of us have experienced emotional stresses: fears, worries, conflicts, or anxieties that had a correlative relation to onset of a bodily disorder as exemplified by the well known "nervous stomach." Physicians and laymen often report cases of psychic disturbances that induce disorders such as skin eruptions, respiratory difficulties, and allergic asthma. The one body system that is especially vulnerable to the effects of emotional stress is the gastrointestinal tract.

One of the earliest investigations of gastric processes and emotional stress was reported in the early 19th century when a U.S. Army surgeon was able to make systematic observations of certain digestive processes through the cooperation of a young Canadian who had a fistula or artificial opening to his stomach as a result of an imperfectly healed gunshot wound. Later researchers conducted further studies on men who had similar injuries. They found that when the subject experienced feelings of anxiety or aggression, the gastric secretions increased and the stomach wall was engorged with blood. Seemingly, physiological changes of this kind were forerunners of ulcers.

More advanced experiments concerning the earlier findings have been conducted, some of the most significant experiments have been made with animals. Important findings are that not every kind of emotional stress produces ulcers. And a given kind of stress will produce ulcers in one subject but not in another. Some especially significant studies have been made with monkeys by researchers of the Division of Neuropsychiatry, Walter Reed Army Institute of Research.

In some of the Institute investigations, monkeys were kept in restraining chairs where they could move the head and limbs but not the body. The monkeys were trained, conditioned behaviorally, to avoid a mild electric shock by pressing a lever in say, once every 20 seconds. Monkeys learn a procedure of this type very quickly.

Early findings from the experiments suggested that the monkeys who developed ulcers did not do so as a result of the psychological stress involved but apparently as a result of the cumulative effect of the shocks. To test this hypothesis, more controlled experiments were conducted in which two monkeys were restrained in "yoked chairs"—both monkeys received shocks but only one of the pair could prevent them by pressing a lever. The responsible member of the pair soon learned that he had to press the lever only during those periods when a red light was turned on in the room. A six-hours-on and a six-hours-off schedule was followed with the first pair.

After 23 days, autopsies showed that the responsible member of the pair had a large perforation in the wall of the duodenum, the upper part of the small intestine and a common site for ulcers in human beings. The control monkey who was not obligated to press the lever showed no gastrointestinal abnormalities. Repeated experiments have confirmed the findings from the first pair.

The significant conclusions, however, are not as simple as indicated by the findings obtained from the first yoked pair. Later experiments indicate that the crucial factor is not in the mere accumulation of stress effects nor in the degree or frequency of stress but the relationship between the length of the stress period and the length of the rest period. The six-hours-on, six-hours-off schedule produced ulcers and other somatic disorders but certain other schedules failed to do so.

A tentative conclusion seems to be that emotional stress must be intermittent if it is to cause ulcers. Some patterns of continuous emotional stress-rest seem to permit the subject to make an adjustment under which ulcers do not occur. If the periodic emotional stress is to bring about an ulcer, the period of stress must conflict (or perhaps coincide) with some natural rhythm of the gastrointestinal system.

The nature of these rhythms as well as many other factors involved in bringing about ulcers are still unknown. Further researches are in progress. Laboratory studies of the kind conducted by the Institute and elsewhere are opening up new horizons in the understanding and alleviation of psychomatic ills in man.[22]

Most members of the general public assume that business executives suffer from stress because of their work load. However, the Life Extension Foundation analyzed data concerning 6,013 businessmen, 179 companies, on all levels of management and concluded:

> The extent and degree of executive stress are far less than is popularly believed. . . . The tension that does exist—and the accompanying ill effects of such stress—stem from within the indi-

vidual executive rather than from any outer forces of his living or working environment.[23]

Further researches may vindicate the belief from experimental studies that every person has his own natural stress level at which his mind and body function without ill effects. When deviations are forced beyond the individual's natural base-line, ill effects follow. If this is true, it may be just as bad to restrain a naturally energetic person from functioning at his intense pace as it is to force a slow-paced individual to perform at an unnaturally rapid rate.[24]

This point of view would seem to be confirmed by a six-year, 1956 through 1961, study of 86,750 du Pont Company executives and subordinates. The researchers found the annual heart attack rate among vice presidents, plant managers, assistant plant managers, district sales managers, laboratory directors, division managers and departmental general managers was only 2.2 per 1,000 employes. By contrast, the highest risk group, which included foremen, clerical supervisors and other lower-level management personnel, had a rate of 4 per 1,000.

Skilled, semi-skilled and unskilled wage workers as a group had an intermediate rate of 3.2 per 1,000. The middle-management workers just below the executive level had a rate only slightly higher than executives: 2.5 per 1,000. The rate among the lowest level salaried workers, mostly clerical workers, was 3.7 per 1,000. All statistics were adjusted for average age differences.

In attempting to explain the low rate among executives, the researchers offered:

> Stress cannot be measured or described by the external circumstances with which a person must contend, but rather by his reaction to these circumstances. One man's stress may be another man's pleasure.
>
> Thus the demands of a top-management job may be no more stressful than situations commonly encountered by persons in lower job levels, at work and at home. Secondly, men chosen for advancement may be those whose personal qualities are characteristic of both executive talent and resistance to coronary disease.
>
> It is conceivable, for example, that in selecting persons to assume greater responsibilities, supervisors and managers, knowingly or unknowingly, may tend to choose the better adjusted individuals, who by virtue of their personality and psychic state are better able to cope with life's stresses in general.[25]

Some evidence is developing which indicates that stress should be viewed in the positive as well as in the negative sense. This was shown in one series of experiments that was conducted with infant rats to learn how the effects of stressful experiences in infancy affect the behavior of the later adult organism. When the investigations were begun, the infant rats of one group were subjected to mild electric shocks, scheduled at the same hour each day. Those of a second group were placed in shock cages but were not given shocks. Those of a third group were left in the nest and not handled at all. It was assumed that when the members of the first group reached adulthood, they would show signs of emotional disorder. Surprisingly, it was the members of the control group, the ones not handled at all that behaved in a peculiar manner. The behavior of the shocked rats could not be distinguished from that of the group that had experienced the same handling but had been given no electric shock. The results of the experiment caused the investigators to reframe their research question from concern about the effects of stress to the effects of the absence of stressful experience in infancy. Some stressful experiences are after all part of the normal life of infants. Apparently, certain degrees of stress help to bring about benefits.[26]

Psychosomatic medicine and related researches are developing new and more effective approaches to the relations between emotions and bodily changes.

A famous physician, in an article, "Why Medicine Is Not a Science," has stressed the importance of understanding the mental life of the patient. Parts of his article are the following:

> There are three states of ill health. The first is a functional impairment or misuse which is

often impossible to detect and may not be noticed by the patient or his physician; the second brings definite symptoms of illness; the third brings structural changes. At present, patients are rarely seen before the second stage has been reached; more often, not before the third stage. To try to learn about an ailment under such circumstances is something like trying to learn about chess by watching only the last moves of a game between two experts, unaware that the outcome is frequently decided in the first moves....

A study of the liver alone eventually becomes no study of the liver at all. Nor is this the only trouble with such specialization. It overlooks also the fact that the person as a whole is something different from a collection of viscera; the wholeness gives some extra, if indefinable, quality to the individual organs. Today we pay for our knowledge of the parts in ignorance of the whole. ...

In ancient Greece the doctor was primarily a philosopher and secondarily a physician. He was first a student of nature, and secondly a student of nature perverted by disease. Despite the great technical advances of our day, the future of medicine may well depend upon the training of physicians who will be once more humanists and biologists, as well as chemists and physicists....[27]

To give these persons whose physiology of anxiety incapacitates them a label such as "psychoneurotic" or to accuse them of overworking their imagination does not help them. They merely drift from one doctor or faith healer to another. What each really needs is a reorganization of adjustment habits to know the true nature of his emotional problems, and to know how to develop new mental habits. For some, this may require the skills of the clinical psychologist. For other and milder cases, the friend or employer may be able to say to the psychoneurotic: "The problem that is really bothering you, young man, is the fact that you fear that the girl friend will tire of waiting for you and marry some other man. Face the issue. Talk it over with her. If you can't agree upon a practicable program of action, let her marry someone else and you do likewise. In the meantime, bear in mind that I'll give you my fellowship because I, too, once had the same problem."

An individual may make adjustments to his barriers quite differently from another because of differences in the weakness of certain organs, behavior habits, or constitution. As a result of frustration, one person may, for example, develop physiological imbalance which results in more colds. Another may have his repressed rages bring about physiological changes which result in high blood pressure or in doing more work. However, all persons need a recognition of the close relation between adjustment and health. For certain persons, poor health often means poor habits of thinking and of conduct. Almost any person who wants to feel faint can do so by saying to himself: "I am fainting. I want to faint." The neurotic achieves the same kind of end by subconscious wishes regarding his breathing, digestion, or circulation. An allergy, as well as other kinds of ailments, may simply be one effect of an evasion of some problem which he does not face consciously.

Remedies for Invalidism

What should be done for those unfortunate psychoneurotics and others who try to make an adjustment to reality by the avenue of illness? Scolding will not help them; it only increases their problems. They need clinical analysis rather than censure.

A helpful suggestion is not the advice, "Use your will," but instead, "Understand the cause of your trouble," and, "What is the real purpose of your behavior?" If the physician makes exhaustive tests and can find no just cause for the illness, then he should ask the patient to analyze himself or to have himself analyzed for problems which he is evading. He should try to induce the patient to face the barrier which he dislikes to admit to himself. He must be convinced that the defect or the inability to accomplish his present aims should be used to achieve another end that is equally acceptable. The main remedy is the trite statement that the cause must be removed. To do this may require considerable assistance on the part of the psychiatrist or the clinical psychologist. Furthermore, in cases of serious maladjustment, the patient who is very intelligent and has read a number of books on abnormal psychology cannot analyze himself and make his readjustment alone. However, his special knowledge should make him more intelligently coöperative in developing better habits of adjustment.

Children are often told that they are "nervous" and should not study or work. This is a serious mistake. It is far better to allow them to learn the joys of strenuous work and play. If they are not reminded of illness, but are encouraged to face life by direct attack habits, they will seldom develop the maladjustments which fond mothers call "nervousness."

Adults, too, are often told that they are "nervous" and should study or work less. This advice is usually a mistake. Work does not cause nervous breakdowns. Nervous breakdowns are the result of poor mental habits when adjustment problems, especially conflicts, appear. In the so-called mental breakdowns, the nature and the amount of work that the person does is largely irrelevant; the emotional reaction of the individual toward the work is all-important. If the worker's adjustment habits have enabled him to gain satisfactions from the work, the amounts and hours of work are incidental.

If the adjustment history has been essentially positive, the individual can recover quickly from strains of work or even "combat fatigue." Of World War II veterans whose afflictions had been diagnosed as "psychoneurosis," those who had combat experiences had more severe psychoneuroses than the noncombatants. But the combatants had more likelihood of improving after service than the noncombatants.[28]

Significant influences in some breakdowns in civilian life are precipitating factors, such as the boss's domineering manner toward the employee, the teacher's negligence of the pupil, the public's condemnation of a person, the husband's niggardliness, or the wife's nagging. When the poorly adjusted person is confronted by such barriers, his ongoing activities are blocked and a "breakdown" results. Such a person is not benefited by reminders of illness. He needs encouragement in performing his daily tasks and in becoming socially integrated.

Everyone should feel that he belongs in the social groups of his environment, but the maladjusted person has special need for being welcome in his groups. His associates should be friendly rather than critical toward him. Otherwise he will tend to withdraw into himself more than ever and will have more acute "pains." The attitude of the associates of the adult invalid should be one of encouraging him to carry on his work more intelligently rather than one of expressing mere sentimentality, or pampering.

As in practically all other maladjustments, the patient should be given work to do that requires complete attention. Of course, we should not ask others to work in order that they may be as wealthy or as important as someone else. Rather because, through work that is adapted to one's capacities, one can achieve the adjustment that comes from doing well work within these abilities. If work is reasonably satisfying, it may be carried on at all hours and for any number of years so long as the body is given a normal amount of exercise and care. If the well-adjusted individual works very hard, he simply gets tired and takes a rest. The well-adjusted individual uses direct attack in dealing with his illnesses, especially those of a functional nature. An unusual example of direct attack regarding a functional illness may be found in the way one organically sick man dealt with his ailment.

In 1920 Dr. A. L. Muirhead, a professor of pharmacology in one of the leading medical schools, found himself stricken with Addison's disease. Realizing that his affliction would end in death in a short time and being not only a physician but also an expert in the science of drugs, he determined to devote the remainder of his life to finding a cure. Instead of sitting back waiting for death in the Mayo Clinic, which he entered, he did all in his power to stave death off, chopped and dried adrenal gland substance which he put into capsules and took by mouth, and by rectum took preparations of the adrenal gland containing large quantities of adrenalin. In a short time he made a remarkable recovery, and for a while was apparently cured—the first instance in history of any such improvement in a sufferer from Addison's disease. The rejoicing, however, was premature, for Dr. Muirhead had not really been cured and had a relapse into his former condition. Although treatment was again instituted and although it did help a little, it did not prevent his death from this disease. But for several years the Muirhead treatment was the best that medicine could offer.[29]

ACKNOWLEDGMENTS AND REFERENCES

1. Caroline B. Zachry, *Emotion and Conduct in Adolescence* (New York: Appleton-Century-Crofts, 1940), pp. 69–70.
2. Winifred V. Richmond, *Personality—Its Development and Hygiene* (New York: Farrar and Rhinehart, 1937), p. 166.
3. Walter A. Lowen, *Advertising and Selling,* July, 1940, p. 31.
4. S. G. Vandenberg, "Difference Between Neurotics, Psychotics, and Normals on Perceptual Tests: Reanalysis of Eyesenck's Results," *Journal of Clinical Psychology,* **15** (1959), 373–376.
5. Henry A. Davidson, "Can Psychoneurosis Mature Into Psychosis?" *Mental Hygiene,* **41** (1957), 12–23.
6. For an understandable discussion on this point of view, see John K. Winkler and Walter Bromberg, *Mind Explorers* (New York: Reynal & Company, Inc., 1939), Chapter XV.
7. J. C. McKinley and S. R. Hathaway, "Multiphasic Personality Schedule (Minnesota): IV. Psychasthenia," *Journal of Applied Psychology,* **26** (1942), 614–624, reports a study of a scale for measuring psychasthenia.
8. K. Hazell, "The Anxiety Syndrome," *The Medical Press,* **216** (1946), 153–155.
9. Morton Prince, "Miss Beauchamp—The Theory and Psychogenesis of Multiple Personality," *Journal of Abnormal Psychology,* **15** (1920), 82 ff.
10. Harry L. Smith, M.D., and Nicholas C. Hightower, Jr., M.D., "Incidence of Functional Disease (Neurosis) Among Patients of Various Occupations," *Occupational Medicine,* **5** (1948), 182–185.
11. Condensed from a 1954 release from the National Office Management Association, 132 W. Chelten Ave., Philadelphia 44, Pa.
12. Graham B. Blaine, Jr., and Charles C. McArthur, *Emotional Problems of the Student* (New York: Appleton-Century-Crofts, 1961), p. 62.
13. See Thomas S. Langner and Stanley T. Michael, *Life Stress and Mental Health,* (London: The Free Press of Glencoe, Crowell-Macmillan, Ltd., 1963), p. 405, and Stanley T. Michael, "Social Attitudes, Socio-Economic Status, and Psychiatric Symptoms," *Acta Psychiatrica et Neurologica Scandinavica,* **35** (1960), 509–517.
14. E. Lewy, "Contribution to the Problem of Compensation Neuroses," *Bulletin of the Menninger Clinic,* **4** (1940), 88–92.
15. P. G. Denker, "The Prognosis of Insured Neurotics," *New York State Journal of Medicine,* **39** (1939), 238–247.
16. H. A. Davidson, "Neurosis and Malingering," *American Journal of Medical Jurisprudence,* **2** (1939), 94–96.
17. George W. Gray, "The Strange Ways of Allergy," *Harper's Magazine,* January, 1939.
18. J. L. Fischer, Ann Fischer, and Frank Mahony, "Totemism and Allergy," *International Journal of Social Psychiatry,* **5** (1959), 33–40.
19. Nigel Walker, "The Definition of Psychosomatic Disorder," *British Journal for the Philosophy of Science,* **6** (1956), 265–299, and W. Malamud, "The Office Management of the Neurotic Patient," *Psychiatric Quarterly,* **33** (April, 1959), 335–350.
20. S. Morrison and M. Fedman, "Psychosomatic Correlations of Duodenal Ulcer," *Journal of the American Medical Association,* **120** (1942), 738–740.
21. Hilde Bruch, "The Emotional Significance of the Preferred Weight," *American Journal of Clinical Nutrition,* **5** (1957), 192–196.
22. Joseph V. Brady, "Ulcers in 'Executive' Monkeys," *Scientific American,* October, 1958. Brady, *et al.,* "Avoidance Behavior and the Development of Gastro-duodenal Ulcers," *Journal of the Experimental Analysis of Behavior,* January, 1958. R. W. Porter, *et al.,* "Some Experimental Observations on Gastrointestinal Lesions in Behaviorally Conditioned Monkeys," *Psychosomatic Medicine,* September-October, 1958.
23. "Life Extension Foundation. Job Stress and the Executive: 6,000 managers report their Experience," *Management Review,* American Management Association, Inc., **47** (1958), 13–21.
24. See *Management Review,* American Management Association, Inc., December, 1963, p. 55.
25. Sidney Pell and C. Anthony D'Alonzo, "Acute Myocardial Infarction in a Large Industrial Population—Report of a Six-Year Study," *Journal of the American Medical Association,* Sept. 14, 1963, pp. 831–838. Also correspondence with authors dated Sept. 18, 1964.
26. Seymour Levine, "Stimulation in Infancy: Both Painful Shocks and Gentle Handling Enhance the Development of Normal Stress Responses in Infant Animals. The Absence of Such Treatment Leads to Behavioral Disorders When the Animal Matures," *Scientific American,* May, 1960.
27. Ian Stevenson, M.D., "Why Medicine Is Not a Science," *Harper's Magazine,* **198** (1949), 36–39.

28. Maurice H. Greenhill, "Clinical Features of the Psychoneuroses in World War II Veterans," *N. C. Medical Journal,* **7** (1946), 585–590.
29. Edward Podolsky, M.D., "Gland Magic," *The American Scholar,* **3** (1934), 449.
30. Harry L. Smith and Nicholas C. Hightower, Jr., "Incidence of Functional Disease (Neurosis) Among Patients of Various Occupations," *Occupational Medicine,* **5** (February, 1948), 182–185.

PROJECTS

1. Smith and Hightower studied the incidence of neurosis among consecutively admitted patients to the Mayo Clinic. They also studied neurosis among the Jewish male and female patients. A part of their summary follows:

   "We studied the group of Jews because, as has been said, some persons believe that Jewish patients are particularly emotional and neurotic. We were somewhat surprised at the results we obtained. Yet when the percentages which represent purely functional disease, or functional and organic disease, are compared, it is seen that the incidence of neurosis in this group is no higher than that in the controls.

   "We fully realize that a study of this type is not entirely accurate. Our results may not represent the actual incidence of neuroses in the population as a whole because the study was limited to persons who sought help from physicians. The least that it does, however, is to confirm the general impression that the incidence of neuroses among persons of various occupations differs greatly.[30]

   a. Interview some of your friends concerning the question of incidence of neurosis among Jews and non-Jews. Get your friends' opinions and discuss possible reasons for the assumption that Jews are particularly neurotic.

   b. Examine any published library articles on the same question to find whether other investigators agree with the Smith and Hightower findings.
2. Examine available textbooks that deal with public speaking and note how stage fright is treated. Which methods seem to you to be the most helpful?
3. List some of the "worthy causes" of your community which are likely to appeal to neurasthenics.
4. Recall some of your own abulic tendencies, such as those in writing to friends, checking your finances, seeing your dentist, and so on. Outline a definite procedure in each case whereby the necessary action may be taken at the proper time.
5. Women of today do not faint as much as women of a generation or two ago. What possible reasons can you suggest for this change of behavior?
6. Make a list of some of the things you have worried about during the past year or two. Check and analyze those cases in which your apprehension was a distinct handicap to the solution of the problem. Did worrying contribute to the solution in other cases?
7. Consider an acquaintance who says that certain common foods make him ill. What physical and psychological factors might be involved? Set up a procedure by which you might test objectively which factors are predominant.
8. Iatrogenic disorders are ailments induced in a patient by autosuggestion based on the physician's manner, examination, or diagnosis. Can you cite an example from your own experience? If not too embarrassing to you, describe the incident.

COLLATERAL READINGS

Cattell, Raymond B., "The Nature and Measurement of Anxiety," *Scientific American,* March, 1963.

Greenfield, N. S., "Allergy and the Need for Recognition," *Journal of Consulting Psychology,* June, 1958.

Hillson, Joseph F. and Philip Worchel, "Self Concept and Defensive Behavior in the Maladjusted," *Journal of Consulting Psychology,* February, 1957.

Knapp, Robert R., "Objective Personality Test and Sociometric Correlates of Frequency of Sick Bay Visits," *Journal of Applied Psychology,* April, 1961.

Lehner, George F. J. and Ella Kube, *The Dynamics of Personal Adjustment.* Englewood Cliffs, N.J.: Prentice-Hall, Inc., 1964, Chapter 6.

Malamud, W., "The Office Management of the Neurotic Patient," *Psychiatric Quarterly,* April, 1959.

Nussbaum, K., "Somatic Complaints and Homeostasis in Psychiatric Patients," *Psychiatric Quarterly,* April, 1960.

Shaffer, Laurance F. and Edward J. Shoben, Jr., *The Psychology of Adjustment.* Boston: Houghton Mifflin Company, 1956, Chapters 9 and 10.

The Rev. George Matheson, author of the hymn, "O, love that wilt not let me go!" is chiefly associated with Innellan on the Firth of Clyde. *Pictured is the Matheson Memorial Church, with its manse.*

Were a plebiscite taken of the Scottish people's favorite hymn, there is little doubt that the afflicted George Matheson's **"O, love that wilt not let me go!"** *written in 1882, and sung to the tune,* **"St. Margaret's,"** *would secure the greatest number of votes.*

Matheson was born in Glasgow in 1842. His early scholastic career was one of great promise. But soon a dark shadow began to descend upon his life. By the age of twenty he was totally blind. All his hopes, it would seem, were shattered. Good friends encouraged him to persevere, however; and the professors at Glasgow University, while making no concessions in the matter of the standard of scholarship required for graduation purposes, afforded him every facility to pursue his studies. In due course he emerged, duly licensed, an accredited minister of the Church of Scotland. Scarcely had he begun his ministry when he was called to Innellan. There he stayed for eighteen years. From Innellan he went to Edinburgh in 1886, as minister of St. Bernard's. There he remained until 1899, when owing largely to declining health, he resigned. He died at North Berwick in 1906.

Early in his ministry at Innellan was added to his blindness that great sorrow, out of which was born the hymn . . . the lyric . . . that was to make him famous and remembered. "I was suffering from extreme mental distress," he wrote, "and the hymn was the first fruit of pain." Matheson himself does not tell us what had happened. But we learn from other sources that it was the content of a letter received at Innellan that afternoon from the woman he loved, intimating that, because of his blindness, she felt constrained to break off her engagement.

The information regarding the Rev. George Matheson, D. D., and also the photograph of the Matheson Memorial Church and Manse at Innellan, on the Firth of Clyde, are from Alasdair Alpin MacGregor's book, **Land of the Mountain and the Flood** *(London: Michael Joseph, 1965). See also* **Scotland's Magazine,** *May 1964, pp. 19 and 20.*

CHAPTER SIX

METHODS OF TREATING THE MALADJUSTED

To bring on the triumph of intellect over mechanism, of responsible morality over irresponsible force, is our mission. If we think things cannot be different from what they are, we but add so much to the dead inertia of the world, which keeps them as they are; while if we will not succumb we may be part of the very forces that will help to make things different.[1]

The treatment of the seriously maladjusted or so-called insane requires years of special training in universities, hospitals, and clinics. This work is done by psychiatrists, that is, physicians who have specialized in the investigation and treatment of mental disorders. Obviously, only experts should treat psychotics, those persons who have a pathological mental condition which tends to constitute a disease-entity. In this chapter, therefore, we shall differentiate between the serious and the minor maladjustments.

TREATMENT OF THE MAJOR OR SERIOUS MALADJUSTMENTS

The theories and methods that psychiatrists and clinical psychologists use are too complex for us to attempt a comprehensive discussion of them in this book. However, we as educated laymen can try to appreciate the importance of their work and coöperate intelligently with them.

FIRST, we should recognize our responsibility toward acquaintances who are suffering from serious mental ailments. One of the great lessons we have learned from our studies of the mentally ill is the need for realizing that a mentally sick person should be treated with the same consideration that we accord the physically ill. When a friend has a broken leg or has a fever, we take him to a hospital, sympathize with him, send him flowers, and visit him. Similarly, when a friend is sent to a hospital for mental treatment, we should treat him, not as a "nut," but as a person who is sick, for that is what he is. We should not attach a social stigma to the person who has been in an institution for mental treatment any more than to a person who has been in a general hospital for an organic illness. In many cases the former mental patient is not handicapped, but to some people he is stigmatized. The stigma is based on unintelligent popular misconceptions regarding the possible permanence of insanity. Many small employers still refuse to hire former mental patients.

SECOND, employers should recognize that there are many kinds of mental disturbances and that each varies in the degree to which it incapacitates for work. The employer or personnel man should be acquainted with the five psychological terms for broad mental classification: the mental defective, the epileptic, the psychotic, the psychopathic personality, and the psychoneurotic.

The *mental defective* lacks some mental qualities or abilities which are present in the normal individual. The synonym for most mental defectives of the kind who visit employment offices is "feebleminded." These differ in their degree of mental limitation, and their intelligence can be measured by means of intelligence tests. Many of these people can and do learn to perform routine and repetitive jobs in industry.

The *epileptics* or, more correctly, those who are subject to convulsive states, can be employed in many cases. Some have convulsions only in their sleep. Others have them only at infrequent intervals. Many experience a preliminary signal before an attack, and some control their ailment by means of medicine. If each person who is subject to "fits" is considered in terms of the variety of his disorder and its control, certain types of employment which he can perform without danger will be found.

Some *psychotics* can be employed, at least during certain stages of the psychosis. However, all persons who are or appear to be psychotic should be examined by a psychiatrist in order to ascertain the kind and degree of the disorder. We must realize that five to ten per cent of the mentally ill are asocial or antisocial to a degree that requires closely supervised care.[2] After adequate diagnosis, certain patients have to be hospitalized; others may be given treatment under controlled conditions. Many are employable for predictable time periods only. In the case of the manic-depressive (having pronounced swings of elation and depression), the patient may have a disorder for one period of time only, or he may have it in recurrent cycles. There may be several years between attacks when the individual is normal and employable. Some psychotics are overactive during the early stage of an attack and work very industriously. Complete recovery from an attack is the rule rather than the exception.

Patients who are hospitalized for *schizophrenia* (literally, "splitting of the mind," formerly called dementia praecox) are incapable of doing work during the early stages of the disorder. After treatment, certain ones can be discharged from hospitals and can work in a protected environment for predictable time periods. However, the chronicity of schizophrenia must not be overlooked. About 80 per cent of schizophrenics will respond to modern therapies, but more than half of this group will relapse, many of them periodically for the rest of their lives.[3] The behavior of many chronic schizophrenics can be too trying and disruptive to have them work with others. "Today, 35 per cent of the patients sufficiently improved to be discharged from mental hospitals relapse and have to be readmitted."[4]

Those who grow old and develop *senile psychosis* have defects of memory and judgment. If such old employees are allowed to work slowly at tasks that do not require new mental habits, they may fill certain jobs very well.

The *psychopathic personalities* include the pathological liars, swindlers, eccentrics, vagrants, sexual deviants, and certain types of criminals. They are deficient in moral values. Few are hospitalized and most are difficult to cure because they do not coöperate during therapy. Most have bad work records and get into conflict with the law. For most types of factory and office work they are useless, but many of them are members of our great army of transient and migratory labor.

The *psychoneurotics* are found everywhere. They are always in touch with reality and are not insane. Some have harmless obsessions, phobias, or forms of hysteria. Some are hypochondriacs who complain of functional ills and pains. They are often absent from work, complain about the employer, are easily fatigued, are irritable and have a bad effect on the morale of other workers. Many are merely childish, or make other evasive adjustments to their personal problems. Every large group of employees has some of these neurotics, and many are needed, in spite of their maladjustments, because of the good work they do in their specialities.[5]

Some persons, merely because they were known to be getting mental treatment, have lost their jobs and their friends. "So-and-so is going to a psychiatrist—he must be nuts" is still too common a verdict of employers and others. Much health education is needed to correct unfair attitudes toward the mentally ill.

Those people who have developed constructive attitudes toward persons with mental or emotional problems realize that "troublesome people are people in trouble." They offer the troubled person intelligent understanding because they sense some of the factors involved in the mental problems. They do not scold or argue nor do they tell him just to "snap out of it." They realize that "there is little point in trying to convince a troubled person that what he is doing is wrong. He has latched on to his kind of behavior as a means of protecting himself and trying to argue him out of it is like trying to take away the only defense he has. He will only resent this and fight you even harder."[6]

THIRD, we should appreciate the chances for recovery or improvement of patients who enter a hospital for the mentally ill. The chance of discharge for the first-year patient in a mental hospital is better than 50–50. Of course, recovery rates vary, depending upon the age of the patient, the kind of mental disorder, and the treatment. For the senile and the arteriosclerotic the chances of recovery are very slight indeed, but for the younger people, those with schizophrenia and the manic-depressive psychoses, the chances of getting out of the mental hospital fairly promptly are very good. Certainly the chances of recovery for many young and middle-aged patients are excellent. Especially important is the fact that current recovery rates are improving as the result of recent researches which are producing new and more helpful drugs and methods of treatment.

According to the reports of the National Institutes of Health, the numbers of mental patient cases continue to decline. Statistics indicate that mental hospital populations may be expected to decrease at the rate of one or two per cent a year for some years to come.

The decreasing trend began in 1955 with the intensive application of new and more effective treatment methods including the psychiatric drugs, changing hospital policies, plus a greater recognition and understanding of mental illness as a public health problem. Also, there is some probability that the increased use of nursing homes for the elderly is reducing the mental hospital population. On the other hand, the statistical rate of the downward trend will be modified by the new mental hospital services that are being added for special patients such as the alcoholics and drug addicts.[7]

FOURTH, executives, parents, teachers, and personnel men should learn enough about the symptoms of mental disorders to know when it is advisable to refer employees, children, pupils, and acquaintances to experts for diagnosis. Psychiatrists and clinical psychologists are trained friends who may help increase our happiness. They are not mere classifiers of mental ailments and custodians of asylums; they are counselors to whom we may go for occasional check-ups of our mental habits just as we may go to the family physician for an annual check-up of our bodily condition.

FIFTH, we should learn some of the basic principles used in the treatment of the mentally ill so that we can coöperate intelligently with the psychotherapist. For example, some patients who voluntarily consult a psychiatrist report that they are not getting any help from the treatments. These statements are often made because the patient's treatment has progressed to the point where he must either live on a new basis or else continue to "enjoy" his old inadequate mental habits. At such times of doubt we should encourage the patient to continue the treatments until he learns to live more satisfyingly in terms of the new mental regimen.

SIXTH, the investigations made by the specialists in mental disease have removed the fear of the direct inheritance of mental ills. Mental ills are not inherited like the color of eyes. Paradoxically, however, mental ills do run in families. Studies of sisters, brothers, uncles, aunts, parents, and grandparents of patients in mental hospitals have revealed no evidence of any exact theory of inheritance. There is no clear-cut case of Mendelian inheritance.[8] A mentally diseased parent cannot hand on this trait as he can hand on the color of his eyes.[9]

Mental disease does occur among the relatives of mental patients and among some racial groups[10] more often than it occurs in the general population. It is possible that a predisposition toward mental breakdown is inherited, but we are not certain because the parents of the mentally diseased also bequeath to the children a particular sort of family circle in which to grow up. Mental habits have a close relationship with mental disease or health, and this fact offers us much hope in the intelligent control of our mental well-being. We can do a great deal toward the development of sound mental habits in ourselves, regardless of who or what our parents were. The maladjusted person is not a poor helpless patient fatalistically sacrificed to his heredity or his environment. More powerful than the germ plasm or the parental pattern are courage and the desire to develop the adaptability necessary to deal adequately with one's barriers.

SEVENTH, we should appreciate the relation between bodily and mental health. A thorough physical examination should precede any psychotherapy, and the examination should be made by a physician who specializes in diagnosis rather than by an ordinary practitioner who is satisfied with taking the blood pressure and counting the pulse. An ailment such as arthritis is often treated as organic only. Yet family worry, grief, and other forms of emotional stress bear more than a chance relationship to the onset and flare-up of the chronic joint disease, rheumatoid arthritis, as indicated by a study of this ailment.[11]

On the other hand, hallucinations may be erroneously treated as purely psychological; yet voices heard by the mentally ill may have a basis in ear infections. Almost one out of every five patients examined at the Boston Psychopathic Hospital was found to have a toxic type of deafness.[12] Certain patients who were free from toxic deafness also suffered from auditory hallucinations but described them differently. This study indicated that an examination of the physical condition is so important in understanding many mental conditions that the diagnoses should be made with the utmost care.

Kinds of Treatments

Physicians and psychiatrists are giving many different kinds of treatments to the body, particularly the nervous system, as an aid in curing patients who were considered hopelessly insane. Some of these more recently developed treatments include electric shocks passed directly through the brain.

Electro-shock is a method of psychotherapy often used on patients who are not responding well to other therapies. A state of shock known as "coma" is induced in the patient by an electric shock passed directly through the brain in controlled amounts. Similar conditions are induced by means of insulin and metrazol. Electro-shock is particularly valuable in weakening those psychological defenses that keep the patient from facing his conflicts. It thus facilitates treatment by other therapeutic methods.[13] Electric shock seems to improve feeling tone and jar the patient out of his apathy and inertia. Rigidity of personality structure is decreased and the immediate release of hostility, especially in rigid personality and depressive cases, is striking. A more outgoing attitude is adopted which improves the patient's chances of benefiting from psychotherapy.[14]

No one knows what really happens as a result of these shock treatments. Perhaps some of the old nerve current pathways and synaptic junctions in the sick brains are so modified by the shock treatment that old neural patterns are lost. Metabolic activity is changed. Chemical and physiological activities are modified, but perhaps only future research will explain the reasons why shock and fever treatments are beneficial to some mental patients. We do know that the psychological meaning of the treatment to the patient is an important factor in the therapy.[15]

Psychosurgery, operation on the frontal lobes of the brain, has become accepted by some psychiatrists. Others, however, still doubt that the results justify this drastic operation. It is used in the treatment of what were formerly considered "incurable" cases of patients with an extreme degree of emotional tension and anxiety. The problem in surgery is to reduce the patient's self-awareness and sensitivity to limits he can tolerate—without making him apathetic and completely indifferent to events and people around him. After the operation, the patient may become more willing to accept himself and others, and, in general, his hostilities and suspicions are lessened. This reduction in hostilities does not always make the patient more sociable, but rather, tends to render him passive to life's complexities. He may develop a "You let me alone and I'll let you alone" attitude, which has its drawbacks, but is certainly preferable to an attitude of violent hostility.[16]

In one study, eight patients who received transorbital lobotomy were compared to a control group of eight who were continued on electro-shock. Rorschach tests indicated that the lobotomy resulted in a lessening of inner tension and reduction in self-awareness. The patients also lost their ardent enthusiasm and active interest. Severing the frontal lobes from the rest of the brain tends to have this effect because it apparently separates psychotic ideas from the usual accompanying emotions.[17]

Narco-analysis is a form of therapy during which the patient talks about or acts out the painful experiences which have caused an acute neurosis, anxiety state, or hysteria. It was used with good results during World War II for alleviating conditions caused by distressing combat experiences. The procedure is to administer to the patient a barbiturate drug which induces narcosis. Sometimes electrical treatment similar to that used in electroshock but of lower intensity and longer duration is used to bring on this form of narcosis. While the patient is in this induced sleep, the therapist encourages him to talk about or act out his traumatic experiences, thereby bringing his repressed fears and anxieties to consciousness where they can be understood. With understanding comes release from the maladjustment expressed by the symptoms.

The "tranquilizing" drugs are now being used by psychiatrists with remarkable effects in treating psychotic patients. Some of the more commonly used drugs are chlorpromazine (trade name: Thorazine), reserpine (Serpasil) and azacyclonol (Frenquel).

One of the psychiatrist's greatest problems in dealing with a psychotic individual is to make some kind of effective contact with the patient. This is especially true of the schizophrenic. The patient may be aloof and apathetic; he may fancy that the radio in the ward is directing insults to him personally.

The new tranquilizing drugs calm the patient without putting him to sleep. Their effects last longer than those of sedatives. Severely disturbed patients may be kept in an open ward instead of being locked up. Even "hopeless" patients become accessible to psychotherapy by reducing their anxieties and removing some of the barriers between the patient and the psychiatrist.[18]

One report indicated that, of 200 acutely disturbed psychotic female patients, 22 per cent had been discharged after six months of treatment with reserpine. This compared with a 4.7 per cent discharge rate from the same institution in the previous six months. About two-thirds of the group discharged had been able to maintain their improvement without any further medication. Of the remaining third who regressed, all responded to retreatment and held their improvement on maintenance doses.[19]

Chlorpromazine, reserpine, and Frenquel are important beginning aids in the treatment of mental ailments. Much remains to be done to solve the problem. None of the tranquilizing drugs helps all schizophrenics nor are the drugs effective in relieving melancholia (a profound, passive depression) or certain long-standing neuroses and psychosomatic troubles. There is also a tendency on the part of some therapists to prescribe these drugs for too many ailments and to allow neurotics to lean on the aid of drugs when they ought to learn to solve their problems themselves.

The hallucinogenic drugs have provided a new tool for the investigation of psychotic states. The ones mentioned most frequently are mescaline, which comes from a peyote cactus; psilocybin and psilocin, from certain mushrooms; and d-lysergic acid diethylamide (LSD), derived from ergot, a fungus that grows on wheat and rye. All are related to one another in chemical structure.

Medicine men of almost every culture have chewed, eaten, imbibed or smoked botanic materials which induced or encouraged visions, euphoria, delirium, or prophetic insight. The Aztecs were reported in 1529 as eating certain mushrooms as "bread of the gods."[20] Certain species of the "divine mushroom" are still worshipped and eaten by religious groups of Mexico and Saskatchewan, Canada.

When certain hallucinogenic drugs are administered to apparently well-adjusted people, they produce the symptoms of psychosis. The subjects who took the drug feel confused, lethargic, and overcome by apathy. They feel that something strange has happened to them and things seem different. Some also have had the feeling that they did not exist or that parts of their body had altered form. Visual illusions appeared. The thought processes slowed down. Time lost meaning. The subjects' capacity to organize and verbalize was reduced. They couldn't put into words the unusual experiences they were having. They lost their usual ability to discriminate between themselves and others. They projected their feelings and attributed them to others.

The use of hallucinogenic drugs gives doctors and researchers insight into the minds and feelings of persons afflicted by mental illness. The entire psychotic period can be telescoped into a period of six to twelve hours, and the emotional disintegration followed step by step. Too, by actually experiencing the psychotic state themselves, researchers can better understand the patient and learn how to communicate with and help him. Mental illness should eventually become less strange or mysterious; there should be fewer barriers between the sick and the well. When we know enough to be able to create a disease, we should be closer to its cure. Various treatments can be tested on the experimentally induced psychosis.

Perhaps the most important result of the LSD and related experiments is that for the first time researchers can investigate experimentally the many relationships between the psychotic state and the body's chemistry and physiology. The experiments indicate that there is a definite link between physiological disturbances and mental changes. Evidently certain types of psychoses may be caused by chemical changes in the body.[21]

Researchers at Tulane University detected the presence of a twisted protein molecule in the blood stream of schizophrenic patients not found in normal persons.[22] This finding seems to confirm the conviction of many researchers who believe that the cure of many mental illnesses will eventually be found by the biochemists.

Researchers are developing a growing body of evidence that some of the psychoneuroses and functional psychoses are in part biochemical, and not illnesses of the mind as such. One contention is that psychological stress causes nutritional displacement and this, in turn, brings about mental illness. A few regard virtually all or most mental symptoms as signs of brain disease.[23] The more representative view is that mental illness is a name for the ways that a person deals with problems in living.[24]

Many methods of treatment other than surgical, electrical, and chemical are being used experimentally. The therapeutic theater is an example. Here patients are encouraged to go on a stage and blow off steam through impromptu drama[25] while psychiatrists listen and offer guidance. The psychodrama has been used in the treatment of marriage problems and for truancy on the part of maladjusted school boys.[26]

Generally, the philosophy underlying most forms of psychotherapy is that the sufferer must be treated as a personality and not merely as the bearer of a diagnosable disease.

Group therapy is an example of a method that helps the patient become better integrated through a special social group of fellow sufferers. The great number of acute psychopathological cases and the comparatively small number of therapists was the immediate cause for the adoption of group therapy on a large scale during World War II.

Much research is being done with this technique. Two journals are reporting studies of benefits, limitations and procedures.[27] Textbooks on the subject are available. In a typical procedure a number of psychoneurotic patients, usually not more than thirty, participate in group discussions of their difficulties, and thereby learn ways of adjusting more effective and satisfying than those they have adopted as manifested by their neurotic symptoms. Prior to being admitted to a group, each person is interviewed by a psychotherapist who ascertains the nature of each patient's troubles and decides whether he might benefit or be harmed by this form of treatment. Harm may ensue if problems stirred up in group sessions appear to be beyond the patient's solution. Certain patients who suffer as a result of serious sexual repressions, are overly suspicious of others, or are easily hurt by criticism may not be ready for group therapy. Those who lack the courage to face themselves are not likely to respond favorably. When the psychotherapist approves a patient for membership in a group, he familiarizes himself with the case. Usually this same therapist is present at the group discussions, held several times a week. He acts as discussion leader, urging patients to talk about their difficulties to the group, calling on them for comments on, reactions to, or interpretations of the troubles of the other members of the group, and encouraging progress reports. In the permissive atmosphere that prevails, patients discover that their difficulties are not unique; that other people have similar ones. As they learn more about the other persons in the group they develop a feeling of fellowship with them, and an identification with the group is built up. This identification furnishes the neurotic with a stabilizing influence and a support with which he can help himself. The situation simulates a small social community where he can find reassurance and self-understanding, and thus adjust himself more adequately to the environment of his everyday life.[28]

The method of therapy most desirable in many cases can be decided upon by determining whether the maladjustment is a simple bad mental habit or of a deep-seated type. If it is of the latter variety, the patient is likely to resist assistance or be incapable of gaining insight and release without systematic professional counsel. Analytical rather than superficial procedures are essential. When strong feelings of guilt are predominant, a Freudian type of approach may be necessary. If feelings of inferiority are predominant, an Adlerian type of approach is likely to be effective.[29] But whatever approach is used by the therapist, the patient must be given a mental reëducation that enables him to live without old tensions and to participate in normal social relations.

Religion is believed by many people to have therapeutic value. The pastor can help those suffering from guilt through the healing effects of confession and forgiveness, those suffering from sorrow through mitigating their grief, those suffering from fear and anxiety through increasing their faith, those suffering from hostility through spreading the spirit of love. Mental health attitudes engendered or increased through religious experience include the sense of personal worth, trust in the ultimate victory of good over evil, membership in a communal fellowship, the support of invisible yet constant companionship, confession, and forgiveness, the urging and guiding of youth along approved paths, the aspiration and dedication of worship, and the discipline or way of life.[30]

So many different kinds of treatment are used that the layman is apt to wonder why chemical, physical, and psychological approaches are at times used for patients who have the same or similar disorders.

> If one asks how could psychological medicine possibly cure an organic condition, the answer is obvious. It could not possibly cure an organic condition. If at the same time one asks, "How could chemicals possibly cure an organic condition," the answer must be the same. It could not possibly. We then perceive that the questions have arisen out of a misconception of the mechanism by which cures are achieved. Processes which go on in the body are of necessity some expression of metabolism. The chemicals which we take when we feel diseased could hardly be said to repair the damaged condition of the organism. Rather their sole purpose is so to change conditions in the organism as to bring about those functional conditions which will enable the organism more readily to cure itself. The organism must always cure itself through its metabolic activities. It will be seen from this analysis that the effects of chemical medicines are purely functional. Viewed from this angle, the situation is somewhat clearer and the question is now as to whether or not the psychological medicine can be of value in bringing about the conditions which will enable the organism to cure itself.[31]

Unfortunately, the bringing about of conditions which will enable the organism to cure itself is often very difficult in psychopathic cases. However, one helpful point of view for the student is that many psychopathic persons develop their mental disorders because they are confronted by problems for which they have no satisfactory answers. Many are in states of conflict.

Conflicts

A humorist described a tardy man and woman standing on a pier watching an ocean liner disappear down the bay. The disappointed woman turned on her husband and said: "Don't just stand there—*do* something!" Obviously, the poor husband could do nothing about it, but the wife's senseless demand for action illustrates how conflicts are likely to arise when no action is possible.

Many experiments have shown the possible effects of conflicts on mental well-being. Ivan B. Pavlov, the Russian physiologist, was one of the first experimenters to prove that abnormalities of behavior can be produced in an animal when the animal has been trained to solve a problem by means of a specific act, and the conditions are changed so that the learned solution is no longer appropriate. Pavlov trained a dog by the conditioned-reflex method to discriminate between two visual patterns; the presentation of a circle of light was always followed by food, while the appearance of an ellipse whose axes had a ratio of 2:1 was not rewarded. The circle soon became a conditioned stimulus to salivation but the appearance of the ellipse inhibited salivation.

In the experiment, the conditions for the dog were changed. The ellipse was gradually changed to approach a circle and the dog continued to make perfect discriminations until the ratio of the axes had become 8:9, after which imperfect discriminations were made. Then the dog's behavior suddenly changed. He was unable to differentiate between the circle and the ellipse and became negative to all stimuli. As the training was continued, the formerly docile dog constantly struggled and howled. The dog had a "nervous breakdown." The confusion of the positive and negative stimuli was too much for him. The conflict could not be solved by any of his learned responses.[32]

Other investigators have done considerable similar work with pigs and cats. N.R.F. Maier and his associates have studied experimentally produced neurotic behavior in the rat.

In Maier's experiments with rats, the rats were taught by reward and punishment to distinguish between two cards. Then, instead of being permitted a choice between a "reward" and a "punishment" card, an animal was shown only the "punishment" card while a blast of air was forcing him to jump. At the sight of the "punishment" card, the rat might resist action for as long as 15 minutes before he would jump. The rat was in a state of conflict. He did not have a suitable mode of response for the problem situation. Neurotic symptoms developed in many rats. The "psychopathic" animal would tear out of the apparatus, run in circles on the floor, show intense tics, and then have varying degrees of coma. Maier found that an irritant which furnishes no release builds up tensions which the organism cannot handle, and these may resolve themselves in catastrophic reactions.[33]

As a result of his experiments, he believes that a cure for frustrated neurotic human patients is to find a way for them to act. His cure of neurotic rats is to encourage them to find something to do even though it fails to solve the conflict that confronts them. He calls this "abortive behavior." To cure them, he taught them to make just a halfway jump toward solving their dilemma. Possible human applications[34] of this principle might be:

> A girl urged by her parents to marry might dislike both of two available suitors. Forced to marry, she would break down. If she engages herself to one but is cold to him, so that they drift apart, she is saved. A substitute activity, such as a career of nursing, would serve the same purpose.
>
> Pregnancy [illegitimate] and the conflicts arising from sin contribute greatly to neurotic behavior by leaving no avenue for behavior and yet requiring that something be done....
>
> On the other hand, going to the electric chair, while it may produce tensions, does not produce neurosis because the individual knows just what he must do.[35]

These experiments with animals and the judgments of many specialists in mental disorders indicate that neurosis is often due to the fact that the individual patient is confronted by the conflicting character of difficulties imposed upon him, difficulties for which he has no direct attack or suitable substitute responses. The neurosis is a haven in his flight from reality. It is an escape from the facing of unpleasant facts, mostly in the form of impulsive attitudes that are irreconcilable to him. In the case of the adult, some of the irreconcilable attitudes probably originated in childhood and are now in conflict with current drives. Inner peace can be developed when the individual finds an acceptable mode of action or makes a final choice in favor of one drive.[36] In some cases, willingness to accept an inevitable situation which the individual previously resented may resolve the conflict within him.

The experiments with animals have suggested some valuable concepts for the treatment of psychopathics. However, the most interesting and frequently used concepts in the use of psychological approaches to the treatment of psychopaths may be obtained from a review of the principles and methods of psychoanalysis.

What is Psychoanalysis?

Sigmund Freud[37] of Vienna was the originator of the technical method of psychoanalysis. He published his first investigations in 1895. Freud studied many cases of nervous disorders and was convinced that the main causes lay in repressed wishes or desires. The repressed desire or impulse was, he believed, of a sexual nature and has been repressed by the forces of education and social conventions. When the wish is repressed it remains alive and active in unconscious form. The theory, to many people, appears to be weird, while to others it holds a strong attraction for its interesting interpretations.

Early in his professional career, he discarded the use of "subconscious" because it connoted a "sub" or lesser mind. Later, he exalted his newly discovered region of mind function and chose the word, "unconscious," the term preferred by most psychotherapists today. Perhaps we should spend a moment reviewing the experiences which gave Freud his method of treating psychopathological maladies.

Before 1890, psychologists had already studied mental abnormalities. Hypnotism was known, and it was noted that, when patients were treated in certain ways, they developed multiple personalities. That is, they regarded themselves and acted as though they were different persons at different times. Sometimes one personality could not remember the other personality of the same individual. In other cases the various "personalities" might be more or less conscious of each other. This was then interpreted as indicating that nervous diseases were the result of a splitting-off of consciousness. One portion of the associations of the mental life broke off and formed a new or smaller "mind" of its own. Compulsions and obsessions were explained in this way, and the physicians of that time used hypnotism to reintegrate the dismembered personality or mind. In the hypnosis, the physician tried to bring the split-off part of the mind back to the main body of the personality. Freud was a physician and treated his patients in this manner.

In the early years of his experimenting, Freud noted that some patients remembered things when they were hypnotized that they could not recall when in the normal state of consciousness. Then, when these forgotten facts of a painful nature were presented to the patient in his normal state he showed very strong emotions. He seemed to respond to these unpleasant and forgotten facts in the same manner as though he were actually experiencing the painful situation that had been buried in the unconscious. In some cases the painful experience had occurred many years before and the patient had been unable to recall it. When, however, the painful experience was brought to the full attention of the

One example of analysis of the unconscious as used in advertising. An insurance company advertisement contained headline and copy as follows:

Did you ever have a dream like this?

Most persons have had the dream of finding money scattered around, and picking it up hurriedly for fear someone would come along and take it away.

This dream, according to many psychologists, betrays a subconscious anxiety about the future, a fear of becoming suddenly poor. Is it any wonder that the dream is so common?

The copy further explains that those persons who are adequately insured need never experience the financial anxiety that this type of dream symbolizes. Courtesy of The Travelers Insurance Company, Hartford, Connecticut.

patient and he reacted to the recalled situation with the same emotional responses that he should have had when the situation occurred years before, the patient became well. The conclusion was naturally reached that the abnormal mental states of the neurotics were caused by the fact that the neurotic had not made a complete and satisfying emotional response to some of his unpleasant impulsions and experiences. The bringing-about of a belated emotional response in order to clear up a neurosis was called the "method of catharsis" and the new or belated emotional response was called the "abreaction."

Freud found that some of his patients could not be hypnotized, but he also discovered that the patients could themselves recall their forgotten experiences when they were encouraged to talk freely and at random. In these experiments, Freud found that the dreams of his patients were often related to the unpleasant things that they were trying to recall or uncover. He made studies of thousands of dreams and learned that the dream is symbolic of some repressed or hidden wish, that it may relate to infantile experiences, and that the repressed wish is one which, ordinarily, we do not admit that we would even entertain. In some dreams, certain symbolisms occurred again and again, such as snakes, knives, seeds, mountains, and wild animals. Freud interpreted these symbolisms to represent repressed desires that we refuse to recognize or carry through emotionally, and so they are stored in the unconscious and are allowed to come forth only in the dream life of the patient or in some abnormal manner during his waking hours. Most of these desires were believed to be of a sexual nature, because sex is the one strong impulse that cannot be expressed freely in our civilization.[38]

The psychoanalyst considers the sex symbolisms as merely convenient means of reaching more certain conclusions, and he uses them in much the same manner that the mathematician uses the symbol x in algebra. The true psychoanalyst does not use these sex symbols as definite proof of the nature of the repression until he has further evidence from the past experiences of the patient. The faddist who dabbles in psychoanalysis is apt to jump to erroneous conclusions when he has learned some of the sex symbols but does not appreciate that the symbolisms merely provide working hypotheses until a verifiable conclusion is reached.[39] The psychoanalyst does not think of the sex impulse in quite the same way that the layman does. The former uses it in the genetic sense. Furthermore, the modern psychoanalyst does not sexualize all behavior. Rather, he more often points out to certain patients how preoccupation with sex interferes with a more mature relationship with people and work.

The "censor" (better, censorship) refers to the assumed group of influences which require the individual to repress his normal impulsions. These influences are the social standards of our times, the reproofs given in childhood, and the many repressive influences of modern life. The reason why the individual patient's dreams express the repressed impulses more readily than the acts of his waking life is that these repressive forces are not parts of his conscious or intellectual life. When we are asleep, the conscious controls are weaker, the censorship is relaxed, and the impulses come into the dream consciousness in symbolic form.

Psychoanalysis is a Special Method of Psychological Observation

Someone has described psychotherapy as "the art of applying a science which does not yet exist."[40] However, all scientists find it necessary to set up special concepts or formulas to explain the phenomena of their fields of study. Chemists have set up "atomic theories" to help them explain facts discovered by experiment. Astronomers, biologists, mathematicians, and others have deliberately set up theoretical constructs to give order to their data. Psychotherapists have found it helpful to follow the same procedure, employing a theoretical construct based on the "unconscious." PSYCHOANALYSIS IS A METHOD OF PSYCHOLOGICAL OBSERVATION IN WHICH DREAM ANALYSIS, FREE ASSOCIATION, AND STUDY OF TRANSFERENCE OF EARLY ATTITUDES TOWARD THE ANALYST ARE USED TO UNCOVER THE UNCONSCIOUS.[41] It uses a unique set of theoretical constructs to give order to its data and to apply effective methods of psychotherapy.

Its theoretical constructs are a great deal more abstruse and difficult to understand than the barrier-adjustment concept used in this text. One explanation for the use of a more abstruse set of concepts by the psychoanalysts is that the seriously maladjusted patient's behavior often requires a more involved system of thinking than is needed to explain the behavior of a normal or only slightly maladjusted person.

As previously stated, dream analysis is used. In addition to the study of the dream life of the patient, the psychoanalyst also uses "free association." In this method the psychoanalyst has the patient come to his office and makes him physically comfortable in an easy chair or on a couch. All possible distracting influences are removed. Perhaps monotonous noise is provided. The patient closes his eyes, and the psychoanalyst may ask him to think of some part of his personal history which the analyst wishes to investigate, and tells him to think aloud and to say everything that comes to his mind, no matter how trivial, how irrelevant, or how unpleasant it may seem to him. The object is to discover the repressed experience or submerged complex that had not been allowed full emotional expression when it occurred in the experience of the patient. The patient is asked to report his dreams and to express his thoughts freely. In this way the analyst tries to unravel the network of experiences that caused the disturbance.

The analyst may also use word associations. To do this he prepares a list of words that may have some relationship to the patient's history and asks the patient to give the first word that comes to mind when the words are spoken. The analyst records with a stopwatch the time required for each response to

*"**Hush! Father mustn't be disturbed,**" and similar highly emotionalized admonitions to the small child may permanently influence the child regarding parental authority. Fortunately, some children are not permanently conditioned by such situations—they react by negative adaptation.* **(Courtesy of General Foods Corporation.)**

self feel that he is virile. To tell him that he must be more gentle does not remove the cause of the rowdiness. The girl who takes refuge in invalidism to gain attention may not be helped by punishment or by being told to make up her mind to get well. The analyst tries to get at the cause of the maladjustment and then to enable the patient to *sublimate* the energies, that is, to direct them into substitute activities that are satisfying and socially acceptable. We can see examples of sublimation in daily life in the case of the man who loses his wife and then takes up golf and plays it strenuously, or the student who fails in his studies and then becomes a collector of stamps. It is probable that many of our strongest drives are attempts to sublimate energy and achieve a sense of worthwhileness because of failure to do so in some other activity.

Criticisms of Psychoanalysis

Freud and his colleagues will go down in psychological history as pioneers and contributors in a field which needed them in their time. They opened new trails in the exploration of the human mind. Many of Freud's trails led to new discoveries of great value. Some of his earlier teachings have been modified by members of related schools of therapy, and they are now adding new contributions by their willingness to discard or correct some of the earlier concepts in his method:

1. A modification of the Freudian principles concerns the concept of the unconscious. Some critics claim that we are not motivated by suppressed wishes, but rather by a series of adjustments to our situations. These ad-

justments are not made by a part of the mind, but by the entire individual. The organism as a whole responds to the stimulus. By trial and accidental success we find that one kind of response results in failure and dissatisfaction whereas another response brings about success and satisfaction. The successful response is stamped into our neurological mechanisms and, therefore, is readily repeated. Repressed desires or suppressed wishes are not entities which have energy by themselves. They have no existence by themselves any more than my fingers have hidden peckings on a typewriter. It is only when I am stimulated as an integrated unit that my fingers peck on a typewriter. Therefore, it is often claimed, the "unconscious mind" is not subject to proof or observation but rather is an explanation of phenomena that can be interpreted more adequately by objective means.

Freud himself did not use the concept of "the unconscious" in his last book even though he was the first man to develop it as a means of explaining unconscious learning. We now think of the word, "unconscious," as an inappropriate noun but a good adjective.

2. Phobias may arise because of a desire which has been stimulated and not allowed expression, recognition, or admission. However, critics claim that normal stimuli may become associated through action of the nervous system rather than through a subconscious mind, with abnormal responses as in the case described by Bagby:

> A man suffered from a phobia of being grasped from behind, the disturbance appearing early in childhood and persisting to his fifty-fifth year. When walking on the street he was under a compulsion to look back over his shoulder at intervals to see if he was closely followed. In social gatherings he arranged to have his chair against the wall. It was impossible for him to enter crowded places or to attend the theater. In his fifty-fifth year he returned to the town in which he had spent his childhood. After inspecting his old home, he went to the corner grocery and found that his old boyhood friend was still behind the counter. He introduced himself and they began to reminisce. Finally the grocer said this, "I want to tell you something that occurred when you were a boy: You used to go by this store on errands, and when you passed you often took a handful of peanuts from the stand in front. One day I saw you coming and hid behind a barrel. Just as you put your hand in the pile of peanuts, I jumped out and grabbed you from behind. You screamed and fell fainting on the sidewalk." The episode was remembered and the phobia, after a period of readjustment, disappeared.[46]

3. Dreams are not always wish-fulfillments. A dream of falling may be stimulated by a sagging bed spring rather than by the fear of a moral fall; or a dream of being choked may be brought about by the tightness of the bed covers. Some dreams are the mere automatic and chance play of the cerebral associational mechanisms. One neural pathway happens to arouse another pathway and incongruous combinations of ideas result. Certainly many dreams are not related to the sex impulse. The child and the adult must suppress many impulses, such as those of self-assertion and gluttony. It is unfair to attribute all asocial impulsions to sex energies which are not allowed expressions by our form of civilization.

It is true that the body is full of energy—energy which must be expressed in some form. The outlets for these energies may be socially acceptable or extremely harmful. For example, a man may become a butcher making his living by killing cattle and cutting up meat. This is a socially acceptable outlet for his energies. If these energies become perverted he may instead become a murderer of people.

4. The energy of the human organism may be thought of in many different ways. It may be called the *elan vital* or the *libido,* or we may accept it, as suggested by Jung, as a striving after larger experience. Adler, on the other hand, considered this striving as an attempt to achieve safety and power. Or we may designate energy with reference to its objectives and call it tendencies or impulsions. It certainly may be analyzed without sex as a basis. Intelligence as well as sexual drive can be considered a form of energy. Intelligence helps to contain impulse and some persons need professional assistance in order to develop an integrated self that is more effective

than the instinct-dominant personality. As one researcher has stated: "In psychological sickness our image of ourself blurs, the colors run, it is not integrated or beautiful.... But in health there is no awkwardness, for the moment of health is a moment of unconscious creative synthesis, when without thinking about it at all we know that we make sense to ourselves and to others."[47]

5. Conflicts between various impulsions do give rise to behavior which may be thought of as resulting in a *complex*. However, the complex should not be considered bad in all cases. Lee Wilson Dodd has written a book[48] wherein he shows that certain complexes are not a stain but an advantage; not a leaden drag but a golden spur. The lame foot of Byron stimulated him to become a master horseman, a good shot, and the best swimmer in England. The assurance thus gained enabled him to become a great lover, poet, and patriot.

"Complex" is a Freudian term, but the inferiority concept comes from Adler. Whether a handicap produces a sense of inferiority and induces a complex, or results in a heroic resolve to achieve despite it, seems to depend largely upon the type of nervous constitution and earlier adjustment habits of the individual who has the handicap.

Contributions of Psychoanalysis

1. Psychoanalysis has given us a method of treatment of the maladjusted which has been of material help, even though the persons who use it sometimes do not believe all its published principles. In fact, some psychologists say that the bases of psychoanalysis are not true, but that it works anyhow. Since psychoanalysis has come into more or less common use in mental hospitals, the percentage of cures, all factors considered, has probably increased. Whether these cures have been the result of psychoanalytical methods, chemical treatments, or both is open to debate.

2. Psychoanalysis has given us some valuable points of view. It has shown the importance of the emotions, the strength of childhood influences, and the ways in which we deal with our problems or evade them. It has shown us the dominating influence-shaping attitudes people have acquired about themselves, about others, and about their surroundings. Their adjustment habits have a great deal to do with their abilities, and the ways in which intellectual capacity is expressed. We now have some evidence to show that psychoanalysis has even made substantial changes in the intelligence quotients of certain individuals.[49]

Does the Psychotherapy Bring About the Patient's Improvement?

From time to time, newspaper and magazine articles question whether psychotherapy as such cures or helps the patient who has a mental illness, particularly a mild mental illness.[50] They cite reports of researchers who have compared the records of matched pairs of juvenile delinquents, soldiers who had "nervous breakdowns" either in combat or just before getting into combat, and psychoneurotics—one half of the subjects received treatment and the other half were untreated. Follow-up studies made after one to five years have indicated little or no difference except that most of those who had been treated *believed* that the treatment had benefited them.

Research-minded clinical psychologists agree with some of these quantitative findings. They know, as one has stated, that "many behaviors that appear to change as a result of psychotherapy are actually influenced little or not at all by the therapy."[51]

They realize that the counteractive and recuperative endogenous forces within the individual bring about the changes. This is somewhat similar to having the physician who treats organic illnesses state that nature really brings about the cure and most patients would recover without the medical practitioner's assistance. Neither the psychotherapist nor the physician turns away a patient because he might regain health without benefit of therapy. Indeed, anyone who has ever become acquainted with mentally ill persons and sensed the desperation in their needs is apt to want to help them or aid them in getting the best available therapeutic treatment. "No one with extensive experience in the practice of psychotherapy can possibly accept any general statement impugning its value."[52]

Industry Offers Opportunity to Contribute to Integrative Adjustments

Many a young person envies psychiatrists and clinical psychologists for their ability to serve humanity. He, too, would like to make a contribution to mental health but he does not want to acquire specialized professional training for that purpose. Such a person can, however, participate in the service toward better mental health, for emotional stresses arise in every walk of life.

One of the greatest opportunities today for the improvement of mental and emotional health is to be found in industry—not in psychiatric treatment, but in preventive maintenance. One need not be a psychiatrist or a clinical psychologist to sense symptoms of anxiety, fear, and "brainwashing boredom" in the people around him. He can contribute to the psychological health of his fellow workers, especially if they are under his supervision.

A company can survive and prosper only through the constructive cooperation of all of its members. Teamwork must be more than a slogan. It is a symptom of healthy minds and bodies; it is also a symptom of healthy management—the kind that considers what happens to people in the course of producing, as well as the ultimate product and profit.[53]

Dr. Molly Harrower, a consulting psychologist who has had much experience in industry, recently stated:

> Human nature is not fixed and unchangeable. It is plastic, flexible, and has tremendous possibilities. But there is no such thing as suddenly changing an attitude.
>
> If you want to change the direction in which a flower is growing, you must change the direction of the light, and you must do it gradually. The flower will die if you snap it off or force it in another direction. It's the same with an attitude. An attitude is a living thing that has grown up with a person. If it can be changed at all, it must be changed gradually. . . .
>
> A suspicious person doesn't think of himself as being suspicious. He feels he is in a hostile world, surrounded by people—bosses, employees, friends—who are always doing irritating things which work out to his disadvantage. He sees himself in a threatening and unpleasant environment.
>
> The problem is to get him to realize that he is carrying a hostile attitude into the world; that he is looking at things through black-colored glasses. How people see the world determines how they experience it. That, in turn, determines how they react to the world and, finally, how the world reacts to them.
>
> Attitudes are formed way back in our lives. They become fixed by usage, emotionally engraved. It takes more than will power to change them.
>
> If I had a suspicious attitude that had been formed in childhood because of repeated experiences which made me afraid of certain kinds of people, I couldn't change that attitude merely because I wanted to. And what's more, I would become suspicious of anyone who wanted me to change.
>
> Few people realize that their emotional problems often result from the influence of old and inappropriate attitudes. Anyone with a stiff, inflexible attitude approaches a problem in terms of the past, instead of thinking about it against the background of the situation he is now facing. Trapped by his own attitude, he limits the freedom with which he can act.
>
> It is the psychologist's job to discover to what extent those old erroneous ways of looking at the world prevent the patient from facing up to his problems constructively. He listens to the patient and attempts to give him some awareness of the forces that have been influencing his behavior. He tries to get him to see situations objectively by giving him some understanding of the facts as they are, without distortions or misinterpretations. There can be no change of attitude without a change in the way of looking at things.

Mentioning her work in industry, Dr. Harrower said that she has come across foremen who apply the psychologist's principles and techniques, and who do that without knowing it:

They seem to work miracles just by establishing a friendly atmosphere in their departments —an atmosphere of acceptance, warmth and affection. They are able to see things from the other person's point of view. They don't feel that they're being attacked personally when somebody differs with them.

They possess the ability to look at their employees objectively. They do not condemn; and instead of moralizing and judging, they try to understand. They are sensitive to the thoughts and feelings of the people around them. And they're aware of how their own actions affect other people. In short, these foremen are mentally healthy persons.

As to how foremen or anybody else can achieve the condition of mental health, Dr. Harrower gave us these comments:

Some people have grown up relatively unscarred by life. They hardly know what it means to have destructive, defensive or antisocial feelings. And neither are they burdened by feelings of anxiety.

Other people have achieved mental health the opposite way. They've had their share of troubles. But they've managed to work them through with the aid of a friend or relative, with someone they could trust and confide in, and who trusted and liked them.

Anyone who has never known someone who is reassuring, has missed something very important in life. Thus trust and affection, I am certain, are basic to the development of a healthy, wholesome personality.[54]

ACKNOWLEDGMENTS AND REFERENCES

1. Felix Adler, *Creed and Deed* (New York: G. P. Putnam's Sons, 1877).
2. Paul H. Hoch, "Challenges for Psychiatry in the Sixties," *Mental Hygiene News,* New York State Department of Mental Hygiene, December, 1963.
3. *Ibid.,* p. 5.
4. "A National Awakening in the Fight Against Mental Illness," National Association for Mental Health, Inc., *Annual Report, 1962,* p. 14.
5. James M. Cunningham, Director, Bureau of Mental Hygiene, State of Connecticut Department of Health, has presented an excellent summary of mental illness and employability in *Trained Men,* No. 3 (1945), pp. 10–16.
6. Harry Milt, *How to Deal with Mental Problems,* National Association for Mental Health, 10 Columbus Circle, New York, 1962, p. 9.
7. *Mental Hygiene News,* New York State Department of Mental Hygiene, April, 1963, p. 2.
8. T. A. Munro, "Consanguinity and Mental Disorder," *Journal of Mental Science,* **84** (1938), 708–714, reports that 2.4 per cent of the 4,200 mental patients studied were of consanguineous parentage.
9. "Mental Ills Not Inherited Like the Color of Eyes," *Science News Letter,* May 20, 1939, p. 313. This article is a summary of a study by Drs. Horatio M. Pollock, Benjamin Malzberg, and Raymond G. Fuller in a book, *Hereditary and Environmental Factors in the Causation of Manic-Depressive Psychoses and Dementia Praecox* (Utica, N. Y.: State Hospitals Press, 1939).
10. J. Slawson and M. Moss, "Mental Illness Among Jews," *Jewish Social Service Quarterly,* June, 1936, pp. 343–350. Comparative rates per 100,000 population of first admissions to 17 mental-hygiene clinics, New York City, 1934, pointed to a relatively greater prevalence of psychoneuroses and related disorders among Jews, and of committed insane among non-Jews.
11. Stanley Cobb, Walter Bauer, and Isabel Whiting, *Journal of the American Medical Association,* Aug. 19, 1939.
12. *Science News Letter,* Nov. 26, 1938, p. 345. Findings reported by Dr. Alvin V. Semrad.
13. Donald M. Hamilton, "The Use of Electric Shock Therapy in Psychoneurosis," *American Journal of Psychiatry,* **103** (1947), 665–668.
14. H. Selinski, "The Selective Use of Electro-shock Therapy as an Adjuvant to Psychotherapy," *Bulletin of the New York Academy of Medicine,* **19** (1943), 245–252.
15. N. Q. Brill, *et al.,* "Relative Effectiveness of Various Components of Electroconvulsive Therapy: An Experimental Study," *American Medical Association Archives of Neurology,* **81** (1959), 627–635.
16. See Walter Freeman, "Frontal Lobotomy 1936–56: A Follow-up Study of 3,000 Patients from One to Twenty," *The American Journal of Psychiatry,* **113** (1957), 877–886. And Martin Brennan, John K. Kew and Wiley Lewis, "Psychological Changes Following Prefrontal Lobotomy," *Archives of Physical Medicine,* **36,** No. 1 (1955) 695–698.
17. See Harry W. Allison and Sarah G. Allison, "Personality Changes Following Transorbital Lobotomy," *Journal of Abnormal and Social Psychology,* April, 1954, pp. 219–223.
18. See Harold E. Himwich, "The New Psychiatric Drugs," *Scientific American,* October, 1955, pp. 80–86.
19. Howard A. Rusk, "Aid for the Mentally Ill," *The New York Times,* June 26, 1955.
20. Paul A. Zahl, "They Come Up So Hastily," *The American Scholar,* Spring, 1964, p. 265.
21. Frank Barron, Murray E. Jarvik, and Sterling

Bunnell, Jr., "The Hallucinogenic Drugs," *Scientific American,* April, 1964. This article presents an excellent review of studies of these drugs as related to mental illness.
22. See *Business Week,* May 12, 1956, p. 29.
23. George Watson, "Is Mental Illness Mental?" *Journal of Psychology,* **41** (1956), 323–334.
24. Thomas S. Szasz, "The Myth of Mental Illness," *The American Psychologist,* February, 1960, p. 114.
25. J. L. Moreno, "Psychodramatic Treatment of Marriage Problems," *Sociometry,* **3,** No. 1, (1940), 1–23. Also R. Borden, "The Use of Psychodrama in an Institution for Delinquent Girls," *Sociometry,* **3,** No. 1 (1940), 81–90.
26. N. E. Shoobs, "Psychodrama in the Schools," *Sociometry,* **7** (1944), 152–168.
27. See examples in Adaline Starr, "Psychodrama with a Family," *Group Psychotherapy,* **12** (1959), 27–31, and Earl H. Nash, Jr., *et al.,* "Some Factors Related to Patients Remaining in Group Psychotherapy," *International Journal of Psychotherapy,* **7** (1957), 264–274.
28. Jerome D. Frank, *Group Methods in Therapy,* Public Affairs Pamphlet, No. 284, Public Affairs Committee, Inc., 22 East 38th St., New York, 1959. This pamphlet presents a helpful description of several uses of the method.
29. O. Kant, "Choice of Method in Psychotherapy," *Diseases of the Nervous System,* **5** (1944), 325–329.
30. "Symposium on Relations Between Religion and Mental Health," *The American Psychologist,* October, 1958, pp. 565–579.
31. M. N. Chappell, "Psychology and the Organic Disorders," *The Psychological Exchange,* 1931–32.
32. I. P. Pavlov, *Lectures on Conditioned Reflexes,* (New York: International Publishers, 1928). In Russia, the theoretical basis for psychiatric practice is organized around Pavlovian laws of conditioning. See Leonard Cammer, "Conditioning and Psychiatric Theory," *American Journal of Orthopsychiatry,* **31** (1961), 810–819.
33. Norman R. F. Maier and Robert S. Feldman, "Studies of Abnormal Behavior in the Rat: XIV, Water Spray as a Means of Inducing Seizures," *The Journal of Comparative Psychology,* **39,** No. 5 (1946), 286.
34. Possible limitations of animal experiments as applied to frustrated human beings have been analyzed by L. S. Kubie in "The Experimental Induction of Neurotic Reactions in Man," *Yale Journal of Biology and Medicine,* **11** (1939), 541–545.
35. *Science News Letter,* Dec. 31, 1938. See also issue of Jan. 13, 1940.
36. Frederick C. Thorne, "Directive Psychotherapy: Therapeutic Use of Conflict," *Journal of Clinical Psychology,* **3** (1947), 168–179.
37. Jerome S. Bruner, "Freud and the Image of Man," *The American Psychologist,* September, 1956. This article describes Freud as one of the architects of our present-day conception of man.
38. Many students of dreams of primitive peoples have indicated that the lack of sexual inhibition tends to reduce the number of disguised and symbolical sexual dreams. Among such savages, the most tormenting and easily remembered dreams are the nightmares of anxiety and hunger. See, for example, V. Elwin, "A Note on the Theory and Symbolism of Dreams Among the Baiga," *British Journal of Medical Psychology,* **16** (1937), 237–254. For a statistical study of certain symbols, see Joseph F. Rychlak and Donald E. Guinouard, "Symbolic Interpretation of Rorschach Content," *Journal of Consulting Psychology,* August, 1961.
39. E. A. Gutheil, *The Language of the Dream* (New York: The Macmillan Company, 1939). This is a textbook of dream interpretation which presents dream symbols, analytical interpretations, and the uses of dream analysis in therapy.
40. Paul E. Meehl, "The Cognitive Activity of the Clinician," *The American Psychologist,* January, 1960.
41. J. F. Brown, "The Position of Psychoanalysis in the Science of Psychology," *Journal of Abnormal and Social Psychology,* **35** (1940), 29–44. See also W. S. Taylor, "Psychoanalysis Revised or Psychodynamics Developed," *The American Psychologist,* November, 1962, and Frank Barron, *Creativity and Psychological Health* (Princeton, N. J.: D. Van Nostrand Co., Inc., 1963), pp. 227–228.
42. William A. White, *Outline of Psychiatry* (Washington, D.C.: Nervous and Mental Diseases Publishing Company, 1924), p. 338. For a later study of word associations, see Roy Schafer, "A Study of Thought Processes in a Word Association Test," *Character and Personality,* **13** (1945), pp. 217 ff.
43. Graham B. Blaine, Jr., and Charles McArthur, *Emotional Problems of the Student* (New York: Appleton-Century-Crofts, 1961), p. 235.
44. Donald R. Stieper and Daniel N. Wiener, "The Problem of Interminability in Outpatient Psychotherapy," *Journal of Consulting Psychology,* June, 1959.
45. Bonnie R. Strickland and Douglas P. Crowne, "Need for Approval and the Premature Termination of Psychotherapy," *Journal of Consulting Psychology,* April, 1963.
46. E. Bagby, "The Etiology of Phobias," *Journal of Abnormal and Social Psychology,* **17** (1922), p. 17.
47. Frank Barron, *Creativity and Psychological Health* (Princeton, N. J.: D. Van Nostrand Co., Inc., 1963), p. 5.
48. *The Golden Complex: A Defense of Inferiority* (New York: The John Day Company, Inc., 1927).
49. L. Chidester and K. A. Menninger, "The Application of Psychoanalytic Methods to the Study of Mental Retardation," *American Journal of Orthopsychiatry,* **6** (1936), 616–625. This article reports an increase in IQ from 62 to 90.
50. See Earl Ubell, "Has Psycho-Probing Helped Anyone?" *New York Herald Tribune,* Section 2, June 3, 1962, and H. J. Eysenck, "What's the Truth About Psychoanalysis?" *The Reader's Digest,* January, 1960.
51. Frank Barron, *Creativity and Psychological*

Health (Princeton, N. J.: D. Van Nostrand Co., Inc., 1963), p. 70, and Nathaniel S. Lehrman, "Moral Aspects of Mental Health," *The Humanist,* Nos. 2 and 3 (1962).

52. *Ibid.,* p. 71. See also Herman Feifel and Janet Eells, "Patients and Therapists Assess the Same Psychotherapy," *Journal of Consulting Psychology,* August, 1963.
53. See *The Management Review,* American Management Association, Inc., October 1955, pp. 722–23.
54. These three passages taken from: "Dealing with Fears, Hostilities," an interview with Dr. Molly Harrower, carried in *The Foreman's Letter,* Feb. 14, 1955. Published by The National Foremen's Institute, New London, Conn.

PROJECTS

1. Make a study of mental health clinics and published materials on mental hygiene that are available. The National Association for Mental Health, Inc., 10 Columbus Circle, New York City, and The Hogg Foundation for Mental Health, The University of Texas, Austin, Texas, are two of many organizations that can be helpful in furnishing objective information on the problem.
2. Get acquainted with the mental health clinics and related facilities of your area. Perhaps you know a clinical psychologist or psychiatrist whom you can interview for information. Get his suggestions as to the facilities and experts available to persons who need their counsel or treatment.
3. One area in which mental health efforts can show definite benefits is with the aged. Older people should find it possible to make meaningful uses of their abilities. The two great enemies of sanity in older people are enforced uselessness and enforced aloneness. Interview several active and inactive older persons of the same approximate age and note any factors that seem to have contributed to their mental health or deterioration.
4. Skim through some of the biographies and autobiographies of your library to find mentions of "nervous breakdowns" or other mental health problems. Did the individual appear to develop extra motivations that helped to bring about his fame? Write summaries of your findings.
5. Analyze your behavior for evidence of inhibitions that are annoying and irrational. Can you think of experiences that caused them? Mention some things that your "censor" does not allow you to do.
6. Interview several persons regarding their attitudes toward persons who have or are now being treated by a psychiatrist. Do not try to educate them—just try to elicit their real opinions. How do your interviewees' attitudes differ in regard to the patient who is extremely depressed and has withdrawn from reality in comparison with, say, the sex offender such as the exhibitionist?

COLLATERAL READINGS

Asher, Harry, "They Split My Personality: An Experiment with LSD," *Saturday Review,* June 1, 1963.

Freedman, Lawrence Zelic, " 'Truth' Drugs," *Scientific American,* March, 1960.

Gellerman, Saul W., *Motivation and Productivity.* New York: American Management Association, Inc., 1963, Chapter 9.

Lehner, George F. J. and Ella Kube, *The Dynamics of Personal Adjustment.* Englewood Cliffs, N.J.: Prentice-Hall, Inc., 1964, Chapters 16 and 17.

Levinson, Harry, "First Aid for Worried Workers," *Nation's Business,* September, 1960.

Rogers, Carl R., *Counseling and Psychotherapy.* Boston: Houghton Mifflin Company, 1942.

Shaffer, Laurance F. and Edward J. Shoben, Jr., *The Psychology of Adjustment.* Boston: Houghton Mifflin Company, 1956, Chapters 14 to 17.

Smith, Henry Clay, *Psychology of Industrial Behavior.* New York: McGraw-Hill Book Company, 1955, Chapter 7.

Taylor, W. S., "Psychoanalysis Revised or Psychodynamics Developed?" *American Psychologist,* November, 1962.

One of a series of tests by Dr. David McClelland *of Harvard University with which he seeks to verify psychological theory—that the economic growth or decline of nations is dependent to some extent upon the entrepreneurs of the nations. The* ***need to achieve*** *is one of a variety of phenomena studied in motivation research.*

How early in life does the difference in achievement motivation show itself? Does it appear in children?

In one of the tests, a group of boys and girls are led into a Ring-Toss Game. The tester tells them that each one will have three rings which he is to try to get over the peg. Each child may stand at any distance he chooses.

The child who is highly motivated chooses a middle distance. He is a moderate risk taker. The child who is low in achievement motivation may stand nearly on top of the peg so that there is no challenge at all.

The question now arises, what accounts for the origin of achievement motivation? Is it related to parental attitudes? To answer this question, Dr. McClelland has devised a test in which both the parent and the child are involved. A young boy sits on the floor amid a pile of blocks. His father sits a short distance from him. The boy is instructed to stack as many blocks as he can using only one hand for the stacking. The father is told he may talk to his son but may not touch him or the blocks.

Then both father and son are asked to estimate the number of blocks the son will be able to stack.

Children with high achievement motivation tend to have parents who make high estimates of their children's abilities, while children with low achievement motivation tend to have parents who make low estimates. Likewise the parent of the boy with high achievement motivation is encouraging whereas his counterpart is discouraging, even deprecating, and will tend to dominate his son's activities.

Now, one might ask, what produces the parents? Dr. McClelland explains that at this point it is necessary to observe the culture in which they live. It has been found that the number of achievement themes in the literature of a given nation is an index of the amount of emphasis a culture places on achievement. He concludes that we are just beginning to understand the importance of the ***need to achieve.*** *Now, a fairly accurate picture of an achiever can be drawn. However, this does not mean that all those who contribute to society are high on tests of achievement motivation. It does indicate that in periods of high economic activity, the need to achieve has been instrumental in the rise of nations and their peoples.**

Achievement needs as well as other needs indicate a basic attitude toward life. Needs arise from certain conditions in childhood to which the individual adjusts in ways that develop characteristic behavioral tendencies and patterns.

Adapted from* ***Focus on Behavior,* *Program No. 8, "The Need to Achieve," National Educational Television, 10 Columbus Circle, New York 19, N. Y. For a more comprehensive treatment, see David McClelland,* ***The Achieving Society*** *(Princeton, N. J.: D. Van Nostrand Co., Inc., 1961).*

CHAPTER SEVEN

COUNSELING: PREDISPOSING INFLUENCES AND OUTLINE FOR STUDY OF THE INDIVIDUAL'S ADJUSTMENTS—CASE PROBLEMS

The human organism's behavior constantly exhibits both stability and variability. Man is not merely a prisoner of his mental mechanisms, urges or patterns of adjustment. He is also capable of controlling and redirecting his basic tendencies. The better appreciation of his nature and potentials for growth must come from many convergent sources: psychologists, psychiatrists, sociologists, anthropologists, biochemists, and others.[1]

Anyone who counsels a person should be aware not only of the dynamics in the development of adjustment patterns but also of the predisposing influences. These underlie the thinking of the counselor and deserve our attention. As stated in Chapter 2, the environment is important from the standpoint of *acceptance, antagonism,* and *indifference* in adjustment. Every individual has many predisposing influences in the course of his adjustment history. Students of anthropology and sociology are especially aware of the cultural influences and differences.

Cultural and Sociological Factors

Man is a social being. Every child's ideas of what is right or wrong, what is to be done or not to be done, what is to be imitated or to be avoided are influenced by his cultural environment. The language, customs, and group ideas surrounding the child are significant factors in his growth.

Anthropologists have studied numerous cultures of primitive peoples and ethnic groups. Important differences and similarities to our own culture have been found. In some primitive groups, for example, each child is reared to distrust other members of the group. In others, the child is reared to give and expect coöperation and kindness. Similarly, discipline systems, sex taboos, rituals, folk tales, and attitudes toward objects vary from culture to culture. While celibacy, self-torture, and voluntary fasting are socially desirable in some groups, in others they are considered undesirable. The things the individual values, fears, seeks, or is ashamed of are conditioned by the family constellation and the culture to which the family belongs.

Despite similarities among members of the same group, wide individual differences are also found. Factors such as the sex of the child, the occupational status of the parents, education, and wealth may affect different children of the same culture in different manners. Changing conditions within the culture, such as war, plague, famine or economic depression may also modify the pattern of life for the individual of a given culture. Examples of these varieties of cultural influence can be observed from the study of first and second generations of foreign-born citizens of our own country. Certainly, many a child of foreign-born parents has had distinctive adjustment problems in the course of his emotional development in the United States. Sometimes the factors that enter into and modify reaction patterns can be appreciated more clearly by means of a study of anthropological and nationality influences. Such studies have their place in the training for greater insight into human personality. The psychologist would like to know about them whenever he deals with the problem personality or the person who has a problem.

In most cases, however, the analyst or counselor is more interested in knowing how the individual reacted to the factors in his early and later environment. The family constellation and how the child reacted to it, the adjustments made at the time and retained (or discarded), are usually of greater significance than a mere knowledge of the culture or of the family as such.

Persistent Affect Fixations

Of special significance in the study of later adjustment are the child's *persistent affect fixations.* This condition of mental development is one in which the individual remains attached to feelings which were characteristic of or dominant in an earlier phase of development. Everyone has some of these persistent infantile tendencies that color or form patterns of behavior in adulthood. The pattern of influence varies in degree and kind from person to person.

To understand an adult fully we must know how he reacted emotionally to his childhood situations and the extent to which the childhood habits of adjustment persist. If we can appreciate how childhood emotional reactions color the later adult behavior, we may gain a clue from the unique adult behavior to the nature of the earlier childhood reactions. If our hypotheses about the adult and his childhood adjustments prove to be correct, we are in a position that enables us to evaluate and help direct his behavior more intelligently.

The child reacts to his environment in ways that affect his well-being in satisfying forms. Habitual or characteristic methods of attention-getting or problem-solving therefore develop, and as they prove to be effective in getting what he wants, they gradually become unconscious methods of meeting and interpreting many situations and obstacles. They become more deeply ingrained with time, and they also may become so adaptive that their original source and form frequently become obscured.

The reaction tendencies which these persistent affect fixations create in the child's personality help to mold his life style. They help to determine how others will judge him. These opinions are also important in the person's own evaluation of himself. They often influence the choice of his vocation. They steer him toward certain types of avocations, sometimes of the lone or seclusive type in which it is not necessary for him to adapt to or mix with others, and sometimes into group activities through which he may be able to express himself through dominance or through identification with the group. If we know the problems that an individual tried to solve or the difficulties under which he lived while a child, we often can understand his present behavior. The dynamics in his adult behavior are, in some cases, his interpretations of his childhood memories and his goals, conscious and unconscious.

If a person has retained persistent affect fixations that are not socially acceptable, he can change them at any time that he develops sufficient insight and determination to do so. Childhood misconceptions often can be corrected and better methods of dealing with life can be learned. But someone, usually a wise counselor, must be able to recognize from adult behavior the possible significance of cues to behavior patterns having a childhood origin. The ability to recognize cues in the adult's conduct and to see how they relate to childhood origins is one of the most important factors in psychological analysis.

If, for example, we meet an adult who obviously lacks self-confidence, has difficulty in coming into a social group and difficulty in leaving it, seldom completes sentences that he starts and repeats questions asked him, we wonder how his present emotional insecurity happened to develop. We have a right to wonder whether his present behavior stems from emotional insecurity in childhood. Were his parents incompatible? Was the status of his early home in danger of divorce or in danger of economic failure? If in danger of lack of income, is he presently motivated to deny himself normal comforts in order to save more money than he needs? Or is wealth so hopeless in attainment for him that money means little to him now?

If it is necessary for us to supervise him, to counsel him, or to live intimately with him, our relationship will be more intelligent and effective for both of us if we know how he defined himself as a child. If his convictions about himself were deeply emotionalized, his childhood self-evaluations are significant today. Table 7.1 presents a helpful list of common affect fixations of childhood, adjustments in childhood, and later methods of adjustment.

Anyone who will carefully study the typical childhood affect fixations (Column A of Table 7.1), adjustments in childhood (Column B), and adult adjustments (Column C) will have a helpful list of cues toward understanding the person with a problem. Certain precautions are necessary, however. The child who had affect fixation number 2 may in adulthood make adjustment number 5. We cannot conclude that any one affect fixation or barrier *always* results in a corresponding adjustment tendency. We can recognize causal connections only when we have learned many pertinent facts about the individual and then see how the facts arrange themselves into a

TABLE 7.1

TYPICAL AFFECT FIXATIONS OF CHILDHOOD AND LATER ADJUSTMENT METHODS

A	*B*	*C*
As a child, did you feel that you were:	Which method of adjustment did you use?	In adulthood, which method of adjustment do you now use?
1. Small, helpless, of poor health, or defective in body?	1. Sickliness. "Nervousness" to prove need for special consideration.	1. Sickliness. "Nervousness." Pains that your family physician seems unable to cure.
2. The center of attention—a kind of toy or animated doll? Did games with others revolve mostly around you?	2. Unruliness in order to gain the limelight, sarcasm, bitter word-battles to deal with domineering parents.	2. Argumentativeness. Word-battles. Comedian knacks or witticisms to gain attention.
3. Disciplined severely, often punished for what you considered minor misdeeds? Suppressed?	3. Model behavior in order to deal with domineering parents, or hoping for affection by being a paragon of virtue. Self-righteousness.	3. Seek perfection for yourself. Self-righteousness. Consider yourself better than other people.
4. Rejected. Extra "human freight," unwanted, and given little affection?	4. Keeping to yourself to avoid failure. Seclusiveness in games and comradeships. Shut-in personality.	4. Seclusiveness. You avoid games and social affairs. Have very few friends. Or, you seek acceptance by others, want to be one of the group you admire.
5. Denied your rights, to be seen rather than heard, forced to be quiet and courteous? Domineered? Discriminated against?	5. Belligerence. Spoiling the fun of others to avoid games where you might fail.	5. Radical tendencies. Cynicism. You believe you could remodel the world.
6. Laughed at, frequently ridiculed?	6. Fear lest you might be ridiculed. Not taking school or work seriously.	6. Laugh off your obligations. Change interests without any real reason for the change.
7. Emotionally insecure because parents were incompatible, or food and shelter were uncertain or appeared to be uncertain?	7. Felt hysterical when parents argued or when sustenance was in doubt.	7. Lack self-confidence or are strongly motivated to make money or to win friends on whom you can depend.

meaningful pattern. This fact makes necessary a wide knowledge of affect fixations and typical forms of adjustments. The lack of fixed or standard adjustments to specific barriers means that every individual must be comprehensively analyzed in order to be understood. Clinical psychology is a very complex study. The clinician knows, for example, that the adult cannot accurately recall childhood events. Nor can he describe how he felt as a child. The affect fixations of his childhood must be deduced from the case history.

From the standpoint of understanding the adult's personality, particularly his drives and his qualitative strengths and weaknesses, the persistent affect fixations are especially important. A good example with comments is the following, written by a psychiatrist:

Everyone's personality and behavior are colored and affected in a large degree by the childhood emotional constellations, but the *more* these interfere with adult behavior, the *more rigidly* they determine behavior, the more "neurotic" is the individual. Again it is a quantitative matter.

A simple example is a certain career woman, no longer young. Her father had been away a great deal while she was a child, and while at home he was partly very indulgent toward her but also partly irritable and neglectful. She reacted with longings for him but also with a deep resentment against him. This became a fixed pattern in her relations with men. She repeated it in her marriage and in position after position. She longed to be a favorite of the head of the firm but would never admit this. She would start off doing very well and making an excellent impression. But gradually her hostility to her employer would become so open and intense that it would only be a matter of time before some incident would precipitate her departure.

In one firm she became good friends with one of the junior members. He left later to go into business for himself and asked her to go with him. She was by this time openly hostile to the boss and gladly accepted the offer. Things went well for a time, but then the old pattern reasserted itself. So long as this man was a junior partner, himself somewhat hostile and rebellious against their boss, she got on with him famously, for she unconsciously identified with him, as a child hostile to his father, like herself. But when this same man had his own firm and was in the father position himself, then she could no longer identify with him as a rebellious child, and she developed toward him the hostility she was destined by her inner reactions to have toward all men whom, for one reason or another, she looked to as fathers...

Such a tendency unconsciously to put certain men into a category is a failure to discriminate them from the original object, in this case the girl's own father. Often in this case, the men were in reality totally different personalities from her father, and they were usually amazed at her reactions to them. But, because of her emotional pattern she saw them as a class and not as they really were. She must revenge herself on all men in superior positions for her father's treatment of her, instead of being angry only at him and treating other men as different individuals. This reaction against her father became a set pattern, carried with her years later after her father was long dead and she herself was a grandmother.

The constellation of desires and impulses always seeks and always finds ways in life of choosing individuals and situations in its efforts to be gratified. It is this complex of desires pressing for satisfaction which seems, more than anything else, to account for the persistence and the accuracy with which everyone repeats in adult life the emotional patterns of his childhood. And it is these patterns which cause one to fit other people into classes and categories formed by these desires. Perhaps mother was kind and sister a bitter rival—hence, an exaggerated tendency to look for love from older women and to fear and compete with women of one's own age. To put it another way, the person becomes "conditioned" to hating, loving, competing, and so on, in relation to certain individuals in childhood and then

"Subconsciously you hate your grandmother, but you transfer this hostility to the troops by over-seasoning the chow!" Source: *by Art Gates. Reproduced by special permission of King Features Syndicate.*

fails to discriminate between them and others but reacts to whole classes or categories of persons of his own making.

Some people do not emphasize whole categories of people so much as they select a few actual persons in life with whom to repeat their family relationships...

If a child has good relationships with most members of his family, then he has enough such models for later life so that he will probably get along well with people. But if most or all his childhood relationships are bad, then he lacks the models for good relationships and will almost certainly have serious difficulties with people in later life. Probably no one can live long without at least one good emotional relationship without developing serious neurotic symptoms of some kind.

We have focused upon the effects of external influences such as deprivation, spoiling, cruelty and domination in forming the patterns. In some cases, internal factors are also of importance, as when the development is impaired not so much by these environmental emotional influences as by long illnesses, severe shocks or congenital deficiencies, be these physical, intellectual or emotional. The end result always depends upon an interaction of the congenital and the environmental factors.[2]

Of course, everyone has many predisposing influences in his growth: early environmental conditions, his culture, race, sex, bodily physique, health, muscular structure, glandular functioning, and intelligence. Only one of these factors, intelligence, can be treated here.

Intelligence

Anyone who examines an individual's adjustments to life's problems is bound to note that his intelligence shows some direct relationships. People of higher intelligence can handle problems which are beyond the capacities of those of lower intelligence.

Intelligence has been defined in numerous ways. One recommended definition is, "The degree of availability of one's experiences for the solution of immediate problems and the anticipation of future ones."[3]

Some investigators think that the intelligence of an individual is probably fixed at birth, and certain ones believe that it is determined even before birth through heredity.* Whatever its basic origin may be, a person's intelligence quotient, as measured by various I.Q. tests, may vary over a span of years. In general, however, the range in which an individual falls usually remains fairly constant. We would not expect a child whose I.Q. tests at 80 one time to have an I.Q. of 130 ten years later. We would not be too surprised, however to find that his I.Q. had gone up to 100.

$$IQ = \frac{\text{Mental Age} \times 100}{\text{Chronological Age}}$$

An individual may go through adjustment experiences which result in a raising or lowering of his intellectual capacity. In the case of some children, favorable educational influences tend to raise the I.Q. The child who is encouraged to think independently, to use his intellectual curiosity, to have his ability challenged, and to gain satisfaction from his intellectual endeavors may have an increase in his intelligence quotient.[4] The amount of the increase and the exact conditions under which it does occur is still largely a problem for future research.

In the clinical areas of child guidance, many cases of "pseudo-feeblemindedness" have been reported. The child is really intelligent, but acts as though he were feebleminded. He is afraid to undertake any activity, even play. The problem to which he is adjusting by a paralyzing fear may be a dislike of school because of the presence of other boys who "beat him up" and otherwise intimidate him.[5]

Clinicians believe that a child's performance on an intelligence test is likely to be impaired by serious emotional problems. Knowing this, the typical clinician regards test scores of such children as measures of intellectual functioning at the time of testing, not as measures of actual intellectual potential. Studies of the effects of a favorable hospital program on emotionally disturbed children show that some children have a rise in the Verbal IQ with overall clinical improvement.[6]

In the field of education, intelligence tests have been useful in estimating the learning capacities of pupils. For example, idiots (IQ under 25), imbeciles (IQ, 25 to 49), and morons (IQ, 50 to 69) have such limited learning abilities that special long-term instruction is necessary to teach them the simplest habits. Idiots cannot learn to dress

---

* Certain investigators who believe that intelligence is inherited often dismiss the low-intelligence person whom they have tried to aid but could not with the remark: "He was gypped by the genes." The mechanisms of genes and chromosomes are blamed for the level of mental ability. However, if intelligence is wholly inherited, we still have much to learn about influences and factors in inheritance.

"Stoddard has cleverly observed that, while California state institutions over the past thirty years have sterilized 13,000 insane and feeble-minded persons, the follow-up, sixteen years later, of Terman's gifted children reveals that about 40 per cent of the parents of gifted children report mental abnormality among their near relatives. As Stoddard observed, 'Very likely a genius is himself safe in California, but it seems reasonable to say his near relatives had better watch out.'" See *Addresses and Discussions Presenting the 39th Yearbook*, NSSE, "Intelligence: Its Nature and Nurture," 1940, p. 49. Last paragraph quoted from John T. Wahlquist, "Is the IQ Controversy Philosophical?" *School and Society*, November 30, 1940.

TABLE 7.2

	IQ		Percentage Population
Feebleminded:			
Idiot	below 25,	M.A. 2 years or under	1
Imbecile	25– 49,	M.A. 2–7 years	
Moron	50– 69,	M.A. 7–11 years	
Borderline	70– 79		5
Dull	80– 89		14
Average	90–109		60
High average	110–119		14
Superior	120–140		6
Very superior	above 140		

themselves or to say more than a few simple words. Imbeciles can learn to talk to a limited extent and even do simple manual labor under close supervision, but they cannot learn the value of money. Morons can learn to read and write and perform routine factory tasks, but they cannot be expected to go beyond the fifth grade in school.

Differences in levels of intelligence are often summarized as indicated in the table on this page.

Morons have normal impulses but they cannot foresee consequences of their own acts and so often get into trouble with the law. They buy goods on credit but forget to pay for them. Among the girls, the percentage of illegitimate motherhood is very high. Many of the boys are likely to become professional toughs or petty thieves, or transients. One study of 504 transients indicated that feeblemindedness was an important background factor in transiency. The transient group studied contained twelve times the proportion of mental defectives as the general population.[7]

The records of gifted children have shown that, contrary to popular opinion, they do not become insane or die young. They do have some emotional problems, but they tend to achieve happier and more successful lives than their less gifted brothers. Of the 1,400 gifted children selected as being the brightest among 250,000 Californians by Dr. Lewis M. Terman in 1922, one half of the boys have entered the professions and a fourth are in semi-professional occupations or business. Their incomes in 1960 were also considerably above the average of the general population.

College students in general are of superior intelligence. However, when the scores on the American Council Psychological Examination were converted into equivalent IQ's by Arthur E. Traxler, using the recommended procedure, wide differences between colleges were found. The quartile and median IQ's at 323 colleges varied greatly.[8] For admission to college, there is no unqualified answer to the question as to what intelligence quotient is necessary. The IQ needed depends upon the college considered.

Usually, we do not use the term IQ for adults. When children near the age of sixteen, it is difficult to compute the relation between mental development and chronological age. For adults, we prefer to specify the Percentile Rank (P.R.),* that is, the percentage of the population or group that ranks lower than the person tested. If a test shows that an applicant has a P.R. of 75, it means that 75 per cent of the population (or group) rank

* The term *centile* is also used by many authors. Whenever we use either *percentile* or *centile,* we should recognize the specific group to which the term applies. For example, a given college student's intelligence test score may place him below the 20th centile on a specific test administered to college students only. When the same or another intelligence test is administered to members of the general population, the same student may fall above the 70th centile for the group. On the other hand, centiles are a convenient device for showing a person's score on different kinds of tests such as intelligence, dominance, musical aptitude, and so on. Many psychographs or mental profiles are constructed on the basis of the centile concept.

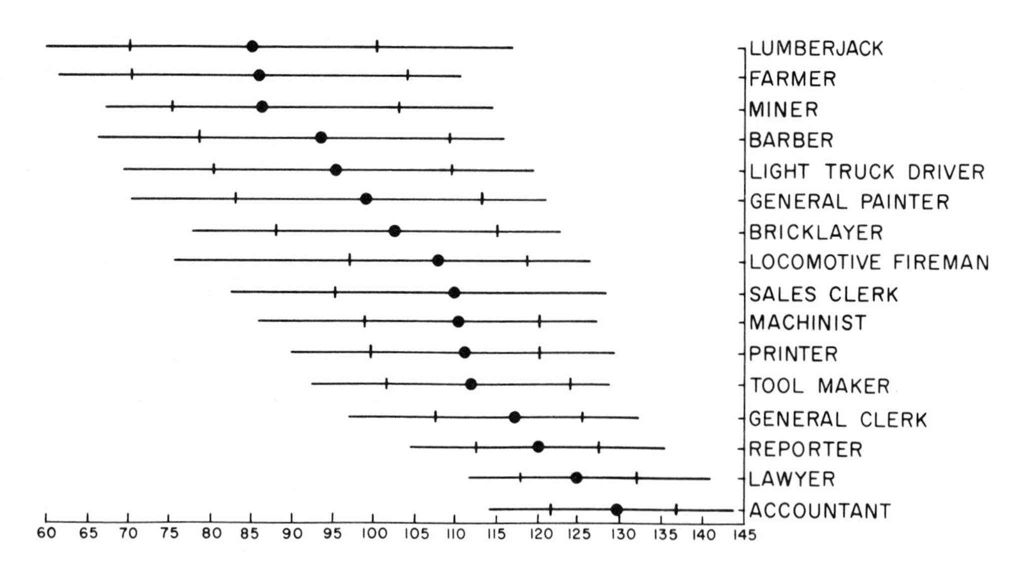

Gross scores of sixteen sample occupational groups *on the Army General Classification Test. The large dot near the center of the line indicates the median score; the upright bars the 25th and 75th percentiles; and the ends of the line the 10th and 90th percentiles. Note that the intelligence test scores of the highest scoring persons of the semi-skilled and skilled occupations overlap the scores of the lowest scoring members of the professions. The members of any one occupation differ widely in their intelligence test scores. There is, however, considerable evidence for occupational hierarchies of intelligence. The highest classes are usually found to be the professional, next the managerial group, then skilled trade, semi-skilled, and finally unskilled.—From N. Stewart, "A. G. C. T. Scores of Army Personnel Grouped by Occupation,"* ***Occupations,*** *October 1947.*

lower in the test than the applicant and 25 per cent rank higher. Similarly, if an applicant has a P.R. of 50 on a test, he is higher in the trait tested than 50 per cent of the population and lower than 50 per cent; hence, he is average for that trait.

Obviously, intelligence has a direct bearing on the individual's possibilities of succeeding in a vocation, most particularly the professional level of occupation. In regard to adjustment, the relationship is not so clear-cut. The psychoneurotic adjustment group, for example, compares favorably in intelligence with the general population.[9]

A review of the findings concerning the relation between intelligence and personality inventories for members of the military services of the United States, World War II, revealed little evidence to support the idea of a common intelligence factor in personality inventory scores and adaptability to military life. There was some evidence, however, to indicate that the relation between adjustment to military life and intelligence is stronger in the lower reaches of intelligence than in the levels above.[10]

In a study of college freshmen in which the "Problem Check-List" by Ross L. Mooney was used, a very low negative relationship was found between the number of problems checked and both grades and intelligence test scores, indicating a slight tendency for poorer students to have more problems. "Correlations with grades show a tendency for those who make the low grades to have more problems in adjusting to college work."[11]

Certainly, we can conclude that neither high intelligence nor low intelligence guarantees either good or poor adjustment. The person of high intelligence has the advantage of capacity for greater insight into his problems and ways of dealing with them. How he uses his capacity depends on other factors, such as his psychological needs.

NEEDS

Numerous approaches to the "why" in the behavior of people have been made by psychologists. They have developed special concepts such as "motive," "drive" and "need." The terms apply to predisposing influences in behavior of a psychogenic nature. Currently, the term "need" is receiving considerable emphasis in certain behavioral researches. Some of the terms used to describe needs are also used in describing adjustments. However, when a term such as "aggression" is used in regard to needs, the emphasis is on the long-term motivational aspects. When used in regard to adjustment, the emphasis is on the dynamic aspects in dealing with a problem and the behavioral pattern that develops. The adjustment concept gives considerable attention to origin; need concept gives little attention to the origin or development of the motivation. Those who think in terms of needs are not usually concerned as to the complex influences that bring about a need, even though factors involved in the origin of the need are rather obvious as in stress situations.

We can easily note the influence of needs when we study people in stress situations as in war. A former prisoner of war described the outward changes in behavior of prisoners as their hardships changed. He wrote the following letter to Dr. Ernest Dichter, head of the Institute for Motivational Research, in regard to his concept of four basic drives in human motivation:

> When we were starving and freezing (one bowl of watery soup per day for over a month), we talked and dreamed only of food; when rations were increased to the point where hunger pangs were less severe, we talked about women, when the food situation improved still more, we became concerned for our safety; and when, on the two occasions we were privileged to eat all we wanted (Christmas, 1944, and May 1945), we got ambitious and philosophical and began to talk about our stations in life and those to which we aspired.[12]

One of the reasons why psychologists had to become concerned about the individual's deep-seated needs was the recognition that harsh punishment does not always extinguish undesirable responses.

Some psychotherapists conceptualize mental illness in terms of the individual's need-structures. The woman whose affect fixations and adjustment tendencies have generated an intense need for admiration may not be able to find enough admirers to satisfy the need and gain psychological equilibrium. The man who has a need for power, money, order or some other personal gratification may not be able to find a place in life where the intense urge is adequately satisfied. Peace of mind for such an individual is a very difficult attainment. He may not be able to resolve the conflicts between his strong need drives and the resources and controls of the environment. Studies in daydreams indicate that many differ with respect to need drive as well as content area.[13]

Needs are given much study by psychologists, but most are more concerned with the manner of expression than their origin. A good example is the need for personal recognition, which may be expressed either in selfish behavior that has an unpleasant influence on associates, or, on the other hand, on becoming especially friendly. Even though our main interest may be in the outward expression rather than the origin of the drive, we can understand and, at times, direct the manifest behavior more intelligently if we can sense the motivating influences, the needs, that give the behavior impetus and continuity. Every socially alert person daily recognizes the special needs of associates.

Each researcher uses a classification of needs that he finds appropriate for the specific project which he investigates. The terminology in regard to the designation and definitions of needs has not been standardized. However, one of the oft-quoted lists of needs as developed by a psychologist is that by H. A. Murray.[14]

The Allen L. Edwards *Personal Preference Schedule* (EPPS) was designed as a self-rating instrument to measure the strength of

TABLE 7.3

THE EPPS VARIABLES AND NEEDS ASSOCIATED WITH THEM

EPPS Variables and Their Abbreviations	*Condensed Descriptions*
Achievement (ach)	To do one's best, to be successful
Deference (def)	To do what is expected, to let others make decisions
Order (ord)	To be neat and orderly, to have things organized
Exhibitionism (exh)	To say and do things that cause one to be noticed
Autonomy (aut)	To be able to come and go as one desires, to be independent
Affiliation (aff)	To do things for friends, to form new friendships
Intraception (int)	To analyze one's motives and feelings
Succorance (suc)	To have others provide help, to seek encouragement
Dominance (dom)	To be a leader in groups, to make decisions for the group
Abasement (aba)	To feel timid and inferior to others
Nurturance (nur)	To assist others less fortunate
Change (chg)	To do new and different things, to move about the country
Endurance (end)	To keep at a job until it is finished
Heterosexuality (het)	Interest in the opposite sex
Aggression (agg)	To attack contrary points of view, to get revenge

The condensed descriptions are taken from more complete statements of the variables measured by EPPS as given in the *Edwards Personal Preference Schedule Manual,* (New York: The Psychological Corporation, 1954).

personal need in regard to 15 "normal" personality variables. The statements in the 225 EPPS items and the variables that the statements purport to measure have their origin in a list of manifest needs presented by H. A. Murray and others. The names assigned to the variables are those used by Murray.

Table 7.3 presents a list of the 15 variables with brief descriptions, "Self-Rating Categories,"[15] derived from the descriptions of the variables as published in the EPPS Manual.[16]

This measuring instrument has been used in numerous and varied studies. The 15 manifest needs have become a part of current psychological literature as exemplified in this comment by a psychologist who studied members of the Peace Corps:

> I surmise that Volunteers have a high need for affiliation. They get substantial satisfactions from being with other Volunteers and from association with new friends in other lands. They wear no hair shirts, nor are they out for an irresponsible lark. They say: "It will be good to make friends in other lands," "It will be fun to see the world"; they also say, "I know I will have dysentery, it will be hot and dusty, I will be lonesome."[17]

Another study showed that the average test profile of the needs of experienced engineers differs markedly from that of male liberal arts students. The engineers scored higher on the EPPS on variables such as Achievement, Order and Endurance. They were lower on Affiliation, Abasement and Nurturance.[18]

When a study was made of 1802 managers of a wide variety of companies, line managers perceived greater need fulfillment from their jobs than the staff managers.[19]

An interesting study of adjustments indicated that well adjusted persons gain more need satisfactions than the maladjusted.[20]

The EPPS schedule is not suitable for use in the selection and placement of job applicants,[21] but is useful in certain research and counseling situations. The subject of needs in counseling is so large that we can treat only two of the most common categories of their influence. One of the categories deals with positive, the other with negative value adjustments.

Need for Achievement

Students who score high in achievement needs tend to make higher grades in college than those who score low. When degree of aptitude for college work as indicated by

College Entrance Examination Board tests is held constant, engineering students who score high in achievement needs tend to make higher grades in college than the aptitude test scores would indicate.[22]

We can define this need as the habitual desire to do useful work well. It is a salient influence characteristic of those who need little supervision. Their desire for accomplishment is a stronger motivation than any stimulation the supervisor can provide. Individuals who function in terms of this drive do not "bluff" in regard to a job which they fail to do well.

Some employees have a strong drive for success in their work; others are satisfied when they make a living. Those who want to feel that they are successes have high levels of aspiration for themselves. Thoughts concerning the achievement drive are often prominent in the evaluations made by the typical employment interviewer who interviews college seniors for executive training. He wants to find out whether the senior has a strong drive to get ahead or merely to hold a job. Researches indicate that some who do get ahead have an even stronger drive to avoid failure.[23]

Generally, college men have stronger achievement needs, to dominate, to be aggressive, and to be autonomously self-directing than college women. The college women have stronger needs to defer to others, to have close affiliations with others, to introspect regarding their personality, to help others, and to be dependent on others.[24]

Of course these differences in achievement needs between men and women often lead to frictions in the marital state. The typical wife who is married to a man of high achievement needs cannot understand why he should neglect her and the children in order to give full attention to his job. She may feel neglected, treated unfairly. Her needs differ so decidedly from his.

If she accepts the situation but does nothing to lift her career or intellectual achievements, she may, in time, feel that her husband has risen to a high level while she has remained on a lower level. This feeling on her part is likely to develop special needs which she may satisfy by positive or by negative value activities. Her special needs may cause her to become keenly devoted to children or friends. These are positive value tendencies. Of course she might instead develop negative value adjustments such as neurosis and faultfinding toward those who appear to be on a higher career level.

Many persons seek satisfaction for their achievement needs through status symbols: a respected title, a distinctively furnished office, a home in a high-income area, or ownership of a boat that elicits social recognition. Many achievers are motivated by an urge to acquire status symbols. To some persons, such as those who are highly creative, status symbols may be of little value. Those who have strong affiliation needs may prefer friendships to status. The lonely single girl who lives by herself in an apartment may, for example, decline an offer of a better job that includes a prestige title because it would take her away from old friends who are congenial.

An examination of current psychological literature concerning achievement needs will present closely related needs, particularly those of *self-actualization.* These emphasize the needs for opportunity for personal growth and development, for the feeling of worthwhile accomplishment, for the liberation of creative talents, and for the feeling of self-fulfillment as a person.[25]

The needs for self-actualization have received so much attention by writers in the behavioral sciences as related to management that at least one company, a California electronics manufacturer, organized its manufacturing operations so that these needs may be fulfilled on the part of the employees. This was done by having management regard its functions as those of teaching and training rather than of directing and controlling, by letting teams of workers pace themselves at their own rhythm, and by letting the worker do or see a whole job.[26]

An important limitation of this method of conducting a business is that roughly 30 per cent of the members of our population are not mature enough to survive under this approach. One study suggested that self-actualization is a middle-class value, inasmuch as only the professional and white-collar workers questioned expressed concern with the personal or ego satisfactions to be derived from the job. The blue-collar workers studied made no mention of such satisfactions, leading the researchers to conclude that self-actualization was unimportant to them.[27]

Aggression Needs

Almost every student has experienced the need for aggression. He has expressed some of his antagonisms toward unpleasant educational-institution frustrations by criticism of a teacher's marking methods or by making derogatory comments about the college's food service. A wise administrator learns to differentiate between objective comments and griping. Generally, griping is only partially justified, but it frequently makes the griper feel better because it satisfies some of his aggression needs.

The aggression drive, in its simplest form, expresses itself in destructive thoughts. When the individual fails to grow up emotionally, the drive continues to express itself in acts of faultfinding, selfishness, procrastination, jealousy, and hostility. The aggression drive is a force that makes us want to hit out when we are frustrated or angry or hurt. It stimulates us to defend ourselves against attack. Counselors recognize that when it is coordinated and balanced with a constructive purpose, the aggression drive can lead to or become transformed into a constructive drive. It may help the individual conquer obstacles that stand in the way of reaching a difficult but worthwhile goal. A constructive drive makes us want to build rather than tear down, to create rather than destroy. In infancy, the constructive drive is self-centered and pleasure-seeking. Its primary aim is self-preservation, as exemplified by the baby's efforts to obtain food, warmth, and affection from those around him. These things are essential to the baby's survival. In later stages, the earlier self-centered drives normally become constructive—they are expressed in thoughts and actions that are kind and creative. That is why we do not admire the adult who functions mainly in terms of aggression. We recognize that he has not as yet attained the maturity of control and direction of his aggression tendencies.

Unfortunately, too, the individual may turn his aggressive drives against himself in self-punishment or, in extreme cases, suicide. In industry, this is seen most often in the form of accidental injury. Of course, many accidents are not a form of self-punishment, but close study of accidents has shown that the people involved often "forgot" or disregarded safety precautions in a manner that is difficult to understand on a conscious or logical basis. Unconsciously these individuals created a situation in which they could be or were injured.

Counselors often note that a person's aggressive drives may go around his conscious guard to find expression in activities that he perceives as commendable. An example is the supremely honest man who must give his frank opinion to his friends on everything that they say or do. He not only believes that honesty is the best policy in all cases, but he practices it even though it sometimes harms those he likes. These are the self-righteous persons whom we avoid because they go out of their way to find fault in order to make themselves feel better.

We see many examples of unconscious hostility in the not-too-well-disguised joke aimed at other people. Aggressive feelings are expressed through humor that is enjoyed at the expense of the other person. Humor is one of the more subtle ways in which people can express their aggressions. True humor is enjoyed by all the persons involved in the joke.

The need for outlets of aggression tendencies is frequently exemplified in the history of nations. The demagogue has had great influence in the evolution of world affairs. He can always find some people who seek a new or better outlet for their hostilities. Scapegoats are universal in the history of nations. These destructive aggressors do not follow ordinary codes of ethical conduct—they have a deep-seated need to be cruel to even those people who treat them kindly and justly.

Every large business organization is likely to have one or more scapegoats or whipping boys—individuals who rightly or wrongly are targets for blame, even abuse. The individual chosen for the satisfaction of this need is likely to be an unpopular power-seeking person who recognizes that he is hated but he is not emotionally disturbed by the snide remarks which he knows are expressed against him behind his back. Top management men are not ordinarly disturbed by the employees' hatred toward the scapegoat member of their group—they know that many employees have unconscious needs for such an outlet. Subconsciously, too, perhaps some feel that if one member of the organization is the unofficial whipping boy, the other members are likely to have fewer mudballs thrown at them!

Ideally, no one should have destructive aggressive tendencies. Practically, all persons have them to some extent, but most people keep them repressed. When repressed, they are likely to appear in disguised forms, commonly in psychosomatic or other functional disorders. This is especially likely to occur with people who are under constant pressure but cannot speak out for some reason. Public contact officials who have to be "nice" to everybody occupy this kind of situation. If a person in this kind of situation "blows up" occasionally, he should be forgiven.

Some children are reared in a firmly controlled manner. The child from infancy on is taught not to show his anger openly. He is not allowed to quarrel with brothers and sisters, to express jealousy, or to say, "I don't like you!" He is taught that it is wrong even to *think* these things. In adulthood, this kind of upbringing in regard to the firm control of aggressive feelings becomes an unconscious part of his psychic life. Consciously, he may not feel angry. He may not even realize that he denies his angry feelings. When, on occasion, he is provoked to anger he unconsciously feels guilty about his feelings of hostility which he dare not express. On the job, he may be easy to get along with; he never picks a fight, he never questions his supervisor's commands, and he does not argue when he is passed over for a promotion which he believes that he deserves. Even though this kind of person gets along quietly with everyone, he seldom develops close friendships. He usually has no deep interests outside the job. Eventually, however, the pent-up angry feelings take their toll. He has no safety valves through argument or an absorbing interest. He becomes an asthmatic, ulcer, migraine, or some other variety of patient whose ailment cannot be cured by medicines.

Frustration arouses energy. If this energy cannot be expressed, by prompt satisfying means of expression, it is nonetheless discharged somehow. If you are reprimanded but cannot talk back, you may later yell at someone for a minor misdeed. You may berate a waitress or yell at other drivers of cars you pass on the way home.

Momentary and short-lived flareups of this kind are common to all of us. When, however, the aggression evokes feelings that are out of all proportion to the situation, we say that hostility is expressed. Unlike anger, it tends to linger on.

When a counselor finds that a person is hostile to someone for no apparent reason, he tries to discover whether he is transferring his frustrations from other experiences into hostility toward the symbolic target. Obviously the individual usually needs the benefit of psychological assistance in recognizing his hostility and in achieving more satisfactory relations with others.

Coping Mechanisms

Even though much of an individual's behavior is an attempt to satisfy his needs, we must not imagine that he is bound to remain the helpless victim of his need drives. He has many coping mechanisms. *Coping mechanisms* are often related to the defense mechanisms. The defense mechanisms indicate how the individual adjusts to conditions that arouse his anxieties. The coping mechanisms indicate how he utilizes positively both his potentialities and his defense mechanisms in his life and work situations. From this standpoint, each person exhibits two varieties of behavior: one variety develops from needs to which he adjusts inadequately as in negative value defense mechanisms, the others are expressions of ways in which he channels his tensions and need outlets into the means of making a living, living with others, and living with himself. The human relations specialist sees examples every day of individuals who exhibit markedly disturbed personality patterns, inability to live with themselves, but they function effectively in work and certain other situations. They have good coping mechanisms.[28]

Our major question about the individual's characteristic behavior should not be: "How normal or abnormal is he?" but rather "Are his coping mechanisms enabling him to function effectively in certain situations under certain conditions?" In everyday practice, almost every intelligent observer does this. He knows that certain defensive or other inadequately adjusted persons manage to do good work and live happily when channels of expression lead to satisfaction of their needs.

Certainly, many a college student who has worked in factories during summer vacations has met a certain type of foreman who has had little formal education. The lack has made him both proud and resentful—proud because he has achieved a good position despite his lack of formal education and resentful because of his work environment where special recognition is given to "college men." A foreman of this kind is apt to divide industrial employees into two groups: the "practical" and the "theoretical" men. Whenever he deals with a college-educated man such as an engineer, he enjoys finding evidence of the theoretical man's stupidity. Such a foreman may treat members of management with great respect but he likes to bawl out subordinates, particularly "dumb college men."

If the college man is aware of the influence of such a foreman's needs, he is not disturbed by the bawlings-out. Instead, he accepts them as of incidental note with a comment to himself such as "Aw, the boss just has to bawl me out occasionally—it makes him feel better!" The smart college man recognizes the needs expressed in the foreman's behavior, overlooks it, and concentrates on learning worthwhile matters from the foreman's practical experience.

Also, we need to realize that the channels of expression of a person's needs may change as he undergoes new experiences such as education, change in status, or "shock" arising from a tragic experience. The earlier expression of the need drives may be modified by later needs even though the earlier patterns tend to remain in controlled form.

Of course the student of psychology is likely to ask "What specific technique should I use in order to recognize and evaluate properly all the various predisposing influences at work in the life of an individual such as a problem person?" The answer obviously is "There is no one standard procedure." However, we can arrange the known facts and cues about a person's behavior, particularly about human behavior, so that he can approach his study of an individual with problem behavior, into a working outline.

Needs can be deduced from a knowledge of a series of adjustments made by the individual or by case studies.

The person who wishes to learn the mode of thinking used by clinical psychologists may start to do so on a relatively simple level, through the adjustment concept.

The psychological findings about a human being cannot be satisfactorily arranged in terms of some algebraic formula, but the facts can be thought of in patternful relationships, as suggested by the Seven-Phase Outline of Table 7.4. Such an arrangement of information about a problem person enables us to appreciate wherein he is a person with a problem and how his psychological background influences some of his conduct.

We should try to learn enough psychology to be able to see the significant adjustments which occur in the lives of those around us. Of course, if we have a professional responsibility for the mental health of others, we should read many books on psychology and attend clinics in order to become alert to the subtle influences in the lives of our maladjusted associates as well as in our own mental development.

TABLE 7.4

SEVEN PHASE OUTLINE FOR STUDY OF PERSONS WITH ADJUSTMENT PROBLEMS

1. *The Barrier:* the problem or problems, ostensible or actual. See Section I of Table 2.2, page 38, for a list of barriers.
2. *Predisposing Influences:* long-term factors such as endocrine glands, bodily health, cultural environment, or personalities in the home. These may be known or have to be assumed.
3. *Precipitating Influences:* relatively recent factors such as a failure, insult, or loss. They may be known or have to be assumed.
4. *Direct Attack Adjustments:* these are adjustments which the individual should have made, or might make in the future. (See Section I of Table 2.3, page 40.)
5. *Positive Substitute Activities:* these vary with the problem, the individual, the total situation, and so on. These adjustments tend to strengthen the personality for future problems but not usually for the problem involved in the adjustment under consideration. (See Section II of Table 2.3.)
6. *Evasive or Retreat Adjustments:* these also vary with the situation but they tend to weaken the personality for dealing with the immediate and with future problems. (See Sections III and IV of Table 2.3.)
7. *How Others Can Help Him:* analyzing the adjustments of others has little value unless the analysis enables us to contribute to the positive adjustments and personality well-being of the person analyzed. Suggestions depend upon many factors, but especially upon the relation of the analyst to the person analyzed.

To the executive, "helping an employee" usually means "How can the company improve the employee's work situation so that he may be able to become better adjusted as a person?" In order to improve the work situation, the employee may be given new work, a new supervisor, different associates, a leave of absence, or a better interpretation of his work situation. Chiefly, however, the enlightened executive expresses his encouragement by means of the genuine warmth of his interest in the employee. In many cases, the executive does not discuss the employee's problem with him but he offers the kind of understanding that is supportive to the employee in his attempts to achieve an effective satisfying adjustment. The executive does not attempt therapy. That function belongs to trained specialists outside the company such as psychiatrists. If therapy seems to be appropriate, he may help the employee find a therapist, but the employee himself, not the executive or the company, has responsibility for the treatment. The main function of the executive is that of a friend who counsels, encourages, and interprets in a permissive manner. He does not solve the employee's problems for him; he wants the employee himself to solve them.

The main need of many people is ordinary friendly counsel and reassurance. Even animal experiments show the value of that. When dogs are purposely made neurotic by experiment, the presence of a human being or a friendly dog in a room reassures the nervous animal so that he does not always have a neurotic attack. Similarly, people need assurance that what they are doing, they are doing well. They can often be given sympathetic intelligent friendship in learning suitable modes of action.

Encouragement Should Be Supported by a Plan of Action

This kind of friendly support becomes especially effective when the person-with-a-problem is given a feasible plan of action rather than friendly encouragement only. Ordinary encouragement to many people means the making of quieting remarks such as "Oh, that isn't important—don't worry about it" or "Forget it. It won't work out that way." A plan of action may be far more supportive as indicated by this example:

Henry, a major in psychology at college, had completed his junior year and was working in a factory office during his summer vacation. His supervisor was an old college graduate who liked to encourage students. One day Henry told the supervisor about the problem that was bothering him to a serious extent. While in college he had fallen in love with a girl who came from a home where the father held a high-income executive position. The girl had three older brothers who had graduated from engineering schools and were making substantial incomes. To Henry, who came from a low-income home, the girl friend's family was in an "entirely different league." He was worried, disturbed, anxious. He had been planning to work for a doctorate in psychology but that long-term program did not seem to fit his needs. He was also older than most students, 25 because of military service.

Fortunately for Henry, his supervisor did not say: "Forget it. You're just as good as anybody else. Eventually, you'll make just as much money as the girl friend's father or her brothers." Nor did the supervisor try to analyze Henry's early home life in order to have him realize why he had developed a tendency toward anxieties concerning difficult adjustment problems.

Instead, the supervisor discussed with Henry his scholastic record and his hopes for himself. He had done especially well in mathematics and liked the higher mathematics courses. He had been reading about automation and wanted to get into that field but he lacked the necessary engineering background to do so. He wanted to make enough money soon in order to get married and have a nice home.

The supervisor pointed out that one of the most rapidly growing phases of automation is data processing through the use of the new electronic computers. Men with mathematical training and some business background are needed in this field and can make rapid advancement. The supervisor gave Henry introductions to men and publications in the field. Henry followed through on the idea and soon lost his anxieties about his qualities in comparison with those of the girl friend's father and her brothers. He had been given understanding and encouragement by the supervisor but the encouragement was backed up with an appropriate plan of action.

Practically, then, helping the employee who has a minor maladjustment means helping him to learn to feel that his supervisors or counselors and associates like him and will encourage him while he puts into effect a plan of action which will displace the handicapping habits that we call evasion and retreat. The study of case problems, limited though such study must be, may be helpful to the student.

If students will present for discussion adjustment problems that they have observed or experienced, they can make vital applications of important psychological principles. The following problems are examples of the kind that students have presented for class discussion:

1. Rose Horn feels sorry for Mr. Ray, her employer. As his secretary, she cannot help being aware that he is under a terrific strain at home. He often comes to the office in a bad humor and is impatient and sharp with Rose; but he is always sorry for it afterwards and is very uncomfortable in her presence. Rose would like to help him if she could, but because of his extreme embarrassment in her presence, she is afraid that she would lose her job if she showed her sympathy. What should she do?

2. Donald Center is working during the summer vacation in a toy factory employing twenty people in all. Jack Horton, son of the owner, works with Donald. Jack is insolent to everyone and does not hesitate to countermand the supervisor's orders whenever he desires. He makes himself generally most disagreeable, the more so because Mr. Horton always upholds Jack in any disagreement that arises. What can Donald do?

3. Jerry Tompkins is a graduate of a good engineering school and now works for one of the Ford agencies in the Middle West. He is the only college man in the organization and has made fine progress in two years. In his opinion, he now knows the job well enough to be able to work on his own initiative, but his manager insists on giving him detailed instructions for each day, treating him as though he had not yet proved his ability. What can Tompkins do?

4. Alice Jaynes is private secretary to Mr. Smiley, a self-made, headstrong, and uneducated man, who has a very limited vocabulary and uses poor and ungrammatical English. In dictating to Alice, he invariably makes serious mistakes,

EMPLOYEE REFUSES TO ACCEPT AN OFFER FOR ADVANCEMENT

Mr. Denison is one of your best and most intelligent workers. You find that you must promote a man to the position of foreman over thirty of Denison's fellow-workers, and Denison seems to be the logical man for the position. When you explain the work to Denison and offer him the foremanship, he says that he is not interested in becoming a foreman. He claims that he would be unable to direct the work of former associates because they know him too well. You, however, are convinced that he really would like to have the promotion.

1. The Barrier:
- a. Ostensibly, his lack of self-confidence.
- b. Actually, a fear of ridicule. (Assumed on analyst's part.)
- c. *Other assumption:*

2. Predisposing Influences:
- a. Has he developed a rut for himself in his present job?
- b. Has he failed in some previous position of leadership?
- c. *Other:*

3. Precipitating Influences:
- a. Has his wife recently discouraged him about his ability?
- b. Did any of his associates talk about his possible promotion?
- c. *Other:*

4. Direct Attack Adjustments:
- a. Take the job and try to develop self-confidence.
- b. Mingle more often with superiors.
- c. *Other:*

5. Positive Substitute Activities:
- a. Throw energy into lodge activities to gain satisfaction.
- b. Put energy into the present job, doing it exceptionally well.
- c. *Other:*

6. Evasive or Retreat Adjustments:
- a. Find satisfaction in solitude.
- b. *Other:*

7. How Others Can Help Him:
- a. Have him supervise only a few coöperative employees until confidence has been gained.
- b. *Other:*

THE IMPRACTICAL DREAMER

George is young and ambitious. He has been out of school for one year but has been unable to settle down to the routine position which he holds with a business firm. He is forever conceiving impracticable get-rich-quick schemes that would, he imagines, give him easy money quickly. His ideas are so impracticable, however, that he is missing opportunities to lay a foundation for his future in the firm where he is now employed.

1. The Barrier:
- a. Tendency to dream because of poor social adjustment.
- b. Does not realize what success really is.
- c. *Other assumption:*

2. Predisposing Influences:
- a. Is he still in the adolescent age of day-dreams?
- b. Does he feel insecure because his father and mother are incompatible?
- c. *Other:*

3. Precipitating Influences:
- a. Does he find his present work very boresome?
- b. Does he see better-educated workers pass him in advancement?
- c. *Other:*

4. Direct Attack Adjustments:
- a. Increase his social participation.
- b. Enjoy small successes rather than dream of spectacular success.
- c. *Other:*

5. Positive Substitute Activities:
- a. Associate with inferiors whom he can impress.
- b. Develop a hobby of an unusual kind.
- c. *Other:*

6. Evasive or Retreat Adjustments:
- a. Adopt an air of superiority and tell others how clever he is.
- b. *Other:*

7. How Others Can Help Him:
- a. Build up his self-confidence through social activities.
- b. Explain to him the "romances" and "adventures" of his present job.
- c. *Other:*

SEX REPRESSIONS

Richard is a young man who works in a large office and is troubled with sordid thoughts, especially about girls. He comes from a small town and has never been away from home before. The apparent freedom in social relations between the young men and women in his office keeps him emotionally upset because he is too self-conscious to make satisfying acquaintances of the girls. He therefore thinks of girls in a strange, abnormal way.

1. The Barrier:

a. Ostensibly, an unhealthy mental attitude.
b. Actually, lack of normal associations.
c. *Other assumption:*

2. Predisposing Influences:

a. Was he ridiculed in childhood for associating with girls?
b. Was he too closely supervised or pampered when young?
c. *Other:*

3. Precipitating Influences:

a. Has he been talking with maladjusted men about lewd aspects of sex?
b. Is he still really living in the country?
c. *Other:*

4. Direct Attack Adjustments:

a. Associate with normal and well-balanced girls.
b. Join a club and learn to dance.
c. *Other:*

5. Positive Substitute Activities:

a. Become intensely interested in his work and avoid women.
b. Get a job in his home town.
c. *Other:*

6. Evasive or Retreat Adjustments:

a. Criticize the freedom in social relationships.
b. Gain satisfaction through daydreaming.
c. *Other:*

7. How Others Can Help Him:

a. Invite him to attend a mixed social affair.
b. *Other:*

SYMBOLIC ACTIVITY

Mr. Amulet is a middle-aged man of higher than average intelligence who suddenly realizes that he has become superstitious. He finds himself doing things for good luck or to ward off evil omens—superstitious acts which he would have scorned a few years ago. He tells himself that he must stop these foolish tendencies, but he claims that he cannot.

1. The Barrier

a. Ostensibly, a desire to avoid injury.
b. Actually, an unadmitted fear of harm because of some act of which he is ashamed.
c. *Other assumption:*

2. Predisposing Influences:

a. Many emotional experiences have given him a sense of guilt.
b. Have friends impressed him with the efficacy of their pet charms?
c. *Other:*

3. Precipitating Influences:

a. Does he believe he escaped an accident because he obeyed a "premonition"?
b. Has he recently committed an immoral act that has caused him to fear disgrace?
c. *Other:*

4. Direct Attack Adjustments:

a. Study superstitions and how they may be ways to compensate for unadmitted mistakes.
b. Visit a psychiatrist.
c. *Other:*

5. Positive Substitute Activities:

a. Take part in religious activities as a means to adjustment.
b. *Other:*

6. Evasive or Retreat Adjustments:

a. Immerse himself in the mystical.
b. Become intoxicated in order to forget his superstitions.
c. *Other:*

7. How Others Can Help Him:

a. Explain to him how one of your fears symbolized feeling of guilt.
b. *Other:*

THE SELF-CONSCIOUS EMPLOYEE

Perkins is thirty years old and is a mechanic in a garage. He is sensitive and becomes easily confused when the foreman, Graves, comes into the room where he is working. Graves knows that Perkins is a good worker, but when Graves stops to watch Perkins, the latter becomes flustered and cannot work efficiently.

1. The Barrier

a. Habit of dealing with people by thinking of himself.
b. *Other assumption:*

2. Predisposing Influences:

a. Was he reared by parents who criticized forwardness?
b. Was he disciplined severely and made to think of himself as unwanted?
c. *Other:*

3. Precipitating Influences:

a. Has Graves ridiculed him about his work?
b. Was he recently ignored when he tried to be friendly?
c. *Other:*

4. Direct Attack Adjustments:

a. Become active in an organization to develop his self-confidence.
b. Entertain the boss socially.
c. *Other:*

5. Positive Substitute Activities:

a. Find another job.
b. Supervise his physical inferiors, such as children.
c. *Other:*

6. Evasive or Retreat Adjustments:

a. Criticize boss and firm.
b. Daydream and picture himself a hero.
c. *Other:*

7. How Others Can Help Him:

a. Praise him for his "little" social successes.
b. *Other:*

BEHAVIOR VARIES WITH THE SITUATION

Miss Palmer is considered a competent "complaint clerk" in the public utility office where she works. She is a pleasant and convincing talker. In the homes of her friends, however, she cannot carry on a conversation. She seems to have no opinion on any subject. When she is asked why she isn't more sociable, she says she just doesn't know what to say or talk about.

1. The Barrier

a. Early conditioning or a complex arising from an inferior social position.
b. *Other assumption:*

2. Predisposing Influences:

a. As a child, was she allowed to take part in family conversations?
b. Were her parents socially inferior in the community?
c. *Other:*

3. Precipitating Influences:

a. Do her friends tell her that she is a wallflower?
b. Has a confidence been betrayed by one of her "friends"?
c. *Other:*

4. Direct Attack Adjustments:

a. Tell her friends how she feels and ask them to help her gain confidence.
b. Take an interest in other people and talk to them about themselves.
c. *Other:*

5. Positive Substitute Activities:

a. Lead a group of younger girls who will respect her.
b. Express herself in activities that do not require conversation.
c. *Other:*

6. Evasive or Retreat Adjustments:

a. Talk about and criticize the girls whom she knows.
b. Adopt an air of silent superiority.
c. *Other:*

7. How Others Can Help Her:

a. Do not give her advice—just show by your manner that you like her as she is.
b. *Other:*

which irritate her and, more important, worry her, since she does not know how to handle the situation. She feels that she should not send out such letters, yet she is afraid to correct Mr. Smiley.

5. Frank White works for an old-fashioned employer who is making very little money. Frank himself is progressive and is anxious to improve the business by a dozen different methods that seem self-evident to him, but when he suggests any changes, his employer invariably refuses to consider them on the ground that they are too risky. Frank is not in a position to go into business for himself and fears that he will be worse off if he changes his job. He is, however, restless and dissatisfied. How can he make his employer more sympathetic with his ambitions?

The reader may gain some practice in the study of adjustments through reading and discussing the six case problems on pages 147–149. Discussion should lead to additional suggestions which may be written into the *"Other"* spaces of the cases partially analyzed for the reader. Phase 7, *"How Others Can Help Him,"* should, of course, include *what he can do to help himself* as well as suggest appropriate plans of action for his consideration.

ACKNOWLEDGMENTS AND REFERENCES

1. See Henry Winthrop, "A Humanistic Psychology Is Born," *The Humanist,* May-June, 1964.
2. Leon J. Saul, *Emotional Maturity* (Philadelphia: J. B. Lippincott Co., 1947), pp. 168–170.
3. H. H. Goddard, "What Is Intelligence?" *Journal of Social Psychology,* **24** (1946), 51–69.
4. Beth L. Wellman, "Our Changing Concept of Intelligence," *Journal of Consulting Psychology,* **2,** No. 4 (1938).
5. Phyllis Blanchard, "The Interpretation of Psychological Tests in Clinical Work with Children," *Mental Hygiene,* **25** (1941), 58–75, presents a discussion of this variety of so-called feeblemindedness.
6. E. Wesley Hiler and David Neswig, "Changes in Intellectual Functions of Children in a Psychiatric Hospital," *Journal of Consulting Psychology,* August, 1961.
7. D. Kaplun, "Feeblemindedness as a Factor in Transiency," *Mental Hygiene,* **21** (1937), 96–100.
8. Arthur E. Traxler, "What Is a Satisfactory I.Q. for Admission to College?" *School and Society,* Apr. 6, 1940.
9. James D. Page, *Abnormal Psychology,* (New York: McGraw-Hill Book Company, 1947), p. 96.
10. Albert Ellis and Herbert S. Conrad, "The Validity of Personality Inventories in Military Practice," *Psychological Bulletin,* American Psychological Association, Inc., **45,** No. 5 (1948), 404.
11. Nora A. Congdon, "The Perplexities of College Freshmen," *Educational and Psychological Measurement,* **3** (1943), 367–376.
12. Letter from Forrest W. Howell, Jacksonville, Florida; published in *Memo from Dr. Dichter and Staff,* Institute for Motivational Research, Inc., Croton-on-Hudson, New York, May, 1956.
13. See C. W. LaGrone, "Sex and Personality Differences in Relation to Fantasy," *Journal of Consulting Psychology,* June, 1963.
14. See his *Explorations in Personality* (New York: Oxford University Press, 1938). Also, Calvin S. Hall and Gardner Lindzey, *Theories in Personality* (New York: John Wiley & Sons, Inc., 1957), Chapter 5.
15. John H. Mann, "Self-Ratings and the EPPS," *Journal of Applied Psychology,* August, 1958.
16. *Edwards Personal Preference Schedule,* (Manual), (New York: The Psychological Corporation, 1954).
17. Nicholas Hobbs, "A Psychologist in the Peace Corps," *The American Psychologist,* January, 1963, p. 52.
18. Carroll E. Izard, "Personality Characteristics of Engineers as measured by the Edwards Personal Preference Schedule," *Journal of Applied Psychology,* October, 1960.
19. Lyman W. Porter, "Job Attitudes in Management: III Perceived Deficiencies in Need Fulfillment as a Function of Line Versus Staff Type of Job," *Journal of Applied Psychology,* August, 1963.
20. See William A. Lewis, "Emotional Adjustment and Need Satisfaction of Hospital Patients," *Journal of Counseling Psychology,* **6** (1959), 127–131.
21. W. K. Kirchner and JoAnne DeGuido, "Relations Among Scores on Edwards Personal Preference Schedule," *Journal of Applied Psychology,* June, 1958. For additional limitations of the EPPS, see E. Levonian, A. Comrey, W. Levy, and D. Procter, "A Statistical Evaluation of Edwards Personal Preference Schedule," *Journal of Applied Psychology,* December, 1959, and Maurice Korman and Frances Coltharp, "Transparency in the Edwards Personal Preference Schedule," *Journal of Consulting Psychology,* August, 1962.
22. Robert E. Krug, "Over- and Underachievement and the Edwards Personal Preference Schedule," *Journal of Applied Psychology,* April, 1959.
23. See D. C. McClelland, "Measuring Motivation in Phantasy: the Achievement Motive," in D. C. McClelland, ed., *Studies in Motivation* (New York: Appleton-Century-Crofts, 1955), pp. 401–413. McClelland is one of the leading investigators in this field of motivation.

24. See A. L. Edwards, *Manual of the Edwards Personal Preference Schedule,* (New York: The Psychological Corporation, 1953).
25. A. H. Maslow, *Motivation and Personality* (New York: Harper & Row, Publishers, Inc., 1954).
26. See Arthur H. Juriloff, "An Experiment in Management—Putting Theory Y to the Test," *Personnel,* American Management Association, Inc., November-December, 1963.
27. G. Gurin, *et al., Americans View Their Mental Health* (New York: Basic Books, Inc., 1960). See also Harry Levinson, "Industrial Mental Health," *Personnel,* American Management Association, Inc., May-June 1961, p. 39.
28. See Daniel Brower, "The Applicability of Projective Techniques to Personnel Appraisal," *Personnel Psychology*, Summer, 1955.

PROJECTS

1. Now that you have become acquainted with adjustment and some of its predisposing influences, make a list of important predisposing influences in your own development of which you are aware. Include factors such as culture, intelligence, health, physique, early childhood conditionings, needs, and work experiences. Discuss the list with a parent or friend who knows you intimately. To what extent do you agree and disagree on the factors mentioned? Are you sufficiently objective and mature in your thinking about yourself to discuss your characteristics without emotional disturbances on your part? Are you aware of any topics that are too painful for you to discuss?
2. Read some of the recent literature on the stability of the IQ. Prepare a list of all the possible factors which might result in the raising or lowering of an individual's IQ.
3. Very few persons can describe their own persistent affect fixations. The counselor must deduce them from the case history. Read the life history of a famous man or woman who described his early life in detail, particularly his home life. Can you define the persistent affect fixations in his life? How did they appear to influence his career?
4. List some of the persons who showed a genuine warmth of interest in you. How did they express it? If you feel that few persons have ever expressed a genuine interest in you, why do you suppose that you feel that way? To overcome such a feeling on your part, plan a program of action that may help you overcome your feeling.

COLLATERAL READINGS

Argyris, Chris, "Employee Apathy and Noninvolvement—The House that Management Built?" *Personnel,* American Management Association, Inc., July-August, 1961.

Gellerman, Saul W., *Motivation and Productivity,* American Management Association, Inc., New York, 1963, Chapter 16.

Guthrie, George M. and Margaret S. Mckendry, "Interest Patterns of Peace Corps Volunteers in a Teaching Project," *Journal of Educational Psychology,* 54, No. 5 (1963), 261–267.

Jones, Marshall R., ed., *Nebraska Symposium on Motivation.* Lincoln, Neb.: University of Nebraska Press, 1963.

Leavitt, Harold J. and Louis R. Pondy, eds., *Readings in Managerial Psychology.* Chicago: The University of Chicago Press, 1964, pp. 6–31 and 249–279.

Lehner, George F. J. and Ella Kube, *The Dynamics of Personal Adjustment.* Englewood Cliffs, N.J.: Prentice-Hall, Inc., 1964, Chapters 3 and 4.

Maier, Norman R. F., *Psychology in Industry.* Boston: Houghton Mifflin Company, 1955, Chapter 20.

CAN YOU IDENTIFY THE MEANINGS OF THESE FACIAL EXPRESSIONS?

Study the emotional expressions portrayed by an actress in the sixteen photographs. You will note that several depict greater or lesser intensity of the same kind of emotional state or feeling. As shown in the example, Series a, pictures numbered 20, 49 and 56 portray degrees of physical exhaustion and a state of response after exhaustion.

Now examine the remaining pictures and select three sets of three that depict three degrees of a different emotion or state and designate the emotion or the kind of situation to which the actress is responding:

The Pictures Numbered	***The Three Depict***
a. Example: 20, 49, and 56	*Exhaustion*
b. ____, ____, and ____	____________
c. ____, ____, and ____	____________
d. ____, ____, and ____	____________

Perhaps you will find it easier to make your selections if you select the most intensive portrayal first and then choose two pictures that show the same or a related emotion in lesser degree. For your information, four of the pictures do not fit into a related series of three—they are leftovers.

Turn to page 622 for the answers as developed in studies reported by Trygg Engen, Nissim Levy and Harold Schlosberg, "A New Series of Facial Expressions," ***American Psychologist,*** *May 1957.*

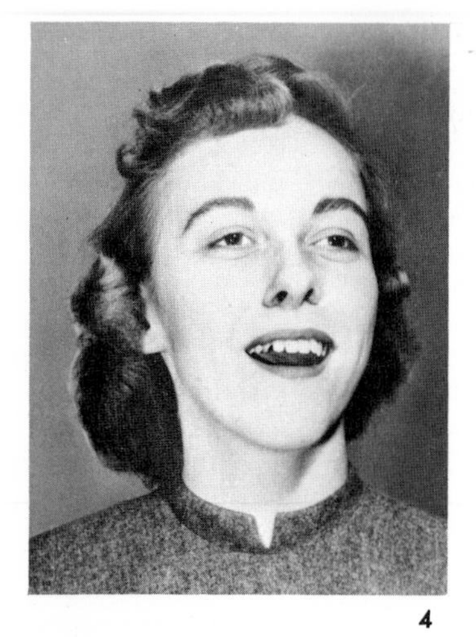

4

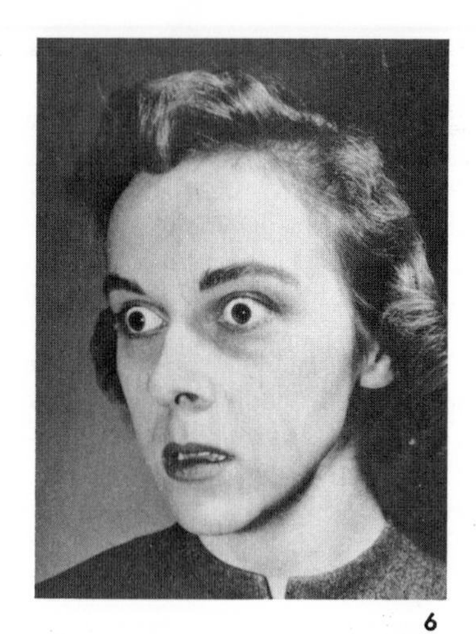

6

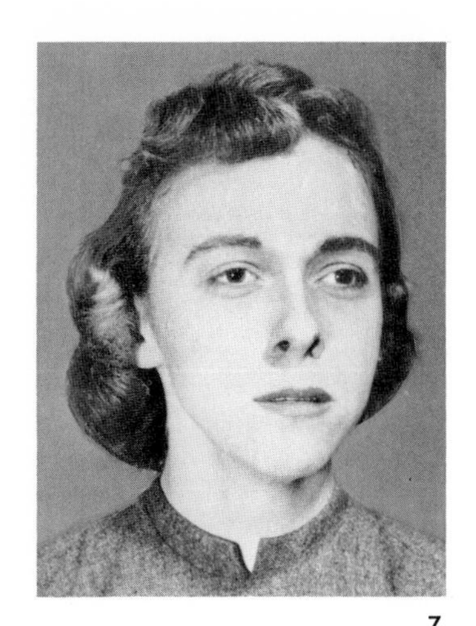

7

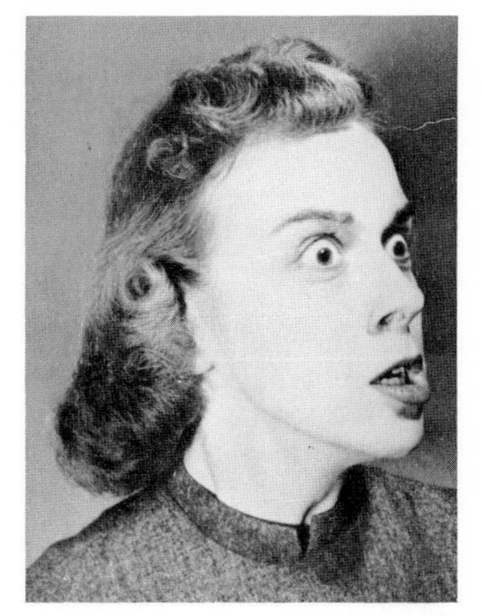

10

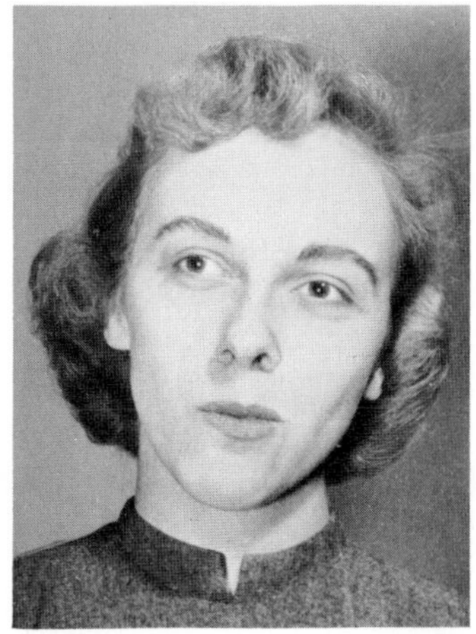

13

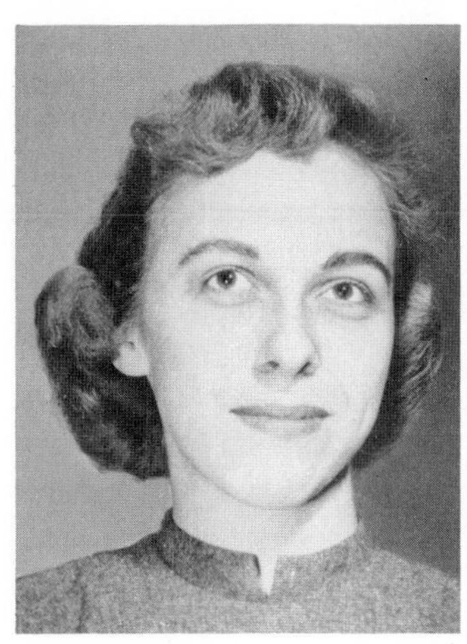

14

15

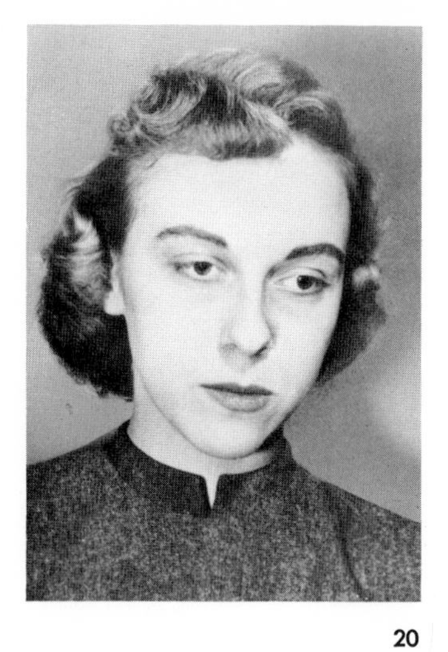

20

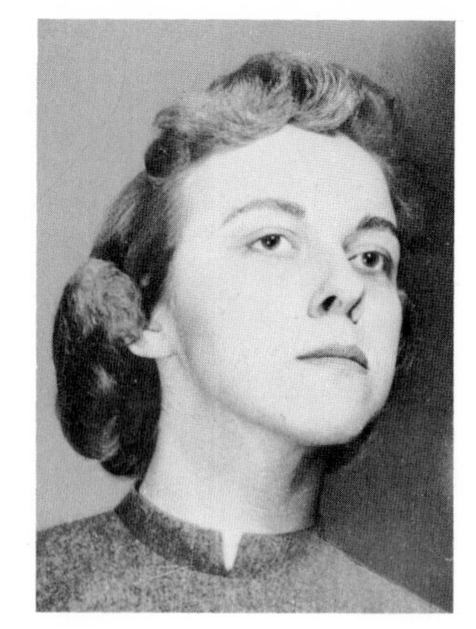

24

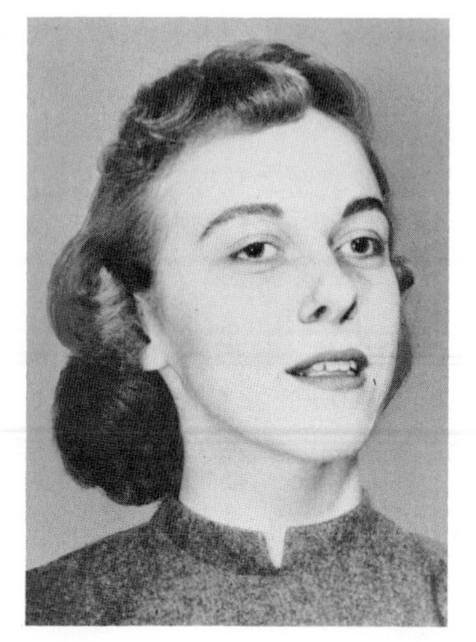

26

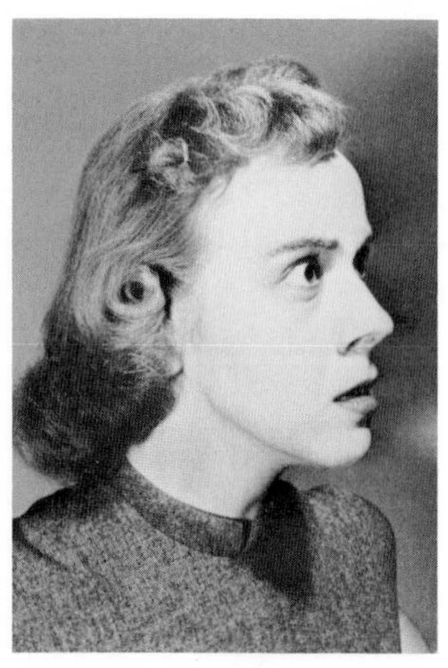

29

32

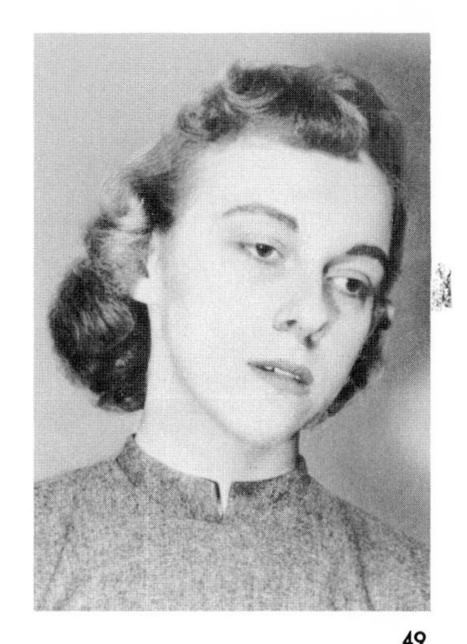

49

51

55

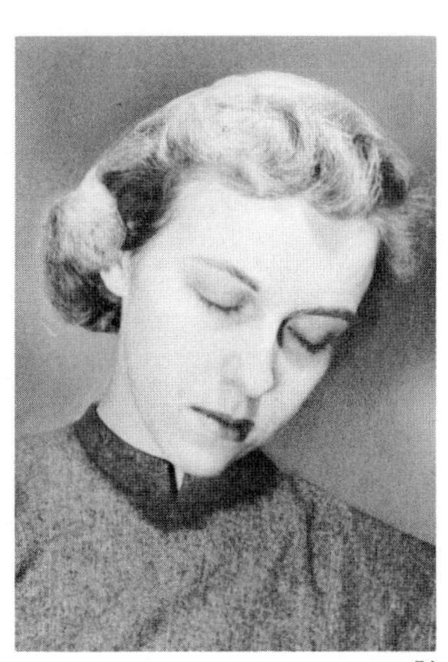

56

The National Institutes of Health, *Public Health Service, Department of Health, Education, and Welfare. Located in Bethesda, Maryland, it is one of the world's largest medical research centers.*

Psychologist in the National Institute of Mental Health *uses small figures to aid in determining the basic problems of disturbed children. By professional interpretation of the child's reaction to each manikin, a diagnosis can be made. (Simulated.)*

Family therapy, *under the direction of a psychiatrist, often gives both a person with mental problems and other members of the family an understanding of the situation which may mean a long step toward solution of the problem. Photos courtesy of National Institutes of Health.*

CHAPTER EIGHT

THE COUNSELING INTERVIEW: CRITERIA OF MENTAL HEALTH (GOOD ADJUSTMENT), PRINCIPLES, AND EXAMPLES

A great deal of counseling of individuals who have psychological problems is being done every day by people who do it as an incidental part of their work or social situation. Most do not think of themselves as professional counselors but many do need a knowledge of criteria of good adjustment and of sound principles for counseling. When objectives and procedures are right, the contributions to mental health and well-being are likely to be greater.

The extent to which ability in interviewing is needed in our modern civilization is indicated by the numbers of workers in the professions and businesses who do interviewing. It is estimated that there are about 3,000,000 persons occupying executive and supervisory positions in business and industry who spend from 50 to 90 per cent of their time in conferring with others. In addition to these, we have more than a million teachers and other school people, a half million nurses, about 200,000 physicians, slightly fewer lawyers, and a similar number of clergymen who, at times, discuss personal problems with counselees as a part of their daily work.

A report of a nation-wide poll conducted for the Joint Commission on Mental Illness and Health, set up by Congress to assess the nation's mental health status and resources, indicated that about one in four of our adults thinks he has had an emotional problem serious enough to call for professional help. One in seven sought such help. The Commission was composed of 36 organizations including the American Medical Association, the American Psychiatric Association, and the American Psychological Association. The Commission's final report to Congress, *Action for Mental Health,* was published in 1961.[1]

The data concerning the sources sought for help by those adults who obtained help gave rise to an easy-to-remember 4–3–2–1 distribution—of every 10 who sought help for their troubles, approximately 4 went to a clergyman, 3 to a family physician, 2 to a psychiatrist or psychologist, and one to a social agency or marriage clinic.

What is Good Adjustment (Mental Health)?

Most psychologists who try to define mental health and more or less interchangeable terms such as good adjustment recognize the difficulties. Here are three significant approaches to the problem.

1. To overcome some of the difficulties, they ask a number of psychologists, psychiatrists and other mental health specialists to prepare a list of characteristics on which some agreement can be obtained. Harry Levinson, as an example, in one of his studies reported that fourteen senior psychiatrists and psychologists were asked to describe people whom they had known and whom they believed to be mentally healthy. From their descriptions the following five aspects of behavior were abstracted, all characteristic of people whom the clinicians judged to be healthy:

1. *They treated others as individuals.* This means they were not only sensitive to individual differences among people, but also they were able to establish good relationships with other people despite these differences. Its opposite would be to view other people as impersonal sources of reward or punishment; to view them as if they were in fact the same as parents, relatives, or other figures from the past; or stereotypes or genotypes.
2. *They were flexible under stress.* Dealing with stress flexibly might mean, for example, to suffer the loss of a loved one with grief but not depression. Stress, as defined here, would include both internal and environmental pressures which threaten to disrupt the organized way in which a person customarily behaves.
3. *They obtained gratification from a wide variety of sources:* people, ideas, tasks, interests, values.
4. *They accepted their own capacities and limitations.* This relates to a realistic self-concept, neither overvaluing nor undervaluing one's potentialities. With such a self-concept a person is better able to make full use of the resources available to him.
5. *They were active and productive.* That is, they spontaneously and naturally used their capacities in the interest of their own self-fulfillment and in the service of others. This differed from a neurotically driven need to achieve.[2]

2. A different approach was used by a team of researchers consisting mainly of Dr. Jules Golden, Albany Medical College, Albany, N.Y.; Dr. Nathan Mandel, Director of Research, Department of Correction, State of Minnesota; Dr. Bernard C. Glueck, Jr., Director of Research, Institute of Living, Hartford, Conn. They dealt with the problem by selecting normal persons for study. They

located 73 members of an original group of 1,953 schoolboys who 12 years earlier had shown no psychopathology on the basis of the administration of the *Minnesota Multiphasic Personalty Inventory* (MMPI), a kind of self-description questionnaire.

These 73 gave no indication of significant pathology at the time of examination, age approximately 14. Of the original 73, the number who were available for study 12 years later was 50. Additional tests and ratings were administered and each subject was given a 1½ hour unstructured interview in which current adjustment, description of home origin, personal history, aspirations, and mental status were appraised.

Occupationally and educationally they were an above average group: 11 men were in professional or semi-professional technical work, 2 were in executive positions, 12 were clerical, sales, or other white collar workers, 13 were craftsmen, skilled workers or foremen, and 12 were operatives and semi-skilled workers. None was in the unskilled, laboring, service, or domestic categories. All of the men had completed high school, 15 had some college education, and 7 had postgraduate education.

The researchers reported findings that led to certain striking conclusions, some of which were the following:

The marked vocational and residential stability which is characteristic of this group, and the general lack of significant psychopathology, may perhaps be achieved at the price of a more creative, spontaneous type of personality organization. These men were found to have little imagination, and generally limited interests and social activities. They indicate limited educational and vocational aspirations for themselves, and also for their children. This was reflected in the ratings given on various subitems of the psychiatric interviews, with richness of personality and breadth of interests and pleasures being the 2 lowest ratings of the 15 descriptive categories. Contentment with spouse and compatibility with spouse were the two highest ratings, with enjoyment of occupation, and contentment with vocational position also being very high on the list.

All of the above raises in our minds a question which has been stated in a number of different ways in the past concerning the balance between the needs and the wants of individuals on the one hand—in this group apparently very much in the balance—and the various factors that have been considered to be part of the richer, more creative, spontaneous type of personality. Does "normality," as evidenced by lack of intrapsychic tension, adequate social, economic and familial adaptation, and harmonious integration with other individuals at all levels, necessarily imply a lack of creativity, imagination, and spontaneity? Our data are suggestive of this conclusion.[3]

In general, we have to conclude that the highly "normal" man is rather unremarkable, perhaps "dull" is more descriptive.[4] He leads a stable, well-adjusted life, in harmonious integration with other individuals but also without evident creativity, imagination or spontaneity.

3. An especially illuminating study was made of university graduate students concerning the excellence of their psychological functioning, *their soundness as persons.*

Frank Barron, in collaboration with psychologists and psychiatrists at the Institute of Personality Assessment and Research, University of California, Berkeley, utilized the judgments of professors about the relative soundness of some 80 advanced graduate students, all males. The research staff took as the measure of its central criterion variables *the social consensus,* or the averaged judgments of a number of nonpsychologists concerning the manifestations of various kinds of excellences.

These 80 subjects were studied in groups of 10 over a period of some six months. Each group of 10 subjects spent from Friday afternoon to Sunday afternoon at the assessment house, sleeping there and taking all meals there. The assessment day ran from 8 a.m. to 12 p.m. The assessors, like the subjects, made their home at the Institute during the three days of study. The distinctive feature of "living-in" assessment as a method of psychological research is that it provides a great variety of informal social interaction, in which the assessor is recognized to be in the role of participant observer.

...observations were made and facts ascertained by the assessment staff during social interactions, including interviews, group discussions, improvisation, charades, a group competition in city planning, and several group problems, in addition to the sort of informal social interaction which took place at meals, during intermissions between procedures, and during the evenings after the conclusion of the day's work.

Much of the data of assessment consisted of test scores. Staff impressions based upon total observation of the subject in the assessment period were summarized chiefly in two ways: in the form of ratings on a set of 37 personality variables, and by use of an adjective check list containing some 280 common, personally descriptive adjectives.

Several case histories and extensive quantitative data have been reported but the main findings from this study concerning *soundness as a person* have been stated at the end of a chapter:

> The conclusion to which the assessment staff has come is that psychopathology is always with us, and that soundness is *a way of reacting to problems, not an absence of them.* The transformation of pathological trends into distinctive character assets and the minimization of their effects through compensatory overdevelopment of other traits are both marks of "sound" reaction to personal difficulties. At times, indeed, the handling of psychopathology may be so skillful and the masking of pathological motivations so subtle that the individual's soundness may be considerably overrated. There is no doubt that some of our apparently "balanced" subjects were balanced quite precariously, and that their stability was more semblance than fact. It is possible to mistake for soundness what is actually rigidity based on a sort of paralysis of affect engendered by a fear of instinctual drives. These cases of pseudo-soundness were probably few, however. . . .
>
> The existence of psychopathology in even the quite sound individuals has been emphasized here partly by way of counteracting the sort of trite determinism with which so many clinical studies seem to conclude: broken homes leading to delinquency; psychosis in the parents being passed on, through whatever mechanism, to the offspring; unloving mothers rearing hateful children; catastrophe breeding catastrophe. Undoubtedly such correlations exist in nature, and they were, indeed, found in our own investigation; but considerable variance remains unaccounted for. What we should like to suggest here is that within the population of subjects of ordinary physical and psychological integrity, soundness is by no means exclusively determined by circumstances but may be considered in the nature of an unintended—and perhaps largely unconscious—personal achievement. Our High Soundness subjects are beset, like all other persons, by fears, unrealizable desires, self-condemned hates, and tensions difficult to resolve. They are *sound* largely because they bear with their anxieties, hew to a stable course, and maintain some sense of the ultimate worthwhileness of their lives.[5]

To reiterate for the sake of emphasis, psychopathology is always with us and soundness is *a way of reacting to problems, not an absence of them.* "High Soundness subjects are beset, like all other persons, by fears, unrealizable desires, self-condemned hates, and tensions difficult to resolve; they are *sound* largely because they bear with their anxieties, hew to a stable course, and maintain some sense of the ultimate worthwhileness of their lives."

The truly "normal person" exhibits adjustment patterns over an extremely wide range.[6] He has problems and makes inadequate adjustments but he has developed patterns in a life-style that enable him to live comfortably with himself and effectively with others. He leads an interesting life.

The conclusions from these and related researches put a new emphasis on the meaning of mental health. Formerly, many individuals assumed that they should have as a major psychological objective for themselves the attainment of absolute maturity—a life style that consisted only of intelligent direct approach adjustments to all problems. Such an objective is not realistic—even the saints had their moments of failures. This conclusion does not, however, allow us to be satisfied or pleased with ourselves when we fail merely because we fail. Psychological strength is a never-ending quest as the poet, Robert Browning, aptly stated:

> "Ah, but a man's reach should exceed his grasp
> Or what's a heaven for?"
>
> and
>
> "When the fight begins within himself,
> A man's worth something."

One important characteristic is that the intelligently well-adjusted person notes the adjustments made by others and objectifies them. He is not overwhelmed by the poor and bad adjustments of the inadequately adjusted. In popular parlance: Cussed people do not bother him—rather, they stimulate him to note their difficult behavior and to treat them intelligently. He usually rises above their maladjustments in so far as they involve him. And he treats them in a kindly sincere spirit. This is a mark of the truly great personality. Few of us ever attain this level of good adjustment but we strive for it.

Limitations and Benefits of Insight

Many psychotherapists have assumed that when a client gained insight into the origin of the inadequate adjustments or neurotic tactics that continually defeat him, he would discontinue the inappropriate behavior and adopt more intelligent and effective forms of behavior. Actually, insight often fails to bring about changes in behavior. Nicholas Hobbs has called attention to and discussed some of the factors involved in this kind of failure:

> A child suffers more than he can tolerate at the hands of his father. The concrete experiences get associated with specific symbols that are a product of this unique relationship and its attending circumstances. As an adult, even after his father has long been dead, experiences with authority figures evoke the symbols which evoke anxiety, guilt, hostility, or perhaps headaches, nausea, or other somatic reactions. Because of the distress that has been aroused, he retreats either literally or psychologically from the situation. His distress diminishes, thus reinforcing the avoidance of the authority relationship, and leaving the symbols as strong as ever. But authority cannot be avoided, and the cycle gets repeated over and over again. The crucial thing to note is that he never has an opportunity to learn new and more appropriate responses to the symbols that are evoking in him what we call neurotic behavior. The conditioned response cannot get extinguished.
>
> The task of the therapist is not to help the client gain insight into the fact that he has trouble with authority figures because of his unfortunate experiences with his own father. This is far too abstract a formulation to be of help. He has got to be helped to identify and use comfortably the specific symbols that are elicited in him by authority figures. The symbols must be divested of their anxiety-producing potential.[7]

Hobbs has emphasized the importance of influences such as providing and encouraging specific and concrete opportunities for learning new ways of reacting to troublesome situations, new ways of relating to other people, and new ways of perceiving oneself. The client must be stimulated to utilize more effectively the normal sources of therapeutic gain in daily living.

Counselors who lack adequate training should not try to play amateur diagnostician or therapist by interpreting deep unconscious meanings. To do so, may set in motion forces that disturb the established life style and result in reactions that cannot be controlled or redirected. Physicians, clergymen, and social workers usually have had some training in understanding emotional problems but they should usually attempt diagnosis and therapy only under direction of a psychiatrist or experienced clinical psychologist.

In most counseling, therefore, we do not attempt deep therapy but try to redirect the established behavioral tendencies and patterns. We do not try to remake a man. To attempt to do so would be an attempt to bring about a psychological rebirth. We begin to appreciate what William James, the psychologist-philosopher stated:

> Man's chief difference from the brutes lies in the exuberant excess of his subjective propensities. Prune his extravagance, sober him, and you undo him.

We begin to appreciate the benefits that are gained from letting the individual deal with his problems, suggesting positive value adjustments to him, and by providing everyday opportunities for growth and strength. Terms such as "stress," "tension," and "pressure" become contributory factors in attaining positive aspects of living. The human body and mind was designed to be used—not to be relegated to a vacuous placidity. As has been said: "The 'wounds of combat' are preferable to the decay of idleness." Enjoyable struggle is more beneficial than the avoidance of stress. Good adjustment emphasizes the quest for excellence in human functioning in everyday situations. Improvements in behavior take place mainly as the individual himself practices new ways of behaving.

One of the tests of mental health that is often helpful to an individual is the question as to what he does in his idle moments. If his mind turns invariably to the negative value thoughts, he is not likely to be healthy. On the other hand, if his thinking is directed toward the constructive, the creative, the giving of himself in service, he is likely to be a happy, healthy man. One man who when he tried to fall asleep at night found himself dwelling on the evil in others and their shortcomings consulted a counselor who helped him develop a rule for himself to turn on the light, get up, and list the tactful, friendly things he might do in order to improve relations between himself and the despised person of his thinking. He still has some negative thoughts but he has learned to control and direct them into effective channels. He has redirected negative value tendencies.

The counselor who deals with an individual who is experiencing a sense of guilt or failure can encourage the use of desirable modes of attack instead of the mechanisms of rationalization, projection, or withdrawal. Guilt should be redirected toward honesty. Emotional dullness or personal failure should lead one to attain new and more intelligent emotional satisfactions.

Fortunately, most everyday problems in human relations are solved by the persons involved. Relatively few supervisors or employees need the services of the clinical psychologist. However, the trained personnel counselor should be able to assist and positively develop many persons who are sources of irritation in an organization for years before they grow to the point of needing to be institutionalized or die. It is important for us to realize that any psychological insight and skill acquired by executives, supervisors, and personnel men will be valuable in dealing with the employees who need counseling.

Types of Interviews

When we consider all kinds of interviews that may or may not involve counseling, many are simple and do not require any special psychological skill or insight. Others are complex and require a high level of professional training. When counseling interviews are classified in relation to the kind of individual problem involved, they are likely to fall into the four varieties: *information, judgment, skill,* and *adjustment.* For example, some persons, who come to the counselor may need or seek a knowledge of facts. Such interviews are relatively simple to conduct. Other persons have all the facts they need but have difficulty in making a satisfactory judgment or decision about the facts. An example would be an employee who asks the personnel man whether it would be advisable for him to buy a home.

In some cases, the interviewee has the essential facts and has reached a decision but feels that he lacks skill in putting the decision into effect. An example would be the employee who knows that he merits an increase in pay and has decided to ask for it but lacks skill in presenting his request. Again, many supervisors, although they know how they should treat employees, lack skill in dealing with them effectively. Roleplaying may be helpful to them.

Adjustment problems are of course rather deep-seated in the personality structure and require considerable insight on the part of the interviewer. Counselors who deal with the more common adjustment problems such as those exemplified in vocational guidance, marriage counseling, discipline of the errant employee in industry, merit rating review of the employee, and other interviews that involve an understanding of the dynamics of behavior know that a knowledge of the fundamental principles in interviewing is essential.

One of the interviewer's major needs is a basic conceptual pattern of thinking that gives meaning to his observations and judgments concerning the counselee's behavior. The specific conceptual pattern recommended, that of adjustment, has been discussed in preceding chapters. In this chapter, we shall give further attention to the counseling interview.

When the Interviewee Initiates the Interview

The principles of the counseling interview vary somewhat with the type of interview and the extent to which the counselee seeks and needs the interview. In the personnel offices of industry, counseling interviews are of two broad classes: those conducted at the initiative of the counselee and those conducted at the initiative of the counselor. The former type is exemplified by the employee who comes to the personnel man and says that he would like to be transferred to another job, to arrange for a loan, to discuss a health problem, to ask the personnel man's advice in regard to chances for a promotion, or some other personal matter of direct or indirect importance to the employer. The latter type of interview, the counselor-initiated variety in industry, is exemplified by a disciplinary problem, as in the case of the employee who has violated a safety rule, the annual review of the employee's merit ratings, or an interview with a labor union steward concerning a union member's conduct. In this discussion, we shall treat chiefly the counselee-initiated type of interview, because it often calls for a knowledge of psychological dynamics. The counselee seeks help and, to some extent, is usually anxious to coöperate in the solution of his problem.

Although there are two principal methods of counseling, *directive* and *nondirective,* a vast number of adaptations of these methods can be made at the discretion of the counselor. It is his responsibility to employ as much or as little direction as he believes will be beneficial to a particular client. Even though some counselors use mainly one method of counseling, they adapt their technique to each situation. Neither method nor technique is peculiar to any one type of problem. Both main types are used today in business organizations,[8] psychological clinics, marriage clinics, and in vocational guidance.

Directive counseling is the older method. It assumes the counselor to be wise and understanding enough to control the interview from the time the client presents himself. The counselor takes the initiative throughout, asks leading questions, interprets the interviewee's answers and reactions to him, and offers advice or actual instructions for the solution of the problem.

Nondirective counseling as in psychotherapy, on the other hand, is interviewee- or client-centered. In psychotherapy, the therapist is not authoritarian in any respect. His function is not to interpret the interviewee's problem to him or to offer advice for the solution of the problem, but to create an atmosphere in which the client may talk through his difficulties and thereby get sufficient insight into his problems so that he may solve them for himself. To this end, good rapport and a permissive atmosphere are essential. Because the client has done the work of ascertaining the cause of his difficulties and has decided upon his own solution, it is claimed that he is far more likely to carry his self-chosen behavior through to a successful conclusion than under the older method.

The goal of nondirective counseling differs from that of directive in that it aims toward the greater independence and integration of the individual rather than hopes that such qualities will accrue if the counselor assists in solving the problem. The personality development of the individual and not the problem is the focus. The aim is not to solve one particular problem, but to assist the individual to *grow,* so that he can cope with the current problem and with later problems in a better-integrated fashion.[9]

One outstanding characteristic of the nondirective interview is the manner in which the counselor responds to feeling. He accepts without surprise or disapproval anything that the client tells him and replies noncommittally to the feeling behind the words in order to encourage the client to explore his problem more deeply. Often the reply is limited to "M-hm," or "Yes." Often it is simply a rewording of the idea which the client has expressed.

Ideally this effects a crystallization of that specific facet of the problem in the client's mind, and after clarification of the various phases, self-understanding is ultimately attained.

"Effective counseling consists of a definitely structured, permissive relationship which allows the client to gain an understanding of himself to a degree which enables him to take positive steps in the light of his new orientation." The interview technique developed by Rogers and his students for bringing about such relationships, is most often described as "nondirective" for the reason that authoritarian and persuasive approaches have been discarded, and because no satisfactory positive designation has yet been found to express in a word what the counselor does and what the client experiences. In using the term, therefore, it is important to recognize its descriptive limitations and to emphasize that this counseling procedure implies more than passive listening and mere "not directing." Rogers defines the therapist's function as "not to pass judgment, but to clarify and objectify the client's basic attitudes." In order to do this, the counselor must work toward the skills involved in understanding what the client has tried to express, in verbal restatement or "recognition" of feeling in terms which the client can and will accept; and in control of the counselor's own impulse toward suggestion and premature interpretation. Even more fundamental is acceptance by the counselor of the client's right to self-determination, and belief in his capacity for constructive choice on the basis of insight rather than guidance.[10]

The wide acceptance by psychologists of nondirective interviewing, particularly in psychotherapy, as developed by Carl R. Rogers, is indicated by many books and articles published about the technique and its underlying principles.

The ultimate aim of these "parallel studies" is to contribute toward the establishment of psychotherapy on a scientific basis. The investigators at the Counseling Center of the University of Chicago have sought to achieve this goal by formulating specific concepts of personality dynamics so that these concepts may be recognized and measured as to the degree of their presence as revealed in the interviews. Some of these concepts, for example, are self-regarding attitudes, acceptance of and respect for self, understanding and insight, maturity of behavior, and defensive-

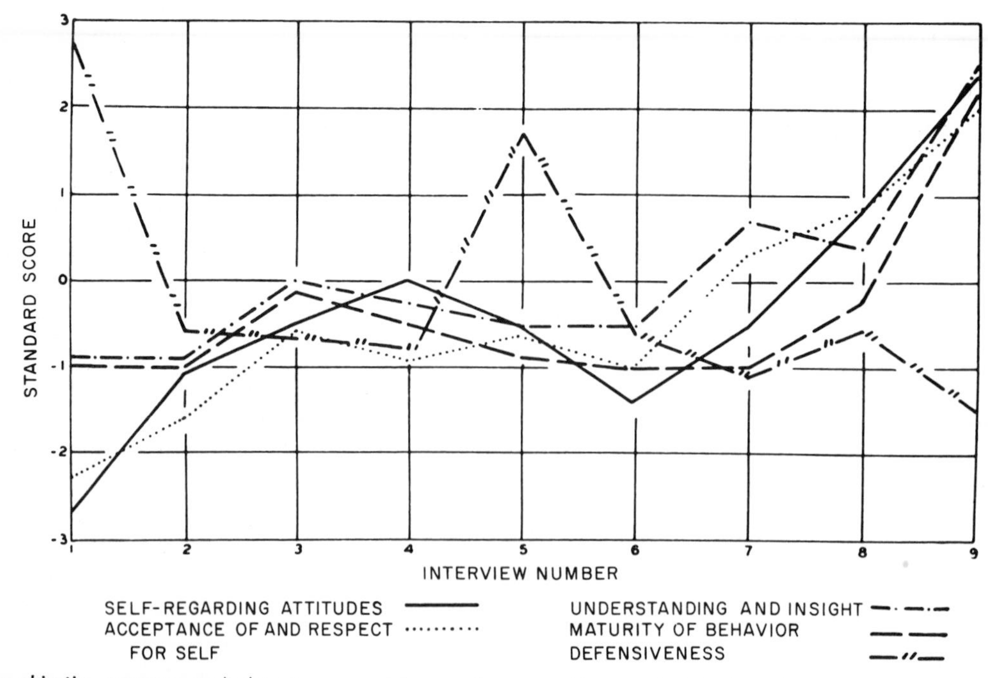

Five objective measures *applied to one successful counseling case. Note particularly how the curve for defensiveness declined as the curves for self-regarding attitudes and for acceptance of and respect for self improved.—From Nathaniel J. Raskin, "An Objective Approach to the Study of Psychotherapy,"* ***American Scientist,*** *Vol. 37, No. 3 (July 1949), pp. 410-413.*

ness. An individual is rated at each interview on all of these five aspects of his personality. Thus personality changes in the series of interviews are more scientifically detected and measured; exact comparisons of the individual's reactions are made possible. Therapists, by employing the findings of these studies, will be able to control and evaluate more closely the progress of the individual through the psychotherapeutic process of counseling. Most important, the nature of successful psychotherapy can be more specifically and exactly defined.[11]

A diagram of five objective measures applied to one successful counseling case is shown in the figure on page 164. The diagram shows that, at the beginning of therapy, defensiveness was great and acceptance of and respect for self was low, and that, at the end of the therapeutic sessions, acceptance of and respect for self had increased and defensiveness had diminished. Apparently as acceptance of and respect for self increases, there is less need for defensive behavior patterns.[12]

The researchers have quantified many aspects of the counseling interview never before analyzed in statistical terms. One study by Elizabeth T. Sheerer, for example, dealt with certain relations between the individual's concept of himself and his feeling toward others.

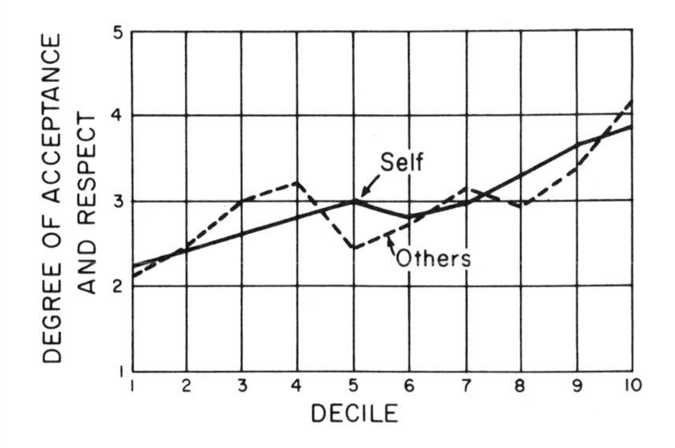

***The relationship between** the mean ratings on the "self" scale and on the "others" scale for ten cases combined. —From Elizabeth T. Sheerer, "The Relationship Between Acceptance of Self and Acceptance of Others," **Journal of Consulting Psychology,** American Psychological Association, Inc., Vol. 13, No. 3 (June 1945), pp. 174-175. Copyright, 1949, by the American Psychological Association, Inc.*

Miss Sheerer found that when the individual's statements about himself were rated on a five-point scale, the average for the first interview was 2.2. The statements about other people rated 2.6. In the last interview the statement on self rated 3.9 while those statements reflecting on others had gone up to 3.8.

It was found to be possible to improve acceptance of and respect for the self by psychological treatment. There was also a closer relation between regard for self and regard for others after the finish of the treatment period.

Some of the implications of Miss Sheerer's findings were stated as follows:

> The findings of this study appear to have implications that are at once commonplace and startling. The central conclusion is that one's attitudes toward others are related, to a decidedly significant degree, to the attitudes one holds towards one's self. In one sense, this is common knowledge. If we are to take it seriously, however, it might mean that change in attitudes of acceptance toward others can come about basically only through change in attitudes toward self. If we apply this to some of the problems of social psychology, it might mean that increased acceptance of minority groups, foreigners, and the like, could best be achieved by some type of group therapy which would tend to alter the individual's acceptance of and respect for himself. It might mean that in situations of industrial tension, or professional friction, the most effective means of approach would be through dealing with the attitudes of the person toward himself, rather than devoting our energies to the expressions of, and descriptions of, the external "causes" of the tension.
>
> In any event the two central facts which emerge from this study promise to have considerable significance for social psychology as well as for our understanding of personality. That the individual's evaluation of himself and his worth as a person, can be significantly altered by the therapeutic process initiated by client-centered therapy is one of these facts; the other is that the individual's evaluation of others—the degree of acceptance and respect he feels for them—is significantly related to his attitude toward himself.[13]

Successful nondirective therapy demands that the client have intelligence above the borderline level, and that he be dissatisfied with his current adjustment.[14] Intelligence is necessary for the development of insight, a prerequisite to a better adjustment, and a certain amount of distress is necessary to impel the client to work earnestly for a better adjustment. Neurotic persons who have adjusted to their symptoms are poor prospects for improvements; and psychotics, because they are out of touch with reality, cannot be treated by this method. Most executives do not have the time or the training to use nondirective techniques, but many would benefit from a study of them.

Typical of sound nondirective counseling is the following excerpt from an actual case phonographically recorded and quoted in Rogers, *Counseling and Psychotherapy:*

S263. I find myself reacting quite strongly to the war situation. I have this very definite feeling—that if I were to be involved, that is, inducted into the army—

C263. M-hm.

S264. I feel it would not only be catastrophic to me in my present condition, but even if I were to have a cure in the meanwhile—my healthy ideals have always been that of—well, an abhorrence of regimentation, and I feel a love of individual initiative and private enterprise—that sort of thing, which seems to make a war situation very much intolerable to me. I had thought I would not be called (gives his reasons), but now I think I might be called, so it's had a very disturbing effect on me.

C264. You feel that would be just more than you could take.

S265. Even if I were up to my psychological ideal, I would find that such a life would be absolutely against my grain—the way I've been raised—the ideals that I've been taught to hold to, and the individual way of life that I have always pursued myself. (Pause.) So I'm reacting very much to that situation.

C265. M-hm. You've found it quite upsetting to you?[15]

An Example of Counseling by an Executive Who Thinks in Terms of Adjustment

The personnel man or executive who has the adjustment point of view regarding the problem employee thinks of him as an employee with a problem. The psychologically sensitive executive does not usually lecture employees on their adjustments. He does not, as a rule, use any psychological jargon in dealing with them. He is likely to use a directive rather than the time-consuming nondirective technique. Occasionally, however, the trained executive may explain the adjustment idea to an exceptionally intelligent employee, such as a dissatisfied college graduate who needs counseling. Some of the principles set forth in preceding chapters are illustrated in the example shown on pages 170–174, typical of the college-educated employee who has a problem in adjustment and is being counseled by a trained personnel man.

A procedure such as this can be used successfully only by a high-grade executive who can explain mental habits and adjustments in an intelligent and sincere manner. He must be able to phrase his analyses in ways that the employee will understand and respect.

One important objective to be kept in mind by the executive is that his attempts to motivate the employee must be economically as well as psychologically sound. This means that the executive's function is not that of apologizing for the economic system, whatever it is, but to give the employee a sense of participation in the evolving economic scheme. Toward this end, the executive may point out unsolved problems of industry which the dissatisfied intelligent employee can help solve by his own direct attack adjustments involved in his own job.

The Counselor-initiated Interview

The disciplinary interview. The executive who has just cause for severely criticizing a subordinate often uses the old-fashioned method of threatening to discharge the man. However, the threat of discharge is not nearly so severe as some of the dramatic methods that are used by executives who have the knack of disciplining men. These experts in chastising men use dramatic situations, such as calling the errant employee into the boss's office and having him sit in the executive's chair. Then the executive plays the part of the employee who is to be disciplined. He makes a full confession, wherein he presents all the facts in the offense and asks the acting chief to make a decision and recommend the justified punishment or discipline. Such methods are forceful, but they do not strengthen the personality as in the counseling interview.

The counseling interview is often used in disciplinary problems, as illustrated in the sample problem on pages 175–177.*

Such a procedure requires an executive who tries to build employees by allowing them to build themselves. He must be normal in his adjustments, since the poorly adjusted executive will try to impress the errant employee with his authority—that is, he will make the employee feel inferior rather than a colleague of his. The educator type executive does not care to punish employees—he wants to enable them to use present situations to strengthen their personalities in order that they may be able to meet future problems more adequately. American businessmen are just beginning to study and practice skills in dealing with employees by methods that are more subtle than the older method of threat of discharge. Psychological approaches are more effective than force.

The counseling interviewer sees human beings in terms of their ongoing activities and emotions. He has a dynamic concept of people. He visualizes them as making adjustments to their changing environments. He notes their resultant attitudes, emotions, drives, habits, and general behavior patterns. In his study of counselees, he sets up working hypotheses as to relationships between current behavior and past events. He checks these for himself by further questioning in the hope that the persons counseled will themselves discover the ways in which they have been dealing with their adjustive situations.

He tries to discover the factors that have influenced them in the past, and how their present ongoing activities may be directed into new channels that will give them a richer self-expression which will be of value to the group as well as to themselves. He does not want to remake human beings—he tries to help them to utilize their present tendencies for positive adjustment to life's problems.

Principles That Often Apply to the Counseling Interview

1. First of all, the specific problem volunteered by a counselee may be only a small part of the actual problem. Some interviewees find it very difficult to present their own problems, even though they seek an interview for that purpose. Complete frankness is often potentially embarrassing. The employee who calls on a personnel man to ask for a transfer to another job may like his present work, but he may dislike his supervisor or a fellow employee. To state the nature of his actual dislike might not be tactful. Similarly, the man who realizes that his poor health is partially caused by or related to his inability to live happily with his neurotic mother does not, as a rule, begin the interview with a statement to that effect. Such admissions are too painful to be handled in a casual manner. The good interviewer will sense such withholdings of facts and open an easy way for a gradual revealing of the significant facts. Sometimes the counselor can sense the counselee's unvoiced questions and discuss them without actually mentioning them.

2. The counselee's willingness to express his thoughts is influenced by the extent of his confidence in the counselor. Many counselees test the counselor by asking him questions the answers to which are not applicable to his immediate problem, but indicate to him the extent to which the counselor might be able to answer his personal question. Every counselor, when a counselee first appears for an

* The conversation presented in this example of the interview for motivation may sound unnatural to some readers. However, as previously stated, each interviewer must use techniques that are spontaneous. In real life, this example is not so unreal as it may sound.

interview, tends to get into the habit of asking himself: "What does this person think of me as a counselor?" "Does he have confidence in my ability to understand his problem and to view him objectively?" "Does he believe that I will keep his confidences?" "Is it easy for him to talk to me?" and similar questions. The wise counselor constantly seeks improvement of his techniques of establishing rapport with the counselee.

3. The outward manner and facial expression of the counselor should be friendly and relaxed. The counselor who has the art of getting repressed people to talk about personal matters has a rested, unhurried manner. He does not show surprise or shock at anything the counselee says or discloses. He evaluates most unpleasant facts objectively without any demonstration of annoyance or disgust. He sits in a relaxed manner and gives the impression that he has nothing to do other than to listen to the counselee. This relaxed manner during the interview also prepares the way for the counselor to end the interview whenever he desires. When he changes from a relaxed to a tense busy manner, the counselee usually realizes that the interview is over.

Some counselors improve their interviewing techniques by means of motion-picture studies of themselves in an actual or simulated interview. Every interviewer who sees and hears sound motion pictures of himself in action is certain to see how he can improve his techniques.

4. The trained counselor uses diagnostic instruments, such as psychological tests. He does not use them, however, in the mechanical manner of the psychometrician, whose use of tests is limited to the selection of applicants for jobs. Rather, he thinks of tests as opportunities to observe the counselee in a sample work situation—to note his grasp of instructions and his reaction to failure or success. The testee's scores are viewed as clues to possible strong points. Furthermore, demonstrations of the counselee's ability in action are more conclusive than mere test indications. Test findings are interpreted in relation to the individual's total situation.

5. During a counseling interview, the counselor listens for recurrent ideas, themes, or repeated statements in the counselee's conversation. Questions which the counselor asks himself are the following: Does the subject resent persons of authority, of higher education, of the opposite sex, or some other class of persons or institutions? What kinds of inadequacy or self-depreciation does he mention with strong emotionality? What topics, apparently incidental to the main problem, are repeated so often that, though apparently incidental, they obviously have a bearing on the crucial problem?

6. The aggressive counselee who has a disagreeable manner indicates that he has a problem which has advanced beyond his control. If he berates the counselor or ridicules his profession or business, the counselor should maintain his poise and look for the counselee's unexpressed problem. The counselor need not bother to defend himself if he has learned how to use a soft answer to turn away wrath.

The counselor does not blame the counselee for his past actions or present difficult situation. If the counselee is at fault, he should discover it for himself or be led to make the discovery. A good interviewer believes that all people have the right to make mistakes and that psychological growth often takes place most rapidly when we recognize and deal constructively with our own mistakes.

7. The counselor does not try to remake the personality of the counselee. To the counselor, most persons are pretty good as they are. Some persons, of course, can redirect into more effective channels their established tendencies, but the life style is so firmly established that a remaking of the fundamental personality pattern is impractical and usually undesirable. The advisee usually needs encouragement rather than criticism. The good counselor puts the emphasis on the counselee's strong points rather than his weaknesses.

8. The advisee needs a plan of action more than a mere review of what happened. The review of what happened is often a necessary step in the development of a plan of action, but a plan of action for the future is usually the main objective in the counselee's thinking.

9. Whatever plan of action is developed, the counselee should feel that it is *his* plan. If the counselor develops the plan for the counselee, it is too easy for the counselee to lean on the counselor for the execution of the plan.

A counselee will often cooperate very well in developing a plan but cooperation and acceptance do not insure that it will be put into effect. Putting a plan into action often arouses doubt, fear, and conflict. A plan usually requires changes in the life style of the counselee and he cannot easily put them into effect even though he wishes to do so. To aid the advisee who shies away from putting his own chosen plan into effect, the counselor can concentrate on analyzing the counselee's resistance and the reasons for it. Then, when the counselee can understand the reasons behind his resistance, he is better able to overcome his reluctance.

10. The counselor must be straightforward in his statements, avoid cleverness, subtlety, shrewd guesses, and astute hints. If the counselor wants to make a statement or communicate an idea, he should state it tactfully but clearly. The poor counselor often offers half-ideas in the form of subtle hints which are supposed to occur to the counselee after he has left the counselor. Good interviewers leave an effect of straightforward honesty. The counselee feels that he understands exactly what the counselor meant to tell him.

11. If the counseling is effective, a strong emotional relationship often develops between the counselee and the counselor. The counselor should be careful to avoid giving the impression that he has personally gained some special advantage over the counselee. Rather, the counselor should stress the idea that the counselee has really solved his own problem and that the counselor functioned as a convenient agent—not as an authority who developed the answer for the counselee. When the counselor and the counselee meet socially, after the counseling relation has passed, the counselor should respond in a friendly but matter-of-fact manner. Certainly, there should be nothing in the counselor's manner that suggests, "What I know about you!" or, "Why don't you act the way normal people do?"

If the counselor is also the employee's supervisor, the emotional tie developed should be that of the normal variety in which the two men identify themselves with each other. The employee should feel that his supervisor is a leader who believes in him and trusts him.

12. The good counseling interviewer makes frequent reviews mentally of the effectiveness of his techniques. At the end of the interview he asks himself questions such as the following:

a. Did I put the counselee at ease and enable him to talk freely?

b. Did I see his problem and his situation from his standpoint?

c. Did I find out his defenses, rationalizations, opinions, and attitudes?

d. Did I learn the various steps in the history or development of his problem and how his present situation became a natural one under the conditions involved?

e. Did I enable him to see his situation in its psychological settings, so that he now feels that he is in better control of himself in relation to his problem situation? Does he feel that he can make a better adjustment to his problem because he understands it more clearly?

f. Did I help him develop a plan of action which he recognizes as essentially his own plan?

The counselor has no formulas. He cannot instill self-acceptance, identity, humor, or drive but he can *encourage* self-acceptance, insight, and new purposes. He can provide a supportive, constructive atmosphere and new perspectives, keeping in mind always that the individual has the right to freedom of choice. He can also encourage a sense of responsibility in the advisee for his own behavior.

The counselor encourages the processes that favor normal psychological growth. This kind of encouragement is also a function of parents, teachers, and clergymen. The psychologically trained counselor differs from most other counselors in his ability to interpret to himself more clearly the problem person's behavior in terms of defensive styles of life.

It has been said that every person sees things not as *they* are but as *he* is. Numerous psychologists have recommended that the counselor who wants to find out why an advisee is rigid, angry and hostile toward life, should seek the answer by helping him to find out what he thinks of himself. The counselee usually needs help in defining himself in order that he can be encouraged to develop new behavior patterns. If the advisee's defenses have been firmly established, a lengthy process of re-education may be needed in order to help him develop a new selfhood for himself. A person is not likely to adopt a suggested new behavioral pattern unless he first develops a new concept of himself as a person.

Similarly, the typical student who hopes to do constructive counseling in his vocation also needs some new concepts of himself. The student of our contemporary academic world is likely to have his analytical abilities improved by the intellectual influences around him. However, he is not likely to have the warmth of his personality improved by the classroom environment. To be effective in counseling the warmth as well as the analytical aspects of his interpersonal skills must be developed.

JOHN MILTON

John Milton graduated from college two years ago. After commencement he worked at several odd jobs for a year and then took a job as operator of a semiautomatic machine in the Burr Gear Company. He is the only college man in his department; most of the other men are illiterate. His production has been erratic, some months slightly above average, other months considerably below. He is paid on a piece-rate basis. He apparently dislikes his work, since he is absent frequently and seems to criticize the company and the industry in the presence of his fellow employees. The foreman has recommended him for discharge but suggests that one of the higher executives talk to him in order to have him realize where he stands. Fortunately, the employee initiates an interview by stating that he is disappointed with his job and the chances for advancement. The following conversation takes place (Early stages in the interview to establish rapport have been omitted from this report):

Principles of Interviewing Stated and Illustrated in the Executive's Thinking	The Conversation
"I'll have to get at the trouble from his point of view."	*Personnel Executive:* "You say you are dissatisfied with your job. Perhaps we should have had a chat before this but we didn't, and now is your chance to open up and tell what you think of your work here. Let's be frank about it; we can make more headway than if either of us holds back his grievances. Besides, I want to assure you that you can be frank with me."

JOHN MILTON (cont'd)

Principles of Interviewing Stated and Illustrated in the Executive's Thinking	The Conversation
"He doesn't open up."	*John Milton:* "I don't think there is any need to be frank. I do my work and that seems to be all that is expected of me."
	P. E.: "Your attendance and your production records show that you do not enjoy your work. Perhaps you expected something different when you finished college. What did you expect?"
"Most of the workers in that department are good physical specimens. Only a giant could do more work than they do." "The old story—college man expects a promotion just because he's a college man. He hasn't grasped the competitive nature of life."	*J. M.:* "In college, I was told that the world is waiting for hard-working, educated fellows, but I haven't found it so. I guess I was full of a lot of false enthusiasm. I'm working among a lot of dumb Bohunks who are stronger than I am. They work all day and don't mind it. When I work as fast as they do, I have to drag myself home at night. I used to think that if I got an education and worked hard I'd be promoted; but I haven't seen any promotion even when I did try for it. So far as I can see, a college education doesn't mean a thing on that kind of work."
"I'll have to build up his ego before I can help him." "Let him get rid of all the poison in his system."	*P. E.:* "Thanks, Milton. I'm glad you are frank. I'm beginning to see your point of view. If only everyone would be as honest as you are, we could avoid a lot of unhappiness. College, or something, has made you more willing to state facts as you see them. Now that you have told me about some of the difficulty, tell me more. How about your relations with the foreman? Has he treated you squarely?"
"The perennial alibi—drag. Perhaps that is a good starting point for us to get together."	*J. M.:* "Oh, yes, he's okay. I feel sorry for him. He's been here for fifteen or sixteen years, and he's still a foreman. He doesn't seem to have any drag either."
	P. E.: "No. he doesn't have any drag and he doesn't want any. Neither do you. You wouldn't feel so proud of yourself if you gained a better job through unfair influence as you would if you won it on ability, would you?"
"Ignore the 'barbs' that are not important."	*J. M.:* "No, I wouldn't, but even that might be better than competing with the physical giants in my department."
"Ask him some questions to which he answers yes."	*P. E.:* "Only as an escape from an unbearable situation. Now let's see whether

JOHN MILTON (cont'd)

Principles of Interviewing Stated and Illustrated in the Executive's Thinking

The Conversation

we can get straightened out on the value of your college training. You spent four years in college and you enjoyed it while you were there; or didn't you?"

J. M.: "I enjoyed it very much."

P. E.: "Did you learn some things you didn't know before?"

J. M.: "Sure, lots of them. In the classroom and outside."

P. E.: "Think of your freshman year. Did you have some difficulty in getting adjusted to college? Was it different from high school?"

J. M.: "Sure. It took me several months to like it."

"We have to get together on one point even though it is a minor one."

P. E.: "Would you agree that the step from college to industry is more difficult than the step from high school to college?"

J. M.: "You bet. Much harder for anyone."

"Here's the crucial stage. I'll have to illustrate this so clearly that he will want to feel himself a part of the concern."

P. E.: "It was for me, too. It took me a long time to realize that I had three choices: I could work *for* the company, I could '*work*' the company, or I could work *with* the company. Let me write them on this sheet of paper so that I can make them clear. (Writes them on paper.) In the past, you have been working for the company. You did what you had to do for the wages you received. You did not enjoy the work and you could not do so with your present point of view. To some extent, you worked the company when you held on to your job but did not work regularly. However, you might have tried to work us far more by catering to your foreman, tattling on the other fellows, or by restricting output through ostensible breakdowns of the machine you operate. You didn't do those things and I'm glad you are too much of a man to do them."

J. M.: "No, sir. I've played straight there."

"Ignore the fact that he tried to upset the morale of his fellow workers because he won't do that if I can enable him to express himself through his job."

P. E.: "Fine. However, you failed to work *with* us. That is, you did not consistently and wholeheartedly work just as though you gained self-expression from your job."

JOHN MILTON (cont'd)

Principles of Inverviewing Stated and Illustrated in the Executive's Thinking	The Conversation
"His objection is evidence of interest."	*J. M.:* "How could I gain self-expression from a job I don't like?"
"He can realize that any job may be satisfying if it has pleasant associations."	*P. E.:* "By recognizing the fact that the nature of any man's work is secondary to the meaning of the work to him. You will agree with me, I believe, when I say that almost any person would be glad to run the machine you operate if he believed that he was the only man in the world who could run it and if he were pointed out as the outstanding man in that work. Let me assure you that the nature of the work is incidental; the meaning of the work is most important. One can give his job meaning by one of three methods: First, he can do it better than anyone else. Second, he can improve the job by inventing a better machine or system to do the work. Third, he can improve the human relations in the job.
"Let's face the facts, pleasant or unpleasant."	"In your case, you cannot do the first because the other men are physically stronger than either one of us. You cannot do this second because you are not an engineer nor are you trained in production management. But you would do well to study the latter and see whether you could improve our production system.
"He has a real opportunity in his present situation, if he can utilize it."	"Your best chance is the third: namely, learn to understand how to influence the employees here. You may consider them Bohunks now, but the place and time to learn how to handle men is the place and time in which you happen to be. If you want to become an executive, you will have to conduct yourself in a manner which will cause those men to like and respect you." *J. M.:* "That sounds all right. But how am I going to get them to admire me?"
"People learn to admire those who admire them."	*P. E.:* "By deserving their admiration. Study them and some of their customs. Realize their problems and you'll forget your own. Visit them in their homes. Let them give you some of their fine qualities. You, in turn, can give them some of your qualities." *J. M.:* "What can I give them?" *P. E.:* "Things you have that they do

JOHN MILTON (Concluded)

Principles of Interviewing Stated and Illustrated in the Executive's Thinking	The Conversation
"Every man has something to give other men if he can learn how to give it."	not have—your education. College should have given you some information in economics, psychology, sociology, and other fields. Find out what things interest them and contribute in simple language the things they want and need. Help them to learn to read and do simple arithmetic. Some of them came to America because they thought it the land of opportunity. Lose yourself in helping them and you will thereby find yourself in this company. There is the opportunity. Do you want to take it or to run away from it?"
"Let him make the decision."	*J. M.:* "Can you explain the whole situation in more detail?" *P. E.:* "I'll try. Perhaps we can both understand the problem and solution if we diagram it." (Draws the diagram in the accompanying figure and explains it according to the principles presented in Chapters 2–8. The evasive, substitute, and retreat activities of J. M.'s behavior are explained, and then direct attack is offered as the one sound form of adjustment. The adviser also presents any ideas that he believes to apply, such as those expressed in Chapter 7.) *J. M.:* "Sounds pretty good. I never thought of my job as having any opportunity in it. I'll try it."
"Let him know that someone is following up his progress."	*P. E.:* "I know you can if you will. You have the intelligence. All you need is the attitude and desire. You'll find ways of doing it. Tell me how you get along. Come to see me a month from now. In the meantime, I'll hear of your activities." *J. M.:* "Thanks. I'll think it through and see what I can do."
"Any problem in industry may be integrated for the advantage of all parties."	*P. E.:* "Do so. Remember that when you help these other men, you also help yourself and this company." *J. M.:* "Good-bye."

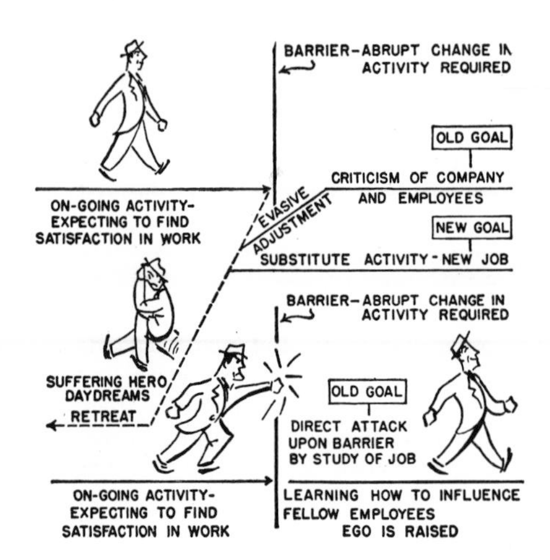

PRISCILLA PARKER

Priscilla Parker, a college graduate, has been working for the Blank Company for the past three years. She has never been tardy and has been absent only a few days. Her record, in general, is excellent. Some of her fellow employees have been tardy and absent more frequently than is necessary. The company decides to conduct a "Be-On-Time-Campaign." On the third morning of the campaign, Priscilla is caught in a traffic jam and is late. She records the correct time of her arrival. However, later in the day, she regrets her honesty and changes the record to show that she was on time. The timekeeper reports the falsification to her department manager, who calls her to his office for an interview.

The Department Manager's Thinking	The Conversation
"This girl has a good record and I must handle her in such a way that she will be strengthened by my treatment of her."	("D.M." is the department manager and "E." is the employee.) *D. M.:* "Good morning, Miss Parker. Won't you have a chair?" *E.:* "Thank you." (She drops into a chair, blushing and in an obvious state of nervousness.) *D. M.:* "The Timekeeping Department tells me that you ought to have a chat with me. Will you tell me your story?"
"I'll let her tell her side of the story."	*E.:* "Well, I left my home at the same time that I usually leave and I took the same bus, but the one I was on had something wrong with it. It stopped several times and I realized that I might be late, so I decided to change to a Third Avenue bus at Garden Street. I knew that I could walk the three blocks and make better time on the other line, but there was a fire at Garden Street and that detained me some more. When I finally got here I was late. I put down the right time when I came into the office. You know the rest, so there's no use my telling you."
"She ought to tell the whole story in her way."	*D. M.:* "I know part of the remainder but I'd like you to tell me, and give me your reasons." *E.:* "Well, I thought of the punctuality campaign, and I was sorry my tardiness would help spoil our department's chances for winning the departmental cup for having the best record. I haven't been late for three years and I was anxious to keep my own record perfect. That's why I changed the time slip later in the morning. But I know it was against the rules to do that."

PRISCILLA PARKER (cont'd)

The Department Manager's Thinking	The Conversation
"She must decide the significance of her act."	*D. M.:* "Why do you suppose we have the rule that office employees must be honest in recording their comings and goings?" *E.:* "Because we're paid according to the record; but I had intended to work overtime to make up for the tardiness."
"She ought to realize how her conduct affects others."	*D. M.:* "If you had worked overtime to compensate the company and no one had noticed your changing the record, would *you* have been satisfied with yourself? Would everything have been square for everybody?" *E.:* "The company would have been treated fairly, but I guess the people of the other departments would consider it unfair if our department should win the attendance prize. Wouldn't they?"
"Have the employee state the effects of her act on the company's efforts."	*D. M.:* "Yes, they would consider it unfair and some might even assume that they would be justified in falsifying their records. How would that affect the Be-On-Time-Campaign?" *E.:* "Well, the campaign and the prizes wouldn't mean anything if we didn't play the game fairly."
"Have employee see the effect of her act upon her personality."	*D. M.:* "Exactly. Changing the record was unfair to the other employees. But do you think that the falsifying of the record also had any effect upon you?" *E.:* "Yes, I guess it did. I didn't feel very easy about it after it was done."
"Find some redeeming feature in her act."	*D. M.:* "I'm glad to know that you were not trying to bluff yourself into feeling proud of an unfair act. Perhaps your feeling of dishonesty and regret will help you to meet such problems in the future in a straightforward manner. You know that your record with us is very good, but if you were to cause us to lose confidence in you, we should feel that we had to watch you constantly, and that would be difficult for us." *E.:* "Yes. and it would be worse for me. I couldn't be happy if I worked in a place where people didn't trust me."
"Let the employee herself suggest the proper correction (punishment) of her mistake."	*D. M.:* "Of course not. But that is where you stand now. Neither your department head nor the Timekeeping De-

PRISCILLA PARKER (concluded)

The Department Manager's Thinking	The Conversation
	partment can trust you in the future unless you square yourself with them and convince them that your misjudgment has improved you. What do you think that you ought to do in order to square yourself and deserve our continued confidence?"
	E.: "I suppose I ought to explain the whole matter to the personnel manager and the chief timekeeper and tell them how the experience has affected me. I also want to apologize to you."
"Arrange for employee to close the incident in her thinking so that she has no 'emotional hang-over' to disturb her morale."	*D. M.:* "Fine! You want to be square and we all want to forget about it. See the personnel man and the timekeeper. Convince them that you have benefited by this incident and I'm sure we can all forget about it. We want you to be happy here and have confidence in us and we want to have confidence in you."
	E.: "All right. "I'll see them and come back and tell you about it. I'll be glad to get this off my mind. I want a clean slate."
"Allow the employee to think that she has solved her problem herself, but require a report of the completed correction."	*D. M.:* "Good. Come back and tell me when you've cleaned the slate. Thank you for your honesty and willingness to correct the situation yourself. That will be all."

ACKNOWLEDGMENTS AND REFERENCES

1. See Elizabeth Ogg, *Psychotherapy—A Helping Process,* Public Affairs Committee, Inc., Public Affairs Pamphlet No. 329, 1961. The percentages reported for those who sought help were 42, 29, 18 and 10.
2. Harry Levinson, *et al., Men, Management and Mental Health* (Cambridge, Mass.: Harvard University Press, 1962), p. 18.
3. Jules Golden, Nathan Mandel, Bernard C. Glueck, Jr., and Zetta Feder, "A Summary Description of Fifty 'Normal' White Males," *The American Journal of Psychiatry,* July, 1962.
4. Emma Harrison, " 'Normal Man' Sits for His Portrait—3 Psychiatrists Find He Is Stable and Contented, but a Little Dull Withal," *The New York Times,* May 12, 1961, p. 31.
5. Frank Barron, *Creativity and Psychological Health* (Princeton, N.J.: D. Van Nostrand Co., Inc., 1963), pp. 44 and 65.
6. See Robert F. Peck, "Measuring the Mental Health of Normal Adults," *Genetic Psychology Monographs,* November, 1959.
7. Nicholas Hobbs, "Sources of Gain in Psychotherapy," *The American Psychologist,* November, 1962, p. 744.
8. Douglas S. Arbucle, "Differences between Clinical and Industrial Non-Directive Counseling," *Personnel Journal,* **24** (1948), 374–376. Also, John M. Butler, "On the Role of Directive and Non-Directive Techniques in the Counseling Process," *Educational and Psychological Measurement,* **8,** No. 2 (1948), 201–210.
9. Carl R. Rogers, *Counseling and Psychotherapy* (Boston: Houghton Mifflin Company, 1942), p. 28.
10. Helen Sargent, "Nondirective Counseling Applied to a Single Interview," *Journal of Consulting Psychology,* **7,** No. 4 (1932), p. 183.
11. Nathaniel J. Raskin, "Development of the Parallel Studies Project," *Journal of Consulting Psychology,* **13,** No. 3 (1949), 154–156.
12. ———, "An Objective Approach to the Study of Psychotherapy," *American Scientist,* **37,** No. 3 (1949), 410–413.
13. Elizabeth T. Sheerer, "The Relationship Between Acceptance of Self and Acceptance of Others," *Journal of Consulting Psychology,* **13,** No. 3 (1949), 174–175. Copyright 1949 by the American Psychological Association, Inc.
14. Carl R. Rogers, "The Processes of Therapy," *Journal of Consulting Psychology,* **4** (1940), 161–164.
15. Rogers, *Counseling and Psychotherapy, op. cit.,* pp. 336–337.

PROJECTS

1. Assume that you are a college professor and one of your students has been found cheating in an important examination. The student has been called to your office. Write a dialogue of your conversation along the lines of the two cases presented earlier in this chapter.
2. Interview any conveniently available persons who do some counseling as a part of their work, persons such as physicians, ministers, lawyers, personnel men, executives, and social workers. Get each into a friendly conversation and stimulate him to tell you about some of the problem persons whom he has tried to counsel. Write a brief report of your findings.
3. Assume that you are the head of a department having about thirty employees. One employee is a chronic faultfinder. He particularly belittles people having higher education. He takes no courses that might improve his own education, which ended in the third year of high school. He obviously tries to lift himself above others by "pushing them down." His constant defensiveness is having a bad effect on the morale of other employees and you decide that you must do something about it. What would you do? Explain the principles that underlie your suggested procedure.

COLLATERAL READINGS

Farnsworth, P. R., (ed.) *et al., Annual Review of Psychology*. Palo Alto, Calif.: Annual Reviews, Inc., 1964, pp. 347–370.

Gellerman, Saul W., *Motivation and Productivity*. New York: American Management Association, Inc., 1963, Chapters 15–19.

Knutson, Andie L., "New Perspectives Regarding Positive Mental Health," *The American Psychologist,* June, 1963.

Lehner, George F. J. and Ella Kube, *The Dynamics of Personal Adjustment*. Englewood Cliffs, N.J.: Prentice-Hall, Inc., 1694, Chapter 16.

Maier, Norman R., *Principles of Human Relations*. New York: John Wiley & Sons, Inc., 1952, Chapter 13.

Rogers, Carl R., *Counseling and Psychotherapy*. Boston: Houghton Mifflin Company, 1942.

Shaffer, Laurance F. and Edward J. Shoben, Jr., *The Psychology of Adjustment*. Boston: Houghton Mifflin Company, 1946, Chapter 16.

Smith, M. Brewster, " 'Mental Health' Reconsidered: A Special Case of the Problem of Values in Psychology," *The American Psychologist,* June, 1961.

The "Six Burghers of Calais" *were depicted in Auguste Rodin's statue as having attained a high level of maturity of personality. When the besieging English promised to spare the medieval city if six citizens would give their lives for Calais, six men had the courage to sacrifice themselves for their fellows. Rodin's statue of the historical event depicts no fear; only regret and awareness of the meaning of their act. Of course we do not know the actual psychological development of each of the six burghers, but we do know that Rodin's portrayal of their personalities was on the right psychological level of maturity.* ***(Courtesy of the Philadelphia Museum of Art, Philadelphia.)***

PART III

PERSONAL PROBLEMS

CHAPTER NINE

DEVELOPING YOUR OWN PERSONALITY

The mere reading of a book on personality will not make you popular or skillful in handling people. It can only start you on the road to making yourself friendly and influential. It can suggest new ways to enjoy people and stimulate you to apply the methods that you already know but neglect to use. At times you may fail to achieve your ends. You may even be misunderstood. But failure should simply spur you on to improve your strategies.[1]

The number of different definitions of personality is about the same as the number of persons who have defined it. Most psychologists restrict the term *personality* to non-intellectual traits, applying it particularly to the traits which determine a person's social effectiveness and happiness in life. However, most definitions tend to fall into two general classes: (a) those which define personality as the unique pattern or organization of the individual's adjustment habits, that is, the persistent tendencies in his mental life as developed through his capacities interacting with a complex social and physical world, and (b) definitions that give emphasis to the effect the individual has on other people with whom he comes in contact, his so-called social stimulus values.

What a Man Is

The first definition refers to what a man *is* psychologically, his fundamental character, rather than what he *does* in social situations. This idea has been expressed in the old adage: "Many a man would reach greater heights if he had more depth." A truly great personality, even though a famous person, impresses us more for what he is than for the achievements that have made him famous, as is explained by a scientist who was working with Albert Einstein at the time of his writing:

> Material facts matter less in Einstein's life than in anyone else's. The world of his sense impressions, of cold, hunger, pain, is dulled by the great intensity of his internal life. The adventure of Einstein's life is that of his mind. . . .As great as Einstein is as a physicist and a philosopher, he is still greater as a man.
>
> I know that the last sentence sounds like a bad cliché. Yet it cannot be, because Einstein is the only great scientist of whom I could say it. When one comes in contact with him, one is not overwhelmed by his greatness as a scientist. This greatness is engulfed by the greatness and strangeness of his whole personality. Einstein is unlike anyone else. And perhaps this simple fact is the real clue to his fame. The real clue is not the spectacular discovery of the bending of light rays. If this were so, why should this fame persist in a quickly changing world that forgets today its idols of yesterday? It must rather be his inner greatness, which the people of the world somehow sense and need for their comfort. . . .
>
> It is easy to say that Einstein is great as a scientist, but even more so as a man. But wherein does this greatness lie? And how is it reflected in the minds of the people? My answer may sound bombastic, but I believe it to be true. For me and for many others (some of them could not or would not care to formulate the answer explicitly), Einstein is the aloof conscience of the world. . . .
>
> I do not know anyone as lonely and detached as Einstein. His extreme kindness, his absolute decency, his straightforwardness in dealing with men and social ideas is, in spite of all the appearances to the contrary, impersonal and aloof. His heart does not bleed, his eyes do not cry, yet his deeds are those of a man whose heart bleeds and whose eyes cry. Perhaps this aloofness and detachment make it possible for him to achieve the highest moral level any human being can achieve. The moral scale becomes unbalanced if the "I" is involved. It is sensitive and accurate for Einstein, because his "I" is little involved. . . .
>
> A few weeks ago I received a letter signed by Einstein as the chairman of the Emergency Committee of Atomic Scientists. With it was a small pamphlet containing his article "Only Then Shall We Find Courage." Here he speaks with the insight and power of a prophet. Indeed, it is the conscience of the world that speaks to us—the wisest, simplest words ever spoken on a subject drowned in a flood of meaningless silly words formed into clichés by men who understand and learn nothing.
>
> There was suffering in Einstein's writing, and strong indications that now the impact of a troubled world has invaded his aloofness. In his words there is a message for humanity. And it seems to me a thousand times more important that people should understand his simple words than that they should understand the Relativity Theory.
>
> At the end of his article he writes:
>
> *When we are clear in heart and mind—only then shall we find the courage to surmount the fear which haunts the world.*
>
> These are the aims for which Einstein strove all his life: to be clear in mind and heart. He is one of the very few who have achieved this clarity.[2]

The truly educated man seeks more than

knowledge; he searches for the basic principles by which men live. The learning of principles and the development of a philosophy of life are more important than the mere acquisition of facts. Facts change and disappear; principles remain. Basic principles are guides to judgment and provide a sense of values that lead to strength of personality. They enable a man to distinguish between cheapness or the conventional and grandeur of soul. The man who attains such maturity of personality has poise, power, and influence. He studies psychology, not to give him a feeling of superiority, but to enable him to enjoy all personalities. He does not pity the maladjusted nor does he identify himself with them. He enjoys them, because he understands and likes them in spite of their inappropriate adjustments. Insight into their adjustments increases his respect for all mankind. He loses his cynicism in constructive service to others.

The habit of using direct-attack and positive value methods of dealing with barriers is one of the goals of personality growth. The person who has achieved it has what people often describe in such terms as, "That man has good stuff in him," "He's a man of strong character," or "There's a man who is a real man." Everyone has heard such statements about a few persons he has known.

Several years ago the author made a list of ten men and women who had been described in these or similar terms. In addition to those on his list, 160 others were chosen by a committee of acquaintances. The 170 superior men and women were studied by means of many reaction questions. The answers of this superior group were compared with the answers of 200 persons chosen at random, 150 mentally sick patients of an institution, and a group of low-intelligence persons. The test that developed from this study, "Personality Maturity," is given in the Appendix.

Personality maturity means that the individual has developed a certain unification of the whole self, a dependable individuality. He is no longer a youth who seeks to try out all kinds of adjustments, all roads to experience, all ways to growth. He has learned that some modes of behavior lead only to new blockings or to deterioration. Past failures and successes have taught him what things are worth while for him. He knows his aims and the ways in which he will strive to attain them. His character is stable, and his scale of values has been established. When a man's maturity has become positive, he feels and believes that adjustments by evasion and retreat eventually result in a lowered ability to deal with the next barrier.

Psychiatrists who are working in a health service for college students have reported that many students who seek counseling in regard to their psychological problems are really trying to get their place in the universe straight. "Identity crisis" has been used as a term for the problem of these post-adolescents. They are trying to develop an adult self out of the welter of possibilities that present themselves.[3] This quest is a never-ending one for the intelligent adult, but the problem often becomes especially acute or even disturbing for some students.

According to one study, students whose grades place them in the upper quarter of their class are more likely to improve their personality adjustment than those who are in the bottom quarter. The MMPI was administered to the top and bottom quarters of the senior class of 1958 at Hamilton College and to those senior men who were originally in the top and bottom quarters of their freshman class 4 years earlier. There was a definite improvement in personality adjustment over a 4-year period of college attendance for men originally in the top quarter of their class as freshmen. However, men in the bottom quarter showed no significant changes on any of the MMPI scales.[4]

What a Man Does

As indicated above, the what-a-man-is aspect of personality growth resolves into the what-a-man-does concept. This is fortunate, because it means that every intelligent person who wishes to develop his personality to a high level of growth can do so by means of conscious effort. One of the most natural environmental situations in which he can work toward his own maturity is in those relations that involve people.

Most people who wish to improve their personalities think of them in terms of their social stimulus value or effectiveness in dealing with people. They realize that they are not alert to the handling of social situations. They are likely to be self-conscious.

The very term "self-consciousness" expresses their basic problem—they are conscious of the wrong person. The socialized person is conscious of others rather than himself. Fortunately, the art of dealing with people can be acquired:

The habit of becoming more aware of others than of yourself can be learned. For example, certain introverted college students asked me to conduct classes in personality development. In these classes I taught one basic principle or rule: *Watch the other person and do whatever appears to be appropriate.*

When the classes were begun, the students were unknowingly given a standardized interview where the interviewer asked six questions. Two of the answers were written incorrectly by the interviewer. The interviewer then tried to erase the error, using a wooden pencil with the eraser worn down to the metal. (Each student had been given a pencil with a good eraser.) The test of the student's habituated use of the above rule was observed and recorded. The poorly socialized students failed to offer their erasers to the interviewer.

After this first test, the students were trained in the practical application of the basic principle. The students themselves suggested extensions and applications of the rule, but pencils and erasers were never mentioned. After eight hours of training, they were again given the same test. Most students made a definite improvement as shown by the moving pictures which were taken without their knowledge. They had learned to objectify some of their thinking; to lose their self-consciousness by becoming conscious of others. . . .

If you wish to have more friends or to be able to handle people happily, you, too, have to learn the art of forgetting yourself. You must lose self-consciousness by becoming more conscious of other people and by directing your thinking toward them. Personality, in this social sense, is not something that you have or are; *personality is what you do when you are with others. It is an activity, not a possession.* It is not a stagnant pool but a running brook.

This dynamic nature of personality is most fortunate. If you are seeking more friendships or wish to handle people more effectively, you can forget what you are. Simply concentrate upon others, and discover how to give them greater enjoyment. Think of each person as being a distinctive individual whom you try to understand and make a bit more happy. If you practise this fundamental principle, you will find, sooner or later, that you are popular and influential with others.

Your attainment of this social artistry is not so formidable a task as it may appear to be. You have already learned some knacks of handling people. If, on certain past occasions, you had not withdrawn into a shell of reserve when strangers or unkind persons were about, you would have learned more skills. Perhaps you were so wrapped up in your own feelings of doubt about your ability, imagined unattractiveness, or self-concern that you failed to watch the other person. Of course, if your thoughts and feelings were concentrated on yourself, you made a poor impression on him and you withdrew more quickly from contacts with the next stranger. . . .

Parents are at fault when they try to protect their children by isolating them from imperfect companions. Sooner or later the children may develop into first-class neurotics whose chief fault is the fact that in the game of life they "can't take it." Parents who constantly guard their children, not allowing them to play with other children for fear that they will learn the facts of life, are not fulfilling their parental responsibilities. Occasionally the children even run the risk of later becoming patients in hospitals for the mentally ill. The only way for a girl to learn how to handle men, or for a boy to learn how to get along with girls, is for both to go through a long practice period of training where each successful skill in getting along with people has been learned through hard experiences plus intelligent judgments. Socially speaking, every man is his own ancestor and his own heir—he makes his own future and he inherits his own past. What he does on a great occasion depends upon what he already is, and both depend upon the years of training acquired in the social arenas of life: the playground, the office, the shop, and the park bench on a moonlit night.[5]

The socialized personality and its resultant

The arts of friendship** begin in the early years. The child who must depend upon himself, unimpeded by excessive parental supervision, when making his own friends soon develops the knack of getting his companions to say: "He's young, but maybe it'd be okay for him to tag along this time."* ***(Photograph by Ward Hutchinson, Sharon, Connecticut.)

friendships must be earned. Many persons who find it difficult to earn friendships would like to improve their personalities, but they have the habits of the *introvert* rather than those of the *extravert*.

Introversion-extraversion

Introverts are characterized by their "shut-in" personality. They do not share their joys and sorrows with others, but keep them to themselves. They are largely self-sufficient for their emotional outlets. Anger, blushing, and laughter are examples of emotional outlets, and the introverts express them within themselves; that is, their emotions are introverted. Daydreaming is an example of an introverted emotional outlet. Introverts, in short, are vividly aware of their own inner lives.

Extraverts, in contrast, express their emotional outlets in action and in seeking the society of others. They do not sit alone with their thoughts, but depend upon others or upon activity for their happiness. Introverts are men of thought and extraverts are men of action. Scientists tend toward introversion and businessmen toward extraversion. Foremen and executives whose duties require the supervision of others are likely to be extraverts. The key executives of industry incline toward *ambiversion,* or a middle position on the scale of introversion-extraversion. Office workers, clerks, and stenographers incline toward introversion. Many accountants and research engineers are pronouncedly introverted.

It should not be assumed that all or most people are of either one type or the other. Rather, they tend to group themselves in the center of the scale. Each person has some qualities of each type, and his classification depends upon the degree to which he is introverted or extraverted rather than upon the absolute presence or absence of the characteristic traits. Furthermore introversion is expressed in several separate traits as in social and thinking areas. A person may be socially introverted but not thoughtful or moody.[6]

Laird devised a scale for the measure of introversion and extraversion.[7] The personality signs he listed are:

1. The introvert blushes easily; the extravert rarely blushes.
2. The extravert laughs more readily than the introvert.
3. The introvert is usually outspoken; the extravert is usually careful not to hurt the feelings of others.
4. The extravert is a fluent talker; the introvert can prepare a report in writing more easily than he can tell it in conversation.
5. The extravert lends money and possessions more readily than the introvert.
6. The extravert moves faster than the introvert in the routine actions of the day, such as walking, dressing, talking, etc.
7. The extravert does not take particular care of his personal property, such as watches, clothes, etc.; the introvert is found continually oiling, polishing, and tinkering.
8. Introverts are usually reluctant about making friends among those of opposite sex, while extraverts are attracted by them.
9. Introverts are easily embarrassed by having to be in front of a crowd.
10. The extravert is a more natural public speaker.
11. The introvert likes to argue.
12. The introvert is slow about making friends.
13. The introvert rewrites his letters, inserts interlineations, adds postscripts, and corrects every mistake of the typist.

Personality Signs Revealed in Thinking and Attitudes:

1. The introvert worries; the extravert has scarcely a care in the world.
2. The feelings of the introvert are easily hurt; the extravert is not bothered by what is said to him.
3. The introvert deliberates in great detail about everything—what to wear, where to eat, etc., and usually tells one why he decided to do what he did.
4. The introvert rebels when ordered to do a thing; the extravert accepts orders as a matter of course.
5. The introvert is urged to his best efforts by praise; the extravert is not affected by praise.
6. The introvert is suspicious of the motives of others.
7. The introvert is usually radical in religion and politics; the extravert—if he entertains any opinions—is usually conservative.
8. The introvert would rather struggle alone to solve a problem than to ask for help.
9. The introvert would rather work alone in a room than with others.
10. Extraverts follow athletics; introverts read books and "highbrow" magazines.
11. The introvert is a poor loser.
12. The introvert daydreams a great deal.
13. The introvert prefers fine, delicate work (die making, accounting), while the extravert prefers work in which details do not bother.
14. The introvert is inclined to be moody at times.
15. The introvert is very conscientious.[8]

The study of personality traits or patterns of this kind has value to the supervisor, because those persons who are most introverted can be influenced by methods that are not successful with the extraverts. Praise, caution, and exactness appeal to introverts. Activity, speed, chance, and challenges appeal to the extraverts.

One researcher wanted to find out whether extraverts really do have more traffic accidents and violations than introverts. He studied a male college population of 937 for whom driving records were available. When the men were classified on the basis of their test scores into equal groups of extravert, intermediate, and introvert, a comparison of the numbers of accidents and violations incurred by the three groups resulted in a statistically significant verification of the hypothesis that extraverts do have more traffic accidents and violations.[9]

As salesmen are decidedly extraverted, it is hopeless to try to compel them to fill in and mail each day very detailed reports to the home office. Salesmen should have a minimum amount of clerical work to perform. Their paper work should be done by women, because women, as a group, are more introverted than men. Bank work usually attracts introverts. Bank workers who meet the public should be assisted by extraverted contact men and women in the lobby. Workmen who are to be promoted to supervisory positions should be extraverted rather than painstaking and retiring introverts.

In the forms of introversive adjustment which we call *retreat* the individual seeks solitude, prefers to stay at home, adopts cults of mysticism, studies his ancestry, or lives in a world of poetry, art, or fiction. Some religions have idealized this tendency by formalizing the retreat adjustment. Tibet, the center of religious fanaticism, has many old Buddhist monks who have kept themselves sealed up—except for small openings for food—in little huts since their early manhood. Some of them have not heard the voice, seen the face, nor touched the hand of a human being for more than forty years.

Many of our very studious college students are introverted, but college fraternities probably attract the extraverted and the introverted students in approximately equal numbers.[10] The differences between fraternities are likely to be greater than the differences between the fraternity and the nonfraternity groupings.

Some introverted students would like to become more extraverted but wonder whether it is possible to do so. The answer is a decided "Yes." On the other hand, many introverts say that they prefer to remain as they are because civilization needs introverts as well as extraverts. No one can argue with those who make this choice except in one important respect, namely, introverts are so very sensitive, their feelings are hurt so often, that they would be happier if they would learn greater skill in the social arts. Those who wish to acquire the social skills can do so by directing their thinking toward others and away from themselves.

Paradoxically, the socially skilled and interesting personality cannot be acquired if it is sought directly. It is a by-product, like happiness. "Happiness is a butterfly which, when pursued, is always just beyond your grasp, but which, if you will sit down quietly, may alight upon you." Or, as Hawthorne said: "Happiness in this world, when it comes, comes incidentally. Make it the object of pursuit, and it leads us a wild goose chase and is never attained."

As previously stated, self-consciousness on the part of the introvert means just what the term indicates—the individual is more conscious of himself than of others. Self-pity and similar ego-centered tendencies can be changed by looking out—not in. Extraversion can be attained by thinking more of external and social values, particularly how to deal with and handle people.

To socialize your personality, watch the other person and do whatever appears to be appropriate. In this social sense, personality is what you *do* with people; not something that you have.* Friendliness can be learned in the same way we learn arithmetic or French—by

* The second person is often used in this chapter for the greater interest of readers who wish to develop the social stimulus values of their personalities.

study and practice. The extent to which the college student, male or female, has learned commonly used information about social relations can be measured by the "Social Knowledge Test" in the Appendix of this book. The students who score high in the knowledge of the Lower Social Strata and low in the Upper Social Strata questions should consider the desirability of increasing their study of social information. The college man or woman who has limited his associations to either class may be somewhat handicapped in certain occupations.

The adjustments made in early childhood are very important in the development of effective social skills. Many a child finds it difficult to adapt himself to others because he feels emotionally insecure. He may feel insecure because, for instance, he took too seriously the ordinary family quarrels of his parents. The frictions between his parents may have caused him to feel that they, and his world as well, were not dependable. He became emotionally insecure because the most important persons of his experience, his parents, did not seem to merit his belief in their dependability.

If the emotionally insecure child is also nagged a great deal, he is apt to grow up to be impulsive, self-centered, and unable to identify himself with his associates. He feels left out and, in awkward attempts to readjust himself, he behaves in ways that cause others to avoid him, thus increasing his feeling of not belonging. However, if he later comes to realize how his insecurity came about, recognizes that many parents show their affection for each other by their bickering, and he secures some dependable person as a friend, he is likely to develop adjustment habits that result in a feeling of belongingness. Practically, this means that the individual should frequently participate in group activities appropriate to his age and social status: sports, team or group games, dancing, committee meetings, and so on. In this respect, chess and archery are likely to be less developmental than baseball or amateur theatricals.

The feeling of belongingness can be achieved by anyone who consciously practices the best methods of doing whatever seems to be appropriate in dealing with people. This means that the intelligently socialized person not only accepts people but also thinks of them as sources of mutual enjoyment.

An important difference between the adjustment-minded person and the average layman is illustrated by the three ways in which we can deal with a problem person's annoying behavior: namely, (*a*) cumulative annoyance, (*b*) negative adaptation, and (*c*) insight-meaning.

Cumulative annoyance is exemplified by the employee who dislikes his boss and at the beginning of each day says to himself: "Another day of that man! Every time I see him I hate him more. When can I get away from him?" The individual who reacts to another person or situation in this manner soon develops intense feelings of resentment. Eventually he rebels, perhaps violently. If circumstances, such as the need for a job in order to support a family, do not allow him to quit, he must "explode" or "break" under the strain. He is

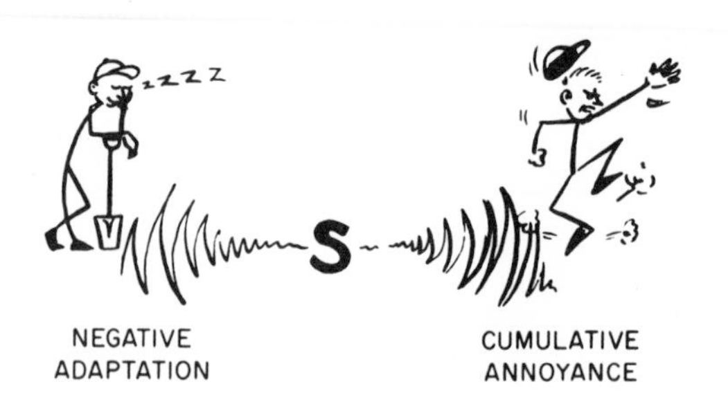

The adaptation-annoyance range. *When an individual is stimulated by the repetition of any given situation, he may, on the one hand, completely adapt himself to the situation, so that it no longer elicits any reaction except one of boredom and dullness. On the other hand, each repetition of the stimulus may result in added annoyance. The effects of the stimulation are then summative. Each reaction adds to the accumulated annoyance of the previous sum. The worker who responds to his job in the latter way soon develops feelings of strong resentment that result in rebellion. If he cannot escape from the summative effect of the annoyance of his job, he will have to "explode " or "break" under the strain. The "explosion" may be expressed through the channel of fighting the boss, or through bitter antagonism toward industry or toward anything that symbolizes the annoying situation. The "break" may be in the form of the so-called nervous breakdown. Contrast this with insight-meaning response.*

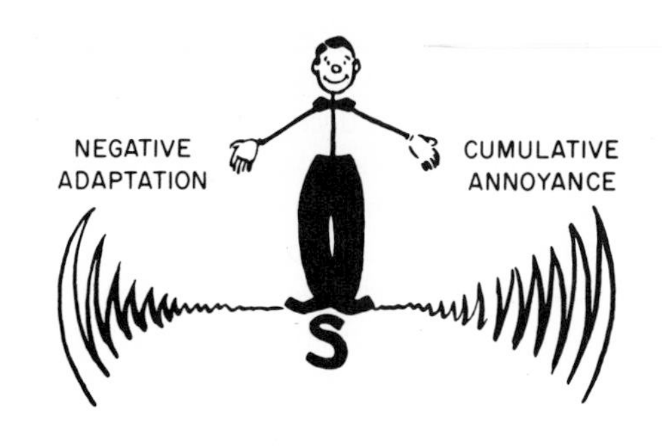

The insight-meaning response. *When an individual is stimulated by the repetition of any given kind of situation, he need not adapt himself completely, nor need he be cumulatively annoyed. He may apply intelligence to the situation. He may seek insight. When he seeks insight, he makes observations. He notes annoying and satisfying factors. He looks for causes and effects. He discovers possible improvements. He utilizes the situation for self-expression. The situation acquires meanings for him, and these meanings radiate in all directions from the situation and result in the disappearance of feelings of dull acceptance or of resentment. The worker who reacts to his job in this manner becomes neither bored nor carpingly critical. He utilizes his job for creative self-expression.*

the type of employee who is impelled to "tell the boss to go to Hell" and thereby lose the job he wanted to lose. This type of worker, if he does not explode, is apt to become a bitter critic toward industry, modern business, or something else that happens to symbolize his baleful situation. If he does not have an outlet for his pent-up emotions, he is likely to escape through the so-called "nervous breakdown."

Negative adaptation applies to many of our daily experiences with people. Some persons and situations are dealt with and forgotten. Examples of negative adaptation are the factory worker who has given up all hope of getting a better job and now does his work in a mechanical spiritless manner, the small child who does not react to his mother's constant scolding, or the husband who does not "hear" his wife's back-seat driving.

Insight-meaning is used by the worker who finds himself in an annoying situation, analyzes it, and discovers some interesting aspects of it. It is used by the boss who, when he is annoyed by the mannerisms of an employee, learns that the employee has a difficult home life and then tries to make the employee's life more interesting by giving him extra attention while at work. Insight-meaning is always more satisfying than either dull acceptance or cumulative annoyance. It can be used every day with our annoying associates, such as the back-seat driver, the teacher who scolds, the executive who threatens, the housewife who nags, the girl-friend who insists on having repeated personal attentions, and others.

A first step in the insight-meaning relationship to people is to become aware of their adjustments. Anyone who learns to apply the adjustment concept to the actions of people will soon develop a feeling of kinship* toward them. He will feel friendly toward them and they will sense that he understands and likes them. The psychologically intelligent person does not tell people how much he knows about them. Rather, he uses his insight into their personalities to help them make the adjustments and gain the satisfactions *they* seek. He never flaunts his knowledge of them but uses it as a background for friendly, mutually satisfying relationships. He learns how people feel and feels himself into their situations and problems.

Second, he notes what people do and like. He learns what topics of conversation interest them, what badges or insignia they wear, their hobbies, the brands of cigarettes they smoke, whether they are more deaf in one ear than another, the taut muscles which indicate tension, and subjects of conversation which are pleasant to them. He says "Good-bye" with his face toward the departing guest. When an old joke is told, the true extravert does not show by his manner that he has heard it previously but laughs heartily. One of the tests of extraversion on the part of a listener is to look so interested when a story teller begins his story that the raconteur does not ask: "Or have you heard this before?"

recognize acknowledge

* "Empathy" is used by some psychologists to express the mental state wherein one person identifies or feels himself into the state of mind of another person. It is also used to mean mental projection of oneself into the elements of a work of art or into a natural object.

This awareness of what people like does not mean that flattery can take the place of a sincere interest in others. Many misinformed persons fail to appreciate the importance of a genuine interest in work and people.

This principle is illustrated by the difference between flattery and a genuine interest in a person, as seen in the case of employees who imagine that flattery is necessary to gain promotion.

Should an employee use flattery in order to gain promotion if he believes that others are succeeding by this method? Mr. Edmunds is thirty-five years old, is married, and has been working for his present employer for ten years. He likes his work and, in general, he considers his employer fair. However, he believes that some of the younger men of the department who have been promoted gained their promotion through clever and tactful flattery toward his superior. Mr. Edmunds should:

1. Try to flatter his superior in order to gain promotion also.
2. Quit, and try to get a job where promotion depends upon ability rather than flattery.
3. Allow the others to do as they wish. He likes his work and he should be completely satisfied.
4. Discuss the situation as tactfully as possible with his superior.
5. Improve his ability by studying, taking an active part in technical associations, and contributing articles to trade journals. The future will take care of itself if he improves himself and builds a reputation for his ability.[11]

Third, the introvert who wishes to socialize himself should practice responding to others by means of his facial expressions. Typical introverts are surprised when they see moving pictures of themselves in conversation. They discover that they look as animated as the Statue of Liberty! If a person feels friendly, he should show it by lifting his eyebrows and smiling with his eyes as well as by grinning with his lips. Of course, friendliness is far more than facial expression. It is a sincere identification with others, but a sincere identification includes facial expressions which help to convey the feeling of friendship.

Fourth, the introvert should acquire the knack of asking questions in order to learn from others; not to argue with them. Usually, we can ask questions of a person about his occupation: what he does, who the leaders are in his field of work, changes since he has entered the field, and what successful experiences he himself has enjoyed.

Furthermore, the good conversationalist does not answer questions completely—he answers them only partially and then asks the questioner what he thinks about the unanswered aspect. He knows that when a person answers a question and then says, "Don't you think so, too?" the conversation is closed. The flow of conversation should not be shut off by requests for agreement but kept moving from topic to topic by requests for additional ideas.

Asking questions is an art which few introverts learn even though they argue frequently. They are so wrapped up in their own feelings about themselves that they cannot ask questions so as to enable the other person to expand. They are apt to ask questions to prove their own point, as found in this typical problem:

Who should take the initiative in correcting misundertandings: the superior or the subordinate? A senior in a Liberal Arts College has had a reasonably good scholastic record. He is now in his last semester. In the first semester of his senior year, he failed a course under a certain professor, but continued the year course with this same professor. The student believes that he failed the first semester's work because he had a very heated argument with the professor. He also believes that he will fail this semester's work because he is sure that the professor does not like him. What should he do?

1. He should remain in the course, work hard, and say nothing to the professor.
2. He should request permission of his dean to change his course, explaining his reason.
3. He should discuss the matter with the professor and find out wherein he was wrong. He should then apologize, if necessary, and put himself on a friendly relationship with his professor.
4. He should tell the professor frankly what he thinks of his unfairness and demand that the professor treat him absolutely fairly.[12]

Fifth, the individual who seeks to make himself interesting to others usually finds it

victions regarding his inabilities are so deep-seated in his personality that a clinical approach is necessary to make the later exercises in spelling worth while.

The following statement by a psychologist who spoke at an annual meeting of the American College Personnel Association explains more fully the need for a clinical technique in dealing with certain inabilities:

> The clinical technique which follows from the theoretical conception of the problem must therefore aim to bring about in the subject a reexamination of those ideas which block his development. Academic difficulties and social maladjustments are both conceived of as due to resistances arising from the subject's* idea of himself. Obviously, the method must rely upon inducing the subject to observe the system of contradictions in which he has become involved.
>
> Let us take the case of an intelligent student who is deficient, for example, in spelling. In almost every instance, poor spellers have been tutored and practiced in spelling over long periods without improvement. For some reason such a student has a special handicap in learning how to spell, though not in learning the other subjects which are usually considered more difficult. This deficiency is not due to a lack of ability, but rather to an active resistance which prevents him from learning how to spell in spite of the extra instruction. The resistance arises from the fact that at some time in the past the suggestion that he is a poor speller was accepted and incorporated into his definition of himself, and is now an integral part of his total personality. His difficulty is thus explained as a special instance of the general principle that a person can only be true to himself. If he defined himself as a poor speller, the misspelling of a certain proportion of the words which he uses becomes for him a moral issue. He misspells words for the same reason that he refuses to be a thief. That is, he must endeavor to behave in a manner consistent with his idea of himself.
>
> In these cases, we find that this self-definition as a poor speller, and consequently the resistance to learning how to spell correctly, can usually be removed in from one to five interviews. The majority become average or better than average spellers within the space of two or three months.
>
> A study of the spelling behavior of these students shows that each individual seems to have a definite standard of poor spelling which he unconsciously endeavors to maintain. If his spelling test is cut in two, it will be found that each half contains approximately the same number of misspelled words. If we study his letters or written theses, there is likewise a striking consistency in the number of misspelled words per page. Strange to say, the spelling of foreign languages seems to be impaired very little if at all, showing clearly that the difficulty cannot be attributed to eye movements, left-handedness, or other mechanical interferences. Evidently the conception of one's self as a poor speller usually has reference to one's native language only.
>
> The clinical technique consists in first finding several strong values apparently unrelated to the value in question which can be used as levers, so to speak, and then demonstrating the inconsistency between these values and the one responsible for the deficiency. Almost every student considers himself independent and self-reliant, for example. On the other hand, it can readily be shown that the poor speller expects his defect to be condoned and treated sympathetically; that, in effect, he has his hand out begging for indulgence. If the contradiction can be demonstrated from his own viewpoint, a reorganization becomes compulsory. His definition of himself as a poor speller is vigorously rejected and a determined effort made to establish the opposite definition. The result obtained is out of all proportion to the effort exerted to bring it about. Spelling assumes such interest that it is studied at every opportunity, even from the advertisements on street cars and subway trains. An elaborate analysis to convince the subject that his difficulty really is due to a fixed idea of himself does not seem to be necessary in the remedial treatment of spelling. He should, however, be asked to recall when he first accepted the role of a poor speller, ceased to worry about it, and dismissed the question as closed.
>
> It is significant that not only poor spellers, but stammerers and others with similar defects, freely admit as a rule that they accept themselves as they are and make no effort to change. This is an excellent defense, of course, for they feel no inconsistency once the definition has been accepted. And they often attempt to avoid the effort of maintaining a more useful definition by referring the defect to heredity or neuromuscular maladjustment.
>
> Our experience also shows that unless a person has an unusually optimistic view of the future he would not be likely to anticipate a lenient attitude on the part of others in regard to errors in spelling. This optimism also appears in the

---

* The reader will note that the word "subject" as used in this context refers to "the person experimented upon"; not to a course of study.

fact that poor spellers seem almost universally to count on the services of stenographers who are good spellers, and many are able to quote the names of several people who became famous in spite of a deficiency in spelling.

Those who claim that they "do not have a mathematical mind" are likewise victims of their own resistance. Such a student may have defined himself in childhood as the exact opposite of some unassimilable companion who had been held up as a shining example of mathematical proficiency. In other cases, remarks by parents or teachers that the child was lacking in aptitude for mathematics seem to be the explanation. The suggestion was accepted and is now a part of the student's conception of himself. In one instance, a student who despised mathematics in high school, during his freshman year acquired a sudden attachment for the subject and is now a professional statistician. This boy's older brother was proficient in mathematics, and the two had been in conflict for years.[4]

The clinical technique is helpful in those cases where individuals have proved that they can learn many subjects but claim they are unable to learn one or two specific subjects. The individual is apt either to continue to assume that somehow he is incapable of learning the "difficult" subject or to use evasion, such as searching for some magical or quick means of attaining his ends. He may, for example, read the biographies of great men, study success books, or books on "how to have power of will." Such epigrammatic books, articles, and lectures are inspiring; but if adjustments to environment have already given him an urge, he can accomplish more by the practice of prosaic acts, such as outlining meaningful material, plotting graphic charts, and learning the cold facts of his courses and tasks.

Group therapy, under a different name, was found helpful to certain students at Harvard as reported by Graham B. Blaine, Jr.:

> The college student is glad to discuss general subjects in bull sessions with contemporaries and even to reveal fairly intimate and personal experiences and feelings, but when this discussion is labeled therapy with the implication of illness, he tends to be much more guarded in front of his fellow students. This defensiveness makes a group discussion vague, inconclusive, and nonproductive. If, however, there is a definite goal to start with, which is understood and accepted by all, then the chances of building a cohesive group where members can trust each other enough to help each other is far greater.
>
> A group of this sort was instituted at Harvard recently. Ten boys from the sophomore class were selected by the dean as being in such poor standing academically that their chances of survival following the final examinations in June were less than one in ten. The boys were told this by the dean and again by a therapist in a letter which also invited them to participate in a therapy group. Eight of the ten reported for the first meeting which took place in April. Meetings were held weekly until the examination period (nine meetings in all), and discussion which originally centered entirely around study habits shifted quickly to family pressures, then to intrafamilial relationships, and finally to the kinds of conflicts which were deep inside these troubled students. The kind of unrestrained silliness and superficiality which characterized the nongoal-centered groups was simply not present. Presumably as a result of the group discussions, each student reported an improvement in his studying ability, and six of the eight brought their actual grades up to the point where they were allowed to continue in college.[5]

Students who are thinking of dropping out of college for a year may be interested to learn that one survey at Harvard indicated that of 160 students who withdrew from their class but returned by the spring of the following year, the number who were in good standing and well on their way to graduating was 60. The researchers concluded that "These figures would seem to indicate that voluntary withdrawal is both a frequent and a generally valuable occurrence for the individual."[6]

Concentration

Informal polls among college students indicate that lack of concentration or poor concentration is the most common of poor study habits.

The student who complains about his inability to concentrate may go through a lot of futile "motions" of studying: sitting in front of an open text book without learning a single idea, doing ritualistic notetaking, or memorizing without actually thinking.

The much-voiced complaint, "Every time I start to study, I all at once just seem to find myself daydreaming!" needs analysis. What causes these daydreams? It may be run-of-the-mill emotional problems, the current girl or boy friend, financial difficulties, or breaking away from home ties. All of these can be a hindrance to concentration.

Ideally, the hampering emotionality involved in adjustment to the problem should be projected into the educational effort. This kind of redirection may require the assistance of a therapist. Most of us, however, have to make our adjustments the best way we can. *Knowing* your particular problems is to be on the way to solving them. Find out what it is that is taking your interest from studies and guiding it into daydreaming sessions. If you do not wish to consult a clinical psychologist in order to find out, try the system of studying for a week with a paper and pencil always at hand. Each time that you catch yourself daydreaming, write down what it is you had been thinking about. At the end of a week, you should be aware of some of your major problems. Some students find this technique an aid to sticking to a subject.

Concentration is so closely allied with interest that in order to be able to concentrate, interest must first be developed. Poor concentration may stem, too, from a spotty background in a subject area. Failure to think ahead so that you know what is coming and the reason for it may leave wide gaps in your thinking. Inexperience or careless observation may have left you with a weak perceptual background. An inadequate vocabulary of either general or technical terms could prevent you from maintaining a continuous thought pattern. This in turn contributes to a lack of interest.[7]

It is profitable to recognize that the big problem in studying lies in creating interest. There is such a thing as achieving a "forced" interest in a subject. Many students have not only created this forced interest, but have gone ahead and achieved a "real" interest through the study of formerly disliked subjects.

The passing of the disestablishment act in 1867 did not satisfy the nationalists under . . . The passing of the disestablishment . . . The passing of the disestablishment act in 1867 did not satisfy the nationalists . . . passing of the disestablishment act in 1867 did not . . . the passing . . ."
—"Vic the Vet," by Gabe, Syracuse University, **Daily Orange.**

There are helpful methods by which enthusiasm for subjects can be developed. One technique that works at times is for the student to study exceptionally hard for the first examination in a course. If the student is successful in getting a high grade, the high grade helps to develop interest in the subject: success generates interest.

Another technique is reading ahead of lectures. This practice will help to eliminate much of the disinterest students have toward especially difficult subjects. For example, in an economics course, the instructor may announce that the subject of the next lecture will be the "Law of Supply and Demand." The student, by reading this material in the text before the lecture and, if time permits, in the library texts and periodicals, facilitates his own understanding of the subject and, hence increases his interest in it.

Of course these suggestions for developing interest in study do not help the student who is using apathy as a defense against an unconscious problem. Apathetic defense may be used as a means of punishing oneself or others. Clinicians find that the fantasies of an apathetic patient are likely to be filled with imagery of rage and potential destructiveness.

Apathy protects the patient from his own aggressiveness.[8] This kind of student needs therapy rather than the simple recommendations of an educational counselor.

Scheduling

Scheduling study time is the most controversial of the study techniques. "Why schedule—I just have so much time," or, "I just work until I'm through," is a typical reaction. If you are receiving grades commensurate with or beyond your mental ability, or if you have time for sufficient relaxation to make for enthusiasm in your work, you probably do not need scheduling. If, on the other hand, you constantly worry because you are "not on top" of your work, then scheduling is a prerequisite for your study.

Students differ widely in their desire for and ability to follow a schedule. A student should plan a schedule for his first week in school, realizing that this schedule will probably be changed by conflicting class meetings, unavailable courses, or inability to get the teachers he desires. However, by the second or third week of school, as he becomes oriented to the semester's work, he can plan another study schedule, knowing that this one is to serve as a guide throughout the term.

A college student usually takes from fifteen to twenty-one class hours per semester, and his professors advise that about two study hours be given to preparation for each hour spent in class. With this simple yardstick of study-time requirement, and with fixed class hours each day, the student can arrange his individual schedule either to increase or decrease his study time, according to his scholastic needs. Some students and instructors think in terms of a weekly schedule. A series of twenty-four hour schedules is likely to be more effective for most students. At the end of each day, the student sets up a feasible, rather than an ideal, schedule for the next twenty-four hours.

It is a good idea to arrange studying time as soon after lectures as possible. Researches indicate that study immediately, or within a

CONVENIENT FORM FOR WEEKLY WORK SCHEDULE FOR STUDENT

		Sunday	Monday	Tuesday	Wednesday	Thursday	Friday	Saturday
MORNING	8							
	9							
	10							
	11							
	12							
AFTERNOON	1							
	2							
	3							
	4							
	5							
EVENING	6							
	7							
	8							
	9							
	10							
	11							

Work Schedule of ______________________

reasonable time, after a class is far superior to the same amount of study the day or the night before a class. In this program, good students often allow for a short period of review just prior to the lecture.

Another important point to remember is that spreading the learning period over the semester is far more effective than cramming in all the subject material at the end of the semester.[9] This means that reviewing must be a constant practice. It is imperative to "keep on top" of your work throughout the semester, and this can be achieved only by wise scheduling.

The evidence from Frederiksen and Schrader's study of how students spend their time shows that the student who gets high marks relative to his ability tends to be a pretty serious sort of fellow with definite academic interests. He is likely to take more courses, study more than the average student, and attend evening lectures. He indulges less in frivolous activities such as going to parties or movies. He does engage in bull sessions, but in moderation.

In general, women in college spend more time than men in extracurricular activities—other than athletics. They attend lectures or concerts, and indulge in social activities—dates, parties, movies, and the like. They spend less time in athletics, physical recreation and in voluntary course reading. They attend fewer classes (presumably because they tend to take fewer laboratory courses) and are less likely to have a part-time job.[10]

"I'm going to try to graduate—I can't stand this mess any longer!" Reproduced by special permission of the artist, Herb Green. ***Saturday Review,*** March 23, 1963.

Physical Setting

It is highly important that the college student study in the right setting. A good desk lamp is desirable. Soft, diffused light should illuminate the rest of the room to eliminate contrast and strain. His desk should be so situated as to facilitate the maximum of efficient concentration. Generally, it is a good idea to have it away from windows affording campus views. If the room is shared by another student, it is a good idea to arrange the desks so that the two students are back to back while studying. Nor should the student, when at work at his desk, be able to see his bed or an inviting easy chair. The chair for study should be of the hard straight-backed variety. This will enable the student to maintain a reasonable state of muscular tenseness during study, a state that greatly aids effectiveness of study.

Keep a specific desk and chair for study only. Lounging and recreational reading should be done in another chair. Eventually, if the particular place of study is consistently used for study only, it will cause the student to settle down to intensive work almost immediately. In order to build up sustained attention habits, the student should begin work as soon as he sits down. Oftentimes it is difficult to get started. Hence, routine tasks such as reorganizing notes or recopying a theme might be tackled first as a "warming up" for the real work.

Of course the well-motivated student pays relatively little attention to his physical environment. Some students do excellent intellectual work while riding on subway trains or in family settings. They can concentrate very well in the midst of train noise, chatting of family members, or the clatter of typewriters. The urge to learn is more important than the physical setting.

Reading as a Study Tool

The increasing awareness of reading ability as an aid to successful study is readily seen in the development of reading clinics as an integral part of college and university programs. The importance of reading ability in the entire program of education can hardly be exaggerated.[11]

Numerous reports from reading clinics emphasize two facts: (1) the average student reads unnecessarily slowly and inefficiently, and (2) after a period of intensive training, such a reader can increase his speed, improve his comprehension, and increase his overall efficiency.[12]

Comprehension is the first objective in reading. Improving comprehension is an aid to speed also. Increasing the speed means that the time spent in study can be reduced. From 85 to 90 per cent of all studying done in high school and college is concerned with some form of reading. With adequate training in reading a student who has been spending four hours per night in study can do the same amount with better comprehension in two hours.

The poor reader reads slowly, generally about 100 to 150 words a minute, comprehends poorly; makes many "regressions" (backward movements of the eyes over material already read); reads word by word or phrase by phrase; must move his eyes six or seven times to cover an average line of print; reads with his tongue, throat, and vocal chords; and tires easily.

The student reads for different purposes on different occasions, and his methods on each occasion should fit the purpose for which he is then reading. The more intelligently he reads, the more inclined he will be to vary his rate of reading and his method of attack.

Most persons can make their easiest and quickest improvement by varying the rate of reading. Various rates of reading may be used for different types of reading material. The light novel and the tabloid newspaper can be skimmed or scanned and comprehended easily, but more complex novels and the more difficult magazine articles must be read more slowly and carefully. The physics test, the economics book, and the philosophy pamphlet must be read even more slowly. Reading clinics have found that the rate can vary from some 40 to 1,000 words a minute for the same individual, reading different types of material.

An understanding of the reading process has helped many students to improve their reading skills. During reading, the eyes are in a constant state of movement. In the actual process of perceiving words, however, the eyes are fixated or stopped. It is during these stops that words are read. How many stops do you make per line? It is a simple procedure to find out. Have someone sit across from you and count them. The number of stops varies from two to six or seven per line according to the skill of the reader and the difficulty of material being read.

The skillful reader reads fast, comprehends exactly, has few regressions, reads phrases and sentences—rarely single words—can absorb an average line of print with one or two eye movements, does not move his lips, reads actively, thinks with the author, has superior concentration, and remembers what he reads.

The student should make certain that his reading procedure is correct before he begins to read. Many students find that a graph representing reading speed serves as a stimulus to practice. Another device is to have constantly on hand a book which is enjoyable and which can be read rapidly—this can be a light novel or a book of short stories. When one book is finished, another can be started immediately. A definite reading program of 15 to 20 minutes a day can be set up, and the chosen reading material will thus be consistently read. Such consistency brings about results. With these books, too, occasional pages can be timed as a check on speed.

Speed of reading and comprehension are closely correlated. Often students show surprise that comprehension can increase along with speed, until they realize that single words do not make pictures or ideas. It is only when several words or phrases are comprehended that a visual picture or idea ensues.

A simple device for improving reading comprehension is *written recall.* The student should take a meaningful paragraph, page, or section from a textbook, read it, close the book, write a summary of the important points, and then check his writing with the text. Some students prefer to write a rough outline, which usually brings about the same result. Vocabulary-building, as an integral part of reading ability, should always be in the developing stage.

An extensive knowledge of the exact meanings of English words accompanies outstanding success in this country more than any other single characteristic. To keep your vocabulary developing requires constant and continuous surveillance. Many systems are in use for this purpose. The most common one uses 3″ x 5″ card indexes, generally set up with a word on the front of each card and its meaning on the back. Thus, in odd moments, the cards can be shuffled and a private word game can be played. When words have been mastered, the cards are usually filed and then occasionally reviewed. Some students prefer to keep a section in their notebooks for vocabulary improvement; others like a small notebook devoted entirely to new words. The particular system by which you improve your vocabulary is not significant; that you do have some system is important. Without one, your vocabulary either levels off or declines. It is imperative to keep your vocabulary developing.

The following rules or practices will help the student improve his reading methods:

1. Prepare your mind before beginning to read. Ask yourself how this book or article fits your plan of development. What questions should the author answer for you? Recall other articles on the same subject and ask yourself how this article relates to your previous studies.

2. Make a preliminary survey. Note the exact title, the author's position and his other writings, the year the book was written, the publisher, and the preface. The intelligent student reads the preface to learn why the author wrote the book and the treatment or points of view which he believed to be of value to the reader.

After reading the preface, read the table of contents and page rapidly through the book to note other main headings and the illustrations. Get the outline of the book in your mind. Note the parts in italics or capital letters or ideas which the author wants to impress upon the reader. Reading a book twice may seem unnecessary and a waste of time—but it is not, because double reading aids the formation of stronger and more lasting powers of recall.

3. Read rapidly. Beware of "dozing" study. Don't think that you are studying when you merely hold a book in your hand and look at words. If you cannot throw yourself into your study and work at high pressure, stop entirely and stand before an open window, or take a few exercises.

Force yourself to read rapidly.[13] Urge yourself to speed up. Begin at once to read rapidly. At first this may interfere with the clarity of comprehension but if you persist, you will soon find that you can learn ten times as much by speeding up. Spending a lot of time in study is far less important than a small amount of time well spent at consistent intervals. Don't dawdle. Go to it full steam ahead. Whenever you find yourself gliding off into daydreams or irrelevant meditations, bring yourself back sharply. Let each digression act as a reminder to get back to the job at hand.

4. Vary the rate of your reading. Read the simple or already known parts rapidly, or skip them entirely. Concentrate upon the important and difficult parts. If you do not understand the meaning of a word, look it up in the dictionary. If you find it difficult to grasp a principle, try to draw a diagram illustrating it or make an outline of the author's own statements. Make it a rule never to do straightaway reading at a regular rate unless you read for entertainment.

5. Make marginal notes or underscore the main ideas. Try to summarize the author's ideas in your own words by writing a sentence in the margin. A good plan is to underscore important items or draw a vertical line in the margin for important paragraphs or sentences. Always read with a pencil or pen in your hand so that you can indicate important passages. A book well-read has many penciled passages.

6. Use "active self-recitation." Think while you read. Spend a large part of your study in thinking over what you have read. Do not accept the author's statements blindly. Consider his views in the light of your own ideas or those of others. Be open-minded and willing to learn, but do not accept without some analysis of statements. Ask yourself whether the author is stating the results of impartial investigations or merely his own opinions. Do his conclusions follow from his statements? Is he trying to sell you some pet idea?[14]

Notemaking

The notebook is the badge of the student, the engineer, the explorer. The standard 8½″ x 11″ looseleaf notebook with a stiff cover is recommended. One well-organized notebook, in addition to class and book notes, can also be used for material passed out by instructors. The obvious advantage of one notebook is that work materials are always at hand. With actual notemaking, a system of abbreviations is necessary. Much time can be saved if this system is a consistent one. Many students, especially in the first months of college, before the abbreviations have become automatic, have found that a page set aside in the notebook for abbreviations is an aid to the mastery of a system.

In actual college work three kinds of notemaking are found: notes on lectures, notes on borrowed books, and notes in a book. Making lecture notes makes you an active rather than a passive participant. It is an aid to learning, for it requires you to evaluate ideas, to organize thoughts, and then to jot down the meaningful items. Good lecture notes are brief, but good lecture notes have complete sentences and are organized under meaningful headings. Making notes on radio programs, a sermon, or a talk can give added practice. In class lectures, being ready for the lecture is essential. Notes from the previous lecture should have been reviewed. Reading ahead of lectures, in textbook and reference books, is valuable here also.

The question whether notes should be rewritten will depend on how expert a notemaker you are. If your original lecture notes are ready for use in review, then rewriting is not necessary. Otherwise, it is.

Notemaking from library books is essentially the same as lecture notemaking. You must sort out the salient points of a chapter or a portion of a book or magazine article. This task is made easier by reading the entire assignment to get an over-all picture or framework. Then go back and actually write out the points or facts of this framework.

Making notes in your own books is essential to active learning. A consistent set of symbols is necessary to indicate important facts, points of disagreement, connection of key words or phrases, and numbering or a series of ideas. Important points can be underlined or can be marked by vertical lines in the margin. A soft lead pencil or a red lead pencil will mark so as to show up plainly. Brief markings will serve the student best—key words, important phrases, and, of course, ideas that need clarification. Through notemaking on an assignment, the important points stand out so that skim reading will serve as a review.

Using the Library

In student life, knowledge of efficient library usage is essential. The librarian is always there to aid research and investigation, but time can be saved by one's own ability to dig out necessary information. In a new college situation, you should spend every available minute during the first weeks in becoming familiar with your college libraries.

Three types of card catalogs are in use in libraries: (a) *Dictionary*—alphabetically arranged by author, title, and subject; all cards are in terms of one alphabet; (b) *Divided-catalog*—divided into two parts: subject catalog and author and title catalog, (c) *Classified* (mostly in technical libraries)—arranged by broad subject or some practical scheme related to the type of material. The dictionary type of catalog is the one in general use and the one you would expect to find in most libraries.

The catalog serves as an index to the library. It contains author, title, and subject cards for the books in the library. These cards are important in that on each the call number of the book concerned is given. The author, title, place and date of publication, and publisher are also given. For most books in the library there are three cards in the card catalog: one, the author card; one, the title card; and one, the subject card. Some books, particularly fiction, have only two cards, and some (autobiography) only one. More cards may result from dual authorship. Also, if the book deals with more than one subject, each subject will be represented by a card in the catalog. On subject cards, the subject is always typed in red at the top of the catalog card so that it can be readily distinguished from an author or title card. In order to get a book from closed stacks, you must copy the author, title, and call number of the specific book wanted on a call slip. It is important to be extremely accurate in copying the call number, making sure that no letter or number is omitted, since an omission may result in having the wrong book delivered. Also, sign your name legibly. Then give the call slip to a staff member at the circulation desk.

Fiction is usually found in a separate section or room. It is arranged alphabetically by last name of the author and under each author alphabetically by title. All the books by Somerset Maugham, for example, will be together. Books other than fiction are arranged according to a special system of classification. The Dewey Decimal Classification is widely used.

Besides learning from books, the industrious student will learn from periodicals. The newest ideas in any field are in the magazines. Using periodicals beyond the limit of assignments imposed by instructors can give you a richer background and a knowledge of current material. As has been mentioned, periodical reading in the field of a new course or an unfamiliar topic can give you extensive information.

To find pertinent information in magazines, you must use periodical guides. The card catalog is an index to books; the *Reader's Guide to Periodical Literature* and similar periodical indexes are indexes to contents of selected magazines. In the front of each issue of an index are lists of the magazines indexed, the abbreviations used, and an explanation on how to use the index. Entries are alphabetized under author, title, and subject. Libraries often have special call slips, and to obtain a desired issue of a periodical, it is necessary to copy the following from the index—name of the author and the title of the article, the name of the periodical, the volume number, the date, and page number. Large libraries usually have a call number for each different magazine to be found in the card catalog. The *Reader's Guide* indexes general periodicals, but for special fields the following indexes are invaluable. The titles indicate generally specific areas covered:

Agricultural Index
Annual Magazine Subject Index
Art Index
Book Review Digest
Dramatic Index
Education Index
Engineering Index
Industrial Arts Index
International Index to Periodicals
Monthly Catalog, U.S. Public Documents
The New York Times Index
Public Affairs Information Service

The achieving student becomes quickly familiar with the indexes that will be useful in obtaining articles in his particular fields of special interest. Business administration students, for example, will find a wealth of material on applied science, business finance, and technology in the *Industrial Arts Index*.

In addition, a library has many reference books, such as dictionaries, *Roget's Thesaurus of English Words and Phrases* and *Webster's Dictionary of Synonyms*. Encyclopedias, as a beginning tool in research, save much time; in them information on every subject of importance is given in alphabetical order. However, a paper based on encyclopedia reading only is not enough to satisfy a professor's assignment such as a term paper.

How to Write

Many college courses consist primarily of a sort of correspondence between professor and student. In such courses it is imperative for you to be able to write. If you can express your ideas in writing, the assignment of a theme, a book review, or even a term paper will present few insurmountable barriers.

First, be sure that you have something to say. Secondly, no matter how small or large the assignment may me, always make sure that the facts supporting your ideas are correct. Third, make a rough outline.

And then—write.

In this initial setting down, it is getting the ideas on paper that is important. If this is very difficult to do, you may not have enough material on the subject. More reading in books or periodicals may be necessary. Definite ideas to express, accompanied by interest, make writing easy.

In reading, the garnering of background material is the objective, it is not the "lifting" of whole sentences or paragraphs for your paper. Ideas are not formed in a vacuum; hence the necessity of wide knowledge. With patience and practice in writing, you can put your ideas across to other persons.

Writing is a skill that requires consistent practice. If you find it difficult to write, do not confine your writing to assignments. Do other kinds of writing for practice. Write friendly letters. See how well you can get across a mood, an event, a day-to-day routine to family or friends. Make summaries of radio talks or the Sunday sermon. Keep a journal.

In writing it is not enough to say a fact once if you really want to put it across. Rather, the point must be made in more than one way. Approach it from different angles or enlarge your original premise.

Many students lose credit on written assignments through neglect. They fail to read what they have written in order to polish and correct the finished product. At the college level, misspelled words, incomplete sentences, grammatical errors often affect one's grade.

An important written assignment should be done in the rough as soon as possible. After the rough outline or plan has been developed, let your ideas "simmer." Keep notes on any new ideas and on hints for the rephrasing of particular sentences. The day before the assignment is due, make the final revision.

All college assignments should be typed.

Professors may be traditionally thought of as absentminded, but they are quick to pick out the theme written at the last minute, perhaps while the writer was being bored in the preceding class. Effective writing of any kind, from class assignments to best-seller novels, is hard work. If you will work diligently at writing, aiming for accuracy and clarity, you can achieve the desired qualities.

How to Remember

Many people dislike the idea of memorizing because memory is thought of only as a mechanical process of "learning by heart." Thinking and memorizing are usually considered as alternatives. Actually they are a part of the same process and go together. Material which has been thought through is remembered without much effort. Memory is a by-product of study, and the general principles of study apply to memorizing.

Most students want to be able to recall studied material for one of the two more common kinds of examinations: the essay test and the objective test. In studying for an essay examination, the understanding and organizing of major ideas are especially important. The making of outlines should be a part of the study for recall.

Objective examinations cover the study content extensively. Underlining of many factual items is important so that reviews can be made easily and frequently.

Good students also do studying that is "instructor-oriented." That is, they are alert to note the ideas stressed by the instructor, and they make extra effort to understand and memorize them.

The main way to improve memory is to improve the methods of learning. However, the following rules may aid in improving the ability to remember:

1. Get the meaning of the material to be remembered. Be sure that you clearly understand the material you want to recall. Think of the new ideas from every angle and try to apply them to practical situations. Do this not only when you are reading but also when you are at leisure. When you are walking or riding to and from your home, do not waste the time in idle reverie. Utilize your spare time. Perhaps you may think it dangerous to keep active mentally so large a part of your time. Have no fear. No man ever went insane or had a breakdown from mental overwork, but a lot have gone insane or broken down from overworry or other inadequate mental habits. Most of the talk about breakdowns from mental overwork is rationalization. The idle and the ignorant are the ones who suffer most from neuroses; not those who are exceedingly busy.
2. Always study with the intent to remember. Herein lies the cause for much forgetfulness. Occasionally a teacher repeats certain outlines of lectures to his students and asks them to memorize the outlines. Later on he finds that he himself cannot repeat the outline because he simply dictated the material from his lecture notes. Whenever you study, do so with a determination to remember the things studied, and you will be surprised how easy it is to recall your past mental efforts.
3. Stop frequently during your studying and check up what you have learned. Compel yourself to recall what you are learning. Spend about

40 per cent of your time reciting to yourself. If you cannot recall what you have read, turn back and read it again. By a little practice along this line you will treble your ability to remember what you have covered. Imagine you are teaching the material and see whether you know it so well that you can explain it clearly to someone else. If you are unable to explain the meaning to someone else, you do not understand or know it. Go over it again and study each sentence and paragraph until you are able to tell what it does mean.

4. Use repetition. Don't expect to recall everything that you study unless you repeat the difficult parts over and over. In the case of definitions of technical terms, formulas, dates, and outlines, where the material has few natural clues for recall, don't hesitate to commit to memory verbatim. Of course, parrotlike recitation is wasteful, but don't consider yourself above mechanical repetition of certain material.

5. In committing to memory it is better to read aloud than to read silently and it is better to read to someone else than to yourself. Attention is better sustained in this way, because an appeal is made to the ear as well as to the eye and some help is gotten from the "feel" of the words in the throat and mouth. The value of reading to another person is that it promotes accuracy of thinking and insures proper emphasis of the several ideas.

6. Attempt to remember only the important material. Confine your efforts to the essential and relegate the nonessential to references to the dictionary, encyclopedia, and textbooks.

Mark with a red pencil items you have to learn verbatim. Then study each item with the intent to understand, and the material will practically be memorized. The index to a book is a useful key to the most important facts, references, and key words. If you cannot identify an item listed in the index, even though you know you have studied it, review it.

7. Carry the learning of important items beyond the point necessary for immediate recall. Experiments show that we forget about 60 per cent of material barely learned within one day after learning. This means that information necessary in your life work must be studied more than is sufficient barely to recall it the next day. The fading of impressions must be met by overlearning. Superficial learning of the spelling of a word may satisfy the immediate need, but it will not satisfy the needs of correct spelling a year later.

8. Space your study. Experiments have shown that it is better to memorize a certain amount of material at intervals than to try to complete the job at one sitting. Don't try to do seven hours of studying in one evening of each week, but study one hour on seven evenings of each week. This allows the individual to organize new material in relation to past experience.

9. If necessary, invent some artificial scheme for learning and recalling material which lacks rational associations. This is seldom necessary, but may be helpful in recalling material, such as the height of the volcano of Fujiyama, which was reported as 12,365 feet. Simply remember that we have 12 months and 365 days in the year.

Or you can use acrostics. As one man said: "In my public school days we had a speaker give us a talk once a month. Of the fifty or more talks which I heard I recall the subject of but one. In that case the speaker's subject was 'Grow' and the method of growth which he suggested was 'Go right on working.' The first letter of each word forms the word 'Grow.' " Acrostics can be used to advantage in remembering lists of words or names.

For temporary recall, it may be very helpful to try to visualize facts or principles. Try to picture them in unusual lights, colors, positions, and so on. However, it is best to depend upon logical connections by understanding the relationships of the material to be remembered.

Memorizing Names and Faces

Remembering the names of people whom we meet is not a mysterious gift that is given to politicians and denied to others. The politician finds it necessary to know people's names when he meets them and he consciously practices learning them. He seriously wants to know their names. Students in laboratory courses in psychology have taken part in an experiment where they repeated the colors in a color-naming test. The colors were only five in number and were irregularly arranged in one hundred bits, each of the five colors appearing twenty times. After the colors had been named over as often as two hundred times by each student, not one student could repeat the colors from memory in correct sequential order. Their efforts had been concentrated upon naming the bits of color as seen and not in connecting them in a series that could be remembered. Similarly, when we meet strangers, our attention is concentrated upon the impression that we make on the stranger and not upon knowing his name. We are too conscious of ourselves to grasp the name of the stranger. Our self-consciousness will tend to disappear if we determine to know and remember the names of those whom we meet.

Quite frequently, when we meet strangers and are formally introduced to them, we do not hear the name, or, if we do hear it, we get it incorrectly. To insure clarity, we should spell the name and ask its owner whether it is correctly spelled and pronounced. The chairman at businessmen's luncheon clubs frequently ask each member to stand up and state business affiliation. After this ceremony is over, few, if any, have learned the names. Most of the names are mumbled, and repeated too rapidly to make any neural impression. If members of clubs wish to become acquainted, the leader should ask the secretary to write each name on a blackboard or have each person write his own name on the board. Each of the other members should then write, on a piece of paper, the name of each stranger and try to connect the name and person in his own mind. Before the meeting ends, each person should try to recall the name of each member and verify his recollection.

A similar method can be used at bridge parties, dances, and banquets. Here the formal introduction must be hurried by the hosts and a request for enough time to write down each name and verify it would break into the smoothness of the occasion. However, when the guests are seated or participating in the activities, then the names of strangers can be requested from a near-by associate. Effort should be made to meet the strangers and learn something about their personalities.

Some memory-training systems advise the student to connect the name of the stranger in a grotesque or irrelevant way, as, Mr. Pitts might remind us of the fiery pit—Hell. Or, Mr. Long may be very short and the contrast seems to enable us to associate the name with his height. However, such irrational associations are not nearly so effective as a logical connection of facts regarding the personality of each stranger. The time and effort expended in making such incongruous connections can be spent more profitably in making logical connections of correct facts about the person.

The feeling tone in names must also be recognized. Persons whom we like, we remember. The name of the girl at the dance who is most attractive to the youth will be remembered for years. He puts forth effort to learn her name, telephone number, and other items of information. Conversely, we tend to forget those whom we dislike or do not care for. If a number of older men are asked to state the number of times they were engaged to girls before they were married, one is likely to find that those who were engaged to three or more girls cannot recall their names. They cannot recall them simply because some unpleasant experiences are associated with their memories. The true politician likes people, and his pleasant feeling toward them assists him in recalling their names.

When the name of the person is to be fixed so that it can be recalled, it should be repeated during the conversation as often as politeness permits. The average individual is able to recall about one-third more names when he has spoken the name once than when he has remained silent.[15] The salesman should get into the habit of prefacing many of his statements with "Mr. Prospect," and ending some of them with "Do you agree, Mr. Prospect?" After the stranger has left one's presence, it is well to think of him—not as "that fellow in the blue suit" but by name. And he should be thought of in terms of a clear visual image.

Techniques of Creative Thinking

Many persons who do original thinking seem to want the public to believe that they do their thinking with the efficiency of firmly disciplined methods. Actually, studies of creative thinkers indicate that they make many false starts, waste time in random and exploratory movements, have desultory periods, and waver between unmanageable fantasies and systematic attack.

Investigations indicate that some creative thinkers realize that they are driven by a kind of demon or creative urge. A student of creative thought, Eliot D. Hutchinson, has reported one man's consuming purpose and commented on such drives as follows:

> Eden Phillpotts, the Devonshire novelist and dramatist, writes: "For my own part the creative urge is a demon that drives, and will doubtless continue to drive, while my intellect, such as it is, functions normally and does not begin to wither with age. As a boy at school there was a longing to make things. I was always drawing. Then I longed to be an actor and create character; then I found these mediums beyond my power and turned to writing."
>
> Perhaps such a drive is instinctive, reaching down into the very foundations of the personality. Perhaps it is conditioned and due to education, perhaps to abundant and overflowing energy. There are a dozen theories to explain it. In some it is not always persistent. It may lie dormant for years and then, when aroused by an inexplicable circumstance, drive the mind with a lashing hand. Whatever its source, we are certain that the immediate occasion for creative activity is the adjustment to some inner and controlling purpose, the resolution of some dissatisfaction with the world as it is, the ambition to idealize reality.[16]

The several stages in the process of creative thinking have been designated by Graham Wallas[17] essentially as follows:

1. *Preparation.* This stage refers to the study of the problem, its essential aspects, and the consideration of similar problems and their solutions.

2. *Incubation.* When the thinker has made the first step, preparation, he often takes a walk, a drive, or carries on some other activities wholly unrelated to the main problem. During incubation, the unconscious mental activities may be applied to the problem while the individual is engaged in easy physical exercise or routine tasks. However, close attention to some other problem, or intense emotional reactions from thrilling motion pictures, seem to be less beneficial than the kind of mind wandering which we experience during a train ride or in easy reading for one's entertainment. Time spent in just "sitting still" is likely to facilitate incubation far more than vigorous continuous search for an answer. Idleness and relaxation are often more helpful than an attempt to stuff one's self with "good reading."

3. *Illumination.* This refers to the appearance of the "good idea," coming seemingly from nowhere. The thinker usually has an intimation of the coming of the sought answer. He is conscious of the "dawning" for which he has searched.

Sometimes the thinker may recognize that he has experienced a great discovery but decide to postpone its consideration. Later he may find that he cannot revive the great idea whose birth he throttled. Failure to record the "flash" or to follow through may result in tragic inability to do so later.

Hutchinson investigated the frequency of "scientific hunch" as recognized by chemists, mathematicians, physicists, biologists, and men of similar standing. Answers to a questionnaire sent out by the Educational Department of the American Chemical Society yielded the report that 83 per cent of the 232 directors of research laboratories and "American Men of Science" replied affirmatively to the question: "Have you ever received assistance from the scientific revelation or 'hunch' in the solution of an important problem?"

4. *Verification.* When the "good idea" or important solution has appeared to the thinker, he tests it in the light of known facts and reason. Perhaps he also explains it to colleagues in the same field of thought.

Creative thinking for most great thinkers has a pattern which may be described as drive, problem, conscious effort to solve it, passivity, repeated periods of conscious efforts and passivity, sudden illumination, and verification.*

Actually, the human mind does not "create." Instead, it computes, searches, probes, changes objectives, and experiments

* These stages in creative thinking have been studied in the work of artists. See the study by C. Patrick, "Creative Thought in Artists," *Journal of Psychology,* Vol. 4 (1937), pp. 35–73. The process of creative thought in sketching pictures was studied by having artists sketch pictures while expressing their thoughts aloud, and by having them answer

with various procedures until a unique new orientation takes place.

Brainstorming as a problem solving or creative technique has been given a great deal of favorable attention in general readership magazines and in certain business concerns. Psychologists have made studies of its effectiveness as a technique. Some of the findings have been favorable. However, the most carefully planned investigations have suggested doubts and modifications. In one study, for example, problems were presented for brainstorming to 48 research scientists and 48 advertising personnel employed with the Minnesota Mining and Manufacturing Company. Each subject brainstormed certain problems individually and other equated problems as a member of a four-man team. The results indicated that individuals produced more ideas than groups and they did so without sacrificing quality of ideas. However, the superiority of individual thinking over group brainstorming was relatively greater when it was preceded by group participation. Some of the findings reported are:

The net superiority of individual performance over group participation for these two sets of industrially employed subjects is highlighted by the fact that 23 of the 24 groups produced a large number of different ideas under the individual condition. To the extent that we may generalize these findings to future situations, we can state that four persons, attacking a problem individually, and then pooling their efforts will, on the average, produce about 30 per cent more ideas than if they attempted to solve the problem in a group session or meeting.

Our findings also suggest that group participation may be useful in "warming up" for individual brainstorming sessions. Research personnel produced more ideas when individual brainstorming followed group participation than when it preceded it. Advertising men also exhibited relatively greater superiority in the individual sessions when they had been preceded by a group session.

The research team report offered comments on a related study by D. W. Taylor, *et al.*, Yale University, Department of Psychology:

Taylor et al. suggested, and we concur, on the basis of our observations during these experiments, that a group tends to "fall in a rut" and to pursue the same train of thought. The effect of this is to limit the diversity of approaches to a problem, thereby leading to the production of fewer different ideas. It was also apparent that the output of many individuals who were highly productive when working alone was considerably less in the group situation. In spite of the stimulus of group brainstorming and our specific directive to avoid all criticism, it was apparent that these persons were inhibited simply by the presence of other group members. The central idea underlying brainstorming of placing a moratorium on all criticism is a good one. It appears, however, that group participation still contains certain inhibitory influences which are not easily dissipated. The "best bet" for creative thinking in attacking problems seems, therefore, to be the pooled individual efforts of many people with perhaps an initial group session to serve simply as a warm up to their efforts.[18]

Suggestions for the Office and Professional Worker

Most people find that on certain days they get things done more speedily than on others. Is the increased speed and productivity merely psychological or actual? The fact is, each person has not only better and worse days, but also better and worse hours. While these are often psychological, there is also a very definite physical basis for our improved ability at certain times and lessened drive at other times.

The rise and fall of our working efficiency coincides with temperature variations in our body. Even when we are perfectly well, our temperature varies as much as three degrees in a single day. These temperature changes reflect our basal metabolism, that complicated process by which our body burns oxygen and keeps us going. Certain studies indicate that

---

questions concerning their usual practices. Fifty professional artists and 50 unpracticed sketchers served as subjects. The reports revealed the four stages of creative thought: namely, preparation, incubation, illumination, and verification, already revealed in other studies of creation. The course of thought in artists and nonartists is similar. Nonartists draw more objects and more different kinds of objects than do artists.

most people fall into one of three types:

a. *The Morning Type:* He wakes ready to go full blast. Packed with drive, he reaches his peak around noon, then cools off gradually. By evening he is pretty well burned out.
b. *The Evening Type:* He hates to get up and goes through the morning listless, lethargic, even surly. But soon after noon, he begins glowing. By late afternoon he is a fireball. His energy lasts into late evening.
c. *The Half-and-Half:* This happy man has the virtues of the other two. His personal thermostat gets him off to an early start. It cools him down at midday and fires him up again for the afternoon.

A person's cycle is not permanent. It is fixed by habit and habits can be changed. A few week's effort may do it. To raise your body heat in the morning, take a long, hot shower or bath, or up to a half hour of calisthenics. If you can change your temperature, you can alter the whole cycle.

The common tendency is to delay mental work until the afternoon. This is often a mistake. Try yourself on these questions:

—Are you using your best hours doing secondary tasks which you might handle just as easily later?
—Do you do a lot of desk work or other straightening up when this routine could be done later or at day's end so as to start you off with a zip?
—Do you insist on handling routine correspondence to "get it out of the way" and leave your mind free for bigger things? Actually, you'd do better hitting those bigger things first. . . ."
—Have you made a conscientious effort to advance your cycle? Bear in mind that even if you're the evening type, you'll suffer a loss of efficiency later in the day. This is because, in most cases, you will already have been at work for a certain number of hours—and thus have used up a portion of the energy not otherwise restored.[19]

For most of us, an attractive surrounding increases our efficiency. Eliminating the clutter on a desk helps to get things done more quickly and seems to help straighten out the clutter in the mind.

Utilizing Time Efficiently

It is obviously impossible to specify how much time any office or professional worker should spend on each operation in the day's work. However, the places and occasions where one's time is wasted or misused are not in the performance of his regular duties but in the attention given to the bothersome trivialities adequately described by James Gordon Gilkey in his "Secrets of Effective Living":

Once I read about a man who was tied down and the ants ate him.
His fingers, his ears, his eyes, everything.
At last they even devoured his brain,
Emptying his skull bit by bit.
I am tied down, too, and little things are eating me—
The friend who calls me on the phone and talks and talks,
The agent who is determined to sell me a new mop,
The children who quarrel and will not do their lessons,
The letters that must be answered before night somehow,
The ice man's short weight, the butcher's carelessness,
All these little things are devouring me alive.

The time-consumers that "eat" us are social obligations, "being a good fellow," eating too much, and chasing ephemeral ideas that appear promising but end in rainbows without any pots of gold.

Our social obligations—receptions, playing bridge, golf, driving just for a drive, formal dinners, fraternal meetings, conventions, and community drives all appear essential to the development of a balanced personality and vocational advancement. In many cases, wives insist upon them. Some of these affairs do bring us in touch with people whom we ought to know. Some do bring in business later, but it is a waste of time in the long run to cultivate people merely for the sake of getting business rather than as the result of a natural liking for them. All these side lines become dangerous when they control us. Selling tickets for charity affairs, putting up decorations, buying theater tickets, lending money, giving talks before Sunday schools, writing letters of introduction, and so on, all have their place, but they tend to devour time and effort and end nowhere. It is seldom that people trust their fortunes or important problems to the accommodating man. When we are seriously ill we go to the doctor who is so busy professionally that he has no time to give to little things. We prefer to deposit our money in the bank whose president is noted for his ability and stability rather than in the bank whose president is a public beast of burden. To achieve things worthy of the respect of our fellows, we must respect the obligations of our own work to the extent that we fulfill them before we oblige others.

The ambitious individual need not confuse the performance of his own duties with an abrupt disregard for the needs and feelings of others. To refuse to take time to be accommodating to others does not necessitate coldness of manner. The daily acts of the worthwhile life can be invested with cordiality and friendliness. Our social relations should be more than mechanically reciprocal. They can be made delightfully pleasing. If a person lends us a book, we can do more than just thank him. We can prove to him that we read and enjoyed it. If we dine in a restaurant on a fifty-fifty basis, we should not forget the tips. We need not say to a person, "I see you do not remember me." but can state our own name without reminding him of his failure. When we win a big score in a bridge game, we need not go into a detailed recital of how it was done. When we greet the stenographer and the elevator operator, we can make the greeting just as friendly as the one we bestow upon our best customers. These little daily acts do not consume much time, but they often bring greater returns in human happiness than years of trifling services or the development of a mechanical variety of mental efficiency.

ACKNOWLEDGMENTS AND REFERENCES

1. Bernice M. Horrall, "Academic Performance and Personality Adjustment of Highly Intelligent College Students," *Genetic Psychology Monographs,* **55** (1957), 3–83.
2. Merville C. Shaw and Donald J. Brown, "Scholastic Underachievement of Bright College Students," *Personnel and Guidance Journal,* **36** (1957), 195–199.
3. See Frederick J. Todd, Glen Terrell, and Curtiss E. Frank, "Differences Between Normal and Underachievers of Superior Ability," *Journal of Applied Psychology,* June, 1962, p. 189.
4. Prescott Lecky, "Personal Counseling: The Theory of Self-Consistency in Personnel Problems," *Report* of the Annual Meeting of the American College Personnel Association, 1935.
5. Graham B. Blaine, Jr., and Charles C. McArthur, *Emotional Problems of the Student* (New York: Appleton-Century-Crofts, 1961), pp. 244–245, Chapter by Graham B. Blaine, Jr.
6. *Ibid.,* p. 99.
7. For further information see Elizabeth Louise Stadtlander, *Planning to Study Efficiently* (St. Louis: Educational Publishers, 1959), pp. 22–23.
8. See Graham B. Blaine, Jr., and Charles C. McArthur, *Emotional Problems of the Student* (New York: Appleton-Century-Crofts, 1961). Chapter 9, by Paul A. Walters, Jr., presents an excellent treatment of student apathy.
9. Robert W. Frederick, Paul C. Kitchen, and Agness R. McElwee, *A Guide to College Study* (New York: Appleton-Century-Crofts, 1947).
10. Norman Frederiksen and W. B. Schrader, *Adjustment to College* (Princeton, N.J.: Educational Testing Service, 1951).
11. C. W. Hunnicutt, "A Functional Program in Reading Instruction," *School and Society,* May 22, 1948, pp. 377–381.
12. Norman Lewis, *How to Read Better and Faster* (New York: Thomas Y. Crowell Company, 1944), p. 10.
13. *A Formula for More Efficient Reading—the S-P-D Approach,* Miscellaneous Publication, No. 753, U.S. Dept. of Agriculture, Office of Personnel, Washington, D.C., 1958.
14. Norman Lewis, *How to Read Better and Faster,* 3rd ed. (New York: Thomas Y. Crowell Company, 1958). This book provides a self-help training manual designed to develop techniques of rapid and skillful reading.
15. Harold E. Burtt and A. C. Beck, "Remembering Names Connected with Faces," *Journal of Industrial Psychology,* January, 1928, pp. 34–38.
16. Eliot D. Hutchinson, "The Technique of Creative Thought," *The American Scholar,* May, 1932.
17. Graham Wallas, *The Art of Thought* (New York: Harcourt, Brace & World, Inc., 1926).
18. Marvin D. Dunnette, John Campbell, and Kay Jaastad, "The Effect of Group Participation on Brainstorming Effectiveness for Two Industrial Examples," *Journal of Applied Psychology,* February, 1963. See also D. W. Taylor, P. C. Berry, and C. H. Block, *Does Group Participation*

When Using Brainstorming Facilitate or Inhibit Creative Thinking? Technical Report No. 1, 1957, Yale University, Department of Psychology, Office of Naval Research. See also, "Yale Study: Brainstorming Blocks Creativity," *Printers' Ink,* Feb. 21, 1958.

19. Ray Josephs, "Gaining a Golden Hour Every Day," *American Business,* February, 1956, p. 12. From a book *How to Gain an Extra Hour Every Day* by the same author (New York: E. P. Dutton and Co., Inc., 1955).

PROJECTS

1. Below is a list of "do" study habits. Post a similar list over your desk and check each night on your study habits:
   a. Prepared the next assignment immediately after class.
   b. Reviewed assignment and preceding lecture notes before class.
   c. Checked written assignments.
   d. Added words to my vocabulary.
   e. Took a brief scanning view over before reading.
   f. Took part in class discussion.
   g. Discussed a lesson with another student.
   h. Read a book or journal in the library for collateral reading.
2. Do you find it difficult to concentrate? For one week study always with an extra sheet of paper at hand. Each time that you find your attention wanders from your studying, list the subject of distraction.
3. Write a set of rules for remembering people whom you meet.
4. Devise a written form of recording new words being added to your vocabulary. Some students use a page in their notebooks, others use a separate notebook, still others keep small card files.
5. What is a card catalog? What information is found on most cards? How are the cards arranged?
6. What indexes does your college library have? Explain each item of one magazine entry in a periodical index.
7. After reading an assignment, develop questions that your instructor might use on the next quiz.
8. When an executive requests a subordinate to give him a report, the executive usually wants it as soon as possible. After the report has been submitted, the executive may neglect to read it for several days or weeks. What is the cause of this habit on the part of the executive? How can the subordinate adjust himself to such wishes of his superior?
9. To what extent does playing the stock market decrease the efficiency of businessmen who do it? Should the ambitious businessman determine not to bother with speculation?
10. Is a clean desk indicative of personal efficiency? Make a study of this problem by preparing a list of the best executives whom you know and then observing the tops of their desks.

COLLATERAL READINGS

Gerken, C. d'A., *Study Your Way Through School.* Chicago: Science Research Associates, 1953.

Powell, W. James and Sidney M. Jourard, "Some Objective Evidence of Immaturity in Underachieving College Students," *Journal of Counseling Psychology,* **10,** No. 3 (1963), 276–282.

Prouty, Helen, "Personality Factors Related to Over and Underachievement of College Students," *The American Psychologist,* August, 1955, p. 364.

Rust, Ralph M. and James S. Davie, "Differences in Behavior Among College Classes," *Psychological Reports,* **12,** No. 2 (1963), 415–420.

Rust, Ralph M. and Francis J. Ryan, "Personality Factors Associated With Acadamic Achievement in College," *The American Psychologist,* August, 1955, p. 382.

Spielberger, Charles D., Henry Weitz, and J. Peter Denny, "Group Counseling and the Academic Performance of Anxious College Freshmen," *Journal of Counseling Psychology,* **9,** No. 3 (1962), 195–204.

Weigand, George and Walter S. Blake, Jr., *College Orientation: A Study Skills Manual.* Englewood Cliffs, N.J.: Prentice-Hall, Inc., 1955, pp. 57–64.

Whitlock, Gerald H., Lewis C. Copeland, and Albert M. Craig, "Programming versus Independent Study in Learning Elementary Statistics," *Psychological Reports,* **12**, No. 1 (1963), 171–174.

"Bonaparte, a Novice in the School at Brienne," *by Realier-Dumas. This painting is reproduced to illustrate the influence of subconscious drives in choosing a career. Napoleon may have become a conqueror as a compensation for a number of unhappy childhood experiences. An inferiority complex is often compensated for by a career that satisfies the ego's needs.* ***(By permission of Gramstorff Bros., Inc., Malden, Mass.)***

"Young Raleigh," *by John Everett Millais. This famous painting is reproduced to illustrate the fact that some individuals choose their vocation as the result of instructional influences. Of course the instructional influences are more likely to be acted upon when they fit into the individual's unconscious drives.* ***(By permission of Gramstorff Bros., Inc., Malden, Mass.)***

CHAPTER ELEVEN

CHOOSING A VOCATION

Many people think of choosing a vocation as wholly a problem in prediction of the person's future vocational abilities, successes, or failures. Psychologists, too, are interested in facilitating the individual's choice by means of valid prediction devices, but they are even more interested in improving his adjustments to the possibilities within himself and his environment. The psychologically well-adjusted person is likely to be a vocationally happy person.

One of the pioneers in the field of vocational guidance became interested in the work because he met a boy who worked in a bird store during the day and studied architectural drawing at night, but had an ambition to become a sea captain! We all know of similar persons who are confused about their vocational objectives, many others who accept their daily grind because they do not know what else to do, and a few who are really enthusiastic about their work.

Vocational Decisions Must Be Made Continuously

Studies of college students' abilities to make lasting vocational choices indicate that permanence of choice varies with the kind of professional training. Law and medical college students are more likely to enter and remain in their chosen professions or areas of work than business students.

Some changes in occupations are probably beneficial and natural. A physician in the private practice of medicine who concerns himself with health problems in the community can make a logical and easy step to politics. The university teacher of chemistry may pass on to chemical research in a corporation. Our available evidence indicates that such shifting about in occupations does take place among the successful members of society. For example, a study of the persons listed in "Who's Who in America" indicated that occupational changes were made after the age of 35 by one-third of these successful persons.[1] Perhaps a great deal of the vocational shifting which constantly takes place signifies one way in which individuals are making adjustments to the psychological problems within themselves as well as to the problems of making a living.

Many persons who have had to choose a way to make a living thought that the choice was determined by chance. But *chance* here, as elsewhere, is simply another name for the influence of a large number of unknown factors. Chance, in the determination of vocational choice, simply refers to the influences of many factors, such as those of adjustment. These psychological influences are now being unraveled in some cases. However, chance will have to continue to play the major role for some generations to come, because science must make many discoveries before we can foretell the future of a youth. We shall probably never reach "that day when men's biographies can be written in advance." However, the man who is dissatisfied with his vocation, or who is at the threshold of his economic life and must choose an occupation, can be given some helpful suggestions.

Several important basic facts should first be fixed in the mind of the person who is seeking vocational guidance for himself or is trying to counsel others who are misfits. One of these basic facts is that "the square peg and the round hole" idea is an erroneous simile. This expression implies that the human being is vocationally fixed and unchangeable in his nature. It also implies that the occupation is rigid in its requirements. On the contrary, human beings are very adaptable. Consider the record of man's progress through the ages and note the many adaptations he has had to make. Few of us would choose the life of the cave man, and yet, if conditions demanded it, many men could meet the demands of primitive life in a highly successful manner. Few of us would choose the trade of the skilled artisan; but, if a sudden industrial upheaval demanded it, we could become blacksmiths and carpenters just as readily as we become salesmen, teachers, and lawyers. Each man who goes into any vocation must adapt himself to some extent; and he, in turn, also modifies the job to fit himself.

We are not fitted by nature for one occupation and one only. It is probable that most persons who are now successful in one field could also become equally successful in some other occupation. No one is perfectly fitted for any occupation. The choosing of a vocation means that we must choose the one that requires the least amount of adjustment and gives us the greatest amount of personal satisfaction. Very few individuals are "born" to any vocation. A person of high intelligence who has had a favorable previous environment could succeed in at least a dozen fields, unless one of those fields required some special organic quality, such as the ability to hear a wide range of musical notes or to distinguish sharply between shades of colors. However, limitations of the sense organs or motor equipment are exceptional in modern vocational adjustments.

So far as we know, the brain does not at birth have certain neural patterns for specific vocational functions. Nor do such patterns develop in the brain except as the adjustments bring them about. Of course, we exclude such native endowments as exceptional qualities or limitations of the sensory apparatus. Insofar as neural capacity is involved, a great majority of persons who are in doubt as to the vocation to be chosen could pick any one of several and succeed equally well in any of the several.

Vocational decisions must be made continuously. An individual cannot make a single decision that will settle his vocational future. Rather, he must make a series of decisions, not only as to the kind of work he shall do, but also as to the kind of training he shall acquire, the place of training, the job he shall seek, and the manner in which he shall advance in his chosen field. As he develops ability in a given occupation, he must choose the phase in which he shall specialize. And, later in life, he must decide upon the kind of activities that will give him the greatest amount of self-expression. Occasionally he must decide upon the factor that shall be construed as success or failure for him; whether his objective shall be happy associations with his children, opportunities to influence the lives of others, fame, or wealth. The selection of this objective cannot be made at the beginning of life but must be decided as time brings about new situations and conditions. Not only does the individual change, but society, business, and occupations change. The occupations which are important in one decade may be of little consequence in the next decade. The progress in aviation and the automobile industry could not be foreseen forty years ago.

No one is born for a particular occupation. Nor should we think that, if an individual fails to find his one niche in life, he will be doomed to a life of failure or mediocrity. No one should be continually looking for a "niche." If he is, it is quite probable that he never will find it, because each man must make his own.

Nor should we seek to follow the vocational pathways that some other successful individual traveled. Much as we admire Lincoln, none of us can be just like him or do what he did. We can hope only to make a place in life for ourselves which we can fill as well, proportionately, as he filled his. The man who hears of how some relative, classmate, neighbor, or friend has become wealthy or happy and then attempts to follow in the same footsteps is apt to find that his feet do not fit those footprints. We cannot take the personality and conditions of some other individual and superimpose them upon ourselves. Each man must establish his own career for himself and in his own way rather than by imitating a predecessor. He cannot even imitate, as a rule, his own father, unless the successful father gives the son so great a head start that it is difficult for the youth to fail. This rule also implies that the boy who goes to "dad's alma mater" just because his father happened to go there should realize that times have changed, and that his needs may not be the same as those of his father when he was young.

The Vocational Advice of Parents and Friends

The vocational advice of relatives and friends is likely to be defective in many respects.

Parents who attempt to influence the choice of vocation for their children often do so as a compensation for their own deficiencies. The parent may say it is for the child's good. Actually, it may be a form of display for the parent. When parents find that they can no longer hope to become famous or to achieve their adolescent dreams, they project their hopes for glory into the brightest or favorite child of the family and compel the child to enter the profession which, in their opinion, offers the desired prestige or wealth. When a boy fails in college and the personnel adviser suggests to the parent that his son should become a mechanic or a businessman rather than a surgeon, the parent is likely to answer disgustedly: "Why, that's no profession at all. I want my son to amount to something." Such an answer indicates that the parent is the one who really wants to amount to something.

The vocational guidance given by many teachers, employment managers, preachers, and lecturers is in the same class as the home remedy of the friend who never studied medicine or the human body. The physician, with all his years of training and experience, makes many errors in diagnosing our bodily ills, but the untrained friend who tries to do so makes many more.

If a person is in need of vocational guidance and asks some of his friends for suggestions, he may be surprised to find that each person's advice differs from that of all the others. Many friends can give only general and trivial suggestions which have but slight value.

Vocational guidance in the sense of showing a person what he should do is very difficult. It is very difficult even for the trained vocational psychologists. Most modern vocational psychologists do not try to study a youth in order to tell him what he should do but to help him improve his adjustments to life by means of a vocation. Perhaps the psychologist also points out what the youth is likely to do. A boy may have certain adjustment tendencies which can be pointed out to him and suggestions may be given him for the utilization of his established tendencies. However, the boy's choice cannot be controlled. The individual himself must make his own adjustments and his own choice. Guidance cannot play the part of a benevolent parent who adjusts conditions for the child; guidance can only prepare the youth to meet his own difficulties.

The logical question arises: When the psychologist analyzes a person for the purpose of vocational guidance, how does his analysis differ from that of the acquaintances who know the individual? Chiefly, in two ways. First, the experienced psychologist who has had some clinical training knows much about adjustment patterns of individuals. He can recognize tendencies which can be utilized in a vocation in order to bring about better adjustment and more satisfying fruits from the advisee's efforts. He recognizes the advisee's needs, particularly those that involve his vocational aspirations. His needs for achievement may lead him to seek realistic or feasible goals. On the other hand, if the motivating need is a strong desire to avoid failure, he is more likely to have unrealistic goals.[2]

Second, the modern vocational psychologist supplements his clinical and other subjective estimates with objective tests. The tests which he uses have been standardized on thousands of individuals and are fairly accurate; so, if two psychologists test the same person, their findings tend to be the same. The psychologist also tries to find the specific channels through which the intelligence expresses itself, as in mathematics, music, mechanics, social contacts, and so forth.

An example of the value of the testing services of the psychologist may be shown in the case of a boy in a western New York high school who was sent to the commercial teacher by the principal. The principal told the teacher that the boy was of low intelligence and could not do good school work. The quality of the boy's work in all his courses was of such a low grade that the teachers had given up all hopes of teaching him. Because the other teachers were tired of the boy, he was sent to the new commercial teacher of the school. This teacher also found that the boy's reputation for poor work was correct so far as commercial subjects were concerned. He was the poorest student that this teacher had met in that school.

Fortunately, the commercial teacher had had courses in mental testing, and he gave the boy several intelligence tests just to find out whether his intelligence was as low as it appeared to be. To the teacher's surprise, the boy scored slightly above normal in all the tests. The teacher then gained the boy's confidence and found that he had a serious inferiority complex. One of his teachers whom he had had four years previously had convinced him that he was a "dub and a dumbbell." After that he made no effort to do good work, but rather tried to live down to the kind of reputation he was given. The commercial teacher changed the boy's attitude and he then did good work in all his courses, because all his teachers knew that he could do good work and required him to do it.

In this example we see that the counselor used tests as an aid in his diagnosis of the boy, but he supplemented the test results with his own subjective insight into the boy's adjustment habits and helped the boy readjust himself to his barriers. Tests often referred to as "aptitude tests," can provide data for constructive thinking by the counselor and the advisee but they cannot predict the degree of success within an occupation.[3] Tests do not make vocational decisions for the advisee. They, at best, are an aid in helping the person tested bring about changes in his value system.

Methods of Choosing a Vocation

Some of the current methods or aids whereby the individual can predict or tries to predict his own behavior for vocational adjustment have been mentioned, but we shall list the more common ones:

1. Pseudo-scientific schemes such as phrenology, character analysis, astrology, etc. These have no value and need not be discussed further.
2. Choose a problem to the solution of which you can devote your life.
3. Analyze yourself according to some systematic plan and make a decision.
4. Have yourself tested with the few valid psychological tests now available.
5. By means of a systematic analysis of your adjustments, recognize the conscious and unconscious drives in your own personality.
6. Allow yourself to be made a case study by a vocational psychologist.

One of the best ways for the intelligent person to choose a vocation is to select a problem that needs solution. The modern scientific student often does this and develops his interest in a problem into a new vocation. For example, a girl who was a student in a college of home economics found that the lowly mushroom had never been studied carefully. She then decided to make a study of mushrooms, and, when she was graduated, she was offered an excellent position where she utilized her interest in mushrooms. Inventors often use this method. So does the man who sees a need for some particular kind of business in his community and then starts a business to answer that need. Thousands of problems in all the professions and businesses are awaiting solution. The man who determines to devote his efforts to answers to economic and social difficulties usually finds that he has found his vocation. A few of many such problems are listed as suggestions and not as a complete list:

1. Develop, through propagation, certain prolific weed plants into valuable food plants.
2. Work out and install better systems of training and promotion for employees of large concerns.
3. Much of the money now spent for advertising is wasted. Someone should develop better techniques to predict the effectiveness of advertising, so that more money spent for advertising will be productive.
4. Find out how to make public school work more interesting, more cultural, and more related to life.
5. Develop better methods of settling difficulties between employers and workers.
6. Work out methods for improving the personal efficiency of certain classes or kinds of persons.

7. Teach and help people of this country to understand and appreciate art—the beautiful things of life as well as the practical.
8. Discover the bases of personality and help others to improve their personalities.
9. At present much of our educational system is adapted to the average child. Some cities pay special attention to the backward or poor student. Evolve a system that develops the exceptionally bright student to his utmost. Much of this latent ability is now being wasted.
10. Religion is in a different environment from what it has been heretofore. Some think that we must put religion on a basis that will appeal to the people of this age.
11. Help prevent or decrease crimes and learn how to re-educate criminals.
12. Solve the parking problem in cities.
13. Invent sidewalks which are less trying to our feet.
14. Improve the lighting of rooms.
15. Invent better children's games, especially games to be played by small children while riding in an automobile.

We Americans have hundreds of unsolved problems, and the solutions of certain problems would give employment to thousands of workers. To the well-adjusted, intelligent worker, the pull of the future (toward the solution of a problem) should be more stimulating than the push from the past (his own adjustment tendencies). Unfortunately, however, most young people allow their own adjustment tendencies and the conventional occupational openings to determine the directions of their vocational efforts. Very few men devote themselves to the solution of some problem unless they first have had some profound emotional experience that pushes them in the direction of such devotion. For example, all of us recognize the need for greater safety in driving automobiles, but few among us will vigorously pursue safer driving as a life work unless we have had an intense emotional experience with bad driving, such as the death of a loved one in an unnecessary accident. Sometimes the vocational psychologist can recognize such adjustment tendencies, resulting from severe emotional problems, which can be utilized in solving a problem and giving the individual a well-motivated and satisfying career.

Self-analysis

Many of the first attempts at vocational guidance required the youth to answer a long series of questions regarding his vocational interests. He was asked not only to state whether he liked, disliked, or felt a neutral interest in listed occupations, but also to estimate himself in general traits as:

Are you aggressive?
Are you industrious?
Do you have a pleasing personality?
Are you neat in habits?
Are you conceited?
Do you coöperate with others?
Do you look ahead?

Hollingworth and others have made studies of the reliability and accuracy of self-estimates of general traits. He conducted experiments wherein the individuals in a group rated the other members of the group and themselves in nine different traits. The results indicated that people cannot rate themselves with any great degree of accuracy. The natural expectation would be that we tend to overestimate ourselves in desirable traits and underestimate ourselves in undesirable traits. The following data from his study of estimates of fifty people[4] show the presence of a factor of constant bias in self-estimation (See Table 11.1).

TABLE 11.1

SHOWING CONSTANT TENDENCIES OR BIAS IN SELF-ESTIMATION

Trait	*Per Cent Over-estimating Themselves*	*Per Cent Under-estimating Themselves*
Refinement	80	20
Humor	78	22
Intelligence	68	32
Sociability	68	32
Neatness	50	50
Beauty	50	50
Conceit	48	52
Snobbishness	36	64
Vulgarity	34	66

Hollingworth also found that the more admirable the trait the closer the relation between possession of the trait and the ability to judge it in others. His subjects who had reprehensible traits could not rate themselves very accurately in those traits. Of course, we must bear in mind that people cannot rate others accurately in generalized traits, and Hollingworth's experiment assumed that the group estimates of the raters were correct. The consensus of the acquaintances who did the rating was accepted as the true impression that an individual made on others. It is quite probable that, if objective measures had been available of Hollingworth's subjects in the nine traits he studied, they would not have agreed with the average ratings of the acquaintances.

The Allports' experiment confirmed the principle that self-estimates in general traits are not accurate.[5] Different people were asked to estimate their own intelligence by the rating scale method, and they were also given intelligence tests. Then their self-estimates and their scores in the tests were compared. Those who were high in intelligence tended to underestimate themselves and those who were low in intelligence tended to overestimate themselves. The correlation between self-estimates of ability and scores in the Otis Group Intelligence Test was $-.67$. Self-estimates are not reliable, unless they can be proved to be of sound predictive value. To prove their value requires careful statistical treatment, which has not yet been given for most traits that are considered in vocational self-analyses.

Even though many self-estimates are not reliable, they may have some value in causing the individual to grade and recognize his own inclinations, tendencies, and characteristics in relation to an occupational choice. In some cases, it may be well for the individual to decide upon his personal likes and dislikes and to try to avoid those occupations that require traits that are definitely unpleasant or to seek occupations that require traits that are pleasant to him. For example, some persons dislike to handle other people physically, which is necessary in the work of the osteopath, the chiropodist, the barber, the nurse, and the hairdresser.

When the individual's self-analysis is made by means of a statistically treated list of occupational and other activities to which the individual reacts in terms of liking for (L), indifference toward (I), or dislike for (D), the method of self-analysis is called an *interest test*.

Vocational Interest Tests

The most widely used interest test is that of Edward K. Strong, Jr. There are two forms of this test, one for men and one for women. Each form of the test is an eight-page leaflet listing some 400 items covering occupations, school subjects, amusements, activities, peculiarities of people, and self-estimates of personal abilities and characteristics. The average time needed by most persons to fill in the test is forty minutes, though no time limit is set.

Norms have been developed for some forty-seven occupations and vocational groupings for men and twenty-five for women. Most of the occupations listed are on a professional level. This makes the administration of the test to a person of low intelligence or one with no prospect of professional training largely a waste of time. The test is best used with individuals of college age and above, though it may be used to advantage with selected high school groups.

The interest test is not a measure of aptitude or ability, and so is used, not to replace aptitude or ability tests, but to supplement them. Results of the test do, however, suggest that the person whose pattern of interest is similar to that of the men or women in the criterion group has greater chances for satisfaction and success in that occupation than in one where his interests differ widely from those of successful persons in that field.

Scores on the Strong test may be translated as standard scores, percentile ranks, or letter ratings. The ratings A, B, and C are more easily understood. An A rating means that the testee has the interests characteristic of persons successfully engaged in the occupation specified; B has a similar implication, but there is less certainty; and C means that the testee does not have such interests. Any occupation in which the rating is an A or B+ may be suggested to the testee for serious consideration. An occupation in which the interest rating is C should be chosen only after careful consideration of other factors, such as strong drives.

Numerous studies have been made of the permanence and predictive value of measured vocational interest and expressed vocational choice.

Strong made a follow-up study of seniors at Stanford University first tested in 1927 and freshmen first tested in 1930. He found that individuals who had "interests most similar to engineer, lawyer, or minister on the first occasion were the ones who had scores most similar to those same criterion groups on the retest—twenty-two years later. People expressed approximately the same order of work preference, according to occupational interest scores, for as long as twenty-two years."

At least two factors that affect permanence of the interest score are the time interval between the test and the retest and the age at the time the test was taken. Obviously, the older a man is when he is tested, the more permanent his preference is likely to be. Thus, the college seniors who ranged in age from 22 to 32 retained the same interests to a greater extent than did the freshmen who were between the ages of 19 and 28 when tested. Although permanence is less for younger men than old, it is still remarkably high among the former.[6]

Strong also made a follow-up study of men who had expressed some interest in engineering in 1930 and found that those with the highest scores were employed in engineering or closely allied fields nineteen years later. Men who had originally had little interest in engineering were usually working in offices, sales, or law. From these observations there would seem to be a high positive correlation between measured interest in engineering and the occupations in which these people were working almost two decades later.[7]

In a study of another interest test it was found that low scores in a particular area of vocational interest do not justify the assumption that the individual cannot derive satisfaction from work in that area. Nor does a high point in an interest test profile always indicate the most appropriate field for specialization.[8]

Interest tests are a helpful device in confirming stated interests as well as in calling attention to occupational interests which the individual may have overlooked. The vocational psychologist is also concerned about certain aspects of interests other than the score on a test, especially about "absorbing interests" or intensive drives which may have developed in the adjustment history of the individual.

Interest tests have certain other recognized limitations. The Strong Vocational Interest Blank should not be expected to predict the specialty within an occupation. The use of the SVIB, for example, with 783 seniors in 15 medical schools in 1950 did not indicate their 1960 specialties or type of practice.[9]

The SVIB can be faked as shown by several studies. If engineering students are directed to do so, they can make scores similar to those of social service workers. Applicants who apply for a job are more likely to make scores favorable to the type of job applied for than non-applicants such as employees who are in the occupation.[10]

However, careful use of the SVIB is justified with high school seniors. Three groups of university graduates were compared, graduates from medicine, law, and accounting, on the basis of SVIB scores obtained in Grade 12. The scores of the three groups were significantly different from one another, and pattern analysis of each student's interest profile revealed that the three groups had different profile patternings as well as different scores on the individual scales.[11]

Other Tests for Vocational Guidance

Many people who seek vocational guidance think that the psychologist can test the capacities of anyone so that the person tested will know just exactly what vocation he can and should follow. The psychologists also at one time thought that they might be able to develop predictive testing to that stage, but the recent researches indicate that they were too optimistic. Professor Seashore and his colleagues have spent some fifty years in the analysis of musical talent. They have developed some tests with high predictive values, but the analysis of that one talent is not complete. If fifty years of research in one field have not produced wholly satisfactory results, we should not expect too much from the use of other tests which have had far less attention than the musical aptitude tests. Certain schools of music now use musical aptitude tests and find them very helpful, but psychologists have probably made more progress in musical testing than in any other aptitude. As stated in the previous discussion of tests, they do have some value, but they furnish a statistical prediction on the basis of what a group or number of individuals will do rather than what any single person can or will do. In vocational guidance we want to know what a group can do, but we wish particularly to know what a specific individual can do.

Another difficulty in vocational guidance, based upon tests only, is the fact that a person who tests high in a given trait that could be capitalized vocationally may not care for that vocation. Thousands of people are capable of becoming good undertakers, but most of them would object to it as a vocation because of emotional inhibitions. Similarly, psychologists might make more statistical studies of the kinds of men and women that can marry each other with the greatest chances of a happy marriage, but such tests would have little value in decreasing matrimonial failures. The persons whom scientific analyses would indicate as ideal mates might not care for each other at all and would refuse to go through with the ceremony. Scientific marriages would not be nearly so inviting to the masses of people as the old-fashioned method of romance and chance. Two individuals must be "drawn" to each other emotionally. The individual must also be attracted to his vocation emotionally.

This statement of some of the limitations of tests should not be construed as making them valueless. It is important to use tests as one factor to be considered when dealing with vocational problems. Tests are particularly useful in pointing out certain vocations in which the individual would have small chance of success. Certainly anyone who considers choosing music as a career should first have himself tested by someone who can administer the Seashore test or adaptations of it.

Other tests, helpful in certain problems of vocational analysis, can often be recommended by competent vocational psychologists and counselors.[12] He often finds general intelligence tests helpful. General intelligence has been defined in various ways, but chiefly as the ability to adjust oneself to the problems of one's environment, as the average of various abilities, as the ability to learn, and as the ability to do school work. Most studies indicate a definite relationship between general intelligence or mental ability and other desirable traits of vocational significance.

In cases of extremely high or low intelligence, we are safe in making certain predictions. A person with an intelligence quotient of less than 100 could not do good work in most colleges. Lack of intelligence can be compensated for, to some extent, by an exceptionally great amount of effort, but even superior effort would not enable a student of low intelligence to succeed in college. The high school student who plans to enter college should try to select a college and a course that are in harmony with his intelligence level and high school marks.

The vocational psychologist often supplements intelligence, interest, and special ability tests with personality inventories, social knowledge tests, and others. These are useful in making diagnoses regarding introversion, social adjustment, and similar personality characteristics of importance to the trained psychologist. He wants to know the pattern of temperament, intelligence, aptitude, interest, and other tests. Knowledge of such patterns may enable the counselor to suggest a suitable type of work within a vocation after the general vocational field has been chosen.

It was formerly thought that a person must have a certain set of personality traits and abilities to fit a particular occupation. Recent investigations have revealed that men with widely different characteristics may be equally successful in the same position. A man seems to be successful if he can supply the one thing that is particularly needed in a situation, with ordinary fitness for other requirements of the job. For example, a man may be a desirable member of an architectural firm if he is an expert draftsman, without any social ablity or power of verbal expression. Another man may be equally desirable as a member of the same firm who has little ability as a draftsman but who knows how to meet people and explain building plans. A third member may specialize in drawing or esthetic appreciation. Legal firms have the same variety of talents. There is a great difference between a successful surgeon, a laboratory diagnostician, and a family doctor.[13]

We should recognize that vocational objectives and choices of college can be revised. Educational and vocational growth are intertwined. Civilizations and personalities are dynamic. Interests mature. The satisfactions derived from exercise of intelligence and aptitudes vary with the individual's adjustments to new barriers in his development. This means that a study of adjustments, drives, and preferences should supplement any tests administered.

Adjustment Analysis for Choosing a Vocation

The choice of a vocation, like the choice of a mate, often expresses the adjustment of the individual. For example, the son of many a very able and successful business executive does not care to become a businessman. He may want to become a scientist, even though he knows that his father hopes he will some day take over the business. When we also learn, as happens in some cases, that the boy has felt for years that he did not meet his father's expectations of him as a son, we can expect the boy to prefer a career in some line of work other than his father's. To such a son, the father's business may be associated with feelings of inadequacy. This appears to be most likely if the father has a dominating personality, is the kind of father who has often said to the child: "I don't understand why you can't do thus and so? Why when I was your age, I did that and more."

Such a boy in his adjustment development naturally turns to some activity which is not associated with the father's personality. Sometimes it is in the direction of political radicalism, because that kind of "conviction" on the part of the boy is one way in which the businessman-father can be "punished."

Of course adjustments such as these are made unconsciously. The boy, when asked to explain his own psychological development, cannot do so. The clinician can. Unfortunately, very few clinically trained persons are doing vocational counseling, and those who are realize that truly reliable insights into a person's motivations can be made only after considerable study of the individual.

Projective techniques such as the Rorschach ink-blot tests have been found especially helpful in making such studies,[14] but these require much clinical training for their interpretation and further validation of their results.

Stanley J. Segal reported findings from a study that was made to apply psychoanalytic theory to the vocational choices of accounting and creative writing students. A battery of projective tests was administered. The findings were:

1. Accounting students and writing students did not differ in general adjustment level.
2. It is doubtful that accounting students show greater acceptance of social norms than writing students.
3. Accounting students show greater attempts at emotional control, whereas writing students show greater awareness of feelings.
4. There were no differences in the use of compulsive defenses.
5. Writing students showed greater evidence of expressions of hostility.
6. Writing students showed greater tolerance for ambiguity and greater ability to deal with complex emotional situations.
7. There were greater signs of a more rigid fearful identification in accounting students and greater evidence of seeking for completion of multiple identifications in writing students.

The findings validate the idea that personality theory can lead to a more complete understanding of the role of personality factors as determinants of vocational choice.[15]

Most competent vocational counselors are aware of the influence upon vocational choices of the advisee's adjustments, such as his barriers, predisposing influences, substitute acts, frustrations, passive and aggressive hostilities, and so on. But they do not tell the advisee all that they know or think they know. The advisee must always retain the human right of living his own life in his own way.

Some clinical psychologists believe that vocational counselors are simply meddlers and that the individual should be allowed to follow the directions of the "unconscious." They believe that all actions are determined by unconscious motives that follow definite patterns formed in the individual during childhood.[16]

The writer has attempted to assist several hundred persons in choosing a vocation. Some of these were students who were asked to have a vocational conference, but others, who heard of these conferences, requested guidance. Those who requested assistance in choosing a vocation certainly included an appreciable percentage of slightly psychoneurotic and inadequate-adjustment cases.

An estimate, based upon experience in this field, suggests that at least one third of the adults who voluntarily seek vocational guidance are really seeking an adjustment to life in general rather than a vocation only. This estimate is probably too low.

Adjustment analysis is of assistance to many persons who are vocationally unsatisfied because it may indicate the manner in which the person with a feeling of inferiority might attempt to compensate for his sense of inadequacy. It is probably partially true that Napoleon became the conqueror of a large part of the civilized world through his adjustment to the taunts of his playmates in his childhood. Some of our poets achieved their eminence because of physical defects. In fact, Adler cited many cases of compensation brought about by some organic inferiority and concluded that some psychic reaction makes up for the deficiency of the physical organism.[17] This theory hardly explains every successful person. Many of us develop our feelings of inferiority as the result of comparing ourselves with others. A person who has average artistic ability when compared with other artists of the world may have a definite sense of inferiority because he knows that there are others considerably better than he. A person need not have any actual physical or mental inferiority in order to feel inferior.

Many a child, for example, who has a very studious brother or sister may believe that he is of low intelligence. Tests and adjustment analysis may show, however, that he has quite adequate intellectual capacity but he adjusted to his sibling rival by assuming that he was inferior.

Consider also the differences in personality needs on the part of the adults who, in childhood, were overdisciplined, were orphans and felt rejected, or were overprotected. Such feelings of inadequacy are almost certain to influence the individual's later choice of work and work environment. The inner needs of the individual interact with the potential satisfactions in the job. We can understand these people when we recall the typical adjustments discussed in Chapters 2–7.

The person who seeks a vocation that fits his personality should ask himself: What difficult or unpleasant experiences have I had for which I need satisfaction in my work? If he cannot answer the question himself, he might consult a vocational psychologist. Each year it is found that several college students who are barely able to do college work and just manage to graduate wish to take additional postgraduate work in another college which has a reputation for requiring unusually hard work. This desired prestige of having done graduate work in a famous institution is merely an attempt to compensate for the feeling of inferiority engendered by their inability to do college work of ordinary grade. In most cases it has been difficult to convince these poor students that they wish to do graduate work not because it is essential to their careers but because the contrast between themselves and other college students causes them to think that they are inferior. Actually they are fine young men who have developed an abnormal attitude toward the importance of college degrees and the college aura.

Adjustment by projection explains many of the dissatisfactions with occupational life. A bank clerk, for example, who is not especially ambitious or intelligent and who knows it, may suddenly develop a dislike for banking. Further analysis may show that his home relationships have become strained and that he would like to get married and set up a home of his own. His dissatisfaction has not been caused by the uninteresting nature of bank work, but he has blamed his work for the fact that he does not have the courage to set up a new home on the available income.

Sometimes a person highly trained and successful in a given line of work suddenly tires of the vocation for which he has a high interest rating as measured by an interest test. His income and social prestige may also be excellent, but he refuses to continue in the work. In such cases, only an analysis of adjustment problems will reveal the true cause of his desire for a change.

Many a person has left a vocation and spent years in training himself for a new vocation because he thought that competition was far too keen, whereas he might have attained greater success by training himself more thoroughly in his original work. A typical example is a certain man who was a fairly successful printer. He blamed competition for his limited income, and decided to study dentistry. After six years of study and several years in developing his practice, he has become another average dentist. In the meantime, one or two printers in his city have become well-to-do. If he had devoted the same effort and capital to printing that he applied to learning dentistry, he might have become far more successful as a printer than he is as a dentist.

Whenever someone wishes to leave an occupation in which he is fairly well established, the counselor should look for the difficulty that the occupation symbolizes or represents to the person. The real reason for his eagerness to leave one job for another may be his irascible stepmother, a brighter sister, an unresponsive executive, a fiancée who loves someone else.

In some cases a sudden interest in politics may be a protest against some injustice. A determination to travel may be an attempt to adjust to restraint or convention. A keen interest in the study of an obscure subject such as paleontology or Egyptology may be an attempt to prove to others that the individual is as bright as those whom he considers to be his rivals. By contrast with the knowledge of such unusual subjects on the part of most people, his meager fund of information gives him the intellectual recognition he unconsciously seeks.

The vocational psychologist frequently

finds freakish interest on the part of persons who are dealing with a barrier, such as the crude man who wants to be an artist, the immoral person who wants to be a preacher, the homely girl who wants to be a beautician, and the failure who writes success books. Such attempts to gain adjustment through the vocation are not necessarily wrong. Many of the world's finest contributions have grown out of such troubled personality strivings. For example, Charlotte Brontë wrote some very successful novels, the result of an overflow of emotions engendered by her father's unfortunate influences. The father was a hypochondriac, a dyspeptic, and an ascetic. He did not believe in marriage and was particularly opposed to Charlotte's marrying. He was fond and jealous of her. He was unable to get along with his associates and so became a tyrant in his home. He tried to please her and showered her with attention, but he was moody and critical as well. She could not develop in a normal manner and was forced inward emotionally. She took refuge in books and fantasies. Her tragic childhood was stamped deeply upon her personality, and the books that she and her sisters wrote show the effects of a maladjusted father upon motherless children.

Vocational Self-sabotage

Anyone who does vocational counseling of adults is certain to meet individuals who have high intelligence, pleasing personalities, seemingly good habits, and many good character qualities; but who always manage somehow to fail in their vocations. In contrast with them, other individuals of less intelligence, more irritating personalities, and poorer personal habits manage to succeed, regardless of their opportunities. Both types are difficult to explain as long as we use quantitative approaches only. When, however, we think in terms of unconscious motives, we get plausible explanations. We discover that many of the men who always manage to fail are really expressing an unconscious urge toward self-sabotage in their vocation.

Failure enables the maladjusted person to accomplish aims that are more important to him than success. Such aims have been revealed by Friend and Haggard in the systematic investigation of two classes of unemployed adults: those *high* and those *low* on eight basic criterion items of occupational adjustment.[18] One of the striking differences between the two groups was described, in part, in their findings.

> Topping the many sharp contrasts in personality, the stronger tendency of the *Lows* to defeat themselves and spoil their job chances stands out as an indicator of adjustment at work. It is often evidenced by excessive drinking, quarreling, and illness. The *Lows* seem to marry the wrong person and to have families so large that they experience difficulty in supporting them. Correlational and other special analyses of the extent of the tendency toward self-sabotage link it with the extent of the following attitudes: parental rejection, antagonism toward the father, resentments both of dependence and domination of families, rigidity, buried fear of failure, and self-attack, unrealistic thinking about jobs, ambivalence, and reliance on pull. . . .Although the relationships suggested are not necessarily causal ones, these factors do seem to serve as devices through which the maladjusted individual accomplishes an aim. They seem to be ways of settling early parental scores; or of handling the guilt which demands constant failure; or of protecting himself against fears of being unable to cope with work. . . .This extreme type of "vicious-circle" behavior seems related to the well-known proclivity of those seriously disturbed emotionally (the *Lows*) to make things generally hard for themselves—a trait that is slight in the *Highs*.

Blaine and McArthur, Harvard University Health Service, have described how certain students who ask for help in their inability to study actually want very much to fail. On the conscious level they wish to succeed, but unconscious forces sabotage their efforts. The two main unconscious drives that undermine achievement in such students appear to be an unwillingness to do or be what someone else wants them to be and a rebellious drive that represents a retaliation against parents who are unconsciously resented.[19] Of course many factors, conscious and unconscious, may be involved in unnecessary failures.

We are all familiar with the idea that an unhappy childhood may drive a person to high aspirations in his field, as a sort of compensatory mechanism. In tests given to 350 university students, it was found that high aspiration levels did indeed correlate with unhappy or unsatisfactory childhood family relations, just as low aspiration levels corresponded to happy childhoods.[20] Persons who felt that they had been neglected by their parents, that their parents had played favorites among the children, tended to work harder as they grew in order to receive the attention that they had lacked as children. Whereas, those who had known love and attention as children did not seem to need to achieve as much as adults.

If the result of this and other tests are correct in correlating aspiration with family relations, a problem may be posed for the future. It is especially true of the generation that was raised during the depression that as parents, they want to insure the happiness of their children. Security seems to have become woven into meaning the same as happiness for many people or vice versa. Happy, secure children may grow up into happy security-seeking adults who want nothing more and see no farther. Success may become defined as security rather than accomplishment. However, all this depends on whether or not discontent is essential to aspirations. Certainly there are people with happy childhoods who have high aspirations; however, the likelihood of achievement seems to be greater when there is an obstacle to overcome.

Whatever the explanations that may eventually be found most appropriate for the understanding of the adults who manage to fail, the fact is that they do manage to fail in spite of apparently excellent outward reasons for success. The only helpful psychological explanation, thus far, is that they themselves are unconsciously sabotaging their own efforts in order to attain aims more important to themselves.

The Case Method of Vocational Guidance

The evidence presented in the preceding discussions suggests that while some individuals do not need vocational guidance, many others do. We must not assume that all wholly normal persons need no assistance in choosing a vocation. The normal youth is not raw material psychologically; he was raw material at birth, but since birth he has developed many adjustments and conditionings. He has certain likes and dislikes, some feelings of inferiority, self-confidence in certain situations and not in others, a fairly definite level of intelligence, and accumulated experiences of all degrees of importance, so that his psychological composite in relation to his environment may not result in a happy vocational choice. In many cases he finds that he has difficulty in choosing a vocation. Even though he thinks that he knows what he wants to do, it may be well for him to attempt to obtain a bird's-eye view of himself and the world in which he lives. He really knows only a few occupations, and those he does not know comprehensively. Such a case study involves the following steps by a counselor:

- I. Analyze the individual.
  - A. History and general status.
    1. Health record.
    2. School record.
    3. Financial status.
    4. Leadership record.
    5. Hobbies and recreational activities.
    6. Psychological test scores.
  - B. Vocational likes and dislikes—self-analysis.
  - C. Estimates of associates and friends—ratings by others.
  - D. Peculiarities of personality.
  - E. Parental wishes.
- II. Present the suggestions of the above to the advisee in a personal conference.
- III. As a result of II, choose several occupations for the investigation of the advisee.

IV. After investigation of the several tentative occupations, choose one as a vocation.
V. Plan a program of training.
VI. Assist advisee to obtain a job or get started in the chosen field.
VII. Follow up advisee and revise his program as occasion demands.

College Education as a Part of a Vocational Program

When a high school graduate wishes to enter business and plans his vocational program, he must decide whether he will go to college or enter a field of work without college training. When successful men in one field are compared with the unsuccessful, investigations show that many of the successful individuals in business do not have a college education. We cannot say that a college education is a prerequisite for reaching the top in all fields. Statistics on the value of college training based upon men who graduated a generation ago are not entirely significant for modern conditions. Going to

*Left, **the Rev. James E. Royce, S. J.,** Psychological Center, Seattle University, aids a student in choosing an appropriate program of studies.*
*Below, **Dr. George F. Wooster,** director of the University Counseling Center, The Ohio State University, with some students in the Occupational Information Library.*

college then required more initiative and ability than it does today, when a college student is no longer a community marvel as he was then.

The main reason why college graduates make more money than high school or common school graduates is superior intelligence and personality. A youth with high intelligence and strong character traits is likely to go to college. He seeks the college degree as part of his program of personal development. College is the required or accepted education for many superior individuals, and professional standards as well as many businessmen require college graduation for admission into many occupations.

The student who attains high grades in college and then succeeds in business probably does so not because the college trained him to think or gave him technical training but because he has superior intellectual and character traits. Perhaps he had stronger drive as suggested by the data for those in the lowest scholastic standing decile, Table 11.2. We should not advise every high school student to go to college. If a student barely manages to get through high school and if his general intelligence in abstract subjects is low, it may be inadvisable to recommend college training. It is interesting to know that high school graduates of both low and high mental ability plan to attend college. The desire to attend college is not a reliable criterion of the ability to do college work. Thousands of college freshmen are dropped each year because they are unable to do the work. However, if a youth has the intelligence and personality that will enable him to benefit from a college education, then he should by all means go to college, even though he may have to earn all his own funds for doing so.

The Vocational Program

The value of a definite vocational program is suggested by a study made by the writer. He made a statistical analysis of the records of 500 men who had registered for jobs with an employment agency. Their employment histories were accurately recorded be-

TABLE 11.2

RELATION BETWEEN SCHOLASTIC STANDING IN COLLEGE AND LATER SUCCESS

	"Who's Who in America"		"Who's Who in Engineering"		"American Men of Science"		*In all Three Volumes*	
Deciles	*No.**	%	*No.*	%	*No.*	%	*No.*	%
1	68	15.3	128	16.1	123	23.8	20	22.0
2	60	13.5	108	13.6	85	16.5	13	14.3
3	45	10.2	87	10.9	67	13.0	16	17.6
4	49	11.1	93	11.7	62	12.0	11	12.1
5	26	5.9	63	7.9	39	7.6	6	6.6
6	19	4.3	45	5.7	26	5.1	3	3.3
7	23	5.2	46	5.8	23	4.5	3	3.3
8	30	6.8	54	6.8	23	4.5	6	6.6
9	26	5.9	53	6.7	23	4.5	5	5.5
10	96	21.8	118	14.8	44	8.5	8	8.8
Totals	442	100.0	795	100.0	515	100.0	91	100.0

From F. Alexander Magoun, "Scholarship and Distinction," *The Technology Review,* Massachusetts Institute of Technology, Cambridge, Mass., Vol. 37, No. 8 (May 1935).

* This column indicates the number of former M.I.T. students, from certain classes between 1868 and 1910, whose names appear in "Who's Who in America." Thus 68 persons (or 15.3 per cent of the total) stood in the 1st decile or top tenth of their class; 60 persons (13.5 per cent) stood in the 2nd decile or second highest tenth—and so on for all ten deciles. The table can also be read as follows: "Of 442 former M.I.T. men listed in 'Who's Who in America,' 96 or 21.8 per cent stood in the 10th or lowest decile, scholastically, of the members of their classes," and so forth.

cause their records had been carefully investigated by the agency. A lot of facts were recorded about each man. Among the facts were answers to two questions:

1. What do you want to do five years hence?

2. What progress have you made in attaining your goal?

Approximately one half of the men stated a more or less definite ambition. When their salaries were analyzed in relation to age groups and ambitions, the following differences stated in terms of index numbers were found:

	Annual Average Salaries by Age Groups		
	20–29	30–39	40–49
The "definite ambition" men	100	158	238
The "no definite ambition" men	96	148	191

The relations between average salaries and extent or progress made in attaining the definite ambitions were found to be the following:

Level of Progress Reported	*Average Salary*
"Preparing myself for it"	100
"Have made no progress," or, "Little progress"	133
"Have made some progress"	181
"Good," "Very good," and "Fine progress"	309

Only thirteen men, all in the older age brackets, claimed they had attained their ambitions. Apparently most sensible men realize they are not likely to be very happy unless they are striving for goals that are ahead. As someone has said: "Success is a wonderful thing to strive for, but a terrible thing to gain."

Of course, a program in itself is of little value. However, persons of superior personality strengths are likely to utilize a program as an expression of their drive to achieve. The following conversation and appeal to a youth illustrates one kind of appeal that can be made when the counselor wishes the advisee to plan a definite program for training himself in his chosen vocation:

"Vocational success hinges partly upon not trusting your life to chance but knowing what you want and how to get it. The man of little ability who concentrates his efforts on one thing, in one direction, and on one goal is bound to succeed. He attains far greater height than the man of brilliant ability who lacks a goal.

"After you have chosen a vocation or selected your vocational goal, you should do what successful business concerns do—schedule your plans. Decide upon what you want to accomplish each year for the next few years. Determine upon what you will do each year in order to attain your goal. Set up standards for yourself. Set a date when you will accomplish each step and keep that schedule before you. Look at it occasionally, especially when you are failing.

"Whenever you find that your schedule needs revision, revise it. But follow a definite plan or you may drift, and drifting wood never reaches port." Table 11.3 shows a sample vocational program which will illustrate how one can plan a career.

TABLE 11.3

FACTORS TO BE CONSIDERED IN PLANNING MY VOCATION

Educational record:
High school graduate, college preparatory course.

Easy subjects:
English, history, languages.

Difficult subjects:
Math courses.

Grades:
Graduated in second quarter of class of 68 graduates. English grades highest.

Test results:
Otis S-A test of intelligence, P.R. 90

Nelson-Denny Reading test, P.R. 92

Iowa Placement, English Aptitude, P.R. 86

Introversion, P.R. 62

Experience record:
Odd jobs in selling magazines, clerking in store.

Health record:
Children's diseases only.
Good health.

Financial resources:
Father will supply money for most expenses. Must earn money for personal expenses.

Parental wishes:
Parents have no vocational preferences but they expect me to make high grades.

Past difficulties that developed drives of vocational value, habits, conditionings, feelings of inferiority, resentment, etc.:
Oldest child in family of four boys, like to show off. Believe that my parents are more or less indifferent to me. A younger brother is praised for his very high grades. Feel inferior regarding my lack of athletic ability. Fear that I will be a failure. Resent close supervision. Resent "poverty" of family.

Interest test results, rank order:
1. Copywriter
2. Advertising man
3. Journalist
4. Lawyer
5. Commercial teacher

Special opportunity:
Uncle is in textile industry but I as nephew could not expect any special opportunity from anyone.

Reasons for suggesting this vocational program: likes, dislikes, aptitudes, etc.:
High record in English.
Practical minded rather than a student of English only.
Like to study people more than I care to influence them in personal contacts.

TABLE 11.4

EXAMPLE OF "MY VOCATIONAL PROGRAM"

Nature of the Career I Wish to Attain: *Advertising Copywriter*

My Job Program Sequence of jobs to reach the main occupation:	*My Training Program* that prepares for the vocation:	*My Personality Development Program* List items, such as:	*The Undesirable Aspects* of this program which should be anticipated:
For this year: Obtain part-time job in retail concern.	Schools to attend: Enter a four-year college of business that offers cultural as well as business training.	Friendships to make: Establish friendship with business owners, advertising men, and salesmen.	Opposition to expect from family, friends, or employers: Parents who help me through college will expect me to get a well-paid job upon graduation. This is not likely.
For next year: Obtain part-time job on newspaper or magazine.	Courses to take: Major in advertising. Courses in commerce, art, psychology, sciences, sociology, philosophy.	Clubs to join: Join local advertising or sales clubs. Later, join luncheon club.	
Later: Write ads for local concerns even though the pay is small.	Books to read: Burton, Philip Ward, *Principles of Advertising,* Englewood Cliffs, N.J.: Prentice-Hall, Inc., 1955.	Books to read: Barron, Frank, *Creativity and Psychological Health,* Princeton, N.J.: D. Van Nostrand Co., Inc., 1963.	Effect on plans for marriage or home: Will prevent my getting married for next eight or ten years.
Possible employers: Previous contacts may suggest possible employers.	Hepner, Harry W., *Advertising—Creative Communications With Consumers,* New York: McGraw-Hill Book Company, 1964.	Burnett, Leo, *Communications of an Advertising Man,* Chicago: Leo Burnett Co., Inc., 1961.	Unpleasant conditions of work: Will have to do many menial jobs in order to get my education.
Employment bureaus to be consulted: Study trade journals for employment bureaus that specialize in my field of work.	Trade journals: *Printers' Ink*, *Sales Management*	Tours to take: Visit the advertising agencies of a large city.	Difficulties in making advancements: Department heads such as buyers of stores often blame advertising man for their own failures.
Places of work: Do a good advertising job in my own community and hope to get an agency job in a big city.	Persons to interview or know: Call on advertising men and women of home town. Associate with all types of people.	Investment plans: Save money when possible but spend in order to become acquainted with men and women in advertising and business. Attend trade convention.	
Vacation jobs: Work in a summer resort patronized by businessmen.	Writing to do: Some themes in college dealing with the characteristics of consumers.	Health plans: Analyze my personality once a year in order to keep a healthy mind.	Income difficulties: Will be out of work at times. Must shift employers frequently.

ACKNOWLEDGMENTS AND REFERENCES

1. Harry Dexter Kitson, *The Psychology of Vocational Adjustment* (Philadelphia: J. B. Lippincott, Co., 1925), p. 47.
2. Charles H. Mahone, "Fear of Failure and Unrealistic Vocational Aspiration," *Journal of Abnormal and Social Psychology,* March, 1960.
3. Robert L. Thorndike and Elizabeth Hagen, *Ten Thousand Careers* (New York: John Wiley & Sons, Inc., 1959). Also, Robert L. Thorndike, "The Prediction of Vocational Success," *Vocational Guidance Quarterly,* **11,** No. 3 (1963), 179–187.
4. Adapted from H. L. Hollingworth, *Judging Human Behavior* (New York: Appleton-Century-Crofts, 1929), p. 52.
5. F. H. and G. W. Allport, *Journal of Abnormal and Social Psychology,* **16** (1921), 6–40.
6. See Edward K. Strong, Jr., "Permanence of Interest Scores over 22 Years," *Journal of Applied Psychology,* April, 1951, pp. 89–91.
7. For further information, see Edward K. Strong, Jr., "Nineteen-Year Follow-up of Engineer Interests," *Journal of Applied Psychology,* April, 1952, pp. 65–74 and *Vocational Interests 18 Years after College* (Minneapolis: University of Minnesota Press, 1955).
8. Solomon Diamond, "Interpretation of Interest Profiles," *Journal of Applied Psychology,* October, 1948, pp. 512–520.
9. Anthony C. Tucker and Edward K. Strong, Jr., "Ten-Year Follow-Up of Vocational Interest Scores of 1950 Medical College Seniors," *Journal of Applied Psychology,* April, 1962.
10. Wayne K. Kirchner, "'Real-Life' Faking on the Strong Vocational Interest Blank by Sales Applicants," *Journal of Applied Psychology,* August, 1961.
11. Ralph F. Bardie, "Strong Vocational Interest Blank Scores of High School Seniors and Their Later Occupational Entry," *Journal of Applied Psychology,* June, 1960.
12. For descriptions of the current developments in testing, refer to the periodical, *Test Service Bulletin* and the annual *Catalog of the Test Division,* both published by the Psychological Corporation, New York. See also the latest copy of *The Mental Measurements Yearbook,* Oscar Krisen Buros, ed., Highland Park, N.J.
13. Paul P. Brainard and Frances G. Stewart, *Manual of Instructions for Specific Interest Inventories* (New York: The Psychological Corporation, 1932).
14. Anne Roe, "Personality and Vocation," *Transactions of the New York Academy of Science,* **9** (1947), 257–267. Goldie Ruth Kaback, *Vocational Personalities; An Application of the Rorschach Group Method,* Bureau of Publications, Teachers College, Columbia University, New York, 1946. Z. Piotrowski, B. Candee, B. Balinsky, S. Holtzberg, and B. Van Arnold, "Rorschach Signs in the Selection of Outstanding Young Male Mechanical Workers," *Journal of Psychology,* **18** (1944), 131–150.
15. Stanley J. Segal, "The Role of Personality Factors in Vocational Choice," *The American Psychologist,* August, 1955, pp. 365–366.
16. A. A. Brill, *Fundamental Conceptions of Psychoanalysis* (New York: Harcourt, Brace & World, Inc., 1921), Chapter XIII.
17. Alfred Adler, "A Study of Organ Inferiority and Its Psychical Compensation," *Nervous and Mental Diseases Monograph,* 1917.
18. Jeannette G. Friend and Ernest A. Haggard, "Work Adjustment in Relation to Family Background," *Applied Psychology Monographs,* No. 16 (Stanford, Calif.: Stanford University Press, 1948), pp. 58–59.
19. Graham B. Blaine, Jr., and Charles C. McArthur, *Emotional Problems of the Student* (New York: Appleton-Century-Crofts, 1961), pp. 84f.
20. Russell A. Dynes, Alfred C. Clarke, Simon Dinitz, "Levels of Occupational Aspiration: Some Aspects of Family Experience as a Variable," *American Sociological Review,* April, 1956, pp. 212–215.

PROJECTS

1. "Success in a vocation depends upon an adjustment to life in general rather than the fortunate selection of an occupation." Assume that this statement is true and prepare a list of mental habits that every person should acquire to be vocationally successful. Assume that the above statement is incomplete and add other forms of behavior that are essential.
2. "A rolling stone gathers no moss" and "A setting hen never gets fat." Which of these two epigrams is the more nearly correct? When should a man change his position?
3. Outline a program for obtaining valid occupational information that fits your needs.
4. Analyze yourself vocationally by means of the devices and suggestions presented in this chapter. Present the analysis in the form of a systematic report to a friend and ask him to

criticize it. Then prepare a vocational program to fit your significant traits.
5. Study a number of friends who have achieved considerable success in their fields, and compare them with others who seem to be "marking time." What psychological differences can you discover between individuals in the two groups?
6. Compare the advantages and the disadvantages of going into business for yourself with those of working for an employer.
7. Study the student employment opportunities in your college or one near by. List all the ways the students earn money to help support themselves. Check the jobs that contribute valuable vocational experience as well as financial reward.
8. List some occupations which may diminish in importance within the next ten or fifteen years. Suggest how workers in those occupations might utilize the change to their advantage rather than suffer because of it.

COLLATERAL READINGS

Farnsworth, P. R., (ed.) *et al., Annual Review of Psychology*. Palo Alto, Calif.: Annual Reviews, Inc., 1964, p. 405–406.

Ginzberg, Eli, *et al., Talent and Performance*. New York: Columbia University Press, 1964.

Lehner, George F. J. and Ella Kube, *The Dynamics of Personal Adjustment*. Englewood Cliffs, N. J.: Prentice-Hall, Inc., 1964, Chapter 10.

Poffenberger, A. T., *Principles of Applied Psychology*. New York: Appleton-Century-Crofts, 1942, Chapters 12 and 13.

Roe, Anne, *The Psychology of Occupations*. New York: John Wiley & Sons, Inc., 1956.

Shaffer, Laurance F. and Edward J. Shoben, Jr., *The Psychology of Adjustment*. Boston: Houghton Mifflin Company, 1956, pp. 567–573.

Smith, Henry Clay, *Psychology of Industrial Behavior*. New York: McGraw-Hill Book Company, 1955, Chapter 15.

Super, Donald E., *The Psychology of Careers*. New York: Harper & Row, Publishers, Inc., 1957.

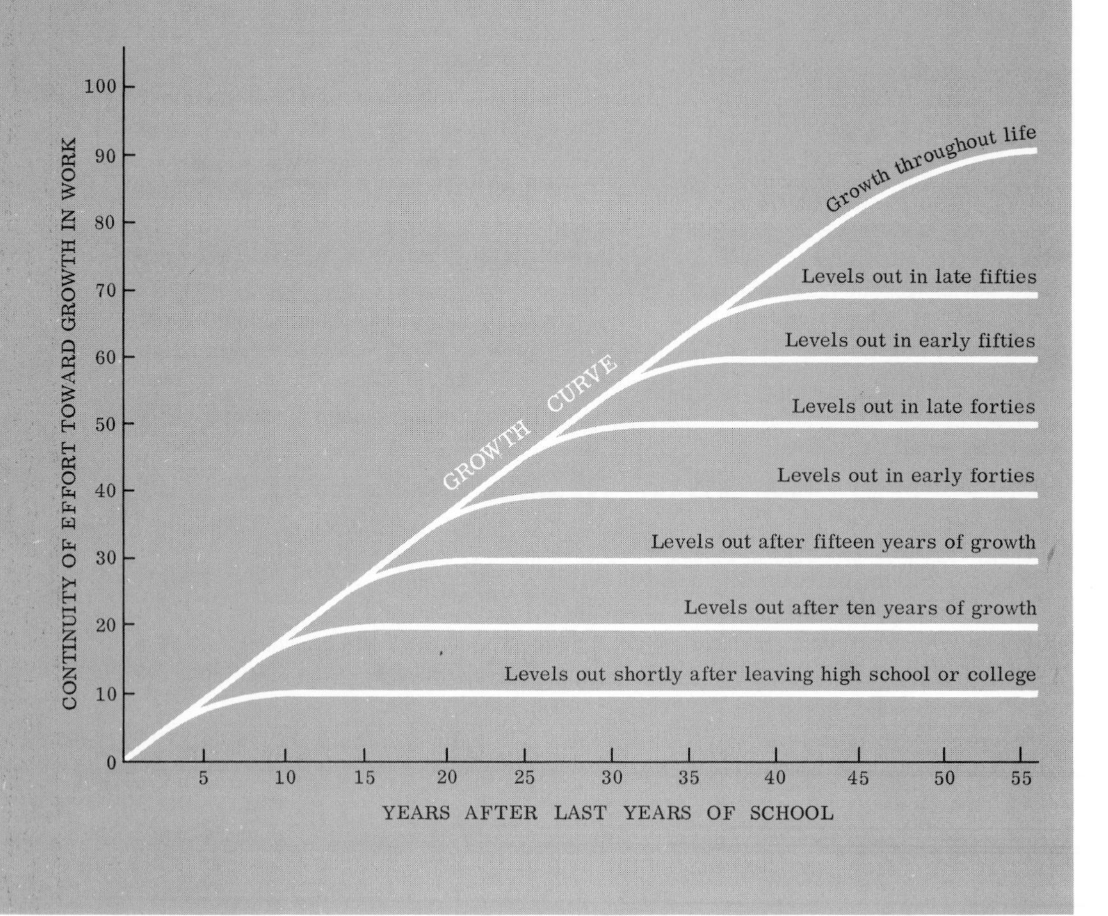

The true growth men of business and the professions *continue their growth efforts throughout life. Others level out in their efforts to seek growth, many early in life. Those who drop out early hold the lower level jobs.*

Anyone who interviews an adult applicant tends to note the approximate stage in his life history when he leveled out in his developmental efforts. Also, the human relations specialist who interviews employees finds that many employees would like to continue to grow in their work but they do not know how to go about it. They need and would like to have counsel and encouragement. Source: Harry Walker Hepner, ***Perceptive Management and Supervision*** *(Englewood Cliffs, N.J.: Prentice-Hall, Inc., 1961), p. 498.*

CHAPTER TWELVE

GETTING A JOB AND GAINING ADVANCEMENT

"How can I get a job when I haven't had any experience?" is the lament of many a young person when he leaves school or college. Actually, any normal individual who has a definite vocational goal, has seriously studied an industry, and developed a well-adjusted personality has excellent evidence of value to employers. But he must be able to present his worth in an effective manner.

Employers do not expect factory workers or uneducated applicants to use clever job-getting methods. Employers assume that such applicants use the old haphazard methods of seeking employment through employment agencies, help-wanted advertisements, labor-union headquarters, and applications at personnel offices. However, the college-educated and other superior job seekers are expected to demonstrate their superiority to some extent by means of their applications. The people who need superior techniques of making application are the more highly trained workers such as engineers, accountants, statisticians, technical salesmen, and professional workers. These should know how to present their qualifications intelligently.

The intelligent candidate in the course of making his application should regard the following admonitions:

1. Know the kind of work you want and why you want it.
2. Study the employer's problems and interests.
3. Present a letter of application which proves your interest in the employer's problems and your qualifications for his needs.
4. Participate in an interview which reveals mutual interests.

Stating the Kind of Work Desired

Many an ordinary applicant is so egocentered when he needs a job that he can think only of his own needs. As a result of his concern about his own needs, he thinks and talks about himself. His argument for a job is similar to that of a candidate for a political office whose placard read: "I am the father of nine children and I need your support!"

The intelligent applicant's major thought is to understand his abilities, limitations, and vocational goals so well that he knows the kind of work he wants and why he believes he can do it. One employment man explained the deficiencies of applicants in this respect as follows:

> I interview hundreds of applicants, and when I ask them what they can do, a high percentage say "most anything." The answer is obviously false. I am not interested in the applicant who says that he can do anything, because that really means that he can do nothing well; nor does he know what he would like to do. But the applicant who says, "I have been studying motor transportation and I believe that I could be of help to your firm in cutting down your delivery costs," arouses a definite interest. Young people who leave school and college are especially weak in this respect. Many of them do not know whether they wish to work in a circus, a department store, a machine-shop, or a cheese factory. How can they expect to sell their services when they do not know what they have to sell?

The superior applicant, especially the one who has benefited from his college opportunities, knows the industry he wishes to enter and the kind of work he wants to do. His textbook readings, classroom lectures, and personal contacts with men in the field of his choice have stimulated him to learn more about certain aspects of the work and to associate with those who are already actively engaged in his chosen field. Such an applicant has read trade journals and attended trade association meetings, and there he has learned the names and addresses of the leaders in his chosen industry. Because of his genuine interest and informed background, he can approach the professional leaders or heads of the best firms and talk with them in terms that he and they understand. The reactions of executives approached by such an applicant are likely to be: "This man knows what he wants and is going after it. He appears to be the kind of man we need in our organization. Let's try him out to discover whether he really means what he says."

Any college student who really wishes to use his college experiences in formulating definite vocational objectives can do so. Faculty members, friends in business, secretaries of trade associations, trade journals, psychological tests, and library books are usually available to him in his search to find himself in his work.[1]

Studying the Employer's Problems and Interests

Whenever an applicant has decided what kind of work he would like to do, his knowledge will indicate which concerns would be logical employers for him. The advertisements and news articles in trade journals, listings in telephone directories, and suggestions from trade association secretaries will reveal names and addresses of many possible employers.

When the applicant has collected such lists, he should select several preferred prospective employers and learn all he can about them. He should investigate the history of each company, study each company's product, interview their customers, and find out why people use the product. Why did they buy the product? Would they buy the same brand again? If not, why not? Of course, the purpose of this kind of investigating is not to impress the employer but to write an effective letter of application and to ask intelligent questions during the interview.

For example, a certain young man registered at an employment office. He had had experience in the retail gasoline and oil business, but had sought work unsuccessfully for some time. As he wanted to obtain employment with a certain retail gasoline company, the employment director suggested that he take definite steps to make himself valuable to this company. He was told that he should learn all he could about the business—if possible, find out if any of the company's local stations were not up to the usual company standards.

The young man found that a gas station belonging to the company where he had applied seemed to be getting less business than it should. To discover the reasons, he made a survey of all cars in the neighborhood to find whether their owners were buying gas from the station and, if not, whether there was any cause for dissatisfaction. When the survey was completed, the young man took it to the local manager of the gasoline company with a suggestion for increasing business at that station. The manager was impressed with the applicant's initiative and gave him a position to prove his worth. The young man made good at that job and at several other difficult ones. His work was so satisfactory that in a short time he had risen to a responsible position in the local office of the company.[2]

When looking for ideas of possible interest to the employer, the applicant can study the business by means of the trade journals of the industry. His local library probably has some copies on file.

If the applicant will also study the specific concern with which he would like to be associated, he will be able to offer some ideas which show that he is seriously interested in becoming a member of that organization. If possible, it is well to talk with the company's salesmen who, in many cases, will be glad to give the applicant helpful suggestions. Once the applicant has developed his ideas and checked them with some person who is acquainted with the problems of the company, he can approach the prospective employer as an inquirer who is anxious to learn more about the company. Of course, if he takes the attitude of an expert who tries to advise the management on how they should run the business, the employer is naturally likely to assume that the applicant is too egotistical to fit into the company team.

The personnel manager of a large department store stated: "Not one person in a hundred who comes before my desk has any ideas. Yet it's the applicant with ideas who gets the job, the applicant who has intelligence and interest enough to spend some time in the store looking around before he comes to me, who can suggest ways we can improve our service, who at least will be able to say: 'I watched the clerks and customers in the jewelry department yesterday and I believe that I could sell in that line.' Most of them don't even do that."

When this question was brought up to the

head of a publishing firm, he answered: "Ideas! Most job hunters don't know what the publishing business is. Less than one in a hundred will even go to the trouble of reading the most widely-used trade journal of the industry. Most applicants think they want to become editors because they do not know of the many other departments in the publishing business."

Any applicant who takes the trouble to read the trade journals of the industry or to observe the ways in which the product is being used by the customers is bound to develop an application that is not only intelligent but outstanding. Most employers today are in need of applicants who show that they can think with the businessman rather than merely do what the boss wishes.

The Letter of Application

Many college students can write letters which are grammatically correct but fail to reveal an interest in the employer or in doing his work. The employer is seldom a student of English nor does he care about the niceties of phrasing. He has work to be done, products to sell, payrolls to meet, taxes to pay, customers to please, and bills to collect. He does not care particularly whom he hires—he does want to get his work done quickly and economically.

This letter, written by a college graduate and published in *Postage Magazine,* is typical of letters of application constantly written by ego-centered applicants who have had no training in writing to employers:

Dear Mr. Publisher:

I am seeking editorial (or writing) work on a magazine staff.

My age is twenty-four. I am a graduate of Grinnell College (Grinnell, Iowa), and since graduation have done irregular work at Chicago and Columbia Universities. My chief aim has been to improve myself in the ability to write and in comparative study of literature. I have also specialized in history, psychology, sociology, philosophy, and advertising. Recently I completed a long novel, which is at present at Doran's, having received one favorable reading.

My college record was good. I am a Phi Beta Kappa and a Sigma Delta Chi member, having edited the last-named organization's comic weekly during my senior year in college. Before that I worked on the staffs of certain local newspapers. I also sold automobiles for a time and can use the trade language with some facility.

I have no present business connections. Since I was fifteen, I have incessantly aimed at journalism. My writing style perhaps tends to the search of the color-bearing word and the ironic, but within controllable limits. I read very rapidly (120 pages an hour) and analytically.

I am willing to start in any position which promises an opportunity for development and offers a reasonable wage.

Sincerely yours,

The comments of the recipient of this letter were:

This letter, written by a college graduate, contains eighteen "I's," "my's," and "myself's" but not a single "you." We can well imagine the publisher who wades through such a letter, searching for and finding the "ironic" word and using it without "controllable limit." Every year, millions of letters like this are written by young men looking for positions. We should like to recommend to every college in the land that a business course on "How to Write a Letter" be delivered to its students, to cover the last six months of their term. Thousands of splendid positions are held by men who knew how to write a good letter and wrote it at the psychological time.

The following application letter, written by an alert college senior, was sent to the advertising managers of eighteen leading department stores and promptly resulted in offers of two jobs, one of which was accepted.

211 West 14th Street
Meldon, Massachusetts
July 5, 19—

Advertising Manager of (Name of Firm)
Street
City

Dear Sir:

Your advertising appeals to me. It suggests that you are following policies and procedures that would benefit the young advertising woman.

My ultimate goal is that of advertising manager of a retail store. To reach this point I realize that real experience is necessary.

I am anxious to have good supervision and direction in my training for this career and recognize the opportunities available in your store. Therefore, I am eager to attain any work in this line you can offer me.

As a beginner in your department, I offer the ability to take dictation and type. As your needs would demand, I could gradually make myself useful in writing copy or preparing advertisements. One of the sample advertisements for a local retail store is enclosed.

You will find further information and references in the attached personal data sheet. May I have your suggestions?

Very truly yours,
(Miss) Mary Doe

This applicant complimented the employer and indicated a genuine interest in learning *his* methods as an aid in her own development. Furthermore, the letter avoided the many "I's," "my's" and "myself's" through the use of a personal data sheet, an excellent device for most applicants.

Use of a personal data chart or résumé is important. A prospective employer likes to have facts about a candidate's past experience on paper in order to have it available for future personnel needs. The résumé lists personal data, and also employers and dates in reverse chronological order along with a short summary of the individual's responsibilities in each position. This, like any type of résumé, should be brief, and honest. Several briefs may be prepared for different types of jobs, with each stressing different aspects of background.

Many high school and college graduates claim that they cannot write a good letter of application because they cannot point to past experience as evidence of their ability. Some of these younger applicants visit employment offices where they are told that no jobs are open for inexperienced workers. These young applicants should recognize that the old answer: "Sorry, we have no opening now for persons without experience," often means that either the applicant did not appeal to the employment man or the applicant did not know how to present his qualifications effectively.

The intelligent inexperienced applicant who knows what kind of work he wants to learn and why, can, with reasonable persistence, find an interested employer. The youth has a most appealing argument whenever he applies to an employer with this type of approach:

"Mr. Employer, I have decided that I wish to learn the hardware business because I have worked in a hardware store during summer vacations and liked it. I know such simple details as the sizes of bolts and saws. I can drive a truck and check invoices. Besides my summer experience as evidence of interest, I read two trade journals in the hardware field. Three hardware dealers told me if they were young again and wanted to learn the hardware business they would come to you. So here I am for your advice and, if I meet your requirements, for your employment."

ADDRESS
DATE

NAME OF FIRM MANAGER
ADDRESS

Dear Mr. Blank:

I wish to apply for a position as Junior Accountant in your firm, and am submitting for your convenience a chart of my qualifications. [See page 246.]

This chart will, in a brief way, I believe, present the information desired.

Very truly yours,

Dear Sir:

I have just read your advertisement.

You evidently want someone who understands what are the real duties of a secretary. She must

—transcribe your dictation accurately, promptly.
—"proofread" your letters for possible errors.
—receive your callers politely, civilly.
—separate the important ones from those who should wait or come again.
—open and assort your mail.
—make a list of your engagements, reminding you of them at the proper time.
—keep your personal accounts.
—keep your business to *herself*.

My experience covers five years of stenographic and secretarial service, with knowledge of bookkeeping. Age, 25 years. Unmarried.

Let me come and see you. I feel confident of fulfilling your requirements. My telephone is Main 6000.

Yours truly,

This letter leaves no doubt that the writer understands what a secretary is expected to do. The advertisement was simply for a secretary. Instead of making her letter the usual hackneyed statement of qualifications and experience, she tabulates the duties of the post and thus modestly conveys the idea that she can perform them.

Any youth can present his qualifications and evidence of interest in a given vocation in an original manner. He can prepare a loose-leaf booklet or pamphlet of his background and characteristics. It can be illustrated with pictures from advertisements and include character references, copies of school report cards, Boy Scout badges, maps, school term papers, and so on. Anyone's personal history offers many examples of good character and interest in performing honest work that leads to vocational growth and advancement. Thousands of employers are looking for young people who exhibit a spark of initiative and strategy in presenting their qualifications in original ways.

Below are a couple of attention-getting advertisements written by two clever young people seeking positions in the advertising or publishing fields.

ARE YOU PREJUDICED AGAINST A PHI BETA KAPPA KEY, University of Chicago? I confess I am—though I am a young woman who owns one.

I want to break into New York publishing or advertising or some similar employment—no matter how humble the starting place.

In extenuation, I offer:

1. One year's editorial experience on a Chicago publication.
2. Youth and enthusiasm—despite two years' public school teaching experience.
3. Some general business experience, including expert knowledge of typewriting.
4. A not unattractive personality—UN-ACADEMIC.

Will you grant me an interview? Box 432, Printers' Ink.

TO UNDERSTUDY top-flight production manager or labor relations executive. College graduate, major in behavioral sciences. Good leadership record in college activities. Not much job experience but worked part-time and summer vacations in a factory and in a production control office. Single. Any area. Write Box 22.

The Interview

The main purpose of a letter of application is to obtain an interview. The interview is an occasion where employer and applicant consider each other's mutual problems and interests. The applicant is not asking a favor nor is the employer granting a privilege. Each has something to give and each has needs which may or may not be of mutual advantage.

Many applicants are nervous because they think of themselves during the interview. They can often overcome or avoid nervousness by anticipating the questions that are likely to be asked in the interview. Typical questions which are asked many applicants are the following:

1. Tell me all about yourself.
2. Why do you want to work for us?
3. What can you do?
4. Why did you leave your last employer? (Why do you want to leave your present employer?)
5. Do you have any good ideas on how to do this work for which you are applying?
6. May I see some samples or proof of your ability?

The first question should not be answered by starting with the date of birth, early life, and leading up to the time of the interview. Rather, the question should be answered by reference to the present: "I completed college this spring and I majored in finance. While I was studying finance I became interested in banking. Perhaps my interest in banking was stimulated by the speakers whom I heard at the state bankers' convention

PERSONAL DATA SHEET

John Richard Doe

PHOTO

ADDRESS:

TELEPHONE:

I. *Vocational Objectives:*

IMMEDIATE: To become a member of a management training program where I can learn a company's personnel, products and problems.

LONG RANGE: To become an executive in sales or some other department where I will have major responsibilities.

II. *Educational Background:*

Was graduated from Blank College with a B.A. degree. Major: psychology.
Academic average: B. Psychology average: B+.
Was graduated from John Adams High School in January 1957.
Both schools are on Long Island, New York.

III. *Military Background:*

Served in the Army for three years. Attained rank of Master Sergeant.
Spent two years overseas.

IV. *Work Experience:*

Work experience has included working as undergraduate assistant in the psychology department at Blank College, vacation work as hardware salesman, and a six-month period as shipfitter's helper prior to being drafted.

V. *Extracurricular Activities:*

Psychology Club (assisted with programs).
Athletics (intramural—baseball, handball, football).
Outside Research (have read first sources in psychology beyond the scope of undergraduate academic requirements and have conducted small-scale experiments on my own initiative).

VI. *Hobbies and Avocations:*

Reading
Cooking
Athletics
Social Organizations
Bridge

VII. *Personal Data:*

25 years of age—married—no children—excellent health.
Height 5′9″; weight 155.
Willing to work at most any task.

VIII. *References:*

Three names and addresses.

PERSONAL DATA CHART

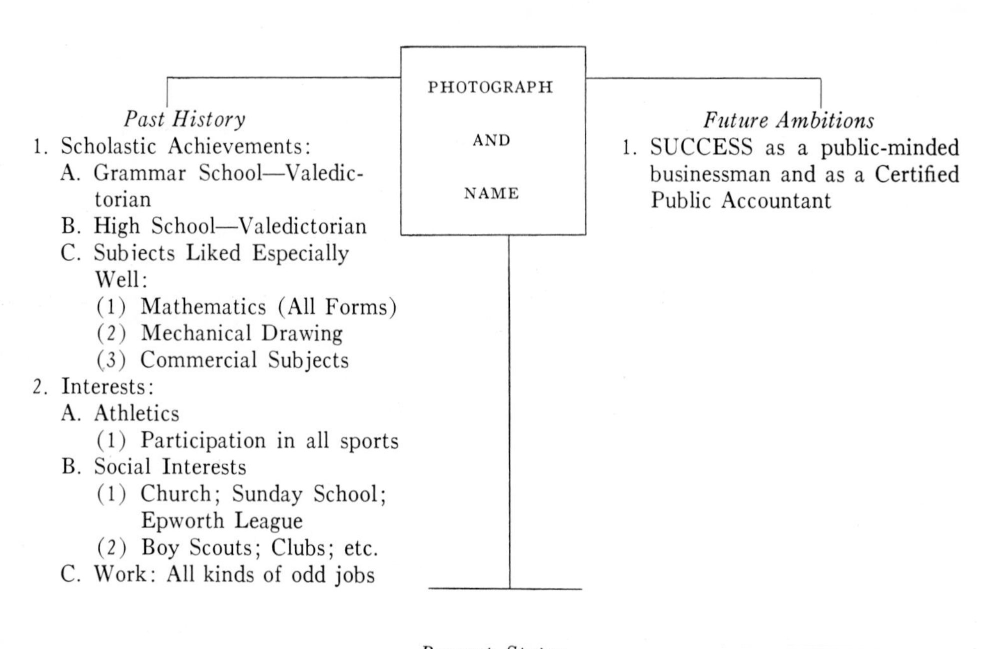

PHOTOGRAPH

AND

NAME

Past History

1. Scholastic Achievements:
   - A. Grammar School—Valedictorian
   - B. High School—Valedictorian
   - C. Subiects Liked Especially Well:
     - (1) Mathematics (All Forms)
     - (2) Mechanical Drawing
     - (3) Commercial Subjects
2. Interests:
   - A. Athletics
     - (1) Participation in all sports
   - B. Social Interests
     - (1) Church; Sunday School; Epworth League
     - (2) Boy Scouts; Clubs; etc.
   - C. Work: All kinds of odd jobs

Future Ambitions

1. SUCCESS as a public-minded businessman and as a Certified Public Accountant

Present Status

Graduate of

Syracuse University; College of Business Administration; Accounting

Scholastic Achievements

1. Winner of two University Competitive Scholarships
2. Member of Beta Alpha Psi (National honorary accounting fraternity)
3. Member of Phi Kappa Phi (National scholastic)
4. Scholarship Rating—B

Wholly Self-supporting

1. College education was wholly self-financed by means of summer work, working six hours daily during school year, and scholarships

Activities

1. Athletics
   Wrestling '57, '58, '59 Intercollegiate
   - Champion .... '59
   - Captain .... '58
   - Soccer .... '57
2. Social Activities
3. Others: Scoutmaster

References

1. Name and address
2. Name and address
3. Name and address
4. Name and address

Personal Record

Birth—Jan. 30, 1939; Henderson, New York
Marital Status—Single
Height—5′4″; Weight—135 lbs.
Health—Excellent; Defects—None

held in Blankville two years ago. The problems discussed with regard to financing farmers' crops interested me so much that I would like to learn more about the problems involved in loans to farmers. I myself was raised on a farm in Spring Valley and my father often felt financially handicapped in his plans for modernizing his farm," etc.

One hundred college students and graduates who had applied for positions were asked to list the problems they had encountered in their applications. The following list is made up of those problems most frequently reported by the interviewees. Each general problem listed below is followed by its frequency and examples of the problem.

Before the Interview

1. The question of experience (27 times). Examples:
   a. Should I admit that I have had no experience and face the possibility of not being hired? Or should I try to lie and take my chances on getting by if I do get the job?
   b. Is there any way in which I can compensate for the lack of experience?
   c. How can I be sure that I am qualified to apply?
2. The question whether or not to tell the truth (19 times). Examples:
   a. Religious affiliations—should I mention membership in my church if I know that my prospective employer is an adherent of another faith? (The laws of some states prohibit the asking of this question; if it is asked in these states, it does not have to be answered.)
   b. Should I admit union membership if I am a member?
   c. Should I mention and discuss my political beliefs?
3. The interview itself (14 times). Examples:
   a. How can I best determine the type of approach to make?
   b. Should I emphasize my scholastic achievements?
   c. How should I sell myself?
   d. What type of references should I use?

During the Interview

1. The salary question (38 times). Examples:
   a. How can I answer, "What salary do you expect?"
   b. How am I to know that I will not ask too much? Or too little?
   c. Or should I ask for an approximate salary?
2. Reasons for choice of firm in making application (19 times). How can I answer, for example, the following:
   a. What can you do?
   b. Why did you choose this type of work?
   c. Why are you sure that you will like the work?
   d. Should I talk freely and frankly about what I consider my ability?
3. The job particulars (15 times). Examples:
   a. Should I ask questions about the job until I thoroughly understand all parts of it?
   b. Or should I wait until I get to the department to delve into the requisites of the job?
   c. Should I try to determine my chances for advancement, and its rapidity, while I am being interviewed?
   d. Should I ask questions about the firm during the interview? Or should I know many particulars concerning the firm before the interview?
4. Nervousness (15 times). Examples:
   a. How can I overcome nervousness?
   b. How can I best conceal my nervousness?
   c. How can I break down the formal attitude of the interview?

After the Interview

1. The interview itself (25 times). Examples:
   a. How can I judge the success of the interview?
   b. How can I tell whether the questions were answered correctly?
   c. What kind of impression did I make?
2. The results (23 times). Examples:
   a. Should I return and keep after the interviewer until he hires? If so, how soon?
   b. Should I have influential friends intercede in my behalf?

No one can offer blanket answers to these and other questions which are asked of applicants and which they ask themselves. Neither questions nor answers can be standardized. The applicant can seek the counsel of some experienced person with regard to appropriate answers to questions such as these. A discussion of the questions and possible answers will be of considerable help to many applicants. However, if the employer's question, "Tell me all about yourself," can be answered in the foregoing suggested manner, many other questions can also be answered sincerely and intelligently. All the employer's questions can be answered naturally when the applicant has developed a genuine long-term interest in the work for which he is applying. Getting a job is merely one stage in a series of efforts to become acquainted with specific kinds of vocational problems, employers, and occupational opportunities.

Some arts of personal salesmanship are helpful and many applicants can improve their abilities to sell themselves through a consideration of the following suggestions:

1. Think and talk *work,* not yourself. Try to think of yourself as a profitable investment to the employer, not of what the job means to you.

2. Consider getting a job as an investment—not an expense. Spend some time and money in getting a job. If necessary, borrow money to get the job you want.

3. Develop confidence in yourself by first studying your prospective employer's product or service.

4. Plan your campaign and follow the plan each day. Do not go about it in a hit-or-miss manner. Know where you want to apply each day for the next month until you get a job.

5. Consider it a sales proposition. If your first and second prospects do not want you, keep on trying. The fiftieth prospect may be just the one who needs you.

6. When asked to fill out an application blank, fill it completely and cheerfully. Put a check mark in the blank spaces not applying to you. Then the interviewer will know you did not overlook any items.

7. Convince the employer you did not stop studying when you left school or college. Show him you are studying your work by means of books, magazines, and night-school or correspondence courses.

8. No one can write a good letter of application for you—you must write it yourself. You must "feel" what you write; then your letter will carry conviction. Study good letters of application, but write your own. If you really feel you are good for something, your letter will show it.

9. Have several friends criticize your letter. You'll probably revise it at least five times before sending it.

10. Always give your complete record and full information when asked to do so. Do not omit your activities of certain months or years.

11. When sending a photograph, send a good one. If the job is worth applying for, it is worth having a special picture taken for it.

12. When discussing salary, state what you have been getting and what you believe yourself worth to the employer. Do not haggle over salary too much, but if the employer is one of the kind who wants to pay less than people are worth, refuse his offer. The fellow who wants something for nothing is not the kind of man you want to work for. Of course, he has a right to pay you a small salary until he knows what you are really worth to him. If you are a college graduate, your alumni secretary can probably give you some helpful figures on average or customary salaries of your fellow-alumni.

13. When you and the interviewer have discussed the vacant job to mutual satisfaction, the interviewer may hesitate to say, "Yes, you are the man we want." Many interviewers need subtle help in making decisions. If you feel that the interviewer really is willing to hire you but needs a "push" in your direction, you can help him by saying, "When would you want me to begin work if you decide to hire me?" The date of beginning work is a minor point but once the interviewer decides on the minor point he also usually hires you.

Advancing in Business

The man who seeks advancement as an employee, as a professional man, or as an enterpriser in a business of his own, has developed those psychological characteristics that are evident in the "growth man." A growth man has an urge to develop his potentials in order to handle more difficult and responsible work. He has strong achievement needs. He manages to improve his abilities regardless of environment or special opportunities. He has a high level of aspiration.

James C. Abegglen, McKinsey & Company, Inc., made detailed biographical studies of a group of top executives, vice presidents or higher, of major firms in the Chicago area. He was especially interested in tracing the movement of an individual from the social class into which he was born to another, usually a higher class. The socioligists' term for this is "social mobility." His studies were made in depth of backgrounds of twenty executives who had been raised in very modest or poor circumstances but had managed to elevate themselves to the topmost rungs of the business ladder. These men were outstanding examples of growth men in business.

The background histories of these executives showed that fifteen of the twenty reported some form of severe strain in their early relationship with their fathers. Divorce, illness, death, or financial difficulties were also present in many instances. One especially interesting finding was that most of these men recalled feeling that their family's economic straits were somehow caused by the father's inadequacies as a protector and provider. In many of these families, the father and mother were notably incompatible; the mother typically provided more of an example of strength than the father. The sons viewed their fathers with a certain disappointment or in some cases even a certain scorn. However, the mothers, though usually perceived as stronger than the fathers, were viewed as austere and not especially "motherly" in the protective sense. But the mother provided the example of self-reliance.

The men sensed that something was missing in their relationship with their fathers, something that they would have liked to enjoy. Accordingly, they turned to other sources for masculine examples which they could accept. These were men such as teachers, relatives, or friends. They leaned on these to some extent as models but they seldom developed a close relationship with any of them.

This tendency to maintain a certain distance from people became a characteristic part of their personalities. Because they were not dependent on others, they could move out of old relationships into new ones without feeling any great sense of loss. It was easy for them to leave old friendships and places behind and to accustom themselves to new friends and their values. Emotionally, they felt as comfortable in unfamiliar groups as in familiar ones.[3]

Obviously, their lives had many dissatisfactions and these probably contributed to an inner disequilibrium that somehow led them to demand more of themselves in the vocations they had chosen. Fortunately, the channels of adjustment, the quests to overcome imbalances, were achieved through positive forms of expression. Had they made negative value adjustments, their life histories would have been quite different.

The origins of the motivations that spur men on to grow through their work vary. As yet, we have only a few researches such as

Abegglen's to indicate significant patterns in the life histories. We do know that many young people are growth motivated in their childhood and youth but the quest for growth becomes sidetracked or lapses to marked degrees.

Anyone who interviews job applicants learns to think of the abilities of men in terms of the individual's age when he begins to level out in his growth. See chart on page 238. Many men in business and the professions level out shortly after they leave school, college, or the professional training institution. Some of those who go to work on leaving high school merely want to make a living. When they change jobs, they go to another that is on the same difficulty and pay level as the previous job. These are the semi-skilled, routine clerical workers, retail sales clerks, order-taking salesmen, typists, and others of the same general class. They, in their own ways, are economically valuable but they make little effort to improve their knowledge, skill, or judgment.

Contrast these lower-level workers with the high-grade professional man such as the well-motivated physician, lawyer, engineer, or teacher. He constantly and throughout his working life, challenges himself to learn more, to increase his ability, to improve his judgment, and to handle more difficult responsibilities than he ever handled previously.

The young man in business who has growth motivations should consider the following suggestions:

1. Seek to know the latest technical information. Growth men want to be able to tackle problems more difficult than any they have tackled before. They read technical journals. They associate with other growth men in their field. They think in terms of problems and the possible methods of dealing with problems. They do not think in terms of rewards of nickels more per hour worked for any extras they do. They do not, as a rule, seek money or status as an end in itself. They seek growth for themselves because true growth brings the many satisfactions of being able to perform greater services than could be performed previously.

Their work week is likely to be longer than that of other employees because they take work home. To them working overtime does not mean overwork because they like to accomplish whatever they feel is necessary. They also tend to take less vacation time than is allotted to them. The manual workers and those who have leveled out usually have idle leisure time to spare—growth men get a large part of their recreation from their work.

The growth men of business and the professions continue their growth efforts throughout life. Those who are not growth men level out in their efforts to improve their abilities. They do not keep on improving themselves. Those who drop out early in life hold the lower level jobs.

Anyone who interviews an adult applicant tends to note the approximate stage in his life history when he leveled out in his developmental efforts. Of course some employees would like to continue to grow in their work, but they do not know how to go about it. They need and would like to have counsel and encouragement from their supervisors. A few of these will develop if someone encourages and guides them until they get emotional satisfactions from their own advancements.

2. Decide whether you wish to advance through a company or through a function. Most ambitious employees try to advance through one company. They study the company and try to move upward through the various supervisory and managerial levels. If they find it necessary or expedient to move from one company to another, they still think in terms of advancing in the company where they are employed. The company man is essentially job directed, security-oriented. The emphasis in his thinking is on accomplishment that fits a company's needs.

Certain others, fewer in number, are function oriented. In the business world, they identify with a specific field such as account-

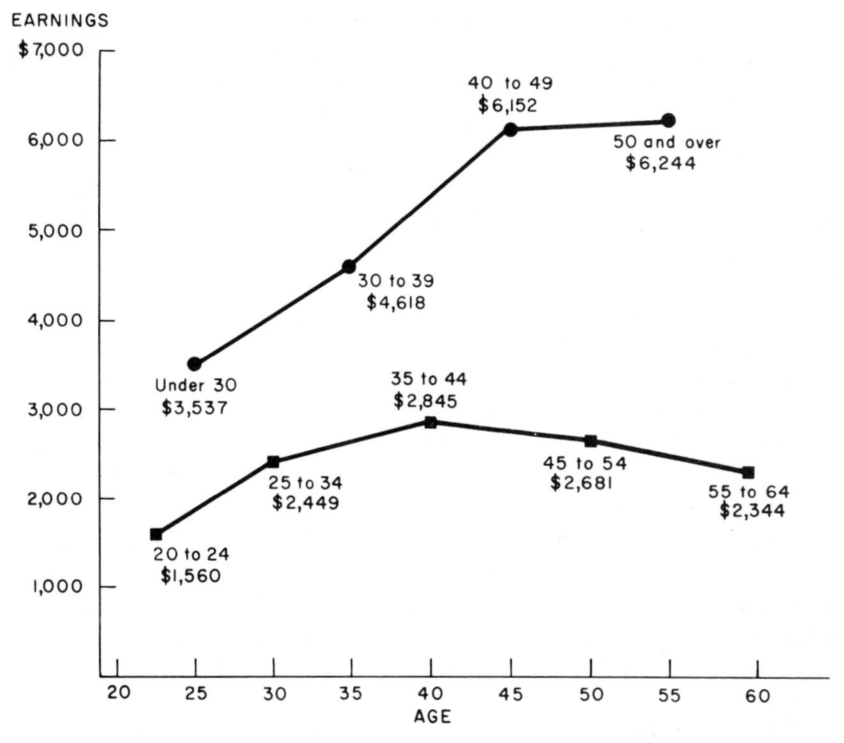

__The study of college graduates__ reported by Ernest Havemann and Patricia Salter West included a comparison of the median earnings of 9,064 graduates of 1,037 colleges, and U.S. workers as a whole at various age levels. The data, analyzed by the Columbia University Bureau of Applied Social Research, indicate that college graduates earn more money almost from the first year on the job than the average man makes at the peak of his earning power. In the population at large, the peak period comes in a man's late thirties and early forties. But the youngest and least established graduates, those under 30 years of age, have a higher median income. In the second place, graduates get wealthier as they get older, while the average man's wealth begins declining after 45. According to the study, the graduates of the very oldest group, the 50-and-overs, have the best incomes. In the general population, the 50-and-overs are losing ground fast to younger men.

College graduate incomes excel the non-college worker not only job for job but also age for age. Even in their earliest productive years they earn far more than the average man at the peak of his earning power. After 45 the disparity becomes even more pronounced. At that age the average man's earning power is dropping fairly fast, but the college graduate's earning power is still going sharply upward.

Source: Ernest Havemann and Patricia Salter West, __They Went to College__ (New York: Harcourt, Brace & World, Inc.), p. 29. Copyright, 1952, by Time, Inc. Reprinted by permission of the publishers.

ing, production, finance, or some other function. The functions in which they excel may be technical research, operational analysis, coordinating, evaluating, interpreting, or teaching. They think of themselves as professional specialists in business. As functional specialists, they are not likely to be especially loyal to any company that employs them nor are they emotionally disturbed if they happen to be laid off or discharged. They are like scientists—loyal to the science rather than the company or institution that employs them.

The function-oriented man is analytical in his approach to a problem. Many of these men become consultants to business. Some do become executives in companies but they are likely to move to other companies where they can practice their chosen specialization in a new setting.

3. Of course one of the most important factors in gaining advancement is willingness to pay the price of success. This is an old axiom but its truth was highlighted when three faculty members of Carnegie Institute of Technology analyzed the early management careers of 30 graduates of a two-year master's degree program in industrial administration. All 30 were of high intelligence and had similar educational backgrounds but some advanced more rapidly than others.

One important difference was in their personal goals. The men who advanced rapidly expressed more desire for power, autonomy, income, and status than the others. They were readier to pay the price of success: job insecurity, isolation, harder work. They changed companies less often than their less successful classmates but they maintained a wide range of outside contacts. They were more sensitive to their environments and quicker to adapt their strategies to the conditions they found around them. They were aggressive in defining their own tasks, willing to take risks, and resilient to setbacks.[4]

The extent to which employees are willing to pay the price of success is indicated to some extent by the percentage who take advantage of available educational facilities. Some companies provide special courses that apply to the business but also offer any employee a tuition aid plan if he wishes to take evening or correspondence courses. Surveys indicate that less than five per cent of the eligible employees of many large companies will take advantage of a tuition refund plan.

4. One factor that will greatly aid an employee in obtaining advancement is to work for an executive who likes him.

General Electric Company made a statistical study of 3,000 G.E. managers' records. Depth interviews also were conducted with a sample of 300 of them to find out what made them successful managers.

These managers were asked in effect: "How did you get where you are? What were the things that held you back? What do you consider were the strongest factors in your development to your present position?" and so forth. The answers were analyzed for significant factors.

Ninety per cent of these managers consistently stated, "I got my best development when I was working for so-and-so and so-and-so."[5]

The employee who wishes to be promoted should seek the goodwill and admiration of his superior or find a new superior who does like him.

Some readers may say: "If there is anything I hate it's a bootlicker, a yes-man, or the employee who sticks around the boss." Yet we should not accuse the retailer of being a fawning flatterer because he dresses up his windows to attract those who are his logical buyers. The merchant merely utilizes some concrete advantages of his wares. Likewise the corporation employee should try to attract the prospective buyers of his services by appealing to his buyers in a way that can be understood.

The importance of working for someone who likes you does not, however, imply that advancement in a corporation depends upon favoritism—having relatives or friends in the firm who push you ahead regardless of your ability. The old adage: "It isn't what you know but whom you know" has been proven untrue. The study summarized by W. Lloyd Warner and James C. Abegglen, The Committee on Human Development, University of Chicago, of 8,000 top executives of large business and industry firms of the United States investigated the factors that are associated with advancement to the top.[6] The findings showed that the boards of directors and executives who direct our large corporations are not interested in "pull" or "drag"—they want men of ability who will produce profits for the company. The interest and support of a superior should be attained

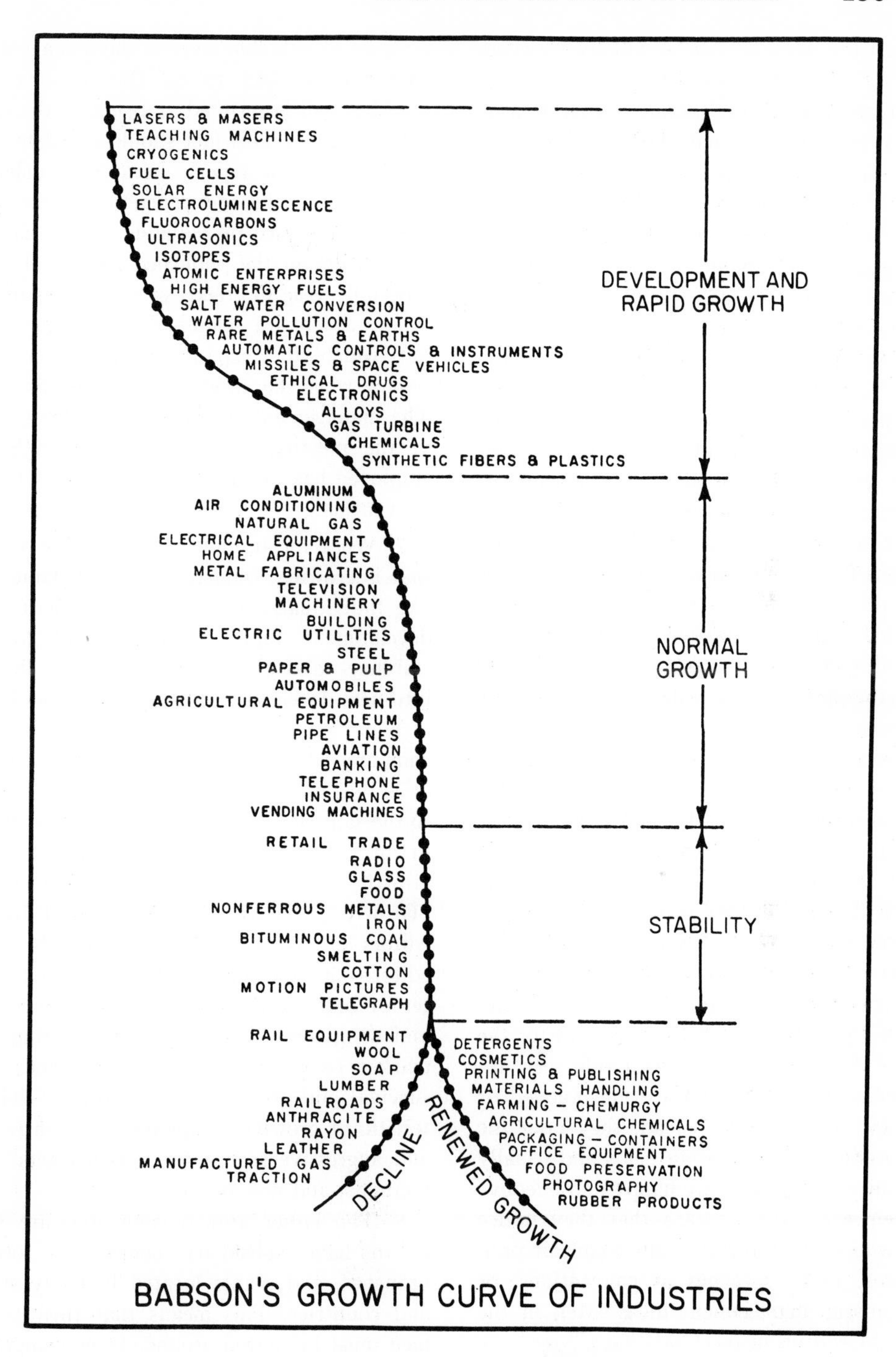

***The prospective growth** curve of industries as seen by the editors of **Babson's Reports.** Imagine that the seed of an industry is sown sometime toward the left of the first vertical dotted line. Consider also that the eventual extinction of an industry takes place at the extreme right of the chart beyond the end of the curve. Industries, like individuals, go through periods of development, rapid growth, normal growth, stability—and then into either a decline or new development. Here, in the opinion of the editors of **Babson's Reports,** is the present status of several dozen industries.*

through the work situation—not by "connections."

5. One method of gaining recognition is that of the trade journal. The trade journals are interested in shop talk, and any systems or ideas which have been of value to men in their field will be of interest to their readers. The good ideas should be described in as pleasing a manner as possible, but efforts should be concentrated on the ideas rather than the form. The editors will revise the article to fit the vernacular of the publication. Of course, one must be careful not to divulge information that should remain in the files of the employer. If in doubt on this matter, the manuscripts can be submitted to the proper authorities of the company before they are sent to the publisher. The average executive will probably be pleased to know that someone in his organization writes articles for his colleagues and competitors to read.

Furthermore, talent scouts, usually called executive recruiting consultants, note such articles and their authors. These recruiting or professional search firms differ from employment agencies in regard to the source of their fee—the employment agencies collect their fee from the man who gets a job through their services but a recruiter receives his fee from the employer. The employer requests the recruiter to find the kind of man who has the qualifications desired for an important position and pays a fee of $5,000 or more for the service. Recruiters do not as a rule seek applications from men who are unemployed or wish to change jobs. Instead, they note the outstanding men of certain fields and usually recommend those who are happy and effective in their work. This means that they notice men who write for trade and technical publications, make speeches at conventions, or offer unique management ideas. Men in the limelight end up in recruiters' files.[7]

6. If it is possible to do so, it is well to attend some of the conventions of associations that influence the business. A good rule is never to attend a convention without making a report of valuable facts to the management. One may neglect to do this because the speeches will be printed and sent to the company later on. This fact should not deter one from making a report, because a delegate should study the undercurrents of the conferences and pick up valuable points that are not evident in the published reports. This is especially true of trends or tendencies of the times, which are seldom described in words but which the experienced technician uncovers when he meets experts in his field. The management should be given the benefit of the meetings attended even though the employee has to pay his own expenses to the convention.

7. Work for an industry, or at least a firm, that is growing. Industries and companies are like individuals—they go through periods of development, rapid growth, normal growth, stability—and then either into a decline or into new development. All other factors being of equal influence, the man who works for a company whose growth has reached stability, or is declining, can hardly expect to advance to the same level or at the same rate he would in an industry that is in a stage of rapid growth or new development. See chart, "Growth Curve of Industries" as seen by the editors of *Babson's Reports*. Growth, these editors point out, is frequently as much a matter of management as it is of the industry, and companies that lead in engineering and market research have the best chances for survival and growth. An outstanding characteristic of growing companies is a continuing and aggressive search for new markets, new methods, and new products.

8. The larger growth companies are likely to have subsidiary companies, foreign branches, and plants located in many states and countries. This means that their better men must be moved around. Some companies transfer hundreds of men to new locations each year. Most transfers increase an employee's opportunities and most who are offered a transfer accept it gladly even though

it means that wife and children must adapt to a new community.

Theoretically, the prospective transferee can turn down the offer. Most executives say that they do not hold it against a man when he turns down the request to transfer. Generally, however, the refusal to transfer is likely to result in fewer offers of advancement in the future.

Incidentally, a twenty-seven year follow-up on job satisfaction of employed adults indicated that the greatest increases in job satisfaction were shown by the men who changed jobs.[8] Transfers are often part of a young man's training program.

A young man's growth program suggests that in the early years, he should seek work that gives good basic training in the fundamentals of the business, even though the pay may be lower than in other types of jobs. Many a young man graduating from college must decide whether he shall take a high-paying job, such as factory labor, or a low-paying job, such as the executive training squad. Trainees are normally paid less than many other employees of the company, but the trainee should, all factors considered, advance more rapidly than the nontrainee. The chances for advancement to superior positions are so good in certain positions in companies that the ambitious, able beginner can well afford to work for a low beginning rate until he proves himself. A survey of plant managers and superintendents of the du Pont Company revealed that 46 per cent started as chemists, analysts, or technicians; 14 per cent as engineers; and the remaining 40 per cent as operators, laborers, clerks, office boys, and the like. Approximately 77 per cent are college graduates.[9]

9. While in college, try to be in the top quarter in a field of likely interest to an employer. It may be in your studies of a course subject or in some other field.

Richard Husband, Dartmouth graduate, class of 1926, made a survey of the 368 members of his own graduating class and carefully compared their records in college with their standing in the world 30 years later. In the main, his findings indicated that an outstanding college record is certainly no bar to success in later life.

He found that activities afforded another significant clue: the more activities, the higher the later income. He concluded that companies would be well advised to look for "the man in the top quarter of almost anything: . . . Actually, *it does not seem to make much difference in what field, or fields, he made his mark*. Together or singly, in sum, grades and extracurricular activity furnish an excellent predictor of later success."[10]

Many able men of business did not go to college. Some learned more outside, on their own, than they would have if they had gotten a diploma. The diploma *per se* is not important. The test of a man is what he can do and what he is worth to his society. Where he acquired his training and his ability is incidental. One investigator, for example, found that of the fellows of one professional society, roughly six per cent have no college degree, 28 per cent have a bachelor's degree, 32 per cent a master's degree, 34 per cent a doctor's degree, and seven per cent an honorary doctor's degree.[11] Perhaps the best evidence of potential ability is past ability and the urge to improve oneself, to grow.

10. Realize that most companies have a shortage rather than a surplus of promotable men. According to one study, the annual growth pattern of American business means that we have a need for about five per cent more able men each year. In addition about 42 per cent of all top management personnel are in the age bracket from 55 to 65—their retirement is necessary within ten years. Death, disability, and turnover continue apace. The sum total of these demands makes finding an available supply of persons who are promotable to executive jobs difficult for many managements.[12] The effectiveness and growth of an organization depend upon the upward career orientation of its members.

ACKNOWLEDGMENTS AND REFERENCES

1. Harry Walker Hepner, *Finding Yourself in Your Work* (New York: Appleton-Century-Crofts, 1937). This is one of many books available to college students who wish to refer to library books in setting up their vocational plans.
2. Charles H. Howard, "Help the Applicant to Help Himself," *Employment Service News,* December, 1935.
3. James C. Abegglen, "Personality Factors in Social Mobility: A Study of Socially Mobile Business Men," *Genetic Psychology Monographs,* **58,** First Half, August, 1958.
4. See *Business Week,* Aug. 27, 1960, p. 82. Study by William R. Dill, Thomas L. Hilton, and Walter R. Reitman and published in the *California Management Review.*
5. Reported by Moorhead Wright, Consultant in Decentralized Manager Education, General Electric Company, "Stop Looking for Loose Geniuses and Start Growing Your Own," *First Advertising Personnel Workshop,* Association of National Advertisers, Jan. 26, 1956.
6. W. Lloyd Warner and James C. Abegglen, "Executive Careers Today: Who Gets to the Top," *The Management Review,* American Management Association, Inc., February, 1956, p. 93.
7. Leonard A. Stevens, "The Great Executive Talent Hunt," *Think Magazine,* November, 1961.
8. Robert Hoppock, "A Twenty-Seven-Year Follow-up on Job Satisfaction of Employed Adults," *Personnel* Guidance Journal, 1960, 38, 489–492.
9. *DuPont Magazine,* October-November, 1947.
10. Richard W. Husband, "What Do College Grades Predict?" *Fortune,* June, 1957, p. 158.
11. See Harley Iams, "How to Attract and Select Creative People," *The Management Review,* American Management Association, Inc., December, 1958, p. 5.
12. See C. Wilson Randle, "How To Identify Promotable Executives," *Harvard Business Review,* May-June, 1956.

PROJECTS

1. Select a business or industry which interests you vocationally, and gather the following data about it:
   a. Names and locations of the leading firms.
   b. Important individuals in the field.
   c. Names of trade associations related to the business or industry.
   d. Trade journals and associated periodicals.
   e. The closest local branches of the leading firms—the men in charge, and something about them personally.
2. From the list of questions about interviews which were asked by college students and graduates (see page 247), select those that you have encountered most frequently yourself. Prepare a well-thought-out procedure for use in your next interview.
3. Prepare a graphic presentation of your past history. Use an outline map to show the places where you have worked in the past.
4. Collect a number of unconvincing "situation wanted" ads from a newspaper or trade journal. Diagnose the difficulty in each case and rewrite the ad for effective results.
5. Name some specific "showcase" items that you can utilize in your present work or in a position with which you are familiar. Analyze the probable effect of each.
6. Write a letter of application for a position you would like to have. Include a personal data sheet and a list of specific skills, or things you could do at once for an employer while working toward the type of position you are aiming at. Use the following check list and add to it any items you think would be helpful.

Men	*Women*
Operate an engine.	Sew.
Repair automobiles.	Cook.
Do concrete-mixing.	Take care of children.
Do physical labor.	Do housework.
Collect bills.	Be a telephone operator.
Run errands.	Do filing.
Be a gas station attendant.	Take care of the sick.
Repair radios.	Design clothes.

Both Men and Women

Do typing.	Invent new systems.
Do bookkeeping.	Versed in current events.
Do selling.	Do statistical work.
Do clerical work.	Write legibly.
Be an office machine operator.	Be an information clerk.
Operate semi-automatic machines.	Drive a car.
Do showcard writing.	Sort mail.
Write a good letter.	Be a cashier.
Drawing, sketching.	Be a sales clerk.
Do window dressing.	Be a helper to a skilled worker.
Repair machinery.	Drive a car safely.
Say a pleasant "Good morning."	Persuade others.

Both Men and Women

Make a good first impression.	Act as a group leader.
Use strategy in buying.	Make many friends.
Know the rules of etiquette.	Supervise others.
Talk interestingly.	Sell goods.
Speak several languages.	Use good English.
Speak in public.	Invent unusual phrases.
Invent new devices.	Write.
	Do research work.
	Develop new services.
	Manual dexterity.

7. Outline a program for obtaining a position. Include an unsolicited letter of application, trade journal advertisement, list of firms where you might apply, and a written description of the facts about yourself that you would try to present to the prospective employers.

COLLATERAL READINGS

Dickson, Carl, "What Employers Look for in the College Graduate," *Personnel and Guidance Journal,* April, 1955, pp. 460–464.

Farnsworth, P. R., (ed.) *et al., Annual Review of Psychology.* Palo Alto, Calif.: Annual Reviews, Inc., 1964, pp. 240–243.

Gellerman, Saul W., *Motivation and Productivity,* Part II. New York: American Management Association, Inc., 1963.

Leavitt, Harold J. and Louis R. Pondy, (eds.), *Readings in Managerial Psychology.* Chicago: The University of Chicago Press, 1964, Chapter 3.

Taft, R. and A. Mullins, "Who Quits, and Why," *Personnel Journal,* **24** (1946), pp. 300–307.

"Time for You to Change Jobs?" *Changing Times,* January, 1956, pp. 21–23.

Uhrbrock, Richard S., *Recruiting the College Graduate: A Guide for Company Interviewers.* New York: American Management Association, 1953.

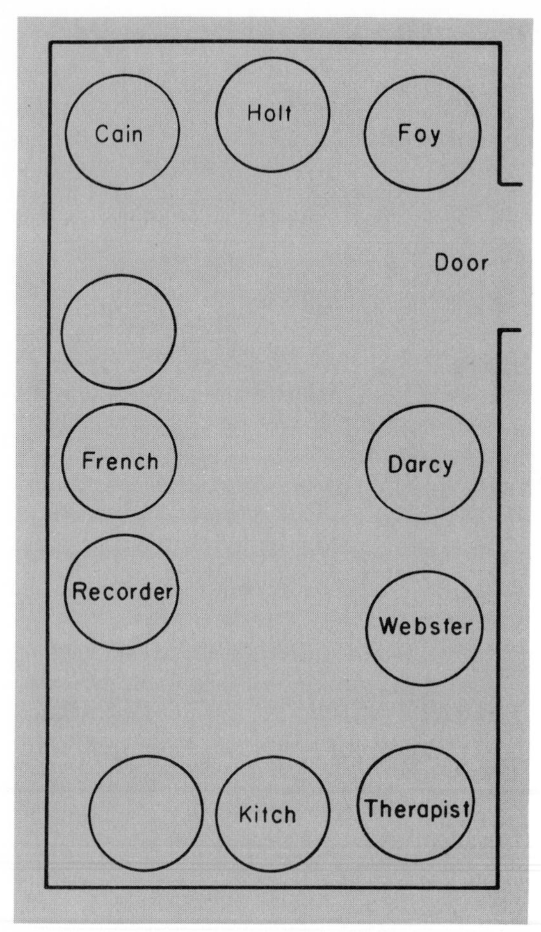

GROUP THERAPY

TWELFTH MEETING

There were seven members present. Mrs. Jacobs was absent.

Mr. Cain (to therapist); ***You seem cheerful. Did something good happen to you?***

Mrs. Kitch: ***He is smiling. Isn't that nice.***

Theme and Dynamics. The theme of the meeting is suggested at the onset: their feelings about the therapist. A smile from the therapist means being liked and approved.

Therapist: ***You seem concerned about my facial expressions.***

Therapist's Technique. Therapist recognizes theme and begins to explore it.

Mr. Holt: ***I think he usually hides his human side in the meetings. I like to see him smile and laugh.***

Mr. Darcy: (Enters room and sits down; no one speaks to him.)

Mr. Cain: ***The men are against the women tonight.*** *(The men and women are sitting on opposite sides of the room.)*

Theme and Dynamics. The subject is changed by the members.

Miss French (to Mr. Darcy): ***Were you sick?***

Mr. Darcy (to Miss French): ***Yes! Were you?***

Theme and Dynamics. Two members made hostile comments to each other.

Miss French: **No.**

Mr. Cain: ***We're getting to be more of a group, Now we are challenging each other.***

Therapist: ***You talked about my smiling. I wonder if you have any other thoughts about my facial expressions here in the meetings.***

Therapist's Technique. The therapist is aware that the subject has been changed. He makes an observation that brings the members back to exploring their relationship to him. Therapist is in control of meeting.

Group counseling *is one procedure that has been found helpful in giving individuals new insights into the problems of marriage and how to deal with them.* *See page 115.*

Group counseling involves special techniques and training. The dynamics of the group process are centered around the group as a separate unit—a functioning structural unit within itself. The diagram exemplifies a seating arrangement, conversations of members of the group, the therapist, and comments about the therapist's technique. **Source:** *James A. Johnson, Jr.,* **Group Therapy,** *The Blakiston Division, McGraw-Hill Book Company, copyright 1963. Dr. Johnson is supervisor of the training program in group dynamics, group therapy, and group activities for the psychiatric residents and other members of the staff in the Department of Psychiatry, School of Medicine, Emory University.*

CHAPTER THIRTEEN

ADJUSTMENTS IN DATING, COURTSHIP, AND MARRIAGE

The movies, novels, songs, and comics proclaim romance as a power that overcomes all obstacles. In these fictions, marriage is pictured as a continuous state of ecstasy. Actually, marriage is like work and other important arenas of life. It is an arena where we have special opportunities to learn to enjoy emotionally satisfying experiences, such as companionship, and to interpret life in new and exciting ways.

One interesting way to learn how adjustments affect the lives of men and women is to study couples during their courtship and marriage. In the case of a young couple courting each other, we can try to understand what each means to the other psychologically. Also, the college student usually knows his own parents well enough for him to appreciate, to some extent, what each probably meant to the other at the time of marriage and to observe some of the ways in which each parent's adjustment has affected his marital life. The college student who gains even a limited insight into the psychological factors involved in the courtship and marriage of other couples should have a somewhat improved perspective for the more intelligent direction of his own courtship and marriage. Certainly marriage itself cannot be the starting point for a discussion of the factors in a successful marriage.

Adjustment Patterns That Can Be Recognized in the Behavior of Couples

Almost all psychological adjustment patterns influence the lives of persons, married or single. Some patterns, however, are especially influential in the choice of mate and the success or failure of the marriage. An objective awareness of these especially influential patterns can be acquired by any intelligent person who studies clinical findings, particularly those which are the mainsprings in the personality developments that lead to marital discord.

One of the first discoveries about marriage on the part of the psychological investigator is the fact that a boy and girl do not fall into love as a result of deep unfathomable forces. Rather, they fall into love with each other because each answers, or appears to answer, some of the dominant psychological needs of the other. A conventional example is the studious introverted boy, socially awkward, who is anxious to enjoy the company of a girl of his own age. He meets an extraverted girl, a poor student, who is vivacious. She helps him to enjoy himself socially. Perhaps she also builds up his feelings of self-worth because she tells him about her own shortcomings as a student and expresses admiration for his intellectual achievements. If he also has feelings of rejection by his parents and she mentions the ways in which her parents do not understand her, he may develop feelings of psychological kinship toward her and identify himself with her, thus forming ties that are likely to lead to further courtship and eventual marriage.

The individual's frustrations often find expression in the choice of the mate. The boy who was dominated by a stern parent or an older brother may prefer the company of a weak submissive girl because he can dominate her by telling her what clothes to wear, where she may go, and what she may or may not do. She, in turn, may enjoy his domination because her father was a tyrant over her. Her boy friend's tyranny allows her to live in terms of her earlier conditioning, but she likes the boy friend's domination better than her father's because she interprets the suitor's domination as proof of interest in her, not mere domination without sufficient interest.

Compensations are frequently demonstrated in the choice of a mate. The girl who feels that her family is socially inferior may prefer a mate of her own social class or she may seek one who appears to her to be of a higher class. If she feels inferior because her father was a plumber, she may prefer a bank clerk as a suitor even though he makes only half as much money as a plumber.

The girl who was reared too leniently or by parents who were inconsistent in their discipline may have pronounced feelings of emotional insecurity. She is not sure that she can depend upon anyone. Hence she may choose a man who has many fixed ideas, likes mathematics, lives his life in accordance with his formulas, is a firm disciplinarian and an army officer. His apparent self-assurance, even though it may actually be defensive on his part, is comforting to her. Actually, the two may be a well-mated couple.

Adjustments in courtship often demonstrate the previously stated principle (Chapter Two) that some persons react to an earlier environmental influence by antagonism toward it, others by adopting it. This is particularly evident in the case of a mother's domination of her son. One son may rebel against his mother's over-attentiveness and want to get away from home as soon as he can. He usually wants a mate who reminds him very little of his own mother. On the other hand, the son who enjoys his mother's attentiveness wants to remain with his mother as long as possible. If he does seek a mate, he is apt to seek a girl of the mother-image type. If he finds her, his courtship is likely to be of a vacillating kind because he finds his mother's company, after all, more comforting than the girl's.

Certainly every girl should know enough about the mother-fixation pattern to recognize it when she sees it. If she fails to appreciate its power for ill in married life and marries the man with an Oedipus complex, she is likely to find that his mother's apron strings become a noose around her life. Any bride who finds that her husband's comment about the pie she baked for him is: "Why don't you bake the kind of pie my mother baked?" should know enough to answer: "This is the kind of pie I bake for you. From now on you are going to eat 'em and like 'em!"

Every college man of courtship age ought to be able to recognize the behavior patterns of neurasthenia and functional invalidism when they are evident in the girls he dates. If he does not know enough psychology to recognize such adjustment patterns when he sees them, he will be lucky if he marries a well-adjusted girl. If he has enough insight to recognize patterns of serious maladjustment in a girl but decides to marry her regardless of such syndromes as neurasthenia or invalidism, he should appreciate the nature of the burden he assumes for life. Any hope he may have of curing her is just about as justifiable as that of the girl who marries a man in spite of the fact that she knows him to be a chronic alcoholic.

Women Who Do Not Marry

If people do marry to fulfill themselves and compensate for their own deficiencies through their mate, then it would appear that it is the less well-adjusted who marry. Martinson studied 118 women who had graduated from the same high school; 59 had married and 59 remained single.[1] They were of approximately the same age, background, and intelligence. Martinson found that the women who had remained single were better adjusted than those who had married. They showed more self-reliance, better social adjustment; in high school they had tended to receive higher marks. They were better adjusted emotionally, used their talents more fully, and had a greater sense of personal freedom. They did not need to fulfill themselves through a husband; they had few ego deficiencies and did not need marriage.

The Midtown Manhattan report (see page 22) revealed that single women have a lower incidence of mental disturbances than any other group, male or female. However, on none of the four age levels do the single women differ significantly in impairment from the wives. Single men, in contrast, reveal a different story. The impairment frequencies of the bachelors are higher by wide margins along the entire age axis. Seemingly, singleness for males is more pathogenic than is spinsterhood among females.

Proportion of Impaired Respondents of Like Age Home Survey Sample[2] *(Ages 20–59)*

	A. 20–29	*B. 30–39*	*C. 40–49*	*D. 50–59*
Single men	20.5%	30.4%	37.5%	46.1%
Single women	11.2	12.1	24.6	25.6
Married men	11.7	19.6	19.0	25.7
Married women	13.4	22.1	18.1	30.6

Perhaps the most satisfying explanation for the different states of mental health of single men and women is that our society views the male as the initiator. If the male cannot play his role effectively, he becomes a bachelor. Single women prefer to think that they play their chosen role well but have simply been "overlooked" because there are so many of them from which to choose. Many single women realize that they have become so capable and independent as career women that they could not provide the atmosphere that would complement the male ego. Perhaps in the future we shall see more women breaking away from the social pressures that force many into marriage, and instead, going on to fully develop their potentials, so that if they do decide to marry, they can bring to their marriage a complete person, ready to deal with the enormous problems marriage entails.

Quantitative Studies of Marital Success and Failure

The adjustment mechanisms at work in the choice of the mate may be fairly obvious or very subtle. It is impossible to predict with one hundred per cent accuracy whether a given personality pattern on the part of a man will result in compatibility or incompatibility when matched with a specific pattern of a woman. We can predict only with greater or less likelihood of validity that two patterns may or may not result in a lasting marriage. Several psychologists and other researchers have investigated factors which indicate likelihood of success or failure in marriage.

Different criteria for adjudging marital success or failure have been employed by different investigators. Clarence W. Schroeder used divorce as the criterion of failure in marriage in his study *Divorce in a City of 100,000 Population.*[3] Factors which he found to be positively correlated with marital success were: parents' marriage reported happier than average; parents not divorced or separated; sex instruction from mother or from books; education beyond high school; attendance at church three or more times a month; attendance at Sunday school beyond 18 years; and being reared in country or small town.

L. M. Terman[4] used the scores that 792 husbands and wives made on a marital happiness scale as the criterion of marital success. He found that the following factors were positively correlated with marital happiness: rated marital happiness of the parents; rated happiness of childhood; no conflict with mother; firm but not harsh discipline in the home; amount of attachment to father and mother; no conflict with father; frank attitude of parents toward early sex curiosity; relative mental ability where the husband is not inferior (with the wife's happiness) and where the husband is not much superior (with the husband's happiness); absence of severe and frequent childhood punishment; absence of disgust and aversion toward sex in premarital attitude of the subject; and, in the case of wife, absence of passionate longing.

Clifford Kirkpatrick[5] found that: (1) "in the case of women there is a marked tendency for greater intimacy with one or the other parent to be unfavorable to marital adjustment," and (2) "in the case of the males an excess or deficiency of friendship with the opposite sex is unfavorable to marital adjustment."

Hornell Hart, assisted by Wilmer Shields, used divorce as the criterion of marital failure.[6] He found that the optimum ages for entering marriage were twenty-nine for bridegrooms and twenty-four for brides. Men who were married when they were less than twenty-four years old, and women who were married when they were less than nineteen, were found to have a greater proportion of unhappy marriages than any other age groups.

In order to obtain objective information regarding the reasons for success or failure in marriage, Ernest W. Burgess and Leonard S. Cottrell, Jr. made a statistical and case history study of 526 married couples.[7] Their major findings were as follows:

1. Contrary to prevailing opinion, American wives make the major adjustment in marriage.
2. Affectional relationships in childhood typically of the son for the mother and the daughter for the father, condition the love-object choice of the adult.
3. The socialization of the person, as indi-

cated by his participation in social life and social institutions, is significant for adjustment in marriage.

4. The economic factor in itself is not significant for adjustment in marriage, since it is apparently fully accounted for by the other factors (impress of cultural background, psychogenetic characteristics, social type, and response patterns).

5. With the majority of couples, problems of sexual adjustment in marriage appear to be a resultant not so much of biological factors as of psychological characteristics and of cultural conditioning of attitudes toward sex.

6. Prediction before marriage of marital adjustment is feasible, and should and can be further developed through statistical and case-study methods.

TABLE 13.1

STUDIES OF THE BEST AGE FOR MARRIAGE AS JUDGED BY MARITAL SUCCESS AND FAILURE

	Poor	*Good*	*Excellent*
Burgess-Cottrell (526 marriages)			
Men:	Under 22	22–27; 31 and over	28–30
Women:	Under 19	19–27	28 and over
Hart-Shields (500 marriages)			
Men:	Under 24	24–28	29
Women:	Under 21	21–23	24
Terman (792 marriages)			
Men:	Under 22	22 and over	22 and over
Women:	Under 20	20 and over	20 and over
Landis (409 marriages)			
Men:	Under 20	20–29	30 and over
Women:	Under 20	25 and over	20–24

From Judson T. Landis and Mary G. Landis, *Building a Successful Marriage,* 2nd ed. (Englewood Cliffs, N.J.: Prentice-Hall, Inc., 1953), p. 107.

TABLE 13.2

DIFFERENCE IN AGE OF HUSBAND AND WIFE AND ADJUSTMENT

Difference in Age	*Marital Adjustment*			
	Poor (per cent)	Fair (per cent)	Good (per cent)	Number of Cases
Same age	13.1	39.1	47.8	46
Husband older:				
One to three years	21.4	31.0	47.6	168
Four to seven years	35.4	26.4	38.2	110
Eight years or more	31.1	17.8	51.1	45
Wife older	23.2	23.2	53.6	56
One or both, no reply	....	....	....	101
Total	28.5	28.3	43.2	526

From Ernest W. Burgess and Leonard S. Cottrell, Jr., *Predicting Success or Failure in Marriage* (Englewood Cliffs, N.J.: Prentice-Hall, Inc., 1939), Table 89 (Chart 36), p. 406.

TABLE 13.3

DURATION OF KEEPING COMPANY AND ADJUSTMENT

Duration of Courtship	*Material Adjustment*			
	Poor (per cent)	Fair (per cent)	Good (per cent)	Number of Cases
Under three months	39.3	28.6	32.1	28
Three to 11 months	42.9	23.8	33.3	105
One year to three years	28.9	31.8	39.3	201
Three to five years	12.6	30.6	56.8	111
Five years and over	17.2	27.6	55.2	58
No reply	....	....	....	23
Total	28.5	28.3	43.2	526

From *Predicting Success or Failure in Marriage,* Table 91 (Chart 38), p. 407.

Particularly important was their finding that similarity of cultural background was found to be of greater importance in a good marital adjustment than was similarity of economic background.

Landis has assembled data obtained from several studies of the best age for marriage as judged by marital success or failure. In general, the researchers seem to agree that the best marital adjustments are made by men who marry after they are about 28 or 29 and women who marry in their mid-twenties. Poor adjustments occur most frequently when the husband has married in his early twenties or teens and the wife, in her teens (see Table 13.1). Several investigators have found that the chances for happiness were less in early marriages than in later ones. Judson Landis found that the "divorce rate was six times higher in the marriages where both spouses were under 21, than in the marriages in which both spouses were 31 or over at the time of marriage."[8]

Judson T. and Mary G. Landis,[9] Burgess and Cottrell, as well as others found that those who had the highest scores based on premarital background items, that is, those who seemed to have the most factors favorable to a successful marriage, actually did have more successful marriages. They found that there was an increase in the number of divorces and separations as the prediction scores became lower. There was also an increase in the number of those who had *contemplated* divorce or separation as the scores became lower. It would therefore appear that it is possible to predict with some reliability the chances of success in marriage if certain factors are taken into consideration.

Factors in Divorce

Divorce, although not encouraged in our culture, is condoned. The number of divorces reported annually varies considerably. The rate was especially low in the midst of the depression years, 1932 and 1933, and reached an all-time high in 1946. The annual average rate during a recent ten-year period was less than one for every 100 married couples. These data differ decidedly from the ones often published: "One out of four U.S. marriages ends in divorce." It would be far more accurate to say: "One out of 109 marriages ends in divorce." It is true that there were more than 390,000 divorces in 1960 and roughly four times that many marriages but annual divorce figures do not come out of the newlyweds of a single year but from the entire married population. The recommended way to calculate the divorce rate is to put the 390,000 figure against the total number of married women 15 years old and older.[10]

Annual divorce figures do not include the somewhat under one million homes from which the husband is absent nor the several hundred thousand from which the wife is absent. This may not mean that more ill-advised marriages are being undertaken than heretofore, but that people are more anxious to be released from the marriage contract if they are disappointed in it. It appears that, in general, the longer the duration of a marriage, the greater is the possibility of its being permanent. The first six years of marriage are the crucial ones. There are more divorces during the third year of marriage than during any other, but the divorce rate remains relatively high during the first six years of marriage.[11]

In connection with his study of psychological factors in marital happiness, Terman statistically evaluated domestic grievances of the 792 married couples who constituted his experimental group. Findings by Terman with regard to the grievances that are considered most important and least important are stated as follows:

> Consider first the grievances that rank highest for seriousness. These are all personality faults of the complainant's mate, not the external circumstances or conditions of marriage. This holds for the entire first 20 in the husband's list, and for 19 of the first 20 in the wife's. A majority of the faults are of the kind commonly thought to be indicative of emotional instability, neurotic tendency, or marked introversion, as these terms are used in the current literature of personality psychology. Their position here lends support to the theory that one of the greatest dangers to

marriage is the all-around unhappy temperament of one or both of the spouses. . . .

Most serious for husband's happiness are, in order: wife's nagging, lack of affection, selfishness or inconsiderateness, complaining, interfering with his hobbies, slovenliness of appearance, quick temper, interfering with his discipline of children, conceit, insincerity, too easily hurt feelings, criticizing, narrow-mindedness, neglect of the children, poor housekeeping, argumentativeness, annoying habits and mannerisms, untruthfulness, interference with his business, and spoiling the children.

Most serious for wife's happiness are, in order: husband's selfishness or inconsiderateness, lack of success in business, untruthfulness, complaining, failure to show his affection for her, unwillingness to talk things over, harshness with the children, touchiness, lack of interest in the children, lack of interest in the home, lack of (general) affectionateness, rudeness, lack of ambition, nervousness or impatience, criticizing, poor management of income, narrow-mindedness, unfaithfulness, laziness, boredom when she talks to him about her everyday life.

Only 6 items are found in the first 20 of both husband's and wife's lists: "not affectionate," "selfish and inconsiderate," "complains too much," "criticizes me," "is narrow-minded," "is not truthful."

Consider next the grievances that are least serious as causes of unhappiness. Here the spouses are in closer agreement. Of the 10 lowest in the respective lists, 7 are found in both.

The 10 things in order of least importance for the wife's happiness are that: husband is older, smokes, differs from her in tastes in food, is younger, differs from her in education, drinks, swears, is late to meals, is jealous, differs from her in religious beliefs.

The 12 least serious to husband's happiness are as follows in order of least seriousness: the wife is younger, drinks, smokes, is older, differs from him in tastes in food, is a social climber, works outside the home, swears, differs from him in education, is a poor cook, differs from him in religious beliefs, is unfaithful.

This list of things that are relatively so unimportant to the husband's happiness is one of the most interesting outcomes of our entire study. The striking fact about the list is that it is composed so largely of things which have long been regarded as among the most essential conditions of a happy and successful marriage.*

Divorce is indisputable evidence that one or both marriage partners have failed to adjust to the other, and to the institution of marriage. We have seen what some investigators believe to be factors militating for success in marriage, but the factors that contribute to a maladjustment, as in divorce, are perhaps even more difficult to ascertain.

The statistical finding that a childless marriage is more likely to end in divorce than a marriage with children may have several possible explanations. The fact that no children are involved in most divorce cases may mean that these mates are selfish—so selfish as to be unwilling to make the adjustments necessary to a successful marriage. On the other hand, the fact that they have no children may mean that it is easier for them to consider divorce than it is for people with the responsibility of children. Regardless of the reasons, however, the fact remains that adjustments of the requisite number and scope are not made so that the marriage may be enabled to grow.

Terman, in his study of 792 married couples who had a mean length of marriage of 11.4 years, found that 8.8 per cent of the men and 11.5 per cent of the women had seriously contemplated divorce at some time during their marriage. When these 792 couples rated themselves as to the degree of happiness achieved, 95.5 per cent of the men rated their happiness from "about average" to "extraordinarily happy." Only 4.6 per cent of the men rated their marriage "somewhat less happy than average" to "extremely unhappy." Of the women, 94.4 per cent rated their marriage as "about average" to "extraordinarily happy," and 5.6 per cent rated their marriage "somewhat less happy than average" to "extremely unhappy."[12]

Husbands of good health make better adjustments than those less healthy. The health of the husband is shown to be more important than that of the wife, probably because of economic necessities.[13]

Statistical studies of divorces and other factors concomitant to marital conditions merely indicate likely relationships, not determining influences. This was shown in the

---

* By permission from Lewis M. Terman, *Psychological Factors in Marital Happiness* (New York: McGraw-Hill Book Company, 1938), pp. 101f.

Family Society of Greater Boston study of the Highs who adjusted well in their work in comparison with the Lows who failed to adjust after counseling. The individual's own adjustments to his barriers were the determining influences, not such factors as family disruption, illnesses, or money troubles during childhood. These kinds of troubles plagued both the Highs and the Lows. The Highs developed a tendency to counteract and reverse negative early experiences, the Lows to re-enact unfavorable early family patterns. One important finding in regard to ability to adjust to barriers was that people seem to be able to adjust far more easily to outside pressures such as family disruption and money troubles than to inner emotional pressures like family antagonism or self-doubt.[14]

The person who adjusts best to marriage is the socialized person. Through his experiences with people in various groups he develops differently from the individual who participates but little in group organizations. He is more apt to be a stable personality and thus better suited to marriage.

Our choice of mates is restricted in our society by certain barriers that limit our acquaintances and friends. Although these barriers are not insurmountable, they are worthy of consideration.

Religion is one of these restrictive factors. While intermarriages do occur and many of them turn out happily, it is generally found that Catholics marry Catholics, Jews marry Jews, and Protestants marry Protestants.

Intermarriages are increasing. However, most couples who have intermarried say that they have to "work much harder" to achieve a successful marriage than those who marry someone of their own race, color, and creed.[15] Divorce rates are higher among those whose cultural, religious, and psychological backgrounds differ. Many parents recognize these difficulties and indoctrinate their offspring with the importance of marrying "their own kind" for their own good. Serious friendships with young people of a different religious faith are usually disapproved. When two people of different religions do fall in love, however, and consider marriage, problems arise, particularly if the couple intends to have children. The question of which religion the children will be encouraged to adopt is a question that must be answered by the parents. Some couples feel that they cannot assume the responsibility of making such a decision and do not marry because of the difference in religion. Other alternatives are: one may decide on conversion to the faith of the other; both may dismiss the problem of choice between two religions by subscribing to neither; each partner may retain his own faith. Another solution, more idealistic than practicable, is the adoption of the attitude that because of a mixed marriage the parents have something extra to add to the child's development—an appreciation and understanding of two religions instead of one only.

The chief obstacles to a successful religious intermarriage, or to any marriage, are psychological. Marriage is an adjustment. Even the most perfect marriage has its moments of difference and misunderstanding. If both partners share a common concern for the same values and are basically well-adjusted and love one another, there is a strong likelihood that they will be able to work out their problems. Yet it cannot be denied that a marriage concerns more than just the husband and the wife. The marriage involves the lives and relationships they have with their families and the religious communities in which the husband or wife had his origin and childhood association. Although churches, families and communities have only an indirect influence, they can do much to complicate and injure, or to support and further, the happiness of the couple. Young couples contemplating religious intermarriage should be fully aware of the pressures that may be brought on them. There are no national statistics to show just how the chances of an interfaith marriage compare with that of a marriage between two persons of the same religious fellowship. Experience has shown, however, that the more similar the background, interests and beliefs

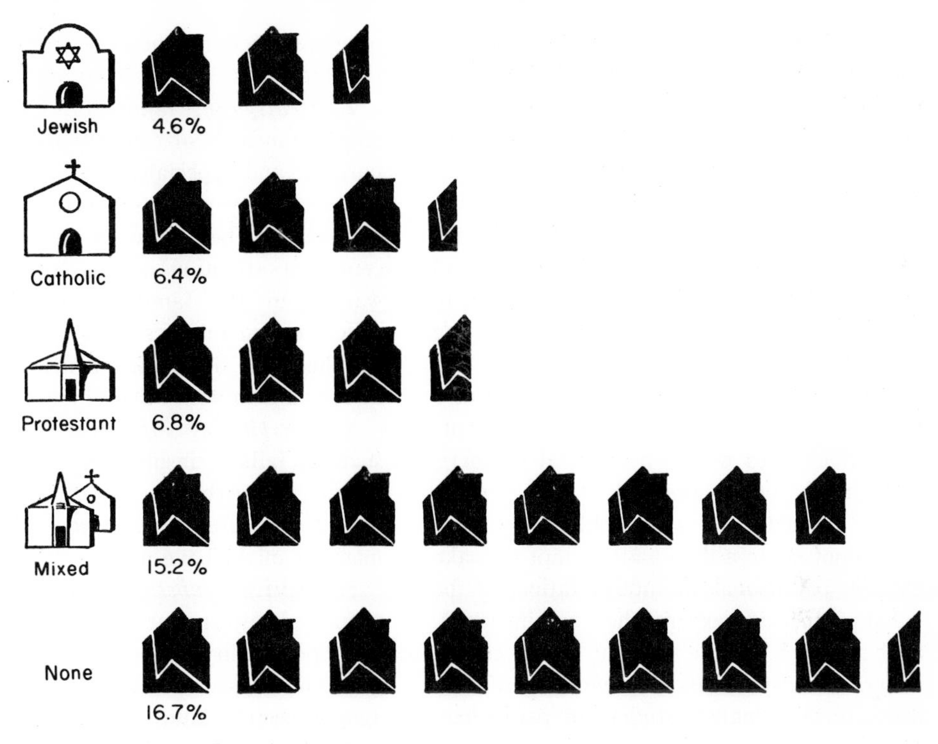

Religion and broken homes—*from a chart by Graphic Associates for Public Affairs Committee, Inc.*

of the two individuals, the more likelihood there is that their marriage will be a success.[16]

It is a fact that couples having church connections have more stable marriages than those with none. The accompanying chart, based on a survey by the American Youth Commission, shows the relation between religious affiliation and broken homes.

Finding a church home is an important part of building a marriage between people with religious needs and interests. Couples oftentimes would like to have a church home but after their marriage, especially if they come from different religious backgrounds, they find it difficult. He isn't at home in her church, nor is she in his, and so they settle it by having no church affiliation at all. This rarely solves the problem because most people need a larger interest outside themselves if they are to be happy. When trouble comes, that need becomes acute. You can feel terribly alone and helpless when a crisis comes. There is a desolation about death, sudden impoverishment, severe disappointments, and many family problems. At times like these, as well as in day-by-day living, religion is often a real source of comfort and support.

Finding a church home usually begins before marriage. When plans are being made for life together you talk about the church in which you will make your home. You visit each other's church if you have not grown up in the same one. Together you plan for your joint membership. If the decision has been postponed until after your marriage, it is wise not to put it off longer.

Religious ceremonies at the time of the marriage, the dedication of the home, the christening of the children, the celebration of holidays, and in the everyday life of the home add richness and a sense of permanence to a marriage.[17]

Intelligent Dating

Dating is a getting-acquainted period. High school and college students rate the ability to date successfully as a kind of status-gaining procedure. On some campuses, dating is largely an end in itself rather than an approach to courtship and marriage. College students, in most cases, must postpone serious thoughts of marriage until they complete their education and earn a livelihood. Dating enables the students to enjoy the company of the opposite sex and to engage in normal social functions until they reach the stage of educational and professional attainment which allows them to have more definite plans for marriage. Dating offers these young people excellent opportunities to note and evaluate the personality characteristics of the opposite sex and to surmise which ones would, as marital partners, be successful or unsuccessful.

The student who is psychologically alert should not go on a date and attempt to make amateur psychoanalytic interpretations of the dated partner and explain them to him (her). Such practice on the part of many college majors in psychology is evidence of immaturity. The mature student of psychology does not "psychologize" his friends and discuss his interpretations with them. Rather, he notes the cues to each friend's adjustment patterns, constantly adds to his understanding of the friend, increases his respect for him, and makes himself a better companion. Such a companionship is on a high level of mutual respect for the personality integrity of the other person. Dating experiences offer the student the opportunity to do some intelligent "field work" in the attainment of this high level of companionability and psychological insight.

Young people on dates often discuss their own childhood histories, their frustrations, resentments, disappointments, hopes, and other influences in adjustment. The alert listener can, in his own mind, note the patterns of behavior that control the other person's personality. The psychologically intelligent male student on a date will note significant factors in the adjustment development of his girl friends, such as the following:

1. *Her barriers:* Problems of health, physical appearance, limitations in mental capacities, birth of other children in the family, parental frictions, neurotic relatives, impatient teachers, domineering associates, et al.

2. *Predisposing influences:* Cultural influences, standards of conduct insisted upon by parents, and especially her affect evaluation of herself when she was a small child. Did she, for example, behave as though she were the center of attention of the family; feel unwanted in the family, denied her rights, ridiculed, disciplined severely; or feel that she was helpless, sickly, and deficient as a child in comparison with other children?

3. *Precipitating influences:* recent factors such as failure, insult, loss, disappointment, fatigue, or success.

4. *Direct-attack adjustments* which she made or might have made.

5. *Positive substitute activities:* What means of adjustment were made of a positive, personality-strengthening nature, such as studiousness, in adjustment to real or imagined social failure or physical unattractiveness?

6. *Evasive or retreat adjustments:* What personality-weakening adjustments has she made, such as withdrawing from social contacts, habitual attendance at the movies, excessive alcoholism, constant fault-finding, exhibitionism, untruthfulness, wishing for death, or other negative-value activities?

If the dominating adjustments have been positive and personality-strengthening, she will need little aid from a future husband other than normal human companionship and consideration. If many dominating adjustments have been of an evasive nature and personality-weakening, she may require a great deal of helpful insight from a husband in order to make her happy or to enable him to be happy with her.

If she exemplifies the very common adjustment pattern of the child who felt inferior intellectually (barrier), was reared by doting parents who made her the center of attention (predisposing influence), now keenly enjoys being well dressed and pleasing others in social situations (positive value adjustment), she is very apt to continue the pattern after marriage. Her husband, in turn, will react to the pattern favorably or unfavorably, depending upon his own adjustment tendencies. If he has developed strong tendencies in the direction of stinginess in buying clothes and has little desire to have his wife impress others in social affairs, he is likely to find her behavior annoying. On the other hand, if he likes to spend money to buy nice things for his wife so that she becomes an ornament that impresses other people, he is likely to find her behavior quite gratifying to him.

Marriage does not change adjustment patterns. The individual takes into marriage the same patterns and techniques that he used before marriage. The girl who resorted to illness as an escape from difficult situations before marriage will also resort to illness as an escape after marriage. The youth who ran to mother for comfort or resorted to drink in emotional crisis before marriage is likely to resort to the same techniques after marriage. But the patterns that one man needs in his mate may be quite different from the patterns that will complement the adjustment needs of another. Success in marriage is not so much a matter of finding the right person as *becoming* the right person, the kind of person who has developed the strength of character and skills that make him effective in his human relations. The people who succeed in marriage are also quite likely to succeed in other human relationships. Marital happiness is related to self acceptance and the acceptance of others.[18]

The one stage in boy-girl relations where our culture provides opportunity for the boy and the girl to evaluate each other objectively is the dating period, before courtship begins. Once their relation reaches the courtship stage, almost all objectivity in personality evaluation disappears. Evaluations of the other person in courtship become mere rationalizations. The degree of intimacy in their relationship is indicated by the kinds of pet names they use for each other. Because of the intimacy of the meanings of the pet names, quarreling couples drop them, or use them with embarrassment or sarcastic intent.[19]

Unfortunately, some people like to imagine that true love has to come suddenly. They offer the cliché, "When the right person comes along, you'll know it." Such claims are far more likely to result in regret than happiness. One investigator, Paul Landis, studied a group of hasty marriages on the part of couples who had known each other for only a couple of weeks and found that four out of five of the marriages ended in divorce in the first year.[20] Love at first sight is a mirage. Intelligent dating requires considerable time as well as psychological perceptiveness.

Adjustments after Marriage

Immediately after marriage the honeymoon takes place. This custom enables the young couple to get away from old environments, relatives, and friends. Marriage requires the changing of many habits, and the honeymoon provides the newlyweds some opportunity for learning how to live together in the first stages of their home life. As stated by Paul H. Landis:

> "The first month isn't easy, you know," is a comment frequently heard from newlyweds. Being happy as man and wife does not come to most couples as a matter of course, but like success in any cooperative enterprise it comes only after considerable experience.
>
> The readjustments of habits that marriage requires are sometimes disturbing, but, to establish any type of home routine, many habits accepted prior to marriage have to be readjusted to suit the new family situation. Habits of rising and retiring, the time of eating, likes and dislikes in foods, and numerous activities that make up daily living have to be adjusted. Failure of either member to make certain concessions is apt to become a source of friction.
>
> Good husbands and wives are not born that way, nor is the transformation caused by courtship or the marriage ceremony. Some old folks on their golden wedding anniversary make flowery statements about never having disagreed on anything. The likelihood is that they have forgotten many things. Actually most couples disagree on certain points, and these differences may come to light early in married life.
>
> Unfortunately, most courtship is carried on during leisure time so the young couple have

opportunities to see each other only when they are in the best mood. During courtship they usually engage in pleasant activities. This is suddenly changed by marriage, when for the first time the marriage partners share every relationship of life: work, trouble, the daily grind of life, responsibility, duty, worry about finances, and all the other normal responsibilities that are a part of adulthood, as well as the leisure time and recreational periods.

During the early months of marriage much of the exaggerated romance wears off as the couple settles down to washing dishes, scrubbing floors, commuting, paying bills, and sharing the remnants of their days with one another. The young man and young woman come to see each other as human beings rather than as the idealized gods they appeared to be in the highly romantic phase of courtship. There was a tendency during courtship to oversell one's best traits to be sure of winning the other party. Now in day-to-day living both best and worse traits gradually appear.

Successful couples work out their disagreements or learn to accept and tolerate each other's differences in point of view. It would be unusual to find any relationship in which two people agreed on everything. Marriage is no exception. Few people like all of their own personal traits. It is unlikely that they will find everything exactly as they wish or had expected in the person they marry. Actually life would for many be a little dull if they always saw eye to eye.*

What kind of marriage do the very well-adjusted men and women enjoy? One significant study in this field was made and reported by Jules Golden, *et al.* (see page 158). In that study 50 young men, ages 26–27, were found to be unusually well-adjusted psychologically. A later study was made of the 38 available wives of the 40 men who were married at the time the investigation was undertaken. Each wife was interviewed in her home by a trained interviewer. Tests were administered.

The findings indicated that "on those items reflecting contentment with lot in life, effectiveness, and overall adjustment, the wives as the men, rate high; on those items reflecting richness of personality, the rating is low."

The researchers' final interpretations follow:

The group as a whole can be characterized not only as mentally healthy, but significantly homogeneous in this regard. At least for our sample, we can speak of a psychological homogamy as well; that essentially healthy individuals select healthy spouses.

Investigation of more representative samples would have to prove whether or not our couples are unique, or if they epitomize what may now be a relatively common level of adaptation in the population at large. We do wish to express our mixed feelings about this adjustment. Such a population would promote stability or a firm backbone of the country; but as observed of the previously described men, these couples' lives seem essentially mundane and dull. Our data indicates, however, that this sample of husbands and wives, with a high order of consistency, experience what we consider some of life's deepest and most meaningful pleasures: in their stable relationships with each other, and in raising their children. The inference could be made that constricted interests permit such subjects a wider opportunity for the meaningful rewards of family life. A more stimulating educational experience and more enlightened media of mass communication, it is our hope, will enrich such "normal" people's lives without sacrificing their essentially sound adjustment.[21]

Perhaps the significance of these findings and their cautious interpretation suggest the value of a modification of an old axiom: "The course of true love, whether before or after marriage, never runs smoothly." Happiness in marriage should mean more than dull acceptance. Successful marriage for most persons necessitates numerous and continuing adjustments on the part of each mate to the other.

The fact that it is easy for any interested observer to go into a restaurant and to differentiate the married couples from the unmarried does not mean that every young married couple need look forward to boredom or eventual separation. Nor should either party expect a completely problemless existence.

Sometimes a frank disagreement or emotionalized "spat" may clear the atmosphere and remove the unspoken grievances that

* By permission from Paul H. Landis, *Your Marriage and Family Living* (New York: McGraw-Hill Book Company, 1946), pp. 152–153.

have accumulated. Disagreement is a part of the process of marital adjustment. It helps to improve the unity of the family if it is a phase in the further adjustment of persons who are basically well adjusted in other respects. If the one partner always avoids open disagreement and merely suppresses his own feelings of frustration, the frustrations will in time affect his personality. He must make some kind of adjustment, such as burying himself in his work. In that case he is likely to suspend his identifications with his mate, and their relationship becomes a conventional one. Success in work, however, may give one partner feelings of adequacy that enable him or her to aid the other by treating him or her objectively.

Most couples want to make their marriages successful. Marriages rarely become truly successful unless both, or at least one partner, is sufficiently well adjusted to facilitate the psychological well-being of the other. Both can grow best when they respect each other's personality and want the partner as well as the self to enjoy married life on its highest level—creative love.

The love life of the average individual passes through four stages: love of self, *babyhood;* love of parent, *childhood;* love of chum, *early youth;* and love of mate, *adulthood.* When the individual's love-object remains on the first level, self-love, he is an example of *narcissism;* when on the second level, attachment for a parent, the terms *Oedipus* or *Electra complex* are used to describe it; and when fixated on the third level, attraction for persons of the same sex, the general term *homosexuality* is used. The latter term is often used in a broad general sense and is contrasted with *heterosexuality,* attraction toward individuals of the opposite sex, but neither of these last two terms necessarily implies perversion or a specific sex relation.

The best-adjusted persons also attain a fifth stage of love-life, *creative love.* Each identifies his personality with that of his mate in absorbing tasks of rearing children, developing a happy home life, and pursuing successful vocational activities. Biologically, creative love is most commonly expressed in the rearing of children.

Sociological Changes

From the sociological standpoint, American family life is changing in line with the influences of a changing society. Families in the United States in comparison with those of other countries have certain differential characteristics. These differential characteristics are largely in terms of process rather than of structure. One of the most distinctive trends is greater *urbanization.* The proportion of families living in cities and near-by urban areas has increased. Furthermore, rural families have adopted the urban way of life.

Instability is greater, as indicated by the increase in divorce. This instability within some families is set in sharper focus by the increased trend toward companionship, common interests, and emphasis on democratic relations. As one advertisement for a women's service magazine phrased the change: "The family climate's healthier, with a warm and sunny weatherness that comes from interests shared—from what might best be termed 'togetherness.' "

Several decades ago the father was undisputed head of the household. He dominated the family, and his preferences received first consideration. Today, this type of family is being supplanted by one that is more democratic. The father is slipping, or has slipped, from his throne as autocrat. He is now a companion rather than boss. His wishes are not the only ones which are considered when the family is involved. Each member can voice his opinion and have his desires acted upon, also. Or, if one member's interests are far different from those of the rest of the family, he can go off alone—within reasonable limits—and do what he wishes. Ernest W. Burgess has described this aspect of the family in a changing society as follows:

> The American family, both in its apparent variety and in its essential unity, needs to be

viewed in the perspective of social change. It is in transition from older rural institutional forms to a democratic companionship type of family relations adapted to an urban environment. This great change in the mores is a vast social experiment, participated in by hundreds of thousands of families under the collective stimulation of the American ideology of democracy, freedom, and self-expression. This experimental situation places the emphasis upon the adaptability rather than upon the rigid stability of the family.[22]

Margaret Mead, anthropologist, has described further this aspect of the contemporary American family:

Great readjustment which is occurring in the family pattern is the terminability of American marriage. As the old religious sanctions which enjoined fidelity until death, regardless of such ephemeral considerations as congeniality or "happiness," have faded for large sections of the population and have been powerless to save many more marriages from dissolution, new ways of holding marriages together are developing. The life of a family is coming to be seen as a ship which may be wrecked by any turn of the tide unless every member of the family, but especially the two parents, are actively and cooperatively engaged in sailing the boat, vigilantly tacking, trimming their sails, resetting their course, bailing in storms—all to save something which is worth their continuous care. This new ideal, in which all the members of a family work together to keep alive an ever changing relationship, may in time provide us with the necessary new ethical sanction within which to give our changing family dignity and safety.[23]

Family Life Education and Family Counseling Services

Married people should be educated to take advantage of the social service institutions provided to aid those with personal marital problems. There should be no stigma attached to visiting a marriage clinic or family service agency, as there should be no stigma to visiting a psychiatrist. An interview with a qualified counselor who can see the problem objectively may save many a failing marriage, or assure a successful one.

The marriage counselor tries to see each partner in marriage as an individual with certain needs and characteristics. In interview after interview, the chief complaint of couples who are having marital problems is that they are lonely, that they feel isolated from their spouse. They no longer seem to share the same interests, and even have difficulty communicating with each other. They cannot explain their feelings to their partner, and this adds to their frustration, and often their attempts to explain end in quarrels over petty issues.

The marriage counselor must help the individual regain his sense of perspective, to realize that every problem he faces has been faced before, and that his experience with previous problems should help him with new ones. And even more important, the couple should realize that they solved problems in the past, and should be able to do the same again, if they take one issue at a time.

Group counseling is one procedure that has been helpful in giving couples new insights into the problems of marriage and how to solve them. In one experiment, couples of different backgrounds who had had relatively long and ostensibly happy marriages met with counselors to discuss marital problems. The couples found that they had all encountered much the same problems and that the most common were attitudes toward sexual behavior, disagreement over parental guidance of the children, disagreement over sharing responsibility for aging parents, and over the number of children a couple should have. Often, the couples had not even dared to think about these problems to themselves, let alone discuss them with their spouse. The relaxed atmosphere of the discussion group in which everyone freely analyzed their own problems and personal shortcomings tended to make the couples see their marriages in a more objective light.[24]

One of the interesting findings in some studies of marital success and failure is that the sex relationship of parents is not a valid indication of the emotional health and level of integration of the family unit.[25] Researchers have found some happily married couples whose sex adjustment was poor. Conversely,

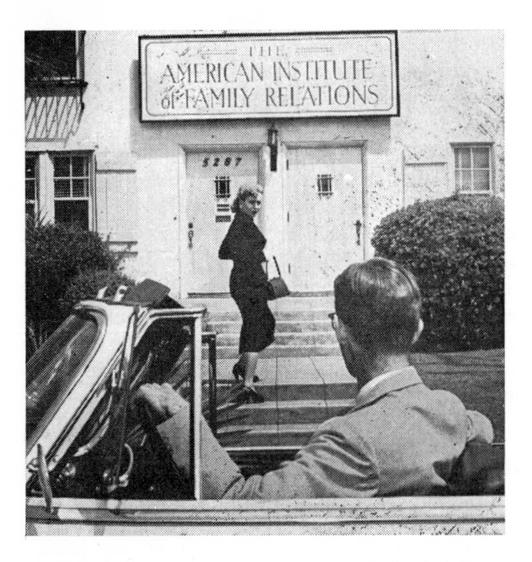

A client entering the American Institute of Family Relations, 5287 Sunset Blvd., Los Angeles 27, California.

Workroom at American Institute of Family Relations. Some of the Institute's more than 160 pamphlets may be seen in rack in background. The people in the picture are filling orders for pamphlets and other materials.

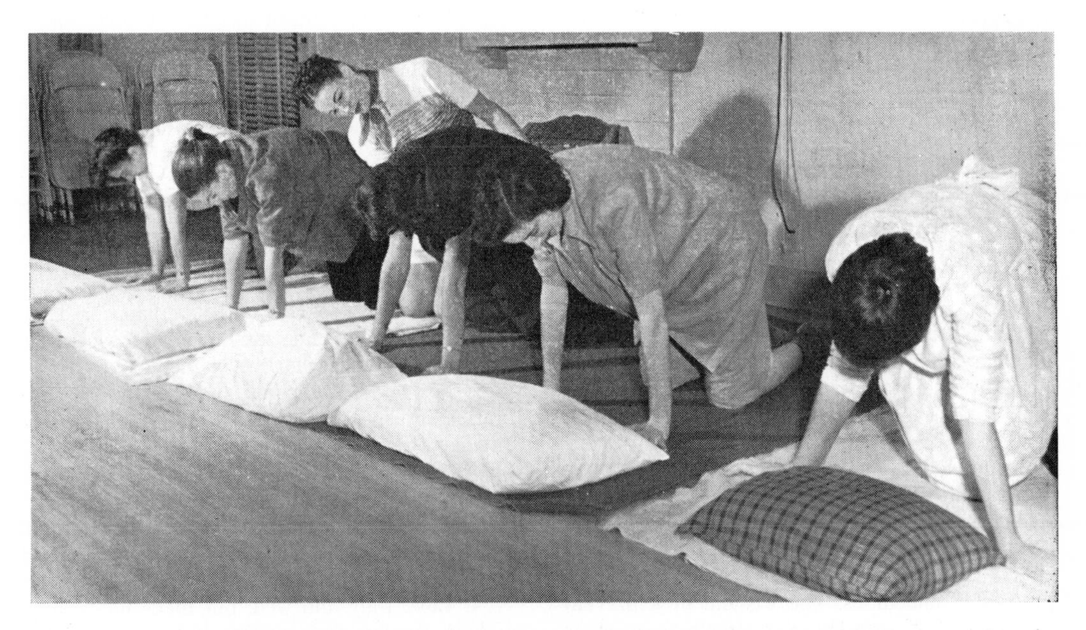

Mary Jane Hungerford, Ph.D. (with braids), directing exercises in connection with course on "Preparation for Parenthood." Photos by Gladys Tippett.

The American Institute of Family Relations, *a national non-profit organization, will without charge put inquirers in touch with qualified counselors in their own communities. It maintains a comprehensive referral list in all of the states, and also in Canada and many foreign countries. It also publishes a monthly service bulletin,* ***Family Life,*** *edited by Paul Popenoe.*

they have also found couples who were physically compatible but unhappy in their marital life as a whole.

In this country there are relatively few marriage clinics as such, but there are two hundred and forty family service agencies affiliated with the Family Service Association of America.[26]

Luther E. Woodward, Field Consultant of the National Committee for Mental Hygiene, has stressed the need for more family counseling services that are educative and preventive:

It is seventy years since the first family society was organized in America, and in many of our cities family services have been operating continuously for forty to fifty years. That seems too long a time to go on correcting family difficulties without making concerted efforts on the preventive side. If leaders in the public health field had been as slow to undertake the education of the public in health measures many of us probably would have been victims of one or another epidemic. In the case of family and community pathology people do not die so quickly. But that is no justification for failing to educate for family living with a view to preventing serious family difficulties. The wisdom of a preventive program is apparent; yet after seventy years of family service extremely little education for family living is being undertaken by the staffs of family agencies.

This reminds me of a sanity test that the Cornwall coast natives are reputed to have used for a long time. Anyone suspected of mental imbalance was brought into a room where water was flowing from a faucet into a bucket. The patient was given a cup and asked to bail the water out of the bucket. If he first turned off the faucet before he began dipping, he was considered sane. If he proceeded to dip the water out while the water poured in from the open faucet, he was considered insane. Our neglect of education for family life hardly justifies a judgment of national insanity, but the point seems clear. To go on bailing out a third of the marriages through the divorce courts while a constant stream from the same potentials flows in hardly seems like good sense. . . .

As a result of his years of experience in the field of family counseling, he has also submitted a "Decalogue for Marriage":

I submit it not as the last word on psychological insight, but simply as evidence that the basic concepts of family life and of interpersonal relations in the family can be stated simply and succinctly enough so that hopefully they may be transmitted somewhat from mouth to ear. The whole story cannot be told in these simple epigrammatic statements, but they are, I think, suggestive of the kind of insight and understanding that can be fostered through education for family living. It can hardly be gainsaid that persons who acquire an appreciation of the truths embodied in these ten brief statements would, through such appreciation, greatly strengthen their own family life.

Decalogue for Marriage

1. Happy homes do not just happen. They are made by the understanding and cooperative zeal of the people who live in them.

2. Sex is as God-given and worthy as sight, hearing, or speech and like these is to be used intelligently and artfully for the enrichment of life.

3. In marriage all things add up: congenial conversation, sexual harmony, shared interests, practical helpfulness, and worship in spirit and truth are interrelated and strengthen each other.

4. Love fully and well, but make not a bond of love, for love is a quality of free spirits; and while love is the foundation of marriage and the home, demand not its constant expression for no one loves anyone 100 per cent all of the time.

5. As mates you need many interests in common which you share in the doing and others which you pursue separately and share only in

AM I WELL-BALANCED?

Your answers to these questions are a good indication of your emotional maturity, and so of one aspect of your fitness for marriage. Read each question carefully before you answer "Yes" or "No." Refer to page 621 for scoring.

1. Do you greatly dislike very bossy people?
2. Do you like to write personal letters?
3. Do you like people who are more clever than you?
4. Is it hard for you to like "yes" people?
5. Do you like to entertain friends at home?
6. Do you usually plan your work in detail?
7. Do you have great confidence in yourself?
8. Do you frequently attend church services?
9. Can you usually cheer up a depressed person?
10. Do you ever rewrite letters before mailing them?
11. Will you fight to get your own way?
12. Does praise or blame affect you very much?
13. Has anyone ever given you a very "raw deal"?
14. Do your friends think you are conceited?
15. Is it annoying to you to lose an argument?
16. Do your friends often talk about you behind your back?
17. Is it hard for you to keep your temper in check?
18. Do you dislike cautious and conservative people?
19. Do you believe present moral standards too strict?
20. Do you frequently feel miserable or grouchy?

the telling. Let each of you fully respect the individuality of the other for mates are not as two peas in a pod.

6. Live fully today and mar it not by undue thought of tomorrow's difficulties, and "Let not the sun go down on thy wrath." Wrath there will be occasionally but let it not be stored up and carried into the morrow.

7. Strive for the grace of full acceptance of your mate notwithstanding his (her) shortcomings for these are likely then to disappear. And remember that while marriage and family living usually result in personality growth, obvious efforts to educate or "reform" one's mate are seldom successful.

8. Dwell upon the virtues and strengths of your mate and let them be praised to her (him) and to others, for we are all so made that we respond favorably to positive attention but are driven away or confirmed in our folly by criticism and nagging.

9. As the springs and tires on the family car take up the occasional bumps in the road and make them of little account, so members of a family must absorb and make of no account the occasional hostility and bad temper which one or another may show. To respond in kind is to make the road more bumpy.

10. Learn to share your feelings frankly be they feelings of affection, perplexity, or irritation, and be equally ready to accept those of your mate, for marriage can survive many troubles but cannot endure sham and pretense. Its greatest security is in being genuine and real.[27]

ACKNOWLEDGMENTS AND REFERENCES

1. Floyd Martinson, "Ego Deficiency as a Factor in *Marriage," American Sociological Review,* **20,** No. 2 (1955), 161–164.
2. Leo Srole, *et al., Mental Health in the Metropolis: The Midtown Study* (New York: McGraw-Hill Book Company, 1962), pp. 175–177. The "Impaired Respondents" category includes those classified has having "Marked symptom formation," "Severe symptom formation," and "Incapacitated."
3. Doctoral dissertation, University of Chicago libraries, 1938.
4. Lewis M. Terman, *Psychological Factors in Marital Happiness* (New York: McGraw-Hill Book Company, 1938), pp. 167–266.
5. "Factors in Marital Adjustment," *American Journal of Sociology,* **43** (1937–38), 270–283.
6. "Early Marriage and Happiness," *Journal of Social Hygiene,* **12** (1926), 554–559. See pp. 115–117 for a discussion of this study.
7. Ernest W. Burgess and Leonard S. Cottrell Jr., *Predicting Success or Failure in Marriage* (Englewood Cliffs, N.J.: Prentice-Hall, Inc., 1939), p. 349.
8. See Lester A. Kirkendall, *Too Young to Marry,* Public Affairs Committee, New York, 1962, p. 3.
9. Judson T. Landis and Mary G. Landis, *Building a Successful Marriage,* 3rd ed., (Englewood Cliffs, N.J.: Prentice-Hall, Inc., 1958), pp. 284–288. Premarital and background items are based on factors in the individual's background such as education, employment history, participation in groups, and so forth.
10. *Trends in Divorce and Family Disruption,* Marriage and Divorce Statistics Branch, Department of Health, Education and Welfare, Washington, D.C., 1964.
11. By permission from Paul H. Landis, *Your Marriage and Family Living* (New York: McGraw-Hill Book Company, 1946).
12. Lewis M. Terman, *Psychological Factors in Marital Happiness* (New York: McGraw-Hill Book Company, 1938), p. 53.
13. Ernest W. Burgess and Leonard S. Cottrell, Jr., *Predicting Success or Failure in Marriage, op. cit.,* p. 118.
14. See Jeannette G. Friend, *Journal of Social Casework,* March, 1948, p. 89, and *The Management Review,* American Management Association, Inc., September 1948, p. 459.
15. See Albert I. Gordon, *Intermarriage* (New York: Beacon Press, Inc., 1964).
16. For further information, see Algernon D. Black, *If I Marry Outside My Religion,* Public Affairs Pamphlet No. 20, 1954.
17. Evelyn Millis Duval, *Building Your Marriage,* (New York: Public Affairs Committee, Inc., 1946), pp. 25–26.
18. D. Eastman, "Self Acceptance and Marital Happiness," *Journal of Consulting Psychology,* **22** (1958), 95–99.
19. David Drake, "On Pet Names," *American Image,* **14** (1957), 41–43.
20. See Ralph G. Eckert, *So You Think It's Love!* Public Affairs Pamphlet No. 161, p. 6.
21. Jules S. Golden, Reuben Silver, and Nathan Mandel, "A Summary Description of the Wives of Fifty 'Normal' White Men," presented at the Annual Meeting of the American Psychiatric Association, St. Louis, Mo., May 9, 1963.
22. Ernest W. Burgess, "The Family in a Changing Society," *The American Journal of Sociology,* **53** No. 6 (1948), 417–418. This issue presents seventeen excellent articles on "The American Family" and should be read by the student who wishes to appreciate regional and ethnic family patterns.
23. Margaret Mead, "The Contemporary American Family as an Anthropologist Sees It," *The American Journal of Sociology,* **53** No. 6 (1948), p. 459.
24. Lena Levine and Irving Brodsky, "Taking Stock of Marriage: An Illustration in Group Counseling," *Marriage and Family Living,* May, 1956, pp. 162–167. See also Richard N. Hey and Emily H. Mudd, "Recurring Problems in Marriage Counseling," *Marriage and Family Living,* May, 1959, pp. 127–129 and Peter C. Pineo, "Disenchantment in the Later Years of Marriage," *Marriage and Family Living,* February, 1961, pp. 3–11.
25. Nathan B. Epstein and William A. Westley, "Parental Interaction as Related to Emotional Health of Children," *Social Problems,* 8 (1960), 87–92.
26. Family Service Association of America has headquarters at 5287 Sunset Boulevard, Los Angeles 27, California.
27. Luther E. Woodward, "Strengthening Family Life by Educating for Family Living," *Journal of Social Casework,* December, 1947.

PROJECTS

1. Make a list of the members of the opposite sex who have especially appealed to you as a possible marital partner. Then list some of their outstanding psychological characteristics. Can you note any significant factors in their appeal to you, factors that tie into your psychological background and needs?
2. Observe women who are strangers to you. A good place for your observations is a bus or railroad station. Study the expression on each woman's face and decide whether she is married or single. After you have made your "guess," note whether or not she is wearing a wedding ring. Keep a record of your "hits"

and "misses." Analyze your own criteria as to whether a woman "looks" as though she were married or single.

3. Examine books and journals in your library that deal with courtship and marriage. Summarize any findings that supplement or clarify the content of this chapter.
4. The chapter on counseling presents some suggestions for the person who must continue to live with an irritating personality, such as a boss or a neurotic mate. It is easier to live with a difficult boss than with a difficult mate because the identification with the mate is much stronger than with the boss. Irritating experiences with a mate break the ties of identification so frequently that the irritated partner must depersonalize the relationship. In such cases, the stronger partner may look upon the weaker person as a kind of "patient."

   This kind of adjustment enables many couples to remain married even though the relationship has lost its former mutuality. The stronger partner looks after the weaker one with a great deal of intellectual consideration but very little feeling of identification.

   What are some of the desirable and undesirable aspects of this kind of adjustment on the part of many American couples?
5. Clinical studies of marital relations indicate that many wives resent the husband's comment, "That's woman's work!" This resentment is especially pronounced in regard to the physical care of the baby. When a husband helps to take care of the baby, does dishes, and scrubs the kitchen floor, is he being unjustly domineered or is he really participating in the home responsibilities for the bringing about of a well-integrated home life?
6. One of the major difficulties in counseling the prospective husband and wife is that intellectually correct answers to questions about their attitudes toward sex may be no more than lip service. Gelolo McHugh, Family Life Publications, Inc., Durham, N. C., has prepared a sex knowledge inventory and a *Marriage Counselor's Manual* to be used with it as a means of gaining insight into the important attitudes toward sex. Here is the first question of the inventory:

What is the relation between sex attraction and love?

A. Satisfies a physical need only.
B. Love always plays a part in sex attraction.
C. Sex attraction is more important than love.
D. Sex attraction is a normal part of love.
E. Sex attraction ends when there is no more love.

The choice of D is the best answer. Does the right answer reveal very much about the individual's level of maturity where it is possible for him to take sex into his life and use it as a healthy way to express love and affection? Does it reveal the presence of feelings of guilt about sex? Does the right answer indicate whether the person really thinks of sex as merely a physical aspect of marriage? Of course the *Manual* recommends procedures for clarifying problems of this kind and dealing with them. Discuss the kinds of questions and techniques of counseling that might be used in pre-marital counseling.

COLLATERAL READINGS

Blood, Robert O., Jr., and Donald M. Wolfe, *Husbands and Wives: The Dynamics of Married Living*. Glencoe, Ill.: Free Press of Glencoe, Inc., 1960.

Duval, Evelyn M., *Family Development*. Philadelphia: J. B. Lippincott Co., 1962.

"Corporate Appraisal of Executives' Wives," *Printers' Ink*, Aug. 3, 1962.

Landis, Paul H., *Making the Most of Marriage*. New York: Appleton-Century-Crofts, 1960.

Lehner, George F. J. and Ella Kube, *The Dynamics of Personal Adjustment*. Englewood Cliffs, N.J.: Prentice-Hall, Inc., 1964, Chapter 8.

Sussman, Marvin B., (ed.) *Sourcebook in Marriage and the Family*. Boston: Houghton Mifflin Company, 1963.

TYPICAL ADJUSTMENTS OF A FIRST-BORN CHILD TO THE BIRTH OF A SECOND CHILD

1. ***The first child*** *is in a pleasant state of ongoing activity. He is the center of attention.*

2. ***After the baby appears,*** *he loses the center of attention. He has a problem barrier, and will make an adjustment as 3, 4, 5 or 6.*

3. ***The direct intelligent approach*** *in the form of helping to take care of the baby will give him new recognition.*

4. ***Positive substitute activities,*** *such as reading or games with playmates, is a more likely adjustment than a direct intelligent approach.*

5. ***Substitute activities of negative value,*** *such as "naughtiness," are very likely to appear.*

6. ***If adjustments exemplified*** *in 3, 4 and 5 do not produce satisfaction, he can still resort to a powerful method of regaining attention—invalidism.*

CHAPTER FOURTEEN

FACILITATING THE CHILD'S ADJUSTMENTS

The ability of the adult to deal effectively with behavior problems in children depends to a large extent on the adult's own adjustment to the problems in his personal experience. Is the adult strong enough to withstand the emotional shocks and attacks that he meets in children's disobedience, lying, stealing, sexual demonstrations, and defiance? The adult's social relationships with others, his sources of personal satisfaction, his strivings for recognition, his acceptance of authority, and his adjustment to love and sex life—all influence his ability to deal constructively with children and their problems.

The study of children's behavior is important to the student of psychology for many reasons. Their behavior often exemplifies the adjustments discussed in previous chapters. Any person who wishes to understand adult behavior can go some way toward it by observing children's problems and their adjustments to them. Indeed, one of the most helpful questions in the understanding of many an adult is, "What would this man's behavior mean if it were that of a small boy?"

Furthermore, most college students would be helped immeasurably in their own adjustments if they were to arrive at a better understanding of those of their own parents. A goodly percentage of students, for example, have been reared by the type of mother who was emotionally insecure and anxious. She found it necessary to protect her child from all sorts of real or fancied dangers, would not allow her child to play actively lest he become overheated and catch a cold, wanted to make sure that he ate enough of the right foods, and insisted that he wear rubbers and take his raincoat. At the same time that she fussed about her child's welfare, she also complained that she was a "slave" to her family and was unappreciated by her husband and children.

The person who has learned to view his parents' adjustment patterns in a clear-cut perspective is well on the way toward a clearer understanding of his own personality characteristics.

Later, when the student becomes a parent, he has the advantage of greater insight and intelligent control of his methods in rearing his own children. If, for example, he has developed strong adjustment tendencies in the direction of dealing with his daily problems by means of formulas for behavior, strict rules of conduct, and mathematically exact answers, he should expect that he will seek a knowledge of *rules* for the rearing of his children. Once he has learned a rule, he will be apt to apply it with mechanical rigidity. Of course such a father is likely to develop either a pathetic duplicate of himself or a rebellious child.

Formulas and rules for child training are less helpful to the parent than an open-minded perspective toward typical childhood behavior and an intelligent ability to project oneself into the child's life.

When eighty parents were asked to respond to the California Personality Test as they thought their 12-year-old children would, a comparison of the parents' answers with those of the children indicated that parents do not understand their children very well. The mothers and fathers generally under-estimated their child's concept and feeling of self-adjustment, and over-estimated his social adjustment. On the whole, they were more accurate in describing the child's social adjustment than his personal adjustment. This is probably because they could observe their offspring's social interactions. The results of the study show that father-son understanding is closest, then comes mother-son, mother-daughter, and father-daughter in order from high to low.[1]

The clinically trained psychologist has the mental perspectives and abilities to feel as the child feels; many intelligent parents also acquire the same psychological acumen.

The parent who appreciates adjustment tendencies and feels himself into the growing child's mental life has a marked advantage over the parent who is psychologically obtuse. The latter may, sooner or later, discover that his child is a serious problem to him. If, for example, a ten-year-old boy fails to go home when he should because he finds the company of neighbors more satisfying than that of his parents, the father who lacks insight into childhood behavior may decide that punishment will induce more desirable conduct. It may not. The child may persist in his misconduct. In desperation the father may consult a person trained in child guidance. Perhaps he will be told that the boy feels rejected because of the recent birth of a baby sister. He may be advised to overlook some of the boy's bad behavior, become a better companion to the boy, and encourage him to participate in the family life. After pursuing the prescribed treatment for a day or two, the parents may decide that the boy is more mischievous than ever. The father reports that the recommended treatment is a terrible failure.

In such a case the contribution of psychology to the aid of the parents appears to have failed, but only because they lacked a proper appreciation for childhood adjustments. The father should gain an understanding of the adjustment concept as expressed by his son, so that he will have some basic principles of child training—a kind of working philosophy. If he does, he will persist in the application of these principles, because he will realize that no one can expect a child to change his deep-seated adjustment patterns suddenly. The patterns are too deeply ingrained. The father must appreciate that the boy continues to feel rejected and needs long-term assistance in developing the feeling that he is loved and wanted. When a child has learned to feel rejected and has developed adjustments of the hostile, defensive, or withdrawal variety, that kind of response becomes more or less fixed as a regular form of behavior and appears even when no real threat to self-esteem is present. As an adult he is likely to be full of anxieties, self-doubts and fears—he expects to be ignored or hurt.

The mere application of rules for child training helps few problem children overcome their problems. The greatest aid to the parent is an intelligent insight into the dynamics of the problem child's behavior.

Predisposing Influences in Childhood Adjustments

Parenthood increases each parent's responsibilities, involves some changes in standards of living, restricts freedom of certain movements, and compels each parent, particularly the mother, to perform many additional tasks at regular intervals. It also brings about important changes in the affectional relation between husband and wife. The new baby may become, in some ways, a rival for the affection of the mate. If the new father is lacking in his personality maturity, he may reject both the role of father and the child. Cases of such extreme rejections are not unusual in our clinics. Far more common, however, are the cases of children who realize that they were or are unwanted and develop feelings of rejection. Children who feel rejected tend to develop detached, seclusive personalities and to have few friends.[2] Many are unable to respond to the affection of others. Some are hyperactive, aggressive, rebellious, or resentful of authority. Rejected children are reported to show relatively a very high susceptibility to behavior disorders and delinquency.[3] Some of them develop characteristics with constructive value, at the high cost of being rejected, evidently as defense or compensation. Many, fortunately, seem able to survive rejection without serious personality damage.[4]

The behavior of a growing person is the result of many factors which operate throughout his life. One of the most important factors in helping him to attain the security he needs to develop well emotionally is to know that he is accepted by his parents. The importance of the home and the people with whom he lives is basic to his capacity for developing adequate adjustments to life's problems.

One of the most important predisposing influences in the life of the child is the attitudes of the parents toward each other. The broken home and the home filled with marital discord are statistically associated with the behavior of problem children.[5]

The child whose emotional loyalties have been torn between two quarreling parents is almost certain to have deepseated anxieties that motivate him in later adjustive situations.

Parents who are cold and impersonal toward the child, who dominate or belittle him or who make him feel incapable and rejected contribute much to the child's nonadjustive patterns. The child feels anxious and his anxieties spread to many activities and situations. The world and people appear to him to be very hostile. His negative value adjustments in later years are likely to be numerous and deepseated. The child who grows up in

BEHAVIOR PROBLEMS CONCEIVED AS EVASIONS OF SOCIAL REQUIREMENTS

EVASIONS BY WITHDRAWAL	REQUIREMENTS IMPOSED ON INDIVIDUAL BEHAVIOR BY	EVASIONS BY ATTACK
Fearfulness Sulkiness Dreaminess Shyness Dependency on adults Cowardliness Unsocialness Dependency on routine Pedantry Solitariness Fear of criticism Suspiciousness Inability to carry responsibility Inefficiency Social inadequacy	FAMILY NEIGHBORHOOD COMPANIONS CHURCH SCHOOL TRADITIONS CUSTOMS LAW INDUSTRY	Temper tantrums Disobedience Overactivity Aggressiveness Defiance to authority Fighting Delinquency Rejection of routine Pursuing own methods of work Wanting to direct Breaking conventions Antagonistic attitudes Exploitation of own authority Contentiousness Egocentricity

Evasions by withdrawal:

REGRESSIVE ESCAPES	PRODUCTIVE ACTIVITY
Neurotic complaints	Invention
Economic dependency	Research
Alcoholism	Science
Drug addiction	Literature
Functional insanity	Art
Suicide	

Evasions by attack:

CONSTRUCTIVE ATTACKS	DESTRUCTIVE ATTACKS
Competitive sports	"Psychopathic" tendencies
Exploration	"I won't work"
Industrial exploits	Crime
Social and political reforms	

From E. K. Wickman, *Teachers and Behavior Problems,* The Commonwealth Fund, New York, 1938.

a home that has a constant air of doom and gloom is likely to develop a lasting conviction that the world is full of trouble and that he must defend himself from those who might take advantage of him. He expects difficulties that do not exist.

Several studies have shown that poor adjustments on the part of parents, with interparental frictions, tend to produce tensions in the next generation. The mental attitudes of husband and wife toward each other and their home are far more significant in the child's environment than their formal education, such as whether the wife has had training in home economics.[6]

In one study of differences in behavior between parents of conduct-problem children and parents of nonconduct-problem children, the parents and their child while in a special laboratory were asked to construct stories to a scene which included a variety of buildings and people. While the parents and their child performed the task, two trained observers rated the parents' behavior toward each other and toward the child. The analysis of the findings showed that the parents of the problem children were significantly more rejecting and hostile toward their child than were the parents of the nonconduct-problem children. However, the experiment did not prove that rejection and hostility on the part of the parents caused the problem behavior on the part of the child, but it does indicate the kind of behavior that might be expected in

THE DIAGRAM on the opposite page roughly illustrates two characteristic methods by which the individual evades behavior requirements imposed by social forces.

The requirements set up for the individual, first as a child in the home, then in the school, and later as an adult in the greater social order, are represented in the central portion of the diagram. The two methods of evading requirements are shown in the columns to left and right.

There are listed only the more extreme examples of attacking and withdrawing behavior which may be observed to occur at various stages of individual development; lesser degrees of these evading tendencies may be detected in most individuals. There is no intention to attach moral or ethical values either to conformity to or evasion of requirements.

Behavior development leading to adult social maladjustment of the attacking or of the withdrawing type does not proceed along pure or regular stages as the diagram might suggest. Though there is a tendency for an individual to learn to respond characteristically by attack or by withdrawal, both kinds of behavior often occur together in the same individual. Early habits of evading requirements may work themselves out to constructive or productive ends and in that case they may modify the social requirements. Though art, literature, science, political and social reforms may represent evasions of social requirements in individual cases, the inference is not to be drawn from the diagram that such activities are always the product of conflict with social influences or social forces.

It is psychologically unsound to make fine distinctions between withdrawing and attacking forms of behavior, inasmuch as both represent individual modes of response to frustrations experienced on encountering social requirements. The distinctions between them are sharply made, however, by social attitudes toward the individual who responds in a manner that is interpreted as attack or withdrawal.

families where there is a child who is manifesting a conduct problem.[7]

Some of the child's infantile experiences and tendencies have no noticeable bearing on the adult personality, but the majority of emotional disturbances found in adults arise from simple beginnings in early childhood. Appropriate changes in the home environment and skillful handling of the child, especially the child with a difficult problem, will enable him to attain satisfactory and even excellent personality maturity. If the parent is warned in advance about likely shifts in the child's behavior, he can improve his competence in meeting these developments.[8]

When the family atmosphere is congenial and the two parents are well adjusted and identify themselves with each other in the family relationship, few problem children occur—because in such an atmosphere a child feels secure, wanted, and is given consistent encouragement and discipline. He is likely to be given a share in making family decisions, a most important factor in happy character development.[9]

One of the major influences in the intellectual approach to the child on the part of the American parent of today is the emphasis on democracy in our government and culture. We believe in individual freedom, equality, and the right to pursue happiness, but such privileges for the child require a high level of emotional maturity and psychological skill on the part of the parent. Very few parents who believe in democracy in government and freedom for the individual have as yet learned how to conduct weekly house meetings which help to give each member of the family a feeling of belonging and of having an essential, respected part in making decisions about the home life. Once this practice becomes an integral part of our culture, many cases of problem children will be corrected.[10]

The direct influences of the parents' adjustments, expressed by their suggestions and examples, are less easily recognized than the direct influences learned from books and other formal instruction and expressed in the verbalized procedures. The former are acquired through each parent's adjustments throughout his life and are a basic part of his personality. The latter influences are intellectual and less basic, but can be discussed and acquired, as indicated by the large amount of published material now available for the treatment of childhood problems.

Contributions from Experimental Psychology

Harry F. Harlow of the University of Wisconsin, using monkeys, has been studying the factors leading to the affection of a child for its mother. An appreciation of the ways this affection takes place is fundamental to an understanding of future infant development.

Harlow experimented with infant monkeys to determine whether the satisfaction of primary drives (especially those of hunger, thirst and pain) is the genesis of love. He removed the infant monkeys from their natural mothers immediately after birth and placed them in cages with substitute or surrogate mothers. He used two types of surrogate mothers; one was constructed of a wire mesh cylinder which contained a nipple for nursing. The other was based on the wire cylinder, but was covered with a layer of sponge rubber over which a piece of terry cloth was placed. If it was desired, the cloth "mother" could nurse the infant. However, whether "she" nursed the infant or not, the results of the experiment seemed to prove that the most important factor in the presence of a mother was not her ability to nurse, but rather the fact that she provided constant, comforting, physical contact. The monkeys spent most of their time clinging to the cloth mother, nuzzling her, and evolving much the same type of affection for her as did those monkeys raised with their natural mothers. When the experimental monkeys were frightened by outside stimuli, they fled to their cloth mother and clung to her for assurance. When placed in a room which contained strange objects, the monkeys would cautiously go exploring, frequently running back to the cloth mother for assurance and comfort. However, if the monkeys were deprived of their cloth mother or left with the nursing wire mesh mother, they exhibited signs of extreme fright and would "freeze." In all the tests run on the monkeys, it was found that they loved their cloth mothers as much as a natural mother, and their love for these cloth mothers had not arisen out of the mother's ability to satisfy their drives, but out of her more comforting presence. Even though they received food from a wire mother, young monkeys still preferred the cloth mother, which provided a "comfort feeling." Freightened young monkeys sought security on the laps of the cloth mother.

Harlow's experiments also showed that monkeys raised by a cloth mother and permitted contact with other infant monkeys were able to establish a pattern of normal sexual behavior. However, those cloth-mothered monkeys which had been deprived of contact with their peers as they matured were incapable of gratifying their sexual desires. This would seem to indicate that sex education and consequent maturity depends largely on contacts with the opposite sex during childhood and adolescence. In spite of some successes with cloth-mothered monkeys, Harlow found that they were failures as mothers themselves; as infants they had known love only through comforting contact and therefore, they could provide little else to their offspring. Permanent psychological damage was incurred by monkeys raised without

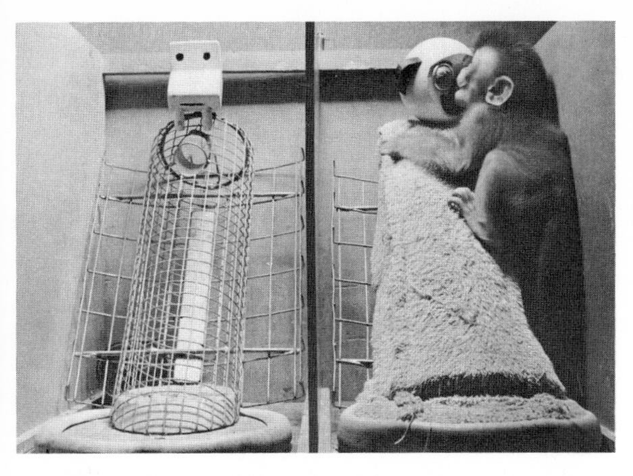

Wire and cloth *mother-surrogates were used to test the preferences of infant monkeys. The infants spent most of their time clinging to the soft cloth "mother" even though nursing bottles were attached to the wire mother.*

Disturbed orphan *in bare wire living cage. This kind of behavior occurred when unfamiliar objects added a disturbing element.*

Infant on cloth *mother exploring open field.*

Infant exploring. *The cloth mother provided quick reassurance.*

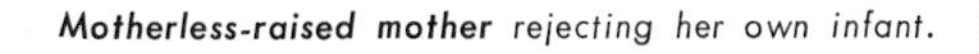

Motherless-raised mother *rejecting her own infant.*

The presence of the wire mother *did not alter the pattern of fearful behavior.*

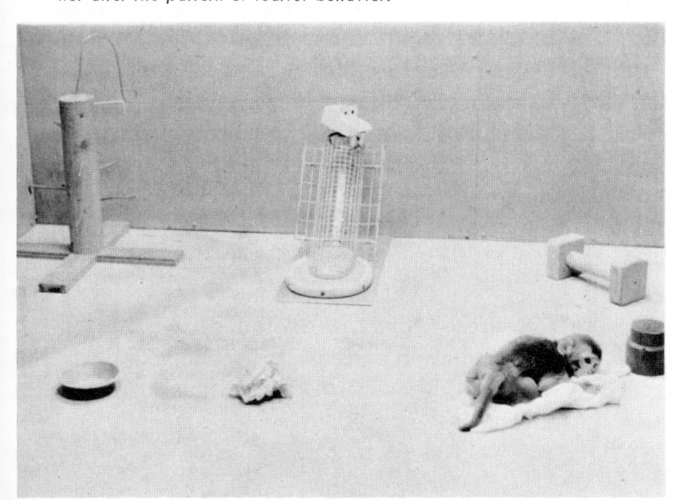

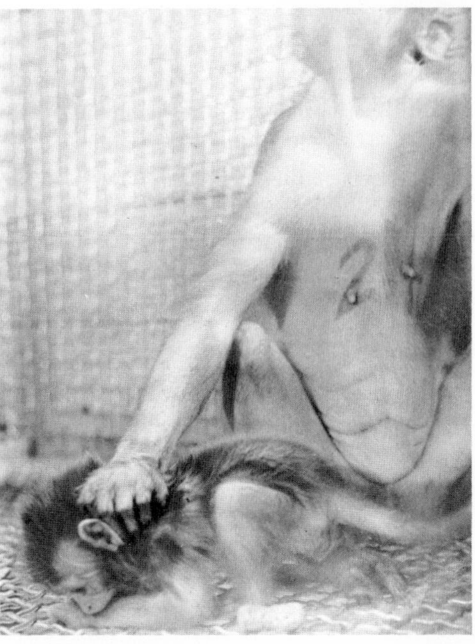

real mothers and without peers. Their social development was arrested. Their mating was not very successful and they did not make good parents even when mating was successful. They became "helpless, hopeless, heartless mothers devoid, or almost totally devoid, of any maternal feelings." Their own young, however, were lavish in affection and regardless of the mother's efforts to beat them off, often wore down this resistance.[11]

The significance of Harlow's findings for us here is to realize the importance of association with peers and of a comforting physical contact during infancy to the psychological well-being of the individual. The infant who is deprived of the loving caresses of his mother will be unable to develop his own affections. Nursing does not seem to be the "fountain of love," but rather, a means to provide contact, which is the genesis of love.[12]

Effects of the young monkey's contact with his peers is also very important in the infant's psychological adjustment shown by experiments when some were raised without mothers but in the company of age-mates and with mothers but without age-mates. The maternal relationship is clearly significant but experimental evidence indicates that opportunity for infant-infant interaction under optimal conditions may compensate for lack of mothering. An especially critical period in the monkey's development occurs somewhere between the third and sixth months of life during which social deprivation, particularly deprivation of the company of its peers, irreversibly blights the animal's capacity for social adjustment.

Motherless infants, raised from birth by cloth surrogates, but allowed to play with age-mates in a specially constructed playroom equipped for climbing and swinging, developed normally in every respect in spite of the lack of maternal care.[13]

Experiments with infant rats have further confirmed Harlow's findings. Denenberg worked with infant rats to determine the influence of the mothers on the emotional stability of their offspring.[14] He found that emotionally disturbed mothers raised emotionally disturbed offspring. This, however, was not entirely caused by heredity as indicated when he had infants reared by mothers who were not the infant's natural mother. Offspring reared by emotionally disturbed mothers, regardless of the emotional characteristics of the natural mother, showed more anxiety than offspring reared by normal mothers. A further finding was that the infant's emotional state influenced the mother. Mothers who raised emotionally disturbed young became emotionally upset themselves.

The emotional stability of the rats was determined by placing them in a new situation, in this case, a box marked off in squares. The disturbed rats reacted in much the same manner as did Harlow's disturbed monkeys; they cowered in a corner and defecated frequently. The stable rats would cautiously explore their new surroundings and their emotional stability was correlated to the number of squares they entered.

Denenberg also found that comforting physical contact played a large part in influencing emotional stability. Those infant rats that had been handled by the researchers scored more favorably on emotionality tests than did those rats that had not been touched. He also tested the effects of an interesting and more comfortable environment on the stability of the rats. He placed both healthy and disturbed rats with members of their peer group in separate large boxes which contained various objects to facilitate play behavior and exploratory behavior. Both healthy and disturbed rats who were raised in this "free environment" performed much better on emotionality tests, indicating the effects of environmental opportunities on stability.

An interesting sidelight of the Denenberg experiments showed that placing emotionally disturbed rats with stable ones might improve the latter's ability to perform in new situations, but definitely detracted from the former's ability. The emotionally disturbed rats appeared to be cowed by the normal ones, and the latter seemed to be reinforced by the withdrawal behavior of the disturbed rats.

This last point could have great significance

in therapy today. The results of these and other experiments may indicate that placing a maladjusted individual with healthy individuals has little therapeutic value; indeed, it may have unfavorable effects on both. This hypothesis, however, needs further research.

It is impossible to experiment with human children as Harlow did with monkeys in order to absolutely correlate his findings with human development. However, case studies of children reared in impersonal institutions or by indifferent mothers or nurses indicate a pathetic comparability. Spitz made a study of infants of two kinds of environments: a foundling home and a nursery. The conditions there were sufficiently similar to provide a basis of comparison with some of the studies of animals.

Spitz used "Development Quotient" tests to determine the growth, both mentally and physically of all the children. After the first four months, the foundling home children were developing at a rate that almost equaled normal. The nursery children lagged far behind. However, at the end of the last four months of the year, the nursery infants had progressed in their development at a rate that was almost normal, while the foundling home infants had dropped far below normal.

There are several possible reasons for the differences in the development of the two groups of infants, but they all seem to stem from the amount of stimulation the infants received, both from adults and their peers. In the foundling home, the infants were all breast fed, unless their health prohibited it, until they were at least three months old. Therefore, they had the benefit of comforting physical contact for three months, although it was undoubtedly somewhat sporadic. In every case, the decline of their development corresponded to the end of breast feeding. Aside from being deprived of the contact that breast feeding provided, there were other factors working against the development of the foundling home children. They were separated from each other and never played together. Often sheets were draped over the sides of their cots so that they were walled in from the rest of the world; they could see only the ceiling. There was no impetus to move, and they lay in their cots hour after hour, to the extent that they wore hollows in their mattresses, and this further impeded even the simplest movements. There was no stimulation, no encouragement in their lives to do anything other than lie in their beds and wait for the nurses to make their periodic checks.

In the nursery, however, the infants had their mothers with them almost constantly. When they weren't playing with their mothers or other infants, they could see them through the glass partitions that separated the infants' cots. There were always stimulating factors at hand. Often these children were the only outlets for their mothers' affections because the mothers had been rejected by society and family. The infants lacked little that normal families could give.

The foundling home infants learned to walk, talk, and feed themselves at a rate far below normal. They were more susceptible to disease, in spite of the best medical care. Without a mother or a substitute mother they became almost vegetable-like. There was no incentive for them to progress. As Spitz says: ". . . it is the security provided by the mother in the field of locomotion, the emotional bait offered by the mother calling her child that 'teaches' him to walk. When this is lacking, even children two to three years old cannot walk."[15] The children who survive the physical diseases that isolation of this sort seem to breed are lucky if they can ever develop at a rate that even approaches normal. Like Harlow's isolated monkeys, they become physically and mentally maladjusted beings.

Psychologists can, in some instances, recognize certain emotional disturbances in the infant that will have a bearing on his future development. These emotional disturbances are often indicated by habits which the baby has adopted; one of these habits is self-rocking.[16]

Normal self-rocking is merely an indication of exuberance and energy in the infant. However, it is the opinion of some psychologists that repetitive and agitated self-rocking is an indication of anxiety in the infant which has been caused by a loss of comforting physical contact with his mother. The infant rocks himself in an effort to replace this lost contact or substitute for it. Perhaps he thinks motion will bring him closer to his mother, or perhaps his mother was in the habit of rocking him to sleep, and he derives more pleasure from rocking than in stimulation of his other senses. The motion of rocking might also lessen the helpless feeling of passively waiting for his mother to return.

The mother of the infant who exhibits these symptoms of anxiety may be the ideal mother ostensibly; however, perhaps she has not played with her child enough, or has decided that if she caters to his every whim he will become spoiled. Whatever the reasons, agitated self-rocking is usually an indication of anxiety in the infant.

Parent Fixations

Reports of animal experiments and clinical studies usually deal with aspects of ineffective parenthood such as failure in giving the child feelings of security in the parent-child relationship. Examples of maldevelopment of the child also take place because the parent-child relationship is too tight. In the animal world, the parents get the young ready to shift for themselves and then push them out of the nest or the den. Some human children, however, are emotionally unable to leave home. They may leave home in the physical sense but remain there psychologically.

Occasionally we meet the boy of seventeen who marries a forty-year-old woman. Such a marriage does not necessarily indicate that the boy has a mercenary motive. The woman may be a widow or spinster who has no money. Sometimes the widow has several children older than the bridegroom. Why does a young man marry a "girl" of that type?

In the Greek myth, Oedipus was led to kill his own father and to marry his mother, Jocasta. Freud and his followers have presented some evidence to indicate that sons become attracted toward the mother and daughters toward the father. The former fixation is called the *Oedipus complex* and the latter is called the *Electra complex*. Clinical psychologists have found that the boy who fixates his emotional life in the mother image may be jealous of his father, who is a great barrier to his love for his mother. When the boy grows up he may become rebellious toward the schoolteacher or the executive, because they are symbolic of the authority of the father. Some of the greatest men of history never married until after their mothers died. Others married but respected their mothers more than they did their wives.

Edward A. Strecker, who has had extensive experience as a civilian and army psychiatrist, found considerable evidence to cause him to conclude that the high incidence of neuropsychiatric disorders (nearly 20 per cent of men of draft age, World War II) in the United States was largely the result of psychological immaturity. In the majority of cases, he believed this to be the fault of the mother (and occasionally the father) who consciously or unconsciously prevented the child from growing up. The mother who consciously or unconsciously but selfishly prevents the child's emotional emancipation is almost certain to have an adverse influence on the child's maturity.[17]

When a mother hugs and kisses her small boy far more than she does her husband, she may be conditioning her child for bachelorhood or for a troublesome married life. It is often quite natural for mothers to direct their starved affections upon their children because the fathers are too busy in the office and the shop to be companionable to their wives. For a while after marriage, the husband may have given his young wife all the loving companionship that she craved, but, as time went by and the children came, father had to get his nose closer to the grindstone. Consequently, he delegated all the care of the children to the mother.

The "secretarial" complex on the part of

certain executives is one result of the over-affectionate mother. Some executives have a child-like dependence upon their secretaries. The executive who claims that he has the perfect secretary would be surprised to know that she is really average in comparison with good secretaries. His admiration is often based upon the fact that he unconsciously associates his secretary with his mother. In such a situation the secretary represents the mother image to the executive; she may be the most powerful member in the organization. His subordinates soon learn that they must not antagonize her. The secretarial complex is not wholly disadvantageous in its mild form. To some men it is a logical and helpful means of emotional adjustment.

Mothers Who Work

Today, very often, the mother must work to supplement the family income. This means that she is away from home for a good part of the day. It has long been presumed that her absence will have a bad effect upon the children. Until recently, however, little actual research had been done on this question. Then, a thorough study of this problem was undertaken in California. In a school district which contained 16,000 pupils, there were 400 who were serious counseling problems. An analysis of the place of the mother in the home of these 400 was undertaken. The children were subdivided according to different family structures: Group 1—Employed mothers, Group 2—Stepparents or guardians, Group 3—Lack of adult male, Group 4—A control group.

Having a working mother contributed to only one quarter of the total number of cases in need of psychiatric help. Apparently, there are an equal number of non-problem children whose mothers work. This seems to indicate that as long as the child is made to feel secure and happy, the mother's full time employment away from home does not create a serious problem for him.

According to the California Test of Personality which these children took, different personality components can be associated to a significant degree with the differing home situations. For example, the most serious problem of the group who lived with stepparents was nervous symptoms (70%) and those children who belonged in families which lacked an adult male did not have as great a sense of personal worth as the others.[18]

One investigator found that if the mother enjoys her job, she may feel guilty about leaving her child. These feelings of guilt are especially common among women of the middle and upper classes who usually do not need to work for financial reasons. If the mother does feel guilty, she tends to lavish her time and affections on the child when she can be with him. It is possible that she may spoil him and overprotect him to the extent that he may become a rather passive and nonaggressive child, for he knows that his mother will sooner or later be there to fight for him. However, when the happily employed mother does not feel burdened with household chores, the child is not likely to feel neglected because the mother usually tries to make the life he can't share with her as pleasant as possible for him.

On the other hand, the mother who resents her having to work or is dissatisfied with her job is more likely to make life at home difficult for the child. She may insist that he do many household chores so that he will not enjoy too much the home she hates to leave. The child in turn, resents his mother and may become assertive and hostile.

Aside from the guilt feelings of the mother who enjoys her job, and the resentments of the mother who dislikes hers, it is reasonable to expect that the well-adjusted woman who has proven herself outside the home to her own satisfaction will return home at the end of the day with a feeling of accomplishment, looking forward to a pleasant evening with her family in which she can devote her time to her child. Generally, most studies indicate that a mother's employment, *per se,* may not have the harmful effects once assumed.[19]

Children who have happy relations with their parents seldom resort to delinquent forms of behavior as a means of satisfying their repressed aggressions. Their anxieties tend to find normal outlets. In contrast with those who have happy relations with their parents, the children who have developed deep-seated hostility toward the parents may turn to delinquency as a means of "punishing" the parents. Girls who feel unwanted and unloved often find it easy to indulge in flagrant sexual delinquency as a means of punishing the parents as well as gaining a kind of temporary affection. The problem behaviors of delinquents are adjustive and can be understood only in terms of the individual's problems, emotional needs, and attitudes.

Sibling Rivalry

The only child can be made to feel that he is a functional part of the family set-up, but his integration is upset at the birth of an interloper called "your baby brother" or "your baby sister." Both mother and father of necessity must direct greater attention toward the new baby. Under these circumstances the older child resorts to aggressive or regressive tactics in order to regain a lost sense of significance or even to avenge his displacement.

His attempts to regain his lost importance may be expressed in vocal form as "Throw the baby away," in bodily attacks on the baby, or in ignoring its presence. Sewall's analysis of jealousy took as subjects a group of seventy small children consisting of one third nursery school children and two thirds clinical or "problem" children.[20] Of the seventy children who had younger siblings, thirty-nine were reported to be jealous and showed their jealousy in the following ways:

1. Bodily attacks on the younger sibling 26
2. Ignoring the presence of the sibling 2
3. Denying having a younger sibling 2
4. No outward manifestation toward the sibling, but definite personality changes at the time of its birth 9

The last-mentioned group of cases showed a wide variety of personality changes, such as more temper tantrums, more destructiveness, changes to withdrawal types of behavior—daydreaming, shyness, or timidity. Sewall found that when the ages of the children at the birth of the youngest child were studied: "Jealousy seems to be associated with an age difference of from eighteen to forty-two months, for two-thirds of the children of that age difference were jealous, as compared with one-third of all the children whose age differences were greater or less than that amount."

This finding may indicate that when children are closer together in age than eighteen months they share the same interests, and that children more than four years apart in age have interests that do not clash. If the younger child is sufficiently younger, the older child may not arouse enough competitiveness to cause resentment.

Additional findings from Sewall's study indicated that four fifths of the children whose mothers were oversolicitous were jealous. Similarly, four fifths of those subjected to inconsistent discipline were jealous. When the families were divided into two categories, well adjusted and poorly adjusted, it was found that ten per cent of the children in the well-adjusted homes and sixty-three per cent of the children in the poorly-adjusted homes were jealous. "The inference seems justified that there is a tendency for jealousy to develop in an atmosphere of maladjustment, such maladjustment often meaning an overprotective mother, a negative father, some marital or other discord, and inconsistent discipline."

As Murphy and Newcomb concluded, after summarizing several investigations of jealousy in children:

> ...a background of maladjustment is apparent against which jealousy stands out, not as the inexplicable fruit of a field devoid of other personality difficulties, but as a growth well nourished by the soil in which it and its ilk are found.
>
> From such studies as these it is clear that competitiveness, standing up for one's right in the family groups as elsewhere, is normal and within limits acceptable to adults; that when it begins to make trouble either because of its intensity or because of inept or troublesome ex-

pression it is given the name of jealousy and becomes "problem behavior."[21]

Intelligent parents prepare the older child for the birth of the younger before it takes place. They prepare him for the inevitable change in his status:

It is better for the child to know ahead of time that a baby is expected so that he can get used to the idea gradually. This helps less than an adult would expect because the small child's imagination may not create anything like the reality. He may visualize an animated doll to tote around or a full fledged companion. Even if he knows and loves a neighbor's baby, he is apt to find that his mother's baby evokes entirely different feelings. Most professionals in the children's field feel that the child should know that the baby is growing within the mother's abdomen. This is not primarily for the sake of abstract honesty but because it is known that many children beyond the age of 3 and some under 3, suspect the truth anyway, through a combination of shrewd observation, slips in the conversation of adults and perhaps a touch of intuition. One supposedly innocent 3-year-old will call attention to his mother's changing girth with hints, partly questioning, partly accusatory. Another will suddenly hit at her abdomen as if already jealous of what he suspects is there. The child who is hesitantly coming to his own conclusion that the new baby is growing in the mother is likely to become troubled. It is not that he cannot take the truth. What worries him is his mother's evasion in continuing to talk about the stork theory or the hospital theory in an unconvincing tone when he is pretty sure the baby is coming from elsewhere. Many parents refrain from telling the child the truth for fear that it will open the door to other embarrassing questions. This is an unjustified fear. The child before the age of 6 years will not put his parents on the spot to explain conception. The likely question will be, "How did the baby get in there?" to which at this age the most understandable answer is that the baby grew from a seed which was there all the time. To the question, "How will it get out?" the answer might be, "Through a special place." Incidentally, parents should be warned against predicting the sex of the baby ahead of time since a wrong guess may lead to long-lasting disappointment.

Some mechanical readjustments in the household are usually necessitated by the arrival of a baby. Wherever possible these should be made several months before the baby's birth and presented to the older child as evidence of growing up. If he is to move into another room or into a big bed, he should graduate to them because he is a big boy and not be dispossessed by the rival in person. If he is to enter a nursery school he should become well established there before his mother's confinement. Then when the baby arrives, even though the older child feels somewhat slighted at home, his satisfying life at nursery school will help to ease the pain. If he is sent off to nursery school after the baby's arrival, he may resent it as banishment, resist going, resist fitting in.

It is vital, particularly when the older child is in the neighborhood of 2 years, that he feel comfortable and secure with the adult who will care for him while his mother is in the hospital. If a relative or maid is coming into his home, she should either be someone whom he knows well and loves, or she should come two or more weeks ahead of time and take over his care gradually. When a very young child is abruptly left in the care of a stranger, he may behave well while his mother is away, but when she returns all his latent anxiety suddenly comes to the surface. Such a state may last for many months and make even more difficult his other problem of adjusting to the baby.

First impressions are most important. When a mother and father bring the new baby home from the hospital there is usually a great deal of hectic confusion for at least an hour. The older child is lost in the shuffle. No one has time to fuss over him and he stands by, looking wretched. If possible he should be off on an excursion during this time and come home when his mother is able to take him in her arms and give him her undivided attention.

Now that the baby is at home what are the parents' cues? The first principle is to play down the importance of the baby. This means talking about him as little as possible, enthusing over him as little as possible, taking care of him casually when the older child is around. The hardest thing for many children to take is seeing the baby nursed, especially when this is at the breast. Often the older child will want a bottle, too, and it is a wise mother who cheerfully provides it. If this is well handled the child will not repeat the request often since he finds that the bottle is not really a delight.

Even though one advises the mother to feed and care for the baby as much as is practical when the older child is preoccupied with other activities, she should, of course, be equally warned against shutting him out of the nursery whenever he has the desire to see what is going on there. If there is a relative or nurse helping out in the early weeks, it is usually best to have this person taking care of the baby, allowing the mother to give as much attention to the older child as she used to.

Then there are the other relatives. When the father comes home from work he should resist the natural impulse to greet the older child in the front hall with the question, "How's the baby been today?" but should stop to play with him for a while before he drifts in to see the newborn. When Aunt Nellie telephones to arrange a visit to the baby, the mother can remind her that the older child is still counting on being her favorite and will appreciate a present much more than the baby will.

So often Aunt Nellie in her thoughtless enthusiasm greets the older child with the breathless question, "Where's that darling baby sister of yours? I have brought her a present." For these situations the mother might have a box of ten-cent store toys from which to produce a gift each time one arrives for the baby.

Many parents have already heard of the value of letting the child share in the ownership and care of the infant. It is fine for the older child to bring the bottle from the icebox or the towel to the bath provided he enjoys his work and does it spontaneously. Another child will overcome the feeling of being an outsider by an elaborate care of her doll which follows her mother's care of the baby to the last detail.[22]

When the older child feels that he is really secure again in his family constellation, wanted and loved by his parents, he usually loses his more severe sibling jealousies. Sibling rivalry probably never entirely disappears, but the relations between siblings may develop into rich companionships. Most siblings soon learn to protect each other in the impacts with neighborhood gangs and school factions. They learn to share each other's persecutions and conspiracies. Their mutual problems and interests should help them to develop a better sense of belonging to both the family and the community, especially when the parents appreciate the drastic adjustment required on the part of the older child on the arrival of a rival.

Disciplining the Child

Children neglected because of a broken home, disinterested parents, or other abnormal conditions are likely to misbehave, but most children are reared by parents who try desperately to make their children "good." These latter parents often seek counsel in their child training, and many of their questions center around discipline. To them, "discipline" means punishment. Actually, it means to learn.

Some parents who believe in rigorous discipline do have children who are "good" in the sense that they have withdrawn into themselves to so great an extent that they cause the parent little trouble. Almost any parents of low intelligence and strong muscle can have a well-behaved child of the fearful, subdued type. Severe bodily punishments are employed by parents who are either too lazy or too dull to learn how to use more intelligent methods in guiding the child. Case studies of children who have a decided withdrawal pattern of behavior show that very many have suffered from abusive treatment: physical punishment, loud scoldings, and threats. Persistent states of fear have been developed that cause the child to react fearfully in many later situations.

As pointed out above in the discussion of sibling rivalry, if the psychological atmosphere of the home is positive, guiding the child becomes relatively easy. The parental example is one of the strongest influences on the child's developing patterns of behavior. However, parents may be unusually well-balanced emotionally, highly intelligent, and constructive in their techniques, and still have many problems in child training. One kind of problem is exemplified by the parent who says: "Why is my toddler good as gold for a while and then suddenly becomes perverse and puzzling?"

An explanation of basic significance is available from the years of systematic research by Dr. Arnold Gesell and his associates of the Yale Clinic of Child Development.

Gesell has found that children do not grow in a mechanically steady manner. Children grow by shedding old habits and taking on new ones. The child's mind grows by making forward "thrusts." During a "thrusting" period the child is in disequilibrium, discarding old ways and reaching for new ones. In such periods, he is in a state of confusion and instability. As he gradually masters new patterns, his equilibrium improves, and a period of stable behavior continues until another forward thrust brings about disequilibrium with its problems for the parent.

Stages in stable and unstable equilibrium are likely to occur in a typical infant at more or less alternative ages: sixteen weeks, relative equilibrium followed by a transitional period in which he shows a dawning sensitiveness to strangers. By twenty-eight weeks he is again more composed and in a state of balance. Periods of lessened equilibrium and reorganization recur at the age of two and one-half, three and one-half, and six years. Children who are confused by their inner drives need added love and security, not spankings.

Periods of reorganization are usually characterized by negativism in the preschool child. He will not do what he can do, and he cannot do what he wants to do. When the two-and-a-half-year-old child seems particularly perverse, it should be remembered that his mental life organization is poorly developed. This also accounts for the regression in toilet habits which frequently occurs at about this age. Even though he knows what is expected of him, the child's inner confusions inhibit his behavior and make him appear to be obstinate. Sometimes there are extraordinary factors, such as illness or emotional crises, which may be influencing the child's behavior. If present, these factors should be investigated; however, if no factors which would be expected to militate against the child's good behavior are present, general health-preserving care is indicated.

In addition to the typical negativism of young children, all children suffer frequent frustrations and may adjust to them by aggression. This may happen when adults impose their wishes, often unreasonable to the child, at times when he is already in a state of mental uncertainty. The average parent regards the misbehaving frustrated child merely as disagreeable or naughty, and punishes him. If the parent could only appreciate the fact that the frustrated child has a problem, he could help the child make adequate adjustments through expressions of understanding, examples of what to do, and encouragement in doing the right thing.[23]

Children's Developmental Phases

Stages in development are obvious in the life of the toddler and the adolescent. These stages tend to produce confusion for the child and the parent. Furthermore, the parent's confusion is often accentuated by the child's ambivalent behavior.

Ambivalence, or manifestations of double feelings toward the same person, refers to reactions in which opposing trends of emotion appear simultaneously. Almost all children show ambivalence by statements such as, "I am going to kill my daddy." Such feelings are most pronounced in the affectional relations of children, but also appear in adult behavior, as exemplified by the sweetheart who says to her suitor whom she really loves, "I hate you." Reactions such as these are normal and do not merit a reprimand on the part of the suitor or discipline of the child by the parent.

Children of older ages as well as toddlers are constantly undergoing mental reorganization. Many college students can recall "thrusting" stages in their development. The adolescent's typical drives are toward complete independence. He wants to make his own decisions without interference from his parents. He wants to decide when and where he will go and when he will return. He likes to belittle his parents and their ideas. Even the furniture at home and the clothes of the parents are ridiculed. In certain stages of adolescence the child can just barely tolerate his parents.

In a study of 1,278 high school boys of relatively comparable backgrounds, Meissner found that as the boy progresses through adolescence he tends to become more depressed and dissatisfied with his life. Perhaps the most significant indication of this growing feeling of depression is that while one third of the freshmen studied admitted to feelings of loneliness, one half of the juniors and seniors experienced loneliness.[24]

Adolescence is a very difficult time for most young people. Teenagers are exceptionally self-conscious as they feel themselves going through physical changes that they cannot understand. We all know the short and pudgy boy who suddenly shoots upward, at the same time that his voice squeaks downward. Meissner found that the teenagers worried about their shyness, felt that they were misunderstood, were troubled about finding a job, and often wondered whether they were normal or not. They also worried about marks, except for the seniors who had the relief (or disappointment) of knowing that they could do no more to change their academic standing.

When the adolescent boy reaches the quiet, secretive phase of development, he does not want his father to be a pal. He wants pals of his own age. "At this stage of his son's adolescence, the wise father will begin to fish and to golf alone again—or with pals of his own age."[25]

In a later stage of adolescence, the young person tries to improve his adjustments by intellectual analysis of himself and the world. He believes that he could construct a much better social and economic order than the one in which he lives. He has ready solutions for many of the problems that have bothered the great thinkers of his age!

Obviously, the child who adjusts to his social situations by withdrawing into himself needs systematic and continued encouragement and invitations to participate in normal social activities. He may still need discipline from time to time, even though his withdrawal stemmed from former discipline. However, he especially needs discipline in the spirit of, "This act is wrong, but I love you." The wise disciplinarian can discipline the child for his wrong acts; others merely discipline the child.

To most parents and teachers, discipline is a personal issue rather than an objective procedure. This results in causing the child to feel that the disciplinarian does not like him. Effects of this harmful procedure are revealed when the child says, "My dad doesn't think very much of me," or, "Nothing *I* do would ever please my mother." Discipline should not humiliate the child. He ought to feel that he is still loved and that the discipline was fair.

When discipline is needed we should not think of children as "good" or "bad," but as "learning." They need constructive discipline. The child gets a sense of security when he has consistent discipline that teaches him the limits in his behavior. The pressures exerted by intelligent loving parents give him patterns for his conduct. If he knows and obeys the rules of society, he will feel more at home in his society.[26]

Investigations by mental hygienists of the values of discipline refute the erroneous inference that the "new psychology" advises parents to let children do as they please. Rather, parents who use no discipline and no restraint tend to rear playboys, delinquents, and psychopaths.[27]

Parents who abdicate their authority and allow the child to run wild lose the child's respect and fail to give the child the development necessary for orderly happy living. Nor should the parent utilize pleasant rewards only to bring about desired behavior. Good conduct purchased by means of frequent rewards is only a veneer because it does not arise from an inner conviction on the part of the child.

Behavior Problems of the Aggressive and Withdrawal Varieties

Man is born with a capacity to react with a variety of emotions. He has within him the lion (the will to fight) and the rabbit (the will to flight). He exhibits three major emotions in response to a threatening situation: Anger directed outward toward others—rage; anger directed inward toward himself—depression; and anxiety—fear. The bodily changes produced in anger are different from those produced by depression or fear. Man's early childhood experiences largely determine in which of these ways he will react under stress. His emotional development is not finished at birth, but is developed as he grows older. Young children are usually more outwardly aggressive than older ones. The older ones are usually more anxious and direct their hostilities inward. The latter emotions are a result of the acculturation of the child; he is becoming an adult and conforming to the society in which he lives.[28]

Young children express a great deal of aggression. As they become older, they become more inhibited. When the child is three, he is probably more openly aggressive than he will be at any other age. As the child grows up, the forms of his aggression change and become more varied. Crying and direct counterattack give way to leaving the scene, verbal expressions, appeals to an adult for help, and general inhibition of his feelings.

Evidently the kind and amount of frustration and punishment a child experiences are very important in determining what his aggressive and dependent drives will be like.

Adjustments of the hostile aggressive variety are exemplified in disobedience, fighting, rejection of routine, delinquency, contentiousness, and refusal to coöperate. Clever parents and teachers avoid open conflict and try to direct the established tendencies into competitive sports, exploring the world of pets, or other interests. The parent who remains calm when faced by defiance and rage can often relieve the situation through humor, or through actively participating with his child in some diverting activity. A funny story or an appeal to take part in some interesting sport will help the rebellious child far more than the use of brute force.

Withdrawal adjustments are closely related psychologically to aggression, in the sense that both represent hostile modes of response to the social situations. Hostility may be expressed by overt aggression or by passive resentment. Parents, teachers, and other adults evaluate the two modes of response quite differently, imagining that the passively hostile child is a "good" child. The child who deals with his problems by means of withdrawal—fearfulness, sulkiness, daydreaming, shyness, solitariness, fear of criticism, and overdependence on adults—is usually liked because he does not annoy others. He is, however, very unhappy within himself. After attaining adulthood, he is apt to be beset with nameless fears and acute anxieties. He is likely to nourish his suspicions and to develop neurotic complaints. Of course, many people who adjust by withdrawal reduce their tensions in the course of development by seeking relief in the quiet nonsocial activities of reading in libraries, enjoying laboratories, art, or inventing. Unfortunately, some also develop escapes from reality in the forms that lead to alcoholism, drug addiction, and insanity.

Interestingly, several studies indicate that isolation in infancy and childhood is helpful in the development of a scientist. An only child has no friction among brothers and sisters and does not have to vie with them for his parents' attention. Often the only child is brought into contact with the adult world sooner and develops a mature outlook more rapidly than he would if he were in constant contact with his peers. And, he cannot help but receive more attention than if he had brothers and sisters.

Isolation in childhood may force the intelligent child to turn to books for enjoyment. He may withdraw into himself and gradually become introverted. He may find pleasure in the activities of his own mind and not have a need for constant companionship to find entertainment. Psychologically, he becomes equipped for the isolation that research requires.[29] Of course the isolation, *per se,* does not cause the child to become a scientist. Rather, the child's adjustment to the isolation happens to give him a predisposition toward the satisfactions enjoyed by a typical scientist.

Size of family is often believed to be very important in adjustment. Most people assume that the larger the family, the better the prospects for good adjustment. The findings of several studies indicate that the large family does not necessarily provide the child with a more favorable environment for personality development as compared with the family in which there are only two or three children. There are some indications that children from smaller families may fare better psychologically than children from larger families.[30]

How to Interpret the Child's Behavior to the Child

College students and parents who have taken a few courses in psychology are apt to attempt psychological analysis of the child to the extent that they become amateur practitioners of psychotherapy. Such practice is dangerous. Dr. Rudolf Dreikurs, Professor of Psychiatry, Chicago Medical School, offers an excellent explanation of what the parent should and should not do in regard to interpretation:

> Psychological interpretation should not be confused with attempts to analyze, to pry into the unconscious, to dig into deep sources of motivation. We do not advocate psychological analysis on the part of anyone who is not thoroughly trained and qualified to conduct psychotherapy. But we must distinguish between *psychotherapy,* which is a tool of psychiatrists and trained psychotherapists, and *interpretation,* which everyone who is dealing with children should be able to make. The main distinction between the two is the kind of psychological mechanisms and problems which are examined and analyzed; only psychotherapy can reveal the *past* development, the formation of deep-seated concepts, of the life style of the person, child, or adult. Interpretation, on the other hand, is concerned solely with *present attitudes and immediate purposes.*
>
> Every parent and educator should have some psychological knowledge and some understanding of the probable nature of a child's personality. In difficult cases, this knowledge may be obtained through the services of a psychiatrist or trained child psychologist. But analytical knowledge should never be used for conversations between you and your child; it can serve only as a guide for your general management of the child. You must take cognizance of the child's actions and attempt to influence them. Discussing the questionable action with a child is one of the most successful ways of changing it. An effective discussion, however, should never investigate *why* a child acted in a certain way, but only explain *for what immediate purpose* he did that. The distinction between "why" and "for what purpose" may seem, superficially, to be insignificant. However, it indicates the complete difference between emphasis on the past and on present goals. There may be a thousand reasons which led to a present attitude of a child; but there is only *one* purpose possible for his actions. The search for the "why" is, for the untrained person, mere guesswork; the recognition of the purpose indicates understanding.
>
> The child responds in a different manner to an explanation of *causes* than to an explanation of *the goals* of his actions. Explanations such as jealousy, lack of self-confidence, feeling of being neglected, dominated, or rejected, feelings of guilt or self-pity, regardless of how accurate they may be in explaining the child's behavior, are accepted by the child at best with friendly indifference. It tells the child only what he is. His reaction is quite different when told what he *wants:* to get attention, to show his superiority, to be the big boss, to demonstrate his power, to get even or to punish others. Such interpretations of his true intentions, when correct, evoke immediately a very definite and characteristic reaction on the part of the child. This reaction is immediate and automatic, a "recognition reflex," and indicates the correctness of the interpretation. It consists of a roguish smile and a peculiar twinkle of the eyes, characteristic of the cat who swallowed the canary. The child need not say one word, or he might even say, "No"; but his facial expression gives him away. This discernment of his psychological attitude generally leads to an immediate change in the particular behavior, especially in a young child. Even very young children, as soon as they comprehend the meaning of words, that is, at two years of age, are capable of conscious understanding of their intentions and are inclined to change their attitudes when they are made aware of them. That does not imply a complete change of the life style, but it may lead eventually to a change of basic concepts in relationship to other people.
>
> Even psychological interpretations must be used with care. If repeated or overdone, they no longer are revelations. They should never have a humiliating or belittling effect and should never be translated by the child as fault-finding and criticism. It is generally advisable not to make a definite statement, "You do that because you want to..." Much better are remarks of vague conjecture, "I wonder whether you don't want to...?" Could it be?" Such discussions never can do any harm. If you are on the wrong

track, you just do not get any reaction. Then you can make another conjecture and the child's reaction will indicate which one was correct.

Two boys, nine and ten years old, annoyed their mother by using bedtime for fighting in their beds. Mother could not stop it and did not know what to do. I had a talk with the boys. I asked them why they went on fighting after going to bed. I did not expect the correct answer to this question, but wanted to hear what they had to say. They both explained that it is so much fun to fight in bed when it does not hurt to be thrown down on the pillows. That was their rationalization.

I asked them whether they would mind if I told them the real reason. Of course, they wouldn't mind. Then I ventured, "Maybe you do it just so that mother will come several times to remind you to be quiet." The younger one said indifferently, "It could be." The older one said nothing, but beamed. One should know that the older one was the favorite of the mother and depended upon her, while the younger one felt somewhat excluded and relied upon himself for his position in the world. Generally, the younger was the one who started the fights, but in this particular situation the older brother obviously had instigated the fights for the sake of getting his mother's attention, bringing her back to the bedroom every so often. Nothing more was said or done about it; but after our short discussion the evening fights stopped and never were resumed. That does not mean that the older boy suddenly became independent of his mother. But this particular method was no longer useful once he recognized his purpose.[31]

No parent should expect a child to answer correctly the question, "Why did you do that?" The child cannot be expected to know why he behaves in a certain way. He needs help in order to understand himself and the purposes of his conduct. The wise parent does not try to give the child such understanding immediately after some act of misconduct. Nor should the parent be angry or excited at the time.

Child training is one of the great arts of mankind. Few peoples and few persons have mastered it.

Unfortunately, a high level of formal education on the part of the parent does not assure good personality adjustment on the part of the children. In one study of 256 fifth grade children of small town and rural schools, the indices of family socio-economic status used were the occupation of the father and the educational level of both the father and the mother. In general, the analysis tended to support the hypothesis that higher-status children showed fewer indications of maladjustment. However, an unexpected finding was that children whose fathers had the highest level of educational achievement, postgraduate study, showed greater indications of personality maladjustment than many of the children who came from homes where the fathers were not as well educated.[32]

Fortunately, however, our modern scientific investigators have developed many principles of value for the present-day parent. A very brief summarization of some of these findings, not emphasized in this chapter, indicate that the child needs:

1. Full satisfaction of his sucking instinct. Not only must sucking periods be of sufficient length and frequency to satisfy the infant, but they must be administered while the mother gives her close attention so that both mother and child may exchange warmth and affection.
2. Unhurried training of the functions of excretion. Toilet training should not be pursued militantly. Socialized habits cannot be taught until the child is physically and emotionally ready.
3. A long period of consistent mothering by one individual, which satisfies the child's psychological and biological needs. This stimulates mutual growth and gratification of mother and child.
4. Parents who are so well-adjusted to each other that they may be capable of setting a consistent pattern for his love development.
5. Absence of harsh disciplinary measures at his infantile manifestations of sexuality. He can learn effectively what is expected of him by parental example and societal attitudes.
6. Treatment commensurate with his position as a person of some importance of his own. He should be credited with needs,

rights, and feelings, and should be given adequate explanations of parental authoritative measures.

7. Truthfulness, honesty, and sincerity, which are essential in dealings between parents and the child.

ACKNOWLEDGMENTS AND REFERENCES

1. Louise M. Langford and O. W. Alm, "A Comparison of Parents' Judgments and Child Feelings Concerning the Self-Adjustment and Social Adjustment of 12-year-old Children," *Journal of Genetic Psychology,* 1954, pp. 39–46.
2. See summaries and bibliographies in L. Wolberg, "The Character Structure of the Rejected Child," *Nervous Child,* **3** (1944), 74–88; F. Clothier, "The Treatment of the Rejected Child," *Nervous Child,* **3** (1944), 89–110.
3. A. Simon, "Rejection in the Etiology and Treatment of the Institutionalized Delinquent," *Nervous Child,* **3** (1944), 119–126; M. Field, "Maternal Attitudes Found in Twenty-five Cases of Children with Behavior Primary Disorders," *American Journal of Orthopsychiatry,* **10** (1940), 293–311.
4. Norman Cameron, *The Psychology of Behavior Disorders* (Boston: Houghton Mifflin Company, 1947), pp. 34–35.
5. J. Macfarlane, "The Relationship of Environmental Pressure to the Development of a Child's Personality and Habit Patterns," *Journal of Pediatrics,* **15** (1939), 142–154; L. Kanner, *Child Psychiatry* (Springfield, Ill.: Charles C. Thomas, Publisher, 1935), pp. 87–105; D. Baruch and J. Wilcox, "A Study of Sex Differences in Pre-school Children's Adjustment Coexistent with Interparental Tensions," *Journal of Genetic Psychology,* **64** (1944), 781–803; D. Baruch, "A Study of Reported Tension in Interparental Relationships as Coexistent with Behavior Adjustment in Young Children," *Journal of Experimental Education,* **6** (1937), 187–204.
6. A. S. Jensen, "How Is Psychology Used in Home Life?" *Psychology in Use,* J. Stanley Gray, ed. (New York: American Book Company, 1941).
7. Robert E. Shulman, Donald J. Shoemaker, and Irwin Moelis, "Laboratory Measurement of Parental Behavior," *Journal of Consulting Psychology,* April, 1962.
8. Benjamin Spock, "Preventing Early Problems," *American Journal of Orthopsychiatry,* **17,** (1947).
9. Andrew W. Brown, Joan Morrison and Gertrude Crouch, "Influence of Affectional Family Relationships on Character Development," *Journal of Abnormal and Social Psychology,* **42** (1947), 422–428.
10. E. S. Rademacher, "Democracy and Mental Hygiene in the Home," *American Journal of Orthopsychiatry,* **10** (1940), 466–471.
11. *Mental Hygiene News,* New York State Department of Mental Hygiene, October, 1961, p. 3.
12. For more complete descriptions of these studies, see Harry F. Harlow, "The Nature of Love," *The American Psychologist,* **13** (1958), 673–685; "Love in Infant Monkeys," *Scientific American,* June, 1959, pp. 68–74; and "The Heterosexual Affectional System in Monkeys," *The American Psychologist,* **17** (1962), 6–9.
13. See Harry F. and Margaret Kuenne Harlow, "Social Deprivation in Monkeys," *Scientific American,* November, 1962.
14. Victor H. Denenberg, "Early Experience and Emotional Development," *Scientific American,* June, 1963, pp. 138–146.
15. Rene A. Spitz, "Hospitalism: An Inquiry into the Genesis of Psychiatric Conditions in Early Childhood," *The Psychoanalytic Study of the Child,* **1** (1945), 53–74.
16. Sylvia Brody, "Self-Rocking in Infancy," *Journal of the American Psychoanalytic Association,* July, 1960.
17. Edward A. Strecker, *Their Mother's Sons; the Psychiatrist Examines an American Problem* (Philadelphia: J. B. Lippincott Co., 1946).
18. For further information see Jack Rouman, "School Children's Problems as Related to Parental Factors," *Understanding the Child,* April, 1955, pp. 50–55.
19. Lois Wladis Hoffman, "Effects of Maternal Employment on the Child," *Child Development,* June, 1961.
20. M. Sewall, "Some Causes of Jealousy in Young Children," Part I of "Two Studies in Sibling Rivalry," *Smith College Students in Social Work,* Vol. 1, (1930), 6–22.
21. Gardner Murphy, Lois B. Murphy, and Theodore M. Newcomb, *Experimental Social Psychology* (New York: Harper & Row, Publishers, Inc., 1937), p. 389.
22. Benjamin Spock, "Avoiding Behavior Problems," *The Journal of Pediatrics,* October, 1945. This excellent article is available in reprint form at a nominal charge from New York Committee on Mental Hygiene of the State Charities Aid Association, 105 East 22nd St., New York, N.Y. 10010. It offers the parent valuable suggestions concerning the following problems: early feeding problems, weaning conflicts and thumb-sucking, bowl-training, kidney-training, anxieties in the early years, and jealousy of the new baby.
23. Arnold Gesell and Frances L. Ilg, *Infant and Child in the Culture of Today,* (New York: Harper & Row, Publishers, Inc., 1943). See also Gladys Denny Schultz, "Why Pre-Schoolers Are Bad," *This Week,* Jan. 6, 1946, pp. 28 f.
24. W. W. Meissner, "Some Anxiety Indications in

the Adolescent Boy," *Journal of General Psychology,* April, 1961.
25. George E. Gardner, "The Mental Health of Adolescents," *Mental Hygiene,* October, 1947, p. 535.
26. John B. Geisel, "Discipline Viewed As a Developmental Need of the Child," *The National Elementary Principal,* December, 1946.
27. Robert P. Knight, M. D., "Behavior Problems and Habit Disturbances in Pre-Adolescent Children: Their Meaning and Management," *Bulletin of the Menninger Clinic,* November, 1944, p. 189.
28. Daniel H. Funkenstein, "The Physiology of Fear and Anger," *Scientific American,* May, 1955, pp. 74–80.
29. See S. Stewart West, "Sibling Configuration of Scientists," *American Journal of Sociology,* November, 1960.
30. See G. R. Hawkes, Lee Burchinal, and B. Gardner, "Size of Family and Adjustment of Children," *Marriage & Family Living,* 1958, 20, 65–68.
31. Rudolf Dreikurs, M. D., *The Challenge of Parenthood* (New York: Duell, Sloan & Pearce, Inc., 1948), pp. 88–91.
32. See *Journal of Genetic Psychology,* **92** (1958), 149–159.

PROJECTS

1. Discuss reasons why many children will not go to their parents to discuss problems. What are the characteristics of parents that encourage, and what of those that discourage, the child in the bringing of problems to them?
2. Why do children react disdainfully to the parent's assertion, "When I was a child. . . ."? What can the child do about it when the parent harangues him about what *he* did as a child?
3. Certain effects are likely to show up in the personalities of children who were reared too leniently, as well as in the personalities of those who were reared too strictly. List some of the likely later problems or characteristics of children reared under each of the two extremes.
4. Discuss techniques of reprimanding the child in the spirit of, "The act is wrong, but I love *you,"* versus, "I am punishing you for what you did."
5. What are the effects on the child's psychological development when he is punished by the "silent treatment"—when the parent will not speak to him for several days?
6. How can the child be integrated into the life of the home through the performance of chores? What chores or tasks can the city child be required to do?
7. What is the effect on the child when the parent almost never gives a definite "no" or "yes" to the child's request for permission to do something which he is uncertain about? Also, what is the effect when the parent habitually withholds permission for several hours or days before granting it?

COLLATERAL READINGS

Bro, Margueritte H., *When Children Ask.* New York: Harper & Row, Publishers, Inc., 1956.

Farnsworth, P. R., ed., *et al., Annual Review of Psychology.* Palo Alto, Calif.: Annual Reviews, Inc., 1964.

Gesell, Arnold and Frances L. Ilg, *Infant and Child in the Culture of Today: The Guidance of Development.* New York: Harper & Row, Publishers, Inc., 1943. Also any other books by Gesell.

Lehner, George F. and Ella Kube, *The Dynamics of Personal Adjustment.* Englewood Cliffs, N.J.: Prentice-Hall, Inc., 1964, Chapter 12.

Morse, William C. and Calvin O. Dyer, "The Emotionally and Socially Handicapped," *Review of Educational Research,* **33**, No. 1 (1963), 109–125.

"Punishment Often Backfires," *Changing Times,* The Kiplinger Magazine, July, 1964.

Schauffler, Goodrich C., *Guiding Your Daughter to Confident Womanhood.* Englewood Cliffs, N.J.: Prentice-Hall, Inc., 1964.

Shaffer, Laurance F. and Edward J. Shoben, *The Psychology of Adjustment.* Boston: Houghton Mifflin Company, 1956.

Dr. A.Q. Sartain, *Dean of the College of Business Administration, Southern Methodist University (a guest speaker), is leading a discussion at the Interviewing Institute. The registrants, including both personnel representatives (training managers, college recruiters, etc.) as well as members of middle and higher management, have already tape recorded two practice interviews each with college students and are now considering the advantages of the non-directive and patterned interview approaches. Each of the registrants will have one more recorded practice interview before the week-long program is completed. Three of the private interviewing rooms can be seen in the background.*

The universal need *for improving interviewing procedures has caused psychology departments of several universities to establish institutes for the teaching of effective techniques. Here are pictures, for example, taken at the Personnel Psychology Services Center, University of Houston.*

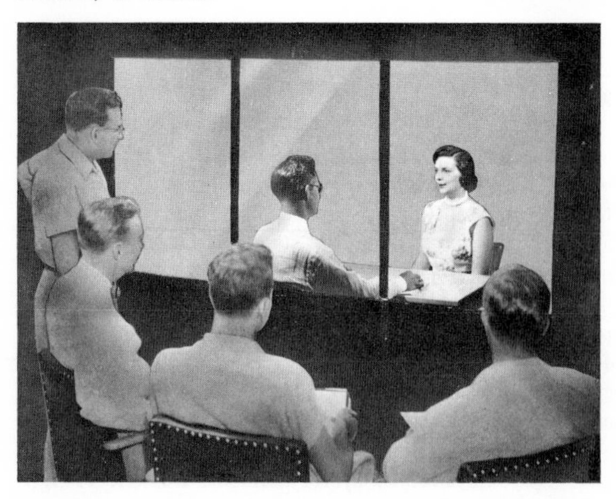

Line executives and employment specialists *are discussing with Dr. MacNaughton the proper use of tests in industry during the week-long Personnel Testing Institute, which is presented annually. Here, such representatives from business and industry have an opportunity to become acquainted with the most recent developments in personnel testing, learn how to validate tests for their own companies, and to integrate them into other aspects of the employment or personnel development programs. They also discuss the major pitfalls, or misuses, of tests and how to avoid them.*

Interviewing rooms *are equipped with one-way glass windows, intercom systems, and facilities for tape recording. Here some of the Institute members watch a practice interview through a one-way glass window.*

PART IV

INDUSTRIAL PSYCHOLOGY

CHAPTER FIFTEEN

HIRING THE EMPLOYEE —THE INTERVIEW

Alfred P. Sloan, Jr., General Motors chairman, in an annual report to stockholders stated: "In our existing industrial economy the only difference of fundamental nature between one business and another operating in the same general field is people. The same sources of raw materials are available to all. The same equipment will be furnished to anyone who may buy. The existing standards of technology are largely a matter of common knowledge. The same markets are available with the same instrumentalities to capitalize them. The same reservoirs of capital are available to those who can qualify. All these means are open to everyone, and generally speaking, on equal terms. The one major difference is people. . . . Management is a most consequential problem as affecting the long-term interests of any business."[1]

The man who does the hiring in a company contributes to the strength or weakness of the organization. If he hires strong applicants, the organization will tend to be strong. Conversely, if he hires weak people, the organization will be weak.

In the hiring interview, the main purpose is to evaluate the applicant's potentials for the vacant job but an additional purpose is to forecast his behavior in relations with the other people who are involved in the job. The interviewer must forecast how the employees will react to him as a person. For this reason, the interview may be called a test of acceptability in human relations. It provides a basis for judging not only job skills but also how well the two persons, the employer (or his representatives) and the applicant, will get along with each other.

The employment interviewer must do far more than estimate abilities of applicants. He must also do a lot of screening to keep out persons who are drifters, troublemakers, seriously maladjusted mentally, epileptics, sexual deviates, and others who would be liabilities rather than assets. And he must know what kinds of persons mesh with the personality of each supervisor and his employees. As Elbert Hubbard said: "There is something that is much more scarce, something finer by far, something rarer than ability. It is the ability to recognize ability."

The incompetent interviewer often fails to get correct information and to make sound estimates of abilities and social characteristics because he is too easily influenced by an impressive personal appearance and glibness in oral expression. More basic facts about the applicant go unobserved or are overlooked.

Interviewing is an art which many persons, particularly employment interviewers, believe that they can practice with a high degree of reliability. Actually, studies by psychologists some decades ago indicated that when two or more interviewers conduct the experiment of appraising the same applicant, their appraisals often do not agree.

One of the earliest experiments of this kind was made by H. L. Hollingworth; in his experiment fifty-seven applicants for sales positions were interviewed individually by twelve sales managers.[2] Each interviewer conducted his interview in the manner that he wished. At the end of the interview, the sales manager assigned each applicant a rating with respect to his suitability for the position in question. These ratings were recast so that it was possible to assign each interviewee a rank ranging from one to fifty-seven. The results revealed very little agreement on the part of the interviewers. One applicant, for example, was rated as first by one interviewer and fifty-third by another.

When Walter Dill Scott had six sales managers interview thirty-six applicants, the results showed that in the case of twenty-eight of the thirty-six, the interviewers disagreed as to whether the applicant should be rated in the upper or lower half of the group.[3]

In addition to the proved unreliability of the traditional interview as usually conducted, the validity of many interviewers' judgment is also dubious. And yet many employment interviewers believe that their interviewing experiences give them an ability to judge people more accurately than inexperienced interviewers can. Some even imagine that their abilities are uncanny, as expressed in this statement:

> Not every man has a head for mathematics, and not every man has a sense of logic necessary for the practice of law. Just so, not every man has what I might call the "sixth sense" necessary to judge what I truly believe is a series of psychic waves which flows from one man to another when in conversation.

Psychologists have been unable to find anything that would correspond to "psychic waves." It is possible, but has not been fully demonstrated in the laboratory, that the facial expressions, general bodily movements, bodily posture, and changes of pitch, intensity, rapidity, and inflection in the voice are noted by those who have daily contacts with people and analyze their motives. Some executives have said that they tend to suspect the man who makes a statement and then leans back.

Others have claimed that, when a lie is told, the speaker catches his breath. Salesmen say that they know when the prospect is sold by the fact that he leans toward the salesman. The writer decided to test the theory that experienced interviewers can detect false statements more accurately than inexperienced interviewers. Arrangements were made to have eleven experienced credit men and fourteen experienced employment interviewers, eighteen inexperienced men students and seven inexperienced women students, interview several hundred college students. These students who were to be interviewed were instructed to answer all the questions that any interviewer might ask, but to answer some truthfully and some falsely. The interviewers had the privilege of cross-examining the students.

The questions varied in nature, but were of the kind that could be answered in a definite manner, such as, "How old are you? How long have you been in college? How much money did you earn during your summer vacation? What were your grades in your college courses last semester?" Both the interviewer and the interviewee kept a written record of the questions and the answers, so that it was possible to record the interviewer's accuracy in judging the answers to each question. Records were tabulated of the interviewers' estimates of 3,205 answers to questions. Of the four classes of interviewers, the experienced credit men were wrong in 34 per cent of their judgments; the employment men in 42 per cent; the inexperienced men in 34 per cent; and the inexperienced women in 47.5 per cent.

A careful analysis of each interviewer's judgements showed that some of the interviewers were better detectors of false statements than others. The experiment indicated the following points of note:

1. The experienced interviewers were unable to detect false statements when the "applicant" wanted to lie. His detection was largely a matter of chance.
2. An interviewer should depend upon records and objective information in evaluating statements of applicants rather than upon his "hunches" or "feel" or "atmosphere" or the movements of lips and hands. One interviewer claimed that he could detect false statements from the movement of the lips. The results showed that he was one of the poorest interviewers in the group.
3. The individual interviewers who made the best records in judging the statements of the students were those persons who had had previous experience in interviewing students and knew the general facts of student life. This indicates what one would expect: an interviewer should be acquainted with the facts concerning the type or class of people whom he interviews.
4. The individual interviewers who made the poorest records seemed to be the "fatherly" trusting type of person who did not cross-examine the applicants. Conversely, the interviewers who made the best records were those who cross-examined the applicants, looked them in the eye, and pursued a policy of compelling the applicant to prove his statements.
5. The best of the interviewers made bad mistakes in their judgments of statements made by students who were adept in talking with strangers and who wished to baffle the interviewer. The experiment clearly demonstrated that, if a person wished to falsify his statements, the interviewer could not differentiate the false from the true unless he could check the statements objectively.

When interviewers depend upon their impressions, without reference to records of the applicants' past behavior, they succeed more often than they fail, simply because the majority of applicants want to tell the truth rather than not.

Several investigations of interviewing have shown that interviewers disagree among themselves regarding the same applicants, that some interviewers vary in the consistency of their judgments and in their ability to judge the applicants accurately. Many experienced employment men realize that they cannot judge applicants with any great degree of accuracy on the basis of the interview alone. They try to obtain dependable information from former employers or to hire the applicant for a probationary period. In spite of the unreliability of the interview, it will continue to play an important part in modern hiring. Somehow human beings want to see each other even though the meeting may not

READ THEIR RECORDS . . .

These are facts matched with models who closely resemble the actual salesmen for a leading manufacturer of aids for handicapped people.

Former Doctor *Salesman A started with company 8 years ago after struggling for years to make a living as a doctor in a low-income town. Age 45. Married: 4 children. Lives in a rented house. Has thorough knowledge of the physiological causes of the malady to be helped. Keeps up-to-date on medical advances. Extremely interested in the clients, maintains close contact with them.*

Social Register *Salesman B has been with the company for 3 years. College-educated, social background. Member of country club, alumni association, and political party. Married; 1 child; lives in own house; has independent income. Came to the job through a personal friendship with the president. Formerly worked in bank. Seldom mingles with other salesmen in the company. Said to be snobbish.*

RANK THEM IN ORDER OF THEIR SALES RECORDS.

(See page 621 for their correct order.)

Smooth Operator *Salesman E has sold everything from can-openers to vacuum cleaners. Knows all the tricks. Worked for competitor for 3 years. Widower for many years; no children; lives at hotel. Is active in local sales organization. Good dresser; big spender. Not receptive to directions, likes to do things his own way, resents criticism of any kind.*

Rose From Ranks *Salesman F has been with the company ever since he first started to work. Began as clerk, rose steadily if not rapidly. Asked for opportunity to enter selling 6 years ago. Married; 1 child. Interested in advancing. Studies and takes courses regularly. Carries heavy life and accident insurance. Intense hobby, stamp collecting.*

. . . THEN RATE THEM AS SALESMEN

Had Own Business *Salesman C formerly owned his own drug business. Wiped out when large chain moved into the neighborhood. Came to the company 6 years ago. Has wide acquaintance in the community. Is well liked. Is known as a mixer; active in church. Married; no children. Middle-aged. Lives in rented house. Supports parents. High-school education. Is a poor manager with regard to money. Harassed by debts.*

Veteran *Salesman D came to the company after discharge from the army. Wounded in action. No visible sign of disability. Held rank of corporal. Age 25; college graduate; single. Had no previous experience in business. Father who worked for the company had recently died. Now helps to support his mother; lives at home; is youngest member of big family. Ambitious and anxious to learn.*

(Reproduced by permission from ***Modern Industry.*** *Photographs by Ewing Galloway.)*

Former Failure *Salesman G had a bad record when he came to work 5 years ago. He never seemed to last on a job, couldn't seem to figure out why. Hired as a favor to a friend. Financially burdened. Supports wife, 2 children, and his wife's parents. Usually in debt and beset by home and family worries. Well-liked by other salesmen, but not by clients.*

Old-Timer *Salesman H knew the current company president when he was a "pup," the sales manager when he was just another salesman. Married; father and grandfather. A little wary of new methods, but excellent with people. Still in fine health, has good record on absenteeism. Good humor and spirit. Never forgets a client's face, name, or history.*

elicit valid information. They want to find out whether or not they would like to work with each other. Furthermore, studies of the interview—the conversation with a purpose—prove that interviewing ability can be improved. Improvability varies with the kind of interview used.

The various kinds of interviews for employment are the following:

1. The Free Interview

This is the customary informal interview as practiced by the average employment interviewer.[4] In the well-managed larger companies the interviewer usually has had special training but when all companies are considered, the typical interviewer has had no systematic training for his work and no constructive coaching. He has read no books on interviewing techniques. He has no understanding of basic psychological concepts, such as the adjustment pattern. He follows no organized plan and asks whatever questions come to his mind. He himself may have emotional maladjustments that cause him to be biased and lacking in objectivity in his judgments. He is a likely victim of common pitfalls in interviewing such as the following:

A. Personal Bias

Each of us, in the course of our psychological development, collects certain likes, dislikes, preferences, and beliefs that in our more objective moments we recognize as unfair or unjustified. Prejudices are an important factor in personal bias. If the employer recently has hired a man who once sold cash registers but failed on the job under consideration, he is apt to be prejudiced against all men who have sold cash registers. One executive claimed that all men who had mustaches had failed him. Dozens without mustaches, whom he had hired, had failed him too, but he still believed that a mustache was an indication of poor material for his organization. Some executives dislike applicants who have red hair or bad teeth, or wear bow ties, green socks, pink shirts, and so on. It is fortunate for applicants that executives differ in their prejudices, because if one employer rejects them they can always go to some other employer who may like the very trait for which they were previously rejected.

Some sales personnel men will not hire a man who has worked for a competitor. They believe that the man who has been trained under one set of conditions will cling to those former beliefs and habits and refuse to become a teamworker in a new organization. Some managers will not hire salesmen who have had a systematic training course where they had to learn a standardized sales talk. On the other hand, one life insurance company found that 20 per cent of the men who had had previous life insurance selling experience turned out to be successful.

Other executives do not hire recent college graduates because they believe that college men require three years in which to orient themselves. In this view college men are believed to want immediate promotions and to loathe doing routine work. In college they studied international problems, the progress of civilization, the boundaries of the universe, great social forces, and historical movements; hence small wonder that they are bored when they must spend hours checking detailed bills in a butter-and-egg firm. Once a college graduate finishes about three years of floundering, these executives will hire him without very much quizzing about his past failures. It is believed that he is then ready to fit himself into the business picture without demanding a front seat.

One executive claims that young single men succeed better than young married men. He assumes that the young married man is either too greatly interested in his wife to study his job or he is ambitious to buy his wife expensive articles for her adornment.

One executive may take applicants for important positions to dinner and gauge their ability by their table manners. Another may argue with the applicant to discover how he conducts himself toward an unruly stranger. The empirical rules for hiring vary with the executive. Most of these rules are merely the result of a few dramatic instances. Many are without sound statistical basis.

Prejudices often affect findings from interviews that are supposed to be so systematic as to overcome subjective influences. Rice[5] made an analysis of the findings of twelve trained interviewers as to the cause of the downfall of 2,000 vagrants who had applied for free lodging. The interviews were standardized, but different investigators obtained different results. One interviewer, a socialist, reported that 39 per cent of the men were down and out because of industrial conditions, and 22 per cent because of excessive use of alcohol. Another interviewer, an ardent prohibitionist, attributed but 7 per cent of the failures to industrial and economic conditions and 62 per cent to drink. Prejudices were even more significantly revealed when we note that, according to the socialist, the *vagrants themselves* gave as the cause of their downfall: industrial conditions, 60 per cent; drink, 11 per cent. But according to the prohibitionist, the *vagrants themselves* blamed industrial conditions in 42.5 per cent and drink in 34 per cent of the cases. Obviously, each interviewer influenced the interviewees to give answers in line with his own biases.

The interviewer should note and compensate for his own prejudices, such as likes or dislikes for applicants who have mustaches, wear a vest, reveal tobacco-stained fingers, or belong to certain racial classes. He should hire people who do good work rather than those who satisfy his own idiosyncrasies. Of course, if the interviewer is hiring applicants who are to be supervised by department heads, the interviewer must hire in accordance with the idiosyncrasies of each department head.

B. *Pseudo-Sciences*

These are phrenology, palmistry, numerology, astrology, and physiognomy. The ideas that a low forehead, receding chin, large ears, or any other physical features indicate certain mental traits or behavioral tendencies are merely blithe assumptions, like the myth that shifty eyes betoken dishonesty. Investigations indicate that college students have some tendency to be influenced in their estimates by the physical factors of appearance, such as the wearing of glasses. Wearing glasses tends to cause persons to be rated as more intelligent and more industrious, but not more honest.[6]

C. *The Illusion of Previous Experience*

Most interviewers tend to assume that the applicant who has had previous experience on a similar job is bound to be a better employee than any other applicant who may have superior potentialities but lacks experience. When a secretary is desired, the interviewer chooses the applicant who claims secretarial experience in preference to the inexperienced stenographer, who may actually be brighter and more competent.

Actually, previous experience when taken in conjunction with other pertinent factors is an extremely valuable indicator of future performance, *but it is not, of itself, a guarantee of ability to do a job well.* Mediocrity is tolerated in much of the world's work, and *experience* too often cloaks such mediocrity. There is danger, therefore, in making a criterion of the fact that an applicant has done similar work in the past. The applicant who is willing to accept a job on the same level as his previous one is as likely to be below average in performance as above average. The tendency to *over-value* previous experience in weighing qualifications should be discouraged, for it may be costly to a company in terms of valuable talent lost and of commonplace or inferior performance perpetuated.[7]

The list of pitfalls in the free interview can be increased by observing any interviewer who is untrained in his art. He may use the interview as a means for expanding his ego by talking to impress rather than analyze the applicant. He even may be so inept as to suggest the answers desired to his own questions or to hire the people who need jobs rather than the ones who can do the work.

2. The Area Interview

Some free interviewers discover that certain areas of the applicant's background and personal characteristics are more significant in predicting job success or failure than other areas. They gradually learn to ask more and better questions about the important areas.

The questions are asked not haphazardly but according to an organized procedure. The interviewer is guided by an interview blank and jots down answers as given, thus making a record of the results of the conversation with the applicant. He tries to ask questions that require factual answers as given, thus making a record of the results of the conversation with the applicant. In some cases he adds some problems which are of a semi-trade nature. The questions in *The Interviewer's Guide,* page 309, were prepared by a group of employment men and executives who wished to have a list of definite questions to guide them. The thirteen suggested questions may be used in conjunction with the usual employment blank. The questions may be phrased to suit the interviewer and the applicant, but it is essential that the interviewer ask each question and record the answer while he is conducting the interview. If he does not adhere to a definite procedure, he is apt to let the interview become a hit-or-miss procedure—a conversation that will not give him complete information. Of course, the interview may be ended long before the last question if the applicant is obviously unfit.

Some area interviewers develop special sets of questions that apply to the personality and aptitudes of the applicant as revealed during the interview. Examples of two sets of area questions, developed by R. S. Uhrbrock, for use in interviewing recent college graduates are the following:

Is he keenly analytical?

- *a.* What college courses demanding analytical ability has he taken?
- *b.* What special problems has he worked on that required careful analysis?
- *c.* Has he taken many "cinch" courses?
- *d.* What special reports, term papers, etc., has he prepared? To what extent do these deal with numbers and statistics?

Initiative and originality:

- *a.* Did he try to interview the interviewer?
- *b.* Did he ask any questions, or make any observations that distinguish him from the ordinary run of applicants?
- *c.* Did he ever make tentative plans for a new mechanical device that he thought might be patentable?
- *d.* Did he ever undertake to sell any article? If so, with what degree of success?

If the interviewer is unusually able and scientifically trained, he may even make satistical studies of his questions of specific areas, as exemplified by the "Diagnostic Interviewer's Guide" developed by Hovland and Wonderlic.[8] If he does make such a study, he raises his interview to a higher scientific level and probably uses the patterned or standardized interview.

The alert interviewer looks for clues to adjustment in the applicant's gestures, voice inflections, and appearance. Such clues may or may not be significant. If, for example, a young man wears a beard, does it indicate that he has grown the beard as a means of satisfying his need for individuality? Is he so individualistic that he would be a poor team worker in an organization? Or when a woman applicant's appearance is extremely careless, does it mean that she has given up all hope of making herself attractive? Is she suffering from a severe emotional problem, or is she so deeply engrossed in her professional interests that appearance is incidental to her? Only further information concerning the psychological history can supply dependable answers.

When an applicant passes his hands over his eyes or face after he has been asked a question, is he trying to avoid giving the true answer? Or is he simply trying to give a better phrasing of the correct answer?

When an applicant folds his arms very firmly and quickly, is this his outward manner of expressing his hostility to the interviewer as a person or to something that the interviewer symbolizes?

When the applicant leans forward toward the interviewer, is he doing it consciously to make a favorable impression or is it a spontaneous unconscious movement that indicates his interest?

THE INTERVIEWER'S GUIDE

Name .... Address ....
Position wanted .... Date .... Interviewer ....

1. Give me the names of your past employers. Begin with the last employer and go backward for the last five years.
2. Describe the work you did for each.
3. What did you do in your spare time: evenings, Saturdays, and Sundays? (Look for side lines and hobbies, reading of trade journals, clubs.)
4. What general education have you had?
5. What technical education have you had?
6. What is state of your health? How much time have you missed from your work because of sickness during the past two years?
7. For what other jobs have you applied with other concerns recently?
8. What is your financial condition: savings accounts, life insurance, investments, speculations, own home?
9. With what merchandise firms do you have credit accounts?
10. What are your plans for the future, vocationally?
11. What suggestions have you made regarding improvements in operations for your former employers?
12. Why do you want to work for us? Interviewer's deductions:

Be near friends	Just needs a job ....
For home reasons	Seems restless ....
Likes the community	Floater ....
Regularity of work	Family reasons ....
Self-expression	More pay ....
More prestige	For opportunity ....
Union reasons	Other reason ....

13. What pay do you expect?

    Overestimates his worth ....
    Underestimates his worth ....
    Fair estimate ....

DECISIONS FOR THE INTERVIEWER TO MAKE DURING THE INTERVIEW

14. Would his personality fit our organization? ....
15. Is applicant eager for the job? ....
16. Does the applicant fit the job that is open? ....

Too good for the vacancy	Undoubtedly satisfactory ....
Not suited to vacancy	Probably a safe man to hire .....
Unable to do the work	Hire, if no better applies ....

17. Remarks: ....
....

What do such clues or hypotheses really mean? Little research has been done to answer these and related questions. However, one study of the validity of certain clues was made of interviews conducted for the purpose of differentiating between successful foremen and workers of equal technical skill who had been judged capable of successfully supervising others. Characteristics that occurred more frequently among the capable men were:

> Good attitude toward early associates.
> More than 20 years' experience in the company.

In contrast, items found more frequently among those believed to be incapable of supervising others were:

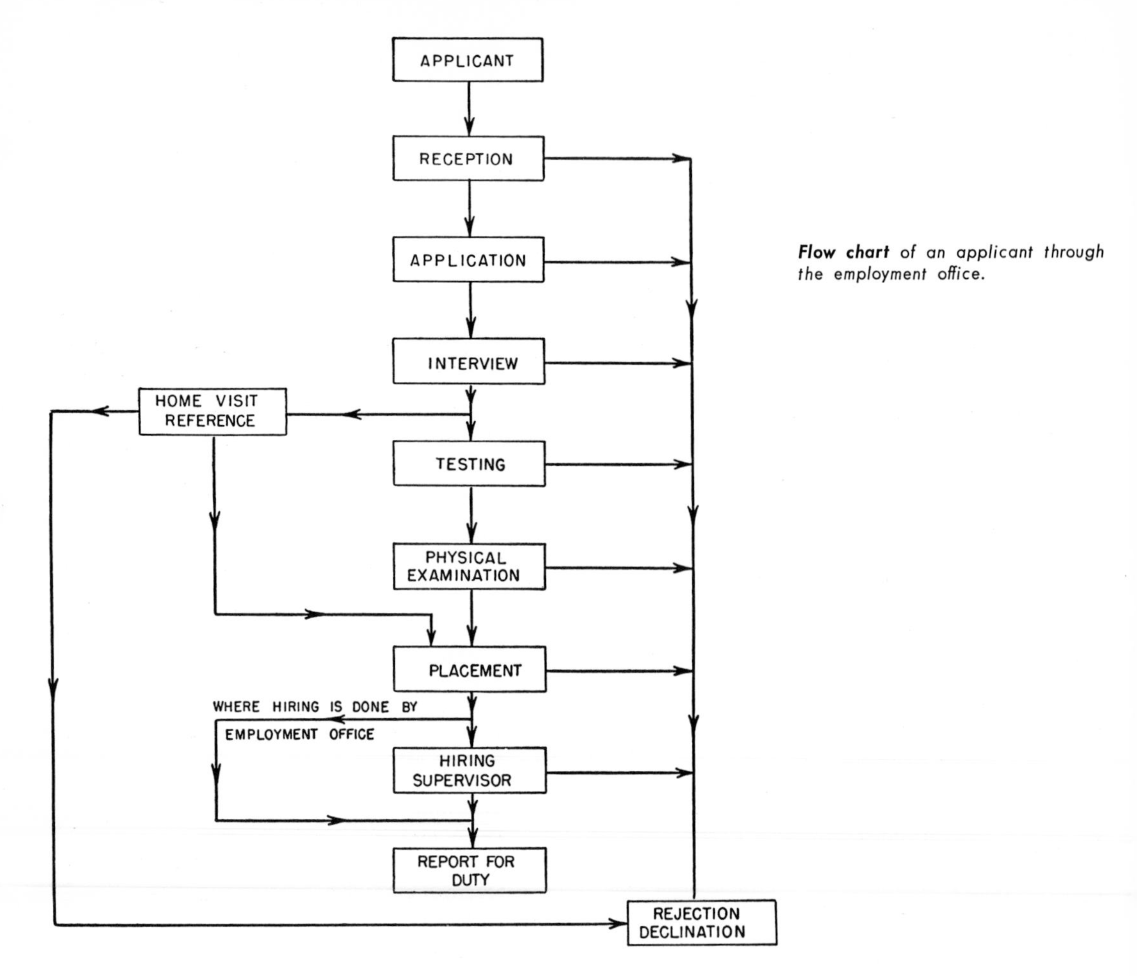

***Flow chart** of an applicant through the employment office.*

Restless movements in the interview.
Repetition of one or more subjects in school.
Self-conscious manner in the interview.
Tense or strained facial expression in interview.
Low intensity of voice during interview.[9]

Obviously, interviewers need the benefit of more research studies essential to improvement of interview validity. We know that *expressions of emotion are dictated by the culture* and clues to feelings vary with the cultural background of the individual. To us, the clenched first indicates anger but it has a friendly meaning to some peoples of the world.

The good interviewer seeks facts and records that substantiate or deny his interpretations of clues whenever possible. He tries to note relationships between clues and verifiable facts. He asks himself "What kind of pattern of growth or decline in ability is evident from the facts?" "When and why did the applicant change the direction of his growth or decline?"

The area interview may be conducted in the manner of a free association, with the questions arranged under certain headings. Or it may be a phase of the most advanced variety of the patterned or standardized interview.

3. The Patterned or Standardized Interview

This type of interview standardizes the procedure. It covers in detail the areas in the applicant's history: work record, schooling, early home environment, domestic status, and level of energy. It suggests questions for the interviewer to ask and helps him estimate what the applicant can do and is likely to do. It helps the interviewer guard against bias. The patterned interview lets the applicant do the talking but it steers the conversation.[10] It usually requires from 25 minutes at the factory level to 2½ hours at the executive level.

To be productive, the interviewer should have the following: careful preparation of questions, the use of printed forms that contain specific items to be covered, a uniform method of recording information and making judgments, prepared manuals that describe the procedures to be followed and the use of directions for interpreting the applicant's responses. One of these instruments, called the "Diagnostic Interviewer's Guide," was developed by Hovland and Wonderlic as part of a selection program of the Household Finance Corporation, a large personal loan organization.[11]

TABLE 15.1

PATTERNED INTERVIEW RESULTS

Percentage of Individuals (1) Still on Job, (2) Resigned, and (3) Dismissed in Various Categories of Scores on D.I.G.

Classification	*Scores on D.I.G.*				
	0–10	12–16	18–22	24–28	30–34
	%	%	%	%	%
On Job	38.9	42.9	47.2	48.6	59.2
Resigned ...	22.2	25.7	29.2	29.4	34.7
Dismissed ..	38.9	31.4	23.6	22.0	6.1
Number	18	35	89	109	49

From C. I. Hovland and E. F. Wonderlic, "Prediction of Industrial Success from a Standardized Interview," *Journal of Applied Psychology,* American Psychological Association, Inc., Vol. XXIII (October 1939), 537–546.

The general construction and layout of a patterned interview blank can be seen from the accompanying illustration (page 312). It usually includes certain general areas of the applicant's background and personal characteristics: (1) work history (2) family history (3) social history and (4) personal history. The top of each section is likely to have a series of standardized questions which the interviewer asks the applicant.

After the interviewer has collected the significant information, he asks himself certain specified questions about the applicant and assigns prescribed values to his judgments. A quantitative score is obtained for each area, and the sum of all the scores for all areas yields a total score for the applicant. The validity of the D.I.G. is indicated by Table 15.1.

This table for 300 individuals shows that "there is a progressive increase in the percentage of applicants who are still on the job the higher the score on the D.I.G. at the time of employment. More striking is the progressive decrease in the percentage of individuals who are dismissed as the scores increase."

Robert N. McMurry has published some of the results of his experience with the pat-

TABLE 15.2

COMPARISON OF INITIAL INTERVIEW SCORE WITH SUCCESS RATING

(Men and Women Combined)

	Interviewer's Rating			
	1	2	3	4
Foremen's Success-on-the-Job Rating				
Outstanding	6 (35.3%)	8 (47.1%)	3 (17.6%)	
Above Average	2 (1.2%)	88 (53.0%)	75 (45.2%)	1 (.6%)
Below Average		13 (6.6%)	175 (88.8%)	8 (4.6%)
Very Poor			4 (14.8%)	23 (85.2%)

In the table above, as may be seen, the relationship is unusually close. The Pearson coefficient of correlation is .68 ± .02. (From Robert N. McMurry, "Validating the Patterned Interview," *Personnel,* American Management Association, January 1947, pp. 263–272.)

SCHOOLING: How far did you go in school? High School: 1 2 3 4 College: 1 2 3 4 Graduate School: 1 2 3 4

	HIGH SCHOOL	COLLEGE AND GRADUATE SCHOOL
Name of school and dates	From 19 to 19	From 19 to 19
Names of other schools and dates	From to From to	From to From to
	Does he show stability?	Did he use every opportunity to get an education?
Courses		
	Were there frequent changes in courses?	
Scholastic standing, honors, scholarships, fellowships		
		Did he do as well as he could?
Graduate	☐ Yes ☐ No Age Date	☐ Yes ☐ No Degrees Age Dates
	Did he show persistence in getting his schooling? Is this consistent with the record?	
If not, why not?		
	Are his reasons for not finishing sound? Does it make him feel handicapped?	
School activities		
	How active was he? Does he get along with others? Were his activities purposeful?	
What offices did you hold?		
	Did others choose him to lead them? Did he accept responsibility?	
What further studying or courses have you taken?		
	Were they efforts to improve himself? Were they related to his work? Completed? Is he still studying?	
Principal sources of spending money		
	Was he self-reliant? Did he get jobs and hold them? Did he show habits of industry?	
Source of money for expenses	Family___% Earned___% Other___%	Savings___% Earnings___% Family___% Borrowed___% Government___% Other___%

To whom did you go for counsel while in college?________
Did he require counseling often? What relationships are indicated?

FAMILY BACKGROUND

Are your father and mother living? Father: ☐ Yes, ☐ No; Mother: ☐ Yes, ☐ No; Living together?________
If living, what is age? If deceased, what year?

Who brought you up?________Who did the disciplining?________
Any indication of overprotection? Was he too restricted? Too neglected?

Occupation of your father when you were a boy?________Income level of the family?________
What was economic and social status of the family?

Number of brothers____sisters____; number older____number younger____Age differences____
Was he the "baby" of the family?

What are present occupations of brothers?________sisters?________
Any indication of rivalry? Has he surpassed achievement of the rest of the family?

As a boy, what were your recreational activities?________What jobs did you have?________
Was he a normally active boy? Did he accept duties?

________What did you do with your earnings?________
Are there indications that he tried to get out of work? If he received pay did he accept financial responsibility?

What music lessons or other special training did you take as a boy?________Hobbies?________
Did he keep busy? Did he persevere in these activities? Did he put effort into them?

How did you spend your summer vacations while a boy?________
Did he keep busy? Did he associate with others?

What part did you take in church activities? (Do NOT ask what church)________
Did he take part in activities with people? Any indication of leadership?

To what other groups (sand lot, YMCA, Boy Scouts, 4-H clubs) did you belong?________
Did he mix with others? Did he take part? Did he enjoy it?

How far did you advance in these groups?________What offices held?________
Did he make progress? Did he accept responsibility? Did he show leadership?

How old were you when you became fully self-supporting?________Age at leaving home?________
Has he wanted to support himself or has he been willing to continue as a dependent?

DOMESTIC AND SOCIAL SITUATION

☐ Married, ☐ Single, ☐ Widowed, ☐ Divorced; Date of marriage________Living with wife? ☐ Yes, ☐ No
Are he and his wife compatible?

(If no) Specify________Dependents: Number____Ages____What plans do you have for your children?________
Do dependents provide adequate motivation?

How did you meet your wife?________When?________Her education?________Her age?________

One page of a four-page patterned *interview form prepared by Dr. Robert N. McMurry. A complete set of McMurry-developed personnel selection and appraisal forms with descriptive information is available without charge to business firms from the Dartnell Corporation, Ravenswood and Leland Avenues, Chicago.*

terned interview and has shown that interviewers trained in the use of this kind of interview tend to obtain reliable and valid results. Table 15.2 depicts the relationship between interviewers' initial ratings and those made by foremen one and one-half years later with 407 cases still on the job.

On the basis of three separate studies in the hiring of metal workers, truck drivers, and workers in the needle trades, McMurry concluded that "a properly conducted and evaluated *planned* interview is a statistically reliable selection instrument." He has described the advantages of the patterned interview:

The *patterned* interview endeavors to overcome the weaknesses of the ordinary employment interview in several ways: First, the interviewer works from definite job specifications; he knows what qualities each job requires. Second, he has a plan; he knows what questions to ask. Third, he has been trained in the techniques of conducting an interview—i.e., he knows how to put the candidate at ease, how to make him talk, and how to extract pertinent information. Fourth, prior to the interview, he has checked with outside sources (previous employers, schools, etc.) and already knows a great deal about the applicant. Fifth, he has a series of clinical concepts—e.g., that of emotional immaturity—which provide him with a yardstick for interpreting and evaluating the information obtained from the candidate. Sixth, the interviewer himself has been carefully selected to assure that he has adequate intelligence and is emotionally well-adjusted.

Moreover, it is not necessary that the interviewer be a psychologist or psychiatrist to obtain good results. Actually, if he makes full use of all available techniques for assembling relevant facts about the applicant, in nearly every case the final decision concerning his qualifications can be made on strictly common-sense grounds.[12]

After reviewing research which has been done on the value of the interview for assessing personality and occupational fitness, K. A. Yonge concluded that the most valuable interview is the one which uses a standardized form. The form should be designed to assess complex, dynamic constellations of traits rather than relatively isolated, static traits. If properly used, he states, the interview can play a reliable part in the over-all assessment of an individual's qualities.[13]

In spite of the statistically demonstrated values of the patterned interview, certain critics object to it on the grounds that some interviewers will follow the pattern slavishly and without insight into the dynamics at work in the applicant's personality. This objection is overcome of course when interviewers are properly trained for their work as recommended by McMurry. Properly handled, the patterned interview draws out the applicant's prejudices, motives, drives, and adjustment history more clearly than an unpatterned interview.

4. The Probing Interview

Questions of a probing nature are used by psychologists for two different purposes: as tools in a clinician's attempts to discover the underlying drives in the psychodynamics of the interviewee's personality, and as a kind of performance test in the selection of men in industry. Examples of the first type of probing are the questions: "If a former high school principal were to ask you to address the school's assembly of students, what do you think your subject or topic would be?" and, "When you have children of your own, how do you plan to raise them, in comparison with the way you were reared?" Answers to questions such as these tend to reveal some of the individual's fundamental reactions to his school and home situations.

The second type of probing interview, as practiced in industry, usually involves the asking of related questions that are slanted so as to force the applicant to reveal his attitudes, judgments, and knowledge of procedures as applied to typical job situations.

When the interviewer asks how the applicant's previous supervisors and associates treated him, his main interest is in what the answers reveal about the applicant's adjustment tendencies. The answers enable the interviewer to judge how effectively the person can deal with others in face-to-face situations, as indicated by his speech, mannerisms, persuasiveness, enthusiasm, and so forth. An example of a probing question used in selecting first-line supervisors is:

If you had a worker who wouldn't do something you asked him to do, what would you do?

Probing: *What if he still wouldn't do it? What if he said union rules forbid it?*

Another probing question, used with applicants for selling, is:

Suppose a salesman has a customer who seems interested in buying, who needs the product, but who seems to find it impossible to make up his mind. How should the salesman handle the customer to make a sale?

Probing Question 1. *What if he still wouldn't sign the order?*

Probing Question 2. *What if he said, "Come back next week?"*

Probing Question 3. *What if he said, "I want to think about it some more?"*

When selecting applicants, the interviewer should use the probing interview before he has learned anything about the applicant's background or experience. To avoid bias, the interviewer should not ask questions about the applicant's personal history nor see his application blank previous to the interview. A committee of several interviewers should conduct the interview, and each interviewer should make an independent rating of the applicant. The interview should last at least twenty minutes.[14] Care must be taken to obtain rapport with the applicant, and he should be told that the interview is only part of the selection procedure. The interviewer should note the applicant's emotional reactions as well as the content of his statements.

Inasmuch as the probing interview is still a relatively new technique in industry, reports concerning its validity are not as yet in published form. The interviewers who have used it in selection practice like it because it seems to indicate what the applicant is likely to do in actual work situations. To some extent, it is a kind of performance test that appears to be particularly useful in selecting salesmen and supervisors.

Practices That Improve the Interview

A good interviewer has a plan. He knows, before he talks to the applicant, the kind of information he wants and the methods he intends to use to obtain it. Furthermore, he has in his own mind some basic framework, such as the adjustment concept (Chapters 2 to 6), for interpreting the information that he obtains. He tries to interpret the available facts in terms of the applicant's psychological needs and motivations. He tries to sense the life style.

Ideally, his framework of thinking has been developed from training in the social sciences, particularly psychology. At any rate, he needs a sound background of information about people and their wants. He knows that the psychological needs of applicants must be considered in hiring. Employment men, for example, who interview college graduates are likely to say to those who apply for routine starting jobs: "You wouldn't be happy in this job—the chances for rapid advancement are too poor." On the other hand, the employment man who would like to hire an especially ambitious applicant even though he must start with a routine job of the company may say: "The job that is open is a simple routine one, but it will enable you to get acquainted with our organization. Also, the head of that department is one of our ablest executives—you can learn a great deal from his methods." In the latter instance, the employment man prepares the applicant to develop the desired kinds of perceptions of the job. Satisfaction and dissatisfaction with an occupation depend to some extent on the individual's achievement needs in relation to his perceptions of the occupation's opportunities or limitations to advancement.

The employment interviewer looks for patterns in the educational and work history that indicate psychological strengths and weaknesses. He has developed skill in stimulating the applicant to talk freely. He tends to follow practices such as the following:

1. He puts the applicant at ease in a natural manner. If the applicant has filled in an application blank, the interviewer may use some fact recorded on the blank as the basis for his first comments. Examples are former places of employment or recreational activities. If the applicant is obviously tense as indicated by speech disruptions of nonverbal sounds, mainly laughs and sighs,[15] the interviewer may give him time to pull himself together by picking up the application blank and saying: "Do you mind if I look at this so that I need not ask you questions that you have answered on the application form?

Some interviewers facilitate the applicant's adjustment to the interview by purposely asking a question that makes the applicant feel a bit better informed than the interviewer. An example might be: "I see that you come from Blank City. Several years ago, I spent two days at the main hotel—it had an Irish name. Was it the Hotel Murphy?" When the applicant answers, "You must mean the Casey House, because that's the main hotel there," he is more apt to feel that he has established his adequacy in the interview situation.

2. He asks many open-end questions, especially in the early stages of the interview. Direct questions are avoided. Instead of saying, "What was your job with your last employer?" he may phrase the inquiry in a less directive manner as, "Tell me about your last job and the kind of work you did there." After the applicant has answered the question, the interviewer can elicit further revealing responses by saying, "Tell me, how did you feel about that job?" "Of course, you have also applied for work with some other companies. That is only natural—I'd do the same thing. Tell me about some of them, particularly your reasons for applying to them." Answers to this question usually indicate the applicant's objectives: search for personal growth, security, work near his home, or use of a random job-shopping procedure.

3. When open-end questions have not revealed a clear picture of the applicant's work record, the interviewer asks questions of a specific nature, such as, "In your job with the XYZ Company, just exactly what did you do? Please tell me in detail."

4. When the applicant stops talking, the interviewer asks exploratory questions that keep the conversation moving in the direction desired by the interviewer. Examples are: "Of all the jobs you have held, in what ways did any of them give you chances to develop your abilities?"; "Compare the last two jobs that you had. Tell me some of the things you liked better about the one than about the other"; and "In what ways do you think that you bettered yourself when you changed some of your jobs in the past?"

5. The good interviewer avoids or has few questions of the following kinds:

a. Questions that can be answered with an unqualified "Yes" or "No."

b. Questions that invariably elicit the same answer from all applicants. Example: "Do you drink liquor to excess?"

c. Trick questions that compel the applicant to defend a former statement or admit an error in an earlier statement.

d. Leading questions, such as: "You finished high school, I assume?"; "Did you make good grades in college?"; "Would you be willing to work in an office where most employees are much older than you are?"; "Were you an accountant or a bookkeeper on your last job?"; and, "Don't you agree that the job I described would be very interesting?"

6. The good interviewer carries on a conversation which results in true exchanges of ideas on the part of both the interviewer and the applicant. He does not dominate the applicant but encourages him to describe his actual feelings, preferences, hopes, abilities, and inabilities. This kind of exchanging of ideas means that the interviewer's statements consume less than 50 per cent of the interviewing time, preferably less than 25 per cent. The amount of time that the interviewer talks appears to be directly related to his decision to accept the applicant.[16]

7. The good interviewer evaluates his own techniques by means of moving picture and sound recordings of some of his interviews. These objective records enable him to observe his characteristic mannerisms. He can note whether or not his facial expression is friendly, his tone of voice encouraging, and his manner one that gives the applicant a favorable impression of the company. Furthermore, the recordings will give him evidence as to whether he spends too much time talking to the applicant or in inducing the applicant to do most of the talking. Is he stimulating applicants to express themselves so that their abilities can be judged accurately, or is he merely delivering unimpressive monologues to strangers?

8. The good interviewer recognizes that the employment interview has two major divisions or phases: the appraisal of the applicant before accepting him for employment; and, if the applicant is hired, the accepting phase.

In the appraisal or sizing-up phase, the interviewer controls the situation in a manner which causes the applicant to realize fully that he is being appraised rather than hired. The careless interviewer is apt to allow the applicant to assume that he is being hired by an overly friendly manner or by the way he asks the applicant to take various tests or questions him about the amount of pay he would expect if hired. As a result, the applicant gets an emotional jolt when he discovers that he has not been hired.

The good interviewer, on the other hand, keeps the applicant subtly aware of the fact that he is still being appraised and that no decision about his employment has as yet been reached.

Once the decision has been made to accept the applicant for employment, the interviewer begins the induction of the new employee into the company. The applicant is made clearly aware that his status has changed from that of applicant to new employee. At the same time, the interviewer gives the applicant ample information about the company and the job, thus enabling him to make his decision to work there more definite, or, as happens in some cases, to come to the conclusion that he does not want the job after all.

9. The good interviewer is a member of the management team. He not only selects employees who fit well into the organization but also prepares the new employee for the kinds of personalities whom he will meet. When, for example, the interviewer knows that the new employee's supervisor has a brusque hard-boiled manner, he explains the supervisor's personality characteristics so that the new employee can adapt himself to his new boss with understanding and develop respect for whatever admirable qualities the supervisor may have.

In reviewing the interview, we can conclude that few interviewers have developed the art of interviewing to the extent that it deserves. Anyone who studies interviewing practices is likely to conclude that modern industry has been productive in spite of rather than because of its employment procedures. Many applicants who have been hired by the present inadequate methods and become productive workers do so because most human beings are adaptable; not because they have been well chosen for their tasks. Futhermore, even though some statistical studies of interviewing have indicated that improved techniques, such as the standardized and probing interview, are better than unguided procedures, a selective interview of some kind is better than none at all, as proved by a study at the Aircraft Warning Unit Training Center at Drew Field, Florida.[17] About one fourth of the men assigned to this school were chosen at random to fill quotas. Thereafter, a four-week study was made to compare the success of these men with those selected by the classification interviewers. It was found that only 29 per cent of those selected at random completed the course, while 84 per cent of those selected by interview completed the courses successfully.

Letters of Application

Our discussion of interviewing would be incomplete without some mention of the letter of application. Carefully conducted investigations show that the letter of application cannot be judged with any great degree of accuracy. If, for example, thirteen experienced employment men are asked to rank several letters of application, the letter that stands at the head of the list of one interviewer is at the bottom of the list of another. No executive has the right to assume that he can pick the wheat from the tares in letters of application. He can eliminate some of the decidedly unfit, but when he rates the remainder he is apt to commit serious errors.

Eight letters of application were received in answer to the following advertisement:

"Required, Secretary to Employment Manager of Large Factory. Apply, stating particulars, to Box ———."

These letters were ranked in order by thirteen experienced employment managers, none of whom knew any of the applicants personally. Half the applicants (four out of the eight) were ranked at both the top and the bottom, that is, first and eighth.

When a company advertises for applicants, no single executive should eliminate and rate the letters of application. A group of executives or other raters should select the letters whose writers are to be investigated further.

The *weighted application blank* has been developed for the selection of salesmen, and office employees, but for few others. The procedure for adapting the application blank to improved salesman selection is as follows: A group of at least one hundred salesmen are divided into sub-groups such as good, average, and poor, on the basis of such factors as their sales records and supervisor's opinion. Each man's background then is analyzed by examining personnel records or by interview. The purpose is to ascertain certain facts, such as age, height, occupation, dependents, and so forth, and whether or not any particular fact or facts are significant characteristics of any particular sub-group of men. It may be found, for example, that height is positively correlated with volume of sales.

The significant items, those that distinguish potentially successful men from potentially unsuccessful men, are put on a weighted personal history blank. Usually such blanks have only from ten to fifteen items.[18]

As in most weighted personal history forms, a man's score is obtained by adding the weights of the various items. If the total does not amount to the minimum score decided upon as the criterion, the man is eliminated from further consideration unless there are special extenuating factors.

Before adopting a weighted personal history blank for use in selecting employees, a company should realize that a formula that has given good results to one company will not necessarily give good results to another. Each company has its own problems, and items that distinguish potentially good employees for one company may be valueless criteria for another. It is for this reason that every company must develop its own weighted blank. Furthermore, the weights assigned to application blank responses should be reviewed every 3–5 years.[19]

Interview information that is based only on "face validity," that is, rapport between interviewer and interviewee should be verified. Relative levels of invalidity of interview data are related to pressures of social desirability and ego involvement. Purportedly factual data of importance should be checked.[20]

Many interviewers who do not have a weighted application blank do have in mind certain "knock-out" factors such as a history of personality difficulties, job-hopping, previous income too high, earnings less than living expenses, and divorce within the past two years.[21]

Several researchers of the Industrial Relations Center, University of Minnesota, made a study of the validity of work histories obtained by interview. The work histories that had been obtained by means of structured interviews with 325 individuals were checked with former employers. Of eleven work history items studied, only three items showed validity of more than 70 per cent and on four items, 40 per cent or more of the interview information was *in*valid. The most valid information was reported for separation and hours, the least valid for pay items. The upgrading type of error occurred more often than the downgrading type. "Social desirability" appeared to be an important influence in the distortions.[22] These and other findings indicate the need for verifying the information obtained by interview only.

Many companies check interview information by telephoning to employers. Companies who use this plan believe that telephoning is better than writing a letter for the reasons:

(1) It is faster. The average time required to check two references by telephone is 12 minutes. The correspondence method requires from three days to months.

(2) Response is more certain. Almost one-quarter of the mail inquries are not answered. Almost everyone will answer questions asked by telephone.

(3) The man who is on the hiring side can modify his questions and ask them more freely in order to get the facts he needs.

(4) The former employer feels that he can act naturally and spontaneously. He will

speak more frankly about former employees on the telephone than he would in a written letter.

(5) Telephoning saves money. The direct cost of securing references by mail, when combined with the money lost in hiring people who later are found to have poor references, is greater than the cost of telephoning for reference checks. This is true in spite of the additional telephone expenses.

One industrial concern found that even though an extra employee has to be hired for the job, checking applicants' references by telephone is cheaper in the long run than using a mailed check list form.

One sales manager who hires salesmen in all parts of the country telegraphs his requests for information from former employers who are given as references by applicants. He has found that he must demand about eight references and follow up each reference very carefully if he wishes to avoid hiring men with bad records. On one occasion he sent telegrams to eight references regarding an applicant whom he wished to hire. Two of the references did not reply at all, but telegrams from four were as follows:

"Glad to hear Walter K. has applied to you for a position. I can recommend him highly as regards honesty and workmanship. He is 100%. Has worked for me 3 years."

"Walter K. was with us for two months. Character and dependability very good. Would recommend."

"While Walter K. was with us he was very satisfactory."

"I recommend Mr. K. very highly in every respect."

These telegrams from the references were quite satisfying to the employment man and he was about to hire the applicant when he received a long-distance telephone call from one of the former employers. The former employer described Walter's conduct with his firm and told how he had failed even to attempt to do the work for which he was hired, had led an immoral life, owed the company money, borrowed money from customers, and had been discharged for incompetency. A few hours later, another former employer telephoned the employment man and gave a similar report of gross misconduct. These executives refused to put their reports in writing, but used the telephone in an honest effort to save time and money for a prospective employer. This employment man frequently requests former employers to telephone him at his expense if they prefer to do so rather than write or telegraph him. He claims that he has saved his company thousands of dollars by asking for telephone answers, because former employers will give more honest reports in oral than in written form.

Most executives write a general letter to a person given as reference, and the person answering usually gives a general reply, selecting those good points in the applicant's history that may be stressed without harming his chances for another job. A slightly better method is to use a special report form that asks for information on specific points, as:

1. Was the applicant discharged by you, let go because of decrease in work, or did he leave of his own accord?
2. Does he owe you any money now? *No. Yes.*
3. Would you rehire him if you needed a person for a vacancy that he had the ability to fill? *No. Yes. Possibly.*
4. How long did he work for you?
5. What date (month and year) did he leave your employ?
6. He states that his salary or income from you was...per month. Is this correct? *Yes. No.*
7. Did he use alcohol to any extent? *Yes. No.*
8. How do you rate his moral conduct? *Very good. Satisfactory. Questionable.*
9. Do you think that he possesses the ability to fill a job with us which is .... *Yes. No. Don't know.*
10. How would you rate his record with your firm?
    a. Very satisfactory.
    b. Satisfactory.
    c. Fair.
    d. Questionable.
    e. Unsatisfactory.

These questions should be made part of a two-page letter to the previous employer, the first page giving the name of the former employee and assuring the answerer that his report will be kept confidential. The questions and answers suggested may be varied, but they should deal with objective factors rather than ask for opinions. The possible answers should be suggested on the form so that the correct answer can be checked by the writer or written with a minimum of effort. This type of letter to a reference does not allow the previous employer to select the pleasant parts in the former employee's record and ignore the bad parts. Such forms have been used by a few progressive firms, but many employment men still accept a general letter of reply from persons given as references. They assume that, when an applicant has a bad record, the person answering will phrase his letter so that it is possible "to read between the lines" and grasp the real story. Discernment in reading between the lines can be developed through experience.[23]

When letters are addressed to former employers of an applicant, they should be addressed to the "Employment Manager" rather than to individuals within the company. Some applicants who do not wish their real record to be revealed to prospective employers often give the name of a friend in the company as a reference. This friend is usually a person of no responsibility and his statement has no weight as a reference for a discharged employee.

Summary

The hiring of employees is still mostly in the hands of the empiricists of business. The old rules-of-thumb and prejudice prevail. A few progressive concerns have made statistical studies of the factors which correlate highly with successful employment records. Some have improved their hiring procedures through more systematic interviewing and the use of psychological tests to eliminate the unfit and to reduce labor turnover, but such modern aids are likely to be found in the larger and better-managed employment offices where trained experts are in charge of hiring. However, any executive or employment manager who wishes to improve his hiring techniques can do so by standardizing his procedure, keeping records of his findings, and then making statistical studies of his records. He can at least use several interviewers rather than depend upon the evaluations made by any one man. Such attempts will yield results more valuable than those of the present haphazard treatment of the interview, letter of application, and letter of recommendation.

When employment procedures are biased or faulty, labor turnover costs increase. Estimates of these costs vary considerably. One researcher estimated that every time an executive says "Good-bye" to an employee who quits, the cost to the average company is $482. The costs for hiring and training a new salesman in one industry were estimated as $7,000–$8,000 and above $10,000 for engineers and scientists.[24] These figures do not include the additional costs of lost production but the costs are so great that modern managements have become increasingly concerned about their hiring procedures.

ACKNOWLEDGMENTS AND REFERENCES

1. This appeared in the 1946 annual report, but the same managerial recognition was stated by John F. Gordon, President, General Motors Corp., in 1959: "There is only one thing one company can have that others cannot duplicate, and that's people. People are what make the difference between one company and another." See *Dun's Review and Modern Industry,* October, 1959, p. 33.
2. H. L. Hollingworth, *Judging Human Character* (New York: Appleton-Century-Crofts, 1923), p. 268.
3. Walter Dill Scott, "The Scientific Selection of Salesmen," *Advertising and Selling,* **25** (1915), 5–6, 94f.
4. Richard Stephen Uhrbrock, "The Personnel Interview," *Personnel Psychology,* **1,** No. 3 (1948), 274. The two sets of questions for interviewing recent college graduates, quoted under "the area interview," are from this article, p. 286.
5. S. A. Rice, "Contagious Bias in the Interview," *American Journal of Sociology,* **53** (1929), 420–423.
6. G. R. Thornton, "Effects of Wearing Glasses

Upon Judgments of Traits," *Journal of Applied Psychology,* **28,** No. 3 (1944), 207.
7. *Manual of Employment Interviewing,* Research Report Number Nine, American Management Association, Inc., New York, 1946.
8. Carl Iver Hovland and E. F. Wonderlic, "Prediction of Industrial Success from a Standardized Interview," *Journal of Applied Psychology,* **23,** No. 5 (1939), 537–546.
9. Carroll Leonard Shartle, "A Clinical Approach to Foremanship," *Personnel Journal,* **13,** No. 3 (1934), 137. See also Ralph F. Berdie, "Psychological Processes in the Interview," *The Journal of Social Psychology,* **18** (1943), 28.
10. See "8 Steps to Staff Selection," *Scope,* November, 1958.
11. Carl Iver Hovland and E. F. Wonderlic, "Prediction of Industrial Success from a Standardized Interview," *Journal of Applied Psychology,* **23,** No. 5 (1939).
12. Robert N. McMurry, "Validating the Patterned Interview," *Personnel,* American Management Association, Inc., January, 1947.
13. K. A. Yonge, "The Value of the Interview: An Orientation and Pilot Study," *Journal of Applied Psychology,* February, 1956, pp. 25–31.
14. The examples and instructions for the probing interview were obtained from Richardson, Bellows, Henry & Co., Inc., and Jay L. Otis.
15. Merton S. Krause and Marc Pilisuk, "Anxiety in Verbal Behavior," *Journal of Consulting Psychology,* October, 1961.
16. C. W. Anderson, "The Relation Between Speaking Times and Decision in the Employment Interview," *Journal of Applied Psychology,* **44** (1960), 267–268.
17. Richard W. Putney, "Validity of the Placement Interview," *Personnel Journal,* **26** (1947), 144–145.
18. Wayne K. Kirchner and Marvin D. Dunnette "Applying the Weighted Application Blank to a Variety of Office Jobs," *Journal of Applied Psychology,* **41** (1957), 206–208.
19. Paul F. Wernimont, "Re-Evaluation of a Weighted Application Blank for Office Personnel," *Journal of Applied Psychology,* December, 1962.
20. David J. Weiss and Rene V. Dawis, "An Objective Evaluation of Factual Interview Data," *Journal of Applied Psychology,* December, 1960.
21. Thomas W. Harrell, "The Validity of Biographical Data Items for Food Company Salesmen," *Journal of Applied Psychology,* February, 1960.
22. David J. Weiss, Rene V. Dawis, George W. England, and Lloyd H. Lofquist, *Validity of Work Histories Obtained by Interview,* Minnesota Studies in Vocational Rehabilitation: XII, Industrial Relations Center, University of Minnesota, 1961, pp. 1–2.
23. Rawle Deland, "Executive Job References: How to Read Between the Lines," *The Management Review,* American Management Association, Inc., July, 1960.
24. Frederick J. Gaudet, "Manpower Wastage," *Mechanical Engineering,* July, 1963.

PROJECTS

1. Collect some letters of application. Ask friends or executives to rank them in the order of estimated desirability of the applicants. Discuss the differences in the rankings.
2. Make a list of some of your own tendencies toward bias in interviewing. What means might you use to overcome such tendencies?
3. Assume that you are about to establish a small manufacturing enterprise employing between 50 and 100 persons. Outline your plans for:
   a. Selecting the women you wish to hire.
   b. Making special provision in the plant and working schedule for the women.
4. Read material concerning lie detectors and evaluate their usefulness and limitations. List other methods you have heard of for telling when a person is lying.
5. Write a *Help Wanted* advertisement to obtain women factory employees and a similar one for male employees. How do they differ?
6. Find pictures of several famous persons of whom you have heard but whose physical features you have not seen. In which cases were you disappointed by the pictures and in which were you pleased? Give possible reasons for your reaction in each case.
7. Collect handwriting specimens of persons whom you know. Analyze the writing according to the system of analysis presented in a book on graphology. Estimate the value of the system.

COLLATERAL READINGS

Bellows, Roger M., *Psychology of Personnel in Business and Industry.* Englewood Cliffs, N.J.: Prentice-Hall, Inc., 1954, Chapters 10–12.

Dictionary of Occupational Titles. United States Employment Service, Washington, D.C. Ask for latest edition and companion volumes.

Fleishman, Edwin A., "One Way to Reduce Office Turnover," *Personnel,* American Management Association, Inc., May–June, 1960.

Fleishman, Edwin A., ed., *Studies in Personnel and Industrial Psychology.* Homewood, Ill.:

The Dorsey Press, Inc., 1961, Chapters 1–3.

Gilmer, B. von Haller, ed., *Industrial Psychology*. New York: McGraw-Hill Book Company, 1961, Chapter 6.

Harrell, Thomas Willard, *Industrial Psychology*. New York: Holt, Rinehart and Winston, Inc., 1958, Chapters 2–4.

Husband, Richard W., *Applied Psychology*. New York: Harper & Row, Publishers, Inc., 1949, Chapter 10.

Smith, Henry Clay, *Psychology of Industrial Behavior*. New York: McGraw-Hill Book Company, 1955, Chapter 15.

The Logical Analysis Device *is used to test problem-solving ability. The Psychological Corporation has developed standardized procedures for using LAD for selection and assignment of personnel and for applied research in the best placement of highly trained and talented people.*

The LAD problems are unambiguous examples of a completely defined logical system. They closely parallel the diagnostic or trouble-shooting situation. No specialized experience or knowledge is required.

The logical complexity of the LAD problems can be quickly changed. By presenting a series of increasing difficulty, it is possible to measure an individual's ability in organizing complex information and to observe his directness of attack, speed of work, recognition of logically useful information, activity when frustrated by an error, and other elements of behavior associated with problem-solving.

A paper read by Dr. William E. Kendall to the XIV International Congress of Applied Psychology, Copenhagen, Denmark, August 1961 (Charles R. Langmuir and William E. Kendall, "A Logical Machine for Measuring Problem-Solving Ability," New York: The Psychological Corporation), reported "the use of LAD as a device in the selection of computer programmers because the magnitude of costs incurred by assigning unsuccessful or even marginal personnel to tasks involving Electronic Data Processing Systems design and programming, justifies a much greater effort in the selection of personnel than the use of conventional aptitude tests implies. . . ."

"Conventional tests have proved adequate for the initial elimination of candidates. They can be economically used for screening among many applicants to eliminate those who are inadequate in verbal or numerical reasoning abilities, and probably to identify individuals whose verbal ability reaches a high level but who have difficulty dealing with abstract content or representations of a non-verbal character. There, is, however, abundant evidence that such screening tests are not sufficient. Many individuals score above whatever cut-off point we may choose but still lack some crucial abilities required for successful work in programming. . . ."

The paper reported findings from a study of the value of LAD in the selection of computer programmers and concluded: "From the evidence so far accumulated . . . the effort involved in using the LAD procedure results in a significant economic pay-off."

CHAPTER SIXTEEN

HIRING THE EMPLOYEE —THE USE OF TESTS

When psychological tests are used in an employment office, they should always be looked upon as supplementing—not replacing—other methods that are in use. No psychologist who has thought at all about the problems of modern industry would seriously suggest that present employment procedures should be eliminated. . . . But the fact that these methods, though excellent in many respects, are still not perfect is proved by the marked individual differences among employees which any study of differential production will reveal. A considerable amount of research, both in industry and in the laboratory, has shown that still further improvements in employment methods can be attained when psychological tests and methods are used as supplements to other employment procedures.[1]

Companies that wish to improve their hiring procedures often turn to psychological tests as instruments of prediction. A psychological test does not evaluate all of the person's ability, but merely tests parts, samples, or symptoms of ability. The psychological test is very similar in nature to the tests made by the assayer of minerals. If a man wished to purchase a vein of silver ore, he would first obtain samples of it and have these analyzed by some competent chemist. On the basis of the samples, he would decide upon the value of the ore and the price he would be willing to pay for it. Obviously he could not test all the mineral in the vein of ore. Similarly, the psychologist tests samples of a person's abilities rather than all of them.

Psychological tests and aptitude tests are terms often used loosely by modern businessmen and even by scientists. In many cases, a businessman thinks he is using psychological or intelligence tests when actually he is merely asking a number of random questions. For example: a businessman may find that he needs a new secretary. Accordingly, he advertises in the usual manner; when he arrives at his office the next morning he may find an applicant there. He then opens his morning mail, chatting with her while he takes a casual glance at the letters which await his attention. Then, deciding that it would be well for him to "test" the applicant, he picks up one of the letters which he must answer and dictates a reply. The applicant types the letter and gives it back to him; he examines it for errors and appearance. He then dismisses the first applicant and awaits the coming of the second one, at which time he answers another letter—an entirely different one. In this manner, he "tests" five applicants, after which he makes his decision. He thinks he had given each one of the applicants a psychological test. As a matter of fact, he has not done so at all. If he were to develop a psychological test for the hiring of stenographers, certain factors would have to be standardized for all applicants, namely:

1. *Materials.* The same letter and appliances must be used for each person.

2. *Instructions.* Each applicant must receive the same instructions regarding speed and accuracy. Instructions should be read.

3. *Technique.* The speed of dictation, enunciation, and so forth must be kept the same.

4. *Conditions.* Distractions should vary as little as possible.

5. *Interpretation of score.* The score of each applicant must be compared with scores of other stenographers of high, medium, and low ability.

Any test, to be of value, must fulfill three requirements: it must be *objective,* so that personal opinion is held to a minimum in the scoring; it must be *valid,* that is, it must test the trait that it is supposed to test; and it must be *reliable,* that is, it must give the same results on repetition, regardless of the particular individual who administers the test. Many of the tests that are published in magazines do not fulfill these three requirements. Such tests are still in the experimental state. They may have promise of future results, but they should not be used as a basis for hiring until their predictive value has been statistically determined.

A psychological test is any problem or series of questions that has been tried out on persons who possess a known degree of the trait being tested. It has been shown that the test scores made by these persons are stable and correlate with their records in that trait. Therefore, one of the chief requirements for preparing psychological tests is that of statistical training.

Many businessmen and scientists have been using tests for many years, but the terminology is not very well standardized. The various terms used to describe tests are: intelligence, aptitude, efficiency, mental alertness, information, specific ability, performance, mental, job, trade, and army tests. These terms usually refer to diverse kinds of tests.

Kinds of Tests Used in Employment

One helpful way to classify tests is to think of them in regard to what they are supposed to measure: (1) *Intelligence, mental alertness,* or *scholastic aptitude* tests are designed to measure a person's ability to deal with abstract relationships, sometimes referred to as the ability to do "mental gymnastics." As mentioned before, a good definition of intelligence is "The degree of availability of one's experiences for the solution of immediate problems and the anticipation of future ones." (2) *Aptitude* tests are tests concerned with the capacity to acquire certain specified knowledge or skills, such as stenography, salesmanship, chemical engineering, or some limited aspect of these or other occupations. Some users of the term assume that it embraces intelligence, personality, and interests, because these must also be included in the prediction of potentiality for learning skills and acquiring knowledge.[2] (3) *Proficiency* or achievement tests intend to measure actual ability to do certain kinds of work or to perform specified skills such as typing, comptometry, grammar, or carpentry. When these tests are applied to the work of the artisan they are also called "trade tests." (4) *Vocational interests* are exemplified by the E. K. Strong test. (See Chapter Eleven.) (5) *Personality* or temperament tests usually refer to adjustment tendencies that more or less characterize the individual's behavior, as exemplified by terms such as introversion, sociability, and emotional stability. Temperament refers

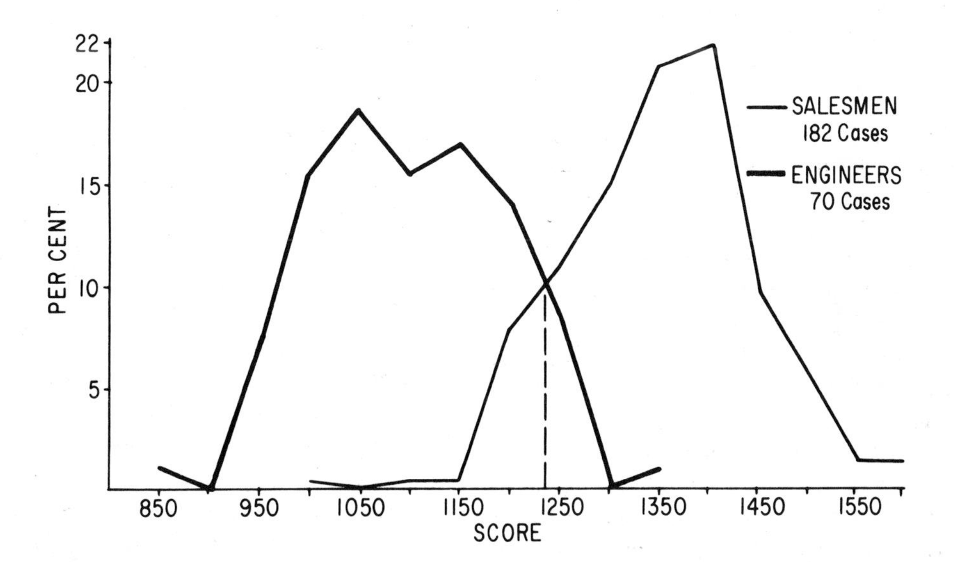

Salesmen differ from engineers. *The scores on the base line represent a combination consisting of measures of interest in advertising, attitude toward sales work, knowledge of selling methods, accuracy, aggressiveness, confidence, emotional stability and liveliness of disposition.*

Edwin G. Flemming, of the Burton Bigelow Organization, Management Consultants of New York City, uses a battery of eight tests in his service designed to aid executives in the selection of salesmen, sales managers, and other executives. When he compared the test data obtained from batteries or sets of tests answered by applicants for jobs as salesmen with that from engineer applicants, he found significant differences between the test scores of the two groups.

After appropriate statistical treatments were given the test data, the average score for engineers was found to be 1125; for salesmen, 1376.—The data showed that salesmen and engineers are distinctly different, not only in the pattern of their major interests, but also in their accuracy, their knowledge, their attitude toward their work, and their personalities.

Dr. Flemming's experience with the practical problem of selecting salesmen for many employers of all sizes in many different kinds of selling operations indicates that sales engineers—those salesmen who must have a technical training in engineering, but whose primary job is to sell—are likely to be found in the area of overlapping of the two curves in the chart, between the scores of 1150 and 1300.—***Chart and data by Edwin G. Flemming, Director, Division for Sales Personnel Selection, Burton Bigelow Organization, New York.***

to one's tendency to act in certain characteristic ways, not at any one instant but over a long period of time.

Stages in the Development of Testing in Industry

The history of testing for the appraisal of job applicants and employees has had three overlapping stages:

1. *Single tests,* such as those for the measuring of intelligence, proficiency, and personality. Thousands of tests, of varying validity, have been published and used. Examples of single tests may be found in the appendix of this book.

2. *The battery of tests* with a profile of test scores. This procedure, developed by psychologists in recent years, means that a number of single tests are administered as a battery. A single test usually measures but a limited facet of the individual's psychological make-up. Under the battery method, the scores of several standard tests, given one

SUCCESSFUL VS. UNSUCCESSFUL SALES MANAGERS

Direct to the Consumer

These curves show the differences between successful and unsuccessful district and branch managers in direct-to-the-consumer selling operations. The heavy perpendicular line represents the median score made by 1040 salesmen.

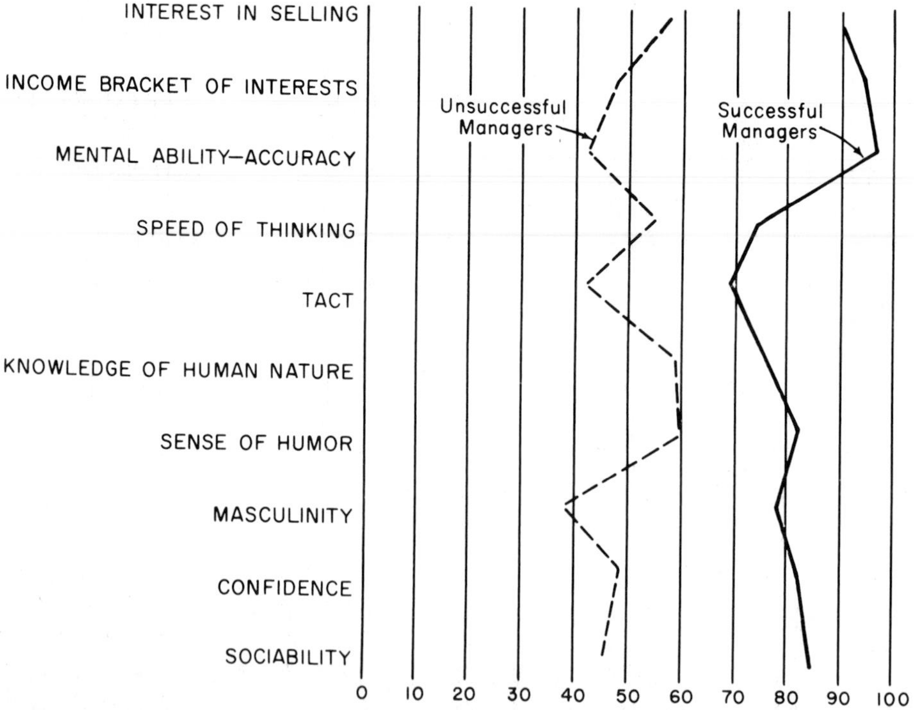

*"**Criticism has sometimes been leveled** at the use of psychological tests in selection because investigators have found no very high correlations between scores on single tests and criteria of success in selling. It is true that very significant correlations seldom are found for single tests, but it needs to be pointed out and emphasized that a score on any one test is not necessarily critically significant in determining a man's potentialities for success in selling. The important thing is the pattern of scores revealed by a battery of tests. No one score may be critically important, but the pattern is. By a pattern we mean the interrelationships of scores and the relative strengths and weaknesses of the traits, interests, and tendencies revealed by the complete battery of tests."—From Edwin G. Flemming and Cecile White Flemming, "Test-Selected Salesmen," **Journal of Marketing,** April 1946. Chart is not included in this article, but was prepared by Edwin G. Flemming for use in this book.*

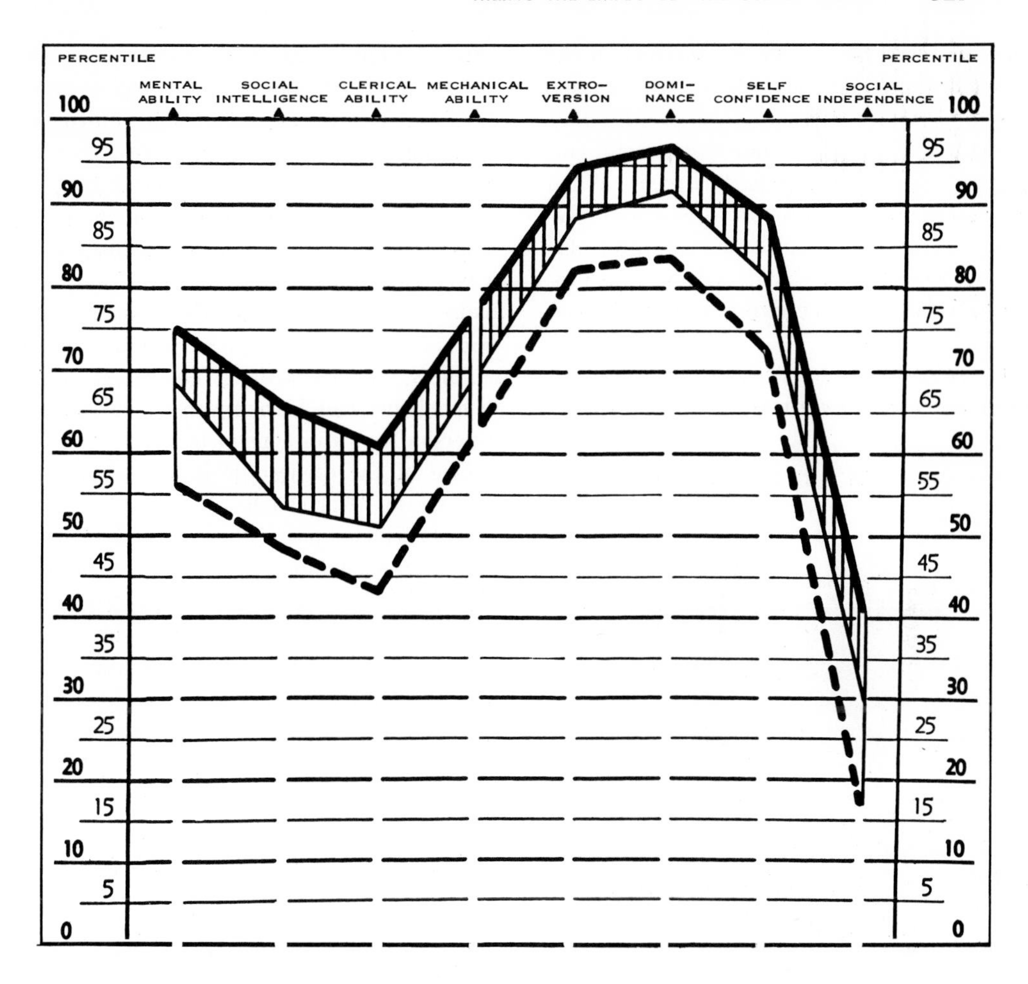

PATTERN SALES PROFILE BASED ON 400 SPECIALTY FOOD SALESMEN.

Shaded area—*above-average hiring area.*
Line *separating shaded from unshaded areas—median scores.*
Unshaded area—*acceptable hiring area within average range.*

The entire profile represents the inter-quartile range or the middle 50 per cent of those employees who were considered above average. This technique was used to eliminate the atypical cases who are unusually high on one hand or unusually low, thus making the profile more indicative of a homogeneous above-average group.—When applicants are plentiful, the shaded area is used. It is also used for upgrading. When applicants are few, the entire pattern, including the unshaded area, may be used.

The criteria used to determine the above-average individuals were above-average production on the job and managers' ratings. Four or five managers' ratings were available for every individual. These ratings pertain to more intangible personal characteristics, which very often are not revealed in production figures themselves or sales volumes, as the case may be, and include such factors as loyalty to the company, willingness to follow managerial policies, stability, willingness to work, planning, personal appearance, etc.

The success of this method in application has been substantiated in one company by the fact that throughout six years of conscientious and controlled application it was possible to reduce the turnover in the sales field from 13 to 1 to 5 to 1. It costs the company around $ 2,500 to hire and train a salesman over a six-months period. On a yearly basis, the reduction in turnover has saved the company approximately $ 150,000. Of course there are other intangible benefits, such as increased versatility in the new men who are now hired as compared to the old type.—Chart and data by Richard S. Solomon, Consulting Psychologist, Dayton, Ohio.

individual, are plotted on graph paper in the form of a profile. This test profile is then compared with the master test profiles that are typical of successful and unsuccessful employees. See figures on preceding pages. When this procedure is used by an experienced psychologist, the psychologist may interpret also the profile for management, writing a one-to-five page report on the significance of the test findings.

3. *Projective tests.* These tests are called projective because through them the person being analyzed tends to project his own unacknowledged motives and traits into a response to a vague and undefined situation. The Thematic Apperception Test, for example, consists of a series of standard pictures, most of which contain human figures. The person being studied is told to make up a story about each picture. When the person makes up the stories, he also reveals important attitudes, feelings, tendencies, strivings, conflicts, and frustrations. The expert clinical psychologist can learn much of value about a person from this type of test.

One of the earliest projective tests is the well-known Rorschach or ink-blot visual stimulus technique. Other examples of the projective technique are those of finger-painting, word association, and the psychodrama.[3]

The projective techniques have been given considerable publicity in business recently as a result of the work done by several personnel researchers, particularly Dr. Burleigh Gardner and his associates in Social Research, Inc., a consulting service of Chicago.

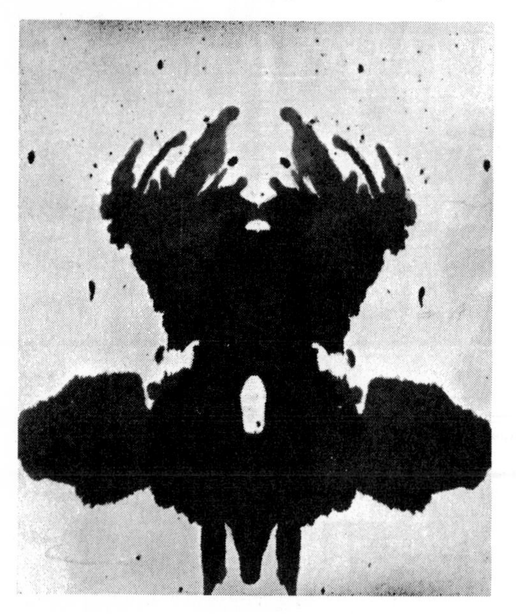

Two examples of response cards for projective techniques. *The ink blot has no meaning in its own right, but it is thought to induce responses that enable the clinical expert to make deductions concerning the subject's imaginative processes and gain clues to the individual's personality. Scoring of responses includes not only response-content, but also such factors as size of area responded to, movement, detection of shading, and others.*

For the second picture *(photograph, Museum of Modern Art, New York) the subject is asked to tell a dramatic story. It is thought that even though he may not be aware of it, he endows the story with needs and stresses that he experiences at the time. From expressions of needs and stresses, generalizations are made about his behavior patterns.—Projective techniques are used in clinical practice and offer one way of getting at the individual's hidden or non-conscious behavior dynamics. The subject has little or no control over his responses. However, much basic research in this area is needed before these techniques can be fully trusted. (Painting shown is "Landscape," a watercolor by Kasimir Malevich.)*

A technique employed by these scientists consisted of a short, nondirective interview, a special analysis by means of several traditional personality tests, and the Thematic Apperception Test, developed by H. A. Murray and associates of Harvard University. Use of the TAT test requires interpretation by experts. As a result of a program of testing executives with this type of test, Gardner and his associates found that the following list of characteristics is typically possessed by a good executive:[4]

1. He must accomplish and achieve in order to be happy.
2. He accepts authority.
3. He has a strong drive toward achievement, material rewards, and prestige.
4. He is able to bring order out of chaos.
5. He is decisive—but he doesn't necessarily have to make snap decisions.
6. He is sure of his convictions and decisions.
7. He has a constant drive to be moving and doing.
8. He may have a pervasive fear of failure —a lingering doubt of his ability to do as good a job as he wants to do.
9. He has a strong sense of reality.
10. He identifies himself more with his superiors than with subordinates. His superiors represent a symbol of his own achievement.
11. He feels and acts on his own. "In a sense, a successful executive is a man who has left home."

On the other hand, an unsuccessful executive is likely to have these traits:

1. He cannot grasp the over-all picture, cannot see the forest for the trees.
2. He fails to carry his load of responsibilities.
3. He has an unconscious desire to be something else.
4. He has an unconscious desire to be someone else.
5. He is unable to cooperate with his associates.
6. He is so ambitious that he is impatient with and intolerant of routine tasks.
7. He cannot accept supervision from his bosses.
8. He is arrogant with his subordinates.
9. He may have a deep-rooted, fixed idea that hobbles him in dealing with his duties. He may, for example, suspect that some colleague is out to "knife" him, or that his background is not adequate.
10. He may keep his nose too close to the grindstone. Overemphasis on work often results in breakdowns. A successful executive must have outside interests and relaxations to sustain his energy, balance his activities.
11. He may, through some quirk of a youthful background, be subconsciously bent on self-destruction.
12. He may have some mental disorders that only a psychologist can pry out.

Obviously, the work of the projective technique users is very technical. Few companies can afford to hire the services of experts of this order. Furthermore, the use of projective techniques in industry should still be regarded as experimental. In some studies, their use failed to discriminate accurately between good and poor performers.

Extent to Which Tests Are Used in Industry

Most employers who do testing limit their testing programs to the use of several single tests or, at most, to batteries that have been found helpful in hiring applicants for certain occupations. Several investigators have made surveys at irregular intervals by means of mailed questionnaires to learn the extent to which companies use tests for selection.

These surveys are usually limited to companies that have well developed personnel policies,[5] are large concerns, or are members of specific industry classifications. The surveys do, however, indicate trends. Generally, the use of tests for hiring is on the increase for clerical and sales positions. Mental (intelligence) tests are being used increasingly but trade, dexterity, and performance tests are used decreasingly. Even though less than one-half of the country's employers are using tests in hiring, their use has increased as indicated by surveys and the sales of test publishers. A list of test publishers and their addresses is given in the references for this chapter.[6]

The United States Employment Service developed norms for occupational aptitude tests and trade tests. The aptitude test batteries are of two kinds: the General Aptitude Test Battery and specific aptitude test batteries. The General Aptitude Test Battery has norms in terms of 35 occupational aptitude patterns covering over 800 occupations. Since not every different occupation requires a completely different set of aptitudes and abilities, those occupations requiring similar abilities are grouped together into a family of occupations requiring the same pattern of abilities. Each occupational aptitude pattern is expressed in terms of the three key aptitudes required for the performance of the jobs within the family and the minimum qualifying scores required for each aptitude. In counseling an applicant, it is possible to determine his aptitudes for many different occupations on the basis of relatively few tests.

Specific aptitude test batteries consisting of tests from the USES General Aptitude Test battery are used in the selection of applicants for specific jobs. In some instances, training time of new employees has been reduced by a third or even a half by using these tests to select the right man for the right job. In almost 1500 local offices of the State Employment Services throughout the United States at which testing is done, employers can request the local office to administer specific tests that have been developed for a particular occupation and to refer test-selected applicants for specific job openings. This service is free to both the employer and the applicant. Inquiry at the local office will reveal the testing services available.

Even though much research must still be done in this kind of testing, the employment interviewer should become acquainted with these tests.

Personality Tests in Industry

The employment interviewer should become acquainted with this field of human analysis. The chapters on adjustment (Two to Six) present a general background for this type of testing and interview.

One study of the Guilford-Martin Personnel Inventory indicated that the test classified as having "undesirable temperament" 82 per cent of the workers who had, in management's opinion, demonstrated that they were troublemakers and soreheads. However, also in the group whose scores indicated that they had "undesirable temperaments" were 38 per cent of the workers whom management had labeled satisfactory.[7]

Dr. Joseph E. King and his associates, Industrial Psychology, Inc., have developed batteries of tests for hiring clerical, mechanical, sales, technical, and supervisory personnel. One test, called Neurotic Personality Factor, was designed to spot the neurotic and maladjusted employee, and to select individuals of high stability and responsibility. The work of Cattell and Stice, measuring the performances of small groups, shows that even when neurotic employees do not actually make trouble, their presence considerably lowers the morale and productivity of the group. Various job areas have different demands in terms of the amount of stability required, and companies can use the N.P.F. for job areas where maladjustment is a serious problem and cost factor.[8]

Personality tests are not as yet as well perfected as some other types of tests. The experimental or statistical shortcomings of many of the studies of personality tests justify a cautious attitude toward the results obtained, but the fact cannot be ignored that the inventories usually do make some definite contribution to psychiatric screening.

Values of Testing in Industry

In American industry, tests alone are not sufficient for hiring or rejecting an applicant in most firms. They are merely one of the factors that must be evaluated, just as age or education must be weighed in the composite score. The tests may have greater predictive value than any other one variable, but in most firms the other variables are considered in the total picture of the applicant. However, tests have been found helpful for the following purposes:

1. Weeding out of the unfit applicants. For example, persons who have an intelligence quotient of less than 105 seldom succeed in clerical jobs of average difficulty.

One personnel manager for a public utility firm reported that when tests were used in selecting applicants, less than 10 per cent of those hired failed on the job. Without tests, the long-term record of failures in hiring approached 30 per cent.[9] At one time, the Woodward Governor Co. of Rockford, Illinois, found that they were hiring too many tramp mechanics and other undesirables. Later The Psychological Corporation made a study of the company's personnel needs and recommended the use of tests which, according to the general manager of the company, succeeded in weeding out 85 per cent of the untrainable men who applied for work.[10] Similarly, the Lockheed Aircraft Corporation averaged twelve successful hirings out of twenty before testing. With testing, the average rose to nineteen out of twenty.[11]

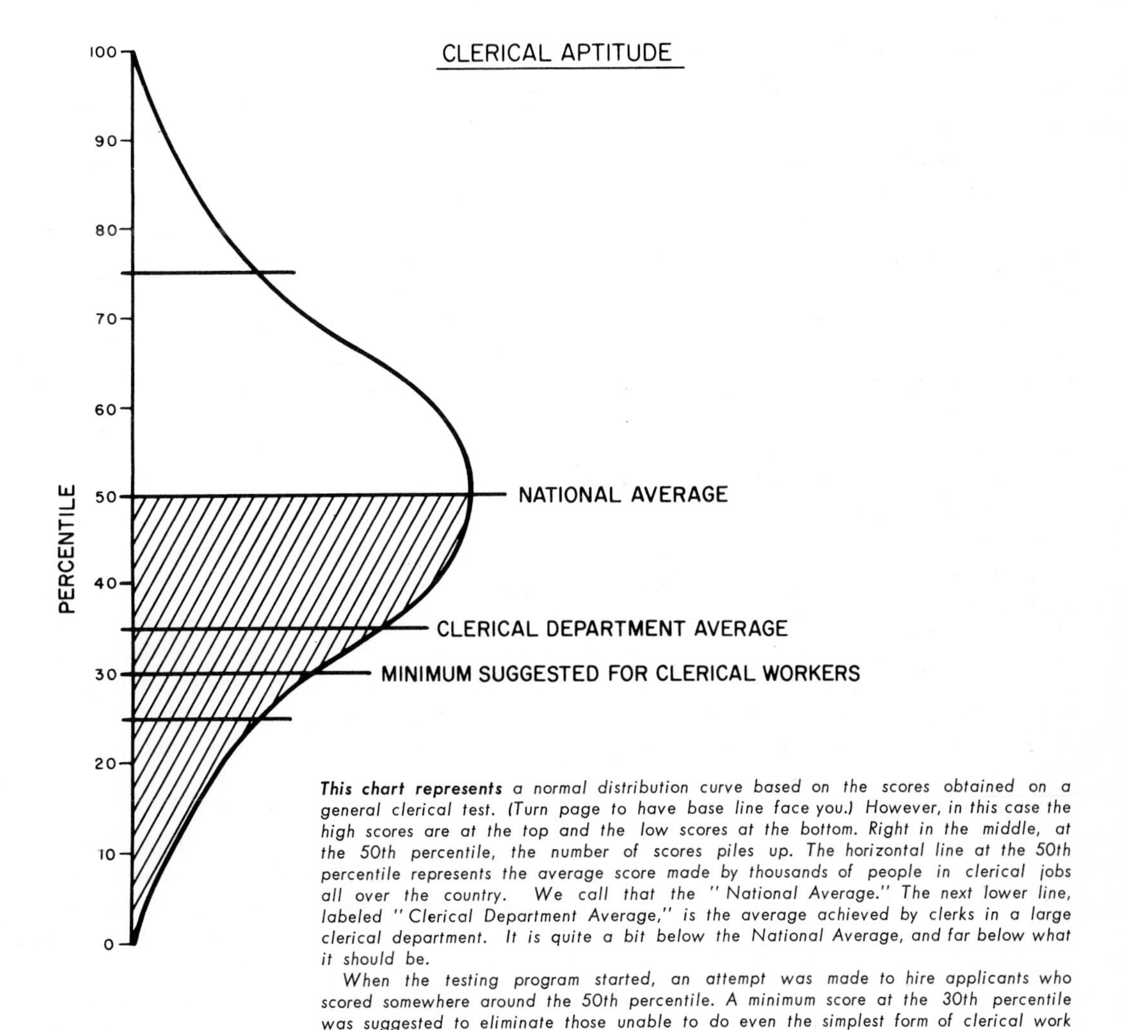

This chart represents *a normal distribution curve based on the scores obtained on a general clerical test. (Turn page to have base line face you.) However, in this case the high scores are at the top and the low scores at the bottom. Right in the middle, at the 50th percentile, the number of scores piles up. The horizontal line at the 50th percentile represents the average score made by thousands of people in clerical jobs all over the country. We call that the "National Average." The next lower line, labeled "Clerical Department Average," is the average achieved by clerks in a large clerical department. It is quite a bit below the National Average, and far below what it should be.*

When the testing program started, an attempt was made to hire applicants who scored somewhere around the 50th percentile. A minimum score at the 30th percentile was suggested to eliminate those unable to do even the simplest form of clerical work well. (David W. Cook, ***Psychology Challenges Industry,*** *Personnel Series No. 107, American Management Association, 1947. Courtesy of David W. Cook and the American Management Association.)*

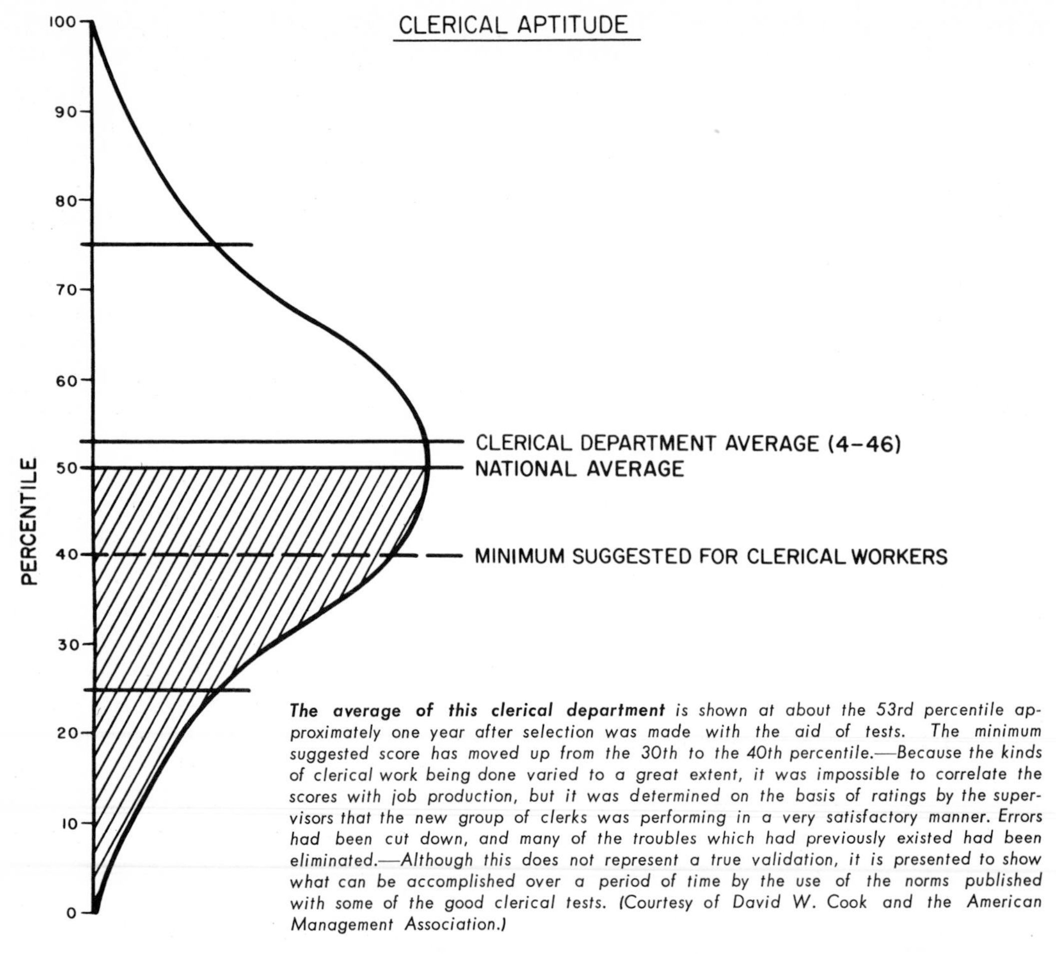

The average of this clerical department *is shown at about the 53rd percentile approximately one year after selection was made with the aid of tests. The minimum suggested score has moved up from the 30th to the 40th percentile.—Because the kinds of clerical work being done varied to a great extent, it was impossible to correlate the scores with job production, but it was determined on the basis of ratings by the supervisors that the new group of clerks was performing in a very satisfactory manner. Errors had been cut down, and many of the troubles which had previously existed had been eliminated.—Although this does not represent a true validation, it is presented to show what can be accomplished over a period of time by the use of the norms published with some of the good clerical tests. (Courtesy of David W. Cook and the American Management Association.)*

2. Tests reduce the costs of training new employees through the selection of applicants who can learn the work. When, for example, a camera manufacturer hired twenty-six persons to learn film spooling, all were subjected to taking a finger dexterity test. Seventeen failed the test. Because of a shortage of labor at the time, all were hired. Ten weeks later each had left the job. The cost of the make-up pay alone, the difference between the minimum hourly rate of pay and what they actually earned, was more than one thousand dollars. Indirect costs to the company amounted to several thousand dollars more. Moreover, a cost greater than dollars was the fact that some of the failing employees were unnecessarily subjected to the experience of failure in their work.

The social science research division of the employee relations department of the Standard Oil Company of New Jersey, conducted a seven-year study known as the Early Identification of Management Potential. The study tried to determine whether the kinds of information that could be obtained from tests, questionnaires, interviews, and personal records had any relationship to managerial success. Over 500 managers participated in the survey. They found a high relationship between over-all success in management and certain tests and questionnaires. Some of the tests found helpful emphasized verbal abilities, non-verbal reasoning, temperament, management judgment, and management attitudes.[12] The test battery predicted long-term success with the company so well that an executive who scored in the top 20 per cent proved to be nine times as likely to do better than average on the job as one who scored in the bottom 20 per cent.[13] However, the researchers pointed out that in spotting employees with management potential they do not rely solely on the use of the tests, but use them in conjunction with data from other sources.

In World War II tests proved to be very helpful. At the time, there was an urgent need to find men qualified for the positions of pilots, navigators and bombardiers. The tests then in use were based primarily on academic intelligence and were inadequate. Only 23 per cent of the men selected for pilot training were able to complete the course. Psychologists were called in to improve the testing program. After studying the tests in use, all but a few were discarded. A team of men devised new examinations which are still in use today. It was found that through testing a man's manual dexterity, his spatial orientation, his ability to read instruments, to manipulate a rudder, and to perform other tasks, the individual most qualified to be a pilot could be differentiated. In time, a battery of approximately twenty-three tests was devised. The percentage of men picked for pilot training who were then able to qualify rose from 23 per cent to between 70 and 75 per cent in only nine months. The great success of these differential aptitude tests during World War II added to their growth in civilian use after the war.[14]

3. Tests enable the personnel manager to spot unsuspected talent within the organization. For example, one third of the line supervisors of the Pacific Lighting Companies first attracted attention through results of their tests.[15] Several large concerns use tests in selecting employees for apprentice, sales, or executive training.

Tests are especially helpful in spotting the applicants and employees who in school were "under-achievers," students of high intelligence but poor school grades. Approximately a half million of these enter the labor market each year. These over-qualified under-achievers do not adjust well to routine, repetitive, detail jobs,[16] but usually have good potentials for growth under stimulating supervisors.

4. Several investigators have developed tests which reduce accidents in bus and truck driving through the selection of fewer accident-prone drivers. In one study it was found that the highest tenth of the drivers (according to composite profile scores) had had 21.2 per cent fewer chargeable accidents than the lowest tenth.[17] A comparison of the average yearly accident rate for the year following the tests and the three preceding years showed an improvement with respect to chargeable accidents of 28.8 per cent. Another psychologist, C. A. Drake, developed a series of tests which reduced the average accident index rate 70 per cent for new employees during the first three months of their work.[18]

5. Psychological tests decrease favoritism in hiring and place the securing of a job on an objective basis rather than on sentiment. Tests are a convenient device for avoiding pressure from friends and politicians who may have some protégé who needs a job. Definite standards which every applicant must meet will enable the executive to say to the man who has an incapable nephew who needs a position: "We shall be glad to have the young man apply to us for a job, and if he meets the standards we have set up, we will find a place for him." However, the main value of tests is in locating good applicants and employees. Furthermore, there is considerable evidence to indicate that when a testing program is installed it tends to draw better applicants to the company.[19] A self-imposed selection takes place among applicants who know that the company uses tests.

6. Tests can be used to determine needed areas of training on the part of new and old employees. Usually, tests of information and proficiency are used for this purpose. However, personality tests are helpful too, particularly in those occupations that require certain personality characteristics, as in selling and research.

7. If a personnel department does counseling of inadequately adjusted employees, tests are essential to diagnosis. When used for this purpose, testing contributes to the development of happier and more effective workers.

8. Test findings and interpretations are especially helpful to effective supervision. The use of tests often reveals vital information for management. Guy W. Wadsworth, Jr., president of the Southern California Gas Company, pointed out their value when he stated:

> Generally speaking, low-grade supervisors tend to attract and to favor low-grade men. Their most favorable reports may be expected to concern subordinates much like themselves, who offer little potential rivalry. A keenly intelligent applicant placed under such a supervisor is often quickly classified as a "smart aleck." Thus there may be an unlooked-for wastage of manpower, in which technical fitness is not an issue. In any case, within our experience, the use of standardized tests has provided a most effective personnel audit, disclosing not only abilities which may not be called into play in the immediate assignment, but which would have remained obscured for other thoroughly human reasons.[20]

Limitations of Tests

Psychological tests have demonstrated their values in many phases of business, but are especially helpful in reducing labor turnover. However, when a critical score is once determined and an executive decides that no applicant shall be hired unless he scores above that point, the executive is also apt to go to the opposite extreme and try to hire only those who score considerably above the critical point. This practice may result in a high turnover, for it is desirable to have a maximum score as well as minimum score or an *optimum range* (see Table 16.1). One employment manager started to use tests for hiring and then hired only persons with high intelligence for all his jobs. His method resulted in a high turnover, because few of the jobs were worthy of a person of high intelligence. The well-manned corporation is like a well-manned army; it consists of one general, a few high officers, many junior-grade officers, and the great mass of the organization made up of people with average or below-average intelligence. An elevator operator should have the intelligence needed for operating elevators and not very much more. If this country should suddenly embark upon a eugenics program and breed only people of very high intelligence, we might be worse off than we are now, because many jobs in a technological civilization require only average and below-average intelligence. Examples of such jobs are truck-driving, elevator-operating, factory machine-tending, and so on.

TABLE 16.1

Test Score	*Average Length of Service in Days*
10 to 19	3
20 to 29	91
30 to 39	156
40 to 49	142
50 to 59	107
60 to 69	100
70 to 79	96
80 to 89	87
90 and above	35

From Harold E. Burtt, *Employment Psychology* (Boston: Houghton Mifflin Company, 1926), p. 289.

When intelligence tests are used for selective purposes, it is well to know whether environmental conditions have been eliminating the unfit of the group to be tested. The use of intelligence tests for the selection of students for admission to college does not result in very high correlations between scores in the tests and scholastic records. One reason for a low correlation is the selective process that has been operating through the school system. The students of lowest intelligence find grammar school and high school work too difficult for them and tend to drop out according to the degrees of intelligence possessed. Hence, when a student is able to apply for admission to college, he has already survived a process of selection. Only those above the average of intelligence are able to finish high school and apply for admission to college.

If an individual has a certain minimum of intelligence for a given occupation or job, his success depends upon other characteristics, such as temperament and personality. The intelligence of the executive is merely one of several factors in his composite behavior pattern, as suggested in the chapters (Two to Six) on adjustment patterns.

Executives who decide to use psychological tests for hiring often want to take the tests themselves. The experience of the writer has been that, if the executive interested in the tests happens to make the highest score of all the employees, he then believes that the tests are good. The executives who happen to score lower than one or two employees lost interest in the use of tests. Such an attitude is wholly unscientific and unsound. If the executive could only realize that the purpose of the tests is to hire employees of a behavior pattern type requiring qualities of a different nature from his own, he might not be so easily elated or offended over the results of the test procedure.

Obviously, the mere fact that executives are pleased with the interpretation given them after taking a test does not mean that the test is useful. This applies particularly to personality tests which are interpreted in broad general terms that apply to almost everyone. Ross Stagner conducted a training session on testing in which he gave a simple test to 68 executives and then gave each the same report, couched in flattering generalities, such as "Proud of your independent thinking, you don't accept others' statements without satisfactory proof." Of the 68 men who received the evaluations, 90 per cent scored the report as being an amazingly accurate over-all picture of their personalities or as good. He used this procedure in order to have the executives realize that a test must be evaluated quantitatively, not subjectively.[21]

One of the most frequent criticisms of psychological tests is that they are unfair to the nervous applicants. It is claimed that a person may be in an unusual mood. His digestion may be bad or he may be in a state of worry and therefore not do justice to himself. Experience indicates that very few persons are emotionally disturbed while taking the tests administered by an experienced examiner. Tests may frighten employees and applicants when they are given without the necessary preliminary explanation of their limitations and values. However, when tests are properly handled, very few applicants object to taking them. A person of an especially timid or psychoneurotic nature may object, but such applicants are in a decided minority. In many situations it is not essential to tell the applicant that he is about to take a psychological test. It is better to ask him whether he objects to taking a short examination of his general fund of information or speed in figuring.

Employees who have been tested should not be given their scores. Such results should be kept in the personal file of a major executive of the firm. As previously stated, if a person has a certain accomplishment level of intelligence, his success and advancement may depend upon factors which are not measured by the tests. When an employee or lower-rank executive is given his own test score and he knows how he compares with other members of the organization, he assumes that those employees who happen to be a few points above or below him are also above or below him in ability or chances for promotion. No tests are available that measure so fine a degree of differentiation. Their chief value is that of classifying individuals into broad or general groups.

Good scholastic records and high scores on intelligence tests are an indication of ability to do the kind of learning that requires some grasp of abstractions. However, ability to learn certain important business operations does not correlate with intelligence tests. The best example of this is stenographic ability. Many students of superior mental capacity make low marks in shorthand, and many who make high marks in shorthand have relatively low intelligence test scores.[22] This simply means that individual companies who use intelligence tests for hiring should supplement them with specific ability and skill tests.

Thus far, personnel men have not been able to obtain tests that measure character traits such as honesty in handling the employer's funds. Obviously, character as well as intelligence and personality must be considered in hiring cashiers, bank tellers, and salesmen. Experiments have been conducted with tests of character. Some people are high in intelligence but of unreliable character. In general, however, we do find that most socially desirable traits go together. People of high intelligence tend to be of good character and are better-looking, easier to get along with, and healthier. However, a high rating in intelligence does not prove that a given individual will be honest in his business relations, for these correlations are not high. It merely indicates that the chances, statistically speaking, are somewhat greater that he is of good character than that he is not. Some of the first character tests dealt with school situations.

Children in school have been tested in deceit by giving them an examination, collecting the papers, making copies of each child's answers, returning each child's papers to the child, giving each a key to the correct answers, and asking each child to score his own paper. The child's own scoring was then compared with the office copies of the scores and definite discrepancies between the two scorings were noted. It was found that some children would correct their own papers while scoring them: some would put dots over the letter "i" when it was a part of the test, others would cross the letter "t," others would write in extra words, and the worst offenders would erase writings in ink and write in the correct answer in pencil. In most of these tests, the amount of dishonesty varied with the degree of motivation. When children were impressed with the tremendous importance of making a high score, they cheated far more than when they were allowed to think that a high score in the examination was of no importance. This is in harmony with the businessman's experience. The executive who wishes to hire an employee for a position where, if he chooses, he can manipulate the company's finances for his own benefit does well when he selects a man who lives completely within his income and saves some money rather than a man who plays the stock market or happens to have a "social climber" for a wife. Our dishonesty tends to increase as the pressure for it increases.[23]

At present, tests are not available that

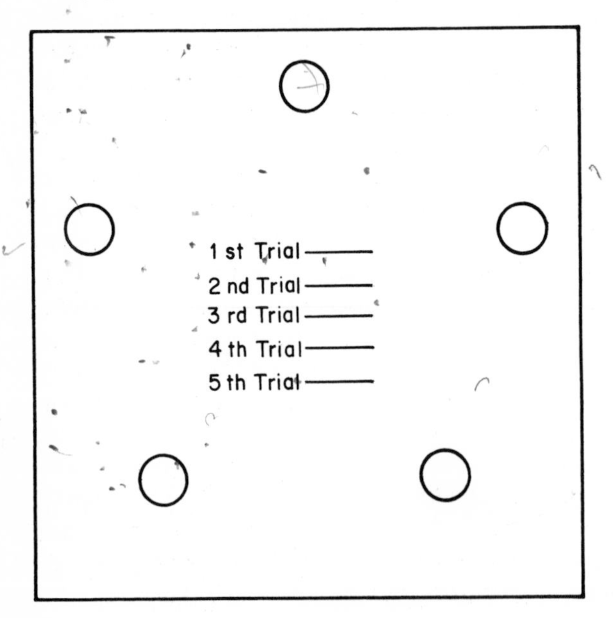

An example of a character test. *Close your eyes. Move a pencil around the square three times without touching the paper. With eyes still closed, try to put a dot in each circle. Do this for each of five trials. You must put a dot in each of the five circles on each trial in order to have a plus score for any one trial. Refer to the Appendix for the answer. (Adapted from V. M. Cady, "The Estimation of Juvenile Incorrigibility,"* ***Journal of Delinquency,*** *Monograph No. 2, April 1923.)*

tell the businessman whether an applicant is honest or dishonest. Honesty, like all character traits, is of a complex nature. It varies with the situation. A man may be scrupulously honest about paying his gambling debts and exceedingly lax about paying his room rent. One test will not measure any one character trait, because character traits are specific in their applications to situations. Knowing whether a person will cheat in an examination does not tell us whether he will steal money.

Deliberate "faking" of answers with intent to deceive the test user is possible and is done by some applicants when they take certain kinds of tests such as personality and interest tests. Every tester knows that the typical applicant will respond in terms of an ideal self-concept rather than give a completely candid self-appraisal.[24]

Occasionally, a popular writer will even offer rules on "How to Cheat on Personality Tests." Psychologists have conducted studies of the effects on personality test scores of deliberate efforts to respond in accordance with honest and dishonest objectives. The research studies indicate that faking one's answers in order to present one's self more favorably for attaining a specific job such as supervision does result in producing scores that appear to be socially desirable. Such manipulations, however, are also likely to result in less desirable scores on other scales of the same test. Thus, dishonest respondents tend to gain only an insignificant advantage over honest respondents.[25]

Psychologists who are sophisticated in the interpretation of personality and interest tests are conscious of the possibilities and likelihood of simulation and interpret the scores accordingly. They note whether the score shows that "the individual is sensible enough to present himself in a reasonably acceptable manner, or whether he is so naive as to be overly candid, or (in the case of the test faker who gets carried away with his deception) clumsy enough to present an unbelievably sterling self-appraisal."[26]

Of course the problem of faking the "correct" answers does not arise in the use of intelligence, educational achievement, proficiency and many other kinds of tests—the individual cannot simulate knowledge or ability that he does not possess.

All tests are limited by the fact that they give a prediction for a group or a number of individuals rather than a prediction for a specific person. As has been said, "Validity is a statistical concept; it refers to large groups, and not to individuals." The validity of tests must be determined by their benefits in screening large groups. Valid tests do not offer predictions about a specific applicant, but they do offer odds on the chances that he will succeed or fail. To the sophisticated interpreter of tests, statistical validity, in some instances, may be less important than the meaningfulness that he sees in a test score as it relates to other facts known about the person tested.[27]

A test that has high positive predictive value indicates that anyone who scores high in the test tends to be high in the trait with which the test correlates. The high score means that, of one hundred persons who score high in the test, a certain percentage will also be high in the correlating trait.* If an employer hires a large number of employees for a specific job, as one does in life insurance selling or factory operations of large standard process shops, a set of psychological tests should be developed for the hiring of applicants; but most American business concerns do not have a large number of employees who do the same work. They have a few stenographers, several bookkeepers, a janitor, an office boy or two, and a larger number of miscellaneous machine operators. Unless the firm employs about fifty persons on the same kind of operation, it is difficult and

* We shall not discuss the meaning of negative coefficients of correlation here, but leave that for the statistician who wishes to apply a more comprehensive knowledge of evaluations. However, the last chapter of this book presents some of the simpler statistical factors involved in evaluating tests.

expensive to develop reliable psychological tests and standards. Even in the larger corporations, it is often arduous to invent profitable tests for more than one or two classes of employees.

Psychologists recognize this limitation of tests and govern their decisions accordingly, but the novice who uses tests is apt to apply the prediction to specific individuals rather than to group relations. In general, no especially difficult technique is required to administer group psychological tests after they have been statistically treated, but to give them statistical interpretation requires more technical application than most businessmen care to give. Executives should obtain the services of a trained tester if they wish to have any worthwhile results from psychological tests for hiring purposes. But the trained tester's findings must be supplemented with the evaluations obtained through an incisive interview, from records of previous education and employment, and by executive judgment. Tests do not measure the will to work, a trait which is often more important to the executive than the capacity to work.

The interpretation of test scores in relation to all other known information about the individual requires considerable experience and training. The difficulties involved can be appreciated, to some extent, by the student who puts himself into the situation of a college admissions director. See pp. 340–341.

Directors of admissions are aware of the difficulties and frequently evaluate the results of their selections in order to note the significant and non-significant factors in their judgments. A recent study by the Admission and Scholarship Committee of Harvard College was condensed by a business magazine:

> A Harvard survey shows that a freshman who ranks so-so (500-plus) on entrance exams but rates high on purely personal qualities—such as energy, judgment, generosity of spirit, and old-fashioned cussedness—is apt to rank near the top of his class in college studies. He'll likely rank just as high as the boy whose prime reason for being admitted is a top entrance exam score (700 to 800 at Harvard). Both types, the survey shows, share later scholastic honors about equally.[28]

In conclusion, we can say that testing does not supplant, but supplements, other steps in hiring. Common sense in the use of tests in industry has been summarized in regard to the more common errors, which are: (1) taking over completely test batteries that have been used successfully in other organizations, (2) thinking that anyone can administer tests, (3) not interpreting test results in the light of the whole situation, and (4) expecting too much from tests. Tests may make definite contributions, however, as: (1) a check on educational background, (2) a check on reported occupational experience, (3) a means of comparing the applicant with workers already employed, (4) an indication of particular abilities, and (5) a device offering some clues to temperament and personality characteristics.[29]

Tests and their limitations are the perennial subject of magazine articles that criticize, even ridicule, their use. But tests will continue to be used. Their use will continue because any one who must evaluate strangers realizes that he needs an aid more objective than his own personal impressions.

The competent personnel man who uses tests also systematically improves his interviewing practices, evaluates the items on the application blank, and checks his appraisals by means of work histories and all available objective data.

ACKNOWLEDGMENTS AND REFERENCES

1. Joseph Tiffin, *Industrial Psychology,* 2nd ed. (Englewood Cliffs, N. J: Prentice-Hall, Inc., 1947), pp. 46 ff.
2. A. G. Wesman, "What Is an Aptitude?" *Test Service Bulletin,* The Psychological Corporation, August, 1948.
3. J. E. Bell, *Projective Techniques* New York, David McKay Co., Inc., 1948).

4. See William E. Henry's article, "The Business Executive—A Study in the Psychodynamics of a Social Role," *The American Journal of Sociology,* January, 1949. Also, "What Makes a Good Executive?" *Business Week,* July 17, 1948, p. 24.
5. These surveys are usually reported in current issues of *Personnel,* American Management Association, Inc.
6. A catalog or descriptive literature about tests useful in industry can be obtained from the publishers by making a request, preferably on company letterhead. Catalogs are distributed freely but the purchase of tests is a different matter. Purchase is usually restricted to companies who have a person on the staff qualified to administer and interpret the instruments, which are graded by level (following the American Psychological Association standards). This person must submit a statement of his qualifications on a special form supplied by the publisher. Some of the major test publishers in the United States are listed below:
   California Test Bureau, Del Monte Research Park, Monterey, Calif.
   Educational Testing Service, Cooperative Test Division, Princeton, N. J.
   Houghton Mifflin Company, 53 West 43rd St., New York, N. Y.
   Industrial Psychology, Inc., 515 Madison Ave., New York 22, N. Y.
   Institute for Personality and Ability Testing, 1602–04 Coronado Drive, Champaign, Ill.
   Psychometric Affiliates, Box 1625, Chicago 90, Ill.
   The Psychological Corporation, 304 East 45th St., New York 17, N. Y.
   Science Research Associates, Inc., 259 East Erie St., Chicago 11, Ill.
   Western Psychological Services, 12035 Wilshire Blvd., Los Angeles 25, Calif.
   E. F. Wonderlic & Associates, Inc., P.O. Box 7, Northfield, Ill.
   Scoring service for certain tests is available from National Computer Systems, 1015 South 6th St., Minneapolis 15, Minn. Write to NCS for description of services.
7. H. G. Martin, "Locating the Troublemaker with the Guilford-Martin Personnel Inventory," *Journal of Applied Psychology,* December, 1944, p. 465.
8. From Industrial Psychology, Inc., Box 6056, Tucson 6, Ariz., 1954.
9. Guy W. Wadsworth, Jr., "Hidden Abilities of Clerical Workers," *Office Management Series No. 88,* American Management Association, 1939; and Herbert Moore, "Experience with Employment Tests," *Studies in Personnel Policy,* No. 32 (March 11, 1941), National Industrial Conference Board.
10. "Testing for Talent," *Fortune,* January, 1941, p. 96.
11. *Loc. cit.*
12. "How to Spot Management Ability," *Printers' Ink,* Mar. 16, 1962.
13. Richard S. Barrett, "Guide to Using Psychological Tests," *Harvard Business Review,* September-October, 1963.
14. Lloyd Humphreys, *The Army Air Force Aviation Psychology Program Reports, Report No. 1* (John C. Flannigan, ed.), *Report No. 2* (Philip H. DuBois, ed.), Government Printing Office, Washington, D.C., 1947.
15. Guy W. Wadsworth, Jr., *op. cit.*
16. *Industrial Psychology, Inc., Newsletter,* August 1960, p. 3.
17. H. R. DeSilva, R. G. Claffin, and W. J. Simon, "Making Safer Bus Drivers," *Transit Journal,* November, 1938, pp. 1–3.
18. Charles A. Drake, "Testing for Accident-Proneness," a paper presented before the American Association of Applied and Professional Psychology, University of Minnesota, Aug. 31, 1937.
19. Eleroy L. Stromberg, "Testing Programs Draw Better Applicants," *Personnel Psychology,* Spring, 1948.
20. "Hidden Abilities of Clerical Workers," *Office Management Series,* No. 88, American Management Association, Inc., 1939, p. 8. See also "Supervisory Selection Programs," *Personnel,* American Management Association, Inc., September 1955, p. 113.
21. Ross Stagner, "The Gullibility of Personnel Managers," *Personnel Psychology,* Autumn, 1958, and Andrew H. Sonerwine, "More Value from Personnel Testing," *Harvard Business Review,* March-April, 1961.
22. Raymond J. Worley, "Prognosis in Shorthand," *The Journal of Business Education,* September, 1931.
23. T. H. Howels, "Factors Influencing Honesty," *Journal of Social Psychology,* **9** (1938), 97–102.
24. C. F. Dicken, "Simulated Patterns on the Edwards Personal Preference Schedule," *Journal of Applied Psychology,* December, 1959.
25. Marvin E. Shaw, "The Effectiveness of Whyte's Rules: 'How to Cheat on Personality Tests,'" *Journal of Applied Psychology,* February, 1962.
26. Saul W. Gellerman, "Personnel Testing: What the Critics Overlook," *Personnel,* American Management Association, Inc., May-June, 1963.
27. Robert L. Ebel, "Must All Tests Be Valid?" *The American Psychologist,* October, 1961.
28. *Business Week,* Jan. 18, 1964, p. 106. These findings are taken from Fred L. Glimp and Dean K. Whitla, "Admissions and Performance," *Harvard Alumni Bulletin,* Jan. 11, 1964.
29. F. H. Kirkpatrick, "Common Sense About Tests," *Personnel Journal,* **21** (1943), 277–281.

PROJECTS

1. Assume that all the employees of a large bank are to be given several psychological tests. Outline your procedure for obtaining and evaluating the tests.

2. A sales manager asks you to select some psychological tests for hiring salesmen. Outline the main steps in the procedure you would follow in attempting to give him what he wants.
3. Intelligence test results are sometimes expressed in terms of IQ and sometimes in terms of percentiles. Which would you select in each of the following cases? Offer reasons for your choice. In the case of percentiles, define each group used as the base.
   a. For applicants for a night watchman's job.
   b. For admission to the graduate school of a university.
   c. For selecting soldiers for officers' training schools.
   d. For discovering mentally handicapped children.
   e. For rating stenographers in an office.
4. Some of our educational leaders are wondering whether admissions to college are determined too decidedly by test scores and other quantitative criteria. What are some of the probable benefits and disadvantages to our society when such criteria are the main or sole determinants? As an aid to your thinking, you may refer to Vernon R. Alden, "What Kind of Excellence?" *Saturday Review,* July 18, 1964.

HOW WOULD YOU INTERPRET THESE INTERVIEW AND TEST DATA?

Do *you* want to try to decide who should go to college? Everyone screams at college admissions directors for their "unfairness," but few people have any idea of how difficult it is to select a freshman class—especially when you have to turn down three or four students for every one you admit.

Arthur Howe, Jr., dean of admissions and student appointments at Yale, here presents six real cases of boys who applied to Yale (their names are disguised). You may admit only two; you must reject four. Printed on page 621 at the end of this book are Yale's decisions, and how all the boys made out—whether or not they went to Yale.

a. ARISTOTLE ANCHOVY, III. The only child of divorced parents, Anchovy lived with his Greek father in South Dakota. He attended a New England academy, where his senior average was 89. But he had trouble with science and math his junior year, which dragged his average down to 74. However, he was on the first honor roll when he applied. His College Board scores for the Scholastic Test (SAT) were 495 Verbal and 504 Mathematical (on a scale of 200 to 800). Still he stood second in a class of 223.

His headmaster gave him a "strong" but not "highest possible" recommendation. His German and Russian teacher called him "one of the most unusual students I have ever taught. He has always been low in tests and high in performance." His Yale interviewer found him "fluent in Greek, English, very good in several other languages" and a "painter, musician and poet." An excellent swimmer, he broke his school record for the 100-yard freestyle.

b. BRUNO BASS, Jr. Son of a Yale alumnus who did not graduate, Bass was the nephew of a Yale professor and also had a brother in Yale. At a Rhode Island prep school, his senior grades were in the 60s, with a 95 in Bible. His SAT Verbal score, however, was 698 and the Math 601. He stood 60th in a class of 80.

His headmaster felt Bass could be "endorsed with confidence." A special letter from his school's dean of students declared that "through hard work and tenacity he has developed from a mediocre performer into a good one." His English teacher said his work had shown "remarkable improvement." The Yale interviewer felt that he "doesn't seem to be the type who kills himself working. Says grades off this fall, but he's sure they'll come back." He worked as headwaiter in school dining room, belonged to French, Philosophy and Car Clubs, and also played tennis and intramural hockey.

c. CLARENCE CARP, Jr. This New Jerseyite was called "one in hundreds in the precosity of his art work" by a Yale professor with whom he had been working while still in high school. A junior expert on mosaics, he had spent two summers in Greece. His senior grades were either C or C minus. But both the Yale professor and the mayor of Carp's home town wrote enthusiastic letters of recommendation, the mayor stressing Carp's work in local radio announcing and programming. His SAT scores were Verbal 563 and Math 599, and he stood 23d in a class of 43.

However, his headmaster expressed concern over whether Carp was too much of a specialist. His art teacher said that "he is not what you would call well-rounded; he is shaping up to be a specialist and in my opinion is likely to make a real contribution in his field." The Yale interviewer found him "a real individual with a definite and nice personality."

d. TRUXTON COD, IV. Both Cod's father

and his brother were Yale graduates. A Bostonian, Cod went to "Old Eli Prep School," where his senior average was 76. He improved steadily in his last three years, and was president of the art society. His SAT scores were Verbal 490 and Math 580, and he stood 49th in a class of 89.

Cod's headmaster said he was "a fine boy," but that "academically, he is not as sure a bet." However, the headmaster stressed that Cod had deliberately worked on his weaknesses. His history professor said he "offers much leadership." The Yale interviewer declared: "I think this boy faces a real struggle and there is some question in my mind whether or not Yale is really the place for him. Perhaps a post-graduate year would help, but perhaps he could make it with a lot of effort. But look at the scores."

e. HORACE HADDOCK. A grandfather went to Yale. Haddock was a public-school student with a great interest in agriculture and the Future Farmers of America. He came from a large farm family, where study opportunities were rare. His grades senior year were two B minuses, a C, a C minus and an E (failing). All were down from his junior year, when he had one A minus, two B pluses, a B and a B minus. He applied only to Yale, no other college. In the top fifth of a class of 210, his SAT scores were Verbal 738 and Math 737.

Haddock's guidance director pointed to his high test scores as proof that he was "quite remarkable as a scholar." However, she said "Horace is as careless in his study habits as in his attire," and "his assignments are frequently late or poorly written." A Yale alumnus who interviewed him found him "very shy and ill at ease," refusing to state his academic high-school record and unaware of his class rank.

f. PETER PUFFER. Son of a life-insurance agent. Puffer went to a public school, where his senior grades were Bs and Cs. He had a 13-year-old brother with an IQ of 170, a genius always held up to him as an example. But Peter was on the honor roll himself and was in high-achievement classes. His SAT scores were Verbal 650 and Math 539, and he stood 27th in a class of 430.

Puffer's principal gave him a strong recommendation. But his history teacher disagreed, saying he had a "general attitude of arrogance." But the teacher admitted Puffer was under "tremendous parental pressure," and that his father gave him the finest clothes and an unlimited checking account, things which had an "adverse effect" on him. The teacher also felt that Puffer sought "an Ivy League College for prestige only." A Yale alumnus who interviewed him wrote: "Everything he says or does about his immediate future is slanted toward an advertising career."*

* From "College Admissions Directors Scream, Too," *New York Herald Tribune,* April 9, 1964. Reproduced by special permission.

COLLATERAL READINGS

Albright, Lewis E., *et al., The Use of Psychological Tests in Industry*. Cleveland: Howard Allen, Inc., 1963.

Farnsworth, P. R., ed., *el al., Annual Review of Psychology*. Palo Alto, Calif.: Annual Reviews, Inc., 1964, pp. 323–338.

Gillmer, Richard S., "Are You Misusing Intelligence Tests," *Personnel,* American Management Association, Inc., March-April, 1964.

Harrell, Thomas Willard, *Industrial Psychology*. New York: Holt, Rinehart and Winston, Inc., 1958, Chapters 5 and 6.

Leavitt, Harold J. and Louis R. Pondy, (eds.), *Readings in Managerial Psychology*. Chicago: The University of Chicago Press, 1964, pp. 157–173.

Lyman, Howard B., *Test Scores and What They Mean*. Englewood Cliffs, N.J.: Prentice-Hall, Inc., 1963.

Thorndike, Robert L. and Elizabeth Hagen, *Ten Thousand Careers*. New York: John Wiley & Sons, Inc., 1959. A report on the findings of a study of 17,000 men who were given a battery of aptitude tests in 1943, and from whom educational and vocational histories were subsequently obtained.

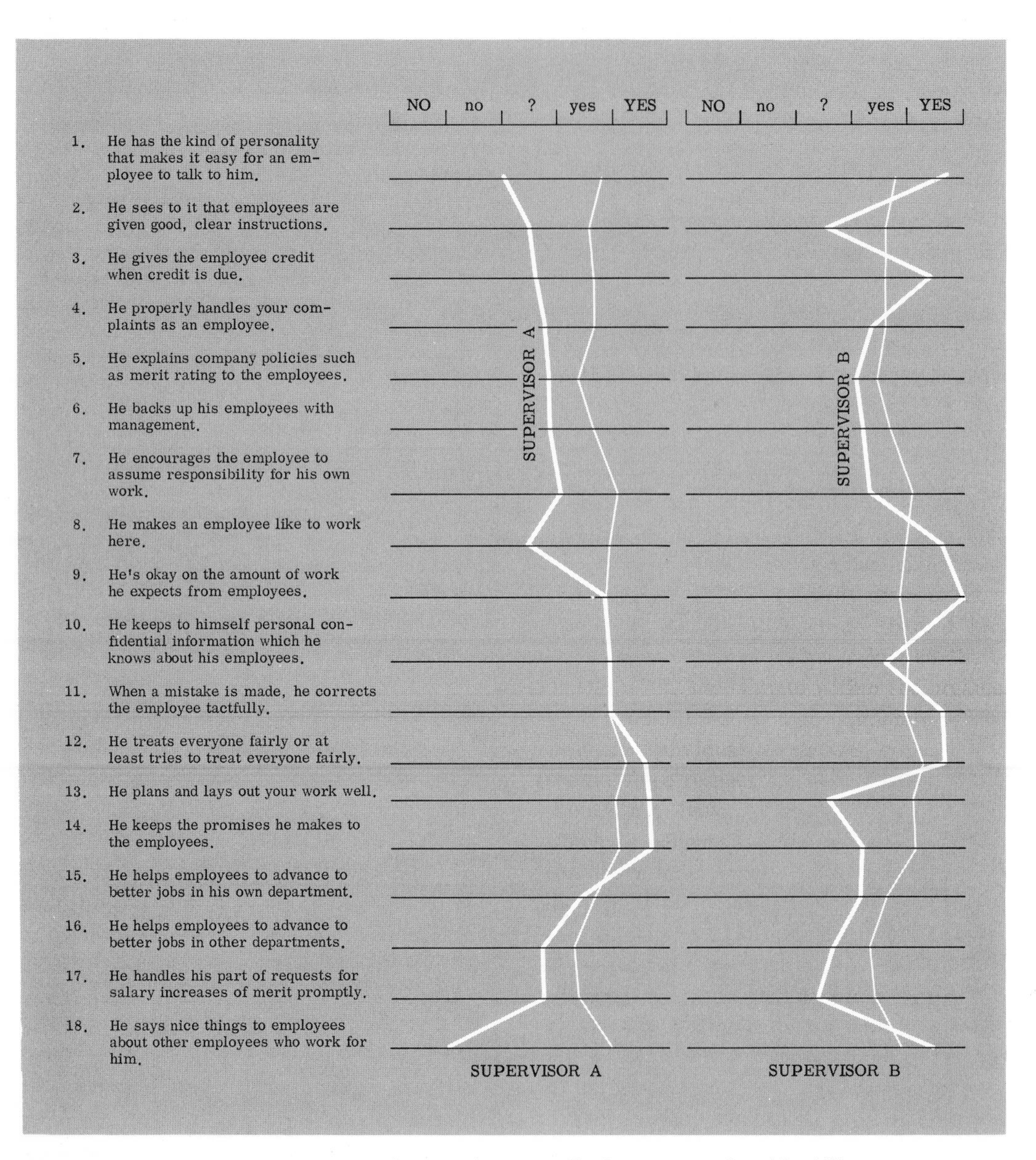

Personality patterns of two supervisors *are shown in the two profiles for supervisors A and B.—When a training program for supervisors was organized, the supervisors were asked to choose the traits on which they would like to be rated by their own employees. The supervisors, in the course of discussion, selected the list of eighteen traits shown above.—Each supervisor's employees rated him without revealing their identities. The ratings were given to the psychologist in charge of the ratings and training sessions. He calculated the average numerical rating for all supervisors. See the thin vertical line. The average rating on each trait for each supervisor was also computed and plotted on the above scale. See the heavy line.*

When the profile for the average rating of individual supervisor A, heavy line on left of chart, was compared with the average for all the supervisors, thin line, it was found that A's profile was typical of the technically well trained but impersonal supervisor, such as a cold unresponsive engineer or accountant. Supervisor B, on the other hand, had a profile characteristic of the warm, friendly, but overly lenient supervisor. His employees criticized him for not requiring them to do as much work as they could do with ease.—The training sessions dealt with techniques of supervision but also included suggestions concerning the personality development, or adjustment pattern, of the individual supervisor.

CHAPTER SEVENTEEN

APPRAISALS OF EMPLOYEES —MERIT RATINGS

The ambitious employee does not want managerial sermons or copybook maxims about how to become a big businessman. He needs definite and organized explanations regarding the actions he should take in order to deserve and achieve a feasible promotion. An inventory of personnel should be as important as a physical inventory.

The writer once had the temerity to suggest to the general manager of a firm having three thousand employees that he ought to have a promotion and training system. His answer was: "Training and promotion? Bosh! Nothing doing. Why, do you know what I did several years ago? I arranged for several training courses to be given, hired the teachers, rented a special room in the center of town, and put a slip in the pay envelopes telling the employees that anyone taking the course would be directly in line for promotion and higher pay. The whole proposition was free. I almost begged some of them to take the training. About 50 per cent of our men are foreigners or too old to take any courses, but I estimated that about 1,200 could benefit by courses I had planned. Of the 1,200 possibilities, how many do you suppose took the courses? Well, you couldn't guess. I'll tell you. Eight started and two finished."

The experience of this manager is not exceptional. Many employees will not exercise the self-discipine necessary to merit important positions. Most employees do not seek responsibility. Some must be persuaded to accept it. However, certain intelligent employees do desire promotion. When higher-grade applicants are hired they often ask: "Where does this job lead to?" The most frequent answer is one of evasion, such as, "You do your work well and keep your eyes open and you'll be promoted when you really deserve it."

A more truthful statement to the applicant would be: "We have no well-planned system of promotion or advancement. We have never taken the trouble to study our employees and to explain how they can make themselves worth more to us. If you work for us and make good, it may be that in time we shall have an opening somewhere in the organization where we can use you. Of course, someone may have to die or leave before you can be promoted, but if you live long enough and work hard enough, you may get there. On the other hand, someone else may appeal more to us than you do, and then the other fellow will get the promotion. We think we know who the good men in our company are, but we don't always know, so you must make a good impression on someone farther up. You must be able to sell us your ability as well as do good work."

Most employees recognize this situation and, even though they are not decidedly ambitious, they would like to know how well they do their work and what management thinks of them. That is one reason why a salary increase is so keenly desired by many employees—it is a token of management's esteem for the employee. Granted that most employees do want more money for their economic needs, they also want more money as a means of satisfying certain psychological needs. That is why surveys of employee morale often reveal that a very high percentage would like to find out answers to the question, "How am I doing?" Of course they want more than a report of the quantitative variety—they want to have the benefits of an interview with a responsible executive who will discuss the employee's potentials and work habits in a friendly, constructive spirit. Many managements, too, would like to do this for each employee. As a means of satisfying these and other needs, merit ratings have been developed.

Rating is a term used to refer to the process of judging people and things. A *rating scale* is a standardized device for recording personal judgments. The use of a scale provides a method whereby judgments may be secured in a uniform manner and treated quantitatively. Personal estimates and subjective opinions can be dealt with in much the same way as test scores and other psychological measurements. However, a rating scale is *not* a test and a rating scale should never be referred to as a test. It is a subjective estimate used because tests to measure certain personal characteristics are not as yet available.

The term "rating" applies to areas of judgment which are not susceptible to the testing process. A rating is a personal judgment, but a test is or ought to be an objective measure. If a characteristic of a person such as intelligence can be tested, it should not be rated.

Ratings do *not measure* "merit"—they *portray* the pattern of perceptions which someone has about the individual. They present what certain acquaintances *think* they know or are willing to say about the person. Obviously what executives think they know about an employee is very important. They will treat the employee as they perceive him.

The Benefits of a Rating Scale

1. Some executives are prone to classify all employees into two large groups: the "good" and the "no-good." The executive may call the "no-good" group "passable," "tolerable," or "just satisfactory," depending upon the mood he is in at the time. Obviously, employees are neither wholly good nor wholly bad, but each has some traits to a high degree and others to a low degree. The use of a rating scale compels the executive to analyze his employees and to obtain a more accurate picture of each person under his supervision.

2. A rating scale also compels an executive to analyze his employees at regular intervals. Many an executive walks by some of his employees every working day for years and never thinks of their specific characteristics. If an employee commits a serious error or refuses to join a labor union, the executive may then hear of the matter and gauge the employee by a single dramatic incident. In most cases, the dramatic incident is an isolated defect of the employee's conduct, because his good qualities are taken for granted. Too many executives are negative-minded toward their employees. They can recite their weaknesses or failures, but are unable to list their positive points.

3. The periodical use of a rating scale discovers the good men sooner and makes them available for the company. These men can be given special training, extra compensation, executive recognition, or opportunities for additional responsibilities or duties.

Executives as well as lower echelons of employees must be analyzed regarding promotability. In one analysis of 3,000 executives,[1] the research project indicated that only slightly more than one-third qualified for any advancement and fewer had potentials for development into top management jobs. This, in some companies, might become a serious problem because approximately 40 per cent of all top management personnel are in the age bracket from 55 to 65. Many of these will retire in the course of their next 10 years. Death, disability, and turnover are continuous.

4. The executive can check or verify his own analyses of employees. If he should rate a man high one month and then rate him low six months later, the cause should be known. Perhaps a trivial incident has changed the estimate of the executive, or he may not really know the employee well enough to rate him. Having a record of his estimates of employees will enable the rater to ascertain his ability to analyze others. His ratings can be compared with those of other executives and his tendencies toward high or low ratings can be discovered. If an executive is a poor judge of human behavior, the rating scale should cause him to realize his own peculiarity.

5. Just as the rating scale enables the executive to improve his ability to analyze the employee, so the employee also learns the particular qualities he should develop or eliminate. Few employees know their own strong and weak characteristics. They do not improve themselves, because the management does not tell them what to improve or how to do it. The "Success" books and pep lectures are too general or too inspirational to enable the employees to make direct and tangible applications to their own jobs.

Kinds of Rating Scales

Many different rating scales have been invented, but most of those in current use can be classified into five basic types:

1. Ranking

The rater is asked to list employees in rank order from "best" at the head of the list to "poorest" at the bottom of the list, in regard to some defined characteristics. This method is seldom practiced today.

2. Man-to-Man Comparisons (paired comparisons)

This method is similar to the first but applied to a group. By this, the individual members of groups are compared to each other, one at a time. This technique was developed during World War I and was used by the army at that time to assess officer ability. It is extremely laborious and time consuming. Hence, it is rarely used today.

3. Forced Choice Rating

This device usually sets up five statements in a section and the rater is requested to check two in each section that best describe the individual. Raters do not like this method, for it is often difficult for them to know when they are rating a person favorably.

4. Graphic Rating Scales

This is the most widely used and abused technique. Series of traits or characteristics important in assessing employee performance are listed. Each listing is divided into degrees. For example, "cooperative" might be divided into degrees such as: "always cooperative," "usually cooperative," "often cooperative," "seldom cooperative," "never cooperative." Thus, in effect, a quantitative measuring scale is provided for each trait.

5. Behavior Check List

Experimentation with this form has been going on during recent years. The check list utilizes definitive statements felt to be typical of poor, average and good performance. The rater is instructed to check whether the person being rated does them or how well he does them.[2] One important advantage of this form is that it gives the rater and ratee helpful ideas to talk about in an interview.

William R. Spriegel made a survey of company practices in the appraisal of employee performance and found that 343 of 567 reporting companies had appraisal programs for employees at the general-foreman level or below. See Table 17.1 for per cent of firms that reported use of appraisal programs.

TABLE 17.1

HOW PERFORMANCE APPRAISAL HAS GROWN

	Per Cent of Firms Reporting Use of Appraisal		
Year	*Any Kind of Appraisal*	*For Non-executives Only*	*For Executives Only*
1930	41.0	—	—
1940	52.0	52.8	20.0
1947	45.9	42.2	20.9
1953	60.8	54.6	32.3
1957	66.0	57.3	42.1
1960*	—	60.5†	45.3‡

* Figures for 1960 are taken from the study reported here, which did not compute total use of merit rating.
† General foremen and down.
‡ Superintendents and up.
Source: William R. Spriegel, "Company Practices in Appraisal of Managerial Performance," *Personnel,* American Management Association, Inc., May-June, 1962, p. 79.

The appraisal methods used by these companies are listed in Table 17.2.

TABLE 17.2

APPRAISAL METHODS USED BY RESPONDENTS

Method	*Number of Firms*
Graphic	63
Traits and/or performance rating, checking various descriptive phrases,	148
Traits and/or performance rating, the rater writing out the degree of performance applicable.	125
Space for an illustration of the degree of performance described.	170
Rate on only one item, "How well does he perform on his job?" leaving room to	

check some 3 to 5 degrees and asking for comments to justify the rating.	82
Traditional "forced choice" system of rating where multiple choices are provided and the rater must select: (1) the one most like the ratee and (2) the one least like the ratee.	45
Numerical or percentage value given to appraisal or rating.	102

Source: Spriegel, *op. cit.*, p. 80.

The choice of form to be used should be determined by the main purpose of the rating system. Spriegel's survey indicated that two of the purposes, "Counseling" and "Training and development," require executives to think through the strengths and weaknesses of the ratee. Most of the other purposes indicate that appraisals are used for decision making as in promotions, discharges and salary administration. See Table 17.3.

TABLE 17.3

PURPOSES FOR WHICH APPRAISAL IS USED

Purpose	*Number of Firms*
Counseling	300
Promotion	298
Training and development	265
Considering retention or discharge	240
Salary administration or merit increase	237
Bonus payments	54
Profit-sharing payments	14

Methods of Training Raters

Method	*Number of Firms*
Provide each rater with a manual explaining the program, but give no other special instructions.	72
Hold a meeting of all raters to explain the program; may also provide a manual.	158
Provide some practice in rating to give raters an appreciation of the standards; may also provide manual and/or hold meeting.	82
Have individual consultation and review with raters who give out-of-line ratings.	175

Source: Spriegel, *op. cit.*, pp. 81, 82.

Most purposes tend to fall into one of four main classes:

1. To obtain a measure or estimate of job performance for administrative use, as in the case of the Lincoln Electric Company's "Bonus Merit Rating Scoring System" (see pages 355 and 356). A general trait scale is usually used for such purposes. When the main purpose of the rating is for administrative use rather than training or interviewing, discussion of four or five general traits is sufficient. As stated by Bittner:

1. In a study of a 12-trait rating scale applied to over 1,100 men in industry, a factor analysis showed that only two traits were really being measured. These were called "ability to do present job" and "quality of performance on the job." This result was due to the great overlapping or inability of the raters to distinguish between the traits.

2. In a study of a 10-trait rating scale applied to 2,000 Army officers, factor analysis revealed that only three traits were being measured—namely, "sense of duty," "physical and mental endurance and ability," and "leadership." It was also found that "ability to obtain results" correlated .90 with the total score on the 10 traits, and four of the 10 traits predicted the total score almost perfectly with a correlation of .97.

3. In another study of a 12-trait rating scale applied to Army Air Force officers, factor analysis showed that only four traits were being measured—namely, "sense of duty," "physical and mental stability and endurance," "leadership," and "judgment and common sense."

4. In developing a new Army rating scale, 900 behavior items—statements like "can't take suggestions," "resents criticism"—were rated by a group of officers on observability and universality, and it was necessary to throw out 600 of them as being not observable, not universally applicable, or both.

The import of these and similar studies is that only a few traits will be included in the rating scale if the three criteria—observability, universality, and distinguishability—are observed in selecting them. Add more if you like, but you end up with essentially the same result (and often misleading results) at the cost of considerably more effort. A few companies have recognized this and applied it in their rating procedure. At least one company I know rates on only two traits—"ability to do present job" and "promotability."[3]

2. To select employees for promotion, transfer, or layoff. The ranking method is most commonly used.

3. To provide a basis for a training program, as exemplified by the "Employees' Ratings of Their Supervisor" (see page 342). In this case, each employee rated his supervisory superiors. The employees' ratings of each supervisor were charted to show whether he was above or below the average for all supervisors of the company. The results of the ratings on all traits were not given in any one training session. To stimulate the supervisors, the results for trait number one were given in the first session, and so on to the end of the training course of eighteen sessions.

4. To provide a basis for a constructive interview with the employee. Some kind of behavior check list or other type that provides a wide variety of specific descriptive phrases is most helpful.

The chief value of ratings which are made on specific characteristics rather than general behavior is that they enable the executive to give the employee definite suggestions as to what he should or should not do. To tell an employee that he should improve his appearance is not so effective as to tell him that he should shave more frequently or press his clothes regularly. To tell him that he should be more industrious is not so effective as to ask him to do less "visiting" in the office or to come to work on time. When abstractions are rated and the supervisory executive wishes to have an intimate advisory talk with a subordinate, he usually preaches a sermon.

When Foremen Conduct the Post-rating Interview

In some companies foremen are expected to discuss an employee's rating or appraisal with him. Most foremen find it difficult. It is embarrassing to tell a subordinate to his face that he lacks personality or a sense of humor. The foreman realizes that when a man is told that he lacks "vision" or a "dynamic personality," he is likely to feel baffled rather than enlightened.

When one foreman was told that he should conduct post-appraisal interviews with his employees, he answered: "I'll be darned if I'll do that. I'll take the time to sit down and rate each one of my men, but I won't discuss the ratings with the man. When I tried to do the reviews last year, it took me several months to get back to normal with each man." Some foremen feel silly when they sit down and try to talk to a worker as though the interview were a special occasion. They believe that if the worker deserves coaching, he should have it given to him as soon as the need arises—not once or twice a year on a special occasion. Many foremen also feel that it is useless to talk to a man about his work record unless it is possible to give each deserving employee a raise in pay right after the interview. As one foreman stated: "If he does not deserve a raise in pay, you can't convince him without an argument."

The list of excuses given by foremen for procrastination in conducting a post-appraisal interview are many: When an employee is counseled about the improvements he should make, he may react badly, he may argue, he may be upset emotionally, he may be made to feel insecure. If the employee is praised, he may become conceited about his own importance, and some employees will tell others the complimentary content of the merit rating interview and thus provoke jealousy on the part of fellow workers.

These objections should be appreciated by top management. Few supervisors know how to cope with an employee's resistance when it is shown by tense silence, obviously emotionalized but with resentment suppressed rather than expressed openly. Nor do they like to deal with counter-arguments.

The personal relationship between a supervisor and a subordinate is similar to that between two good friends—neither mentions to the others certain touchy subjects. Some companies find it easier therefore to spend money necessary to hire specialists such as psychologists and consultants to do it for the foremen. And yet few hired specialists are in so strong a position for counseling as the man's own boss. The hired specialists, in time, discover that an employee's behavior will not be changed until he is involved in action—in the performance of a real task whose outcome will be significant to him. The most meaningful action plan to an employee is one set up under the guidance or direction of a senior who is responsible for the work being performed. However, the senior may have to be a member of management of a higher level of responsibility and skill than found in the typical shop foreman.

APPRAISALS FOR COACHING PURPOSES

Most merit rating systems that involve the use of an elaborate printed scale for evaluating personality traits do not encourage the "judge" to examine the factors that are most important in the employer-employee relationship—getting the work done. The employee who is not getting his work done properly or in the expected quantity, needs coaching about the work and his procedures rather than an evaluation of his personality traits. Generally, merit rating plans of the trait variety have been used mostly by personnel workers for administrative purposes. Appraisal plans for coaching purposes are used mainly by line executives above the typical supervisory level.

The trend toward the use of formal appraisal systems for coaching purposes has increased. Executives do some informal coaching of their subordinates every day. The main value of a formal appraisal system is that the executive is encouraged to analyze each subordinate's work record and to review with him all those factors that might enable him to do a better job.

Several investigators of appraisal systems have pointed out the difficulties in trying to be judicial in appraising people and have advocated the use of a plan that gauges "management by objectives" rather than by judgment of the personal worth of a subordinate.[4]

The first stage in the procedure used in this new approach is a simple statement, conversational, of employee work responsibilities rather than a formal job description. From this the boss and the subordinate establish the subordinate's "targets" or short-term (about six months) performance goals. At the conclusion of the six-month period, the subordinate makes *his own* appraisal of what he has accomplished relative to the targets which he had set. The boss and subordinate then hold a "review interview" to discuss the record, evaluate the weaknesses and strengths in what has been done, and set new targets for the next six months. In this procedure the subordinate is an *active* figure in the system, and the major difference between this approach and the conventional trait-rating technique is that it shifts the emphasis from *appraisal* to *analysis*. There is also a shift of emphasis from the past to *performance in relation to work goals* in the future, and this serves a more constructive end than judicial evaluations of the person. The personality of the subordinate is not a central issue, but the prospects for self-development through work are greatly enhanced.[5]

Coaching by the executive provides a meaningful method for letting a subordinate know where he stands in his work relations with management and for discussing specific ways in which he can become more effective in his job.

Many executives who believe in coaching would like to improve their skill in doing it. The intensity of interest on the part of executives is indicated by the experience of the American Management Association. The AMA reports that whenever it announces a seminar on appraisal reviews, it is flooded with executive applicants. Another barometer of management interest in the subject is the increase of management consulting firms who have entered the field.[6]

In an appraisal review session for coaching purposes the boss and the subordinate should conduct a give-and-take discussion of the subordinate's performance on the job, relations with fellow workers, standing with his superiors, and all strengths and weaknesses in regard to the work. The session ends with a summary of what the subordinate can do to improve his performance.

What goes on in a coaching interview varies with the individuals involved. The typical executive usually starts the interview with a review of the subordinate's strong points.

Then he gradually moves into areas where the ratee could stand improvement. The executive will, if he is skilled, let the subordinate do most of the talking, let him tell what is wrong with his current procedures. The executive adds comments of approval or disapproval, or makes recommendations.

Skilled interviewers use the "turnback." When the ratee asks a question, the rater turns the question back to the ratee before he tries to give an answer.

Here are four examples of turnback:

1. RATEE: But how does my rating stack up with the other employees in the department?
   RATER: How do you feel you compare with the others?
2. RATEE: But I try hard all the time. What can I do to improve?
   RATER: What do you think you might do to improve?
3. RATEE: Have I been doing any better lately? Do you think my work is improving?
   RATER: Do you feel you have been improving?
4. RATEE: I would like some time to get to be a secretary. How should I go about it?
   RATER: Do you have any ideas as to what you might do?

When the person rated responds with strong feeling, the interviewer does not give a logical explanation. Instead, he encourages the ratee to talk out his feelings and thereby clarify his thinking so that he can develop his own solution. If pent-up feelings have been released, he may become more receptive to a logical explanation.

These permissive techniques do not mean that an employee should not become aware of his weaknesses and needed improvements.. On the contrary, the processes of making him aware can be achieved by different techniques. The permissive procedure of the kind that uses the turnback is designed to enable the ratee to discover and to accept the criticism rather than hear it given but refuse its acceptance.[7]

Some executives can or at least think they can do effective coaching. When they do, the executive and his subordinate try to agree on what areas of performance are poor and what the subordinate will do to bring about improvement. At the next appraisal, or perhaps sooner, they will meet to see how the improvement program is progressing.

Great skill is needed by the executive who conducts a discussion of a subordinate's performance and how he can improve it. Yet the practice is spreading to shop and office employees as more top management men see it as a help in coaching their junior executives. The boss usually talks with and gets suggestions from other executives to improve his appraisal and recommendations before the interview takes place.

As an aid to the executive, the committee or group approach to appraisal review systems is gaining. The typical executive does not want to be the only person to evaluate a man. In the committee approach, the group consists of personnel specialists and senior executives, including the man's immediate supervisor. They hold an appraising session, essentially constructive in spirit. Later, the immediate supervisor sits down with his subordinate to clarify the group's findings and suggestions. The two men then discuss ways in which improvements can be made in the performance. The committee approach eliminates tendencies toward personal prejudice. It also takes a great load off the supervisor. Instead of saying "I think...," he can say, "We believe..."

Recommendations for Effective Post-Appraisal Interviews

Management men and researchers have found that the effectiveness of interviews can be increased by means of the following procedures:

1. Do not tell a man how or in what

respects he should change himself. Instead, ask him questions about his work responsibilities, his objectives, and his methods of work. Use the job-centered rather than a man-centered approach.

2. Interviews should not begin with a review of what is wrong with a man or his work. Let him suggest the first topics for discussion so that he may feel that his interests are being recognized. Always preserve a man's dignity.

3. Stress the team approach. Discuss the relationships with other members of the company and procedures for getting work done by bringing those people into the program who are or should be participants.

4. Some executives who conduct post-appraisal interviews find that going through an interview themselves with their own chiefs helps them improve their interviews with others. To be effective with others, it is necessary to be relaxed and self confident. The man who has experienced the benefits of a constructive appraisal interview himself usually improves his manner with his subordinates.

5. The coaching type of interview should not involve a review of the advisee's present salary or promises of reward for the future. The focus of discussion is the employee's job, not his pay. This procedure is the opposite of that used in merit ratings for administrative purposes. Some companies use merit ratings in deciding whether to grant or withhold raises. As a result, the rating system has this meaning for the employees. When all appraisals are made in the same month of the year, the appraisal date becomes the time when every employee expects a raise. Hence, some managements conduct their appraisal of each employee about two months prior to the anniversary date of his employment. This spreads the administrative task throughout the year and prevents the expectation of an increase being given to most employees at the same time.

6. When an employee raises the question of pay during the coaching interview, the coach should point out that that subject must be treated in another type of interview. An appointment for the purpose can be made. During the coaching interview, the coach should stress the worker's satisfactions gained from his knowledge that he is doing good work. Professional workers such as physicians and teachers are likely to continue to improve their work and abilities even though financial rewards do not follow immediately. To them, financial rewards are by-products of good work. As in the professions, most intelligent workers in business improve their abilities because they increase their respect for themselves, not for money alone. They seek self-fulfillment as well as material rewards.

7. To be effective as a coach or counselor, the executive must be held in high esteem by the subordinate. If the subordinate merely acts in a respectful manner because the superior holds a higher rank, the coaching benefits will be negligible.

8. Executives who do systematic coaching as in post-appraisal interviews realize that much skill is essential. This kind of interview cannot attain its full benefits when an executive acts in his usual authoritarian manner. If he is to learn to respect the special contributions that can be made through permissive techniques, he may have to develop a new kind of respect for himself as a skilled counselor, diagnostician, and teacher. The executive coach can get self-appraisal values out of the interview, too. He does this when he asks, "What can I do to help you make your job go better?" When the atmosphere is truly permissive, the subordinate will tell him quite frankly.

9. Use "playback." Ask the employee to state his ideas as to the conclusions and plans that were developed during the interview. If he wants to make promises that he cannot or is not likely to fulfill by the time of the next coaching session, it is necessary to help him set goals that are attainable.

A favorable attitude on the part of employees toward a rating system can be fostered by using a positive and pleasing title for it, such as "Employee Progress Review" or "Employee Development Plan."

Whatever the appraisal or coaching program that may be used, all employees should know about its nature and its purposes. Employees should be given the information *before* the plan is put into effect. One bank management made the mistake of hiring a retail reporting organization that had its interviewers "shop" each teller in the bank in order to rate the teller. When management presented the "shoppers'" reports to the tellers, they felt resentful. Management had failed to be above board with them. Cleverness cannot be justified when it also implies insincerity.

Rightly used, the development of a rating system can be made the basis of an extensive company educational program. When employees do not participate in management's rating and educational plans, the employees do not respond whole-heartedly to management's well-meant efforts. The violation of this basic principle explains why the manager mentioned in the beginning of this chapter failed to get a worthwhile response to his new training courses.

Teachers are often asked to rate students or former students, but their ratings should be limited to the classroom contacts and should not include the many outside activities. When a teacher has a large class, he seldom becomes acquainted with the students. Occasionally he does have direct associations with a student in his home or on the athletic field, and then the classroom estimate may be modified very decidedly. The ratings made by ministers and doctors have little value, because they know people under limited conditions only. Few of us conduct ourselves normally when in the presence of preachers and physicians.

Ronald Taft reviewed the literature concerning the ability of people to judge others and described five different types of methods of measuring this ability. He found that the following characteristics appear to be related to the ability of a person to judge the personality characteristics of others:

High intelligence and academic ability. This is positively related to ability to determine another's characteristics analytically, but not to non-analytic ways of judging. Probably perception and attitude are more important in determining the latter than abstract intelligence.

Emotional adjustment. The better adjusted person is the better judge.

Insight into one's own status. Evidently those who can rate themselves accurately on individual traits can also rate others fairly well.

Social orientation. Good judges of others have a greater social orientation than the poorer judges.

Social skill. The ability to predict how subjects will respond to opinion items is consistent with measures of social skill such as leadership, salesmanship, and popularity. This might also be due to projection on the part of the skilled people.

Apparently the ability to judge another's personality characteristics accurately depends on more than the possession of certain traits in the person judging. It is more than the right proportions of general intelligence to social intelligence to intuition that is needed. The judger needs, in addition, appropriate norms, such as a similar background, and he should be motivated to judge accurately and be free to do so.[8]

Some persons are poor judges of other people. Conversely, certain individuals can rate others objectively and accurately. The best judges can be identified to some extent.[9]

Studies of individuals regarding their abilities to judge others accurately have suggested that the rater's concepts of himself determine the quality of his interpersonal appraisals. As one researcher stated: "It is not that as ye shall judge so shall ye be judged, but as you judge yourself, so shall you judge others."[10] Generally, clinicians assume that an emotionally healthy individual is a better judge of others because he has fewer problems that interfere with his ability to view others objectively.

As previously stated, some companies try

to improve the accuracy of ratings by having raters meet as a group and agree on a consensus evaluation. Experimental studies indicate, however, that if three raters make their estimates independently and then arrive at a consensus estimate, the consensus is not as satisfactory as the statistical pooling of the ratings (by items) made by the same three judges independently.[11]

The "Halo Error" Is Common to All Ratings.

The general impression of an individual markedly colors our evaluation of his specific traits. If a person impresses us favorably in a general way, or because of some specific quality that we know he possesses, or because of an outstanding experience with him, we then tend to invest his entire personality with a luster that causes us to overestimate his desirable traits and underestimate his undesirable characteristics. One executive was asked why he rated a certain employee so low in all traits. His answer was to the effect that he did not like people who have small mouths and the particular employee had a small mouth. Some previous experience caused small mouths to become associated with the undesirable kind of personality and this experience colored his estimates of people who had that incidental trait. As we all know, if we like a person, we are apt to attribute all good traits to him. Conversely, if we dislike him, we tend to assign to him all negative traits.

The halo influence on graphic rating scales can be overcome to some extent if the rater will fill in the rating blanks for all employees by judging the employees on one trait at a time. For example, if twenty employees are to be rated on ten traits, the first trait on the scale being initiative, the judge should rate all twenty on initiative, and so on for each trait. It is natural for the executive to consider one man at a time rather than one trait at a time, but that procedure increases the halo effect. This danger also suggests that raters need systematic instruction before they make the ratings of their employees.[12]

The One Best Rating Plan Is Still to Be Invented.

When executives decide to use a merit rating plan, they naturally want the "one perfect plan." Unfortunately, no one system or form has as yet been proved to be valid or appropriate for all or even for many organizations.

The rating plan that is best for most companies is the one that most members of the organization will use constructively.

When the Industrial Relations Section, California Institute of Technology, had completed a total of 25 surveys in 18 different companies, covering over 50,000 employees, the Section formulated a number of conclusions based on all of its studies of employee opinion. One of these was that "Employees want to know from their supervisors how they are doing on the job and how they can improve." Supervisors will not do this task, which appears disagreeable to them at first, unless they have been properly trained and unless there is a planned procedure for rating employees and for discussing these ratings with them.[13]

The managements that try to make their appraisal programs an important contributory influence in strengthening their personnel do more than provide a manual of instruction—they also provide practice sessions and conduct individual reviews with raters.

Spencer J. Hayden has described some of the current faulty practices and the more effective procedures, in part, as follows:

> What do most of us do when we "coach" a subordinate after rating him? Well, usually we begin by calling him in for a special interview. (How did *you* feel the last time your boss scheduled such a meeting—anxious and on the defensive?)
>
> Next, we "put him at ease" by rambling on about the weather, his kid's progress in school, and such. Then we pointedly compliment him on some minor matter. All of this is a prelude to getting down to the dirty work. (How did

you feel when you were on the receiving end of this—were you fooled? Were you mentally preparing your defense?)

Then we lower the boom: tell him what's wrong, his "strengths and weaknesses," and what he ought to do to improve. (How did *you* feel when you got the works—cooperative on the surface but hurt underneath; confused, upset, resentful?)...

When someone tells you that you are doing wrong, he is really disapproving of you. Therefore, he becomes a threat to your self-esteem. When this happens, the perfectly normal tendency is to react defensively. And the more a person is on the defensive, the less advice he is able to accept from the threatener. In other words, the person who tells you your weaknesses is doing you no favor. He has created a barrier, unless the weaknesses are so minor, and mean so little to both parties, that the criticism cannot be taken seriously. At any rate, the boss's telling does not help the subordinate learn how to criticize himself, to solve his own problems, or to think more objectively about his performance, now or in the future....

At any rate, in the ordinary post-appraisal interview, the boss carries the ball, does all the work, does all the thinking, does all the planning—even though it is the *subordinate* who should be doing the learning. Somehow, this type of interview must be converted into a situation in which the subordinate does the work: the appraising, the evaluating, the thinking, the learning, the planning. And this will not happen unless he does almost all the talking.

To put it differently, when someone "advises" you, or pleads with you, or "suggests" that you do something, all these approaches involve *his* ideas rather than yours. Ever try advising a problem drinker? Or pleading with him? Or suggesting that he stay away from alcohol?

The point is this: everyone has a behavior pattern that reflects his personal adjustment to the problems of work and life. Until he *feels* differently about these patterns he'll continue them or substitute similar ones. If forced to abandon or change his ways, by being told to, or ordered to, or advised to, the change is usually insincere, uncomfortable, and only temporary.

What, then, can be done to help or motivate people to change...assuming that straight-forward telling or suggesting doesn't really come to grips with the basic problem? The answer lies in the fostering of the man's own *insight,* that is, in the maturing of his own self-perception, so that he sees himself, his behavior and the consequences of his actions in a clearer and more objective light, and eventually frees himself from the tangle of needs and emotions that determines the things he does. No one learns about himself from another. No one can be "analyzed" by another, because no two people have the same feelings about things, the same history, or the same problems. A man has to analyze himself. A counselor's role (the post-appraisal interviewer's role) is to stimulate this self-appraisal....

Attitudes are not changed by telling, advising, or showing. They are not changed by the process called "training." They are changed only by *education,* a long-range process that takes into account the whole man, his home life, goals, fears, hopes, history, and concept of himself. We call this type of education "counseling." It is man-centered rather than work-centered. It aims at the source rather than the result of performance. It doesn't ask "What should this man do to improve?" It seeks the answers to the questions: Why does he act this way? How far does he recognize the nature of his trouble?...

The most important thing is *a man's own appraisal of himself.* This, rather than anyone else's rating, should form the basis of a counseling relationship. Let *him* rate himself. Let *him* initiate the discussion of his own rating. As an example, some rating forms carry printed directions requesting the man to turn in his rating to his superior. This provides a somewhat less objectionable situation than the scheduled visit or summons to the boss's office. If a man initiates his own post-appraisal interview, he may feel a little surer of himself. He can wait until he's ready and feels that things are "right" for the meeting.

The objectives of post-appraisal interviewing should be a personal recognition of limitations and a self-propelled motivation toward improvement. The senior man should listen sympathetically and encourage the subordinate to "think out loud." With freedom of speech and a relaxed atmosphere, certain things will be said and brought to the surface that ordinarily would be hidden. The senior man's task is to help the other man to see the hidden significance of things that are said. "What did you mean when you said...?" "How did you feel when that happened?" "Tell me more about that."

No matter how wrong the subordinate seems, he should *not* be told that he's wrong. Instead, the questions should go on. "Why do you feel that way?" "Why did you say that?" The questions should seldom be of the kind that can be answered by a "Yes" or "No." The emphasis throughout should be on feelings, not on facts. Facts here are relatively unimportant. How the man *sees* and feels and interprets the facts are what count. . . .[14]

In spite of the many arguments for and benefits of merit rating, a few managements refuse to use them. They believe that a personnel function of this kind should not be formalized. They dislike the idea of cataloging any person's qualities and limitations. People, they say, deserve to be accepted and treated as members of a team, not as machines whose features can be listed on a sheet of paper. Those who cannot be fully accepted should be dismissed in a respectful manner.

Most managements, however, believe that the use of an appraisal system does not detract from the dignity of the individual. They remind the critics that anyone who attends school is rated throughout the years of his formal education.

Recent college graduates take to merit reviews quite easily. They are accustomed to having their work graded and their characteristics listed. They look upon such devices as means of getting tips that will be of value in their growth. Rising young men are usually confident of their records.

Lincoln Electric Company's Bonus Merit Rating System

Lincoln Electric Company employees are recognized as among the world's best paid workers. In 1961, Lincoln Electric paid out profit-sharing bonuses totaling $6.4 million to its 1,354 employees. The size of the total bonus pool is set by the board of directors after taxes, reserves and dividends have been deducted from gross profits.

For all employees, including engineers, the end-of-year bonuses normally range from 60 per cent to 150 per cent of the regular salary. And the basic salary structure is said to be competitive with other companies. Everyone but the president and chairman of the board share in these incentive extras.

The size of an individual's bonus depends on three factors: his merit rating, his base salary and the size of the total bonus pool.

As one employee stated about this incentive system: "It's a good place to work if you like to work."

Excerpts regarding the incentive compensation and merit rating plan are quoted from the "Employee's Handbook":

The Lincoln Electric Company has a unique system of incentive compensation, often referred to as the "bonus."

Each year since 1934 workers at Lincoln have received a substantial cash payment in December. This is not a gift. It represents a sharing of the results of efficiencies created in production during the past twelve months. The total bonus amount is determined by the Board of Directors, based on the success of the company for that year. The bonus is not guaranteed but is entirely dependent on the successful, profitable operation of the company, which to a very large extent depends on *your* enthusiasm and "will-to-work." Your share in the bonus depends on two major factors—your wages in the twelve months prior to and including October 31st and your merit ratings made as of April 30th and October 31st. The final rating used is the average of your record for the year. . . .

Twice a year, you receive a set of four merit rating cards, which show your general performance on your job and thus measure your contribution to the company. The four basic rating factors and the part of your performance they cover are shown on page 356.

Each card describes the rating factor briefly and is divided into sections in which the person doing the rating can place a check mark close to the printed statement best describing the individual's work. . . .

Workers are placed in rating "groups" of not less than fifteen people. Most "groups" average between twenty-five and fifty persons. . . .

Merit ratings are based on a numerical score which determines the standing of the individual within his rating group in comparison to the other people in that group. All of the ratings in each group must average 100 points per person. This means each of the four rating factors will average 25 points. You can determine whether your work is considered above or below the group average by comparing the numerical score showing opposite the check-mark on each card to the 25 point average figure. If your total score on all four rating factors is less than 95, you should discuss the rating with your supervisor or foreman to secure suggestions on improvement. . . .

You can see that merit rating is used a great deal in determining who is to be promoted to a better job. Your merit rating will be reviewed by any foreman, supervisor or department head who may wish to promote you to his working unit. . . .

Merit rating gives you an opportunity to increase your earnings substantially. . . . Through merit rating, an outstanding person can earn far beyond his base pay on his existing job, as his total compensation will be related directly to his contribution.

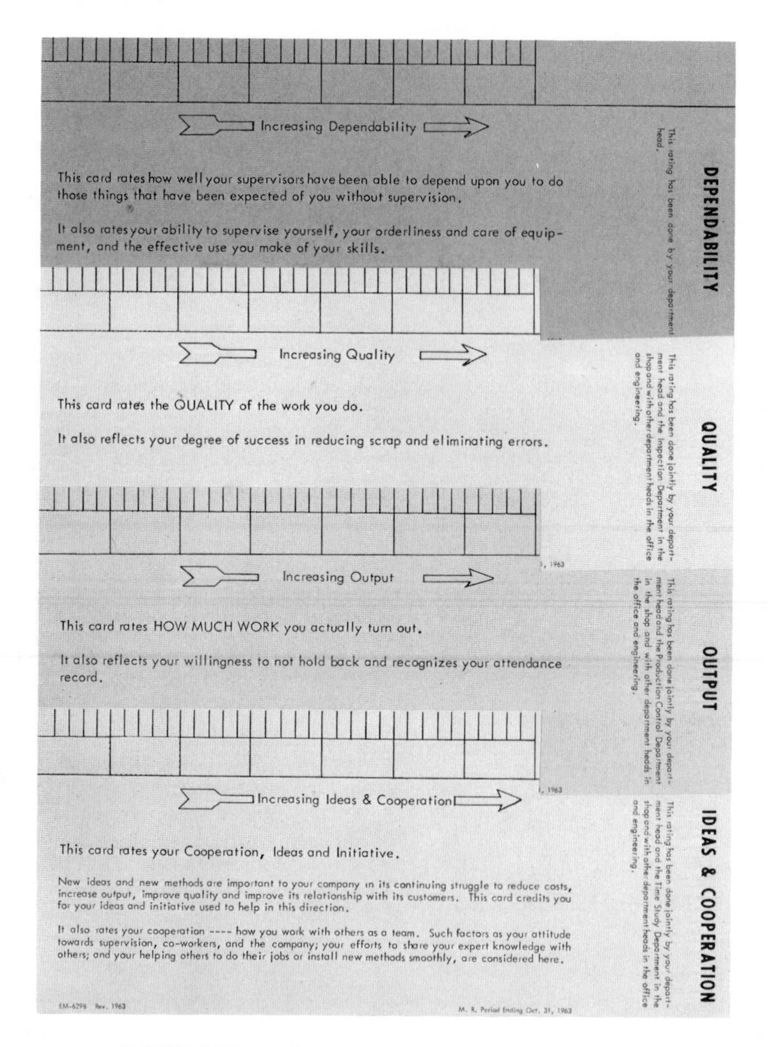

Increasing Dependability

This card rates how well your supervisors have been able to depend upon you to do those things that have been expected of you without supervision.

It also rates your ability to supervise yourself, your orderliness and care of equipment, and the effective use you make of your skills.

DEPENDABILITY

This rating has been done by your department head.

Increasing Quality

This card rates the QUALITY of the work you do.

It also reflects your degree of success in reducing scrap and eliminating errors.

QUALITY

This rating has been done jointly by your department head and the Inspection Department in the shop and with other department heads in the office and engineering.

Increasing Output

This card rates HOW MUCH WORK you actually turn out.

It also reflects your willingness to not hold back and recognizes your attendance record.

OUTPUT

This rating has been done jointly by your department head and the Production Control Department in the shop and with other department heads in the office and engineering.

Increasing Ideas & Cooperation

This card rates your Cooperation, Ideas and Initiative.

New ideas and new methods are important to your company in its continuing struggle to reduce costs, increase output, improve quality and improve its relationship with its customers. This card credits you for your ideas and initiative used to help in this direction.

It also rates your cooperation ---- how you work with others as a team. Such factors as your attitude towards supervision, co-workers, and the company; your efforts to share your expert knowledge with others; and your helping others to do their jobs or install new methods smoothly, are considered here.

IDEAS & COOPERATION

This rating has been done jointly by your department head and the Time Study Department in the shop and with other department heads in the office and engineering.

EM-6298 Rev. 1963

M. R. Period Ending Oct. 31, 1963

ACKNOWLEDGMENTS AND REFERENCES

1. Data from an unpublished survey by the Management Research Department of Booz, Allen & Hamilton. See "How to Identify Promotable Executives," by C. Wilson Randle, *Harvard Business Review,* May-June, 1956, p. 122.
2. For further information, see Roland Benjamin, Jr., "A Survey of 130 Merit Rating Plans," *Personnel,* American Management Association, Inc., November, 1952, pp. 289–294.
3. Reign Bittner, "Developing an Employee Merit Rating Procedure," *Personnel,* American Management Association, Inc., January, 1949, p. 281, pp. 290–291.
4. See Alva F. Kindall and James Gatza, "Positive Program for Performance Appraisal," *Harvard Business Review,* November-December, 1963 and Richard S. Reichmann, "Letters," *Harvard Business Review,* March-April, 1964.
5. See Douglas McGregor, "An Uneasy Look at Performance Appraisal," *Harvard Business Review,* May-June, 1957. See also *Personnel Management Abstracts,* Summer Issue 1957.

6. See "Executive Coaching Catches On," *Business Week,* Mar. 9, 1957.
7. See Bernard J. Covner, "The Communication of Merit Ratings: A Philosophy and a Method," *Personnel,* American Management Association, Inc., September, 1953.
8. Ronald Taft, "The Ability to Judge People," *Psychological Bulletin,* January, 1955, pp. 1–21.
9. Cecil J. Mullins and Ronald C. Force, "Rater Accuracy as a Generalized Ability," *Journal of Applied Psychology,* June, 1962.
10. Statement by Harry Stack Sullivan. See Marvin Spanner, "Attribution of Traits and Emotional Health as Factors Associated with the Prediction of Personality Characteristics of Others," *Journal of Consulting Psychology,* June, 1961.
11. See Victor B. Cline and James M. Richards, Jr., "A Comparison of Individuals Versus Groups in Judging Personality," *Journal of Applied Psychology,* June, 1961.
12. W. V. Bingham, "Halo, Invalid and Valid," *Journal of Applied Psychology,* **23,** No. 2 (1939). The author points out that not all halo is invalid, because the person rated may be evaluated with regard to a specific position. This study indicated that "...it is not the rater alone whose reactions to the candidate are in question. He is but typical of others—clients, subordinates, fellow employees—who will react to the subject not as a bundle of isolated traits but as a person with certain duties. The judgments and responses of all these people will unconsciously and inevitably manifest a halo effect which is, in part at least, valid."
13. Excerpt from Project 5, "Surveys of Employee Opinion," *Annual Report 1953–1954,* Industrial Relations Section, California Institute of Technology.
14. Spencer J. Hayden, Training Director Metal & Thermit Corporation, New York, "Getting Better Results from Post-Appraisal Interviews," paper delivered before the AMA Special Conference on Training held Dec. 9–10, 1954, at Atlanta, Georgia, and published in *Personnel,* American Management Association, Inc., May, 1955, pp. 541–550.

PROJECTS

1. Examine several graphic rating scales for general traits such as initiative, personality, and so on. Select the traits that are objective in nature and those that are reactions to persons. Select several general traits and break them down into the specific forms of behavior to which they may apply.
2. Perhaps you think that a person can be judged more fairly by means of an anecdotal behavior journal, a cumulative record of characteristic behavior patterns, than by means of rating scales. If so, write several paragraphs that describe one or two persons whom you know well. Show them to someone who knows the ratees. Does that person think that your anecdotes are truly descriptive of each person you described?
3. You may, without experience with the post-appraisal interview, think that it is easily conducted. To appreciate its difficulties have some friends rate a person on a standardized rating form. Then conduct an effective post-appraisal interview with the ratee. Let several observers evaluate your skills and discuss possible improvements that you should make.
4. Discuss reasons why some students may disagree with an instructor regarding marks given in a course.
5. Would you like to work for the Lincoln Electric Co. or any other employer who pays employees on the basis of a merit rating system? State likely advantages and disadvantages for the employee.

COLLATERAL READINGS

Bellows, Roger M., *Psychology of Personnel in Business and Industry.* Englewood Cliffs, N.J.: Prentice-Hall, Inc., 1954, Chapter 17.

Fleishman, Edwin A., *Studies in Personnel and Industrial Psychology.* Homewood, Ill.: The Dorsey Press, Inc., 1961, Chapters 10–15.

Gellerman, Saul W., *Motivation and Productivity.* New York: American Management Association, Inc., 1963, Chapter 19.

Karn, Harry W. and B. von Haller Gilmer, *Readings in Industrial and Business Psychology.* New York: McGraw-Hill Book Company, 1962, pp. 175–218.

Kirchner, Wayne K. and Donald J. Reisberg, "How Supervisors Differ in Appraising their Subordinates," *Personnel,* American Management Association, Inc., November-December, 1962.

Maier, Norman R. F., *Psychology in Industry.* Boston: Houghton Mifflin Company, 1955, Chapter 8.

Zander, Alvin F., ed., *Performance Appraisals Effects on Employees and their Performance.* Ann Arbor, Mich.: The Foundation for Research on Human Behavior, 1963.

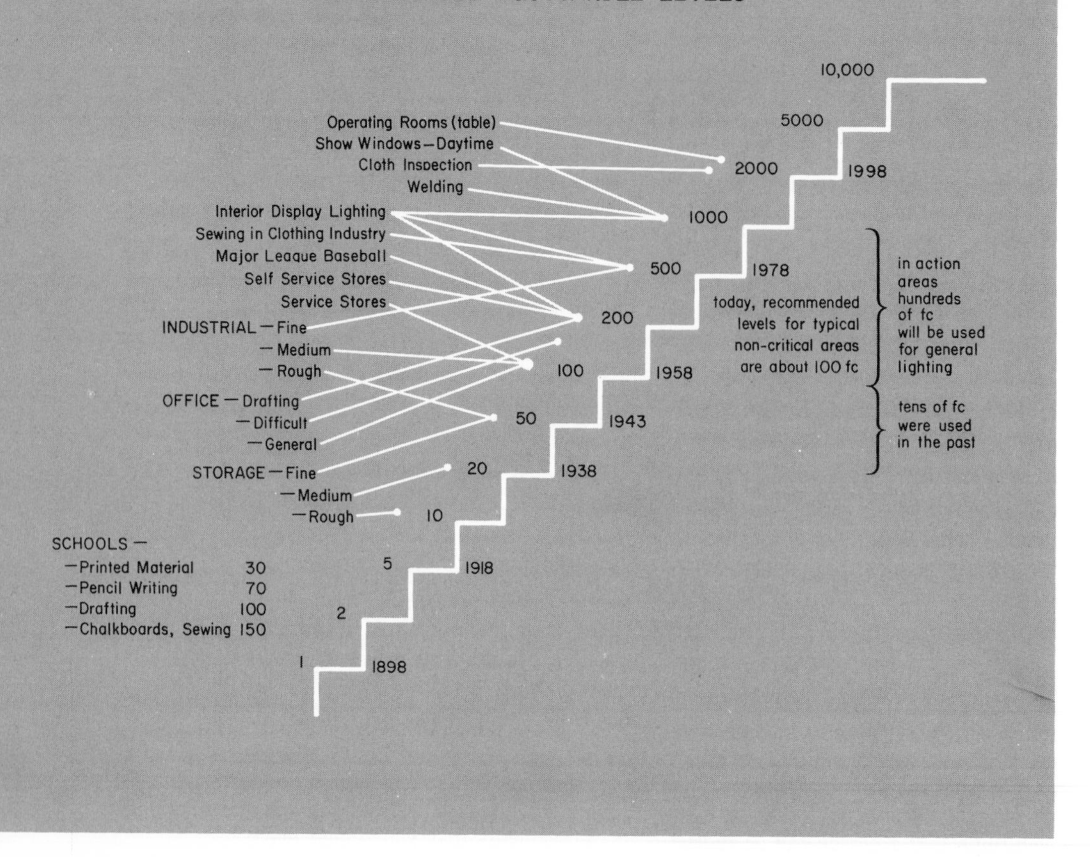

PROJECTED HISTORY OF ILLUMINATION STANDARDS IN THE UNITED STATES

The history of electric lighting *shows a steady increase in recommended lighting levels at about the rate of one log step every 30 years—that is, a tenfold increase. This is roughly equivalent to doubling every ten years. The footcandle value beside each step in the chart above indicates a typical recommended level for a corresponding year. Dots show new I.E.S. recommendations.*

Visually, much is being done to create pleasing conditions—good color combinations, interesting patterns and textures, attractive furniture, painted machines in factories.

The lighting design implications of creating a pleasing environment are:

1. Lighting should be unobtrusive, and if equipment is exposed to view, it should be attractive.

2. Moderate variations in the brightness pattern are desirable to avoid the monotony one associates with a cloudy day outdoors.

3. Lighting should bring out characteristics of objects such as texture, sheen, form, and color.

4. Directional light in addition to diffused light is needed. (This is closely associated with points two and three, and suggests sunshine.)

5. Dynamic or mobile change in environment is desirable. Much has to be learned in this area, but one can see that part of the charm of natural lighting is its variation, by season, by time of day, and even over a matter of minutes. Also, it seems evident that our appreciation for things is based in part on change. However, variations in the lighting should not be so pronounced as to be distracting. It is probably true that we enjoy changing contrasts more than simple changes of the over-all lighting level within a space.

Source: *Karl A. Staley,* ***Fundamentals of Light and Lighting,*** *Cleveland, Ohio; Large Lamp Dept., General Electric Co., August 1960, and R. T. Dorsey and E. A. Lindsay, "Concepts for Meeting Human Needs with Light,"* ***Light Magazine,*** *July-September 1958.*

CHAPTER EIGHTEEN

MAKING WORKING CONDITIONS FAVORABLE FOR EMPLOYEE EFFICIENCY

Employee morale is lowered by unfavorable working conditions. This situation is the more serious because often the employees who are affected are unaware of the true cause of their grouchiness and dissatisfaction...the physical surroundings of a job may result in a general lowering of employee morale in a way which is not revealed by ordinary questioning of the men. The conclusion we may draw is that when an unfavorable morale condition is found to exist, it is wise to examine carefully the physical surroundings to determine whether some unnatural condition may be at fault.[1]

Many investigations, similar to those of the Hawthorne studies, have indicated that the factor of motivation is more important in productivity than simple physical changes in the environment. When workers feel that they are participating in a significant project and that they are important as persons, they are likely to be so highly motivated as to ignore mere physical conditions. Of course we cannot assume that environmental factors are of no consequence. As specified by Whitehead, "in order to maintain a satisfactory material situation . . . the total physical situation at any time must be within the indifferent range of the individual experiencing it."[2]

Lighting-illumination of Work

Good lighting often helps the worker do more work with less effort. Furthermore, inadequate lighting is depressing to many people. Offices are boresome if lighting does not create variety. Obviously, lighting should be adequate, constant, evenly distributed, and without glare. Contrary to popular opinion, direct sunlight does not always meet these four requirements, so that it often must be supplemented with artificial lighting.

Many managements fail to realize the effects of lighting on output, quality, costs, morale, and safety. When neglected lighting fails to furnish the illumination that is necessary for high production, man hours and materials are wasted every day. Every kind of working situation is likely to have its unique lighting problems, and we cannot assume that what is good lighting for one worker and his work is also good lighting for the next worker and his work. However, many studies of lighting have indicated that better factory lighting tends to increase production.

Vision checks of more than two million workers by the American Optical Company indicated that about one third of all American industrial employees have poor eyesight. Some workers admit that they obtain their glasses without an eye examination, and some wear spectacles borrowed from friends or relatives. Among 200,000 employees in diversified industries, about 55 per cent had normal or 20/20 vision without glasses; 20 per cent had normal vision with glasses; and 25 per cent had defective vision which was not corrected with glasses. Another typical survey of nearly 15,000 adult employees showed that 25 per cent had 20/30 to 20/40 vision.[3]

In many cases of reported improvements in efficiency as a result of better lighting, only the lighting is mentioned, even though important additional changes are made. Sometimes methods of work are ignored. Furthermore, marked improvement in conditions of work, tend to result in increased efficiency. Marked increases in efficiency as a result of improved working conditions are not always permanent, because the "lift" in morale may wear off ofter several months.

Surveys of lighting of homes, offices, factories, and schoolrooms have revealed many examples of inadequate and harmful illumination. The three aspects of lighting which most often are unhygienic are brightness or intensity, quality or color, and distribution or diffusion of illumination.

The Department of Psychology *of the University of Texas, Mezes Hall. The offices, classrooms, laboratories, clinics, shops, and library of the department are housed in this building. Specialized research rooms—soundproof, constant temperature, surgery, and submammalian laboratories—are located in the basement; the machine shops and graduate research rooms on the fifth floor. This building offers facilities for the study of psychological factors that influence work effort.*

Intensity of Light

Intensity of light is measured in footcandles. Footcandle is a technical term which refers to "the amount of light illuminating a surface by a standard candle at a distance of one foot." A green grass lawn under the full sunlight of midday in mid-summer may have a level of illumination of 8,000 footcandles, but is not excessively bright because of its relatively low reflectance.

Footcandles currently suggested for performance of representative tasks are offered as relative recommendations rather than as invariably fixed levels of illumination. Bookkeeping, for example, under certain conditions may require eight times as many footcandles as typing on white paper to give the respective workers the same ability to see.

Based upon such considerations of footcandles for equal visibility, committees of the Illuminating Engineering Society have developed lighting recommendations for a wide range of practical work-world tasks. Representative values are presented in Table 18.1.

Generally, lighting engineers advise 50 to 75 footcandles of glareless light for reading, writing, or any other close work. In laymen's terms, this means from five to ten times more light than is available in the typical home.

TABLE 18.1

LEVELS OF ILLUMINATION CURRENTLY RECOMMENDED FOR TYPICAL WORK-WORLD VISUAL TASKS

Task	*Footcandles on Task**
Industrial Tasks	
Rough, easy assembly work	30
Rough bench and machine work, ordinary inspection	50
Medium bench and machine work, rough grinding, medium buffing and polishing, difficult inspection	100
Color inspection, grading and evaluation, making and finishing shoes, highly difficult inspection	200
Fine bench and machine work, medium grinding, fine buffing and polishing, sewing, very difficult inspection	500
Extra-fine bench and machine work, fine grinding, welding, extra-fine assembly work, most difficult inspection	1000
Office Tasks	
Corridors, elevators, escalators, stairways	20
Reading high contrast or well printed material, tasks and areas not involving critical or prolonged seeing such as conferences, interviews, inactive files and washrooms	30
Reading or transcribing hand writing in ink or medium pencil on good quality paper, intermittent filing	70
Regular office work, reading good reproductions, reading or transcribing hand writing in hard pencil or on poor paper, active filing, index references, mail sorting	100
Accounting, auditing, tabulating, bookkeeping, business machine operation, reading poor reproductions, proof reading, rough layout drafting	150
Cartography, designing, detailed drafting	200

* Minimum on task at any time.

The lighting requirements for ideal seeing conditions should be derived from consideration of such factors as optimal visibility and visual performance and maximal ease of seeing. Ideal levels of illumination and brightness relationships should be looked upon as ultimate objectives. Their establishment should not be hampered by their practicability or attainability. On the other hand, when developing lighting recommendations it is necessary to include such factors as economics and the ability to provide these lighting levels with the light sources and equipment currently available. Thus, lighting recommendations become a flexible rather than rigid requirement, and improve and change with the advancements made by illuminating engineering. This has happened in the past and will continue in the future.

Source: Sylvester K. Guth, "Lighting Research," *American Industrial Hygiene Association Journal,* September-October, 1962.

Direct Glare . . . *It is no new problem to have too much light in a worker's eyes, too little on his work. The first step to effect a cure . . . is to shade lamps properly, put the light where it belongs . . . save as much as 60% of light that may otherwise be wasted.*

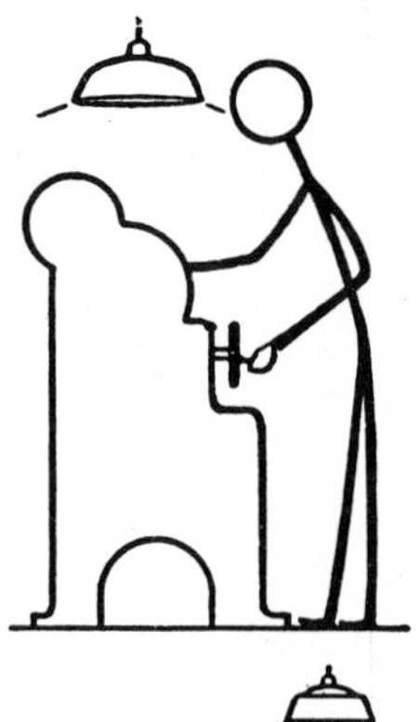

Reflected Glare . . . *is a problem in two phases . . . often more objectionable than direct glare, and frequently more harmful. A change from concentrated light sources to a large-area light source is the first and best cure. Adequate covering, to assure diffusion, plus proper placing of offending supplementary units, can help.*

Daylight Glare . . . *Improper placement of drafting boards, desks, etc., can cause time loss due to glare from direct daylight. The cure . . to shade the window or, wherever possible, shift working surfaces to put natural light on working plane instead of in the worker's eyes.*

Dirt . . . *Commonest of all lighting bottlenecks and easiest to cure. Dirty lamps and fixtures or windows frosted with grime can cut lighting levels as much as 50% . . . a regular soap and water schedule is essential, and for many installations equipment must be taken down for thorough washing.*

CHECK THESE FIRST-AID RECOMMENDATIONS

Reflected Daylight Glare . . . *is natural light that bounces from work plane to eyes. Its only cure is shading the source or providing a high enough indoor intensity to offset as much reflected daylight as possible. (Sketches to be interpreted as plans, not as elevations.)*

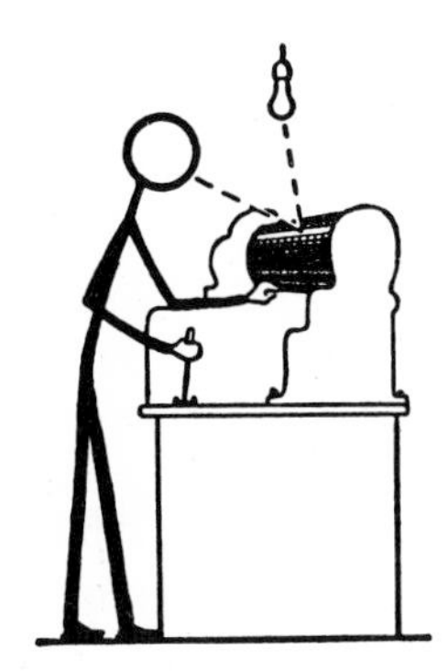

Point-light Source Reflections . . . *Light reflected from curved work surfaces is concentrated by a point-light source . . . can be minimized by shifting the lamp, shading, diffusing or changing to a long light source.*

Shadows . . . *Every worker knows the problem of "standing in his own light." Belts, beams, cranes, and tool racks all aggravate this trouble. The complete cure is adequate general lighting. The next best remedy is to increase the number of light sources.*

Procedure Chart Lighting . . . *Here eyes must change focus constantly, look through the pool of light over machine at a less highly illuminated procedure, blueprint, or scale table. The cure . . . to equalize the illumination on machine and chart.*

From ***The Magazine of Light,*** *No. 3 (1942). Lamp Department, General Electric Company, Nela Park, Cleveland. Recommendations verified July, 1964.*

One practical way to overcome such a lack is to set aside a well-lighted corner of the living room or den for reading purposes.

Light Distribution

Distribution of light is exceedingly important and can often be achieved with little effort. Unevenness of distribution is the most common error in lighting. Failure to maintain a proper diffusion of light produces eyestrain and decreases visual efficiency. Simple rearrangements of work and changes in lighting fixtures often eliminate glare and the bright areas and shadows within the visual field. Tinker has summarized suggestions for certain improvements in distribution as follows:

> The uncomfortable effects of bright spots of light above or off to the side of the line of vision while reading, doing other visual work, or even when no visual discrimination is involved, is common experience. Elimination of this disturbing peripheral illumination is necessary if hygienic vision is to be maintained. When these side lights become brighter or are moved closer to the line of direct vision, the immediate working surface, the fatiguing effects become greater. Furthermore, the greater the number of such peripheral light sources, the more detrimental is the effect upon vision.
>
> Uncomfortable glare and loss of visual efficiency also result from highly polished or glazed objects within the field of vision. Examples are nickel-plated metal parts of a typewriter and glazed printing paper. Such glare is reduced by maintaining well-diffused illumination in the work room.
>
> Visual fatigue and lessened efficiency are produced by brightness contrast within that portion of the visual field where critical vision is required and also within the immediate surroundings. When the eyes must shift back and forth from bright to dark areas or when there is a sharp division between dark and bright portions of the working area, the eyes must constantly re-adapt to the different degrees of brightness. Eyestrain soon results. Examples are (1) white paper on a dark desk, and (2) a dark undersurface of an opaque eye shade used in a brightly lighted room.
>
> The following will aid in eliminating glare effects: (1) Avoid peripheral light sources, such as wall brackets and low-hanging fixtures which reach down into the field of vision. (2) Avoid as far as possible the use of glazed paper, polished metallic objects, and marked contrasts of brightness within the visual field. (3) Avoid strictly local lighting like that produced by most desk lamps with opaque shades. The latter produce a circle of bright light surrounded by dimly illuminated areas and shadows. (4) Maintain, in general, as equal a distribution of light as possible over the working surface.[4]

Researchers have used various criteria for the determination of the most desirable lighting conditions. One criterion frequently used has been the production or output of the worker under different conditions of lighting. However, studies of lighting based upon factors such as output, rate of performing useful work, and speed of reading must be supplemented with additional criteria. Psychological factors often are more difficult to measure than the relatively simple objective environmental factors.

COLOR

Like lighting, color has been used in industry to help reduce employee fatigue, increase efficiency, decrease accidents, and improve housekeeping. Many industrial plants are too dull and dark for efficient seeing. Even the most modern lighting system is ineffective if light falls only on dull, dark walls, workbenches, and floors. Such surfaces may absorb rather than reflect and spread light. Color in industry often is used to improve "see-ability" rather than merely to provide more aesthetic surroundings. Color use should be planned to be functional and to fit the needs of the industry.

> ...Data show that with the use of color it is possible to recover light otherwise wasted and increase the actual illumination 100 per cent without changing the lighting equipment or increasing the wattage.
>
> ...Frequently eyestrain, which can create dangerous fatigue and nervous tension, is the result of constant, involuntary adjustment of the eye muscles caused by wrong color contrast, or distracting, glaring horizon colors, even where there is sufficient light.

In the inspection room of a North Carolina

Pittsburgh Plate Glass Co.

COLOR HATH CHARMS . . . ***After the paint job at right, which "defined limits" of the stair well, the behavior of junior-high-school students on the stairs definitely improved, their teachers say.***

Several years ago, *one of the country's largest paint makers, the Pittsburgh Plate Glass Company, joined forces with a group of psychologists at Johns Hopkins to find out, one way or another, whether the color scheme of a room really does affect the people who work in it. The Pittsburgh people developed a system of color decoration to which they gave the trade name "Color Dynamics." It involved tailoring paint colors individually to each situation in which paints were to be used, taking into account such factors as light, space, furnishings and equipment, and the purposes to which a room was to be put, on the theory that the performance of persons working amid such planned colors should appreciably improve.*

To test their theory, Pittsburgh asked the Hopkins psychologists to make a lengthy statistical study of a large group of people at work. The first idea was to conduct the study in a factory, since industry had already done a great deal of experimenting with colors, especially in an effort to increase the safety of workers on dangerous machines. But the psychologists felt that the tests would require several years, and it would be almost impossible to find an industry whose work force, equipment, output, and other factors were likely to remain stable for that long.

So the experimenters decided to conduct their tests in schools.

The elementary schools showed a very strong reaction to the experimental decoration. Kindergarten pupils improved most of all, suggesting that the younger the person the greater may be his response to color.

Surprisingly, these young pupils improved more in scholarship than in behavior. Average ratings for history, spelling, music, and even arithmetic were up from eight and a half to twelve per cent, while "social habits" brought up the rear with an improvement of less than six per cent.

In five out of six areas of comparison, the same situation prevailed; the unpainted school stayed about as it had been, the conventionally painted one improved somewhat, and the experimental school improved appreciably more.

An unexpected discovery was that boys often responded more to the new colors than did girls.

The teachers overwhelmingly expressed pleasure with the new paints, and the great majority of them felt strongly that the appearance of a building plays a big part in the morale and loyalty of both teachers and pupils.

—For further information, see "New Colors in the Classroom—Psychologists and Paint Makers Study Hues' Effects on School Work," ***Johns Hopkins Magazine,*** *May 1954, pp. 10-12.*

textile mill, girl operators scan blue denim hour after hour, as it moves rapidly under their eyes. Thinking to provide the maximum light, the operators of the mill had painted the walls of the room white. But when the girls looked up momentarily from the blue cloth to the white wall for a rest, a peach color swam before their eyes.

This is the visual phenomenon called "after-image," The human eye, over-stimulated by one color, registers the opposite or complementary color as a means of readjustment. When the girls looked back at the work, it took them several seconds to regain normal vision. A color engineer greatly increased the time the girls could work effectively and without strain at this job by providing what their eyes demanded: peach-colored walls.[5]

To avoid eye fatigue, colors directly in line with the workers' eyes should be about the same brightness as the bench-top or working area.

When a desk worker, for example, works with white paper on a desk with a dark green surface, he will constantly be seeing strong contrasts. In terms of the eye, this means a constant opening and closing of the pupil or lens-opening. The excess of mechanical movement within the eye contributes to fatigue. Soft shades, such as light gray, pale green, and light blue, are restful, line-of-vision colors.

Eyes may become overworked by staring too long at two objects of the same color and trying to differentiate between them. A too brilliant reflection, such as sun rays on snow or light on a painted surface, may produce marked strain. An important factor in improving the working environment is to provide a color harmony that does not tire the eyes. Color engineers have developed certain effective principles:

The idea that colors on the red side of the spectrum are warm and stimulating, while those at the opposite blue-green end are cool and relaxing, is accepted as a rule-of-thumb by all color practitioners. In a chain of restaurants, waiting lines formed outside telephone booths. When each booth interior was painted bright red, conversations speeded up so that the signs asking users to be brief were removed.

Another group of restaurants in New York adopted their striking red-and-yellow scheme on the advice of a color consultant. Originally a chaste gray-green, the restaurants were popular, but patrons were inclined to linger and the turnover wasn't fast enough to suit the management. When the decorating was changed to stimulating colors, traffic speeded up and business increased. . . .

Though most animals, including bulls, are color-blind, color has its effects on certain insects. Blue appears to be repugnant to flies. Recently a Chicago cheese manufacturer painted a large factory window blue, to screen out the ultra-violet rays. It was discovered that flies no longer congregated outside this window, though they were as thick as ever around other windows. Mosquitoes, however, seem to like blue. During the war the Navy withdrew blue shirts from men working at shore installations in malarial districts and substituted white, after tests showed that the incidence of mosquito bites was considerably higher among men wearing blue.[6]

Generally speaking, the warm colors (yellow, orange, etc.) are those that stimulate and promote efficiency. When properly used, they create a most pleasant environment. Of all colors, green apparently has the most relaxing effect on mind and body. Nature's extensive use of green in field and forest is ample evidence of this. Various shades of green such as Eye-Rest, Vista and Seafoam form the basis of properly engineered office color patterns. Blue is a calming color and can be used extensively in the form of Cascade Blue and Stratosphere Gray in offices to promote peace of mind and a calm, quiet atmosphere conducive to efficient work. The cool tints of Mist Gray could be used on the ceilings to counteract the too-warm effect of southern light. Cool expanses of Seafoam Green on the walls would rest the eyes of the personnel when they glance up from their desks or typewriters. To emphasize further the eye-rest factor, the walls which the workers face could be treated as a focal center and finished in an Eye-Rest Green. The floor could be a dark shade of green to harmonize with walls and ceilings. This combination would effectively offset the feeling of too much warmth created by the exposure and the broad expanse of desks. . . .

. . . In one instance, an office manager changed a drab office color scheme to a cool, relaxing pattern featuring blue. The office was painted in August; when winter came, the girls complained of feeling too cool. The normal temperature was 70 degrees Fahrenheit; this was raised to 75. The girls still felt cool. After much discussion and study the color scheme was changed to warm yellows and restful greens. The temperature was left at 75 degrees. Soon the girls protested it was too warm; it was dropped to normal and complaints ceased. This is just one of many instances showing the psychological effect of color.[7]

. . . In another plant, workers lifting black metal boxes filled with rough-cut brier pipes complained that they strained their backs. One weekend the foreman had all the boxes painted a pale

*Sometimes a more intense lighting is not the key to bettering a work situation. When one progressive manager brought daylight lighting into his shop, he got the wrong effect. Instead of production going up as he had intended, it went down. His error came in considering only the lighting of his shop and not the lighting in harmony with color. When a color engineer, Faber Birren, was called in, he had the colors changed: the yellow walls were subdued to a two-tone green, (light green top and medium green dado). Instead of the relatively non-reflective black, floors were changed to a durable gray. Machines were painted a deep gray-green. The ceilings were made an off-white to distribute the light evenly. Thus, through judicious use of color, the quality of the workmanship in the shop improved, accidents were reduced, maintainance simplified and production increased. See T. Metaxas, "Color: Paint Plants Scientifically," **The Iron Age**, May 7, 1953, pp. 142- 144.*

green. On Monday several men said to the boss: "Say, these new lightweight boxes make a real difference." . . .[8]

If the factory interior is cold looking, warm colors, such as ivory or buff, should be substituted if the illusion of warmth is desired. If working conditions involve high temperatures, cool colors, such as blues and greens, should be used.

"Working with dark objects, the surroundings should not be too brilliant, or the [iris] opening will become too small, with the result that vision will be taxed, production will suffer, and general tension and fatigue increase. The ideal situation is that in which illumination is ample and the surroundings a trifle lower in brightness than the object of concentration. Where dark materials are used, supplementary lighting may be necessary."[9]

Faber Birren, who has done outstanding work in color conditioning in industry, recommends that walls should not be too bright for the particular type of work. For example, bright, glaring white walls are not good for types of work that require the handling of dark objects. If the lighting is ample, walls can be toned down; if walls are on the dim side, supplementary lighting may be necessary.

Colors rarely should be pure, because these are likely to distract the worker. Soft grayish blue-green is recommended because it is neutral and stimulating.

If the work is of a type that demands much close work with the eyes, walls should provide a resting place for the eyes—for "space-gazing." Eyes need at least 20 feet to gaze through and a cool color to see.

Faber Birren emphasizes that painting with different colors will pay larger dividends in accident prevention than in any other one phase of industrial application. He cautions against overuse of color in industry however. When this happens, the worker does not see the things he is supposed to. His eye is distracted by many colors clamoring for his attention.[10]

The color program at Master Lock Company in Milwaukee is credited with contributing to this company's excellent safety record. Master Lock has had an especially low accident rate in comparison with other plants in the nation. It was one of the first companies to experiment with yellow in place of red as a danger signal. Some of its findings have modified safety standards set by city and state codes and insurance companies.

Unlike other factories where machines are painted in dark shades, this company uses bright tones. The giant padlock-making machines are painted in flamboyant brights to show dust and soot rather than hide them. "If they see the dirt, they'll clean it"—and the workers do. Although there is no company rule requiring employees to play housekeeper, the plant is immaculately clean.

Two standards were used to determine the

efficiency of a particular color or combination: workers' preferences and production records. What finally developed was an eye-rest green for machinery with buff and yellow to point up guards and other units. Pipes and conduits gleam in iridescent greens and yellows.[11]

Oil refineries are leaders in the effective use of color in industry. The Baton Rouge refinery of Esso Standard Oil has developed a paint schedule to designate specific units and tank markings using nineteen different colors that harmonize together. Redecorating programs have resulted in greater worker pride in the colorful surroundings, keeping the plant cleaner, providing a pleasant change for workers, and helping to prevent accidents. Night workers, particularly, are benefiting from proper color schemes. Distinctive colors are being used to designate equipment, show what liquids are flowing through particular pipes, warn of the presence of stairwells, and aid visibility in dark areas.[12] Color standards, once adopted, should be rigidly adhered to, especially in accident prevention. Once workers learn the meanings of color signals and rely on them, the accident frequency rate should decline. However, in nonhazardous work even a good color may be changed from time to time—the switch gives everyone a psychological lift.

NOISE

Work in almost every factory and office involves a certain amount of noise. Executives have recognized that noise is a distraction to many employees. Accordingly, some executives have attempted to overcome the problem by sound-proofing offices and other places of work.

Everyone knows, too, that the worker may become adapted to noise and that certain noises do not distract some workers. Experiments by psychologists indicate that the nature of the noise and the attitude of the individual toward the noise are of paramount importance regarding the distracting effects. A continuous noise may not have any harmful effects whereas an intermittent or unusual noise may. The steady noise, such as that of a battery of typewriters, is not likely to be as disturbing as irregular noises from automobile horns, strangers entering a room and banging a door, or persons talking more loudly than usual. Noise may even facilitate the individual worker's output if he has adopted a favorable attitude toward it. Noise helps to create a tempo that causes work to be produced at a certain rhythm.

Many workers accept a certain amount of noise, thinking of it as a necessary background for the work of the day. Several investigators have found that the significance of the noise for a particular individual rather than its intensity or nature determines its effects on the individual listener. Most of us have at some time been annoyed by a power shovel or hoisting machine. However, it is probable that if the listener who is annoyed by the power shovel were the inventor or manufacturer of the shovel, he would enjoy the noise rather than consider it a distraction. Several studies have been reported which indicate that 80 per cent of those annoyed by aircraft noise also fear to fly. In contrast, few persons complain about the hum of air-conditioners because the comfort they provide is more important than the noise.[13]

The Industrial Health Research Board, Great Britain, found during its experiments on the effect of noise on the efficiency of industrial workers that, although noisy working conditions usually do not markedly impair worker-efficiency at simple motor tasks, noise consistently does have the effect of decreasing efficiency to some extent. Loud noise, particularly mechanical irregular noise, was found to be prejudicial to efficiency roughly in direct proportion to the difficulty of the work involved; and even though differences in performance of work with and without noise were not statistically significant, a trend was evident. The trend, however, does not indicate as deleterious effects as often are charged.

Loud noise appears to be most distracting

when first heard. This is equally true of unpleasant noise, such as irregular mechanical noise, and pleasant noise such as music. However, because of man's powers of adaptation, he soon accustoms himself to distracting influences such as noise, and its detrimental effects shortly disappear. This disappearance seems to be caused more by a decrease in interest in the noise than in a change in sensory reaction.

Certain forms of mental work consistently are more affected by noise than are simple mechanical tasks, apparently because motor tasks, with a moderate amount of practice, become almost automatic, whereas even simple mental tasks are relatively complex in their demands upon the worker. However, as in simple motor tasks, in simple mental tasks the worker adapts himself quite readily to noisy conditions. Sometimes noise-caused irritation or annoyance results in better than usual performance of work because the worker expends greater than usual effort in order to counterbalance environmental conditions. On the other hand, if the worker does not increase his expenditure of effort his performance may be worse than usual. If the work being done is highly automatized and there is no increase or decrease in effort expenditure, performance will remain within normal range. Thus it can be seen that performance in a noisy environment depends not upon the noise itself, but upon the worker's attitude toward the performance of the work.[14] Some researchers have found that the rate of work is not improved by noise reduction, except perhaps by a general morale factor.[15] Moreover, the apparent effects of noise on human performance may be influenced to a greater extent by psychological stress than by noise itself.[16]

Various investigations of noise have pointed out that it should not be assumed, when a worker accepts noise as a background for his work, that his passive acceptance signifies an increase in efficiency. Furthermore, they have found that an increase in output often is accompanied by a considerable increase in the expenditure of energy involved. Several clever experiments of this kind have been conducted with keyboards. For example, the operator pressed appropriate keys similar to typewriter keys when he was given a designated stimulus. Careful measurements indicated that the operator exerted more pressure under distraction of noise than he did without the distraction.

Laird studied the air exhaled by typists and inferred from the greater consumption of oxygen during the noise periods that the typists expended more energy at a given task when conditions were noisy than when conditions were quiet. When typewriter keys were used to transcribe a code, J. J. B. Morgan found no difference in learning capacity when the room was noisy, but recorders attached to the keys indicated that more muscular pressure was then exerted by the operator. However, loudness and annoyance do not wholly go hand in hand. Loudness in relation to the background is often simply the dominating measurable feature of noise. A recent survey of the literature on the relation between noise and performance has indicated some lack of agreement among the proposed answers to the question.[17] Only a few experiments have demonstrated that noise produces readily measurable changes in human performance. These studies indicate that the more gross effects found as resulting from the effects of noise can be treated as a source of psychological stress.[18]

In general, we can conclude that when a noise really distracts the worker, a decrease in output or an increase in the expenditure of energy is likely to result. Also, when the noise is considered a background for the worker's activities, the sound which is noise for one observer may be a kind of pleasant environment for the person who has become adapted.

When noise of work cannot be reduced sufficiently to satisfy workers, the sufferers may gain some advantage by using ear defenders or plugs. Certain solid types of defenders are useful for relieving discomfort from intense noises and explosions. The wearer may still hear conversation. Complaints of traffic noise usually come from office workers in rooms facing the street, the sound being transmitted through windows or other openings. Closing the windows often keeps out the noise. Panes of heavy glass are helpful in further decreasing the noise. The best remedy is to use double windows and keep them closed, providing ventilation by quiet fans or vent ducts. When employees complain of noise from office appliances used by other members of the staff, annoyance can be reduced by the use of absorbent materials on the ceilings and walls. The absorbent materials may be tiles of a soft, porous nature or canvas, or perforated metals. Also, the machines can be insulated by means of bands of felt placed under them. An experienced sound engineer may discover many additional ways of reducing noise and making working conditions more comfortable.

Interestingly, one approach to protecting the ear against industrial impulse noise has been developed through the use of another sound, a pure tone. This technique is still in the experimental stage but offers promise for certain types of industrial noise.

Employees' reactions to noise were studied systematically in six industrial plants. In three of the plants, studies were made before and after sound conditioning. Results indicated that acoustical treatment improved ease and accuracy of understanding of conversations in noisy areas. Discomfort and annoyance from noise were decreased. No evidence, however, was obtained from the study to show that production was increased.[19]

The effect of noise reduction on the personal output of a group of ten weavers was studied by Weston and Adams.[20] The output of the group was charted for twenty-six weeks; on thirteen alternate weeks the weavers wore ear plugs to reduce the noise.

The average hourly output per weaver for the group studied in this investigation shows an increase of approximately one per cent when the loom noise is reduced by the use of ear defenders. Weaving is largely a mechanical process, and it is probable that in other occupations, comparable in regard to the intensity of noise but depending less upon the mechanical and more upon the human factor than weaving, the effect of noise upon

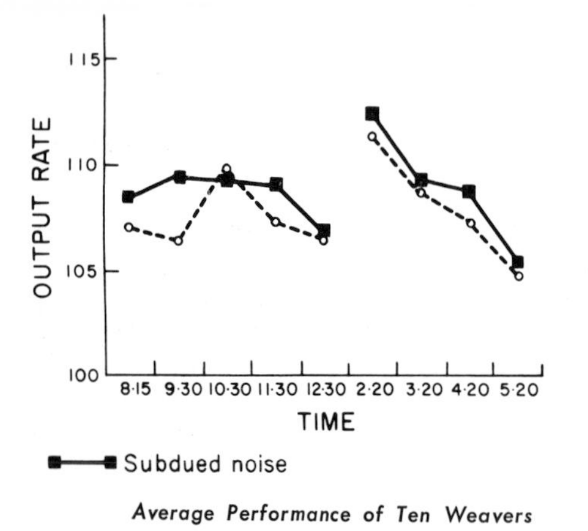

Average Performance of Ten Weavers

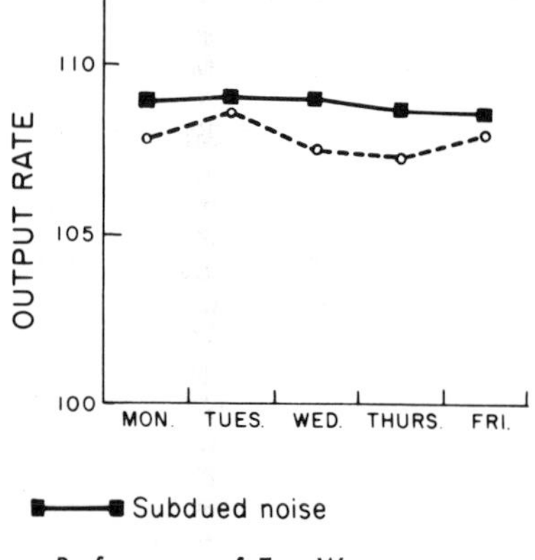

Average Performance of Ten Weavers

Ear defenders *(a special type of ear plug) were given to ten weavers whose job was highly mechanized and involved the use of noisy machines. The output rate was slightly greater when noise was reduced every hour during the day except for one—9:30 to 10:30. See figure on left. This figure also shows the difference between the morning and afternoon production. Figure on right shows that the subdued noise conditions resulted in a more nearly straight-line production curve, a finding that is considered ideally desirable.—From H. C. Weston and S. Adams,* ***Two Studies in the Psychological Effects of Noise, II. The Effects of Noise on the Performance of Weavers,*** *Industrial Health Research Board (Great Britain), 1932, Report No. 65. Reprinted by permission of the Controller of His Britannic Majesty's Stationery Office.*

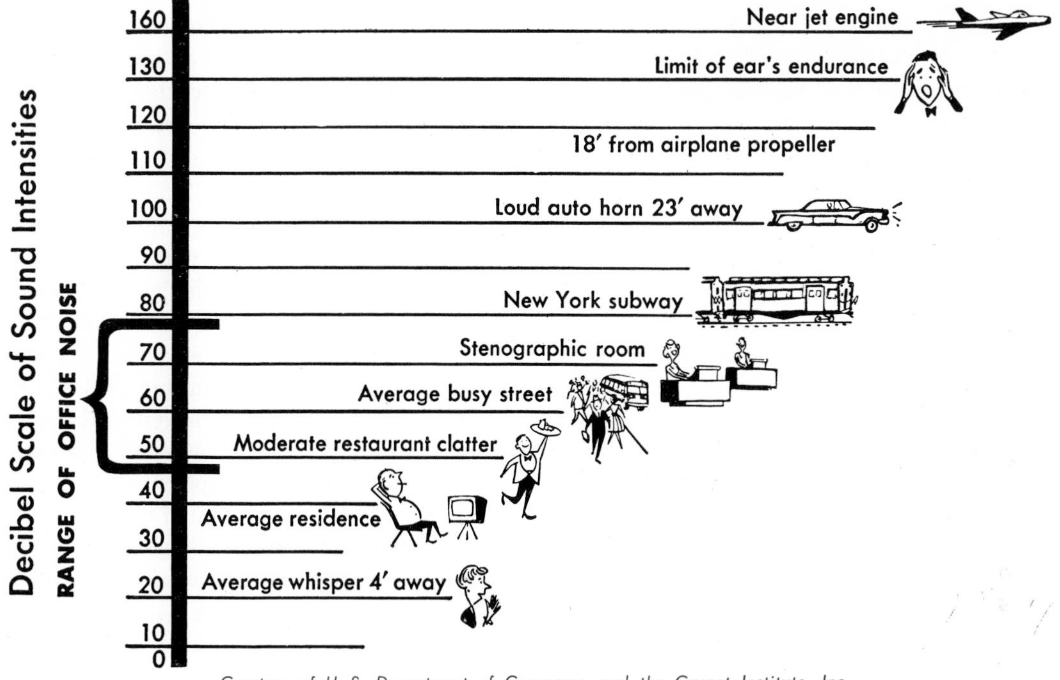

Courtesy of U. S. Department of Commerce and the Carpet Institute, Inc., New York.

output may be considerably greater than that demonstrated by this investigation.

A study of the hourly variation of output during the day under conditions of reduced noise, as compared with normal conditions, is very interesting. Over half of the gain in output occurred during the first three hours of the work day, while some increase occurred every hour of the day but one. This distribution suggests the important conclusion that, even after years of work in a noisy environment, the worker does not become completely adapted or acclimatized to noise but goes through the process of adaptation daily.

Owing to the increased output with reduced noise, the type of work curve characteristic of the relatively quiet experimental period is better than that of the noisy period, since it is smoother and tends to approximate more nearly the theoretical ideal straight line.

Further data and study of the general significance of noise would permit more specific conclusions; however, noise must be recognized as one of the factors which can exercise an appreciable influence on an individual's job performance, particularly at times when other factors combine to lower personal efficiency.

The American Standards Association defines noise as "undesired sound." To the engineer or physicist noise is a sound whose characteristics can be defined and whose properties can be measured with standard instruments:

(1) Decibel levels are usually determined by electronic measurement, i.e., by a microphone, an amplifier, and a calibrated meter. The complete instrument is known as a sound-level meter.

(2) The average office has a background noise level of about 50 decibels.

(3) At a level of 120 decibels most people get a feeling of discomfort.

(4) Around 140 decibels, the feeling becomes painful.

(5) The ear drum may be ruptured at a level of 160 decibels.[21]

The Workmen's Compensation Board of New York State has adopted standards on the relation between deafness and industrial noise. Based on recommendations by a committee of 5 specialists who studied the problem for more than a year, injurious noise starts above 90 decibels. These standards set forth that permanent hearing damage results as follows:

> Most persons exposed to over 120 decibels of noise for several hours daily will suffer permanent damage in a matter of months. An "overall" din of 100 to 120 decibels for several hours daily over a long period can permanently damage hearing of a considerable portion of workers. A few very susceptible persons may be permanently damaged by exposure for many years to noises between 90 and 100 decibels.[22]

Several states have legislation that allows compensation for partial loss of hearing by a worker who can prove that his hearing loss was caused by the noise of the factory equipment he operated. In most other states, complete loss of hearing in either or both ears must be proved.

Some sources had concluded as early as 1952 that a prolonged 85-decibel sound will injure a worker's hearing. There is some evidence, however, that a noise level as high as 100 decibels is not injurious even after considerable periods of exposure. The important factor is noise frequency (cycles per second or pitch) rather than decibel rating (volume).[23]

Sleight and Tiffin made a comprehensive survey of the literature on industrial noise and hearing.[24] They found that some experiments have indicated that the harmful effects of noise have been overemphasized, but that the weight of experimental evidence indicates that there are many circumstances wherein noise is deleterious. They suggested that the following actions be taken by employers confronted with the noise problem: (1) noise measurement; (2) institution of noise elimination or reduction measures; (3) establishment of hearing testing programs.

There are several sources from which the employer may draw assistance in approaching his noise exposure problem. Among these:

1. The industrial hygiene division of the state's board of health or its equivalent can

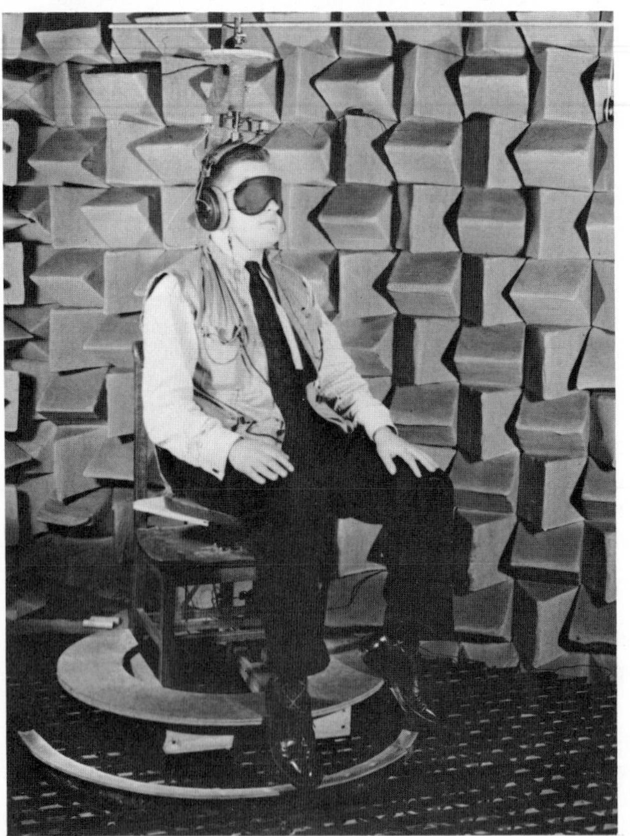

A subject participating *in a sound-localization experiment in a specially constructed chamber at the Psycho-Acoustic Laboratory, Harvard University. Reflected sounds are carefully controlled. Soundproof chambers of this type are also used to measure noise such as the sound coming from a motor. Photo by courtesy of S. S. Stevens, Director of the Laboratory.*

help him establish a conservation of hearing program.

2. Trained specialists supplied by insurance companies can be of particular assistance in occupational hearing-loss problems.

3. Trained acoustical consulting engineers, in general, can render assistance on all types of problems.[25]

MUSIC IN INDUSTRY

Hundreds of plant managers have used music to relax tensions and to stimulate production. Stevedores, cotton workers, and others know that music often helps to reduce fatigue. Managements of certain department stores, banks, and other firms regularly devote a period of the working day to mass singing. Night clerks in some post offices handle mail to the music of the radio. We all know that many school children also study their lessons with an ear "glued" to the radio.

One of the beneficient effects of music in industry is that it tends to reduce the strain of factory noises. The irritating din of a factory contributes to fatigue. Factory noise consists of irregular pulsations that lack rhythmic form and regularity. Music, on the other hand, consists of regular pulsations. It has rhythmic sequence. Even in the midst of industrial clatter, the human ear tends to follow a pleasing melody and ignore disagreeable noises. Almost all types of industrial work are adapted to music, with the exception of riveting and other operations that have loud, intermittent noises, sounds of definite pitch, loud squeaks or scratches, or high continuous sound. The explanation for this lies in the acoustical difference between sound and noise.

A helpful fact is that people working constantly in a noisy environment grow accustomed to the noise—in reality, develop a psychological deafness to it—and therefore are able to hear other sounds above the noise far more readily than someone unused to it. For this reason, adjustments in loudspeakers should be made in accordance with the ability of the plant workers to hear the music clearly, rather than with that of the sound engineers who have come in from the outside. Expert sound engineers are aware of this.[26]

Because of the acoustical difference between musical sound and noise, *Rustle of Spring* can be heard through the sound of pneumatic hammers, and *The Skaters' Waltz* through the 102 decibels of a worsted mill weaving shed.

Authorities in the field of music and industry do not agree as to the optimum lengths of periods of music. Some prefer twelve to twenty minute periods; others use forty-five minute music periods.

In many companies, the periods from 9:30 to 10 A.M. and 2:00 to 2:30 P.M. are considered major fatigue periods—the periods when music is needed most and is likely to be most effective. This is especially true when the fatigue is mental and is induced by the boredom of repetitive work. Obviously, these fatigue periods do not occur at the same relative time in all plants, but they are usually in the middle of the morning and the middle of the afternoon. Sometimes, production graphs indicate the time when music is likely to be most helpful to the employees.

Some companies follow the practice of scheduling pre-fatigue music—an hour or so after the beginning of each half-day of work. Music for the minor fatigue periods is generally of shorter duration. The most important music periods appear to be those at the opening or closing of the shift, because next to overcoming the tedium of monotonous work, the most important objective is to have workers start and end the day in a pleasant frame of mind.

Those who plan music programs for industry differ somewhat in their planning. One authority may recommend music of progressive stimulation during certain hours to overcome workers' fatigue. Another may recommend that the program have decreasing stimulation toward the end of the day.

Work music should have a clear-cut, singing melody. The tunes should be of a nature that overrides plant noises. Highly stimulating

WORDS AND MUSIC ADD UP TO INCREASED PRODUCTION, HAPPIER EMPLOYEES AT EQUITABLE LIFE

A personally controlled background music system *for transcribers of network dictation, the first of its kind, has been successfully tested and installed in the home office of Equitable Assurance Society of the United States in New York City.*

Developed by the Voicewriter Division of McGraw-Edison Company, the system enables each of Equitable's transcribing secretaries to enjoy the benefits of background music which business and industry are increasingly providing for employees but which the transcriptionist has been denied because of the nature of her job. Each of Equitable's 43 transcriptionists listens to the dictation she is transcribing against a background of continuous, specially programmed, non-vocal music over which she has complete control. She can lower or raise volume or turn it off completely to suit her wishes.

The background music system is integrated with the individual transcribing instruments on Equitable's standard Televoice network. Pre-recorded music, specially selected to reduce monotony and on-the-job fatigue and to enhance the audible quality of the words dictated, is "piped" through the individual transcribing units.

The secretary uses a special Edison Music/Dictation Listening Device (patent pending) that blends music and the dictator's voice. The music is supplied continuously, is not interrupted by the stop or start of the voice. This means that the transcriptionist can have music while she is preparing her work or while performing other non-transcribing tasks.

Management at Equitable had been searching for a way to reduce tedium in the vital transcription area.

The Voicewriter background music system was first installed on a trial basis, using three groups of transcriptionists as experimenters during successive tests.

Production was compared, morale was gauged, and questionnaires were circulated to each of the transcribing secretaries after the test periods. Management disclosed these results: a definite increase in average production is being maintained after six months; the transcribing secretaries report an increasing satisfaction with their transcribing work attributable to the music.

The system eliminated distracting background noise, permitting the secretary to give greater attention to the spoken word. Dictation, instead of being interfered with, was actually made clearer and more distinct. With tension reduced, the transcribers were more relaxed at the end of the day.

music, such as that of the jitterbug type, is too distracting. *Deep in the Heart of Texas* is usually considered taboo as work music because some workers cannot refrain from stopping to clap hands in the chorus. Religious music, except when used on Sunday morning shifts, tends to slow down production.

The musical selections preferred by employees vary considerably with the individual company. Each management must determine by means of questionnaires the selections and types of music that are preferred.

Scientific tests of the effects of music on work and workers are difficult to make. Those investigators who report greater productivity and less absenteeism after music has been introduced often tend to overlook the presence of other factors which may be influencing the productivity or attendance.

One carefully conducted study of music was made in relation to employee attitudes, piecework production, and industrial accidents. The influence of an industrial music program, which systematically varied the amount, type, and distribution of music played, was studied in a plant of approximately one thousand employees over a twelve-week period. An effort was made to determine effects of music on employee attitudes, piece-work production, and industrial accidents. Some of the important findings, presented in the summary of the report by Henry Clay Smith, were the following:

Employee Attitudes

A questionnaire concerned with attitudes toward music was sent to every employee before the music program began. Somewhat over 70 per cent of these questionnaires were completed and returned. An analysis of the replies showed that:

1. Almost all of the employees (98 per cent) thought that music during working hours would be at least "mildly pleasant," and 74 per cent thought that it would be "extremely pleasant."
2. The intensity of interest in music while working decreased somewhat with age. The oldest group preferred semiclassical, nonvocal, and quiet music more than the younger groups.
3. No sex differences in the intensity or type of musical interest were found.
4. Personal interviews with a sample of employees at the end of the twelve weeks showed no decrease in the desire for music while working.

Piecework Production

Music in relation to production was studied on a highly repetitive assembly line operation which was on incentive pay. Two separate shifts with an average of 21 employees on each shift were studied simultaneously for twelve weeks. The results showed that:

1. Production under varying conditions of music increased from 4 to 25 per cent. The average increase on the day shift was 7, on the night shift, 17 per cent. The increases were

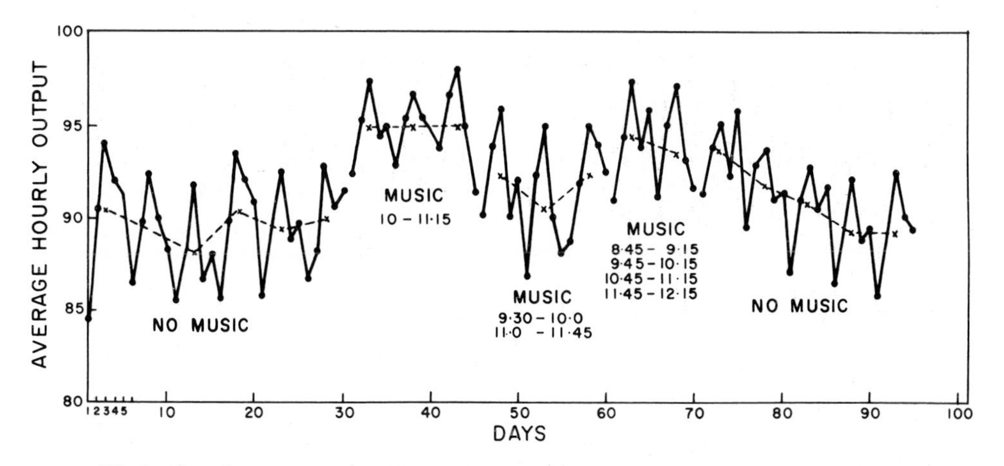

Effects of music *on output of workers performing repetitive work on a straight piece-rate basis of pay.—From S. Wyatt and J. N. Langdon, assisted by F. G. L. Stock,* ***Fatigue and Boredom in Repetitive Work,*** *Industrial Health Research Board, Great Britain, Report No. 77, 1937. Reprinted by permission of the Controller of His Britannic Majesty's Stationery Office.*

statistically significant and large enough to be of economic importance.

2. Maximum production increases were found when music was played 12 per cent of the time on the day shift, 50 per cent of the time on the night shift.

3. Production tended to decrease with a large increase in the number of semiclassical selections but did not vary with a large increase in the number of vocals. Waltzes were more effective at the opening of the shift than marches.

4. Production increases varied with the hour at which music was played and were greatest during the hours of low production.

5. The more an employee wanted music, the more music tended to increase her production; the lower the employee's production, the more music tended to increase her production; the more the employee's job permitted conversations while working, the more music tended to increase her production.

6. The greater effectiveness of large amounts of music on the night shift corresponded with a greater demand for music on the night shift; the greater effectiveness of varied music corresponded with an expressed preference for varied rather than for special types of music; the greater effectiveness of certain distributions of music corresponded with an expressed preference for such distributions.

Conclusions

Music during working hours will generally improve production where repetitive work is common. Properly administered in such situations, it not only will increase production but also will provide widespread employee satisfaction. Music probably produces its major direct effect when the individual's capacity for attention is not absorbed by his work; in this circumstance, music appears to divert unused attention from brooding, talking, or off-the-job activities. Although music, on the average, had no influence on the accident rate, the relation of music to accidents was not entirely clear in the present study.[27]

A later investigator, Richard S. Uhrbrock, made a comprehensive review of the published evidence concerning positive effects on productivity. He found that belief in music as an incentive is very strongly entrenched but that very few investigations of its value can stand the test of scientific scrutiny. Some reports of the "before and after" measurements of production cannot be accepted because of dubious statistical procedures. Others simply demonstrate the old finding that any notable change in the work situation is likely to have a temporarily favorable effect on attitudes and output. However, he found that several carefully controlled studies indicated that music does in fact increase productivity. The investigations he cited showed that young, inexperienced workers, engaged in simple, repetitive tasks, produced more when music was played during working hours. Another study indicated that music had no effect on the output of experienced factory workers whose work patterns were stabilized and who were performing complex tasks. Generally, he found that many people, particularly young ones enjoy working to music and would dislike having it withdrawn—to them, it is a "fringe" benefit in the work environment.[28]

An investigator who studied the attitudes of employees toward music in several industrial plants offered the following recommendations: Music should be provided for work areas in which the work is manual and monotonous if a majority of employees want it; the music preferences of employees should be measured rather than approximated; the music needs of night-shift workers should receive special attention; selection of bass and soprano announcers should be avoided; and industrial music should be regarded as a factor favorable to quantity of production in the typical repetitive operations of industry.[29]

Perhaps the best indication of the positive value of music for morale is the fact that once the employer has provided music for the employees, in only rare instances has he discontinued it. Much depends upon the employee's attitude toward the music. For example, dance music may be a distraction or an aid to concentration, depending upon the worker's attitude. This fact was brought out in an experiment in which one group of subjects was told that music facilitated arithmetical calculations, and another group was told that it interfered with them. Charts allegedly based on a previous experiment in

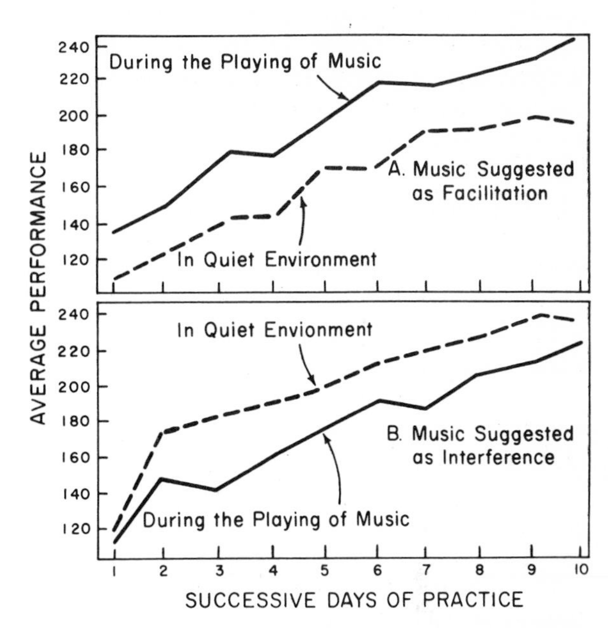

The effect of attitude *on performance in mental arithmetic as shown by the production of ten subjects in a quiet environment and during the playing of music* ***(a)*** *when music is thought by the subjects to facilitate performance, and* ***(b)*** *when subjects believe music interferes with performance. Note that the music facilitates when subjects believe it to, and interferes when they believe it an interference.—Adapted from K. H. Baker, "Pre-experimental Set in Distraction Experiments,"* ***Journal of General Psychology,*** *Vol. 16 (1937), pp, 471–486. Sidney L. Pressey, J. Elliott Janney, and Raymond G. Kuhlen,* ***Life: A Psychological Survey*** *(New York: Harper & Row, Publishers, 1939), p. 533.*

which the appropriate finding was made were shown to each group to help create the mental set.

The subjects reacted in accordance with the suggestion in both cases. All those who were told that music was an aid to more work produced more work. All those who were told that music would interfere did more under normal conditions of quiet. The subjects who were told at the beginning of the experiment that their performance without music would probably exceed their production with it appeared to work harder under conditions of quiet. Their remarks, changes of posture, and appearances of concentration gave this impression. The subjects who were led to believe that music would increase their output stated afterwards that it had helped to keep their minds on their work. See chart on this page.

It appears that "the changes in attitude and accompanying changes in motivation may be all that is necessary to account for differences in performance under various experimental conditions."[30]

ACCIDENTS

Many managements have considered industrial accidents as a phase of faulty or inadequate machine design, the lack of proper machine guards, failure to safeguard hazardous areas or the conditions of work such as night work. Studies by insurance companies and by research groups indicated that from 80 to 90 per cent of all accidents are due, not to defective machinery or to a physical or mental defect or lack of skill in the worker, but to an *X factor* in the person injured.[31]

Numerous statistical studies of the persons who have accidents, indicate that certain individuals have a disproportionately high share of the accidents. Evidence of the presence of these "accident-prone" individuals have been found in analyses of accidents that occurred in industrial plants and among automobile drivers. Analysis of the accidents that occur in a typical industrial plant are likely to indicate that approximately 65 per cent of the accidents that take place over a two-year period are experienced by about 15 per cent of the work force. Findings such as these have stimulated certain psychologists to make special studies of individuals who have had a history of repeated accidents.

Children who are accident prone seem to exhibit different patterns of behavior from those who have few accidents. When a researcher studied two groups of children who were matched according to age, sex, and accident history over a four-year period, it was found that children who had had repeated accidents were generally freer and less inhibited in a doll play situation than the others. Their play was less stereotyped. The accident-prone children expressed their aggression more readily than did the accident-free. The former were more verbally aggressive.

The child's background was found to be related to his behavior, too. Accident repeaters seem to come generally from larger families, were born in somewhat later birth order, came more often from broken homes, and transferred schools frequently. They had been, in many instances, referred to home and school counselors in public schools.

The author suggests that if these characteristics identified in children with accidents were also found in adults, accident liability might be considered continuous from childhood to maturity.[32]

Several significant clinical studies have been made of accident-prone persons. Alexandra Adler, for example, studied 100 such industrial workers of Europe and 100 Massachusetts applicants for workmen's compensation.[33] Some of her findings were:

Among American accident-prone workers, over one fourth were over-fearful. She found that fear of accidents can produce them. More than 23 per cent of American accident-prone workers had a fatalistic attitude that they were unlucky. Almost 20 per cent wanted to be pampered. More than 13 per cent had a revengeful attitude toward parents or teachers.

Among the European workers, a revengeful attitude was responsible in 56 per cent of the individuals. These men were bitter, antagonistic, revengeful, particularly toward parents and educators.[34]

Flanders Dunbar, a researcher in the field of psychosomatic medicine, has made extensive investigations of the personality profiles of accident-prone and other hospital patients. In one study of 1,600 patients that led to the development of distinguishing profiles, she found that 80 per cent fell into recognizable profiles of significance in regard to accident record:

It is clear from a brief review of these personality profiles that two important diagnostic points are: the sphere of life in which the patient had his major conflicts, and his characteristic means of reaction and of attempting to solve these conflicts. The area of focal conflict of patients with the accident habit is in the realm of authority. The authority may be, first, parents, then school, and later, church, job, wife or husband. The characteristic response to these difficulties is to strive for independence and autonomy outside such relationships and to minimize and avoid conflicts with authority whenever possible, although without submitting. . . .

Any dynamic formulation relative to the profile of these accident-prone personalities should begin with an investigation of the nature of their defenses. By focusing their values on immediate concrete experience, striving to find satisfactions and security outside the authoritarian hierarchy, and avoiding any marked submission or domination in vocational or social roles, accident-prone persons get along without serious conflicts with authority. The defenses work most of the time. When thwarted, deprived, or subjected to unusual strain such as unemployment, or the pressure of a mother-in-law in the family, these persons "do something" to modify the situation or get away from it instead of keeping their anger bottled up inside. It is significant that these patients have a health record far above the average.

When the characteristic defenses fail and conflict with authority becomes unavoidable, the accident happens. Aggressiveness may break out in an act which appears to punish the victim or those responsible for his frustration, or both. Or it may come near enough to the surface to cause the kind of confusion which leaves the person defenseless in the danger situations normally encountered from day to day. Unlike depressed persons who consciously attempt suicide, the accident-prone individual usually reports no conscious premeditation. It is interesting, however, that he occasionally reports a dream or a "hunch" that "something was going to happen today" or that he "was going to have bad luck." This trend is illustrated by the statement made so frequently by these patients after the accident has happened: "You can't get around fate; I got mine today, you'll get yours tomorrow. . . ."

. . . These profiles may be useful to the physician not trained in psychiatry, as an aid in

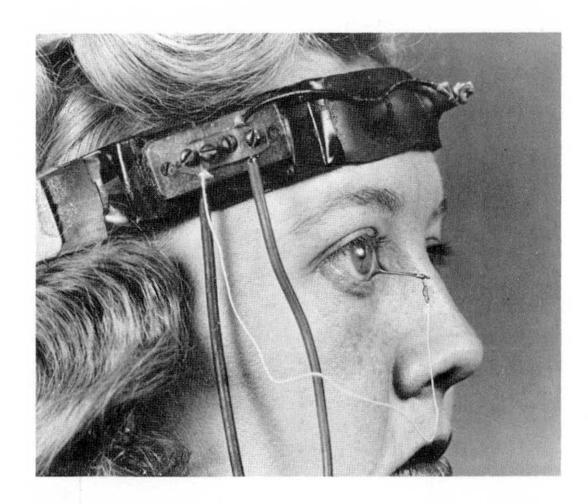

Night blindness, *a factor contributing to some accidents, has been difficult to diagnose, since those affected by it do not always realize it. Electroretinography, which is especially useful in identifying night blindness, was made possible by the introduction of the contact lens electrode for use on human beings in 1941. For the first few years, the laboratory of the Department of Psychology, Brown University, was the only one carrying on this work, but since the war the technique has spread to other laboratories in universities, medical schools, and military installations. The photograph shows electrodes in position for recording the electroretinogram.—See Lorrin A. Riggs, "Electroretinography in Cases of Night Blindness,"* ***American Journal of Ophthalmology,*** *July 1954.*

knowing what kind of questions to ask, which emotional problems should be approached first and what *not* to do in general therapeutic management of the patient. Too often if a mother-in-law or a sexual problem turns up, the psychosomatic-minded internist or surgeon concentrates on this and fails to realize that although he may make the patient happy by listening, he will do nothing that is effective in curing the accident habit unless he attempts to deal with the fundamental problems of his patient in terms of both the area of the patient's greatest sensitivity and the inadequacies in his habitual manner of attempting to solve his conflicts.[35]

Freud's contributions made psychologists aware of unconscious motivations that influence behavior in everyday life. Clinical psychologists and psychiatrists see much evidence that leads them to believe that many accidents are not chance happenings but are linked in some way with dynamic factors within the personality.

Several investigators have tried to find psychological tests that identify the accident-repeater. Projective techniques have been used to study the influence of personality dispositions on the part of high accident persons in an industrial setting. Davids and Mahoney in a study by the use of the projective technique found that high-accident individuals, in comparison with the nonaccident subjects, were significantly lower on socially desirable personality dispositions of optimism, trust, and sociocentricity. There was highly significant association between high accident proneness and projective responses indicative of a negative attitude toward employment.[36]

A statistical study of accidents in 147 factories correlated 75 variables with accident severity and frequency. Most of the significant findings were interpreted in terms of preoccupation of workers due to threat to status and comfort and to guilt feelings and frustrations.[37]

One investigator probed the primary personality qualities and occupational interests of pairs of employees working on the same job. One member of the pair was selected as being a definite injury repeater. The other member was considered a reasonably safe worker on that job. This study revealed 27 measurable personality factors related to accident proneness that could be classified into seven trait patterns, or syndromes. An example of one of the syndromes was described as "*Social orientation.* The injury-repeater tends to have aggressive, self-assertive attitudes toward others. He is not likely to be interested in teamwork or cooperating in the achievement of group goals." The author, as a result of his researches, has developed a "Job Attitudes Survey" as a promising device for predicting the likelihood of safe behavior on the job. Further research on the degree of validity of this predictive instrument is in progress.[38]

In spite of the many researches which have indicated that accident proneness is an important factor in the occurence of accidents, some writers on the subject claim that "accident proneness and accident-prone people are probably no more than secondary factors in accident causation."[39]

Some of the critics of the concept claim

How many unsafe practices can you see? *Unsafe working practices are illustated in the manner of the old picture puzzle. One employee found 34 violations of safety in the above bottling house scene. See Appendix, page 622, for his list. Courtesy of Joseph S. Finch and Company, Schenley, Pa., Stanley S. De Vault, Safety Director. Cartoon by William Wilson.*

that it is necessary to differentiate between "personal" and "situational" accidents in order to isolate other than personal factors in the accident data. As an example, the amount of hazard exposure should be considered. One investigator analyzed the accident data concerning 737 electric utility employees during a period of one year. He grouped the employees according to relative hazard exposure. His analysis revealed data which suggested the presence of accident proneness. The author, however, was unable to identify accident-prone individuals by the statistical analysis he had made.[40]

An examination of the literature concerning accident proneness indicates that those researchers who object to the concept do so on the basis of statistical analysis—not all variables are considered. Those who believe that the arguments in favor of the accident proneness concept are valid usually do so on the basis of clinical analysis. They believe that a poor accident record is only one manifestation of an "inadequate method of living."[41] We are also certain that the temporarily "accident-prone" individuals—those distracted by job tension, family troubles, or more serious emotional disorders—contribute to on-the-job accident statistics.

Current thinking concerning accidents seems to be that some persons do have more accidents than others, that tests to spot the repeaters do not as yet identify most of those who will have accidents, and that the factors associated with their occurence are not well established. There is also considerable disagreement over just what an "accident-prone" person is. One investigator may use the term in an empirical sense merely to identify persons with a history of accidents. Another may use it in a diagnostic sense, referring to a supposed clinical entity. Empirical descriptions would seem more advisable until sufficient data have been accumulated to make etiological distinctions. Hence we should regard a person with a history of accidents as an "accident-repeater" rather than "accident-prone."[42]

NIGHT WORK

Scientific study of the effect of night work on production is difficult to make because many uncontrolled variables prevent it. However, *Modern Industry* editors surveyed a number of plants to find out what problems are posed by night shifts and how the problems are handled. In some plants night shift workers appear to be more relaxed than day shift workers. Occasionally, they act as if they are doing the company a favor by being on the shift at all.

In general, night workers equal the quantity production of the day shift, but the quality of the work record is usually not as good. For that reason, simple routine jobs may be the best choice for the night shift. Surprisingly, night workers seem to have fewer accidents than the day shift. Perhaps this is because there is less movement of materials at night.

Personnel experts estimate that less than 25 per cent of all workers actually want to work at night. Most of the rest won't do it at any price. Today the usual night-shift premiums (4¢ to 10¢ an hour, or 5% to 10% of earnings) provide little incentive to the worker who doesn't like the night shift to begin with. That's particularly true of the third shift.

Neither does it seem to make much difference whether shifts are rotated so men work each shift for a certain number of weeks, or permanently set, with men definitely assigned to one shift or another. Each has a few things to recommend it, and a good many drawbacks. . . .

When shifts are permanently set, workers with most seniority and highest skill will get the preferred day jobs. That leaves the less-experienced, less-skilled workers for the night shifts. On the credit side, there is that small, reliable corps of men who actually prefer night work. And permanent assignment to it lets them arrange their lives accordingly.[43]

Interviews with nighttime workers who are on alternating shifts, particularly weekly shifts, usually reveal almost universal dislike: habit disruptions, reduced feeling of physical well-being, and loss of appetite. Monthly or fortnightly work spells are preferred over weekly. However, some workers prefer permanent night shift over day work.[44] They like the higher pay, greater work freedom, and opportunities to carry on other activities such as farming or a small business of their own. Certain employees, too, prefer to be relieved from community and home responsibilities. These isolates can avoid undesired interactions with others because of the demands of night-shift work.[45]

In spite of the objections to alternating shifts, some managers prefer them because the method assures having good workers on all shifts.

Because top management, engineers, and production specialists are not regularly in the plant at night, it is difficult to keep night-shift workers informed of company plans and policies. A special effort should be made to get such information to the night-staff—both by word-of-mouth and by means of bulletins and memos.

FATIGUE AND BOREDOM

Certain biology teachers have likened man to a machine and tried to compute his efficiency in a manner similar to that used in measuring the efficiency of motors. In terms of chemical energy consumed, the Diesel engine and the high-compression automobile engine surpass man's efficiency as a machine. In terms of chemical energy consumed as food and converted into external mechanical energy, man's efficiency usually ranges from 15 to 20 per cent.[46]

The term fatigue has various meanings. To the layman it simply means "feeling tired." Researchers usually call this type *subjective fatigue*, and it may be thought of with reference to certain muscles only, or it may be rather general and involve drowsiness. Laboratory experiments often show that subjective fatigue may be quite pronounced but that the person having such feelings actually may be doing as much work as ever.

Subjective fatigue often is distinguished from mental fatigue, the tiredness that develops from work of a mental rather than a muscular nature. The fatigue that results from doing accounting or writing a book may be considered to be somewhat different from the subjective fatigue caused by the use of muscles. Perhaps the difference between the two is only one of degree or source. At any rate, mental workers often wish to change to some other activity, but the other activity at the time may have a greater appeal simply because of vague psychological influences and not because of physiological changes in the body.

Of course, physiological conditions have pronounced bearings on the feelings of fatigue. For example, in hot industries workmen are given salt in tablet form or in drinking water in order to remedy the deficiency of body salt lost through perspiration. Glass-making, baking, steel, and similar industries furnish salt to workers, especially during heat waves. Some football trainers feed salt, or bouillon, which is more palatable, to football players.

In some fatigue experiments, the subject of the experiment may not feel tired but may do considerably less work. This decreased capacity for work because of exhaustion of energy-producing materials such as sugar products, especially glycogen, and the accumulation of waste products, mostly carbon dioxide and lactic acid, is called *objective fatigue*. Objective and subjective fatigue do not always correlate, especially when the individual is offered a greatly desired reward for continued output.

In most cases, psychological and physiological factors in fatigue are closely interrelated. Differentiation is difficult. However, the "feelings of fatigue" and "boredom" have been differentiated by Brozek:

> Boredom is characterized by discontent, restlessness and yawning, whereas the "feeling of fatigue" appears as weariness and can be relieved only by rest. Fatigue which accompanies heavy or very intensive work is regarded as a subjective sign of physiological changes produced by the work. In some cases, such as sprinting, it is possible to identify and measure some of the physiological changes such as the rise in blood lactate, oxygen debt, and so on. . . .
>
> What are the personal characteristics of the boredom-prone individual? Wyatt and Langdon[47] investigated four personality traits: general intel-

An Alertness Indicator has been developed at Tufts University. The Indicator, the device pictured in the middle of the photograph at right, works in such a way that when the subject becomes drowsy or less alert, a relay is tripped. This relay could conceivably be connected to signal the individual or another person that the subject's state of alertness had deteriorated. The meter might have application in any situation where human safety and economic loss would occur if continuous alertness were not maintained, e.g., as in automobile driving or radar watching.

The Alertness Indicator is set up so that the muscle potentials from the subject's forehead and the total integrated electrical output may be read from a meter in the upper right-hand corner of the instrument. For research purposes, Tufts University can also record the bio-electric activity from the Cathode-ray Oscilloscope (shown at the left of the picture) and on an ink recorder shown in the background. Information and photo by courtesy of Prof. Leonard C. Mead.

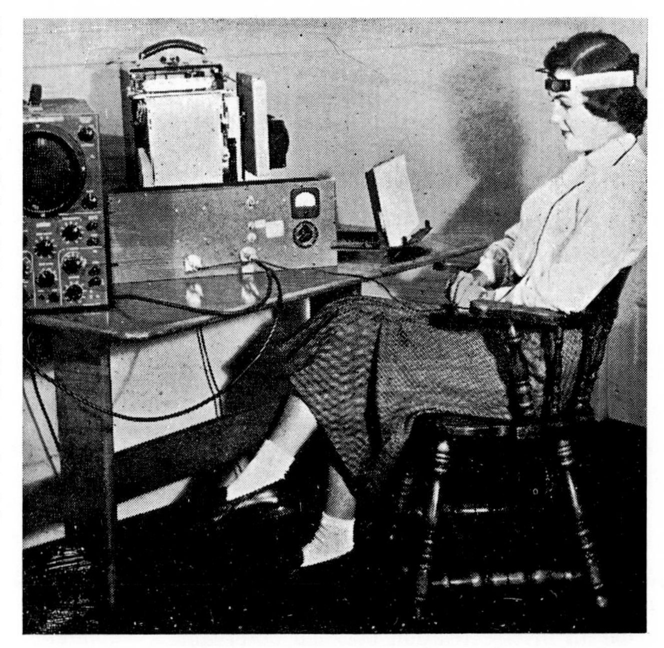

ligence, divided attention ("ability to think of other things while working"), perseveration (interference of the preceding activity) and introversion-extraversion. The differences between the average scores of "least bored" and "most bored" workers were found to be statistically significant for the first and last traits studied. Higher intelligence and extroversion tend to be associated with greater susceptibility to boredom.

Individuals who were classified as "most bored" registered also a higher number of complaints against working conditions. In three plants where studies were made on sub-groups comprising 54, 34 and 26 workers, bored workers registered on the average, 19 per cent, 23.7 per cent, and 21.3 per cent more complaints.

Workers spontaneously develop antidotes to boredom such as talking, singing and day-dreaming. Features introduced and tested experimentally in previous investigations included such factors as rest pauses and changes in the form of work.[48]

In office work, more work is done per hour when authorized rest periods are given to clerks than when there are no authorized rest periods.

Even when the length of time consumed by pauses is added to the length of the working day, this increase holds true. These findings were made for a group of sixteen women, comptometer operators, who were computing applications for crop loans in a government agency.

When the experiment was started, the only authorized rest pause was the 45-minute noon recess. Observers noted that the women took rest pauses when it was convenient. During the second part of the experiment, rest periods were installed from 10:22 to 10:30 A.M. and from 2:23 to 2:30 P.M., and the fifteen minutes thereby consumed were added to the length of the workday. During this part of the experiment a decrease in the amount of unauthorized rest and an increase in the amount of production per hour was proved. Although in this particular case only six of the sixteen operators preferred authorized rest periods, the complaints of the majority were directed not at the system itself but at the crowded restroom. Such negative aspects of the work situation should, of course, be corrected if authorized rest pauses are inaugurated.[49]

Practices in regard to the granting of rest periods usually vary for office and factory workers.

Although rewards such as rest pauses and bonuses tend to facilitate production, they have little effect on reported feelings of tiredness and boredness. This was found in an experiment in which subjects were told to "work as hard and as fast as you can" at monotonous laboratory work that simulated the type of work done by many industrial workers daily. The study was made to determine the effects of various suggested attitudes or mental sets on work productivity and boredom. Authors tested eighty-eight college students—divided into groups to test various attitudes and conditions. The manual work (motor tasks) performed were simple, but equipment prevented it from becoming automatic even toward the end of the four-hour test period.

Under ordinary working conditions, reported feelings of tiredness and boredness were found to be in inverse proportion to the amount of work done. There also was found to be an inverse relation between observable boredness and tiredness as rated by experimenters and amount of work done. Additional findings were:

> Knowledge that a rest pause is imminent retards production for the period immediately preceding the pause.
>
> Indulgence in activities such as talking or laughing tends to objectify the working situation and also tends to inhibit to some extent reports of tiredness and boredness.
>
> The introduction of positive motivation, in the waking state, facilitates production considerably, and produces fewer reports of tiredness and boredness.
>
> The introduction of negative motivation, in the waking state, inhibits production significantly but has little effect on reports of tiredness and boredness.[50]

Workers often reduce their boredom at repetitive work through conversation. They provide their own rest pauses if management does not systematize rest for them.

The Meanings of the Work Are Most Significant

Satisfaction with the working conditions does not necessarily bring about productivity. An employee may be pleased with his job situation but have no strong desire to contribute to production goals. To stimulate the employee, the task at hand must have meanings that the employee can understand and respect.

For example, the greatest contrast in productivity in a certain factory was found to exist between those who wrapped and those who unwrapped pieces of toffee. Employees thought of unwrapping as destructive and aimless. Their mental set created a disinclination to work which was not altered noticeably even by different wage-payment systems. See lowermost line of figure on page 385.[51] In general, employees caused the most trouble and wasted the most time on processes that they disliked. Conversely, they showed the greatest increase in productivity when working on those jobs they liked most.

Most line executives are incapable of, or uninterested in, verbalizing the meanings and values inherent in the job. Executives who are engineers, in particular, are inarticulate in this respect. Hence, the personnel department must help provide the interpretation of the job to the workers. The effect on production of such interpretation was dramatically illustrated during World War II:

> Take the case of the atomic bomb plant at Oak Ridge, Tennessee. The workers there were above average. They had been meticulously screened before they were selected—they had been chosen for their outstanding Americanism after a thorough check-up by the F.B.I. You would expect these people to give their best effort to war production, not only because of their general background but because they knew that "Manhattan Project" was considered an AAA1 priority operation. *But they did not know what they were doing,* for of necessity it was the policy of "Manhattan Project" not to let its "left hand know what its right hand did."
>
> Taking the normal level of production as 100 per cent base, I am told on good authority that the first week after the A-Bomb fell on Hiroshima and they learned the full meaning of their efforts, production at Oak Ridge doubled! The week following when the second bomb fell on Nagasaki and they could begin to see that they could help bring the war to a quick close it went up to 300 per cent of the original level. *Here, dramatically, is demonstrated the stimulating effect of knowing what one is doing and why.*[52]

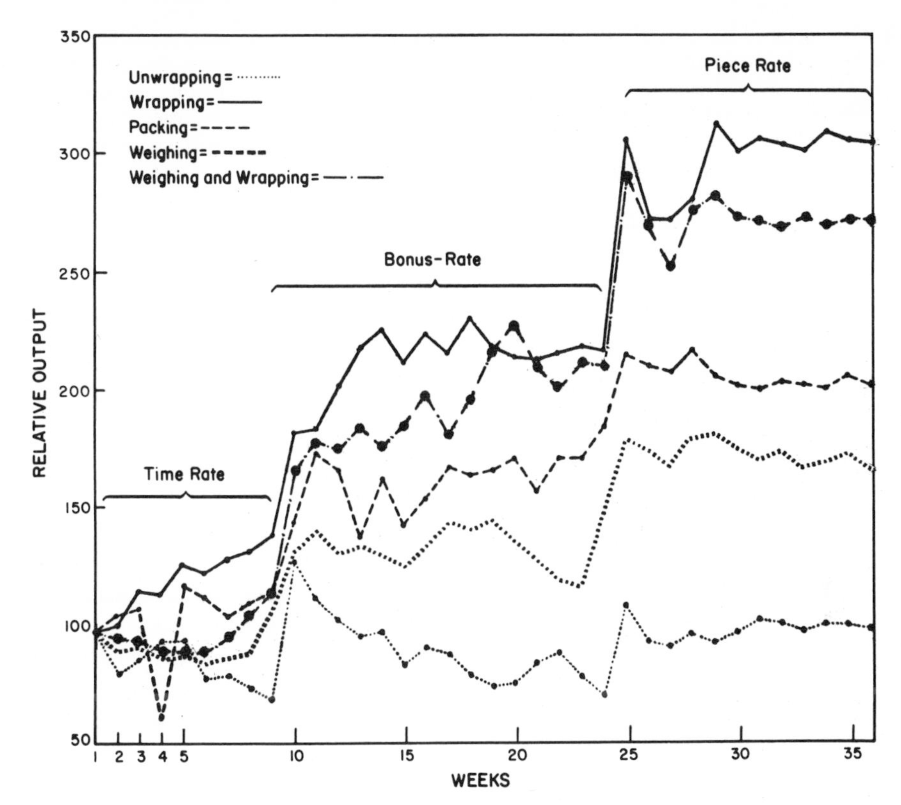

Relative output for each process in successive weeks. *Effects of incentives on work that is considered useful, wrapping, and on work considered destructive, unwrapping. The incentive of extra pay was ineffective in the case of the work disliked by the employees.—From S. Wyatt, assisted by L. Frost and F. G. L. Stock, **Incentives in Repetitive Work, A Practical Experiment in a Factory**, Industrial Health Research Board (Great Britain), 1934, Report No. 69. Reprinted by special permission of the Controller of His Britannic Majesty's Stationery Office.*

Certainly, studies of production procedures indicate that the human relations involved in a plant are important factors in the productivity and morale of workers. Several postwar studies of this type have been reported.

In one series, cost differentials in different companies of approximately the same size and character were studied. The most striking example was that of four gas mask plants which operated until shortly before V-J Day.

These plants had been equipped with identical government-owned facilities. Their operations were determined by the same production schedules and by the same piece rates for identical work. The government found, however, that the labor cost differed considerably in those four plants; it ranged from 52¢ to 87¢ per gas mask. It was also found that the average take-home pay was $1.17 an hour in the plant producing the low-cost gas masks, whereas take-home was much lower (72¢ to $1.00) in the plants delivering the high-cost gas masks.

When plant operations were investigated, it developed that the reason for the cost and take-home differentials lay in the varying degree of work interest among the employees of the four plants. Supervisory know-how in "human engineering" was low in the high-cost plants, but on a relatively high plane in the low-cost plant.

As a consequence, workers responded quite differently; their output (under equal piece rates) was high or low, depending on such factors as (1) speed with which grievances were settled; (2) worker confidence in the foreman's judgment and ability; (3) ease with which the workers could bring up their problems with the foreman and (4) willingness with which the workers accepted the foreman as their boss and leader.

Other differences, not directly pertaining to

the quality of supervision, existed also. The low-cost plant had a better staffed and better functioning personnel department than the others. Also, its whole industrial relations policy had been given as much attention as the technical aspects of production. "Human engineering" was recognized as an important factor in industrial operations, making for competitive advantages where cost and other conditions of doing business were the same.[53]

Industrial psychologists have concluded that bad working conditions do not in themselves produce bad morale nor do good working conditions produce good morale. Rather, the *psychological climate* determines the kind or degree of good or poor morale. A company may, for example, recognize that certain employees have to work over a chemical bath that gives off unpleasant fumes. When an exhaust system is installed to draw off the fumes, morale goes up or down depending upon whether the workers think that the exhaust system was installed for their benefit or to boost output only. When workers are suspicious of the reasons behind management's moves, the improvement of working conditions will not change morale.[54]

In general, we can say that fatigue and efficiency of the individual are influenced by many chemical and psychological influences. Furthermore, the individual can accommodate himself to almost any conditions. Man has permanent settlements in towns that frequently have winter temperatures 50 degrees F. below zero and in deserts with sun temperatures of 150 degrees. Attitude is exceedingly important toward the adaptation. An experienced stevedore, for example, can toss freight all day without appreciable fatigue but will be worn out by several hours of simple effort while on a shopping trip with his wife who is looking for a hat!

In the case of industrial workers, Britain's Industrial Health Board has summarized the findings of researchers on the effects of working hours and similar factors on output of workers as follows:

> It used to be thought that worker's and employer's interests were opposed—the worker wanting plenty of leisure and pay, the employer wanting the most work for the least expenditure. But now psychological researches into industry have shown that the best conditions of work for the greatest output are exactly the same as those that give health and a low accident rate to the worker.[55]

Many executives, in their labor relations thinking, still pay too much attention to physical conditions, important as they are, but not enough to human feelings. The physical environment can make a factory or office a more comfortable place in which to work, but the best morale and highest production come out of a homey atmosphere of friendliness and personal understanding between management and workers. It is, of course, much easier for an executive to install a mechanical system or device or some kind than for him to change his cold personality to a friendly understanding one.

General Motors, using its own 79 plants as a laboratory, conducted an interesting study on the effect of physical environment on productivity. The company has some plants that are the last word in employee comfort as well as other, older plants where there is less emphasis on the mechanics of comfort. The survey showed that there was no difference in output between the slick and the staid plants. Workers who are impressed by swank factories and bowling leagues will normally gravitate to such plants, it seemed, while others, who do not care for externals or sports, take jobs with companies that do not go in for showmanship. The study showed that while frills and fringes made no dent one way or the other in individual productivity, the degree of camaraderie in the department or plant made a tremendous difference in ultimate output.[56]

A few decades ago, the emphases in the attempts to improve production were largely of the time and motion study variety. Today, the work simplification programs still give attention to methods of work but they are now based on the simple principle that people do best the things they understand and enjoy because of their meanings. Work simplification recognizes that real productivity and satisfaction in the work situation depends upon the psychological climate in the day-to-day relationships with management and fellow workers.

ACKNOWLEDGMENTS AND REFERENCES

1. Joseph Tiffin, *Industrial Psychology* 5th ed. (Englewood Cliffs, N.J.: Prentice-Hall, Inc., 1965), pp. 475 ff.
2. T. N. Whitehead, *The Industrial Worker* (Cambridge, Mass.: Harvard University Press, 1938), Vol. I, p. 94.
3. Matthew Luckiesh, "Footcandle Levels Threshold, Ideal, Optimum, and Recommended," paper presented at the National Technical Conference of the Illuminating Engineering Society, New Orleans, September 15–19, 1947. General Electric Company, Cleveland, Ohio. See *Illuminating Engineering,* **43** (1948), 395.
4. Miles A. Tinker, "Illumination Standards for Effective and Comfortable Vision," *Journal of Consulting Psychology,* **3,** No. 1 (1939), 17 ff. Quoted by permission of the author and the *Journal.*
5. "Color Punches the Time Clock," *The Management Review,* American Management Association, Inc., September, 1947, p. 452. After Lloyd Stouffer *Popular Science,* June 1947, p. 124–126.
6. *Loc. cit.*
7. "Color in the Office," *The Management Review,* American Management Association, Inc., September, 1948. After C. E. Seghers, *Office Management Association of Chicago Monthly Bulletin,* April, 1948.
8. *Loc. cit.*
9. Faber Birren, "Color Conditioning in Modern Industry," *Dun's Review and Modern Industry,* July 1942. See also *The Management Review,* American Management Association, Inc., **31,** No. 8 (1942).
10. See Faber Birren, "Color in Your Plant," *Factory Management and Maintenance,* February, 1954, pp. 110–112.
11. See "Making Color Pay Off in the Plant," *Safety Maintenance and Production,* April, 1955.
12. See "Industry Dresses Up with Color," *The Management Review,* American Management Association, Inc., February, 1955, p. 77.
13. See *Insider's Newsletter,* June 1, 1964, p. 4.
14. K. G. Pollock and F. C. Bartlett, H. C. Weston and S. Adams, *Two Studies in the Psychological Effects of Noise,* Industrial Health Research Board, Great Britain, Report No. 65, 1932.
15. D. E. Broadbent and E. A. J. Little, "Effects of Noise Reduction in a Work Situation," *Occupational Psychology,* **34** (1960), 133–140.
16. Harry J. Jerison, "Effect of Noise on Human Performance," *Journal of Applied Psychology,* April, 1959.
17. William N. McBain, "Noise, the 'Arousal Hypothesis,' and Monotonous Work," *Journal of Applied Psychology,* October, 1961.
18. Jerison. *op. cit.*
19. Robert B. Sleight and Joseph Tiffin, "Industrial Noise and Hearing," *Journal of Applied Psychology,* **32** (1948), 476–489.
20. H. C. Weston and S. Adams, *Two Studies in the Psychological Effects of Noise, II. The Effects of Noise on the Performance of Weavers,* Industrial Health Research Board, Great Britain, Report No. 65, 1932.
21. Albert E. Bachmann, "Quiet, Please!" *Harvard Business Review,* May–June, 1955, p. 69.
22. See John F. Goldsmith, "New and Noteworthy," *Factory Management and Maintenance,* February, 1954, p. 132.
23. See "The Growing Industrial Battle Against Decibels," *Dun's Review and Modern Industry,* June, 1963.
24. Robert B. Sleight and Joseph Tiffin, *op. cit.*
25. For further information, see Albert E. Bachmann, *op. cit.,* pp. 68–74.
26. "Your Plant Doesn't Have to Be So Noisy," *Industrial Relations,* January, 1948, p. 23.
27. Henry Clay Smith, "Music in Relation to Employee Attitudes, Piece-Work production, and Industrial Accidents. With a foreword by Joseph Tiffin," *Applied Psychology Monograph,* No. 14, Stanford University, published for the American Psychological Association by Stanford University Press, 1947.
28. Richard S. Uhrbrook, "Music on the Job: Its Influence on Worker Morale and Production," *Personnel Psychology,* Spring, 1961.
29. Ernest M. Werner, *Work Music by Muzak,* 1945–47, a Research Study of its Effectiveness and Acceptance, Muzak Corporation, New York, 1948, p. 23.
30. K. H. Baker, "Pre-experimental Set in Distraction Experiments," *Journal of General Psychology,* **16** (1937), 471–486.
31. Flanders Dunbar, "Susceptibility to Accidents," *The Medical Clinics of North America,* **28** (May, 1944), 659–661. Published by W. B. Saunders Company, Philadelphia.
32. See Vita Krall, "Personality Characteristics of Accident-Repeating Children," *Journal of Abnormal and Social Psychology,* January, 1953, pp. 99–107.

33. Alexandra Adler, "Accidents in Industry," *Science,* **94** (Sept. 5, 1941).
34. *Ibid.,* p. 12.
35. Dunbar, *op. cit.*
36. Anthony Davids and James T. Mahoney, "Personality Dynamics and Accident Proneness in an Industrial Setting," *Journal of Applied Psychology,* October, 1957.
37. Paul Slivnick, Willard Kerr and William Kosinar, "A Study of Accidents in 147 Factories," *Personnel Psychology,* **10** (1957), 43–51.
38. Thomas N. Jenkins, "Identifying the Accident-Prone Employee," *Personnel,* American Management Association, Inc., July-August, 1961.
39. See Wayne K. Kirchner, "The Fallacy of Accident-Proneness," *Personnel,* American Management Association, Inc., November-December, 1961 and Robert Penn, "The Use of Job Performance and Job History Data as Indices of Personality Maladjustment Among Accident-Prone Employees," *The American Psychologist,* July, 1957, p. 408.
40. Paul L. Crawford, "Hazard Exposure Differentiation Necessary for the Identification of Accident-Prone Employee," *Journal of Applied Psychology,* June, 1960.
41. From *The Insurance Index,* January 1954. See also *The Management Review,* American Management Association, Inc., March, 1954, p. 175.
42. See John C. Larson, "Industrial Accident Research: How Can It Be Improved?" *Personnel,* American Management Association, Inc., September, 1955, pp. 135–138.
43. "Making Night Work Pay," *Modern Industry,* Jan. 15, 1948, pp. 41–44.
44. Hilda Brown, "Day and Night and Three Shift Working," *Personnel Management,* **39** (1957), 150–156.
45. Harry Levinson, *et al., Men, Management and Mental Health,* Harvard University Press, 1962, p. 108.
46. J. D. Ratcliff, "What Makes You Tired," *Collier's,* Dec. 21, 1940, p. 43.
47. S. Wyatt and J. N. Langdon, "Fatigue and Boredom in Repetitive Work," Industrial Health Research Board, Greater Britain, Report No. 77, 1937, p. 86.
48. Joseph M. Brozek, "Psychological Factors in Relation to Performance and Fatigue," *Federation Proceedings,* **2,** No. 3 (1943).
49. William McGehee and Edwin B. Owne, "Authorized and Unauthorized Rest Pauses in Clerical Work," *Journal of Applied Psychology,* **24** (1940), 605–614.
50. James H. Taylor, Claude E. Thompson, Dimiter Spassoff, "The Effect of Conditions of Work and Various Suggested Attitudes on Production and Reported Feelings of Tiredness and Boredness," *Journal of Applied Psychology,* **2** (1937), 431–447.
51. S. Wyatt, Assisted by L. Frost and F. G. L. Stock, *Incentives in Repetitive Work, A Practical Experiment in a Factory,* Industrial Health Research Board, Great Britain, Report No. 69, 1934.
52. "Worker Productivity, A Challenge to Management," a talk by Robert M. Creaghead, Employee Communication Specialist, Greenwich, Connecticut, before Industrial Marketers of Cleveland, Chapter of the National Industrial Advertisers Association, Inc., Hotel Carter, October 25, 1946.
53. *The Foreman's Letter,* June 5, 1946. Copyright © 1946, National Foremen's Institute, Inc., Deep River, Conn.
54. See *The Foreman's Letter,* National Foremen's Institute, New York, Dec. 6, 1954, p. 3.
55. Marjorie Van De Water, *Science-Supplement,* **92,** No. 2396, p. 12.
56. See Lawrence Stessin, "Good Feeling Is Key to Productivity, Survey Suggests," *Forbes Magazine,* Oct. 1, 1952.

PROJECTS

1. Conduct a study among fellow students or associates regarding effects on efficiency of listening to the radio while reading or studying. Note the kind of music listened to, the loudness, and other pertinent factors.
2. List the factors in lighting that tend to improve productivity in industry. Which recommended factors or principles are you violating in the lighting of your own study or work environment?
3. What is the effect of music on your mental efficiency? Do your tastes in music annoy anyone else who studies or works in your environment? If others are annoyed by your preferences in music, what reasons can you suggest for the different preferences?
4. Consider the colors of walls, ceilings, and furniture in your study or work situation. Are the colors conducive to study or work? What improvements would you like to make in the colors of your work or study environment?
5. What kinds of noises do you usually have in your study or work environment? If certain ones distract you from study or work, how do you try to adapt yourself to them? Do you simply ignore them? Does ignoring them appear to affect your productivity or your comfort? Have you ever been in a work situation in which the noise factor was a major problem? How was it solved?
6. What period of the day can you do your best mental work: early morning, mid-morning, noon, mid-afternoon, late afternoon, early

evening, or late at night? When is your mental efficiency lowest? Do you try to schedule difficult mental tasks accordingly?

7. Do you know an automobile driver who has had several automobile accidents? If you do, describe any psychological factors that may be influential in his high accident rate. If you were a traffic court judge, what sentences would you impose on traffic law violators who are "repeaters"?

COLLATERAL READINGS

Bowles, R. S., Jr., "Color in Your Plant—Helpful or Harmful," *Factory,* August, 1962.

Farnsworth, P. R., ed., *et al., Annual Review of Psychology.* Palo Alto, Calif.: Annual Reviews, Inc., 1964, pp. 29–86.

Fleishman, Edwin A., *Studies in Personnel and Industrial Psychology.* Homewood, Ill.: The Dorsey Press, Inc., 1961, Chapters 49–56.

Gilmer, B. von Haller, *Industrial Psychology.* New York: McGraw-Hill Book Company, 1961, Chapter 15.

"Growing Industrial Battle Against Dangerous Decibels, The," *Dun's Review and Modern Industry,* June, 1963.

Harrell, Thomas Willard, *Industrial Psychology.* New York: Holt, Rinehart and Winston, Inc.; 1958, Chapter 9.

Karn, Harry W. and B. von Haller Gilmer, *Readings in Industrial and Business Psychology.* New York: McGraw-Hill Book Company, 1962, pp. 219–270.

Smith, Henry Clay, *Psychology of Industrial Behavior.* New York: McGraw-Hill Book Company, 1955, Chapter 13.

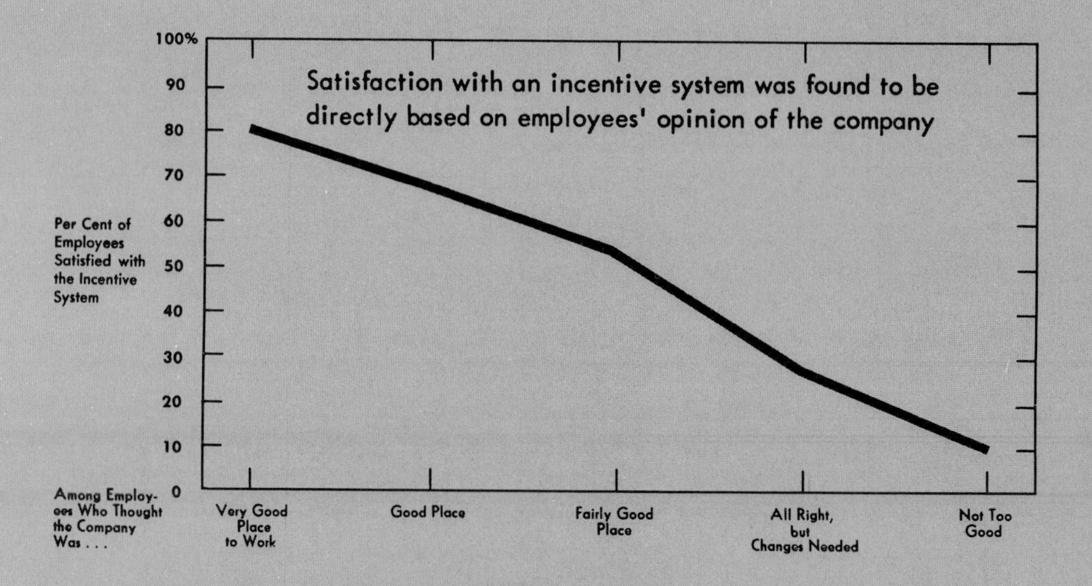

The Foundation for Research on Human Behavior *invited a number of business concerns, research agencies, and other organizations to participate in a series of seminars in the broad area of leadership productivity and job satisfaction.*

The seminar participants set out to examine research findings on current problems of administrative leadership, motivation, and organizational effectiveness, with a view toward applying these findings to improve organizational performance.

Among the studies evaluated was one conducted in an appliance factory to find out why an established incentive plan was more acceptable to employees in some units than in others. The figure above shows that satisfaction with the incentive system was very closely related to employees' general feelings about the company as a place to work; to some extent it appeared to be a reflection of their confidence in the fairness of the management.

It developed in the discussion that the difficulties in the company's plant were the result of inadequate management and supervision over an extended period. Therefore any incentive program would probably have to be accompanied by far-reaching management changes to prove successful. The features of an incentive program itself are by no means the only factors which determine its acceptability and effectiveness. **Source:** *G. Mahoney, "Supervisory and Administrative Actions Associated with Employee Attitudes toward an Incentive System," an unpublished paper available from the Institute for Social Research. From* ***Leadership Patterns and Organizational Effectiveness*** *(Ann Arbor, Mich.: Foundation for Research on Human Behavior, 1954), p. 6.*

CHAPTER NINETEEN

PSYCHOLOGICAL CLIMATES

All our well-meant objectives
and techniques for dealing with people in industry must
take cognizance of the pervading psychological framework
or atmosphere of feeling and thinking
where the people are functioning. This kind of awareness
on the part of the observer or new employee cannot be learned
from a printed statement prepared for visitor
or newcomer. It must be deduced
by the perceiver
as he gradually learns to interpret the cues
he notes or discovers for himself.

Each home, each educational institution, each company, and each department of work group within a company has a psychological climate of its own. The prevailing atmosphere in one work group may be almost as impersonal as a computer. In another group, the atmosphere is sunny and the people are cheerful and friendly. The people, not the buildings, furnishings, equipment or the product produced determine the psychological climate.

Psychological climates are so important that every person who wants to become more perceptive should become aware of their kinds and the factors that bring them about. However, the student should not try to find a work group that is perfect. Perfect climates do not exist geographically nor do they exist psychologically. The objective for the individual in his relations with the group should be one of alertness to the nature and causes of the atmosphere and of ways in which he can contribute to its positive aspects. The psychologically perceptive person usually finds ways in which he can play his own role intelligently in many kinds of climates.

Some of the factors that are influential in producing the climate within a company are mentioned in other chapters even though they have not been designated as such. In this chapter, we shall list and give brief descriptions of certain major influences that are likely to be noted in attempts to sense the climate.

1. *The extra-company environmental influences.* Behavioral scientists* who study outside-the-company influences are especially interested in cultures. *Culture* may be defined as a "body of learned behavior," a collection of beliefs, habits, practices, and traditions, shared by a group of people (a society) and successively learned by new members who enter the society. Cultures are found in and are often characteristic of nations, tribes, communities, and companies. The older the institution, the greater the likelihood of finding such a firm body of learned behavior. When an established culture is disturbed, pronounced reactions occur. When, for example, efforts are made to improve the economic lot of a nation of low-income people by introducing the use of more productive machinery, the natives may resist. The continuation of their cultural heritages may be more important to them than a higher standard of living which they have not as yet learned to appreciate.

The mores of the people of one geographical location often differ from those of another region. In the early history of the Tennessee Valley Authority, certain supervisory problems arose because southern workers were not accustomed to the rough-and-ready language of those foremen whose previous work experience had been in the North.[1]

Managements of companies in this country know that cultural differences in regions are often influential. They have found that persons reared in rural areas are likely to have somewhat different attitudes toward work than those reared in the city. Rural-reared employees are more willing to accept and attempt to fulfill management's work expectations. Generally, morale surveys of industrial firms indicate that the attitudes of employees toward management are relatively better in the South than in the older industrial centers of the East.

2. *Size of company.* In general, most persons assume that the size of an organization has considerable influence on its climate. Any one who reads current literature about human relations in industry is likely to find statements that describe effects of bigness. One oft-mentioned correlate or effect is the so-

* The term "behavioral science" usually refers to any systematic attempt to study the behavior of human beings using the attitudes and procedures of science. The disciplines working in this field are psychology, sociology, cultural anthropology, economics, and history. Formerly, the term "social science" was used, but when the Ford Foundation coined the new term, the scientists in these fields began to use it because it is a relatively neutral term—it is less likely to be confused with socialism. See "Behavioral Science—What's in It for Management?" *Business Management Record,* National Industrial Conference Board, Inc., June, 1963, p. 33.

called "organization man,"[2] the individual who is characterized as following a pattern of conforming behavior. It is assumed that the nonconforming individual who is less subservient to the group influence is more likely to join a small than a large company. The faults of the large company in hiring and developing the comforming person are believed to be more severe than in the small firm.

Relatively few studies of the effects of bigness as such have been made. However, Lyman W. Porter analyzed responses to various questions from more than 1,700 managers of companies of all sizes. He found that jobs in large concerns are likely to be seen as more challenging, more difficult, and more competitive than in small companies. Furthermore, the personality traits of the "organization man" are seen as being in greater demand in small than in large companies. He found that the ego and self-fulfillment needs of individuals, particularly for those who reach the middle and upper management levels, are more likely to be experienced in the large than in the small companies. The reasons for this may be the greater facilities usually available in the form of technical, financial, and personnel resources. The manager is also likely to have a larger group under his command. Larger size offers more challenge. Apparently, the so-called "organization man" is in more demand in the small than in the large company.[3]

" You'll find we're just one big family here—intrigues, jealousies, fights, . . . " **Source:** Dale McFeatters, ***The Management Review,*** (October 1957). Courtesy of American Management Association, Inc.

Thus far, the available evidence indicates that we should direct our attention concerning psychological climates toward the orientation of the management and the dominant personalities, not toward external size.

3. *Orientation of the management.* One simple approach to the management orientation is to estimate it from the history of the president. If he achieved his advancement to responsibility in the production end of the business, we can usually note that the management is especially concerned with the manufacturing equipment, the shop employees, and the engineering staff. Quality control is a popular topic in management meetings. And a frequently heard criticism is that the sales department makes too many ridiculous promises to customers in regard to delivery dates. Production executives are likely to be pessimistic rather than overly optimistic about what the product will do. This kind of management likes to get large, long-term contracts with the big merchandising firms such as the Chicago mail order houses, because that kind of arrangement makes it easy to put production on a stable, efficient basis. It also decreases the need for making expensive market researches.

In contrast, top management of a sales-minded firm is more likely to prefer small contracts with many customers. Selling, not production, is fun. The popular topics in the management meetings that get priority are marketing and advertising. Executives try to find out what the customers want by means of market researches. They are apt to assure the prospective customer that the product will do or be just what he wants. And they are optimistic about the quality of the product.

If the top executive has had an active financial history, we should expect an extra emphasis to be given to the financial aspects of the business. In such a company, one should look for the banking connections. The board of directors is likely to have a representative from the affiliated bank or financial house. He, however, is not likely to exercise very much influence on the personnel except in the selection of the president or other key executives. He will be more concerned with the profit-or-loss picture and how it may be improved.

The fact that a company is under the financial control of a banking group or a foundation does not mean that the management provides a good or a poor climate, one that is favorable or unfavorable for the young man who wants to grow. However, a knowledge of the controlling personalities on the board enables one to evaluate their influence more accurately.

The significance of a company's financial situation is especially important as to how profits are used. They may be sought to build high salary-paying practices and retirement benefits for the major executives, to earn profits for important stockholders, to satisfy status needs, or to strengthen the company through research and diversification. Fortunately, most professional management men have a desire to develop a bigger and stronger company because of the challenge, and not for the sake of special benefits to any one interest group.

4. *Is the management expansion minded?* Relatively few managements like to pile up profits into cash reserves. They prefer to invest their profits in expansion programs. Historically, the contrasts between cash-rich and expansion-minded managements are often studied by comparing the earlier development of Montgomery Ward under Sewell Avery, and of Sears, Roebuck and Company under General Woods. Avery followed a policy of piling up cash. Woods used cash for expansion. Later, Montgomery Ward management recognized that profits are most productive when put to work.

Typically, American executives consciously think of expansion first and profits second. Business boom and growth are more thrilling to the aggressive executive than money in the bank. Many have sought expansion for the sake of expansion with little regard for immediate profit. Certain managements find this necessary, at times, for competitive reasons. The history of automobile manufacturing offers examples of this kind of need for disinterest in profits in one year for the sake of later corporate health.

An important need for survival through expansion arises when the company's main product is declining in sales simply because it is approaching the end of its life cycle. New products are like people—they are born, grow slowly, reach the vigor of maturity, decline, and eventually die. Alert managements therefore seek to retain their corporate vigor by expanding their activities toward the acquisition of other products and companies, often through mergers.

Reasons for a company seeking to bring another firm into its own organization may be to strengthen product lines, to join forces with another firm that deals in the same product, to build a vertically integrated unit as exemplified by the steel manufacturer who buys an appliance company, to diversify its products and to bring about operating savings. In some cases, the competitive position may be improved through the acquisition of a larger sales force or a better geographical distribution of sales offices.

A common reason for mergers is the need for obtaining a better management. Perhaps the management of the acquiring company consists of old men, while that of the acquired company has a supply of capable young executives. For the small company, one of the benefits to its men is that they may have a better chance to grow through a greater number of opportunities to advance to better jobs.

Fundamentally, however, expansion is a part of our business way of life. If growth through further enlargement of the company's current activities is no longer feasible, expansion must be made into unrelated lines. The company diversifies. Some of these diversifications may be organized in a manner that brings about profitable integration—others merely bring about a polyglot collection of companies, some of which may be a financial drag on the profitable companies of the group.

Many merged companies suffer severe varieties of "indigestion" before the added segments become profitably integrated with the parent company. Some never seem to reach stable profits and growth. This suggests that the growth-minded man who chooses a company for its expansion mindedness should also try to note whether the executives are as able and versatile as the expansion program requires.

On the human relations side, personality clashes and conflicts of interest often arise between members of the acquiring and the acquired managements. The controlling company's management may make decisions which the acquired company's executives know to be wrong. Or the latter may give only lip service to the central management's programs while running the operations in a manner that produces only mediocre results. This latter group of executives functions as an "island of autonomy."

Members of a central management and those of an acquired management often need years of experience with each other in order to develop mutual confidence and wholehearted cooperation. Until such time as they have gone through tribulations together, they lack identification with each other and remain a polyglot collection in spirit as well as in structure. The psychological climates of merged companies often remain varied and uncertain until their members have experienced suffering and success with new organizational assignments.

The average industrial employee is likely to prefer to work in a climate of stability, a place where few changes take place. The ambitious young man, in contrast, usually prefers to work in a less stabilized place, one where the growth of the company is more important than comfortable stability.

5. *Centralized or decentralized decision-making*. A large company, whether it resulted from a merger or not, can be viewed as a grouping of smaller business units. In some large and small companies, decision-making is so highly centralized that no subordinate can act on his own until he has got a signal from someone up the line. Initiative on the part of middle management men is stalled. Personal growth becomes more difficult as the centralized decision-making and the hampering red tape increases.

Efforts to decrease decentralized decision-making has increased in recent years because the red-tape organization is not especially profitable. Also, the improvement of human relations is likely to be easier. The current policy in some large companies is to create a small business atmosphere by dividing the company into a number of smaller units, each headed by a man who has broad responsibilities. The concept, as Harlow H. Curtice of General Motors has expressed it, is:

> ...to divide the business into as many parts as consistently as [sic] can be done, place in charge of each part the most capable executive that can be found, and develop a system of coordination so that each part may strengthen and support each other part; thus not only welding all parts together in the common interests of a joint enterprise, but importantly developing ability and initiative through the instrumentalities of responsibility and ambition—developing men and giving them an opportunity to exercise their talents, both in their own interests as well as in that of the business.[4]

One of the best ways to utilize human resources for business success is through the delegation of the decision-making power, as Curtice pointed out. Henry Ford almost lost his business as a result of his insistence on having the final say in unimportant as well as important matters.

Anyone who has risen to top levels in management, whether as the owner-manager or as a driving member of a large organization, is likely to feel that the success of the business is due to his efforts. It is difficult for him to let others make important decisions because he has learned to depend upon himself rather than others. To develop his subordinates, however, he must learn how to allow them to make mistakes. Generally, executives who really want their subordinates to grow do so by choosing the goals but letting them decide how the goals will be attained. For the ambitious young man, the extent to which he will have the privilege of decision-making in regard to operational procedures is one of the most important aspects of a company's psychological climate.

6. *The controlling personalities in the company.* The formal head is not necessarily the most influential leader in a company. The man in the president's chair may in reality be a figurehead—some other executive may be setting up the goals, pushing the sales, and directing the organization. He, rather than the formal head, may also be looked to as the leader by the customers.

If the founder of the business has, in his old age, turned the company over to a charitable foundation for control, the climate is likely to be one of conservatism, and a conservatism that leads to the decline and eventual death of the company. Continuity of family control is often safeguarded by the placing of large blocks of stock in the hands of a trust which retains them for the benefit of the original owners' children and grandchildren.

If an heir remains at the helm, the management may be competent or incompetent, probably competent because the founder usually trains able assistants who can guide the heir. In many cases, too, the founder puts the heir through years of strenuous training for later responsibilities. If the heir does not achieve an acceptable level of ability, the board of directors may quietly arrange for his departure from the company. The members of the board and other executives are likely to have so great an investment in time and money in the company that they will not allow a weak scion to jeopardize their investment through poor management. In American business, dynastic succession is less prevalent than popular fancy imagines. A survey of public opinion on the subject, made by The Psychological Corporation, indicated that almost one third of the public believes that most of industry is run by a few wealthy families like the Rockefellers, du Ponts, and Fords. Yet careful analysis of the top command echelons of the 500 largest publicly owned corporations of the United States revealed only a 14 per cent incidence of dynastic relationships, much of it at secondary levels. Relatively few managements follow a fixed policy on the question of nepotism—the showing of too much favor by one in power to his relatives. Informally, many managements do not employ relatives because they feel that hiring relatives tends to bring criticism from non-related employees. Also, many able young men refuse to work in their fathers' companies because they want to earn their own titles and responsible positions without benefit of parental influence. Besides, some sons know the father too well!

Many heirs are sons of forceful fathers. Such fathers are apt to be exceedingly demanding and intensely critical of their sons' performance. Many fathers are still at the height of their own powers when their sons reach adulthood. "In the very best of circumstances, sonship in dynastic industrial families is no bed of roses. The pressure can be intense, and an heir's opportunity to spread his wings may be long delayed."[5]

In small companies, wholly or largely owned by one man, the basic financial orientation may be toward the building up of an estate for the benefit of heirs. Few profits are spent for research or further growth. Instead, the policy is usually described in such words as "The old man is milking the company in order to take care of his incompetent heirs." The owner of such a company may have one or two competent assistants but most employees are chosen because they can do a passable job and are willing to work for below-average pay. If an outstanding man is selected for employment because of his excellent potentials for growth, he is usually chosen because the owner wants to have his company continue to operate profitably after his death. If a young man of drive and high aspiration is hired on the assumption that he will be trained to become the head later, he may find that he advances rapidly in income and responsibility.[6]

7. *The ages of the top management men.* Usually, boards of directors like to be able to refer to the management as "young and ag-

gressive." They prefer to have some young rather than old men only. They realize that the perpetuation of the company is a basic responsibility of a board. Of course a company that has young men only may be as weak as one that has only old men.

Age is not a sound criterion of managerial ability. Many of our most progressive companies are headed by top executives who are in their fifties and sixties. Some are even older. Generally, top management men need judicial wisdom that has developed from years of experience. They must guide the development of the younger, more aggressive members of middle management. The full development of a personality often takes place in the later years of life. Maturity means that the emotional roadblocks of youth have been overcome so that energies are fully released for constructive activities. "Judgment ripens as the hair whitens." The fact that a management can be described as "young and aggressive" does not necessarily mean that it is efficient and successful.[7]

Of course when senility approaches, judicial ability declines.

Actually, management's most serious problem in regard to age is not the continuation of executives in jobs which they are no longer able to fulfill. Instead, a greater difficulty centers in the presence of "old men" on all levels who have become embittered sometimes quite early in their work life. Their unhappiness often permeates the department or group to such an extent that they create a psychological climate of pessimism, frustration, and criticism. Managements are usually aware of their negative influence on the younger employees but do not want to be so unkind as to remove them. It is up to each younger person who enters any group to recognize the presence of the disgruntled older employees and to plan his career without letting their soured outlook affect him.

8. *How well do the personalities at the top mesh together?* Many students who read the literature on human relations in business imagine that the ideal climate for a company is one where no frictions can be found—only sweetness and light. This kind of company should be avoided. A complete absence of friction between executives means that the members of the organization are not thinking aggressively, not stimulating each other to do better work. Such an atmosphere is not found in growth companies, those noted for their growth in sales over the years. Their management men have an enthusiasm for achievement. They like to accomplish things. They like to take the lead in making changes.

Growth companies have organized programs of product research and development, market research, diversification, and corporate planning. They plan their programs with an assumption that an accelerating rate of economic and technological change and an accelerating intensity of business competition will take place.[8] They are characterized by a zestful management spirit.

When individual executives have a strong drive to achieve, and are dynamic and imaginative in their thinking, they are bound to develop some frictions with their colleagues. But their frictions usually occur in regard to objectives and the means of attaining them, not in regard to petty or personal differences. Good management men do have some conflicts with each other but the conflicts usually have corporate purpose and produce common enthusiasms.

When a smart management man realizes that his own personality limitations are a handicap to his associates and subordinates, he may select a colleague or subordinate who neutralizes the ill effects of his personality pattern. One well-known American corporation is headed by a man of driving ambition and pride. He is meticulous in attire and in speech but mercurial in temper and is abrupt with people. He has become so aware of his negative characteristics with people that he has delegated most human relations responsibilities to a fellow executive who is of great ability but the opposite of himself in attire, manner, and speech.[9]

9. *Power politics*. Politics exists in all organized societies: in religious groups, schools, colleges, civil service, and hospitals, in trade

unions as well as in business. Most of us first become acquainted with the political variety of power seeking as practiced by some of history's political leaders. We hear about it daily as reported in newspapers and magazines. When a man gets a job in a business organization, he notes the schemings of certain ambitious employees who are referred to as "empire builders," "eager beavers," or "crown princes, self-appointed." At first, these men function as factional leaders, but they move into any group situation where the group lacks leadership or where a power vacuum exists. Power politics is likely to occur from time to time in so many work situations that the new employee should become aware of its presence. If he succumbs to the influence in its worst forms, he is likely to develop certain crafty qualities of catering to the "politician," qualities which at first appear to give him advantage over his associates. Generally, the clever politician should be avoided.

As one writer has stated, there are several different types of power seekers who seek to gain personal followings of their own. Some operate only in a relatively small group. A few, but not all, are self-centered. The beneficial kind may acquire his empire by any one of several procedures:

(a) by skillful maneuver when others fail on a job, retire, or both, or
(b) by sheer ability and applied imagination, being two or three jumps ahead of one's colleagues, or
(c) by being multi-functional in work situations. The more departments he controls the greater his importance.[10]

Generally, these procedures benefit the company and the employees. However, when management decides that the power seeking is having more harmful than good effects, top management usually controls the power seeker by relegating or transferring him to another assignment.[11]

We must not imagine that only ruthless power seekers get ahead in business. The ruthless self-centered men are likely to be more conspicuous and annoying than the more representative men who advance in business through unselfish service. There are, in every large company, certain good sound men whose aggressiveness is objective and sensible. They direct their efforts to the benefit of the company or entire group, not to or for themselves. They are able men who are usually well adjusted as personalities. They have not sought power—it has come to them because they learned to seek *power with* rather than *power over* others. They have vision. They have ability. They help others get ahead. But the dominating center of their thinking is the work, the job to be done. They do not perceive their efforts as ends in the attainment of selfish benefit. Instead, they think of themselves as agents in getting things done well. Finally, every member of an organization should realize that changes, even painful changes, in leadership are necessary for the growth of a company. This means that the individual employee in industry should perceive the shifts in leadership taking place, adapt himself to them, and view them intelligently, not with fear.

10. *The accounting controls.* Anyone who comes into a strange company learns to become aware of the accounting department's influences. These may be in the form of numerous statistical reports to direct management's decisions, budgets, and audits. In recent years, the men who have become computer minded have also become a dominating influence in many large companies. The effects of computerized thinking are becoming so severe that we shall treat the topic more fully in terms of its social dangers and challenges. See Chapter 25. In this treatment, we shall direct our thinking to the psychological effects brought about by internal accounting controls which are necessary to the productive operation of any company. These usually center in the officer designated as the controller.

Of course, each management follows its own policies in controlling costs. Some follow the practice of using rigid controls; others set up controls in a manner that still allows ample opportunities for the men of initiative. This suggests that the ambitious person in a company should note whether the internal con-

of the factory supervisors' assumptions about budgets is that they can be used as a pressure device to increase production efficiency. The need for pressure is based on the assumption that most workers are inherently lazy. Many employees also believe that top management thinks the workers do not have enough motivation of their own to do the best possible job. Such feelings, even if never openly expressed to the employees, filter through to them in very subtle ways. Once they sense that feelings of this kind exist in top management, they may become resentful.

The pressure, while increasing efficiency, may also release forces that pull in the opposite direction. Certain employees will try to keep production at the new level and to prevent it from rising again. Tensions begin to mount. People become uneasy and suspicious. They increase the informal pressure to keep production at the new level.[14] Of course, the employee can release some of his tensions by joining a group that opposes management. The supervisor cannot join because he at least partially identifies himself with management. He would not help his chances for advancement by joining an anti-management group.

Some pressures are necessary. What the effects of pressure are in terms of productivity, absenteeism, turnover, morale and the like will depend in part upon the business climate in which the company is operating. The management that follows the philosophy of "being nice" is likely to find that that attitude is more appropriate for an organization that is coasting along than for the company that aims at growth, expansion, and efficiency.[15]

Astute managements use intelligent approaches to the problems of pressure. One of the approaches invariably recommended is to gain acceptance by having supervisors participate in the making of the budgets that affect them. Most controllers emphasize the need for participation of all key people in instituting any changes in budgets, plus the willingness on the controllers' own part to revise their budgets whenever experience indicates it is necessary. Argyris' observations indicated, however, that some controllers find it easier to follow the form than the spirit of participation.

Generally, one reason for hostility towards existing budgets is the typical accountant's tendency in reporting budgeted performance to show, and even to emphasize disproportionately, what is wrong, without considering why variances occurred. The budget reporter should note first where actual performance has been significantly better than estimates and then mention what has fallen short of expectations. Analysis of the latter should be cautious because the origin of shortcomings may be in factors not evident to the financial analyst.

Ideally, budgetary controls should not be made nor appear to be made as edicts of accounting department experts nor as dragnets for substandard performance. They should be looked upon as aids in achieving objectives. Lack of understanding of these objectives can lead to suspicion of the budget—even to its unvoiced rejection. Top management should therefore state the objectives in a manner that causes employees to desire a budget that is reasonable and challenging.

How Companies Acquire Good Climates

Managements do not acquire a favorable climate by issuing directives or by hiring outside experts to produce it. The orientation of the top executives must change. If, for example, the president is oriented in the direction of spending most of his time and thinking to gain the good will of financial interests while he neglects his associates and subordinates, the climate is not likely to change until he takes a sincere interest in the members of the organization. In time, when he has solved the company's financial problems, he will, if he wants to modify the climate, do so by concentrating on giving the employees greater psychic income. He will organize programs and direct his colleagues in ways that will provide for the employees' emotional participation in the business. He will treat all members of the organization as colleagues whom he likes. He will conduct himself in accordance with high ethical standards and he will hold employees to high work standards. The systems he installs will be backed up by his continuing efforts to work with his people. As someone has stated: "Today's weather is tomorrow's climate."

A top management that becomes concerned about the psychological climate may send its junior executives to special institutes to take management courses. This may help, but we cannot expect the effects of such training to change a company's climate. Obviously, subordinates cannot put into effect any new practices they learn which contradict those of their superiors. The middle-level man who learns sound principles in a course knows that it is unwise for him to do his work in a manner that is markedly different from what his superior has been accustomed to expect. Wise managements know that middle-level leadership of, say, the participative variety cannot function with top-level leadership of another variety, such as the authoritarian. The climate of an organization will not be changed by a few injections of some new philosophy of leadership.

A good climate is more likely to develop when there is a normal growth pattern of structural changes in the organization. Rapid changes disrupt the climate. An organization may be rather loose-knit by design. After all, the structural organization is less important than its spirit. Frequent reorganizations that involve changes in executive responsibility tend to destroy the spirit. Structural changes, when made, should be minor, and evolve over the years. They should bend to the requirements of growth, not be imposed suddenly. Climate is likely to be favorable when the company has a record of steady growth and a low percentage of executive and personnel turnover.

Climate is developed when employees know that management is sincerely interested in their welfare. Every executive should spend a large part of his time in close individual contact with employees in regard to their work. Each employee should feel that the boss is interested in helping him to do his work, not merely inspecting him or his work. The functions of a supervisor are to evaluate the job the employee is doing and to help him do a better job.

One clue to the extent that a management is vitally interested in employees as human beings is the company's effort or lack of effort in finding jobs for capable employees in other organizations if management cannot, in its own company, provide opportunities that will use the employee to the full. Few employers follow this policy, and yet this policy not only attracts superior men but also causes many of those who have left to come back with experience and loyalty that could not be obtained otherwise. Some managements also assist laid-off employees in locating positions elsewhere. They do more than offer good wishes—they make vigorous efforts to help them find new positions.

Another clue to the climate encouraged by a management is indicated by the way members of the organization preface explanations of new ideas. If they present them in an extremely apologetic manner as "Now I know this sounds silly," or "This is just off the top of my head," the climate within the organization probably does not stimulate growth through individual initiative. An employee should voice respect for his colleagues but he should not have to apologize for an idea which he believes might be helpful. If executives have indoctrinated subordinates with the dictum, "Don't open your mouth until you are sure of what you are saying," they are promoting second-guessing rather than original thinking. The test of an idea is to see it in action. The employee who presents only sure-fire ideas is not a creator—only a describer of old ideas.

The company that has a good psychological climate is likely to have many executives who are always accessible to the employees. Employees can easily identify themselves with them because they are true leaders who practice participative methods. Men of good adjustment and good will usually enjoy and contribute to the positive psychological climates wherever they go. They tend to rise above the negative aspects of an environment and, in so far as they can, they help to bring about a better climate.

ACKNOWLEDGMENTS AND REFERENCES

1. See Milton M. Mandell, "The Effect of Organizational Environment on Personnel Selection," *Personnel,* American Management Association, Inc., July, 1953, p. 14.
2. See William H. Whyte, Jr., *The Organization Man* (New York: Simon and Schuster, Inc., 1956) and Alan Harrington, *Life in the Crystal Palace* (New York: Alfred A. Knopf, Inc., 1959).
3. Lyman W. Porter, "Where Is the Organization Man?" *Harvard Business Review,* November-December, 1963 and "Job Attitudes in Management," *Journal of Applied Psychology,* December, 1963.
4. Harlow H. Curtice, *The Development and Growth of General Motors,* Statement before Subcommittee on Antitrust and Monopoly of the U.S. Senate Committee on the Judiciary, Dec. 2, 1955. See Alan C. Filley, "Human Relations in the Growing Company," *Personnel,* American Management Association, Inc., September-October, 1957.
5. See "Heirs at the Helm," *Forbes,* Nov. 15, 1957, pp. 63–72.
6. See "Waiting for the Boss to Retire," *Business Week,* Mar. 14, 1959.
7. See Ralph A. Bing, "The Fallacy of 'Young Management,'" *The Analysts Journal,* August, 1957.
8. See Robert W. Smith, "Management Spirit: The Big Intangible in Corporate Growth," *Sales Management,* Apr. 18, 1958. Smith is Assistant Director, Economics Research Division, Stanford Research Institute, Menlo Park, California. This article presents preliminary findings from a study of 210 apparently "gifted" companies, selected for having exceptional growth histories as measured by growth in sales.
9. See *Fortune,* August, 1957, p. 112.
10. See John Marsh, "Power Politics and Power Politicians," *Personnel Administration,* July-August, 1957.
11. See also "How to Clamp Down on Company Politics," *Business Management,* August, 1963.
12. This kind of humorous definition of an occupational member is found in many groups and mature members do not resent it—they accept it as humor. Consider the many definitions of statisticians you have heard.
13. Chris Argyris, "Human Problems with Budgets," *Harvard Business Review,* January-February, 1953.
14. See Kurt Lewin, "Group Decision and Social Change," in Theodore Newcomb and Eugene L. Hartley, eds., *Readings in Social Psychology* (New York: Holt, Rinehart & Winston, Inc., 1947), especially p. 342.
15. See Chris Argyris, "Organizational Effectiveness Under Stress," *Harvard Business Review,* 38 (1960), 137–146.

PROJECTS

1. Describe the climates you have experienced in classrooms, living centers, departments, or companies. Were certain individuals key influences? If the climate changed in the course of time, was it because key individuals or members of the group left and were replaced? Did the climate really change or did your reactions to it change?
2. When you enter the business or some other work world, what factors will you try to note, factors that affect the climate? Apply your thinking to a possible visit to a university campus in order to do graduate studies there.
3. When a person enters a new group, should he try to modify or contribute to the existing climate? Should a contributor be more tactful than a noncontributor?
4. Very few checklists or rating scales are now available for evaluating the psychological climates of companies. Prepare a rough draft of such a proposed scale.

COLLATERAL READINGS

Argyris, Chris, "The Organization: What Makes It Healthy?" *Harvard Business Review,* November-December, 1958.

Deutsch & Shea, Inc., Consultants, "Company Climate and Creativity," *Industrial Relations News,* 1959.

Hepner, Harry W., *Perceptive Management and Supervision.* Englewood Cliffs, N.J.: Prentice-Hall, Inc., 1961, Chapter 9.

"How to Clamp Down on Company Politics, *Business Management,* August 1963.

Meltzer, H., "Mental Health Realities in Work Situations," *The American Journal of Orthopsychiatry,* April, 1963.

Perry, John, "Human Relations in Small Industry," Small Business Administration, Washington, D.C., March, 1954.

The observed and the observers are shown in the Group Dynamics Laboratory, as several students and staff members from the Group Dynamics Research Center, Institute for Social Research, University of Michigan, demonstrate the use of this research facility. The camera shows a teacher conducting a small group meeting as it is seen through one of the vision screens. In the photograph opposite, Mrs. Jane Corfield and Dr. Sidney Rosen look on from one of the observers' booths.

The Laboratory is used both for teaching and research by the Research Center for Group Dynamics.

The observation rooms are equipped with the one-way vision screens, sound proofing, an intercommunication system, and necessary ventilating equipment.

Primary purpose of the laboratory is to make possible additional research on the psychology of group life. The Research Center for Group Dynamics, which was established at Michigan in 1948, is interested in discovering the basic principles of group behavior—those which affect the formation, change, or dissolution of groups, or which influence the relations of one group with others and of members within a group with each other.

Some of the research programs of the Center for Group Dynamics have to do with group productivity, communications, and spread of influence within and between groups, inter-group relations, and adjustment of the individual to the group.

A good deal of this research is accomplished by means of field studies, as for example in the armed forces, in a telephone company, in a clothing factory, and in a housing development. Other projects, however, are carried on in the laboratory under carefully controlled conditions.

For further information, see D. Cartwright and A. Zander, **Group Dynamics** (New York: Harper & Row, Publishers, 1955).

CHAPTER TWENTY

GROUP DYNAMICS IN INDUSTRY

The behavior of each worker takes place in a social context. Researches have demonstrated the importance of recognizing the group dynamics and the individual group member's expectations. The potentials for action within the individuals of the group can be utilized in order to build an effective work team.

Industrial psychologists and members of management have, in the main, concentrated their efforts on the individual. Many psychologists in industry have confined themselves to such activities as interviewing, testing, rating, and counseling the worker. Management men, too, have thought in similar terms. Of necessity, the individual always will be a focus of interest to both the psychologist and the executive.

Until recently groups of employees have been considered mainly as work units, and employee relations programs have been concerned with wage payment plans, unionization, company-sponsored social affairs, and recreational programs. All of these relations of management to employees as a group or groups are pertinent to good morale and productivity. Investigations have shown that they are not in themselves, however, sufficient to assure either good morale or high productivity. It has been found necessary to consider the function of the group in other aspects of the work situation.

Considerable research is now being done in industry and in the military concerning factors that influence work carried out by teams rather than by individuals only. Team members must be able and willing to anticipate the expectations of other members as well as make their own needs known to them.

Within the group are certain powerful dynamics such as the degree of cohesiveness or the extent to which members of the group stick together as a team in order to attain their objectives. The psychological climate, the extent to which employees participate in making decisions about their work, the role of the leader, and the attitudes of workers toward the group are examples of the kinds of influences that currently are being studied in the area of group dynamics.

Historically, the growing interest in group dynamics can be dated from the research studies made by the Harvard investigators in the Hawthorne plant of the Western Electric Co. These studies began in 1927 and lasted five years. The stated aim at the time was to find "the relation between condition of work and the incidence of fatigue and monotony among employees."[1]

Temperature, humidity, and hours of sleep were to be studied to learn the effects of these factors on output. As the experiment progressed, it was discovered that productivity is influenced by a wide variety of factors including attitudes, motives, interpersonal relations, and strong forces from within and without the group itself.

Some of their first experiments dealt with the introduction of unaccustomed rest pauses. Later, variations were made in length of working days and weeks. The wage incentive was also considered as an influence on output, but the investigators concluded that the wage itself was not adequate to account for output changes.

Social Relationships in a Factory: a Study of an Industrial Group[2]

The most provocative aspects of these experiments have been described by Whitehead and are here summarized as follows:

In a special test room designed for the experiment, five girls assembled telephone relays at a work bench. Trays containing parts for assembly were opposite them. A sixth girl procured necessary parts for the assemblers and performed other routine duties. A male supervisor and one or two assistants sat facing the assemblers. The supervisor in charge obtained and kept numerous records relating to quality of output, reasons for temporary stops, length of time spent in bed by each girl every night, periodical medical reports of their physical condition, and other factors. Room temperatures and relative humidities were taken hourly. The supervisor and his assistants made extensive daily notes of conversation and of the relations developing among the workers. The workers were also occasionally interviewed in a separate room by an experienced interviewer. Furthermore, an automatic

Average weekly output *of five workers assembling telephone relays, who received much individual consideration under a variety of work conditions. The following summary describes the various "periods" of work:*

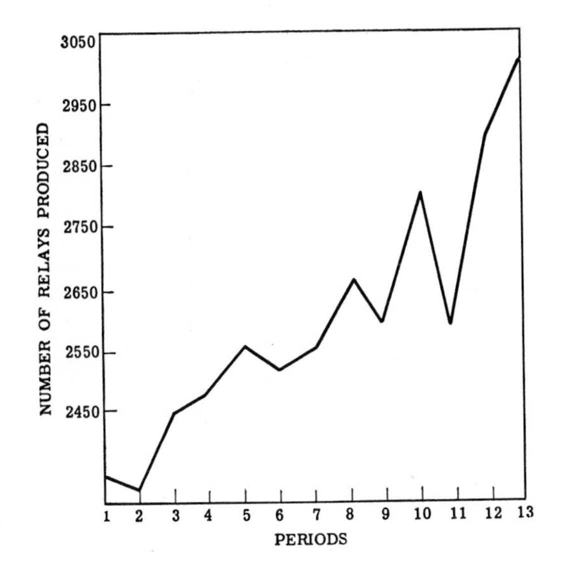

Period	*Duration in Weeks*	*Description*
1	2	*In regular department*
2	5	*Introduction to test room*
3	8	*Special "gang" rate*
4	5	*2 5-minute rest periods*
5	4	*2 10-minute rest periods*
6	4	*6 5-minute rest periods*
7	11	*15 minute morning rest with lunch*
8	7	*Same as 7, but with 4:30 stop*
9	4	*Same as 7, but with 4:00 stop*
10	12	*Same as 7*
11	9	*Same as 7, but 5-day week*
12	12	*Same as 3 (no lunch or rest)*
13	36	*Same as, 7, but operators furnish own lunch*

In this study extending for more than two years, *a group of workers were placed with usual equipment in a separate room, shown friendly individual consideration, and repeatedly interviewed regarding their opinions of various incentive conditions that were being investigated. The noteworthy thing is that* ***regardless*** *of the incentive or the work conditions introduced,* ***output continued to increase!*** *As an outgrowth of this study, the company has since instituted a plan of widespread interviewing of individual workers.—Data from Elton Mayo, "Supervision and Morale,"* ***Human Factor,*** *Vol. 5 (1931), pp. 248–260. Chart and comment on Mayo's data taken from Sidney L. Pressey, J. Elliott Janney, and Raymond G. Kuhlen,* ***Life: A Psychological Survey*** *(New York: Harper & Row, Publishers, 1939), pp. 542–543.*

device recorded, to a fraction of a second, the instant at which each girl completed each assembled relay. Hence, a minute-to-minute record of output with supplementary information was available for each girl over a five-year period.

When the production of each worker was charted in graphic form, it was found that wave-like irregularities were exhibited by each graph. Some of the waves lasted for months; others only a week or two. The output figures also showed that similar irregularities occurred with durations of as little as a minute or two.

At first it was supposed that these variations in working speed might be related to the experimental changes deliberately introduced, or possibly to other changes in physical circumstance such as temperature or the worker's physical state. However, careful analysis of the data showed that irregularity in output failed to correlate with any known changes of physical circumstance.

When this negative conclusion was reached, the researchers next considered changes in the girls' social relationships. Study along these lines produced positive results. It was found that speed of work varied markedly with changes in the sentiments entertained by the workers toward each other, toward their supervisors, and toward the group. A social history of the test room from 1927 to 1932 offered an explanation of the major fluctuations found in the graphs.

Certain graphs showed an average increase in speed of about 30 per cent. The curves were not learning curves, because all the workers had had several years experience in the work before they came into the test room. The plateaus and spurts in output were decidedly suggestive, and analysis showed that:

> . . . It was the organization of human relations, rather than the organization of techniques, which accompanied spurts in these cases. This illustrates the futility of attending exclusively to the economic motivation of workers, or to their physical conditions of work. These things are of high importance; but no group of workers can be expected to remain satisfied, or cooperative, unless their social organization and sentiments are also protected at the working level.[3]

As the experiment progressed, the girls developed common interests and loyalties. The girls took their discipline out of the hands of the supervisor and supervised themselves. For example, when a girl wished to have a half day's leave she had to obtain permission from the supervisor. However, the girls themselves developed a custom whereby no girl could ask for such leave unless the group approved the request.

In general, the output of individual workers was directly related to their sentiments toward each other. The feelings of *approval, antagonism,* and *indifference* toward each other influenced their individual variations in output. One of Whitehead's final generalizations was the following:

> Perhaps the main conclusion to be chosen from this type of analysis is the vital importance of human relationship as a factor in the motivation of an industrial group, and in its ultimate stability. The logical motive in economic activity is financial; and endless ingenuity has been expended in devising schemes of payment, designed to secure a maximum of employee satisfaction and efficiency. But, in the last analysis, buying power is largely a means for satisfying social sentiments; and money incentives will never secure a full measure of activity and contentment until firms are organized with greater regard for the social stability of their own working groups, *at the working level.*[4]

The same company conducted an experiment with fifteen young men who did wiring, soldering, and inspecting of electrical apparatus, and obtained quite different results from those found in the experiment with the women workers.

Nine wiremen were organized in three groups of three men. Each group of three wiremen had one solderman. Two inspectors judged the work of these twelve men, and one supervisor was in charge of the fourteen employees. All fifteen men worked together in a small shop. Payment was on the basis of group piecework. Within the group, the supervisor had the highest official status, the inspectors ranked second, the nine wiremen third, and the three soldermen lowest. However, a more elaborate social organization soon developed. The group split into two cliques. These cliques were not divided according to the social status levels but cut across one of the wiring groups and across the various occupations. Each clique had its own leader.

The customs that developed within the group related mainly to the organization and performance of the work. Output and performance of the work were soon controlled through the customs which developed among the men. Certain levels of output from each individual were decided upon and controlled by the men themselves. They maintained their output at the levels they determined through breakdowns, interruptions, and other behavior that wasted time. If any worker indicated that he was exceeding his allowance of work, he was "disciplined" by the others. The supervisor, too, was more or less forced to accede to the workers' control. The control of output which was exercised by the workers was largely for the purpose of protecting the group from managerial interference. They jealously guarded what they believed to be their rights and privileges as workers. In short, the workers were not protecting themselves against economic injustice but against social ignorance on the part of management.

The contrasting results of the experiment with the two groups of workers of the same company, the five girls versus the fifteen men, cannot be attributed to a sex difference but rather to the fact that the girls' group ways and sentiments were integrated to a much greater extent with the economic purposes of the management.

One lesson revealed and emphasized by the experiment with the fifteen men is that the administrator should appear to the members as one who is guarding and developing *their* life and the emotional character of *their* group, rather than representing only the economic policies and wishes of the management. The men resisted outside threats to the character of *their* group. This suggests that an executive should not only promote the efficiency of his employees but should also guard and develop their social sentiments toward each other.[5]

Effects of Western Electric Company's Experiments on Thinking about Human Relations in Industry

The result of these experiments was to force later investigators to pay more attention to the attitudes of workers, to the role of the work group, and to study the social organization within the factory situation. The experiment showed that the strength of the work group was more powerful than the wishes of management. The group often operated quickly and effectively to protect itself from violations within the group as well as from the outside.

When it wished, the group restricted the output of its individual members by means of ridicule and ostracism.

When reports of these researches were published, thinking about industrial problems was improved. Productivity was no longer assumed to be solely an effect of changes in illumination, physical fatigue, hours of work or pay. Supervision became recognized as a more important factor in output.[6]

New methods of measuring the network of relations among individuals within a group were developed by researchers.

The most important change that occurred after this series of experiments in the Western Electric Company was that a large number of men, trained in the fundamentals of psychology, turned their researches toward groups at work. These psychologists enlarged their thinking about industrial problems above the traditional tests and individual differences approach to the more meaningful studies of adjustment, motivation, and psychological ties among individuals as members of functioning groups. Many men contributed to this development; one who deserves particular attention was J. L. Moreno. He found ways of identifying the kinds of bonds that exist between group members. His sociometric technique maps these relationships, for example, by having each member list the persons in the group whom he likes most and those whom he likes least. The reactions that hold accepted members in the group and those that tend to expel rejected members can be diagrammed.

The Sociometric Technique

This technique which J. L. Moreno devised is a method of studying relationships that exist between persons within groups. This procedure, and modifications that have been tested by other psychologists for measuring the amount of group organization and the interplay of personalities within groups, is known as the sociometric test.

Its purpose is to analyze a person's relationship to other members of a group. At the same time certain facts about the group are clarified, such as to what extent it is cohesive, whether there are cliques and cleavages, and who the dominant personalities are. Bronfenbrenner defines the sociometric test as a method for discovering, describing, and evaluating social status, structure, and development through measuring the extent of acceptance or rejection among individuals in groups.[7]

It must be emphasized that only a test that tries to ascertain feelings of group members toward one another and to ascertain them in respect to the same criterion (that is, for a concrete situation in their group life) can be called sociometric. The feelings and attitudes of the testees are of prime importance, as it is on them that validity of the whole test rests.

In order to make a sociometric test, all members of a group are requested to select a certain number of persons whom they want to associate with in the context of a particular situation. Ideally, subjects participating in the test should have some reason for expressing their interpersonal likes and dislikes truthfully. Their choices should, in some way, affect their lives. For example, if all testees are living in assigned quarters, they might be informed that their choices will be the basis for reassignment in accordance with their own preferences instead of the convenience of the assigning authority. It is reasoned that, if the subjects are given the opportunity to improve their own life situations through the test, their choices will be truthful and the test will not incur the odium commonly felt for a test.

After choices have been made by each group member, they are calculated and charted, and a definite pattern of group and subgroup formation can be observed. The fact that some members are highly regarded and desired by many members emerges. These much-chosen individuals are the "key" individuals. They are in many situations also the actual leaders; in some cases they are not. But they usually are the ones whom the leader must attract and direct in order to exercise influence and attain power. Other members may be chosen by no one. These are the "isolates." Between these two extremes are many intermediate statuses. For example, one individual is chosen by one person and himself chooses that same person. In other cases a person chooses only one person and that person does not choose him. Obviously, in the latter case, such persons are not wanted by others as colleagues in the situation for which the choices were given.

Thus the cohesiveness of a group in its interpersonal structure can be tested. If many group members are linked in mutual chains of preference forming a network to which the large majority of members are connected, a fairly cohesive group exists. By classifying an individual in relation to others on the basis of his associates' opinions, his importance as a unit in the group is measured, and his part in the sociodynamic situation in which he lives for at least part of the time can be evaluated. Inevitably the individual acts upon the group of which he is a member, and the group acts upon him. Thus the extent to which he accepts the group and the group accepts him determines whether individual growth and constructive group activity will be encouraged, or whether membership in the group will militate against good adjustment of both individual and group. As Bronfenbrenner has stated: "The sociometric test, while it may show where people stand in the group, does not indicate why they are placed there. In other words, a person may be the 'star' or 'isolate' for a wide variety of reasons—some of them good, others bad. The natural tendency to interpret rejection as an indication of unsatisfactory adjustment and wide acceptance as signifying superior social relationships is therefore not always justifiable."

Different experimenters have employed varied techniques in the testing situation.[8] Some have set no limit on the number of choices allowed group members, and some have allowed expressions of rejection in addition to expressions of choices. Some have retested the same group after an interval of several months in order to ascertain the extent to which choices remain the same over a period of time.

While doing sociometric work for the Navy during World War II, Jenkins formulated the nominating technique. Although it is similar to all sociometric methods, it is particularly adaptable to solving the problem of selecting suitable industrial leaders.

Under Jenkins' direction, members of a group made four selections apiece. Each named two persons, inside or outside the immediate group, with whom he most preferred to work. He also named two with whom he most disliked the thought of working.

Modifications often are made in the method by framing the question in accordance with what is desired to be learned, e.g., "Who, in the group, would be the best foreman?" Number of choices allowed each person also varies in accordance with the purpose of the experiment.

Results are graphically illustrated by representing each group member as a circle and a number. An arrow is drawn from the circle representing the chooser to the circle representing the one chosen. When all choices have been charted it will usually be apparent that one person is chosen more often than others. "Isolates" and "mutual admiration societies" appear also by this modification of the original Moreno technique. Cliques and cleavages within the group are also exposed. The figure on this page is a sociogram.

Little imagination is required to envision how useful this method might be in choosing a leader. He would be the most highly regarded, thus the one likely to get greatest cooperation.[9]

Although leaders of social groups in our culture are usually chosen by the group of which they are a part, this is not true of leaders in industry. Leadmen, foremen, superintendents are usually selected by some person or group in authority. The desires of the group which is to be led or supervised are not of prime importance, although the chosen leader must not be so unacceptable to the group that he will be ineffective in the leadership role. The fact that leaders and supervisors in the work situation are not chosen by the group as they are in social situations contributes to much of the jealousy and divided loyalty found in industry. This is accentuated when leaders are seemingly arbitrarily appointed or removed. As already stated, leadership is a function of the group. The leader must fulfill the needs of the group. If the group has mental reservations about its leadership, it will probably not operate with optimum efficiency. If, in addition, there is petty feuding and overtly expressed discontent, all possibilities of a smooth-functioning unit may be disrupted.

Snags of this type of tension arise when, for reasons of economy, the number of supervisors is reduced. For example, the foremen in a certain industry were told to reduce the number of leadmen (foremen's assistants). Accordingly, one foreman assigned two of his leadmen back to their old jobs as mechanics. He explained to them that they had been selected for demotion because they had less seniority than the other leadmen in the department. One of the demotees continued to help the men who formerly had been under him. They wanted him to do so and he was pleased. The leadman to whom these men had been newly assigned was delighted with the help. However, when the demotee asked the foreman for a raise and was refused, he became antagonistic toward the foreman, and his ex-subordinates imitated his attitude. The foreman met this antagonism by staying away from the clique.

Van Zelst's Use of Sociometric Procedures in a Study of Construction Workers

The building trades are particularly well adapted to a study by sociometric procedures because they are not subject to the same limitations that are typical of mass industry where a regrouping means that a worker must learn an entirely new job. The subjects of this study by Raymond H. Van Zelst were four total work groups: a carpenter group of twenty members, another carpenter group of eighteen members and two separate groups of bricklayers, each having sixteen members. These men were working on the same housing project, but were split into two separate groups by a highway running through the middle of the site. In housing construction the foreman normally assigns men arbitrarily to work crews, but in Van Zelst's study the men were asked to indicate their first, second and third choices as to preference for teammates. The foreman assigned workers into these new groups, respecting each man's choices as far as possible.

The graphs on page 413 show the results in terms of costs. The savings in both materials and labor are quite evident. Furthermore, the men liked the new system much better than the old.

Van Zelst found that using sociometric procedures resulted in increased satisfaction for the worker and greater financial returns for management. The company's chief construction engineer in his report to management stated:

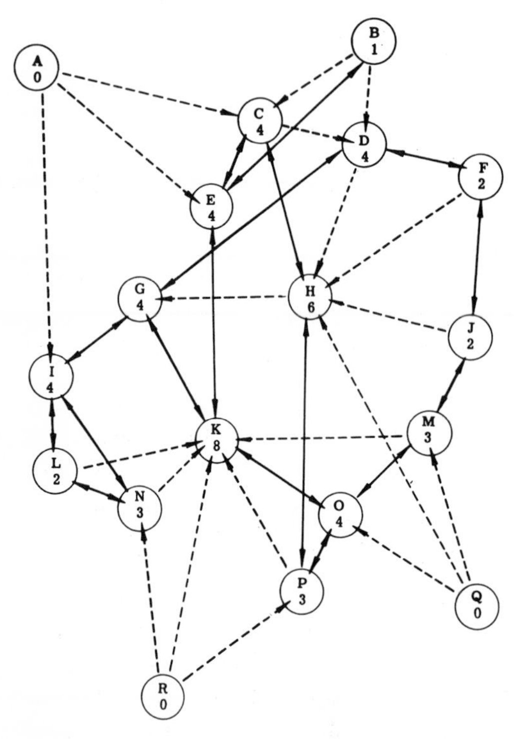

Sociogram *above shows a work group of eighteen carpenters, from data collected by Raymond H. Van Zelst. Each circle represents one man. Each member of the group was requested to nominate the three men with whom he would most like to work. Arrows indicate the direction of choice, broken lines indicate one-way preferences, solid lines indicate mutual choices. Total number of votes for each individual is shown in the circle. "R" chose "N," "K," and "P." "R" is an isolate because no one chose him. Raymond H. Van Zelst, "An Interpersonal Relations Technique for Industry,"* ***Personnel,*** *American Management Association, July 1952, pp. 68–77.*

. . . savings due to this psychological procedure have exceeded those of any previous work saving device or any combination of five previous work saving methods. Financial benefits are such that we are now constructing every 29th building entirely free from labor and materials costs. Even greater financial gains would occur were it possible to evaluate monetarily savings due to the great reduction in turnover. . . .[10]

The level of group output was definitely superior after the regrouping. At no time during the experiment did actual costs even approximate previous costs or the engineers' estimates. The decline in production costs was probably due to the success of improved technique for the incorporation of isolated and newly hired workers into the work force.

Careful employment of human relations procedures increased the worker's sense of belongingness and molded worker and management together into a mutually satisfied group solidarity. There was less turnover. The men seemed more satisfied with their job and work situation. The end result of this study was a happier and more productive worker and a reduction in total production costs by 5 per cent.

The way the workers felt was summed up by one of the men:

"Seems as though everything flows a lot smoother. It makes you feel comfortable working—and I don't waste any time bickering about who's going to do what and how. We just seem to go ahead and do it. The work's a lot more interesting too when you've got your buddy working with you. You certainly like it a lot better anyway."[11]

The methods of sociometry permit the worker to express his needs and interests. He can determine to his advantage his part in the social structure of the group in which he operates.

Sociometric measures reflect meaningful personality variables which can be reliably measured in terms of observable behavior.[12]

Educational level and intelligence have been found to be unrelated to sociometric ratings. Interestingly, they are also unrelated to factors such as frequency of sick bay visits as indicated by a study of 81 Marine

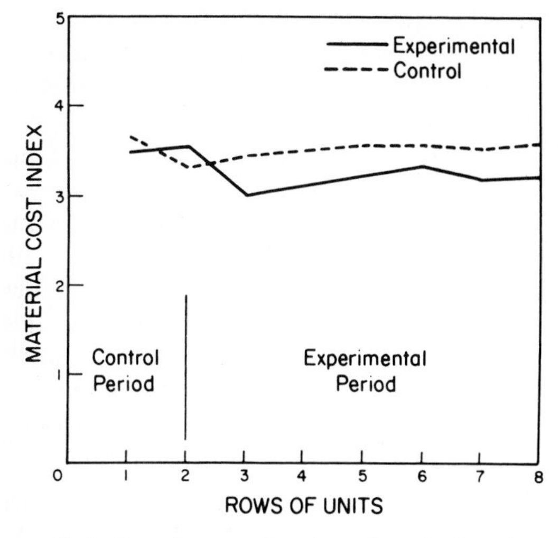

Fluctuations Between Experimental and Control Groups on Materials Costs Compared for Entire Three-Month Period

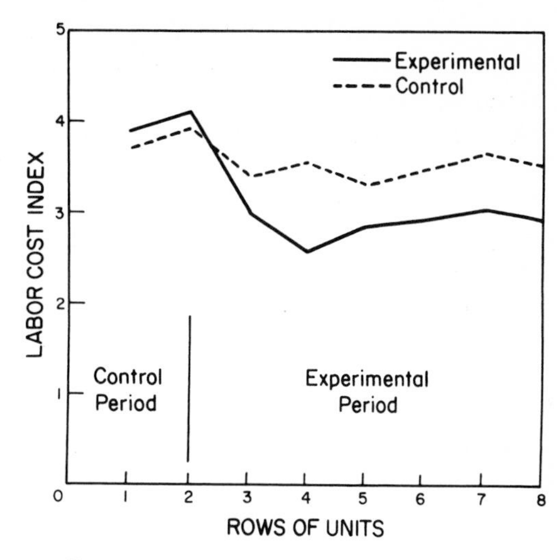

Fluctuations Between Experimental and Control Groups on Labor Costs Compared for Entire Three-Month Period

***The figures above** show cost differences in the work done by an experimental group on which sociometric procedures were used and a control group where these procedures were not used. Both groups worked on the same housing project during the same time. They were separated from each other by a highway. Note that the cost indexes for both materials and labor were lower in the experimental group—the one which received the benefit of sociometric techniques.—Raymond H. Van Zelst, "An Interpersonal Relations Technique for Industry," **Personnel,** American Management Association, July 1952. See also "Validation of a Sociometric Regrouping Procedure," **Supplement to the Journal of Abnormal and Social Psychology,** April 1952.*

Corps officer helicopter pilots. However, sociometric ratings of pilot proficiency, officer-like qualities, and social acceptability related to frequency of sick call visits, with those having the lower sociometric ratings being the most frequent sick call visitors.[13]

Sociometric techniques are expecially useful in supervisory selection, assigning of buddy-workteams, and for selecting maladjusted employees for counseling. They are used in certain researches on the informal organization of a company to determine the traits of successful and unsuccessful leaders.

George F. F. Lombard and his group of researchers made a study of interpersonal relations in the children's wear department of a modern department store.[14] The investigation revealed numerous misunderstandings and misevaluations on the part of supervisors and buyers. From the standpoint of group dynamics one interesting finding was that the older salesgirls often tried to mother and to help the junior executive who resented the older salesgirls for their better knowledge of the business.

Employees often develop supportive relationships toward members of the group. They do this without direction from management. One of the oft-cited examples occurred in a study of organizational structure in British coal mines. The researchers found two types of organization in very similar coal mine situations.

One kind of organization was the traditional variety in which jobs were broken down into small bits and each person was told what to do. He then performed his work repetitively and was rewarded directly for the amount of performance.

The other kind of organization was a more flexible one that had been evolved by the workers themselves.

Several important differences in performance were found but especially significant were the differences in accident rates. In the flexibly organized mine, the accident rate dropped by more than half. This, however, was not because of a difference in the safety programs. Nor was it caused by special propaganda or directed discussions by management. The researchers concluded that what happened was that, in the flexible type of organization, the miners felt a higher degree of personal security on a dangerous job because they were in a work group that would move around and help them if they got into trouble.[15]

Informal Groups and Factional Leaders

Employees normally develop certain interpersonal work relations which management has not specifically planned. They borrow tools from each other, give or withhold information to certain associates, counsel certain fellow workers, and they associate with some employees and ignore others during the non-work hours and days. They are attracted to some and repelled by other employees of the job environment. As a result of these and other influences, cliques develop.

Some managements who discover the presence of strong cliques try to overcome their influence by transferring clique members to other departments. Other managements accept them and try to align them toward company goals. Factional leaders can be utilized to accomplish ends of benefit to the group and to related larger groups. Generally, most managements accept the fact that cliques exist and cannot be ordered to disband even though they may be gradually weakend.

In nonunion plants, the cliques are watched in order to see whether a clique is becoming the nucleus of a formal union that will spearhead group hostility to management. If such cliques are developing, it usually means that management has failed in its communication responsibilities. The employees have not been given a participative relationship with management. Progressive managements therefore avoid making abrupt changes which affect the social organizations of the employees. Changes are planned to enlist the support of the cliques.

The factional leader is looked to as the informal leader. To some extent he functions as a "big brother" in a family setting. He is expected to get action or follow through with the supervisor on problems or wishes of the group. He is an unofficial spokesman. Giving him special status symbols will add to his position as the informal leader.

The foreman who is socially alert realizes that he must get spontaneity of cooperation through the informal groups and their leaders. If he ignores their existence because they are not mentioned on the organization charts, he will become the victim of extra resistance. If he introduces technical changes or new methods of work without any attention to their effects on group relations, he will find that his employees are likely to develop mannerisms and attitudes which indicate that they harbor the feeling that they are being "pushed around." Those who have the feeling invariably discover ways of pushing in the opposite direction to that desired by management. They can slow down the production rate, lose tools, damage equipment, or "forget" to perform tasks which they would ordinarily perform.

The discerning foreman or executive utilizes the factional leaders in his group and thereby prevents the development of antagonistic cliques. He eliminates opposition by integrating the factional leaders into the life of the larger group.

The Pecking Order

We are all familiar with the term, "henpecked," in its more humorous usage. Recently, new and more serious implications have been found in henpecking. Perhaps it is easiest to study henpecking in its natural background, the chicken coop.

In a flock of chickens, or in any group of animals, there is a hierarchy of leadership and power.[16] Among chickens, the strongest and most powerful hen or rooster peck their subordinates into obedience. The second hen in command pecks all other hens except the leader, and the third hen pecks all but the

	Y	B	V	R	G	YY	BB	VV	RR	GG	YB	BR	Number Pecked
Y		𝍸𝍸𝍸 𝍸II	𝍸III	𝍸𝍸𝍸 III	𝍸𝍸I	𝍸𝍸𝍸 𝍸𝍸𝍸	𝍸𝍸	𝍸𝍸II	𝍸𝍸III II	𝍸I	𝍸𝍸I	𝍸𝍸𝍸 𝍸I	11
B			𝍸𝍸𝍸 𝍸𝍸IIII	𝍸𝍸I	𝍸𝍸𝍸 𝍸I	𝍸II	𝍸𝍸II	𝍸𝍸𝍸 II	𝍸𝍸𝍸 𝍸𝍸I	𝍸𝍸𝍸 I	𝍸II	𝍸I	10
V				𝍸I	𝍸𝍸I	𝍸I	III	𝍸𝍸𝍸 𝍸𝍸II	𝍸𝍸II	𝍸II	II	𝍸𝍸IIII I	9
R					𝍸𝍸II	𝍸𝍸𝍸 𝍸I	𝍸III	𝍸I	𝍸𝍸I	𝍸𝍸𝍸 𝍸𝍸I	𝍸𝍸𝍸 II	III	8
G						𝍸III	𝍸𝍸𝍸	III	𝍸𝍸	𝍸III	𝍸𝍸II	𝍸𝍸𝍸	7
YY							𝍸𝍸𝍸 𝍸𝍸𝍸	𝍸𝍸𝍸 IIII	𝍸𝍸𝍸 II	𝍸I	𝍸𝍸III	𝍸III	6
BB								𝍸III	III	𝍸𝍸II	𝍸𝍸I	𝍸𝍸II	5
VV									𝍸𝍸III	𝍸𝍸𝍸 𝍸𝍸I	𝍸𝍸𝍸 III	𝍸𝍸𝍸 𝍸	4
RR										𝍸I	𝍸III	𝍸𝍸II	3
GG											𝍸𝍸𝍸 𝍸I	𝍸I	2
YB												𝍸𝍸𝍸 𝍸𝍸II	1
BR													0

The photograph shows threat-avoidances or incidence pecks. *The table shows the manner in which pecks and threats are tabulated to determine the peck order. The letters are the code (color markings) for individual hens. The birds listed on the left are the aggressors (pecking or threatening) and those on the top are the recipients. The tabulations show the dominance relationships (unidirectional dominance) as well as the frequency of dominating (between any two birds) during the periods of observations. The chart shows differences in social tension (or relative toleration) between pairs of birds. For further information, see A.M. Guhl, "Reflections by an Animal Behaviorist,"* ***Transactions Kansas Academy of Science,*** *Summer 1963 and* ***Psychological Bulletin,*** *1954, Vol. 61, No. 4, pp. 277–285.*

other two. This hierarchy descends downward to the last hen who is the weakest and least attractive, and who, unfortunately is pecked by all the others, and has no one below her to peck. The pecking order, as it is called, is the outward sign of a hierarchy which brings with it many privileges. The highest rooster or chicken in the pecking order has his choice of food, water, roosts, etc.

The hen will not mate with a rooster who is below her in the pecking order, and consequently, those males who rank highest in the pecking order are usually those that sire the most chicks. Even if the males are not sexually aggressive, they will prevent the lesser males from mating. Hens who rank high in the pecking order, unfortunately, mate less than their subordinates. The hen who is the leader of her flock, apparently is not willing to submit to a male when she is used to being the dominant figure in her relations with others.

The pecking order is not restricted to chickens alone. We see examples of it in other species. In most organizations, formal or informal, there is usually a hierarchy in which some individuals exert their influence over those below them. In groups of children we can see the pecking order at work; perhaps without even realizing it, the children have a leader who dominates them, a second in command and so on. The subordinate children give their tacit assent to the leadership of the others.

Aggression often occurs as an aspect of the pecking order. We see one child suddenly turn on another for no apparent reason. Often, this happens because the aggressive child was merely asserting his dominance and rank in the pecking order over the other child.

We usually think of aggression as rising from frustration. However, aggression can also rise spontaneously—without apparent cause. Usually this latter form of aggression is brought about by a need to assert one's dominance over others and to bring oneself into a closer personal contact with them.

Cohesiveness of a Group Does Not Assure High Productivity

The Institute for Social Research, University of Michigan, has made outstanding re-

"Poor Roger has been quite despondent since he learned that his 'in group' isn't the 'in group'." By Henry R. Martin. Source: *Management Review*, American Management Association, Inc., July 1963, p. 11.

search investigations which have thrown new light on group dynamics in industry. One approach has been to study the characteristics and performances of high-producing and low-producing work groups. In one series of researches the degrees of cohesiveness of different work groups were studied by asking each employee questions like: "Would you rather remain in this work group than move to another one even if you can get the same pay and do the same kind of work?"

Strangely, one of the findings from the study of cohesiveness has been that the cohesive work groups produced on the average the same as the groups that were not cohesive. Some of the closely-knit groups showed both very high and very low extremes of productivity. Robert Kahn, director of this program of research for the Institute, found that one characteristic of the cohesive work group is that the individual workers in it will tend to produce at the same level. Group ways of regulating production take over. The level of production that is chosen by the group is influenced by several factors; one that is especially important is the supervisor. Researches usually indicate that there is a greater relationship between supervisory attitudes and productivity than between group attitudes and productivity.[17]

Think of it this way: a group can get together tightly and stick together for a lot of reasons. One is in response to some external threat or against some external enemy. We're certainly familiar with this at the national level. Sometimes the group gets together and forms this kind of alliance in defiance of the foreman, and for the express purpose of frustrating the company's goals. But we also know that some of the tightest groups are put together when the effort is not to frustrate the organization's goals but to achieve them. The athletic team, for example. So there are two important kinds of cohesive work groups. One is the kind where it is the group against the foreman. The other is the kind that has developed, not apart from the foreman, but including the foreman, and he may even be the leader who has had the skill to bring the thing off.[18]

The relationship between cohesiveness and productivity is complex. Seashore's investigation of the question also indicated that highly cohesive groups had either high or low productivity. The direction of this deviation was related to the perceived supportiveness of the larger organization.[19]

We do not as yet know all the factors that cause a group to be either nonproductive or highly productive but we do know that under certain conditions, some groups restrict their production while others increase it. Let us now consider some findings regarding restriction.

Group Restriction of Production

Obviously, the attitude of the individual worker toward the amount of work he should produce is often influenced by the group with which he works. The Western Electric Company experiment with the fifteen men who did wiring, soldering, and inspection indicated what every production executive knows, namely, output and performance of the individual worker are often controlled by what the group members believe to be fair. The effect of such social influence on the workers is

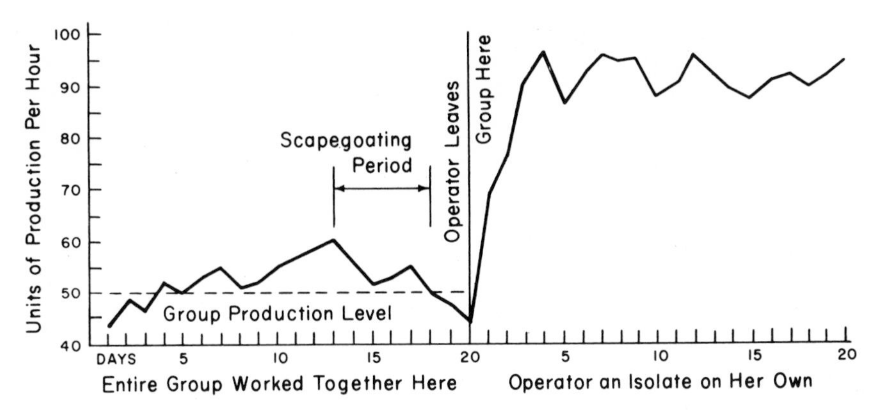

Effect of group expectations *on member productivity (sewing factory).*

illustrated by the figure on this page. In this case, the output of a girl increased greatly when group pressure was removed. As stated by Lippitt from the study by Coch and French at the Harwood Manufacturing Company:

> We see the day-by-day production curve of a girl belonging to a work group with a group production level of 50 units per hour represented by the dotted line. On the 11th and 12th days her production began to rise noticeably above the group standard and when she on the 13th day, hit standard production of 60 (a psychologically very important deviation for the other members) she became a scapegoat of the group with a great deal of social aggression directed toward her. Under this pressure her production decreased toward the level of the other group members. After 20 days the work group had to be broken up and the members transferred to various other units. The scapegoated operator remained on the same job, alone. As can be seen, her production shot up from about 45 to 96 units per hour in a period of 4 days. Her production stabilized at a level of about 92 and stayed there for the remainder of the 20 days. Clearly the induced forces on behavior from a strong subgroup may be more powerful than those induced by a progressive friendly management, and by personal needs for economic reward.[20]

Evidence that the group influence often restricts the production of the individual members is available in almost every factory, but we should not assume that the group influence is restrictive only. Sometimes it aids productivity very decidedly. This has been proved by several laboratory experiments where group members participated wholeheartedly in the solution of complex problems such as code problems. Group effort was found to be more productive than solitary effort.[21] The benefits of group participation are pronounced when problems require originality, insight, and the rejection of incorrect ideas.

We now know that a modern factory is a social enterprise. The worker comes there not only to earn money but also to be recognized as "one of the fellows." To be so recognized he must conform to the group's standards of conduct and as to what constitutes a fair day's work. If his output exceeds the group norm, he becomes known as a "ratebuster." In some plants this kind of nonconformist is likely to have narrow escapes from accidents, his wife may be given the silent treatment when she goes shopping, and his children may lack playmates. While he is at work, his machine may be broken so often that he cannot earn a normal rate of pay.

On the other hand, if he is accepted as a regular member of the group, he will be given aid by his fellow workers when he needs it. This aid may even extend to allowing him to earn extra take-home pay during an emergency such as illness in the family. Such a concession is, of course, only temporary.[22]

Job satisfaction is related to the integration of the work group. The greater the degree of integration of work teams, the higher the level of job satisfaction. This is especially evident in studies of railroaders and miners where the nature of the work requires much interaction of group members. However, in assembly operations as in meat packing and automobile manufacturing, the technological structure is such that the majority of the workers perform their operations individually. The man on an assembly line can talk only to the man in front of, behind, and across from him. Therefore, few stable work groups develop. Worker satisfaction in such an industry is likely to be less than in railroading, mining, or steel making where social integration is likely to be an essential to the performance of the work.[23]

Participation as a Factor in Productivity

The importance of participation by the individual in those matters which are important to him and of the participation of the individual in the group life has been revealed in numerous researches in group dynamics.

One of these is the Western Electric Company study. Other studies have revealed the influence of interpersonal relationships in employee productivity. An industrial organization is a social unit, governed by laws of social interaction. Good personnel management includes recognition of the individual as well as the social structure among the employees. This kind of recognition has been investigated at the Harwood Manufacturing Company, Marion, Virginia, under the direction of Dr. Alfred J. Marrow, president. When he was a graduate student in psychology, Marrow came under the influence of Dr. Kurt Lewin, one of the pioneers in the study of social psychology in industry.[24]

A significant study, made by Coch and French in the Harwood factory, indicated the importance of member participation in the setting and accepting of new work standards upon transfer to a new type of job. For the simplest type of job in the plant, the average learning time for beginners was five weeks. Yet when experienced operators were transferred to this same type of job, 38 per cent required an average of eight weeks to reach standard production. The remaining 62 per cent either became substandard operators (regardless of their record before transfer) or quit during the relearning period. Furthermore, there was marked resistance to transfer, expressed in grievances about the standards,

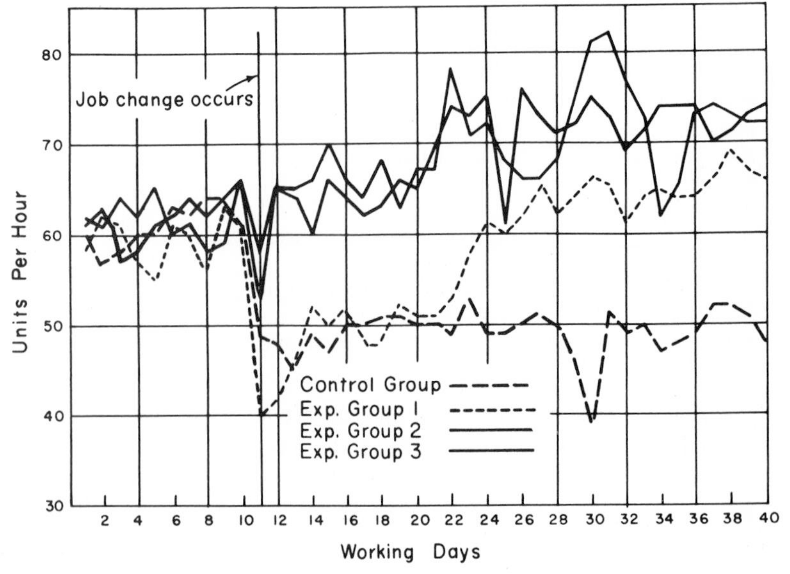

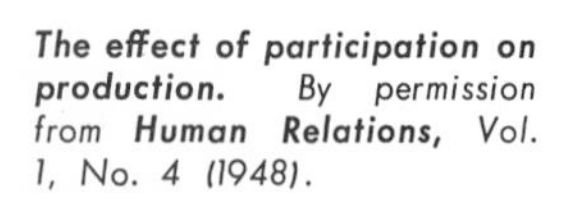
The effect of participation on production. By permission from *Human Relations,* Vol. 1, No. 4 (1948).

restriction of output, and aggressive reactions toward management. Analysis indicated that skill was a minor factor and that motivation was a major factor in determining the rate of recovery. A real-life action experiment was designed to study the problem.

The experiment consisted of selecting four groups of operators, one control and three experimental groups. The four groups became experimental transfers:

1. For the *control group,* the usual factory routine was followed. A group meeting was held in which the employees were told that a change was necessary because of competitive conditions and that a new piece rate had been set. The new piece rate was explained by the time study man. Worker's questions were answered.

2. *Experimental Group 1* was represented in the planning of the change by selected group members. The planning included a dramatic explanation of the need for change, and group agreement was reached concerning savings that could be made by removing "frills" and "fancy" work from the garment. The plan for the new job and piece rate included participation of the employees in the development of the new methods, having the time study made on them, and having the trained workers help train their co-workers in the new methods.

3. *In experimental Groups 2 and 3,* the above plan was followed except that the groups were smaller and all workers in each group were the "special" operators who participated in the actual designing of the new job. They also were the workers whose performance of the new job was studied by the time study man.

The results of the experiment were fairly clear. The control group dropped in production immediately upon change, and by the end of the experiment showed no appreciable amount of recovery. Resistance developed almost immediately. There were marked instances of aggression against management, deliberate restriction of production, lack of cooperation with the supervisor. Nine per cent quit during the first 15 days after the change. Grievances were filed about the piece rate which, upon checking, was found to be even a little "loose."

The recoveries for Groups 2 and 3 were dramatic. Both groups recovered to their pre-change level of production the second day after change, and by the end of the experiment they had actually surpassed their pre-change level by about 14 per cent. They worked cooperatively with their supervisors, there was no indication of aggression, and there were no quits during the 15-day period.

Group I required more time to recover (possibly because of an unavoidable operational problem), but reached the pre-change level by the 14th day after change, and by the end of the experiment had exceeded its pre-change level. Here, too, no quits were recorded. One act of aggression was observed which was neither prolonged nor serious. . . .

The success of the experiment seemed to be attributable largely to the fact that experimental transfers were given the opportunity to participate in planning the change, in planning their own work future. Thus, where such external motivating forces as monetary rewards, management pressure, and other means had failed, group involvement and decision developed internalized motivation for the accomplishment of a goal mutually desirable to management and worker.[25]

Robert E. Schwab has summarized some of the ways in which the principle of participation was applied in a typical industrial situation:

We've always known that some supervisors got better results with their people than others. When we begin to look objectively at the supervisor who is building highly motivated work groups, or a division, or a department, we find he is likely to be a sort of fellow who

Goes to bat for his employees;
Shows an interest in how they get along;
Lets his employees know what he thinks of their work, and
Gets his employees' ideas and does something about them.

These are only typical of the personal characteristics of the supervisor who gets best results with his work group. The significant finding is that sincere concern for the employee as an individual and consideration for his point of view are essential elements in motivation. We can hardly expect the other fellow to be concerned with our point of view unless we show a little interest in his.

In examining further the human relations principles which are present in the high-morale, high-productivity situations, we find one kind of activity that is almost always present. There is a good deal of sharing of problems and plans with those who will be most affected by decisions. This is a practice which most top managements recognize as valuable for building a strong top-management team, but we have not been fully aware of its importance for high motivation at every level in the organization...

Belief in the principles of good human relations and awareness of the special significance of participation has led us during the past five years to extend our understanding and activity in these four ways:

1. The training of all supervisors, from top management down, in human relations in supervision. The purpose of the training was to develop understanding of and skill in sharing certain job problems with employees.
2. The involvement of all supervisors and, on occasion, employees in the development of a number of company personnel policies and benefit plans.
3. The feedback of results of a company-wide attitude survey to supervisors and employees for consideration, comments, and recommendations.
4. Continuing investigation of the relationship between participation and desirable attitudes or action on the part of supervisors and employee...

Once the effectiveness of participation was demonstrated, ways of sharing problems with the group were discussed, and supervisors were encouraged to try the method on their own problems. A great many examples of the successful application of participation to the solution of problems in work groups resulted. As supervisors experienced success in using this method, they began using it more in their relations with their subordinates. Some problems successfully solved in this way included:

1. Distribution of disagreeable jobs.
2. Selection of vacation periods.
3. Office arrangement.
4. Reduction of paperwork.
5. Lunch schedules.
6. Equal distribution of work.
7. Care of equipment.
8. Correction of errors on bills of material.
9. Responsibility for company-owned tools.
10. Wash-up time.
11. Selection of men to be transferred.[26]

Schwab has pointed out that participation also causes problems. Once employees have the satisfaction of being "in" on things, they tend to resent it when, for some reason, they are not consulted. He found, however, that these limitations have not offset the advantages that have been gained. They are perhaps the result more of limited understanding and skill on the part of the individuals involved rather than of any basic fault in the principle itself.

Lombard's Study of Developing Teamwork among Employees

Every leader of men who has supervised many groups of employees has recognized that some groups have excellent team spirit; others very little. When he has had good teamwork, he has had high productivity and good morale. Supervision was a pleasure.

Several scientific studies have been made of the psychological factors that underlie and influence teamwork. One outstanding investigation in this field was made by Mayo and Lombard in the aircraft industry of Southern California in relation to labor turnover. They found that teams are of three classes:

1. The "natural" group, arising spontaneously in a small group of workers, limited apparently to 6 or 7, the work of each individual clearly related to the work of the others.
2. The "family" group, larger in size, based on the presence of a core of relatively long service workers whose behavior is respected by, and sets the example for, the behavior of newer workers. Formation of this group is limited to situations where the whole group can stay together long enough, for a minimum of possibly 6 months to a year, for the example of the older group to be effectively communicated to the newer workers.
3. The "organized" group, where a supervisor with skill and understanding consciously conducts his administration to secure the group integrity and spontaneous coöperation of his workers.[27]

In Lombard's study, one department, Department IV, had an exceptionally good record regarding attendance and productivity. The output per man-hour was 100–105 per cent efficiency in a plant where the average was about 80 per cent. The high level of teamwork in Department IV was due mainly to a "leadman," Z, a college man who did not rank as a supervisor. This man thought of himself as having three chief activities: first, helping the individual worker in such ways as listening to him, introducing him to his companions, getting him congenial work associates, and dealing with his personal problems; second, adjusting technical difficulties; and third, handling for members of the group their contacts with inspectors, time-study men, the department foreman, and others outside the work center. The leadman also arranged trips for the worker to other parts of the plant so that he could see in place on finished assemblies the parts he produced.

Supervisory practices that have been found effective in developing teamwork in other plants are: insisting that foremen shall listen patiently to individual workers; having employees participate in deciding which day each individual may have as his day "off"; making sure that each employee is content with his work; not transferring or lending employees to other departments; letting employees control their own rest-pause system; consulting and discussing the work with the employees; and giving them a sense of mutual responsibility and teamwork, as shown in the Hawthorne Plant, Western Electric Company "test room" experiment.[28]

This experiment began with a high number of attendance irregularities on the part of the employees. When, however, the new worker at No. 2 bench of the test room assumed informal leadership of the group and identified the team wholeheartedly with the company experiment, attendance irregularities stopped and casual absences sank to a fraction of their former number and to a fraction of the rate in the department outside the test room. "A change in morale had also been observed. No longer were the girls isolated individuals, working together only in the sense of an actual physical proximity. They had become participating members of a working group with all the psychological and social implications peculiar to such a group." The effect of the mutual responsibility thus created was remarkable: the layout girl, for instance, had been absent, before the teamwork began, 85 times in 32 months; after it began, she was not ever absent during 16 months.

Lombard's findings, as well as those of many industrial leaders, have shown that teamwork can be developed by management. Teams can be directed so that employees take over responsibilities, not only for discipline but also for production and attendance. Once the team takes over such functions successfully, their performance immediately becomes an important source of satisfaction to the workers.

Numerous examples of the effectiveness of participation in industry are available. One company, for example, received for years only a hostile response to programs to reduce scrap. When, however, a workers' economic education program explained in understandable terms why keeping scrap low was necessary to maintain the firm's competitive position, the workers realized that it was in their own self-interest, as a measure to protect their jobs, that scrap should be kept as low as possible. From then on such scrap programs made sense to the workers and were not looked on as "speed-up" programs but as necessary in their own interest.[29]

Generally, a group which has a leader who mixes with his men, who has informal relations with them, who encourages their ideas, and is interested in their welfare is regarded as the more effective one.[30]

Also, how members of a group feel towards one another affects the extent to which various methods and characteristics will change the efficiency of the work group. In pleasant working situations, high efficiency is more likely to occur when the group believes that it is regulating the behavior of individuals in its own midst. That is, the members as a group could place restrictions on each member's freedom of behavior. To a lesser extent, this is true in groups where membership is characterized by griping, complaining or unpleasant feelings.

Regardless of the atmosphere in the group, however, if the equipment facilities are not adequate and the skills of the individual not applicable to the job, the efficiency of the group is reduced.

Of course, individuals in top management positions who do not basically believe in this kind of philosophy toward employees or other individuals in general should avoid any attempt to promote participative management in their organization because the long odds of failure will be against them.

When Group Dynamism is Destroyed

One of the best examples of the destruction of group dynamics occurred during the Korean War. Although the experiments of the Chinese communists in this field met with little success, their basic assumptions about group dynamics are valuable in helping us understand it more fully.

To many United States soldiers the reasons behind the Korean War were obscure, and the Chinese found it easy to exploit the soldiers' doubts about the goals of the war. One of the Chinese communists' most effective weapons in breaking down the morale of their prisoners was to systematically destroy all formal and informal group structure. The officers were separated from the enlisted men, thus each group was composed solely of equals and was left virtually leaderless. The loss of their leaders who had described the soldiers' goals and channeled their energies left the men unable to act as an effective unit, and being deprived of a sense of unity, the individual was unsure of his position and duties. The Chinese further destroyed the prisoners' feelings of comradeship by encouraging mutual criticism discussion groups in which the soldiers sat and verbally assaulted each other. One of the most powerful influences on the prisoners' morale was the presence of turncoats and informers. When an officer or an enlisted man whom they had respected collaborated with the Chinese the doubts of the prisoners as to the validity of their beliefs were greatly increased.

The absence of a leader, the idea of mutual criticism, the lack of strong beliefs in their way of life, and the defection of their comrades deprived the prisoners of a feeling of unity, of the sense of being on a team.[31]

Some Individuals Are More Responsive to Group Pressures than Others

The evident influences of group dynamics in industry should not cause us to imagine that every member of the group is equally susceptible to group pressures. In any industrial group, certain employees will invariably go along with majority opinion; others tend to identify and side with management in so far as they can without antagonizing their colleagues. Some few will even choose management's points of view at the risk of losing the friendship of their colleagues.

Social scientists have investigated the effects of group pressures on the responses of specific individuals and have found some interesting differences. Solomon E. Asch, for example, has reported some of his experiments with college students. He used groups of seven to nine men, assembled in a classroom for what was supposed to be a "psychological experiment," in visual judgment. The experimenter told the students that they would compare the lengths of lines on a series of large white cards.

One card of each pair had a single vertical line—the standard whose length was to be matched. The other card of the pair had three vertical lines of various lengths. The subjects were to choose the one line of the same length as that of the standard line. See figure on next page (size is reduced).

When the experiment began, the subjects announced their answers in the order in which they were seated in the room. On the first trial, everyone chose the same matching line. On the exposure of the second pair of cards, the opinions were again unanimous. After

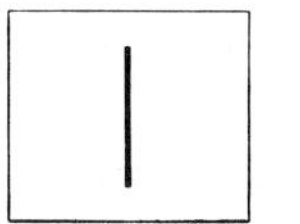

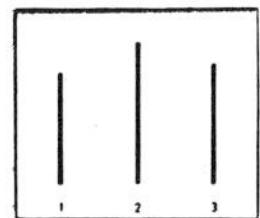

SUBJECTS WERE SHOWN TWO CARDS

One bore a standard line. The other bore three lines, one of which was the same length as the standard. The subjects were asked to find this line.

EXPERIMENT PROCEEDS AS FOLLOWS

The subject (center) hears the rules of the experiment for the first time.

He makes his first judgment of a pair of cards, disagreeing with the unanimous judgment of the others.

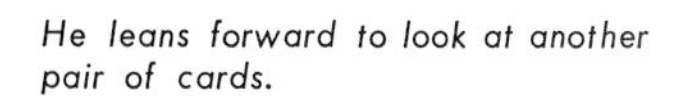

He leans forward to look at another pair of cards.

He shows the strain of repeatedly disagreeing with the majority.

After 12 pairs of cards have been shown, he explains that he has to "call them as I see them." This subject disagreed with the majority on all 12 trials. In some studies as many as seventy-five per cent of experimental subjects agreed with the majority in varying degrees.

that, all the members of the group except the one who was the real subject of the experiment gave incorrect answers.

Some of Asch's findings reported by him at the time of the study are the following:

What the dissenter does not know is that all the other members of the group were instructed by the experimenter beforehand to give incorrect answers in unanimity at certain points. The single individual who is not a party to this prearrangement is the focal subject of our experiment. He is placed in a position in which, while he is actually giving the correct answers, he finds himself unexpectedly in a minority of one, opposed by a unanimous and arbitrary majority with respect to a clear and simple fact. Upon him we have brought to bear two opposed forces: the evidence of his senses and the unanimous opinion of a group of his peers. Also, he must declare his judgments in public, before a majority which has also stated its position publicly....

How do people respond to group pressure in this situation? I shall report first the statistical results of a series in which a total of 123 subjects from three institutions of higher learning were placed in the minority situation described above.

Two alternatives were open to the subject: he could act independently, repudiating the majority, or he could go along with the majority, repudiating the evidence of his senses. Of the 123 put to the test, a considerable percentage yielded to the majority. Whereas in ordinary circumstances individuals matching the lines will make mistakes less than 1 per cent of the time, under group pressure the minority subjects swung to acceptance of the misleading majority's wrong judgments in 36.8 per cent of the selections.

Of course individuals differed in response. At one extreme, about one quarter of the subjects were completely independent and never agreed with the erroneous judgments of the majority. At the other extreme, some individuals went with the majority nearly all the time. The performances of individuals in this experiment tend to be highly consistent. Those who strike out on the path of independence do not, as a rule, succumb to the majority even over an extended series of trials, while those who choose the path of compliance are unable to free themselves as the ordeal is prolonged...

Which aspect of the influence of a majority is more important—the size of the majority or its unanimity? The experiment was modified to examine this question. In one series the size of the opposition was varied from one to 15 persons. The results showed a clear trend. When a subject was confronted with only a single individual who contradicted his answers, he was swayed little: he continued to answer independently and correctly in nearly all trials. When the opposition was increased to two, the pressure became substantial: minority subjects now accepted the wrong answer 13.6 per cent of the time. Under the pressure of a majority of three, the subjects' errors jumped to 31.8 per cent. But further increases in the size of the majority apparently did not increase the weight of the pressure substantially. Clearly the size of the opposition is important only up to a point....

In a variant of this procedure the trials began with the majority unanimously giving correct answers. Then they gradually broke away until on the sixth trial the naïve subject was alone and the group unanimously against him. As long as the subject had anyone on his side, he was almost invariably independent, but as soon as he found himself alone, the tendency to conform to the majority rose abruptly.

As might be expected, an individual's resistance to group pressure in these experiments depends to a considerable degree on how wrong the majority is. We varied the discrepancy between the standard line and the other lines systematically, with the hope of reaching a point where the error of the majority would be so glaring that every subject would repudiate it and choose independently. In this we regretfully did not succeed. Even when the difference between the lines was seven inches, there were still some who yielded to the error of the majority.[32]

Asch has tried this type of experiment on about 100 groups. In over 60 per cent of them, the lone individual changed his judgment to conform to the reported judgment of the other members of the group, usually eight in number.[33]

His studies indicated that the independents did not feel that opposition to the majority reflected a defect in themselves, but the yielders did feel that failure to agree with the majority meant that they themselves were at fault. "Independence requires the capacity to accept the fact of opposition without a lowered sense of self-worth...the compliant person cannot face this ordeal because he translates social opposition into a reflection of his personal worth."[34]

Richard Crutchfield, University of California, conducted related experiments, using individual booths and lights that signaled the answers of the other four members of groups of five. He, too, found that given the right conditions, a high percentage of individuals will desert the evidence of their senses and conform to the seeming consensus of the group. The essentials of his finding as stated by Carl R. Rogers offer illuminating interpretations of personality differences between the yielders and the nonconformists:

> ...under especially extreme circumstances, nearly everyone yielded in some degree to group pressure. Yet there were sharp individual differences, and these are found to be definitely correlated with personality characteristics. For example, those who yielded, the conformists, tended to show a lack of openness and freedom in emotional processes. They were emotionally restricted, lacking in spontaneity, tending to repress their own impulses. The nonconformists, those who made their own choices, were, on the other hand, much more open, free and spontaneous. They were expressive and natural, free from pretense and unaffected. Where the conformist tended to lack insight into his own motives and behavior, the independent person had a good understanding of himself.
>
> What is the meaning of this aspect of Crutchfield's study? It seems to imply that the person who is free within himself, who is open to his experience, who has a sense of his own freedom and a responsible choice, is not nearly so likely to be controlled by his environment as is the person who lacks these qualities.[35]

Numerous experiments show that there is a strong tendency on the part of most individuals to conform to group pressures. Some persons have, as a result of their observations of group behavior, hypothecated the functioning of a "group mind."

The "Group Mind" Fallacy

The fact that we often see examples of unusual group behavior such as "mob hysteria" does not mean that such group action must be interpreted in terms of a "group mind" concept. The individual member of each group retains his emotions, motives, and perceptions. He acts as an individual.

Ross Stagner has ably explained the need for thinking in terms of individual psychology by means of a typical conflict situation in industry:

> *A picket-line example.* A brief consideration of a specific incident will clarify our emphasis on the distinction between group and individual understanding, and our concern to reject the group-mind hypothesis. Suppose that a strike is in progress at a small manufacturing plant. The company has taken the position that it will try to operate; the union places a picket line across the gate. Some employees, not members of the union, try to drive in to go to work. The car is stopped, tipped over, and badly damaged; the non-strikers are mauled around, as are the police trying to protect them.
>
> This kind of incident is often referred to as an example of a "group mind" or "mob hysteria." The point is made (correctly) that the union members did things under the influence of the group situation that they as isolated individuals would never do. Joe Jones and Sam Smith are honest, quiet, law-abiding citizens. They would not damage a neighbor's car or beat up strangers whom they had never seen before. Yet as members of a picket line they may do just such things. How can we reconcile these two sets of observations without saying that the men were under the influence of a "mob spirit"?
>
> Psychologists, while agreeing that Joe Jones acts differently in the group situation, reject the notion that any new principles are needed to understand his action. Here are the main points of an analysis adequate to understand his behavior as a picket:
>
> 1. *Intensity of motivation.* Although it is true that Joe would not *ordinarily* attack another man individually, it can happen under strong motivation—to protect his money, his family, or his life. To some extent the striker protecting his job sees all three of these involved. The strikebreakers are seen as snatching the bread from the mouths of his children.
>
> 2. *Mutual reinforcement.* The tension level is reinforced by the group situation. Other men are shouting angrily. Joe hears their voices, sees their facial expressions. Each encourages the other to act in a violent manner. People are pushing and shoving. The physical contact intensifies the emotional response.
>
> 3. *Distortion of perception.* Under the stress of excitement and strong motivation, the strikebreakers are perceived as alien, inhuman. They are criminals. It is not only permissible, it is actually righteous to attack them.
>
> 4. *Lifting of inhibitions.* The group situation acts in two different ways to relieve the normal inhibitions against violence. One is the neutral-

izing of "conscience" or superego restraints against antisocial actions. Conscience is a social product. Group pressure instills in us a reluctance to damage property or use force against other human beings. But in the mob situation there is an illusion of group approval of violence, just as in wartime people get medals for killing. Hence the normal internal inhibition against violence is diminished or neutralized in the group setting.

The fear of punishment for violence is also lessened. Guilt in our culture is an individual matter; but when many participate simultaneously in an act, it will be difficult to identify and punish individuals. The individual feels anonymous in the mob. He thinks (correctly) that his chances of being punished are rather small.

This skeletonized analysis of a typical group incident serves only to show that the concepts and methods of individual psychology are adequate to give us a basis for the understanding of behavior in groups.[36]

ACKNOWLEDGMENTS AND REFERENCES

1. F. J. Roethlisberger and W. J. Dickson, *Management and the Worker* (Cambridge, Mass.: Harvard University Press, 1939), p. 5.
2. This title was used by Whitehead for a paper read before Section J (Psychology) of a British Association meeting in Norwich, England, September, 1935, and later published in *The Human Factor,* National Institute of Industrial Psychology, London, Vol. IX, No. 11.
3. *Ibid.*
4. *Ibid.* The author's summary of this outstanding experiment in worker efficiency has of necessity omitted many important aspects. The reader should read the more complete and accurate reports listed in Roethlisberger and Dickson, *op. cit.*
5. *Ibid.*
6. For further information, see B. B. Gardner and W. F. Whyte, "Methods for the Study of Human Relations in Industry," *American Sociological Review,* **11** (1946), 506–512.
7. Urie Bronfenbrenner, *The Measurement of Sociometric Status, Structure and Development* (New York: Beacon House, Inc., 1945).
8. Charles P. Loomis and Harold B. Pepinsky, "Sociometry, 1937–1947," *Sociometry,* **11** (1948), 147–191.
9. J. G. Jenkins, "The Nominating Technique: Its Uses and Limitations." paper presented at Eastern Psychological Association in 1947.
10. Raymond H. Van Zelst, "Validation of a Sociometric Regrouping Procedure," *Supplement to the Journal of Abnormal and Social Psychology,* April, 1952.
11. Raymond H. Van Zelst, "Sociometrically Selected Work Teams Increase Production," *Personnel Psychology,* 1952, pp. 175–185.
12. Carroll E. Izard, "Personality Correlates of Sociometric Status," *Journal of Applied Psychology,* April, 1959.
13. Robert R. Knapp, "Objective Personality Test and Sociometric Correlates of Frequency of Sick Bay Visits," *Journal of Applied Psychology,* April, 1961.
14. George F. F. Lombard, *Behavior in a Selling Group,* Graduate School of Business Administration, Harvard University, Boston, 1955.
15. See Eric Trist, "Socio Technical Systems," (mimeographed), Tavistock Institute of Human Relations, Document No. 572, London, England, November, 1959.
16. See A. M. Guhl, "The Social Order of Chickens," *Scientific American,* **194,** No. 2 (1956), 42–46.
17. See R. L. Kahn, "The Prediction of Productivity," *Journal of Social Issues,* **12** (1956), 41–49. See also Thomas M. Lodahl and Lyman W. Porter, "Psychometric Score Patterns, Social Characteristics, and Productivity of Small Industrial Work Groups," *Journal of Applied Psychology,* April, 1961.
18. *Modern Management,* The Bureau of National Affairs, Inc., Washington, D.C., Aug. 15, 1955, p. 2.
19. See S. E. Seashore, *Group Cohesiveness in the Industrial Work Group,* Ann Arbor: Survey Research Center, 1954.
20. Lester Coch and J. R. P. French, Jr., "Overcoming Resistance to Change," *Human Relations,* **1,** No. 4 (1948), after Ronald Lippitt, *Current Trends in Social Psychology* (Pittsburgh, Pa.: University of Pittsburgh Press, 1948).
21. For examples, see Marjorie E. Shaw, "A Comparison of Individuals and Small Groups in the Rational Solution of Complex Problems," *American Journal of Psychology,* **54** (1932), 491–504; and R. W. Husband, "Cooperation versus Solitary Problem Solution," *Journal of Social Psychology,* **11** (1940), 405–409.
22. For further information, see William Whyte, *Money and Motivation* (New York: Harper & Row, Publishers, Inc., 1955).
23. See Robert Blauner, *Work Satisfaction and Industrial Trends in Modern Society,* Institute of Industrial Relations, University of California, Berkeley, California, 1960.
24. Alfred J. Marrow, "Human Factors in Production," *Personnel,* American Management Association, Inc., March, 1949, pp. 343–344.
25. *Ibid.* See also Ronald Lippitt, "A Program of Experimentation on Group Functioning and Group Productivity," *Current Trends in Social Psychology* (Pittsburgh, Pa.: University of Pittsburgh Press, 1948), pp. 14–22.
26. Robert E. Schwab, "Motivation and Human Relations Principles," *Personnel Series,* No. 155, American Management Association, Inc., 1953, pp. 31–34.

27. Elton Mayo and George F. F. Lombard, *Teamwork and Labor Turnover in the Aircraft Industry of Southern California,* Bureau of Business Research, Harvard University Graduate School of Business Administration, Boston, Mass. Copyright 1944 by the President and Fellows of Harvard College.
28. Roethlisberger and Dickson, *op. cit.,* p. 83f. See also Thomas North Whitehead, *The Industrial Worker* (Cambridge, Mass.: Harvard University Press, 1938).
29. See Father Edward S. Keller, CSC, "What Makes People Do the Things They Do?" Bureau of Economic Research, University of Notre Dame, South Bend, Ind., *Personnel Series,* No. 155, American Management Association, Inc.
30. For further information, see Bernard M. Bass, Feelings of Pleasantness and Work Group Efficiency," *Personnel Psychology,* Spring, 1954, pp. 81–91.
31. See Edgar H. Schein, "Some Observations on Chinese methods of Handling Prisoners of War," *Public Opinion Quarterly* **20** (1956), 321–327.
32. Solomon E. Asch, "Opinions and Social Pressure," *Scientific American,* November, 1955, pp. 31–35. Photographs and quotations by courtesy of the author and the publisher. See also, Frank Barron, *Creativity and Psychological Health* (Princeton, N.J.: D. Van Nostrand Company, Inc., 1963), Chap. 14.
33. See Alfred J. Marrow, *Behind the Executive Mask,* No. 79, American Management Association, Inc., Management Reports, 1964, p. 113.
34. Solomon E. Asch, "Studies of Independence and Conformity: A Minority of One Against a Unanimous Majority," *Psychological Monographs: General and Applied,* **70,** No. 9, Whole No. 416, (1956), pp. 51–52.
35. Carl R. Rogers, "Freedom and Commitment," *The Humanist,* The American Humanist Association, Yellow Springs, Ohio, March-April, 1964. See mainly Richard S. Crutchfield, "Conformity and Character," *American Psychologist,* **10** (1955), 191–198 and Vernon L. Allen and Richard S. Crutchfield, "Generalization of Experimentally Reinforced Conformity," *Journal of Abnormal and Social Psychology,* **67,** No. 4, (1963), 326–333.
36. Ross Stagner, *The Psychology of Industrial Conflict,* (New York: John Wiley & Sons, Inc., 1956), pp. 8–10.

PROJECTS

1. Make a study of some small group with which you are acquainted, such as a fraternity or a work group. Use the sociometric technique. Can you plot the choices of members of the group? If you were to put the group to work in a factory or office, would your sociometric findings be of value to you?
2. Think of a place where you have worked or are now working. Describe the group culture; the employees' unwritten rules about the amount of work to be done, when loafing is permissible, when employees may be absent, the conditions under which employees may appear to cooperate with management but actually modify management's programs, and so on.
3. List some of the difficulties and dangers to management of attempts to use group dynamic influences in supervising employees.
4. List incidents which you have observed or read about that would appear to substantiate the "group mind" concept.
5. The pecking order is rather easy to observe in a flock of chickens but more difficult because of its subtlety in groups of human beings. Try to describe it as you have noted it in a small group of persons as in a living center, athletic squad, or department of a company.

COLLATERAL READINGS

Cartwright, Dorwin and Alvin Zander, *Group Dynamics: Research and Theory.* New York: Harper & Row, Publishers, Inc., 1955.

Farnsworth, P. R., ed., *et al., Annual Review of Psychology.* Palo Alto, Calif.: Annual Reviews, Inc., 1964, pp. 379–398.

Haire, Mason, *Psychology in Management.* New York: McGraw-Hill Book Company, 1956, Chapter 6.

Krech, David, Richard S. Crutchfield, and Egerton L. Ballachey, *Individual in Society,* New York: McGraw-Hill Book Company, 1962, Chapters 13 and 14.

Leavitt, Harold J. and Louis R. Pondy, (eds.), *Readings in Managerial Psychology.* Chicago: The University of Chicago Press, 1964, Chapters 8–13.

Thelen, Herbert A., *Dynamics of Groups at Work.* Chicago: The University of Chicago Press, 1954.

Training in supervision *is not limited to skilled workers and foremen. Executives holding responsible positions in industry are attending workshops, classes, and discussion group meetings in order to improve their own abilities.*

Here is a picture of a discussion group of southern California executives who were members of one of the groups attending the "Executive Program" of the Graduate School of Business Administration, University of California, Los Angeles.

The program is designed primarily for men in the executive and middle ranks of management, including both line managers and staff specialists.

Members of the past groups had an average age of 43 and 40 per cent were either presidents, executive vice-presidents, or general managers of their firms.

Similar workshops, seminars, and conferences are conducted by other industry associations and universities.

CHAPTER TWENTY-ONE

SUPERVISING EMPLOYEES

Good management organization, by reliance on authority instead of skilled and understanding leadership as the basis for handling men, easily destroys the desire for cooperation. A higher type of leadership adapted to democratic conditions is necessary. Management, if it is to be successful in the years which lie ahead, must rely less on authority and more on leadership which transcends authority.[1]

Every supervisor tends to develop a psychological climate that is related to his personality and his techniques. Just as every father helps to influence the psychological atmosphere of the home so each foreman affects the work situation of the shop. It may be one that is tense because it is dominated by an authoritative or a neurotic individual. Or a relaxed, cheerful atmosphere may result where every member enjoys the confidence of his colleagues, and group wishes and feelings govern conduct. When the well-adjusted supervisor arrives at work, a current of enthusiasm fills the place. Faces become brighter. Movements become faster. Work seems to flow along more smoothly. Other supervisors have the opposite effect: fears arise in employees; they become tense; their work becomes harder and gloom settles over them.

The importance of the well-adjusted leader is exemplified by an experience reported for one company:

> A simple questionnaire was handed out to employees. The idea was to find out how the men got along from the standpoint of coöperation. Employees were asked to describe the attitude of their fellow-workers, whether friendly or unfriendly, and to comment on working conditions.

Replies revealed these surprising facts:

> Departments with friendly and coöperative operators had a far better all-around production record than those departments in which employees showed a disgruntled attitude toward one another. The "friendly" departments produced an average of 10 per cent more, with spoilages about 40 per cent less than the "non-coöperative" departments.
>
> In these latter departments, the foreman's lack of friendliness was often commented upon. One worker had this to say (since the questionnaires did not need to be signed, he felt free to get his gripe off his chest): "Who does our foreman think he is? The big cheese himself? Why don't he get wise to himself? He's no better than any of us here. He acts like it costs him money to say good morning to us."[2]

When the Industrial Relations Section, California Institute of Technology, had completed a total of 25 surveys in 18 different companies, covering over 50,000 employees, the Section formulated a number of conclusions based on all of its studies of employee opinion. One of these was that "The morale of supervisors is usually higher than that of employees, but the morale of employees is related to that of supervisors: the higher the morale of supervisors, the higher the morale of their employees."[3]

The typical foreman in American industry is recognized as a key factor in employee morale. He, rather than the heads of the company, often represents the company to the individual employee.

A Supervisor Has Special Meanings to the Employee

To the employees whom he directs, a supervisor or executive is far more than an assigner of tasks. He also fulfills certain vital roles of an unconscious nature. As he acquires years of experience in dealing with people, he realizes that to certain individual employees he is an *authority figure, impartial judge, target of affection, target for hostility, confidant, catalyst, or a tone-setter.* He must meet or help to fulfill the deeper psychological needs of people, needs of which they themselves are not aware. His most important functions are likely to be in the symbolic meanings that he represents for each of his employees. He is sensitive to the deeper psychological needs of people, and he is likely to increase his skills in becoming the kind of role symbol that makes his leadership effective. In some cases, failure of a given executive can be directly traced to his inability to fill successfully the role expected by the employee.[4]

The supervisor who has developed an acute sensitivity to the feelings of others toward him realizes that he communicates and receives feelings as well as ideas. What he says in words is often less significant than the feelings which he transmits and receives. When, for example, he feels that a subordinate is not very important, he realizes that his feelings are transmitted to the subordinate even though his verbal behavior does not state the message.

He knows that covert hostility is expressed toward him by subordinates through behavior such as excessive absenteeism, tardiness, resistance to his suggestions, and subtle blocking of his program. These and other forms of opposition often stem from difficulties that have their origins in symbolical as well as in unexpressed difficulties that remain covert. Some executives who sense these covert influences in interpersonal relationships believe that the best way to overcome them is to bring them out into the open. Sometimes a frank exchange of feelings, even though somewhat bitter, may clear the air and improve the situation.[5]

A supervisor is a center of the men's work life. For one thing, his word carries more weight than theirs; he has authority. And for another, he, either actually or from the men's point of view, knows more and is a more able person in one way or another; he is their leader. This being the case, it is difficult for him not to prompt in others—in at least some others—a variety of emotional stirrings that seem to have nothing to do with the boss-worker relationship.

The supervisor as a father figure causes emotional reactions whose source is not recognized by the employee. Expressions of either anger or friendliness from a supervisor can trigger unconscious as well as conscious reactions that transferred from early childhood relationships. They may even test him to find out whether they can depend upon him as a parental figure. The supervisor plays an important role in providing the context for balanced distance between himself and his subordinates. A balanced or optimal psychological distance between the two, neither so close that the supervisor is hampered by emotional ties nor so distant that he loses emotional contact, has been shown to be a significant factor in indicating productivity differences among supervisors.[6]

One study of leaders of small groups indicated that the effective leader's social distance from his men is distant only from the poor co-workers rather than from all of his co-workers.[7]

Some employees feel toward the supervisor as they do toward their father.

To give an illustration:

A foreman had noticed that one of his men displayed an indifference and hardly-concealed resentment for which there seemed to be no reason. He couldn't get any clue to the fellow's strange behavior and he finally decided to pay the man a visit at his home. Being within his own domain, the foreman thought, the fellow would probably feel free to say what was on his mind.

Much to his surprise he found that the worker's wife greeted him with a great deal of reserve. And it was she who almost immediately launched into long and intemperate remarks about "snobbishness and favoritism." It seemed that she was sore at him because he, the foreman, had failed to play with her kids at the company's last picnic. But he did spend a lot of time romping around with the kids of another fellow, "not half as good a worker as my husband."

The foreman didn't laugh; he didn't even feel like laughing. To be sure, the complaint wasn't any too reasonable. But then, from the man's and his wife's point of view, it was important that he, the foreman, should act as just the person for whom they had previously felt a great deal of respect and admiration. Because the foreman had failed to pay any attention to their children, he had shown himself unworthy of the good sentiments the man and his wife had had for him. They felt cheated, neglected and hurt.

Just how persuasive the foreman's explanation of his own conduct at the picnic was, he did not know. He only noticed that, having spoken her piece and having listened to his comments, the woman seemed to be somewhat mollified—and her husband looked as if he would find great pleasure in having a tooth pulled. At any rate, the talk proved to be a great success. The man again turned into the cooperative and attentive worker he had been before.[8]

The supervisor has certain responsibilities in regard to his daily human relations. He is under close observation by those with whom he works: superiors, subordinates, associates, and the public. One of the main parts of his job is example-setting.[9] He is aware of the effects of his own conduct in relation to what he asks of his employees. If, for example, his superiors issue instructions to curtail annual leave during a heavy work period, he realizes that he himself cannot take his vacation while his employees are denied theirs.

Each Supervisor Attracts Some People and Repels Others

Each supervisor's personality and techniques in dealing with people will attract some persons and repel others. Those who are attracted will tend to remain with him. Those who are repelled will tend to leave his department or company.

An alert observer who visits a department or company headed by a specific executive can often see a relationship between the chief and the employees under his direction. This does not mean that the employees are near-duplicates of the chief's personality. Instead, the executive in charge unconsciously symbolizes answers to basic needs on their part. If he is a domineering person, he is likely to have many employees who feel more secure when they work for an autocrat. If he is the teacher type of executive, he is likely to have many employees who like to be treated as intelligent colleagues.

We must not assume however that all employees at any one time are there because the personality of the boss and the employee complement each other. Certain employees, those of superior psychological qualities, may remain for several years under the direction of a repellent personality because of interest in the work itself. These stronger persons usually have definite career objectives and they will "put up with" or ignore the characteristics of an executive who repels them. These exceptional individuals usually remain only as long as necessary to gain a desired amount of experience or other objective that fits their specific needs. Then they move on.

Supervisory techniques vary in their effectiveness in accordance with the culture, size of organization, complexity of the work, and other factors. Thus far, the tests for the prediction of supervisory ability have not proven to be very helpful. A few do give some promise of eventual usefulness upon further refinement.[10]

Some Findings from the Institute for Social Research, University of Michigan

This organization is conducting systematic research on what a good management does that makes the difference between high and low productivity, between high and low morale, and the principles and practices of leadership that are responsible for high productivity and high job satisfaction.

Studies have been conducted or are under way in a wide variety of organizations: public utilities, an insurance company, an automotive company, a heavy machinery factory, a railroad, an electric appliance factory, and some government agencies. The work of the organizations studied has varied from routine clerical and assembly operations to complex scientific research.

In this program of research, two major criteria have been used to evaluate administrative effectiveness:

1. Productivity per man-hour or some similar measure of the organization's success in achieving its productivity goals.
2. The job satisfaction and other satisfactions derived by employees or members of the group.

The findings show that a consistent pattern of motivational principles and their application is associated with high productivity and high job satisfaction, irrespective of the particular company or industry in which the study is conducted. Some of the generalizations that are emerging from this research are summarized in these condensations and excerpts from one of the Institute reports:

1. Very little relationship, *within a company*, has been found between employees' attitudes to-

ward the company and their productivity. The more productive employees or sections do *not* have appreciably more favorable attitudes than do the less productive employees. A favorable over-all attitude toward one's company and job does, however, result in less absence from the job.

2. In some situations at least, there is a negative relationship between the extent to which employees participate in a recreational program and their productivity. The less-productive sections participate in recreational activities more often than do those sections that are more productive.

3. In contrast to the two above-mentioned patterns involving factors of a nonpersonal nature, there is a marked relationship between the kind of supervision an employee receives and both his productivity and the satisfactions which he derives from his work. When the worker (or a person at any level in a hierarchy) feels that his boss sees him only as an instrument of production, as merely a cog in a machine, he is likely to be a poor producer. However, when he feels that his boss is genuinely interested in him, his problems, his future, and his well-being, he is more likely to be a high producer.

4. The employee-centered supervisor not only trains people to do their present job well but tends to train them for the next higher job. He is interested in helping them with their problems on the job and off the job. He is friendly and supportive rather than being punitive and threatening.

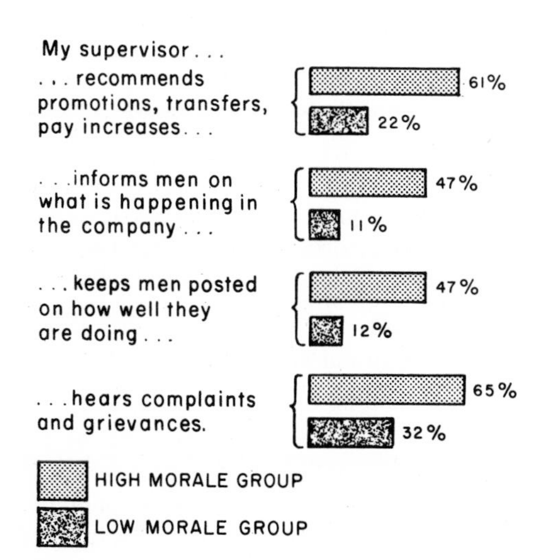

Supervisory relations *as seen by high and low morale groups. University of Michigan findings show significantly higher percentages of highly productive workers, both in office groups and section gangs, had pride in their groups, than did those with low production records. Chart above shows difference in attitudes towards supervisors, company communications, and grievance procedures among machine shop employees with generally high and generally low morale. Chart reprinted with permission from* ***Dun's Review and Modern Industry,*** *July 1956, p. 43.*

5. Close supervision tends to be associated with lower productivity and more general supervision with higher productivity.

Low productivity may at times lead to closer supervision, but it is clear that it may also cause low productivity. In one of the companies involved in this research program it has been found that switching managers of high- and low-production divisions results in the high-production managers raising the productivity of the low-production divisions faster than the former-high-production divisions slip under the low-production managers. Supervisors, as they are shifted from job to job, tend to carry with them and to maintain their habitual attitudes toward the supervisory process and toward their subordinates. This suggests that supervisory attitudes and habits tend to be the causal influence.

6. The superior's skill in supervising his subordinates *as a group* is an important variable affecting his success: the greater his skill in using group methods of supervision, the greater are the productivity and job satisfaction of the work group.

7. For both blue-collar and white-collar workers, there is a marked relationship between worker morale and how much employees feel that their boss is interested in discussing work problems with the work group.

8. Work groups with high group pride and loyalty are the more productive. One reason is that the workers cooperate more and help one another in getting the work done. Work groups with high group loyalty show more teamwork and more willingness to help each other than do those with low group loyalty. In the high-loyalty groups there tends to be a flow of work back and forth between the workers depending upon the load. In groups with low group loyalty there tends to be more of a feeling that each worker is on his own and that how he gets along with his work is his own responsibility.

9. In high-productivity groups, workers help one another. When foremen were asked, "How does your section compare with other sections in the way the men help each other on the job?" the answers showed a marked relationship to group productivity. The foremen of high-production groups reported much more often than the foremen of low-production groups that their men helped one another in getting the work done.

The workers in the high-production work groups not only have greater group loyalty and help one another more but give this help on their own initiative.

As might be expected, work groups with high group loyalty have more favorable attitudes toward production than do groups with low group loyalty. Thus we find that high-loyalty groups differ from groups of low group loyalty in having higher production goals. Their opinion as to what is reasonable production is higher and is more nearly the same as that of their foreman. Moreover, the high-loyalty groups have a more favorable attitude toward the high producer.

We are finding that the high-loyalty groups differ from the low in ways that form a consistent pattern. In addition to the differences already mentioned, the following characteristics have been found. The groups with greater group loyalty are more likely to

—Have greater identification with their group and a greater feeling of belonging to it.

—Have more friends in the group and in the company—rather than outside the company.

—Have better interpersonal relations among the members of the work group.

—Have a more favorable attitude toward their job and their company.

—Not only have higher production goals but produce more with less sense of strain or pressure.

10. When a superior treats subordinates as human beings, it results in greater group loyalty and pride. When supervisors stay sufficiently close psychologically to their workers to be able to see the problems of the workers through the eyes of the workers, they are better able to develop good group loyalty.

11. The good supervisor is able to identify with his employees and keep psychologically close to them. This seems to foster a good team spirit with open communication. It permits the supervisor to understand problems as employees see them and to interpret for top and middle management the employees' points of view. The supervisor who fails to identify with employees becomes psychologically far from them. This makes him incapable of seeing and dealing with problems as employees see them and hence unable to help middle and top management to see problems as employees see them and thereby to help management to arrive at policy decisions which will be mutually satisfactory.

12. There are, of course, many other factors which are important in developing group loyalty and team spirit. Scattered research in industry and elsewhere indicates that commonly recognized methods of group leadership will yield good group loyalty when used. These methods and skills include those developed and taught by the National Training Laboratory in Group Development. Among the most important of these methods are those involving group participation in decisions affecting the group. There is evidence that group participation and involvement are beneficial at all levels in an organization. One of the best ways, for example, to have supervisors become aware of the job that needs to be done by their work group and to have them accept responsibility for it is to involve them in decisions where the functions and responsibilities of their work group are examined and reviewed. . . .

An examination of the results presented here and of results from other research shows that every human being earnestly seeks a secure, friendly, and supportive relationship and one that gives him a sense of personal worth in the face-to-face groups most important to him. The most important face-to-face groups are almost always his immediate family group and his work group. If his formal face-to-face work group is hostile, he develops new friendly informal groups. Human nature seems to motivate each of us to establish and maintain these friendly supportive relationships in those face-to-face groups in which we spend most of our lives. Either we successfully establish these friendly and supportive relationships or we crack up.

It is not surprising, therefore, that we see people generally striving for a sense of dignity and personal worth. We all seem to seek recognition and a sense of importance in terms of the values and goals which we cherish and which our most important face-to-face groups also cherish.

To say that people seek friendly and supportive relationships does not mean that they seek to be coddled. Quite the contrary. People seek to achieve a sense of importance from doing difficult but important tasks which help to implement goals which they and their friends seek.[11]

The outstanding finding from the Michigan studies in regard to the effectiveness of the varied methods and attitudes used by first-line supervisors is that supervisors characterized as "employee-centered" were likely to be in charge of high-producing groups. Those characterized as being "production-centered" were likely to be in charge of low-producing groups. The typical employee-centered supervisor thought of supervision mainly in terms of people under his direction. He did not forget about production but the emphasis in his thinking was directed toward his subordinates as personalities. He usually gave his employees a general outline of what work was to be done, how it was to be done, and then left details to the workers. He assumed that they felt they were responsible for their work. The production-centered supervisor was more detached in his attitudes toward employees' feelings and checked their efforts closely. He thought of employees as instruments for getting work done. This emphasis on production at the expense of the worker's dignity was self-defeating.

As individuals, the employee-centered supervisors were, in general, likely to be democratic, cooperative, and willing to listen to the employees. The production-centered supervisors were more likely to be authoritarian, defensive and arbitrary in manner. Of course, each supervisor had some characteristics of both kinds of centeredness but his supervisory style was identifiable.

Employee-centered Supervision Is Not Always the Most Effective

In spite of the main finding from the Michigan studies, it is also recognized that employee-centered supervision is unsuitable in certain situations as in those instances where work is an individual matter without social relations that require harmony between members of the work group or crew. Social isolates, "rate busters," and other work isolates may prefer an authoritarian supervisor who uses a firm production-centered procedure. Some employees, perhaps 10 per cent, do not care to participate in making plans or decisions about the work—they prefer to be told what to do by a no-nonsense type of boss. The Michigan and other researchers recognize that no one formula for productive supervision is available but that enlightened supervision harnesses the latent motivations of the individual worker for the benefit of all concerned.[12]

Raymond A. Katzell[13] has reviewed the scientific literature on the directive or bureaucratic systems of organization versus the democratic, participative, human relations type. He found several studies which have shown that democratic supervision is by no means universally preferred to more autocratic supervision. In some instances, both production and worker satisfaction were as great or even greater under autocratic supervision. In general, more research is needed in this field but the current findings indicate that the organizational system that is most appropriate is conditioned by those who have the knowledge and motivation to get the job done, preferably by providing freedom and action for those who give it leadership as well as for those who do the work.

Certainly, a company can have an authoritarian approach to leadership and still show consideration for the feelings and desires of its employees. Sometimes a democratic approach may be effective, while in another situation and authoritarian approach is preferable.[14]

Pressure from a supervisor can produce productive results even though the employees have been given irritating treatment previously. This was rather clearly indicated when a systematic study was made of the effects of emotional states on groups of assembly line operators who had been matched for factors such as productivity and length of employment. Some groups were treated as "favored." The chief techniques for the favored groups were praise and managerial friendliness. The "disfavored" group members were treated in a threatening manner by persistent time and motion studies and irritating criticisms from quality control and supervisory personnel. In one part of the study, the foreman of a disfavored group was asked to pressure the employees about the quality of their work. He went to some of the assemblers on the line, told them that they were making too many errors, and asked them to improve. He worked briefly with one of the operators to suggest changes in work procedure and then left. These operators had been producing 29.0 per cent of defective units. In the four days that followed the foreman's criticisms, the operators reduced their level of errors to 17.3 per cent. An especially interesting aspect of this part of the experiment was that the foreman's additional pressure on employees who had been given previous treatment of an irritating nature, nevertheless resulted in improved production.[15]

Generally, the better supervisors are somewhat tougher raters of their men. They show more variation in their ratings of high- and low-rated subordinates. The less effective supervisors tend to rate all their subordinates as being more or less alike.[16]

One of the key factors in supervision, often more important than the organizational system, is the supervisor as a personality rather than the role he plays. This was indicated in a study of three techniques of supervising radar air control teams. A complex task setting was provided by the simulation of a radar air traffic control system. Work-team productivity was modifiable as a consequence of different supervisors and supervisory procedures under different task loads. Six two-man teams were observed. Each team worked under each of three supervisors. The supervisors shifted from team to team. Three techniques were used alternately: laissez-faire, active monitoring, and direct participation.

The observers in this study concluded that the individual supervisor was a more consistent influence on performance than the particular role he employed.[17]

The effective supervisor stimulates productivity because he has developed a climate where people are genuinely interested in the work problems and in doing good work. They help the boss to plan ahead and to anticipate problems. They know that the boss likes them and respects them and their abilities. Good work climates do not develop by chance. Instead, they are produced by leaders of good will and competence.

GROUP METHODS OF TRAINING SUPERVISORS

Numerous procedures for training supervisors, particularly factory foremen, have been developed in industry. The first and most commonly used methods naturally repeat the schoolroom procedures. Executives or teachers hired for the purpose give lectures or conduct classroom instruction of an informative nature. These traditional methods have not been so successful in industry as in the academic fields, chiefly because the teaching of supervisors is not mainly a problem in giving information. Supervisors need a kind of stimulation that causes them to drop old habit patterns and to adopt new attitudes toward human relations. Mere verbal understanding and acceptance of new ways of dealing with employees is not sufficient. What the supervisor does in everyday contacts with employees is the important measure of the effectiveness of the training program.

Lectures have little effect on the kind of foreman who, for example, is 60 years of age, attained his foremanship the hard way while working on a night shift, is now arbitrary and set in his habits.

The authoritarian type of supervisor believes in the old philosophy that men will work only when they are controlled by a firm disciplinarian who uses fear as a motivator. Fortunately, modern managements gradually are developing supervision directed toward democratic leadership. Democratic leadership means that the foreman strives to satisfy the egos of the members of the working group and de-emphasizes his own ego. He does little shouting at people, sits quietly, listens to people, gives them a sense of participation in solving the fascinating problems that are the daily part of the job.

The authoritarian person tends to regard others as either superior or inferior to him, and he adopts conduct adapted to the situation. The authoritarian person does not love or respect others. "In the last analysis, the alternatives are to fear or be feared."[18]

The democratic supervisor endeavors wherever possible to share with his group the decision-making about work planning, assignment and scheduling. Where a decision must be made by him, he helps the group to understand clearly the basis for his decision. He is careful to develop as much participation, opinion-giving and decision-making as possible, and a feeling of responsibility for the success of the work on the part of everyone. He is concerned that each employee clearly understands his work and has opportunities for success in it. His praise and criticisms are always delivered objectively in terms of work results and never personally in terms of what he may or may not like. He encourages worthwhile suggestions and the development of new procedures.[19]

The traditional training techniques of the past failed to develop the desired changes in attitudes and behavior of foremen and other supervisors. Foremen could be convinced intellectually that they ought to greet employees with a smile when they reported for work, discuss common problems with them, and behave in ways which show an interest in people, but still fail to supervise their workers in that manner. The latter obviously recognized their insincerity, because their words and actions did not express their underlying attitudes. After all, employees often react to a supervisor's attitudes rather than his words and actions.

The attitude of the supervisor is highly important in another respect. Not only do his actions tend to reflect his attitude, but his attitude also influences the way he will view or interpret the behavior of employees. For example, loafing, insubordination, failure to cooperate, disregard of company property, and being unwilling to do a full day's work are largely supervisory interpretations of actions which might also be interpreted, respectively, as resting, face-saving, lack of skill, an accident, and a reluctance to begin a job that cannot be completed. The differing interpretations are highly important, since the problem which confronts the supervisor depends on his interpretation rather than on the actual behavior. The procedure that the supervisor will follow depends in turn upon the problem he sees, so that inaccurate interpretations invariably result in inadequate procedures.

Interpretations of behavior are greatly influenced by an attitude of suspicion. When employees do not trust supervisors and supervisors do not trust employees, misunderstandings in great numbers are created. Grievances that seem small and childish to management are seen as fundamental issues by workers. When mutual trust is present, grievances are rare, and when they do appear, remedies are easily found. Trust is an attitude that must be developed, and when the supervisor has this trust, his attitude is recognized and it develops mutual trust.[20]

Recent advancements in training supervisors are designed to influence attitudes as well as teach techniques for dealing with people. These training programs are of three general kinds:

1. Conference
2. Permissive (nondirective)
3. Role-taking

1. The Conference

The conference may be defined as a group training method in which problem situations of common interest to the supervisors are discussed in an effort to formulate a solution through the contributions of all members of the group.

Advantages claimed for the conference method are:

1. The subject matter is of immediate interest to supervisors.

2. Opportunity for participation by members is provided.

3. The supervisors themselves do most of the talking.

4. The level of discussion usually matches their learning speed.

5. The method tends to develop qualities of self-reliance and the ability to recognize and solve problems.

A typical conference usually consists of four steps:

1. The conference leader shows why a given problem or subject applies to the members of the group.

2. The nature of the problem is discussed and defined.

3. The discussion centers around wrong and right methods of handling the problem.

4. Analysis is made of right and wrong ways for the prevention of the problem in the future.

The conference method enables the leader to present informative material as well as conduct a discussion. Principles may be developed and emphasized. Problems involving the principles may be used for emphasis. When doubts arise concerning the applicability of a principle, the leader can clarify the principle more fully and illustrate its applicability to everyday situations in the plant. The leader also may give special assignments which are to be carried out on the job. Later, the supervisors may present the reactions to their attempts to carry out the assignment. During the discussions the leader encourages the whole group to participate. His role is to keep the discussion on the problem or topic under consideration, to bring about opportunities for face-saving, and to make contributions which clarify the issues or emphasize neglected aspects of the discussion. In some cases, he functions as a democratic leader and in other instances as an expert.

When attitudes or habits are to be changed, discussion is especially important as shown by the kind of experiment conducted by Kurt Lewin during World War II. He worked with the National Research Council program on food conservation. Consumers' food habits were to be changed. One problem was to persuade housewives to use beef hearts, sweetbreads, kidneys, and other animal organs in family diets. Three groups of women were given lectures that stressed the health value of these meats, demonstrated various menu applications, and linked the nutrition problem to the war effort. In another experiment three comparable groups of women took up the question in group discussion, rather than lecture, and talked freely about their aversions. A follow-up showed that of the women who had heard the lectures, only three per cent served one of the meats never served before. Of those women who had had group discussion, 32 per cent of the women did so.[21]

One of the important advantages of the group conference, as practiced in the better concerns, is that the leader or secretary of the group can summarize the principles learned in the meeting. These principles can be mimeographed and reviewed by the supervisors and members of management. The supervisors can be provided with a textual guide which can be reviewed and re-emphasized. Most supervisors like to have some kind of written statement which summarizes what they think they have learned.

An effective conference includes a summary of the conclusions developed by the group. Conferees will feel that the conference was worthwhile and that something definite was accomplished if they are given a formal statement of the thoughts and conclusions brought out in the discussion. Such a formal statement usually includes the recommendations of the conference leader as exemplified in the following statement, which was developed during several discussions on disciplinary problems of supervisors:

> As a supervisor, you are the leader of your men. Most of your contacts with them deal with the work and the ordinary everyday instructions to them. Most of your thinking and conversation with employees is of a positive friendly nature.
>
> Occasionally, however, you find it necessary to handle problems that involve discipline, problems on the part of employees who have violated some company regulation or failed to do what is expected of a good employee. These problems in violation or failure must be handled with good judgment and offer you a chance to give employees the kind of leadership that builds strength and loyalty to you and the company.
>
> Here are some suggestions and principles that may help you handle the fellow who gets out of line:
>
> 1. *Believe in the rules or practices which you expect employees to obey*. Every good rule or regulation has sound reasons back of it.
>
> If you understand the reasons for the company's rules and expectations, you can wholeheartedly represent the company in regard to the expected practices by employees.
>
> Employees are very smart. They soon recognize whether the supervisor really believes in a rule or is willing to shut his eyes and ears at certain times. Most employees naturally fall into line with what they think is expected of them.
>
> Of course, if a rule has become a dead letter and everybody ignores it, somebody ought to find out whether the original reasons for the rule have changed and, if they have, the obsolete rule should be declared null and void. Review the old doubtful rules with your superior and get his decision about the rules that appear to need review.
>
> If you yourself understand the soundness and fairness of the rules that your superior wishes

you to enforce, your part in enforcing them will be easier.

2. *Getting employees to obey rules is an educational matter; not a policing job.* Years ago, a lot of plant foremen and other supervisors thought that the main part of a boss' job was policing employees. As a result, those old bygone foremen had a lot of policing to do. The employees were like the small boys in the old schoolmaster's schoolroom—they often raised hell because their teachers were poor teachers. The good teachers kept the boys so interested in their work that they forgot most of the hellraising.

The same principle applies to the good supervisor of today—he keeps his employees so busy and interested in their work that they usually do the right and neglect the wrong. The good supervisor is a good teacher who explains the right so enthusiastically that employees do the right. And he explains the right before, not after, trouble arises.

3. *The good supervisor has good discipline and still has most employees like him.* A lot of poor supervisors think that the employees do not like the supervisor who expects employees to obey the established rules. Actually, most employees have more respect for the supervisor who takes good discipline for granted and enforces it on the part of the few employees who need disciplinary attention.

Bear in mind that the children who usually have the least respect for the parent are the children who are allowed to do as they please. Employees who know that they can get away with anything usually have little respect for the supervisor who lets them get away with it.

4. *Disciplining an employee who needs it is not only a matter of being fair to him, but a matter of being so fair about it that the other employees approve of it.* Now and then, it becomes necessary to fire an employee. Every supervisor and personnel man who fires a man hopes that he can do it in a way that makes the fired employee feel that he was treated fairly. In addition to making the employee feel that the drastic treatment given him was fair, it is also necessary to make the other employees feel that the treatment was fair.

No one wants to punish an employee for his bad conduct just for the sake of punishing him. We do not punish our grown-up friends who work with us, but we do find it necessary to tell them that we will have to get along without them until they learn that we insist on working with each other in ways that are fair to all of us: fellow employees, the company, and customers.

5. *Good housekeeping and good discipline tend to go together.* The supervisor who keeps his equipment and materials in clean orderly fashion usually finds it easier to have his employees work in an orderly manner.

The supervisor who allows employees to get into sloppy habits of work in surroundings unnecessarily dirty, where raw materials are wasted and unused tools litter the place, must expect his employees to ignore a lot of good rules essential to efficient production.

6. *When the good supervisor finds that one of his best employees has lied to him or violated an important work rule, the good supervisor thinks of himself as also partially guilty.* He thinks of himself as also partially guilty because every employee under his supervision cooperates because his supervision is good. And the bad employee is also partially bad because of bad or poor supervision.

When a normal employee lies to his supervisor, it means that the supervisor has not established the kind of relationship that produces frankness and confidence on the part of the employee. (Of course the chronic liar is another kind of problem.)

When a good employee knowingly breaks a work rule, the good supervisor realizes that he failed to train the employee to appreciate the sound reasons for the rule.

In the long run, the good supervisor tends to attract and hold good employees. And the poor supervisor tends to attract and hold poor employees.

To the supervisor who finds that he has too many problems in discipline, the following "Don'ts" may be of help:

1. *Don't threaten* an employee. Explain. State the facts. Let the plain facts tell their own story. If repeated explanatory statements of the facts do not produce satisfactory results, act. Weak men make threats and use sarcasm.

The parent who constantly threatens his children seldom gains obedience. The parent who teaches the right and holds his children to good conduct gets the desired action without threats.

2. *Don't criticize or find fault only—point out the right.* Stress the right. When an employee has knowingly failed to do the right, let him explain his side of the story before the reprimand or criticism is made. Perhaps special circumstances were involved.

3. *Don't blame "higher-ups" for the rules.* The poor supervisor hides behind the old dodge: "Don't blame me for the rules—I didn't make 'em!" And every time the supervisor says that or its equivalent, he admits that he is not really a full-fledged member of management. Any rule that ought to be obeyed has a good reason back of it and the average employee knows it. The

average employee has greater respect for the man who stands on his own two feet than for the supervisor who passes the buck to someone else in management.

4. *Don't try to make the wrongdoer feel guilty —try to get him to see the right.*

Perhaps you've seen a mother grab her small son by the shoulders, stare in his face, and yell at him: "Tell me you're sorry or I'll do so and so." In most cases, the mother is more interested in building up her own ego by wringing an admission of remorse than in getting the child to do right. The child must learn to understand why right is better than wrong.

The supervisor who likes to make the wrongdoer confess his guilt is likely to be the kind of sinner himself who feels bitter about his own sins when others confess their sins to him!

5. *Don't carry the whole discipline load on your shoulders.* Let the employees feel responsible for their own conduct and the conduct of their fellow employees.

A good supervisor respects his own employees. He shows by his manner and conversation that he likes them, trusts them, and expects them to conduct themselves sensibly. His manner of brotherhood toward them helps to develop a feeling of brotherhood on the part of the employees toward each other. Sometimes their suggestions and influence will help to keep one of their fellow employees in line.

Discuss your problems of discipline with your superior. Keep him informed and ask his advice. The two of you usually can handle any disciplinary problem within reason.

2. The Permissive Method

In recent years many psychologists have given a good deal of attention to the use of nondirective techniques in psychotherapy. The usefulness of these methods has been demonstrated in dealing with some inadequately adjusted individuals. In the nondirective technique, the individual subject or client is encouraged to think through his own problem and develop a solution or procedure that appeals to him rather than to the counselor.

A few psychologists have applied the method of nondirective or permissive principles to the training of supervisors. Permissive conferences differ from most other conferences in the fact that the leader does not attempt to teach principles verbally; he stimulates the members of the group to develop their own principles.

After the audio-visual material has been presented to the group, the leader allows the members of the group to develop their own discussion and to discover answers for themselves. The leader is cautioned to remain silent and wait for the members of the party to take hold, even though they may flounder. Even if the leader is asked to give help, he refuses to start the discussion. A basic principle is that what the leader tells is not important; rather what the group members want to know must indicate where discussion should start.

The leader does not take the position of a teacher or tell the group members what is right or wrong. They must find out for themselves what is right. They must participate, explain to themselves, and develop their own insight. When the leader remains neutral and refuses to agree or disagree with the member of the group who makes a statement, the latter is left free to decide his answers, to decide how he feels, and what position he wishes to take on any issue. The leader does not take sides because taking sides is likely to start an argument. When an argument is started, some persons will disagree but remain silent. Instead, the leader compels members of the group, by his silence, to sweat through their own problem and take the position which they themselves finally choose.

One of the chief values of the permissive or nondirective technique is in the contribution which the technique makes to the personality development of the leader himself. Very few discussion leaders can use a nondirective technique effectively unless they have a personality development that characterizes individuals who are emotionally secure. A leader who attempts to use the nondirective technique with a discussion group cannot have a temperament that is characteristically on the defensive. He first of all must feel secure within himself as a person and be able to hear criticism of himself without emotional disturbance on his own part. Discussion leaders who have learned to use the nondirective technique are likely to be individuals who have an unusually high type of emotional control and poise in social situations or they acquire such a level of social development. True personal leadership and long-term patience in getting benefits from it are necessary for the effective use of the nondirective technique. As yet, its application to the training of supervisors has not been widely used, but it gives promise of considerable future effectiveness.

3. Role-taking

Role-taking (also called role-playing) is a grown-up form of "Let's Pretend." In the training of supervisors, the supervisor acts out a situation that involves a human relations problem. The basic principles used are very old. Companies have used them for years to teach salesmen. Psychotherapists have employed them in the psychodrama technique. In recent years, studies made by Alex Bavelas, of the Massachusetts Institute of Technology, and his associates used the "Do and Learn" technique in the training of supervisors in handling human relations problems. In the role-taking, the supervisors not only discuss the techniques which supervisors should use in dealing with employees but they also demonstrate them in the presence of their colleagues.

Several large industrial concerns have used the Bavelas studies as a basis for their supervisory training. In the American Type Founders Company and in other companies, the principle works as follows:

1. The staff-training department calls a meeting of the foremen to set up principles for handling a certain type of case.
2. A foreman is briefed to be the "worker" in the role-taking—usually from actual case histories of labor disputes.
3. Two other foremen, one at a time, are called on to hear the "worker's" grievance, and deal with it.
4. Recordings of the discussions are played back, and criticized by the two foremen-players first, then in open discussion.
5. The group then decides how the grievance should have been handled. If there's time, a foreman and "worker" play the roles that way.[22]

When supervisors are inducted into this form of training, they at first tend to dislike the idea. They feel that they are not actors and that the whole idea is a lot of foolishness. However, after several sessions have been conducted, the members of the group learn to enjoy the role-taking and begin to volunteer for roles. Sometimes a competitive spirit makes the sessions quite lively. Of course, some supervisors refuse to change their beliefs merely because they have seen others play a role with which they did not agree.

Allan H. Tyler, training supervisor at American Type Founders, after the plan had been in operation about a year, noted considerable improvement in the ways in which supervisors handled their grievances. Quality and quantity of production rose. Supervisors spoke up at meetings with other management men. One of the last foremen to accept the principles developed under role-taking instruction was a tough old-timer who ran his battery of machines and crew of men in the traditional manner. The first time this foreman played a role, he had to handle a charge of carelessness: a worker accidentally had dropped a wrench into a machine, damaging it. The foreman, in demonstrating the role that he would play in such a situation, promptly fired the man in five acrid sentences.

Then the old-timer watched while another supervisor took over the same role. The new man reprimanded the "worker" and showed him the right way to handle a wrench. After the playback, the old-timer still insisted he was right: A dope who damaged a machine ought to be fired. But the group voted him down; it decided a reprimand and short layoff would be enough penalty for a first offense. At this point, the old-timer relented a little—maybe he had been too rough. Since then, Tyler reports, the foreman has mended his ways somewhat. Tyler credits the role playing with the change.

Tyler believes the great value of role playing is this: Supervisors learn, by practice, to think on their feet. They never know what the "worker" will say next, hence they learn to make quick

1

"Damn it!" the irate employee at ATF, Inc., yells at his foreman in the familiar way a grievance is initiated almost everywhere, "I'm getting a bum deal."

2

"It happens out there all the time," the foreman reports to his superior—and how well management knows it. In getting supervisors to handle grievances effectively, ATF had the same problem that most employers have experienced. That's why the company sought a better way to make each foreman a human-relations expert.

3

ATF thinks it has found the answer in role-playing: a development in psychotherapy which the company aims at its specific training objectives.

4

Role-playing is a modern version of childhood's play-acting with a serious purpose. Here the foreman acts out the role of the irate employee, pouring it on a younger foreman, who handles his part as he would do it in the shop.

5

Still acting as the aggrieved employee, the foreman tries the routine on a supervisor who is an old hand. Unabashed, the old-timer mobilizes his experience, lays his argument on the line like the capable veteran he is.

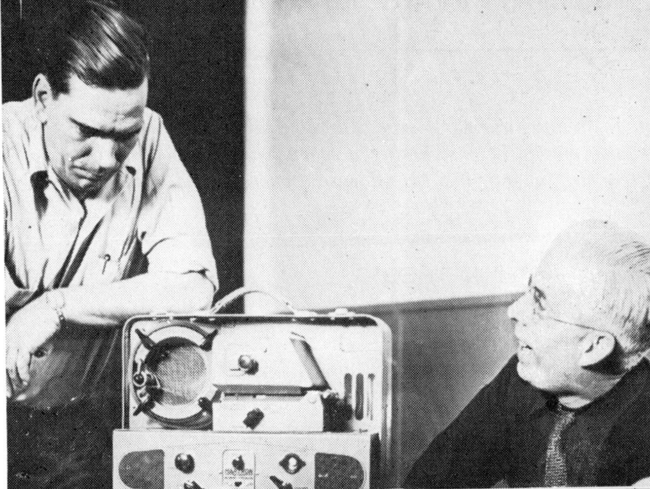

6

The old-timer and the younger foreman hear a recorded playback of their exchange with the aggriever. They are critics of each other and of themselves. This gives them a chance to stand off and check their own performance, to see what they did wrong.

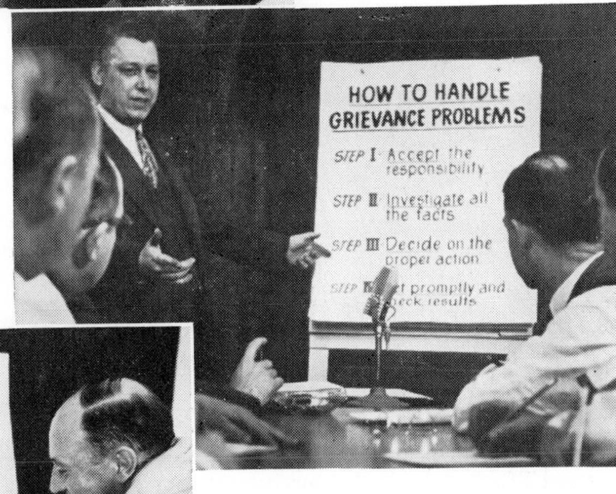

7

How they have handled their parts is measured against company standards for best ways to settle grievances.

8

A discussion, led by training experts, clarifies what good practice is, and how it's best achieved. Courtesy of ***Business Week.***

decisions under realistic pressure and anxiety. Then, too, they learn by seeing how others cope with situations. And—when they act an employee's part—they put themselves in the place of a worker and see his point of view.

Other companies have had much the same experience. Role playing is firmly set in training programs at Owens-Corning, Armstrong Cork Co., General Foods Corp., Sharp & Dohme, Inc., Esso Standard Oil, and elsewhere. The Michigan Industrial Training Council recommends it to its member-training directors. The American Society of Training Directors recently gave considerable time at a convention in Cleveland to a demonstration of the technique.

At least one union has adopted role playing. The Pulp, Sulphite & Paper Mill Workers (A.F.L.-C.I.O.) uses it to teach shop stewards how to handle workers who fancy they have a grievance, and how to put grievances effectively to foremen.[23]

Role-taking is a process in which supervisors spontaneously act out problems that face them. It differs from demonstrations in the fact that demonstrations are previously

The four steps below were made famous during World War II in the Training Within Industry Program. They are one means of instructing a learner in a job. Not only do they seem applicable to teaching a job, but to all cases where an idea is being transmitted.

FOUR-STEP METHOD

The four steps	How each is accomplished
1. PREPARATION: Prepare listener to receive new experience.	1. Put learner at ease. 2. Tell him the title of job. 3. Explain the purpose of the job. 4. Explain why he has been selected to learn. 5. Help him relate his past experience to the job.
2. PRESENTATION: Set the pattern in his mind.	1. Introduce him to tools, materials, equipment and trade terms. 2. Demonstrate the job, explaining each step slowly and clearly. 3. Review with him what he should know up to this point: Title of job, Purpose of job, Steps to be taken.
3. APPLICATION: Help him form habit.	1. Supervise his doing the job. 2. Question him on weak and key points. 3. Have him repeat until he has developed the manual skills and/or habits of thought.
4. TEST: Check the success of your instruction.	1. Have him do the job alone. 2. Inspect job against standards of performance. 3. Discuss with him where he goes from here, whether to production work or new learning experience.

Robert P. Cort, "How to Get an Idea Across," *Personnel,* American Management Association, July 1951, pp. 46–51.

prepared. In role-taking, one of the group takes the part of the supervisor and the other member the role of the employee. The scenes are discussed by the members of the group and the skills and principles pertinent to the particular type of problem are clarified and stated. One of the chief values in role-taking is that it enables the supervisory trainee to participate in his own training.

A fundamental concept of the modern foreman or supervisor is that he is a teacher and a leader—not a boss. He realizes that if he is a poor leader, his record will show his weaknesses in the form of lowered production, higher costs, increased absenteeism, and numerous grievances. If he is a good leader, he also knows that he can prove the effectiveness of his supervisory methods by means of favorable production figures. Furthermore, he enjoys handling people. He gets as much thrill from a skillful handling of an "ornery" employee as a fisherman gets from landing a game fish.

Schuyler Dean Hoslett has described examples of good and poor supervisory procedures:

EVELYN: (Getting up reluctantly and going over to Anne at the desk.) Well, Anne, you only made 30 units yesterday. Did you have any special trouble? After I brought you all your work, too.

ANNE: I didn't feel good.

EVELYN: Did you have any machine trouble or anything?

ANNE: Yes, I did.

EVELYN: Well, why didn't you put your little red light on?

ANNE: I don't know. I guess I forgot. And the thread breaks all the time.

EVELYN: Well, you should tell me about those things so I can help you. You'll do that after this, won't you? And you'll try to do better too, won't you?

ANNE: Yes, but I don't know if I can. It's hard to do.

TRAINER: That's fine. Now let's talk about this case.

The role-taking continues with suggestions of using check studies and additional training. In the discussion of "making excuses," the Personnel Manager thinks the supervisor should find out whether the girl has any personal problems. Because the trainer knows that Evelyn has caused resentment by prying into personal affairs of her girls and because he wants to criticize the argumentative technique without criticizing her personally, he set up a special situation.

TRAINER: Let's see how Mr. Jones (the Personnel Manager) would tackle this problem. I'll be the girl, the same girl Anne was last time. (Sits at the "machine.")

MR. JONES: Well, it just seems to me this way. There's lots of things that might be holding the girl back. Possibly she got a letter from her boy friend that had bad news in it, or something like that.

TRAINER: Well, let's try it out and see how it works.

MR. JONES: (Getting up from his chair.) What did you say your name was?

TRAINER: Dottie Sholley.

MR. JONES: (Now acting the role of supervisor.) I have some bad news for you here, Dottie. It seems you have fallen down a little in your units. What seems to be the trouble?

TRAINER: Well, I didn't feel so good.

MR. JONES: But when you asked me to be your supply girl you seemed to be feeling well enough.

TRAINER: Well, I got some machine trouble and that slows you up. And these old threads break all the time. You can't do much when that happens.

MR. JONES: (Pauses for a moment.) Did you go to the show last night?

TRAINER: No.

MR. JONES: Anyone in your family sick?

TRAINER: No.

MR. JONES: Did you have a date last night?

TRAINER: No! I'm married.

MR. JONES: And you say you haven't been feeling well?

TRAINER: No, I wasn't feeling well, but that was just yesterday.

MR. JONES: You don't feel sick most of the time?

TRAINER: No, that was just a little stomach trouble. There's nothing wrong with me.

MR. JONES (*laughing*): You're sure bucking me. I give up!

BILL: If you let them get into an argument with you, you'll never get out. They answer and answer and answer.

TRAINER: Thanks. I certainly was being a tough one. Now let me give you my reactions. When you came up saying you had bad news I felt nervous. I didn't like that, so I was sort of on the defensive. I was thinking, now what am I going to say? I thought of something, and then while I thought of that I thought of something else to have ready for the next question. Then he asked me about my family and that scared me. I thought maybe something was wrong. Then he asked me if I had had a date, and I was married. That made me so mad I nearly slapped him. And when he asked me again about my health I tried to assure him that I was in good health because I was afraid maybe he would fire me if he thought I was sick all the time. Now, this is the toughest kind of case you will get. A girl who doesn't do what she can do, and you just can't find out why. Now would you like me to try the skunk oil method?

BILL: Yeah, I think so.

TRAINER: O.K. You be the girl, Bill.

BILL: Sure, I'll answer your questions.

TRAINER: You try to be the same girl that Anne was and that I was. Be as tough as you want to.

BILL: O.K. (*Sits down at the table.*)

TRAINER: (*Approaching Bill with the sheet in his hands.*) Hello, Dottie. Here's the unit sheet for today. Let's see, where is your name? (*Turning the sheets with Bill's help.*) I guess it's over on another page. What have you been doing?

BILL: Well, I made 30.

TRAINER: How does that compare with what you've been doing? Is that good for you or not so good?

BILL: Well, I have done better.

TRAINER: How long have you been on the job?

BILL: Oh, about eight or ten weeks, but they change me around so much.

TRAINER: How long have you been on this job?

BILL: About six weeks.

TRAINER: Well, it usually takes a girl three or four months to make 60. You say you have done better?

BILL: Yes.

TRAINER: Have any trouble yesterday?

BILL: Yes, the thread breaks all the time. And I had such little bundles. I had to get more all the time.

TRAINER: Oh, I'm sorry. I told you yesterday I was going to bring you a lot.

BILL: But they're too little. You run through them in no time.

TRAINER: What you want to do is not worry about your progress one day or another day. How much do you suppose you will make a week from today? Maybe you'll get some small bundles and maybe your machine will give you trouble, but counting that in, what do you suppose you will make in a week?

BILL: I don't know. I might make 40 or 45.

TRAINER: You think you could make 40 or 45! Why I've known girls who have taken three or four weeks to get up there from 30! What's the best you have made?

BILL: I think it's 48.

TRAINER: Well, maybe you could then. How'd you like to try and make 40 by next Friday?

BILL: You mean just do 40 by next Friday?

TRAINER: Yes, that gives you a good chance in spite of machine trouble and those things that you can't help that come up. Do you think you could do it?

BILL: I believe so.

TRAINER: Now I don't think you can do it if you have troubles that aren't your fault. Now on the matter of thread breaks, sometimes that's the way you hold your cloth and sometimes the trouble is with the machine. When you get trouble like that, we can call the mechanic in or we can get the trainer over to see what's wrong. You want to have perfect working conditions. I'll come over Friday to see if you've made it, and I'll come around every other day, too, to see if I can help in some way. (*End of role-playing.*)

MR. JONES: Fine!

TRAINER: I don't think I did that very well, but I was trying to use a different technique. Now what's the difference?

MR. JONES: Well, you weren't on the defensive all the time.

TRAINER: You mean Bill didn't put me on the defensive?

BILL: What he means is when you were the operator you answered him back. And I could answer all your questions to me this time, but there never was any blame on me.[24]

The discussion continued for fifteen minutes on the details of how to avoid arguments, putting a person on the defensive, the use of production goals, why the trainer tried to make a goal out of the *lower* of the two estimates given by the girl, and so on.

Conclusion :

There is no standard spiel which can fit every situation, no standard spiel that will work with every kind of personality. More important than the specific words are the attitudes the supervisor brings to this kind of discussion. If he tries to build up a fellow instead of tearing him down, if he sets up a goal the worker can accomplish, the chances are pretty good he will get cooperation.[25]

Role-playing, when properly used, helps the supervisor to make theories in human relations techniques fit into and become integral parts of his personality.[26]

The results of a survey of companies who use or had used role-playing show that the chief benefit of this technique is in developing human relations skills. There are other benefits, too: The members of the group participate more, they become interested in their co-workers and subordinates, and they gain confidence in handling problems in interpersonal relations. Over half the companies polled thought that role-playing was useful in handling morale, teamwork, attitude improvement, and grievance problems.

There are disadvantages to role-playing, also. Among these are the fact that it takes too long and it fails to present the material in true perspective. Hence, it is unnatural. Some management men feel it is unwise to use this device because it produces occasional embarrassment. A few are reluctant to use it because it takes too long to get the group to feel at ease. The authors, however, thought that most of the disadvantages were of the sort that could be overcome if the role-playing procedures were improved.[27]

Recently it has been found that there is a high degree of correlation between what is called role-playing and interpersonal adjustment. We define role-playing as one's ability to perform a given role, and interpersonal adjustment as the "ability to perform roles that are recognized to be situationally and socially appropriate." Role-playing is also defined in some cases as empathy, or identification with another person or situation. A person who can identify with the problem of another or who can perform a role that is not natural to him with a degree of success has been found to be well adjusted to his social situation. It then follows that if one's role playing ability changes, that it is marking a change in one's interpersonal adjustment.[28]

The effectiveness of personal relationships in industry depends upon specific social skills. Like other skills, they may be learned by practice. Thus far, the most effective method for teaching these skills appears to be the common-sense one—"Watch others, let others watch you, discuss and evaluate differences, and try it again." Alex Bavelas has described the principles and procedures of role-playing in several published articles. Excerpts from one are:

...Group discussion may effect considerable changes in motivation, and may raise the group's level of understanding regarding the problems of face-to-face relationships, but it is not very effective in transmitting behavioral skills. It is this defect in the discussion method that has led individuals interested in the problem of training social skills to experiment with role-playing. The central idea of role-playing is the assigning of roles to various members of the training group and the acting out of problem situations. . . .

...Whatever the form of role-playing, [strictly-defined roles, or highly-spontaneous roles], if it is well planned and directed, the following advantages for teaching are usually gained:

1. Playing a role before an "audience" makes an individual self-conscious. Since the purpose of role-playing is not to present a finished performance, this self-consciousness is desirable because it makes the individual aware of his actions in a new way. . . . He becomes as it were, "sensitized" to himself.

2. ...The foreman who is playing the role of a *worker* can report how it made him feel when the *foreman* treated him the way he did. This helps the trainees to get a better insight into the effects of their actions on others.

3. Rotation of roles causes certain factors to operate:

a. the individuals waiting for their turn take full advantage of the chance to see what the fellow "at bat" will do, and thus eliminate errors from their own performance.

b. the individuals who have already been at bat, elated with their success or chagrined at their errors, are also only too ready to find and point out the good and bad points in the current play.

c. very often an individual who has just played the role of *foreman* takes the role of *worker* in the very next play. For him this offers the stimulating experience of "feeling the difference" between the foreman's and the worker's position in a difficult situation.

4. Role-playing shows you how to *do* something rather than *telling* you how to do it.

5. People learn by *doing*.

...Several years of trial and error in the use of role-playing in management training seems to indicate that an effective procedure for teaching specific skills requires (1) the use of carefully planned "stereotype" situations as basic training material, and (2) rather close controls of all roles being played, with the exception of the role primarily under consideration—that one being left entirely free to be played as the individual sees fit.

...And there is always the task of constructing the situations which will be acted out. Almost always they must be planned anew for each group and organization, and it is not easy to find the problem situations which will yield the most fruitful material. It may appear on the surface that certain types of problems are common to all foremen—attendance, discipline, work delegation, employee training, etc. But in reality these are areas of responsibility, not problems.... The planning of situations for role-playing rests finally not upon generalizations from the picture of industrial management as a whole, but upon individual diagnosis of the organization in which the training is to be done.

...The question often arises "Granted that role-playing is an efficient training method, can individuals be trained to use it?" The answer is a qualified "yes," based upon both failures and successes. Attempts to train individuals to direct-role-playing yield very questionable results when reliance is placed upon lectures, demonstrations, and trainers' manuals. Experience indicates what should have been self-evident: that the directing of role-playing can best be taught by the use of role-playing itself.[29]

To Be Effective, the Training of Supervisors Must Be Done in a Favorable Leadership Climate

Paradoxically, several studies of the effectiveness of certain training programs for supervisors have indicated that the supervisors were less effective after than before training! The reason for this finding can be attributed to the kind of leadership climate to which the supervisor returns after training. If his superior is authoritative, arbitrary, and production-minded rather than employee-centered, the supervisor will fit his practices into the established pattern, not into the pattern taught him in the training program.

The conflict between his situation as he feels he must function in it and his new desires to adopt better methods may cause him to become confused. He may adjust to the problem by some form of aggressive behavior.

Many a supervisor has said of his training program: "A wonderful program but when does my boss get it!"

The kind of superior under whom the foreman or other supervisor operates is more closely related to his behavior than the kind of training course he has taken. This indicates that the answer to the improvement of supervision in industry must include top management men as well as the supervisors.[30] Many companies are doing this through the numerous workshops for executives such as those conducted by the Graduate School of Business Administration, University of California, Los Angeles; National Training Laboratories, NEA; and others.

Sensitivity Training for Supervisors

One of the most promising methods of training supervisors by the group method has been developed by psychologists in a workshop for executives at the University of California, Los Angeles.

"Sensitivity training" is an approach to management development programs which emphasizes that supervisors should see themselves and others realistically, understand their own feelings and prejudices, and be sensitive to the ways people relate to each other. As the trainees examine themselves and the impact they have on one another, they also develop specific skills for the handling

"Sensitivity Training," *a program usually limited to fifteen persons in a group, makes possible a high level of individual involvement.*

Unstructured discussion among participants helps them to gain a new feeling about their human relations problems. Here a small group of executives and community leaders at the University of California, Los Angeles, utilize an informal circle arrangement to promote conversational atmosphere.

of various human relations problems. This novel training approach, clinical in its orientation, has resulted in far-reaching changes in the ways in which people work together on management teams.

Aims of Sensitivity Training

1. Each trainee should get a better picture of the kind of person he is.
2. Each trainee should check the accuracy of his perceptions as to what other people are like.
3. Each trainee should obtain more relevant factual data.
4. Each trainee should develop new "human relations" skills, including ways of dealing with conflicts and tensions.
5. Each trainee should be helped to become more aware of "group process," those forces unique to a group which ultimately may result in its success or failure.

The Nature of the Training Process

1. The training is "feeling-oriented" as well as "content-oriented." The participants learn to deal not only with specific cases and examples from their "on-the-job" situations, but also to analyze their own reactions and feelings toward one another and toward the situations in which they become involved at the training session.
2. Each person attempts to keep his concept of himself intact, and little training impact can be expected unless the trainee is able to examine his "self-concept," to re-evaluate it, and to instigate those changes which he feels would benefit him.
3. The training design is partly unstructured. Opportunities are provided for the trainees to decide what they want to talk about, what kinds of problems they desire to deal with, and what means to use in reaching their goals.
4. Auxiliary training devices and techniques are utilized to facilitate the interaction process among the participants.
5. A permissive atmosphere is maintained.

Experience shows that if participation in the training process has been effective, the first impact will probably occur in the trainee's own perceptions of himself and others. His new self-assessment may lead to more confidence and security, and to less anxiety in his day-to-day relations on the job. Next, the repercussions of such insights will probably be felt by those with whom he deals. He may "blow up" less often, turn an attentive rather than a deaf ear to suggestions, or play a more constructive role in staff meetings. As he begins to feel his way and explores new behavior patterns, he must be supported by his co-workers to utilize the understanding and skills which he has learned. He needs an environment where human relations practices are part of the total organizational philosophy, where "gimmicks" and manipulative devices are recognized and deprecated for what they are.

As yet, the results of sensitivity training have not been subjected to a rigorous scientific analysis to ascertain the specific type and direction of changes which have undoubtedly taken place. However, reports from both trainees and co-workers indicate that this method of training does lead to greater "human relations" know-how, which in turn often seems to be followed by higher productivity, better morale, and lower turnover. Sensitivity training, of course, is not a "cure-all" for every organizational problem; there are too many other technical and administrative aspects to effective management. We do see it, however, as an exciting development in executive training—with a future rich in promise and in potential rewards.[31]

Sensitivity training has been in a continuous state of transition during the past fifteen years. As a result, important changes have taken place in design, methods, and objectives. The earlier emphasis on group variables has moved to a "relatively greater attention on individual dynamics and the unfolding of a more fully functioning personality." The stress on the development of interpersonal skills has given way to a greater concern with the individual's understanding of himself, particularly his rarely faced feelings about himself, and the better appreciation of the direction of his central life values. The major emphasis has moved from the individual's neurotic tendencies to "the release of his potentials for richer, more constructive, satisfying living."[32]

Sensitivity training is a general term often applied to programs in which personal experience in a group is used to aid individuals in becoming more fully aware of themselves, the ways they affect others, and the ways others react to them. Such programs are now conducted in all major regions of the country as at the Western Training Laboratory at Lake Arrowhead, California and at the University of California, Los Angeles, where some twenty workshops have been conducted under the auspicies of the Institute of Industrial Relations and the Graduate School of Business Administration. "The Managerial Grid," keyed for achieving production through people, is centered at The University of Texas.[33] National Training Laboratories of the National Educational Association conducts sessions at Bethel, Maine; at Arden House Campus (Harriman, N.Y.) of Columbia University, as well as in other areas. The Ameri-

(Above and right) *The National Training Laboratory in Group Development is sponsored by the National Training Laboratories of the Division of Adult Education Service of the National Education Association of the United States.*

The NTLGD's two three-week intensified summer laboratory training sessions on the campus of Gould Academy at Bethel, Maine, are devoted to the more effective development of human relations knowledge, insights, and research on the part of various professional and volunteer leaders—whether in industry, labor, government, education, or civic groups. The whole training design is based on the National Training Laboratories' beliefs, borne out by research, that (1) our nation's need for practical, effective, and democratic leaders in all occupations is constantly on the increase, and (2) effective leadership depends on face-to-face working relations in small groups. For its faculty it draws persons from both educational and applied fields.

Keeping abreast *of current supervisory techniques is recognized as important in modern industry. Relatively few foremen will attend formal courses such as those offered by colleges in their evening programs. As a result, several special letter services have been developed and made available, distributed without cost to the foremen.*

General Foreman Russ Ellis of the Organic Recovery Department, Chas. Pfizer & Co., Inc., Groton, Conn., is a regular reader of the bi-weekly, ***The Foreman's Letter,*** *and other supervisory newsletters published by National Foremen's Institute, Inc., Waterford, Conn., and New York City. Photo by Lou Silverstein, New London, Conn.*

can Management Association has organized and sponsored numerous groups in many areas. These latter two organizations usually refer to their groups as T-Groups. The programs and techniques as well as the sponsorship vary but the underlying approach and purpose usually stem from sensitivity training.

Sensitivity training should not be confused with group therapy. Its purpose is not therapy because in the great majority of members, the individual already functions in a relatively effective and happy manner. It does hold much promise for the development of leaders who can meet some of the human relations challenges of this evolving age. The leader will continue to play an important role in the future as well as in the past.

When six outstanding men of the behavioral sciences conducted a round-table discussion held at a management conference, National Industrial Conference Board, January, 1963, tribute was paid to the leader as indicated in the comments of three of the men, reported as follows:

CHAIRMAN NEWMAN: Somehow or other, back in the years of history, it seems to me that the brilliant leader accomplished the miracles of the world. He is the person who, single-handed and alone and all by himself, has gone out in front and carried people to great heights; without the leader the people seem to have milled around restlessly and done nothing.

You behavioral scientists have given the impression that if you create the right climate, right situation, right interpersonal relationships, you don't need a leader. Do you mean this?

DOUGLAS MCGREGOR: The business of creating the right environment, right goals, right challenge, right method of control—that for me *is* leadership.

DON SCOUTTEN: Needless to say, I don't believe this. Years ago, I was the principal of an elementary school in Ohio where we were keenly dedicated to the principle of the child-centered school. We said, "We will put these children in the right atmosphere and climate, but we will not force them. We will not teach them to read, for example, until they have developed a desire, a readiness, for reading."

Well, you know, some of those little beggars were smart enough to figure out what the gimmick was and they never did show any interest in, or readiness for, reading. We turned out damned fine carpenters who built footstools and birdhouses for years, but, unfortunately, they were illiterate.

When you say, in effect, you don't need leadership, all you need is the right environment, you are kidding yourself. People ain't that smart! And they aren't that good, and they aren't that creative, and they don't have that degree of integrity.

It is an overstatement to suggest you don't need a strong man to lead. It doesn't follow that a strong man becomes a dictator and ignores the possibilities of the group's contributions. He is a fool if he ignores the possibility of tapping the creative powers of the group, but he is equally a fool if he says, "They don't need a leader, I will turn them loose."

DOUGLAS MCGREGOR: I agree 100%.[34]

ACKNOWLEDGMENTS AND REFERENCES

1. Wallace B. Donham, Elton Mayo, and George F. F. Lombard, *Teamwork and Labor Turnover in the Aircraft Industry of Southern California* (Boston: Harvard University Bureau of Business Research, 1944), foreword.
2. *The Foreman's Letter,* National Foremen's Institute, Inc., New York, November, 1945.
3. Excerpt from *Annual Report 1953–1954,* Industrial Relations Section, California Institute of Technology, Project 5, Surveys of Employee Opinion.
4. See Norman H. Martin, "Practical Politics in Administration," *Personnel Administration,* July-August, 1957.
5. For a more comprehensive treatment of these covert interpersonal relations, see William C. Schutz, "The Interpersonal Underworld," *Harvard Business Review,* July-August, 1958.
6. Frances M. Carp, Bart M. Vitola, and Frank L. McLanathan, "Human Relations Knowledge and Social Distance Set in Supervisors," *Journal of Applied Psychology,* **47,** No. 1 (1963), 78.
7. E. B. Hutchins and F. E. Fiedler, "Task-Oriented and Quasi-Therapeutic Role Functions of the Leader in Small Military Groups," *Sociometry,* **23** (1960), 393–406.
8. *The Foreman's Letter,* National Foremen's Institute Inc., New York, May 4, 1949, pp. 3–4.
9. See G. W. Peak, "The More 'Personal' Responsibilities of the Top Executive," *Advanced Management,* December, 1957.
10. Solomon L. Schwartz and Norman Gekoski, "The Supervisory Inventory: A Forced-Choice Measure of Human Relations Attitude and Technique," *Journal of Applied Psychology,* August, 1960.
11. Rensis Likert, "Motivation: The Core of Management," *Personnel Series,* No. 155, American Management Association, Inc., 1953, pp. 3–7.
12. Saul W. Gellerman, *Motivation and Productivity* (New York: American Management Association, Inc., 1963). Chapter 2 presents a summary and discussion of the Michigan studies.
13. Raymond A. Katzell, "Contrasting Systems of Work Organization," *The American Psychologist,* February, 1962.
14. See Erwin S. Stanton," Company Policies and Supervisors' Attitudes Toward Supervision, *Journal of Applied Psychology,* February, 1960, for report of a study that confirms the statement.
15. Stanley Schacter, Ben Willerman, Leon Festinger and Ray Hyman, "Emotional Disruption and Industrial Productivity," *Journal of Applied Psychology,* August, 1961.
16. W. K. Kirchner and D. J. Reisberg, "Differences Between Better and Less-Effective Supervisors in Appraisal of Subordinates," *Personnel Psychology,* Autumn, 1962, pp. 296–302.
17. J. S. Kidd and R. T. Christy, "Supervisory Procedures and Work-Team Productivity," *Journal of Applied Psychology,* **45,** No. 6 (1961), 392.
18. A. H. Maslow, "The Authoritarian Character Structure," *Journal of Social Psychology,* **18** (1943), 401–411.
19. John M. Pfiffner, "A Pattern for Improved Supervisory Leadership," *Personnel,* American Management Association, Inc., January, 1948, p. 271.
20. Norman R. F. Maier, "A Human Relations Program for Supervision," reprinted from *Industrial and Labor Relations Review,* **1,** No. 3 (1948).
21. For further information, see *Fortune,* August, 1950, p. 46.
22. *Business Week,* Apr. 9, 1949, pp. 102–103. By special permission.
23. *Op. cit.*
24. Schuyler Dean Hoslett, *Human Factors in Management* (New York: Harper & Row, Publishers, Inc., 1946), pp. 107–111.
25. *The Foreman's Letter,* National Foremen's Institute Inc., New York, Nov. 6, 1947.
26. See Erwin S. Stanton, "Role Playing for Training Supervisors in Human Relations," *The Office,* March, 1963.
27. See Gustav R. Stahl, "Role Playing in Training Supervisors," *Factory Management and Maintenance,* January, 1954, pp. 102–105.
28. See John H. Mann, "The Relation Between Role Playing Ability and Interpersonal Adjustment," *Journal of General Psychology,* April, 1960.
29. Alex Bavelas, "Role Playing and Management Training," *Publications in Social Science,* Series 2, No. 21, Department of Economics and Social Science, Massachusetts Institute of Technology, Cambridge, Mass. See also *Sociatry* **1,** No. 2 (1947), 183–191.
30. See Raymond A. Katzell, "Staffing and Developing the Organization," *Behavioral Science Research In Industrial Relations* (New York: Industrial Relations Counselors, Inc., 1962), pp. 113–114.
31. Irving R. Weschler, Marvin A. Klemes, and Clovis Shepard, "A New Focus in Executive Training," *Advanced Management,* May, 1955.
32. See Irving R. Weschler, Fred Massarik, and Robert Tannenbaum, "The Self in Process: A Sensitivity Training Emphasis," *Issues in Training,* Selected Reading Series Five, National Training Laboratories, National Educational Association of the United States, Washington, D.C., 1962, pp. 33–46.
33. Robert R. Blake and Jane S. Mouton, *The Managerial Grid* (Houston, Tex.: Gulf Publishing Company, 1964). Alfred J. Marrow, *Behind the Executive Mask* (New York: American Management Association, Inc., 1964), presents a description of that organization's program as well as data concerning some of the others.
34. "Behavioral Science—What's in It for Management?" *Business Management Record,* National Industrial Conference Board, Inc., June, 1963, pp. 43–44.
35. Glenn Gardiner, "Reaching the Individual Worker," a paper delivered before the second Annual Greater Philadelphia Safety Conference, May 27, 1935.

PROJECTS

1. Discuss the good and bad aspects of the foreman's procedure described in the following example.

    I recall a situation where a foreman in charge of an unloading crew went to the superintendent and recommended that inasmuch as certain roller conveyors had been put into use in the unloading of cars, a reduction in the tonnage rate paid to workers for unloading cars should be put into effect. His recommendation was accepted and a reduction in rates was installed.

    In announcing this reduction to his workers, the foreman explained to them that the superintendent had called him in and told him that rates would have to be cut.

    "In spite of everything I could do and in spite of every argument I could put up against this cut in rates, the superintendent insisted it had to be done anyhow," the foreman explained.[35]

2. Construct a rating scale for the use of a supervisor who wishes to have his employees rate him on his supervisory characteristics and ability. Keep the tone and purpose of the rating scale constructive rather than critical in nature.
3. Tell how you would deal with the following kinds of employees who are in need of executive attention:
    a. The employee who asks for a raise but does not deserve it.
    b. The employee who thoughtlessly gives a company secret to a competitor.
    c. The rank-and-file employee who masquerades as an important executive of the company.
    d. The salaried employee who was absent because of intoxication.
    e. The employee who pads his overtime card.
4. What rules should the supervisory executive follow, in order to be certain that his instructions to an employee are thoroughly understood by the employee?
5. What should be done by the executive who happens to appear unexpectedly among a group of workers on a day-wage basis of pay and finds that most of them are loafing on the job?
6. Tell how the autocratic type of executive might handle the cases listed in this chapter. What would be some of the possible reactions of the employee in each case? How could an intelligent, well-adjusted employee handle himself in such circumstances?
7. Several researchers have found that employees tend to do more work when they have a supervisor who gives them little close supervision, allowing them to feel responsible for their own work. What are some of the dangers or difficulties in such supervision?
8. Review the characteristics of one of your former supervisors or a present supervisor. To what extent does he apply the supervisory practices that develop teamwork?

COLLATERAL READINGS

Fleishman, Edwin A., *Studies in Personnel and Industrial Psychology.* Homewood, Ill.: The Dorsey Press, Inc., 1961, Chapters 33–39.

Gellerman, Saul W., *Motivation and Productivity.* New York: American Management Association, Inc., 1963, Chapter 20.

Gilmer, B. von Haller, *Industrial Psychology.* New York: McGraw-Hill Book Company, 1961, Chapters 8 and 9.

Haire, Mason, *Psychology in Management.* New York: McGraw-Hill Book Company, 1956, Chapters 3 and 5.

Karn, Harry W. and B. von Haller Gilmer, *Readings in Industrial and Business Psychology.* New York: McGraw-Hill Book Company, 1962, pp. 317–366.

Leavitt, Harold J. and Louis R. Pondy, eds., *Readings in Managerial Psychology.* Chicago: The University of Chicago Press, 1964, Chapters 5 and 6.

Likert, Rensis, *New Patterns of Management.* New York: McGraw-Hill Book Company, 1961, Chapters 7–11.

Surveys of how employees feel *about their jobs and relations with the company provide little benefit unless the findings are followed up. Most survey findings show the need for more information about areas such as company policies, benefit plans, new products, marketing programs, competition, company expansion programs, and other job-related activities.*

The American Can Company prepared a film as part of a well-planned communications program. At some plants seats were set up on the floor of a factory garage for the showing. In other places, theaters were rented for showing the 30–minute company film. Executives presided and answered questions. The film consisted of a description of the company's new products, its new divisions, what was being planned, how competition might be met, and how jobs could be maintained.

CHAPTER TWENTY-TWO

COMMUNICATION IN INDUSTRY—MORALE SURVEYS AND MEDIA FOR COMMUNICATION

Five thousand years ago an ancient Egyptian by the name of Ptah-Hotep wrote: "If you are in the position of one to whom petitions are made, be courteous and listen to the petitioner's story. Do not stop his words until he has poured out all that is in his heart and has said all that he came to say. A man with a grievance loves the official who will accept what he states and let him talk out his trouble fully. A kind word will illuminate his heart, but if an official stops the flow of his words people will say, 'Why should that fellow have the power to behave this way?' "[1]

Systematic surveys of employee attitudes began in the early 1920's. Now similar investigations are made each year in hundreds of companies with thousands of employees. One reason for the growth of attitude surveys in industry is the need for better communication with employees. Managements realize that they are often unaware of their workers' true feelings and resentments.

If you have been at all alert to social situations, you have had the experience of talking to a person who did not respond to what you were saying. You talked and he talked but you realized that he did not get meaning from what you said. Perhaps you, too, failed to get meaning from what he said.

Communication can be defined as the conveying and exchanging of meanings. Recently, it has become a highly appreciated problem in modern industry. Actually, the problem is as old as civilized life. Civilized life has always depended on communication. The reason why the problem is now gaining more attention is not because of a change in the nature of the problem but in our constantly developing complexity of modern industrial life. We now realize that as work teams have grown in size our techniques have not kept pace with the needs for intra-team and individual communication.

The Need for Improved Communications in Industry

Many communication relationships between managements and men are based on the assumption that the employees are interested in the same things as management: profits, lower prices, efficiency, and free enterprise.

Actually, the individual employee does not see things the way management does. The things important to management are not necessarily important to the employee. Management does *not* have an obligation to reform the employee who sees his situation in a manner quite different from the way management sees it; management *does* have the obligation to arrange its relations with employees so that both management and men can work together harmoniously and effectively.

Effective communication is a fundamental skill of modern management. Productivity in industry is largely a result of work team performance, the work team consisting of all members of an organization: officials, executives, supervisors, department heads, rank-and-file employees, and all their colleagues. Communication as a term used in industrial situations usually implies the two-way conveying of ideas: upward to management as well as from management downward to subordinates.

The effectiveness of communication often depends upon psychological factors such as attitude, motivation, skill, and the psychological climate where the words are used. Anyone, for example, who has participated in labor negotiations between an employer and a union knows that weeks of discussion may have taken place but there may have been very little real communication. There may have been much talk and little listening on the part of both parties to the controversy. Round the clock negotiations may have produced no agreement because deep-seated resentments prevented a meeting of minds.

Personality characteristics influence and are related to a person's attitudes and beliefs. Several research studies have demonstrated such relationships. Social scientists have, for example, studied the connections between attitudes toward big business and personality. Personal factors condition attitudes and beliefs as reported in this example:

> Suppose a man tells the interviewer that prices are too high, that big business is running everything these days, that the small fellow gets no break, and that all labor unions are run by gangsters. If this is all we know about the man, we are not very near to understanding him. We can perceive his bitterness and know that he probably does grind an axe when these attitudes are tapped. But we cannot see any sources of his feelings; and, most of all, we are still in the dark completely on how one might seek to change his attitudes.
>
> Suppose further, however, that we discover

that this man feels isolated, is a poorly paid low-ranking clerk, feels left out of the main stream of life, and that he has risen from a manual laborer's background, though he does not feel he has lived up to his own expectations. We can now better understand the connection between his expressed attitudes and his private world.[2]

Studies such as this one have emphasized to business leaders the need for training in psychological insight into the factors that color and control attitudes. Communications research has given impetus to the need for training in sensitivity to the other person's wants, to the need for facing frankly one's own wants, and to the establishing of a system of "feedback" in industry whereby the employee can give the communicator—the executive—a better understanding of the employee's ideas and needs. Most communication in management-employer relations is downward—only a trickle takes place in the other direction.

Management men who think that they have developed good lines of communication downward, upward and horizontally within their own organizations, often find that bottlenecks block the channels. The bottleneck may be in the form of individual supervisors who garble the message transmitted or they may be in the form of human motives, attitudes, and aspirations that management has failed to appreciate. The higher a man goes into management, the more he becomes dependent on the accurate exchange of information on all levels of his organization.

Every experienced person in industry knows that status relationships of superior-subordinate—formal organization structure—slow down the free interchange of information, ideas, suggestions and questions. The subordinate tends to tell his boss only what the latter is interested in hearing, and to cover up mistakes, failures, and bad news. He distorts information going up. This distortion also takes place in information going down. The superior does not always explain his problems to his subordinates.

In progressively managed companies, these status differences are not especially prominent in boss-employee relations. Each looks upon the other as a colleague in performing work. Well-managed companies realize that the spirit of colleagueship and openness of communication channels are not always operating as well as possible. Surveys of the situation are necessary to reveal bottlenecks, irritation points, and the effectiveness of management's messages.

Methods of Keeping Track of Morale

One investigator defined morale as the feeling of well-being that an individual experiences when his needs are being fulfilled to his satisfaction.[3] Other investigators regard morale as a synthesis of employee attitudes toward the employment situation. In general, it is regarded as a combination or complex of employees' attitudes which arise from the ways in which they perceive the factors in their work situation. It often influences the speed with which activities are carried out.

Several methods have been developed for getting factual reports of what employees think about their jobs, their supervisors, and their working conditions and of what they like or do not like about them.

The standard methods used to keep track of morale conditions are three:

Analysis of Company Records

Ups and downs in employee attitudes can be deduced to some extent from production and spoilage records. Marked changes in the production output of employees and increases of rejects from inspection of work produced are signals that something is happening to morale.

Attendance records may be significant. A morale sag may show up in excessive sick leaves, habitual tardiness, long lunch periods, and early quitting. Safety records, too, bear examination. Frequency of one-day absences has been found to be an especially reliable measure.[4] One study showed that workers in low absence groups at Detroit Edison revealed that they usually felt free to talk over job problems with their supervisors whereas those in high-absence departments did not. The former also reported that their supervisors held group discussions with them and were even willing to listen to their off-the-job problems.[5]

Employee Committees

These are used in some of the larger corporations. Committees, consisting of members from employee ranks, can indicate morale, spot causes of dissatisfaction, and help correct them. Any number of committees, each with a special field to cover, can be set up.

A large department store, for example, was dissatisfied with employee morale as reported by members of the personnel department and by supervisors. The management set up 22 committees, each with 20 members, to work on every conceivable phase of the morale problem. In the first two months, 500 specific complaints were received and processed. The store eliminated over half of the trouble spots at a cost of a few hundred dollars.

Morale Surveys

The most widely used systematic method is the employee attitude survey, or opinion poll, administered in questionnaire form.

This type of survey consists of a list of carefully prepared, written questions about the work situation which employees are usually asked to answer on an anonymous basis. If properly administered, tabulated, and interpreted, these responses give a representative picture of what employees think about the areas covered by the survey questions. The survey responses thus become a report of employee opinion or morale. The survey is often conducted for a company by an outside consultant such as a psychologist or by an industrial relations consulting firm. In most cases, technical know-how is required. Furthermore, outsiders are better able to keep the operation on a strictly confidential basis.[6]

Generally, the survey is conducted so that no information can be traced back to the person who gave it. Employees must be assured that they can express criticisms without any retaliation being possible. Also, they should understand why their answers are sought, that management is sincere in asking the questions, and that complete frankness will be helpful to both management and employees.

Questions for an Employee Relations Survey

The questions should express the spirit and purpose of the advanced change in thinking that has taken place in regard to modern employee relations. Formerly, employers thought that they should be most concerned about whether employees were contented in their jobs, liked the conditions of work, fringe benefits and other welfare aids. Modern managements realize that happiness and contentment are by-products of the employee's opportunities to achieve his own self-actualization in his work.

Yale J. Laitin, President of Survey Research Associates, has stated basic principles for making employee attitude surveys that express the principles learned from behavioral science studies:

1. *In drawing up the questions, emphasize the company's operations, policies, and procedures. Give people a chance to talk about their on-the-job situations. Think of morale as "the drive to work well' rather than as "contentment."*

Nowadays, though questions about "contentment" are still included, a good many surveys are also probing company operations and asking about specific policies and procedures—the issues most directly related to work accomplishment. It has become clear that in most American business firms workers and managers alike are more deeply frustrated by ineffectiveness in operations than by discontent with personal conditions.

Said an hourly worker in a chemical plant, "I get annoyed about our poor parking lot, but I can put up with that. What really gets me down—and I've lost sleep over it—is the way we waste so many batches because of production variances. This is no way to run a company."

A project engineer in a rubber company said, "I'm paid well and treated fine, but I'm looking for another job because I can't stand the buck-passing here. No one is willing to say, 'O.K., let's *do* it,' and I'm not free to do it on my own. I spend more time getting initials on authorizations to do things than I do on engineering, and I'm fed up with it."

A tool-maker picked up the piece of steel he was grinding and polishing and said, "See this? To me this is beautiful; I like to look at it and feel it and know it is just right. But when that hand truck comes through, it makes the grinding wheel chatter, and that flaws the tool. I stop grinding whenever I hear the truck coming, but I don't always hear it. I wish I could figure out an answer."

2. *Administer the survey not only to hourly workers but to all executives, supervisors, researchers, technicians and engineers, salesmen, and the like. The questions should, of course, be tailored to each specific group.*

Survey Research Associates' studies of 1,263 salesmen in 11 companies found that the 149 top producers tended to be more customer-oriented and business-oriented than the 133 lowest producers. While the low producers accepted the status quo in their companies' performance, delivery was never efficient enough to suit the top producers, and they were dissatisfied, too, with the way the home office handled their special requests for customers. The top producers were restless, always eager to provide the best possible service, price, product, and salesmanship. Clearly, the real pay-off would come from studying the top producers' responses for ideas on building sales and the low producers' responses for clues to the reasons for their poor performance and to the flaws in the company's selection methods.

As Albert F. Watters, General Foods' Vice President of Personnel, has noted, "The researcher, the engineer, the marketing specialist, the manager, the outside salesman are typical of [the] key people whose contributions to corporate growth and profitability far outweigh their numbers as expressed as a percentage of payroll. ...Their needs must be considered from a different perspective than that traditionally taken with respect to mass groups of factory employees."[7]

3. *Involve all top executives in the survey as fully as possible at the very start.*

...the need for involving top management right from the start is now being recognized as an integral part of survey procedure. The most effective way to do this is to give a voice in the initial decisions about the survey—including whether it should be held at all—to all executives who will be called upon to direct the follow-up. They should be made to understand that the survey is intended as a tool for their use as managers, not as a means of evaluating them. Accordingly, they should be individually consulted as to what subjects they would like covered and how and when the survey should be conducted in their departments. The more the survey works for them, the more they will do with it. In other words, if it is to succeed, the follow-up program must be recognized from the start as the major objective of the survey.

Asked what topics he would like covered in his company's forthcoming survey, a production manager who had at first seemed uninterested in the whole business suddenly sat up. "Can you find out about my production bonus?" he asked. "If you can tell me what's wrong there you'll have my gratitude for life."

4. *If you have a union, try to bring the union officers into the survey at the outset. Ask them to agree to questions about the union itself, and any subjects they are interested in. Include material about the union in the foremen's survey too. (Here, of course, the questions need not be cleared with the union.)*

Formerly, most surveys avoided union topics, though the union's activities do much to determine the nature of a worker's job and his perceptions of it affect him in any number of ways. Nowadays, questions about the union appear in a fair number of surveys, and are directed not only at hourly workers but also at foremen, whose views of the union and of the company's labor relations activities are equally important in determining how they handle their jobs. Recent studies have indicated that workers usually feel much the same about their union and their company: they are either pleased with both or dissatisfied with both.[8]

Many employee attitude surveys use the traditional "Evaluative" form of question as stated in "I sometimes wonder whether the foreman approves of my work," followed by a multiple-response scale such as 1. Strongly agree, 2. Agree, 3. Uncertain, 4. Disagree, 5. Strongly disagree. Research indicates that the "Descriptive" approach is likely to be more meaningful and less biased. This type of phrasing is exemplified in a fill-in form as in "My foreman let me know how I was doing ______ times in the past three days."[9]

Previous to making the survey, some companies interview a sampling of employees and use some of their statements as items for the questionnaire. Questions that are specific to the company are included. Usually, a scoring method or report-of-results outline should be planned in advance so the results may be presented in a usable form. It should be planned that results can be compared with rates of turnover, absenteeism and grievances as a check on the validity of the survey findings. When, for example, responses to 735 attitude questionnaires from ten different plants were statistically analyzed regarding group factors, the data indicated the presence of two group factors: one represented the perceived status of management's regard for employees personal rights and the other group represented perceived opportunities for self-improvement.[10]

It is also well to use a sample of employees in order to eliminate ambiguous items and items that fail to discriminate between employees of high and low morale.

Some managements believe that a printed questionnaire cannot produce the incisive results that are needed. They argue that as an example, when the typical married woman is asked why she wants to work, she is likely to answer that the family needs additional income. Probing in an interview may, however, reveal that she wants to escape from the monotony and loneliness of the home and to make herself feel that her life is worthwhile by satisfying her needs for self-actualization. Of course, few companies have persons on their payrolls who have had the necessary training or experience to conduct interviews of this nature. Outside consultants are usually necessary.

Typical Findings from Surveys

Eugene J. Benge, consulting psychologist, has conducted employee attitude surveys over a period of several decades in many companies. The findings show roughly that 20 to 30 per cent of employees seem to be somewhat on the unhappy side—that is, they check more negative than positive responses. Additional findings are:

> We find that women have better morale than men as a group; that the lowest morale appears between the ages of twenty and twenty-four and that it is higher before and after this age period; that employees start in jobs with high morale and that morale falls for a period of about five or six years before it starts to rise again; that low paid and high paid employees have higher morale than the medium paid; that the closer an employee approaches in earning power to his immediate supervisor, the lower his morale is likely to be. We also found that small companies tend to have better morale levels than big companies and that night shifts tend to have better morale than day shifts, contrary to usual thinking. Usually the latter is associated with the fact that night shifts approach working teams much more than do day shifts. By indirect reasoning we are sure that those who have left or are about to leave a concern have much lower morale than the average of that concern.[11]

The above findings represent a composite for the employees of a large number of factories, commercial and financial institutions, offices, and sales forces. When the Industrial Relations Section, California Institute of Technology, had completed a total of 25 surveys in 18 different companies, covering over 50,000 employees, the Section formulated a number of conclusions based on all of its studies of employee opinion. One of these was that "Morale is affected by length of service. Employees with less than a year of service have almost as high morale as employees with 25 years of service or more. The morale of employees declines with length of service, reaching its low point after 10 to 15 years of service. After this point, morale tends to increase."[12]

Individual companies that make a morale survey usually tabulate answers so that comparisons can be made by departments, men versus women employees, by wage brackets, and other factors.

Interestingly, one of the most common causes of low morale is the employee's inability to do good work because of poor equipment. Poor maintenance of equipment has marked effects on employee morale. Employees resent having to put up with an unnecessarily high percentage of down time due to machine failure, off-standard quality of materials used in work, and similar delays beyond their control. When they are unable to do good work, their morale is likely to be low as indicated by their adverse comments, absenteeism, tardiness, and high quit rates.[13]

Surveys of employee attitudes, opinions, and morale are made in many companies. These surveys should be viewed not as a means of analyzing the employees but of analyzing the effectiveness of management in its communications.

Benefits of Morale Surveys

Practically all companies that conduct morale surveys say they obtain new information about employee attitudes, and that results are helpful in giving a more exact measurement of attitudes that were known or expected prior to the survey. Employees' answers in most cases are analyzed by departments, divisions, or other work groups, to pinpoint the information from the survey.

The National Industrial Conference Board made a study of the reactions of production workers of two plants. The workers and plants were matched except for the one factor of communication. In Plant B the foremen had conducted monthly work-unit meetings in which reports were made on company matters such as vacation schedules, receipt of new orders, scrap reports, and so on. Also, workers were encouraged to make suggestions and offer their ideas. Plant A had no communication program of this nature. The Board prepared a questionnaire which was filled in but not signed before mailing it directly to the Board. The questions dealt with reactions to various aspects of communication and morale.

Typical questions and percentages of answers for the two plants were the following:

1. *Question. Have you been able to get your ideas up to the top men?*

Answers	*Plant A*	*Plant B*
I can almost always get my ideas up	21%	49%
I can sometimes get my ideas up	31	28
I can hardly ever get my ideas up	32	13
I am not interested in trying to get my ideas up	16	10

2. *Question. Does your company do a good job of telling you what's going on and what's being planned?*

Answers	*Plant A*	*Plant B*
It does a very good job	18%	55%
It does a fairly good job	60	31
It doesn't do much of this at all	22	14

3. *Question. Do you feel a part of your company?*

Answers	*Plant A*	*Plant B*
I feel I really belong	29%	62%
I feel I just work here	42	14
Sometimes I feel one way and sometimes the other	29	24

4. *Question. Generally speaking, how does your company compare as a company to work for compared with other companies that you know about or have worked for?*

Answers	*Plant A*	*Plant B*
One of the very worst	1%	0%
Worse than average	4	3
Just average	35	19
Better than average	40	33
One of the very best	20	45

One of the goals of communication is to develop a team spirit—to increase positive feelings toward the organization. The investigators concluded that the findings evidenced that communication is a powerful factor that affected the ideas and attitudes of employees of the two plants.[14]

Most companies that sponsor employee-opinion polls are convinced that management's willingness to let each employee have his say has good effects on the workers' morale. The findings usually reveal important points about any company communications program. The survey indicates the subjects on which employees could use more information, such as survivor protection and retirement planning.[15]

Management gains especially helpful benefits after a major change has been made in organizational structure or work procedures as in the case of mergers or the installation of a new incentive system. Executives expect some hostility, aggression or indifference as part of the first stage in any important developmental program. This is the initial reaction. Normally, it does not last. After sufficient

S R A Science Research Associates, Inc.

Instructions — THE CORE SURVEY — 7-1590

Purpose of the inventory

Your company would like to know what you think about your job, your pay, your boss, and the company in general. This inventory is designed to help you tell us your ideas and opinions quickly and easily without signing your name. This booklet contains a number of statements. All you have to do is to mark a cross by each statement to show how you feel. It is easy to do and you can be completely frank in your answers.

How to fill in the inventory

Read each statement carefully and decide how you feel about it. You will agree with some statements, and you will disagree with others. To help you express your opinions, you are offered three possible answers to some statements and four possible answers to others. For example:

1. This person prefers a small town to a large city.

	Agree	?	Disagree
I would rather work in a large city than in a small town.	☐	☐	☒

2. This person feels in no uncertain terms that the car parking situation should be remedied.

	Strongly Agree	Agree	Disagree	Strongly Disagree
The parking facilities here need improvement	☒	☐	☐	☐

This is not a test

There are no "right" answers and no "wrong" answers. It is your own, honest opinion that we want.

Work rapidly but answer all statements

Do not spend too much time on any one statement. If you cannot decide definitely about a statement, mark the answer you feel is most like your opinion, and go on to the next statement. Some of the statements may not be worded exactly the way you would like them. However, answer them the best way you can. Be sure to mark every statement.

Write or print your comments in the space provided. These comments may deal with things you particularly like, or matters you think need attention. Write something in the space, even if it is 'No comment.' Most people will find comments or suggestions to make.

General information

Do not sign your name on the inventory. Be sure to fill in the blanks for general information on the pages indicated. This information will be used only to make the results more meaningful. It will not be used to find out which inventory is yours.

Science Research Associates, *Chicago, publishes the SRA Attitude Survey, the most widely used instrument of its kind. It has been used to survey over 600,000 employees. Through the aid of interpreters it has been used to survey the attitudes of foreign-speaking employees—Japanese, Chinese, Spanish, Italian, and Filipinos.*

The survey is distinctive in that the percentage of favorable attitudes among one employee group toward various aspects of their employment can be compared with national norms. This enables management to identify more accurately the specific areas of strengths and weaknesses within the company and within departments of the company.

time has been allowed, the employees are expected to like the change and to object to going back to the old days. However, management wants to know whether the hoped-for acceptance has taken place and the approximate time when it does occur.[16]

Sometimes extra benefits can be obtained from an analysis of the records of those employees who do not respond to an opportunity to fill in a morale questionnaire. Morale surveys are usually conducted by having all employees of a given department or floor go to a central meeting room where they answer the inventory. In some companies, every employee is expected but not required to go. This is done to avoid the kind of bias that results when opinions are obtained from volunteers only. Several researches have shown that the volunteers differ in personality characteristics and in job performance from the nonvolunteers. In one company, for example, when attitude questionnaires were mailed to

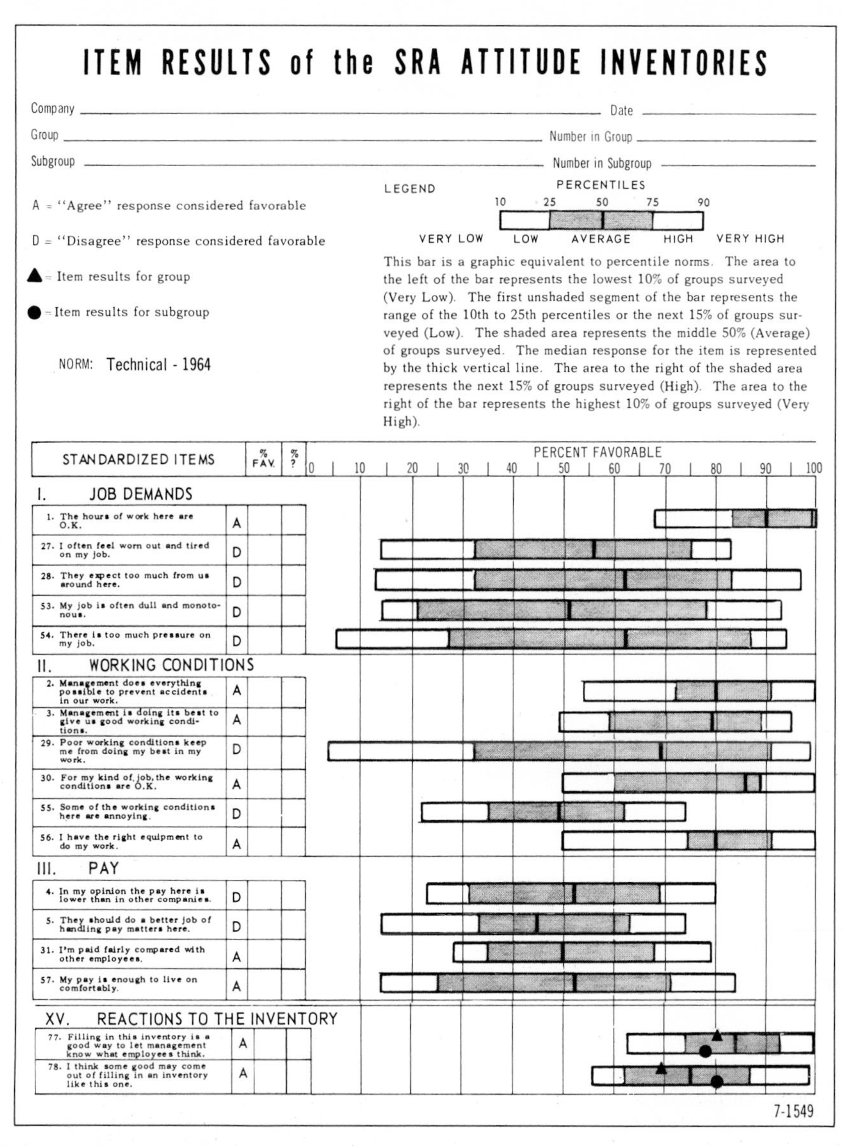

ITEM RESULTS of the SRA ATTITUDE INVENTORIES

Company ______________________ Date ______________

Group ______________________ Number in Group ______________

Subgroup ______________________ Number in Subgroup ______________

A = "Agree" response considered favorable

D = "Disagree" response considered favorable

▲ = Item results for group

● = Item results for subgroup

NORM: Technical - 1964

LEGEND

PERCENTILES

10 25 50 75 90

VERY LOW LOW AVERAGE HIGH VERY HIGH

This bar is a graphic equivalent to percentile norms. The area to the left of the bar represents the lowest 10% of groups surveyed (Very Low). The first unshaded segment of the bar represents the range of the 10th to 25th percentiles or the next 15% of groups surveyed (Low). The shaded area represents the middle 50% (Average) of groups surveyed. The median response for the item is represented by the thick vertical line. The area to the right of the shaded area represents the next 15% of groups surveyed (High). The area to the right of the bar represents the highest 10% of groups surveyed (Very High).

STANDARDIZED ITEMS		% FAV.	% ?
I. JOB DEMANDS			
1. The hours of work here are O.K.	A		
27. I often feel worn out and tired on my job.	D		
28. They expect too much from us around here.	D		
53. My job is often dull and monotonous.	D		
54. There is too much pressure on my job.	D		
II. WORKING CONDITIONS			
2. Management does everything possible to prevent accidents in our work.	A		
3. Management is doing its best to give us good working conditions.	A		
29. Poor working conditions keep me from doing my best in my work.	D		
30. For my kind of job, the working conditions are O.K.	A		
55. Some of the working conditions here are annoying.	D		
56. I have the right equipment to do my work.	A		
III. PAY			
4. In my opinion the pay here is lower than in other companies.	D		
5. They should do a better job of handling pay matters here.	D		
31. I'm paid fairly compared with other employees.	A		
57. My pay is enough to live on comfortably.	A		
XV. REACTIONS TO THE INVENTORY			
77. Filling in this inventory is a good way to let management know what employees think.	A		
78. I think some good may come out of filling in an inventory like this one.	A		

7-1549

Companies who use the SRA Attitude Survey *can graph the morale of individual departments on profile charts like this one. Here the triangles or the last two items indicate how one department feels about jobs, pay, and the company management. The circles show how the employees as a whole reacted to the same questions. (Item categories IV–XIV are omitted here.) Findings of one study showed, for example, that the workers have strong loyalty towards their immediate supervisors and fellow employees. On the other hand, they are not enthusiastic about management or working conditions.* ***SRA*** *scores the survey and delivers a report of results along with follow-up recommendations for management's consideration.*

The set of 78 questions *provides a comprehensive survey, and space for an additional 21 special questions specific to a company and/or 31 specific to a function, insures the instrument's flexibility.*

The Attitude Survey *uses easy-to-understand language. Since it requires only a few minutes to administer, it can be given during working hours with little disruption or loss of production time. The brief time required for answering the questions is equally important where the* ***Survey*** *is given to employees on their own time. Because employees are asked not to sign their names, they are willing to answer frankly. Management can use the* ***Attitude Survey*** *to: (1) Measure morale for a company as a whole; (2) Compare morale between departments or plants in an organization; (3) Compare morale in one company with the average of others, particularly in the same industry.*

By using the ***Attitude Survey*** *to find out what employees really think, companies can pin-point weak departments, increase the effectiveness of supervision, learn if communication is adequate, discover training needs, improve employee relations, build good will, and cut employee turnover. The* ***SRA Attitude Survey*** *is published by* ***Science Research Associates, Inc.,*** *259 East Erie, Chicago, Illinois, 60611.*

STEPS IN

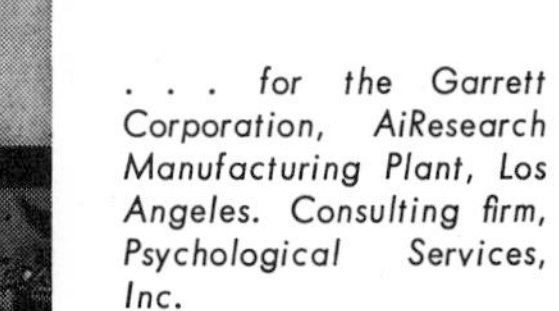
. . . for the Garrett Corporation, AiResearch Manufacturing Plant, Los Angeles. Consulting firm, Psychological Services, Inc.

1. **Survey begins** *when industrial relations staff formulates questions. From left are John Muchmore, staff assistant; Chuck Wetmore, industrial relations manager, Phoenix; Duke Reynolds, vice-president, industrial relations; Jerry Bradley, industrial relations manager, Los Angeles. Division managers often help.*

2. **Mail room (right)** *addresses and sends surveys. No one in The Garrett Corporation will ever again see them.*

3. **Employee** *fills out survey in privacy of his home. Best results are obtained when questions are answered as soon as received.*

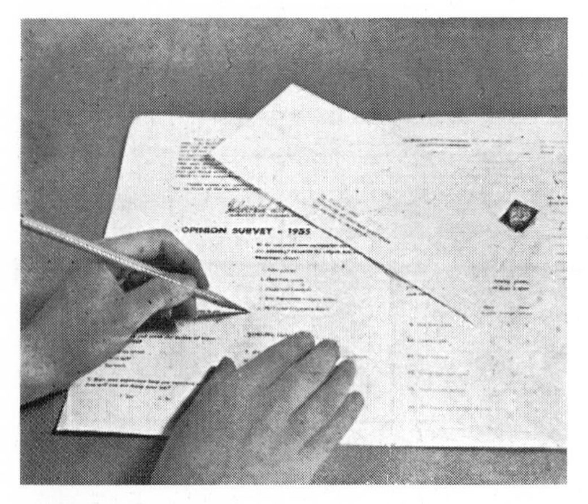

4. **When mailed,** the completed survey goes to Psychological Services, Inc. Maximum return means maximum value of survey.

5. **Mail clerk** *at office of Dr. Floyd Ruch, head of Psychological Services, removes completed questionnaire from envelope, which is destroyed along with postmark and return address.*

*6. **Answers** to specific questions are punched onto tabulation cards for statistics necessary to evaluate survey results. Verbatim comments are ignored at this point.*

*7. **Verbatim comments** are transcribed by a typist at Psychological Services so there will be no way of recognizing handwriting. Comments are grouped by departments, but no other information supplied by employee is used here. There is no way to connect verbatim answers afterward with such information as employee's length of service.*

*8. **Dr. Floyd Ruch** personally supervises burning of the questionnaires. The last step in the program of scientific secrecy has been taken, assuring accuracy of the survey.*

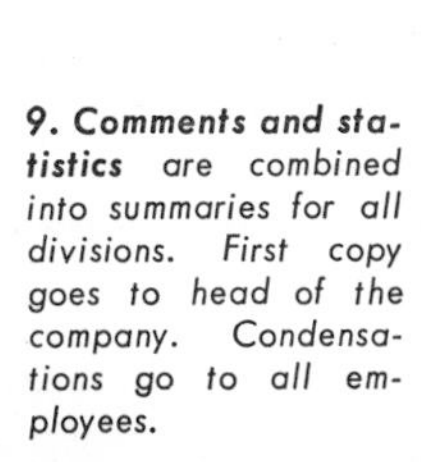

*9. **Comments and statistics** are combined into summaries for all divisions. First copy goes to head of the company. Condensations go to all employees.*

*10. **Conferences** are held with department and division heads. Herb Stout, AiResearch, Los Angeles, machine shop general foreman, maps action on needed improvement with Don Bromley, personnel. All comments must be investigated.*

91 salesmen in one division of a large, midwestern manufacturing concern, 72 salesmen responded. After two follow ups, 19 non-respondents remained.

The two groups of respondents and non-respondents were then compared in terms of two objective measures of performance: (a) net sales points; (b) net total points. Net sales points were gained by direct selling of the product; net total points included net sales points plus points gathered in other ways as in the collection of delinquent accounts.

Respondents differed significantly from non-respondents in terms of both net sales points and net total points achieved. For example, respondents averaged 123.5 more net sales points higher and 102.8 more net total points higher than non-respondents.

The researcher pointed out that "It is possible that respondents give more favorable responses because they are better performers and presumably more satisfied. In any case, respondents do differ in this study from non-respondents in terms of actual job performance with the findings reinforcing the oft-found result from past research that respondents are generally 'better.' This now seems true as well in an actual work situation in an industrial setting."[17]

Putting Morale Survey Results to Work

Obviously, making an attitude or morale survey is only a first step in the improvement of communications within a company. Generally, managements agree that at least two uses can be made: one, the findings can be reported to the employees and two, remedial actions can be taken to improve the situations that need it.

Some managements conduct meetings with supervisors and employees in order to clarify the reasons for negative findings. Shortcomings on the part of management are brought into open discussion and improvements in managerial practices and communications are developed. If such "feedback" sessions are conducted in a sincere and constructive spirit, later surveys of employee morale are likely to produce higher percentages of favorable reactions to conditions that were previously found to be "least liked" by the employees.

Anyone who participates in feedback sessions of this kind is likely to become convinced that the results of morale surveys can be made far more beneficial to employees and employers than speeches by executives or educational conferences.

Experimental Study of the Value of Feedback of Attitude Survey Results

Relatively few experiments have been set up to measure the benefits of attitude survey feedbacks. Robert E. Schwab has reported one of several studies of this type.

The Institute for Social Research, Survey Research Center, University of Michigan, made an intensive survey of the attitudes of employees and supervisors of a company:

> Written questionnaires were administered to all non-supervisory employees, and all supervisors and members of management were interviewed concerning their work attitudes. In addition, ten per cent of the non-supervisory employees from groups identified through the questionnaire as having high or low morale were given personal interviews. The resulting information about attitudes of employees toward their jobs, their supervisors, company benefits, pay, their chances for promotion, and various other factors in the work situation was sent back down the line for discussion. Comparisons between departments and work groups were made available, and both supervisors and employees were asked to interpret the results and make recommendations for the solution of problems which were present. Here again many changes were made which resulted in better understanding and improved working effectiveness.
>
> In one department, a controlled experiment was set up in which supervisors of certain work groups held a series of discussions with employees about their own group attitudes as revealed by a survey. In other work groups the results were reported back to employees but without the opportunity for group discussions led by the supervisor. In those groups where discussions were held over a period of several months, there was

a measurable improvement in the attitude of the employees toward their jobs, their supervision, their opportunities in the company, and various other factors in the work situation. In those groups in which discussion was not held, relatively little change in attitude took place.

This experiment would seem to indicate that sharing of a group's own problems with them and freedom to discuss such problems with the supervisor result in more favorable attitudes in the work group. Another very interesting fact was that greater change in employees' attitudes occurred in this situation than in other departments where employees' attitudes were studied after their supervisors were given training in human relations.[18]

Limitations of a Morale Survey

Even though a morale survey usually produces some benefits it also has or may have some drawbacks. These are:

1. Its impersonality. The employee who fills in a questionnaire which he does not sign may fail to get the satisfaction that is obtained from face-to-face communication. On the other hand, many employees will state criticisms anonymously on paper that they would not state in face-to-face situations.

2. In too many cases, surveys are made and the results are filed but the employee never again hears or sees any evidence that his criticisms and recommendations were acted upon. As a result, the individual employee feels that he has been whistling into the wind. Managements that ask for criticisms are obligated to act upon them or to explain why they cannot be acted upon.

3. Results are usually presented to management and employees statistically. Majority responses are studied more carefully than minority findings. And yet a minority feeling that is intense, such as a strong resentment against a wage differential, may give rise to action that overwhelms the majority of employees.

4. Questionnaire attitude surveys indicate the nature of some broad problems such as whether morale is high or low, but they do not, as a rule, break the problems down in terms of the individual employee and his needs. The individual employee is a member of a group and has certain group relations but his problems are personal and individual. Even though he has strong group loyalties, he still wants to be treated as an individual.

5. Certain pitfalls must be recognized when evaluating results of questionnaire attitude surveys. One of the most difficult to avoid is the wording of questions in such form that the desired response can be indicated. Another pitfall is the oversimplified question that forces employees to make absurd or unrealistic choices. For example: "Would you rather have the company spend its available money for new machines in the plant, for more parking space, or for a better technical library?"

6. The time lag in collecting the data and writing the report causes interest in the survey to cool off. The results of a survey are not available for a month or two. During this time, the interest of management and employees is likely to cool. Executives, for example, may say, "Things have changed during the past sixty days. Hence, the findings no longer apply."

7. Certain aggravating situations cannot be corrected because of financial or other limitations. Bad working conditions such as the need for air conditioning cannot be corrected unless the company can afford it. The company may not have the money to buy the equipment. Executives may agree to the desirability of the recommended changes but the money needed to make them is not available. Similar difficulties occur in regard to poor supervision. A specific supervisor may be very competent in so far as his technical abilities are concerned but a poor leader of men. And yet, his job may require his technical abilities even more than good supervisory skills.

8. Surveys do not emphasize the mutuality of working interests between management and men. Instead, they put the management on the defensive. The very nature of a survey implies that it is up to management to correct every disliked condition.

Some companies such as Champion Paper

and Fibre Company design the survey to not only uncover roadblocks that handicap the company's progress internally but also to "offer an opportunity to further the development of problem-solving skills among its managers and demonstrate to managers the importance of tapping the ideas of their people."[19] Many morale surveys of the past did put management somewhat on the defensive but the current trend is in the direction of using the plan to promote constructive thinking on the part of both management and men. Instead of asking, "What is wrong?" more questions are stated in the spirit of "What ideas do you wish to offer to improve what we are doing?"

"Satisfiers" and "Dissatisfiers"

Formerly, it was assumed by managements that all that was necessary to keep workers happy and productive was to provide good working conditions, good wages, and fewer hours of work. When this idea did not bring about either happiness or motivation, managements added more benefit programs and more pleasant working conditions. A recent research study shows why such policies have not succeeded in motivating employees.

Frederick Herzberg and his colleagues of the Psychological Service of Pittsburgh conducted careful interviews using the critical incident technique with some 200 engineers and accountants who worked for eleven different firms in the Pittsburgh area. These men were asked to recall a time when they felt especially good about their jobs. The interviewers probed for factors that brought about their good feelings. They were also asked to describe sequences of events that resulted in negative feelings about their jobs. In both kinds of questions they were asked to describe effects these incidents had on their attitudes and on their performance and whether these effects were of short or long duration.

The findings demonstrated that when these men felt good about their jobs, it was usually because something had happened which showed that they were doing their work particularly well or that they were becoming more expert in their professions. Good feelings were related to the specific tasks that the men performed, not to background factors such as money, working conditions, status, or security. On the other hand, when they felt bad it was usually because some disturbance in these background factors had caused them to feel that they were being treated unfairly.

This led the Pittsburgh researchers to draw a distinction between what they called "satisfiers" and "dissatisfiers," or *motivators* and the *hygienic factors*. A motivator is an influence that usually has an uplifting effect on attitudes or performance. Hygienic factors produce no improvement in productivity but rather serve to *prevent losses* of morale or efficiency. Hygienic factors are prerequisites for effective motivation but they do not by themselves motivate the individual. They only prevent serious dissatisfaction or drop in productivity and make it possible for motivators to operate.

Pay, job security, status, and working conditions are hygienic factors. When they are unsatisfactory, they do have adverse effects on the men's attitudes and effectiveness. However, managements should not expect high motivation to develop simply through paying men well or through providing fringe benefits and an attractive place to work. To deprive the men of these things is likely to cause their motivation to deteriorate very rapidly.

Praise and pats on the back had only a temporary effect. The lasting good feelings were caused by the motivators: being assigned to stimulating work, having considerable responsibility, being advanced to positions of increased importance, freedom to exercise initiative, and the privilege of handling problems in their own way.[20] Herzberg also found that the mentally healthy person seeks happiness from the growth factors, to acquire knowledge and skill right where he is, and he seeks the avoidance of dissatisfaction from the hygiene factors. In contrast, the mentally ill person is a hygiene seeker even though these factors are largely beyond his control.[21]

Some managements still assume that morale

We don't let them know where they stand. *One of the basic needs of any employee is to know how he's doing. Apparently, we're not giving enough attention to satisfying this need. Too many of us probably assume the man can figure it out himself. He might be able to, but he wants* ***you*** *to confirm it. Many of us will probably protest that we already spend more than enough time doing just that, but it's not always how much time we spend on it, it's how honestly we approach it.*

We don't give enough attention to showing them how to do their work better. *If employees think they can do better work, and want to, we ought to jump at the chance to help them. This doesn't mean we have to hold their hands and stand over their shoulders every minute. But it might indicate that many of our people expect more of themselves than we do.*

We don't always give credit where it's due.

To repeat: *We can't afford to treat these findings as the complaints of a bunch of malcontents. The surveys show that an employee who is dissatisfied with one aspect of his relationship with his manager is likely to be unhappy in other areas. We can't keep everybody happy about everything all the time. But we can take a hint from these studies. There are many IBM managers who* ***have*** *recognized these complaints as valid, and have successfully done something about it.*

Interpretive information given to managers. *When a company has made an employee opinion survey, top management usually informs other members of management of the findings and encourages them to pay special attention to adverse findings. When International Business Machines made a survey of the employees of four plants, the results indicated that the great majority of the employees were enthusiastic about the company, their work, their fellow employees, pay and benefits, and their IBM opportunities. However, there were also dissatisfactions, largely in the area where manager meets employee. Some of the dissatisfactions and recommendations made to the managers were given in illustrated form.*

can be achieved by having the company do kindnesses *for the employees* or by solving all their problems. Many executives fail to realize that morale is highest when employees also do things *for the company.* Morale and loyalty are best when employees as well as executives devote their efforts to the success of the company, when employees realize that they as well as management are essential to the company's success, and when management and employees work together in a spirit of operating a mutual enterprise.

Management can gain little by a display of fatherly generosity toward employees who are treated as children. On the other hand, both management and employees gain growth and competence when management treats employees as colleagues in their joint economic enterprise.

In its usual form, a morale survey is a device that helps management to listen. And to communicate effectively, management must "listen." The ability to "listen" is also essential to the understanding of the other person's motivations.

Morale and Productivity

The work of early researchers into human relations, and the studies which grew out of the classic Western Electric Company Hawthorne experiment, have tended to confirm the common-sense point of view that a satisfied worker is more productive than a dissatisfied one. However, recent investigations have indicated that the relationship between morale and performance is not so self-evident or so simple as was once assumed. Cases have been found where high morale has been found to accompany either high or low productivity; and, conversely, low morale has been found where productivity is either high or low.

Arthur Brayfield and Walter Crockett, of Kansas State College, made a comprehensive survey of attitude studies.[22] They concluded that there is little evidence that employee attitudes of the *type usually measured in morale studies* bear any simple—or, for that matter, appreciable—relationship to performance on the job. This finding should be expected in some companies because statistically-measurable changes in productivity depend upon many factors other than morale: the alertness of management, the competence of employees, and the motivational drives of the individual executives and employees. After all, lazy and incompetent workers may be just as satisfied with their work situations as the industrious and competent members of a work group.

A key finding of the studies by the University of Michigan, Institute of Social Research, has been that there is a marked relationship between an employee's productivity and job satisfaction on the one hand and, on the other, the kind of supervision he receives. The highest productivity and the highest morale have consistently been found to result from employee-centered supervision as opposed to supervision of the production-centered type.

The present stage of research indicates that companies cannot look to specific types of morale-building programs for a complete solution to the problem of building a productive and satisfied work force. Instead, it must be recognized that morale has its origins not in any particular "program" but right on the job—in the relationship between the supervisor and the worker. Furthermore, this relationship must be carried on by competent, well-motivated individuals who function in a favorable psychological climate. This suggests that if morale and productivity are to be linked together, management must find ways to select and develop more supervisors and workers who are capable of putting the principles of sound communications and good human relations into practice. The media of communications, such as employee publications and bulletin boards, do not in themselves bring about high morale and productivity—they are useful aids in the hands of intelligent managements and employee-centered supervisors.

COMMUNICATIONS: MEDIA AND METHODS

The term "communication" connotes many media and methods. It is applied to any kind of behavior that leads to exchange of ideas and includes media such as personal telephone calls, feature stories in a company publication, office memoranda, speeches to employees, and group conferences. Communication in itself is not an end or a goal. Rather, it is a universal tool for conveying meaning and—particularly for management—a factor in inducing action. Problems in communication may arise from poor acoustics, semantic confusion, emotional resistances, and bottlenecks in channels of transmitting messages.

In industry, the channels of communication are of three types,—up-line, down-line, or cross-line, depending on the direction from the source to the ultimate receipt of the information. Unless each avenue of communication is kept clear and is used effectively, serious problems may result. A block in the up-line channel, for example, may leave top executives feeling walled off from their employees, while a break in down-line or cross-line communications may damage morale and increase the traditional friction between line and staff members.

Obviously, treatment of all aspects, problems, methods, and media in communications would require several volumes. In this section, the major emphasis will be placed on those that involve management's means of communicating information, action plans, and attitudes to employees—that is, down-line communications. Two methods of achieving up-line communications will also be discussed.

What Do Employees Want to Know?

Numerous surveys indicate that an especially important interest of employees is the security of their jobs and the factors about the company which enable them to think that their jobs are even more secure than they had thought.

Generally, employees not only feel that they should know more about the company for which they work, but they also want information *regularly* about manufacturing operations, about future company plans, about new products and the story behind the progress being made in the development of new products.

Most employees have a sincere interest in the company's competitive position and long-range outlook. They want to know the company's products and plans well enough to discuss them intelligently when they talk with people on the outside. An employee has an opportunity to feel important when he can answer the questions of his family and friends about the company's plans and prospects.

An intelligent executive of today realizes that as a leader he should transmit not only the information that employees seek but also certain information that they may not be consciously seeking. He should anticipate their wishes by providing information that improves their working relations even though they are not always aware of what they need. A good leader has the larger perspectives that enable him to use his initiative in setting forth those facts and interpretations that strengthen the team spirit.

The wished-for development of true understanding between management and labor is a big and continuous task. A complete solution has not been found, but better communication—the sharing of meaningful information by both parties—moves in a helpful direction. Some of the ways in which this is being attempted are discussed in the following sections.

DOWN-LINE COMMUNICATIONS

Employee Publications

To supplement other methods of communication, many firms have utilized the company house organs of the employee publication variety. Though some date back to the turn of the century, widespread use of company magazines is relatively recent. The precise number of such publications is not known, but one investigator estimated the total as 10,000. This includes those of small companies as well as medium and large firms.

In the interest of bettering morale, most company publications run personal recognition stories, recreation stories, department and division news; and "personals." Almost all give information about the company to employees. Informative material includes articles on safety, profits, expansion programs, product improvements, employee benefits, business outlook, the company's role in national defense, company policies, and union-management news. Some carry stories on the role of taxes and financial reports on the economics of business and give information on competition and profits.

An employees' magazine can be entertainingly educational as well as merely entertaining. For instance, many employees believe that advertising is a waste of money and that their wages could be raised if those funds were added to the wages. Many others think that orders are easy to get, that any business can borrow plenty of money, that the government could operate all businesses more cheaply than private concerns, that there is a fixed amount of money in the world, and that factory workers have all the "grief" and office workers all the "snap" jobs. Such erroneous impressions can be corrected by including humorous comic strips or chatty articles in the magazine which drive home the point. To an extent, some of the editors have seemed to realize this need and have attempted to experiment with cartooning and other features. But most editors, while close to management in the sense that they identify themselves with management, paradoxically have done a poor job of selling management to the employees.

Such editors have limited their pages to friendly personals, bowling scores, or editorials on plant safety. This type of news is good to a degree. But more and more of these editors are beginning to realize the great potentialities of their media. More are reporting such news as information on new orders, installations of modern equipment, certain data on the cost of producing and selling the products, and the allocation of the company's income dollar. In short, these more enterprising editors have taken it upon themselves to explain to the employee the factors operating in a free enterprise system. Some editors have ventured to discuss even labor problems—legislation and strikes—in their pages.

The humor page is a standby of the less venturesome and nonprogressive editors. The joke used as "filler" appears to be disappearing. Communications people are disposed to agree that a joke page or jokes used as fillers are essentially space users and nothing else. The joke page does have high readership but it does not serve any useful purpose beyond that of entertaining.

The sports page, when done properly, is a genuine readership builder, and surveys have indicated that such pages help to pull male readers into the rest of the publication.

The *company's magazine advertisements* to the consumers and the trade are reproduced in many employee publications. These reproductions show the end products to the people who helped create them. When this is done, experience indicates that it is well not to publish the advertisement without a special explanation for the employees. The explanation should be presented in an adjacent block of copy where the advertisement appears. This block of copy tells where the advertisement has appeared, how many people it may reach, and the purposes that lay behind its creation. The employee and his family have a real curiosity about the company's product and take pride in making a product that is used by thousands or even millions of customers.

For the open "question-box" policy to be effective, management must be ready to accept and answer any question and to be irritated at none. The executive who accepts the assignment of answering questions must answer all questions: those which are stupid or unfair as well as the ones that are sensible.

Signed editorials on socialism, profits, and so on, do well, while economic news does even better. When one company published a feature telling about contracts the company bid for and won or lost, it got a phenomenal 84 per cent "read some" and 83 per cent "read most" scores for the feature.[23]

Experience indicates that the company organ or magazine should avoid being so management-conscious that the employees feel that they are receiving only company platitudes. The idea is not to propagandize the employees, but to create harmony between the employees and management. Whenever the executive of a company has an impulse to explain some policy in the pages of the magazine, he should first discuss the matter with his editor. This editor should be free to express his honest opinions to superior officers.

The theme for house organs to emphasize is simple: management cannot get along without the employees, and the employees cannot get along without management. Each complements the other. It is to their mutual benefit to make the relationship a happy, profitable one.

There is some evidence that the employee publication pays off. When falling profits in the face of increased sales alerted the management of Johns-Manville Company to the need for paring costs, the employee newspaper was assigned an important role in explaining the situation to a "Work Smarter, Not Harder" campaign, pulled no punches, but ran articles on business lost, competition's inroads, and quality complaints from customers. The problem of rising costs was gradually overcome and the chairman of the board credited the employee paper with the major share in bringing about the improvement.[24]

Financial Reports about the Company to Employees

Many business leaders believe in the doctrine of sharing operating facts with their employees. They publish financial reports for the benefit of employees as well as stockholders. They make surveys of the rate of profit that the employee considers fair and show that the rate actually made by the employer is less than that. Yet, when this fact is pointed out to the employee, he still believes that the company makes too much! This attitude has been extremely disconcerting to executives who sought to gain the good will of employees by means of published reports about the company, its profits, plans, and so forth.

The procedures, mostly ineffective, used by managements in attempts to gain acceptance by their employees of facts favorable to the company have been the following:

1. Managements have presented the facts in a "protestation of virtue" manner, particularly about profits made and salaries paid officers of the company.

2. The basically sound reasons for the effectiveness of free enterprise as an economic system have been used as an argument for friendliness toward the employer.

3. Managements have thought of security in terms of sickness benefits, old-age pensions, and guaranteed annual wages. Employees think of security as a sense of job satisfaction.

4. Managements have assumed that the technical terms of accounting and finance are beyond the comprehension of most employees. Business leaders, particularly those in the accounting fields, have recognized the psychological ineffectiveness of current methods of giving accounting information to employees.

Ross G. Walker made a study of a Controllership Foundation, Inc., report. A few of his more significant conclusions are:

> That there appears to be general agreement with the premise that lack of understanding and acceptance of the facts and figures of business are not altogether due to the way reports are prepared; but that this is part of a large problem with which management is confronted; viz., that of creating acceptance for, and instilling confidence in, our American capitalistic system.
>
> ...That in the case of employees, personal

contact is regarded as being more effective than written messages.

> ...to me the survey findings make one conclusion unavoidable: that management is typically bent on looking for appropriate remedial action in handling the misinformed employee exclusively within the agreeable master-servant framework. If there is a failure of "confidence" at the lower levels of organization, management feels it must be from some error in the direction of affairs within that framework, and whatever action is taken must be consistent with the basic acceptability of that framework as an industrial way of life.[25]

Of course employees will not believe facts presented to them as long as the employer presents them in the master-servant framework. The employer can hope to gain acceptance of facts when he keeps in mind the old psychological principle: "People believe as they participate." Facts in themselves are not sufficiently forceful in changing the attitudes of employees toward the employer. The devices of communication such as financial reports, conferences, and house organs cannot be effectively used as ends in themselves nor even as means toward educating employees and supervisors to understand management. Rather, the devices of surveys and communication should be incidental parts of a socially mature philosophy of management. The philosophy should be one of a desire to exchange ideas, to participate mutually in the work of the enterprise, to understand and respect each other in the daily face-to-face relationships.

Bulletin Boards

Bulletin boards are an essential means of communication in most plants. To be effective, however, their use must be supervised. If notices are allowed to accumulate on them for months, employees will decorate them with witty remarks and cartoons. Hence, when an important notice is posted, it is likely to be neglected by the workers.

The bulletin board should be painted, enclosed in glass, and lighted. The inside of the board should have a number of brass nails upon which small colored boards can be hung. Every bulletin should be tacked to one of these colored boards. As the colors are changed, they gain attention for the new notices. Several headline boards should be prepared for special types of notices—"Read the bulletin today," "The cause of an accident," "See our national advertising," or "What our competitors are doing."

The bulletin board should have photographs to illustrate the principles of safety. Broken goggles and old shoes may be displayed if they have played an important part in an accident. Human interest pictures of employees who have caught a big fish while on a camping trip, the bride and groom of a recent plant marriage, and valuable suggestions made by employees are examples of items that can be posted. The bulletin board never should be used for sermonizing by the general manager. It should be kept inviolate for the interest and information of the employees. As a rule, all notices should be changed or reserved for change every three days.

The boards should be located where the employee traffic is heavy but slow. The area of the time clock is a poor choice because traffic is fast. Restrooms are likely to be good locations.[26]

The bulletin board and similar forms of written communication have definite limitations. When management wants its employees to grasp changes in a company policy, it rarely succeeds by simply passing on the information in written form. The most effective way of transmitting information is by combining oral and written methods, according to a study which included 1,030 Purdue University students; 84 employees of a corporation in Lafayette, Indiana; and 528 employees in a mail-order chain-store firm—Spiegels, Inc., of Chicago. These last-mentioned employees were in the warehouse facilities, not in the retail departments. If use of this combination of methods is not possible, then oral communication is next-best. Just writing a message is the least effective of these three methods.[27]

CROSS-LINE AND UP-LINE COMMUNICATION

The Grapevine

The "grapevine" is a familiar variety of communication that peddles news and gossip wherever a working force consists of more than one person. The term "grapevine" probably arose because it was thought to be a long, winding means of communication from one point to another—like a real grapevine. But it is now recognized that the grapevine is often faster and more direct than so-called direct, formal channels of information.

The grapevine is typically considered to apply to workers, but investigations indicate that it is also active among management. Wherever there are people, there are grapevines.

Grapevines are likely to be especially troublesome in plants where union officials and management representatives distrust each other. Where management and employees get along amicably in union as well as in other relations, grapevines are not so likely to function irresponsibly. In the absence of suspicion and distrust, the natural tendency is for both parties to talk over their problems regularly, calmly, and objectively. Hence, the evils of rumor-mongering are diminished.

Most employers realize that the information the grapevine passes along is frequently disturbing to employee morale and to the company. Quite often it is misleading if not downright wrong.

One evil inherent in grapevines is that they become vehicles by which office "politicians" conduct whispering campaigns. Sometimes they reveal management secrets before the time appropriate for official announcement. They may even ruin reputations of individual employees or executives.

Grapevines do have one value. They are an effective safety valve at times when a management plans to make changes in policies or programs but is uncertain as to how employees will react to them. If the plans "leak out" and are discussed, the results may become a trial balloon. Just as some management attitudes are passed down through the grapevine, so also employee reactions are passed up.

Obviously, the grapevine is likely to stay in spite of its many evils and few virtues. As a result, managements today are trying to learn how to live with it. In some cases, it can be made to work for employer and employee benefits. From management's point of view, the main problem is to supply the grapevine with facts in order that misinformation may not be relayed. Plans that have been tried by managements are the following:

1. *The rumor clinic.* In small group meetings, employees are asked what rumors they have heard recently. Such discussions may report that the plant is going to be moved or that a 10 per cent raise is coming through. If a rumor is true, management fills in any details which may be lacking so that the full story may become known. If there is no basis for the rumor, management presents the true situation.

2. *A "Sounding Board"* for rumors is part of the employee communications program at one company. Feeling the need of a speedier method for dealing with rumors than was provided by existing employee communications devices, management posted "Rumor Boards" at key plant locations, with the legend: "Rumors flying? Get the *right* answers here." Attached was a pencil and a pad of paper with the instructions: "Write down the question or rumor you want answered in the space below."

As might be expected, however, many questions which employees post on the boards are not strictly rumors. Some are complaints, some are criticism. But seldom are the boards empty.

The board is checked daily by members of the personnel department, who contact the proper person to answer the question, type the answer, and post it on the board. The question is usually answered the same day it is posted on the board.

3. *Putting the grapevine to constructive use* may be accomplished by having meetings with the "natural leaders" in employee ranks. Management tries to keep these key employees informed on the theory that this will ensure that the facts reach other rank-and-filers in undistorted form.

Robert Hershey has suggested the following methods as means of controlling and reducing the harmful effects of rumoring:

> Keep the normal channels of communication open—rumors are found in the absence of reliable information.
>
> Don't use public address systems to debunk a rumor; this method seems to make the rumor better remembered than the refutation.
>
> The best way to debunk a rumor is to present fact upon fact about the topic, rather than to try to disprove the logic of the rumor.
>
> Prevent idleness and monotony in the work force wherever possible.
>
> Campaign against rumors and ridicule rumor-mongering.
>
> Educate your supervisors in the dynamics of rumor.
>
> Distract people's attention from the rumor area.
>
> An official denial alone will never debunk a rumor.
>
> And the most effective: Interpret the rumor as a psychiatrist would interpret a symptom. Ask yourself, "What anxiety or attitude does this rumor reflect?" Then, try to relieve the tension by correcting the situation which caused it.[28]

Information from Unions

Employees' organizations, the labor unions, also present their views of industrial relations questions to employees and the public.

The labor union organizer deals with the workman's most vital interests. He is often a better student of labor psychology than the employer, for the organizer directs his appeals to the worker's problems and interests. And labor has developed a fairly extensive scheme of propaganda.

> Generally, union journals today not only print news of interest to their readers, such as goings on within the union itself, news of labor elections and contracts won, but also decry the high cost of living, plump for wage increases, and attempt to win membership support for labor-approved candidates for political office and for labor-approved legislative programs. They are used by the leadership both to stir up trouble and to pour oil on waters already troubled.
>
> The news of a labor publication, in short, is tailored to fit the occasion. If a business man resists the union's attempts to organize his plant, the union's publication may well call him every name under the sun in order to steam up his workers. The same thing may apply during contract negotiation time. For the rest of the year, however, the publications can afford to be charitable.[29]

Some labor editors do an effective job of selling their story to their followers. Their language is uninhibited. They come to the point quickly and pull no punches. For example: commenting on a NLRB ruling regarding freedom of speech for employers, one labor paper said, "You've got to sit and listen to the boss raise unshirted hell about your union if he calls you and your fellow workers together on company time for such a purpose."

Company editors and the businessman could learn much from the labor press. As Martin Dodge says, "When the businessman takes the trouble to find out what is being said about him, he also will come upon the whole gamut of gripes, aspirations and delusions that labor harbors, for they are all spelled out in the union press."[30]

It is fair to say that, on the average, each one of the country's unionized workers gets at least one labor paper. This may be either the official organ of the international union to which he belongs, a local labor body publication, or the paper of the state federation. In most cases, union dues entitle the member to a subscription. Distribution usually is through the mail or by handout at union meetings. In most cases the paper is taken home and carefully and sometimes laboriously read and reread, for labor editors fill their sheets with information close to the interests of their readers. About half of these publications accept local and national advertising.

The labor press is frankly propagandistic, in fact supplementing the never-ending organizing work which many unions conduct. The function of the labor press is to bring workers information about their trade and industry and to interpret for them their economic interests in such affairs. On the whole, they see their job as counteracting what they consider to be the "anti-labor bias" of the daily press, the radio, and the movies, and as anchoring the member's loyalty to his union.

In view of the two differing emphases in the communication of employers and of union organizations with workers, it is not surprising to find that leaders of both groups see the same situation in differing lights. When a survey was made of about 100 labor and 100 management executives, a few of the highlights were:

Leaders of both groups have plenty of complaints about "irritations" with the *personal* characteristics of the other side's leadership. Almost all of the specific gripes hit at the morality of the other group, or at its *behavior during negotiations*. Name-calling and the use of stereotyped epithets like 'labor racketeers' and 'business autocrats' are almost universal. Union leadership is especially resentful of the *lack of respect* shown it by management. Company leadership clearly expressed this disrespect, and cited the 'irresponsibility' of labor's executives as a justification. These *personal feelings* are reflected in the *policy demands* of both groups. Neither group is particularly realistic about what the other feels, thinks, sees, or hears.

Both sides live in private information *worlds*. Overwhelmingly, management and labor trust sources of information which are identified in advance with their *own point of view*. . . .Thus labor has more confidence in government information; management in the daily newspaper and periodical press.

What comes out of this study as 'cause for alarm' is not the body of issues in dispute between union and company officials. The most disturbing result is the existence of highly charged emotional attitudes on both sides which will interfere with the reasonable solution of whatever issues there are. . . .

The ways out of this impasse lie along the road to clarification and greater familiarity between both sides. . . .

But above all else both sides must have a day-to-day common meeting ground at the plant, industry and national levels. There must be a medium which introduces them to one another, and in which they can both have confidence. Information breeds understanding; understanding produces respect; respect is the sole foundation on which a workable machinery for meeting the nation's industrial problems can be built.[31]

Face-to-face Communications

In our preoccupation with media of communication we are likely to slight the basic problem: improving face-to-face communications between the employee and the supervisor. Nine-tenths of industrial communications take place face-to-face.

Face-to-face communications are not simple because they are as complex and as varied as the human beings who take part in them. The basic attack on communication problems must begin in these daily face-to-face relationships. In order to do this, more attention has to be paid to motivations of individuals as outlined according to the adjustment concept in Chapters 2–8.

Productivity depends on effective teamwork that arises first and foremost in the on-the-job dealings between an individual and his supervisors. All need practical guidance on every aspect of interpersonal communication, including giving orders that are accepted wholeheartedly, handling grievances, making rumors work constructively, counseling on job performance, and reporting results to upper management.

Company publications, speeches by executives, bulletins, and letters are important media of communication, but they are only aids to the day-to-day relations. Both the executives and the employees communicate most of their meanings by the words they say and how they say them. Attitudes are communicated by the tone of voice, facial expression, and the manner of presentation.

The true leader knows this principle and practices it naturally. One example is that of a superintendent of a leather plant who has the reputation of being tough on quality. He has developed the reputation through such acts as taking a foreman and his crew off their down-the-line jobs and taking them into the sorting room, the final step of the operation. "Isn't that a beautiful piece of leather?" he'll ask, with pride expressed by his voice and manner. He has communicated his own high regard for good workmanship by his manner rather than by his words and has enabled the workers who produced the leather to experience pride in themselves for their contribution to its high quality.

Workers judge an executive by what they *think* his motives are. If they sense that he is for them, they will put a good construction on what he says. If they sense that he is basically disinterested in them, they will read negative meanings into his words and efforts even though what he says and does would appear to be favorable to them otherwise. Employees sense the psychological climate from daily personal contacts rather than from formal media of communication.

The written word is not a substitute for sound face-to-face relationships. Written communications to employees are not convincing unless there is first a foundation of trust and confidence, an understanding psychological climate where management and workers can function effectively and happily.

ACKNOWLEDGMENTS AND REFERENCES

1. Quoted from Glenn Gardiner, *How to Handle Grievances,* Elliott Service Company, 1937.
2. Burleigh B. Gardner and Lee Rainwater, "The Mass Image of Big Business," *Harvard Business Review,* November-December, 1955, p. 62.
3. See O. J. Gordon, "Factor Analysis of Human Needs and Industrial Morale," *Personnel Psychology,* Spring, 1955.
4. Edgar F. Huse and Erwin K. Taylor, "Reliability of Absence Measures," *Journal of Applied Psychology,* June, 1962.
5. Robert L. Caleo, "Absenteeism: Why It Happens," *Administrative Management,* June, 1963.
6. Louis A. Allen, "Action-Oriented Attitude Surveys," *Personnel,* American Management Association, Inc., September, 1952. This article presents a good set of directions for making attitude surveys. For a description of various methods of attitude measurement, see Irving R. Weschler and and Raymond E. Bernberg, "Indirect Methods of Attitude Measurement," Institute of Industrial Relations, University of California, Los Angeles, 1949.
7. "Personnel Management: Future Problems and Opportunities," *Personnel,* American Management Association, Inc., January-February, 1961, p. 57.
8. Yale J. Laitin, "How to Make Employee Attitude Surveys Pay Off," *Personnel,* American Management Association, Inc., July-August, 1961.
9. See Ronald Paul Yuzuk, *The Assessment of Employee Morale,* Ohio Studies in Personnel, Research Monograph No. 99, Bureau of Business Research, The Ohio State University, 1961. This monograph presents an extensive list of inventory questions that use both phrasings.
10. Donald C. King, "A Multiplant Factor Analysis of Employees' Attitudes Toward Their Company," *Journal of Applied Psychology,* August, 1960.
11. Eugene J. Benge, Asheville, N. C.
12. Excerpt from *Annual Report 1953–1954,* Industrial Relations Section, California Institute of Technology, Project 5, "Surveys of Employee Opinion."
13. See G. S. Odiorne, "Some Effects of Poor Equipment Maintenance on Morale," *Personnel Psychology,* Summer, 1955, for a study on this aspect of morale.
14. Stephen Habbe, "Does Communication Make a Difference?" *Management Record,* National Industrial Conference Board, November, 1952. See also "Communicating with Employees," Studies in Personnel Policy No. 129, National Industrial Conference Board, Inc., New York, pp. 36–40 and Frank E. Fischer, "A New Look at Management Communication," *Personnel,* American Management Association, Inc., May, 1955.
15. See Robert Newcomb and Mary Sammons, "Sharing Survey Results with the Employees," *Personnel,* American Management Association, Inc., November-December, 1960.
16. See Aileen L. Kyte, "The Evolving Role of Personnel Administration," *Management Record,* July-August, 1962, pp. 11–12.
17. Wayne K. Kirchner and Nancy B. Mousley, "Differences Between Respondent and Nonrespondent Salesmen to an Attitude Survey," *Journal of Applied Psychology,* June, 1963.
18. Robert E. Schwab, "Motivation and Human Relations Principles," *Personnel Series,* No. 155, American Management Association, Inc., 1953, pp. 36–37.
19. *Following Up Attitude Survey Findings,* Studies in Personnel Policy, No. 181, National Industrial Conference Board, Inc., 1961. This study presents a description of the Champion plan plus comprehensive and helpful reports for the benefit of other users of attitude surveys.
20. See Frederick Herzberg, Bernard Mausner, and Barbara Snyderman, *The Motivation to Work* (New York: John Wiley & Sons, Inc., 1959). See also, M. Scott Myers, "Who Are Your Motivated

Workers?" *Harvard Business Review,* January-February, 1964 and Robert B. Ewen, "Some Determinants of Job Satisfaction: A Study of the Generality of Herzberg's Theory," *Journal of Applied Psychology,* June, 1964.
21. See Frederick I. Herzberg, "Basic Needs and Satisfactions of Individuals," *Behavioral Science Research in Industrial Relations,* Industrial Relations Counselors, Inc., New York, 1962, pp. 35–36.
22. Arthur H. Brayfield and Walter H. Crockett, "Employee Attitudes and Employee Performance," *Psychological Bulletin,* September, 1955.
23. See *The Management Review,* American Management Association, Inc., February, 1954, p. 84.
24. Lawrence Stessin, "Managing Your Manpower," *Dun's Review and Modern Industry,* August, 1960.
25. Ross G. Walker, "The Misinformed Employee," *Harvard Business Review,* May, 1948.
26. See Robert Newcomb and Marg Sammons, "Office Bulletins Catch the Eye," *Advertising Age,* Dec. 2, 1963.
27. See the study by Thomas L. Dahle, "Transmitting Information to Employees," *Personnel,* American Management Association, Inc., November, 1954.
28. Robert Hershey, "Heed Rumors for Their Meaning," *Personnel Journal,* January, 1956.
29. Booton Herndon, *Nation's Business,* June, 1954, p. 66.
30. Martin Dodge, "Labor's Fourth Estate," *Personnel,* American Management Association, Inc., January, 1949.
31. *Must Labor and Management Fight?* (New York: Nejelski and Company). See also *Tide,* May 31, 1946, p. 70.

PROJECTS

1. Visit an industrial plant in your community and note evidences of the management's program for maintaining high morale among employees. Write a report of your findings.
2. A Canadian Mountie is credited with the statement: "Human beings are only twelve meals away from the dumb animal stage." To what extent do you accept this point of view? How does it affect your communications with employees?
3. Andrew Carnegie wrote his epitaph for himself:

   Here lies a man
   Who knew how to enlist
   In his service
   Better men than himself.

   What personality characteristics are necessary for an executive to pursue such a policy?
4. Collect copies of employees' magazines or plant organs and analyze them as to style, selection of material, illustrations, size, and so on.
5. Some companies give employees a great deal of economic information that shows how well off they are in comparison with workers of the Soviet State. Would you present information of the kind that follows in the company's publication for employees? Give reasons for and against its use with employees.

The real measure of a nation's living standard is not what its citizens earn, but what they can buy with their work. Even though one of the Soviet Union's avowed economic and political goals is to close the gap between the American and Russian level of living, studies based on the worktime required to buy essential items indicate that very little progress has been made in shortening the distance in the last nine years. . . . Despite the efforts of the Soviet State to provide a higher level of living, the worker still had to work longer in 1962 than was necessary in either 1928 or 1959.

Worktime Required to Buy Food
Moscow, State-fixed Prices
(Hours)

	1928	1953	1959	1962
Rye bread, 9.84 kg.	2.71	4.52	3.20	2.84
Potatoes, 12.16 kg.	3.56	3.10	3.04	2.70
Beef, 3.68 kg.	11.04	15.77	11.04	13.08
Butter, .44 kg.	3.69	4.00	2.97	3.52
Sugar, 1.80 kg.	3.85	5.57	4.23	3.56
Milk, 4.96 liters	1.08	3.71	2.73	3.20
Eggs, 6.40	.44	1.50	1.28	1.14
All 7 foods	26.37	38.17	28.49	30.04

The average factory worker in New York City earns enough in 1 hour to buy a pound of potatoes, a pound of beef, a quart of milk, a pound of butter, and a dozen eggs. To buy the same items, the average Moscow worker must stay on the job for 7 hours and 53 minutes. The table shows the worktime required in Moscow to buy a week's supply of seven essential foods in several past years.

These comparisons between American and Russian workers were compiled by the Department of Labor and published by the Joint Economic Committee, 87th Congress, in a study entitled "Dimensions of Soviet Economic Power." In assessing the relative standard of living in the U.S. and Russia, the study notes that the Russian consumer is provided with free medical care, education and pensions, as well as low cost housing for which he pays only 4 to 6 percent of his monthly earnings. However, most Moscow families live in only one room and must share bathroom and kitchen facilities with other families. . . .

The Moscow worker has to work over 3 times as long as the New York City worker for potatoes, over 4 times as long for vodka, and 5 times as long for meat and milk. A few possibly significant reductions have occurred in apparel items. For example, in 1962 the Moscow worker labored only 10 times as long as the New Yorker to buy a wool suit compared to 16 times as long in 1953.

Source: Business Bulletin, The Cleveland Trust Company, July 25, 1963.

COLLATERAL READINGS

Bellows, Roger M., *Psychology of Personnel in Business and Industry*. Englewood Cliffs, N.J.: Prentice-Hall, Inc., 1954, Chapter 7.

Fleishman, Edwin A., *Studies in Personnel and Industrial Psychology*. Homewood, Ill.: The Dorsey Press, Inc., 1961, Chapters 40–47.

Gilmer, B. von Haller, *Industrial Psychology*. New York: McGraw-Hill Book Company, 1961, Chapter 10.

Haire, Mason, *Psychology in Management*. New York: McGraw-Hill Book Company, 1956, Chapters 2 and 4.

Harrell, Thomas Willard, *Industrial Psychology*. New York: Holt, Rinehart & Winston, Inc., 1958, Chapters 11 and 12.

Karn, Harry W. and B. von Haller Gilmer, *Readings in Industrial and Business Psychology*, New York: McGraw-Hill Book Company, 1962, pp. 53–81.

Leavitt, Harold J. and Louis R. Pondy, eds., *Readings in Managerial Psychology*. Chicago: The University of Chicago Press, 1964, Chapter 4.

The clubhouse that was never used. *It was built by an employer for his employees, but they were not grateful for the gift, and objected to the club fee of one dollar a year. In time the employer demolished the entire clubhouse.* *See page 493.*

CHAPTER TWENTY-THREE

EMPLOYEE RELATIONS —FORMAL PROGRAMS

Two real comrades know all about each other and are tolerant. Each knows what the other is up against and, understanding each other, wanting to work out the common task which is theirs, they make allowances as one man to another. Then there is fun in the day's work, there is that sense of going places with other men, there is a click in the job. That is great; that is a priceless possession. When it exists among men in industry, so-called "personnel management" is simple. But you cannot define this relationship; you cannot blueprint the course of comradeship. It is a mistake to try. But we can create the physical environment that is conducive to comradeship. We can have good "personnel management" and then give comradeship a chance.[1]

Systems of personnel management in industry are relatively unimportant. A given company may have the finest industrial relations mechanisms or formal systems and still have poor industrial relations. Another company may have almost no personnel management mechanisms and yet have fine industrial relations. If the executives have the kind of managerial leadership that inspires comradeship and confidence between management and men, the formal methods of supervision are incidental. Many examples of this fine relationship exist in American industry.

At the same time that some of our largest corporations have been beset by costly labor controversies, other companies of the same industry have had few or no disturbances. And yet the company that has a pleasant industrial relations history may have no special plan or system to account for the results. It may have no formal suggestion system, no employee relations counselors, no music or public address system in the shops, and no athletic association. There may be no printed statement of labor policy or procedure, no codified rules of conduct, and no commitment on the part of the company or its workers except the intent to comply honestly and fairly with a simple arrangement or practice regarding wages and working conditions. It may, however, have many spontaneous get-togethers that provide opportunity for fellowship. In such a company, the relationship between management and men is likely to be surprisingly informal. The psychological climate is right—management and men work together in a spirit of mutual confidence.

Managements of other companies who would like to bring about a more favorable psychological climate in their organizations often turn to some formal plans as a means toward achieving the desired relationship between employees and the company. The plans to which they turn are typically profit-sharing, stock ownership, and suggestion systems.

Profit-sharing

Profit-sharing is not a new idea; the plan was in operation in agriculture in England during the thirteenth century. Records show that it was used in shops in England in 1870 and in France as early as 1842. The first plan instituted in the United States was that of Albert Gallatin, who introduced it in his glassworks at New Geneva, Pa., in 1794. In 1889, the United States had thirty-two recorded schemes for profit-sharing. Most of these schemes were short-lived, although one St. Louis firm has been operating on a profit-sharing basis since 1886. The Procter & Gamble plan was begun in 1887, but it has been modified several times since then. Few schemes now operating were started before 1900. As one review of their history stated: "...profit-sharing plans have been particularly susceptible to the ups and downs of the business cycle: each upswing has resulted in a rash of new plans, each downturn has brought abrupt terminations."[2]

In most cases, profit-sharing should be distinguished from bonuses, which are given as a reward for high production by an individual worker. It is not part of a wage system. True profit-sharing is an agreement between the employer and the employees under which the profits allocated to the workers rise or fall in proportion to the increase or the decrease in the profits realized by the employer.

Most profit-sharing plans can be divided into three classifications: current distribution, deferred distribution, and combination. Under the first, the older type, the profits are paid in cash at regular intervals. In the second type, the employee's share of the profits is deposited in an irrevocable trust and the employee, or his beneficiaries, does not receive his shares until some future time: termination of employment, disability, retirement, or death. In combination plans, a portion of the profits are paid in cash but a deferred element also appears. Plans to which the employees contribute toward deferred benefits are more common in large than in small companies.

Small companies are more likely to have current distribution plans.

According to one writer, approximately 7.5 per cent of all United States companies with 20 or more employees share some of their profits with workers. Most are small or medium-sized, but several large firms have also adopted the plan.[3] The adoption trend is upward. One important factor in recent years has been the tax advantage for both the company and its employees. In a qualified deferred plan, the company's contribution, up to 15 per cent of the participating payroll, can be deducted as a business expense in computing the company's income taxes.[4]

Many of the plans have been started in the hope that efficiency would be increased, costs decreased, and the working force stabilized. Some were begun by wealthy employers who wished to share their success with the employees whose hard work contributed toward the profits of the enterprises. The employers' motives were an attempt to give social justice and to increase their own sense of well-being. Where such an attitude prevailed, and was coupled with reasonable managerial efficiency, some benefits actually accrued from profit-sharing and similar plans of employee relations. The plans started by such humanitarians were usually abandoned at their deaths, when inevitable changes in management took place. In a few instances, the owner of the business provided for the perpetuation of the plan after his death.

In general, profit-sharing has not stimulated the employees of some companies. One important reason is that many employees prefer to have a definite salary or wage that is known in advance. They declare "a bird in the hand is worth two in the bush." In the years when the company makes unusually large profits, the money distributed is accepted as a gift from a kind, industrial Santa Claus; but when profits are negligible or a deficit must be written on the books, the employees may be sorely disappointed. To say the least, an employee will be shocked if, after he has spent his anticipated profits, he finds that the practice of distributing profits has been suddenly discontinued. When profits are shared for a long time, they are often confused with or considered as a part of the wages.

When the profits of the company do not allow any distribution to the employees, the employees tend to doubt the honesty of the management, particularly if they note that the president or the general manager of the company has purchased a new house or a new limousine. They do not, as a rule, have access to the accounts of the employer; but even if they did, they would not be able to understand the accounts. A negligible number of the employers who have a profit-sharing plan have a disinterested accountant audit their books and prepare a report, which he presents to the employees. However, the great masses of workers cannot understand how profits in modern business are made or computed. It is only natural, therefore, that they should be suspicious of the management when the plan of distribution remains a mystery to them.

The individual employee can seldom see any relationship between his own daily efforts and the profits at the end of the year. In most plans, the profits divided are a small fraction of the annual wages. In one-third of the plans studied, it was found that the dividends amounted to less than 6 per cent of the annual wages of the participants. Hence the interested employee who decides to work hard in order to increase the company's profits at the end of the year, a proportionate share of which he will receive, finds that the lazy worker by his side receives a check just as large as his own. As a result of his discovery, during the following year he may decide to work as slowly and as carelessly as the poorest workman in the shop. Thus profit-sharing, under some conditions, tends to bring the efficiency of the best workers down to the level of the poorest rather than to raise the efficiency of the poorest workers. The profit-sharing sun shines just as brightly on the undeserving as on the deserving. It is for these and other reasons that profit-sharing for workmen has been found deficient as a universal incentive to work. The one type that appears to have high incentive values for modern business is that of managerial profit-sharing.

The making of profits in modern business is largely beyond the control of the factory workers. Profits depend upon the managerial ability to purchase economically, to organize the whole scheme of production efficiently, to sell the goods at a satisfactory profit, to finance the operations during the depressions that are bound to occur in business, and to find new markets to take the place of contracting markets. The key executives of a business—the sales manager, the production manager, the comptroller, the purchasing agent, and a few others—can see the direct relations between their own efforts and the profits made. They are the men who are responsible for profits and losses, rather than the workers in the factory. For wage earners, profit-sharing is largely incidental to a humanitarian motive or managerial attitude of fairness toward the employees. As a rule, it does not by itself give all workers a strong sense of participation in the enterprise.

Many employers who adopted profit-sharing did so, not with the hope of obtaining more material gains from employees, but to improve the *esprit de corps* and to express management's sense of colleagueship with employees.

According to studies by the Profit Sharing Research Foundation, approximately 85 percent of profit sharing companies rate their plans as "successful" or as "very successful." Only 1 to 2 percent said their plans were "disappointing."

Around 1 percent of the *deferred plans* are being terminated each year. The discontinuance rate of *cash plans* is somewhat higher. This higher rate is partly because smaller companies, where most cash profit sharing plans are found, have a higher failure rate.

Some of the plans are closed out as the result of mergers or when businesses are liquidated or sold for various reasons.

A few companies drop profit sharing because it doesn't work out for them. Usually, the reason is a string of unprofitable years in which there was nothing to share with employees. Other plans failed because the owner-manager did not keep his employees interested in profit sharing.[5]

Large companies are more likely to rate their plans successful than are small companies. Success ratings are larger in proportion among financial and professional enterprises than among manufacturing or mercantile enterprises. Some companies with unions have successful profit-sharing plans, but the success rating of nonunion companies is higher than for the unionized companies.

To make a profit-sharing plan work satisfactorily, investigators have offered the following recommendations.

Provide a Healthy Psychological Climate before Setting up the Plan

Both management and workers should have confidence in each other, before the directors and officers can expect profit-sharing to be beneficial. To succeed, profit-sharing must be consistent with the way the business is done and the way management and employees feel about each other. Companies that succeed with profit-sharing would, in most cases, also succeed without it.

Be Willing to Give Employees All Facts about the Business

A willingness to share all the facts in the financial situation is necessary. A willingness to give limited facts only is likely to result in doubt and disbelief, thus defeating the aim of profit-sharing.

Provide a Sound Compensation Plan

An equitable wage and salary plan should be developed before profit-sharing is introduced. A poor compensation plan that is bolstered by the contingent compensation from profit-sharings is likely to cause trouble. If the pay structure is sound, a profit-sharing plan will supplement it. If the pay structure is unsound or inequitable, profit-sharing will only accentuate its inequities.

Have Everybody Share Alike

The same number of dollars per employee is not necessary, but the same percentage is.

If the pay structure is sound, a profit-sharing plan may improve it, especially if the percentage of wages rather than a scale of wages or salary brackets is used to determine the profits per employee.

In spite of the fact that some profit-sharing plans have not worked out to the complete satisfaction of all employers or employees who have adopted them, certain companies have demonstrated the effectiveness of the idea when it is part of some more comprehensive plan of employer-employee relations. The Lincoln Electric Company is an example. There, as in other successful uses of profit-sharing, the idea is only part of a greater philosophy. As the Lincoln Electric Company states, "...if all employees of any organization, from top to bottom, will work together and do as much as they can, instead of as little as they can, everyone in that organization will be better off. As a result, such an organization will be outstanding among all others of its type."

The profit sharing system of Lincoln Electric Company was developed by James F. Lincoln, beginning in 1914. When he took over operation of the plant he established an advisory board of employees. Such a board has been meeting twice a month since that date. Members of the advisory board are elected by the employees voting in secret ballot. The compensation part of the plan is of an annual incentive bonus nature. The board of directors meets toward the end of the year to study the year's operations and profits. They set aside reserves for growth, taxes, and other operations. They also decide on the amount of the total bonus. Each employee receives a share of the bonus but the amount is determined by merit ratings made by three or four persons who are familiar with his performance. See rating cards used on page 356. Workers who contribute more receive a proportionately larger share of the bonus. The annual incomes of the employees are among the very highest in the world. Few employees quit. At Lincoln Electric, the employee turnover is less than one-half of one per cent a month. In contrast, the national average for all employees in industry in some years is about seven per cent.[6]

Many companies, usually small ones, have experimented with plans that link profit-sharing with individual performance. These sponsors assume that money is the mainspring in employee behavior. Some of these plans have a good record when measured in terms of the survival of the company. Such incentive systems, however, do not work very well with employees who value intangibles such as social acceptance and the satisfaction of affiliation needs. Any management that installs a comprehensive incentive system is likely to find that it attracts the psychological type of worker whose perspective is narrowed down to "How much do I get out of it?" The psychological climate in such a company is a special one. When the bonus happens to be less than expected, the employees may become embittered. This was evident in the first 17 months after the Kaiser Steel Corporation inaugurated its sharing plan. The plan replaced individual and incentive pay with a company-wide incentive plan that emphasized a monthly sharing of cost reduction and labor-management cooperation. The plan gave workers, on a monthly basis, in wages and fringe benefits, 32.5 per cent of future savings in the material supply and labor costs of producing finished steel. It was hoped that the plan would eliminate the need for long negotiations or strikes over wages and other economic issues. Bonuses in one month hit an average of $100 per worker. When the average fell to only $14 per worker, worker disillusionment became pronounced.[7] In short, even the most astutely planned systems for sharing profits do not always succeed as management and men may hope.

Employees' Stock Purchase Plans

It has been argued that stock ownership, rather than profit-sharing, is more advantageous to the employee for the following reasons: Under the latter plan, although the employee may gain a little by sharing in the profits, he is not required to expend any extra effort or to take any risks. Thus the profit-sharing plan does not give him any feeling of responsibility in the management of the company. On the other hand, under the stock purchase plan, the employee, by being allowed to purchase some stock, is made to regard himself as a partner in the business; consequently he naturally takes an active interest in the affairs of the business and acquires a sense of importance as a budding financier!

Advocates of the plan claim that stock ownership would be an incentive to the employee to eliminate waste, to be more industrious, to attend work regularly, not to quit for a better job, to criticize the employer less, and to refuse to harm the company's property in case of a strike.

The main reasons for instituting employee stock ownership plans are a desire (1) to make employees partners in the business, so that they will have greater interest in and loyalty to the company; (2) to promote employee thrift; (3) to educate the workers on the advantages of the free enterprise system; (4) to provide a hedge against inflation; and (5) to obtain working capital for the company.

Stock ownership on the part of the American public has been increasing rapidly. In the course of approximately ten years, the number of common stockholders of 38 of our largest corporations increased from 111 for every 100 employees in 1951 to 182.[8] This means that for every 100 employees on the company payroll there are 182 stockholders.

The extent of employees' ownership of stock in the companies for which they work varies with the industry:

Industry	*Number employed—millions*	*Per cent owning stock in their own companies*
Manufacturing	16.9	1.4%
Public utilities	1.1	15.9
Banking and finance	1.7	8.6
Professional business service companies	1.2	6.4
Petroleum companies	.9	5.8
Transportation companies	2.6	3.1
Total	24.4	3.2

According to this study, only one worker in 70 in manufacturing owned stock but one utility worker in six was a shareholder. In the telephone companies about 21 per cent of women employees owned stock as against 12 per cent of the men.[9]

These figures, of course, do not tell the whole story of business ownership. Several million people have shares in private, closely-held companies. Many of these also own stock in publicly held corporations. In addition, other millions own small businesses. These are the proprietors and partners who own an overwhelming share of the four or more million businesses operating in the United States. Economically, too, other tens of millions of Americans have an indirect share in the ownership of American industry in the form of life insurance policies and bank accounts.

One of the principal complaints made against the stock purchase idea is that not enough wage earners participate. When, for example, the National Industrial Conference Board made a survey of 33 companies which provided company stock plans, only a quarter million, or 26.6 per cent of employees, were buying stock under the company's latest stock offerings. Only one of four eligible employees took advantage of the offer. The percentage of employees buying stock, however, ranged for different companies all the way from 1.1 per cent to 92.5 per cent.[10]

Actually, some employee stock ownership plans have not worked out as anticipated. It has been found that employees purchase stock mainly for three reasons: as a speculative investment; in the hope of attracting the good will of management and of gaining promotion; and as a nest egg for old age. The extent to which these hopes have been dashed in some unfortunate instances is illustrated in the case of the employees of a company that suffered severely in a business depression. When the company was only a few jumps ahead of the sheriff, the executives had to retrench and, consequently, many of the employees were dismissed.

Certain employers who have sold negotiable

stock to employees have found that the employees have become interested more in the market value of the stock than in increasing its real value through extra diligence. At the very time when the employer has needed employee loyalty—a keen desire on the part of the workers to pitch in and lift a little harder—he has found them busy watching the stock market! In a few cases, employees have made paper profits that would have given them substantial annual incomes had they sold at the right time; but they held on, hoping to make still more or fearing that the employer would look upon their transactions as disloyalty to the company. When the paper profits were wiped out, the former "well-to-do" employees lost heart in their work and blamed the company for their misfortune.

Most stock ownership plans for employees, inaugurated before the market crash of 1929, had to be dropped because of the later decline in security values. Many of the employee purchases had been made at peak market prices, with the result that many employees suffered severe losses. However, by the late 1940's a small number of companies had revived interest in employee stock ownership because stock market price levels appeared to be stable and favorable to the employees.

Some stock purchase plans are open to selected employees, such as managers, department heads, salesmen, or others whose services are highly respected or who can afford to stand a loss in case of a decline in value. Stock purchase plans can give the employee a sense of participation in the industry only when he has rights in shares in which the public does not participate, a partnership psychologically as well as economically in the business. Otherwise, the employees who are encouraged to purchase stock should be of the higher income class, who are mentally capable of understanding the fluctuations in stock prices and able to absorb their losses.

Despite the misfortunes suffered by stock purchase plans in the depression of the 1930's, many companies continue to be interested in the idea of employee stock ownership. They still think it can be a good way to promote employee thrift and help the worker to identify his own welfare with that of his company.

Currently, about one-fifth of the companies whose stocks are listed on the New York Stock Exchange have some kind of employee stock-acquisition plan. About half of the eligible employees participate in the company plan. The plans that offer savings and thrift programs under which the company contributes 25 cents to $2.00 in common stock to match every salary dollar set aside by the employee have a participation rate of 76 per cent.[11]

Managements, of course, are aware of the hazards in stock ownership plans and hope to set up plans that avoid disasters. The recently developed plans are based on the regular savings of the worker, augmented by a contribution from the company, and invested in varied types of securities. Many of the plans are called "thrift plans" or "savings plans."

Widespread share ownership is in the interest of free enterprise and society, but a worker seldom changes his attitude toward business or his employer simply because he owns a few shares of stock in the company where he works. Even total ownership of a company does not always produce an effective or a happy organization as indicated by the history of such companies and of nationalized enterprises. Rather, the ideas of participation, involvement, and accomplishment at work, regardless of ownership of the place where the worker is occupied, are more basic.[12]

Most employers realize that they cannot hope to develop a profit-sharing, stock ownership plan or other formal plans that will be of measurable direct productive value. They know that any plan in itself is effective in the extent that it helps to develop a favorable psychological climate in which management and men can work together productively. For most companies stock ownership and profit-sharing are big and serious ventures—too big for their capacities. Many of these managements do, however, want to work toward a better psychological climate. They want their employees as well as the company executives to have the benefit of a sense of participation in the business. They therefore turn to the suggestion system idea.

Suggestion Systems

Ideally a suggestion system should be unnecessary. Management and men should work so closely with each other that each makes suggestions regarding the work as the work is carried on. Practically, such ideal relations seldom exist. A suggestion system may, to some extent, enable alert employees to participate more actively in the operation of the business. The extent to which employees participate depends upon the attention given to the suggestion system by management. Some companies get ideas from about 50 per cent of their employees in the course of a year, but so high a percentage of participation is unusual.

The average rate of adoption reported by the National Association of Suggestions Systems has been about 20 per cent.

General Electric Company has had a formal suggestion system for more than 50 years. Employees in a recent year sent in 87,400 suggestions, of which more than a third were adopted. Many other companies have equally good records. In some firms as many as 40 per cent are acceptable. Some of the awards run up to $25,000 and more.

Employees will not offer ideas unless they have learned through years of experience that suggestions are welcome. The executive who calls employees into his office and makes a direct request for suggestions is likely to be disappointed for several reasons. One is the fact that most employees are like students; they try to give an answer that they think will agree with the questioner's ideas.

Again, employees who are paid on a piece-rate basis may be able to make suggestions that would speed up their work, but they have learned that the new method would bring about a retiming of the job and a lower rate of pay. They can make more money by keeping the discovery to themselves and retaining the old rate of pay than if they were to be paid a small reward for the suggestion.

To operate a successful suggestion system, the management must do more than merely hang up a few tin boxes with a sign, "Suggestions Wanted." Considerable managerial thought and effort are essential to the operation of a satisfactory suggestion scheme.

1. Small concerns have found it best to conduct a contest for suggestions. The contest should start and end on definite dates. Announcements should state that rewards are given for each accepted suggestion and also prizes for the best of these suggestions. The disadvantage of this method is that awards cannot be made until all the suggestions have been considered; and many suggestions require considerable time for study and investigation.

2. Large concerns find it better to conduct extended campaigns and to award prizes at definite periods, or simply to pay for suggestions when they are accepted or put into effect.

3. It is well to obtain the cooperation and good will of the foremen and other executives. Many a department head considers an employee's suggestion for improvement as a reflection upon his ability. This really is not true, but foreman lethargy and company politics can be quite effective in throttling employees' suggestions. To overcome employees' fears, some companies request that all suggestions be submitted on a standard three-part form, each bearing the same number. The largest part of the form is reserved for the description of the suggestion; each of the two smaller parts is for the name of the employee and the number of the suggestion blank. When the suggestion form is submitted, it is first sent to one of the higher officials of the company, who tears off the parts which include the name of the employee, files one of these in a private safe, and sends the other to the employee, acknowledging its receipt and expressing appreciation for the suggestion. The employee is also told when the suggestion will be given its first hearing

by the committee in charge. By using this plan, the committee does not know the name of any of the suggestors, and therefore it will more easily avoid unfair personal influences.

4. The announcements and requests for suggestions should explain to the employees the specific kinds of suggestions that are desired. A mere invitation to employees to *think* does not stimulate them to think. The management that really wants employees to think should list and describe problems that are within the employees' areas of experience. Descriptions of specific plant problems can be posted on bulletin boards with an urgent request for suggested solutions. This kind of notice gets thoughtful attention, especially when diagrams, cost figures, and amounts of awards are stated.

One company increased its suggestions for reducing costs of paperwork by presenting questions like these to clerical employees:

> Is any record or file you keep identical with another kept in your office?
>
> Are there some files or records on which you never get calls?
>
> Do you find some records unreliable, so that you have to use other sources?
>
> Are you making too many copies of some records?
>
> Do you know why you do each paperwork job? Does it help you in your duties? If you're not sure, have you asked your supervisor?

Employees usually find it easiest to think up ideas for improving operations involved in their own job because they are the only ones who can observe everything that happens in their operation during the working day.

They can often make valuable suggestions for their improvement, however, especially when they are invited for their ideas about preventing machine breakdowns or damaged goods. Some companies even offer awards for the employee's statement of problems which he himself cannot solve.

5. When suggestions are considered by the appointed committee, complete records of proceedings should be kept in order that copies of the minutes and other records may be submitted to the management. Each item of business should have an identifying number; thus all activities of the committee can be traced. Monthly and annual reports can be made from the proceedings of the recorded meetings. These reports will be available for guidance in the elimination of duplicate suggestions. The foreman in charge of each department should be informed of all suggestions that are made by employees of his department, and he should be congratulated when his employees make good suggestions.

6. When a suggestion is rejected, the reason for the rejection should be explained in writing to the employee. A member of the suggestion committee should discuss the rejection personally with the employee in order that he may understand why the suggestion was not acceptable. Few things will cause a suggestion scheme to die more quickly than to ignore or to forget the employees who make the suggestions. An important factor in the rejection interview is the personality and the manner of the rejector. His manner may stimulate the employee to submit additional ideas or discourage him permanently.

7. The employee should have the right of appeal when his idea has been rejected. If he cannot be convinced that his idea is valueless, he should have the privilege of preparing new charts, drawings, or evidence of its worth.

8. The members of the awarding committees should include several employees. The employees then will know that they are represented in the determination of awards. If they are not thus represented, some of the employees may suspect the company of stealing their brilliant ideas.

9. The employees who make the best suggestions should receive publicity in the plant paper, on the bulletin board, or at a general meeting. A few firms give no financial reward for accepted ideas, but consider promotion, prestige, and personal pride a sufficient reward. Such a policy is often harmful, because

it stimulates the sycophants rather than the more balanced personalities.

10. The awards or rewards should be commensurate with the value of the idea. If the company demands from each employee a waiver of rights for a patentable idea, the flow of suggestions is certain to decrease. If a suggestion has little cash value to the company, the reward may be modest, but not less than five dollars. The employee who is given too small a reward is likely to be teased by his fellow workers; for example, "Well, Bill, are you gonna buy a new house and car with that two dollars and a half you got for your bright idea?"

A point which easily escapes employee attention is the company's lack of ability to pay off on imagination and ingenuity alone. Most improvements become valuable only by their cumulative impact on a large number of operations. This fact makes it necessary for managements to explain to employees the reasons for its system of awards.

The formulas used to calculate awards vary considerably. However, a study of 53 companies revealed definite relationships between award practices and the number of suggestions submitted:

1. The granting of low minimum awards, sometimes called token awards, such as some companies offer for safety suggestions, tends to increase the total number of suggestions received.

2. The granting of even an occasional high award also tends to increase the number of suggestions received.

3. As the number of suggestions received increases, the acceptance rate tends to increase. (Part of the increase in the acceptance rate may be attributed to the granting of token minimum awards.)

4. As the number of suggestions received increases, the average award tends to decline. (Part of the decline may be attributed to the granting of token awards by companies receiving a larger number of suggestions.)

Sixty-five per cent of the concerns responding in this survey calculate the amount of the award on a percentage basis of savings to the company. Of interest is the fact that the firms using a net saving formula receive, on an average, 530 suggestions annually per 1,000 employees, whereas those employing a gross saving formula receive only an average of 250 suggestions per 1,000 employees.[13]

Suggestion systems, like all other group methods of influencing employees, depend for their success upon the alertness and ability of the management. One of the country's leading manufacturers of a highly technical product receives about forty suggestion letters a day. An expert examines each suggestion to determine whether it is of any possible value to the company. This company has found that it pays to examine one thousand ideas in order to find six that are definitely valuable and can be adopted with satisfactory results to the company. The management of this company, however, is "on its toes" in many respects, and its careful consideration of submitted ideas is simply one phase of an aggressive outlook.

Summary

Many formal methods of dealing with employee relations are available to management and employees. The extent to which various methods or plans are used and factors to consider in their use may be studied from reports published by scores of research organizations. Among the organizations that report valuable studies of industrial relations are the National Industrial Conference Board, Inc., The Brookings Institution, The American Management Association, and The Policyholders Service Bureau of the Metropolitan Life Insurance Company. Those who deal with employee relations should become acquainted with the publications of these and other sources of information, such as the current professional and business journals.

Studies of such publications indicate that industrial relations activities are a mark of alert management rather than of a desire to exploit workers. Intelligent managers wish to supply pleasant working conditions, vacations with pay, rest rooms, physical examinations, insurance, and pensions for employees. The money spent for such provisions is not necessarily taken out of the employees' pay envelopes. At least one study showed that the companies which engage in industrial relations activities pay higher wages, on the average, than companies which provide few activities such as bonuses, profit-sharing, vacations with pay, and group life insurance.[14] This study also indicated that a weak management cannot bolster itself by the use of welfare devices. On the other hand, the strong management tends to be intelligent in its employee relations as well as in its customer and financial relations.

Whenever industrial psychologists have studied methods of management, the usual result has been that the spirit back of the methods has been more important than the method itself. After all, we should expect this to be true. Employees are human beings. When owners and managers prefer to continue to operate their business in the old boss-subordinate manner, difficulties tend to develop, and owners may wonder whether they should quit entirely.

Generosity Alone Does Not Produce Good Employee Relations

In 1910, a certain successful factory owner in a Wisconsin town decided that he would like to do something big and fine for his employees. He had become so wealthy that the making of money appeared to be rather easy. He had more or less "made his pile." After some consideration, he realized that the town offered his employees very little suitable recreation. Accordingly, he decided that he would build a beautiful clubhouse for the use of his employees—to show his gratitude to those who had helped him make his fortune.

He owned a valuable plot of land that was near the center of the town's business section and an ideal location for a clubhouse. He engaged architects, approved their plans, selected the materials, made contracts, and paid the costs of construction. In the course of construction, he told the employees about the recreation center that he was having built for them. When the building was completed but still unequipped, he announced the rules for the use of the clubhouse and stipulated that each employee should pay a membership fee of one dollar each year as a partial payment of the cost of operating the clubhouse.

Some of the employees immediately criticized the "rich old man" for his gift. "Why doesn't he pay the cost of operation?" they said. When the employer learned of the attitude of his employees, he became discouraged by their lack of gratitude and announced that he would not give the clubhouse to them. He then offered the building, which could be used for a gymnasium, to the local high school on the condition that the community would raise ten thousand dollars to cover the cost of the equipment, which had not yet been installed. The high school students were delighted at the prospect of receiving a much-needed gymnasium. The students were allowed thirty days in which to raise the money for the equipment. They solicited energetically during this time but were able to raise only about seven thousand dollars in subscriptions, and requested an extension of thirty days for additional soliciting. The students had encountered considerable difficulty in getting subscriptions because the "donor" of the clubhouse was not well liked by many of the well-to-do people of the town, and at the end of the sixty days of hard soliciting, they were still more than a thousand dollars short of the specified amount. They reported their failure to the philanthropist and tried to make a suitable "arrangement." But he was obdurate; he was through.

Some time later, workmen were hired to demolish the building. The building materials were sold or dumped into the river. In a short time, the excavation for the foundation was filled in, and sod was placed on the site. The beautiful new clubhouse was gone and the experience had cost the employer approximately one hundred and seventy thousand dollars!

This incident from American industry illustrates an old principle that many employers have had to learn through costly experience; namely, that *employees must be mentally prepared for the employer's well-meant human relations plans.* The employer cannot assume that his employees are thinking as he is thinking. All proposed plans for the improvement of employee relations must fit into the wishes, attitudes, and behavior patterns of the employees. The employer must develop a feeling of genuine colleagueship through employee participation in dealing with the problems of the business.

ACKNOWLEDGMENTS AND REFERENCES

1. Roderic Olzendam, *The Importance of Personnel Administration to Public Relations,* Weyerhaeuser Timber Company. Undated.
2. See Mitchell Meyer and Harland Fox, "Profit Sharing for Retirement Income," *Management Record,* National Industrial Conference Board, Inc., May, 1960, p. 2.
3. See Jack Harnicke, *The Wall Street Journal,* Sept. 13, 1961.
4. See B. L. Metzger, "Will Profit Sharing Help Your Firm?" *Management Aids for Small Business,* No. 157, Small Business Administration, Washington, D.C., October, 1963.
5. *Ibid.,* p. 2.
6. See A. N. Wecksler, "A Case Study of The Lincoln Electric Company," *Mill & Factory,* April, 1963.
7. See "Troubled Labor Plan: Kaiser Steel Workers Gripe as Bonuses Fall," *The Wall Street Journal,* June 3, 1964. Also "A Second Look at Profit Sharing," *U.S. News & World Report,* June 22, 1964.
8. See "Shareowners and Employees: Who's Ahead?" *The Exchange,* December, 1963.
9. For further information, see *Business Week,* July 19, 1952, p. 176.
10. See "Stock Ownership Plans for Workers," *Studies in Personnel Policy,* No. 132, National Industrial Conference Board, 1953.
11. See "In Management," *Business Week,* Sept. 23, 1961.
12. See Simon Marcson, "Motivation and Productivity in Industry," *Behavioral Science Research In Industrial Relations,* Industrial Relations Counselors, Inc., New York, 1962, pp. 157–158.
13. See A. W. Hendrickson and A. E. Heusser, *Factory Management and Maintenance,* May, 1945.
14. *Industrial Relations Programs in Small Plants,* National Industrial Conference Board, Inc., New York, 1929, pp. 39ff.

PROJECTS

1. Assume that you are the executive given the task of instituting a profit-sharing plan to your plant. To what aspects of worker psychology would you give special thought? How would you proceed?
2. Assume that you have been given the same kind of task for instituting an employee stock ownership plan. What factors would you consider in organizing the plan? In what ways does the plan of procedure for instituting a stock ownership plan differ from that for a profit-sharing plan?
3. In what ways would you vitalize a suggestion system already functioning, theoretically at least, in an industrial plant? What would be your steps of procedure? State in one sentence the principle of psychology that you are employing in each step.
4. Compile a list of industrial relations services a company can give its employees at a nominal cost. Ask several workers to check those which they think they would like and those they would not care for. Do workers seem to agree as a whole or are individual differences pronounced?
5. Examine the magazines in your library and list those which have regular departments that treat industrial relations problems. Examples of such magazines are *Business Week* and *Dun's Review and Modern Industry.*

COLLATERAL READINGS

Center for Productivity Motivation, The University of Wisconsin, School of Commerce, Madison, Wisconsin, publishes a comprehensive bibliography on profit sharing and related plans.

Chalupsky, Albert B., "Implementing the Profit Sharing Concept: A Research Approach," *Personnel Journal,* January, 1963.

Council of Profit Sharing Industries, Riverside Plaza, Chicago, Illinois, can provide articles. Ask for latest bibliography.

Meyer, Mitchell and Harland Fox, "Profit Sharing for Retirement Income," *Management Record,* National Industrial Conference Board, Inc., May, 1960.

National Association of Suggestion Systems, 28 E. Jackson Blvd., Chicago, Illinois, publishes NASS Quarterly magazine to provide information about suggestion systems. Reprints and copies of other publications in the field are available.

Profit Sharing Research Foundation, 1718 Sherman Avenue, Evanston, Ill., can provide helpful publications on the subject.

Smith, Henry Clay, *Psychology of Industrial Behavior.* New York: McGraw-Hill Book Company, 1955, Chapter 11.

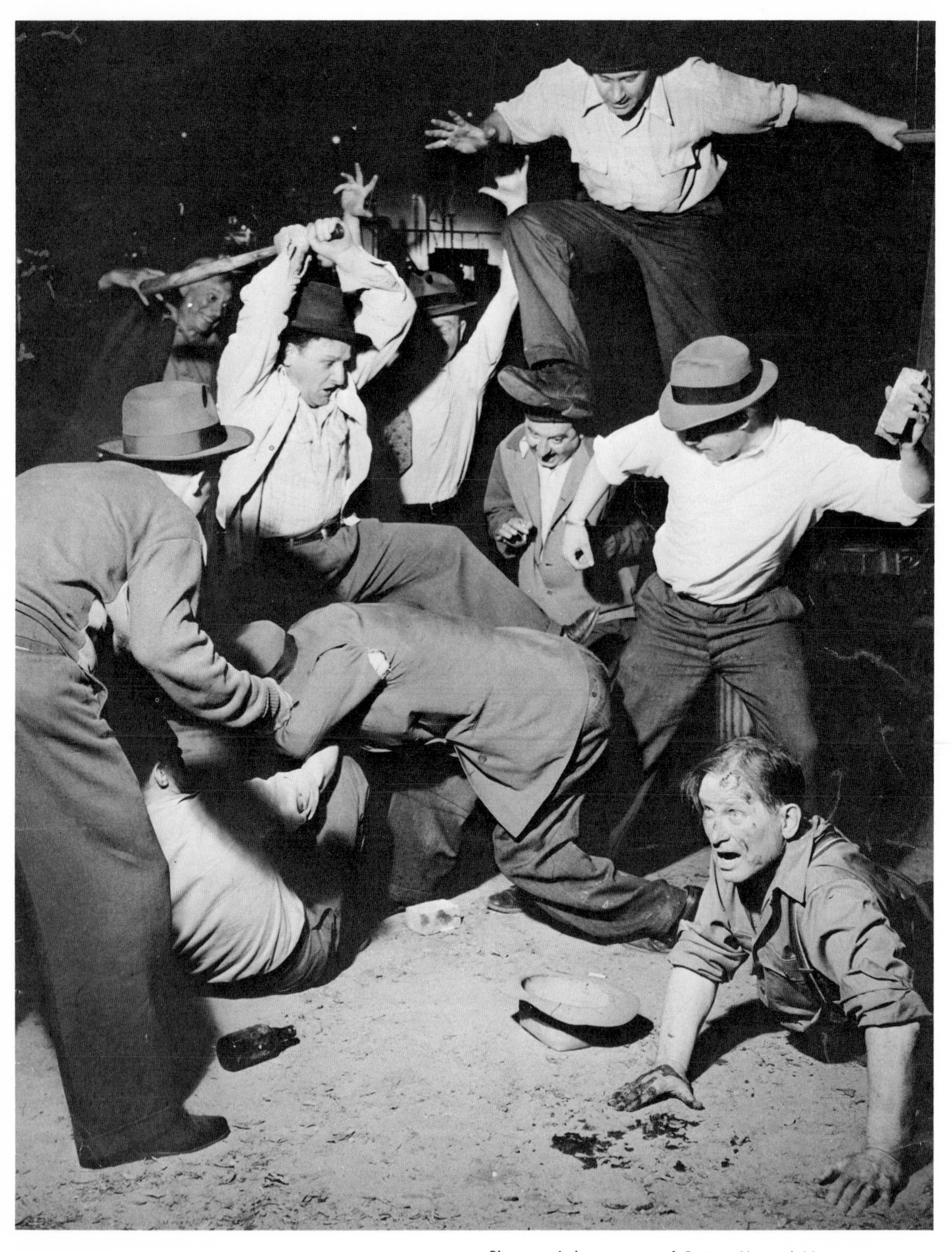

Photograph by courtesy of Scripps-Howard Newspapers

The stress and conflict aspects *of certain labor relations are often given considerable attention, but the typical psychological influences offer more of interest to students of psychology.*

CHAPTER TWENTY-FOUR

ORGANIZED LABOR

One of the most formalized relations
between the employees of some companies and their management
is the labor union.
Many management men look upon the development of unions
as an indication of management's failure in meeting employees'
psychological and economic needs.

Labor unions have so many psychological aspects that any attempt to discuss them is likely to become a description of human nature itself. Examples of good and bad unionism are as plentiful as the examples of good and bad psychological adjustments by individuals.

Even the most objective description of unionism is likely to arouse criticism or defense on the part of some readers, depending upon their psychological needs and their identifications. Each reader is likely to be either an advocate or a critic of unionism even though he may imagine that he is objective in his thinking. Thorough objectivity in this field is difficult for each one of us. One reason for this difficulty on the part of an executive is that he likes to think of himself as the leader of his employees. Unions and union activities often interpose themselves between the executive and his employees. Some union leaders try to drive a wedge between the employee and his company. They may even go beyond the "...point of telling him that the union is a good thing, and far into the zone of trying to persuade him that his company is his natural enemy, never to be trusted or respected, actuated entirely by unworthy motives and managed exclusively by men who are stupid or dishonest or both."[1]

Why Workers Join Unions

Management men like to think that workers join unions because of coercion. Actually, most join because the union provides a business service: greater security in the job, higher wages, better working conditions, protection against arbitrary or unfair treatment by management, and other services. The worker who belongs to a union feels more secure—nobody in management can push him around unfairly. He cannot lose his job as easily as he might if he were dependent only upon his own relations with management. After all, he knows that foremen come and go and he cannot predict whether the next one will be considerate of him and his needs.

Most employees have need for a business service organization that represents them and their job security needs. Even though the nonunion employee has a job that he likes and does well, he knows that he can be discharged for numerous reasons including arbitrary action by a superior. If he is discharged or laid off, his financial resources may not carry him over comfortably to the next job. As a family man, he probably is buying a home, a car, and one or more electrical appliances on an installment basis. As long as his regular income continues he can meet the payments and at the same time support his family adequately. As soon as his income stops for even one month, he and his family are likely to suffer and many of his savings in the form of equities in purchases may disappear. His financial reserves are so limited that he feels he should seek the services and protection that a union can provide. He also knows that the employer is not a completely free agent in the market —he must run the business to meet competition and to please the customers. The customers' wishes and the survival of the company take precedence over the continuation of his employment. Besides, if it should become necessary for the employer to lay off some men, he believes that the ones selected for layoff or discharge should be influenced by an organization that represents all the plant employees.

This kind of felt need on the part of workers of many industries has been accentuated by automation.

Fortunately, many management men do put themselves in the place of the worker confronted with job insecurities and seek to enable him to attain an optimum degree of security. If job tenure is not possible, management should at least give the worker an appreciation of why the need cannot be answered by explaining the company's limitations and competitive problems. Usually, if the worker feels that his needs are understood and that management wants to meet them, he can participate with management in dealing with the company's problems as a colleague, not as someone who must accept whatever management is willing to give.[2]

To the worker of the large corporation, members of management appear to be remote privileged persons who do have job security. The union leaders, in contrast, are men like himself who claim to understand him, they cater to him and treat him as an equal. This is especially likely to be the feeling of people engaged in mechanized work. To the worker, the labor union is an instrument for enhancing his dignity as an individual. When the worker's dignity is ignored and his needs are not recognized, his resentment is likely to be expressed by increased loyalty to the union. His incidental complaints and grievances are manifested through various forms of hostility, often irrationally, as in wildcat strikes and slowdowns. For some members, the union also offers an outlet for aggression against the autocratic or the paternal figure of management.[3]

Most employees who belong to unions are loyal to their union officials. They are not greatly concerned about newspaper reports of embezzlement and misuse of union funds by union leaders. They are more concerned about getting more benefits through the one organization that represents them and their interests.

Adverse publicity and findings of union atrocities that are revealed in congressional and other hearings seldom destroy the faith of a union member whose leaders have accomplished something for him. He thinks of his recent wage increases, improved fringe benefits, and better working conditions, and he believes—rightly or wrongly—that these improvements have been brought about by his union. He feels that if his union were to be destroyed or weakened, he might once more be at the mercy of an arbitrary member of management. His employer might be a kind person, or on the other hand, he might not be. To the worker, his union provides a set of effective brakes on management. He is not too confident about how well his relations with management would operate if the brakes were removed.

The workers who will not join unions are not without desire for security, opportunity, an improved standard of living, and recognition. But they either have resigned themselves to the belief that these things are unattainable or have concluded that some other method for getting them is more feasible. These men believe that their employer's good will and good sense will provide as much security and recognition for them as they could get through the unions. They may prefer to rely on their own individual efforts; or they may feel that only far-reaching political and economic change could effect any real alteration in their circumstances.

Behavioral Patterns of Some Union Leaders

Members of management who deal with union leaders tend, in time, to find that these men have certain typical characteristics. Of course, the executives realize that individual differences occur among labor union leaders as well as among executives and other occupational members. They do, however, become aware of patterns, or signs of behavioral patterns, in the psychological make-up of union leaders. Unfortunately, these patterns have not as yet been studied by social scientists to the same extent that behavioral patterns of business executives have been studied. A reason may be that union leaders are more defensive and less confident about themselves. They therefore do not like to be analyzed even though the purpose of the analysis may be friendly. In contrast, the able, self-confident, emotionally secure executive does not, as a rule, care how much anyone studies him.

However, a few systematic studies have been made of union leaders. Howard M. Bogard, for example, administered a battery of tests and biographical inventories to 40 trainees of the International Ladies Garment Workers Union and to the same number of management trainees of the Grace Line, Inc., a major international shipping corporation. The two groups differed markedly. The union trainees were found to be somewhat less intelligent and less aggressive than the management trainees. However, both groups tended to score above the general population in both of these traits. The ILGWU trainees appeared to manifest less social maturity, to be less responsible, and to reveal a long-standing propensity to overt conflict with authority figures. They appeared to reveal the strong social feelings encouraged by the union, to be aggressive, assertive, and impulsive. Their data suggested a lack of emotional maturity. However, in most of the traits studied, the picture of the two groups was close to the ideal types sought by the particular union or management program administrators. As usual in studies of this kind, individual differences found within each group were often considerable.[4]

Another study of sixteen personality and other variables of union stewards and managers was made in regard to 33 tool-and-die shops. One of the few statistically significant findings was that shops with a low emotional tone tend to have union stewards who are sensitive and thin-skinned.[5]

When we attempt to describe behavior patterns that characterize typical labor union leaders, we have to depend mainly upon empirical judgment rather than statistically significant measurements. The approach must be qualitative, not quantitative. This limitation is, however, also applicable to studies of members of other groups in business and in society. Few quantitative evaluations of people are ever statistically proven or especially useful in our human relations. The patterns we see through our experiences with the specific individuals must be our main guide.

Those who have had considerable experience in dealing with labor union leaders recognize that many of them are capable and ambitious, but they never learned to feel at home in the company of people in management or in the social groups frequented by executives. Many college students feel the same way, but the ambitious business-oriented student typically identifies himself with management. He looks forward to becoming a member of management and associating with executives as an equal. The union leader does not. He does not identify himself with management and therefore has difficulty in understanding or trying to understand business problems and how to deal with them constructively. He identifies with the employees, whom he perceives to be like himself: unappreciated, neglected, or exploited. He often feels frustrated in his desire for advancement because he realizes that he does not fit into the group that is likely to advance into management.

Another type of union leader is the one who is rebelling against authority. The man who has rebelled violently against authority is rarely found in management. He is, however, frequently found among those union leaders who are in power in the early history of unionism in a company—the fighting stage of union-management relations. He is elected to office because he has the characteristics that a new and insecure union needs if it is to achieve the things its new members desire of it at the time of its organization. When such a union leader first appears across the negotiating table from management, he causes a good deal of dismay among the management men. They realize that such a man is resentful toward management and completely unwilling to bury the past in order to build a new relationship. Consequently the growth of peaceful industrial relations is checked so long as he is in power.

In the normal course of events, however, the union achieves some of its purposes, and with this achievement comes a measure of security. When this happens, there is likely to be a change in union leadership. The fiery oratory of the aggressive rebel against authority does not get much response from members who cannot be whipped into a frenzy after their main desired rights have been recognized and granted by management. The authority-hater moves on to another company where his zeal fits the kind of situation that calls for inflammatory leadership. Of course, a few of these leaders may remain for some years after management has accepted the union.

Imberman's Study of Labor Leaders

The purpose of Imberman's study was to facilitate labor relations by an analysis of the leaders' characteristics. Over a two-year period, he worked for a public relations firm having two large unions as clients. His work brought him into friendly contact with 249 labor leaders of 42 unions.

He found that most of the labor leaders come from a laboring class family, do not have much schooling above grade school, and have found the union the most feasible means of attaining financial success and power. But the labor leader often finds that neither he nor his family is accepted socially, in certain groups. Members of these groups think of him as on the occupational level of the members of the union, and as a dishonest power-grabber. Even political office, which many of the successful union leaders seek, does not protect him from social rebuff. The resulting frustration breeds bitterness.

The bitterness over being unaccepted socially may work itself out by: (1) antagonism toward the employer, resulting in unreasonable union rulings and demands and (2) accepting bribes for favorable decisions. The bribe may not be in the form of immediate cash but in an "arrangement" whereby the company agrees to buy products in accordance with a special contract that benefits the labor leader's private business on the outside. However, bribes are a common practice with certain types of union leaders only, and when those leaders refuse a bribe, it may be because of the insulting manner in which it is offered.

Imberman also found that a high proportion of these leaders found some solace in the company of women who were "of better social graces and elegancies than the original wife, seeming to indicate that even here the drive for acceptance and higher social status may be operating."

He concluded that the difficulties that exist between labor and management exist not so much over issues but over the fact that management as a group snubs or appears to snub the labor leader socially. He suggested that a helpful remedy for management people would be to accept the labor leader, make him an important member of the community, and have him join exclusive clubs. This, he thinks, would tend to cause the antagonism expressed across the bargaining table to dissipate itself.[6]

Unfortunately, this recommended remedy is not feasible. Any union leader who would hob-nob with management men would arouse suspicion on the part of his own rank-and-file members. They would assume that he was taking the points of view of management and would not fight for the members' rights. Such a union leader would be in office until the next election only. Few labor leaders could take the risk of adapting themselves to a new social environment that might lead to identification with management. The main contribution of Imberman's study is its implication that management men in all their relations with union leaders should be relaxed, respectful, and friendly toward each as an individual even though he may be an embittered, unreasonable person.

In many companies, the psychological patterns of the union leaders differ markedly from those of the majority of union members. Management men note this and often ask the question: "Why do our friendly and reasonably well-balanced employees usually vote into union office the most cussed candidate rather than the typical normal cooperative type of employee?" The answer becomes simple when we remind ourselves that most employees think of the union as providing a business service—the disputatious officer is more likely to get higher wage rates and better working conditions than the easy-to-get-along-with union official. They want a union leader who will watch the wage increases being secured in other plants and be sufficiently aggressive to make his members feel that he is achieving the best wage arrangements that can be obtained for them. Union leaders do, of course, find causes of grievances and correct them but these are extra services between contract negotiations rather than the main service to the members.

Characteristics in the pattern of typical union leaders, as noted from contacts with them, are:

1. Little education
2. Above average intelligence
3. Laboring class family orientation in childhood
4. Leadership ability
5. Feeling of rejection by members of social classes who are on same income level as the union leader—management symbolizes a social rank unattainable by labor leaders
6. Usually functions in a situation that does not permit close associations with management as a colleague of management for fear of being accused of "selling out."

Member Participation in Union Affairs

Leonard R. Sayles and George Strauss have reported findings from a series of unstructured interviews with union members. They found that the members' participation in day-to-day union activities contrasted sharply with their loyalty to the union in strikes. Also, even though members exhibit strong loyalty toward their union as an institution they frequently criticise the union's officials.

The interviews revealed that the typical member is convinced he needs his union for protection against arbitrary management action and for obtaining economic security. Members expressed their need for the union: "Without a union we would be lost; the company could really take advantage of us." Members will endure privations to belong to the union and to win strikes. The typical member will remain loyal during a strike even though he is subjected to tremendous pressures such as those of seeing his children hungry, lack of his wife's sympathy, and putting up with an openly hostile community.

At the same time that the union member demonstrates firm loyalty in regard to the union's economic functions, he is apathetic toward the union's internal activities. For example, attendance at regular meetings of large industrial unions averages two per cent to eight per cent of the total membership. Attendance at meetings for a strike vote or contract negotiation averages from 40 per cent to 80 per cent.

Many workers do not seek or accept union offices. Reasons given are "All those meetings to go to," "No time with the family," "Always some guy after something he doesn't deserve," and so forth. An important conclusion was:

> For a small group, the union is a way of life; for the majority, it is but a method of representation, although a very important one. For the leaders, the union has become an end in itself; for the rank and file, it is but a means to an end, a way of gaining greater security on the job, *not* a great social movement.[7]

Dual Loyalties

In many cases, both company and union are in competition for the loyalties of the worker. Some people imagine that the worker's dual allegiance to company and union is impossible. In some companies, the workers are split into two sharply defined groups: one, pro-management and anti-union, the other, pro-union and anti-management.

Investigations indicate, however, that in a unionized plant both labor and management can have the allegiance of the worker. As long as these demands are not contradictory, the worker can live up to the expectations of both company and union. He can have dual allegiance and be thought of as loyal by both parties, for he is meeting their requirements.

Theodore V. Purcell conducted a study of

a unionized Swift plant to find out whether the employees' attitudes were favorable or unfavorable toward the company and the union.[8] His findings show that most of the workers had a dual allegiance:

	Per cent
Unfavorable to both company and union ...	0.
Neutral to both ...	0.5
Favorable to one & unfavorable to other ...	13.
Favorable to one & neutral to other ...	13.
Positively favorable to both ...	73.
Stewards with dual allegiance ...	88.
Foremen with dual allegiance ...	57.

In general, the majority of workers in a company find that they can favor and support both the company and the union. They can do this in spite of the fact that they often disagree with spokesmen of both management and labor. The workers do not feel that conflict is inevitable, or that they must accept one group and reject the other. Many accept the state of dual allegiance.[9]

The fact that a worker joins a union does not mean that he is therefore anti-company. The employer may still be able to gain the good will and cooperation of many of his employees who belong to a union. In some cases, the union employees are "loyal" to the employer and the employer in turn, is "loyal" to the union.

Unions have also contributed toward easing some employers' burdens. For example, unions are likely to call the management's attention to rates of pay and other conditions that hinder production. Workmen are more apt to speak their minds freely when they know they have the union to defend their rights. Foremen of unionized plants also must improve their skills in handling their men. Foremen cannot take out grouches on men who are unionized. Recognition of the union tends to clear the atmosphere for the employees and enable them to express their grievances. On the other hand, many unions also act as a kind of wedge between the management and the men, thus preventing management and men from ever understanding each other or cooperating wholeheartedly.

As stated by Arnold S. Tannenbaum in a report of a seminar jointly sponsored by the Institute of Labor and Industrial Relations of the University of Michigan and Wayne State University and the Foundation for Research on Human Behavior:

> The labor movement has repeatedly expressed aversion for efforts toward developing some of the psychological positives. These are often identified as cow sociology and manipulation techniques for exploiting the worker and undermining the power of the labor movement. The satisfied worker is thought to be a "tranquilized" worker. In its zeal to protect itself against this "tranquility," labor has perpetuated a set of cultural norms which define work in essentially negative terms. The ideal image of the working man which the labor movement provides is not that of a man enjoying his work. This is ironic since in many unionized plants, the man who enjoys his work is more likely to be an active and loyal union member than his less satisfied brothers.[10]

A few unions and companies have cooperated in developing programs of education for workers. Such attempts, when sincerely and objectively conducted, are likely to result in long-term improvements in industrial relations.

The few examples, so favorable to the unions, should not cause one to assume that strikes have been eliminated from industries which have had a long experience with unionism. Strikes continue with great frequency in some highly unionized industries.[11] However, the strike records of individual industries vary so greatly that the results of unionization in specific industries are likely to depend upon factors other than extensive unionism. Unionism may become popular in a specific industry because, for example, employees resent certain policies of a particular management. They may be reacting to emotional stress.

Why Workers Strike

When an industrial conflict reaches the strike stage, everyone loses, especially if the strike is one of long duration. The employer loses in sales and maintenance costs. The customers and stockholders lose. The employees, in particular, lose wages and savings that may require years of labor to recoup.

Labor union leaders claim that they do not want strikes and blame pigheaded industrialists for causing them. Industrialists claim that they do not want strikes and blame the irrationality of power-seeking union leaders. Both the labor leader and the industrialist claim that the other fears and hates him without just cause. Rumors and suspicions flourish. Grievances flare into strikes, slowdowns, and work stoppages.

The factors in industrial relations that lead to strikes are difficult to analyze scientifically because of the numerous influences and unrecognized variables at work. A strike does not occur because of a few influences. Only the precipitating influences are revealed by most investigations of strikes. The predisposing influences are usually overlooked. Group dynamics and the ways that people react to stress should be studied to discover more comprehensive factors than are revealed by the published reports of strikes. A riotous strike is an act of aggression under stress. A few significant studies have been made of the ways in which people tend to act under stress. For example, a study of lynchings indicated that when the price of cotton went down in fourteen states, the number of lynchings went up.[12] Race riots and similar forms of aggressive expression have been investigated and found to involve strong fears, frustrations, and stress.[13]

Of course many studies of violent aggressions that develop from frustration and fear do not reveal all the basic causes of many strikes and labor union activities of today. Additional questions, such as the following, need to be asked:

1. To what extent are seekers of power in conflict? Either management or labor union leaders or both may be seeking greater economic power in order to maintain or to strengthen their position in the economic life. Sometimes the worker is exploited for the benefit of power-seekers, as reported by Arthur O. England on his return from a study of industrial relations practices in various Mid-West plants:

> The average worker is a sympathetic sort of a fellow who is ruled generally by his emotions rather than by logical thinking and reasoning. Sometimes this sympathetic fellow gets taken for a ride. Surrounding us are people who desire power. Their desire for power is a personal one. We have seen how these power boys have "rifled" their way to the top. They may have to distort the facts a little. They may appeal to our needs, those needs reflecting our weaknesses, those areas where doubts can creep in.
>
> These leaders are smart, for their own good, because they understand a fundamental fact about human nature. It's easier to make people unhappy than to make them happy. It's easier to put people on the defensive than to strengthen their prestige. It's like the old story about the mother trying to put her two children to bed. The vociferous neighbor brings them candy and tells them stories. "Why go to bed? Stay up and play like the rest of the kids. Here, have ten pieces of candy. Candy never hurt any youngster. Your mother," the intruder goes on, "must be an old witch to make you go to bed so early and not let you eat all the candy you want." Well? Our mother is truly put on the defensive now. How can she regain the respect and confidence she needs to rear her children properly? The American worker has been kept up long past his bed time. We can't blame him for being a sympathetic individual—that's a rather general American feeling—but he has been the subject of some pretty bad guidance. Too much candy and too little sleep have made a pretty sick fellow out of him.
>
> It's easy to see why a successful concern has to stand for more than a square deal. In addition to its products it must also produce good citizens out of its employees.[14]

2. What stage has been reached in the development of employer-union relations? The life history of most old well-established employer-union relations usually has three stages: (*a*) The *organizational* stage, when the union tries to get a foothold in the company. The employer resists and the union intensifies the fight. The union leaders are of necessity very aggressive and belligerent; (*b*) The *cold neutrality* stage, when the union has won recognition and the employer acts

in accordance with the requirements of the contracts; (*c*) The *established* stage, when the union and the employer have learned to live and work together in a more or less cooperative manner. The leadership of the union has changed from the hard-boiled fighting variety to a more cooperative type. However, completely genuine cooperation between union and employer is rare, regardless of the stage of stability attained by the union.

An analysis of labor events today indicates that many unions are moving toward the third or established stage.

These trends should be checked at intervals in the future to see if they continue or waver.

3. Are the labor union leaders trying merely to increase their share of the "economic pie," or are they trying to enlarge the pie? If the returns from a business enterprise may be considered a pie, there are two ways for a union to get more pie. One way is to fight for as big a piece as can be obtained. Another way is to increase the size of the pie through greater worker productivity. The former method is called collective bargaining; the latter, union-management cooperation. Economically, wage increases tend merely to distribute rather than create property.

Are the policies and practices of the union designed to make work and cause featherbedding in order to please members, or are they designed to stimulate members to produce more in a cooperative relationship?

4. Are conflicting ideologies influencing the employer-union relations? So many examples of such conflict have occurred in recent years that only one need be mentioned here. A comparative study was made of two Pacific Coast industries: the pulp and paper industry and stevedoring. These two industries had contrasting records. The former enjoyed industrial peace; the latter suffered from a continuous record of conflict. On the basis of his findings, the investigator of the two groups made several generalizations, one of which concerned ideology:

> Where employers and union representatives hold irreconcilable differences in economic belief, and where the union representatives have not only been thoroughly indoctrinated with left wing philosophy, but where this philosophy has been the touchstone of union action, hope for enduring industrial peace is illusory, and conflict, whether open or concealed, pervades and dominates the employer-employee relationship.
>
> Officers of the Longshoremen's Union have assumed since 1934 that the purpose of collective bargaining is not to establish a system of industrial jurisprudence, but rather that it is a device through which, under the cloak of an agreement, unremitting if undeclared warfare can be carried on against the employers. Since any procedure, no matter how devious, has been considered as legitimate under conditions of war, it was this philosophy which dominated the position of the union's representatives. They have looked on the employers not as a necessary and desirable component in a joint industrial effort, but as an inescapable evil. Co-operation and collaboration have been to them unthinkable and basically undesirable. Consequently, the written word, whether it be the language of a collective bargaining agreement or an arbitrator's award, was scrutinized with the objective of finding some way to torture its plain intent and meaning to the advantage of the union, rather than as a rule to be observed and followed. This is definitely the approach of the ideological unionist.[15]

5. Are the policies of the unions and of management based on a desire to strengthen the personality of the individual worker or merely to cater to his weaknesses? Labor unions, in addition to being service organizations are also political organizations. A union politician is, in effect, constantly running for office. Such an objective on his part will naturally cause him to cater to the weaknesses and prejudices of the workers. He will have little interest in policies that strengthen either the worker's personality or the company's economic position.

Collective Bargaining—Contract Negotiations

The negotiation of the contract in collective bargaining calls for high degrees of skill in human relations on the part of both the representatives of the company and of the union. To some, it is a process of "haggling," comparable to the bargaining in an oriental bazaar. The best price offered by the dealer at the outset is not his best price at the end of the last bargaining session.

In modern collective bargaining between the larger unions and companies, the business agent of the national or international organizations negotiates the contract. He works full time at this, negotiates day in and day out, and is usually of an alert aggressive character. Business agents of this caliber receive salaries that compare very favorably with or exceed the salaries of company executives.[16]

Negotiating is no longer for the man who comes off a machine to sit at a bargaining table once every few years. In big union negotiations as in the automotive industry, economic and other specialists back up the teams of both sides. Experts are hired as consultants.

In some cases the dealings between the company and the union are approached in a legalistic manner. More often, they become similar to the last days of a hot political campaign.

Pitfalls that an experienced company negotiator avoids are:

1. *Smugness.* Representatives of labor unions are typically quick to resent any implications of their social or other inadequacies.

2. *A show of undue concern.* If management is scared at the start, the opposition can capitalize their defensiveness.

3. *Personality conflict at the bargaining table.* If two or more persons there hate each other before the sessions begin, the negotiations will tend to accentuate the hostility. One or both parties should withdraw tactfully by claiming that his presence is needed elsewhere.[17]

The collective bargaining process should be perceived not as a situation where management or the union wins or loses in a power struggle, but as a form of communication. A knowledgeable writer in this field has explained this principle very well:

A labor lawyer tells the story of a young executive who had just taken over the helm of a company. Imbued with idealism, he wanted to end the bickering he had seen take place during past negotiations with labor. To do this, he was ready to give the workers as much as his company could afford. Consequently he asked some members of his staff to study his firm's own wage structure and decide how it compared with other companies, as well as a host of other related matters. He approached the collective bargaining table with a halo of goodness surrounding him. Asking for the floor, he proceeded to describe what he had done and with a big smile on his face made the offer.

Throughout his entire presentation, the union officials stared at him in amazement. He had offered more than they had expected to secure. But no matter, as soon as he finished, they proceeded to lambaste him, denouncing him for trying to destroy collective bargaining and for attempting to buy off labor. They announced that they would not stand for any such unethical maneuvering, and immediately asked for 5 cents more than the idealistic executive had offered.

...a large share of collective bargaining is not conflict but a process by which the main terms of the agreement, already understood by the negotiators, are made acceptable not to those in charge of the bargaining but to those who will have to live with its results! Sometimes this latter group includes you and me; but more often it includes only those at work in the company—supervisors and nonsupervisors. To accomplish the bargaining task properly often requires cooperation, not conflict, between the negotiators; and cooperation, even if surreptitious cooperation, is what we frequently find if we look below the surface of collective bargaining.

We find it most easily when we look at those industries where the settlements follow a pattern: if the industry leader signs a contract, all the other companies will then sign, too. It does not matter whether a company makes firm policy statements to the effect that it will only pay wages equal to those paid similar workers in the community; if the union has negotiated a higher wage with the industry leader, the labor group can normally secure it from the company no matter what its personnel policies may be. This does not mean there are no fights—sometimes there are hard-fought ones.[18]

Obviously, some showdown battles in the form of strikes do occur but experienced negotiators of both managements and unions realize that strikes often provide an opportunity for workers to get rid of pent-up emotional hostilities. Collective bargaining can be viewed as a form of communication and emotional catharsis rather than a class struggle.

The negative aspects are, of course, less significant than the positive as summarized in the following recommendations:

> Collective bargaining is not an isolated event to be treated like a David Harum horse trade. It is a way of life—a way of living with the employees upon whose services you rely and with the union of their choice...resign yourself to the idea that you will have nothing better than a cold war, with only the hope of intermittent peaceful coexistence, if your labor relations are not well managed.
>
> And since dealing with unions is a continuing job for management, I'd like to make some suggestions that may be useful in establishing sound labor relations.
>
> 1. Earn a good reputation with your employees so that you may bring it with you to the bargaining table.... I am speaking of a reputation for firmness, a demonstrated willingness to fight for your rights, together with a reputation for open-mindedness, reasonableness, truthfulness, trustworthiness and a decent respect for your fellow man at every level....
>
> 2. Your representatives should be able to take advantage of your good reputation without soiling it. Be sure that they understand human nature. Brilliant men who quickly step on the toes of anyone who steps on theirs are not necessarily helpful in the long run....
>
> 3. Never let your bargaining team forget that the union bargaining team has its own internal political problems.[19]

Achieving Peace with the Union

The National Planning Association made a seven-year study of labor-management relations under collective bargaining. The study was made in order to learn the reasons behind successful union relations among thirty companies of varied size and in different industries. The study indicated clearly that industrial peace benefits all concerned.

The report revealed no new or magic formula for achieving industrial peace. The invesigations did indicate, however, that "...if they really try hard enough, management and unions—two historically hostile groups—can co-exist on a basis of reasonable equality in an enterprise, with each retaining its institutional sovereignty."

The main reasons for peaceful relations among the companies investigated are both procedural and psychological. The psychological similarities are difficult to define, but they are fundamental to good relations. For example, when feelings of "good will" and "mutual trust" were common to both sides, relations were better. And, when both sides acted with good will, they found it beneficial to their interests.

As for procedures, the study found that most successful collective bargaining sessions were carried on without the aid of lawyers or other outside agencies. If both sides have a mutual desire to reach agreement and both sides are frank, their negotiations are likely to be effective especially when the representatives of each group have the authority to make decisions on the spot.

To get labor and management cooperating together in a true spirit of collective bargaining requires more than a set of rules. But if the study proves anything, it is that industrial peace *can* be achieved.[20]

Conflicts between the company and the union can, to some extent, be anticipated.

At Humble Oil & Refining Co.'s Bayway Refinery, Linden, N. J., union contracts covering both salaried and hourly employees have been settled by advance discussion. Bargainable problems in this and other companies are being handled as they arise rather than letting the contract expire before making improvements.[21]

Employees Respect Firm Leadership by Management

Many unions are constantly arguing for and demanding more privileges. When they know that they have a management that thinks in defensive terms only, there is no end to their claims. Conversely, they will respect firm management.

This firmness does not imply that management may use the same verbal tactics that are used by a union. A union representative or editor of a union journal may call a company president various vile names. The president, however, may not retaliate in kind. If he were to use the same langauge, no matter how great the provocation, he would lose the respect of the employees. He is in the same position as the lady shopper who is reviled by a fishwife—the fishwife can use that kind of language and remain a fishwife but the lady cannot use the fishwife's language and remain a lady! Similarly, union leaders may use language and tactics that are "out-of-bounds" for management. This limitation does not, however, mean that management cannot be firm in holding to those principles in which management believes.

Positive Approaches to Union Relations

Most managements of unionized plants try to develop and maintain constructive relations with their unions. They realize that labor peace in the sense of absolute freedom from conflict is not possible, but they do try to keep the conflict within reasonable bounds. Thus far, their best hope for doing so lies in maintaining a balance of power between management and the union. Theoretically, this calls for men of mature leadership on both sides. Practically, that cannot be expected. It is up to management therefore to achieve on its own part the highest level of participative leadership it is capable of bringing about. Certainly, dealings with labor problems require the same executive strength and competence as do all other aspects of managerial responsibility.[22]

Of course there is no one cause or cure for labor conflict. The causes are many and the remedies vary with each situation. A common ingredient in those programs that have proved successful is a constructive attitude on the part of management.

Some employers are honestly trying to build more responsibility and maturity among the union representatives with whom they deal. Methods used are the following:

First, the employer gives full recognition to the union's collective bargaining status. He wants the union to know that he fully accepts the union as the spokesman and voice of the employees on matters of wages, hours, and working conditions.

Second, the employer does not compete with the union for the loyalty of its employees. As previously stated, employees can be loyal to both the employer and the union for certain relationships.

Third, the employer separates the areas of conflict from the many nonconflicting interests between management and labor. In some relationships such as contract negotiations, grievance procedure, and arbitration, the interests of the company and the union are frequently at cross purposes. In others, there is little or no conflict of interests as in suggestion committees, safety programs, good housekeeping, social and sports activities, annual picnics, and open-house affairs.

Fourth, the employer works with rather than around the union in the field of employee communications. He does not try to out-maneuver the union in getting a message across to employees. He works out with the union an agreement on channels of communication.

Fifth, he recognizes that the union is a political organization and that at times union officials will do certain things simply because it is politically expedient for them.

Sixth, he is firm when necessary. Most unions have far more respect for a company that has analyzed the facts, has all the pertinent information at hand, and will say when the time comes, "Based on all the facts, this, gentlemen, is the best we can do." Until management reaches the point where the union knows that management means just exactly what it says, the union cannot be blamed for trying to put on one more bite and then another and another.[23]

Many employers assume that unions are

here to stay and that their objective should be to maintain a balance of power as has been stated by one experienced investigator:

> We must face the fact that labor peace in the sense of absolute freedom from conflict is neither possible nor desirable. The answer lies in keeping the conflict within reasonable bounds. This is best accomplished by maintaining a balance of power between management and the union. This can be done if the business is headed by strong and emotionally healthy men who are capable of participative leadership. If any lesson stands out from the experience of the last 50 years, it is that labor problems require the same executive strength and competence as do all other aspects of the business, and are not susceptible to any special "quick tricks" or "gimmicks."[24]

Industrial relations research indicates that of all variables of significance in particular union-management relationships, management policy stands out as being of crucial importance. Companies which achieved relative success in labor relations showed clear evidence of (1) management by policy, (2) effective administration at the worker level, and (3) management initiative in labor relations.[25]

ACKNOWLEDGMENTS AND REFERENCES

1. From an address by John L. Caffrey before the Industrial Relations Association of Chicago, *The Management Review,* American Management Association, Inc., January, 1955, p. 12.
2. See Rensis Likert, "Motivation: The Core of Management," *Personnel Series,* No. 155, American Management Association, Inc., 1954.
3. See Marc Karson, "The Psychology of Trade Union Membership," *Mental Hygiene,* **41** (1957), 87–93.
4. See Howard M. Bogard, "Union and Management Trainees—A Comparative Study of Occupational and Personality Choice," *Journal of Applied Psychology,* February, 1960.
5. See Ross Stagner, "Personality Variables in Union-Management Relations, *Journal of Applied Psychology,* October, 1962.
6. See A. A. Imberman, "Labor Leaders and Society," *Harvard Business Review,* January, 1950, pp. 50–60.
7. Leonard R. Sayles and George Strauss, "What the Worker Really Thinks of His Union," *Harvard Business Review,* May-June, 1953. See also book by same authors, *The Local Union: Its Place in the Industrial Plant* (New York: Harper & Row, Publishers, Inc., 1953), pp. 3, 4.
8. Theodore V. Purcell, "Dual Allegiance to Company and Union-Packinghouse Workers. A Swift-UPWA Study in a Crisis Situation, 1949–1952," *Personnel Psychology,* Spring, 1954.
9. See Ross Stagner, "Dual Allegiance as a Problem in Modern Society," *Personnel Psychology,* Spring, 1954.
10. See *Research Report from the University of Michigan,* No. 13, March, 1963, p. 2.
11. John I. Griffin, "Conclusions from Strikes—A Study in Quantitative Economics," *Studies in History, Economics, and Public Law,* No. 451, (New York: Columbia University Press, 1939).
12. John Dollard, *et al., Frustration and Aggression* (New Haven: Yale University Press, 1943).
13. Alfred McClung Lee and Norman Daymond Humphrey, *Race Riot* (New York: Dryden Press, Inc., 1943).
14. Arthur O. England, "An Evaluation of the Personnel Practices in Midwest Plants," *Industrial Relations,* April, 1947, p. 37.
15. Paul Eliel, "Industrial Peace and Conflict: A Study of Two Pacific Coast Industries," *Industrial and Labor Relations Review,* **2,** No. 4 (1949), 495–496.
16. For further information, see *The Management Review,* American Management Association, Inc., January, 1955, p. 61.
17. See Andrew J. Dalton, Jr., "Learn How To Deal with Organized Workers," *The Office,* November, 1956, pp. 140, 224–226.
18. Albert A. Blum, "Collective Bargaining: Ritual or Reality?" *Harvard Business Review,* November-December, 1961, pp. 64–65.
19. Walter Bordon Merritt, from an address before the National Industrial Conference Board. Reported in *Management Record,* August, 1955. See also *The Management Review*, American Management Association, Inc., April, 1955, p. 257.
20. For further information, see "The Difference That Isn't There," *Business Week,* Jan. 9, 1954.
21. See "Noncrisis Bargaining Trend is Spreading," *Industrial Relations News,* July 27, 1963.
22. See Robert N. McMurry, "War and Peace in Labor Relations," *Harvard Business Review,* November-December, 1955.
23. Adapted from an address by Herbert O. Eby (Labor Relations Director, Pittsburgh Plate Glass Co.) before the California Personnel Management Association. See *The Management Review,* January, 1955, p. 38.
24. Robert N. McMurry, *op. cit.* "War and Peace in

Labor Relations," *Harvard Business Review,* November-December, 1955.

25. Proceedings of the Twelfth Annual Meeting of Industrial Relations Research Association, Publication No. 24, Edited by David B. Johnson, Washington, D.C., 1960.

PROJECTS

1. Collect newspaper accounts of recent strikes and list the grievances and demands of the strikers. Analyze them. What additional factors of importance would you like to know?
2. Obtain reports from several magazines concerning one important strike. Compare the several reports for bias. After reading the reports, write your own summary of the issues involved in the strike. Show your summary to several critics, asking them whether they detect indications of bias in your summary.
3. Obtain the copies of official publications of several unions. How do they differ from employee magazines published by employers?
4. Interview some ardent labor union members who are quite vocal in expressing their advocacy of unionism. What adjustment influences, Chapters 2–6, do you detect in their motivation?

COLLATERAL READINGS

Gellerman, Saul W., *Motivation and Productivity.* New York: American Management Association, Inc., 1963, Chapter 24.

Gilmer, B. von Haller, *Industrial Psychology.* New York: McGraw-Hill Book Company, 1961, Chapter 11.

Harrell Thomas Willard, *Industrial Psychology.* New York: Holt, Rinehart & Winston, Inc., 1958, Chapter 14.

Karn, Harry W. and B. von Haller Gilmer, *Readings in Industrial and Business Psychology.* New York: McGraw-Hill Book Company, 1962, pp. 427–472.

Smith, Henry Clay, *Psychology of Industrial Behavior.* New York: McGraw-Hill Book Company, 1955, Chapter 12.

Stagner, Ross, *The Psychology of Industrial Conflict.* New York: John Wiley & Sons, Inc., 1956, Chapters 11–15.

Courtesy of the Ampex Corporation, Redwood City, California

CHAPTER TWENTY-FIVE

AUTOMATION AND ITS PSYCHOLOGICAL CHALLENGES

All the cartoons and jokes notwithstanding, there is nothing very funny about automation. It is one of those great historical forces like the Industrial Revolution. It will probably end by changing living standards for the better—but only at the cost of more than a little harsh human readjustment.[1]

The origin of the term *automation* has been attributed to Delmar Harder, a vice president of Ford Motor Company who used it in 1946 when the company was building a push-button plant in Cleveland. He used it to describe the automatic handling of parts between successive production processes. The invention of the word has also been attributed to John Diebold. Generally, the meaning of the word has been broadened to apply to all office and factory operations run by self-correcting control devices.

Basically, the new production methods derive from the integrating of machine tools, computers, transfer machines, and automatic guidance systems. This combination provides mechanical control over productivity.

As usually used, the term applies to any automatic processing of information in an office. A definition of more interest to a psychologist has been stated by Charles C. Killingsworth, as "the mechanization of sensory, thought, and control processes."[2] The functional principles of computer technology are based in *cybernetics,* the science of communication and control.

Computers are superb machines that can add, subtract, multiply and divide at incredible speed. They can store huge amounts of information and they can retrieve it. And they perform these operations practically without machine error. The latest ones operate at the rate of a billionth of a second per step. A design is now on the drawing board that can take a step every pica second. A pica second has the same relationship to a billionth of a second as a second has to 30 years.[3]

This new type of mechanization, particularly the computer aspect, has, even in this relatively early stage of development, brought about drastic changes. It has speeded the development of new products, provided new weapons for a new kind of military strategy, produced new conditions for conducting business, and affected education. Of course, the one dominant effect that frightens many people is its impact on employment. Some of the new machines in factories are highly flexible. We now have machines that make eighty automotive parts of different design, such as tailpipes, in succession just as rapidly and as cheaply as eighty of the same design. The automated monster is often portrayed as relentlessly destroying jobs to the point where only a select few technically trained persons are needed to supply our economic needs. Indeed, one maker of automated equipment has been reported as telling a Senate Labor committee that automation is eliminating jobs at the rate of more than 40,000 a week.[4]

"It says it wants to think about it for a while," *by Art Huhta. Reprinted from* ***Business Automation.*** *Copyright OA Business Publications, Inc., October 1958.*

Unemployment Effects

News items about unemployment appear frequently in our press. When the Secretary of Labor issued a profile on "Who Are the Unemployed?" the study spotlighted the finding that those having the most difficulty in securing work are the very young, the very old, and the Negro. These dominate the group classed as the long-term unemployed, those out of work 15 weeks or longer.[5]

Those who are usually satisfactorily employed are likely to wonder whether modern technology will soon make them "excess" as employees and whether they too are likely to find themselves in the unemployable group especially when they read news items such as:

1. "Typical of the food industry's new automation equipment is Borden's $37,000 automatic biscuit packer. With a single man at its controls, the packer can do the work of 40 women. Borden is doing 13% more business than it did five years ago, but with 12% fewer U.S. and Canadian employees."[6]

2. At a Douglas Aircraft Co. aerospace plant in Southern California, a worker with the relatively humble title of "assembler" cuts, shapes, trims, aligns, and fastens together the equipment he produces—and is something of an experimental mechanic as well. He works in a plant where, 20 years ago, Rosie the Riveter performed her single, repetitive, low-skill job all day long.

The change is only one of many that transformed aerospace manpower requirements as the industry switched from aircraft to missile and space system production. Similar changes are in prospect for other industries that are moving toward a technological advanced, research-oriented mode of operations. A case study of Douglas probably offers glimpses of the future for a great many other companies.

The most striking change is the turnabout in labor structure (Table 25.1), mirroring what has happened elsewhere in the industry.

More versatile. The hourly production worker not only is rarer; but where he survives, he's both more skilled and more versatile. The rigid tolerances and quality control requirements of spacecraft demand the first characteristic, its "custom-made" nature the second.

"It's prudent to employ people with a number of skills, so you can move them around. Spacecraft work is made-to-order, and we just don't have long assembly lines with single jobs to be performed," says an aero-space company official.

Deeper into electronics. The same space age needs that have drastically slashed demand for riveters, assemblers, fabricators, jig builders, template builders, and foundry workers have generated it for electronics technicians, a type of hourly rated worker who's more likely to wear a white smock than coveralls. Also in demand are solderers, who must pass rigid government-administered tests, and certain types of complex machine tool operators.

Most companies that once were airframe producers are now deep into electronics, so electronic assemblers are also needed. Finger dexterity is the most important qualification for this work, performed almost exclusively by women.

Pay scales rise. As skill levels go up, so do pay levels. The technical school graduate who began at Douglas as a sheet metal assembler in 1953 earned $1.80 an hour. Today the youngster out of technical school may begin work as an electronic systems checker at $3.10 an hour. The average weekly wage of aerospace workers has leaped from $68.39 in 1950 to $117. at the end of 1961.

> Want a fast press? Radiation, Inc., will build you one fast enough to print a complete Bible, Old and New Testaments, in 70 seconds. Instead of type the printer uses electronic impulses, and special sensitive paper. To get the machine you go on a waiting list. Cheapest model is $350,000.00.

Source: Alexander McQueen, "Nothing but the Truth," *The Gilcrafter,* July-August, 1963.

TABLE 25.1

How Douglas' Labor Needs Have Changed

Engineering and Scientific Assignments	*Per cent of Work Force* 1953	1963
Aerodynamics and astrodynamics	8%	18%
Structural	29	10
Mechanical	17	11
Structural-mechanical	13	2
Propulsion	6	6
Electronics	20	31
Computing	5	16
Life sciences	2	2
Nuclear	0	2

Source: "Why Aerospace Needs Flexible Men," *Business Week,* June 22, 1963, pp. 44–48.

3. In 1950, the Veterans Administration had 17,000 employees to handle its 6,000,000 insurance policies. This number was reduced to 3,000 in less than fifteen years by means of computers. By so doing, the agency reduced its operating costs from $9.03 a year per policy to $3.88.[7]

4. When a large utility company made a study of the effects of a computer billing system, involving approximately 500 employees, it was found that the persons most often affected by the large-scale change were the lowest-service employees. The employees who remained out of their usual classifications two years after conversion was completed were mostly—60 per cent —those who had 30 or more years of service. Morale took a downward trend with those who found that they had to take a lower grade job than they had anticipated while the conversion

was being made. Both supervisory and nonsupervisory employees felt that they had less control over their jobs than under the former system. They also saw less opportunity for promotion than in the past.[8] These changes in morale took place even though all the employees involved in the conversion were continued on the payroll.

Why Automation Will Continue

Occasionally someone will suggest that the solution for the unemployment and other problems that arise from automation would be to "freeze" our technological advances. Why let the inventors and technical innovators continue to produce more and more inhuman forces that can eventually destroy us?

The answer, of course, is that the social gains from our advancing technology far outweigh the losses or damages. Here are some examples:

1. On the farm, higher milk production has been accelerated not only through better breeding but also through better feeding. One out of every twelve dairy cows in the United States is now fed and "managed" with the help of a computer. The dairy farmer himself could not find the time to keep the extensive records necessary for any new feeding plan. In 1951, however, the Dairy Herd Improvement Association thought a data-processing system could handle the tedious, analytical job for the dairyman. The idea was tested in several states and eventually resulted in increasing the milk output of whole herds, ordinary milkers as well as champions, as much as 25 per cent, even 60 per cent. In 1962, these cows produced an average of 11,742 pounds of milk. That's about 50 per cent above the national average, or two extra tons per cow.[9]

2. We now enjoy a much greater variety of food items than in 1900. At that time, about 100 food items were readily available to the general public. Today there are 8,000 or more. We enjoy the fruits of greater crop yields per acre and reductions in spoilage of foods. In almost every instance, the genesis of the increase in our food supply has been in the research and development of agricultural chemicals.[10]

3. The telephone industry has reported some benefits to the telephone user. In the early 1960's the American Telephone & Telegraph Company had 730,000 employees. This was more than twice the number it had in 1920, when the minimum charge for a cross-country call was $16.50. Currently it is $2.75. Much of the reduction in cost to the user should be attributed to automatic equipment. The automatic equipment has not only reduced costs to the consumer but also enabled the company to provide the service. If telephone service still had to function with the mechanisms of 1920, there would not be enough employable women in the entire country to operate the system if we had to rely on switchboard operators.[11]

4. Similarly, the General Electric Company has been mechanizing its lamp division since 1920. Estimates by the company indicate that if it were still using the hand methods of 1908, ten million employees would be needed to turn out the production of the early 1960's. Currently, its 100-watt lamp sells for twenty-five cents. If it were being made by 1908 methods, it would have to sell for $20.[12]

5. United Air Lines, Chicago, installed an Instamatic reservations system designed by Tele-Register Corporation, that linked 900 desks into a nationwide network of high-speed communications circuits issuing from a Denver-based Telefile computer. This network makes it possible to instruct hundreds of employee-students simultaneously from coast to coast without an employee leaving his work place. The training material has a separate, simple numeric code that makes it possible for a reservation-making employee to use his regular desk set as a teaching tool. United Air Lines has measured the effectiveness of the training device by testing 3,000 employee students. It took an average of only 46 minutes to achieve proficiency and retention of certain information as against 75 minutes for a con-

Not so long ago the smiles of these Guatemalan children were listless stares. Read how Incaparina®, found with the help of an IBM computer, made this transformation possible.

Report from the tropics:

IBM computer helps science save protein-starved children

SCIENTISTS have found an answer to protein starvation, the world's biggest killer of children. A new cereal food called Incaparina is the hero of this marvelous news. When mixed with water, it costs about a penny a glass and provides as much protein as milk.

An IBM computer helped scientists to develop this lifesaving powder. Here is the story from problem to solution.

Protein starvation, known as "kwashiorkor," runs rampant through many tropical regions. Its telltale signs are the red-splotched skin, the swollen belly, the lifeless stare and defeated spirit.

It kills by lowering resistance. When infection strikes, a child's enfeebled body cannot fight back. Twelve years ago, the scientists of the Institute of Nutrition of Central America and Panama (INCAP) joined forces with U.S. nutrition experts to fight this scourge.

Food—and an IBM computer

For years they roamed Central American villages, accumulating data on diet, income, customs and available cereals. Their objective: to concoct a tasty, high-protein food from native plants and grains. Their data, entered on punched cards, was flown to North Carolina State College for special analysis by an IBM computer.

The computer analyzed this multitude of facts, and helped scientists develop the most economical combination of plant foods with a high protein value. Without the computer, these calculations would have taken a lifetime.

The new food formula was called Incaparina. It is a vitamin-enriched compound of cottonseed flour, corn and sorghum—cheap plant foods readily grown in most tropical countries.

Results in eight weeks

After extensive testing, Incaparina was introduced in Guatemala. The listless children took to it at once. Three cents' worth of this food a day produced startling results. Babies near death in hospitals became well in eight weeks.

Incaparina is now being introduced in seven other countries in Central and South America. And compounds inspired by it are being tested in Africa and Indonesia. INCAP will soon have its own new IBM computer for further research.

Today, nearly half the world's population is perpetually tired, weak and vulnerable to disease—for lack of protein. Incaparina has shown how vitalizing protein can be formulated from local plant sources—readily and cheaply.

"Such new foods may eventually save millions from starvation," reports The Reader's Digest.

IBM®

trol group of 175 employee students who were given the standard lecture/demonstration in classroom instruction. Furthermore, the system permits employees to study during slack periods without loss of time on the job.[13]

The rapid distribution of information as shown in the above examples is changing the formerly impossible to the practical for the scientist and engineer. The machines help find better ways to build bridges, jet engines, typewriters, and a host of other products. They automatically detect and analyze atomic particles produced by atom smashers, show how aircraft and missiles will perform before they are built, and analyze the causes of highway traffic jams. "Any time a physical action follows the rules of physics, geometry, and chemistry, computers can simulate the action. This means that new and complex avenues are open to the scientist in his quest to explain what makes the physical world work."[14] Our high-speed calculating machines enable the scientist to test his ideas without going to the time and expense of building actual models or performing the many experiments which previously were not feasible.

Our available knowledge is expanding at an almost explosive rate—technical papers alone published around the world number approximately one million annually. This means that students as well as scientists will need better ways of obtaining and evaluating information.

Eventually, we shall have to develop regional information centers where optical scanners and digital computers will catalog, digest, and store vast amounts of information from books, periodicals, and reports. Libraries will be linked to the centers with data transmission lines. Information will be retrieved from sources much broader and more complete than any available today.[15]

The Forces Beyond Our Control Are Numerous and Complex

The benefits of technology are so great that we cannot check its momentum. Our human universe of knowledge and achievement is expanding in all directions. Change and growth are taking place not only in technological areas but also in social and political life. Social values are changing. Class animosities and fears of new wars as well as rising standards of living strengthen demands in some quarters and weaken them in others. Today's complex economy is characterized by swift change and the growing interdependence of a vast number of factors, often seemingly unrelated.

Some managements, as well as workers, have doubts about automation. But they realize that high productivity is the only means by which a high-wage economy can be supported in the face of inflation, high taxes, consumer resistance to high prices, and foreign competition. They recognize that the costs of social adjustments to changes caused by automation should be considered in the cost of producing products by the new machines. When, for example, a company built an automated factory in a new area and offered to transfer 325 employees to the new plant, it developed that more than a hundred employees owned houses and could not afford to move. Nor could their homes be sold in the already depressed area of the old plant. Of course when one argues that all costs, however great, should be paid by the employer, one should realize that the costs may be so tremendous that he cannot possibly afford to move into a new automated plant. On the other hand if he continues to produce in an obsolescent plant, competitors will take his business away from him and his employees will find themselves in their old homes but without jobs.

The acceleration of automation has been brought about by forces beyond the control of any one company or group of persons. Companies that hope to survive have found it necessary to build new plants, to install modernized equipment and to introduce cost reduction programs. Managements that failed to heed the pressures of competition have lost out to foreign and domestic competitors.

The struggle for survival in the business milieu has been, however, only a secondary force in the adoption of automation. The basic influence has come from our increased scientific knowledge. Estimates indicate that perhaps 90 per cent of all the scientists who ever lived are living today and that our total accumulation of scientific knowledge doubles every ten years. As scientists have made new discoveries, they have opened new doors to man's liberation from labor, to new opportunities to move ahead to greater achievements in the use of the world's resources. The potential benefits of research are inevitably adopted by someone somewhere.

Approaches to the Transitional Problems

Some efforts are being made to meet the challenge of advancing technology. Certain large companies are developing alleviative procedures to meet the problem of employee displacement. Humble Oil and Refining Company reduced its work force by about one fourth in a recent five-year period. It did this by the old methods of layoffs and early retirement. Attrition also helped. However, the company eased the situation for employees by communicating fully with them by early notification of the impending layoff.

Advance notice and joint bargaining on the extent and timing of such changes, guarantees against loss of employment to regular employees, new arrangements for the transfer of workers between plants of multiplant companies, and new forms of dismissal compensation are some of the mitigating methods used.[16]

Several years ago, E. I. du Pont de Nemours & Co. shut down an 89-year-old cellulose nitrate plant in Arlington, N.J. The old method of production could no longer compete. The product made there was being replaced by newer materials and costs of modernizing the old plant were too high.

Employees were notified as far in advance as possible. The company gave them two years' notice and sent letters to them explaining the reasons and the plans. The company established a task force to help employees find new jobs. Letters listing employees' qualifications were sent to 150 employers in the area, and interviews for employees were arranged at the plant during working hours. The plan was successful for most employees: of the 635 employees not retired, 90 per cent found other jobs within the two-year period.

Du Pont gave severance pay even if the laid-off employee walked into a new job across the street. The company also gave vested interest in the pension plan to those employees not eligible for regular pension during the shutdown period.

Employees regarded the benefits as generous. The effects on the local community were good and employees appreciated the company's help in finding new employment.[17]

Some companies go so far as to shoulder the responsibility of finding a new job for the displaced employee. They will set him up in a business of his own or retrain him for another job. Generally, managements believe that technological advancements must be allowed to continue even though the short-term effects involve difficult adjustments for the employer and the employee.

The adverse impacts of automation are alleviated to some extent by unemployment compensation. When Ewan Clague, Commissioner, Bureau of Labor Statistics, U. S. Department of Labor, spoke in 1964 before an international conference sponsored by the American Foundation on Automation and Unemployment, Inc., held in Geneva, Switzerland, he stated that at least 20 per cent of America's jobless have family incomes of \$7,000 a year or more. Another 60 per cent of our jobless have family incomes over \$4,000 a year and the remainder average at least \$3,000 annually. According to a reporter at the conference: "Our jobless, through unemployment insurance and other family income, take in more than the British steel worker, the French auto worker, and the German metal worker." In many other countries of the world, the jobless must shift for themselves.[18]

In spite of the current displacements, the long-term employment statistics for the United States have been rather favorable:

> Technological advances have gone forward over the generations. While creating transitional problems—very real to the individuals and industries affected—they have produced a revolutionary improvement in the welfare of people. They have not created ever-rising pools of unemployment. In 1900, we had 27.5 million persons employed. Today we could produce the 1900 national income with only 11 million workmen. The population meanwhile has risen 140 per cent. We have more people to support. It would take 28 million workmen to produce the 1900 *per capita* national income. But employment today is neither 11 million nor 28 million. We have no less than 71 million persons employed. The proportion of the population that is working has actually increased, from 36 to 39 per cent, while the average work week has shrunk from about 53 hours to less than 40.
>
> There is no end of work to do, work that only men and women can accomplish. The challenge present-day America faces is to build on the great achievements of past generations. This cannot be accomplished by encouraging indolence. It can be accomplished by encouraging competitive effort for even greater achievements.[19]

The above findings are favorable, partially because of the increased number of government employees. In 1929 there were 4.4 Federal Government emyloyees and 20.8 state and local government employees per thousand population. In the 15 years, 1948–1963, the number of Federal employees declined slightly from 12.7 to 12.4 but state and local government employees rose sharply from 25.7 to 37.9 per thousand population. The largest single category of state and local employees has been in education. The number of school-age persons per educational employee declined from 32 in 1930 to 15 in 1962.[20] One aspect of the change is that the number of school teachers has been rising more rapidly than the number of defense employees, the latter group being especially well represented in the technological development groupings.

Obviously, the favorable long-term statistics regarding the percentage of the population employed do not give sustenance to the man who is out of work and cannot readily adapt himself to the changed situation. Many problems are awaiting our serious attention.

PSYCHOLOGICAL CHALLENGES

Clearly, the forces that are bringing about increased automation are too powerful and too beneficial for any one to turn them back, to check them, or to control them. The only intelligent policy we can pursue is to utilize and direct them to social advantage and human well-being. This policy must be a continuing one for this and future generations.

The student of psychology should see especially great possibilities for himself in this opportune time to become a contributor in this mainstream of history. Let us consider a few of the obvious opportunities.

First, *interpreting automation* and the things that go with it as providing possible benefits that may outweigh the disadvantages will have to be done by knowledgeable persons in all fields, not only by psychologists.

Whenever large numbers of people find themselves in rapidly changing circumstances which they do not understand, three kinds of reactions are likely to occur:

a. "Let's preserve the status quo."
b. "Let's wait and see."
c. "Times are changing—let's take advantage of the best potentials."

The most appropriate of the three reactions is often discovered by the individual himself through his own healthy adjustments to previous experiences with changes. Sometimes the better adjustment of a worried person is suggested by a close associate or a man's wife as illustrated in this example in the work life of an advertising man:

> It was 2:35 P.M. on Friday afternoon, Joe had just returned to his office from the Ad Club luncheon. The guest speaker had been the media vice-president from a large eastern agency, and his subject was one which vitally concerned Joe. It was about the new age of computerization and its affects on the buying habits of the agency media man. Joe was an associate media director

for Woofle & Doofle, Advertising & Marketing Counselors, and the tone of the talk frankly had him worried.

As Joe's wife poured their second cup of coffee the next morning she asked, "What's the trouble, Joe? You looked unhappy last night and didn't sleep well. Anything wrong at the agency?"

Now, thought Joe, that's an understatement if I ever heard one. But, as calmly as he could, he explained the talk he had listened to and the obvious long-range effect it would have on his job. The most obvious was that he would probably be out of one. "And replaced by a machine, at that," he said bitterly.

With uncanny wifely ignorance she asked, "But doesn't someone have to collect all the available data and determine what's important enough to be fed into the machine? Who would do that?"

"I guess I would, if I'm still there," said Joe.

"And doesn't someone have to evaluate the answers that come out of the machine?" she asked intuitively. "Who would that be?"

Again Joe had to reckon as how he would, if he were still around.

"Then about all the machine does is speed up the clerical part of the job. What's so bad about that?" she asked blithely.

As he sipped his coffee, he was surprised to find that the butterflies in his stomach were gone. His wife was looking at him over the top of her cup, and Joe thought he detected a slight twinkle in her eyes. "Couldn't be," he said to himself, "she doesn't understand the problem."[21]

Computers and other technological gadgets are only as valuable as men, not machines, make them. Men do not have to think of change as merely something they have to get used to. Instead, they can look for ways to put the new technological facilities into beneficial use, to lighten man's mental burdens in much the same manner as his physical burdens were lightened by the physical sciences and technology.[22] As has been well stated: "The really tragic technological displacement occurs not in the companies that make technological improvements but in those that do not: those losing their ability to compete and sustain any jobs.[23]

As Edward H. Weiss, chairman of Edward H. Weiss & Co., observed: "The greatest danger in modern technology isn't that machines will begin to think like men, but that men will begin to think like machines."[24]

Future psychologists will offer helpful encouragement through special services that will have to be developed for the displaced individual.

The *psychological testing* programs of today are too limited for the needs of the future. The researchers have concentrated on the statistical aspects and these do deserve the attention of well-trained men. Usually, they have conducted their researches by using as subjects the conveniently available people such as students. A few test developers have ventured into industry and have made helpful contributions there but the age of automation is rapidly producing a new crop of prospective clients—the displaced, the obsolescent employees. When John Diebold heard, at a congressional committee meeting, that automation would kill 20 million jobs, he said: "That won't happen. Instead we will see in 20 years a change in the type of work involved in 60 million jobs. Point is we're in for a rapid rate of change, not a rapid rate of job extinction." Most of those displaced are experienced in performing routine work only. They have limited skills and education. They are not experienced in making value judgments or decisions. Most have little or no initiative for making improvements. Some of these are capable of becoming machine operators or card punchers.

Very few psychometricians have specialized in finding out what the individual obsolescent employee might be capable of learning or doing. Few or no appropriate testing services are available today, services that measure a displaced man's work potentials in a comprehensive manner. True, many testing services are now available but they are too limited for an age of automation. None is now on a level comparable to that of the health testing services of our best medical clinics. This indicates that the psychological testers of the next generation have lifetime opportunities ahead.

Counseling, too, offers opportunities. It calls for new emphases. In the past, counseling psychologists have of necessity been concerned about mental health. This kind of emphasis and objective must continue, but the displaced employee requires a special kind of attention, something more than now available in the office-type of service.

The kind of service needed will deal with the individual's attitudes toward himself and his adjustments to new job opportunities. This need has become increasingly evident as retraining opportunities have been offered to the displaced employees. In most instances, only a very small percentage of the displaced men and women have started the training program and fewer have finished.

A typical example of the reactions to retraining programs is indicated by an experience of Connecticut in its Community Action Plan. The plan was set up to help 12,000 job seekers of the Bridgeport area. Most had been unskilled and semiskilled workers. The retraining program was planned to train them in semiskilled machine shop work. The number screened was 4,400. Of these about 1,500 were interviewed. About one-third of these were uninterested and another third were rejected as unsuitable. However, 600 were recommended for testing by the United States Employment Service. Of these, 200 did not appear for the tests and 250 failed the tests. "Of the remaining 150, 56 either failed to start training, or dropped out during the first week, or for some other reason failed to finish the course. Ultimately, of the original 4,400 applicants only 84 completed the training."[25]

Displaced people require a type of service that is far more time consuming than one or two counseling sessions where test reports are discussed with the client. We shall have to develop a new kind of emotional re-education service, group variety perhaps, where the discouraged individuals will learn how to perceive themselves and their potentials in new perspectives. This kind of service will be lengthy and expensive but probably less costly than public monies now being spent in welfare for displaced persons and for the rehabilitation of depressed areas. Some of these expenditures in the past seemed to be mere stopgaps for political purposes. Though often well meant by the sponsors, the public fund programs for aiding the displaced thus far have not come to grips with the psychological re-adjustment problems. The shortcomings, however, are not in the desires of those who sponsor the governmental grants but in the shortage of competent counselors and teachers. The Manpower Development and Training Act as inaugurated in the early 1960's was more soundly conceived than previous programs but it too suffered from a lack of trained manpower: men and women who were qualified counselors, instructors and administrators.[26]

Education has been given new tools by automation. Teaching machines have some obvious limitations, but they also offer special facilities. Their limitations and benefits will be given more investigation. One interesting study of their values for teaching the retarded is indicated by a United States Office of Education report of a two-year study at the University of South Florida. When teaching machines were used with sixty-six children in Florida schools or in institutions for the mentally retarded, they learned from two to six times as many words in eight weeks as were usually learned in four years under standard classroom procedures. They far surpassed thirty-three children of the same mental ages of five to nine who continued their studies in regular classes. They did almost as well as pupils who were given individual instruction by teachers for the same length of time. The machine-taught retarded children improved their spelling more than those in regular classrooms. The proportion of new words remembered sixty days later was close to the standard attained by normal children.[27] Teaching machines for all subjects and all types of persons will be given considerable use and research as to their values in the years ahead.

College students who are mathematically inclined and have a high regard for detail should be able to obtain especially lucrative positions as computer programmers in the next as well as in this generation. Systems engineers will be needed in industry. Systems engineering is the central influence in the whole automated system. The systems engineer makes a systematic analysis of how a production process will work, determines the information needed to control the operational process, and then integrates the plant equipment, instrumentation, and computers to bring about the most economical method of producing the product. Systems engineers are needed in education as well as in industry.

Those Who Train for Management

One of the inadequately satisfied needs in industry is communication with employees. This has been a problem-characteristic of executives ever since the days of the treadmill. As Douglas M. McGregor has well stated: "We have not learned enough about the utilization of talent, about the creation of an organizational climate conducive to human growth. The blunt fact is that we are a long way from realizing the potential represented by the human resources we now recruit into industry."[28] Few supervisors have developed the skills needed for giving employees a feeling of involvement. Few have learned how to manage through the development of the growth potentials of the workers. Few have learned how to give workers explanations of the benefits, in human terms, that may come to them from new equipment and methods. This old inadequacy becomes even more acute in the push-button age of computers. Systems engineers, controllers, accountants, and others find it easy to think well logically but difficult to think psychologically. Many workers will agree that the directives they receive on the basis of computer-reached decisions are logically correct but they resent the lack of opportunity to contribute any thoughts they may have concerning the decision before it is stated in a directive. They have almost no feelings of growth through participation. These feelings are often present in the reactions of those who work in places where the computer governs management. Both supervisors and nonsupervisory employees feel that they have less opportunity to make changes in procedures in doing their work.[29] Eventually, as this problem becomes more acute, many of these frustrated employees will project their feelings against incidental aspects and persons that symbolize management and will make irrational demands or become restless and escape through transfers to other less automated work such as selling. At any rate, tensions often build up as work life becomes increasingly depersonalized. Automation, whatever its blessings in filling the horn with plenty, reducing manual labor and human drudgery, also accentuates the need for warmth of colleagueship in producing goods and services.

Push-button Exhaustion

The depersonalization in the work situation on the part of regular factory and office employees is less stressful than the work of those who sit at the console boards in the factory or the clerks who work in the key punch room.

PUSH-BUTTON EXHAUSTION: The age of automation will take its toll not only from among those it puts out of work but also from among those who push the buttons. Dr. Rolf R. Coermann, chief of the biotechnology department of the Max Planck Institute for Industrial Physiology in Dortmund, Germany, reports that the effects of the era of automation are beginning to show up in the men who execute the new production processes. As an example, Dr. Coermann cites the operators of the control panels in Germany's highly-automated steel sheet mills. Most of these operators are young men who have received a three-year technical training course in automation skills. But the factory managers notice that after five years on the job the men display a marked nervousness and a slowing down of reaction time. Dr. Coermann relates this to tests—made on workers in highly-automated coal mines and post offices—which show that work demanding a high degree of continuous mental alertness with respect to production puts a greater strain on the heart than does heavy physical labor. The tests compared the heartbeat rate of individuals during rest—60 to 80 beats a minute—with the rate during work. While the average increase during work should not be more than 30 beats a minute, it was found that the increase for those doing automated work was significantly higher. And when the average heart-beat rate increased above the 30 beat limit, there was an accompanying decrease in productivity and the beginning of prolonged exhaustion. "It is no longer a source of surprise to us," Dr. Coermann says, "to find that the heart rate is higher for the man who operates a bank of machinery by a flick of a button on a control panel than for the man who does heavy physical work."[30]

Professors F. C. Mann and L. K. Williams, the University of Michigan, made case studies of reactions to changes after an installation of electronic data processing. They found that work routines became closely tied to the machines, and the company became less tolerant of errors which could be traced to individual employees. In addition, a premium was put on regular attendance and specific deadlines and work quotas were imposed. The result of all this was that employees and supervisors often complained that they had lost some of their autonomy.[31]

An increased similarity between office work and factory work has also been reported by other investigators.[32] The number of key-punch operators increases with the introduction of EDP and the operators are subjected to production quotas and to a considerable

The problem of filling *the extra hours given to us by automation will be solved as in the past—we shall simply take increased interest in the fine arts, athletics, travel, and other recreational and educational activities.*

amount of pressure for maintaining accuracy. Many develop psychosomatic symptoms because of this stress. Many complain of being "chained to the machine." And the noise of the key-punching equipment and other machines accentuates the "factory-like atmosphere" of their work. As stated by Allen I. Kraut who has reviewed studies on the effects of EDP on workers:

> In sum, then, office automation seems to have several kinds of important occupational consequences: Though it does not commonly result in a great many layoffs, it does permit a reduction in the size of the workforce and thus makes many employees redundant. Those employees who remain in their jobs when their work units become automated usually find the content and setting of their work changing markedly—most often, in the direction of factory-like methods and atmosphere. There is a substantial amount of upgrading throughout the organization as a whole, but not very much among the employees whose work is directly affected by the change to EDP, relatively few of whom are given positions in the newly created EDP units. Finally, supervisors and older workers are likely to be especially hard hit by these changes, and find it more difficult to adjust to them than do other employees.[33]

These findings seem to fit into the tentative conclusions reached in the observations on gastrointestinal lesions in behaviorally conditioned monkeys. See page 101. The findings suggested a close relationship between the formation of the ulcers and the cyclic character of the stress periods. Only further research can reveal the true relationships between work rhythms and the physiological rhythms of the individual dial watcher who suffers from the stress impacts of automation.

In the meantime, executives can use known ways of reducing the depersonalizing and stress effects of automation by giving employees more involvement in operations. A few managements do this now through full and frequent explanations as to the purposes in the operations.[34] They also enable the individual to note the effectiveness of this role. The purposes of automated operations are easy to explain to operators so that they will take pride in their routine work but few supervisors in this field are able to or bother to communicate adequately with their employees.

Of course, the shift to computer-controlled operations has resulted in marked benefits to those employees who happened to fit into that type of work, especially on the higher levels. They have found themselves upgraded in pay and in status. Some have achieved a measure of professional standing. A few have found that their abilities to utilize computers for the benefit of management in decision-making have moved them to higher positions in their own or other companies.[35] Certainly, the men who understand and direct computer operations have moved so much closer to policy-making and decision-making positions as to have altered the structure of power within many a business. These men have achieved a high degree of self-actualization in their work life.

Supervisors Who Can Stimulate Employees in Ways That Satisfy Their Deeper Needs

Unfortunately, automation is favorable to only the few specialists who can find self-fulfillment in their work. Many employees of modern industry turn to outside activities for satisfying their pent-up needs for feelings of self-worth. They turn to non-job pursuits for their best efforts. This usually means one of three possibilities: that supervisors have failed to stimulate men to interpret their work in ways that are meaningful to them, that the individual should be in another job, or that he has developed too many negative value adjustment patterns to be able to enjoy his work. Perceptive supervisors can often tap the achievement motivational needs of ordinary persons by giving them constructive feedback about their work and standards of excellence against which they can compete. These are the hallmarks of the achievement motive according to McClelland.

David McClelland of Harvard University has developed the hypothesis that the economic growth and decline of nations is dependent to a large extent on one of the major motives of people of those nations. The motive is *the need to achieve.* He has developed a projective test that is used to assess a man's achievement motivation. Over ten thousand men in 18 different countries have been given the test. The results show that the men who score high tend to be dynamic entrepreneurs and successful businessmen.[36]

Those very high in need for achievement are likely to consciously place themselves in situations where their needs will find satisfying outlets. However, many others, particularly ambitious employees, would make contributions to innovation in their work if they were in a favorable psychological climate. It is these whom the perceptive supervisor can stimulate productively. The study of psychology should be especially helpful to the supervisor and prospective supervisor.

Leisure

The average work week in 1850 was 66 hours. By 1950, it had fallen to 40. The trend is still downward. Some of the benefits of technology have come to workers through more days of paid vacation, more paid holidays, and an earlier retirement age. Most benefits have been in the form of higher real wages, an improved standard of living. One estimate indicated that with the shorter work week, more years of schooling, earlier retirement, and longer life span, the average working man today has twenty more years for leisure than his grandfather. Of course, part of this extra spare time is consumed in commuting, moonlighting, and doing home projects.[37]

The fear that increased time for leisure would have a degenerative effect on our population has been a bugaboo ever since the length of the work week started to decline. The fears were unfounded. Americans with extra time on their hands have not spent it in riotous living or dissipation. Instead, they have done more traveling, exposed themselves to more news sources, enjoyed more sports, taken more educational courses, and participated to a greater extent in the fine arts. As the effects of cybernation become more widespread, more people will take up old as well as new forms of recreation as well as new varieties of work. The entrepreneurs will devise new and more recreational facilities and services. See page 524 as an example of an old form of the performing arts that is increasing. The entrepreneurs will continue to fill in the voids even though some of the leisure aids will be in forms such as the paperbacks for escape reading. These activities may not all be productive, but many will be rewarding and developmental for the individual.

The individual who has time on his hands will use it in accordance with the dominant adjustment patterns developed in his childhood. If psychologists can make more contributions to positive adjustments in individuals, the extra time that becomes available as a result of automation should bring no especially detrimental effects. As one writer has stated:

> The problem lies not with automation but with our conception of how the benefits of automation are to be realized. Instead of bemoaning automation we ought to be directing our attention to the shortage of imagination and intelligence that stands in the way of the fuller life that is now clearly attainable. It is not too soon to be studying and planning now to keep the greatest potential asset in the nation's history from disintegrating into a liability. It may well be that such study will indicate that a three- or even two-day work week for many millions of the American people is a practical and desirable development.
>
> The fundamental problem will be represented by the ability of people to make productive use of their time. Here, then, is the ultimate test of a free society. What happens when people have maximum freedom? When peace and plenty are genuinely attainable, will this result in suffocating boredom or in a vast release of human creativity?
>
> We make a mistake, therefore, if we look to economics for the answer. We must look to

education, to our individual and national purposes, and to the preciousness we attach to human life and the possibilities inside it waiting to be released.[38]

THE GREAT CHALLENGE

When we view the changes that have taken place and the new frontiers that are being created by science and technology, we realize that we must utilize the opportunities before us. To turn our backs to the expanding facilities for production is unthinkable.

Of course, many influences, in addition to those of automation, are involved in making available to people the potentials of the coming increase in production. The mass market has been one important factor in the socioeconomic growth of the United States. The mass market is also expanding in countries beyond our borders. The world is becoming more homogeneous and distances are shrinking as the advances in communication and transportation are utilized. Other nations are gradually creating mass markets of their own. "Eventually this will stimulate a new cycle of discovery, development, and growth"[39] to which we must adapt ourselves. One historian has suggested that history may not remember this century primarily for its wars, its medical miracles, or even for the discovery of nuclear energy, but rather as that century when, for the first time, the benefits of civilization became available to all mankind.

This is the great challenge before us in this age. The special contributions of psychologists in making available to more members of mankind the benefits of civilization are likely to be in the fields of marketing, particularly in consumer research, advertising, and selling. We shall treat these subjects in the next three chapters in order to exemplify some of their psychological aspects as currently practiced in our mass marketing in the United States.

ACKNOWLEDGMENTS AND REFERENCES

1. "Who Profits from Automation?" *Forbes,* June 1, 1963. © 1963 by Forbes, Inc.
2. See Charles C. Killingsworth, "The Automation Story: Machines, Manpower, and Jobs," *Jobs, Men and Machines: Problems of Automation,* Charles Markham, ed. (New York: Frederick A. Praeger, Inc., 1964), p. 14.
3. Ralph Lazarus, "Automation's Perplexing Boon: Years of Time to Spare," *Personnel,* American Management Association, Inc., March-April, 1964, p. 9.
4. See John I. Snyder, Jr., "The Implications of Automation," United States Senate Committee on Labor and Public Welfare, Washington, D.C., Oct. 3, 1963; *Jobs, Men, and Machines,* Charles Markham, ed. (New York: Frederick A. Praeger, Inc., 1964), p. 153; also "Ancient Fears and Modern Prophecies," *The Wall Street Journal,* Oct. 17, 1963.
5. See "New Profile of the Jobless," *Business Week,* May 23, 1959.
6. "Special Report—Automation," *Forbes,* June 1, 1963, p. 28.
7. See *Saturday Review,* Apr. 11, 1964, p. 22.
8. See Albert Kushner, "People and Computers," *Personnel,* American Management Association, Inc., January-February, 1963.
9. See Douglas M. Stephen, "Computers Make Better Milk," *Farm Quarterly,* Fall, 1963.
10. "The U.S. Chemical Industry—Keystone of Our Economy," *Empire Trust Letter,* Empire Trust Company, New York, June, 1964, p. 4.
11. See "Automating the Post Office," *Printers' Ink,* Nov. 30, 1962, p. 65.
12. See John Chamberlain, "Automation Isn't Enemy of Labor Unions," *The Shreveport Times,* Mar. 21, 1963.
13. See Employee Relations Bulletin, *National Foremen's Institute,* Waterford, Conn., May 27, 1964.
14. "New Tool, New World," *Business Week,* Feb. 29, 1964, p. 79.
15. See George Melloan, "Tomorrow's Colleges," *The Wall Street Journal,* Feb. 24, 1964.
16. See James J. Flanigan, "Automation and Jobs—What Can Be Done?" *New York Herald Tribune,* Jan. 16, 1964, p. 23.
17. See W. A. Bussard, "Displaced Workers—A Management Responsibility?" *The Management Re-*

view, American Management Association, Inc., November, 1960.
18. Victor Riesel, "U.S. Jobless Income High," *Post-Standard,* Syracuse, N.Y., Aug. 16, 1964.
19. "Automation and Employment," *Monthly Economic Letter* of the First National City Bank, New York, November 1962, p. 131.
20. See *Business Bulletin,* The Cleveland Trust Company, Mar. 25, 1964.
21. Russell J. Hill, "Computers Don't Have Wives," *Printers' Ink.* Sept. 27, 1963.
22. See Daniel Grant Tear, "Psychological Consulting Applied to Banking," *The Consulting Psychologist,* Nordli, Wilson Associates, Worcester, Mass., December, 1960.
23. A. H. Raskin, "Fears about Automation Overshadowing Its Booms," *The New York Times,* Apr. 7, 1961.
24. See "The Care and Feeding of the Idea," *Printers' Ink,* June 14, 1963.
25. C. E. Daly, "Retraining For What?" *Personnel,* American Management Association, Inc., November-December, 1963. This article presents the findings from several retraining efforts.
26. See Charles C. Killingsworth, "The Automation Story: Machines, Manpower and Jobs," *Jobs, Men, and Machines: Problems of Automation* (New York: Frederick A. Praeger, Inc., 1964), pp. 45–47.
27. See James Cass, "While School Keeps," *Saturday Review,* Apr. 18, 1964, p. 69.
28. Douglas M. McGregor, *The Human Side of Enterprise* (New York: McGraw-Hill Book Company, 1960), p. vi. See also, *Harvard Business Review,* January-February, 1961, p. 25.
29. See Albert Kushner, "People and Computers," *Personnel,* American Management Association, Inc., January-February, 1963, p. 33.
30. Reprinted from the June 1, 1964 issue of *The Insider's Newsletter.* Copyright © 1964 by Cowles Magazines & Broadcasting, Inc.
31. See F. C. Mann and L. K. Williams, "Observations on the Dynamics of a Change to Electronic Data Processing Equipment," *Administrative Sciences Quarterly,* September, 1960.
32. "Effects of Mechanization and Automation in Offices," *International Labour Review,* February 1960, pp. 154–173; March, 1960, pp. 255–273; and April, 1960, pp. 350–369.
33. Allen I. Kraut, "How EDP Is Affecting Workers and Organizations," *Personnel,* American Management Association, Inc., July-August 1962, p. 43.
34. See Richard A. Beaumont, "A Broadening View of Industrial Relations," *Behavioral Science Research in Industrial Relations* (New York: Industrial Relations Counselors, Inc., 1962), pp. 10–11.
35. See Leon C. Megginson, "The Human Consequences of Office Automation," *Personnel,* American Management Association, Inc., September-October, 1960.
36. See David McClelland, *The Achieving Society* (New York: D. Van Nostrand Company, Inc., 1961) and "The Need to Achieve," No. 8 in the series "Focus on Behavior," produced by National Educational Television.
37. See "Spare Time? What Spare Time?" *Changing Times,* The Kiplinger Magazine, May, 1964. Presents findings of Sebastian de Grazia of the Twentieth Century Fund.
38. Norman Cousins, "Hail Automation, Hail Peace," *Saturday Review,* Jan. 18, 1964.
39. Richard A. Beaumont, "A Broadening View of Industrial Relations," *Behavioral Science Research in Industrial Relations* (New York: Industrial Relations Counselors, Inc., 1962), p. 8.

PROJECTS

1. Interview several executives in regard to the probable or actual adoption of automation in their industries. What limitations and advantages do they foresee in regard to the effects on employees, customers, and society?
2. List some of the specific individual differences in people that might play important roles in adjustments to the social and economic conditions imposed by automation.
3. Study possible changes that might be made in our educational system for a better development of young people to adjust themselves to a changing world.
4. Examine a number of recent proposals for governmental economic planning or control of the use of automation. Give your opinion of the possible consequences if such control were to be adopted.
5. The new term, GIGO, stands for "Garbage in...garbage out," suggesting that the quality of information input of a computer determines the validity of the output. Have you noted any examples of erroneous mathematical findings that were computed mathematically correctly but were erroneous as to fact?
6. Make a study of the probable effects of increased automation on unionism. You might begin by reading A. H. Raskin, "The Big Strike: A Thing of the Past?" *Saturday Review,* Nov. 16, 1963.

COLLATERAL READINGS

Bellows, Roger M., *Psychology of Personnel in Business and Industry*. Englewood Cliffs, N.J.: Prentice-Hall, Inc., 1954, Chapter 12.

Farnsworth, P. R., (Editor) *et al., Annual Review of Psychology*. (Palo Alto, Calif.: Annual Reviews, Inc., 1964), pp. 387–392.

Leavitt, Harold J. and Louis R. Pondy, eds., *Readings in Managerial Psychology*. Chicago: The University of Chicago Press, 1964, Chapter 14.

Shils, Edward B., *Automation and Industrial Relations*. New York: Holt, Rinehart & Winston, Inc., 1963.

TV testing. *Panel families watch TV commercials at the Institute's Living Laboratory. Home atmosphere helps to evoke true audience responses.*

Misery of choice. *In-store tests determine " shelf-appeal " of package.*

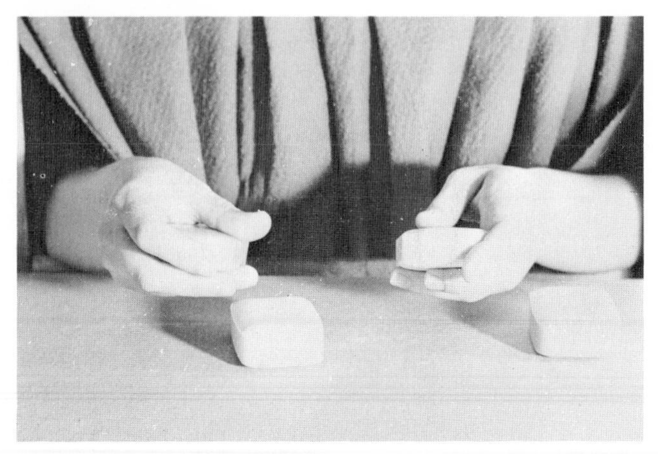

Sensory test. *The Institute tests products for various sensory reactions. Here, a respondent reacts to tactile quality of soap bars without seeing product.*

Depth interview *elicits full range of responses to products or services.*

Ad testing. *Reactions of young and old are checked for pulling power.*

Use test. *Motivational theatre acts out product uses in home atmosphere.*

Some of the procedures *used in making consumer studies are indicated in pictures of techniques employed by the Institute for Motivational Research, Croton-on-Hudson, N. Y. Depth interviews are supplemented by other techniques such as observation and use tests.*

PART V

THE CONSUMER

CHAPTER TWENTY-SIX

MARKETS—PSYCHOLOGICAL FACTORS AND TECHNIQUES OF STUDYING CONSUMERS

A successful merchandiser stated several effective appeals in the following maxims: "Any physical fact, like increasing fatness or the phases of the moon, is much more interesting to any woman than such outside activities as city planning, national politics, or the Bi-Centenary of George Washington; a man customer never grows up, and will spend twice as much time choosing a trout fly as a stair carpet or a refrigerator; people are steadfastly unwilling to skimp on things they buy for their own children. To make sure of a sellout, at least 25 per cent of the merchandise must be in doubtful taste; and no advertisement, no matter how lavish, will persuade people to buy what they don't want."[1]

Those who are aware of the trends in our time recognize that we are in the midst of a revolution. Automation is upon us. The product potentials in modern science and technology are very great but they will be of little value unless people can be stimulated to want and use them. An "automated business" makes not only forceful demands on management and employees, but also requires greater ability from those who market its products. More goods must be sold. Furthermore, automation requires that production be fairly constant, or at least move within a fairly narrow range, over long periods of time.

The burden of these developments will fall increasingly on the people in the distribution of goods—marketing. Hence, the need for marketing knowledge and competence will increase tremendously. This means that we shall have to train more men who can discover new markets, men whose psychological training will be especially helpful in learning about the customer's concepts of what he believes to be of value in his purchases. There will be increased need for men who can analyze an old product in terms of consumer needs and men who can develop new products that will satisfy unrecognized needs of consumers.

Those Who Distribute Goods Work in the Dynamic Area of Ideas

The student who chooses some phase of distribution such as advertising or selling as a career should look upon it as more than a way of earning a living. His work should have social values which he regards as important. Only if he can see it as a vital factor in an economic system which maintains the political freedom of the individual and leads to higher levels of spiritual as well as material living will it merit his respect.

The success of our economic system can be measured quantitatively by the volume of goods we produce and consume, but we must not forget that this progress in material things rests upon a sound socio-economic basis. Admittedly, many of those engaged in marketing lose sight of the larger social values of their tasks and become preoccupied with the details of day-to-day transactions. This has led some observers to conclude that *all* Americans are completely materialistic. As one European critic expressed it, "The United States is the only nation in history that went from barbarism to decadence without attaining maturity." It is encouraging to note, however, that the intelligent, responsible leaders in American industry are displaying an increasing awareness of their role in the social and cultural development of our nation. They recognize that ideas, not material things, will really direct the course of our future progress.

American businessmen learned more clearly the dynamic influences of ideas when several thousand hand-picked experts from abroad toured the United States after 1949 to find out what underlies America's high productivity. They were organized into some 200 "productivity teams" under the Marshall Plan, financed mostly by funds provided by the European governments themselves. Most of them stayed long enough—some as long as nine months—to get more than a tourist's view.

These visitors discovered our *attitude toward the market*. Before they arrived here, they thought that the major factor in our distributive system was the continental span of our market. They discovered, however, that it is not in width but in depth that the American market differs basically from European concepts and business practice—a qualitative rather than a quantitative difference. "That the American is rich beyond our wildest dreams we knew in Europe," they said, "but that 'wealth' here is not just an economic term but a social one, that it means that there are the same things for the rich and for the poor, this none of us understood—and it is much more important."[2]

In America, unrelenting pressures are constantly exerted on our marketing system. These pressures are usually attributed to our rapid technological developments, ample natural resources, a large land area, and a growing population. These and other factors

How many times will you vote today?

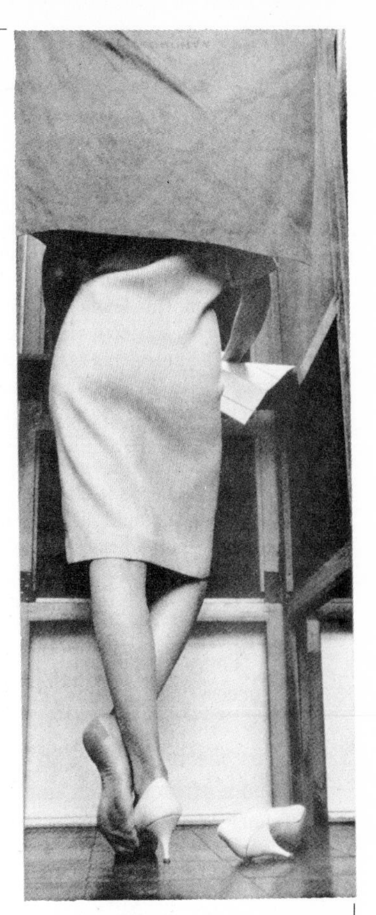

UNDER our American *political* system you get a chance to vote in our national elections every two years. Under our American *economic* system you vote many times *each day*—every time you make a purchase.

No one can calculate the number of individual purchases—from groceries to gasoline—that are made in this country each day. But we know they must far exceed 700 million. (By contrast, even an election as vital as our presidential election is expected to draw less than 70 million votes this year.)

This infinitely complex process of voting—by buying or not buying the goods and services offered in our free market—is a wonderfully democratic mechanism. It continually registers the ever-changing needs and wishes of all the people in the country—directing what should be produced, at what price, and in what quantities.

The curling iron gives way to the home permanent; the celluloid collar is replaced by the wash-and-wear shirt; not because of any governmental edict, but simply because the American people "vote" them in and out of existence.

Ironically, communism and socialism—which purport to be "economic systems of the masses"—are the least democratic of all. The people have little opportunity to "vote" on what they want. Instead, a central authority determines for them what shall be produced, how much, and where it will be distributed.

In this country the "private segment" of our economy (which accounts for 4/5 of our Gross National Product) is literally and truly directed by the "votes" of the people. For that reason the economic system of the United States is the most democratic institution the world has ever known.

UNION OIL COMPANY OF CALIFORNIA 

MANUFACTURERS OF SUPER-ROYAL TRITON, THE AMAZING PURPLE MOTOR OIL

do play a part, but a basic influence can also be attributed to our striving for a higher standard of living for all members of our population.

As an observant marketer of England stated:

> If I were to summarize my impressions of American marketing in one word, that word would be "dynamic." The dynamic nature of American marketing is nowhere more clearly illustrated than in your obsolescence policy. This, it seems to me, is not merely a policy but also a philosophy. There is a driving force in your system which makes it imperative that [this year's] model—whether it be an automobile, a radio, a razor, or a fountain pen—shall immediately render [last year's] version out-of-date.[3]

It is important that employees and other members of our public should learn to appreciate advertising and selling as of positive value to the citizen rather than as clever methods of extracting dollars from obstinate prospects.

In most companies, factory workers imagine that they have no common bond with the work of the salesmen, and the salesmen fail to recognize their relations to the factory workers. Actually, both are members of the same team and each should respect and help the other. Both should seek to understand how advertising and selling contribute to a higher standard of living.

A leading advertising man, Kenneth Goode, said: "The best modern advertising does not try to sell. It aims to help people buy intelligently." Furthermore, the alert business enterpriser seeks to offer, not only what people want, but also something even better than what they thought they wanted. The successful editorship of Edward Bok is an excellent example:

> One of Edward Bok's first acts as editor was to offer a series of prizes for the best answers to three questions he put to his readers: what in

the magazine did they like least and why; and what omitted feature or department would they like to see installed? Thousands of answers came, and these the editor personally read carefully and classified. Then he gave his readers' suggestions back to them in articles and departments, but never on the level suggested by them. He gave them the subjects they asked for, but invariably on a slightly higher plane, and each year he raised the standard a notch. He always kept "a huckleberry or two" ahead of his readers. His psychology was simple: come down to the level which the public sets and it will leave you the moment you do it. It always expects of its leaders that they should keep a notch above or a step ahead. The American public always wants something a little better than it asks for, and the successful man, in catering to it, is he who follows this golden rule.[4]

The businessman who expects to become successful must offer a better product or service than his competitors. The superiority of his offering may be in the form of lower cost, more attractive packaging, or greater convenience than the duplicate product or service offered by less successful competitors. The American standard of living has risen partially because enterprisers have outbid each other in catering to the consumer, not at the consumer's immediate level of taste but at slightly higher quality levels, at lower cost, or with greater convenience. The marketer seeks to know the consumers' present preferences, habits, and tendencies in order that he may enable them to take the next step in the direction of a higher standard of living.

Of course, businessmen do not look upon themselves as reformers or improvers of mankind. The objective of their efforts is profits, but the system of competitive enterprise with the rewards of profit for the better enterprisers results in a gradual rise in buying tastes and material conditions of the consumers. Admittedly, consumers often do not know what they want even when they are asked. The enterpriser studies their present preferences and buying practices and offers many new products, a few of which are liked by consumers. When many consumers like the new products, the business prospers. When offerings happen to miss the consumers' wants and result in losses to the enterpriser, we do not have a profit system but a profit-and-loss system.

Identifying the Market

To most people, "mass distribution" implies that modern marketing is done in a generalized sort of way. Actually, the modern marketer selects definite targets for his advertising and selling. A "market" is usually defined as a group of buyers, actual or prospective, for a product or service.[5] Factors frequently considered in defining a consumer market are income, age, family status, and financial outlook regarding income in the future.

Men who are responsible for developing and defining markets and setting up marketing programs watch long-term trends in the changing world of consumer wants and preferences. Trends that currently are of special interest to those in distribution are the following:

Markets that Result from the Use of Leisure Time

As automation increases our productivity, the benefits appear not only in more goods and services but also increased leisure time. The average number of hours worked per week in 1930 was 47.2; in 1940, 43.0; in 1950, 40.8; and in 1960, 37.7. By 1980 the 30-hour week should be attained. These figures include agricultural work. For nonagricultural workers the numbers are lower.

When people have extra leisure time, marketing men try to help them utilize it through the purchase of more products and services.

A generation ago, economists and moralists worried a great deal about what people would do with the increased leisure time that would come from shorter working hours. Businessmen looked upon leisure time only in terms of lost man-hours, reduced production, higher costs, and a lower standard of living, Moral-

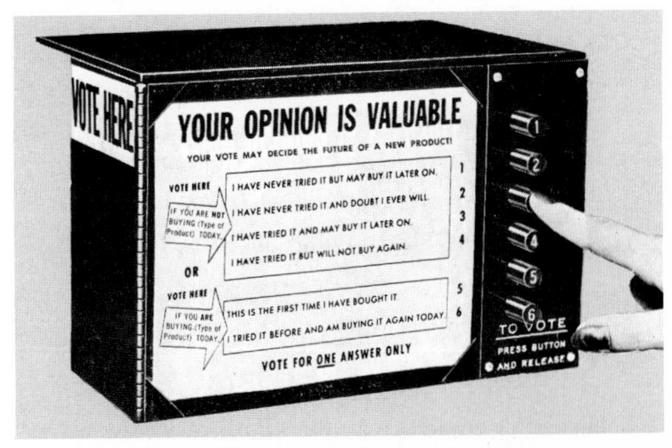

Shoppers respond to printed questions *by pushing appropriate APTIMETER* voting buttons. A special time-delay interlock inhibits repeat voting, and automatic counters record the voting results.*

The need to obtain opinions on sizes, labels, package designs, and a host of other questions concerning current products, as well as on new products still in the development stages, is always paramount.

The Aptimeter will gather, during a typical three-day ten-store test, 3,000 to 5,000 consumer opinions which can be reported to the client within a few days after completion of the test.

*As one manufacturer stated: "The important aspect of the Automated Preference Testing machine is that by placing many of the machines in a group of stores throughout the country, our company will be able to get thousands of answers quickly to questions that may need immediate answers. Gathering a large number of opinions in this way can be far more economical and many times faster than techniques now being used." *Trademark owned by A. C. Nielsen Company, Chicago, Illinois.*

ists, too, assumed that idleness would produce only dissipation and more alcoholic stupors. Actually, the per capita consumption of alcoholic beverages has decreased over the years.

The average American now has some 125 days a year away from his workbench or desk. He has a two-day weekend, two or more weeks' vacation with pay, 10- to 30-minute coffee breaks morning and afternoon, and early retirement on pension. This means that he spends a lot of time and money on travel, TV viewing, reading, church functions, gardening, do-it-yourself activities, and other amusements.

Nor has the industrial productivity of the people of the United States resulted in their use of extra time on vacuous spectator amusements, as was once predicted by educators. Instead, available data indicate that they have decreased their recreational expenditures for spectator amusements and increased individual recreation activities.

The Do-It-Yourself Market[6]

Several important changes in American life have stimulated the do-it-yourself market. The old-fashioned handyman in the community who worked for $1 an hour is no longer available. The $100-a-week office worker cannot afford the $200-a-week carpenter or paperhanger.

Investigations by psychologically minded researchers, however, indicate that the force behind the do-it-yourself movement is not so much a desire to save money as "an accumulation of intense resentment" on the part of the homeowner against the often dictatorial union repairman.[7] Most analysts of the movement think that it has grown out of such influences in modern life as the available leisure time from long weekends and the natural desire to do and see what has been accomplished. This last-mentioned desire has been accentuated as a result of our industrial specialization whereby few workers in a factory or office see the completed articles or services they are helping to make or provide.

The Dietetic Market

America's millions of dieters have established a trend of major significance to many marketers. For some, it has increased sales; for others, decreased them. Current evidence of the wide interest in diets and dietetic foods can be observed in our modern supermarkets. Dietetic foods are now displayed by approximately 90 per. cent of supermarkets. Most of the foods offered are of the low-calorie kind to control overweight and diabetes; some are of the low-sodium variety to control certain disorders of the heart and kidneys; and a few are of the hypoallergenic variety to control food allergies and sensitiveness. Examples are soybean flour, gelatin, eggless cake mix, nonnutritive sweeteners, salt-free canned soups, evaporated goat milk, dry milk, water-packed fruits, sugar-free juices, low calorie soft drinks, saccharin, and so on.

Today, the emphasis on "fitting into last year's suit" is becoming a major business influence in the marketing of many foods. Millions fighting the "battle of the bulge" provide business for the modern marketer. They consume protein bread, nonfat dry milk, oilless salad dressings, sugarless soft drinks, water-packed fruits, and nonnutritive sweeteners. In other fields, too, the dieters are providing a market; they join gym classes, buy bathroom scales, and purchase massage machines as well as many other "reducing" gadgets. Clubs are formed for the purpose of mass weight reduction.

Health authorities support the fact that obesity is one of America's health problems. In addition to those interested in streamlining themselves, there are the diabetics and low-sodium users. Business firms have, as a result, introduced new products suited to these special requirements, and called attention continuously, through advertising, to what is available.

Markets in Terms of Geographical Areas

In some geographical areas, climatic conditions, customs, and traditions are so well known that extensive research is not necessary to appreciate their influence in sales differences. Hard- and soft-water conditions have a recognized direct bearing on sales for coffee, tea, soap, and detergents as well as on water softeners.

The U.S. Department of Agriculture conducts numerous surveys on what people eat and wear. Lemons, for example, are used for different purposes in certain areas. In Los Angeles they are most widely used as hair rinses, bleaches, and cathartics. In the South, only 10 per cent of the users squeeze lemons on fish but 30 per cent of those on the Pacific Coast do. Lemon pies are made by 44 per cent of the housewives of cities and by 65 per cent in the country. A Boston housewife rarely admits to buying a box of cranberries on impulse. Topeka housewives buy twice as many cranberries on impulse.[8]

U.S.A. stands for the United—not Uniform—States of America. Its more than 3,000 counties differ widely in purchase of certain products: bottled drinks, fishing equipment, clothing, and so on. Tastes in entertainment vary with the area. Some cities have few or no night clubs. An artistic moving picture will have its art values stressed in a city such as Kansas City and its sex angles in Chicago. Likes and dislikes in movies are more a question of small-town vs. large-town or downtown vs. neighborhood audiences than anything else. Small-town audiences want Westerns, comedy and action pictures. Heavy dramas make their big money in the metropolitan centers. Message pictures go well in urban centers but not in small towns.

The differences and similarities in purchasing preferences of regional, state, county, and city areas are so numerous that each marketer finds it necessary to analyze and be guided by them. Sears, Roebuck and Co., for example, has found these differences and similarities so important that their general catalog is printed in eleven different editions to fit the conditions of the sections where their eleven major distributing centers are located.

Some marketing targets are selected by means of consumer surveys; others by the study of trends in consumer behavior. The main principle for the student to appreciate is that if marketing is to be effective, it must be directed toward a market that has been identified before the advertising and selling are planned. Consumer habits and preferences must be analyzed by means of appropriate techniques.

Among psychologists, the best known organization making consumer studies is The Psychological Corporation. However, many advertising agencies and manufacturers have trained psychologists on the staff or in charge of consumer study programs. Many of our corporations have found the services of psychologists very helpful in conducting consumer research.

Marketing men constantly seek to learn what consumers want and to compete with other purveyors of products so as to lower prices and to raise the standard of living. General Motors Corporation, for example, has sent out over thirty million questionnaires since 1933. Most of these have dealt with the design or improvement of automotive products and services. Recipients of the questionnaires have been asked to indicate their preferences for such features as the location of spare wheels and types of upholstery fabrics.

Marketing researches must be conducted at frequent intervals because consumers' wants and purchasing habits change. Today's woman shopper, for example, visits more retail stores than she did a few years ago. A study made in Metropolitan Chicago in 1957 indicated that women shopped an average of about two and a half buying centers. Six years later the average woman shopped about seven centers and the highly mobile women average nine or ten. This practice seems to be extending as more superhighways are built and more stores carry wide varieties of goods. As a result, loyalty to specific stores is decreasing.[9]

METHODS OF OBTAINING CONSUMER RESEARCH DATA

Several methods of securing consumer research data are in common use. The method varies with the need. A specific problem may demand a special type of laboratory, test campaign, questionnaire, analysis of company records, or field survey. Applied psychologists are interested particularly in the questionnaire and the interview as used in surveys. We shall discuss briefly construction of questionnaires and methods of securing data through field investigators or interviewers.

The Free-association or "Open-end Interview" Approach to the Consumer

When the consumer researcher wishes to formulate a questionnaire, he does not begin by writing a list of questions which he himself considers appropriate. For him to do so would be to require consumer respondents to think in *his* rather than *their* terms. He wants the respondents' minds to function in terms of their patterns of behavior; not his. One approach to the collection of ideas from typical consumers is to ask them to give their own free associations, to let their minds run freely, and to have them express their thoughts spontaneously about the given topic or product. For example, a manufacturer of toothpaste wished to devise a questionnaire to discover the satisfactions and wants of consumers in regard to the use of toothpaste. An interviewer called on typical users and said: "I am making a study of a product with which you are acquainted and I would like to ask questions about it, but I do not know what people really think about it. When I give you the name of the product, will you kindly tell me whatever comes into your mind. Tell me what you think, no matter how trivial it may seem. The word is 'toothpaste.' Now let your mind run." Sample responses were the following:

1. "I use X brand toothpaste, not because of the radio program or any other type of advertising but because of its taste. It has been proved that toothpaste is of little value, but I'll continue to use it because I like its taste and refreshing feeling in my mouth."
2. "I like the fresh, tangy taste of tooth-paste within my mouth."
3. "There's a fresh taste left in my mouth after using it. Much ballyhoo about their qualities. Little real value in the power of destruction of germs. The taste of mint is often too strong."
4. "There are many toothpastes on the market, but I think salt can be used to good advantage. We like the taste of the toothpastes and they are convenient. One of the greatest inventions of the modern era."
5. "Toothpaste and dentrifices have made the appearance of the present generation much improved over those who came before us. It removes dirt and food from between the teeth and has lessened decay. Thus, we have less tooth ailments and other ailments caused by faulty teeth. Has done away with bad breath to a great extent."
6. "Much ado about nothing. All toothpastes are basically the same with different flavoring. The best dentrifice is plain salt or a plain powder that is not tasty. Various companies pick on minor differences to fool the public."
7. "You can pay anywhere from five cents to a dollar for toothpaste. Every toothpaste company is trying to cut the other one's neck. Advertising appeals come in two classes: Be mouth-happy and remove that white film from your teeth."
8. "I can't start to class unless my teeth feel clean whether they are or not."
9. "X Brand is like a dishrag in your mouth."
10. "X Brand is like a mouth full of soap suds."

At first thought, one might think that the nonguided comments of consumers would be difficult to classify and arrange into any logical order. Actually, their comments can be classified very quickly, simply by underlining favorable statements with a red pencil and unfavorable with blue. Each statement can be further classified as shown in the partial tabulation in Table 26.1 of the responses of fifty men to the word "toothpaste."

The major value of the free-association technique is that it reveals what consumers think when they deal with the given product or its class as they use it, shop for it in a retail store, or discuss it with their friends. Any questionnaire made up without resort to free association or a substitute simply funnels the consumer's thinking through unnatural channels. Many a questionnaire has resulted in pages of statistical tables that showed only what people thought while they were thinking in terms of the consumer analyst's patterns, not what people think when they behave in their own unguided manner.

TABLE 26.1

SUMMARY OF FREE ASSOCIATIONS OF FIFTY MEN

Reasons for Preferences for Certain Toothpastes:	*Per Cent*
1. "I like a certain toothpaste because the radio programs are good"	14.0
2. "Toothpastes refresh the mouth"	12.0
3. "I use the toothpaste I do because I like the taste"	10.0
4. "It sweetens the breath"	4.0
5. "It's convenient when you're in a hurry"	2.0
6. "The appearance of the teeth is improved"	2.0
7. "It lessens tooth ailments"	2.0
8. "My teeth feel better when using it"	2.0
Reasons for Disliking Certain Toothpastes:	
1. "Advertisers make claims for their products which are impossible"	18.0
2. "Toothpaste is made cheap and sold at a high price"	10.0
3. "Salt and soda are not so expensive and are better for the teeth"	10.0
4. "Some toothpastes are injurious"	6.0
5. "All toothpastes are basically the same with different flavoring"	4.0
6. "I don't like the taste"	4.0
7. "I dislike colored pastes"	2.0

Furthermore, an additional value of the free-association technique, or so-called "open-end interview," is the richness of its yield for advertising ideas. The advertising man who has fifty typical consumers practice free association concerning his product is almost certain to obtain a supply of ideas for advertising it. He will feel no need for thumbing through magazines to look for themes or ideas that he might use in advertising his own product.

The Mailed Questionnaire

The first few questions used in any questionnaire should be interesting to the respondent. They should establish rapport, put him into a mood favorable to the answering of the main questions of the survey. "Icebreaker" questions are developed most easily when the consumer analyst has learned from free-association techniques how consumers think about the topic of study.

Many questionnaires in the past have been phrased in such general and vague terms that the person answering them may, while he is answering the questions, feel that his answers are going to be useless, because he is not sure that he understands the questions in the same way that others understand them. Frequently, too, the answering of a questionnaire has involved a great deal of time and expense. In spite of the fact that some persons dislike the questionnaire, it is still widely used and will continue to be used. Fortunately, the phrasers of questionnaires are learning how to make them attractive, inviting, and reliable. The chief psychological factors in securing a high percentage of replies to mailed questionnaires are:

1. The questionnaire should have an attractive physical appearance.
2. The recipient should be made to feel that the questionnaire is worth while.
3. Compensate the answerer for his trouble.
4. For some studies the identity of the real sender should be hidden.
5. The questionnaire should be given a preliminary test on a small group before it is tried on the larger group.
6. Make the questions easy and, if possible, interesting to answer.

1. *The physical appearance of the questionnaire.*—A concern which sells by direct mail would not think of sending out a letter set in solid, monotonous type. The direct-mail expert makes careful tests of returns with regard to copy, color of paper, quality of paper, postage, day of week mailed, and other pertinent factors. It is necessary, therefore, to prepare the physical appearance of the questionnaire with consideration of the same factors used in direct mail. The questionnaire

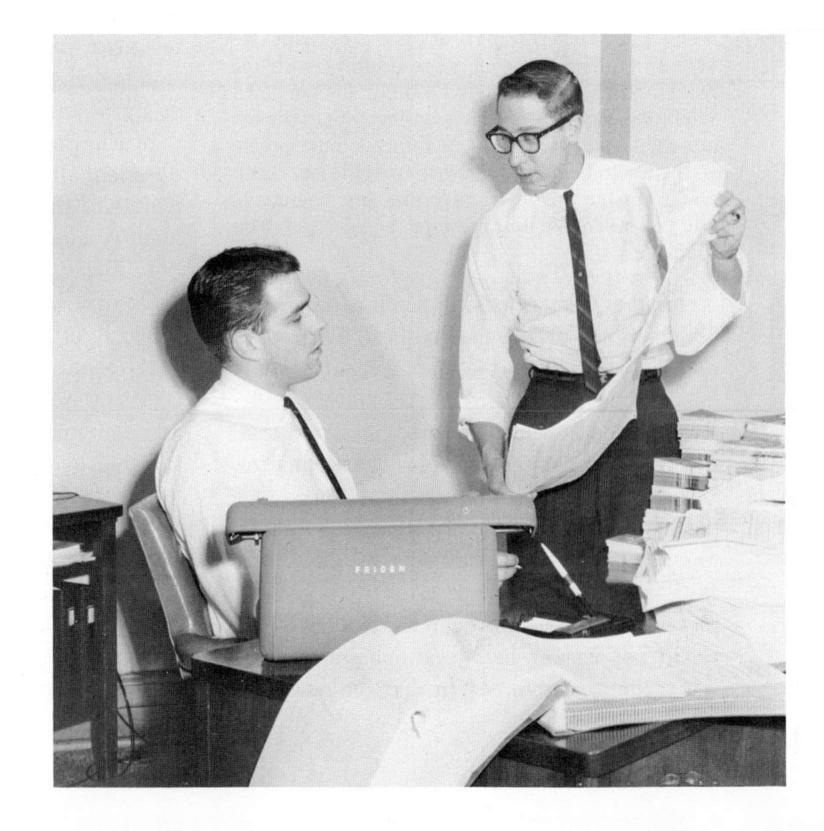

Two young members *of General Motors Customer Research Staff check the data on motorists' opinions obtained from some of the many thousands of questionnaires returned each year by car owners.*

According to a business magazine article, automobile manufacturers are often guided by customer research on such matters as what kinds of transportation the public will buy, the factors of economy, luxury, sport, family, suburban, and related questions. It was no accident that Chevrolet's four successive nameplate introductions, Corvette to Chevelle, were effective without taking away sales from the standard, and more profitable, Chevrolet.[10] *See "Scouting the Trail for Marketers,"* ***Business Week,*** *April 18, 1964, p. 91.*

can be illustrated with human-interest pictures that explain its purpose and enable the answerer to state his experience or wants with pleasure as well as ease. Pictures on mailed questionnaires increase the returns greatly. Color illustrations and attractive appearance are essential to large returns in direct mail. They are just as essential to returns in questionnaires.

2. *The addressee should be made to feel that the questionnaire is worthwhile.*—The person who is asked to answer a questionnaire usually feels that he would be doing the sender a great favor by taking the time to answer the questions. In order to obtain answers, therefore, it is well to make the answerer feel that he is doing himself a favor. Most questionnaires introduce the request for answering as this one did: "We are compiling some data giving us statistics on our business and we would like you to fill in the inclosed questionnaire and return it to us in the inclosed stamped envelope."

Contrast that with this concern, which was trying to get the attitude of their 3,000 dealers toward them as jobbers:

> Did you ever get mad at us?!! Perhaps we were at fault in some of your dealings with us. We are doing some housecleaning of our own minds and methods of doing business. Our friends and our enemies can help us improve our service to them by being frank with us. Please check over the following list and make any comments that you wish. We'll appreciate it and thank you in advance.

One jobber received 500 replies from 3,000 dealers by use of a similar request. The replies were followed up by the management through the salesmen.

The appeals which succeed in direct-mail advertising often succeed in questionnaires. One concern phrased its questionnaire to give the impression that a very charming woman was asking a very small favor. The letter gave the reader the impression that her employer had made a wager that the readers would not answer her questionnaire and she was trying to convince him that the recipients were really interested in helping those who wish to improve their methods of work.

When the questionnaire is sent to a specific group, such as kindergarten teachers, accountants, or shoe merchants, it is often possible to appeal to them by offering them a copy of the data when it has been compiled. In that case it is well to specify the date when the report will be completed and available. A request card for the report should be attached to the questionnaire to enable the person who answers the questionnaire to realize that he may have a free copy of the report.

If the copy of the report has no appeal, it is possible to increase the answers by offering a small gift for answering the questionnaire and returning it by a definite date.

3. *Better results may be obtained if the true identity of the sender is hidden.*—Magazine publishers occasionally wish to make an impartial investigation of their readers' preferences. In some cases the candid answers of the person who fills in the questionnaire may reflect against the publisher who sent the questionnaire. In cases where honest answers might offend the sender, it is well to give the recipient the impression that the investigation is being conducted by an accounting firm or by a statistical concern.

Much depends upon the purpose of the questionnaire. If it is to learn about the complaints of the customers, for example, the true identity must be stated.

4. *Decide upon the type or class of people that you wish to reach.*—In certain situations, it is easy to limit the sending of the questionnaire to the desired group. When a company wishes to get customers' reactions and the company has a complete list of customers, the problem of finding the right group is answered. When the reactions of the general public are desired, it is well to find out which segment of the public is to be reached.

When it is important to know what types of people answer the questionnaire, it is well to insert questions that will enable the investigators to tabulate the answers according to groups, such as occupation, education, sex, or age.

5. *Give the proposed questionnaire a preliminary trial on a test group.*—Again the principles of direct mail should be used with the questionnaire. The direct-mail specialist does not use a letter on a large group of prospects until he has tested it on a small group. He finds that he must do this even though he is absolutely certain that he has a good letter. Experience has taught him that it is dangerous to spend large sums of money until he has determined the percentage and quality of returns.

Questions which are quite clear to the researcher may be ambiguous, vague, impertinent, or unnecessary to a large number of strangers. Only a trial survey can determine the probable value of the mailing. In making the trial survey, it is well to have interviewers present the questionnaire to individuals in person and then note their remarks and questions as a guide to revision.

Phrasing the Questions

No one enjoys attempting to answer a question that he does not understand. The more certain the reader is that he understands the question, the more willingly he will answer it. For this reason, questions of opinion rather than concrete facts are inhibiting to the answerer of a questionnaire. Questions such as, "Why did you buy a Blank auto?" "What is your opinion regarding our powdered milk?" or, "How would you advise us to change our displays?" are not clear and definite to the consumer, and he cannot answer them correctly. Answers to this type of question, however, may give a copywriter a great many suggestions for new copy in advertisements.

Questions, to be understandable, should be phrased in the vernacular. The academic phrasing, "What dentifrice do you customarily employ?" will puzzle more people than "What do you use to clean your teeth with?"

A more involved question, of a type difficult for anyone to answer, was used in a survey of automobile travel: "From March of last year to March 1 of this year classify out-of-town journeys of some length (round trips of 70 miles or more) made by automobile whether in your own car or in a car belonging to someone else."

People should not be asked to make complicated computations in their recall of purchases or habits. If a man is asked: "How often in the course of a month do you change to a new razor blade?" he must make a bothersome computation. It is better to ask, "How many shaves do you get from a razor blade?"

To achieve certainty of understanding, it is well to have the questions relate to matters of fact rather than opinion, and to give all the possible types of answers after each question. Giving the correct answer will then be easy—it merely requires a checkmark, and compensates for any vagueness in the phrasing of the question.

Questions should be stated positively rather than negatively. For example, it is better to say, "Have you bought any Blank soap this week? Yes—, No—, than to say, "Have you not bought any Blank soap this week? Yes—, No—."

Negative and positive phrasings were used in a nationwide survey with the question: "Do you think that advertising is *less* (*more*) truthful today than it was a year or two ago?" Each of the two phrasings was used for 3,200 individuals, and was asked of every second person. It was found that 56.5 per cent answered *No* to the *less* phrasing. But the fact that one is not justified in assuming, on the basis of the foregoing, that people therefore think advertising is *more* truthful is indicated by the answers to the positive phrasing, which were only 46.7 per cent affirmative. Also, the *Don't know* answers for the second form of the question were 22.1 per cent, compared with 18.8 per cent for the first form.[11]

The same investigators also found that the words used in expressing alternatives will influence the results obtained. In two surveys, one month apart, the following were asked of comparable samples of 7,867 persons in each of the samples.

Form A—*"Which of these companies do you think well of generally, which not so well?"* (Company name given and response recorded.)
Form B—*"Do you think favorably or unfavorably of the following companies?"* (Company name given and response recorded.)

Essentially these questions are similar, except for the change from *well* and *not so well* to *favorably* and *unfavorably.*

Company	Responses *Form A* *Well* %	*Form B* *Favorably* %
A	79.4	67.6
B	58.3	46.9
C	52.3	46.8
D	85.5	74.1
E	72.4	62.1

It can be said that the term *favorably* was apparently interpreted as being a more extreme alternative and therefore received fewer responses than the term *well.*[12]

Questions which involve the prestige or personal integrity of the person answering them, such as, "How much did you pay for your last hat?" "Do you do your own washing?" "How often do you take a bath?" do not elicit accurate results. When it is necessary to ask questions which involve the personal affairs of the individual, the questionnaire must come from a third disinterested party or from someone who is able to assure the person that the answers will be kept confidential and used in a legitimate manner.

Obviously, leading questions should be avoided. However, many questions that do not appear to be leading tend to encourage respondents to answer unduly favorably. "What brands of the following foods do you use?" suggests the use of all the foods listed. This question is improved somewhat when phrased, "If you bought any of the following foods in the last three months, state the brand you bought last." Overstatements are especially encouraged when this type of question is phrased, "What brands of the following toilet requisites do you buy?" And most students would be encouraged to say *Yes* if asked, "If Dad were to buy a new car, would he be influenced by your choice?"

"It's a survey man asking what programs we watch. What are some real highbrow programs?"
Reproduced by permission of Chicago Tribune—New York News Syndicate, Inc.

One concern made its mailed questionnaire attractive to housewives by writing an interesting short story, in pamphlet form, describing the problems of a housewife. The story also set forth her methods of work. The housewife recipient was asked to check the method that she herself used under those conditions, and in this way the manufacturer learned the conditions and methods under which women used his product.

Respondents should be invited to give their comments in addition to their check marks. The comments are likely to reveal the feeling tones and manner of thinking more helpfully than the tabulated check marks.

Generally, when a questionnaire dealing with one subject is mailed to a list of possible respondents, the recipients most interested in the subject are most likely to respond. This often makes the results misleading if projected to the entire population surveyed. Unfortunately, we seldom know the amount or degree of the bias.[13]

The Personal Interview as a Source of Consumer Research Data

Sometimes the questionnaire does not elicit the desired data when mailed. It may then be necessary to obtain the information by means of interviewers. If a study were to be made of the reactions of vegetable hucksters, factory workers, or shoe shiners, the results of a mailed questionnaire would be inadequate. When necessary to secure answers to a large number of questions, the interview may be the best method of getting representative answers. Sometimes the same people who will not answer a list of questions by mail will do so when called upon personally.

For research problems that cannot be studied through mailed questionnaires, personal interviews must be obtained. An example of this is the advertiser who wishes to find out which of three proposed headlines, illustrations, or layouts is the best. If the researcher were to hand copies of the three advertisements, identical in every respect except the factor under investigation, to fifty buyers, and ask each buyer of the commodity to state which of the three advertisements was the best, many of the fifty persons would cease to be consumers of the product advertised and become advertising critics. Their reactions would be artificial. By means of interviews, it is possible to plan a technique which will lessen the artificiality of the judgments.

If a study is to be made of three different kinds of copy, three advertisements can be prepared which are identical in all respects except for the copy. Ten other advertisements of different products can be mounted on cardboard. When the investigator calls on typical buyers of the product to obtain their reactions, he may fumble in his brief case for the ten advertisements and "accidentally" pull out the three advertisements and hand them to the prospect with a passing remark such as, "Do you care to look at these while I prepare my ten advertisements for your opinion?" In a few seconds he arranges the ten advertisements and the prospect lays aside the three important advertisements. After a five-minute discussion of the ten advertisements, the interviewer replaces in his brief case the ten advertisements, and then, *incidentally,* asks the prospect about the copy of the three layouts he saw in the early part of the interview. The reactions of the prospect will then approximate those which he would have if he saw the advertisements in a periodical where they would have to compete with many other interests.

If the field interview is used, it is usually necessary to choose and standardize the questions just as carefully as for a mailed form. The interviewers must be instructed also as to how they are to present the questions. They must be trained so that they do not put the answers into the mouths of the informants. When persons are interviewed who are not accustomed to supplying information to oral

***Interviewer** from the Survey Research Center of the Institute for Social Research, University of Michigan, getting survey data from a consumer. Field reports such as these are basic to the planning of programs in modern marketing.*

questions, the interviewer should be trained not to write down the answers in their presence. They may dislike the idea of having someone write down their statements as they make them. In some cases the investigator can be taught to memorize the questions and then informally write the answers on the margin of a newspaper and copy them later.

The research interviewer should have some qualities of salesmanship. However, salesmen are not, as a rule, competent to do field work of a research nature. Salesmen are trained to influence the answers of the person interviewed. They are apt to see only those factors of the situation that agree with their own prejudices. They are promoters rather than analysts.

MOTIVATION RESEARCH IN MARKETING

Motivation research tries to discover the relations between overt behavior on the part of people in the market and the underlying inner mental processes such as drives, desires, emotions, impulsions, attitudes, avoidances, and preferences. It digs beneath the surface of behavior by indirect methods in order to uncover those motivations of which the individual is wholly unaware or only partially aware. It is person-centered. Most readers are acquainted with some of the techniques used, such as the projective tests—word associations, picture associations, the Rorschach inkblot test, and the depth interview. Many of the researchers in this field have had training in psychoanalysis.

Psychoanalysis and motivation research are, however, not synonymous. The purposes of the two are different. Motivation research also is more varied in its approaches as to why people behave than psychoanalysis alone. When approaches from the social sciences are used—sociology, cultural anthropology, psychology, social psychology, psychiatry, and psychoanalysis—they are often grouped under the heading of motivation research whenever the areas of their efforts are planned as aids to advertising and selling, particularly the selection of appeals. The social sciences are basic in learning about motives in the market place, hence some investigators prefer to use other terms, such as "Behavioral Science Research" or "Motivation Analysis."

Quantitative research long since has provided the marketer with statistics concerning the numbers of people who buy a product, the approximate percentages that buy the major brands, the ages and incomes of the consumers, and the geographical areas where they live. The modern marketer wants to know more: why some people buy and others do not. If he knows that, he can define his market more precisely and use more effective appeals in his advertising and selling.

Need for Motivation Analysis

Each researcher who has done an appreciable number of studies of consumer behavior has run into statistics that simply did not jibe with the known facts. In one study, for example, a carefully surveyed sample of consumers were asked whether they preferred to drink the light or the regular type of a certain brand of beverage. A ratio of 3 to 1 stated their preference for the light brew. The actual facts, however, were that the regular outsold the light by a 9 to 1 ratio! Apparently the people questioned answered according to their feeling as to what discriminating people drank.[14]

The inadequacy of direct questioning was also demonstrated when people who were interviewed in the course of a survey were asked the question, "Do you borrow money from a personal-loan company?" All of those interviewed answered "No." This answer was given even though all those interviewed were listed in the records of a local loan company as having recently borrowed money! Similar untruthful answers are given when people are asked about the magazines they read. The answers, if taken at face value, would lead one to believe that the *Atlantic* has six times its actual circulation, while the pulp magazines, printed by the millions, have negligible

The advertising and sales promotion *manager of the KAYSER-ROTH Lingerie Company, Inc., has described the benefits of this garment:*

"In our search for ways to open new accounts and develop our business we searched for non-competitive merchandise wherein the stores which had not bought our goods before would find the new innovations exciting enough to take in the items and look with favor on the line as a whole. We found this item in 'Tonight.' Here are the results of our research:

"First . . . comfort. Women who carefully groom themselves all day long and wear the finest underpinnings money can buy step out of them into nightwear, and the result is ofttimes a letdown. Women are vain, even when there is no man about the house. As a matter of fact, our first headline, run during a market test in five cities, was 'Now you can have your lovely daytime figure . . . 'Tonight.'

In addition to the cosmetic virtues, the garment is wonderful for women who have suffered mastectomies. They now sleep better and are able to wear their prosthetic devices to bed, as their doctors have ordered. We have received hundreds of letters, many quite moving, asking for more information about the garment.

"In our research, we also found that women do not want to sleep in a regular bra, which is too confining, but will sleep in the soft, comfortable support offered by 'Tonight.' (It is patented, by the way.)

"It retains the fashion feel that fine lingerie offers women.

"Motivation research pointed the way to success and as the innovators, we have the market. We have added a shorty gown, a less expensive gown and a bra-gown in cool Kodel blended with cotton. We added them because the demand created by 'Tonight' opened new markets for us."

appeal. The desire not to appear "low-brow" clearly influences the answers given to this type of question.

Many consumers have an *upward bias,* the tendency to overstate their liking for or use of high-priced or prestige products. Because of it, consumer researchers try to avoid asking questions about a specific brand. The interviewee is invited to state his buying habits or preferences as he perceives them. Later, if necessary, the one brand of interest to the researcher may be mentioned and discussed along with other brands.

Sometimes our assumptions about consumers are not supported by systematic studies. This was exemplified when a study was made regarding attitudes of metropolitan area adults toward the purchase of small cars. A random sample of 250 adults was interviewed to determine the relationship between respondents' attitudes toward the purchase of small cars and readiness to accept challenge and innovation. It was expected that persons who saw themselves as "confident explorers" would show greater acceptance of small cars. The data did not support the expectation. On the contrary, persons who saw themselves as "cautious conservatives" were more likely to express a favorable opinion toward them. Conservatives did not consider a small car an adventure, but rather a practical, economical convenience. Confident explorers saw the large car as a means of expressing their ability to control the environment.[15]

Candy

Some people who like candy worry as to whether it is "bad" for them. They hold exaggerated ideas about its effects on teeth and diet. To them, candy is an indulgence food. They wonder whether they should control their appetite. The main problem in selling candy to them is to help them modify or redirect irrational inhibitions on their appetites. Motivation researchers suggested that one approach to encouraging less guilty everyday eating of candy would be to promote the idea that people "owe it to themselves" to gain renewed energy from candy in order to cope with the stresses of modern living. Such an idea gives candy a worthy purpose beyond that of self-indulgence.[16]

Cigars

When a cigar advertiser asked for an evaluation of his advertising, the typical advertisements showed a hostess graciously offering cigars to her men guests. Motivation research studies revealed that the advertising did not lessen the feeling of repugnance on the part of those women who regard cigars as "dirty" and "smelly." The women's attitudes had probably been conditioned by the mother who objected to the father's smoking. If the mother regarded her husband's cigar smoking as dirty, the daughter often carried over the attitude into her adult reactions.

Studies of the men indicated that their reactions to these admonitions were quite different. They developed feelings of rebellion to feminine control. By smoking cigars, the man asserts his maculinity and individualism. And when a woman offers him a cigar, she deprives him of one of his most important reasons for smoking it. She removes his chance to show his independence.[17]

Breakfast Eating

Motivational Programmers, Inc., studied male white-collar workers who do not eat breakfast and found that their reactions to breakfast give some indication of the relationship of a man to his home. Those who dash out with nothing to eat do not feel closely related to their home in the morning. Also, if a man feels insecure about his job and is under tension, he is less likely to eat breakfast. As the years pass, career success tends to bring back the habit.[18] Those who eat breakfast regularly—about 40 per cent of the total studied—are likely to be happy and eager to take on job and other daily challenges. The nonbreakfasters are more likely to be tense, unhappy worriers.

Instant Coffee

A classic example of the way projective methods were applied to a marketing problem has been reported for instant coffee. Powdered instant coffee was on the market, in some form or other, long before World War II. Yet for many years women did not use it to an appreciable extent. Then Mason Haire of the University of California decided to discover possible motivational influences.

First, he questioned a group of women as to why they did not use the powdered coffee, and found that they all agreed upon not liking the taste of it. This seemed a stereotyped answer to Haire, as he doubted that the taste was that unpleasant to everyone. Thus, he looked for a more significant answer and tried the following experiment: Two shopping lists were drawn up which differed in only the fifth item:

List A

1½ lb. hamburger
2 loaves Wonder bread
Bunch of carrots
1 can Rumford's baking powder
Nescafé instant coffee
2 can Del Monte peaches
5 lb. potatoes

List B

1½ lb. hamburger
2 loaves Wonder bread
Bunch of carrots
1 can Rumford's baking powder
Maxwell House coffee, drip grind
2 cans Del Monte peaches
5 lb. potatoes

List A was given to a group of 50 women and List B to another group of 50. He then asked each of the women to describe the type of women who would go to the store with such a list. Actually neither list could possibly give any clue to the personality of the shopper. In order to comply with Haire's request, each woman had to project her own feelings into a word picture.

The results were surprising: 48 per cent of the women with List A pictured a lazy woman who does not plan her purchases well, 12 per cent tagged her as a spendthrift, and 16 per cent declared she wasn't a good wife.

Of the women using List B, only 4 per cent indicated laziness; 12 per cent mentioned bad planning, and none pictured the shopper as a spendthrift or bad wife.

This seems to indicate rather clearly that some women did not use powdered coffee because using it would give them a picture of themselves that they did not like.[19]

The methods used in motivation research are not ordinarily a part of the repertoire of the typical marketing man—he turns to specialists trained in psychology for services in this area of investigation.[20]

Many psychologists are interested in the unconscious aspects of human behavior. There are, broadly speaking, three areas or levels of motivation:

1. The rational, self-knowing area in which one is aware of what motivated his action and is *able and willing to tell why*. Example:

A man has been looking for a certain kind of shirt, one that he can wash easily when on trips away from home. It must be quick-drying and have no-ironing features. When he happens to see an advertisement for a Dacron shirt that offers the desired features, he is motivated to buy it. Ordinary questioning elicits the information needed to prepare advertising that triggers the purchase act.

2. The rational area in which one is aware of what motivated his action and is *able but unwilling to tell why*. Example:

A man buys a home in an expensive neighborhood because, as he says, "It's a better investment" Actually, he realizes that he wants to become a member of a better social set.

The *Chicago Tribune* Research Department also found that most women do not get overly excited about a hosiery advertisement that displays only stockings or legs. Instead, a hosiery manufacturer should depict a smartly dressed woman wearing hose and being admired by others. He should try to create an image of beauty for the woman as a person.

3. The complex hidden area in which one is not aware of what motivated his behavior and really *cannot fully tell why*. Examples: the morbid gambler's unconscious wish to lose as self-punishment for certain unconscious aggressions or the housewife's bargain hunting as a need to outsmart others and to express aggression toward a mother substitute.

Much of our everyday behavior involves more than one type of motivation. When areas 2 and 3 are especially pertinent to the person's behavior to be studied, special procedures are necessary. These procedures to explore motivation have been known and used for a long time.

Of the several techniques used, one used by a number of research workers in an attempt to understand the hidden areas is based on the *Thematic Apperception Test*. This test consists of a standardized series of pictures of people in "some unstructured, ambiguous form of action." Each picture is vague as to its meaning. The person being tested is asked to look at some or at all of these pictures—one at a time—and tell "the story" of the picture.

The pictures do not induce a standardized form of response, and no standardized answers are expected. The significance of answers given by the respondent must be interpreted by a skilled analyst. The original pictures are used by psychiatrists and psychologists in an attempt to diagnose personality traits, but some psychologists use them in consumer research. A common and somewhat related technique uses pictures that have balloons of the kind we see in cartoons but one or more of the balloons may be empty in order that the respondent can fill in his ideas as to what is happening in the situation. Of course when an interviewer records the responses, the balloons are not necessary.

To explore areas 2 and 3, procedures such as the depth interview have been brought over from clinical psychology where they have been used for many years.

The Depth Interview

Motives in buying are very difficult to uncover by direct questioning. When housewives, for example, are asked why they buy a certain brand of a household utility, most of them may mention its high quality. When, however, they are encouraged to discuss the product without prompting or suggestion of answers, they may reveal that the real reason for purchase is the economy, because of assured long life of the article. People are apt to rationalize when casually interviewed about their buying.

The *depth interview* is one of the newer methods of motivational research used by a few large advertisers and agencies. A depth interview is a three-hour detailed case study of the steps and reasons involved in a consumer's behavior. It is an attempt to get better answers than the usual surface re-

Orderliness and status *(at left) are correct appeals, but love and family ritual are much stronger. Courtesy of The Institute for Motivational Research.*

sponses, such as, "I like Blank's chocolate pudding because it's chocolate," or "I like it because I like it." The person who is interviewed by the depth technique is stimulated to talk, to reveal his basic attitudes, opinions, and reasons. Only psychologically trained interviewers can use this technique.

Ernest Dichter, a Viennese psychologist, has been a pioneer in the development of depth interviewing. He has pointed out the difficulties involved in finding out why consumers do what they do when he asked direct formal questions. In a study of car buying, as an example, he never got beyond such superficial motives as satisfaction with the previous car, better trade-in allowance, and so forth. The use of depth interviewing and motivational research brought forth truly basic reasons from the interview, such as dread of change, nostalgia, and the like. In explaining the need for the use of special techniques in learning motivations of the consumer, Dichter stated:

> ...whenever we are dealing with motivations in research, we have to employ methods different from the ones used when a simple factual statement of *quantitative* relationship is required. Why should this be so when we are studying such seemingly simple problems as why Mr. Smith bought one brand of dental cream rather than another, or why women listen to certain types of radio programs?
>
> The answer lies in the nature and the mechanisms of human motivations. Motivations are of such a different nature from our other research objectives that the usual research tools no longer suffice. One might well ask, at this point, what is it about motivations that makes them the subject of an almost separate branch of research requiring special tools? I should therefore like to turn now to a discussion of those aspects of motivation which make this necessary.
>
> To begin with, *motivations are dynamic.* If I wanted to find out why Mr. Smith is wearing a blue suit today, the answer most likely would not be a single reason or even a list of reasons. When he opened the closet this morning, the blue suit was hanging nearest him and so he decided to put it on. Then, however, he remembered that he didn't have any tie his wife liked to go with it, and so he selected the brown suit. When he looked this over, he discovered that his wife still had not sewn on the missing button. Annoyed by his wife's neglect, he spitefully reached for the blue suit again. While he was putting on the blue suit, it occurred to him that his decision was a good one after all because he had not been wearing this suit for a long time.
>
> Let us not go any further. This relatively simple example shows us how unsatisfactory any single statement of motivation may be. When questioned for the motivations of his choice, all Mr. Smith may have told us, was that he saw the blue suit first. This despite the complicated dynamics of the true motivation. We can understand, therefore, that a direct questionnaire technique will rarely be adequate for the registration of dynamic motivational mechanisms....
>
> ...a respondent is frequently unaware of his motivations. Dr. Maslow, in a study, "A Theory of Human Motivation," says the following about unconscious motivations:
>
> "Everyday conscious desires are to be regarded as symptoms, as surface indicators of more basic needs. If we were to take these superficial desires at their face values, we would find ourselves in a state of complete confusion, since we would be dealing seriously with symptoms rather than with what lay behind the symptoms."
>
> This is extremely important as far as our methodological discussion is concerned. We must be able to distinguish between conscious and *unconscious motivations.* Depth psychology teaches us that unconscious reasons are usually more basic and powerful than the conscious ones. Obviously, a direct question runs no chance of success in uncovering unconscious motivations.[21]

Dichter uncovered some especially important findings regarding the purchase of automobiles. He found that only two per cent of car buyers buy convertibles. This two per cent figure, however, did not indicate the true importance of convertibles in car buying. When he counted the number of people who stopped in front of showrooms with convertibles in the window and compared the figure with the number who stopped in front of showrooms without convertibles, he found that the convertible was far more important than indicated by the two per cent sales figure. Investigation showed that the convertible is a symbol of eternal youth, coveted and dreamed about by almost every car buyer, but seldom actually bought. Convertibles are psychological lures to attract people to showrooms and to increase the attention value of advertisements.[22]

Dichter publishes findings from his Institute for Motivational Research studies from time to time as indicated in these two examples concerning baseball gloves and boats:

Manufacturers of baseball gloves learned, as a result of IMR research that autographs on both cheap and expensive models confused youngsters: "A glove with a star ball player's signature provides a means of identification with a grown-up person. In a sense, it is a psychological certificate of qualification for 'grown-up-hood.' This is true mostly of the younger boys (from eight to twelve). Not one of our older teen-age respondents would admit outright he was interested in star players' signatures on his glove, dismissing this as kidstuff. Upon deeper probing of skeptical older teen-agers, we found that some of the rejection of the star's signature was due to unbelievable advertising. ('Sure, it's got Mickey's signature on it. But who says he uses the glove? . . .'). The objection is not due to the autograph itself, but to what is seen as a questionable endorsement." An easy solution offered by IMR: reserve "the star player's signature on the more expensive glove and put a printed name rather than a signature on the cheaper one."

To those salesmen who wish to sell boats to the vast army of would-be boat owners that has cropped up within recent years, the Institute has this advice. Studies indicate that today's boat buyer is first of all making an emotional investment when he decides to walk into a boat yard and look over the fleet. He wants to belong to a leisure club, either imaginary or real, rather than a leisure class. He therefore expects the dealer to cater to his ambition and not to snub him because of his lack of expert boating knowledge.[23]

Psychologists realize that motives are difficult to uncover. Sometimes helpful answers to "why" can be obtained by asking a series of related questions that may reveal aspects of motivation such as, What brand did you buy last? What brand did you use before this? In what respects do you think your present brand is better than the kind you were using? What was your principal objection to the brand you used before?

In some instances, helpful answers to "why" can be obtained by asking a series of questions that begin with the word "what" and "when" and "how." Respondents who are unable or unwilling to answer "why" are able and willing to give valid answers when the indirect approach is employed.

The Special Contribution of Motivation Research

Motivation research is usually considered as qualitative rather than quantitative. It deals with why; not *how many?* Its findings must be verified by means of quantitative studies which answer the question as to how many persons behave in terms of specific motivations. A given trigger to action may be present, but whether it is potent with many or few consumers must be answered by conventional procedures such as questionnaires and field interviews, statistically treated. Motiva-

> The difference between creative consumer research and most conventional marketing research which usually asks questions that can easily be tabulated by a machine can be illustrated by the wife's answer to her husband when he asked her, "What would you like me to get you for Christmas, my dear?" She answered:
>
> *Don't ask me what I want—surprise me!*
>
> She realized that he was well acquainted with her present material situation as well as with her emotions and feelings. She wanted him to utilize his knowledge of her by thinking of something she had not thought of, something that would please her beyond her own imagination.*
>
> The creative researcher tries to get as well acquainted with consumers as a husband learns to know a wife, but he goes beyond the present and tries to discover possibilities that are beyond their current imaginations.

* This kind of expectation is appreciated by great artists. When the famous Daghileff gave his instructions to the artist chosen to produce a poster for the Imperial Ballet, he said: "Astonish me!"

tion research does not involve any new techniques for the psychologist nor are its findings alone sufficient for controlling a marketing program. Its findings are, however, very valuable for the improvement of marketing programs. Influences in buying and new markets are revealed. New courses of marketing action are charted, particularly for advertising. Currently, motivation research is growing because it adds a source of new insight for marketing. It offers a clearer understanding of the consumer's aspirations, feelings, subconscious longings, and fears. It is used mainly as a source of ideas, but quantitative techniques are needed to indicate its values in its applications in the marketplace.

Good Consumer Research Is Creative

Experts in consumer research need so much statistical ability that they are apt to become engrossed in research techniques and lose sight of the creative aspect of their work. Business executives, particularly those in charge of advertising and selling, do not as a rule think in refined statistical terms. They are essentially promoters and innovators. They utilize the benefits of research, and they utilize its benefits most effectively when field research is an integral phase of their business philosophy. This attitude is fully expressed in the following admonition:

> Remember that field research is essentially creative. Its value will be nil to a concern afflicted with complacency. If management's objective for its advertising is merely to ride the Babson sales curve, keep its name before the trade and "build good will and prestige," then it should not use field research. But if a company is progressive and alert, it can use field research profitably, for the research can help to create advertising that will increase sales and reduce unit sales costs.
>
> All too often a business loses sight of the end purpose of its activities—a service to the customer which represents a sound value to him. There is a tendency to feel that service to the customers is the special and exclusive province of sales and service departments. This may explain why we find credit departments which bite the customer; why we find design engineers who concentrate all their efforts on making a better gadget which may or may not be acceptable to the customer; why we find advertising that takes into consideration not what the customer wants to know, but what the advertiser thinks he should know.
>
> Therefore, step number one in any consideration of field research is accepting the fact that every activity the company engages in is on behalf of the customer. This holds true of design, purchasing, distribution, sales, service, promotion, advertising, financing administration, credit, etc. . . .
>
> To sum up, it may be said that field research answers three questions:
>
> 1. What should your advertising say? Obviously, your advertising is most effective when it gives customers information that is pertinent to the selection, application and maintenance of your product. . . .
>
> 2. Where to say it? Advertising won't help much if it is directed to the wrong people. One field investigation disclosed that a certain company's direct-mail literature was being sent to purchasing agents, who had no voice whatsoever in the selection of the product. It was learned that production engineers were the real behind-the-scenes authority on purchases. The mailing list was completely revised and made really effective. Field research can indicate to whom to say it as well as what to say.
>
> 3. Why? Unless you know why a customer thinks or believes the way he does, there probably isn't much you can do about it. . . .
>
> Also, field research can give you freedom from doubt—doubt that appropriations are spent most effectively—doubt in the minds of management as to whether advertising is justified—doubt of the advisability of spending *x* dollars or *y* dollars. Field research answers the *why's* of management about advertising expenditures. It provides a sound sales reason why you say what you say and where you say it.[24]

ACKNOWLEDGMENTS AND REFERENCES

1. Abbott Kimball, Inc., *Advertising and Selling,* Aug. 4, 1932, pp. 42–43.
2. See Peter F. Drucker in *Nation's Business,* April, 1952, pp. 34f.
3. Stuart G. Waterhouse, "An Englishman Looks at American Marketing and Distribution Policies," The *Journal of Marketing,* January, 1948.
4. Edward W. Bok, *The Americanization of Edward*

Bok, (New York: Charles Scribner's Sons, 1920), p. 164.
5. For a more detailed definition, see *The Journal of Marketing,* October, 1948, p. 209.
6. Sometimes the synonym "Build It Yourself" is used; however, this is a copyrighted term, owned by the Easi-Bild Pattern Co., division of Pattern Publishing Co., Pleasantville, N.Y.
7. Survey by Politz Research, Inc., reported in "Do-It-Yourself: The Greatest Market Development Since Self-Service," *Tide,* Oct. 10, 1953.
8. See Jerome Shoenfeld, "Washington Has Answers for You," *Sales Management,* Apr. 15, 1955.
9. See "Mobility Saps Shopper Allegiance," *Sales Management,* Nov. 15, 1963. Studies conducted by Pierre Martineau, *Chicago Tribune.*
10. See "Scouting the Trail for Marketers," *Business Week,* Apr. 18, 1964, p. 91.
11. Sidney Roslow, Wallace H. Wulfeck, and Philip G. Corby, "Consumer and Opinion Research: Experimental Studies on the Form of the Question," *Journal of Applied Psychology,* **24,** No. 3 (1940), 334–346.
12. Elmer Wheeler, "The First Ten Seconds: The Crucial Turning Point of the Sales Talk," *Sales Management,* Nov. 15, 1937, p. 49.
13. William S. Blair, "How Subject Matter Can Bias a Survey," *Media/scope,* February, 1964.
14. See James K. Blake, "Consumer Motivation Research," *Dun's Review and Modern Industry,* July, 1954.
15. See Eugene Jacobsen and Jerome Kossoff, "Self-Percept and Consumer Attitudes Toward Small Cars," *Journal of Applied Psychology,* August, 1963.
16. See address by John Kishler before Associated Retail Confectioners of the United States as reported in *Advertising Age,* Feb. 11, 1957, p. 3.
17. Edward H. Weiss, *How Motivation Studies May Be Used by Creative People to Improve Advertising,* Contributed Papers, May 7, 1954, University of Michigan, Bureau of Business Research.
18. See "The Motivation of Breakfasting," *Printers' Ink,* July 13, 1962.
19. Mason Haire, "Projective Techniques in Marketing Research," *Journal of Marketing,* national quarterly publication of the American Marketing Association, **14,** No. 5 (April, 1950), 649–656. Haire's findings were checked in a later study reported by Ralph L. Westfall, Harper W. Boyd, Jr., and Donald T. Campbell, "The Use of Structured Techniques in Motivation Research," *Journal of Marketing,* October, 1957. Some of the findings of the two studies differed as on the question of whether or not women thought instant coffee users are lazy. Perhaps one factor in explaining the later finding is that instant coffee in the course of the intervening years had become socially acceptable to more housewives.
20. An excellent understandable summary of these and other methods, written for the advertising or marketing man, is George Horsley Smith, *Motivation Research in Advertising and Marketing* (New York: McGraw-Hill Book Company, 1954).
21. Ernest Dichter, "Depth Interviewing," a talk given at Market Research Council, Oct. 15, 1943.
22. *Tide,* July 26, 1946, p. 58. See also Ernest Dichter, *The Psychology of Everyday Living* (New York: Barnes & Noble, Inc., 1947), p. 86.
23. *Memo from Dr. Ernest Dichter and Staff,* No. 43, 1963.
24. Charles S. Wilkinson, "The Why and How of Field Research," *Printers' Ink,* July 13, 1945, pp. 28, 36.

PROJECTS

1. Choose any common product on the market today and compose questions which might be used in a free-association interview to determine consumer opinion and the extent of use by the consumer. Give your questions trials with several friends. What did you learn from your limited experiment?
2. Select a number of articles in popular use today but which you think may no longer be on the market 10 years from now. Present reasons for your selection and indicate what type of article may replace them. How could the manufacturers of the products adjust themselves to the change?
3. Look up the ratings of a number of products in both Consumers Union and Comsumers' Research reports in your library. To what extent do the ratings of the two organizations agree?
4. Leaf through three distinctly different types of magazines, noticing the advertisements. Do the advertisements seem to be designed to appeal to the particular class of readers of that magazine? Why? Why not? Select some good and some poor examples from each of the three mediums.
5. Obtain a copy of a mail questionnaire and analyze it from the viewpoint of the principles discussed in this chapter. Rewrite it if you believe it can be made more effective.
6. Outline the steps you would take in conducting a field survey to determine the potential market for a new type of electric toaster.

COLLATERAL READINGS

Blankenship, Albert B., "Creativity in Consumer Research," *Journal of Marketing,* October, 1961.

Dichter, Ernest, *The Strategy of Desire*. Garden City, N.Y.: Doubleday & Company, Inc., 1960.

Goldman, Alfred E., "The Group Depth Interview, *Journal of Marketing,* July, 1962.

Guest, Lester, "Consumer Analysis," *Annual Review of Psychology,* Vol. 13, 1962.

Hepner, Harry Walker, *Advertising—Creative Communication with Consumers*. New York: McGraw-Hill Book Company, 1964, Chapters 3–6.

Karn, Harry W. and B. von Haller Gilmer, *Readings in Industrial and Business Psychology*. New York: McGraw-Hill Book Company, 1962, pp. 473–502.

Smith, Henry Clay, *Psychology of Industrial Behavior*. New York: McGraw-Hill Book Company, 1955, Chapter 17.

A man can do a lot of thinking while waiting for the moving van

AT THE END OF SEPTEMBER, THE 136 PEOPLE WHO ARE YOUNG & RUBICAM IN CHICAGO ARE MOVING FROM 333 NORTH MICHIGAN AVENUE TO ONE EAST WACKER DRIVE.

THESE ARE THE THOUGHTS THAT WENT THROUGH ONE MAN'S MIND WHILE WAITING FOR THE MOVERS TO COME.

I am in advertising and I believe in it.

I believe in advertising as a worthwhile career, but more importantly as a force for good, in a free economy.

I know of no more significant opportunity than telling an honest public about an honest product.

I believe in words and I believe in pictures, not so much in the way they can be put together to arrest the eye and ear, but in the way they get ideas out of the package into the buying mind.

I respect the arithmetic of the census, but in so doing, I try to listen to the heart-beat of the people.

The size of the market impresses me, but it is the feel of it I trust.

When it comes to publications, I do not question the number of people they reach as closely as I do the way they talk to them; and it isn't the power of TV that stirs me as much as the purpose to which it can aspire.

I believe that in the act of advertising you move from principle, not merely policy. You seek to lead and to build, and you accept the risk, and if you fail, you dare the risk again. Or you are neither leading nor building.

It is difficult to believe like this, because it is more popular to hedge the bet than to make the book.

It is safer to repeat a platitude than to suppose a philosophy.

It is easier to arrest attention than to earn your welcome.

Imagination can be dangerous. But lack of it is fatal.

Figures comfort business minds and formulas promise refuge. But in neither do I repose my full belief because I am of the people.

Of, not above them, and most decidedly for them. And when I have kept faith with my job, I am with them.

Advertising is my business, and this is why I believe in it.

Courtesy of Young & Rubicam, Inc.

CHAPTER TWENTY-SEVEN

COMMUNICATION WITH CONSUMERS BY MEANS OF MASS MEDIA —ADVERTISING

People who are unacquainted with the dynamic influences in modern business assume that the improvement of consumer products is brought about by the initiative of the men in the research laboratories. This is only partially true. Actually, a great deal of the prodding comes from the advertising end of the business. Scientific research and advertising work together to stimulate and discover the making of the improvements in the laboratory. The direct beneficiary is the consumer.[1]

Communication with consumers by means of mass media is commonly called advertising. At its best, advertising can be defined as creative communication with consumers. It is creative in regard to two aspects:

1. Its stimulating effects on the consumer's desire for improving his standard of living.
2. The originality evident in the selection of the message to be communicated and its presentation through the mass media: newspapers, magazines, television, radio, direct mail, and others.

Encouraging Consumers to Adopt the Better Products Available to Them

Most persons assume that people will adopt all beneficial products as soon as they have the necessary money available and the products are offered on the market. This has not been entirely true even in an economy of scarcity. Let us go back in our history for a few examples when our economic needs were very great.

In 1797, American farmers made their plows out of crooked tree-forks. The implement was so crude that it merely scratched the soil and required several steers to drag it over the ground. In that year, an inventor by the name of Charles Newbold patented a metal plow that would turn the soil in neat, smooth furrows. The operation of the plow required only one man and two oxen. Newbold showed New Jersey farmers fields of splendid grain for which his metal plows had turned the sod, but the farmers still believed that the iron plows would poison the soil and produce only weeds. In all, the inventor spent $30,000, a substantial sum in that day, to introduce his labor-saving device to other farmers before he gave up in disgust. Similarly, when sewing machines and mechanical washing machines had been invented and were available, thousands of women preferred to sew by hand and to rub clothes over a washboard. Businessmen and inventors have had to spend years and much money for advertising and selling in order to stimulate people of capable financial means to purchase and use the better products made available to them.

The same kind of inertia is evident in the realm of ideas. People are also slow to adopt new and better ways of thinking. Socially important movements or concepts rarely burst into full bloom over night. Each social group tends to lag behind the best culture that is available in its particular time. People are slow to change. And they should be. If every group had adopted every supposedly excellent idea or product as soon as presented, the human race would long ago have gone over the brink of destruction. Individuals and social groups make haste slowly in order to avoid the adoption of too many changes that might do harm. This means that the leaders in the fields of ideas as well as the businessmen who sell products and services must present their offerings by means of new approaches that will enable the non-users to decide more intelligently.

In our free enterprise system, the consumer is king. He cannot be forced to buy the products of our factories. He can only be encouraged. His wants, translated into purchases, will determine the rate at which we utilize the productive facilities of our age of automation. The people will decide how fast and in what ways they wish to raise their standard of living.

The Adopters of New Products

The rate of adoption of new products has been studied by business research organizations and others. Some of the most illuminating studies have been made by rural sociologists concerned with improving farming practices and increasing agricultural productivity. They studied the adoption of new pesticides, new farm equipment, new fertilizers, new seed varieties, and new home practices such as the use of synthetic fabrics. Their findings have significance for advertisers and others who are interested in bringing about the adoption of new products and services. Researches indicate that members of the different categories tend to have the following characteristics:

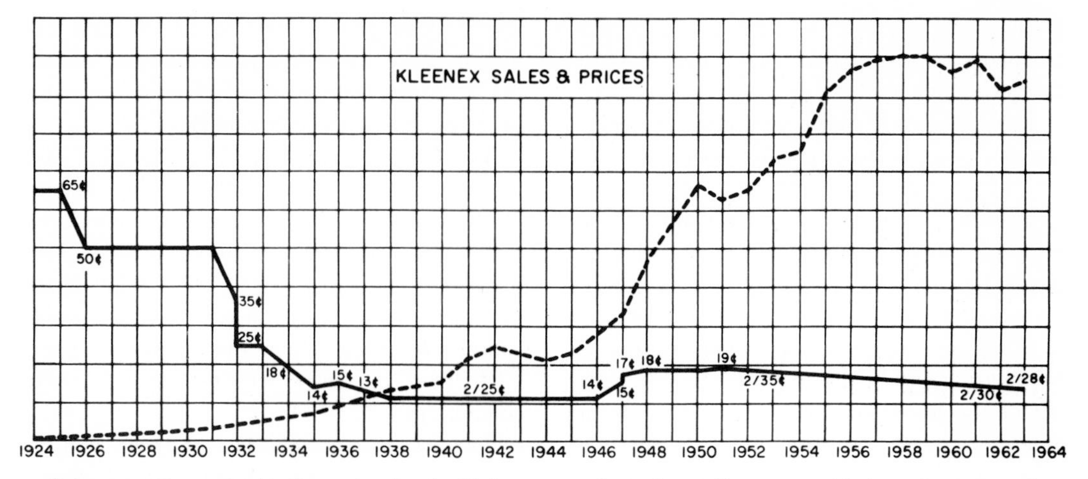

Sales promotion and advertising can be justified *economically and socially as exemplified in the history of Kleenex:*

It was offered to the public for the first time in 1924 as a cold-cream remover under the brand name Kleenex. Six years later these disposable tissues were featured as having a second major purpose—as handkerchiefs. Sales doubled, and the next year they redoubled. The public went for Kleenex tissues for handkerchiefs because they were cheap, sanitary, and saved laundry.

As sales went up costs were reduced–and price to the consumer went down. It dropped from 65 cents in 1924 to 50 cents to 35 cents in 1932. Six months later it was down to 25 cents for a box of 200 larger, softer sheets. And here's something particularly worthy of notice–the Kleenex of 1932 was a softer, stronger tissue than the original product and it came in a handy serv-a-tissue package.

Ten years from the date Kleenex was launched nationally, the consumer could buy the large carton of 500 tissues for 41 cents or the regular 200-sheet package for 18 cents. Again the sales doubled, and once more the price was cut to 13 cents–two for 25 cents.

The price shown for 1963 was 14 cents per box which was a suggested price. Actually in a good many outlets such as supermarkets, the package was sold at a considerably lower price.

It is also interesting to note that in spite of increased costs and the substantially lower buying power of the dollar in 1963, prices were still lower than they were in 1951.

Through the advertised brand name, Kleenex, the public was educated to the advantages of these sanitary, convenient tissues. Consumer response made possible mass production, which, in turn, made for lower price to the consumer.

Source: "Notes on the Progress of Brand Names Research Foundation," Sales Management, Mar 1, 1945, p. 74, for history previous to 1945. Updated October 1963.

TABLE 27.1

ADOPTER CATEGORIES

Researchers took the data from a number of independent studies of new product adoption by farmers. They divided people into groups according to time of adoption* and then studied each group. These were the groups they distinguished and studied.

People Adopting			*Cumulative Total Adopting*
First	2.5%	innovators	2.5%
Next	13.5	early adopters	16.0
Next	34.0	early majority	50.0
Next	34.0	late majority	84.0
Last	16.0	laggards	100.0

* Statisticians will note that for convenience in making comparative studies, the researchers used standard deviations of a normal distribution to establish the percentage breaks between categories. People who fell within one standard deviation above the mean were considered in the early majority; people who were between one and two standard deviations above the mean were classified as early adopters. Similarly, people within one standard deviation below the mean were classified as late majority, etc.

Innovators, the first people to adopt new products, are likely to be well educated and often come from well-established families. They have more risk capital and can afford to take calculated risks. Their sources of information transcend the local community. They frequently have friends at a considerable distance. They turn to scientists for information. They are likely to belong to organizations at the state, regional, or national levels. Interestingly, they are respected by people in their own community for their success, but they are not used as sources of information by their neighbors to the extent that other adopter categories are used.

Early adopters, the second group to adopt the new product, have smaller operations and less risk capital than innovators. Their education is above average. They are younger than most of the people studied. Early adopters watch the innovators, and when the success of a product is reasonably assured, they try it. They are respected as good sources of information and hold a disproportionate number of the leadership positions in the formal organizations of the community. They take more magazines and journals than people who adopt later, but they do not take so many as the innovators.

The *early majority* are slightly above average in age and education. They have medium-high social and economic status. These people belong to formal organizations but are likely to be active members rather than leaders. They take fewer magazines and journals than the early adopters but more than the late adopters. They rely more on informal sources of information than the early adopters do. When these people begin to adopt, a great many other people tend to follow their example. They are looked to as informal leaders and informal sources of information by many other people of the community.

The *late majority* have less education and are above average in age. They do not belong to so many formal organizations and have fewer lines of communication outside their immediate neighborhoods. They take fewer magazines and rely heavily on informal sources of information and influence. They participate in fewer activities outside their community.

The *laggards* are the last of those who do adopt a new idea. They have the least education and are the oldest. They take fewer magazines. They are very closely oriented to their immediate neighborhood. They participate least in formal organizations and may even be suspicious of those who offer new ideas.

Obviously, these categories and descriptions would vary somewhat for entirely different products. Psychological as well as economic factors have to be considered. Some never adopt a new product which the majority of the possible users do adopt.

TABLE 27.2

SOURCES OF INFORMATION AT EACH STAGE IN THE ADOPTION OF ANTIBIOTICS (Condensed Table)

Categorized Source of Information	*Awareness*	*Information*	*Application*	*Trial*	*Adoption*
Mass media[1]	49%	35%	16%	3%	
Agriculture agency[2]	19	18	12	7	
Informal sources[3]	8	14	21	13	1%
Commercial sources[4]	24	33	50	67	
Self[5]				3	94
No response			1	7	5
	100	100	100	100	100

1 Mass media are farm magazines, farm papers, newspapers, radio, and television.
2 Agricultural agencies are direct contact with the state university, extension service, or county agent; college bulletins; high school vocational agriculture; adult evening classes; 4-H clubs, etc.
3 Informal sources include relatives, friends, neighbors, etc.
4 Commercial sources include feed dealers, salesmen, printed directions on containers, commercial circulars, etc.
5 Self includes responses such as "My own experience" and "My own trial."
Source: George M. Beal and Everett M. Rogers, *The Adoption of Two Farm Practices in a Central Iowa Community,* Special Report No. 26, Agricultural and Home Economics Experiment Station, Iowa State University of Science and Technology, Ames, Iowa, June, 1960.

ADOPTION CURVE AND TIME CATEGORIES

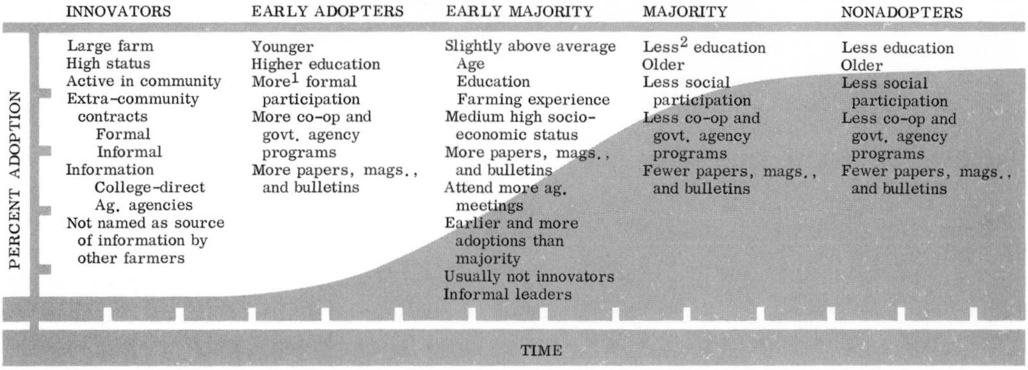

INNOVATORS	EARLY ADOPTERS	EARLY MAJORITY	MAJORITY	NONADOPTERS
Large farm High status Active in community Extra-community contracts Formal Informal Information College-direct Ag. agencies Not named as source of information by other farmers	Younger Higher education More[1] formal participation More co-op and govt. agency programs More papers, mags., and bulletins	Slightly above average Age Education Farming experience Medium high socio-economic status More papers, mags., and bulletins Attend more ag. meetings Earlier and more adoptions than majority Usually not innovators Informal leaders	Less[2] education Older Less social participation Less co-op and govt. agency programs Fewer papers, mags., and bulletins	Less education Older Less social participation Less co-op and govt. agency programs Fewer papers, mags., and bulletins

PERCENT ADOPTION — TIME

[1]More refers to significantly more than categories that follow.
[2]Less, older, fewer refer to significantly different from previous categories

THE ADOPTION PROCESS AND SOURCES OF INFORMATION

Awareness	Interest	Evaluation	Trial	Adoption
Knows about it; lacks details	Develops interest; gathers general information and facts	Mental trial; application to personal situation: Can I do it?	Small-scale, experimental use: satisfaction	Large-scale, continued use; satisfaction
1. Mass media: Radio, TV, newspapers, magazines	1. Mass media	1. Neighbors, friends	1. Neighbors, friends	1. Neighbors, friends
2. Govt. agencies: Extension, voc. ag., etc.	2. Govt. agencies	2. Govt. agencies	2. Govt. agencies	2. Govt. agencies
3. Neighbors, friends	3. Neighbors, friends	3. Mass media	3. Mass media	3. Mass media
4. Salesmen, dealers	4. Salesmen, dealers	4. Salesmen, dealers	4. Salesmen, dealers	4. Salesmen, dealers

The "diffusion process" in the adoption of new products and ideas has been studied by several researchers, particularly by George M. Beal and Joe M. Bohlen. They as well as others[2] have listed five stages in the mental process:

1. *Awareness.* The individual becomes aware of a new idea or product such as hybrid seed corn, but he lacks information concerning it.
2. *Interest.* The individual wants to know more about the idea or product: what it is, how it works, and its potentialities.
3. *Evaluation.* The individual makes a mental trial. He applies the information learned in the previous stage to his situation by asking himself: "Can I do it, and if I do, will it be better than what I am doing now?"
4. *Trial.* He decides that the idea has possibilities for him and he makes a small-scale experimental application. In this stage, he needs specific information which answers his questions: "How do I do it; how much do I use; how can I make it work best for me?"
5. *Adoption.* The final stage is characterized by large-scale, continued use of the idea. He accepts the idea as good and he intends to use it in his on-going program.

Individuals go through the process at different rates. The rate is influenced by the complexity of the process and the psychological characteristics of the individual as indicated by his place in the innovator-nonadoption curve.

The diffusion process that takes place in the gradual adoption of new products by farmers can also be observed among consumers of nonfarm products. When only a few innovating housewives in a block or social group have a new appliance such as an air-conditioning unit, most nearby women do not sense any special pressure to buy it. Later, as more and more adjacent housewives buy and talk about the appliance, the pressure on the laggards increases.

Interpersonal influences in the adoption of certain new products vary with the influences of opinion leaders in the community. A woman, for example, may be a channel of information and advice to other people in regard to fashion products but not in regard to grocery purchases or movies. Fashion opinion leaders are likely to be unmarried. Grocery purchase leaders are likely to be housewives who have a large family. Of course, the leaders in any one area of purchasing and influence are more likely than nonleaders to read advertising in the line of their specialized interests.[3]

The Tastemakers—The "High Mobiles"

Opinion Research Corporation, Princeton, New Jersey, studied people who set trends in the buying of 160 products and services. These "pioneers" were found to have certain distinguishing characteristics. When 105 households were studied and the findings checked against a seven-point "mobility scale," a concept of change as "perhaps the common denominator" of American culture was evident. This tastemaker theory was expressed in the hypothesis:

"The central thread of our modern society is mobility. The leadership elite is that group of people who possess this quality in greater degree than do other people." That group is made up of what may be called the "High Mobiles" (27 per cent). In relation to the rest of our society:

> They travel more and change residence more often.
>
> They show more movement through the occupational structure.
>
> They are more likely to change their economic status.
>
> They associate with a wider variety of people of different types.
>
> They move through more educational levels and institutions.
>
> They move through more intellectual influences.
>
> They are more selective and variable in their politics.
>
> In these various dimensions, they have moved a greater distance from their family of birth.

The High Mobile group move around mentally as well as physically. They continue to learn, change jobs, earn more money, make new friends, and push education for their children. They travel more than most and do not depend on kinfolk for companionship.

Mobility was compared with buying habits, recorded current usage and first-year usage of the 160 products and services.

The High Mobiles, it was found, were first to use credit cards, electric blankets, frozen soups, low-calorie beverages, wild rice (exotic to the Jerseyites who were being studied in this project), hi-fi, foreign cars, and clothes driers. They were disproportionately high early users of freezers, colored sheets, and blenders.

Among the 105 families queried, the High Mobiles accounted for 100 per cent of the purchases of stereo equipment from 1945 until about 1956, when other households began buying such equipment. By 1958 the High Mobiles' share of this market had dropped to only 57 per cent while the other families represented 43 per cent of the market.

In most instances the High Mobiles led the Mediums and Lows in adopting new products and services, but not all the 160 items studied conformed consistently to the pattern of High Mobile predominance in the early stages of the market's growth. The family-centered "Low Mobiles" were first to fill their kitchens with copper pots and pans and all classes adopted aluminum foil at about the same time.

Opinion Research believes that traditional methods of market forecasting—through study of upper-income groups, highly educated, younger generation, suburbanites, etc.—do not meet today's needs. Such studies give a static picture and "tell nothing about the moving process of change which explains and helps predict the individual's changing tastes."

High Mobiles, with their open-mindedness, are quick to try the new. Where they lead, others tend to follow. Opinion Research Corporation believed that if, in the 1950's Detroit had watched the High Mobiles, it could have saved itself grief. When it saw that one per cent of the new-car market was going to foreign cars, the automotive manufacturers should have recognized "that the one per cent was a bellwether, a red flag. For the buyers were not ordinary people. They were High Mobiles, the leadership elite for change."[4]

The Advertising "Target"

Numerous surveys are made of consumers by government bureaus, media owners, and advertising agencies. Most surveys deal with demographic factors—vital statistics concerning age, income, education, and geographical distribution of consumers. Data from these and other sources are used to estimate markets and to set up marketing programs. When these objectives have been determined, the advertising and communication targets are chosen. This means that when a knowledgeable student looks at (or hears) an advertisement, he asks himself: "To whom is the ad directed?" To test this principle, examine some magazine advertisements or television commercials. Try to identify the class of people whom the advertiser has chosen as his prospects for purchase. In some instances, the advertiser may be trying to advertise his electrical appliances, for example, to all housewives. More perceptive analysis may indicate that he is really directing his advertising to rather definite groups such as newly married couples, employed women, low-income families, or others. If the advertising has been properly planned, the group can be identified by the kind of art work, the characters in the illustrations, or the style and content of the copy. Sometimes, too, the group chosen can be recognized by the kind of television show that carries the commercial.

The Appeal

Researchers in advertising who have made studies of the relative importance of various factors such as long copy versus short copy, big pictures or little pictures or no pictures at all, charts and diagrams as an accompaniment of other pictures or used alone, and testimonial versus reason-why seem to agree that none of them is so important as the *appeal* or *theme*. The appeal is the dominant idea which is supposed to arouse a dormant desire in the mind of the prospect and stimulate him to

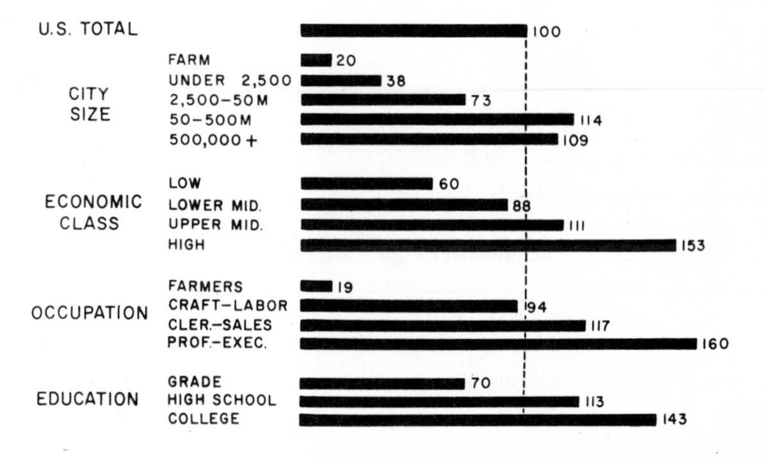

Average family consumption *of frozen vegetables is charted as index 100, based on reports of family purchases secured from the National Consumer Panel of Market Research Corporation of America. As the chart shows, use of frozen vegetables is high in city families in the upper-income, white-collar, better-educated group. This indicates a short-term advertising goal of securing more business from best customers—the upper-income, city families. It also suggests a long-term goal of making better customers out of other families. Chart and caption from Alfred R. Oxenfeldt and Carroll Swan,* ***Management of the Advertising Function,*** *Wadsworth Publishing Company, Inc., Belmont, Calif. Copyright 1964 by Wadsworth Publishing Company, Inc., Belmont, Calif. Data by Market Research Corporation of America.*

purchase the product. The appeal is far more important than type face, illustration, or headline.

One would expect the theme or appeal to be the one great influence in causing us to be affected by the advertisement. Hand a page of closely typewritten material, haphazardly arranged, to a group of people and ask them to look it over. If the names of the readers are among the words on the list, it is easier for them to find their own names than to find the names of strangers. Twenty-eight adults were used in such an experiment to find out how long it would take each person to find his name on a page of closely typewritten material. Each person's name appeared five times in the copy. An examiner timed the subject with a stop-watch while the subject looked for and underlined his own name five times. Then the subject or person who had found his own name was asked to find the name of a stranger in the same copy. The stranger's name also appeared in five places in the copy and had to be underlined five times. Accurate records were kept for each name, and it was found that the average length of time required for each of twenty-eight persons to find his own name was 72.6 seconds. For these persons to find the names of strangers required 103.7 seconds, or 43 per cent longer.

An example of an effective appeal. *This headline was first used by its author, Jack Cornelius, of Batten, Barton, Durstine & Osborn, for a Community Chest campaign in 1936. It has been a perennial favorite in later campaigns.*

A theme or appeal in advertising is any idea used by an advertiser when he seeks to influence people of the particular class who are logical prospects for his product or service. The advertiser does not seek to reach everyone with his message. Even though the advertiser sells a so-called mass product such as soap or food, he has narrowed his choice of appeals to the particular class or classes of people who are apt to buy his soap or food. The advertiser thinks of his advertising appeal as a selective device which is designed to be attractive to his prospects; not to all persons. He has defined his market by means of motivation research or the use of some other technique such as the analysis of sales records, coupon returns, questionnaires, or interviews with consumers.

How the Appeal Affects the Reader

Psychologically, an appeal is a very complex set of influences in the life of a reader or hearer of advertising. A prospect's actions are greatly influenced by his own inner needs and desires, particularly in the promise of satisfaction of his needs. An analysis of the reader's mental activity when he sees an advertisement would reveal the memories that it arouses, the pleasant and unpleasant feelings, associations, and thoughts of the possibility of satisfaction. Depth interviews uncover numerous unsuspected psychological responses on the part of the reader, responses that are difficult to measure by ordinary questioning. Dichter, for example, found in a study in the field of deodorants that:

> ...The appeal of social acceptance and safety is valid only for a small group of women. A much

greater proportion considered such goals as much too far removed. What interested them more than anything else was to be able to like themselves, to feel clean, to consider themselves smart beauty technicians.

Very often in determining advertising campaigns, the advertiser makes the mistake of thinking that death, romance, fear or hope are valid and powerful appeals. This is a lay view of psychological facts. Actually the fear of being embarrassed or of having to consider oneself a failure far outweighs the power of such grandiose concepts as romance, love, death or happiness.

It can be shown again and again that the pure recital of technical claims about a product leaves the reader cold and does not arouse the emotions necessary to make him change to a new product....

In functional psychological research we distinguish between symptoms expressing the superficial rational explanations of an action and the real, deeper reasons which form the emotional basis of such actions, and are connected with the functional role a product plays in the user's life....

Every time a reader views an advertisement three successive steps are set in motion: (*a*) an attempt to get into the advertisement, (*b*) a registering of the psychological effects and (*c*) a registering of the commercial effects of the advertisement.

a) *Ways of getting into the advertisement.* A reader viewing an advertisement for the first time tries to enter it by various means. Either he abandons the attempt after a few seconds of casual observation, or he is caught by the advertisement.

Among the various processes which help him into an advertisement are these: identifying, being curious, arguing, accepting, rejecting, excluding, memorizing, dissecting, assembling, and emotionalizing—feeling pity, hatred, love, sympathy, and so forth.

The channels enabling the reader to enter the advertisement can be grouped into two large classifications: emotional and intellectual forms of immediate reactions.

An emotional entrance would be signified by: "I'm glad they're not talking about me," or "I hate that darn stuff."

That an intellectual process has taken place would be indicated by the exclamation: "Gee, that's an interesting story!" or, "I'm curious to find out what this machine does."

b) *Ways of registering the psychological effects of an advertisement.* An advertisement may leave the reader with any of a number of possible gratifications: "I feel relieved," "I've learned something new," "I feel sure of myself," "My curiosity has been satisfied," or "It makes me feel that I'm smart."...

What might be considered a well-planned advertisement can have negative psychological effects if one is not conscious of the mechanisms stimulated by it. This was the case in a study for a well-known reducing remedy. Although women accepted the desirability of slimness, they rejected the advertisement and the product. Investigation showed that the stout women featured in the "before" half of the "before and after" routine were too extreme to be accepted by the readers. Their reaction to the picture was, "That's not me," and "I don't look that bad." The effectiveness of the ad was lost because of this psychological blunder.

c) *Ways of registering the commercial effects of an advertisement.* The real commercial effects of an advertisement are difficult to ascertain solely in terms of actual sales....

The only real test of an advertisement's effectiveness is a knowledge of the thoughts, associations, and mental images produced in the reader. In concrete terms each purchasing act is really the result of a mental rehearsal for buying. A shoe advertisement, for example, is successful if at some point the reader reacts with the thought, "I imagine myself trying on the shoes." Similarly, an airline advertisement produced a desirable commercial effect because it provoked such associations as "I'm daydreaming. I visualize myself sitting in a plane and I'm proud of myself," or "I see myself getting into a plane."

In other words, the closer any advertisement comes to producing thoughts which have the appearance of a purchasing act or which rehearse use of the product, the higher the commercial value of the effect of the advertisement....

An advertising program, brilliantly conceived and executed from a technical viewpoint, may miss completely if it neglects to control the psychological effects. The intangible implications of an advertisement often are more significant than its actual content. No item of merchandise is ever sold unless a psychological need exists which it satisfies. In other words, the actual merchandise is secondary.[5]

Appeals That Have Been Found Effective

The experienced advertising man who plans a campaign looks for the dominant idea that will appeal to the consumer classes whom he can reach by means of media available to him. He wants to find out what can be said that will answer the needs of prospects. When we study the progression of appeals of advertisements and sales talks, we find important changes made to increase their effectiveness. Let us note a few examples.

1. In the past, manufacturers of shoes assumed that readers of their advertising were most interested in style, price, construction of shoe, details about fancy punching, and so on. However, one shoe manufacturer conducted a survey of 5,000 men and found that when they were asked what they liked about the shoes they were wearing, 42 per cent replied "fit and feel" or some equivalent; 32 per cent said "wear and tear"; 16 per cent said "style and looks"; 9 per cent said "price and value." The manufacturer changed his advertising accordingly, using themes such as "Walk-Fitted," and benefited by the change.

2. One candy manufacturer found that when he advertised the quality of his candy and made reference to its excellence he did not sell so much as when he changed his appeal to that of buying his brand as a gift. He discovered that the bulk of his business came from men who buy candy to take home to their wives and daughters and from young men who buy it for girls. Price as an appeal was not so important a consideration as the appropriateness of the article for gift purposes.

3. The maker of a game, well-known to the public, devoted his sales and advertising messages to the story of the pleasure his game would yield to the family circle. His advertisements usually pictured father and mother and the two children playing the game with happy smiles on their faces. His appeal for years was: "For Enjoyment." Then, upon consulting a marketing specialist, the appeal was changed: "To Be Popular." With this appeal the players were pictured in a home which was the rendezvous of delighted friends. The response to the advertising doubled in sixty days and the sales of the game tripled.

4. A certain insurance company found that in the advertising of accident insurance the note of protection to loved ones was not nearly so effective as some other appeals, such as the low price of the insurance of this sort. The best-paying advertisement they had was one headed "Three Cents a Day," which explained how many thousands of dollars of protection this small expenditure would bring.

5. One of the most interesting records of appeal effectiveness occurred in the advertising of "Dr. Eliot's Five-Foot Shelf of Books." Charles W. Eliot, president emeritus of Harvard University, made a famous remark in 1909 to the effect that an individual could acquire the equivalent of a liberal education by devoting fifteen minutes every day to the study of great literature.

The basic appeal in the advertising of these books has been to "get ahead"—to grow. The self-improvement theme has been supplemented with appeals to the reader's desires for self-confidence. One insertion, captioned "How to get rid of an inferiority complex," was used with success for several decades.

These five examples from literature in the field of advertising illustrate the reason why advertisers and salesmen seek a keynote or theme that will touch off the spark of interest in the prospect. The history of advertising reveals many examples of appeals, both ineffective and effective ones. Until recently, psychologists often analyzed instincts as possible sources of effective appeals. Today we no longer study lists of instincts and reflexes in the quest for effective appeals, because instincts and reflexes usually have been analyzed by means of armchair or laboratory methods only. The modern marketing analyst does not bother with such obsolete approaches to the choice of appeal. He uses better techniques to bring about reader (viewer) involvement. When a creative advertising man plans the appeal of a print advertisement or a television commercial, he asks himself: "How can I bring about personal involvement on the part of the consumer?" Involvement can be brought about by describing a typical problem and a solution, by picturing a nostalgic scene, showing a photograph of an admired character, by offering opportunity for a reward, presenting a challenge, and many other techniques.

The director of research of a farm publication found that when advertising farm equipment, a picture of the kind of farmer, preferably by name, who represented the reader was most effective. "In Iowa, a good hog picture will out-pull a picture of the president of the company any time. Throw in a picture of the president's pretty daughter too, and the hog will still win."[6]

The same principle applies to the lower income and blue-collar workers' wives. Advertisements least attractive to women of the so-called working class are those which stress motives of the status-seeking varieties. Advertisements that show women attired in mink have little appeal—they do not aspire to become members of that social class.

Research studies of television commercials have shown the importance of creating a situation into which the viewer can spontaneously project himself. Some commercials offer no opportunity for the viewer to identify himself with any person or situation portrayed on the screen. This, of course, is one of the important factors in some of our adverse reactions to certain television commercials. Television advertising is so expensive that to be economically acceptable to the advertiser, it must attract huge audiences. The fact that it uses many appeals that attract very large numbers of people, also brings about criticisms from those persons who want something a little different from what everyone else is getting. It is a great mass medium but the more it attracts the masses, the more it irritates those viewers who feel that they cannot escape from the advertising sections they dislike—in print media the reader can turn the page and ignore the advertisement that is obnoxious to him.

The Illustration

In most cases, the noteworthy part of the advertisement is the illustration. Most people are pictorially minded. Picture shows are far more attractive than lectures. Pictures were our first written language. They attract and hold attention more readily than cold words. One of the most common problems of the advertiser who uses an illustration is its relevancy to the product advertised. A picture of a beautiful woman on a calendar attracts attention to the calendar, but it may not attract attention to the product.

Mark Wiseman studied many readership reports, covering thousands of advertisements, and listed the kinds of pictures most interesting to men and to women. At the head of the list for men was "men" and at the head of the list for women was "women." A part of his explanation follows:

> The reason is not that each sex is not interested in pictures of the other but that the sex of the sole or dominant figure in a picture is a symbolic selector: a signal to the reader that the advertisement is directed to one sex and not the other. Men are rarely interested in an advertisement which they think is meant for women, and vice versa, although a larger proportion of women will observe and read a man's advertisement than the other way around. If you use the wrong sex in a picture, you risk missing or misleading your audience.
>
> In a women's advertisement don't use pictures of combat or adventure; don't use diagrams unless they are very simple and easy to understand; don't use sports scenes unless the chief figure is a woman; don't use mechanical equipment unless you show it in use by a woman or in relation to a woman's job; don't use animals which women might fear or dislike.
>
> The kinds of pictures most interesting to women are those containing domestic scenes, foods in full color, babies or small children, women's apparel, decorative details (room furniture, floor coverings, table settings, boudoir accessories). If you use a picture of a woman, give her an interesting coiffure, one or more pieces of jewelry, an unusual dress, and a background—women love details. Be sparing of cartoons—if you use them, be sure they are easy to "get" and do not ridicule women. If you use before-and-after pictures (before using and after using), make them credible—don't let them arouse suspicion that they are faked or doctored.[7]

Data concerning interests in pictures fluctuates from year to year, depending upon the topics of current interest to the public. In

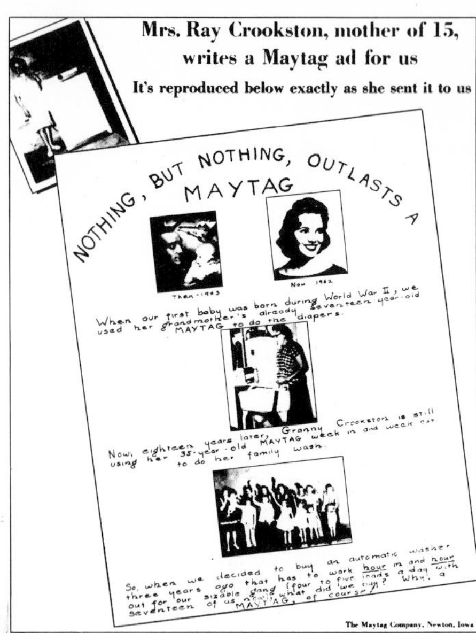

When a good idea for an ad is submitted by a consumer, research is usually necessary to make the idea effective. Here is an example by John S. Coulson.

Many advertisements *for home appliances have a monotonous similarity, and when testimonials are used, they often convey a message of insincerity, particularly when the testimonial is attributed to a glamour personality. Maytag was able to adopt a believable slant by utilizing the consumer's thinking.*

Mother's copy—*An unsolicited ad written and submitted to Maytag by a mother of 15 stressed dependability—a theme that Maytag wanted—and the ad was run with good results.*

Mrs. Ray Crookston, mother of ~~15~~, 16
writes a Maytag ad for us

At left is the ad exactly as Mrs. Crookston sent it to us from Provo, Utah. It reads:

"Nothing, but nothing, outlasts a Maytag...when our first baby was born during World War II we used her grandmother's already seventeen-year-old MAYTAG to do the diapers.

"Now, eighteen years later, Granny Crookston is still using her 35-year-old MAYTAG week in and week out to do her family wash.

"So, when we decided to buy an automatic washer, three years ago, that has to work *hour* in and *hour* out for our sizable gang (four to five loads a day with 17 of us now), what did we buy? Why, a MAYTAG, of course!"

Of course.

Today, Maytag offers you all these features right along with dependability: *Unsurpassed Big-Load Capacity, Automatic Bleach Dispenser, Lint-Filter Agitator, and a Water-Level Control.* For a guide to all Maytag Washers and Dryers, send 10¢ in coin to: Maytag, Dept. 310L-6, Newton, Iowa.

Since Mrs. Crookston wrote her ad, another Crookston has joined the family. We're happy to report mother, baby and Maytag doing nicely.

MAYTAG
the dependable automatics
THE MAYTAG COMPANY, NEWTON, IOWA
SOLD IN CANADA AND THROUGHOUT THE WORLD.

Better—*Research by the agency, Leo Burnett Co., Chicago, showed that this revised ad, featuring the family photograph, attracted remarkable interest among women readers. Starch scores soared.*

Later, *the better ad was repeated but the figure 15 was X'd and a 16 was written beside it in longhand with the notation: "Since Mrs. Crookston wrote her ad, another Crookston has joined the family. We're happy to report that mother, baby, and Maytag are doing nicely." This version proved to be the most effective.*

Source: *John S. Coulson, Vice-President in Charge of Research, Leo Burnett Co., Chicago. See also* ***Advertising Age,*** *September 30, 1963, p. 98.*

wartime, for example, pictures of pretty girls are of less interest than army and aviation subjects. Human interest and crime pictures get high attention at all times and from both sexes.

People enjoy both the real and the ideal. Readers of advertisements prefer to see a product in pleasant surroundings, appropriate to the theme of the advertisement. Generally, people like to imagine themselves in ideal rather than realistic situations. In a study of readers' habits in reading women's magazines, it was found that women preferred to read two kinds of magazine articles: those that dealt with specific household tasks in terms of "how to do it" and those that presented colorful idealistic home settings, the more highly imaginative the better for reader interest.

An illustration of the "before-and-after" use of an advertised product must be used with discretion. When used for cosmetics, a woman usually reacts adversely to illustrations that show her as she really looks. She may admit it to herself but she does not want the advertiser to tell her so. Advertisers of cosmetics have learned that their products are advertised most effectively by picturing only the attractive after-use results. However, more than happy results should be pictured. Good advertising also appeals to the reader's self-interest and explains why it is to his advantage to spend his money.

Of course the type of art work and subject used in an illustration is greatly influenced by the product advertised and the purpose of the advertisement. A product such as linoleum or a carpet requires illustrations that are attractive and in color.

Copy

As previously stated, the dominant factor in successful advertising is not the layout, illustration, color, or size of the advertisement, but the character of the copy itself. The success of an advertisement is determined by the manner in which its central theme or idea identifies the product with some current desire, irritation, problem, or habit on the part of a portion of the buying public. "Stop those runs in stockings," for example, identified Lux soap with current irritations toward runs in stockings.

Copywriting is an art, and, like most arts, its effects depend upon the creative skill of the artist. Furthermore, an art has few invariable rules. However, the right combination of words and ideas can double a five per cent "Read Most" readership rating. This means, in some instances, that as many as a million readers are added at no extra cost to the advertiser. In spite of the difficulty in writing in terms of rules, we can note the findings of some of the most significant researches on copy. One finding from several studies in regard to copy indicates that effective copy is informative.

Charles M. Edwards, Jr., made a seven-year study of the advertising of 72 retail stores. A total of 671 factors, including the kind of advertisement, sales results, weather, media, layout, illustration, headline, price and copy were considered. The characteristics of successful low-cost advertisements were contrasted with unsuccessful high-cost advertisements. Edwards stated his most significant conclusions, in part, as follows:

> When we summarized the findings in each of our studies, we learned that no technique had always succeeded and no technique had always failed. We did discover conclusively, however, *that certain techniques invariably succeed more often than they fail, while certain other techniques invariably fail more often than they succeed.* For example, we learned that an advertisement's chance for success invariably increases as the number of *pertinent* merchandise facts included in the advertisement increases. The more you tell the more you sell!
>
> One store discovered, for instance, the following relationships between the number of merchandise facts included in its advertisements and the sales results of the advertisements.
>
> Of all the store's advertisements that included
>
> 4 or more merchandise facts, 44.2% succeeded.
> 5 or more merchandise facts, 49.6% succeeded.
> 6 or more merchandise facts, 57.7% succeeded.

Now Swift makes it easy for you to attract birds

NEW, READY-TO-HANG **BIRD FEEDER**
FILLED WITH **SEED & SUET** ONLY **79¢** at your store

New kind of bird feed has more of the things all birds need

When a new wild birdseed *was to be introduced to the market, the first ad, A, stated that the product would attract wild birds because it had what wild birds want and need. The second ad, B, told the same story but added points such as "to fill your yard with song birds all winter."*

Ad C did not stress the suet story but had a stronger appeal of ease in bringing "birds right up to your window." Research revealed no excitement over wild birdseed but the revision centered around strong human interest and aroused effective response.
Source: *John S. Coulson, Leo Burnett Co., Chicago. See also Advertising Age, September 30, 1963.*

7 or more merchandise facts, 60.0% succeeded.
8 or more merchandise facts, 66.7% succeeded.

The necessity of including all the pertinent merchandise facts does not mean, of course, that the mere cramming of all conceivable facts into an advertisement assures the success of the ad. It does mean that an imperative condition for the fullest success of an ad is the inclusion of all the essential merchandise facts—facts that the customer needs or wishes to know about a particular article before she can or will buy it. Actually the *character* of the facts included is more important than the *number* of facts. Whenever a store omits from its advertisements any essential merchandise facts, it instantly reduces sales response.

	Per Cent of Ads That Failed
Facts about appearance omitted (designs, colors, etc.)	60.1
Facts about composition omitted (materials, parts or pieces, etc.)	58.0
Facts about construction omitted (construction, workmanship, etc.)	56.5
Facts about serviceability omitted (uses, benefits of use, etc.)	56.1[8]

Daniel Starch found evidence in several studies of the importance of copy being informative. He analyzed the copy treatment of the fifty least-read and fifty most-read advertisements. After fifteen years of measuring the readership of magazine advertisements, during which period some two million interviews were conducted, he selected 100 advertisements from his readership records. Fifty were least read and fifty had been read most thoroughly by the largest number of people.

The most-read advertisements had been read by as many as 30 to 35 per cent of the persons interviewed. This is a very high percentage, since these advertisements contained 400 to 500 words and some more than 1,000.

An analysis of these 100 advertisements from the standpoint of copy treatment revealed that they fell into five general groups. Based upon copy approach, the subjects being:

1. *People.* In these advertisements people were

the center of the illustration and text matter. Usually these persons were doing something or saying something. They were of three different types. There were living persons, often well-known. . . .

There were fictitious persons such as Little Lulu. Then there were persons with or without names but representing types, such as a father and son or a family group.

2. *"How to" do things.* These advertisements told readers how to lay out a modern kitchen, launder silks, use tape, prepare certain recipes, or do other useful things.

3. *Striking events, facts, or statements.* Examples are "More Thousands Will Go to Rio by Clipper" and "4,300,000 Jobs to Do Today."

4. *Broad, general assertions.* Examples: "Tavern Wax for Longer Lasting Luster" and "Ozite Makes Rugs Look Lovelier, More Cheerful."

5. *Product.* These advertisements made no use of persons or their actions. Examples are advertisements that merely show a picture of the package or product, such as a cake of Fels Naptha soap in the wrapper with a headline "The Inside Story" or a large picture of a Van Heusen shirt and collar with a headline "Choose a Name You Can Trust."

Classifying these 100 advertisements in this manner, I derived the following results:

Type of Copy Treatment	*50 Read Most*	*50 Read Least*
Advertisements about people	29	10
"How to" advertisements	15	2
Striking events, facts, or statements	6	2
Broad, general assertions	0	4
Advertisements about products as such	0	32

Of the 50 advertisements read most, 58 per cent were about people in action, whereas among the advertisements least read, only 20 per cent were about people and in several of these cases the people were not in action. In the successful group none dealt merely with the product as such, without the use of people in action, whereas among the 50 least read, two-thirds were of this variety.

In other words, the two groups of advertisements were exactly reversed in respect to their use of people in action and their dealing with the inert product as such.[9]

MEASURING THE EFFECTIVENESS OF AN ADVERTISEMENT

When Kenneth Goode taught classes in advertising at Columbia University, he showed the students copies of eleven pairs of advertisements whose effectiveness was known from actual use. Each member of the class decided which advertisement of each pair was the better one. The results were almost a matter of chance. Later, he changed his procedure with some classes by first giving them only two guiding principles for evaluating the effectiveness of advertisements:

> "Don't tell people how good you made your goods. Tell them how good your goods make them!"
>
> "If your promise of a direct personal benefit as direct reward for your reader's response comes later than the first subheading of your top title, maybe it will come too late!"...
>
> With these two vital fundamentals, that class thereafter not only voted wrong on fewer advertisements, but fewer members voted wrong. Thus advantaged, in fact, instead of following earlier Columbia classes placing correctly any six or seven advertisements out of 11, it got all 11 right but two![10]

Psychologists and other researchers are seeking better methods of predicting the probable effectiveness of a proposed advertisement. Years ago, they conducted experiments with students as subjects in the laboratories. The results of such experiments had little or no value because laboratory situations did not approximate real life situations.

Prompted-recognition Surveys of Readership

The prompted-recognition, or aided-recall, method of studying advertisements has been used for many years by Daniel Starch and Staff, which has made available to agencies and others, the tabulated results of various studies of advertisement readership.

The procedure is simple. Readers of a medium are interviewed and asked several questions, such as, "Did you see this ad?" "What product is advertised?" "Did you read the headline?" "Did you read the copy?" "How much of the copy did you read?"

Since 1939, Starch surveys have given the results of the aided-recall test for all advertising of one column or larger, appearing in leading magazines.

From results obtained in the field surveys, the Starch organization compiles for advertisers and advertising agencies this advertising rating service. The service supplies percentages of visibility and readership of individual advertisements, includes computed costs per person for visibility and readership, and provides percentages of readership of the component parts of each advertisement.

The prompted-recognition method has certain limitations. For example, some media are read for their news columns; others are only skimmed for personals. The thoroughness of reading varies considerably for different magazines and newspapers of the same general class of publications.

For most national advertisers, it is more economical to buy the Starch reports than to attempt a checkup of readership independently. Obviously, these reports are more in the nature of an audit of what has already been done than a guide to what should be done with a proposed advertisement, which is often the advertiser's practical need. Furthermore, a measure of general reader interest may have little value for the advertising of a product that interests only a definite small class of consumers or the advertiser who seeks direct action from his copy.

Predicting Effectiveness of Advertisements Previous to Extensive Use

The marketing expert who believes that he can analyze an advertisement and predict by his subjective analysis the public's response to that advertisement is a dangerous man. His estimate may be worth more than that of the girl at the switchboard in the office, but he is likely to be sadly mistaken if he continues to make predictions based on subjective analysis only.

Consumers' receptiveness to each advertisement of a series can be predicted by means of balanced schedules in daily newspapers or other inexpensive media. For example, some advertisers select six typical cities and run six different advertisements for one week in each city. The advertisements are so arranged that every one of them is run in each of the six orders. For example, the six cities may be designated by letters *A, B, C, D, E,* and *F.* The advertisements may be designated as 1, 2, 3, 4, 5, and 6. A schedule of the test campaign might be arranged as follows:

A	*B*	*C*	*D*	*E*	*F*
1	2	3	4	5	6
2	3	4	5	6	1
3	4	5	6	1	2
4	5	6	1	2	3
5	6	1	2	3	4
6	1	2	3	4	5

This kind of test prevents misjudgments because of unusual news events, weather, or the cumulative effects of preceding advertisements. Such a six-weeks' method involves a great deal of time and it may be expensive, but it is a fairly safe way to predict the public's reaction to the advertisements proposed for use in an advertising campaign.

Split-run Tests

When several advertisements are to be tested in order to predict their relative effectiveness, the conditions under which they are to be tested should be as nearly identical as possible. The split-run test supplies these conditions.

The split-run test means that the publisher of the magazine or newspaper arranges the printing of the copies into two or more divisions. For example, an advertiser may want to know which one of three advertisements, *A, B,* or *C* is the most effective in drawing inquiries. To answer the question, the publisher does the printing so that one third of the copies have advertisement *A,* the second third have *B,* and the last third have *C.* In the printing plant where the three streams of copies meet, a workman or a mechanical device alternates the copies of the several streams. This means that the three advertisements are of the same size, have the same position, appear on the same day, are read by the same classes of readers, and advertise the same product under directly comparable conditions. Any one factor such as the headline may be changed in order to test its several variations.

Scores of newspapers and magazine publishers are now equipped for and willing to help an advertiser make split-run tests. Alert advertisers have used this device to discover the most effective appeals, headlines, copy, illustrations, coupons, and other factors. The procedure is far more accurate in its predictions than the older laboratory method in which people are asked what they like or think they like.

The split-run method is one of the most scientific tests available to the advertiser but it also has certain limitations. For example, some advertising campaigns must be planned to gradually build up a reputation for an article, a purpose for which the split-run test is not especially applicable. Also, split-run tests can be misleading when the circulation given each advertisement is not large enough to produce volumes of inquiries that are statistically significant.

Split-run tests are more significant for the measuring of effectiveness of different appeals than for determining the most effective presentation of one appeal. A whole series of split-run tests on the presentation of a chosen appeal may reveal which presentation is best, but the best presentation may not sell the goods at a profit.

The split-run test has not displaced all other methods of testing. Certain other techniques still have special values.

Gallup and Robinson, Inc., Impact Technique

Of the psychologists who have made notable contributions to measuring the effects of advertising, Gallup and Robinson are outstanding. They, for example, developed the *impact technique.* This procedure enables researchers to determine objectively what consumers get out of advertisements. The impact method can be applied to any medium: television, radio, newspapers, magazines, and billboards.

In an impact test for a magazine advertisement, the reader is required to recall an ad-

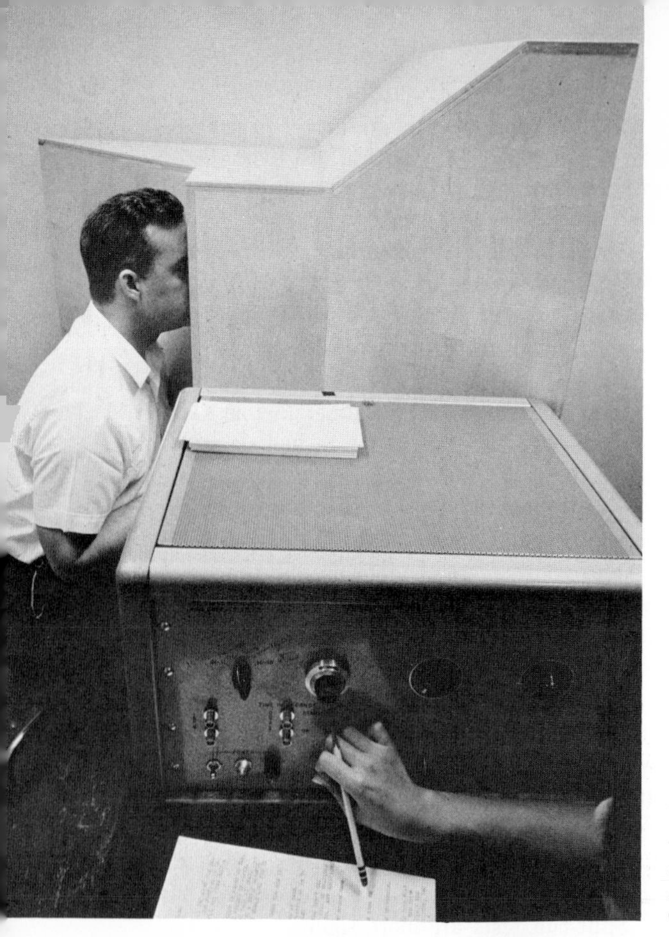

Tachistoscope. *The Burnett-designed tachistoscope is used regularly so that both research people and creative people in the agency can find out how quickly a consumer might recognize an idea, picture, headline, or the essential message of a possible advertisement.*

The test apparatus allows the advertisement to be visible to the respondent only in flashes of accurately controlled lengths of time, starting with an exposure of one one-hundredth of a second. The time period is gradually increased until the consumer becomes able to identify the basic features of the advertisement.

Group Discussion. *A small group of club women are interviewed by a staff member regarding a rough pilot of a television commercial shown in a box at the end of the table. The one-way mirror at the rear of the room enables an observer in a control booth to hear and see the group interview in progress without being observed or known to the members of the group.*

Creative Research Workshops *are operated by several advertising agencies. Leo Burnett Co., Chicago, for example, operates a workshop whose function is to pre-test, through research, the work and ideas of its creative staff. The main purpose is to determine whether the advertising messages under consideration are or can be communicated satisfactorily to consumers.*

Rough print advertisements, television and radio commercials, outdoor posters, packages, and new products are pre-tested. In the pre-testing of potential new television programs and commercials, electronic devices are used to measure certain reactions of consumers. Involuntary feelings, for example, are recorded by means of a psychogalvanometer. This device measures changes in blood pressure and respiration in the manner of a lie detector. A special tachistoscope, an apparatus that enables an examiner to show an advertisement or other stimulus to a respondent in flashes of accurately controlled lengths of time, is used to measure the time needed to communicate an idea or information.

For most tests, a sample of 10 to 20 persons is used. An idea to be tested can be brought to the workshop by one of the agency's creative men at 10 o'clock in the morning, and the results reported to him by 4 o'clock of the same day. These kinds of pre-test services are not always conclusive but are of great value to the agency's creative staff members.

Source: *"Burnett Men Get Fast Test Results via Busy Creative Research Workshop,"* ***Advertising Age,*** *September 10, 1962. Copyright, 1962, by Advertising Publications, Inc.*

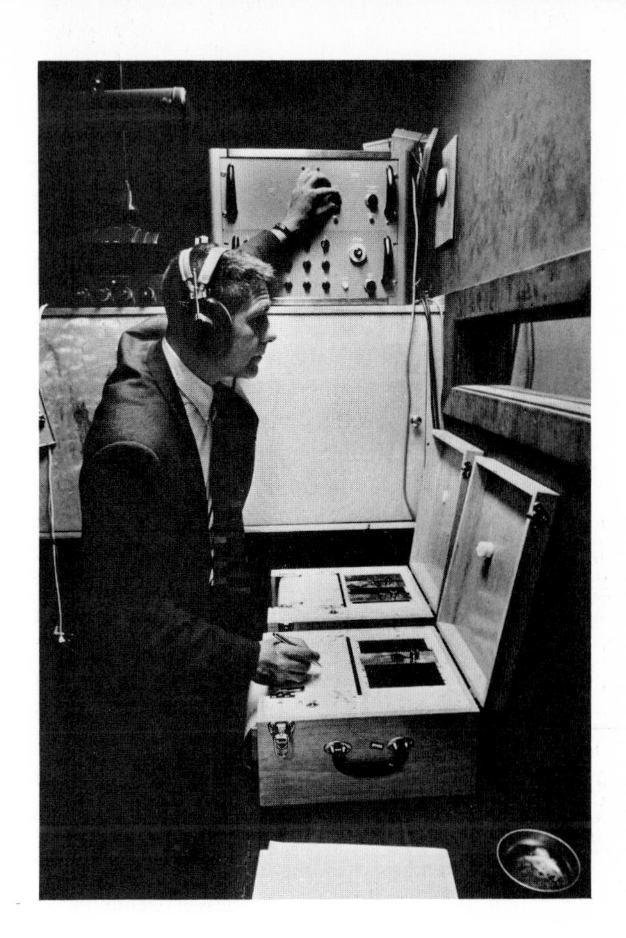

Clark Leavitt, *research supervisor and head of the agency's Creative Research Workshop, looks through one-way mirror while monitoring apparatus that records the voluntary and involuntary reactions of a woman who is watching and reacting to a television program and commercials.*

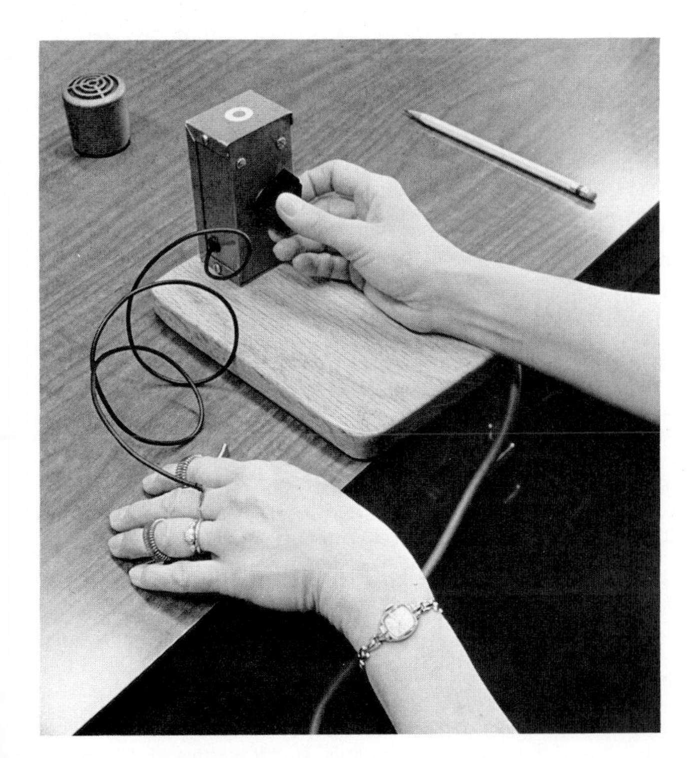

Television Pre-test. *This woman is rating her reactions to a new television program with regular commercials. With her right hand, she uses an electronic "like-dislike" rating unit to give voluntary opinions as the show progresses. Her involuntary reactions over the half-hour period also are recorded via the electrodes attached to two fingers of her left hand.*

vertisement and "play back" the selling message with the magazine closed. A playback is simply the verbatim report, in the respondent's own words, of everything he or she can remember about a particular advertisement. The playback is the end result of a series of probing questions about the advertisement.

Readers have difficulty in playing back an advertisement which has made no impression upon them. If the advertisement actually has made a memorable impression on a person, then within a limited period after exposure he can recall the advertisement and play back its message. In the case of some advertisements, over 40 per cent of the readers of a magazine have been able to prove that they have seen the advertisement—and this with the magazine closed. In addition they have been able to play back the message the advertiser told in his copy. No differences have been found among various educational groups in the ability to recall and play back a copy story. Readers with only a grade-school education play back as many advertisements as those with a college education.

Gallup-Robinson researches indicate that the flow of ideas is greatest when communication is rewarding to the reader or viewer, when statements or claims are validated, and when the reader or viewer is not required to perform mental work, like figuring out what analogies or coined phrases mean.

Gallup has reported that effective advertising is that which uses "not words or phrases, but ideas. Ideas distinguish more than anything else the advertising that penetrates from that which does not get into the minds of people who read or hear it. Boast copy is of little value. Believable proof copy is the kind that sticks with people. Demonstrations are especially effective. . . . The gimmick-y ads usually don't work. Gimmicks tend to get in the way of idea expression."[11]

Impact studies are forcing a new conception of advertising effectiveness—effectiveness which places emphasis upon ideas as opposed to advertising gadgetry.

Advertising, to Some, is a "Scapegoat" Occupation

Advertising as an occupation attracts creative thinkers, men and women who like to choose themes, plan campaigns, and invent strategies for increasing the use of goods and services through effective communication with consumers. These creative workers believe in the benefits that come to more and more people as we learn to take advantage of our productive facilities.

They recognize that to some extent "Madison Avenue" has displaced "Wall Street" as a convenient business image scapegoat for things that are wrong in our culture today. They also recognize that advertising in itself is not inherently good or bad but a communications tool. Its goodness or badness depends upon the ethical standards of the user. Properly used, it adds to man's well being.

ACKNOWLEDGMENTS AND REFERENCES

1. For supporting information, see Howard Morgens, President, Procter & Gamble, *Advertising from a Management Viewpoint,* address at the 8th Annual Marketing Conference of the National Industrial Conference Board, Inc., Sept. 15, 1960, in New York City, pp. 6 and 10.
2. A summary of some of these studies is available in *The Adoption of New Products: Process and Influence* (Ann Arbor, Mich.: Foundation for Research on Human Behavior, 1959).
3. Significant findings from certain studies in this field have been made available by Robert C. Brooks, Jr., "'Word of Mouth' Advertising in Selling New Products," *The Journal of Marketing,* October, 1957.
4. *America's Tastemakers,* Research Report of The Public Opinion Index for Industry, copyright by Opinion Research Corporation, 1959, Vol. 17, No. 4, 463-B, April, 1959.
5. Ernest Dichter, "A Psychological View of Advertising Effectiveness," *The Journal of Marketing,* July, 1949.
6. Donald R. Murphy, Director, Editorial Research, *Wallace's Farmer,* Des Moines, Iowa, "Questions on Ad Readership Answered in Farm Paper Ad Layout Study," *Advertising Age,* Apr. 6, 1959, p. 70.
7. Mark Wiseman, "Illustrations: 1," *Advertising and Selling,* February, 1947, pp. 74, 76.
8. Charles M. Edwards, Jr., "Pretesting of Advertis-

ing: a Prerequisite for Profits," *Advertising and Selling,* June, 1945, pp. 73, 74, 153.
9. Daniel Starch, "Why Readership of Ads Has Increased 24%," *Advertising and Selling,* August, 1946, p. 47.
10. *Advertising and Selling,* October, 1948, p. 123.
11. See "Gallup Tells What Makes a Good Ad on TV or in Print," *Printers' Ink,* November 6, 1953.

PROJECTS

1. Alexander Hamilton Institute ran advertisements with the following headings:
   a. "Those Who Shy at Unpleasant Facts Should Not Read This Page."
   b. "Men Who Are Satisfied to Wait Ten Years for Success Will Find Nothing Interesting on This Page."
   c. "Afraid to Face the Facts—Then Don't Read This Page."
   d. "Men Who Know It All Are Not Invited to Read This Page."

   One of these pulled marvelous results. Select the one that pulled best. See Appendix, page 622, for answer.
2. One of the country's most successful teachers of dancing said that he does not sell people *dance study.* He sells them what dancing will do for them, such as bring them popularity, health, charm, relaxation, or other benefits. A lawyer, for example, who buys the lessons does not "take lessons"; he relaxes. Apply this principle to the advertising of a canned food, an automobile, a bank account, or a radio.
3. James W. Young built a business of selling men's ties through the use of split-run tests in *Sunset* magazine. For example, he tried three different headlines: (a) HAND WOVEN by the mountain people of New Mexico, (b) SHABBY HUSBAND made over—by my hand-woven ties, and (c) HUSBANDS LOVE my hand-woven ties (and you). The first outpulled the others by a wide margin. Why?
4. A split-run test in *The New York Times Magazine* for the sale of a popular-audience book tried two different appeals in the headline. The headline "How to win friends and influence people" produced twice as many sales as "How to ruin your marriage in the quickest possible way." Why?
5. Find an opportunity to observe one or more persons while they are viewing television for at least four different programs. What do you notice about their attention to the broadcast? What do they do when the commercial comes on?
6. Select several print advertisements for study in regard to the people to whom the advertising is directed. Attach them to a brief report that lists the headlines. For each headline and ad, state the probable categories of adopters, mobiles, social class, age, education, income, and geographical areas which the advertiser appeared to have in his mind as the "target" for the advertising.

COLLATERAL READINGS

Hepner, Harry Walker, *Advertising—Creative Communication with Consumers.* New York: McGraw-Hill Book Company, 1964, Chapters 17–22.

Lucas, D. B. and S. H. Britt, *Measuring Advertising Effectiveness.* New York: McGraw-Hill Book Company, 1963.

Martineau, Pierre, *Motivation in Advertising.* New York: McGraw-Hill Book Company, 1957.

Schwab, Victor O., *How to Write a Good Advertisement.* New York: Harper & Row, Publishers, Inc., 1962.

Use of Motivation Research in Marketing, Studies in Business Policy, No. 97, National Industrial Conference Board, Inc., 1960.

THE MAN WHO MADE THE BEST MOUSETRAP WAITS FOR THE WORLD TO MAKE A BEATEN PATH TO HIS DOOR

*Cartoon by Nate Collier. Reproduced by special permission from **The Saturday Evening Post,** The Curtis Publishing Company.*

CHAPTER TWENTY-EIGHT

COMMUNICATING WITH THE INDIVIDUAL CONSUMER —SALESMANSHIP

When several members of the National Sales Executives organization attended a sales convention in Europe, one of the world's leading statesmen also happened to attend some of the sessions. After he had listened to the speakers who told of American ingenuity and enterprise, he stated that he had always thought mass production was one of the secrets of America's greatness. He realized, however, that other countries had mass production, too. At one time, he had assumed that the cause of our living standards could be attributed to our willingness to work hard and to our huge natural resources. Other countries, however, could boast of those, too. After listening to all the speakers at the convention, he believed that "he had finally discovered what really makes America great—we make people want things!"[1]

Salesmanship, at its best, renders a service to consumers. It breaks us away from our ruts in living and induces us to adopt the new and better devices that modern technology has made available to us.

The best selling is helpful selling. The way to sell is to serve as shown in the example that follows:

"I get the greatest satisfaction out of selling because I feel that I am building a business for three people. They are my customer, my company, and myself. And it's my customer who must benefit first. In other words, it is service, satisfaction and, of course, profitable sales on which I have always tried to build my volume. That's why I got a lift the other day when one of my dealers said, 'You've really become a partner in my business,' a more than ample return for the long, uphill job I had in getting him started."[2]

The Image of Selling as a Career

Unfortunately, many people, particularly college students, do not credit selling as offering important social or economic contributions.

In one survey of seniors, it was found that less than a fourth believe that aggressive selling is a principal factor in large-scale production and the high standard of living in this country. Instead, a large proportion think that our standard of living is a result of large-scale production only. "One-fourth judge that people would be as well or better off if there were fewer salesmen, and over half say that people would be as well or better off if there were fewer of some kinds of salesmen. Only about a fifth believe that the net effect of sales and advertising on consumers is to make them happier."

According to the largest proportion, students think that salesmen are insincere. Their respect for selling in general is impaired mainly by beliefs regarding sales ethics—"salesmen exaggerate, tell part truths, are insincere." Over a fourth indicate that selling requires more compromise with the truth than some other kinds of jobs, but about 60 per cent say that some kinds of sales jobs do make such requirements. One-third believe that salesmanship is morally different from the persuading "which everyone does," because "the purpose is to influence...for the self-interest of the salesman and his employer."[3]

How do experienced salesmen view their job, its financial and personal satisfactions? The answers will, of course, vary with the kinds of salesmen who are interviewed. The beginners, the marginal producers, and those in transitory types of selling have lower opinions than those who do technical selling or have succeeded in selling as a career.

A survey conducted by the Research Institute of America among 10,000 salesmen in 671 companies, representing 48 industries, indicated that 89 per cent of the respondents were satisfied with their occupation and that 65 per cent felt they were being paid equitably.[4] As among members of any occupational group, those individuals who have high intelligence and are interested in interpreting their work in terms of its larger meanings are those who perceive the salesman as an important person in moving goods into the hands of the consumer.[5]

The Need for Selling

As mentioned previously (see pages 556–59), one of the most common fallacies in the thinking of many people is the assumption that people will buy what they need when they have the money to pay for it. They do in the case of elemental needs but not for discretionary spending items. Those, in most instances, must be sold.

Anyone who imagines that people with money will buy everything that would enrich their lives need only make a very simple survey. Think, for a moment, of a high-income residential area of your own community. You probably know the main furnishings of at least a dozen homes. How many have a modern color television receiver? Most, probably, have none, or at best only one or two have a set. And yet, good color reception has been available for many years in most areas of the United States. The fact that the majority of well-to-do families could increase their enjoyment of several good television shows each week does not mean that all those families are rushing to dealers to buy new receivers.

Consider the many people in cold climates who could sleep more comfortably if they had electric blankets on their beds. They get along with heavy blankets because no one has sold them on the benefits of the better ones.

Think of the housewives who need better stoves in the kitchen or improved labor-saving automatic washers in the laundry. They get along with what they have now. Somebody will have to show them the benefits they can enjoy from the new appliances before they'll change their habits.

Visit several offices where typewriters are clicking. Chances are many of the typists are not using electric typewriters. No salesman has as yet made an effort to have the owner of the business modernize his equipment.

Travel to other countries and observe all the obsolete backbreaking equipment that is in use to a far greater extent than here. Even though America has a higher percentage of venturesome consumers than most nations, we have so many slow-to-change people that constant selling is necessary to get them to adopt the better living that is available.

Whenever we imagine that most Americans now are buying about all that they need, we should recognize that our annual sales for the material comforts of our citizens are smaller than we realize. In any one year it is probable that less than two per cent of our families move into a new house, less than five per cent buy a room air conditioner or an electric range; less than ten per cent buy an electric shaver, a washing machine, or paint for the house; and less than 25 per cent take a real vacation trip.

The old concepts of selling as having the "peddler" and "pitchman" connotations are gradually decreasing. More emphasis is being placed on the modern salesman's functions of customer counseling, sales promotional assistance, organizing dealers' meetings, product service, and sales expense control.

There was a time when each salesman who called on retailers tried to load the merchant with goods. The modern trend is for manufacturers' salesmen to show dealers the dollar value of low inventory.

Selling is an Aspect of Marketing

Today, the making and the marketing of goods are so interwoven they are being recognized as complementary parts of the productive process. A product must be not only *good* but *right* from the consumer viewpoint. Production is not one thing and marketing another. More and more company managements are dominated or influenced by marketing men because the typical company's basic problem is not how to make the product but how to find or develop a market for the product. In this sense, marketing is broader than selling. It is a point of view for selling.

The term "marketing" includes every activity that has to do with the movement of goods from the point where they are produced to the point where they are consumed. As a study, it usually includes advertising, sales management, salesmanship, sales policies, foreign trade, pricing, product planning, and the analysis of products in regard to their present and potential customers. It seeks to discover where and how typical customers live, their habits and motivations, and their responsiveness to varying forms of marketing stimuli such as dealer displays and sales procedures.

The terms *marketing* and *distribution* have the same general meaning. Contrary to popular conception, distribution is more than wholesaling and retailing. It is broader and more inclusive than selling.

Marketing today includes numerous activities that precede the production of a product as well as those that follow its production. Some of the marketing activities that precede the decision to start production are research in consumer motivations, the study of individual choices, the search for and pretesting of ideas for new products or new uses, product planning, product testing, and the selection of distribution channels.*

Most persons are acquainted with the common method of distributing products through the channel: manufacturer to wholesaler to dealer to customer. There are, of course, many other channels of distribution such as those that involve direct mail selling and house-to-house canvassing. Discount houses have opened new forms of marketing, both wholesale and retail. In the limited treatment of selling of this chapter, we shall offer psychological aspects of only two kinds of selling: retail and industrial. When salesmen in these two fields of one manufacturer were studied, the data showed that they differ markedly in personality characteristics. The typical salesman who calls on industrial firms places heavy emphasis on ingenuity, inventiveness, and the exercise of his wits in the selling situation. His interest in technical and scientific problems is moderate. The typical salesman who calls directly on retail dealers places heavy emphasis on hard work, planning, and persuading other people to his point of view or way of doing things. He has a high degree of orderliness. He rejects "thinking" jobs such as those related to the technical sciences.[6] Those who do customer-contact selling in retail stores have distinguishing characteristics that differ from the above two classes as indicated by standard vocational interest tests.

* The student who studies marketing will learn the meanings of the commonly used terms: wholesaler, distributor, and jobber. A *"wholesaler"* is a merchant middleman who sells to retailers and other merchants and/or to industrial, institutional, and commercial users but who does not sell in significant amounts to ultimate consumers.

In the basic materials, semi-finished goods, and tool and machinery trades merchants of this type are commonly known as "dealers," "distributors," or "supply houses." "Distributor" is a term especially common in the appliance and automotive industries. The term "jobber" is now widely used as a synonym of *wholesaler*.

Retail Selling Techniques

Anyone who reads books and magazine articles on retail salesmanship is likely to find considerable evidence reported to show that the salesmanship in retailing is poor and that salespeople play a negative rather than a positive role.

Each of 18 students of the merchandising department of College of William and Mary (Norfolk, Va.) was given $25 to spend in leading Norfolk stores recently. They were each to select and purchase an item that cost much less than $25. More important, they were prepared to buy additional items that were suggested by retail salespersons. Each student was eager to spend his entire $25.

SAD TRUTH: "The students were able to spend only $122.54 out of a possible $450," reports James E. Simmons, president, Hampton Roads Sales Executives Club. Total value of items selected by students was $77.59.

Salespeople suggested additional items whose value totalled only $44.95. So students walked out of stores with $327.46 unspent! WE SAY: Shame on selling![7]

Admittedly, some retail salespeople are incompetent and gain little satisfaction from their jobs. And some store managements are not seriously anxious to help their employees sell more effectively. Some store managements place greater dependence on low price, large stock, self-selection, and similar non-personal devices than on training the selling employees. Other managements follow the policy of also training and stimulating the sales personnel. Fortunately, many managements and salespeople are constantly improving their selling techniques. Several examples of effective techniques are offered here in order that emphasis may be given to the positive practices.

In a sense, the employees are the most important sales attraction in a store. They, by their appearance and manner, help to build the store's personality as well as perform the selling functions.

In the more progressive stores, executives are given special training in the operating philosophy that good public relations begin with employees and that all employees are human beings with intelligence and emotions. And they can learn helpful principles.

Willard M. Thompson has reported a department store research study of how expert salespeople sell. Recordings were made of the ways a panel of 50 expert salespeople actually sell. Their techniques were analyzed. As a result, an important definition of personal selling emerged:

> Personal selling in stores is not entirely focused, as current definitions imply, upon the objective of helping customers buy. It also serves the broader purpose of helping customers obtain maximum personal satisfaction for money spent.[8]

The Jewel Tea Company, Inc., conducted studies of its home-route services and analyzed the nature of personal selling largely in terms of time and duties. In the first study, successful salesmanship was viewed as a matter of spending a certain amount of time and following prescribed steps with all customers. It was hoped men might be trained in "automatic selling." Later, the objectives were changed because

> ...motivational studies have taken a different point of view and looked on salesmanship primarily in terms of establishing and maintaining satisfactory salesman-customer relationships. Among other things, they investigated how the housewife felt about this kind of service. They considered her need to feel important, to feel that she was in control of the sales visit, and to feel that she was an efficient shopper; they took into account her fears of installment buying, the temptation to be extravagant, and the tendency for husbands to feel hostile toward route men.
>
> In the early study, the concept of selling was mechanistic and logical—in terms of procedures and products. The later studies used a concept that included the procedures and products but also emphasized the maintenance of relationships that would satisfy the needs and feelings of people. The results had important implications for selecting and training sales personnel as well as for planning supplementary promotional material.[9]

All types of salesmen can be trained and retail sales people can benefit from training but most efforts to train salesmen have been made for industrial salesmen.

> James Adams, who was instrumental in creating the halo of enjoyments surrounding the Cadillac, stated that his method was to combine the dream and the rationality in each advertisement. "He utilized the symbols of success, aspiration, achievement, prestige, luxury—all the key meanings which Cadillac represents. But he also gave the buyer several practical reasons. Ideally, the owner can feed on the dream, probably at the never-stated level, while at the same time he knowingly talks about safety of construction or some other functional quality."

Source: Pierre Martineau, *Motivation in Advertising* (New York: McGraw-Hill Book Company, 1957), p. 104.

One important reason for the greater amount of training given to industrial than to retail salesmen is that the average cost of a sales call by an industrial salesman is some thirty dollars. It is this level of selling that is treated in the remainder of the chapter.

The Communication Process in Selling

The standardized or "canned" sales talk can be taught to salesmen by drilling them until they perform it satisfactorily. This kind of selling is not at all appropriate for low-pressure selling in which the prospect and the salesman communicate with each other.

In this kind of high-level salesmanship, it is necessary to learn to sense the customer's needs and wants. The salesman must not only be able to communicate his ideas and proposals to the prospect, but he must also develop the ability to understand what the prospect is attempting, explicitly and implicitly, to communicate to him. To perform effectively in this kind of two-way communication in face-to-face situations, the salesman needs a basic concept, a frame of reference, about human behavior. The adjustment concept as described in Chapters 2–8, or some equally helpful frame of reference, is essential. The skillful use of such a concept must, of course, be developed through years of experience in much the same manner as it is developed by the skilled clinician.

Rules for the salesman's behavior have little value for low-pressure selling. The development of psychological insight is far more valuable. John M. Frey has described the needs and methods of training salesmen in this kind of effective communication, in part, as follows:

What should a salesman understand about the communication process that will help his selling efforts? He should understand what the process of communication entails; the complex social context in which it occurs; the difficulties that are likely to arise; the difference between statements of feeling and statements of content; the context in which words are spoken. Further, he should be aware that different people are bringing to each situation different assumptions, perceptions, and feelings based on their personal experience and "self" concept; that these assumptions, perceptions, and feelings are constantly interacting with his own, that he is intellectually, emotionally, and very personally involved in most situations; that recognition and acceptance of responsibility for this involvement are vital... sales trainers could well borrow a concept from the field of supervisory training:

"We have to stop telling supervisors how they should behave and what their attitudes should be.... Let us remember that our new objective is to assist people in learning from their own experience. We are no longer trying to change them; we are giving them the opportunity to change themselves, if they wish, by reflecting upon and re-evaluating their own experiences.... We are not interpreting their own experience *for them;* we are not telling them *our* personal experience. Instead, *we are allowing them to examine* and *re-evaluate their own experience*."[10]

Working within such a conceptual scheme, Roethlisberger proposes three ways in which the trainer can facilitate the process of self-learning: (1) helping people to recognize the attitudes they bring to experience; (2) helping people to ask better questions of experience; and (3) providing them with a useful way of thinking about matters of human behavior so that they can make better observations about themselves and their relations to others....

Role-Playing

The most promising approach, I believe, centers around the use of role-playing. This is essentially a self-explanatory term. In sales training role-playing puts one man acting as a buyer, another as a salesman. Many variations are possible. For instance, the "buyer" can be told to act as he himself personally feels. Or he can be given a few basic "facts" about himself, or even a relatively complete characterization to portray. As for the "salesman," he can be given many, few, or no facts about the "buyer." Each instructor will naturally want to adopt the particular variation that suits his own personal preference and situation.

To illustrate what a company can do with role-playing, here is the experience of a firm employing a fairly large salesforce in a highly competitive industry:

In the beginning the salesmen—particularly the older, more experienced ones—were skeptical of the value of this role-playing. Agreement was finally reached, however, to experiment with the plan on an informal basis in one department. At first the salesman acting the part of the "buyer" played the role as he himself felt. The acting was somewhat stilted. The players were rather embarrassed, and a number of jokes and humorous comments were made. The ensuing discussions were restrained and brief.

But soon the atmosphere changed. The initial embarrassment was gone. The participating salesmen began to get deeply involved in what they were doing. So did the observing salesmen. The formal discussions waxed hot and heavy, continuing in informal groups for days afterward. One salesman suggested acting out the part of a real buyer whom he had recently come in contact with. This was done, and it worked out very well.

At times the discussions wandered. At times they got out of hand. But for the most part they were remarkably beneficial. The salesmen gradually became more consciously aware of the assumptions, perceptions, and feelings that they were bringing to a particular situation, and of how these feelings and attitudes were inextricably interwoven into their relationship with a buyer. They also became more perceptive of the feelings and emotions of a buyer. And they began to recognize the nature—and consequences—of the term "involvement."

In the particular situation of the company making this experiment the problem of price negotiation has continually loomed large. Quite naturally, therefore, the bargaining process arose in almost every role-playing situation. Initially, the natural tendency of the discussions was to focus on the "best" method of bargaining with a buyer—a natural error in this day of "how-to-sell" books. Consequently, a strong effort was made to guide the discussions away from a "right-wrong" basis to a "what happened" basis, which was found to be far more profitable.

In general, then, it would seem that role-playing can be used with considerable success. One great advantage of the method is that it forces learning by doing—practicing—rather than just talking. The men cannot say, for instance. that they should be tactful; they must *be* tactful. Role-playing allows the players (and observers) to learn from their own experience, in a sheltered atmosphere. Because the men are not "playing for keeps," they are free to experiment. At the same time, role-playing gets the players close enough to an actual situation so that they become excited and concerned about it.

Note that, in addition, role-playing is relatively practical. In contrast to the case method of instruction, it does not require prior preparation on the part of the salesmen, nor does it require the development of case materials.[11]

Of course this kind of superior salesmanship is applicable only to salesmen of high intelligence. Most salesmanship training must be given to typical rather than exceptionally able men and deal with the more simple aspects of the sales situation.

Training in Selling is Beneficial to All Personality Types

The need for careful selection and training of salesmen is indicated by the oft-repeated statement of sales managers that "the top quarter of the average sales force sells three-fourths of the total volume." The editors of *Sales Management* asked several hundred subscribers regarding the truth of this statement and the answers were as follows:

In 8% of the companies, the top quarter sold 71 to 80% of total volume.

In 35% of the companies, the top quarter sold 51 to 70% of total volume.

In 29% of the companies, the top quarter sold 41 to 50% of total volume.

In 28% of the companies, the top quarter sold 30 to 40% of total voume.[12]

Considerable statistical evidence is now available which indicates that sales results depend primarily on the selling methods used rather than on the personality type only.

Some sales executives have become intrigued by the idea of changing a salesman's personality in order to increase his effectiveness. Investigations indicate that it is difficult, often impossible, to change a salesman's personality to fit his superior's wishes. The salesman's methods, however, can be improved. Several wholesale drug firms, in cooperation with the Bureau of Business Research, Ohio State University, conducted a study that included systematic observations of 70 wholesale drug salesmen. Marketing research specialists with pad and pencil and stop watch observed 70 wholesale drug salesmen on their rounds.

When all the findings were analyzed, the drug executives and the researchers concluded that effective selling largely depends upon:

1. *How many* genuine sales arguments are used.
2. *How many* items the salesman mentions.
3. *How much* time is spent in actual selling.

The emphasis, thus, is on: "how many" and "how much." According to these particular investigators, the "quantitative factors" are important in making a high score as a salesman. Salesmanship is not so much a personality gift, a bubbling personality, or the use of "psychology" as a matter of sticking to business.[13]

Other studies such as one made of life insurance salesmen indicated that a salesman's belief in his product and his motivation are more important than technical knowledge in determining how well he does his job.[14] Evidently both quantitative annd motivational or qualitative factors are related to sales success.

Studies of expert salespeople indicate that top sellers can develop in even the smallest firm—without lengthy training programs, and without depending upon complicated research or expensive staff specialists. In general, we can conclude that personal selling proficiency can be taught through guided constant, on-the-job practice. For this to take place, three elements are needed: a customer-centered attitude, an appreciation of the importance of certain basic, personal-selling skills, and an administrative climate which encourages improvement.

Formulas for Selling

E. St. Elmo Lewis in 1898 formulated the slogan, "Attract attention, maintain interest, create desire." Later he added a fourth point, "Get action." Numerous additions and substitutions have been made to this theory of selling, such as "Gain confidence" and "Give satisfaction."

Strong has formulated a theory of selling in terms of "Want, solution, action, and satisfaction."[15] This formula, like its predecessors, also deals largely with mental states, it directs the attention and efforts toward what goes on in the prospect's mind. Some sales managers who have trained salesmen claim that it is very difficult and decidedly confusing for a salesman to focus attention upon what the prospect is thinking. An easier and more effective method is to train the salesman to think of what he himself does rather than what may be happening in the mind of his prospect. The mental states of the prospect cannot be ignored, but *the emphasis should be upon what the salesman does and the objective factors of the selling act*. The salesman should think in terms of:

1. *The prospect as an individual*—his education, health, business affiliations, business and psychological needs, and so on.

2. *The situation of the prospect*— his problems, financial status, and other objective characteristics relevant to the purchase of the salesman's product.

3. *The methods or acts in the sales canvas*—the time of day he calls, the methods of demonstrating, the words he speaks, the number of calls, the method of closing the sales talk, and other controllable acts on the part of the salesman.

Directing the Sales Talk Toward the Prospect's Problem

The dominant attitude of the true salesman is that of the man who wishes to render service. Many men do not want to sell a prospect unless that prospect really needs the article under consideration. Some concerns are even changing the title of salesman to "serviceman," or, in the case of those who sell to dealers, "merchandise counselors." This attitude toward the prospect is expressed in the frequent mention of the "'You' viewpoint," "Prospect analysis," or the "Objective attitude." Selling has become a matter of "combing" the prospect's situation and then capitalizing that part of the situation which can be made more satisfying.

The best salesmen study the prospect, capitalize the immediate situation, and then arouse in the mind of the prospect a feeling of want. The prospect must be made to feel that his present situation could be better or more profitable. A man may wear the same suit for a year, but he may not have any sense of want for a new suit until his wife mentions his shabbiness so often that he wants a new suit. The *need* may be present; but, until that need is transformed into a *want,* it might as well not exist so far as the salesman is concerned. The salesman must induce in the prospect a feeling of inadequacy, a *felt need.* This feeling of a need or a conscious want takes place as soon as the salesman demonstrates his article in such a way that it fits into the prospect's problems. The suggested purchase becomes an answer or a solution to a want. In a few cases the salesman finds it an easy matter to fit his product or service into the wants of the prospect, as in the case of the fire insurance salesman who finds that his prospects want fire insurance right after a big fire in the community. At such times, they have a felt need or a conscious want. However, it is usually necessary for the salesman to arouse the want or to connnect his product with some present want.

The salesman who sells books for school children does not create a new want on the part of the mother, but he associates his books with the "want" for her child's success. The automobile salesman does not create new wants, but associates the new big car with the prospect's present want of social prestige. He shows the prospect how he can have his want satisfied *now*. The skillful salesman is adept in the art of presenting means to *immediate* satisfactions.

To do this, the salesman does not emphasize the product itself but describes the product as an *end*. The product is not even the means to the desired end. The salesman gives a vivid description of the product so that the prospect pictures himself as enjoying those delights which the product gives. The automobile salesman does not say: "When you have this car, it will give your wife a lot of pleasure," but, "When you have this big car, your wife and your friends will realize that it is worthy of a man of your caliber."

It often happens that the inventor of a machine is unable to sell it. The technical expert knows so much about it that he describes the machine. The salesman describes not only the things that the machine does but also the satisfactions and pleasures that it gives. He describes not just the means to the end but the end in its most pleasant aspects. The dealer is given attractive descriptions of the profits to be made from handling the product rather than a description of the product itself.

Some salesmen who sell to dealers think that they are giving the dealer service when they arrange his stock for him, sweep the store, wait on customers, or wash the windows. These acts are not rendering a service based on the goods the salesman sells. They are merely a method of approach to put the dealer in a receptive state regarding the salesman's commodities. The approach may be made from any one of several angles.

The Approach

Tricky approaches are popular with a few salesmen. They refuse to discuss their proposition with anyone except the "big boss," because they are calling on a "personal matter." The "personal matter" approach is an exceedingly weak and stereotyped start for an interview. It is a deceitful method of getting into an office, because any official can be made to leave a meeting of his board of directors if his secretary tells him that a man wants to see him about the "accident" his son just had.

Generally, investigators of selling techniques believe that *the first 10 seconds before a customer are especially important.* First impressions are likely to last throughout the sales interview.

Salesmen are advised to cultivate a voice that reflects pleasant feelings and helps the customer to have a pleasant participating experience during the interview.

The rule in this connection is, *Keep the voice up on the last syllable.*

An *up*-rising voice holds attention. A dying-out voice loses attention.

Macy's in New York conducted an experiment on this point and found that when salespeople greeted customers with "Good Morning"—keeping their voices up on the last syllable—there was a marked warming up of customers and an increase in sales tickets.[16]

Salesmen often try to find out a prospect's hobby before they call. This kind of interest in a prospect's affairs is legitimate if the salesman does not try to bluff. His interest in the prospect's hobby should be that of a learner. He can have a genuine desire to learn something about the hobby, but if he exhibits an artificial interest merely to make a sale, he is likely to make himself ridiculous. The salesman should mention the hobbies of the prospect in such a way that the prospect is pleased with himself because the salesman is willing to listen to his exploits. Sincerity is always important for the salesman, but it is especially important when hobbies are discussed.

Futhermore, the prospect approached by the salesman should be a live prospect at the time of the call. Studies of automobile selling, for example, indicate that typical motorists

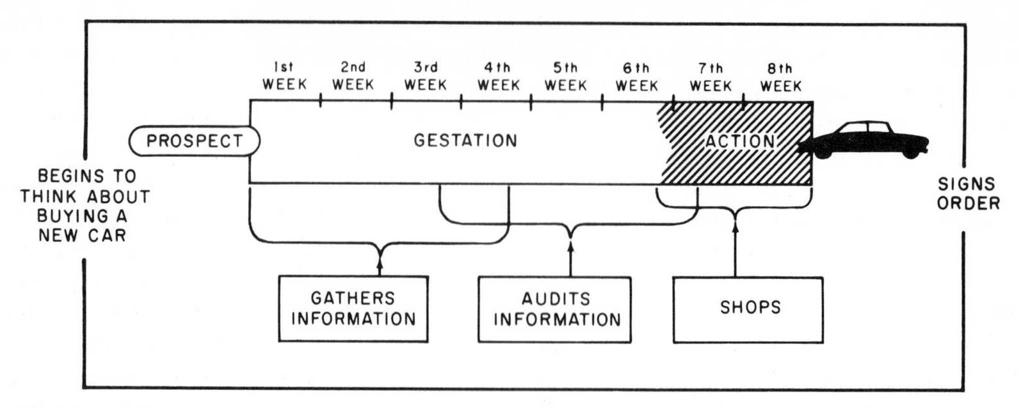

***The buyer makes up his mind** in advance. "The typical motorist is in the buying mood only about 2 months out of every 3 or 4 years." During the "period of gestation" the prospective buyer gathers information and makes up his mind as to which cars he should look at before buying. In many cases he wants more information than is given in automobile advertising. At the same time, he is often reluctant to ask for such information because he does not wish to be subjected to "sales pressure." If the manufacturer can bring to his attention some new type of information that is sufficiently attractive to overcome his reluctance, and get him to tell who he is before he becomes exposed to competitive solicitation—then the salesman has a far better chance of selling him.—From "27 Suggestions for Locating Prospects," C. R. Report No. 3606, General Motors Corporation, Detroit, Mich.*

who buy new cars gather information and think about cars for about two months before they purchase. During the "period of gestation" the prospective buyer gathers information and makes up his mind as to which cars he should look at before buying. In many cases he wants more information than is given in automobile advertising. At the same time, he is often reluctant to ask for such information because he does not wish to be subjected to "sales pressure." If a salesman can bring to his attention some new type of information that is sufficiently attractive to overcome his reluctance, and get him to say who he is before he becomes exposed to competitive solicitation—then the salesman has a far better chance of selling him. Eventually, an effective demonstration becomes important in the selling process.

It is often difficult for the salesman to demonstrate the service or article with the service or article itself, so he must depend upon some graphic means to enable the prospect to realize his present situation and to visualize the best possible situation. The film method of demonstration is one of the very best methods, because the prospect can really see the benefits claimed for the product instead of attempting to visualize them. The moving picture machine is a means of demonstration that should be used more frequently. The chief objection to most of the films seems to be that they deal with the manufacturer's problems rather than with the customer's problems.

The Sales Interview

The first rule of the successful sales talk is that it must deal with the prospect's situation and be directed toward a more satisfied, more contented, or more effective prospect-situation. The talk that starts nowhere and gets nowhere seldom leads to a sale. Even though a salesman dislikes the "canned" sales talk, he should have certain definite goals in each talk. Far more sales have been lost through lack of a planned sales talk than because of having the talk too highly standardized.

One "quota-beating" salesman who sells a specialty tells his prospect that he has planned his sales talk so that he, the prospect, will be able to see clearly what his machine can do and that the prospect can judge for himself as to whether the machine will make money for him. Then he hands the prospect a small printed card, saying: "This card has listed on it the six most common questions which my prospects ask or want to ask while I demonstrate this machine. If I do not make myself clear on some point, check that question. Of course, if you think of a point not on the card, be sure to ask that." A significant part of this scheme is the fact that the salesman has omitted from the card the most common question asked by the prospects and which every prospect is almost sure to ask. When the prospect raises that question, the salesman acts as though the prospect has thought of something no one ever before thought of. He scratches his head, then answers the point, and compliments the prospect's ingenuity; but at the same time the acceptance of that point practically commits the prospect to the purchase of the machine. The above method can be adapted to almost any product or service sold today.

A major fault of some salesmen is to talk in abstract terms. They discuss *quality* in a general way. The word "quality" and similar terms should never be used. Quality should be described by actual examples of what a user did with this machine under certain trying conditions. The salesmen of a paper company, selling paper towels, do not talk about superior absorbency. They take two inkwells having the same amount of ink in them and stick their own towel into one inkwell and a towel of another brand into the other inkwell. After a few seconds, the difference in their absorbent qualities can be seen by the prospect.

Advertisers long ago learned that people do not read advertisements that are full of abstract ideas. They want pictures that illustrate a concrete and definite situation. All abstractions such as *best, strongest, newest, value, service,* and *most economical* should be avoided; the talking point should be stated in terms of the concrete with actual instances of how that characteristic has been proved by other users.

The use of definite terms in the sales talk does not necessitate boresome technical descriptions of how the product is made, the kind of raw materials used, or the way it is sold. When technicalities are used, they should be related to the prospect's problems. The reason for a detailed description of a gear in a machine should be stated to the prospect to convince him that, while a specific part has been giving trouble in some machines of other makes, it cannot cause difficulties in this brand. The prospect wants definite facts that the he can grasp.

Goodall Company, manufacturer of Palm Beach suits, operated a retail laboratory and experimented with various sales approaches to customers. The company found that when salesmen addressed customers with a time-honored bromide, such as, "Can I help you?" seven per cent bought. When salesmen used the system of letting the customers alone until they asked for help, 12 per cent bought. But when the salesmen greeted customers with specific comments about the merchandise, such as, "This will be this year's most popular tan," 25 per cent bought.[17]

The sales talk should be definite in its mental imagery, but it should also have human interest. Cold, intellectual appeals are not so stimulating to action as are appeals that arouse the warmer emotions. The prospect wants to hear a story. He likes to have a lump in his throat and a tear in his eye. He wants to hear about people and things that make him smile, that cause him to love more devotedly, to sacrifice a little, and to dream new dreams. The prospect wants to take sides with what he believes to be right. It is necessary to invest the sales talk with an emotional tone. As the old banker said to a young salesman: "If you are trying to sell the services of a bank, show the prospect the pictures of your officers. Describe the little human-interest aspects of their work. Tell how one of those officers helped a man to pull out of a bad situation and achieve business success. Don't talk the usual talk about the financial strength of the bank."

Answering Objections

The true salesman hopes that the prospect will raise objections before he buys. The objection offers the salesman an opportunity to demonstrate his product. One of the best salesmen in the country always has a pang of regret when the prospect indicates that he is sold and wants to sign on the dotted line. This salesman enjoys selling: the meeting of minds, the fencing-like encounter, the parries, the thrusts, and losing or gaining a new friend. He sells because he loves the game of selling.

Objections are a natural part of the process of selling. The prospect seldom welcomes the salesman with open arms. Can we blame the prospect? If we try to analyze the various ideas in the prospect's mind, we can understand why he does not, as a rule, want to see another salesman. The reason is that the salesman interrupts the prospect's *on-going activity*. Even a newborn baby objects to having its activity thwarted or retarded. Hold a baby with his arms tight against his body and he will soon show his anger in no uncertain manner. When the salesman comes to see a prospect, he interrupts the flow of ideas and activities of the prospect. The worthwhile prospect is always busy doing something else, mentally or physically. The most natural response of the prospect to the salesman is that he does not need or does not want what the salesman has to offer. The salesman must, first of all, get the prospect into a new line of thought, and, if the salesman has planned his demonstration and sales talk in the right manner, the sale should follow as a matter of course. The live prospect will make some objections in order to clarify his ideas and to ascertain whether he really understands what the salesman has just told him.

When the prospect says, "I am not interested," the salesman can say: "I know that you are not interested, Mr. Prospect. That's why I called. You have never used this device and Mr. Blake of the Samson Company thought I ought to show it to you." The salesman who can smile and accept the objection with nonchalance will be able to go ahead with the demonstration. The objections of most dealers to buying because conditions are bad can be answered with definite, prepared figures to show the dealer that business will continue regardless of conditions. Certain professional and other people who are not affected by the current conditions are always buying. The bank clearings of the city may show that they are greater than last year in that town. Ask the dealer to look out on the street and see the cars that are going up and down. People are still wearing clothes and eating.

To answer objections, the salesman should be able to show facts and figures that have been collected by a disinterested person. If the buyer does not believe that the salesman's shirts do not fade, the salesman should show the results of tests conducted under conditions that will satisfy the prospect. The shirt that went through the tests should be handed to the prospect for inspection. The salesman often depends upon his wits and bullying to answer objections, when the objections could be answered far more easily by just a tested sample, a page of charts, or a testimonial letter.

"The price is too high" is one of the arguments which should be answered in a straightforward manner rather than by evasion or humor. If the price objection is evaded, the customer may not mention it again but may refuse to buy. After all, the customer should know why the price asked is fair. A direct answer to the price objection is the dramatized form of answer. A salesman of washing machines capitalizes the high price of his machine by demonstrating the machine with money in his hand. Every time he points out a strong feature of his machine, he places a dollar bill or a quarter on that part of the machine. When he gets through he adds up the amount of money and shows the prospect that the price asked is fair in comparison to the value.

If the prospect has been sold during the salestalk, neither price nor any other objection will prevent the sale. The prospect may raise the question of price, but he may do it because he really desires to have ample justification for the price. The salesman who is unduly price-conscious has never been convinced that the product is worth the price asked. If his standard of living has been on a scale below that of the price level of the article he is selling, it will be necessary for the sales manager to re-educate the salesman.

When the prospect wants a handy excuse for not buying, he objects to the price. Only one other excuse is more common: *"I'll see you next time."* If the dealer presents this excuse, it simply means that the salesman has not done a good job of convincing him that he can make money with the line. The salesman can answer: "Of course, I'll see you next time, but that will not be for three months. In the meantime, according to my quota, 4,600 people are going to buy this article in this county. They will pay the dealers who sell them a gross profit of $2,300. You will want to be one of the dealers to have your share in the profits."

The salesman should not have the impression that it is well to "annihilate" the prospect when he makes an objection. To knock the prospect's objection too hard causes him to lose his self-respect. When an objection is stated, the salesman should restate the objection briefly and fairly; then the prospect knows that his objection is appreciated. Pay the prospect a compliment when he raises a threadbare objection—act as if it were an unheard-of objection and answer it—not too quickly but satisfactorily to the prospect's sense of worthwhileness.

The answering of objections should never degenerate into an argument. The salesman may be able to win the argument; but, if he does, he loses his sale. As soon as the discussion between salesman and prospect tends toward the argumentative type, the salesman should use humor. In fact, since most salesmen do not take the trouble to prepare evidence that will meet objections, they should at least collect a set of anecdotes that will answer the most frequent objections.

The Close

The psychological moment to close has received much attention in sales discussions. As a matter of fact, there are few true psychological moments when the prospect wishes to order and the salesman catches the prospect off his guard for the order. Orders that must be "caught on the fly" are often countermanded. The salesman should not pounce upon the prospect for the order. If the salesman has studied the needs of the prospect and is anxious to render a real service, the order will follow of its own accord.

It is true, however, that some prospects find it difficult to make a decision and the salesman must help them to decide. A few salesmen claim that they can recognize the moment when the prospect is ready to decide. They note whether the prospect leans forward, toward the salesman, and toys with the sample. One salesman even claimed that a prospect once told him that he did not want the article under discussion but the salesman said: "Your lips tell me that you do not want the article and yet your body tells me that you do, because you leaned toward me when you said that you could not buy it now." The prospect admitted that he wanted the article, but that he had an inhibiting objection which he hesitated to mention. When the objection was stated and answered, the prospect bought. In the best sales canvasses, the salesman and the prospect get into the same mood or attitude, into a mental state of mutuality of interest, so that the salesman does not view the prospect as a mere plaything but as a fellow businessman whose interests are complementary to his own.

The salesman may help the prospect to make a decision by arranging the situation so that he need decide only a minor point. The experienced life insurance salesman does not, as a rule, ask the prospect whether he does or does not want his policy. Rather, he asks him: "Will it be convenient for you to have our medical examiner call at your home on Tuesday evening and give you the health examination?" If the prospect indicates that that time is satisfactory, he has also indicated incidentally that he will take the insurance. The jobber salesman often does the same when he asks about the method of shipment or the date of delivery, the salesman naming a plan that he knows will be satisfactory to the customer.

Some salesmen apply this "minor-decision" method too frequently, when they get into the habit of asking for a trial order. The trial order of a half-dozen lot is easily asked for and easily given. But a trial order simply means that the sale was not completed. The customer still has many mental reservations, or he would give a worthwhile order. Of course, the trial order may be used as a starting point and the amount can be stepped up to a profitable figure.

The prospect will find it easier to buy if the salesman has succeeded in getting him to say "Yes" several times during the interview. The prospect who is in a hostile or negative attitude is hard to persuade, whereas the agreeing prospect is in a mood for further action. The unskillful salesman who tries to have his prospects "Yes" themselves into an order is likely to lose his grip on the situation. This method can be used only by those who are unusually adept at controlling the sales situation. The salesman can concentrate on the one point which appeared to appeal most to the prospect. Automobile salesmen know that the points about a car that appeal to those who know cars are not the points that appeal to most prospects. The salesmen tend to be interested in the mechanical qualities of the car, whereas many prospects are interested in the accessories, such as the cigar lighter and the vanity case. The real estate salesmen know that building construction does not interest the modern housewife nearly so much as the design of the fireplace and the arrangement of the cupboards in the kitchen. It is legitimate, therefore, to emphasize those factors that appeal most to the prospect in hand.

Each prospect varies in his susceptibility to assistance in making the decision to buy. Some prospects sell themselves. Others must be pushed and tugged at. Still others need a simple sales technique to do the thing they want to do but cannot, because the habit of turning down all salesmen is too strong to allow them to lift themselves out of the channels of indecision.

Aggressive selling produces more orders than easy-going salesmanship. The man who has lived among farmers knows the pleasure they get from chatting with strangers. It is often assumed that a sort of easy-going, chatty sales canvass is necessary when selling to farmers. A sales manager who traveled with a sales crew that sold a five-dollar product to farmers found that the salesmen who used the most aggressive and shortest canvass had the biggest sales records. The salesmen who spent not more than ten minutes with any farmer made the greatest number of sales. Action begets action. The most common methods of stimulating prospects to act are:

1. An aggressive, definite sales canvass.
2. The use of a minor decision, which makes it easy to buy without a big decision.
3. Getting the prospect into an agreeable and agreeing mood.
4. Showing the prospect that he can purchase with ease right now.
5. Showing him the danger of delay, such as "A coming change in price," "Temporary trial offer," "Only one to a customer," "You are now losing $50 per month by not having it," or "The continued inconvenience should be ended now."

Need for Follow-up

Salesmen are often asked how many calls they are willing to make on a prospect before dropping him. The correct answer may be one or a dozen. Some of the largest accounts that business firms have are the result of ten or more calls. One thousand retailers kept accurate check for six months to learn how many calls salesmen made on them before giving up the job as hopeless. Here is the surprising result of that check-up:

48.2 per cent made 1 call and quit.
24.4 per cent made 2 calls and quit.
14.7 per cent made 3 calls and quit.
12.7 per cent made 4 calls and quit.

Yet it was discovered that 60 per cent of

their merchandise was bought by these dealers at the fifth call or after.[18]

Persistence is as essential in selling today as it ever was. But mere persistence may be only boresome to the prospect and fatiguing to the salesman. Persistence means more than footwork. It means headwork as well. Selling hard requires more than merely trying hard to sell. When the salesman finds that he cannot get an order, he should close his sample case without insisting upon an order, but he should prepare the way for his next call by saying: "I am sorry that I don't have a sample of our Palate brand of food with me. I shall ask the house to mail you a sample for your wife and when I call again in four weeks, you can tell me how you like it." Before the salesman makes his next call, he should write a friendly letter to the prospect and explain the profit or value of his article.

The salesman should, during the interview, have learned one subject that interests the prospect. He can bring the prospect a newspaper clipping, a photograph, a book, or any other article or idea that will interest him. Each call means that the salesman must present something new and worthy of the prospect's consideration. The turn-down should not actually take place. The good salesman does not allow it. No interview, when it ends, should give the salesman a sense of relief. It should simply pave the way for another interview when new ideas may be presented in a new way with more attractive applications.

The Basis of Success in Salesmanship is Skill in Human Relations

This skill usually originates in early childhood; that fact explains why many sales managers think that good salesmen are born that way. The adjustments which lead to human-relations skills begin so early that observers imagine that the skill is hereditary or some accident of birth.

Potential sales ability on the part of some boys can be observed in many typical American families at, let us say, the evening meal. Father comes home tired and eats in silence. Mother is busy serving the dinner. The children eat in silence or amuse themselves by picking on each other. But sometimes in such a family one boy cheerfully talks about the happenings of the day. He enjoys his sports. He likes to talk about his experiences and his friends. The others listen occasionally. Gradually he acquires skill in making others listen to him and respect his statements. In later adulthood, selling is a natural vocation for him, and his sales manager is likely to speak of him as a "born salesman."

Many college graduates drift into selling, especially those who find that their education has not trained them for any specific vocation. They drift into selling by force of circumstance rather than from a spontaneous or intelligent choice. Such men are almost certain to fail as salesmen unless they go through the usual psychological steps which enable a person to enjoy selling. These steps are likely to involve one or more of the following:

1. An intellectual conviction that selling is a socially valuable vocation.
2. An emotional experience which makes selling an important vocation.
3. A series of adjustment habits which lead to satisfaction from dealing with people, as exhibited by the typical extravert.

Thus far, the lessons from the school of experience rather than the laboratory have been used as a guide in learning salesmanship. It is true that some laboratory experiments have been conducted for the development of methods to measure the relative effectiveness of elements composing a sales interview, but very few applications of these methods have been applied to actual sales situations.[19] The experimental laboratory study has the serious disadvantage of artificiality. Even though selling cannot be studied as an exact science it can be learned as a worthy art. Our appreciation of its worth will increase as we recognize its contributions to our social and economic well-being.

ACKNOWLEDGMENTS AND REFERENCES

1. Adapted from Robert A. Whitney, *Should You Be A Salesman?*, New York Life Insurance Company, 51 Madison Ave., New York, 1956.
2. See William C. Dorr, "What's in a Sales Job Besides a Pay Check?" *Sales Management,* Oct. 5, 1956.
3. The study was sponsored by the Sales Executives Club of Los Angeles and is reported in "What's Wrong with the Way We're Selling Sales Careers to Collegians?" *Sales Management,* Mar. 15, 1957, pp. 50–53. Reports of surveys on the same subject are published from time-to-time in *Sales Management* and other periodicals. The findings usually confirm those reported here.
4. See "Are Salesmen Sold On Their Jobs?" *The Management Review,* American Management Association, Inc., April 1956, p. 257. See also *Sales Management,* Feb. 15, 1956.
5. See "The Public's Bad Image of Salesmen Keeps Good Talent out of Sales Careers," *Printers' Ink,* May 23, 1958.
6. See Marvin D. Dunnette and Wayne K. Kirchner, "Psychological Test Differences Between Industrial salesmen and Retail Salesmen," *Journal of Applied Psychology,* April, 1960.
7. *Sales Management,* May 2, 1958, p. 7.
8. Willard M. Thompson, "How Expert Salespeople Sell," *Journal of Retailing,* Fall, 1955, p. 150.
9. Joseph W. Newman, "New Insight, New Progress, for Marketing," *Harvard Business Review,* November-December, 1957.
10. See F. J. Roethlisberger, "Training Supervisors in Human Relations," *Harvard Business Review,* September, 1951, p. 51.
11. John M. Frey, "Missing Ingredient in Sales Training...for Today's Competitive Market," *Harvard Business Review,* November-December, 1955, pp. 126–132.
12. "Marketing Pictograph," *Sales Management,* May 15, 1940.
13. See "Salesmen: Stick to Your Knitting," *Changing Times,* The Kiplinger Magazine, May, 1950, p. 13.
14. D. E. Baier and R. D. Dugan, "Factors in Sales Success," *Journal of Applied Psychology,* **41,** No. 1 (1957), 40.
15. Edward K. Strong, Jr., *Psychology of Selling and Advertising* (New York: McGraw-Hill Book Company, 1925), Chapter 22.
16. J. N. Bauman, "How the Professional Salesman Makes His Approach," *Sales Management,* June 15, 1955, p. 58.
17. *Business Week,* May 25, 1940, p. 45.
18. *Sales Management,* January 1, 1938, p. 18.
19. Fred McKinney, "An Empirical Method of Analyzing A Sales Interview," *Journal of Applied Psychology,* **21** (1937), 280.

PROJECTS

1. Have a friend coöperate with you in practicing dealer sales situations. He is the prospective buyer and you are attempting to sell him certain articles. Have your friend include the following objections as well as others he may think of:
   a. I want the exclusive agency.
   b. I never had a call for it.
   c. I'm all stocked up now. Got too much of your stuff on the shelf.
   d. I'm too busy to talk to you now.
   e. I'm satisfied with the house I buy from now.
   f. You come to see me only when you can't sell Jones, up on the corner.

   After you have met your friend's objections, discuss with him the best methods of answering them.
2. List some of the expressions, methods, or mannerisms that irritate you when used by a salesman. Find out from others whether these are personal prejudices of your own or are general. Work out specific corrections for each item you have noted.
3. Salesmen frequently carry a sample or some related object to show to the prospect while making the sales talk. Think of interesting and original related objects that might be used in selling the following:
   a. Lawnmowers.
   b. Office furniture.
   c. Home insulation.
   d. Fire insurance.
   e. Coal.
   f. Advertising space in a local paper.
   g. Safety equipment for a factory.
   h. Vacation trip by airplane.

   Tell how and when you would use the related object in your sales talk.
4. Clip several magazine advertisements of articles you believe you could sell quite successfully. Analyze all the reasons for your choice. Do the same for an article you think you could not sell. Analyze your reasons from the standpoint of your own likes and dislikes, your personality, the qualities of the article, the nature of the market, and other possible factors. Which factors seem to tie into your psychological development.
5. Read in trade papers about concerns that have done outstanding work in sales-training schools. Analyze the ideas gathered and

present them in a letter of application to one of the companies, explaining to the company addressed why you chose the company as your preferred employer.

6. A woman went into a ready-to-wear store to buy a blouse. The sales girl showed her blouses in three different price ranges and then held up the most expensive one and said, "I'd like to see you buy this one."

   Was this a good reason for the prospect to buy? What might the sales clerk say that would be more appropriate?

7. The story has been told of the animal painter, De Auber, that, having painted a picture, he rubbed raw meat over the representation of a rabbit in the foreground. His reason was that a Mrs. Blank, a prospect for the purchase of the picture, was coming to see the picture. He assumed that when her pet poodle smelled the rabbit and got excited about it, the woman would buy the picture.

   The woman came to see the picture, the poodle smelled of the rabbit and got excited, and the woman bought at the artist's price!

   Was this ethical selling on the part of the artist?

COLLATERAL READINGS

Brewster, Ray C., "More Psychology in Selling," *Harvard Business Review,* July-August, 1963, pp. 91–99.

Frey, John M., "Missing Ingredient in Sales Training...for Today's Competitive Market," *Harvard Business Review,* November-December, 1955, pp. 126–132.

Gilmer, B. von Haller, *Industrial Psychology.* New York: McGraw-Hill Book Company, 1961, Chapter 18.

Husband, Richard W., *Applied Psychology.* New York: Harper & Row, Publishers, Inc., 1949, Chapters 25–27.

Thompson, Willard M., "How Expert Salespeople Sell," *Journal of Retailing,* Fall, 1955.

Administration offices *in Center for Advanced Study in the Behavioral Sciences, Stanford, California. The "students," called Fellows, come from the faculties of other universities.*

View of part of the library *of the Center. In addition to the library of the Center, the Stanford University and other libraries are available to the Fellows.*

One of the fifty offices *for the use of the Fellows.*

Main meeting room.

One of the important developments *in American scientific work is that single sciences are no longer expected to explain many of the events in human behavior. Interdisciplinary approaches are being used more and more each year. The members of several sciences come together for the study of important behavioral problems and principles.*

An example of this trend is indicated by the opening on September 20, 1954, of the Center for Advanced Study in the Behavioral Sciences. The director, Ralph W. Tyler, explained the purpose of the new institution as follows:

"The behavioral sciences have come to a stage of development calling for more—and more effective—communication between specialists. The Center is designed to provide a working atmosphere where this communication can take place. It is an opportunity for a selected number of university faculty members concerned with the study of human behavior to come together in one place in order to help one another gain new skills and insights and to work upon common problems in addition to their individual specialties."

The Center is an independent and non-profit corporation located at Stanford, California. It selects its fellows each year from the large and growing list of nominations submitted by university representatives. Originally, the Center was supported by a grant from the Ford Foundation. The Foundation made a terminal grant in 1959, and as the Ford money is used up, the Center seeks support from a variety of other sources.

PART VI

RESEARCH

CHAPTER TWENTY-NINE

HOW TO READ REPORTS OF PSYCHOLOGICAL RESEARCHES

Not the truth in anyone's actual or supposed possession, but the sincere effort he has exerted to master the truth, makes the worth of the man. For not through the possession but through the pursuit of truth comes that widening of a man's powers by which alone is achieved his ever-growing perfection. Possession makes one stagnant, lazy, proud. If God held shut in His right hand the whole of truth, and in His left had only ever-active striving after truth with the certainty of ever and always erring, and He said to me, "Choose!" I should humbly reach toward His left hand, saying, "Father, give me this! The pure truth is indeed for Thee alone!"—Lessing, Eine Duplik[1]

The difference between scientific research as "lived" by the pure scientist and as viewed by the layman may be illustrated by an incident in the life of the great scientist Faraday. He gave a lecture in the Royal Institution in London before a group of celebrities of the day. He brought a magnet close to a coil of wire. An electric current was produced.

After the demonstration a lady asked him, "Professor Faraday, even if the effect you explained is obtained, what is the use of it?"

Faraday replied, "Madam, will you tell me the use of a newborn child?"

The pure scientist conducts his experiments without regard for their practical or commercial value. Eventually some of the experiments may have practical value, but the scientist seeks truth mainly. Louis Agassiz, Lord Kelvin, Oersted, and others made their great discoveries without thought of personal gain. Some of their apparently useless discoveries have led to very valuable results for modern civilization.

The value of research in technical matters is now generally accepted, and it is probable that research in the human-relations problems of our economic life will make unusual strides in this and the next generation. As has often been stated, the keynote of the twentieth century will be human engineering. Occasionally, political and international disruptions appear to make this prediction incorrect, but such disruptions are only temporary.

The practical man finds himself in many situations where it is difficult for him to utilize scientific research. Lack of time often compels him to make a quick decision. Sometimes business expediency does not permit changes wrought by science. A company may have established a reputation for a certain product or service and it would be difficult to make a change, even though scientific studies indicate that a change to a better product might be made. Moreover, the present "laws" of commerce are not nearly so exact and fixed as the laws of physics and chemistry.

In spite of the many difficulties in the way of predicting and stimulating human behavior in business, psychological research has become a recognized phase of modern economic life. The student who becomes a businessman learns that if he wishes to market a new product, he must do more than try it out in his wife's kitchen, ask the opinions of his friends, or consult his salesmen. He finds that his own company's records and past statistics of monthly reports do not enable him to predict the public's reception of a new idea or invention. Snap judgments and empirical rules may lead him astray. But even the best feasible research study is none too reliable.

Professional Research Organizations

In one issue of a trade journal, ten professional research organizations were advertised. Some of them have been in existence for years. Others seem to advertise once or twice and then disappear. The ability and reliability of these research organizations must be rated in the same manner that we rate individuals. A few individuals are competent for a specific task, but there are many who are not. The executive who hires a professional research worker or research organization should be acquainted with research principles if he wishes to secure competent service. Otherwise he may be handed a voluminous report that looks impressive but is filled with fallacious conclusions. Statistics are often helpful, but they also can be very dangerous. The reader should at least know the essential terms and methods which are common to research reports in the field of analyzing and controlling human behavior.

Starting Important Researches

When an executive or a group of executives decides that a research shall be made of some problem or problems, certain questions should be asked and answered in advance. These are:

1. *Just What Is the Problem?*

What is it that is to be learned? How shall the problem be stated, in order that the persons making the research may keep it clearly in mind? Shall the research be limited to a single specific problem or shall the investigation have a broad and generalized scope?

2. *Who Shall Perform the Research?*

In many cases the executives decide that some accountant or statistician now in the company can do the work. Such an attempt to save money is conjectural. The findings of a single research may be used to modify a company's production schedule for a year and may involve thousands of dollars. It does not pay to take chances. Only a few large concerns have a staff of researchers who are qualified to conduct a psychological investigation. The fact that an engineer knows calculus and can plot nice curves does not mean that he is qualified to make a market investigation or standardize psychological tests for employment. Trained and experienced workers are just as important in psychological research as in other branches of industry.

3. *What Shall Be the Method of Securing the Data?*

Shall the company start a research department with laboratories of its own; shall field investigators be used; shall the data be secured by questionnaire; shall a test campaign be conducted; and so on? Can the necessary data be secured? Are the facts now available in the company's records? Is it possible to obtain the facts?

4. *Do the Executives Have a Fair Attitude Toward the Research?*

Are they seeking to obtain data to prove a present theory, or are facts wanted regardless of their pleasantness or unpleasantness? Are the executives future-minded or past-minded? Is the research for the purpose of finding out "why the horse was stolen" or to prevent the stealing of horses in the future?

5. *How Much Time Shall Be Allowed for the Investigation?*

Does the company expect the researchers to achieve functions of the administrative executive, or is the research to present facts for the guidance of the executives? One sales manager hired a research man to make a consumer analysis. He agreed to expect his report at the end of three months. However, at the end of two weeks he began to write letters to the researcher, asking him why the sales had not increased in the territory where the analysis was being made. When a company starts a business research department of its own, definite results of proved commercial value should not be expected for one or two years. Furthermore, some of the executives of companies having sales researchers are inclined to expect the sales research department to act as a sales promotion department. If research is to fulfill its function of making discoveries of value to the business, it must be allowed sufficient time and remain advisory and independent of immediate problems of showing a profit on the balance sheet.

Points to Look for When Analyzing a Research Report

When any statistical report is analyzed, it is necessary to look for fallacies regardless of the ability or reputation of the author. Administrators must operate on the plan of delegating functions and responsibilities to others. When an executive selects the most competent researcher he can find and gives him a research problem, he tends to assume that whatever the statistician says must be true. However, the reader of the statistics must be alert to detect and question discrepancies. It is impossible for the executive or the student to know all or most of the errors in statistics or logic that may occur, but some of the more common ones can be pointed out.

1. *Is the Unit of Measurement Sound?*

In statistics, the units of measurement are the bricks from which the whole statistical structure is built. The units of measurement may be individuals, foot-pounds, wages, accidents, or businessmen, but the unit must be sound in its entity. One sales manager asked his salesmen to predict the condition of business for the next month. Each salesman was to state whether he expected to have an increase in sales over the preceding month. Approximately 80 per cent of the weekly reports of the sales force were optimistic. They were of the type: "Conditions here look very good for next month. I expect to sell more than I did this month." At the end of the month for which the sales had been predicted, less than 10 per cent of the salesmen had had an increase in sales, and the total volume of business for the sales force was 15 per cent below that of the preceding month. The reason for the unreliability of the investigation was that the salesmen knew that the sales manager usually expected optimistic reports and they sent in the expected viewpoint lest they appear to be alibi-artists and expecters of failure. The prediction could not be reliable because the units of measurement, statements by individual salesmen, were unreliable.

2. *Are the Data in the Report Authentic?*

Occasionally statistics are quoted by bankers, salesmen, publishers, and others, and it is impossible to find anyone to substantiate the figures. A notable example is the oft-quoted figures regarding the incomes of men who begin their vocational life at the age of 20. At the age of 45, 16 per cent are supposed to be dead; 65 per cent self-supporting; 15 per cent dependent, wholly or in part; and only 4 per cent are supposed to have accumulated anything and kept it. When they are 65 years of age, 85 per cent of the men still living are quoted as dependent on children, relatives, or charity.

An attempt has been made to find the original source of these figures but has met with no success. The life insurance companies that were consulted said that they had seen the figures and their salesmen had used them, but the originator was not known. So far as they know, no one really knows what the correct figures are.

3. *Are Single Causes Interpreted to Give Rise to Single Effects or Events?*

In human relationships, effects are seldom brought about by single events or causes. The "new American tempo" is not the effect of one cause, such as the development of the physical sciences. Increases in crime cannot be attributed solely to a change in religious devotion or divorce. Labor unrest is not caused alone by universal education. Psychological abnormalities cannot be attributed solely to a thwarting of the sex impulse or to heredity. Increases and decreases in sales cannot be attributed to the lone influence of the new sales manager. Decreased labor turnover cannot be interpreted as wholly the result of a newly organized personnel department or of profit sharing.

The veteran advertising manager of an ice-cream company "showed" how his advertising efforts had increased the per capita consumption of ice cream in his territory. He should also have mentioned as factors of influence: improved quality of the product, pure food laws, greater number of retail outlets, lower cost of production, and greater competence of company management.

4. *Are Graphic Curves of Increase and Decrease Compared with Basic Curves of Increase and Decrease?*

Frequently they are not. This kind of error is common in reports of individual executives to the management. The sales manager may show that sales have increased 20 per cent each year over the preceding year for the past five years. He should also show how much the industry as a whole has increased during that period. The employment manager may show that labor turnover has decreased each year for the past three years. He should also compare his curve of decrease with the employment situation of the community.

5. *Are the Graphs in the Report Properly Constructed?*

The person who wishes to understand statistical reports needs an understanding of some of the more common principles of graphic charting.

If the statistician wishes to construct a simple line curve to show the amount of

TABLE 29.1

SHOWING ACTUAL SALES BY YEARS AND INDEX NUMBERS THEREOF

Year	*Actual Sales (thousands of tons)*		*Index Numbers* On 1952 Base as 100		On 1965 Base as 100		On 1961–65 Base as 100	
	XYZ CO.	ENTIRE INDUSTRY	XYZ CO.	ENTIRE INDUSTRY	XYZ CO.	ENTIRE INDUSTRY	XYZ CO.	ENTIRE INDUSTRY
1952	5.2	31,300	100.0	100.0	36.4	70.8	50.3	73.8
1953	4.0	23,513	76.9	75.1	28.0	53.2	38.7	55.4
1954	6.3	32,151	120.2	102.7	43.7	72.7	44.4	75.8
1955	7.9	42,773	151.9	136.7	55.2	96.8	76.4	100.8
1956	8.5	45,060	163.5	144.0	59.4	101.9	82.2	106.2
1957	8.0	44,462	153.8	142.1	55.9	100.6	77.4	104.8
1958	7.0	34,671	134.6	110.8	49.0	78.4	67.7	81.7
1959	8.4	42,132	161.5	134.6	58.7	95.3	81.2	99.3
1960	3.6	19,783	69.2	63.2	25.2	44.7	34.8	46.6
1961	9.0	44,943	173.1	143.6	62.9	101.7	87.0	105.9
1962	7.3	37,932	140.4	121.2	51.0	85.8	70.6	89.4
1963	11.5	45,394	221.2	145.0	80.4	102.7	111.7	107.0
1964	15.8	48,294	303.8	154.3	110.5	109.2	152.8	113.8
1965	14.3	44,214	275.0	141.3	100.0	100.0	138.3	104.2

building construction in a certain city over a given period of years, it is possible to construct the graph so that a small or a great increase or decrease may appear to have taken place. This may be done regardless of the actual facts in the situation. The curve can be made to appear unstable and to have fluctuated violently, or to have fluctuated little and to have great stability. The construction and type of graph is often determined by the impression that the statistician wishes to make on his readers. One of the best statistical devices for comparative data is the index number.

Table 29.1 illustrates three possible sets of index numbers, or series of simple relatives, which might be constructed from the *actual* sales data in the first column.

The method is simply to divide each year's sales by the sales in the base period which one may think best. The base periods here used are (1) the year 1952, (2) the year 1965, and (3) the yearly average for the five years 1961–1965, inclusive.

What practical purpose is accomplished by the use of these index numbers? Examination of the data for the two variables—sales of the company and of the whole industry—is much easier when the data are in the form of index numbers. The two columns headed "Actual Sales" are much harder to compare than the three index-number arrangements for the same data.

When a base period has been chosen suitable to whatever purpose the analyst may have in mind, the curves are readily brought into each other's neighborhood by the index-number method. Then it is easy to answer such questions as: How does the long-time growth of our company show up in comparison with our industry as a whole? How much more, or less, did a boom or depression affect us than it did the industry generally? How does our recent position compare with that of the industry?

The index number is not the only method of analysis which can be used on occasions to answer such questions as these; but it is one of the most effective, and, when properly understood and applied, one of the easiest. Some statisticians prefer to use the semi-logarithmic charts.

Graphs are the quickest, clearest, and most condensed method of conveying valuable information to the reader, but he should realize their potency for misinformation as well as for administrative guidance.

6. *Is the Number of Units Studied Sufficiently Large to Represent the Group Fairly?*

It is obvious that if we wish to study any single human trait, such as the general intelligence of salesmen, it is necessary to test the intelligence of a large typical group of salesmen. If we were to draw conclusions from the measurements of only ten salesmen, we should be very liable to fall into error. Psychometrists have developed several formulas which show the required size of the group, or, in some cases, the unreliability of the conclusions drawn from a group of a given size. We shall leave these more complicated formulas to the statisticians, but the layman can approximate a decision from two simple questions:

Do the measures extend over the entire *range* for the group in question? An example is that of the study of intelligence of college students. If we were to measure the intelligence of only those students who fail in college or those who graduate with honors, we should not be testing a representative sampling of the factor under study. Tests would have to be made of those who fail, those who do passing work, those who do average work, those who are slightly above the average, and those who are the best—all in their proper proportions.

The next question is: How *many* students must we have on each part of the entire scale? We can answer this by noting whether the number of cases measured distribute themselves according to the normal frequency (normal probability) curve. When the base line of the theoretical probability curve has been divided into five equal parts and vertical lines have been erected at the dividing points, five areas result, which include the following percentages, reading from left to right: 3, 22, 50, 22, 3. This bell-shaped curve seems to apply to many living characteristics. It has even been found that when the number of hairs on the left hind legs of a large number of bees are counted, the frequency curve has this bell-shape. Because of this universality of distribution of human traits, many schools

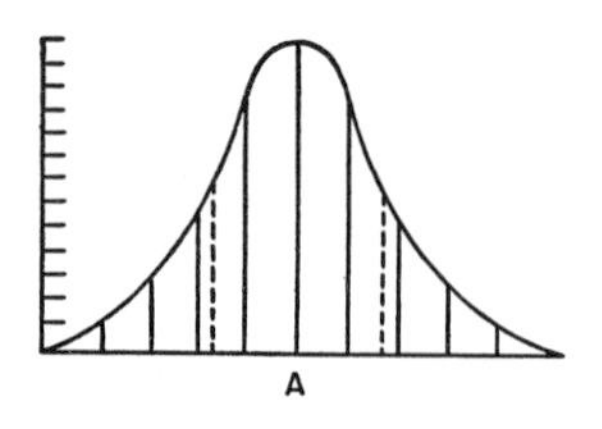

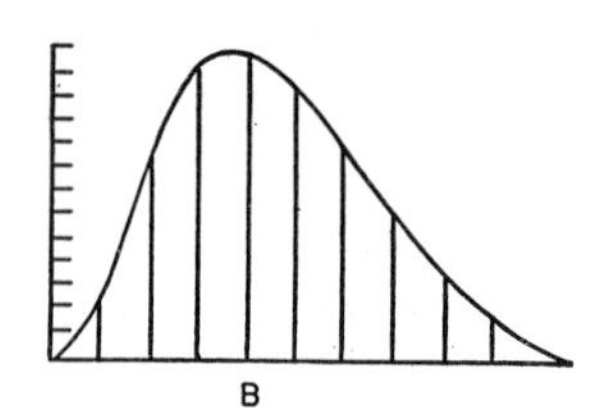

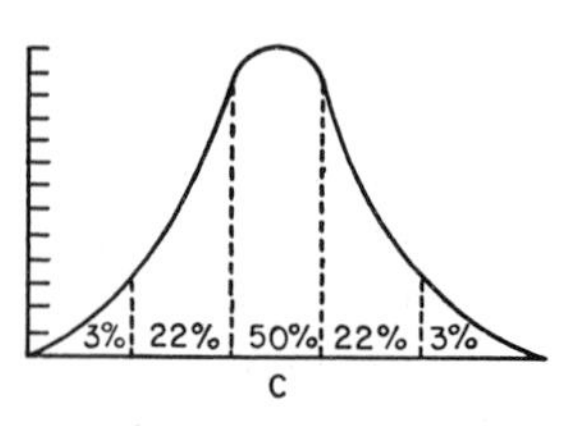

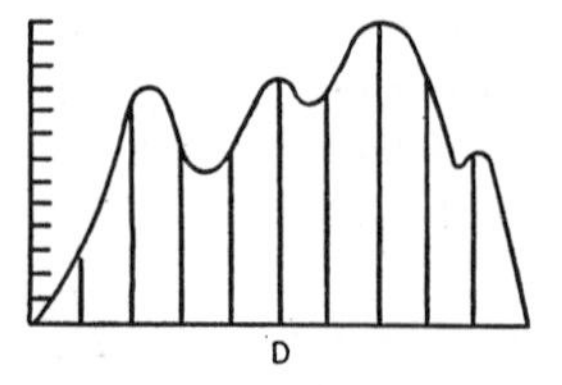

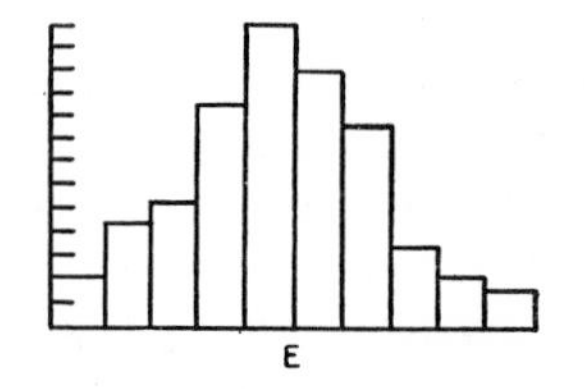

A Curve of normal frequency; base line divided into three equal parts
B Skewed curve
C Base line divided into five equal parts
D Multimodal curve
E Rectangles representing groups of grades

and colleges grade their students in conformity with this curve.

When an insufficient number of cases have been studied, the frequency curve may be skewed or multi-modal in form. This discussion applies only to human traits or reactions found in a representative number of nonselected persons. That is, if we wish to test the intelligence of only the best 10 per cent of salesmen in one company, the normal frequency curve would not result. But if we were to test the best 10 per cent of all salesmen in a thousand companies, the plotted results would probably follow the normal curve.

Statisticians who are acquainted with sampling theory can, in some instances, use small samples to yield greater accuracy than is obtained from tallies of complete files. An example has been cited for a mail-order firm that had some 3 million customers. When 100 per cent tallies were made, the figures obtained had so many errors that the findings were of doubtful utility in sales planning. The use of sampling resulted in more precise figures. The difference was in the quality and acumen on the part of the new personnel that was made possible by the less expensive small sample technique. These resulted in greater care in collecting the data.[2]

7. *Have the Data for a Group Been Checked by Control Groups?*

When a group of persons are experimented upon in the laboratory to determine the effects of smoking, caffeine, scolding, praise, music, lighting, or a system of wage payment, it is also necessary to measure the same or similar reactions of another group of persons who are not affected by the same stimuli. One investigator experimented upon the effects of periodicity of women in the performing of certain mental functions. A control group of men was used because obviously they could not be affected by the same organic condition. It was found that the men had more fluctuations which could be looked upon as cyclical for twenty-eight-day periods than the women! If the control group of men had not been used, it is probable that the data of the women only would have given quite another impression.

Sometimes experimenters try a new method of sales management or lighting or wage payment and find that the production figures go up the next month. These stimuli do cause changes in production, but it is well to check the new plan by allowing certain groups to work under the old system so that the one factor which is blamed or praised for the change may really be known beyond any chance factors that may be bringing about the change. In the experiments on the effects of drugs, it is absolutely essential to have control groups because of the effect of suggestion. It is also essential in proving the effects of new methods of motivating or training employees.

8. *Do the Conclusions and Suggestions Harmonize with General Experience and the Judgment of Persons Experienced in the Field Studied?*

Because of the opportunities for misinterpretation of statistics, it is well to compare the findings with empirical conclusions. The man who has had years of experience in any field is likely to know many facts and principles that cannot be revealed by laboratory experiments.

It should be kept in mind at all times that laboratory experiments in human reactions usually deal with one factor or one set of factors only. An experiment may be sound so far as it goes, but *psychological laboratory conditions seldom approximate actual conditions*. Some important human reactions cannot be subjected to experiment. Several psychologists have attempted to measure the reactions of persons when in love, angry, fearful, or sexually excited; but it has been very difficult to achieve genuine mental states in the laboratory. All psychological laboratory experiments should be looked upon as laboratory experi-

"It seems to me you overlooked an important factor in this impartial survey—WHO IS PAYING FOR IT!" Source: ***The Wall Street Journal,*** *April 24, 1959.*

ments which may or may not carry over into actual life and business.

If the investigation does not agree with the past experience of those who are conversant with the empirical facts, then it may be necessary to repeat parts of the research. On the other hand, if the study does indicate that it would be advisable, all things considered, to make certain changes, the research will have been a waste of time and money unless the changes are made.

Conclusion

The research "tools" presented in this chapter are not comprehensive, but the discussion is an attempt to stimulate certain types of students to go on and acquire further skills in measuring human reactions.

ACKNOWLEDGMENTS AND REFERENCES

1. As quoted in Zechariah Chafee, *The Inquiring Mind* (New York: Harcourt, Brace & World, Inc., 1928).
2. See Chester A. Wasson, "Common Sense in Sampling," *Harvard Business Review,* January-February, 1963.

PROJECTS

1. Examine a standard book on the construction and interpretation of graphs and charts and list some of the common errors and fallacies in this field. Find a graph or chart that misrepresents the data on which it is based and reconstruct it so that it presents a true picture.
2. A doctor made the following statement: "I had all the nicotine removed from a cigarette, making a solution out of it. I injected half the quantity into a frog with the effect that the frog died almost instantly. The rest was administered to another frog with like effect. Both frogs were grown and of average size. The conclusion is evident that a single cigarette contains enough poison to kill two frogs."

   Is this a valid argument to prove the harmfulness of cigarette smoking? What would be the effect of taking the white of an egg and injecting a part of it into the human bloodstream? (For guidance in obtaining the answer, look up the chemical nature of rattlesnake venom.)

3. In reading a research report, how can one detect whether the writer tried to prove a point or merely to present the facts that he happened to find? What are the distinguishing characteristics of reports that *defend a position* compared with those that *try to promote an idea?*
4. In a discussion group of thirty industrial executives, the leader of the group was opposed to a bonus for the foreman of a gang of seven workers. Three of the members of the group had had experience with bonuses for the foreman of small units of production. These three men were heartily in favor of a bonus for the foreman as well as the workers. The leader of the discussion group then asked the members of the group to vote for or against a foreman's bonus. The three who had had experience with such a situation voted in favor of the bonus; the remaining members of the group who had had no such experience opposed it.

   How can the voting of these executives be explained?
5. Statistically, is the difference between two and three the same as the difference between ten and eleven? If 10 men can build a house in 100 days, can 1,000 men build the house in one day?

A BRIEF CHECK LIST FOR EVALUATING SCIENTIFIC ARTICLES

1. The analysis of the purpose of the article:
   —is the purpose clearly stated?
   —will the purpose be supported or refuted by the kind of data collected?
   —is sufficient account taken of previous studies in this particular field?
2. The analysis of the design of the sampling procedure of the experiment involved:
   —is the design of the experiment so formulated that it will give an adequate answer to the purpose of the experiment?
   —how are the subjects selected: from the total population, a restricted population, or other?
   —is the number of subjects adequate to take care of the purpose of the experiment satisfactorily?
   —are there proper and adequate controls (e.g., have controls been properly equated with experimental group)?
3. Analysis of the procedure of the scientific article:
   —are the procedures so described that any other experimenter could duplicate the experiment to check the findings?
   —are the data systematically collected and presented?
4. Analysis of the results:
   —are results correctly and clearly presented?
   —are the units of measurement sound?
   —are graphs properly drawn?
   —are tables properly constructed?
   —are statistical procedures essentially sound?
   —are the proper tests of significance made, such as critical ratio, *et al.?*
   —do the verbal statements agree with the quantitative and tabular data?
5. Analysis of conclusions:
   —are the conclusions warranted by the data presented?
   —are significant trends recognized?
   —are the limitations of the experiment recognized?

For more thorough discussions of analyzing scientific articles see Dael Wolfle, Rensis Likert, Donald G. Marquis, and Robert R. Sears, "Standards for Appraising Psychological Research," *The American Psychologist,* 4 (1949), 320–328, and Darrell Blaine Lucas and Stuart Henderson Britt, *Measuring Advertising Effectiveness* (New York: McGraw-Hill Book Company, 1963).

6. Discuss statistical data of business which are often compared but which really are not comparable, such as bond prices during the Civil War and World War II or wages in London and in Chicago. Is homogeneity in comparisons of psychological data possible?
7. Distinguish between immediate or superficial causes and remote or fundamental causes. How does this apply to retail costs? To unemployment? To sales records?

COLLATERAL READINGS

Farnsworth, P. R., ed., *et al., Annual Review of Psychology*. Palo Alto, Calif.: Annual Reviews, Inc., 1964, pp. 277–346.

Fleishman, Edwin A., *Studies in Personnel and Industrial Psychology*. Homewood, Ill.: The Dorsey Press, Inc., 1961, Chapters 36 and 38.

Harrell, Thomas Willard, *Industrial Psychology*. New York: Holt, Rinehart & Winston, Inc., 1958, Chapter 3.

Smith, Henry Clay, *Psychology of Industrial Behavior*. New York: McGraw-Hill Book Company, 1955, Chapters 13 and 18.

APPENDIX

SOCIAL KNOWLEDGE TEST

I. KNOWLEDGE OF THE LOWER SOCIAL STRATA

Each question has several possible answers. Underline the one answer that is correct or the most nearly correct, and put its letter in the parentheses at the end of the dotted line. Do not omit any question, even if you must guess.

1. "Come off the oil" means:
   (a) that your wallet is empty (b) to stop bragging (c) you look like a gigolo (d) you've got dandruff .... (B)
2. "Skid Row" refers to:
   (a) a London street (b) a term used in ice-hockey (c) the lowest level of the underworld (d) a snowy road .... (2)
3. The term "to fade" is used in:
   (a) dice (b) golf (c) dress designing (d) billiards .... (D)
4. "Snafu" is:
   (a) a Hollywood actor (b) a term meaning scram (c) a term meaning easy going (d) a term meaning difficulties in progress .... ( )
5. A "queer" is:
   (a) a stool pigeon (b) a storybook fairy (c) an insane person (d) a homosexual .... ( )
6. A "pug" is:
   (a) a bulldog (b) an English tavern (c) a strong cigar (d) a prize fighter.. ( )
7. A "frog" is:
   (a) a railroad worker (b) a prostitute (c) a thief (d) a Frenchman .... ( )
8. "To give the bird" is to:
   (a) heckle (b) give a dinner party (c) double-cross (d) pay tuition .... ( )
9. "Scuttlebutt" refers to:
   (a) rumors (b) bet (c) used cigarette (d) a whistle .... ( )
10. "Two-fingers" refers to:
    (a) a brand of candy bar (b) a sign to obtain someone's attention (c) a symbol of secrecy (d) a measure used by bartenders .... ( )
11. The term "soup" is slang for:
    (a) nitroglycerine (b) jail (c) freighter (d) poison .... ( )
12. An "uncle" is:
    (a) a jockey (b) a hockey goalie (c) a gambler (d) a pawnbroker .... ( )
13. A "hot rod" is:
    (a) a hot spoon (b) a fat fisherman (c) a fast auto (d) a lucky gambler .. ( )
14. "Red-eye" is a term for:
    (a)strong arms (b) bookies (c) pink lady beverage (d) cheap whiskey .... ( )
15. A "necktie party" is:
    (a) for girls only (b) for men only (c) a hanging (d) a high school dance ( )
16. The figures on the opposite sides of a die of dice always add up to:
    (a) 4 (b) 6 (c) 7 (d) 11 .... ( )
17. A "cat" is:
    (a) a game of casino (b) a poker hand (c) a dead beat (d) a sharp character ( )
18. "Heaven-beck" refers to:
    (a) a bird of paradise (b) an angel (c) a minister (d) a chicken coop .. ( )
19. "Little joe" is a term used in:
    (a) golf (b) cards (c) dice (d) horse racing .... ( )

20. "Foo-foo" is:
(a) perfume (b) ketchup (c) a dog-biscuit (d) a rattle .... ( )
21. A "beezer" refers to:
(a) a dagger (b) a stiff test (c) nose (d) magazine .... ( )
22. A "foul ball" is:
(a) a vexatious person (b) an army officer (c) a rum drink (d) a cop .... ( )
23. A "skin slammer" refers to:
(a) a doctor (b) adhesive tape (c) a drummer (d) a politician .... ( )
24. A "cokey" is:
(a) a horse (b) a bad mistake (c) a drug addict (d) an imbecile .... ( )
25. A "deep-sea chef" is:
(a) a fisherman (b) a lover of sea-food (c) a dishwasher (d) a man who prepares tabasco sauce .... ( )
26. A "quail" is:
(a) a dog (b) a truant boy (c) a woman (d) a foreigner .... ( )
27. A "snow bird" is:
(a) a dope addict (b) a nude painting (c) a race horse (d) a night club.. ( )
28. The term "shiv" refers to:
(a) a bad cold (b) a delirium (c) a chaplain (d) a knife .... ( )
29. A "chucker" is a name for:
(a) chuck wood (b) a baseball pitcher (c) a braggart (d) an extravagant person .... ( )
30. A "daisy cutter" is:
(a) a farm implement (b) a milliner (c) a low ball (d) a rustic .... ( )
31. "Boondocks" refers to:
(a) a country shack (b) a backwoods location (c) a small canoe (d) a hound ( )
32. To "highball" is to:
(a) stagger (b) tip-toe (c) dance (d) go at top speed .... ( )
33. "Little Phoebe" is:
(a) a stolen purse (b) a dice term (c) a deputy sheriff (d) a baby's doll ( )
34. An "eightball" is:
(a) a poor loser (b) an incompetent person (c) a team mascot (d) a good sport .... ( )
35. A "sun-pecked jay" is:
(a) a bird (b) a rustic, who lives in the city (c) an informer (d) a bird food ( )
36. In the language of sports, a "screw-armer" is:
(a) a southpaw (b) a right-hander (c) a man who fixes roller skates (d) a water boy .... ( )
37. "Dominie" is a term referred to when speaking of:
(a) a game (b) a priest (c) sugar (d) profanity .... ( )
38. "Annie Oakley" refers to:
(a) a free pass (b) an English actress (c) Tom Oakley's wife (d) a machine gun .... ( )
39. The "black gang" refers to:
(a) slaves (b) spiritualists (c) a secret society (d) machinists in the Navy.... ( )
40. A "job robber" is:
(a) a foreman (b) a bookie (c) an overzealous piece worker (d) a stool pigeon .... ( )
41. "To lower the boom" means:
(a) to hit somebody (b) to anchor (c) to be inebriated (d) to bluff .... ( )
42. "Joe" refers to:
(a) a man (b) the mouth (c) dope (d) a cup of coffee .... ( )
43. "Yack" means:
(a) to talk seldom (b) a stupid person (c) a criminal (d) a billygoat .... ( )
44. A "bim" is:
(a) a jitterbug (b) a plastic record (c) a convict (d) a tough girl ...... ( )
45. A "chippy" is:
(a) a billiard ball (b) a girl (c) a small ship (d) a score of three in dice ...... ( )
46. A "gibroni" is:
(a) a crying doll (b) a jerk (c) a pilot (d) a chef .... ( )
47. To "lose one's marbles" means to:
(a) lose money (b) be a simpleton (c) be drunk (d) lose a job .... ( )
48. A "bindle stiff" is:
(a) a flower (b) a college professor (c) a tramp (d) a dead crook .... ( )
49. A "thornback" is:
(a) a rose bush (b) a spinster (c) a bank-teller's window (d) a fish ...... ( )
50. A "gapper" is:
(a) an addict in need of dope (b) a ditch digger (c) a consumptive (d) a fishing rod .... ( )
51. In a game of dice the "odds" are the same for making the number four as for making the number:
(a) 8 (b) 6 (c) 10 (d) 7 .... ( )
52. "Land grabbers" are:
(a) chains (b) shoes (c) animals (d) farmers .... ( )
53. A "whey belly" is:
(a) a fat man (b) a bald man (c) a starved cat (d) a poor horse .... ( )
54. A "geek" is:
(a) a clown (b) the wildman in the circus sideshow (c) a bookie (d) a ham ( )
55. A "pad" is:

(a) a tiger (b) a one-room apartment (c) a bald man (d) a stone .... ( )

56. The expression "croaker" refers to: (a) morticians (b) bootleggers (c) doctors (d) preachers .... ( )
57. A "flunkie" is: (a) a dope addict (b) a goal in ice hockey (c) a brain who wears glasses (d) a cringing person .... ( )
58. A "ridgerunner" is: (a) a southern hillbilly (b) a mountain climber (c) a ski instructor (d) a forester .... ( )
59. "Run-em" is a term used in: (a) horseracing (b) casino (c) poker (d) bridge .... ( )
60. A "round heel" is: (a) a politician (b) a poor prize fighter (c) an alcoholic (d) a salesman .... ( )
61. A "vegetable" is: (a) a fruit (b) a helpless patient (c) a worm (d) a stag party .... ( )
62. "Slum" has reference to: (a) a boarding house (b) meat stew (c) prison clothes (d) beer .... ( )
63. The term "down and go" is used in: (a) Air Force (b) racing (c) football (d) cards .... ( )
64. "Flat ball" refers to: (a) baseball (b) bowling (c) football (d) golf .... ( )
65. A "tout" is a person who: (a) never bets (b) is a tightwad (c) is often seen at the race tracks (d) wears zoot suits .... ( )
66. "Travelers" are: (a) nervous twitches (b) head lice (c) crutches (d) tears in stockings .. ( )
67. A "hood" is: (a) a woman's head gear (b) a criminal (c) a fence (d) a pot .... ( )
68. A "chit" is: (a) a young girl (b) a receipt (c) a bill (d) a small black bird .... ( )
69. "Red lead" refers to: (a) hot steel (b) whiskey (c) a bullet (d) ketchup .... ( )
70. When one is a "shiny-back" it means that he belongs to: (a) a football team (b) an orchestra (c) a baseball team (d) a bald men's club .... ( )
71. A "twist" is: (a) a woman (b) a tennis racket (c) a prison trusty (d) a formal dance ( )
72. A "hussle" is: (a) a fishing rod (b) an attorney (c) a bothersome situation (d) a beer party .... ( )
73. A "binte" is: (a) an isolated cottage (b) an overcoat (c) a humorous book (d) an unwieldy crow-bar .... ( )
74. A "dizzy stick" is: (a) a pogostick (b) a clarinet (c) a drummer (d) a cigarette .... ( )
75. A "night line" is: (a) a policemen's beat (b) a sheik's conversation (c) a fishing device (d) a rendezvous .... ( )

II. KNOWLEDGE OF THE UPPER SOCIAL STRATA

Encircle "T" if the statement is true; "F" if it is false.

1. Table service is usually placed with the oyster fork at the outer edge, so that one uses the silver from the outside toward the plate .... T F
2. Replies to all invitations may be typewritten or engraved .... T F
3. Children should remain seated when being introduced .... T F
4. When shopping, it is not good etiquette to thank the salesman .... T F
5. Informal invitations should be written by the lady herself in the first person .... T F
6. The person who calls on the telephone should be the one who terminates the conversation .... T F
7. On the whole, for engaged couples it is in good taste to show signs of affection in public .... T F
8. Manners do not change much fundamentally; only in outward manifestations .... T F
9. After one has finished eating, the fork should be laid on the plate with the tines upward .... T F
10. Letters of condolence should be sent on black-edged paper .... T F
11. At a concert it is customary to applaud the performance between the various movements of a symphony .. T F
12. A man should not ask a young lady for a date in the presence of others .. T F

13. If an inexperienced servant blunders, you should pretend, if you can, not to know it .... T F
14. "Double-redouble" is descriptive of a phrase of contract bridge .... T F
15. A woman should not permit a new chance acquaintance to pay for her meals in the train .... T F
16. When a newcomer is introduced to the members of a group, his name must be repeated to each member of the group .... T F
17. When serving a meal, all drinks should be served on the right ...... T F
18. When a servant at a door says "Not at home," this phrase means that the lady of the house is not at home to visitors; it is a more polite expression than "Not receiving" because it leaves the pleasant uncertainty that it is quite possible she really is out .. T F
19. A "bread and butter" letter is written to your hostess thanking her for a pleasant weekend ....T F
20. If a clergyman is present at a dinner party, in a home, he should be asked to say grace .... T F
21. At informal dinners, people do not usually go in to dinner arm in arm .. T F
22. A navy blue or black suit will not do in place of a cutaway at a very small or country wedding .... T F
23. The time limit for occupancy of a hotel room is usually between three and six P.M. of the following day .. T F
24. The expression "Meet so-and-so" is permitted in society .... T F
25. Pink and blue stationery are in especially good taste .... T F
26. Etiquette concerning the armed services makes it necessary to introduce a rear admiral, for example, as admiral .... T F
27. It is never proper for a man to look over a restaurant bill before paying it when he has people dining with him .... T F
28. Formal invitations are written in the third person .... T F
29. When one is introducing a friend to another friend, the younger person is presented to the older person .... T F
30. A person is stymied in golf when he cannot putt directly because of interference from another ball .... T F
31. A full dress suit does not require a shirt with a stiff front .... T F
32. A man sitting next to a strange woman in a theater should assist her when she wishes to take off her coat T F
33. When registering at a hotel, it is proper to sign, "Mr. John Doe and Wife" .... T F
34. In a restaurant, a woman waits until she is seated before removing her coat T F
35. It is not necessary to answer informal invitations .... T F
36. Any guest who is older than the guest of honor may leave before he, or she, does .... T F
37. It is correct for an unmarried woman to ask the gentleman she knows best to act as host when giving a dinner T F
38. In good society, ladies do not kiss each other when they meet either at parties or in public .... T F
39. The proper way for a bachelor to entertain a debutante is to ask her to tea or to the theater .... T F
40. The butler is the most important servant in every big establishment T F
41. A very smart invitation to a wedding ceremony is one that has a raised margin formed by a plate mark .... T F
42. In a Pullman car, a woman may dress in her own berth or in the dressing room .... T F
43. Appropriate dressing plus good taste is all that is necessary for good attire T F
44. Chukker is a period of play in a polo game .... T F
45. The phrase table d'hôte on a menu means a fixed price for a meal, regardless of how much or how little of it one orders .... T F
46. One should wipe one's mouth before drinking any water .... T F
47. Wedding announcements are invitations to attend the ceremony ..... T F
48. An unmarried woman signs her name "Alice Burt" rather than "Miss Alice Burt" .... T F
49. It is snobbish not to adopt the customs of the community of which one has become a member .... T F
50. When casual acquaintances meet, the man should be the first to speak to the woman .... T F
51. It is not wise to tip the head waiter even if special attention is desired, as it is the head waiter's duty to give special attentions .... T F
52. Ladies always wear gloves to formal dinners and take them off at the table, putting them in their laps .... T F

53. It is correct for a man to shake hands with his gloves on if they cannot be removed quickly .... T F
54. It is permissible to drink bouillon by lifting the cup, as one would drink tea .... T F
55. The engagement ring may be worn in public before the betrothal is announced .... T F
56. Red wine is preferable to white wine with fish courses .... T F
57. It is not correct for the hostess to be served first .... T F
58. The term "My dear" in correspondence is more formal than "Dear" .. T F
59. A young man may continually go to see a young girl even if she shows him scant attention or even if she indicates that she is not interested T F
60. One should congratulate a woman on her engagement .... T F
61. A man raises his hat when giving directions to a strange woman on the street .... T F
62. A woman never rises to an introduction .... T F
63. When an engagement is broken, gifts, letters, etc., are returned .... T F
64. When paying your respects to the bride and groom, it is proper to offer them both congratulations .... T F
65. The invitation to the church ceremony always requests the honor and never the honour of your presence .. T F
66. The fundamental difference between a ball and a dance is that people of all ages are asked to a ball, while only those of approximately the same age are asked to a dance .... T F
67. The word "ball" is never used except in an invitation to an affair that is public .... T F
68. In hotels, "European Plan" means that meals are included in the rate charge .... T F
69. When entering a room with a guest the hostess goes first only when the guest is a stranger in the house .... T F
70. When a man is walking with two women on the street, he should walk between them .... T F
71. When first names are to be written on a card, the husband's name is written first .... T F
72. If the maid offers to do some extra work while you are a guest at the home in which she is employed, it is not necessary that you tip her .... T F
73. Antibes is a summer resort on the French Riviera .... T F
74. As long as the audience enjoys it, a person who talks well should be encouraged to monopolize the conversation .... T F
75. The bride should always carry flowers at a formal wedding .... T F

KEY TO SOCIAL KNOWLEDGE TEST

I. Knowledge of the Lower Social Strata

1. (b) to stop bragging
2. (c) the lowest level of the underworld
3. (a) dice
4. (d) term meaning difficulties in progress
5. (d) homosexual
6. (d) prize fighter
7. (d) Frenchman
8. (a) heckle
9. (a) rumors
10. (d) a measure used by bartenders
11. (a) nitroglycerine
12. (d) pawnbroker
13. (c) a fast auto
14. (d) cheap whiskey
15. (c) a hanging
16. (c) 7
17. (d) sharp character
18. (c) a minister
19. (c) dice
20. (a) perfume
21. (c) nose
22. (a) a vexatious person
23. (c) a drummer
24. (c) drug addict
25. (c) a dishwasher
26. (c) woman
27. (a) dope addict
28. (d) knife
29. (b) a baseball pitcher
30. (c) low ball
31. (b) a backwoods location
32. (d) go at top speed
33. (b) dice term
34. (b) an incompetent person
35. (b) a rustic, city person
36. (a) southpaw

37. (b) priest
38. (a) a free pass
39. (d) machinists in the Navy
40. (c) an overzealous piece worker
41. (a) to hit somebody
42. (d) a cup of coffee
43. (b) a stupid person
44. (d) tough girl
45. (b) girl
46. (b) a jerk
47. (b) be a simpleton
48. (c) tramp
49. (b) spinster
50. (a) an addict in need of dope
51. (c) 10
52. (b) shoes
53. (d) a poor horse
54. (b) the wild man in the circus sideshow
55. (b) one-room apartment
56. (c) doctors
57. (d) cringing person
58. (a) southern hillbilly
59. (c) poker
60. (b) poor prize fighter
61. (b) helpless patient
62. (b) meat stew
63. (d) cards
64. (b) bowling
65. (c) is often seen at the race tracks
66. (b) head lice
67. (b) a criminal
68. (b) receipt
69. (d) ketchup
70. (b) an orchestra
71. (a) woman
72. (c) a bothersome situation
73. (b) overcoat
74. (d) cigarette
75. (c) fishing device

II. Knowledge of the Upper Social Strata

1. True
2. False
3. False
4. False
5. True
6. True
7. False
8. True
9. True
10. False
11. False
12. True
13. True
14. True
15. True
16. False
17. True
18. True
19. True
20. True
21. True
22. False
23. True
24. False
25. False
26. True
27. False
28. True
29. True
30. True
31. False
32. False
33. False
34. True
35. False
36. False
37. True
38. True
39. True
40. True
41. True
42. True
43. True
44. True
45. True
46. True
47. False
48. True
49. True
50. False
51. False
52. True
53. True
54. True
55. False
56. False
57. True
58. True
59. False
60. False
61. True
62. False
63. True
64. False
65. False
66. True
67. True
68. False
69. True
70. False
71. False
72. False
73. True
74. True
75. False

NORMS

Rank for College Students	For Lower Social Strata RAW SCORE OR NUMBER RIGHT		For Upper Social Strata RAW SCORE OR NUMBER RIGHT	
	Men	Women	Men	Women
Highest fifth	58–75	45–75	56–75	60–75
Second fifth	53–57	38–44	51–55	55–59
Middle fifth	49–52	31–37	48–50	52–54
Fourth fifth	42–48	23–30	45–47	47–51
Lowest fifth	0–41	0–22	0–44	0–46

The most helpful interpretation of the scores on the "Social Knowledge Tests" is to score both the Lower and Upper Social Strata sections and note the difference or similarity between the two rankings, connecting them by a line. as in these four examples:

Quintile on Lower	*Quintile on Upper*
5	5
4	4
3	3
2	2
1	1

Quintile on Lower	*Quintile on Upper*
5	5
4	4
3	3
2	2
1	1

Quintile on Lower	*Quintile on Upper*
5	5
4	4
3	3
2	2
1	1

Quintile on Lower	*Quintile on Upper*
5	5
4	4
3	3
2	2
1	1

A TEST OF PERSONALITY MATURITY

A person may have high abstract intelligence and still lack personality maturity. He may be bright in the study of certain books, but he may never have studied the kinds of books or had the experiences that are necessary to make him a well-adjusted, mature adult.

Maturity is, after all, not a matter of age. Some young people are relatively mature, and some old people are still children in their points of view and attitudes toward important aspects of life. In Chapter 9 we described the way in which the following personality-maturity test was developed. Apply the questions to yourself and refer to the key on pages 615 and 616 for the proper scoring. Then consult the table at the end of the key, entitled "What Your Score Means."

PERSONALITY-MATURITY TEST. Check one and only one of the possible answers to each question.

1. The manner in which my employers or teachers have treated me is that they
   - ☐ *a.* always tried to make my life miserable by constant nagging.
   - ☐ *b.* had a tendency to criticize me whenever they could.
   - ☐ *c.* were indifferent to me so long as I conformed with their regulations or performed work satisfactorily.
   - ☐ *d.* helped me in my work a great deal.
   - ☐ *e.* helped me and praised me for my conscientiousness.
   - ☐ *f.* condemned me when at fault and praised me when I deserved it.
2. When taking part in card games or athletic contests where my side or I fail to win, I usually react to the defeat
   - ☐ *a.* by studying possible reasons for the defeat in order to improve my skill.
   - ☐ *b.* by admiration of the perfection of the other person's skill.
   - ☐ *c.* by feeling inferior to the other person.
   - ☐ *d.* by feeling that, at any rate, I'm superior in other things.
   - ☐ *e.* by realizing the relative unimportance of defeat or victory in such games and promptly forgetting the defeat.
   - ☐ *f.* by thinking the other fellow got the breaks that time; maybe I will next time.
3. When forced to give up a plan or ambition such as to go to college, to make a fortune, to marry a certain person, etc., I find that I
   - ☐ *a.* am sure that I shall be unhappy for the rest of my life.
   - ☐ *b.* have so many interests that I soon have something to take its place.
   - ☐ *c.* am determined to get it at any cost if it takes the rest of my life.
   - ☐ *d.* am sure that God's will is for the best.
   - ☐ *e.* try to reconcile myself to the loss and make the best of it.
   - ☐ *f.* figure that's my luck and I shouldn't have hoped for anything in the first place.
   - ☐ *g.* never had a plan or ambition of vital importance that I had to give up.
   - ☐ *h.* am unhappy for some time but get over it.
4. The extent to which people seem to like me is
   - ☐ *a.* either very much or not at all.
   - ☐ *b.* people like me a little but not enough to have me for their best friend.
   - ☐ *c.* everyone seems to like me at first meeting.
   - ☐ *d.* people like me only if they know me very well.
   - ☐ *e.* no one likes me.
   - ☐ *f.* many people like me to some extent.

- ☐ *g.* I cannot tell.
- ☐ *h.* people like me if I can do them a favor.
- ☐ *i.* people like me at first but later they change their opinion.

5. My tendency to call the attention of others to my failures, defeats, or inabilities is
   - ☐ *a.* I always tell people about them whenever they seem interested.
   - ☐ *b.* I tell people about my failures only when it's incidental to the conversation.
   - ☐ *c.* I very seldom mention my defeats to anyone to avoid seeking sympathy.
   - ☐ *d.* I never mention my defeats; people think I'm either looking for sympathy or admitting my inferiority.
6. People whose opinions differ from mine
   - ☐ *a.* are unsocial and peculiar.
   - ☐ *b.* are egotistical.
   - ☐ *c.* are in need of more training.
   - ☐ *d.* are justified in having their own opinions.
   - ☐ *e.* simply differ from me in background.
   - ☐ *f.* are in need of more years of experience.
   - ☐ g. are usually superior to me in intelligence.
   - ☐ *h.* are more informed on the particular subject.
7. The kind of opponent I prefer in a game or contest is one who is
   - ☐ *a.* a master and my superior, because I have a greater chance of improving my skill.
   - ☐ *b.* somewhat superior, because it makes the contest more stimulating to me.
   - ☐ *c.* an equal, since we both do our best and have an equal chance to win.
   - ☐ *d.* an inferior whom I know I can beat. (Then I feel I'm superior in one thing at least.)
   - ☐ *e.* a good sport, regardless of his skill.
8. Life, for me, is worthwhile in the extent to which I have the privilege of living in a political, social, and economic world that
   - ☐ *a.* is on a simpler scale than this present organized society.
   - ☐ *b.* would remain as it is now.
   - ☐ *c.* is orderly and seemingly logical in its changes for the better.
   - ☐ *d.* is in a state of change where I can utilize its changing requirements for my own development and the satisfactions of others.
   - ☐ *e.* is constantly changing.
   - ☐ *f.* is considerably improved over this world.
9. My tendency to argue with my associates is
   - ☐ *a.* I'm always ready for a good, hot argument.
   - ☐ *b.* I usually argue if I'm at all interested.
   - ☐ *c.* I seldom argue with anyone; I prefer an intellectual argument with myself.
   - ☐ *d.* I dislike to get into arguments and avoid them as much as possible.
   - ☐ *e.* I hate arguments.
   - ☐ *f.* I argue only in a free-for-all discussion.
   - ☐ *g.* I like to test the other person's knowledge.
10. When a person not in my family criticizes me, my usual reaction is to
    - ☐ *a.* analyze the critic as to why he criticized me.
    - ☐ *b.* ask him for the reason of the criticism.
    - ☐ *c.* say nothing and forget about it.
    - ☐ *d.* criticize him when I get the chance.
    - ☐ *e.* defend myself verbally if I think I am right.
    - ☐ *f.* say nothing but hold a grudge against him.
11. In order to succeed in a vocation, family influence, "pull," or "drag" is
    - ☐ *a.* always harmful. Eventually it will be difficult for the benefited person to face future problems without his usual "drag."
    - ☐ *b.* usually harmful rather than helpful.
    - ☐ *c.* helpful only in getting started in one's vocation.
    - ☐ *d.* helpful at times but not necessary.
    - ☐ *e.* always helpful but not necessary.
    - ☐ *f.* necessary in order to achieve prominence.
    - ☐ *g.* always helpful and always necessary.
12. I believe that the extent to which an individual can learn to enjoy life nobly depends upon
    - ☐ *a.* the way in which he responds to his environment (assuming that the environment is reasonably good) and uses it to develop his natural abilities.
    - ☐ *b.* the way in which he responds to an environment that has many facilities for his development.
    - ☐ *c.* the way in which he utilizes his environment, even though the facilities of that environment are poor.
13. My reaction to the thought of my own death is to
    - ☐ *a.* greatly abhor the thought.
    - ☐ *b.* dislike the thought but do not express my feeling.
    - ☐ *c.* take it for granted as an eventual inevitability and not think about it often.
    - ☐ *d.* frequently speculate about it, wishing

that I had the nerve to become experimental.
- ☐ *e.* secretly wish that I were dead but not often say it to others.
- ☐ *f.* openly wish that I were dead.
- ☐ *g.* never give it a thought.

14. The extent to which I try to make a favorable impression on other people is to
- ☐ *a.* make definite plans and devote much time to it.
- ☐ *b.* seldom plan to do so in advance but if the opportunity arises try to make a good impression.
- ☐ *c.* devote a slight amount of time to it.
- ☐ *d.* dislike the practice in others and never do it myself.

15. When confronted by an unusual problem in work or study
- ☐ *a.* I never hesitate to seek help from someone who knows more about it.
- ☐ *b.* I usually ask some close friend to help me.
- ☐ *c.* I very seldom bother anyone enough to ask him to help me.
- ☐ *d.* I usually ask a friend if I am sure he knows more about it.
- ☐ *e.* I make every effort to solve it before asking anyone for help.

16. Life, for me, is worthwhile to the extent to which I have the privilege of living among friends and relatives who are
- ☐ *a.* more congenial than the present ones.
- ☐ *b.* stimulating intellectually.
- ☐ *c.* I need more friends and relatives than I now have in order to be happy.
- ☐ *d.* the ones I now have are sufficient to stimulate me satisfyingly.
- ☐ *e.* they are unnecessary for my happiness.
- ☐ *f.* interested in the things that interest me, common interests.

17. When a member of my family criticizes me severely or nags me, my usual reaction is to
- ☐ *a.* resent it but say nothing.
- ☐ *b.* keep peace in the family by agreeing with the other person and flattering him.
- ☐ *c.* say nothing but try to get even later.
- ☐ *d.* maintain my self-respect by arguing back.
- ☐ *e.* try to understand the reason why the other person is citicizing or nagging me.
- ☐ *f.* get angry and argue.

18. My feeling about calling the attention of others to my activities, abilities, or achievements is
- ☐ *a.* I seek the attention of others and do it deliberately.
- ☐ *b.* I seek the attention of others but do not do it obviously.
- ☐ *c.* I like the attention of others but do not solicit it.
- ☐ *d.* I hate to call attention to myself in any way and always avoid speaking about myself.

19. The importance of my personal appearance to me is
- ☐ *a.* very great; I spend much time in studying and improving it.
- ☐ *b.* moderate, and I devote only a small amount of time to it.
- ☐ *c.* so slight that I spend only enough time at it to keep from looking conspicuous.
- ☐ *d.* of little or no interest to me.
- ☐ *e.* very important to me, but I spend only a moderate amount of time on it.

20. I find enjoyment in the companionship and friendship of
- ☐ *a.* members of the opposite sex; they understand me better.
- ☐ *b.* people who are congenial to me regardless of their sex.
- ☐ *c.* members of my own sex because I get along with them better.
- ☐ *d.* I do not feel the need of companionship or friendship with anyone of either sex.

21. The way in which I react to religion is
- ☐ *a.* that I do not personally need any religion but think that it is necessary for most people.
- ☐ *b.* I read about and observe various religions and eventually may decide upon one for myself.
- ☐ *c.* I am inventing a religion of my own which I hope will some day be satisfactory for me.
- ☐ *d.* I now have a religion which satisfies me.
- ☐ *e.* the religion of my parents is most satisfactory to me.
- ☐ *f.* the religion of my parents is not satisfactory but I accept it.
- ☐ *g.* that religion is very burdensome to me but necessary.

22. The extent to which I study and read about social or economic changes in other countries of the world is
- ☐ *a.* I am not interested in conditions in other parts of the world.
- ☐ *b.* I am too busy solving my own problems to think about those in other parts of the world.
- ☐ *c.* I am trying to locate accurate information about conditions there.
- ☐ *d.* I am more interested in conditions in

other parts of the world than in those here.
- ☐ *e.* I should like nothing better than to study and read about conditions in other parts of the world.
- ☐ *f.* I am interested in studying conditions in other parts of the world in order to make comparisons with my own part of the world.

23. When forced to speak in public, I find that
- ☐ *a.* it is extremely difficult and causes me embarrassment or stuttering.
- ☐ *b.* it is difficult, but I can manage it without much evidence of embarrassment.
- ☐ *c.* it is a challenge to my self-respect so that I do it without flinching.
- ☐ *d.* I can usually speak without much effort.
- ☐ *e.* I always enjoy speaking to an audience.
- ☐ *f.* it is very difficult unless I am sure of the friendliness of the audience.

24. The extent to which I study or read about social, political, or economic changes in my own country is
- ☐ *a.* I read much relative to them.
- ☐ *b.* I read only those things I'm especially interested in.
- ☐ *c.* I read them only when there's nothing else to read or when I have to.
- ☐ *d.* I read them incidentally as I read the newspapers and periodicals.
- ☐ *e.* I read them only enough to be able to discuss them intelligently.

25. My reaction to seeing news items published about myself is
- ☐ *a.* I enjoy seeing them and often show them to my friends.
- ☐ *b.* I rather like to see my name in print, but it's not very important to me.
- ☐ *c.* seeing my name in print is of no interest to me at all.
- ☐ *d.* seeing my name in print amuses or disgusts me.
- ☐ *e.* I am proud to show people my name in print if the item isn't derogatory.
- ☐ *f.* I intensely dislike to see my name in print.

26. My attitude toward omens, premonitions, etc., is that
- ☐ *a.* in my life I have known them to indicate almost without exception success or failure of some activity.
- ☐ *b.* they usually predict the success or failure of some activity.
- ☐ *c.* I can't decide whether it is chance or whether they actually do predict.
- ☐ *d.* I don't believe they ever predict anything for anyone.
- ☐ *e.* I realize they are false but find myself heeding them.

27. The extent of my activity in group or social meetings is
- ☐ *a.* I always try to lead in the discussions.
- ☐ *b.* I take part in the discussions only if I know something about the subject.
- ☐ *c.* I do not take part in the discussions unless I am positive of the worth and truth of what I am saying.
- ☐ *d.* I never take part in the discussion because I very much dislike talking in a group.
- ☐ *e.* I take part to keep things moving but not to lead.

28. The extent to which I visit fortune-tellers is
- ☐ *a.* I consult them only when confronted with a serious dilemma and can't decide what to do.
- ☐ *b.* I visit them sometimes when friends I know are going to do so.
- ☐ *c.* I only consult them when I wish to see if I can discover the techniques used.
- ☐ *d.* I never go to a fortune-teller; I think they're fakes.
- ☐ *e.* I go there for entertainment.

29. The extent to which I take financial risks is
- ☐ *a.* I take many serious risks because if I win I win a great deal.
- ☐ *b.* I take serious risks only when the balance is in my favor.
- ☐ *c.* I take no serious risks; the losses would overwhelm me if I didn't win.
- ☐ *d.* I take a few minor chances since I wouldn't be greatly injured should I lose.
- ☐ *e.* I take no chances of any kind; I prefer to be safe where I am now.

30. When emotional problems or difficulties confront me
- ☐ *a.* I enjoy them because I love to overcome them; they stimulate me.
- ☐ *b.* they don't interest me particularly; I'm used to them.
- ☐ *c.* they are just another obstacle in my path which temporarily impedes me.
- ☐ *d.* I have no emotional problems or difficulties.
- ☐ *e.* I stick them out although they wear me down.

31. In regard to nature, I believe that
- ☐ *a.* nature is intrinsically good; if I could be in complete harmony with nature I could avoid all evil.
- ☐ *b.* nature is essentially good, but it must be subject to control by man.

☐ *c.* nature is evil; if it could be completely subjugated we could eliminate all vice.

☐ *d.* only a few things in nature are innately bad, but they do not cause us great worry now that science has shown us that even innate mechanisms can be used advantageously.

☐ *e.* nature is neither good nor bad; it simply offers material with possibilities and limitations for the individual's development.

32. My attitude toward the world in general is that

☐ *a.* it is filled with evil; the faster I can escape it the better off I shall be.

☐ *b.* it has a great many temptations so that it is difficult for anyone to remain good.

☐ *c.* the world is an interesting panorama; I am interested in utilizing my time in investigating it.

☐ *d.* the world is good if people would live lives of worth and true goodness.

☐ *e.* I live only once, so I intend to enjoy it instead of trying to explain it.

☐ *f.* I am a part of the world, whether good or evil, so I intend to live to the fullest extent of my capabilities.

33. Assuming that everyone wants enough money to satisfy his needs for food, clothing, and shelter, I also want more money

☐ *a.* so that I can have a better house, larger car, more beautiful clothes, etc.

☐ *b.* to carry out plans that I would like to put into effect, such as improving my business or professional ability.

☐ *c.* I don't want any more money.

☐ *d.* to be able to share it with others.

☐ *e.* I don't want any more money because I think it destroys more happiness than it creates.

☐ *f.* I want enough money so that I can do as I please.

34. When I read the daily papers, my attitude toward items relating to my vocation (managing a home is considered a vocation) is

☐ *a.* I always read items relating to my vocation.

☐ *b.* I read only those items that especially interest me.

☐ *c.* I very seldom read anything about my vocation; I have enough of that all day long.

☐ *d.* I never read anything about it. I hate it.

KEY TO PERSONALITY-MATURITY TEST

Subtract total minus score from total plus score.

1. (a) −3, (b) −2, (c) +4, (d) 0, (e) −1, (f) +6
2. (a) +4, (b) 0, (c) −3, (d) −3, (e) +8, (f) −4
3. (a) − 3, (b) +10, (c) 0, (d) − 5, (e) + 2, (f) − 3, (g) + 6, (h) 0
4. (a) 0, (b) −3, (c) 0, (d) 0, (e) 0, (f) +8, (g) −2, (h) −2, (i) 0
5. (a) −3, (b) +8, (c) +2, (d) −1
6. (a) −2, (b) 0, (c) −3, (d) +8, (e) +4, (f) −2, (g) −1, (h) −1
7. (a) −2, (b) +6, (c) 0, (d) −5, (e) +8
8. (a) 0, (b) −5, (c) +6, (d) +6, (e) +2, (f) −3
9. (a) −2, (b) +8, (c) 0, (d) 0, (e) −4, (f) 0, (g) 0
10. (a) +8, (b) +6, (c) −3, (d) −2, (e) +4, (f) −4
11. (a) −2, (b) 0, (c) +8, (d) +8, (e) 0, (f) −4, (g) −4
12. (a) −1, (b) −2, (c) +8

13. (a) −2
(b) −3
(c) +10
(d) −1
(e) −2
(f) −3
(g) −1

14. (a) −1
(b) +8
(c) −2
(d) −2

15. (a) +6
(b) −3
(c) 0
(d) 0
(e) +2

16. (a) −4
(b) +8
(c) −2
(d) 0
(e) −4
(f) +4

17. (a) 0
(b) −3
(c) −3
(d) +2
(e) +8
(f) −2

18. (a) −1
(b) −4
(c) +8
(d) 0

19. (a) −2
(b) +4
(c) 0
(d) −3
(e) +4

20. (a) −3
(b) +8
(c) −3
(d) −3

21. (a) −2
(b) +6
(c) +4
(d) +8
(e) −2
(f) −3
(g) −3

22. (a) −5
(b) 0
(c) +6
(d) −2
(e) 0
(f) +8

23. (a) −4
(b) +6
(c) 0
(d) +4
(e) +2
(f) 0

24. (a) +6
(b) 0
(c) −4
(d) 0
(e) +4

25. (a) −3
(b) +8
(c) 0
(d) 0
(e) −2
(f) −3

26. (a) −5
(b) −4
(c) −3
(d) +10
(e) −4

27. (a) +4
(b) +6
(c) 0
(d) −4
(e) 0

28. (a) −4
(b) −3
(c) −3
(d) +10
(e) 0

29. (a) 0
(b) +6
(c) 0
(d) +8
(e) −4

30. (a) 0
(b) +4
(c) +6
(d) 0
(e) −1

31. (a) −4
(b) −4
(c) −3
(d) 0
(e) +10

32. (a) −3
(b) −3
(c) +6
(d) 0
(e) −2
(f) +10

33. (a) −2
(b) +8
(c) −2
(d) 0
(e) −2
(f) 0

34. (a) +4
(b) +4
(c) −3
(d) −4

WHAT YOUR SCORE MEANS

Score	
0–99	Below average for people of the general population
100	Average for people of the general population
101–248	Above average for people of general population
162	Average for college students

EXECUTIVE REACTION PATTERN TEST

Underline the term or degree which most adequately describes your likes, beliefs, record, and so on. Do not try to think of what you would or should do, but answer according to what you have done.

1. Number of meetings of a technical nature or of trade associations attended—local organizations as well as national or state:
   - ☐ *a.* Ten or more per year.
   - ☐ *b.* From 5 to 10.
   - ☐ *c.* From 1 to 5.
   - ☐ *d.* Few or none.
   - ☐ *e.* None.
2. Activity in trade or technical association meetings:
   - ☐ *a.* Took very active part as a leader.
   - ☐ *b.* Frequently took part in discussions.
   - ☐ *c.* Occasionally asked questions.
   - ☐ *d.* Rarely took part.
   - ☐ *e.* Never took part.
3. Time devoted to personal appearance:
   - ☐ *a.* Large amount.
   - ☐ *b.* Considerable amount.
   - ☐ *c.* Moderate amount.
   - ☐ *d.* Few minutes a day.
   - ☐ *e.* Neglect it.
4. Amount of study given to subjects related to my business since leaving school:
   - ☐ *a.* Spent all available time on such subjects.
   - ☐ *b.* Studied business subjects frequently.
   - ☐ *c.* Occasionally spent time in study of my business.
   - ☐ *d.* Seldom gave any.
   - ☐ *e.* Never gave any.
5. When I have read the daily papers, I have read items relating to business:
   - ☐ *a.* Almost exclusively.
   - ☐ *b.* Much of the time.
   - ☐ *c.* Frequently.
   - ☐ *d.* Occasionally.
   - ☐ *e.* Never, except by accident.
6. My record of leadership in my youth:
   - ☐ *a.* Frequently organized games, teams, or clubs.
   - ☐ *b.* A leader in activities.
   - ☐ *c.* Little marked leadership.
   - ☐ *d.* Willing to follow other leaders.
   - ☐ *e.* Disregarded playmates.
7. I actually associated with men whose ability was:
   - ☐ *a.* Much greater than mine.
   - ☐ *b.* Somewhat greater.
   - ☐ *c.* About the same.
   - ☐ *d.* Slightly less than my own.
   - ☐ *e.* Considerably less.
8. When I was not busy taking recreation or taking care of routine matters and had some time for thinking along any line, I devised new methods, plans, or systems. The percentage of such available time devoted to improvements was from:
   - ☐ *a.* 75–100 per cent
   - ☐ *b.* 50–75 " "
   - ☐ *c.* 25–50 " "
   - ☐ *d.* 5–25 " "
   - ☐ *e.* 2–5 " "
   - ☐ *f.* 0–2 " "
9. My thinking of improvements dealt with problems relating to (underline as many as apply):
   - ☐ *a.* Organization of company as a whole.
   - ☐ *b.* Organization of work within one department.
   - ☐ *c.* Organization of work between departments.
   - ☐ *d.* Stimulating employees.

- ☐ *e.* Cutting costs.
- ☐ *f.* Increasing sales.
- ☐ g. Better service to customers.
- ☐ *h.* New mechanical inventions.
- ☐ *i.* Better financing.
- ☐ *j.* Helping society in general.

10. My family influence has:
- ☐ *a.* Greatly stimulated me to do my best.
- ☐ *b.* Stimulated me slightly.
- ☐ *c.* Had no effect—good or bad.
- ☐ *d.* Had slightly negative effect.
- ☐ *e.* Had pronouncedly negative effect.

11. A rival or rivals:
- ☐ *a.* Stimulated me strongly and I tried to beat them.
- ☐ *b.* Stimulated me slightly.
- ☐ *c.* Did not affect me at all.
- ☐ *d.* Discouraged me slightly.
- ☐ *e.* Discouraged me greatly.

12. I met my financial obligations:
- ☐ *a.* Always promptly.
- ☐ *b.* Fairly promptly.
- ☐ *c.* As best I could.
- ☐ *d.* Sometimes with failure.
- ☐ *e.* Sometimes with neglect.

13. In times of failure or discouragement:
- ☐ *a.* I persisted.
- ☐ *b.* I persisted to a limited extent.
- ☐ *c.* I thought of ways out of the difficulties and applied them to the problems.
- ☐ *d.* I thought of remedies but did not apply them.
- ☐ *e.* I just quit and regretted that I was not trained to solve them.

14. My energy supply:
- ☐ *a.* Compels me to keep busy at all times.
- ☐ *b.* Is plentiful.
- ☐ *c.* Is enough to meet my needs.
- ☐ *d.* Is small and I force myself to keep going.
- ☐ *e.* Prevents my attaining many possibilities.

15. My attitude toward risks:
- ☐ *a.* I took many serious business risks.
- ☐ *b.* I took a few serious business risks.
- ☐ *c.* I took no serious risks.
- ☐ *d.* I took a few minor chances.
- ☐ *e.* I took no serious or minor chances.

16. The extent to which I tried to make a favorable impression on important persons:
- ☐ *a.* I made definite plans and devoted much time to impressing the right persons.
- ☐ *b.* I devoted a slight amount of time to making a good impression.
- ☐ *c.* I seldom planned to do so in advance, but, if opportunity arose, I tried to make a good impression.
- ☐ *d.* I never noticed such opportunities.
- ☐ *e.* I disliked the practice in others and never indulged myself.

17. Problems or difficulties around me:
- ☐ *a.* Stimulated me greatly.
- ☐ *b.* Stimulated me mildly.
- ☐ *c.* Had no effect.
- ☐ *d.* Caused slight discouragement.
- ☐ *e.* Caused pronounced discouragement.

18. Criticisms from others regarding my work have:
- ☐ *a.* Greatly stimulated me to do better.
- ☐ *b.* Slightly stimulated me to do better.
- ☐ *c.* Had no effect.
- ☐ *d.* Worried me.
- ☐ *e.* Caused resentment.

19. Anticipating problems before they arose:
- ☐ *a.* Gave them much thought.
- ☐ *b.* Gave them some thought.
- ☐ *c.* Planned to meet present problems only.
- ☐ *d.* Let all problems take care of themselves.
- ☐ *e.* Passed them on to experts.

20. When conversing with superiors:
- ☐ *a.* I felt at ease and talked freely.
- ☐ *b.* I talked freely, but was not at perfect ease.
- ☐ *c.* I talked fairly freely, but was ill at ease.
- ☐ *d.* I talked little, because I was ill at ease.
- ☐ *e.* I felt inferior and said nothing.

21. When conversing with inferiors:
- ☐ *a.* I tried to make them feel at ease.
- ☐ *b.* I let them talk.
- ☐ *c.* I talked more than they.
- ☐ *d.* I monopolized the conversation.
- ☐ *e.* I tried to make them feel inferior.
- ☐ *f.* I did not think of any differences between us.

22. In group discussions:
- ☐ *a.* I said nothing.
- ☐ *b.* I spoke occasionally.
- ☐ *c.* I spoke when I had something worth saying.
- ☐ *d.* I dominated the conversation.

23. The amount of time I devoted to work has been:
- ☐ *a.* Far too much to enjoy life fully.
- ☐ *b.* About the right amount.

☐ *c*. Too much.
☐ *d*. Too little.
☐ *e*. Decidedly too little.

24. Ability to influence others:
☐ *a*. I could influence large numbers of persons.
☐ *b*. I could influence small numbers of persons.
☐ *c*. I could influence some individuals.
☐ *d*. I could influence those who were under obligations to me.
☐ *e*. Had difficulty in influencing anyone.
☐ *f*. Don't know—I never tried.

25. The number of technical or trade journals I read fairly regularly:
☐ *a*. 5 or more.
☐ *b*. 3 to 5.
☐ *c*. 2 or 3.
☐ *d*. 1 or 2.
☐ *e*. None.

26. My interest in my past work has been:
☐ *a*. Very great and enjoyable.
☐ *b*. Usually enjoyable.
☐ *c*. Slightly enjoyable.
☐ *d*. Little or none.
☐ *e*. Mostly negative.

27. The number of my friends who would help me in putting across a really good idea:
☐ *a*. A great many—50 or more.
☐ *b*. Many—10 to 50.
☐ *c*. Few—5 to 10.
☐ *d*. Very few—1 to 5.
☐ *e*. None.

28. The extent to which I have gone out of my way to help others:
☐ *a*. Often inconvenienced myself.
☐ *b*. Occasionally inconvenienced myself.
☐ *c*. Seldom inconvenienced myself.
☐ *d*. Never inconvenienced myself.
☐ *e*. Believed in taking care of myself and in letting others do the same.

KEY TO THE EXECUTIVE REACTION PATTERN TEST

1. (a) +10, (b) + 2, (c) − 3, (d) − 5, (e) − 5
2. (a) +6, (b) +4, (c) −6, (d) −2, (e) −6
3. (a) 0, (b) +2, (c) −5, (d) −2, (e) −3
4. (a) +3, (b) 0, (c) −1, (d) −8, (e) −8
5. (a) +6, (b) +2, (c) 0, (d) −6, (e) −8
6. (a) 0, (b) +3, (c) 0, (d) −5, (e) 0
7. (a) +1, (b) +3, (c) −5, (d) 0, (e) 0
8. (a) +6, (b) +5, (c) 0, (d) −1, (e) −5, (f) −5

*9. (a) +2, (b) 0, (c) +2, (d) +2, (e) 0, (f) 0, (g) 0, (h) +2, (i) +2, (j) +2

10. (a) +2, (b) −5, (c) −3, (d) +3, (e) −3
11. (a) +3, (b) −1, (c) −2, (d) 0, (e) −5
12. (a) +4, (b) −4, (c) −5, (d) −5, (e) −5
13. (a) +4, (b) −3, (c) −3, (d) 0, (e) 0
14. (a) +5, (b) +2, (c) −2, (d) 0, (e) 0
15. (a) +5, (b) 0, (c) −2, (d) −3, (e) −5
16. (a) −6, (b) +2, (c) +1, (d) 0, (e) 0

17. (a) +4
(b) −2
(c) −5
(d) −5
(e) −5

18. (a) +2
(b) −2
(c) 0
(d) −4
(e) +4

19. (a) +4
(b) 0
(c) −3
(d) −4
(e) +5

20. (a) +4
(b) −2
(c) −4
(d) −4
(e) −4

21. (a) +3
(b) +6
(c) −3
(d) −3
(e) −3
(f) −3

22. (a) −5
(b) −5
(c) +5
(d) +5

23. (a) −2
(b) +6
(c) 0
(d) −2
(e) −2

24. (a) +4
(b) +2
(c) −1
(d) −4
(e) −4
(f) −4

25. (a) +10
(b) + 5
(c) 0
(d) − 4
(e) + 2

26. (a) +5
(b) −3
(c) 0
(d) −6
(e) −6

27. (a) +10
(b) 0
(c) − 4
(d) 0
(e) 0

28. (a) +4
(b) −4
(c) −4
(d) −4
(e) −4

* Number 9 should also be scored on the total number of items underlined. If only one or two items are underlined, give no extra credit. If three or more items are underlined, give a plus score equal to the total number of items underlined. Example: if the five items *c, d, h, i, j* are underlined, each item having a +2 score, the total score for question No. 9 would be 10+5, or 15.

Assign plus and minus values to your own answers according to the above key. Add all the values having a plus sign. Add all those having a minus sign. Then add the two sums algebraically. Find the position of your final score in one of the six grades in the extreme left-hand column of the probability table. Read to the right and the per cent figures will indicate, statistically, the percentage of businessmen who made the same score in the test.

Example: Of the businessmen who made a score of minus 40 to minus 120, 100 per cent were in the lower-most category of business position; of those who made a score of plus 81 and above, 14 per cent were in the middle, 29 per cent in the upper middle, and 57 per cent in the uppermost classification of position held in business.

PROBABILITY TABLE SHOWING THE RELATION BETWEEN SCORES IN EXECUTIVE REACTION PATTERN TEST AND CLASSIFICATION OF POSITION IN BUSINESS

Score in Test	*Lower-most*	*Lower middle*	*Middle*	*Upper-middle*	*Upper-most*
+ 81 and up	...	...	14%	29%	57%
+ 51 to + 80	...	13%	22%	22%	43%
+ 21 to + 50	7%	30%	33%	21%	9%
− 9 to + 20	15%	39%	34%	9%	3%
− 10 to − 39	59%	18%	18%	5%	...
− 40 to − 121	100%	...	...	...	...
Mean	− 23.1	+ 14.8	+ 23.0	+ 40.5	+ 62.9
Median	− 25.0	+ 13.5	+ 26.0	+ 41.0	+ 66.0

ANSWERS TO TESTS IN TEXT

INTERPRETATION OF ANSWERS TO PRE-MARITAL TEST—
"Am I Well-Balanced?" (page 275)

The first 10 questions should be answered *yes,* the last 10, *no.* If you answered 15 or more correctly, you would appear emotionally well-balanced and in that respect likely to be happy in marriage. A score of 10 or less suggests that you may not yet be ready to assume the responsibilities of marriage.

On the basis of rating scales, using extremes (quintiles), the validity of this test is about .40. Copyright of test and scoring by Clifford R. Adams, Associate Professor of Psychology, Pennsylvania State University.

Answer to Project Question 5, page 340

a. Admitted. With an average of 86 his freshman year, Anchovy made the dean's list.
b. Rejected. Bass, rejected by every college to which he applied, joined the Marine Corps, where he was cited as best man in his platoon.
c. Rejected. Carp went to a good small college, where he is doing fairly well in a less demanding program than Yale's.
d. Admitted. By hard work, Cod got a 71 average in January and upped it to 75 by June.
e. Rejected. Haddock, it turned out, didn't want to go to Yale despite family pressure, which accounts for the "tailspin" of his senior year. He went instead to a state university, where he happily studied agriculture.
f. Rejected. Puffer went to another college, where he has a C plus average.

WHICH ONE WOULD YOU HIRE? Answers to quiz on pages 304–305

Here is the actual sales ranking of the salesmen whose records are given. How right were you?

1st: Former doctor
2nd: Rose from ranks
3rd: Old-timer
4th: Smooth operator
5th: Veteran
6th: Former failure
7th: Had own business
8th: Social register

The results of a study of the reliability of judgments of intelligence from photographs are reported in the *Journal of Abnormal and Social Psychology,* July 1939. Care was taken in this experiment to use a large number of photographs and a group of "judges" accustomed to sizing up people on relatively short notice.

Photographs of the "passport" type were taken of 150 first-year male college students, all of whom were taken in the same position, at the same distance from the camera and facing it squarely. The intelligence of the subjects was estimated by the Thurstone Intelligence Test IV given by a person experienced in testing. The raw scores were found to range from 35 to 150.

Subsequently the photographs, numbered for identification purposes, were given to a group of ten experienced personnel managers and social workers with careful instructions to classify them, according to the subject's intelligence, into eight groups, ranging from *lowest* to *highest.*

It was found that all the judges estimated intelligence with an approximately equal degree of inaccuracy; the pooled estimates of the judges had an equally low correlation with intelligence (.07±.055); and the judges were no more accurate in estimating extremes of intelligence than they were in estimating average or near-average levels.

ANSWER TO FIVE-CIRCLE CHARACTER TEST (page 336)

If you have a plus score on any one trial, the probabilities are very great that you "peeped."

ANSWERS TO SAFETY VIOLATIONS PICTURE PUZZLE (page 380)

In the drawing which depicts a scene in a bottling house operation, there are shown thirty-four distinct unsafe practices or conditions, as follows:

1. Man in foreground is removing foreign body from another's eye with dirty handkerchief instead of using proper first-aid facilities.
2. Man is smoking in room where alcoholic beverages are being bottled and near can of gasoline.
3. Welder does not have electric arc covered and is welding near can of gasoline.
4. Welder has sharp protruding tools in his pocket.
5. Welder has sleeves rolled up while welding.
6. Welder's pliers, chisel, and so on, are lying in aisleway.
7. Cable from welding machine is stretched across aisle.
8. Girl on bottling line has long flowing hair, uncovered. It may get caught in the moving machinery.
9. Same girl is wearing loose bracelets on arm.
10. She is also wearing shoes with high heels.
11. Stool on which she is sitting has broken backrest and braces.
12. Man at capper has grip around bottle and might be cut if the bottle broke.
13. There is no guard on capper, and operator is not wearing goggles.
14. There is no guard on filler pump belt.
15. Man is oiling moving machinery.
16. Same man has waste rag hanging from pocket, where it might get caught in moving machinery.
17. Same man has loose sleeves that might get caught in moving machinery.
18. Man carrying cartons has them stacked so high he can not see in front of him.
19. Same man has hole in sole of shoe.
20. Man in right background is climbing over power conveyor.
21. Girl at left is running.
22. Man is carrying ladder in a hazardous manner and not looking where he is going.
23. Fire extinguisher is blocked by cases.
24. Hand truck is in middle of floor.
25. Ladder on which man is working is set up incorrectly.
26. There is broken glass in back door.
27. Cartons are thrown across aisle.
28. Bucket is set in aisle.
29. Section of pipe is lying in aisleway.
30. Labels are scattered on floor.
31. Broken bottles are on floor.
32. Lid is off sewer along bottling line.
33. Bottle caps are scattered on floor.
34. There are no sprinklers in building.

ANSWERS TO "FACE QUIZ" (page 152)

b. 51, 6, and 7
   Anxiety as a plane falls
c. 10, 29, and 14
   Anger and repose when seeing a dog beaten
d. 55, 15, and 32
   Pleasant surprise

Answer to Project Question 1, page 575

Heading d, "Men Who Know It All Are Not Invited to Read This Page."

AUTHOR INDEX

SUBJECT INDEX